A WHITE RADIANCE

"The One remains, the many change and pass;
Heaven's light forever shines, Earth's shadows fly;
Life, like a dome of many-coloured glass,
Stains the white radiance of Eternity,
Until Death tramples it to fragments....
That Light whose smile kindles the Universe,
That Beauty in which all things work and move...
Burns bright or dim, as each are mirrors of
The fire for which all thirst; now beams on me."
                              Shelley, *Adonais*

"And Coleridge, too, has lately taken wing,
    But like a hawk encumber'd with his hood,—
Explaining metaphysics to the nation—
I wish he would explain his Explanation."
                    Byron, *Dedication to Don Juan*

By the same author

Awakening to the Light
The Fire and the Stones
A Mystic Way
Selected Poems
The Universe and the Light

A White Radiance

*The Collected Poems
1958 – 1993*

NICHOLAS HAGGER

ELEMENT
Shaftesbury, Dorset • Rockport, Massachusetts
Brisbane, Queensland

© Nicholas Hagger 1994

Published in Great Britain in 1994 by
Element Books Ltd
Longmead, Shaftesbury, Dorset

Published in the USA in 1994 by
Element, Inc.
42 Broadway, Rockport, MA 01966

Published in Australia in 1994 by
Element Books Ltd
for Jacaranda Wiley Ltd
33 Park Road, Milton, Brisbane, 4064

Cover design by Max Fairbrother
Design by Alison Goldsmith
Typeset by Alison Goldsmith
Printed and bound in Great Britain by
Biddles Ltd, Guildford & King's Lynn

British Library Cataloguing in Publication
data available

Library of Congress Cataloging in Publication
data available

ISBN 1-85230-489-8

CONTENTS

CONTENTS

CONTENTS

CONTENTS

THE PILGRIM IN THE GARDEN 1973 – 1974

THE NIGHT-SEA CROSSING 1974

VISIONS NEAR THE GATES OF PARADISE 1974 – 1975

CONTENTS

CONTENTS

CONTENTS

CONTENTS

CONTENTS

CONTENTS

CONTENTS

CONTENTS

A FLIRTATION WITH THE MUSE
1992 – 1993

CONTENTS

CONTENTS

ANGEL OF VERTICAL VISION 1993

INTRODUCTORY NOTE BY THE POET

These 1,272 poems represent all my finished works to date. They are grouped in 27 "volumes", the titles of which head each section. They are in broadly chronological order to reflect my growth, with three qualifications: sometimes dating is approximate; sometimes there is overlapping as two poems were worked on simultaneously; and sometimes a poem has been added to an earlier group for thematic reasons. The juvenilia are thus at the beginning; the Light is first properly opened to in *The Silence* and *The Gates of Hell,* which are the turning-point; the gain is consolidated in *The Fire-Flower*; and the fully mature work, such as *A Rainbow in the Spray* and *Question Mark over the West*, is therefore towards the end.

Like any artist, I have grown through different periods and styles, some of which I would not practise now. I have left these as they are as this is a historical presentation of works from different times of my life when I was growing into the person I am now. Where a poem has been revised I have sometimes given both versions; when I have not, the revision has always been within the idiom of the style that applied at the time the poem was first drafted.

For a full account of the life from which the poems arose, see first my long autobiography *A Mystic Way*, which includes many references to particular poems and quotations from all my *Diaries*; and secondly *Awakening to the Light*, Volume 1 of my *Diaries* which covers 1958-1967. These two works account for many of the influences on my work, for example my thoughts about the Roman poets who influenced my poems during the 1970s, and my growing metaphysical perspective and declaration of the Metaphysical Revolution, which has already entered philosophy and the sciences and which now enters poetry with this collection. In this respect, the second version of *A Metaphysical in Marvell's Garden* is clearly an important poem.

In art, the metaphysical manifests as the Baroque, as it did in the 17th century. My Baroque and metaphysical perspectives are outlined in the two *Prefaces* at the back and in the *Metaphysical Commentary* that follows them. It will be helpful for the reader to know at the outset that Baroque poetry combines the Neo-Classical (social situations and attitudes in rational statement) with the Neo-Romantic (emphasis on inner feeling and mystical contact with Reality in image). Neo-Baroque poetry blends statement and image, and unites both strands of 20th century: the active and contemplative lives, and sense and spirit. It will help the reader to know that just as Bernini shows St. Teresa swooning in a sexually suggestive pose, so the new Baroque sometimes presents the Light of Reality and inspiration in contemporary sensual imagery.

As a sometime Existentialist and now Universalist poet, I have sought to reflect the Reality behind the universe in poetry. The Baroque Revolution – the manifestation or emanation of the Metaphysical Revolution in poetry which results in a Poetry Revolution – presents hints and glimpses and chinks of this One Reality in everyday situations. Universalist poems blend experience and tradition; they relate the poet's inner experience to the 5,000 year old Universalist tradition which I have stated in full in Part 1 of *The Fire and the Stones* and in *The Universe and the Light*, and references to which can be found in the *Metaphysical Commentary*. Universalist poems offer perceptions and eternal truths about the universe (and the energy of the Light) in imagery that draws on or is associated with the tradition of the last 5,000 years.

1st February 1994

THE POEMS

A WELL OF TRUTH

1958 – 1963

DEAR SIR

Dear Sir, Your Will, with reference to,
State the position, have a word,
Account payee, inform trustees,
Say it again – he never heard!
He's b—y useless, give a call.
Still at lunch? Upon my soul –
That blasted phone, I'll wring its neck,
Yours very truly, extension please.
It's in the strong room, not the box.
What sort of interest, on the list,   10
In Common Law, that Statute Book.
Was that my buzzer, see cashiers.
Let's do some work, send in Miss Smith.
She's knitting? O God, what is this firm!
Good morning ma'am. The gentleman
Is not at home. Pink carbon, sir!
My God this thing. O she can wait.
Too early for – what does he want?
Entailed interests, settled land,
A bonus issue, without doubt.   20
Bob, get this file, and now for lunch.
Deed of Appointment, Hell! I'm bogged.
Right, thanking you, require our costs.
Roll on the dinner! Let's be friends
For one whole evening in the year.
Then back to work, where it's each for self.
The Queen and Bedford Row will persevere!

1958

A DREAM SO VAGUE

A dream so vague, a touch so far,
A softened hand, a longing look,
All are but shadows that obscure
With pain this sobbing heart you took.

I touched, I held, I looked so close:
Such bliss, such joy, ecstatic hope.
I toss, I turn, and am morose:
"Such tedious hours, such grief," I mope.

Dear woman, so innocent, so game,
Yet so experienced in love,
To hear you call me by my name

And squeeze my hand, and smile above,

Soothes all my sorrows, removes care,
Gives my heart to your restful ease.
Turn my sighs of separation
Into sighs of loving, please!

WHY SO DEJECTED?

Why so dejected? Up! Arise
And shake off gloom's persistent lour.
It is only natural to surmise
On pleasure's retrospective hour.
No sullen misery, no sad sighs,
No wistful longings, nothing sour!
Forget those futile, anguished cries
For readmission to her "bower".
As surely as Time steals past away,
He steals towards another day.

LINES WRITTEN IN THE DEPTHS OF DESPAIR

I sigh and turn my wretched track
In vain towards my pointless goal.
How futile and aimless to lack
A motive force, a "directive soul".
It is so purposeless to live
In blissful harmonies of peace
When all too soon we stand the sieve
Of our delights aside, and cease.
No cure for Melancholy's attack
In trade agreements, women's charms,   10
For Time is cruel and snatches back
Our Love's delight from tender arms;
So blissful moments glide away
And plunge us into muddy now.
Such doubting aftermath's delay
Impels the hand on Fortune's plough
Towards my end. Furrows. It cleaves;
My distracted heart, resolved on Fate,
Is thrown in an abyss of drifting leaves
Which swoop and curl, settle too late.   20
They serve their purpose, withering fast:
A living death, a dying life.
We are figments, illusions, cast

3

Into a pool; the dual strife
Of Hope and Gloom. The unseen eye
Of perfect values, hidden Light
Will mirror the flow. We toil, we sigh
For the impersonal infinite,
But as a watcher on the hills
Leaves scars of longing on the slope,   30
Our dull existence, Godless, void
Bereft of zeal, inspires a hope:
End it all, you are already destroyed.

EPITAPH

Mortal he was: mortality overtook him.
Before his manhood, the universe forsook him.
He had laughed and cried, he had seen and
          smiled;
He had looked and touched, he had willed and
          wiled,
He had loved and lost, he had lived and died.
He lies in a narrow grave with a measure of
          pride.
Mortal he was, the Fates span out their thread.
Mortal he was: mortality lay dead.

I KNEW A BOY

I knew a boy of a happy birth
Who thoughtlessly used to run and play.
His warming smiles were full of mirth –
No hint of sorrow on a coming day.

He used to laugh and run and smile,
He looked so bravely at the sun.
He played marbles in a church aisle,
So heedless of what the Fates had spun.

The years flowed by like an Essex stream,
A darkening shadow crept up near
The feet and knees of his morning dream.
A destiny, and grim despair.

MEDUSA

In mid Ocean, tugged by the heavy ground
          swell,
Alone in the vast expanse of glittering blue
Whose reflection delights in Heaven's glassy-
          dome,
Beyond reach of voice stands a rock, joined to
          a reef.
The sea's kissing rote, perpetual, laps
          listlessly

At his sun-drenched sides, trying endlessly
To draw him gently into her deep bosom.
He stands fast, looking disdainfully down
At the down-running wavelets always
          doomed to failure
But refusing to accept the truth. The friendly
          sun   10
Drowns the cool breezes beneath the deep's
          dark loins.
God-forsaken, bereft of man, scorning
The sensual swell, the rock weeps tears of
          pearl.

Between the beginning and the end lie painted
          pictures
Which Medusa shuts in stony shield to deter
The seeker. Sphinx-like, she is always on the
          verge
And behind her is no open-bosomed valley
Sighing the solution, but only a mirage
Of reclining statues, still-born, two in one
Another's arms, one piece, one heart, all
          false.   20

Though turned to rock, a seeker can make
          pearl.

                              Summer 1959

ON BEING ACCUSED OF EMOTIONAL MATERIALISM, I.E. OF KNOWING WHAT HE WANTS

Who else will bury thorns? Who else will
          walk
In this leafless night, smile at shrivelled
          fingers,
Or laugh without help? Who else will leave
          the cold
Urchin on the lichway to read the stone
Inscription by the ash? Who else will stare
At chill waters, watch the hour-old dragonfly
Die over its lifeless lava in the slime?

It is mine to affirm. Let those who will
Deny, let those who will malign. I am firm.

                              Autumn 1959

THE OATH

If you should ask me why I seem so proud,
Why wrinkles have belied my beaten brows

Or why I no longer join you, to carouse
My time away with laughter and your crowd,
I'll tell you of an oath to Beauty, that I vowed.

But if you wonder why I turn aside
With self-reproach and anguish, to unwind
My traitor-soul, in which my senses twined,
You will see my body stained, but not by
    pride;
My body, soulless, by my soul denied.

A LIFE'S THEME IN AN IMAGE
(A FRAGMENT OF A DESTROYED POEM)

"Hell and damnation," cried the crowd.
On strove the lodestar, touchstone-finding
    ship....

THE DOUBLE

Two eyes spat at me when I looked,
And when I went away they stayed.
When I looked again they met mine
So harshly that I turned them down.
Then I saw the chain and they were hard
While I was kind. I kissed the gold.
But when they saw, the cross was stained
And fell in two. I looked, it was whole.
I laughed, but they burned. I fell forward.
They moved up and bit. I cried out
But it held firm, although they tried
Until I heard a voice. And when I went
Away, they were gone too. And I was kind.

STALLION

I serve a stallion that I chase in vain
Through the black night, bright with the fire
    of a world
Whose might is lost to day. Its essence sears
My eyes which are still searching for a
    shadow –
Just a light to reassure – and burns whole
    moments
From your hot embrace, until it fades to a
    glowing
Cinder in your flickering face, a burnt-out
    shell;
But not too late it comes again, bright-white
In the phoenix-heat, licking my loins to death
And giving me life to feel outside your arms,
To span whole aeons in a second's breath

And ride its flowing flanks in a phantom-
    dream
Less real than its phantom-source, only to fly
From your charms into the pale milk-white of
    your throbbing
Heart and my quivering thighs. The moment
    is now
But still I serve, for you are the fire that burns
My parts, and you I have found.

AT THE GRAVE'S EDGE
(A FRAGMENT)

OLD MAN: This is the place, your mother's
    grave, where I
    Come yearly to minister to your
    sorrows.
    This is the place, and this bough
    with full leaves
    Hangs through sun and snow
    darkly to point the way.
    And this stone has the inscrip-
    tion. Stoop and read.

GIRL: I can just trace the figures with
    my finger
    But I cannot follow it to the
    end, for the dust
    And the wind have taken their
    toll.

OLD MAN: You do not need
    To look beyond this letter. Read
    to here.   10

GIRL: I cannot. I can trace the signs,
    but the stone
    Is too worn. It must be a very
    old stone.

OLD MAN: It is many years since your
    mother died,
    Too many years for you to
    remember,
    Many years. You cannot know
    how many.

GIRL: The stone is very old. It is eaten
    By the wind. See, these fossil
    holes have chipped
    This letter from its hold.

OLD MAN: You cannot know.

GIRL: Why will you not tell me who
    my mother   20
    Was? I have asked you many
    times, but you

OLD MAN:
Laugh and shake your head.
Every year I ride
Across the sea in my small boat
to look
At this grave. Every year when
the leaves begin
To fall, and the sea looks up to
winter,
I stand and stoop and trace the
inscription.
Every year I pluck a leaf from
this bough
To save and watch. It is no
ordinary leaf.

GIRL: You make me feel afraid.   30

OLD MAN:
And now, you have
Ridden across the high sea-
horses, and
The tugging foam. It is as it
should be.

GIRL: Will you not tell me who my
mother was.

OLD MAN: Your mother was my wife. And
this is her grave.

GIRL: Your wife. Then you must be
my father. You
Are my father. You are very
old. Are you
My father?

OLD MAN:
I am your father,
and now,
Now that you have searched the
stone with your finger   40
And crested the white sea, now
is the time
To tell you of your old mother,
so old
And wrinkled there beneath that
you would fear
Her fertile body, cracked and
gnarled as an oak.
She bore you on the old four-
posted bed,
Bore you without propagation,
bore you
Out of her dead limbs. She was
my mother,
And now she is your mother,
and I your
Father. She was older than the

mossy
Wall that runs beside the sea,
over the hill.   50
And this is her grave. She is not
beneath,
She is too old for that. The
white of her bones
Have long passed into dust,
riven like an oak.

GIRL: I, born from a dead woman?
Then who am I –
What witchcraft is this? Was
my mother
A bride of the Devil, that she
was so old?
Answer!

ANGELS

Who mortal can see beyond the drape-veil's
Phosphorescent mesh? The shadowy wings
Startle with stillness like a clock's silence
Or a vase in silhouette. The Forms are points
Of will and cast their shadows on us. They
Call to us, asking us to renounce our wishes.
The glow of the candle throws outlines
through the mesh,
Like moths on a wall. We grasp with frozen
fingers
Paralysed by our blindness, perpetually
Beating towards the candle, far from
lovers,   10
And we beat with the will-less fury of moths
At insubstantial Form-wings, radiant
With suffused dimness. Our senseless struggle
Makes the death-love harder, in freedom and
bliss.
Death is our friend. We see him in a child's
last cry,
We see his delight in one too quiet to
converse,
Too deep to catch the surface splash of wit,
Too tired to grasp the word, where to exist
Is to speak. Sluggish thought and barren
knowledge
Have not found me, or locked my tongue.
Friends are   20
Of the moment, they fill their desolation
And mine with fragments and vain pursuits.
Now
I can review my heart with self-control.

6

Does serene being lie beyond, through the
    mesh spiral
Of discipline? Can I transcend the whorl?

ON REVISITING THE GREEK ISLANDS

The hawk fixes his eye and swoops with a
    firmness,
While the pearl-white sun is eclipsed with
    tarred smoke.
Vibrating engines din out the dance-music.

The satin-blue swell has fled the grey sand-
    ripples,
The horn beats on islets too coarse for houses.
A cigarette floats in the grey wind-waves,
The demoiselle forgot to alight at Hydros.
The rowing-boats at the tidemark are out of
    reach.
The air is flecked with salt and incense, and
    the sound of bells.

The rocks are black when they plunge beneath
    the still,
The cleaners have found a drinking-straw on
    this deck.
The sun is a point of light over the hill
But I have no shadow. The wake cuts three
Receding lines through the silvering water.

While a shaft of golden wave-light runs with
    me
To the low mist, I review my unlived past.

August 1960

ELEGY ON A NEGLECTED GRAVEYARD IN SCIATHOS

Let us pause above this town, breathe the salt
    rote
A cliff's face beneath us, see the skiff's tee
And trace the scrub down to the white walls.
    Above
The silent church trusts strangers. The violet
Harbour swell dances with yachts and
    sparkles.

Past the water pool and the white stooping
Caryatids filling jars, up towards
The light where stones are more jagged, we
    climb.

Here, by the bright lich-gate, let us pause and
    look
At the neglected graveyard with open tombs,

Crouch and stare through the dandelions at one
More wise than you: coffinless skeleton.

August 1960

CHOPPED-UP PENTAMETERS

My feelings are like a shabby
Worn-out hat.

Only two years back, I felt
The backward glances of strangers
Waiting to listen
Waiting to judge
In Regency rooms.
When their eyes became blind
So were mine.

On the heath I was content
To play. I caught butterflies
And labelled them.

Here?

Greek faces on silver
Were my lovers.
I caressed them with fingers
And polished them with milk.
I put Ithaca on the map
And discovered Troy.

August 1960

BLIND

Now I demand the right to state: to compare
Is to betray. Why should I not say, "Look, I
Have lost my sight?" Must I be "like
    Oedipus"?

The man is sitting in the sea, thrashing
The heart of a small octopus across
A stone. The tentacles are limp in his hand.
If you ask, he may say, "His eye offends me."

The stone also held the prickled urchin.
Now dry and dead, it clung, vulnerable.
I, looking at that stone, that octopus eye,
Feel the darkness from the wavelets surround
    me.

I WILL CALL ON MY LOVE AGAIN

I will call on my love again
And holding her by the hand,
I will pour out this gathering pain
And ask her to stay in England
And not leave me sitting on this sand.

Yes, I will call on my love again
And holding her with my eye,
I will swoop her through corn-stooks and
    heaps of grain
And ask her to stay in England
And not to leave this hand
But always to remain close by.

YOUNG AND OLD

He was a young young man
And he loved a hundred women
And his shirt was the colour of pilchards.
He was a young young man
And he fractured fifty hymen
And terrorised the willing wilchards.

He was an old old man
And he mourned a hundred women
And his beard was the colour of sea-foam.
He was an old old man
Who remembered fifty hymen
And stick-tapped a far death-roam.

THE HOUSE OF UNREASON

See in night-blue the nestling lattice light,
Star-stung and new above the shadowed
    château's height.
Run on in dawn-thrust to know the ruined rust,
The musty house of louse-infected, dead and
    deathly dust,
Head into the darkness of floor-infested
    fust
Before the lightning dawn-birth destroys the
    fearful sight.

Give in night-black a heart to sightless eyes.
Revere the sorrowing stair where cobweb
    blind surmise
Feels foot by finger, draws back and racks
    unreason's bare
Unthinking host, gropes through moon-lit
    pools to hear

The mixed music, lumbering up alone to
    silence sorrow's lair
And crack a black flood of feeling with his
    axe: the prize.

Give in night-blue a mind to patient pain,
Frown at the faltering, down-haltering
    disdain
When blind surmise laughs at the door barring
    bands,
Mocking the unformulated rock-quivers of
    motioned hands;
Break hard at dawn-thought, lock out thought-
    shorn fairylands
And catch at sunrise the captive in his ball
    and chain.

TWO SONGS FROM
THE MOLTEN OWL'S SONG

1.

When the sun's warm ray sighs under the
    ground
And Beauty's bound in winter snow,
I'll make no more hay by my dead love's
    mound,
I will sing to you my song of woe.

2.

I'll strew my flowers upon your grave
And fill your glass with ashes.
For you have drunk the mind's dark wave,
And worn life's molten lashes.

Spring 1961

THE PERSISTENT WOMAN

Indeed, I like to talk to you at night;
I am never bored. No, Heaven forbid.
But though I like to taste your company
There are so many other things to do.
You yourself do not deny that you are cold,
And though I am charmed, I cannot give you
    much.
You must believe I would like to, but I can't,
It's in my nature not to. No of course
There is no other, but I stay too long.
I will miss the Prologue. That would never do.
So au revoir, I will be seeing you.
And you, you understand, I hope? I hope so.
And as the sun smiled low through the

Western sky,
The white earth glowed in the thickening night.

ODE TO A PROSPECT FROM A WINDOW FRAME

I sat in wonder at the window edge
And breathless watched the peace of day recline
Over the still green hill. The soft grass sedge
Waved to the fleeing evening beneath the pine,
And oh what glory in that dying light!
My heart leaped clear. There were streaks of russet cloud,
My mind fell free and walked with unscaled eyes
Down flimsy-paper streets at triple height
And peered through panes. My body was a shroud;
The wilting world wept at my spirit's size.   10

But then the cooling window froze to night;
There was no noise to disturb the sleeping grass,
No chirp of bird or insect. I had no sight
To glimpse a moonlit movement, for – alas –
Too soon my tingling nerves grew calm and sour;
I saw my hands caress a picture-frame,
A wilderness of art in nature's paint.
My heart was heavy in that shrouded hour,
An artifice that left the feeling lame,
And left the well of knowledge to the saint.   20

Would there were a well of Truth that all might see,
A well of clean and lasting Light to soothe
The souls of all who dip their hands, to be
A cure for all whose hearts are like a sound-proof booth.
That picture will soon be in winter's sprawl
And slow Decay will sing the frost of time
And the slow dance that sighs the grave's embrace
For years to come, for aeons past my fall
To a lich bed, beneath the hoar-frost's rime,
Beyond the eternal smile of Beauty's face.   30

But, to capture beauty now should be our aim,
Not to be darkened by the shadow thrown by death
Across the water-lilies, which evening breezes tame
And whip to fury with their dying breath.
Who has not stood and looked into the lake,
And seen the dancing pictures flow and fade
Deep in the grey pool's heart? We must not despair. Each one
Will dance again. Our sensibilities must make
The fleetest shadow special for it might be Beauty's shade.
Behind each shadow reigns a glorious sun.   40

NUDITY OF HEAVENS AND MAN

Nudity of heavens and man, bridged by a tree
That I cannot climb, is all life's harmony.
Here in the stark stillness of middle winter,
Dull in the deep pool's dark surface, I tread
Near a tree that fades with the fall of each child-leaf
Until the shock has subsided, and the two are at one.
Here is the union of dead horse chestnut bark
And its living copy, which reaches out to receive
The image it has barely cast off, clutching in the gloom.
One stone, and it is finished. I am like that tree.

And just as this wintry picture is but a copy
Perhaps I, and man himself, like the source of the tears
That splash and ruffle this calm, are also copies
Of a reality whose divine power can be guessed
From this watery grave? Where is my invisible essence?
Bareness, bareness. The lambent light lingers on my lips
White-grey, kisses my barren cheeks with deadness.
Nudity of heavens and man, do not shine on me.

9

EXTERNALS

The loadstone's lure allays
The mind's decaying fear;
The serpent praise betrays
What inner minds can hear.
The unreal wheel of days
Turns with the sun's sol-air
And burns the body's bier.

Stone eyes survey the tomb
And crack in its decay;
Weep-hearts staked to the womb   10
Bewail the still-born day.
No self-in-self can bloom
To scent sweet sorrow's spray,
Destroy destruction's play.

The severed soul alone
Will spurn the wheelless cart,
Sharing the carter's groan
It clasps will to knotty heart
And, offering tears of bone,
Truth's star-quiet plays the start   20
Of Truth's cold and distant part.

TWO MEN HANGED

They took us to a crowded room.
I had never seen a Court before.
They talked a lot about my "doom"
And said, "This man defied the law."

They sentenced two of us to die,
And one for life, and Jim went free.
And people laughed when they saw me cry,
"Have no sympathy. Did he?"

They took me to a furnished vault
And set me down upon the bed.   10
"This will teach you to assault
A lover, hit him on the head."

I haven't seen my friends since then.
The Minister refused my plea.
I had two weeks to use my pen.
Two weeks have passed, and it must be.

We killed him in the darkened lane,
We had spent our money in the bar.
Our only thought was a little gain.
I pushed him down and went too far.   20

I know that I deserve to hang,
I'm young, and old enough to know.
But Tony never touched the man,
He did not even aim a blow.

I laughed and joked when Elsie came
And asked if she would keep the child
And often loudly took the blame,
But secretly, I am afraid.

The chaplain said, "Believe in God,
His mercy is great, he will forgive   30
Even you." I do not give a sod
For his Heaven. I want to live.

And now the bell is tolling nine.
The door has moved, I see the rope,
And now I'm standing on the line.
The rope is new and greased with soap.

And now at last I see the sun
And faces turned the other way.
And now my knees and arms are bound.
What should I think? What should I say?   40

"I know that I deserve to hang,
I'm young, and old enough to know.
But Tony never touched the man.
O God, why can't you let him go?
Please God, please can't you let me go?"

BEAUTY

The seisma. The sensation and the cenotaph.

I have touched sienna faces in the heat,
Bitten magenta grape-lips, ashen and red,
Trodden in glaucous pits and heard
    crepuscular feet.

THE LONE SAILSMAN IN EXILE

The friendless foam follows my boat. Island
Mists float and weep. No more is the
    Kingdom for me,
Only the grate and boom and the wind's bite.
I do not know where I go, whence I come.
The sail shines to the moon, and I must share
Salt on eyes and a heavy chest. I talk
To no one. Wet, cold, I head for the ice-floes,
The curse of my father's will seething the foam

Behind me as the gull swoops. Empty space
Awaits, when the dark cliff looms from my
    sleep.

STRATFORD

The swans nestle in the dark straw,
The actors huddle in their Avon nest
And riot a retreat in pairs.
Around us was the smell of love
From opening legs, and I was surprised
By the lying mirror, which told
I was not too old for this, to touch a skirt.
Never has the temptation to fall in love
Been so hot, live at home, have our room.

I, watching my youth flow by,
With memories of childhood games
And too great a respect to rape,
Went single out of Heaven with a sigh.

LAMENT OF THE FARRASH

The glad years have fled, the good-hearted
    years
When I, a dignity, dried the King's socks,
Drove his flocks – with what care – to the
    artesian springs,
Content and peaceful beneath his sceptre,
Paying homage to his many-ringed hand.
Then, one bloody day, wonders barbarous!
And I, driven by burlap buckram, barefoot
Over the sand, to beg, a barbarian....
Now I, a farrash, walking-crouch, wash floors
For feet to violate with mud from the rains.

Ma-leesh!

Autumn 1961

THE NEW MAN

He prays for his aspiration
And continuity.
His gift is for his situation –
And the soul's alchemy.

To aspire to talent and forge a mite
Is silver to the soul.
To find one's furnace and miss its Light
Is the hallmark of the fool.

It is the Age of leaden ears,
The wise have golden tongues.   10

Only the old wear woollen years
But he has golden lungs.

You can forget the tongues of flame,
Their fire will soon die down.
Against the Age, his soul is the same
As a round, golden crown.

On Babel's flimsy tower he stands,
Where Satan purrs commands.
He heals with Pentecostal hands
And seals all dead demands.   20

He wears a golden scourge of thorns
And none will drink the blood.
No more ritual. This philosopher warns
That magic was drowned in the flood.

From the corpse of the man he calls
A paean that shaped the ape,
Shakes kings who recline by astrologers' walls
And allows the stars to escape.

On a hill the New Man is born
And grows and suffers and dies.   30
His mind is a stone its philosopher will turn
Into gold, like a water sunrise.

FACES OF THE AGES

I have seen you, faces of the Ages,
On skulls and abstract art, pleading from
    walls,
Dark in my dreams, dead and sightless sages
Bone-white in the night-lights of darkened
    halls.

I have seen you, faces of the lost years,
And I do not hesitate to judge you.
Tonight I saw your silence, understood your
    leers,
How, at the old year's death, you will make
    nothing new.

I have seen you looking at your watches,
Heard your anguished cries in your crackling
    fire.   10
Nitch on your staff your life's sharp-edged
    notches,
Throw "shamrut assa" – ask "How far" as you
    desire.

11

I have seen you smiling through boiling
　　blood,
Heard the crackling cry of your whimpering
　　masks.
I have seen you praying for a new flood
To quench the fire of desire that always
　　asks.
I have seen you, faces of the Ages,
Burning so brightly in your pleading
　　pain.
Racked with remorse at your flickering,
　　flaming rages
I have foamed in fury at the race of Cain.　20

SUNDAY MORNING

I dreamt I saw the altars
Burning in the night
And in the Christian rafters
Shone education's "light".

I dreamt I saw the people
Groping in the dark
And on the blazing steeple
Sang a dawning lark.

I dreamt I saw the sunrise
Burst upon the land
And in the smouldering embers
Lay many a priestly hand.

I woke and saw the people
Follow to the bell
And underneath the steeple
There was an illumined Hell,
And no one dared to tell.

CHIAROSCURO

Yes, we are all of us in the dark.

Tree-shoots, green, and newly mown grass,
A ripe girl, a white gale of clouds,
An ocean-seeking stream –
All illuminated this afternoon
The chiaroscuro of my shaded being
Like brief beacons in the dark night
Of our impermanence, lights that were pure.

As the sun went in, I inhaled the smell
Of smoking manure.

Autumn 1963

SUN-LIGHT

Is that all for the brain, to grow and sun-ripe
　　shine,
And fall like a Newtonian apple?
Is there no purpose? Are the cave shadows
After all, then, real? Is there no Light
For the inner eye, from within? Is there none?

O body-bud brain, at last to ungrateful man
Have you yielded the secret of your being?
Dark, dark moon-tidal force, have you
　　reduced
The spiritual and the material to earth?
If you Darkness is true, let us worship great
　　men.

It is false, there cannot be absence of Sun.

Autumn 1963

EARTHQUAKE

I too once dreamt of friendship and success,
The warmth of fires, the understanding face,
Comfort and work, and children's happiness,
Of ordered lives, achievement's irreligious
　　grace.
I awoke in a city of smoke and tumbling
　　towers;
I groped aghast and shouted to a shape,
And then the rumbling road gaped wide and
　　sighed,
Walls yawned and crashed, dust rose, and
　　writhing bones
Groaned within the smouldering graves and
　　died.
Their hopes were but a level waste of stones,
Their pride mourned only by one shock-
　　crazed ape,
And the wind which swept behind the two
　　sharp showers.

Autumn 1963

A STONE TORCH-BASKET

1963 – 1965

THE EXPATRIATE
(A DRAMATIC MONOLOGUE SET IN JAPAN)

ὦ δώματ' Ἀδμήτει' ,ἔν οἷς ετλην εγὼ
θῆσσαν τράπεζαν αἰνέσαι θεός περ ὤν.

Euripides, Alcestis 1-2

I. WHEEL
In our Gethsemane,
In the full moon of May,
Let us watch and pray.
A shadow glides beneath the gingko tree,
By the stone lotus; darkness swallows deep
The pool, the peace, the pleasure-woman's cry,
And in a silver sweep the roses die
In incidental scent for their release.
I too would now be there, had I not met you.
I joke – I only came to drink of course,   10
That is for others, drink's enough for us,
And lilies, and the intellectual moon.
We have the night, stranger; and they, the
      night has them,
By the stone lotus. They burn bright and fade,
      while we –
We glow and know our doom in our Bhodi-
      garden.
I joke of course, I joke about my life;
I joke like any fool who's left his wife.
Another shadow glides beneath....Your
      question,
The haiku brought me and I stayed too long,
      that's all.
I joke, stranger. And I provoke.   20

And yet, as you are a discerning man,
I can confess, I am not what I seem,
Am at odds with something – an alien,
An alien pagan in an unreal dream.
My home? Oh no, I've no regret for that,
I don't miss England – that, too, is just a
      dream:
The Saturday shopping-spree, the cricket bat,

The City bells and the Forest, and Sunday tea.
That ringing laughter, by the willow-tree.
No. She had nothing for me to share,   30
Except....
            We were a very different pair.
No, I've no regrets; no smouldering leaves
      burn in my heart.
No, no, they're evergreens of winter, cold
Photogenic scenes, cheap holiday slides to
      while away our May:
The party, and after, until the break of day.

Another shadow....I joke, stranger, I joke.
I cannot hate the East. You see, my choice
Demands acceptance, yet another voice
Invokes: "You are apart from other folk."

A hundred births and deaths return through
      smoke.   40

II. MIRROR
I can confide – come closer – other men
(Not you of course) corrode me with disgust.
(I felt the same when I was only ten.)
It is not just – ahem! – those fires of lust
(Pace Augustine), something more august:
Self-love and self-interest, hypocrisy,
Deceit and superficial pettiness,
Egoistic craving and vulgarity.
There is no doubt, mankind is in a mess.
Take Harmon at the office – he's my
      senior   50
(Junior in age) he....No, Ivor Tate,
He was worse; a brash con-man who boasts
And never listens; "he's a must for hosts."
He has a manner.
            Once, in former days,
She knew him. There was a fire through the
      window-panes,
And then I was lost in the frost; and there
      were bicycle stains.
Another time there was a broken glass,
And two cigarette-ends stubbed out on the
      grass.

13

I envy no one who is out for praise.

Have you known what it is to suffer that
        apart   60
With gutting gas-lamps huttering in your
        heart,
And thunder in your spleen?
                You understand,
You too have seen it – don't you loathe
        mankind,
And long to strip aside his rusted blind,
Or long to rip behind his rusted blind?

I have endured a bitter, bitter dream.
I am a slave to other men's conditions.

But there's another question I often ask:
What is the point of all this menial farce,   70
Of papers on a desk – or an office dance?
Midwives, and brides; promotion, and
        success,
Are mocked to menial meaning by my death.
And what of children; running up the road
        from France.

I wear a mask: to myself I am a stranger
For all my intellectual positions.
I know; I fear. And Harmon does not care.
I know but do not show.
             No I despair,
I cannot see my enemy   80
I cannot find him anywhere.

My life – my life is not sufficient.
In what – in what am I deficient?

III. CINDERS

Another shadow glides beneath the tree
By the stone lotus. No, I have no creed;
I envy you your simple certainty.
I cannot deify the living dead.
I am a pagan of a needing breed;
Not daily bread.
              I can erect no proof: 90
A trillion star-leaks trickle through my roof
And drown my differential coefficient.

And yet, you see that garden-temple's light
Just this side of the pleasure-lazaret?
There's still a light in my stone torch-basket.

I've not despaired; it may not burn that bright,
But it does burn, for something – some region
Glimpsed in clumsy silhouettes, my Zion.
In that kingdom of superconsciousness
There's no negation, I know a quiet peace,   100
I glow with meaning that I can't express
And happiness I never want to cease;
It doesn't matter that I've no redress,
To exist – exist! is no macabre caprice,
It is divine, that brief release,
Those dragging hours of timelessness.

But I have known another time, a cry
Within, a din, a shunting-ring of sound,
Of passions – not impressions – whirling
        round
With hunting appetites, and in vain I try   110
To gain control and ask them: Who am I?
Last night – last night my life dripped from a
        tap.
Tell me, did the earth shake at five?
        Seismology
Is now my hobby.
              And sometimes I deny
All rational order as a brilliant lie,
And long to die.
             Last night, I lotus-sat.
There was a mewing cat. Six year's austerity
With five, then curds; and then the Bhodi-
        tree.   120
But not for me. Just words, Gethsemane:
Awake, alone, the flames behind my dome,
And eyes of coals that burn and yearn to
        weep,
Aslake for sleep, asweat for dawn to creep,
And a deep deep dread of going home.

These summer nights I'm apt to disintegrate,
But dawn pieces me together. If ever I kill
Myself, it will be to make my reason still.
And yet, I would rather be me than Ivor Tate.

I am attached to something that I hate.   130

IV. DAWN

I must leave you – this is my alleyway.
No, I see no one. Her? Oh that woman,
She's just a neighbour. Not an imposing
        place,
I do agree: a little too animal.

But see, the night is giving birth to day –
See in the palms how pale the moon-lamps
    hang –
A vast cave-chasm of indifference;
Another spasm – there it is, the face,
Ablaze with your Master's graveward grace –
    what sense
But this sense can consent to something so
    irrational?   140
Now go and kneel and be intentional.
I serve; but I will never make pretence.

> The loveless man from another
>   home
> Is lost within his "neighbour's"
>   room
> And loves himself in his neigh-
>   bour's womb.

THE SEVENTEETH CENTURY PILGRIM

"Wyrd oft nereth unfaegne eorl thonne his ellen
deah."

Beowulf

Once I complained of many bitter facts,
Of ruins and epitaphs on empty hopes,
That I was born to die despite my acts
Or the futile benedictions of the Popes.
Yet as I watched the seasons ebb and flow
I saw the tides that swirled across my brain
In fickle flood and moon-fall – παντα ῥει;
No self of mine felt constant agony.
And I resolved to evolve from pointless pain
(My Hell) and grow a Paradise that I could
    know.   10

Since then I have journeyed through rocks
    and pines,
I have sat by rivers in the summer sun,
I have watched timeless dawns flush golden
    Eastern shrines,
And knelt to my shadow when the day is
    done.
I am still a sequence of moments;
But my abiding eye of strict assent
Nakedly loves the underlying Power
That pulses through existing's every hour.
Don't ask me where I'm bound. It brings

    dissent
To analyse perfection's senseless sense.   20
And yet I know from the wild wind's sound
I too will rot to nothing underground.

BINSEY GREEN

O Binsey Green, I knew you in my youth,
I knew your river, your heath, I knew your
    swans.
And now, just smoke. You are the same,
    but I –

All's changed. No longer do I seek your peace
Among frustrations; no longer do I need
Your peace, now that I am doing what I want.

I am as far from you as this Tokyo.

AND SCHOLARS WILL ASK

And scholars will ask
"What was it like,
Living in the breakdown of Western
    civilisation?"
Knowing we wear
A Republican Roman's mask.   10

And they will read themselves
Into our accurate chronicles,
Researching in academies of Mongol
    materialists,
Like unread scriptures
From buried Roman shelves.

No Tacitus, but taciturn,
I bequeath an image
Reflecting the sickness of White Man's
    degeneration,
Like a cracked mirror
In a catacomb urn.

Open-mouthed, as in post-Periclean Greece,
He ambles, our equal,
Sprawling past the hoarding, our Master-
    Consumer,
Or vacant at the bus-stop,
Ape eyes at peace.   20

ODI ET AMO

Vulgar, I said.
See how he moons moronically past the

church,
Gaping vacantly: don't you realise
Our culture's founded on his clumsy eyes,
Our civilisation's quest is his head's search?
He should be dead.

Tragic, I said.
Hear how he died: "sitting with his mother
When the train crashed," or in agonies of
     pride
Captured on the Congo, or burnt or crucified.
As in my dream I wept, my naked brother
Shot through his head.

He, the Eternal Victim,
Odi et amo;
I, knowing myself in him,
Have a long way to go.

THE NOMAD

Unlimited, unfree the nomad stalks,
Trekking and choiceless:
Thonged feet carve tracks of sand
Through thronging voices,
Disembodied and broken
Near the shadow of the broken totem;
Dusty and rusty from his gnarled hand
Hang three Judgement-hawks
And a broken compass.

Unaspiring, unattaining lies the nomad,
Mirage-broken, hermit-thirsty
On the baking sand:
Dead, and by the pole-star's eyes
From inner fountains could arise
A beckoning hand,
From inner fountains driven mad.

THE PRIEST REFUSES DEATH

Dark are the trees: dark is my heart's lake,
Waiting beneath the mistletoe
For a priest I know
To pluck the bough and break
The Guardian of the nation with a deathblow,
For their sake.

And that they perish not – shall I consent,
Turning in moon-glow,
The moon-gleaming blow,
Shall I accept? Shall I prevent

The dark anguish of my priestly foe
For their assent?

Withered corn-stalks, a plague on the land,
And blood on my hand.

TWILIGHT
(FIRST VERSION)

In the twilight of this dwindling Age
I dream of men of stature, images
Of contemplation, self-creation:
Our stone-devoiding century has destroyed
Established images of soul direction,
Those crystal images of saintly ages;
Can modern idols modern saints assuage,
Those stone-avoiding seekers in our void?
What remains but pagan self-perfection?

I glimpse him there, the prophet incarnate, 10
Squatting in firelight, mocked by meaner men
Who ring the flickering cathedral square:
Fire-flitting effigies of stone tower round –
Priapus, Bacchus, Mammon and a host
Of hostless single-visioned pioneers:
All else is twilight: uttering no sound,
Oblivious of their deeds, their creeds, their
     gibes
On the firelit flagstones he describes
Gigantic struggles of mortality
And crystal victories: before his mind   20
Whole eras pass and fall, and looking out
Over the ruined altar, looking far
Into the blackness of the beyond, his eyes
Shine with conviction: ask not his intent –
The radiant "Yes" of his silent detachment
His perfect eyes of purpose will confess
The senselessness of self-development.

TWILIGHT
(SECOND VERSION)

In the twilight of this dwindling Age
I dream of men of stature, images
Of slit-eyed contemplation, self-creation.
Like a man born blind who gropes and denies
     the sun,
After tight-lipped gropings over old idols
And careful pronouncements they are on
     stone,
Our logic-chopping century has hewn down
Established images of "soul-direction",

The pitted cross-on-wheel from saintly ages.
Can lunar ash, or dust from Heelstone
    clock,   10
Put out the burning "madness" in those eyes
Which seek a solar vision in this earthen Urn?
What remains but pagan self-perfection?

I glimpse him there, the prophet for our time,
Squatting in firelight, mocked by meaner men
Who ring the flickering cathedral square.
Fire-flitting effigies of stone tower round –
Priapus, Bacchus, Mammon and a host
Of hostless single-visioned pioneers,
Cold monuments to conquerors of the
    stars.   20
All else is twilight. Uttering no sound,
Oblivious of their deeds, their creeds, their
    gibes
On the firelit flagstones he describes
Gigantic struggles of mortality,
And crystal victories. Before his mind
Whole eras pass and fall, and looking out
Over the ruined altar, looking far
Into the blackness of the beyond, his eyes
Shine with conviction. If you verbalise
The radiant "Yes" of his silent detachment 30
(The flickering eyes of his great Fieriness),
His perfect eyes of purpose will confess:
"The senselessness of self-development."

THE OCEANOGRAPHER
AT NIGHT

"To be in heaven is to steer."

Once anchors comforted me,
Like stillness within motion:
But by the gull, hindward hovering,
By the shifting surface of the ocean,
By the crucifix across the moon
And the crow's nest eclipsing,
I know we drift imperceptibly.

    The Oceanographer knows too well
    The stillness of his tomb.

For certainty I tried to fix   10
Whole continents within rotation:
But, by the rote on rugged slopes,
By the rift in the crust of this ocean,

Like icebergs in a perpetual flow,
I know the mantled continents move,
Even the mantle-rock is in a flux;
Imperceptibly I know we drift.

    The Oceanographer knows too well
    What the continents prove.

Elsewhere I have dropped an anchor,   20
Have sounded cliffs within erosion,
Founded whole continents on another rock:
But by the moon's eclipse,
By each tremor and each tidal wave,
By each measured "iceberg" top,
I know the currents of a shifting base,
And, unstill in an unstill ocean,
I know I imperceptibly drift.

    The Oceanographer knows too well,
    The Oceanographer knows he is in Hell. 30
    Will the Oceanographer discover
    The centre of his retrogression,
    The source and goal of all progression?

POSTSCRIPT TO BRUEGEL IN
TOKYO: DREAM AND
REALITY

Their faces, pocked and putrid bones, it was
That impressed me. Then I realised, by
Their radioactive rot, disintegration
Was on their sickness, plague and pestilence.
The human condition grinned. And I could
    smell
By my smouldering skin, I too would burn.

I woke to rain. We cannot walk in the garden,
The radio says, as the leaves drip with hot
    dust
From yesterday's Chinese test of an atomic
    bomb.

WINTER IN NARA
(AN INVESTIGATION OF THE
RELATION BETWEEN CULTURE
AND DEATH, CIVILISATION AND
ETERNITY)

Here I sit, sheepskinned in an open slop shop,
Blowing on my left fingers, while madam
Pokes the cold charcoal brazier with the iron
    chop

17

Stick, brews a loud-mouthed kettle for her
    silent Adam.
She wears a white peasant smock and clogs.
    The air
Nips, and, as this is Nara Park of the pines,
Opposite, statue-still, stare the fawn deer.
High over the hill, the Tempyo shrines.

For fourteen months I have shirked this
    obligatory trip,
Made excuses. But everyone's asked, again
    and again   10
If I have been, and so…in this winter nip
I have come for a day and a half by the new
    train.
At Horyuji I met the well-drilled hordes,
Standing unsmiling before cameras, freeing
Handfuls of yen for the Buddha, such
    generous lords,
And clapping hands to bow and watching who
    was seeing.

I asked myself, would it have been the same
After the clang of the gates at sunset?
Or is it that shrines leave me feeling tame,
As I know so little of the eighth century? And
    yet,   20
Though I could not feel in those coachload
    crowds
The spirit in those time-hewn blocks of wood,
All day I have been pondering among the
    clouds
Till, after the death-stones down those steps, I
    understood:

All culture is a brazier against the dark.
Man in the Forest erected trophies
To light and heat the dusky world of bark.
The élan and thrust of a fine old temple is:
First a shining defiance of the dark of death
Through the civilisation of a treasured work
    of art,   30
Then a warming conquest of all loss of breath
Through the enduring symbol of an eternal
    peace of heart.
January 1965, revised December 1974

CHRIST OF THE SEA-SPRAY

Who is this turbulent man who looks out of
    his time,

Stooping in khaki, intense eyes indrawn,
Cheeks hollow and tubercular? Why does he
    judge
This bustling, concreted city with that frown?
On Edogawa Bridge there is nothing amiss.
Proud polyphony! I hear the green canal
Swirl once and disappear by the empty
    warehouse
Where at twelve the church-bells chide lifted
    skirts,
And echo past busy ears in pachinko-dens –
    the pastoral
Of a Westernised building-over of this native
    earth.   10

O let me descend into the pit of the heart
Of this city, and cast out its snakes! O horror!
I see a city that is a harlot of falsehood.
O modern men in leather jackets,
O modern girls in Western make-up
Who will not wear your kimonos,
O modern hostesses in bars
And businessmen in borrowed cars,
O sensei in your honoured Chair,
And students, you who put him there,   20
What has become of your traditional customs,
Why do you live like souls you are not, so
    falsely,
Why do you allow this foulness to nest in
    your hearts?

I said, I will leave this sprawling city to its
    sickness.
Discordant faces, fevers like images
War in my dying limbs. Each labyrinthine
    room
In this faded palace wears an ugly mask.
I said, I will look for welled rainwater and fire
In the unspoilt villages on the fishermen's
    Pacific.

A snow-waste. Five miles of night-tracks up
    the sky,   30
Under the frozen star-tree in this green
    twilight.
Hishinouma sat in his village, mending
His nets near the well. His wife planted paddy
In the horseshoe valleys, and the motorcycle
Roared, bringing his son from the city,
    scarred

And drunk and educated, and in the rotten log
The hornets hummed. Hishinouma stood up
And walked to the shrine his ancestors built
Five centuries ago, and the echoes
Of the motorbike clanged the temple bell.   40

Hishinouma, meaning "water chestnut", had a
    thatched well.

I stood on the beach under the Milky Way.
The sea flung spray far into the Nobe night,
And I heard them dancing a sea-ritual,
Hishinouma and the rest, clapping and singing,
And I felt that man was too great for the
    universe
Not to be a god.

          That night, I played a late
Beethoven Quartet, my paper doors open
To the booming sea. The agony of the
    strings,   50
The resignation, the quiet ecstasy!
I was ten thousand years away from a daimyo
Who stood upright, crew-cut and chewing
    gum,
Watching his wrapping paper float down the
    canal,
This citizen of the Pax Americana,
I was ten thousand years away from any
    trouble
While the final darkness gaped and swallowed
    us
And a freezing gust blew across a heap of
    rubble....

I, Christ of the sea-spray, stand on Edogawa
    Bridge
And look in vain for the spirit in Edo's
    child.   60
My divine consciousness foams for all who
    have yet
To make the journey from the lower mind
To the heights of a union in a shrine
Or under the Milky Way, when the sea is
    wild.

SONG OF THREE
THAMES–DAUGHTERS

"Order *has* been restored,
We have reconstructed our broken land

And buried our ruined continuity
Under new estates and new towns;
The centre is now repaired,
Some other mouth may be as fair as ours
But a crashing blast now brings
Barely remembered frowns."

"We can make our land more just,
Sequestrate the estates of Dukes;   10
Otherwise we have no social purpose
But to maintain the status quo.
Washington is the new Rome,
And New Britain, at last alone,
A Hellenistic rally into Europe,
Like an old lady dying
In her rich son's home."

"Ours is the vicarious generation;
Neither lost nor tragic, no longer angry,
We live at one remove   20
Like a bedridden old lady,
Watch others discuss our fate,
Read of others' exploits and decisions
Or lose ourselves in television heroisms,
Courting a garish world,
Unnourished by its synthetic opiate."

ALL:
    "As good a time as any
    To find our way back to the spring
    Of real consciousness within."

THE EARLY EDUCATION AND MAKING OF A MYSTIC

(IN 42 FORMATIVE SCENES)
FRAGMENTS OF A SPIRITUAL ODYSSEY

1965 – 1966

1. FOLKESTONE

All morning we clamoured to go down to the
    sea,
I chanted "Miss Whitworth's in the ba-ath"
Knowing there would be no ogre to chase me;
At the bedside of the paralysed neighbour
I pulled a face and made the others snigger;
But when, tears in her eyes, she squeezed my
    hand
I was well-behaved. Being immortal
I found her wrinkles funny, and her silent room
Like an agonised church.

          On the promenade   10
The prophet squatted and raked his glowing
    embers
Of potash, carbon, tugging his mariner's beard
And pointing a scrawny finger at a red-hot
    omen.
My aunt tried to hurry me past, but I broke
    away,
Joined the small group, waited for him to
    speak,
Read the boarded feature from *The Daily
    Express*:

PROPHET CYCLES BLINDFOLD TO FIND
    WRISTWATCH.
He spoke in a grating voice through clods of
    earth,
"Verily, I say unto you, my experiment shows
God died in his bed after a long illness,   20
God is dead."

So can't God curl down like a genie and spy
Through the window?
"God is dead."
          No one cheered. With un-
    comfortable smirks

They dispersed. I stayed, aghast.
          The sea
               fell
                   away
Into the sky.   30
"Is God really dead?" I asked my flurried aunt
As she dragged me away.

2. HOLY GREY

As we came round the may-hedge in our
    Sunday suits
He was parking his bike at the end of the
    road,
I said, "It's Grey," and we both laughed
    excitedly
As he carefully knelt in the centre of the
    T-junction
And clasped his hands in inaudible prayer.
"Will God make sure that the drivers don't hit
    him?"
Remounting, he pedalled with an old man's
    rhythm –
"Quick," I said, and we scuffled a stone past
    the centre half;
As he drew level he wobbled and got off,
There was grey down all over his shiny
    pate   10
And fire and brimstone in his holy eyes.
"Yer can't play football on Sundays," he
    declared,
"Yer irreligious urchins."

          On a squally afternoon
I looked in the local bookshop window, and
    saw
His face frown behind me like a morning
    moon;
He leaned his bicycle against the old brick
    wall

And opened his saddlebag: fifty new prayer
    books,
Which he had bought out of his earnings as a
    navvy.
"Here," he said, not recognising me, "have
    this."   20

Years later, I turned the stairs in an evil house
During a blackout, groping after a lighted
    match,
And saw a thin little man hands folded, eyes
    shut in prayer.
Grey had been dead a decade. And now I too
Have seen the light they both saw, one on the
    stairs,
The other kneeling in the middle of the street.

3. CRICKET CAPTAIN

I was cricket captain of four elevens.
I recall the coach for match day, and the smell
Of rain on my sweater, of linseed oil
On my golden bat. I still hear the jingle of
    pads,
The willow-smack from the square. I still
    tremble with fear,
If I fail to score fifteen, what if I fail?
A summer evening drenched our roasting
    field,
Threw long shade from the chestnuts. The
    chapel
And library dome were afire, and the Hall
    clock
Showed six-thirty. Seniors stood in a ring,   10
Waiting for our last over, their last pair in,
Stonewalling for a draw. Six blocks to make,
And I, weighing the leather between our fast
Bowler and leg-spinner, prefer guile to force.
All round a shock, a groan. But was not pace
A little too obvious? Should one not be
    subtle?
Six teasing arcs, six angers and disgusts.
I lead in the team, deaf to their mutters.
What independence I showed in those
    days!   20
How crucial those decisions were in those
    days,
How unimportant now, like fagging-lists.

4. NEW YEAR'S EVE DANCE

I was fifteen. Strangled in a dinner jacket,

I went to the New Year's Eve dance in my old
    school hall
Near the nature-table, where the percussion
    band
Played. The jungle-jim still stood on the
    frosty lawn.
Adolescent among childhood objects
And sleek young bloods, and mirth and
    mistletoe,
I miserably prayed, "Please, no foxtrots
Or Paul Jones." I felt wall-flower ugly and
    proud.
Across the parquet floor sat the fat girl
In a boned dress, plump-armed from the
    dancing classes.   10
I should go over, for at Ladies' Invitation
She would ask me. She looked at me,
    entreating
Between the waltzers, piteous were I not
So blushful and proud. The next one, I said.
When all go, choose and act, and do not
    dither.
The waltz stopped. "Ladies' Invitation."
    Smooth
Men preened. I shuddered, rose, sloped up the
    stairs,
Out to my coat in the cloakroom of shoe-bags.
I shall say I went to look at the jungle-jim.
And looking at the moon through the old
    window   20
I yearned for this agony to be taken from me.

5. HISTORY LIKE THE RUSHING DEE

Asquat in a cloaca one Easter
I poked my trowel among its Chester tiles
For remnants of Roman sewage. I was
    sixteen,
The dust filled my nostrils. Then the trench
    sank;
Clay caked my boots, among surveying-poles
I tramped, seeking a lost legion. I was free
From home and the twentieth century for a
    week.
On my last day the sun beat fiercely down,
The sap smelt in the leaves, quickening my
    blood.
I could imagine the fatigue of digging.   10
I hurried round the cemetery down to the Dee,
Rocks cut its rushing flow, it was frothy

Under the bridge arches, shallow, alive.
I threw myself on the grass bank, giddy
With the yellow-white glare, and watched
The provincial men and the summery girls,
   while
The rush of the Dee hissed over the wet
   stones
I savoured the scholarship of Wace's
   Mycenae:
Each ramp-stone and lintel as accurately
Measured as the lineages in my two charts 20
Of Greek myth heroes and Roman Caesars.
I lay there until sunset, dreaming of the foam
Of history, of ancient times, and I felt
The rush of the years and empires on a power
That was as peaceful as the absent breeze.
So I dreamt until, glutted with Mycenae's
   stones,
I awoke in the ruins of Phaestos Palace.
The guide asked for a comment in his book.
I wrote: "To be is more important than to
   have."

The window. I bent double. My pack bumped
On my back as I crossed the gap. I ran, boots
   clumping.
I hugged the hedges, gasping till I reached
The cliff and safety. My boots were damp.
Crouching, I packed my beret, my belt, my
   lunch,
And then my sopping gaiters. Then I walked
To the edge of the cliff, peeled off my itching
   khaki.
Behind, the war was on: smokescreens by
   scrub,
The gleam of brass in the sun, remote orders
And obedient bursts of fire. On drying turf
I lay down, two hundred feet over dazzling
   blue,
And the wash of the indifferent sea on the
   granite teeth
Of the Stack Rock. Soon the sun was very
   hot,
And a quiet bloomed under the clover, and the
   humming bees.

6. CORPS CAMP

On Field Day we broke away and hid in
   ditches,
Put apples on the end of our rifles,
Fired blanks so they curved in an arc and fell
On our Captain. And in the Armoury later,
Studying toy warfare on the sandtable,
We buried villages behind his back
With one squash of a thumb. But this Corps
   Camp
Was different: we put up tents on a hill,
And slept on duckboards. There was an awful
   storm,
I woke in water, I was soaked, I was
   chilled   10
To the marrow. Then bugles and blanco,
The early barking of army NCOs
And the chatter of machine-gun volleys
Up distant valleys.
          It was two miles to the sea.
We were to have a war in the clifftop lanes.
Standing on waste ground for roll-call
   ("Sergeant"),
We were told, "Fall out for lunches and
   rifles."
I sidled up for my paper-bag. Quick – now!
Like a shot, I was behind the shed, under 20

7. MURDER IN THE DARK

The Christmas game: as the Fellowship
   Leader
Prepared lots, settling on the arm of a chair
She looked so proud, aloof and independent,
And above such things, with a full, round,
   breast
And languid gaze. Her looks went everywhere
But did not notice me. And how many nights
Through wind and rain had I followed or
   waited,
Wanting only a smile? Crouching under the
   coal-scuttle
I prayed for recognition.
          Up the darkened stairs,   10
In each bedroom there is an expectant silence
And whispers from a wardrobe, a quiet
   giggle.
Shapes behind doors, or lurking in corners,
Waiting for a creaking board, a prowling
   tread,
And the ugly thrill of a coldly deliberate hand
Closing slowly round the neck, or like a snake
Striking swiftly, quickening the blood with
   dread
And fascination, subduing the resisting breast;
Waiting for a scream. With gleaming eyes

22

A gloating adolescent waits to spring,   20
Tormenting his victim in his isolated mind,
Stripping her naked, stabbing her with a knife,
Transformed by the dark and the power in his
     pocket…
How far removed from my routine attack,
The feeble rape of fumbling fingers,
Her token scream, and the indignant scorn
In her bodily recognition!
 During the glaring inquisition
By the detective under the sitting-room
     searchlights,
I vowed to redeem that moment.

8. LEAVING SCHOOL

Between masters and praefects, the standing
     throng
Listens intently to the end of term address,
An advertisement for direct grant public
     schools.
Leaning like a groundling, Freeman does not
     hear
His name mourned as one who will be
     missed,
Not having excelled in leadership or public
     spirit.
The posthumous farce of summer arrange-
     ments
Brings a disrespectful yawn.
                    Amid flying feet,
And bawling, breaking voices, wandering, 10
He passes the boredom of the upper studies.
And if a master, stopping, asks, "What is the
     cause
Of your unnecessarily premature departure?"
Would you say, "What is the point of staying
     on?"
As if there were little to choose between
     staying and going?
Wheeling out of the bike shed, I pedal off
With a year or two to kill, and nothing to do
After a visit to Rome, and the Sicilian
     Madonna.
When I reach home I go for a walk to the
     shops,
Hands in forbidden pockets.   20

9. ETNA

And the satin swell grew dark; as we dipped
     our oars

The Catania lights glimmered from the shore,
And above us, in the silence, with each
     muffled splash,
Gratuitously stark in the sharp green dusk,
Etna towered higher; sitting in the stern,
I felt its scorn like the scorn in a dead man's
     absence
And I shuddered: hugely existing, but not
     alive,
It dwarfed me; it threatened me with its
     permanence,
Its dead existence crushed me, and with
     horror
I saw the earth in the post-human era.
Then from the prow rang out Lorenzo's tenor,
A paean of happiness rising up to the night,
"Sa-an – ta-a Nu-u-ci-i-a":
And as I thrilled, with a great spurting of red,
Falling away in an arc, the mountain burst
In a wild ejaculation.

10. OFFICE LOVE

In this office, faded yellow parchments
And torn files behind glass, on the tables,
Bound with old tape. The partner calls,
Clerks scurry from their holes, and stand and
     wait
While he telephones, and click their false
     teeth
Or nibble nervously with their rodent jaws.
Under the electric light in a bustling world,
Peeking out from my shell, I pretend to
     examine
An abstract of title.
                    Her footsteps echo,   10
Heel upon heel, dragging down my tautened
     nerves.
Prepared, I skulk under the rim of my collar
And rehearse the passing tugging of her skirt,
Between each tread, savour the perfumed air,
Peep up behind me. At the grimy window
In olive-green she peers anxiously, and
     cranes,
Scanning the gaslit street for the ordered taxi,
Eager to see the senior partner's back
And run downstairs to meet her wealthy lover.
She starts, I turn. Her steps recede, pulling 20
Lumps from my bleeding heart. No dreaming
     now
Of meeting her by chance in the musty strong-

room,
Unmocked by the assured. Despair beckons,
Oblivious of the signatures, the final cup of
tea,
Pointing forward to the lone tube journey
home
And evening in my room.
From eight to ten-thirty,
The trial of law books, the tedium of living.
I have not forgotten you, evenings of torment!

11. THE LONDON HELL

What sap unites these dry and splitting
branches?
Under the iron cathedral an autumn wind
Blows fallen leaves past the graveyard to the
tube.
Pressed in a pile of sere and crinkled faces
I could not imagine the time they had burst
into bud
On green, tender, supple, unifying boughs.
And in this condemned part of the decaying
stronghold
There is an agony of awareness in the
sepulchral gloom;
Among unburied fragments of equestrian
opiates,
Smith grimly costs betted moments on his
adding-machine;   10
Having awakened from a nicotine dream
Janes strains to surpass himself by the grimy
window,
And Davis weeps for an unrepeating freedom,
Dying and redying on the dungeon dicta-
phone;
Davis weeps at his repetition
Checking and rechecking his dictaphone.

On Tower Hill
I saw the will of man rise from its chains:
Supine on an olive groundsheet, ringed by a
crowd,
In ring-mail, he was bound, and four swords
thrust   20
To the throat of his Balaclava helmet.
While the coppers fell he writhed and
wriggled,
Striving to be born like a snake from a useless
skin
Or a perfect image from its chrysalis,

And with what speed he, lithe as an acrobat,
Leapt from the pile, bare arms and neck
unscarred,
And received his acclaim, exultant under his
sweat
With a master's scorn!
                    Smith, Janes and Davis, from
                         my room,
Costing and straining and clicking that dicta-
phone,   30
Crinkled faces waiting for a resurrection.

12. A DESTINY

In a Westgate boarding-house, I listened to
the rain.
I felt a strange peace.
On the Guildford golf-course, I dreamt of
fame,
And when I got back at sunset, and sat alone
And pushed aside my books, and pulsed with
purpose,
What, after the closing of a cupboard door,
Could have prevented me from resuming my
destiny
For four whole years of classics and the law?

On this fist and arm if a High Road
Five churches like congealed scabs   10
Each commemorate the same blood, which
you missed.
Through two maternal ancestors who were
preachers,
Freeman's allegiance is to Wesley, at the
wrist.
"I was turning out some books the other day
For the Jumble Sale, and it struck me some
Might be of interest to you; so here's a
bargain,
I'll reserve them until you've been and had a
look.
Sixpence each."
                    A destiny refound,
New altar-rails and new communion cloths 20
Where, no scholars, unaware of "dark Satanic
mills",
All bleated Blake like sheep and praised free
love.
I hid my antennae beneath my wig,
After the dislocated table-chatter
And the desperation of hysterical games

I scurried for a hole, rolling an image
Between my feathered legs.
I, who skulk, could be a cross-bearing god!

13. THE UNDERGROUND DEAD

Clackerty tickety pickety clapity clack.
Under the City, suspended breathless
Between bowler hat and sweaty make-up,
Among blank faces, writhing, stale armpits
Under an advert for deodorant, hear
The rustle of an impeded *Evening News*, or
    sighs,
Or the distant rush of a wind siroccoing
Down different tunnels.

        Before we jolted on
I heard, in silence, someone say my name, 10
Turned as towards a ghost. "Strange friend," I
    said,
"My neighbour in the Latin class last March,
You who cribbed on your knees under the
    dome,
How art thou come to this dark coast
    unburied?"
And he in heavy speech: "Articled by
My father in a black office, ill fate."
As though I talked he talked, insensitive
To frowns and ears, and unpocketing Sartre,
Concluded, "To be free", unaware of
My thought and theory, or of Trust
    Accounts, 20
Or the indignant mutters of comfortable
    corpses
In window-seat graves.
           As we rushed past the
    cemetery,
I said to myself, "There must be a
    resurrection,"
And a thousand sparrows flew up from the
    angel stones.

14. AN AWAKENING IN LONDON

(For Colin Wilson)

Digesting Sartre on a Chancery Lane platform
I saw a concave poster, PHILOSOPHY,
And should it not be my free choice for the
    day?
I memorised the address as the tube rushed in.
In a room off Haymarket, I was reborn;

For two enthralling hours I heard one
    message:
"Not by reasoning, or words, or learning from
    books
Is a wise man wise, but by observation,
Awareness of habit, command of experience.
Be more conscious."   10

        On the top of a London bus
I sought enlightenment, in a City suit
I broke the circuit of fragmentary dreams:
First I relaxed, then I commanded 'Stop all
    thought',
Then, one by one, I observed the senses,
Saw the seat in patterned red and green
And the platinum streak in the middle-aged
    woman's head,
Heard chesty wheezings under the diesel
    engine
And inane non-sequiturs on foul-smelling
    breaths,
Felt the weight of my body like a tired
    machine.   20
And after, the world was rich in varied
    detail,
It was as if I had been living in a waking
    dream,
And I glimpsed a future superconsciousness
Whose shadow crossed the yob in the front
    seat.

And Amos came up from the country and
  spoke against Baal
        And town-bred Isaiah listened
            Before Tiglath-Pileser pushed
            West;
And modest Jeremiah came up from his
  village and spoke against Baal
        And cataleptic Ezekiel listened 30
            Nineteen years before the fall
            of Jerusalem.
There was ferment in the Fleet Street coffee-
    bar,
You could see it in everyone's eyes, the old
    repudiated,
The new a question; a time of transition,
Few saw we'd settled down into a quiet
    decline.
When *he* came in we applauded, when he
    went

We stood in a ring near the empty beer bottles
And, battered with books, we scratched our
  heads and puzzled
Over his angry message, "Our civilisation
Is in spiritual decay."   40
          But I knew,
From the unreal limbo, there is descent down-
  wards,
To the earthy real, and ascent upwards
To self-surpassal in consciousness;
I knew ὁδὸς ἄνω κάτω ,
The way up and the way down are the same.

And I knew that nothing could ever be the
  same.

15. CRIMES AND VIRTUES

In this black office, faded yellow parch-
  ments....
And I knew that nothing could ever be the
  same.
O the kindness and sacrifice that had to be
  smashed,
So that I could surpass myself with an Isaiah's
  power.

Satutes and blackened stone
Restrain a mystic's dream;
Restraint and bad conditions
Are a good discipline
But an artist must be a professional;
Among Angry intellectuals   10
Or alone by a Forest stream
I approached a decision:
"I oppose the bourgeois sin,
There must be a revolution."

In an unrepeated dream I read the accusations
Before the marriage-bed: "Notwithstanding
Your kindness and love, which is bounteous,
And sacrifice and selfless devotion,
You committed domination by excess of
  security,
Preferring business to artistic risk,   20
Quoting your choirs and orchestras as
  precedents;
And you committed judgement by Puritanic
  standards,
Forced ecclesiastical attendance in the name
  of discipline,

Frowned on scholastic misdemeanours, or
  attractions,
Instilling shame of wine or women or song.
You committed conformism, by extension
  from these,
Esteeming trichine smartness and social
  charm,
Classy symbols and christenings and
  extroversion,
Opposing deviation with insecure fears.
And you committed organisation, substituting
  arrangements,   30
Kind interference, for spontaneous affection,
Freezing my feelings with frightened
  investigations
(Especially at greetings) from an outgrown
  parenthood.
Then you committed deception, compensating
  a relationship,
And I am defiant, amoral, rebelliously
  individual,
Ridiculously shy, honest, resentful of
  demands.
But you are not to blame, only the marriage
  system...."

A few years forward, and these crimes are
  virtues.
I work, am teetotal, and probably Christian,
I venerate the disciplines of our tradition.   40
But now I have the benefit of having found
  myself.
Then I was lost in the unreality of a legal
  prison.

16. THE POWER BY THE LAKE

No missing breakfast that week. I was down
Early, searched the pigeon-holes daily, until
My father's envelope came. I left the Lodge,
Walked past the Cottages to the College
  gardens,
Meandered to the lake, sadly detached
From my doom, the entire future pressing
And I observed my feelings, free
Yet foreordained. Could I abandon Law
For Literature? Under the stone arch, alone,
I opened it, swallowed the broken
  surrender,   10
"I consent", and some great shadow of
  authority

Shattered into fragments. Sun-flecked,
    lawless,
Free, I wept.
          The early morning blazed,
Trees of every green linked earth and blue-
    white sky
In the lake. Adazzled, a great power filled me.
Purified, I grew, head sun-scorched, feet
    earth-rooted,
Stomach pulsing water-trees; I towered
Giddy, vast as God, I had always existed,
Earth-trees-sky would die, not I, the life-
    beat   20
And order, the permanent sole meaning.
I knew without understanding, as now
Without thinking, I know my own surname.
All creation was me, a pounding power,
And infinitely good.
            Breakfastless in my room,
I pondered the impure sleep of my lake-like
    mind
Which, when woken with such purified force,
Could be transformed by such a mystic
    power.

17. THE CRICKET CLUB DANCE

Shattered into fragments, my chains fell off,
My inner war against all that restrained me
Had ended, requiring a readjustment:
I poured my energies into Milton
But still there was a surplus, like a premature
    peace.
Between my breaking-out into action,
And my withdrawal into contemplation,
My unstable being would ejaculate
With hysterical exultation.
           In the cricket pavilion   10
I stood suspended between past and future,
Mourning the empty bluster in Derek's words,
And reading the adverse judgement in
    Chegwedden's eyes
While cricket colleagues waltzed with YC
    girls
Or ground out raucous laughter behind beer.
That black-haired one. Why else the shaggy
    hair and Italian
Buskins? Or else confess to cowardice,
Admit you are saddled with a stable
    personality

Unchangeable if unliked, go home con-
    temptuous
From typists and navvies you need never see
    again,   20
Not one of whom was born with samba
    knowledge,
And no breaking-out for dreading a shake of a
    head....
Become that businessman striding to the
    gents.
I said to Chegwedden, "Shall I really tell
    them?"
As if I could squash it all under my heel.
"Let's go," I said, and I drank up and went out
And the solitude under the stars was like a
    choice:
Turning my back on the remote saxophone
I felt exhilarated, I was intense,
And before we had lurched half way up to the
    station   30
And gone into a field to pee, I could pick
Star after star, biting each to the core.
"Are you there, God?" I called drunkenly,
    free,
And I roared out into the universe that I was
    free,
The power was sparkling from the tips of each
    hair
On my head as I shouted down the telephone
Of the night: an "I" that had to be overthrown.

18. A TEARFUL SURRENDER

And Freeman yawned in the upper circle.
Beside him in the dark, a lady six weeks ripe
Scathingly made remarks above the sound-
    track,
Ignoring the mutters of thick-stockinged
    ladies
And thin-skinned men in buff mackintoshes.
At length, charged with celluloid
    suppressions,
"I can't stick any more," she said, rising,
And Freeman stood and pushed past
    unyielding knees,
And escorted her back to her basement
    bedsitter
In the Iffley Road.   10
           Before the gasfire
The lady fell to luf-talkyng, waiting
For the kettle: "sir, 3if 3e be Wawen."

And Freeman, caring for his cortaysye on the
    carpet,
"pa3 I be not now he pat 3e of speken."
And she: "3e are welcum to my cors." Then
    quop
Freeman, trembling for his trawpe, "What
    would
Your lord say?" And, ringless, in silence she
    undressed
And opened her white arms to him, urging,
"In the tobacco tin, but it doesn't matter,"   20
Hurrying to forget her absent lover.
But, paralysed, the fumbling Knight delayed,
Nakedly nervous, too suddenly demanded,
And suddenly, the high-born lady wailed,
"Oh what am I doing?" Hopeful Freeman:
"Would you rather not?" She: "It's too late
    now,
No, continue," weeping. Humiliating tears
Splashed down her surrendering cheeks. He:
    "By my pite
pat passe3 alle poynte3, I release you,"
And he twisted aside. "You're so noble," she
    blubbered,   30
"You needn't have done that."

19. HITCH-HIKING BACK FROM GREECE

After the fifth week I wanted to return.
She said, "How selfish, just because I was ill
And you'd seen everything before I came,"
Ignoring our arrangement. I gave in.
Knowing I was eking out six pounds, she
    would say,
"I don't think you've given me back all my
    change,"
Eat steak, and suggest we stayed at a five star
    hotel.
Five times a night she would wake me and
    say
"I can't sleep – talk to me," or, "I've wasted
    my life,"
Or, snapping Emily Bronte, "What I dislike
    most   10
Is your vulgarity."
             Beside a dusty track
For three days we sat in the baking heat,
Eating nothing while a dozen cars bumped by,
Mocked by the Macedonian military.
Her spiky fingers clawed my consciousness,

And all through the misty mountains the
    Erynnes
Sat by my shoulder, until, on Dubrovnik cliff,
Cymbals beat in my temples, bats whirred and
    crawled
In the shadows of the glare, and with a final
    shriek   20
I nearly flung my twanging nerves into the
    sea.
On the boat I hid, and from a vantage point,
    saw
Her squash a reserving hat in a deck-chair,
Witnessed the indignant friends, the exchange
    of blows.
I did not interfere.
             She is dead now.
A few years later we scuffled through leaves
In the Forest. She was bare-footed. She took
    her life
Near where we saw antlers in an Essex
    stream.

20. A TWIRLED STEM

And Freeman sat hunchbacked over Bishop
    Wulfstan
Near hair-greased bricklayers and sporty
    spivs,
Coterie-cornered by the two mechanics,
Christmas-Eve-grievous, Mackeson-mourning
The meaningless mouth-gaping of the ghostly
    throng.
Carols wafted from the radio. Past Jeanie,
Who was mopping tables, lolled in the upper
    saloon
A bunch of Young Conservatives, gentyl
    knightes
And faire maidens, weary from sports cars,
Elegantly unthirsty, carelessly conversing   10
In City-English: "Comdidacomdi,
Comdidida."
             Apart, bored, the black-haired
             one,
Idly twirling a Pymm's stem, unattended,
Drumming with her fingers on the shiny table.
And should I go over, fearless of their
    formulations,
Vanquish all to my will, and subjugate
Them as subjects? Should I assertively ask,
"I'm doing market research, what does
    'Godes yrre'

Mean to you?" And I was shattered into
    fragments   20
Of broken glass, a cluster of half-truths
In the deceptive spring. I saw two leave,
She with her lined face and her Italian hair,
I heard her voice chanting "Amore", and then
I heard gulping pipes; then a creaking stair.
And did you not take her down to the Quad
And when she asked "Come with me to the
    Lodge,"
And you replied, "I can't – I'm in my
    slippers,"
Did she not say, with a scornful toss of her
    head,
"How can anyone so logical have
    emotions?"   30
And did your mind not ripple? I saw you part
Abruptly. And did she not have to be quiet
And less assured?
        And in the singsong
On a Saturday night, a dying traditional life
Calls to a black-haired girl who is unattended,
Who twirls and retwirls her stem, wishing she
    were
With the long-locked fellow who fingered his
    Mackeson.

21. DRUGTAKING

Lawless in Hinksey, the Gipsy crew reveal
Their arts to rule the working of men's brains.
Couples lie on tattered pads, and pat to
    Charlie Parker,
Dig the cool rhythms of gently sighing thighs.
At the broken desk, dressed like some
    Kerouac,
A mental traveller takes another pill
And travels on at forty lines a minute.
Then someone said "Who's for turning on?"
And all at once they sang, "Crazy, man,
    we've
Nothing else to do."
        Under a naked bulb
I knew the infection of the twentieth century.
I knew how Romans wore barbarian manners
And perished at forty heartbeats a minute.

22. A COFFINED COUNTERPANE

Freeman compulsively groped through
    mythology:

The return of Cain, the wandering Prodigal,
And his destruction of the saintly Abel,
Secular stoicism and loss of faith.
But who *was* he, that first of obsessive priests,
Driven by slow apostacy to fiery death,
That wooden eunuch to his dead father's
    will?
You did not know, locked in his furious
    embrace.
Nor did you recognise the futile fugitive,
Exiled for butchering his father's beasts,   10
Returning to find out if he was forgiven,
Outwardly self-sufficient, impenitent,
But reluctantly leaving the glowing hearth,
Turning his back on Abel's sad widow
To despair at Eastern dawns like some
    wanderer.
He was sustained from nothing by pagan
    virtues,
By courage and enduring independence.
You did not know you had anticipated
A lifetime's conflict.
        But you needed someone   20
To share it when, returning at nine, you saw
Candles in the windows between the curtains,
When you tottered down the path, stumped up
    the stairs,
Heard a Nocturne trickling through her open
    door,
And her gentle voice, "Would you like some
    coffee?"
You fell on the bed, befuddled, and you stared
At the knobbled coffins on the counterpane,
You smiled, watching her clink a spoon in
    black,
"If I make my divan I must lie in it,
If I dig my grave..." She had a geography
    man,   30
But one chance-moment, a joke, and you
    betrayed,
Opening the Providential door to your
    betrayal.
Was it Abel or Cain, lying on that coffined
    counterpane?

And would you live it, suffer it all again?
Yes, if you could have a retrospective
    knowledge,
Go back with hindsight and share a forward
    vision,

Yes, a hundred times yes! To repeat the death
of Cain,
And relive the resurrection of a redeemed
Abel!

23. A GRUBBY SOUL

Dreaming of empires and the law of Beauty
Freeman wrote: "In the green dusk lay
another day."
And when he went to the pay-desk at La Roma
The fuzzy youth said, "You'd better watch it
mate."
Constantia turned and looked the other way.
In the passage between two shop windows,
Pressing on glass, Freeman wrote out a
cheque,
His Parker Fifty-one in his right hand.
Said the youth with three pals, "That is my
bag."
Said Freeman over his shoulder, "Don't be
funny."   10
Then he was jerked round onto his knuckle-
duster,
He was going back, his head hit the window
glass,
Then he rebounded onto fuzzy hair,
Which butted his jaw, he bounced back to a
swinging fist.
Then all was silent, save for their running feet
And Constantia's scream.
                    Three days later,
Pondering how Saint Augustine found the
Light
In his soul, he went into Constantia's room,
And there sat the fuzzy, waiting for her
friend.   20
"Aha," said Freeman, "there is justice in
Providence!
Are you going to take it standing up, or
sitting?"
He raised his fist, the fuzzy cowered and
begged.
But irony was a thicker stick, by far!
"In the Dark Ages of your memory,
Can you recall a Paradise?" he asked,
And disregarding his "Ay?": "Did *you* take
To your heels and become an unwilling exile
And dream of moving in from the raw
autumnal cold
Of your outer darkness to a peace within

morning mist?   30
Your need to wash your grubby soul in calm,
Then darn it with the needle of my
forgiveness.
Here, have some tea."
                    And when, emerging later,
He heard his future settled, all confirmed,
He was calmly unimpressed.

24. AN AMATEUR FORTUNE-TELLER

A cluster of prismatic mirrors
And a roomful of hidden events.
Kneeling on a floor
Miss Swain said, "I'm a Norfolk witch;
Once I took a photo of my mother in a
churchyard
And over her shoulder you could see a
transparent skull."
With an incredulous murmur, clearly very
impressed,
Freeman sipped lemon tea and scratched an
itch.
And seeing her coiled and squinting in a ring
of cards,
I saw her floundering in an invisible web-like
net
Whose toils she span herself in a musty
corner;
I thought, Should I set her free with one puff
of breath,
With one sweep of my hand? But who was
deluded
When, having explored each pre-determined
chance,
Having absorbed each predestined head, she
said,
"I see golden and black together: that is ill-
starred"?

25. BOOKSTEALING

And Freeman strolled into a Charing Cross
Road bookshop
And stood beside a friend from school, who
said:
"Once I stood alone, without so much as a
raincoat
Or camouflaging newspaper. Four assistants
Kept watch, one for each wind. It was in a
basement.

I took down two books, whipped one under
    my left arm
Inside my jacket, and replaced the other.
Then I took a cheap one and sauntered to the
    till,
Singing with freedom."
              Through the lighted window 10
The dead stood patient in an ordered line
Watching for the crime with expressionless
    faces,
Watching the anthologies of French
    symbolists
With the inquisitive concern of a London
    crowd,
And no breath stained the transparent glass.
Seeing him poised, Freeman whispered, "You
    should be careful –
That browser under the mirror, he's been here
    all day,
And those bifocals, can't you see they're the
    latest telescopic?
If it's a matter of a couple of pounds, it's
    better to pay."
When he turned, his eyes shone with
    significance,   20
And he murmured, "Do not imagine I have to
    take it;
Only that I cannot be restricted, and least of
    all by habit,
For every moment could prove me a complete
    master,
Chooser of my destiny." He walked straight out,
And only the indignant dead, chattering on the
    pavement,
Drew attention to the empty space in the
    lighted window.

26. PRIVATE EYE

Freelance debt-collector and private eye,
Freeman investigated the relations
Between a Polish Lady and a Mister Bly.
"I live here with my sister and no one else,
Now get out," she screamed; Freeman swiftly
    complied,
Pausing to strike an attitude by the shelf,
Lingering pertinently by the blackened pipe.
Outside, Higgins, old lag, revved up his bike,
Expressed pecuniary thanks for the
    information;
Freeman said nothing in a TV imitation.

27. AN ISAIAH INFECTED

And blind Amoz ruled with a broken sceptre:
"Did Lear not require an hundred retainers,
Am I not entitled to one?" Around
His sickcouch in the night's unchearefull
    dampe,
His dependents trembled. "He has rebelled
    against me.
Should he who denied us so much deny us
    this?
I say, accursed be he and his associate
Who has led him astray."
              After the twelfth stroke,
And lo! the wishèd day is come at last,   10
The Prodigal spits out his breath-freshening
    spearmint,
Trips on the step, wrongly turns the handle,
Then enters the throne-room with meticulous
    care,
Stands like one mistaken near the Venetian
    glasses,
Blinking with beer. Rising on his elbows,
    Amoz:
"Not to speak of chits and wenches, or
    ungodliness,
Or dishonour through disattire, your wasted
    years
And disregard of our concern, or social
    esteem,
Your ecumenical arrogance and dependence
    on our pocket,
And rejection of the security for which we
    sacrificed   20
A decade's sweat, your attitude to your blood
Is disgraceful." And he arose, shaking,
And stood, tottering, pointing a finger
Before the empty glasses.
              And I, Isaiah, recite:
Woe is me! I am a man of unclean lips,
And I dwell in the midst of a people of
    unclean lips.
I, who have foreseen the Fall of Judah, have
    been infected
By this sinful nation.

28. SMALLPOX ALLEY, BAGHDAD

On either side of the sewer and the rotting
    sheep
Is the timeless slumber of shaded Turkish

courtyards.
Above the paddling children on the chaikhana
    wall,
A portrait of the Leader and a bloodstained
    hand.
Over the babble of a medieval market
The blue and yellow erection of a gilded
    minaret.
Passing Lurs strain under office wardrobes,
Past a careering cartwheel.
 And here is their prison.
I walk through this unattended gate to this
    compound,
"Losing my way," looking for two students.
In the open air, on hands and knees they peep
From waist-high zoo cages.
 Hooked beaks and hooded crows.
Around the broken body mourn screaming
Nuns, who devour the holy carrion,
Tearing doctrine from the loving bones....
O Baghdad! You are infected by noxious
    germs.
Would I could squash them all under my heel!

29. A PRIEST AT THE AMBASSADOR'S

In the floodlit limbo, the Ambassador's
    garden,
A thousand perfumes hang like tobacco
    smoke
And perforate my nostrils like withered roses;
Here in all their aggressive opinionation,
The foreign company are heatedly agreeing,
Shaking the universe with their scholarship,
Mosquitoes whine and drink in forbidden
    female places,
Gat-toothed old hags flaunt tarted-up faces
And I observe each tragi-comic scene
Before the toast to the Queen.   10
            Seeking the real
I prowl like a Third Secretary over the turf,
Pretend I'm neither a beetle nor a god,
Neither flinch from clichés, nor scorn a
    human voice.
Glimpsing Jeanie, I wheel and use my elbows,
And there, soaking up whisky, sprawled the
    priest.
I knew I would feel tense until I'd talked with
    him,
As I always do with priests, I got straight on

With my ghastly tale of brain physiology,
And listened for a refutation that never
    came.   20
Slopping his drink, he muttered obscurely,
"The horror of existence without God," and
    wandered off,
And all round shadows flickered in the night,
And I was superior to the Ambassadress, and
    to Jeanie
With her black-lace stockings.

30. DOVER SOLE AND A WHISTLE

And Freeman went on an outing to Gorringes.
Squeezing a slice of lemon on his Dover sole
He cocked a detached ear to his swollen wife
While his mother caught the waitress's
    attention,
Asked black-haired Jeanie for a jug of water.
Later, in a murky shop with flaking walls,
He witnessed the sale of his moth-eaten suit,
Then greeted the two half-termers, and
    absorbed
The gilded paint on Buckingham Palace gates.
Returning under a scaffolding, he bristled   10
At a workman's whistle.
            In Victoria Station,
For the platform gates were closed, and the
    pregnant must sit,
Barred from the platform, foetally considerate,
They rested on a bench near waddling
    pigeons,
After an independent purchase of a fashion
    magazine.
And Freeman refused the kindly proffered note
But took his fares. And all round, another
    world –
A sharper, a down-and-out, the girl by the
    Gents –
Churned with the chaos beneath their
    chatter   20
And safe shutters, which he could never
    share.

31. THREE CLOSENESSES

For two hours we sat alone in the corner,
Sipping pints between intimate question and
    answer,
And each experience he gave me from himself
As if to say, "I've saved it for you – take it,"

And taking each twitch of his eyebrow, each
    tremor of his hairlip,
I felt so close to his sensitive sufferings,
I nearly sobbed with joy. After we had peed,
He hung on my shoulder.
               And was it any different
After the vacant seat, when I came in
With intense eyes and a distracted air,
Sat by the ironing, ignored TV,
Recited regrets for my absence, ruffling my
    hair
And watching confidences splash into your
    tea?
Or when I reflected on what had been said
    while you sucked me dry?
Nor was I conscious that Saturday, my love,
Listening to your chit-chat in the suburban pub,
Exhausted with creation, and fulfilled,
Barely listening to your blind encouragement
Or lack of concern at my diminishing credit,
Your contempt of class, your fingers in my
    shaggy hair,
And feeling unaccountably euphoric
Like an aching schoolboy after a hard match
In a steaming bath.

             Later I had an illicit drink
With your sick father in a sitting-room
Once denuded by pawnbrokers. He became
    maudlin.
"I won on the Yankee."
         "And so?"
              And so whatyouexpect,
Since the house's coming down, and every-
    one's on my back,
And I haven't got a penny."
          We became reflective.
He told me his mother stripped herself naked
On her death-bed, while his father slept with
    the maid.
Then he stumbled up, embraced me and wept,
    "My son."

Three closenesses like outgrown suits.

32. QUARREL WITH A FRIEND

In a smoky pub off Leicester Square
An angry tension strains the atmosphere.
With Cambridge honesty, Chegwedden
    prefers

Psychology to philosophical ideas
About the universe, which make the hero tick,
Observes the motives in relationships,
Why the eponymous prig is so dynamic
Or why he's so hysterically manic,
Through whose eyes the work is seen, and
    who's a bore,
Why they all talk, not what they all aver;   10
Says, "Who cares if the universe is irrelevant,
Who cares if it's balanced on an elephant?"
Then, with realistic eyes, and cold despair,
He abjures all art as a life-enhancer,
Objecting to one pessimistic author,
"You don't get anything out of a mirror,"
Declares himself indifferent to perfection
Through organised perceptions in a pattern –
Why sweat for satisfaction from ordered rules
When there is satisfaction in easing
    bowels?   20
"Listen," he says, "I am growing bourgeois.
I am cautious, secure, lacking in adventure,
I have narrowed down my interests
To girls and social confidence, and the test
Of my weekly job. Our meetings are dead-end
    devices
To pass the time. I prefer other vices,
I no longer make the same demands on life
That you do. Discuss your demands with your
    wife."

Slumped in a vast and empty station, Freeman
Is disillusioned with this sometime friend: 30
Initiator and exhibitionist,
I traded my experience for his ideas on art.
Demanding no more, I encroached on no
    weakness,
Which led him to like me for my tact alone
Until, accepted, no longer having to impress,
He rebelled against his role as my touchstone,
And followed the secret counsels of his heart.

On an electric train he wept trickles
Of blood, sitting deadpan-faced and alone.

33. A DEATH

This room on the first landing is unfriendly.
Beneath the laboured breathing of the dying
    man
I can hear the nocturnal ravings of a brother,
The rustle and silence of French au pairs,

And my father's quaver from the dark dark
    corner
As he told me I wouldn't rock my sister any
    more.
(And I was filled with importance, confided
    in.)
In the door I wonder whether to disturb him;
Out of the window the stark indifference of
    lights
In his Council Offices.   10
         The last drink,
The ritual Guinness in the pewter tankards
To pledge recission of a lifetime's dis-
    agreement.
I raise him, put a pillow under his shoulders,
Then pour slowly to preserve the richness.
(Not too much froth, says his glazed, critical
    eye.)
He stutters, then his trembling hand reaches;
Disregarding aid, with shaky defiance
He gulps, then splutters. His breathing is
    convulsed.
He labours. I snatch his tankard. He
    conquers.   20
Then disintegrates, crying incoherently in the
    dark
"I don't want to die"; groping for my hand,
    gripping
The living, clutching. And I was all and
    helpless.
"This is the end," he sighed, baffled, angry,
And downstairs the television tube went
And the picture shrank to the size of a postage
    stamp.

And looking at the moon, he understood:
From one single cell during a gleam of
    sunlight,
Into night and silence, man came and swelled
    and went.
From the end of priceless existence, he saw
    through: 30
An icy cinder, in an endless night.

Later my mother said, "Look there's nothing
    frightening
About death," drawing back the sheet in that
    stillness.
I lingered on alone near his grey still face,
Fascinated yet afraid in that awful stillness.

34. THE SPLITTING OF THE DARK AT THE STRAWBERRY HILL POND

In the late autumn I took my last look
At the pond. By the fallen tree I happened to
    exist,
In the sunlight I stood bereaved in an inner
    dark
In the disturbed reflection.

Ah, but the darkness split;
In the late autumn sun I thrilled to the point of
    the plan,
The pond blazed in an unknowable revelation.
The silver birch caught fire, then I lit up,
The white branches flared up in a living
    scheme,
Licked and glowed and crackled into flame,
    burned   10
Up the blue sky. Mallards and water boatmen
Bobbed, throbbed and sizzled in the roasting
    orb,
Generation after generation, caught
In a spiralling dance of consciousness,
Whirling round and upwards and up, evolving
To the fire-like power of a higher
    consciousness.
I thrilled with order, I knew why it all meant,
I turned and left the spreading furnace of my
    heart
And walked back through the beeches to
    Robin Hood Lane,
And a deep calm and peace filled my
    bereaved dark.   20

35. DEMIURGE AMONG THE BIKINIS

And here's Brunetto, that dying man,
Blown out twenty years more by his allergy
Against himself, brooding on his death,
Brooding on the alternative, the madness of
    cortisone,
Lonely in cities, buttressed up by despair.
Slouching into the shadows of Nichigeki
    doorways
He seeks a shifty man in darks who flits,
A peddler of films. A Rabelaisian Puritan,
Followed by Freeman.
         In a purple haze,   10
Rose-tinted, neoned and pop-blaring, through

a door
To the subconscious, see, twisting, many faire
    urges
Shrieking in welcome, bursting in bikinis,
A place pickt out by choice of best alyve
That nature's work by art can imitate.
Dodging thighs that drip with frozen sweat,
The dwarf brings beer. They poetaste,
Preferring rhythm to false-eyed Jeanie,
And Freeman is created by his imaged
    demiurge
While all the while, right over him she
    hong,   20
Ogling a likely Paramoure. Said Brunetto:
"Not to speak of your meddling intellect, or
    control,
Or confusion of art and essay, your simplified
    complexity
And constricted flow, or fallacious continuity,
Art is born from the whole being: be wholly
    whole."

He paid the bill, and like some paternal ghost,
Generous in failure, wandered out into the
    dark street,
And with scorched face, resumed his despair.

36. ADVICE TO A STUDENT

A year I tubed back from that University
With a Japanese student who wriggled her hips
As we clattered into stations. Then she grew
    quiet,
She felt full, swollen and proud. On Tokyo
    station
She asked me to drink coffee and listen.
Two months ago, she said, she loved her
    teacher.
Impatient for knowledge she broke her seal
In Kamakura. He said, "I love you,"
And went to Paris for six months, an ego
Of thirty with a hundred scalps. "Advise
Me, sensei," she said, with quivering lips.
"Regret nothing," I said, "the law-givers
Don't know, only you can only learn. Drain
    life dry.
Can a child smell throbbing, a Rechabite
    gin?"

And was she a stranger when you turned
    again,

And did a new love begin?
Or wondering who she thought you, did you
    shudder,
As the birds flew up and the one-eyed train
    nosed in?

37. AN AMERICAN PROFESSOR

They had a pre-prandial skirmish over
    "moral":
Freeman could not understand him because he
    spoke
American, he thought Freeman was being
    petty.
And, reclining in silence, Prudence Wine,
Geographically neutral, impartially observed
The English distaste for generalised
    assertions,
The self-evidence of some American
    assumptions
And a particular American reluctance to
    consider
From every side. After carving the joint,
    Scholander
Imperiously praised Yeats' "imagery",   10
"He had a good imagination." Said Freeman,
"To us imagery is more than imagination."
Bristling, Professor Scholander poured
    scorn,
Sighing to Heaven at Freeman's dis-
    agreement.
Over brandy he declared, "Elizabeth the First
Was greater than St. Teresa." Said Freeman,
"Can they be compared, a politician, a saint?"
And Scholander turned with a lambasting
    fury.
When he said, "Auden told me he went into
    the Church
Because the Christians can make a good
    H-bomb,"   20
Freeman laughed, knowing the date of
    A New Year Letter.
Ignoring his hostess's anxious admonitions,
Scholander assailed personally, until
Freeman asked, "What's the purpose of your
    existence?"
Expecting no answer. Misunderstanding,
Scholander pronounced it insolence. Deeming
A facile idea original, he left.
Walking behind him with Prudence, Freeman
    said,

"A perfect example of how ideas
Can rest on emotions. The man's un-
   married."   30

And in the taxi he talked to her, not him,
Till she got out a Shinjuku Station.
Then Scholander ceased to conceal his
  attraction
From himself, his aggression turned to
  affection.
His hand touched Freeman's knee as he gave
  his card,
Said, "Would you like to come back to my
  flat near Ikebukuro,
And listen to some medieval music?"

38. PARADISE VALLEY

I said to myself, "Despair has clogged up my
  eyes,
I need clearing out, I need to know I exist."
So I turned my back on the sea and took my
  stick
And the path up into the horseshoe valleys.
Shrieking cicadas crawled up the walls of my
  skull
Trying to get out through my ears like a
  swarm of bees
And each whoop of my heart echoed in the
  giant bamboo
Like a long-tailed bird.
Ducking bulging spiders in red and blue,
Passing a peasant bending over her paddy, 10
I crossed the old planks. My blood quickened,
Ascending to Paradise.
     Above this secluded valley
In silence, shrikes circled with outstretched
  wings,
Casting their shadows on brilliant butterflies.
I trod warily, armed, but nothing struck
Like an arrow from the hedge. At the stony
  bank
I turned at right angles, scanning the under-
  growth,
Each limb tensed to recoil, seeking the
  Horror.
When I reached the end I felt disappointed 20
With undischarged tension. A slither – I
  turned:
Two yards away and still – a black snake;
  erect

But quite still; my whole being watched for its
  fork
As, poised, we stood our ground in con-
  frontation.
I pounced with my forked stick and pinned its
  neck
And examined the monotonous markings of a
  killer.
Then as I leapt back it turned and writhed
  away.
Looking up at the shrikes, I felt exhilarated,
I was flushed with life, I was cleansed; going
Down to the world I ran and danced for
  joy.   30

39. A GARDEN TEMPLE

The chanting has stopped, only the flying
  beetle
Disturbs the hot night's silence.
The rows of seekers are silent,
Bare soles upward on cramped thighs, knee-
  caps down,
Both thumbs at the navel.
Chests rise, noiselessly breaths fall on the
  stillness
And soon the half-closed lids begin to droop
As each one sinks away from blurs and
  shadows
Into the darkness of his well.
     At the third bell 10
Smashing the silence, summoning to koans,
I reached a state where nothing surprised me.
Not even the shout "Kura, kura", the smack
Of the stick on a sleeper's back could distress
  me.
I said to myself, I will sit before a mandala
And, working inwards, I will pass each con-
  centric ring
Of my experience, until I have reached the
  centre;
Then, when I have reconciled my con-
  tradictions
I shall know what is unreal, I shall know my
  Self.
I know the complexity of simplified
  diaries,   20
That I cannot grasp myself whole in one
  moment
In any convenient synthesis, that my Self is
  the knower;

My Self is not; timeless, it can only be known
    through experience,
And what is known in one moment may be
    different the next,
For the forms of Self are continuously in flux
    and accretion
Like a Japanese garden and a pile of weeds.
I will see nothing in the centre for I am doing
    the seeing.

Fine rain of Rosan and the tide of Sekko.
When I returned it was just the same as when
    I first left them.
I am in familiar places, but I have
    changed.   30

40. SATORI

As I tortured my body
In satori's outer form
An amorphous shadow obscured the polished
    floor
And spoke to my self from a future dawn.
On Tower Bridge, I felt gravity snap,
I fcll headlong into space; I was alone
In a vast and indifferent universe, waiting
To die and not-exist for ever, not knowing
    why:
A smallness in an eternal silence without
    purpose
While hostesses served drinks and pickled
    prattle.   10
And not the lanterns in the gnarled pine trees,
Nor the dark outline of fishermen's boats by
    the road,
Not the phallic lanterns in swollen Shinto
    shrines
Nor the bamboo rustling in the breeze could
    deceive me.
But now all was different. "You have begun
    to grow,
Unlike those somnambulists who have
    tumbled
To the painless quiet of a cottage grave.
Now, sitting alone and asking whether you
    knew
And wondering why you should expect to
    know,
Sitting one evening alone in your sunlit
    room,   20
You have renounced all why, and found your

being's ground.
No more will you ask anxiously, with a touch
    of dread,
'Am I mature?' Now, if you clench your eyes,
You will stare on the fires of a thrilling white
    vision,
As when the bottom of your reason fell away
Into a deep abyss, and you were suspended
Before you floated down to a new terrain
Where no depression rises like any fog,
No bat-eared priests with fangs and vulture-
    wings
Swarm in the drains or wheel patiently in   30
The empty sky."
              My soul is a white light.
Amid lazing bodies on the roasting beach,
I was discontented. Excess of energy
Clenched my fingers among the dried sea-
    weed.
I left my family and friend for the timbered
    house.
Nothing swooped with curved talons round
    my windy head.
The cicadas were singing like wires in a sea-
    gale,
With tension fed by scorn for pretence and
    lies,
Unsociable with that being of comfort and
    night –   40
Fixed, not developing from or towards, not
    discovering –
I calmed myself and tortured my closed eyes,
A purblind moth flying round and round the
    light,
A moth flying round and round a barely
    glimmering light.

41. ANDRIZESTHE

Chatting with a chamberlain in the corridor,
Strolling with the Prince down a Palace
    sidewalk
I shuddered over my shoulder for enemy
    planes
While the souls of his ancestors chirped in
    their nesting-boxes.
I thought, I will be free from all my past
    attitudes,
And a free act rioted through the universe
Which cracked down the centre, like a
    dropped egg.

There was a crack down the sky, and in the
    bathroom
I was flooded with golden light. I slept
And sat on after lunch in a Turkish
    restaurant.   10
Then the earth shook, the wind of the East
    broke
And the next day I was filled with a round
    white sun
Which dazzled.
                    In the centre of the universe
Like a sun holding a galaxy in whirling place
All opposites and pluralities were held
    together
And there was a pole star between life and
    death.
And suddenly the tunnel ended.
Ruin, once I was an unwilling exile,
Once, betrayed by an ingratiating ape,   20
I moved in from a raw autumnal cold
And wondered how a small seed could
    become an oak,
But now I understood, the centre of the
    universe
Was a Power as big as this Golden Flower,
This four-faced sun, shining on each wind of
    the compass.
"Ἀνδρίζεσθε," I told him, "be a man."

42. A VAST PALACE AND A CHIMING CLOCK

In this suburban hall, the dust resettles
On warming pan, on gong and padded stick,
On dumbbells, on the broken barometer,
On treasure-chest and silver visiting-plate.
Ghosts of aproned maids and side-burned
    butlers
Glide in the cluttered stillness of neglect.
In the sitting-room window, on a summer
    evening,
I put on the hands of a clock that will not
    start,
I am free from historical progression.

Now I am like an improvising actor severed
    from my plot.   10
That old man, waiting on the village bench,
Has he taken possession of himself, or does
    he know only
Fragments of broken moments, fragments of

himself?
I said to myself, I must occupy my
    experience,
For to know one's past is to know one's
    present,
And unescorted at the exhibition
I could not connect each arbitrary fragment,
Each marble head or faded painting. In no
    deserted hall
Could I relate myself to a pattern,
Juxtaposition denied the development   20
On each wall. I said to myself,
I must explore each chamber, for I am like a
    stranger
In a vastly complex palace of my own
    construction
Near ivied walls rippling in a distorting
    mirror.
I ask the wind: a stranger, or a prisoner?
Do I repeat myself according to a pattern?
Who is the agent in my self-creation?
I skulk under the rim of my collar.

Self-discovery is a self-uncovering,
To know one's past is to know one's
    present,   30
And the past is a complex image of oneself,
Which is only to be known through
    experience,
And to know oneself is to cease to be
    surprised
Both by what one does and what one never
    suspected oneself capable of
    doing.
To know one's past is to know one's present
And intensify one's everyday consciousness,
And intensification is the beginning of
    affirmation.
I am the quality of my states of mind,
I am the intensity of my consciousness.

Art leads us back to ourselves: like a hall
    pendulum.   40
This sudden chiming of the childhood clock.

THE SILENCE

1965 – 1966

(A MEDITATION ON A QUEST FOR MEANING AND SELF-DISCOVERY)

To Mr. F. T.
This string of baroque pearls,
To be told like a rosary

1. DYING: SHADOW

Walk, my shadow,
Down these lanes of the mind. Let us take wing
And swoop down Cornish hedgerows, wheel past furze
To the sea-cliffs. We have the freedom of these hills,
Let us soar to the Black Head of Trenarren.
There flutter down. Far on the sullen rocks below
The sea boils from the angry years.
Here my shadow let us remember the young Freeman.
Let us remember his torments.
I have a "necklace" in my pocket. We will watch mo-   10
-ments spill through our fingers, and then,
We will tell waves like threaded gems and show
An age like wind and foam.

Freeman stood
Near an Essex church. The sun stretched his shadow years
Across a gravestone where, as across a mirror,
Flitted a congregation. Vicar came by and said,
"Hello Milton, how's the office? When are you off to Oxford?"
Freeman scowled.
                And now in Whitehall, an autumn State,   20
And a sour mood, a mood sour as murder, or a Great Power's fate.
An exhausted Christendom.
Round an iron tree
Bruised and rotting cubes from an old élan,
Blackened rails and mouldering masonry,
Decay like the rancid moon –
A windfall city like a cemetery.
Under a sepulchral sky the once prosperous sit on after dinner,
And see how slowly, slowly, their exhausted, ribbed lungs fill –
And now like a flower unfolding, quickly, see,   30
The walls are crumbling, their skeletons break up;
On after dinner, having talked first to the right and then to the left, saying
"We are like needles on a lighted Christmas tree,
Members of an evergreen Greatness. What shall we discuss?
Whatever it is, let it not be anything morbid."
That silence under the wind contains the House of Windsor,
It contains the bones of a thousand Empires.
Senile lips dribbling, veterans shuffling through museums.

Wandering at dusk in a forum of broken statues I shuddered,
For what if our seeds detonate in a crimson cloud?   40

The young Freeman   From this Monumental height, the stone-pile is alive
perceives with a   From a provincial life like an exhausted stone-strewn field.
vertical vision, a way   Said Freeman, "Look at that crowd. Who are those people? What are
of looking that fills   they?"
him with terror, and   See, crawling robots, remote-controlled computers
he longs to see   Commuting like run-down clockwork to grimy windows.
meaning.   Let us stop them and descend. Let us walk among them.

On a horizontal plane, they are like sunflowers in an unhealthy soil,
And we are united by our roots and our common metal –
He was groaning in the gutter, imploring in the dark,
And when a headlight lit his stump of an arm, and he shrieked, we
                   wept;   50
Or as the aircraft slewed round, and the red smoke from the wings hung
                   like dust,
A cheer went up, they had crashed safely, and we ran over the airfield.
But what of this other agony – lying awake under stars,
Alone in a deep silence, utterly beyond others, waiting,
Breathing the last, now silence, mouldering flesh and cinders,
Waiting in icy terror under the stars? Do they know that?
And what of their response to it, turning away from chatter
To strive alone after dinner in a silent room,
To fix the moment in a Persian carpet
And glimpse a meaning that fills with peace   60
And leaves one unalarmed? Do they know that?
Have they seen the smallness of "I" and now within the pattern?
See, under the stars their crowns are of different heights, like city trees.
What vertical do they share? What makes them grow?
Let us move them on and ascend and resume the vertical vision.
         Said Freeman, "It is a problem of perception,
         Look at the consciousness of this nation."
         The chaffinch in the almond blossom.

Freeman recalls   Sid Frampton, "efficient" entrepreneur,
examples of the   Took his foreman on an inspection tour.   70
nation's perception.   In the corrugated hangar, piecework-Joe
He feels that it is not   Hammered the malleable metal and intoned
enough to live at the   "'It 'im on ve 'ead wiv a fatted ba-nana."
level of everyday   "Sweeping" chips and metal shavings near the door
social triviality.   Albert called "'Ts 'e ol' man." In overalls Freeman drove

The final rivet in the hundredth frame, with a placid fury.
In a timid Essex drawl the boss directs
"Come over 'ere and bust up some of these boxes."
Assigned to help, bus-driver Harry Luscombe,
Part-timing for his nipper's education,   80
Pulls on the pincher handle, and extracts
A curved six-inch long nail, and pants:
"You won't want ter know me when yer at Oxford."

Having added a ha'p'ny to the district rate
By catapulting a hundred and eighty street-lights in one night,
Albert draws a nail near Freeman's bike,
Says "Hi say, hain't you goin' to defend yower property?"
Joe grinned, and his soul, beloved of a collective God,
Boggled in his opaque eyes.

                        Victims Joe and Albert Lee,   90
I want to weep, but is it burnt flesh I can smell,
Or a scratching of fleapits, before afternoon break for tea?

      Smears and dirty panes:
      Before the looking-glass
      Jeanie cakes on a face
      And, deaf to the wooing gram,
      Dreams of the brand new Jag
      That Charlie Weemack will race
      Down streets that have forgotten
      The whine and shattering blast   100
      To the war memorial;
      Where, parked with a greasy smile,
      He will lubricate her parts,
      Ignite her and rev her up
      And, under the sputtering lamp,
      Switch off when she's overhot
      And pour in cooling rain.
      From Peking Man to Yeats
      We struggled to create
      Her serviceable yawn   110
      And, immune against the past,
      That china-poodle taste,
      That mechanised embrace.

      Echoes and empty rooms:
      After calling in her "pussy"
      Twice widowed Mrs Hall
      Stands by the gas and broods
      On her Portslade property
      And the man who rented her body
      And built it round with a wall   120
      In a jealous, free-hold decade
      And nightly knelt at her grave
      And paid her a monthly due
      And lived respectably,
      And who narrowed down her head
      To an occasional trip into town
      And fear of a burglar's tread
      Or a crash in real values
      Or a sudden fuse.
      Quasars and galaxies   130
      Sent light for millions of years

To help cheated Mrs Hall
Brew twenty thousand tears.

The TV crackles in a thundery silence;
And as he renounces weapons I can hear
The scraping of a knife and tensely exhaled breath;
Not looking, Freeman turns the evening paper.
Then the Wing-Commander spoke, trying to provoke:
"Anyone'd think he'd had some experience, the cowardly traitor.
What is the country coming to if it's that soft?   140
My God, if I had my way I'd have dropped the Bomb years ago,
And I'd lock up every long-haired idealist.
They're a menace to society." (Freeman does not stir.)
Unsatisfied, he asserts himself on the dogs,
Angrily making them bark with a false alarm,
One of the Few who fought in our finest hour
For an unheroic age of education,
Who saw too clearly past the Second Empire,
Who could not see beyond conserving the status quo
And who would not disarm the status of Great Power.   150

At last the inheritor invades the blackened stairs,
Noctambulist Fosdick from a consultation;
And, dreaming of flaking walls like peeling loins
And of groins that are bare beneath a petticoat
He furtively reclimbs a darkened Soho stair,
And, turning the handle to his office room
Barks timidly at his secretary to resume his role.
And watch *this* ailing Knight of a Merrie day
Extend a sagging hand and fall into a chair;
An exhausted Tory, spawned in a tired tradition   160
One of the unlevelled gentry, with an unlevelled air!
After confirming the "approximate" acreage
Of the pre-1810, unregistered estate
They agree the "estimated" annual rents;
Among decomposing Pharaohs, in Phaestos ruin
Freeman is disturbed to preserve the established order,
To wall out chaos with a "statutory" return.
Are they real, or are they waxworks from Tussauds,
These comfortable corpses in share-lined graves?
Lord, let them choke in a disinherited terror   170
Before they leave for backgammon at the St James!

The sun rose
Red and majestic
On the formal garden
White paths
Misty fountains
Dark grass
Empty couples

On idle glasses

The red sun rose,   180
Throwing a judgement on a squandered night.
Reclining on the pillared wall, His Acred Lordship
Regally received his departing guests,
And, mid crinolines turning for the last quadrille,
Tickled the crumpled bottom of his latest trollop.
Say what you will, thought Freeman, blue blood once swung in trees,
And reassured, superior, strode over and shook hands,
Looked through the smile to yellow-ochre eyes
And seeing, beyond, the perception choked with names
Said "It was nice" like an epitaph, saw the surprise   190
And smelt the decay.

Six purposeless futures for a savage "saint",
Lower consciousnesses he will not imitate.

On a London bus he becomes aware and sees with his higher or spiritual consciousness.	On the top of a London bus I was withdrawn, In a City suit I broke the circuit of fragmentary dreams, I awoke to my presence on the chesty engine, And watched my breathing like a tired machine And observed the puce flush of a strenuous dawn.

And might not twenty years
On tensely bended knees   200
Take one to the meaning
Of a schoolgirl's bleeding thighs,
Or a stranger's red-rimmed eyes,
Or a swelling universe,
Or a nation's thrust and disease?
Or, scaling a self till it's nothing,
To the reason why two twisted lungs should breathe?

At a church jumble sale he feels that Christianity has nothing to offer him.	"I believe in the Resurrection of the body, and the life everlasting." In this sepulchral part of the decaying stronghold Answers are chanted in an absent-minded dream 210 While Mrs Purkiss, Vera Styles and Lady Black Turn in their pews with insinserious smiles Or put up a hand to adjust a hat.

And squared by trestle-tables in this Essex hall
A hundred ladies contract for merchandise,
See how they thumb with concupiscent touch,
Give ungrudged pennies with meretricious smiles.
Freeman refuses a glass of orangeade,
Agrees with ladies in hat-veils and gloves
Who soliloquise on new collection-plates,   220
Avoids the bored reporter from the local rag,
Awaiting the Minister, who is scoffing cakes.
"Would you like another piece of *child's flesh*?"
Suddenly the parquet heaved, dwarfs crawled up

With tattoed biceps, swarmed up pleated skirts,
And tore and rucked in struggling, churning thighs,
Then flung aside and burnt, deaf to the screams.
Freeman went outside.
                       Virtuously undressed!
O generation of virtuous coquettes,   230
Go to the brothel and be virtuously honest!

Nor has the Essex
way of life.

No sap united the splitting English tree,
Feeling no connection, the final fruit broke free;
Beneath the iron cross lay a congregation.
A sinful nation, through lack of opposition:
What great dreams will you have, Jeanie,
In visionary ecstasy outside the record shop?
And, thanks to the nocturnal struggles of kneeling authorities,
What shattering insights will be flashed on your screen, Mrs. Hall,
To make you blink after five hours' vibrant surrender?   240
What great choice will you make at the church bingo, Dolly Jakes,
Putting yourself in question with one creative stake?
And, disturbed by an arresting mural, Mr Parks,
Will you feel the night gape like a bailiff's laugh?
          Screaming gods and hoardings;
          In a decayed time, unreal states;
          Where is there any purpose,
          If not in the silence of saints?

Freeman rebels
against society and
glimpses the form
which he believes
can bring meaning to
his life: a future state
of himself as a high-
er consciousness
which perceives
meaning.

Said Freeman, "I have rebelled," and arrogantly stood alone,
Opposed to the drifting High Road, parting shoppers like a stone.   250
But what dream hung over the church, what surpassing image
Like the dream of a fallen seed in a dying season,
What dream like a twilit moon?

                       In a broken life-line
Is a sunset in a library, when, laughter in veins,
What could prevent if one had the belief, what save one's own will?
          To a violin's scales
          I made a renunciation;
          Weeping arpeggios
          I unchose my self for a Law routine.   260
But now in the electric light each man's shadow spread years before him;
And can they not see, looking through the Hobbies, the motor
                          magazines,
Can they not see that each is awaiting creation,
Awaiting the features of a giant or dwarf?
Do they not know they are sculpting themselves,
This one his drooping jowls, that his sparkling eyes,
Can they not see that every second carves the future idea?
O Shadow, can I not ascend to you? Who are you,
Out there in the future like an inscrutable sage?
          The vision faded like a dream   270

Into foggy air;
An artist's quest began again,
A Tammuz resumed his despair

2. IN THE UNDERWORLD: MOON ON THE NORTHERN DEAD

Before he can begin
to grow towards his
Shadow Freeman
must first complete
his rebellion against
society. Watching an
escapologist he
realises he must free
himself from the
chains of his back-
ground, and choose
himself anew.

Swollen in decaying
Soil and stone
Snugly fermenting
In a fertile bed,
Painlessly dreaming
Of a painless spring
On Tower Hill, I saw the will of man rise from its chains: 280
Supine in ring-mail, ringed by a crowd,
Writhing to be born from his useless skin,
With what speed he, lithe as an acrobat,
Leapt from the pile, bare arms and neck unscarred,
And, exultant imago, with a master's scorn received his acclaim!
But underneath, in a packed and silent tube,
Hearing a stranger call his name,
He turned to a forgotten face from school
Who said "I've chucked the office, what are you doing?"
Who talked as though he talked, calling him to choose again. 290
"Freeman," he said, "*you* chose that anxious look,"
(After I came out of the warm wood and waded through primroses,
When I took to my heels and ran down past the churchyard)
"*You* chose that false image of yourself, *you* are to blame."
Before the ascent to light
And the upward thrust of the shoot
There must be a descent into darkness
And the slow riving pain of downward driving roots.

First, he decides to
give up playing
cricket.

Said Freeman: "I will unchoose falsehood: cricket."
In the pavilion a gentle class undresses, 300
Predicts the wicket, visits the stinking gents,
Sits on the splintery wood under a row of pegs
And tensely tugs on reeking socks and vests.
Oiling varicosed veins, the eldest reminisces,
Varying gossip with historical recitations.
Then some wag said for the twelfth consecutive week "Jim's putting his
strap on,"
And each face split in a strong, conditioned laugh
Of well-oiled length, the nervous shibboleth
Of a corporate member.
Remote in the roasting sun, 310
A flurry of dust and five hundred hands react.
"*Oh, well beheaded.*" Putting down Shelley,
Freeman advances,
Passes the returning corpse with his head under his shoulder,
Takes middle and leg from the sweating umpire.

45

Shall I do a dance or streak across the square?
Freeman crouches at the crease, the bowler trundles in,
Ball swings, Freeman hooks to leg,
First bounce into the Ladies Tea Committee. Polite applause.
What did I do? Did I suddenly bring hope to the lives of hundreds?
Frowning, the bowler tries again. Something dislodges a bail.   320
"'Owzat?" shouts the keeper, and as the umpire raises a finger,
"I'm sorry, you're out. Hit wicket." Said Freeman, "It was your pad."
And he stood his ground, ignoring his captain waving from the boundary.
And later, walking back, he thought, serene,
"That was my last innings. I have better things to ask myself
At weekends than, 'What does this cricket mean?'
I will find a girl."

And should one, sitting near greasy mechanics
Or elegant Young Conservatives, carelessly conversing,
Should one scrutinise each for a twirling stem   330
Or the drumming of tawny fingers on the shiny table
And cross and solipsistically sit
And ask with dread, "What does your life mean?"

He meets Jeanie and takes her home.

In the dry cellar a long blue wail
Speaks for the dispossessed. With a languid air
Men slowly rise in Chelsea disattire,
Take taken for granted girls with distant eyes
And sadly pivot to the thumping dirge.
The threadbare sofas are nearly empty, all
Are moving clockwise in the circular funeral dance,   340
Each heart-beat adjusts to the ruling feet,
No-one notices Freeman drooping in sweater and jeans
Near the bored, black-haired girl in a with-it smock.
And can one disturb the heaviness of *those* thighs?
At length Freeman advances to Jeanie, on her evening off,
Extends an awkward hand in the mournful coda
Which, rising, she ignores. And what eyes stopped and multiplied
As his first unpractised steps confessed, and what nightmare amplified
The sudden silence and Jeanie's titter?
    On the rebound   350
    Jeanie drank coffee
    In Freeman's lounge
    Against his mother's wish:
    "She can't even speak
    The Queen's English."
She had nothing to say – she had no curiosity,
For nothing concerned her.
Crossing the railway bridge I thought 'Are you punishing yourself?'
For watching her clear away the dirty plates
And noting her tarty hair-do, her rounded shoulders,   360
I did not mistake her vagueness for independence.In the tube she said "O
look, my hair-spray." I smelt B.O.

Passing the butchers
In the moonlit street
Freeman remarked
On the price of meat.
She said: "Ay?"

Then he rebels
against his father by
giving up Law and
choosing himself as
an artist.

Having returned from Counsel,
A trifle too slowly
Freeman stirs his tea and observes   370
A future rise and exhale
Alone in Fosdick's window,
Imagines he, too, remembers
Gnats on a limpid stream,
Walks in a lush green forest,
Questions in a flaming sunset
And, in an impossibly twilit graveyard,
Despair, and an artist's dream;
And that Fosdick sighs as he turns
And is lost to his codicil   380
Before, with an ectomorph's nerves,
He takes down to his waiting client
A long surrendered will.
Said Freeman, "I have rebelled, and my Shadow calls to my will,
Yet I consent to serve the statutes of a father's law
And preserve the sins of the established order."
Said Freeman, "I have rebelled, and nothing can fetter my will,"
And with an unfeeling frown, he slammed his future's door;
And as he opened the college gate and went through the stony arch,
Some great shadow of authority shattered into fragments   390
And the sun scorched the backs of his eyes as he towered over the lake;
Then an outlaw began an autonomous descent
While priest-headed birds screamed for blood on the farther shore.

As an undergraduate
at Oxford, reading
an Arts subject, he
is free. But he
has thrown off
discipline, and his
misuse of the will
leads to a riotous
summer among
modern Maenads
who nearly tear his
emotional life to
pieces, and he
continues to be ruled
by his Reflection; his
social ego.

Are those Maenads like garbage on the new carpet?
Seeing Orpheus stump in, I want to warn him,
This Playhouse bar is for those who have lost their direction,
Abandoned lives, οἱ βάρβαροι transferred
To the ranks of a Western internal proletariat.
No increase of consciousness, but reduction. Turn back.
"Come on," he said, and he drank up and lurched forward into a
                                        nightmare: 400
He was elated – he scrumped stars and bit them to the core,
Laughed and roared out "Are you there, God? Are you there?"
He stood beside statues of saints in the winter dusk;
Police stood patient in an ordered line
Waiting for a crime with expressionless faces;
Requesting strangers' beds in a foreign city
Like a prisoner jumping on the bars of his cage;
"These stables once belonged to a monastery
And I know your Tut-ankh-Amun is a dark power;"

Slooshed beer into a scorner's face and can hear   410
The turbulence in a drunken corridor
And a soothing voice, "He was sometimes so emotional,"
Like a nurse allaying fear, rushing waters
And the swirling flush of a surly lavatory bowl;
Faces peer cautiously from darkened doors –
Bawl, and pouting goddesses grin with common sense under empty skies.

Reeling images twittered in my belfry;
In the 2 a.m. dark, men yawned and raved and rotted away;
I made no choice, I just wanted to get away.
Yet for one who has seen in dreams a hanged man's eyes   420
Bulge on the ends of strings, he was deliberate,
Noosed on the chair and testing the iron ring,
Until, one arm staying in warning, a white-haired apparition
Whispered from a future morning, "Die not from the world, but from your
'will'."

        Freeman, he said, *you* chose...

        O choice,
        Did you betray me,
        Have you left me without a voice?

Freeman's rebellion
has led to emotional
paralysis and mean-
inglessness.

        No Shadow strolls
        through these stone nudes   430
        or blackened bones;
        in cotton-wool clouds
        that slot-machine disc
        shines on rubber trees
        and on icy fingers
        in a paralysed wind
In the hot month
Having dawdled down canvassed walks
And admired the floodlit cottage walls
Which are to be restored when funds permit   440
Having displayed women like new weapons
Or new Rollers
In the big marquee
Arranged in a rich hierarchy of meaning
Commem Committee carefully in the centre
With Lords and Ladies, then proceeding outwards
Like a mandala
                        In the outer circles
Justly acknowledged by wealthy smirks,
At a round table sprawls a scornful rebel   450
Sharing a plate of turkey bones with rugger-men
Who spew and reminisce with podgy gestures
And wear their raucous laughs like college shirts;
Unnoticed, too, his comment sitting beside him

THE SILENCE, 1965 – 1966

Amid the chatter of country-life and future plans,
A painted mask to hide a mother's face
And a glittering dress to hide a madam's thighs,
                                        And loss of meaning.

<table>
<tr><td>He sells programmes
at the Soho Fair dur-
ing a vacation.</td><td>As I stood on the corner accosting the bourgeois
She touched me sleeve and said, "If anyone asks you
Send them to 15A." She said I'd get a good commission.
"On the right," I said to the man in the panama hat
And I drank up and picked up my pile of programmes.
What did his wife in the country matter to me?
Newsvendor Pete called, "Hey mate, seen the K man?"<br>"No," I said. And on he roamed unrecognised,
Like a windowland Vollard.
A rising god. Lounging in the playground,
I saw him stumble from the Cathedral porch
With organ-chords and silence streaming from his wound.</td><td>460

470</td></tr>
</table>

He sells programmes
at the Soho Fair dur-
ing a vacation.

As I stood on the corner accosting the bourgeois
She touched me sleeve and said, "If anyone asks you   460
Send them to 15A." She said I'd get a good commission.
"On the right," I said to the man in the panama hat
And I drank up and picked up my pile of programmes.
What did his wife in the country matter to me?
Newsvendor Pete called, "Hey mate, seen the K man?"
"No," I said. And on he roamed unrecognised,
Like a windowland Vollard.
A rising god. Lounging in the playground,
I saw him stumble from the Cathedral porch
With organ-chords and silence streaming from his wound.   470

He is aloof from his
family at the seaside.

Freeman sunbathed in a striped deck-chair. The fierce sand smouldered,
Scorching the midday squatters near shadeless beach-huts,
Burning lobstered men with knotted handkerchiefs,
Searing shivering swimmers traversing stones,
Cauterising the entreating queue at the landing stage,
Consuming the coach-party eating candy-floss
And the chattering crowd chasing the whirling standard.
In the babble rites are discussed: paddling, then putting,
After we've seen the sea knock down our castle
And eaten our scones and gone and got our ices.   480
And looked askance at the undesirable couple
With slightly sing-song accents. Freeman's opinion is asked.
Interrupted when dreaming of higher things,
He grunts his agreement, spoiling the holiday spirit;
Reproached for not attending, he simulates enthusiasm;
Perceiving ghosts, he clutches images of the real:
The whores in the Ramblas slipping their hands in the pepsis,
And the jellied blobs on Malaga's greasy beach.
And slowly a scowl spread from the horizon
And obliterated the sun, and a sharp gust of wind   490

Rattled the ring of skeletons reading their papers.
Freeman grinned.

Freeman glimpses an
escape from mean-
inglessness through
experiences of inten-
sified consciousness.

                        A ringless lady
                        With a swollen belly
                        Vociferously scorned
                        The nun's habit;
                        Between cool knees
                        In the dress circle
                        Her full womb yawned.
She brought me a rose she'd filched from someone's garden   500

And struggling for the expected emotion, I had nowhere to put it.
But she returned,
Disturbing the Sunday silence with a wooden tread,
And, washed with sunset,
Reclined in the bay window and turned up a taunting head.
And in this drowsy evening, all are awake.
Supine on the carpet, six bodies stir,
Only to breathe. The MJQ have stopped.
But no hand moves, to check the needle's clicking.
The black reefer droops. In a slow monotone   510
One asks: "Which is more, nem con or unanimous?"
And after a long delay, some slowly giggle.
I groped back, groped back, and found the eternal in patterns,
In geometric shapes and alien forms,
And projected on the wall from my buried self
Was a film of young memories and vivid dawns.
Keeping a vigil in the green-smelling haze,
Freeman ponders the spark from heaven, knowing those Goths
Strong but to destroy, else have they left no trace,
Hears their heavy whispers, "Man, am I high,"   520
And mourns, "What I seek can't be learned here,"
And in despair, sinks down, holds out his hand,
And soon his ego leaves his weary limbs,
Floats up an industrial chimney like crematorial smoke,
Soars above traffic-jams, drifting on a dry wind,

Scattering soot on silent queues and milling station-crowds,
Wafted in aetherial wisps, dissolving in cloudy images
Over stony spires.

These glimpses
recall him to the pos-
itive side of his
quest.

And, rebel against
A rather nebulous foe,   530
Remember what you forgot,
Remember those silent saints;
Our symbols have been lost;
Heathen, who made a vow,
For the purpose you barely know
Wear this golden cross.

At Christmas he
shocks a crowded
pub. Thrown out, he
goes to a Forest pond
and sees his reflec-
tion on the ice. He
feels a need to die
away from his self-
assertiveness.

"And when Parks stood up, 'e 'ad a stain on 'is flies" –
Mrs Purkiss shrieked and threw her head onto Joe's shoulder.
In the corner, under the mistletoe,
Fixing the nervous laugh that did not belong,   540
Freeman drank his beer, and mourned
The meaningless mouth-gaping of the gibbering throng;
While carols, blaring from the radio,
Swung paper-bells in ballerina twirls,
Like Jeanie's buttocks to the wet-lipped businessman.
Then Freeman rose and bawled, "Silence, ladies and gen'lemen, I want
                                        silence,"

And when slowly all were dumb, smouldering with scorn:
"You've made a mockery of your church, let's see it BURN."
Shocked and with one accord they muttered out against him.
And God-fearing Hades of the Sicilian wife pushed through   550
And said "Ma hoose is a guid hoose; bloodie gang awa,"
And as he chucked him out, the hour struck, and Christ was born.

               Outlawed under the moon,
               In the icy pond
               A tired rebel
               Sought a dead image
               Of a lawless will
               And a rescuer's arm.

               In an unrepeated dream
I read the accusation until, with outstretched arms,   560
She changed into an eternal with long black tresses
And glamorous as a film-star, drew me down and gratified my desire.

               Reason that old whore
               Opened her legs to any idea
               And rotted with gonorrhoea.

Nearing the end of his studies, he feels he should marry. Although he barely realises it, he connects the idea of a wife with the subrational depths of himself, which he must now cultivate (and be cultivated by).

Rejecting abstract ideas
For the living actual,
Seeking beyond his years
Education in the sensual,
Freeman said of the artist's wife   570
(Forgetting his nervousness)
"I must root myself in life –
All art is meaningless
That is not felt or does not
Grow out of experience";
A lesson he often forgot,
Idealising tarts
With a puritan's prurience,
A resolve he remembered
With all the dedication of a dismembered heart.   580

               Freeman and American Joe
               Drank their way round Jericho.
               Dust, darts, and heads filled with rubbish.

He meets his future wife,

But then, I got back early and *you* were there, alone, dressed in black....
Among the black candles, before the gaping grate and the narrow flue
I took a man's part, it was something I knew how to do.
At first I didn't recognise your golden hair,
But when, in flowing cloaks of blue,
We floated along the church-ruled shore
And the drowned girl revived by the monk's fire   590
Turned black and, burning, tortured a golden bride,
Then, bride and devil, secretly I knew.

Near a coastguard's cottage on the harbour wall,

Freeman said: "I will leave this netherworld, I will go abroad."

and acknowledges
his need of her,

In a naked winter, vibrant with direction,
Dramatising his scorn for the "indifferent herd"
And exaggerating its nihilistic contagion,
Knowing it said "His manner is absurd,"
Freeman recognised his limitation,
Admitting what, though seeking, he had ignored,   600
Admitting his independence was a compensation,
A camouflage for gaucherie, a fraud:
   By a moon-green canal
   And on a spray-damp jetty,
   Announcing his exile,
   He turned fearfully
   And lingered, feeling a presence near that glowing hearth.

And from my corner I knew what was real,
Seeing another turn and turn
Beneath the indifferent pose of her reputed lovers,   610
Addressing her body to all men, poised and colourful,
Made vivacious by others' admiration,
Gaily cynical, always existing in the minds of others.

and chooses to marry
her.

At closing time he said, "Let's go up to the pond."
Ascending through cerebral trees in the misty dark,
His silence bowed under his vast decision.
But as, in the uterine hollow, he chose to marry her,
The night rocked riot, split, and with a shattering of laws
The moon broke full on the water. And when the universe had settled
       down
There was a shadow on the rippling silver black   620
Like the drowned image of a rescued reflection
And, enslaved to a moment's freedom, he had changed.

He takes her to meet
his grandmother.

A quarter stirs and musically resounds
With a lost century's languor,
The echoes curl with soporific yawns
And relapse in slumber;
Motes of dust resettle on cluttered walls
In this subconscious hall.
In fading light, three generations are engaged in scrabble.
Having approved her grandson's choice of bride   630
Materfamilias, with a determined glee,
Triumphantly builds OLDEN, and defies
Her daughter to consult the OED.
And in a brown background, on the wall I espy
Harmonious maidens in an ideal family.
With a handful of Xs, the cynosure declines
Her orthographic ordeal, and draws a Z.
And should I lay down that word, in no-one's dictionary,
Say, "Even now it could float through the window and flutter to the
       floor,"

Or, "I have studied post-war graffitti on expectorated doors"   640
As though worms should squirm and hang from my bulbous eyes?
I see harmonious maidens in an ideal society,
And forfeit the victory.
              Abiding alone,
              Writhing to be born,
              A seed less like a stone
              Than a dying corn

                Dead image

He marries her,

Within St. Clements the gathering guests
Trade immediate recognition with unfamiliar relatives,   650
Stare across the aisle with hostile curiosity
At well-dressed strangers, read class or contours,
Threatened by unpredictable faces,
Or decorously whisper, protecting images,
And then, restored by clichés, condescend to praise
Th'exampled Paire, and mirrour of the bourgeois race.
And listen, listen, can you hear
The shifting of a foot, the scraping of a heel
And the tense rustle of a straightened hem
As, with clenched eyes, each recreates the atmosphere;   660
Until, chanting Lambeth love and vision, all blaspheme
Against satanic altars, in a green and pleasant hymn?

and feels he has sur-
rendered his self-
assertiveness to her
subrational depths.

        That ageless fertility goddess
        With the swollen breasts
        Awaits an impersonal embrace
        From a priapic son
        Who, after the totem feast,
        Will die in a whole tribe's place
        And in a bursting caress
        Sow fields of golden corn,   670
        Descend to the dark origin
        Of a matriarchal race,
        Ascend to the Virgin image
        Of a single face.

But, he takes a teach-
ing job in Iraq
(Tammuz's land,
now ruled by a dicta-
tor) and finds that his
chaotic inner life has
been subdued by an
authoritarian dicta-
tor. He is not grow-
ing as he wished.

But Freeman had said: "I will go and live abroad."
And, Cubist in the refracted heat, trachomatous cripples
Snot and spit in the narrow, sewered street;
Paddling children and the Arab in the pit
Disturb the Turkish courtyards' shaded sleep;
Over the gaping market ulcerously swells   680
The blue and yellow erection of an infected minaret.
Next to this horned goat, let us take a seat.
He swung into them, felling them with his feet,
Just as I came through the gate, and then they fought
Only a day after the killing outside the Dean's door,

And I couldn't see any armoured cars, or militia,
I shouted "Stop this" and everyone went, and I was supreme.
Grinning with power the Leader's Dean cracked nuts,
Proposed that the President be tried for crimes against the State
And, sweeping the shells aside, belched, then proscribed: 690
Confinement in a cage.
                                        And when the Leader entered,
I knew him from my dreams, that gaunt tyrant
Who ruled with hated order in my unruly being.

            Ziqqurats and fir-trees
            and the northern dead;
            the sweating coach disgorges
            into the garden tomb,
            there is no resurrection
            growing in my head   700

only the moon in the bottom of the screeching night
or the beating of storks on a caravanserai
or the swirl of two brown rivers under drifting smoke;
and gliding through silent palms in the setting sun
I thrilled to a wading reeder's warbling song.

In the floodlit limbo, the Ambassador's garden,
A thousand perfumes hang like tobacco smoke
And perforate the nostrils like withered roses;
Gat-toothed old hags flaunt tarted-up faces,
And I observe each tragi-comic scene, before the toast to the Queen.   710
When I saw him in the centre I had to confront him –
He was like a meaning, that sprawling priest,
Bowed over an empty glass and slurring out: "I thirst."

            Through a dusty haze
            On the horizon shimmer
            Pools of glistening glass
            Like a broken mirror
            And bits of a single face

                        Empty space.

He returns to   Robots and computers   720
London, and, still   In an English winter:
static, for a short Before this walled mandala
while succumbs to   With an empty centre,
Mechanism. This   And under a blood-red sun
period coincides with Freeman refused to despair of the One.
the first illness of his Until the flickering lights
father, and the birth Of an octopus of steel
of a child.   Threw a round image
                     On an empty screen

And reduced a haemorrhage 730
And a wringing pain
To the electric nightmare
Of a bulbous brain.
A flash, and the light went out in a Stoic's scream.
Venetian blinds hung over a father's eyes
As over hotel rooms with forgotten memories,
And angry fists pounded his murky temples
Like a cell-door tumult in a penitentiary;
Plugged into an EEG, he knew nothing
Of a foetal thrash into theta and delta being, 740
Lying in the ill-lit ward like a fused machine.
A groan from the bed, a wail, and a daughter's born....
That screwn-up face
Will crawl,
Will scoop up frogspawn
And also walk through snow with a doctor,
And drink in the Ball and Mace.
                              (And Vera Styles, stinking of gin
Your father flirted with an auburn lady
Whose gaping laugh contained the new Estate. 750
I went and had my pee and when I came out, they'd gone
And trudging through the snow I passed
Steamed-up windows, and rubbers like icicles,
And the running of plugged-in leads.)

                    O decomposing age,
                    Does this blue crocus wither
                    For lack of voltage?
                    Or is it not rather:
                    A creaking of infirm walls,
                    A rattling of dirty panes, 760
                    Then a silent wind
                    Over a fissured brain?

He takes a temporary
job as a park garden-
er. His existence
being static, life
seems futile.

And Freeman worked in the open air.
Trudging with a wheelbarrow and an awkward hoe
I saw a mouldering graveyard in the grey distance.
When I met Armstrong he said, "Ready for some 'ard graft?"
Dislodging sorrel in the Berlin roses
I ignored the mackintoshed white-collared mourners.
Dolly passed and said, "You'd better dodge ve guvnor,

He's got ve rats, and 'e'll be along on 'is bike in a few minutes." 770
In a Council shelter, I refused to despair:
On five bob an hour, I said to the abyss in my stomach,
"So what, and were there rainbreaks or roses in Belsen?"
But staring at the brown gutter by the tufted lawn,
And watching each frothy illusion float and explode
Against a wrecked hull of crumpled paper,

Solitary and damp and cold,
I felt withered tufts on the sodden crust of my brain.
"Come on," said Gordon, "it's stopped raining now
And you 'eard what 'e said about firing us if 'e finds out."   780
And the Nissen split in a revved-up roar.
The music in my heart I bore....

Freeman decides to
leave the West once
more.

    Leaves like tears, tumbling,
    From the inexhaustible spring
    I shed a few illusions.

"Sweeping" the paths of a glass-fronted comprehensive,
Freeman succumbed to the New Town atmosphere,
Flung down his broom, slumped down head between knees
And stared, stared at nothing, in numb despair.
Then from the other side of denial grew rejection,   790
The complex pain and hope of a new life,
Not wanting to go but having to find the freedom,
Shattering familiar deaths for a Shadow's voice
Yet clinging as to a home marked out for demolition,
Choosing the possibility, not making the choice.
There was no resolution in that vacillation,
That "outcast's" fumbling for exile from "an indifferent land",
Before the bawling order, "'Ere, get up and
Give us an 'and with these bleedin' roses."

His father has
another stroke, and
his suffering and
death seem
meaningless.

What is that scream from the summer roses   800
Like an unbearably beautiful pain?
And what disturbance in the condemned men's ward
As madness raged in a provincial's bleeding brain,
As with terrible logic he proved his tormentors wrong,
What triumphant shriek like a discordant chord
And then silence and the patter of rain?
In a lucid moment, lying in the bottom of a bed,
He groaned, "What have I done, what is the reason?"
And seeing him fall apart into a collage of bones,
I could not shake my head and say, "It is all in vain."   810

In the lush serenity of a sultry hollow
A distant rumble closed a prayer, and echoed
When will all this suffering reach an end and serenity follow?

In the angry autumn a storm came,
Breaking summer defiance,
Licking down from heaven with a white-hot tongue,
Leaving behind
A blasted bole in the after-calm,
And a charred inside.
Weary, he resigned his pride,   820
Surrendered a slurred confession to his inquisitors

And heard the twitter of migrating birds
In evening skies.
At nightfall in the unfriendly room,
Baffled by the indifferent lights of a lifetime lost,
He sighed at the yawning nothing round the flimsy moon
"This is the end," and shivered at the early frost.

And looking at the moon, he understood:
On a blind and slumbering retina, one flicker of light
And a universe; was no more: 830
Man, nothing and all.
He saw through, saw through.
An endless night.

He cried out – panting, labouring, groaning, he cried out –
    groping for my hand, grasping, clutching,
        clutching the living, gripping, gripping
           under the lamp
And I was all and helpless; while downstairs

The TV picture shrank into a
        postage stamp.

      Night.   840

He believes the   Then suddenly the sunlight stopped and we groped into the womb
Essex people who   And, following the shouldered coffin, I could see
attend the funeral   Rows of withered sunflowers in unnatural stillness
have been affected   Attesting the family's roots in their community,
by the barrenness of   Committee members and urban dignitaries
contemporary   From a provincial life like an exhausted stone-strewn field.
Western culture. He   Was it in vain, his driving of roots through slag
connects his futility   Into the unnourishing darkness of a rubble tomb?
and his nihilism with   Has it prospered us, I thought, to fasten into stone,
this barrenness. He   Have bricks and mortar filled us with vital sap?   850
had thought he could   At the party they talked of trifles and future plans,
grow by opposing it,   Attesting my roots in the family, not seeing
but it is like the air   I wilted like a block-fed shoot in a worn-out land.
he breathes.   Lingering in the Forest, I said "I don't want to belong,"
  But I was already rejected by a fallen beech's brittle unfriendly
           hand.

    Ah, was it just a dream,
    That warmly fertile sleep
    And the tumescent turmoil,
    And did the roots not feed,
    Did no moisture seep   860
    Into that Western seam?
    Uproot this stemless seed,
    And plant it in a healthier soil.

3. RISING: REFLECTION ON THE CLOUDED GROUND

Temples on the pine slopes, red carp in a shoal....

Freeman is now a
Professor in Japan.

Withdrawn from a Professor's role,
Behind the outer smile,
Is as present a silence
As round a microphone;
Centuries of contemplation
The Western sneer derides   870
Have fertilized this valley
And peep through a worker's eyes;
Here let Eastern silence feed your soul.

His feeling of being
different from other
people is more
pronounced, and he
begins to live behind
his social "I".

Walking past noteless bars of telegraph wires
And the rattling of metal balls in pachinko dens
I passed under the twilit metal web
Whose cruel threads had trapped an exhausted tram
And on the trembling bridge I inhaled the smell
Of the drifting layers of scum on the green canal,
I connected the tang with oyster shells, and rejoiced in the banal.   880
But watching him while he acted out his expected role,
I knew he was a stranger who did not belong,
I heard them whisper, "With what disarming charm
He walls himself within the language barrier,"
Or, "See how loosely he wears his position
Yet see how he pulls it round him when alarmed,"
I knew what they respected with their questions,
I knew their code.
                              In the train,
I did not have to hide my dislocations   890
Or alienate to an awesome distance;
Openly strange, I felt an expatriate's peace.
And when I came out of the station I couldn't get a taxi
And the great sweep of the Milky Way was frozen and crisp
And my heart welled out and flooded the universe.

On a beach at night
he realises that the
stars are meaningless
without man.

The sea sighed like a lover,
Explored the face of the shore with webbed fingers,
Blind in the dark phase. And in a glittering sweep
Some of the hundred thousand million suns
In one of a hundred thousand million galaxies   900
Whirled on in a fiery band, shot out rays
To traverse the silence for a hundred thousand years
And beam on the man who crouched by a whelk-shell.
On a Japanese beach, my terrestial illusions shattered,
I fell headlong into a deep, dark silence

And floating like an astronaut, I shuddered – for I was nothing.
Suddenly a great flood of being surged in me,

Streamed out into the stars, brightened their fires
And released affirming voices in my blood:
"Without your creating eye would they exist, those cinders,   910
Without your moist cheeks would they have meaning?
Beside one creator, what are space or number or time?"
While the sea reached and tenderly smoothed away my footprints.

He receives an image   After days of intense thought
of a work of art   My energy flung up
which offers him a   An image of a search;
meaning: he can cre-   It swelled into a work of art,
ate himself as an   Creating its creator
artist.   Into the form it sought.
      It might have found its form   920
      In a Parliament or Church.

And what dream

He meets a nun who   Seeing the priest at cocktails I felt tense.
is living authentical-   But when she came in like a vision,
ly,   And led me to the chapel, whispering on silence,
      Her gentle beauty a reflection,
      Her hard, clear eyes
      Shining like pebbles in a pellucid stream
      That flowed from a deeply forming spring
      Born in muddied digging and discipline   930
      And patient agonies,
      I felt unclean:

and he reconsiders   That nun with contemplation's eyes,
his rejection of   That nun believes in lies,
Christianity in rela-   That "man" who knows the "truth"
tion to the life of the   Is too shallow for a questing youth.
spirit.   Before that fake icon
      That nun found realisation,
      Gave her being's source
      To a transforming cause;   940
      Bracket out the symbol,
      There is still the spiritual.
      Recreate the symbol
      And realise potential.
      Live by metaphor
      Confirm the spirit's law;
      Enjoy that inner Light
      In eternity's despite.

That is Eternity's delight.

For God's sake, stow your rational proof: 950
That ruined academy,

59

The foundations crumbled, not the leaky roof.

Freeman, listen to me:
Are you a saint in a rose-window
Or a rebel who must be free,
Reflection or Shadow,
What is or what will be?
Or are you an artist – do you receive and show
Symbols of Eternity?

You have a choice: 960
To be an actor, or a disembodied voice.

In a university,
Freeman rationalises
away his interest in
religion,

Washing his hands in a university, Freeman said to the mirror:
"And did you not dramatise disbelief
Into a Great Tragedy, in a Humanist Age,
Forgetting different ages need different ideas?
And did not a Minister symbolise
The impossible saint's ascent,
And does not any priest, and do you not repeat
With them your refusal, to apologise
Or justify with science your dissent,   970
And do you not recreate them as apostates
To prove that you, the existential saint, are right?
And are they not your conscience in disguise,
And are you not arguing with your higher self,
And have you not failed to substitute art for spirit?"

and sees his
obsession with
priests in terms of
his father-figure.

And yet, behind the confessional I have heard
The imploring cries of an unforgiven sinner
And the statutory volley of a firing-squad.
You sought your father in a world of whores,
But did you not know, he knelt in meditation   980
Behind hallowed doors?
                              Four unforgiving fathers,
Dying in agony on barbed and rusty wires.

Reject, I said, and cease your repetition,
Write them no more, these emasculated fathers.
Reject, you have outgrown what you have written.
Reject, I said, and burn your repetition.
Reject, I said, and cease your repetition.

Writhing in agony on barbed and rusty wires.

This leads him to
discover, at an open-
air cocktail party,
that he has been
repeating himself in

With "unified" vision I rose to the surface   990
And, dripping insights over the clean carpet,
I stumbled down the path to a hollow world.
And later, drinking in the lanterned garden,
Stomaching an American's wit while others laughed,

60

his relationships.
I had nothing to say –
Could I play a seeker's role among bankers' masks?
Dreaming of Jeanie I turned and saw
A red silk trousered, ageless, black-haired whore.
So it's all in the mind, then;
Scanning their faces, I find actors for seven roles: 1000
Shadow and intellectual, priest and fallen father,
Jeanie and madam, and loving bride.
And the impromptu play is merely an inner drama,
The meanings projected on a hollow cast,
And perhaps some players do not fit the robes
And perhaps I chose again to refuse them parts
Or perhaps my whole life is just a nightmare
Dreamt through me by the minds of others,
My action mere reaction, and my freedom
A Third Act cry of blindness at the Arts?   1010
And, egotist to whom, alien as stone,
Others were unwitting counterparts in an unwitting dream
Dreamt by seven flagellants in a lurid room,
When, yielding to an unknown hatred,
You slooshed beer at another, making drink the excuse,
It was, perhaps, yourself, in part, you hated?

But after judging a
drama contest, he
realises that at the
same time he has
changed.
Yet who is this intruder among the judges,
Humped wilfully in old cords,
Hair over his collar
"It doesn't look as though he's had a wash,   1020
There must have been a mistake."
After the first play I could bear it no longer,
I leant forward and shared his derision;
But when, united against the hall, we walked outside,
And he said "I have rebelled," I shivered,
I was repelled as by a dead image in the concrete light.

A dozen attendants bowed and gestured me forward;
And turning the corner, I checked myself in the middle of a step
For the figure I saw in the mirror was unreal.
In the limousine I averted my eyes from the chauffeur's mirror   1030
And we purred past choirs of silent angels until we saw
The moated majesty of the bouldered Palace walls,
Obsessing like the centre of a mandala.
Turning the corner, what happened, for weren't you anti-Establishment?
In the centre,
Arranged in a rich hierarchy of meaning,
I glimpsed myself as a meditating Buddha.
Withdrawn from dark suits, why shouldn't he sit in a dark suit?
In a microcosm of art and meditation
There is neither time nor energy to rebel   1040
Against the macrocosmic outward form.
And the form I saw in the mirror had become unreal.

He cannot reconcile
his contradictions.
By the sea he falls
into despair.

Dark-suited Buddha and priest,
Does man change or repeat?

And is this the end of the quest, is this all,
Is there only this uncontainable complex whole,
This pattern of Becoming, and nothing more?
This carpet on this floor?

I shall sink to the floor so, and tear out tufts of hair.

Poet of the Self,
You who gave your youth to questioning despair,   1050
Stare in the mirror, and question each greying hair.

In the early spring,
Observing a sea-slug spinning a yellow thread
I transcended my yearning:
XYZ,
It exists; there is no why; it might be dead.

Sunlight on a wrinkled sea.
The jumping of exploding diamonds and the sparkle of crystal,
I flashed jubilation like a white hot mirror:
Might be dead.   1060

Turning in the seasons of my sunlight
I shall continue to seek,
Transcending the indifference of will-less fatalists:
A luminous sapphire-cell expiring on the beach.

He tries anew to dis-
cover himself; first
in terms of psycholo-
gy, and the repeti-
tions that determine
him,

Ah, they said, there is no discovery,
Only presenting questions to oneself.
Like an antiquary seeking a submerged mosaic
Freeman uncovered the centre of a vast pattern:
A suckling presence with a maternal face
That reconciled four cornered contradictions: 1070
The turbulent son, repeating a rebellion,
Like the projecting *husband* on the ambivalent bed,
Dominating to disguise dependence,
Destroying what he loves with an exile's dread;
The *seeker* of a return to a projected presence
In the warm, dark cave of a summer universe,
And the anxious, unknown poet with a grandiose vision,
Despising the trivial with a solitary's fear,
Itching for the protection of his warm, dark room, an infant saint.

Or was it a ruling presence with a forbidding face,   1080
And was that son seeking a father's benison
To end an exile he could not endure alone,
And was he seeking an unshattered shadow,

THE SILENCE, 1965 – 1966

And was the poet anxious with guilt, a prodigal saint?
A seaweed Janus with a reflecting face.

Osiris, he said, *you* chose

                                        And then he saw

and secondly in
terms of change and
his drive towards the
Shadow.

A faceless Shadow with an objective stare;
That turbulent *son* has won identity,
That exiled *husband* security for his vision,   1090
That *seeker's* gnosis knows maturity,
That *poet* with an ectomorph's restlessness,
Confirming a hostile world, his image at stake,
And itching to retire and contemplate
The wobbling images in the rippling lake,
That poet is anxious with dedication –
A seer, a visionary artist, not a saint.

He understands him-
self as an artist.

In a balanced time, we learn;
The artist paints two wheels
On his yellow judgement urn,   1100
One for a form that is real;
He is a maker who heals with his brush,
Not a tramper of farms;
When the streets are all arush
Or the preachers wave their arms
He goes to the window and stares,
Leaving his drying pot;
He smiles or scowls at the cheers,
Then lets the curtain drop.

Like a pieced togeth-
er Osiris, he suc-
ceeds in reconciling
his contradictions.
Walking among
shop-windows he is
confronted by his
Reflection, the nor-
mally taken for
granted embodiment
of the repetitions
whose dictatorial
rule has impeded his
growth. He rejects
this Freudian devil's
static and repetitive
view of himself for
the Shadow's
dynamic view of
himself, and affirms

Reflection and Shadow   1110
Man can repeat *and* grow
An upward striving stem
Splitting a resisting shell.

I met my tempter in a wilderness of windows,
A gaunt Reflection like a repetitious bourgeois,
Evasive like *Ambroise Vollard*. "You know
The outer real reflects your dream here,"
He said, "your self-important fantasy;
You fear the adjusted, you must cling to your idea
As secretly you know by your desperate vow,   1120

You poor, neurotic exile from reality.
Accept your average self."
                          In a London shelter
Refused to despair; wounded by neon,
He bled to death in a foreign square?
                    I countered:
"I reject you. With absurd belief I hung

the importance of the artist"s role in society.

A lamppost at the end of my future self
Like a moon at the end of a deserted street;
I have my purpose and so I progress.   1130

Do not expect me to live like those consumptive men,
Coughing their fatalistic disbelief
And infecting such as you with their "normal" breath;
Undiagnosed in an unreal world, they need
My solitary journey, to know their lack of health.
My place is apart from their consuming ease.
I will pour my being into this outer dream.
I gaze to realise, not preserve, belief.

　　　　　"It is too late
　　　　　To accept the mediocre;   1140
　　　　　I cannot live by Freud:
　　　　　There in his mirror
　　　　　I cannot create
　　　　　A towering image of man against a void."

The revolution seems over. Caught up in a Festival, he is jubilant, until he again sees the stars with meaningless and frightening immediacy.

He melted down the window and trickled to the gutter....
And with a great cry of jubilation, the hot night burst –
To tumultuous applause and triumphantly marching, they came, the
　　　　　　　　　　　　　　　　　　　　dancers,
Their sequins glittering in the many-coloured falling snow.

There was a great health, and when the cymbals clashed, sobbing,
I put on my mask and joined them, crying "I will, I will,"   1150
And I was stamping among hot thighs, smelling of earth, faster, faster
And when the god came into me, in a great shudder of joy, I howled
Until I staggered and spun and fell
　　　　　　　　　away
　　　　　　　　　　　　　　　　whirling
To be violated by silence and the rustle of leaves,
And the terror of broken assurance and blindness, the terror,
Under the cold blades of the inexplicable stars.

In a Zen temple Freeman is confronted with the spiritual world and with the irrational basis of his existence, the metaphysical ground of his being.

　　　　　In the meditation hall
　　　　　Each breath is unreal;
　　　　　There on the silence
　　　　　As the dawn shadows fall   1160
　　　　　The empty seekers feel
　　　　　Empty and full existence;
　　　　　As when the ruffled surface calmed –
　　　　　Beyond your reflection
　　　　　You saw the clouded ground
　　　　　And the towering depths around your rational question.

And when I emptied myself and looked beneath
I was speechless, speechless –

There were no foundations in that darkness,
I understood nothing, confronting that silent ground. 1170

He feels divided. It was all round me, like a cloud of exhaled smoke
And later in the twilit air I knew it would enfold me again,
Rising like a haze from a subterranean furnace, and choke
Me with questions, I knew I must live with it, and live in pain.
Under a scaffolding of rusty girders,
I heard a whisper, as if from a lunch-time stroller,
"Now you will always be two unless you refuse;"
And, queuing for damnation in a mirage of heat and fumes,
And switching off the engine, have you never inquired
"Who is this 'I', intruding on silence?" 1180
And seen your two profiles split in a mirror of cubes?

                    red viscera and black
                    in impenetrable dark
                    could be a Janus-priest
                    in a golden wheel
                    or, invalid and seer,
                    victims of earth and air,
                    the chiaroscuro twins,
                    red king and black queen
                    under a cocktail sun and a lonely moon 1190
                              Through the cracked glass

On a railway plat- They were like husband and wife waiting for a train
form he accepts the In a grey and bleeding dawn,
irrational depths of Hands clutched by the androgynous central child,
himself. Like a Divider and reconciler of their scarred disdain.
reclaimed Tammuz Watching the white orb boil in a platform puddle
who understands and While, adjusting darks, she said, "Isn't it like a moon?"
accepts Inanna's I knew why, I knew why she completed me, what I had projected
role, he is about to And what, as from a priest or nun, received,
escape his As when, turning the wheel and lowering sunlight, 1200
Underworld, I drew a shattered reflection from the moon-dark well.
And I knew I must live between, in the child's place,
And, turning to a stranger by the wall,
As to a Reflection who would not abdicate,
I said, "I accept my inner being, I accept it all,"
And saw him slope away, disconsolate.

                    I perceive, falsely,
                    A Reflection that is *me*;
                    To smash it is to be.

and it seems to him Leaving the station, I groped down empty streets 1210
that the power of his Until, near the stadium, I went down a yawning stair
Reflection is finally And lost my way into a hall of Buddhas.
broken. I saw them, my thousand selves in tiers
Like a football crowd at prayer;
Lost in a labyrinth of plaster whores

I panicked, but there,
Beneath the central image, confirming a brawl
I had no fears.
                    The lift went down a well
Into a mine of gleaming diamonds   1220
And golden gods with Egyptian heads were drawn past my closed eyelids.
Through falling masonry I rushed up into the shaking street –
And seeing the city crumbled into a thousand ruins,
And the dancing dead, I did not cry out or weep,
Wandering in the girdered rubble of an old personality.

He undergoes a per- And when i awoke, i was a floor below my thoughts,
sonality shift from   Looking out at the dawn as from a tiled bungalow –
his Reflection to the And suddenly, nourished by silence
irrational depths of   My seed-case burst into a thousand I's
his inner being. He   And a central stem broke through the tiled crown of my head.   1230
experiences illumi-   Hallelujah! in a dazzling universe i had no defence,
nation,   round that round white light, life and night were one
                      and i was afraid, for i did not know
                                          if the sun reflected
                 my reflecting sun

and perceives the   and in that four-sided garden
unity of the universe   rock and sea and sand
and is face to face   mountain and cloud and earth
with the divine world   mirrored in an empty mind
and with metaphysi-   reveal a refutable truth   1240
cal Reality.   between stone and stone
                                in an arbitrary frame
                                there is no difference, all is one
                                still or moving, all existence is the same

                                An Eastern sage tempts:
                                "(+A) +(-A) = Nothing,
                                The Absolute is where there is no difference."
                                The Being behind Existence

Rationally he resists   the stone garden reflects
the prospect of per-   what you want to see   1250
sonal immortality,   a mirror of
first in terms of   subjectivity
death,   and on this hill
                     bristling with monuments to synthesis
                     gape, earth, and reveal
                     a thousand insights into the abyss
                                     and, backslider, do
                                          you now deny
                                between system and finality
                                          there is no difference?

and secondly in   A blossom of white light

terms of his fellow
men.

illuminates the cosmic night, 1260
  my heart welled out –
a volley, and three men bowed low like acrobats
and under this ghastly sky, the condemned of all nations
are limping and crawling and groaning up the scorched hill,
writhing, screaming, feel their chopped bleeding, be faithful – Freeman, be
     faithful to your fellow men;
see – some are ignorant of such matters
but that spurting flesh is yours, you're one of them
  and whoever they are, would you abandon one?
  between man and man there is no difference. 1270

And when a headlight lit his stump of an arm

In a graveyard he
retreats from the
metaphysical, and
for the time being
rejects immortality
as a privilege he
has yet to come to
terms with, and
immediately stakes
all on existence,
which he now
perceives with
meaning. He sees
things as they are,
objectively, without
interference from
his sense of "I". He
perceives Being as
opposed to
Becoming.

In a graveyard of uniform stones, I looked for the stars,
No matter what escaped old bones, I stood by my fellow men.
I thought: 'If just one is damned or dealt extinction,
I will be too, and if all men are a part of One
And all shall be eternal, without exception,
Then without effort all are guaranteed,
And I reject a truth that ends all striving.'
And when I had shaken my head, my mind was calm,
In a long rhythm of shadows, of days and nights 1280
Like the scudding clouds on the unruffled moon-centred pool,
I mirrored the glory,
I was all existence in the silence of that stone garden.

  Darkness within
  Throws a chaotic waste on the empty screen;
  A disc of white-hot will
  Throws an orderly meaning on the sunlit screen;
  And the centre of the universe is in the self
  When only what one is is seen.

  A red-winged ladybird
    in sunlight, 1290
A meaning of gullwings by the turning tide.
To be
Is to perceive the world
As a stone-like unity.
Therefore, "percipere est esse",
To perceive truly is to be.

I was all "I", Becoming,
Before the Journey;
Now I share the sky
i perceive truly
  and feel all Being flow like a surging tide. 1300

I saw them at the break of day,

All my exorcised ghosts, sullenly skulking away.
And from the baked land joyously burst a prepuced palm.

And I was weary, weary – I prayed for rest, knowing
(+A) + (-A) = nothing;
Between red and black, the blaze of azaleas
And the dignified weeping of a dying piano,
In a disintegrating summer I became nothing,
I surpassed myself, on my way to becoming nothing.

And I was at peace.   1310
                                                    And I had liberated
A great tide of will I did not want to cease.

As a result he is unit- I turned the corpse with my toe, then climbed on up the iron tree
ed with his Shadow   Until our stony land spread out in the Western evening;
and he glimpses his   Then my Shadow obscured the sun at my feet
future task: he must   And spoke retrospectively from a future dawn:
communicate his   "Now that you have overcome and nothing but time divides us,
vision to his inau-   And know you are real, that your soul is eternal,
thentic Age.   I can reveal what is in store for your generation.
                         Through your rejection of social ego, which history has taken,   1320
                         And static Freud, already discredited,
                         And of reduction of all existence to partial, rational terms,
                         And of the will-less image of man which destroyed your fathers,
                         Who, lacking the forward vision, accepted defeat
                         Or reacted in historical transition,
                         You will escape. And what you will rebuild,
                         The 'new' form your age needs for ancient energy –
                         History will take that too, but you will have lived.
                         Your growth, not an enduring form, will be your goal.
                         Therefore turn the wheel."   1330

                                        To outgrow all ideas
                                        Save the important one,
                                        The upward thrust of the sap
                                        To a form of pagan height
                                        And the quiet, stout-timbered shrine,
                                        Or in the fading light,
                                        At one with his fellow man,
                                        The giant Buddha's calm;

                                        to begin in inner silence
                                        behind the outer smile   1340
                                        as empty as the stone garden
                                        between central stem and Shadow
                                        in the mosaic
                                        between child and irrational woman
                                        like the four-faced striking clock
                                        that woke me as a child

                    and measures an exile.

    I heard a cry from the old Professor's darkened room,
    "The Age of Analysis is dead!"
    Books lined with dust, a buzzing fly....   1350
                            While, naked on the petalled lawn,
    A new Baroque age is born.

                            Member, fingers,
    Hands, lips, mouth, hair, eyes, nostrils, crown, face – WHOLE.

Freeman now sees   "O fool, fool," said Freeman, "I have been a fool
himself first and   For I, a metaphysical, have clung to reason.
foremost as a meta-   I gaze and show my Age, and the way to live.
physical artist.   I have been tempted away from my true work, my art.
                        I am a maker, not a changer in a school;
                        I show man, and all the dreams and contradictions in his heart.   1360
                        I have two lives. I grieve, but I am apart.
                        I am a detached artist; I do not preach.
                        He who yearns to act and revitalise his Age
                        Learns action destroys vision and the window-gaze.
                        I am not a leader of movements, I am an artist with a frown.
                        I oppose the sick 'I', but a decade is a scudding cloud.
                        Let others nurse this body into a church.
                        My action is my gaze, and the clay-kneader's art.
                        I bear truths from the spirit, and images
                        I will fix into a pattern on a well-glazed jar   1370
                        So action and contemplation are held in balance.
                        Like a streetcorner artist, I am apart."
                        And he died away from a preacher's dream
                        Into the Orphic self of a healing art.

Freeman no longer   On Edogawa Bridge
perceives with mean-   In the noon glare I saw my shadow lengthen
ingless immediacy.   Into a self completed; a vast illusion,
He now takes stock.   Like a glimpse from ten years' solitude in mountains
His self-discovery   Or in Nitria, hearing more certainly the living word.
and the knowledge   I am my consciousness: always in the now,   1380
he has won will carry   Inextricable from a situation,
him forward.   I was a succession of states of mind.
                        Wandering at dusk in a forum of broken statues, I shuddered,
                        I was severed from my past, I had no meaning,
                        Like a Caesar severed from his plot, I had no meaning,
                        And at night, woken by silence from confused dreams,
                        I felt like a stranger in a vast museum.
                        Freedom breaks history, but does not give us knowledge.
                        Now I have taken possession of myself, have occupied my life,
                        I have strung moments like beads on a Catholic's necklace,   1390
                        I have ordered images in the Louvre of my soul.
                        And so wandering at dusk in a forum of statues – hurrah! hurrah!

                                    69

I felt a wind blowing my past into future.
That old man waiting on the village bench, he sees the now
Like petals dropping on water, like petals rising
From the stream of a quietly flowing Year.
Or as wave succeeds wave against the Trenarren peninsula.

Freeman, I said, there has been a real development
Between withdrawal endured and withdrawal chosen;
Vowing and defying, you seized your own,   1400
Knowing only a rebel can create himself,
For vitality is only won from opposition.
Now you are mature and know what is real,
Now your soul is an eternal, silent glow,
And to know your inner Being is to know your possibilities;
You have found peace and a real way of looking,
But like an improvising actor with a knowledge of Act One only,
Remember, the forces which control your present
Are forces which determine but are not unbreakable,
Just as a free act only enslaves until its revocation,   1410
Creates a system that only limits freedom
If, by absence of denial, it is daily rechosen:
That yard of heads and torsos behind the exhibition.

Despite a vision of   "No crumbling forces are unbreakable," Freeman had said.
the ruin which is   Grass sprouted from these rotting roofs and walls
eventually in store   But, dictating progress reports, nobody noticed;
for European civili-   And from this Monumental height men are crawling like ants
sation,   Hither and thither in a pile of rubble and iron,
Hither and thither without a unifying idea
In a heap of crumbled machinery and falling spires   1420
And, exhausted by aimlessness, drag weaker, falter,
Watch from now smouldering compost in the hard, clear dusk,
As with slow, regular flight,
A steel bird soars towards the crimson sun,
And fall, now burning; and, in a crimson conflagration,

                                        expire.

the meditating   The angry years, an age like wind and foam.
Freeman glimpses   Let us leave this inner kingdom, let us awaken to that blur.
Reality near   A skylark twittering above the wheat,
Trenarren and is able   Cows on green fields, primroses in the hedgerow.   1430
to affirm.   Let us dip back into the mind and fly to Trenarren.
Rejoice from this headland, my Shadow, let us rejoice
At this sea pounding these rocks, at these sparkling waves, this tide.
Now let our eyes open to this sparkling, dancing sea,
This watery stone garden, lapping round still rocks.
It images: the starry universe, whose waves
Of cosmic radiation fill the blue sky,
And all Existence enveloped in Being;

THE SILENCE, 1965 – 1966

The one ocean of manifesting Being;
The Void of unmanifest Non-Being   1440
Behind it; and the One which contains both
For $(+A) + (-A)$ = zero,
Great nothing, the Infinite.

       Let us be

The blue meaning of the foaming round the rocks.
Let us be the fourfold sea!

My Shadow sees
With a metaphysical eye.

Let us be the sea!

January 1965-June 1966,
revised August 1970, 25-26 July 1974 and later

THE WINGS AND THE SWORD

1966 – 1969

ARCHANGEL

"Oh, we will convince them that only then will they become free when they have resigned their freedom to us and have submitted to us....And they will all be happy, all the millions of creatures, except the hundred thousand who rule over them. For we alone, we who guard the mystery, we alone shall be unhappy."

                                        Dostoevsky

I

Like domes of a cavernous mind
These groined and frescoed vaults
Over pictured pillars and walls
Dream out a recurrent theme
In this Kremlin mausoleum:
Grand Dukes and palaced Tsars
As haloed, Orthodox Saints
Pursue a spiritual quest
In an unequal Christendom
While apart from the rich man's feast   10
Are rebellions of the starving,
Bread-fisted Leaders and skirmish,
And, as in the nearby palace,
The future tyrants of well-fed Peoples'
        States.

Like a collage of propaganda in a self-divided
        brain;
Leave these bare-footed porters and gaping
        bars,
The tapewormed squatters under the
        blackened Hong Kong church
And, shaking your head at this exhausted,
        ellow earth,
Cross over the guarded bridge between
        decaying rails,
And then, to triumphal singing, sweep past
        laughing girls   20
Who wade in green-brown water, or till fertile
        fields,
Pass whitewashed walls to a blue-clad,
        virginal city

And the dark, censored silence round puritan
        Kwangtung;
Or, well before midnight, in a dim-lit
        nightmare,
Pass pocked and terraced, ruined Berlin
        turrets,
And, after the dark waste and the row of
        searchlights,
The final river, approach the "protective" wall
Until, near the floodlit gate and the out-
        stretched angel,
The blaze of jumping neon thinks unrepressed
        words.
Behind those squinting eyes is a schizo-
        phrenic's mind;   30
How but by containing both sides, can we
        heal
This split down the mind of Europe and the
        world?

There is a disease within
And Revolutions breed
Like resisting antibodies
In an infected blood,
To exterminate the germs,
And leave the body healed;
Shots from the Winter Palace,
An absent Chief Commander,   40
A Tsarina's doting on
A haemophiliac son,
A faith-healing lecher –
Were these responsible for
Or were they symptoms of
The sickness that angered and drove
These thick-coated workers
In the queues at the bakers' shops
To strike processions and shots?
And, after the abdication,   50
Before the Sverdlovsk blood,
On the second disguised return
And after Kerensky's flight,
To storm the Winter Palace
And hail the Smolny cure?
Or, after a crusader drank gold leaf,

And a hundred day's reform,
Were an imprisoned Emperor,
An "Old Buddha's" mistaken scorn,
And, after the indemnities,   60
A retirement "with sore feet"
And reprisals for a bomb,
Were these responsible for
Or were they symptoms of
The sickness that compelled
These thin-ribbed peasants
In their landlord's cropless fields
To arm for a republic?
And, after a twelve year old's twelve day
    rule,
Warlords and a Sun-set,   70
Butchery under a hill
And a march against a traitor,
After the temple meditation
Through to the great idea,
And the three-sided war,
And after Chiang's escape,
To storm Nanking Headquarters
And hail the Tien An Mien cure?
And how can one proclaim
It is better to be diseased?   80

When the reactionaries triumphed, there were
    groans from the Party seats,
To sombre music, they were flogged to
    execution, the anti-bourgeois
    rebels,
But then Marx and Lenin shone up on the
    funereal drape,
And as the light streamed from their heads,
    the broken army recovered,
With shining eyes, they pledged faith in their
    undaunted Leader,
And, with flags and rifles, rushed across the
    stage to bring great victories,
And when the proud imperialists and their
    lackeys were finally driven into
    the sea
A great cheer went up, all applauded, and as
    the orchestra joined in,
With one accord both choirs stood up and
    sang out
While soldiers with joyous faces gathered
    under the red banner   90
And laughed and hugged peasants laden with
    fruit from a bumper harvest

And there was Paradise under their Chairman
    Leader's blessedly streaming
    head.
As the students crowded round me, laughing
    among the magnolias,
I felt a great singing in me, I wanted to sob for
    happiness
For I had gone back to a dawn and was with
    an original man;
But when, at a woman's command, eight
    hundred children burst into
smiles and applauded,
And, after clambering like guerillas round the
    barbed wire in the playground
And shooting imperialist bombers out of the
    amusement centre sky,
When five year olds danced "Embroidering
    the Saviour's portrait" –
I knew they had put the smiles on those faces,
    and, for the sake of the future,   100
Taught them to be joyous and grateful at well-
    rehearsed signals
As if they were dogs, trained to salivate at a
    bell,
And although I could not say "Insincere", for
    can saliva be,
I said "No" to their Party, and I knew their
    Saviour was an enslaver of souls.
"Yes" said the former landlord in his pig-stye,
    and, when jogged, added
"I am grateful to the Commune for permitting
    me to be a member,"
And he left the barn and stood outside his
    former house
While the peasants gawped in a silent arc, as
    if round a belled leper;
"Yes" said the Shanghai capitalist in his
    unliberated mansion,
"I came to see that capitalism should be
    detested,   110
These Americans call it brainwashing, but it is
    only the process
Of seeing things in their right perspectives,"
And his eyes seemed confused, as though a
    lobotomised mind
Had been dictated over, and bits of the old
    remained;
"Excuse me," said the official in the sacked
    ruins of the Summer Palace,
After the board of eligible "voters" for the

unopposed Party
And the barred library on the purged and
    deserted campus,
"Our history books say the concessions were
    seized in 1949,
And Romanization will not change a thing,
I know that Confucius was in a fairy tale." 120
And, staring into the green pond in the
    Empress Dowager's Garden,
Where, marble walks and bridges and tea-
    house pavilions,
The world was a circular quest, as on a
    meditating mind,
I was back in a past like the diseased Saints'
    Western Hell
Where children dance a plague song, and jeer
    and scowl
When the bell tolls for their Saviour's funeral,
Where an infectious idiot reviles Trafalgar
    Square
And, unremoulded, votes out a clever fool,
Where no historians expurgate our accounts
Or claim Suez was given away when the
    troops withdrew, 130
Where truth is in libraries and one's reflecting
    self
And we are here for more than bread and
    smiles
And no "protecting" Parties enforce our
    "health".

II

That cry for human justice that smashes the old
And heralds in a decadent, equal age –
That Leader's cry of horror deserves our
    praise
Despite our cry of horror at the murdered
    Tsar;
But, despite counter-revolution and
    foreigners,
The oldest pretexts for "protecting" power,
Now those bellies are full, the struggle is
    over, 140
And that other howl, at masters, cannot last
Long after the masters have been overthrown,
And those full-bellied Leaders on Lenin's
    mausoleum
Have known no masters, save among them-
    selves;
That floodlit corpse may seem indestructible,

But what of the bustless grave under the
    Kremlin wall,
And are not Ramesses' laws now unread
    hieroglyphics
Round the cracked vellum of his "immortal"
    form?
And one condition is changeless; as those
    Saints were aware,
Interrupting night, the People; are no
    more, 150
And that long curving queue across the
    cobbled square
Will see itself in an unimmortal image,
And will need those sad-eyed, uncollectivised
    Tsars;
And that causeway across the cobbled
    approach to Heaven,
And the cloud of dust that tactfully obscures
The distant gate and goal of an earth's
    endeavour.

Those ancient scholars knew:
Like a Roman aqueduct
Those four crumbling arches
In that square Nanking pavilion   160
Sign to weary horsemen
To dismount and bow
Before the solemn procession
Through the marble carvings
That guard the chambered hill
And the rich imperial riddle
Of the rebel Ming founder's
Hidden sarcophagus;
And the end of the quest:
After an immortal lust,   170
Before a noose on Coal Hill,
A doubted divinity,
A hastily sealed coffin
And Wan-li's unembalmed dust.

The children joyously waved flags under the
    Ching arches
And, eyes shining, applauded at the ringing
    command,
And as I walked among them, imagining how
    Christ would feel,
I saw a lone figure turn away under the distant
    trees
As though He had despaired of finding souls
    in this happy material.

Outside the church gates, some old men sat
    and huddled,   180
And within, all round the kneeling woman,
    were fourteen agonies
As He stumbled under his cross, jeered by
    soldiers and peasants,
And, defined in blood and thorns, he was an
    individual.
As they stepped, one by one, from the
    Kremlin Armoury door, and
    frowned,
Watching each face, I thought I was counting
    the purged
As if, still bewildered, each corpse were
    entering Hell,
And before the wall and the blindfold and
    Nothing, each was an individual.

    This forward slump concludes
    The march through a dawn mist,
    The proud stand at the post   190
    Of a "traitor" to the State.
    What fundamental value
    Should a Leader venerate?
    Into night and silence
    We came and went,
    Me and my brothers;
    No value before man.
    Within an eternal dark
    Each single man must choose
    What he will revere;   200
    The wise man feels, and sighs,
    "Existence is my all,"
    And, between the eyes of his neighbour,
    "That man, too, faces the wall,
    And what he may sacrifice
    No belief or Leader may take."
    No Raskolnikov or Mao
    Can rationalise away
    His feeling of horror
    At a Napoleon's vow   210
    Or the smash of a Party bullet
    Or, after a scalpel's scraping,
    A desympathised citizen
    With a Party's brain;
    No less if the victim has,
    Like a cold Beria
    Who never learnt to feel,
    Taken the side of evil,
    And threatened the lives of others;

    The ideal Blakean "should"   220
    Of "every thing that lives"
    Is always preferable to
    But more impractical than
    The practical Cromwell's "can't"
    Of "cruel necessity",
    Or of limbs in Saigon billets
    Or torsos in Haiphong
    Where what is threatened is
    The existence of the State:
    The insolent soldier inside the Felpham
    gate.   230
    No value before man.

That Leader may value those men before the
    wall,
But, worker and boss, peasant and landlord,
To feel the world as a whole, he must struggle
Away from his group or class to a knowledge
    of all men's beings;
And can a Leader know all if he does not
    know himself,
If he is bewildered, as in an exhibition of
    disconnected pictures
And, never relating them, has never located
    that centre
Wherein he is a part of all men's silence and
    all men are brothers,
And if he has never related the whole of him-
    self to the history of man –   240
Can a man see the world as a whole if he is in
    fragments?
Hence this Saints' Cathedral: among images
    of tombs
These murals and icons tell first of a buried
    mind,
And, after completion, when studied and
    understood,
Reveal the full meaning of memories made
    whole,
And, as on either side of Cuba, like Kennedy
    and Krushchev,
In two glowering faces, reduce to opposite
    pictures
The brotherhood of man and the wholeness of
    the earth.

III

The old men huddled, the woman slunk away;
And, standing at dusk on the crowded

People's Square   250
As on the grey cortex of a great remoulded
     brain
While, like happy slogans, obedient faces
Wandered painlessly round and round against
     sterilized museums,
I knew, only in such nightmare cities of
     ordered streets
And thoughts like lighted windows in
     Ministry hotels,
Could that cross be a centre, like the
     Forbidden City –
Like the Archangel Cathedral within the
     Kremlin wall
The Church must be denied to contain
     Christ's vision.
Otherwise, established ally of that Welfare
     board,
In a dwindling parish of tired, habitual
     aims   260
And loudmouth individuals whose only quest
Is for a group of skirts near the broken kiosk,
The vicar raffles liquor in the crumbling
     porch,
And the visionary walks apart in deep forests;
And where, oh where, is that spiritual way of
     life
That takes for granted icons and sad-eyed
     Saints,
And could drive all those howling slogans in
     Trafalgar Square
And shame to shallowness the Red inquisitors
Who, in agonised compassion, wade in blood,
And then, to save the many from their own
     tormented brains   270
Degrade them beneath the values of
     compulsorily happy States?

Indifferent Tsars and tyrants,
Compassionate inquisitors;
Can nothing bring together
Enslaving Leader and Saint?
As I stared at the murals' centre
In this Cathedral-tomb,
The Archangel became a Shadow
With a sword and wings outstretched,
And I saw in the second icon   280
The future of the West,
From the Atlantic to the Urals:
Into the People's Square,

From the Cathedral gates,
File in the morning rush-hour
An élite of self-made Saints
Each still on the last hour's quest.
They reach the central banner
In the forum of statues and graves,
The great mazed mandala   290
Under which the supplicants wait;
Decades of contemplation
Show in their white-haired peace
As, trusting to perfect feelings,
They value each equal they greet;
Until, whispering on silence,
They glide to the Leaders' Hall,
Their hearts, with a World-Lord's
     wholeness,
At the centre of life, of all,
Their hearts where all past and future
     meet.   300

An outstretched angel of Paradisal vision,
And a dream of an escapist dreamer in an
     impossible heat.

BLIGHTY

"Something is rotten in the state of Denmark."

                 Hamlet

"Blighty – England, home, after foreign service";
"blight – disease of unknown or atmospheric
origin."

           Oxford English Dictionary

Aching in every limb, near-blind in this
     cluttered room,
I feel as if I am falling apart into a
     dismembered corpse:
My lungs tear on my ribs, and, straining to
     hold this rotting flesh together,
My spine stretches and threatens to snap into
     a heap of bones;
Like the monotonous cog in that old and
     rusted clock
My head throbs with the squelchings of a
     reluctant heart
That ticks lethargically towards the jangling
     alarm.
What is wrong? What has gone wrong? Is it
     just this greying hair,

Is it the natural breakdown after the turbulent
time,
Like the broken-handed flutterings from an
Edwardian spring,   10
Or is it some cancer? Sometimes, in the
autumn sunset,
These cells rise up against me, clogging and
multiplying –
They respect nothing and will be subordinated
to nothing –
And I feel I am being strangled by my own
ill-disciplined growth.
Or is it, far worse, that self-visited running-
down,
Like an abandoned ticking towards the
snapping of a rusted coil,
Whose end is contained in the initial winding
up?
Inevitability is a torture under a tomb,
But this is not "just flu", and if I shan't
recover, I want to know.

For the decline in my social position, I have
always apportioned blame   20
And defended myself with excuses, some of
which may be true:
All right, I have said, before my two children
quarrelled
I was the most respected in this snobbish
district
And everyone feared me because I was a
successful tycoon,
But haven't I always preferred to live at
home,
Was I ever very interested in my rotten
fortune?
And while I was doing my good works,
preaching and teaching the town-
kids,
And, taking advantage of my change of life,
the district turned against me
And ungratefully called me a speculator, a
dirty profiteer,
Wasn't I ready to give it all away, wasn't I
scrupulously generous,   30
Didn't I treat them all like human beings,
putting my interests last?
I won their good opinion, didn't I, didn't I
keep my friends,
And don't they still come to my house and sit

by my bed
And express their gratitude for my
philanthropy
Just as they expressed their gratitude for my
scrupulosity?
No one hates me, and my house is always full
of well-wishers,
And aren't I even now being supported by the
syndicate over the road?
And what's wrong in that, after all I've done
for others –
Should one be blamed for having wealth, and
then for giving it away?
And who's to say I shouldn't pamper my
body and have things a little
cushy,   40
Isn't a woman of property entitled to a spot of
comfort
Even when times get bad? And what if I
haven't worked as I should?
It's not easy to work for a living when you've
been used to having it good.
I have always made excuses, but now I
seriously wonder,
Although I didn't know it, wasn't the
surrender an act of exhaustion,
A symptom of the late latent phase of a
possibly malignant disease?
If so, I can account for the inertia of my
present condition,
If so, it's all very well to say "You should pull
yourself together,"
But how can you pull anything together when
you're perpetually out of sorts,
And where do you start when you don't even
know what's wrong?   50
And anyway, what's the use, if I must
continue this decline to the death
While this lovely old house is turned into an
electrical shop by my newfangled
son
Or by those grasping creeps in the terraces
over the road?

A plastic, American heart
That pumps a low-pressured blood,
Driven by compressed air
And connected by nylon tubes,
Can, when sewn under the skin,
Make a decayed system thud,

And, on an electrocardiogram,   60
Shew that I am a machine.
Will it prolong my life?
Like a diseased culture
I decay with progress –
Health centres round my heart
And a comprehensive head
Do not make up for vision;
And these congealed scabs like churches,
Recall a throbbing circulation
That ripened this crabby womb: 70
Sucked by these parasites,
Down my clotted arteries
A thick, European blood
Pumps jumbled images
Into this nightmare room.

The doctor said "Come off it, Blighty, you're
    seeing things,"
But I know what he's keeping from me, I
    know what's in store,
The paralyzing strokes, the hardening arteries
    to a near-blind brain,
I know what the getting of prosperity does,
    the delayed reckoning
Like a payment for the pleasures of a riotous
    youth.   80
There are no sores on one's body when one's
    breasts begin to swell,
Not until one goes out and gives oneself to the
    backward and unclean,
And even then the fairness without hides the
    rotting mess within;
But, like a spot of decay in a shining enamel
    tooth,
It festers and spreads, until, bursting through
    the outer complacency,
Long after the promiscuous pleasures have
    been forgotten
A chankrous nemesis brands the suppurating
    skin.
And since, despite my rotting inside, my
    exterior is still fair,
Since times are bad and I have not yet lost my
    glamour,
It is natural I should think of opening my legs
    in my own home, instead of
    working for a living;   90
I have as many entrances as my clients have
    wishes,

And when I seek relief in dreams, all kinds of
    lusty fancies spring up in my
    brain.

Or is it also the consequence of one disastrous
    stroke
That went unrecognised in the crack-up of the
    turbulent time
And the killing strain of the last, exhausting
    quarrel,
As if my body had said "Why should my grey
    cells govern and not the white?"
And a long rule was broken, a strong brain
    paralyzed?
If this is so, isn't it useless to seek to subdue
    these cancerous cells
With a strong nightmare of Ironside authority,
For wouldn't the flesh resist, saying
    "Shouldn't my limbs be free to
    fall apart?"   100
And besides, what use is will-power if the
    body is old and cancered
And inexorably visited with irreversible sins,
For if the brain is healthy, then will the body
    be so too?
No, rather, who will operate on this cancerous
    body, to prolong my life,
For if the body is healthy, then will not the
    brain be so too?

Conflicting voices, I go nearly mad
With the confused babblings of opposite
    opinions –
It's as though I had conflicting doctors for
    each identity,
For I am my son's neglected mother, and the
    one opposite the terraces,
And the philanthropist's ghost, and the dying
    whore;   110
What is certain is, I shall never recover my
    property,
And never again will I be number One in the
    district;
I must watch my prestige shrink to these four
    rooms, to this one room,
And, if I recover, I can only hope to get in
    with those bores over the road,
Or perhaps persuade my tasteless son to
    support me for old times' sake,
Even though he no longer listens to me. And

why shouldn't he, he's stinking
    rich.
Otherwise, I am nearly blind, and I can see
    nothing in the future
Save a stay-at-home's bitter decline to the end,
Staring at the grandfather clock among the
    latest gadgets,
Growing flowers, thinking about the next
    meal, humming the latest pop, 120
Eking out the overdraft on all sorts of
    trivialities.
Nothing much will happen – what can you
    expect if you're almost dead?

What does it matter that, before she finally
    decays,
This right old schizo, dressed as a mini-
    skirted whore,
Imagines her cancerous body a chankered
    corpse in a bankrupt's grave?

AN INNER HOME

"The forest which surrounds them is their godhead."
(From a review by Mr Geoffrey Gorer of *Wayward
Servants*, a book on the Mbuti pygmies in the Ituri
rain forest, N.E. Congo)

I have followed the Waltham stream:
Winding through sunny meadows,
Stilled by lilies and reeds
It seems a long way from
King Harold's rough-hewn bridge
And Edward's two arches,
Till under the Abbey's tower
On either side of stone
Under two modern humped bridges
With a sudden tugging of weed   10
The stillness overflows
To plunge in a cascade down
And froth into gentle channels
And trickle underground
And I turned away in a panic,
There was weed in my hair and toes.
That child, who, sick from fleeing a baying
    form,
Lay on the humming Stubbles near the
    Witches' Copse
Like a sacrificial victim near Stonehenge,
And, seeing a six-spot burnet, suddenly felt

secure,   20
Walled round and alone in a forest enclosure;
That child seemed a long way from that
    adolescent
Who, sick at having seen the universe
In a string of bubbles blown through a child's
    wire-ring,
Stood in Loughton Camp among writhing
    pollards
Like nerve tracts rising to a memory rooted in
The skulls of Boadicea's unconscious dead,
And, under the dark grey cortex, distinctly
    heard
The silence beneath the distant hum of cars
And knew himself under the patter of falling
    leaves;
And that young man, who, retching at one last
    sigh,   30
Stood where he fished as a child with sewn
    flour-bags
And skidded to the island on an icy slide
And stared past his reflection in the gravel pit
As if seeking an image in an unconscious
    mind,
Until his darkness split, and in the autumn sun
The pond blazed in an unknowable revelation,
He said Yes, and, looking back through the
    blinding leaves,
He longed to be a statue between the two ponds
And gaze for ever on the thrusting of those
    trees;
Or that poet, who, sick with impending
    exile,   40
Having driven round Lippitt's Hill to
    Tennyson's estate,
Crunched broken glass in the littered Witches'
    Copse
Alone in the centre of a living mandala,
And knew, although before him was
    approaching stone,
Like a hermit enfolded in a godhead he
    projects
He would always be enfolded in this Forest,
In this unchangeable image of an inner home.

Like the tree-enfolded face a still stream
    reflects
Below humped bridges where waving weed is
    pressed
Before it plunges down and is lost in foam. 50

THE CONDUCTOR
(OR: AT THE ROYAL ALBERT HALL)

Under lights which hang like planets from the
    dome
A banked society, in tiers to the highest gods,
Is appalled at the orchestra's changing tune:
A diminuendo that chilled a hundred moods
Before it froze our frowning generation's
"Barbarian" breaking down; bar new soloists,
All's finished in the mind on the podium,
On whose fighting gestures every eye is fixed.

Like a demogogue appealing to the pit
In Rome or Athens, he varies old themes,   10
Then takes his bow, as if for a Cabinet;
Standing in a crisis crowd in Downing Street,
Brooding on Empires and a European Queen,
I wished we had a centre, like these seats',
With a fixed prospect: when he leaves his
    podium,
Society will be a crowded street.

Like a Saint he has turned his back on the still
    tiered throng;
But, seeing a drinking orchestra playing parts,
Now simpering, now with a lambasting
    scorn –
A scowling generation wearing grotesque
    masks   20
That have been worn a hundred times before –
I knew he was the Reflection they played to,
    for applause;
And seeing him as the tyrant who makes false
Should we not cry "Rise up, orchestra, and
    drive him to the door"?

The orchestra plays false parts but what it
    plays
Is real; the Artist wears a high priest's mask
And, reciting ritual, rips back the altar-veil,
Makes initiates reel at a hacked-out human
    heart;
Art, like revolution, bleeds in decay
A dialectic the Red Guards don't know: 30
If the Artist were the centre of this banked,
    tiered place,
Only he would wear the Reflection's Leader's
    robes.

The Leader who waves his arms in a roaring
    square
Blusters down the deafening Way of Action;
The Saint who stops his ears, retires, and
    hears
A chord, glides up the Way of Contemplation;
But this Artist does both; see, with screwn-up
    lids,
He quivers at an unheard crescendo,
And yet, with impatient hands, he acts, to the
    fingertips –
Without him the orchestra could not play a
    note.   40

And I have glimpsed, in mirrors in different
    rooms,
One not unlike that Flash Harry tyrant
Who directs a hundred reflexes in a stale old
    tune,
And a Shadow of that masked Artist or Saint
Who summons a hundred memories along
To roll and pluck and screech and clash and
    blow,
And transcend themselves in a unified
    ensemble,
And fill with rhythms and phrases this great
    decaying dome.

TWO MORAL LETTERS AFTER HORACE
AN EPISTLE TO AN ADMIRER OF OLIVER CROMWELL (ADVICE TO A YOUNG REVOLUTIONARY GOING INTO POLITICS)

There's "going to be a revolution," and you say
You will "be another Cromwell, or at least an
    Ireton".
You are going into politics to "emulate the
    great man"
So that you can "bring in anarchy and storm
    out the Windsors".
I do not argue with your ability to wreak
    confusion:
We live in a hurricane Age, and chaos is
    never far away,
If it isn't an oil crisis that is ruining our
    civilisation
Then it's bombs, murders, strikes, kid-
    napping,
And these days only a tiny gust of cruelty will
    snuff

Out a monarch. And who knows, so many of
 our people   10
Are discontented that the whirlwind may find
 followers enough.
All I ask is: have you the right motive? Is it
 your country
You "wish to save", or, thwarted, are you
 succumbing
To personal ambition? For it is one thing for a
 nation
To rise out of the ashes, another for it to be
 shattered by an ambition.

Of course, I do not say you are such a man.
But consider your hero. Before leaving his
 glebe house
He, too, championed his poorer neighbours,
But once he was a Calvinist, he was too
 concerned with the present
To scheme the Protectorship, and he was
 surprised   20
By his own advancement, which was "guided
 by God",
And due to "sudden providences in things".
 Historians say
His sincerity and integrity are beyond
 question.
He felt he was a tempest in the winds of a
 high power.
Consider: after the passing of the Grand
 Remonstrance
Of what the nation had suffered under Charles,
He said that if it "had been rejected, I would
 have sold all I had next morning
And never seen England more." And when
 the fight for sovereignty began
Between King and Parliament, and the
 Royalists were winning,
When Cromwell was Lieutenant-General of
 the Eastern Association 30
Under "sweet meek" Manchester, whom he
 blamed for Newbury,
Consider: he himself proposed the Self-
 Denying Ordinance
To reorganise the army, he himself raised the
 idea
That no member of Parliament should hold
 military office.
By his own proposal he ended his military
 career.

He could have prosecuted Manchester, and
 replaced him,
In place of this legal barrier to his own
 employment;
He did not know that Fairfax would petition
 Parliament
To prolong his command, that he would win
 at Naseby
And Langport, that Oxford would capitulate
 and end   40
The First Civil War save for little sieges.
Consider: when the Church was reorganised,
 and the Presbyterians
Allied with the King to restore him to
 sovereignty,
And when the army, unpaid, petitioned him,
 he did not listen,
Fearing anarchy. But when the Presbyterians
 invited in
The Scots, and the army mutinied, then he
 listened,
To prevent anarchy, with a strong hand.
If he had wanted to revolt against Parliament,
 why did he leave it so late
And consider: when he had appointed a
 Council to negotiate
And had won the concessions the army
 wanted,   50
He was for re-establishing the monarchy,
 again to avoid anarchy,
And when the soldiers submitted "The
 Agreement of the People",
Whereby Parliament was to be set aside by an
 appeal to the people,
He opposed them, persuaded them that
 Parliament should judge
The King. Only when Charles escaped to
 Carisbrooke
And intrigued with Scotland, and refused the
 ultimatum
Of Parliament, did he announce that the army
 stood by Parliament
Against "an obstinate man whose heart God
 had hardened".
Only then did he favour setting aside the
 King.
Consider: when the "Commonwealth's-men"
 urged the trial of the King, 60
He kept himself "in the clouds according as
 Providence should direct",

And so little did he dream of ruling England
that he planned
To marry his eldest son into a family of no
standing.
And consider: even after the Second Civil
War – after Poyer's revolt
And the defeat of the Scots at Preston and
perfidious Charles
Had met Parliament at Newport and promised
Presbyterianism for three years
"Merely in order to my escape", as he wrote –
when the Army
Demanded punishment for the "grand author
of all our troubles"
And seized the King and took him to
Hampshire,
And Pride purged the Presbyterian majority in
Parliament,   70
Cromwell, though "not acquainted with this
design", approved,
But was for sparing the King's life. Only
when all compromises
Failed, and the King, refusing to plead,
Preferred death to surrender, only then
Did the military revolution proceed: "We will
cut
Off his head with the crown upon it."

                    Cromwell never sought
The Protectorship. He opposed the resignation
of Fairfax,
Which made him Captain-General and
Commander-in-Chief
Of the Commonwealth. "I have not sought
these things," he wrote,
"Truly I have been called unto them by the
Lord. He will enable   80
His poor worm and weak servant to do His
will."
Consider: after his victory over the Scots and
young Charles
When he had the power to dissolve the Long
Parliament
That delayed reforms, he refused until the Bill
For a New Representative, which the army
opposed.
Consider: after he had closed the Long
Parliament with musketeers,
And was expected to crown himself as the
only authority left,

Being Commander-in-Chief by Act of
Parliament,
He resolved to curtail his power, and called
A little Parliament of godly men.   90
Consider: when Lambert offered him the
crown he refused,
And he "did not know one tittle of
the resignation" of the Little
Parliament,
And though again he was in possession of the
dictatorship he had not sought
He accepted the Protectorship to place his
power under
A Council or Parliament, and was installed
not in a general's
Scarlet but in plain black citizen's coat.
And after the moral crusade, the Sunday
observance,
The punishing of swearing, and the closing of
alehouses,
After the tolerance to all worshippers and the
victory over Spain,
After the twelve Major-Generals acted as
police,   100
After Sindercombe's plot against him, when
Parliament offered him the Crown
Again, he refused once more, but accepted the
Protectorship
As the people's man, rather than as the army's
nominee.
"There is not a man living can say I sought
it," he said,
"No, not a man or woman treading upon
English ground."

And after the agued end and the succession of
his son,
And Monk's readmission of the Presbyterians
Pride expelled,
And the Restoration – the flowers and
swinging bells,
The tapestries in the streets, the three carcases
On the triple tree at Tyburn, the three
heads   110
In Westminster Hall – after the return to
before
The Civil Wars – what of his life's work then?
It was as if he had never existed.
                    No, your hero
Refused power at every turn.

And in those times revolution made some
    sense!
My advice to you is: if you are going into
    politics, deal
With everyday necessity, and leave the Dark
    to Providence!

EPISTLE TO HIS IMPERIAL HIGHNESS, ON HIS BIRTHDAY

Imperial Highness, on your birthday,
Spare a thought for the poor of the world.
Use your influence like your father; end
Their suffering; for your seeds have over-
    flowed.

As I drive to your reception in your
    chauffeured car,
I think of the Hiroshima your father
    remembers,
Not the garden town I have just returned
    from.
I think of charred wood and ashes, of your
    children
Under droning planes, the orange flash and
    blot,
The wind over a smoking, flattened plain. 10
I see a slag-heap and a towering mushroom,
And in an underground shelter, a brave
    Emperor
Outspoken: "I cannot bear to see my people
Suffering any longer, I cannot bear it." Do not
    forget that.

On the new Tokaido line, skimming through
Black chimney smoke towards your Eiffel
    tower,
Swooping low over the curly-tiled roofs
Of the sleepy outskirts of the largest city,
Glimpsing the red sun on your misty
    mountain,
Fujisan, I felt like a Second Coming. Later 20
The city was like an upset box of bricks
In the petrol haze. O your new fly-overs,
Your great buildings! O the money in your
    Maronouchi!
I passed the Bank of Japan, above whose
    vaults
I sit once a week, I went straight to JETRO.
From the top of its windows, the US Embassy
Was drenched in a blood-red light, and I knew

Japan has risen again, the Japanese sun is
    rising,
Japan is again poised for empire, only this time
A peaceful one. Yet what have you done for
    Asia? 30
What aid have you given? Great economic
    power,
Like a banknote, has great responsibility on
    the back,
And material advance a spiritual mission.
Gone are the days of isolation and trade-
    barriers,
Of narrow nationalism. You are the world's
    uncle now.

How are empires created? We have read of
    the rise
Of all of them, you and I, sitting upstairs
In your secluded palace. We both know that
    some
Spill over, like copper suds from a full
    granary,
An overflow from material prosperity, that
    others 40
Spread outwards like an epidemic that is out
    of control,
The catching germs of an ideological fervour.
Your people do not want to emigrate, they are
    not like
The British who have open minds, who would
    open up
A new world. They enjoy a full storehouse
At home. O I know there are still things to be
    done.
Your surpluses are nothing, one crisis
Will scatter them into the Pacific. You have to
    build
A chamber that is proof against the "black
    mist"
Of men who make a profit for themselves. 50
You need green parks and fresh rivers
Whose fish are not poisoned by mercury and
    other waste.
These considerations rightly concern you, but
    do not forget
The sufferings in Asia of peoples of your race.
Look at South and North Vietnam; look at the
    two Koreas;
Look at Taiwan and China; Malaysia,
    Indonesia,

Look at India and Pakistan. We need peace
In our world, we need Asia to unite as a
    prelude
To world government by the world. And for
    that we need
Prosperity in Asia. Your economic empire, 60
Your spill-over, should pour grain into the
    Bank
For Asian Development. You have learned
    from your mistakes,
The butchery of thousands is behind you now,
    though it can never
Be erased from your tradition: the Bushido
Contempt for surrender, the living skeletons,
Sick, starving, throughout Asia put to the
    sword,
With an "It was difficult to cut today, but in
    Hokiji's
Demonstration, the neck was cut perfectly."
And death for your father was the height of
    glory.

O the contradictions of the last twenty
    years!   70
O the opposition in this sultry, backward
    region.
O the conflicts in your own uncertain bosom!
Walking at dusk near Nichigeki, I have seen
The unpitying frown of a pow camp
    commander,
The pitiful scars of a Hiroshima victim;
I have greeted industrialists, and an Asian
    banker,
And I have wondered how you will unite
    these opposite dreams.

O, there is unity. The other day
I sat with the President of an international
    bank,
Discussing Ahriman and Ahura Mazda,   80
The dark-light of Zoroaster which are
    eternally apart,
And he said, "Yin and Yang, our dark-light,
    or 'yo' in Japanese,
Are united by Tao." And he mentioned the
    "Yi King" –
Our I Ching – which came out of the Tao
    circle,
The "Great Extreme" being rolled out into
    one line,

Or so some say. (Others say it came from a
    map
Given forth by the Yellow River, a map that
    has perished
In which Yin comes from the moon and Yang
    from the sun.)
He fished in his briefcase and found fifty
Bamboo sticks, which he shook over his
    head   90
To foretell the future, saying: "Originally we
    found
The hexagram by heating a tortoise shell
Until it cracked, but now we ask Heaven
To give an answer through the bamboo sticks.
But remember, there is no absolute answer,
For yin is contained in yang, and vice versa,
And each hexagram can be reversed." And
    behind the changes
I glimpsed the One, the Tao, in which all
    conflicts
Are reconciled. It was like the one Heaven-
    Man-Earth,
That unites your ikebana, or the one force 100
Behind the pebbles and rocks in your Ryoanji
    Zen garden.

And again the other day, I saw your opposites
Dancing in harmony. You invited me
To see the imperial Gagaku
On a stage with two flame shields supporting
Spoked sun and moon. After the wind and
    string,
The reeds between the thumbs like a boy's
    coarse grass,
A red quartet with broad sleeves appeared
    from
Behind the left flame drum that held the sun –
The Yang – stood one in each corner, and
    danced   110
A "samai" dance in slow unison. They looked
So gentle, but after a Mongolian beast
In a brown mask danced with a knobbled
    stick
Like a bone, they reappeared in true form:
In helmets, carrying Gothic shields, spears
And swords. They were hostile to each other,
They shook their weapons; but danced to one
    tune,
A slow, stately, grave dance that held them
    together,

Just as your father, the Son of Heaven,
Held the sun and moon together among these
     flames.   120
So it is with your identities, with the powers
     of Asia.

Your first kamikaze pilot, one of the few to
     live,
Cashes my cheques at the Hongkong and
     Shanghai Bank.
National conflicts do not last. No Reign
Of Virtue or Terror lasts, and the Red Guards
Across the water proclaim: Communism too
     will pass.
The Vietnam War is a conference away from
     its end,
Nations will settle, as Malaysia and Indonesia
     have settled
And where once they persecuted your people
     will restore,
I petition your Highness to work for the
     world's good.   130
When I went to see Kabuki, it was *Kanjincho*.
A yamabushi, a monk travelling
The countryside to raise funds for a temple.
He was told he must have a subscription scroll,
I solicit funds for the temple of the world.
This parchment on which I write is my
     "kanjincho" scroll.

Now at your birthday party, the only
     foreigner,
I stand in a dark suit, drinking with your
     Household
And guests. You are surrounded by men you
     could influence.
Japan has risen from the ruins. You are
     neutral, peace-loving.   140

Sound the trumpet, beat the drum,
The Imperial birthday's come.
Put on your morning coat and bow,
Honour the divine son now.
Imperial Highness, on your birthday
Spare a thought for the templed way.
Sound the trumpet, the Gagaku drum,
Honour now the Saint's wisdom.

I lament over scholars and chamberlains
     flushed with wine

Until suddenly all stand to attention and sing
     the anthem: 150
Kimigayo wa
Chiyo ni yachiyo ni
Sazare ishi no
Iwao to narite
Koke no musu made.
May your glorious reign
Last for ages, for ten thousand years
Till the tiny pebbles
Grow into mighty rocks,
And hoary moss covers them all.   160

Imperial Highness, on your birthday,
Spare a thought for the poor of the world.
Use your influence like your father; end
Their suffering; the wind is rising; let your
     seeds be scattered and whirled.

1966, revised 1974

A WELL-GLAZED JAR
(A FRAGMENT)

Freeman, listen to me:
Are you the saint in the rose-window
Or the rebel who must be free,
Reflection or Shadow,
What is or what will be?
Or are you an artist – do you merely show?

You have a choice:
To be an actor, or a disembodied voice.

    In a diseased time, we learn,
    The artist paints two wheels   10
    On his yellow judgement urn,
    One for a form that is real;
    He is a maker who heals with his brush,
    Not a tramper of farms;
    When the streets are all arush
    Or the preachers wave their arms
    He goes to the window and stares,
    Leaving his drying pot;
    He smiles or scowls at the cheers,
    Then lets the curtain drop.   20
"O fool, fool," said Freeman, "I have been a
     fool.
I have been tempted away from my true work,
     my art.
I am a maker, not a changer in a school;
I show man, and all the dreams and con-

tradictions in his heart.
I have two lives. I grieve, but I am apart."

After Philip the Second
Spain began a long decline,
Became creatively fecund:
The bold Baroque line.
Late Romanov Russia,   30
Third Republic France –
The urns blaze red with pictures
Of a throbbing totendanse.

In a Trafalgar Square crowd Freeman said: "I
        am apart;
The man who yearns to act and revitalise his
        Age
Is the destroyer of the window-gaze. Action
        destroys vision.
A Yogi's dream will cure this unreal body
And carve a giant Ramesses to attract its
        living,
A self-image to hang on the dawn of our Year,
But I am not a leader of movements. I am an
        artist with a frown.   40
I oppose this sickness, but a decade is a
        scudding cloud.
It is for others to nourish this body and nurse
        it into a church.
Whether of choice or defeat – and who has
        not been defeated,
Since the higher we rise, the longer gapes the
        grave –
My action is my gaze. And the clay-kneader's
        art.
I still bear truths from the spirit, but I live by
        images;
I will build them into a pattern on a well-
        glazed jar.
My role is to disturb with images; I will not
        harangue these people.
Action and contemplation can only be in
        balance
In the images we live by, or on a jar. Like a
        streetcorner artist, I am apart."   50

Said Freeman, "Pro and con, pro and con,
        I am apart."
And he died away from a preacher's
        dream
Into the detached self of his art.

A HERESY

"Today we are all seekers. Our work is a kind
        of tea-break in our quest –
Three times a day I leave the 'Cathedral' for
        the 'People's Hall';
Our Leaders have given priority to the soul
And, officially at least, there is no hatred or
        cruelty or war.
Yes, man has come forward. He has
        never been more noble, he has
        transcended himself,
Though he has not transcended death. Man
        has come forward, but I am not
        happy.
Oh yes, man will always dream up Republics
        and Utopias and pray for Paradise,
But let me tell you, man does not want
        Paradise, man does not even want
        to be happy.
Man must always be moving, he yearns for
        truth yet dreads finding it,
As an exile dreads the warmth of his home.
        He fulfils himself by striving
And not by attaining. So, too, must man
        always be discontented:
He longs for peace, but, like Lucifer, will
        destroy himself to escape it.
Man is a paradox who gladly acts against his
        best interests.
That is why I am not satisfied. Man will
        always rebel,
And out of boredom with this 'Transhuman
        Era', I have risen up and rebelled.
That is why I am going home now. I have
        finished with the 'Cathedral'.
They will say I am sick, they will lock me up
        and try to change me.
I shall tell them that human nature is constant.
        'Man dreams,' I shall say,
'But there is no progress in his soul.' Man
        must be free."

A SHRUB AND SMILING LEADERS

Gasmen climbed out of the trenches and
        waddled across a misty desert,
And suddenly the earth rose into an
        unflowering shrub, then fell away,
Dropping limbs and tin helmets round the
        barbed wire,

And then there was a pit, and among the pile
of corpses
Lay one that held a cross and twitched at the
lips and fingers,
And then men with bandaged heads and slings
hobbled behind swaying waggons
And clockwork men quick-marched heaps on
stretchers
Through a dazzling rubble of ruined
cathedrals,
Until, decks groaning with wounded, a
requisitioned steamer
Turned down its bows and slid into a dark,
cold sea.
And, seeing the smiling leaders reviewing
their material,
Hornpiping and tapdancing like puppets,
I knew I was better off than their dying men,
It was better to be Little and broke than be
Great and laugh with Haig,
And, even as thousands beat drums and gongs
in the Peking cold
And cheered a cloud like a shrub because it
made them "great",
And peasants sweated blood in a broken
Saigon shade,
I thought, 'Look to the limbs and FEELINGS
in your State.'

THE RUBBISH DUMP AT NOBE, JAPAN
(AN INVESTIGATION OF NATURE AND HISTORY, PATTERN AND MEANING)

A seaside village, thatched fisherman's huts,
Paddy fields, pines, threshers, a light that cuts.
I stare at this rubbish dump, under this hill:
A heap of litter by the dusty track, still
Boxes, rusty petrol cans, panniers below
Old timber, wrapping paper; red cannae, a
mallow,
A purple flower that blooms only at sundown;
Pine-bristles, wire-bars; a mess that makes me
frown.

Cicadas, like a sawmill, go fee-fee-fee-fee-
feeee.
Ants crawl up and down a bamboo cross.
See,   10
This mess is in the pattern that includes the hill,
It relates to its design, two sweeping curves

that thrill.
Like the Cro-Magnon skull, pattern is
relation –
Nature's, of seasons; history's, of evolution
And empires. This mess is in a rhythm of
birth and decay,
And discarded things – dead leaves, old bones
– pondered on today.

The rhythmic long-short pattern of rise and set
Is like the stressed and secondary colours on a
carpet.
The meaning of "dieu" requires the
enlightenment of French,
Or it is a four-letter pattern by a school-
bench.   20
"Nature" has no meaning to unillumined eyes,
There is patterned "isness" only, sunset and
sunrise.
Like "history", she springs and falls and is
gone,
Like a mallow in a field, or a Napoleon.

But seen with the Light, the vocabulary book
To the divine language, "nature" has the look
Of a whole process framed by these sliding
doors;
A fountain of seeds and years, a power that
pours
Love through all things, and unites all
contradictions –
Storms, wars, murders – just as all our
passions   30
Are united by our calm spirit. We see one
Power
Teem through nature and history and mind in
this and every hour.

The most important question of philosophy,
"The meaning of life", has been defined as
"me"
By men who say their search for truth is truth,
That "meaning" is in the jaw like a bad
wisdom tooth.
But this Power transforms the mess of a
rubbish heap
To the rich purpose of a waking up from
sleep,
The Divine, loving Superman! Just as its
Light

Redeems these bits of jelly from primeval
    sludge and night.   40
1967, revised 1974

HAIKUS

You were permanent,
I was just waves. O where is
My breakwater now?

White magnolia
Tumbling like snow under a
Blue sky. I am lost.

Dragonflies, forest
Ponds. Rosy shepherd's clouds. Will
I ever be whole?

The Zen master calls
For koans in Japanese.
I answer silence.

This cherry blossom,
I glimpsed my hair streaked silver.
Petals on night sky.

You stood, a pale white,
The sun goldening your hair.
Men littered the grass.

TANKAS

O generation
Of vipers, you have cared a-
-bout your cheque-book, I
Have seen you drive through the rain
With speeding windscreen-wipers.

Gulls and fishing smacks,
Ploughed fields and one lapwing. As
The wind blew and the
Wan sun went in, the chopping
Of a heavy axe!

Golden October.
A blackbird sang from willows.
My heart leapt with light.
Green water. I forgot my
Sorrow in a green delight.

Seagulls and wagtails
Bob among the rocks by the

Broken harbour wall.
Bombed-out cellars, purple flowers.
Flies spatter windscreens: rejoice!

SAKURA-BA

Oh, Sakuraba came down in the lift
With a hey-ho and a scrape, scrape, scrape,
Oh, Sakuraba came down in the lift
And his pockets were stuffed with cake, cake,
    cake.

Oh, Sakuraba came down in the lift
With a hey-ho and a clunk, clunk, clunk.
Oh, Sakuraba came down in the lift
With his armfuls of British junk, junk, junk.

Oh, Sakuraba came down in the lift
With a hey-ho and we were first, first, first.
He bowed to the door thinking it was the fifth
    floor,
And I bowed back, though I could have burst,
    burst, burst.

A CHAMBERMAID LIES ON THE BEACH IN A WHITE MINI AND LAMENTS

The sea is like an eiderdown
Kicked back from a rucked-up bed,
And, yawning at that rock's moist tongue,
My womb beats in my head;

And scorns the stiff brass lighthouse
As dead as a bedstead knob,
Until, blood-red, it flashes out
And the dark begins to throb;

And, creaking this four-poster,
What hotel guest will flop
On these stones, lift this skirt above these
    knees –
And, letting the white hem drop,

Slide up a hand and whisper,
Leering across the bay,
"The foam is like a petticoat frill
In a sundown cabaret"?

AN INCENSE CONE BURNS IN A STORM

And after that came the storm;

Like a hot wind tossing a tree
That whirled all night, shook off and blew
Teardrops of willowy leaves,
Like the throbbing cock that crew
Up the night-blue urn of the dawn,

One torrid, blood-bated breath
Rustled that twitching limb
That, like a red incense end,
Sheds years to a cupboard crypt;
When vein and synapse distend
They crow to the tear-throwing death.

A battered tree in the calm
Sighs for the wind, and mourns
That flaked out incense balm,
And the ash that burned in the storms.

BLOOD IN THE EYE

The rain splashed like a sprinkler,
I looked upon my wife;
Through the watery, flower-shop window blur
She held a rippling knife.

The blood wept in my conjunctivae;
In the rain her oatmeal hair
Rustled like a field of rye,
I was bones in a cromlech prayer.

The rain moaned as the night sea sighs,
My wife was a bladderwracked skull;
Before night dropped on my swimming eyes
I drowned in a sea-green hull.

NIGHT: CATHEDRAL AND TOWER

O tiny tiny grub man
Under great Cathedral rungs,
Can't you climb to the chicken coop fan-
Light, get that yoke pumping round your
    lungs?

O look look up at that tower
Like a farmer's silage hut: on
An upward-pointing finger,
Bells like four sleeve buttons.

O glow glowworm in the dust
Near-squashed by a cruel god's shell,
Will you ever see what you're trying to bust?

Dawn broke with a peal of bells,

And with a great shell-splitting spring
The giant bird stretched its neck
And beat its silver wings,
And devoured me with one peck.

I HAVE SEEN

I have seen green water splash in the
    muttering rain,
A pond jumping with fish, like a doubting
    heart;
Murky, opaque; no lanterns or bamboo
Danced in the surface of that stagnant brain,
Just ice-white moonlight, the mirrored art
Of a lost self bruised by chatter, and untrue.
I prayed for quiet, for vivid still of dreams.
Now eight miles under the wing, the blue sea
    gleams,
Is veined like blue sand after a rippled ebb,
Still like the waving rhythms of an EEG
    trance,
Rhythms breathed and pumped along a poet's
    arm.
Now this light is golden, within this calm
It bursts me like a boil pricked with a lance,
I am spilt red on a snow-white cloudy web.

HIGH OVER CALCUTTA: A CASTLE IN SPAIN

Like a few small rocks on the shore
The mountains of Bengal range;
While the parched Ganges delta
Is a child's sandcastle grange,

And the 5 a.m. rags and bones
In bundles on every kerb
Like sandworms under stones
In a diamond-sparkling blurb;

I would that I were God
On a garuda's neck, over hell;
She would lift her wings and brood,
But, armed with a bucket and shell,

I would dig my heels in her teats,
Swoop down from this heavenly nest,
Scoop up the Calcutta streets
For a sandpie Everest.

1967

89

STEAMED UP

As I looked out at the snow,
At the bleak white roof and the tears,
A mist crept up the window
Like a sea-mist from twenty years

And the Abbey National "hat"
Grew round in my red-hot brain,
And a boy, I was scribbling at
A bandstand in the rain;

Then it turned to a Mormon temple
In a snow-streaked blur, in the cold,
And the stars drifted down like confetti,
The moon died like a marigold.

Hands clasped, I lay in my death,
On a slab, five fire-blackened bones;
And I cursed this flurry of breath
For blinding these two icy stones.

A POET READS THE FIRE

There is a fire in my heart
And two red lumps that burn
The heaped-on truths that smart,
That the crackling flames will turn

Into specks on the mind's black wall;
Shoot sparks up the sooty flue
To catch and wriggle and crawl
As under a groundsheet do

Nipped worms and maggots and lice
When the frost still glazes the cars;
Then, in a thrilling trice
The sootflakes glowed like stars

And jumped and wriggled and shot
Like shooting stars over a bay,
Crawling for all they'd got
In a sooty Milky Way.

O grub, black universe,
What fire will I impart
When the sun is three cold cinders,
My burnt-up eyes and heart?

THE GREENFLY AND THE MONEY SPIDERS

On the pink and crimson roses

Black money spiders spin
A web near where a greenfly feeds
On a sky like a biscuit tin;

Shaking the sticky lace mat
Like a midge on a yellow Dutch cheese,
Bruegel crawls up the moon
And dies of two broken knees.

O greenfly, pest to the petals,
Through your wings I could scale the
        moon;
If you hadn't nibbled their roses,
Would the spiders still crunch your cocoon?

STORM AND FIRE

My father frowned at the storm,
The flashes fused and blew
Round my childhood window,
I shuddered and longed for you.

On a blue chapel's slab
My father descended to fire,
And now, again a child,
I await your crackling desire.

JOHNSON McVITERS

Johnson McViters'
Name hung on the Catholic church lamp-
        post.
No fouling of footpaths.
He was Clerk of the Council
Till he was given his gold watch
And pensioned off to the coast.

Johnson McViters
Lived in a large red-curtained room
In a seaside hotel.
He spoke to the echo
Of his slippers on the purple felt
Of a twenty-guinea tomb.

Johnson McViters
Walked to the dogpound every day
And stood by the netting.
He is not there now.
Behind drawn red curtains he lies,
Between two candles, hands folded,
And the gold watch stopped ticking when
The young priest knelt down to pray.

A SMALL BOY LOOKS AHEAD DURING HIS SUMMER HOLIDAYS

Our seven league boot thuddings
Are thunder to the roach,
And the worms in the hollow apple
Cower in their pumpkin coach,

Let us swing upside down on the rainbow
And fall like a clobbered knight

Then we'll lie on the grass and puff at
This chewed-at acorn pipe
Till the sun frays its string and floats away
Like an orange balloon that is ripe,

And the sky feels alone and begins to cry –
Till your windwipe chokes in the night.

NONSENSE RHYMES FOR CHILDREN

1.
Green green leaves
Hung over a red berry.
Nadia said
"That's very very
Dan-ger-ous,
It's poi-son-ous."
Daddy said, "Yes."

2.
O riddle me ree
O riddle me ree
Nadia's duckers
Are up in the tree.

3.
Little old Nan
Put her blood in a can.
She said, "Look at my bones,
They're as dry as stones.
I must buy some swiss rolls
From the Otani van."

4.
The star is white,
The star is down,
Over the chimney,
Under my crown.

I am the King
Of this big town.

5. THE MUEZZIN
Mohammed said Mohammed
Had coal black eyes.
Mohammed said Mohammed
Had watched the sunrise.

Mohammed said Mohammed
Had his nice new flower.
Mohammed said Mohammed
Would be back in half an hour.

Mohammed said Mohammed
Had not washed his hair.
Mohammed said Mohammed
Had gone to Tripoli Fair.

Mohammed said Mohammed
Had a broken nose.
Mohammed said Mohammed
Had picked a crimson rose.

Mohammed said Mohammed
Wanted to brew black tea.
Mohammed said Mohammed
Lost the teapot in the sea.

Mohammed said Mohammed
Had lost his white skull cap.
Mohammed said Mohammed
Had dropped it in his lap.

Mohammed said Mohammed
Had a swollen eye.
Mohammed said Mohammed
Had been to his pig-stye.

Mohammed said Mohammed
Was resting near a sheep.
Mohammed said Mohammed
Would drink himself to sleep.

Mohammed said Mohammed
Had made the mosque go off.
Mohammed said Mohammed
Was a blue and white show-off.

Mohammed said Mohammed

Was chewing a poppy-stalk.
Mohammed said Mohammed
Was training a sparrow-hawk.

Mohammed said Mohammed
Was snoring in his bed.
Mohammed said Mohammed
Had bumped his head.

Mohammed said Mohammed
Had eaten the pepperpot.
Mohammed said Mohammed
Had met the army and been shot.

6. SOLDIER
He's a great big soldier with a hat upon his
    head.
It looks like a lamp shade when he's lying
    back in bed.

Oh I look just like a soldier with a lamp shade
    on my head,
And when I've been tucked up at night, I'm a
    soldier gone to bed.

7.
Marble statues on a tomb
Do not leave me any room;
If I lie down in the aisle
I can be buried in some style.

Marble statues on a tomb
Fill my heart with dreadful gloom.
I will lie down in the aisle
Where children pass in single file.

BARBARY SHORES
(THE EXILE)
Over those yellow sands the black sea creeps.
I see Italian skiffs, the Castle cannons
Spurt orange through their knightly slits...
                   A dream
Slides through this courtyard of Roman jars
Where a corsair walked up stone steps,
    through arches
To a meal. From alcoves rushed angry men,
    swords curved.
They washed their hands in that large bowled
    fountain.
Over the banana trees, see the hareem.

Up, up, and perhaps *that* night burst into
    streamers   10
Of fire, over blue water. We are a flock of
    sheep
In the desert. Here in this shade let me
Foam and fling.
             Shh, sea washes on laval
    black,
On sandstone canyons – splosh – until it
    trickles
Out on the yellow yellow sand. Who is he,
This stepper-ashore? Rags drenched, dripping,
    on that
Concrete jetty? Near Italian bootprints?
What has he done? Behind him the sea rolls
Like a creaking deck. A man like an exiled
    god   20
In an open-necked shirt, damp patches under
    his arms
Between ship and nowhere near the gharries
    of the old souk.
What is he doing, staring at those pebbles?
Those women, one eye peeping through white
    sheets,
Those squinting women – he….But let him be.
It is the yawning hour, the ghaffirs are
    slumped in their folds,
Listening to garden taps, ready to stretch an
    old sacking
Among sheep-bran and beans. Round the next
    bend
A line of small tanks drones. But now – let
    him be.

I think of home. Not wistfully. Like a
    school,   30
Woodwormed noticeboards, punishments
    under springs like trap-jaws,
Gulleys in red brick where I kept cave
While plimsolls thudded on swing lockers.
There H. D. was sacked and died of aspirins,
"Nowhere else to go." Home like a red-brick
    wall,
A porch scratched with initials. Green gates,
Green porch doors, an umbrella stand, a
    grating
Smelling of cellar. Home.

OLD MAN IN A CIRCLE

(A VISION)

1967

"The year is the prototype of all cyclic processes (the day, the span of human life, the rise and fall of a culture, the cosmic cycle, etc.)...The year (or the wheel of the Zodiac) is usually represented by the figure of an old man in a circle."

J .E. Cirlot, *A Dictionary of Symbols*

I. UNCLEANNESS AFTER THE SUNSET

The spring has gone, and the hot sun
Has grown a crop of glass and iron
Among the Gothic spires of Europe.
Steamboats have carried steel harvests
To ore-rich jungles, capitalists
Have driven loin-clothed gangs to chop
And wound the earth with mines and
    railways,
And guarded their investments: the flag flies.
But in the centre of this Wheel of Life, a
    plump
Old man with ape legs weighs   10
Sun and moon like a juggler with bent knees,
And now, with an earth-shaking bump
Like a balance-pan weighed down, the Year
Turns towards Aquarius. And see, under
A rising moon lie the ruins of ten
Western empires like palaces
After an earthquake. The spires are in pieces,
All is multiple, mirrors and stone. Then
Pale and sickly abstract faces. In the middle
Hands clutch round a courtyard fire. All
    huddle   20
For the long dark night of the Year's return
At Pisces' end and a new age's dawn.

From the heels of Europe, a low black cloud
    of dust
Hung like a shroud across a blood-red
    Greenwich sun,
And in a New York noon men counted bags
    of gold
While a white-flagged convoy steamed over a
    crimson ocean;
And now, under planes that hang like flies in
    a billowing smoke,

In a ghastly, red-brown light, the scorched
    horizon glows,
The Prince of Wales sinks, the Midway
    victors cheer,
And now, in smouldering ruins, while Red
    tanks crawl,   30
The protector of Europe waits like a butler on
    the American elbow,
Waives his indemnities under a boiling
    mushroom cloud;
Shivering in snow, in a power-cut early dark
A threadbare rationed people queues for
    coal –
I see lorries leaving Greece, and GIs trundling
    in,
I see flurries of dollar bills, like autumn
    leaves, in eighteen cities,
And flights of Allied planes heading for
    Berlin,
I see lights going on in Hindu and Moslem
    India, in Ceylon and Burma,
I see lights going on in Palestine and Iraq, and
    the sun setting over Africa,
I see a servant saying "Careful" in Korea, and
    piqued at his master   40
For befriending the plaintiff who lost him his
    fortune,
I see twilight in Malaya, in Cyprus, in Suez,
And a dolled-up Cnut stopping the night with
    a policeman's palm
And his master saying "Fool, can an old man
    stop the earth?
Wind up the clocks, for your dark is our
    morning."
I see a black cloud advancing from the East,
    and eyes turning West,
I see a giant and a shrivelled dwarf under a

93

Bahaman sun.
I see deserted streets and skeletons shuddering
    at a car backfire,
Trapped far from Cuba between orange and
    white night,
I see a black cloud racing up from the
    South   50
And thirteen lights going on in Africa, as in a
    block of council flats,
In Gold Coast and Nigeria, Tanganyika,
    Sierre Leone,
In Uganda and Kenya, Zanzibar and
    Nyasaland,
In Zambia and Gambia, Bechuana- and
    Basuto- and Swazi-land,
I see lights going on in Algeria, the Congo,
    Libya,
I see a thundercloud over the western horizon,
Over Jamaica and Trinidad, over British
    Guiana,
I see twilight in Aden, in Rhodesia, and
    frowns in a conference chamber,
I see Hindu and Moslem embrace under a
    hammer and sickle,
I see Common Wealth leaders flinging dollars
    to their poor,   60
I see Marlborough House a museum, and,
    outside the wall of Europe,
A suffering servant in motley, rejected of men
Talking to himself, saying "Careful in Hanoi,"
    as, with one last shaft,
On the Falklands and Fiji, Hong Kong,
    Mauritius, and the Rock,
The curved orb slid into the sea, and the land
    grew suddenly dark.
Northern Ireland, Mozambique....Panama,
    Iraq....

The golden sun set and a moon tinted all
    silver.
I heard a voice cry, "Watchman, what of
    the night?"
"Rise and fall," the watchman said, "rise
    and fall:
The morning cometh, and also the
    night –   70
The Habsburgs rose and sank into the
    night,
The British rose and shone against the
    night."

O Churchill.
There is silence in Whitehall
Save for the muffled drums;
The flag-draped gun-carriage crawls;
Sailors with reversed guns;
The launch moans up the river,
The cranes dip in homage
Under a fly-past to Rule Britannia   80
And the passing of an Age.

Put another nickel in
In poor old Winnie's treacle tin
Screeched "a Jutland veteran" with a black
    peg leg
And all down Piccadilly, the indomitable
    Grand Fleet steamed,
71 battleships and battlecruisers, 118 cruisers,
147 destroyers and 76 submarines;
And on the dreadnoughts our guardian angels
    sang
"Rule Britannia, Britannia rules the seas."
O 15 St James's Square, O Edward the
    Seventh,   90
Clyde, Scott and Franklin, Burgoyne and Lord
    Lawrence,
Like a gallery of summer ghosts in the winter
    dark.
Ah Palmerston! Leaving the HQ of de
    Gaulle's Free French,
Sauntering down the Waterloo steps
And meandering along the Mall to the
    Admiralty Arch –

skyyyyboltbluewaterstreaktsrtwoooo,
A pair of F-111s skimmed like swallows
    underneath
Where Vulcan and Victor, coupling blue
    steel wings,
Droned towards the warning web at
    Fylingdales,
And, near Holy Loch and closed down
    shipping yards,   100
Disregarded the fish with the independent
    fins,
The Polaris sub with the interdependent
    scales.

Aegospotami and Midway. Ah the maritime:
One blink and a whole armada is knocked to
    bits

Or sold abroad, or stored, as "obsolete",
And shipless Admirals' voices float from
    aerials
To 4 aircraft carriers, 2 commando ships,
2 cruisers and a few destroyers and frigates –
O Senior Service.
As I left Downing Street during the Seamen's
    Strike,   110
Big Ben peered over the trees and pulled a
    face
And Nelson raised an arm.

In an angry crown of cotton and motor
    workers
As I waited for the "grim-faced" union
    leaders,
Sighing over the Times front page, while, on a
    transistor,
A newscaster told of uproars in Parliament –
As I shook my head
An NAB man twitched my sleeve, and
    said:
"We're much better off now than we were
    after the war, mate.
Look at them all these days, with their mini-
    skirts and their records.   120
We went to Austria again this year, on the
    cross-channel steamer,
Why, I got a hundred quid taperecorder last
    week,
And we'll soon have made the last payment
    on the car,
And now our Jimmy's left school he's
    bringing in twelve pound a week
And that means Vi can go to the bingo parlour
    now and again for a little flutter,
She couldn't do that just after the war, you
    know, not bloody likely.
Empire meant nothing to ninety per cent of
    us, except wars.
I had a brother. Killed in Cyprus, he was, and
    what good the Empire do him?
No. the Empire was a drag, mate, and we was
    lucky to chuck it,
And you don't wanta worry about what's
    happening here, this is just
    stop-go.   130

No, we're all right, mate, we're more
    prosperous than we've ever been."

But round the corner on the blackened
    Treasury wall
Alongside RHODESIA WHITE I saw
MENE, MENE TEKEL PERES, and I was
    appalled.
(Many, many shekels – perlease.)
    "The-Tax-man's-tak-en-all-my-dough
    And-left-me-in-my-state-ly-home,
    La-zing-on-a-sun-ny-afternoon,"
Sang Lord Roberts the landowner with
    shoulder-length hair.
Beside him, under the equestrian statue in a
    packed Trafalgar Square,   140
Slouched Sir Eric Porter, the civil servant's
    son,
And, yawning with one hand limp on an ND
    banner,
The Marxist grandson of a Tory Chancellor,
Toby Long, a praefect at Winchester;
"Up the workers," shouted Roberts, "up the
    Viet Cong,"
And nearby a scowling nobody with a
    spurned and rejected air
Cocked his *Look Back* with a revolutionary's
    stare –
"'Vous vous étes donné la peine de nâitre,'"
    he sneered,
"Screaming Lord Roberts with your shoulder-
    length hair."

    Said Roberts, "Could you spare three
        pounds?   150
    There'll soon be nothing to do except
        wandering round."

From the air lighthearted London
Was like an orange star
On a holiday camp restaurant.
St. Paul's dome bristled
With a Beatle's haystack hair,
Eros wore Carnaby gear,
And Queen Victoria bustled
From where a hook-nosed Sheikh
Followed a crooked finger   160
Into a flesh boutique;
Near a Soho discotheque
Two minidollies strummed
"We export sixteen per cent
Of our gross national product;
Hovercraft and reactors,

Vertical take-off planes,
Computers and farm tractors,
And expensive British brains –
We export sixteen per cent,   170
We are not decadent."

Ya, ya, ya-ya, smashed kiosks and seafront
    windows,
Ya, ya, ya-ya, deck-chairs chucked in the sea,
And a horde of youths broke under the Palace
    Pier
And swarmed up the shingle with barbarian
    ululations,
Burst through the railings, dragged a man
    from his machine,
Poured across the road into the coffee-bar,
Overturned the tables and trampled on the
    leather-jackets,
Then swept out after the Duke, jumped on
    four hundred scooters
And kicked and, like a cloud of hungry
    locusts, clacked away   180
To rip at concrete slabs, coils of wire and
    metal
And drop them over the bridge before the
    distant smudge of a train.

Ring a ring a roses –

O how is this faithful city become a harlot.
As under purple flowers rooted in basement
    cellars
Your memory still shudders at a siren's whine
And breathes fresh air beneath your festering
    wounds;
But now you are charcoal and bubonic black,
    and you are weary, weary,
The skin on your face is peeling, like
    mildewed yellow parchment,
You are full of sores, and germs scuffle under
    your crumbling spires,   190
Foreign bodies clog your veins and choke
    your aorta,
Fevers throb hot and cold in your indecisive
    brain,
The whole head is sick, and the whole heart
    faint,
Your coins show an outline Queen, here are
    smudged Churchillian crowns,
And you burn to the pealing rooftops with

rosy rings;
Ah London, your sins are as crimson, your
    silver like impure snow,
Your moons rise on feasts of indulgence, all
    varieties of vanity,
Two decades your ingrown flesh has turned
    grey and rotted with dirt,
Wash you, make you clean.

O how the Assyrians advance from the
    East....   200
I see the peoples of Eastern Europe take to the
    streets,
I see the Russian empire crumbling into dust,
O the Cold War. You resisted

While you rotted in bitter freedom.

Make you clean.

II. PURGING UNDER THE MOON

Outside Horse Guards a Solicitor greeted a
    General;
"They live for pleasure," he said, "because we
    have lost our way,
A doctor earns less than an unskilled factory
    worker,
And I know an exporter who only gets
    sixpence an hour overtime;
It doesn't pay to swot or set up on your own
    these days,   210
And I have to say 'Pine er bi'er' if I want a
    drink;
And what will our sons do? Will they
    emigrate,
Or will they stay and be taxed into debt in a
    school-leaver's paradise,
And be sneered at for having brains and be
    kept out of power
By a grubby group of blunderers who
    couldn't govern pussy,
And who are wrecking all that made us great
    for the sake of a few blacks?
And what about the two per cent, and
    their "nursery of lust and
    intemperance"?
If anyone's to pay, shouldn't it be them rather
    than us?
We aren't respected, and I'm telling you, if

democracy can't value us –"
"Yes," muttered the Major-General, "if
    there's still an Army,"   220
And as they grasped hands I saw a malcontent
    smirk and move away
And marching bands of frowning Puritans
    tramp.
    Between statues of Charles and Cromwell,
    Outside the Banqueting Hall
    I saw the impossible,
    I saw the second wave. All
    Foaming, a Puritan crowd
    After an overtaxed decade
    Jostled Earl Roberts, loud-
    -ly chanted, "Down with the Govern-
    ment,   230
    Seize country estates for trade,
    Vive le Popular Movement."

I see shouting men. They rush through the
    streets and tear down the statues.
I hear blanks burst with an echo. I hear live
    rounds whine.
They smash into boutiques and discotheques,
    there is smoke over Buckingham
    Palace.
Yes, a life of ease and privilege has been torn
    to pieces.
See, there swings the hated dummy of the
    ancient regime.
I see the city smitten: a city of graves.
And ahead is a time when we must live in
    darkness,
Neglected like other former centres of the
    world.   240
As surely as the Hordes of the Golden Khan,
    these things willhappen.
Unless....

Is this the only cure, these bands running
    through the streets –
Does there have to be this scuffling with
    parasitic germs?
O the pain, the pain. And must we close our
    eyes to the broken heads,
Must we stop our ears to the wails of the
    exiles at the landing-stage,
Their gnashings of teeth as their palaces blaze
    and crumble,
Must we stop our ears to the groans of the

earth
As each hectare of lawn and grouse moor is
    put to the plough?
O the agony when an old system is flushed
    away. Feel for the redeployed 250
As centres are renewed in a dozen Industrial
    Townships,
Feel for the work-teams of women, feel for
    those coffee-bar toughs
As they strain to renew themselves like cells
    in a decayed body.
Ah, if it could only stop at that, with a return
    to a National Assembly
And the scholar-revolutionaries going into
    quiet retirement.
If only there were not the final fever, when
    the head throbs
And nightmare images
              drip down
                    the bulging walls
And swell into bubbles and burst   260
Into judgements ringing through dank and
    gloomy halls,
Into soldiers hustling across a frosty park
And prayers muttered like bluebottles through
    darkened windows
Until, at a groan from the rooftops round the
    "sandy square"
The crowds press against the police at the foot
    of the black scaffold
And stop stop stop chop
            under the minstrels' gallery
            window
Lies the headless trunk, floats the frosty
    breath of the last Windsor –
If only there were no extremist coup, like
    Pride's
Pulling the body apart; no purge to pull it
    together,   270
No house-owners dragged from their beds and
    shot outside the Health Centre,
Until, with a final destruction of tissues, the
    fever itself is spent
And a cleansed and exhausted city
    convalesces,
The genitals throb, bells swing, for a lusty
    Thermidor.

    The body can be renewed
    With another cure

That leaves the head ice cool
And free from all fever:
        "prayer".

In a great spurting of iron we scattered
    ourselves, like spilt seed;   280
On ground stained russet we were enfeebled,
    as after an orgy,
We were empty, empty, even in the depths of
    vesicle and duct;
Ah, did we not learn late that too much expan-
    sion of blood is a spending of self
Until the limbs hang limp as over the sides of
    a bed?
Oh yes, when the Nazis came in we pulled our-
    selves together and put up our fists –
Like a Cup-tie giantkiller, men become great
    in the teeth of the insuperable
And, rising above themselves, fight with a
    godlike belief;
But after the giddy victory, did we not relax
    with the memory,
Did we not sink back into a torpor in a sauna
    room
Until, the spending and the strain having
    lowered our resistance,   290
The "sickness" set in? What should we do,
    then, what should we do?
Let there be a peaceful cleansing. To wash the
    body,
To deny the seed, the belly, and then to purge
    the self;
Not "I do right" but "I am cleansed". And
    then the right will follow,
For to be purified is to have a globe inside
    one's head
That shines through every limb. And this
    Dark Night.

"Ya-ya-ya-ya," sang Duke, as he flicked a
    comb through his hair;
I sat on over my coffee in a contemplative
    trance.
Should I go over to the juke-box, smash it,
    say "Duke, you're asleep,"
And, as he turns away in the silence and stares
    in the window,   300
"Remember your bones?" The silence
    stretches years beyond light-years.
Should I say, "Look at the wasted time," and

as he weeps,
For the shoppers are dying of years and trivial
    chatter,
"Wake up from your blindness, see colours
    till your eyes crack?"
His reflection shatters, scattering bits of other
    people,
And the rooftops shine out in pure, assenting
    light,
And, shuddering with joy, Duke smites his
    brow and cries,
"O the wasted years, the waste, when this
    sleeping giant
Snored through this dream, this automatic
    lullaby.
O the waste, what must I do to keep this self
    awake?"   310

You must climb, I say, and where are your
    roots?
Do you know your own past, let alone your
    civilisation's?
Connect yourself with your life, and your
    inheritance;
Each day you must snap yourself in a
    situation,
You must study the prints for a pattern, learn
    your repetitions
And then you must go through the pain of
    discarding your scaly shell
Until your being is like a spring dawn
And then you will see the entire universe in a
    yellow ball of fire.
Then you will grow towards the sun;
Look, I say, that old visionary in this
    suburban lounge,   320
He is like a many-sided prism, he has the
    universe in his soul.
To his sun and moon eyes this moment
    contains all history
Like the rise of man in a glass museum.
Do you think he was born with that
    understanding, that serenity?
Nine chairs are taken, the tenth is yours,
    I say.

    I started to and became aware
    Of Duke singing "Ya Ya Ya,"
    And flicking a comb through his Ya-hoo-
    ha hair.

As from a Yogi's head
A regulated breath   330
Will redeem a decayed body
From an unreal, nightmare death;
In each village of the muscles
There shall be cells of ten
Fed by red corpuscles
And invisible oxygen;
From a few's creative glow
"Fused" neurones shall burn and strain
To recreate the Shadow
In the new towns of the brain.   340

O purified Messiah,
O single-minded mystic who is not wrong,
Will the weak accept
A Shadow for the strong?

The Yellow Year turns on,
Dying from its King's head down
Through zodiac and backbone
Into a black, aimless clown;
Can a footward decline
Be an ascent to the brain,   350
To a golden-headed Goddess
And a snake biting its tail again?

Because the creative few
Found an image for the Fire
Our civilisation grew
With the thrust of a Gothic spire;
The descent round the old man's light side
To the ape-feet turn of the Year
Went though a Sistine giant's "pride",
A bull burnt in a square,   360
Through a root and branch Puritan,
A Copernican measuring-rod
And men made of steam and iron
To a static, fairy-tale God.
Carved images in Chartres
Attract no energy,
The Cathedral has lost its art
To inspire growth in the many,
And with such aimless leaders
And grey-suited diplomats   370
And doubting philosophers,
What could we do but contract?
We must reject them all
And dredge up for our dying Age
The tight-lipped growth ideal

Of the Fire-gazer's message
To carry it in its ascent
Up the old man's dark left side,
Up the backbone ligament,
Back to the bearded, Byzantine pride.   380

III. DAWN OVER MOUNT BROCKEN

As I grieved by night over a graveyard of a
      city
A twisted veteran dragged himself up the hill
And, squatting on the stumps of his legs, said,
      "If there's a plague in the city
Is it the fault of the city? If drunks dance on
      the ashes
And the poor sleep in the streets, should you
      pull down the walls,
Should you pull down the banks and the
      country-houses and shoot all the
      rich?
What of the self? Can one not turn away,
Can one not ascend the mountain of oneself,
Can one not conquer oneself in a village pew?
It is not their environment you should change,
      but the self.   390
What is the man-made macrocosm at any
      time, but a reflection of the self?
What are pyramids or ferro-concrete buildings
      but projections of the self?
Look at that City of Mirrors. It has no soul;
See how it reflects the face of this empty
      generation –
It is as dead as an upset box of bricks;
And this switch that makes the trains rush
      round and round, this repetitive
      neon,
This electric life that comes from the selves of
      the few
Who made their cities 'healthy' by pouring
      their being
So that the late-night offices suddenly burst
      into light
And threw a glow into the sky, far over the
      dark horizon,   400
Until it is spent and they grow dark again, like
      this, and rot –
Where will they be then, where will the
      system be,
Where are the Minoan trade figures beside
      one Homeric vase?
Cromwell, Robespierre, Lenin, Mao – they

cleansed and lit my cities,
They loved me enough to hack me up, and for
　　that I honour them;
But they treated me as a cipher in a system,
　　they denied my self –
When I cried out for a Shadow they gave me
　　their portraits,
They 'flushed my head clean', they filled my
　　head with slogans,
So that I did not exist outside their lit-up
　　offices,
And man must exist. Stunted under their smiles,
　　I rebelled and was mutilated.　　410
Do not mutilate that city, do not make blood
　　gush in the gutters.
For my sake, rather let the dying be. They
　　exist.
Under the hoardings the people are empty.
　　Make them real.
Therefore, turn the wheel."

In this Wheel two Ages hang in the balance,
And in between is an anguish, like the Black
　　Death
And war and schism between manor and
　　court;
O the dust as the nations crash like falling
　　walls,
O the wailing as a settled system crumbles
Like a bombed-out Archduke's palace or
　　Cathedral,　　420
O the rage as tormented, questioning men
Shake fists at crown and flag and tradition
Like "barbarians" jeering at "Gothic".
Dynasties have crashed, empires have
　　crashed,
And over the rubble of nations, near the
　　Ministry
With the seventh-floor lights in the Brussels
　　snow,
Towers a skyscraper with a giant beam,
The Cathedral-Hall, the Lighthouse of Europe
Whose new system mirrors a reborn soul,
A Counter-Renaissance; we are the
　　rebuilders.　　430
After the Mannerist sickness, our images
Throb with Baroque, with the whole of Being,
We are the new mystics.
I heard a cry
From the old Professor's darkened room,

"The Age of Reason is dead";
But the deaf stared on, intent on measuring
　　the moon.
Compasses, dividers, and rules to measure
　　yawns;
We have flown over mountains like chopped,
　　veined cubes,
We have seen angular deserts under green
　　Siberian dawns.　　440

From a sun-wheel cross
White rays stream in arcs
Down the Cathedral ladder
In perfection's mottled glass;
The "I" falls with a clatter,
The purged self stands free;
Saints' heads shake like apples
As he climbs up the rose-wheel tree;
An undoctrinal Luther
Whose will was like a claw,　　450
Who nailed the inner eye
On the Wittenberg church-door;
Whole man with a whole vision,
Philosopher-scientist-saint,
Climb on, climb on, climb on,
As if to a summit – paint
How in a crescendo
The organ swelled, and the sun
Burst through the red rose-window
And stained a swooning nun.　　460
With the conquest of the moon
The mystic claim has shone:
The metaphysical man,
An illumined Reformation!

From the mountainside I saw a giant Europe
　　burst into light;
Descending, I walked in the neon-streets of its
　　automated cities:
London, Brussels, Paris, Amsterdam, Berlin,
Rome, Vienna, Prague, Warsaw, Budapest,
　　Bucharest;
They throbbed with a dull pounding, as if
　　from an iron lung,
And, as from a plastic heart, conveyor belts
　　carried things　　470
That were fed into glass tissues by arms and
　　shoots and slides:
The people were calm and gentle, and there
　　was a peace in the air.

Then I came to a City of Images, and I stood
    in the station
And stopped a passer-by who looked like
    myself.
"Our time?" he said, recognising me, "Things
    aren't all that
Much better than in other uniform times, I
    shouldn't imagine.
Oh yes, there has been progress in the
    macrocosm – these machines and
    amenities;
There has been amelioration, and everyone is
    cared for now;
But nothing lasts. Buildings decay, machinery
    crumbles; money gets short,
    squalor sets in.
Cities sink into the earth. Rise and fall, rise
    and fall."   480
I closed my eyes in Whitehall and sighed:
O the Treasury wall, O the broken spires,
Black black black is the skin of this dying
    city;
O the agony in the body, the sores, the sores
As old John Bull dies away from his greatness
    like a sick ego,
And, mid dreams of dreadnoughts and distant
    fires,
Hears remote voices like leaves shaken in the
    wind;
O the torture as the factories run down for
    lack of oil,
O the anguish of blasted out city-windows –
O Israel, O Portugal.   490
O the torment in this dying, before it is
    understood!
Did not Harold weep when he prayed before
    the Waltham stone?
O this giant Europe, these nations as federal
    states.

    Time has gone beyond
    Winged Kairos with the scales;
    On the golden zodiac clock
    On Anne Boleyn's rose-web gate;
    The black hand with the sun
    Has crept up the dark Year,
    Like a blood clot that will stun   500
    An old man's unpurified stare.
    But, at the first glimmer of dawn,
    While the winter sun is low,

Above the windbeaten watchman
On the rocky mountain brow,
High over the East-West border,
On the cloudy skies of Europe, newly
    born,
Raising his arms like a Conductor
With a cleansed Archangel's scorn,
A lone huntsman hails the future: 510
The giant Brocken Shadow sounds his
    horn!

O the giddy hopes as a civilisation gathers its
    spirit together,
O the grandeur of the new God it throws
    across the heavens!
O the sadness of the far-seeing huntsman, as
    undeceived,
He blows the last post for the eventual
    extinguishing of the Lighthouse
    beacon!

THE GATES OF HELL

(PART 1 OF SONNETS AND LYRICS FROM A DARK, DARK NIGHT, A RECORD OF A VICTORIOUS OVERCOMING, A TRIUMPH OF THE SPIRIT)

1969 – 1972

ORPHEUS ACROSS THE FRONTIER

At five, hens squawked, dogs barked. I was
    woken by shots.
There were more shots at six, at nine the
    Tripoli street
Was deserted, the police had gone. Idle knots
Of people on the corners held radios, a
    discreet
Armoured car dropped soldiers who aimed at
The sky. Then someone said, "There's been a
    coup."
And the shooting....For a day we crouched in
    our flat
While the bullets whined, then we were
    allowed out to
Shop. Army men fired shots in the air every
    hundred yards,
In the supermarket, soldiers shouted, "No
    beer."
They wore plimsolls, they crept in, our
    "freedom's guards".
The skull-capped greengrocer muttered,
    "King good man here."
So history changes by stealth, and lacking the
    power or
Will to crush it, the West's frontier contracts a
    little more.

PROVIDENCE WHICH TAKES

Does will, accident or Providence rule our
    lives?
I could have gone to Teheran instead of
    Tripoli.
At our child's school, a mother asked us to a
    party;
Her act traps me in a chain of events that
    deprives.
A hot Libyan night under curfew. Black

houses, dark sand.
Your birthday. I poured champagne saved
    from before the coup,
Our child danced. We hung our arms round
    our shoulders, you
Sang, "We're a happy family." She giggled in
    bed, and
Snake-bitten, you will not be touched.
Poisoned, Eurydice has no warmth at present.
And your friend in her red trouser suit, I could
Have found it as she lay, as on a bed, and
    clutched
The cliff near the Phoenician ruins...Is there
    no accident,
But Providence which takes what is not for
    our good?

A BANGED DOOR AND A STRONG GIN-PUNCH

A party in defiance of prohibition:
Our guest made punch in the kitchen,
    muttering
While her friend quarrelled with his mistress,
    and banging
The door, flung out. Our guest's hand was
    position-
-ed over the bowl, adding gin. Of her own
    volition
She emptied the whole bottle and ran out,
    holding
Up her skirt, her chain of events touching
Mine. The party passed out, I was in a
    paralytic condition
On the floor. You, temptress, fondled my hair.
    "If you
Want me, I'm free after the houseboy goes
And before the children get in from school,"
    you said.
Faces swam down, I drowned. Then *she*

floated through,
Said "I caught you." We reeled home through
   curfew, suppos-
-ing we would be shot. White wolf-dogs
   snapped at my godhead.

WELL, DRIED GRASSES, DEAD BUTTERFLY

Now I have begun the next of my descents
Like that foul old Arab down this clogged
   well.
Here I am, at the end of a decade, of an
   expell-
-ed regime, thirty, having put up homes like
   tents
And torn them down, trapped in this
   turbulence,
The wrong side of the *limes*, in a barbarian
   citadel.
I want to settle by the spring of life, dwell
There, not roam thirsty in this affluence.
I need to dig out the health in myself, exhume
It, unblock the source of this parched seaside
   life,
This Mediterranean sloth. It has made you
   droop.
Today a butterfly flew round our sitting-room,
Settled in my dried grasses and died. Like a
   wife
It is still lodged there, a painted lady in mid-
   swoop.

LUMP LIKE A CANNON-STONE

Corinna,
Your pomegranites were red that blue day;
I crept up your drive, your piano warbling,
I tiptoed in, straight back rising you flung –
Teeth gleaming in a Spanish smile – two
   hands. My
Heart, when you touched my chest, burst into
   blood.
I was raw, I sang like wind in telegraph wires.
There were no clocks until the bell rang in
   your ears.
Who squats by you on that red pouffe now?
   Who should?

Now, under liquid stars, the pye-dogs howl,
Sad army lorries drone.
With a rumble of thunder, curfew comes

crashing down,
As it did for me when you spoke of your
   French class and drove
Off in your blue car this torrid afternoon,
Leaving, in my lungs, a lump like a cannon-
   stone.

TWO DAMNATIONS

After lunch, I drove you down to the sea.
We swam on the Homs Road beach, you lay
   in the water,
We paddled, then we waded with our
   daughter.
She dived from my shoulders, like a water
   baby
In her wings. The beach shimmered with heat
   waves, we
All lay and roasted in the heat for a quarter
Of an hour. How different from that shorter
Visit, after your sobbing. What heavy
Hearts on the low rocks beyond the American
Base. The waves came in like generations,
We walked among sparkling glass, near sea-
   lavender,
I bent and picked up two Roman-Libyan
Coins, said, "Like us, green and corroded."
   Two damnations.
Two pearly tears rolled down your cheeks, so
   tender.

SPARKLING PAVEMENTS AND RED ROSE-HIPS

Yes, like the best of them, I must will to be
   poor;
These carpets and beds and rooms of yours,
   Corinna,
They are too unlike rocks, foam, bladder-
   wrack;
Glass in park litter-bins, green sleeping-bags,
White tile reception centres, a man behind a
   sliding door –
These are what stir me, like sparkling
   pavements, keener
Mists, blowing on knuckles that show the
   bone, black
Tea in a corner-house, elbows and cuffs in
   rags.
Through the window is what I left behind,
   turned my back on.
You can keep your furs, your crystal glasses,

your cars,
Your comfort in the hour after lunch when
    you are alone –
I want none of them; only the hungry grin of
    the boy with two guitars
Who stands outside the London Arts Lab,
    licking his lips,
His belly rumbling, his mind the red tint on
    wild rose-hips.

HOPELESS

You are like a ghost to me, Corinna;
When you are not by me, you haunt me
Like a Maundy face, dominating me outside
    your body,
Pure woman in this that you are! You say you
    are
Maimed; having been raped by your father at
    five,
Feeling no real contact except with your son;
You say you see only me when I am with you
    – no one
Else – but when I leave the room you say it's
    as if I am no longer alive.
But for me, I need you. I want to be with you.
    I admire
You. Yet you have children, I have a wife,
This wraith who would not come in to bed,
    this tiresome girl;
Now over the palms a thundercloud dusk
    begins to swirl.
I feel hopeless, you are so far from my life,
Like the red skull-capped spy outside who sits
    and warms his hands at an orange-
    flickering fire.

A NOTHINGNESS

As I lingered near her door, Corinna said,
"Don't go." Then the children rattled on the
    blind.
I stayed. "My husband loves your wife," she
    said,
"He said so last night when we were reclined

By the fire." I did not believe her. When I
    went home
You were asleep on our double bed. It was
    hot.
You woke and said, "You're late,"
    apprehensively.

I said who I had been to see, how she was not

Sure – how she was worried about her
    husband, and you said,
"I want to talk to you," over the ironing-
    board,
"This is serious...." And then it dawned on
    me.
"I'm marrying him," you said, "I've
    promised. We'll live abroad."

Now I sit numb at my desk, too shocked for
    tears.
You have made a hot water-bottle and gone to
    bed.
Our child says, "Daddy, I know what eight
    sixes are,"
And I wish I were a nothingness, I wish I
    were dead.

THE DEATH OF OUGHT

I see how it all happened now. He was
Infatuated with you and whispered to you
    then
Before the log fire and by the candle.
    "Because
I love you," he said, "I'll leave my wife and
    children.
We will live in London, I'll be your security."
At first you shook your head, but later
    listened,
And, cleaning our flat floor, you let the
    committee
In your mind vote for his obtaining a key
    from a friend....
You met him when I was at work; and talked
And loved him over lunchtime, so that when
    you met
Me in the car, and we had driven home, and
    walked
In our garden, your flaxen hair was wispy.
    Yet
Though I see how it happened, I am
    distraught:
We will not recover now, this is the death of
    "ought".

FEAST: SKULL ON A BEACH

You are living with me, we have switched
    partners and laze

In bed. We had a nerve to leave them, to
    sweep
Out together for "our affair". It was a bit
    steep!
You said you would give anything for a few
    days
With me. I am too upset to argue with your
    ways.
You cook for me, drink with me. I drink
    myself to sleep,
Obsessively pick over the same deep
Ground. This compulsive talking! This mental
    blaze!
You came so I could get you off my chest,
To fill the emptiness of the Feast. I needed
    speech.
In one night you became all to me: mother,
    little girl, lay,
Wife, mistress, bird. You are a courtesan, the
    best!
Yesterday morning, a skull lay on the beach.
It could have been a sheep's. It has been
    swept away.

MARQUESS

I am as weak as a clapped-out Marquess.
In the dusks, I lie on this double bed,
A great work hangs above me, like an Arab
    head-dress,
Yet, hands flopped limp, I go on gazing like a
    dead
Man, and never manage the effort of taking it
    down.
Then, when I feel I can make it, in haste
I lie beside you, Corinna, lie back with a
    frown
And watch as your hair tumbles round your
    waist.
Kneeling, deliciously you simper a sweetness,
Savouring me like sugar-plums with a red
    flush,
Leaving me calm. I would not have it
    otherwise.
I love your soft fingers. They are those of a
    true mistress.
Later I feel detached, as after a hot bath, while
    you blush.
Now the blue sea tears in near the
    coastguard's bell, and think what I
    must revise.

GEISHA

You are like a geisha. You ran a bath, shout-
-ed, "Come here," stepped in with me, soaped
    my tingling skin.
Then we tossed and writhed, two mindless
    forces within
One panting Being that quite banished doubt.
"Three explosions," you gasped, "a bursting
    out
Of stars. Perfection...." Then you went quiet,
    hand on chin,
And said you are going to Spain to begin
Anew. And I am a prisoner here, there is no
    doubt
Of that, for government servants are not
    allowed
To break contracts, have exit visas. I cannot
    speak,
You want the Perfect Man, but you want to be
Independent, and keep your children. You
    have vowed
As much. You are slipping away from me.
    This week
Was supposed to clear my chest, but you have
    conquered me.

MUFFIN MAN

A week has passed, you have missed your
    children, not
Wanting my wife to look after them up at that
Villa of yours. You put on your leopard-scarf,
    sat
And said you were going back. My wife has
    got
To stay with friends. This is your last night
    here. What
Next? At four you are asleep, I pace round
    this flat.
Black, black, all utterly black. A wall. I stare at
The air-rifle I bought, the pellets. One shot
Through my eye, I will be six feet down, a
    mere spine.
I am futureless. Now you are woken by
    barking dogs....
Three hours later I drive you back, now I
Visit you at dusk with my bootleg wine,
Eat coquilles in front of steaming, hissing
    logs.
Your son croaks, "Here comes the muffin
    man," and I want to cry.

GATES OF HELL

Now you say you cannot see me. You sigh:
"If the police find out, he will be deported. He
Will lose his job, I my maintenance." Can't
   you see
You are shutting me out? I feel it in your eye
As I take you round the crowded *suk*. You
   buy
A round brass tray, and on the way back we
Pass secret policemen – you look uneasy –
Standing like lamp-posts for Nasser. Some
   tie
Palm-fronds on the telegraph-poles. Fear stabs
Me as you say, "We should not meet until
   Christmas Day."
And will we then? Sullenly I drive through
   snags,
The streets are crowded and white skull-
   capped Arabs
Clamber over arches like Gates of Hell. They
Hang bunting. Gates clang in the gaze under
   your two-starred flags.

AU REVOIR

Last night I visited you here, till you went
   back
To the unironed "diapers", your cheeks
   flushed crimson
With passion, femme fatale that you are! I
   stayed on
Till he returned the children, opening the door
   a crack,
And pulled out a wobbly tooth with a
   handkerchief, and knack,
And said, "Fairies will come." Now all that
   has gone.
I have come up to your villa for my last "Bon
Voyage", and you say that, confused, he
   wants you back.
And I hope that Carlotta....Now I must say
   good-bye.
We make arrangements for six months' time,
   and so
"I love you," I breathe, kissing you, "courage
   will tell,"
And I walk the path to the car. It is a deep
   blue sky
And a blinding glare, and the sea is a bracing
   indigo,
Tearing towards the yellow coastguard's bell.

A WHEELED-AWAY STAIRCASE

A dawn thunderstorm. I drive to the airport,
   stalk-
-ing you. In the American car, your silhouette
Shines in my headbeams, with each lightning
   flash, wet
Through my running windows, like a bobbing
   cork.
At the airport I stand with our child. We talk,
Then you come over and say, "Look after
   yourself," like a threat.
And leave me for your Hell. And now I sweat
In a glaring sun, and watch the plane. You
   walk
Quickly, wave from a porthole. I roast near a
   wing.
Pluto stands behind me on the tarmac in
The vicinity of a boarding staircase, in the
   shade
Of steps that go up and lead nowhere,
   deceiving.
You go like a dolphin crossing a sea, one
   fin
Downward and wake like a frothy decade.

THE GOOD-BYE

You say it is over between us, Corinna. I
Hear that friend of yours has told him your
   secret,
Which I foolishly let slip after taking a tablet
Of valium, that you feigned with him, gave a
   false cry
Of pleasure. And now you have written to say
   good-bye.
Two weeks ago I saw you, before you caught
   your jet
Back to the States with your four children.
   You let
Yourself promise to live with me in Spain, a
   lie
I believed. So much for your promises! You
Made advances when I was paralytically
   drunk,
Not knowing the punch was neat; you
   broached an affair,
You proposed a time and a rendezvous.
And now, after destroying my marriage, you
   have slunk
Off. Destructive, selfish woman, I am well rid
   of you. So there!

WRECKED

Now is a time of great sorrow. I patter round
This flat, make my dinner, sit, stare. Nothing,
    this mess.
She is in love with him. If I show forgiveness,
Ring her, accept her back, will she come?
    Will she sound
The new Carlotta, or the one who never
    frowned?
I love her, *but*…I contemplate the bleakness
In a Hell of dreaming of my own creation. I
    confess
How happy we were last summer, before we
    drowned,
Without knowing it! Now I feel broken up, I
    escape
Into wine, valium, the radio, work, anything.
They endure through courage and heroism in
    Hell.
I know I must encounter the Protean shape
Of my dead self, get to know my heart, my
    feeling
About her, gouge these limpet eyes, this
    stopped-up sea-shell.

DESPAIR LIKE BELLBIND

Despair is the weed, the illusion that winds
Round the heart. I must be choked by a Hell
Of anguish and strangling conflict which
    bellbinds
The peace of Paradise like the bluebell.
I must droop in hopelessness, and sink low,
Touch the bottom, I must surrender my youth
To it. Then it will slip off, wither, and go.
I must be alone and confront its choking truth,
Then I will value air and Orpheus will feel
Himself as a mystic soul, forget the "outer"
Stranglehold, slip its tentacles, being real
Through this self-stripping, forget the doubter
For the desert flower which sheds delusion.
Take heart: despair is a withering illusion.

A SMALL GIRL'S CURFEW

My daughter, I hear you have been locking
Your grandfuhrer in his cellar.
In your Wellington boots, you have been
    heaping snow
For a fort – like an Arab guerilla.

Here in this barbed wire garden,

The poinsettias russet red,
You pedalled your jeep and took the salute
Like a Colonel gone in the head.

Here in this Alamein desert
You stoned boy commandos;
And your "pow pow pow" at the soldiers
Was spray on a fisherman's rose.

But now this winter grapevine drags
Its trawl of autumn stars,
And the wind in your bedroom echoes round
Your doll's house wars, my scars.

A DROWNING IN ANGUISH

He is broken like his promise, in his dressing-
    gown.
He says he stayed with your parents. He is
    alone,
Struggling and thrashing with a soul of
    smashed pelvic bone.
He pours me wine, we chat. He strips himself
    down.
"I don't think we're going to make it" – here a
    frown –
"I still love her, but I've found out I miss my
    own
Children. I'm going back to the States." And I
    have always known,
Deep down, you will soon be free. Watching
    him drown
In anguish, I ask him to ring and let you know.
He insists on "waiting till London" – he goes
    there
At the end of the month. If I go first, will you
    be fonder
Of me? Will you believe me? Will you let me
    go
To see you? And our families….It's better
    you should hear
From him first. Do I want you? I will go to
    Egypt, and ponder.

CAIRO

I am in a limbo, between wanting you and
    know-
-ing it is hopeless. I must not rush, be too
    swift.
I sit, knowing this wretchedness should be a
    gift,

And watch ghosts flit through the passages of
my bro-
-ken mind. This balcony overlooks the Nile's
flow.
Guns thump from Dahshur. Sandbagged
bridges. I shift
And watch the curved white sails of the boats
drift
Like dorsal fins along the silver-green river.
Slow
Eaglets soar overhead. At night the streets
make sense:
There is blackout, windows and headlights are
painted blue,
Without street-lightss this city is a ghostly Hell,
Faces loom and fade in eerie silence.
In this dark tide the permanence of you,
And a damned soul drowning near the
Purgatory Hotel.

WAY OF LOSS

I stand in a hotel filled with clutter:
Ceilings, walls, curtains, furniture, tea-
Cups, carpets, music, Scotch, radio, TV,
Luxurious lifts, an at-attention waiter,
Girls, books, newspapers. Outside in the street
There are pavements, restaurants, distractions,
cars,
Museums, dance-halls to fill in time, and
bars –
Where are the sand and stars? I cannot meet
Nature in a city round of social drinking,
Culture and prattle. I live in delusion,
This Western cluttering, endless thinking.
I must go to the desert and strip each illusion
On a Way of purifying Loss, and temple-sleep
Till I see my soul with a head-scarfed
Tuareg's timeless peep.

GHADAMES SPRING
(POEMS LIKE BUBBLES)

I drive through the desert, two days of sand
And Czech lorries, till I reach the necropolis
Of Ghadames – a hill of tombs, palms and
Tuareg who live underground in this oasis,
In a Hell of chambered tunnels. Near the Hotel,
Glory! I sit by the spring, on polished stone
Steps: clear water, and green weed; a square
well
And bubbles wobbling up in the sun. A lone

Tuareg peeps through his head-scarf's slit,
and I know
That at last my hopelessness is over. As old
As the Great Pyramid, this overflow
Fills Roman baths where toga-ed citizens still
hold
Court. I have found the forgiving spring in my
heart
Whose Divine bubbles pour up into art.

EURYDICE LOST:
EXPECTATION AND A TEAR

Oh hurry, they are at the airport gate,
I run to her, kiss her Malta lips.
Now surely she's come back. A tear
Trickles to her chin, and drips.

Is it a tear of happiness?
In the car I turn and hold her hand,
Peer for her letter behind her dark glasses.
She takes away her hand.

What is up? Now, in my whitewashed room,
Screwn expectation in the grate,
Head bowed she sobs near her tearful womb,
"We must separate."

THE FALL

I read of Eve and how she pleaded to go
Alone to the rose-garden, ignoring Adam's
war-
-ning, his "Go; for thy stay, not free, absents
thee more,"
Even though he knew she would be tempted –
even though.
I think of how you pleaded to go out on Malta
Without me, how I warned you and gave in to
your frown,
And how you fell, and, like Adam, I was
dragged down
From the promise we made before the
marriage altar.
You were responsible. I warned you twice.
O perfidious, blind woman, so unaware!
I, Adam, now stand on the edge of Paradise
And must needs find my way, find my way
back, for there
I grew. O awful freedom of the innocent!
That allowed my Eve to ruin us with her
discontent.

THE SPECTRE

We go to the Roundabout, and who
Is that spectre at the Malta bar?
Sitting squat and bald while I talk
And laugh and joke, looking so far

Away, as if to the future?
Our hostess goes and talks to him,
Who is he, sitting on his stool,
Whispering while you look so grim?

Ahead is a melancholy time,
A spectre looking in a car
Outside the house where I had a place.
Who is this spectre at the Malta bar?

LIKE A FRUIT MACHINE

We sit in a great airport. We have done
All we can. This is our last time together,
Perhaps. I make a plea: "Are you really
    uninvolved?
How much did you mean of what you said
    earlier?"

"About a half," you say. Behind you there
Is a steel fruit machine. You are like it.
You have three moods – aggressive,
    depressed and
Elated – like three whirling discs. I hit

The lever. If they say Yes together, oranges
In the centre, there is a rushing of squeezed
    pips
In the metal till. If they are all separate,
Nothing. Sadly I kiss other people's lips.

DANGER

Once again I seek out danger.
In this stadium the Leader speaks.
I stand on benches with workers
Only forty yards from where he shrieks.

The workers in barracans and skull-caps
Indignantly turn and stare at me.
I feel cruel hands pin my elbows,
I am bundled away ignominiously.

Two men with guns pat my trousers,
Remove my dark glasses from my
Pocket. They thought it was a gun.

Why do I seek out danger? Why?

I attended the rally in the streets
When a volley of shots crackled through
The air. Am I trying to destroy
The part of me that hankers for you?

A DEATH

I drank bootleg wine late at night in an austere
Villa. The bell rang, a secret policeman
    said, "I
Want you to come to prison." A large car was
    parked nearby,
A young Arab in a suit and a cruel sneer
Drove me to a villa like a graveyard, gave me
    beer,
Then said, "We have had this 'evolution' to cry
Out that Libya is great. You are a spy.
I am in charge of executing journalists here."
And he went for his Luger. To shoot me, he
    had to choose.
He sat across the table with wild eyes,
Sipping his whisky. Dying, I felt a peace,
I thought, 'He who loveth his life shall lose
It', I stopped clinging to life, serenely realis-
-ing you and our child were safe. Oh, what a
    release!

ON THE WATERFRONT

I walk on the waterfront, after the Libyan coup.
Arabs sit in the cafés, the sea splashes.
I walk tensely to this latest rendezvous.
I am a target. If I am shot now, my ashes
Will be "the remains of a Westerner who was
    rushed,
Who represented a decolonising power
That has been liberal when it would once have
    crushed."
I am its response. At a dark, secretive hour
I wait for the car, the hand that will give me a
    wad
So I can go to the supermarket and drop the
    bright
Notes among tins; enough to buy a squad
Of men for a civilisation that has lost the will
    to fight.
I am a lost mystic, who should be kneeling in
    a church,
Not loitering here on the waterfront, on the
    Devil's research.

109

THE ESCAPE

The day before I leave this hole there is a hue
And cry. My ghaffir points to the grapevine,
holds five
Bunches of grapes. The skull-capped green-
grocer, conniv-
-ing, moans: "He say you stole these. For
sure, I see you
Last night, ten o'clock. These police take you
to
Prison." Two uniformed ghosts, both armed,
arrive.
In vain I protest I was out till four, that "I've
A right" to them. "No, they Revolution's
grapes for true."
Then I know this charge is an infernal
detention order,
Fleeing to my car, I roar for the gates....I steal
Back at night, pack among shades, sleep my
farewell
At a friend's, creep out for my passport, drive
to the border.
Pale guards drive nails in a tyre, I change a
wheel
In the desert, but I have escaped that circle of
Hell.

KINGDOM OF WINDOWS

The sea is violet, the hills are as green as her
ribbon,
The sun-waves shimmer off this Tunisian
sand,
I stare in, as at a travel poster through a wet
shop window,
Cracked down the middle, a blurry wonder-
land.

There is a crack down the sky of my being.
Like the brown egg I saw dropped on the
grocer's floor,
I leak transparent liquid down my shell,
The golden yoke is secure, but I am raw –
A golden afternoon on deserted Libyan sand
When I oiled *her* tawny back, then in the water
She clung round my neck and laughed,
laughed
As I bent into a springboard for my daughter.

The sun-gold ball hurts easily, I am glad
This green-ribboned fraulein is the other side

of glass.
She knows the damaged shelf, she eats a
bruised apple, sad
In this Kingdom of windows, where the Gates
are impossible to pass.

ORAN: HELL REMEMBERED AGAIN

Once again, sitting in a restaurant, my eyes
have let me down!
I am wet for you, you, whoever you are,
Whichever, rather. Wet. Would it were further
down
Instead of this public sniffing and blinking,
people thinking I am a pop star
On drugs, because of my hair (my Samson's
hair she called it,
Wanting to shear it, turn me into a man, a man
with burns for godsake, but a
man).
Let them look, let my eyes trickle, let the
waiter lie down and have a *fit* –
Nothing can change this artery of grief in my
neck, this river
Not run from, though in my mind I flee its
blood-red, love-wet pit.

DESPAIR

After dinner it should be love, that's what *we*
said;
But here in this port, the girls are more
difficult than in London,
The man in the bank told me, and to love with
the head
Is as bald as to love with the body – no heart
or soul in an automaton.
So my tigress – my hotel room;
I shall get up from this white-papered table,
loiter in the humid street, then
quietly climb the empty stairs to
bed.

RAIN AND SUN: A BEING LIKE A SNOWMAN

It rains, my being leaks like a wet Sunday,
I look for a room in Kensington and can't find
one.
I have no home to go to, Carlotta is "not in"
when I ring her.
After dark I get through. She says, "I'm

110

getting married, there's nothing to
discuss."

At my mother's in Essex, I cry myself to sleep
in my old room.
In the morning I wake with the sun on my
cheeks.
My being immediately opens, I trickle away
like a melting snowman.
One thought of you, Carlotta, and I pour like
that snowman I made you both
when it thawed
in this hot sunshine.

FACES IN SMOKE

Writhing by the phone box in Sloane Square
I wait for my wife to float up from her home
And mutter if we are to live together
Or if she is going to haunt another region in
this catacomb.

Like faces in smoke, the actors in the King's
Arms.
I play a tearlessness, held together with shirt
buttons. I try not to choke.
She plays regret, she shakes her false head.
"He's going to marry me," she says, a painted
face in smoke.

Smoke, the years are like shapes behind a
bonfire.
Driving away, I see her wandering forlornly
to the car park
The other side of Sloane Street. Opposite that
aunt of hers we visited.
I stop and watch her. She does not see, walking
slowly in her daylight dark.

CHAMBER IN HELL

Everything's changed.

I knock at a house near Harrods, a Jew with a
cigarette-butt between his lips
Wheezes up stairs to the Fire Exit, and a room
of glittering silver.
"The last girl was French – she covered the
walls with foil, she was kinky."
I stare at the fanlight, like a coal-hole. I could
not be happy in this walled-in
chamber in Hell.

A week later I return, to a room lower down
with French windows, facing the
Gardens.
I sit and look at the plane tree, boil coffee and
read the papers, while next door
the whore shouts.
At breakfast next morning I sit among
wrecked people in a tortured
basement.
The drunken slut of a housekeeper shrieks at a
West Indian girl for being late
with her rent.

Oh Carlotta, everything's changed, like the
grime on these windows or my
three-legged bed.
Our feather-dusted peace is now a whore
swearing between the silences
through the wall.

What shall I do?

THRONE

I think of the deed by water that brought me
here.
It is just as wrong today, yet you smile at me
As if the flow of time could make a wrong
right!
Some things are wrong for all time, for
Eternity.

Absolute wrong! Our century dethroned
That concept like a high tide submerging
where
There was an Egyptian palace. Now the flood
goes down.
Absolute wrong! A little damp, but there.

Behind us on the river are landmarks
Of wrong. You look ahead, you do not want
to see
Our Abu Simbel: why "stare at that dead
stone"?
Have I forgiven? Only partially.

ME

I am alone again on this side of the pub.
A girl passed in the street, but I did not pick
her up.
They are playing a song I do not want to

hear.
This is what I am escaping from, this lonely
    cup

Of sorrow, shaped like a pint beer-glass. She
    rang
Me at 5 a.m. from the airport, but I was out.
The potgirl has her hair in girlish bunches.
She is chatting to a man who does not know
    doubt.

Next to me three men are talking business.
I want to go to the girl with bunches, and flee
Into her, away from myself. I can telephone
Five women, but none are here now, and I am
    me.

THINKING COLD

I stagger drunkenly in Leicester Square
And stare at restaurant couples killing time.
Birds scream in the trees as they did that day
We ate in *that* steakhouse, before your crime.

Cheap music hall creeps from this basement
    bar,
America blares from that. I sway on, hands
In pockets, looking at cinema pictures
As I did as a boy, slipping away from the
    sands.

A sailor asks me the way to the station.
I shout across a distance, speaking Morse.
I am like a policeman. The paper he carries
Says, "Hero of Peking Sued for Divorce."

Think, I told you, think. You will have gone
    for ever
This time next week, leaving me facing an
    Old
People's Home. Killing time, I roll to the
    "Yankee
Bar", open my head to the twanging guitar,
    and think cold.

SAILOR

Worthless!

I am like a mindless old tar wasting myself on
    worthless girls.
I pester this black-haired piece, she says "I

don't even know you."
Carlotta, I would not have been seen dead
    with her if you were at home.
And she rejected me! Oh why this reef-knot in
    these blue veins, this nightly
    tightening?

Wind in the sails. Scrubbers. Old slags.
    Worthless!
But isn't it better than being like these
    detached ones,
Feeling nothing at the bodies in the street?
    And aren't I usually successful?
I look into the sun and take a sailor's
    consolation:
At the centre of the greatest brightness there is
    a blackness like a woman's
    tongue.

THE WIND

Climb up a lightning flash,
Thresh corn from the rippling sea,
Scrump the stars from Heaven,
Grow a rose from a chestnut tree –
    And never, never
    Will you find
    A woman who blows more constant
    Than the wind.

As for me, I destroy myself with drink,
I rush out into other people.
I look through eyes like tunnels
At the absurdity of old men sitting
As if it were worth doing.
I cannot sink any lower.

John said, "Fork up rubbish and some will
    smell,"
But I know I will never never find
A woman who blows more constant than the
    wind.

ORPHEUS-PHILOCTETES AT HIGH BEACH

The leaves turn red, around High Beach
Are beechnuts, toadstools; in Turpin's Cave
The coal fire glows faces, in the grave
Of my love dark phantoms screech.

I twine long hair round a tree nymph's breast,

In a dark glade whisper "Greensleeves!"
And clasp *her* on these fallen leaves,
Shed tears, a highwayman obsessed.

She sits up with leaves in her hair, the moon
Is caught in a forked bare beech tree.
Back at the house my little sleeps peacefully.
Tied to the big clock-tower is a yellow
    balloon.

I tuck her closer, stroke her hair.
Tomorrow we'll go to Robin Hood Hill
Where oyster mushrooms cling to logs, and
    she will
Show me her red-veined leaf from the garden
    pear.

3,2,1. AGING: AN AUTUMN LEAF AND HOLLY

Out in the Gardens this decaying day
Three boys try to catch an autumn leaf.
Leaf flutters, they push each other out of the
    way.

Yesterday I walked in the Forest with my
    daughter.
Holly with red berries. "Pick two pieces," she
    said,
"One will be lonely, like the lily in the water."

Carlotta loved autumn, and the breaking leaf,
And so I sit alone over a sprig of holly.
Oh sad season that looks forward to winter
    ribs with a petalled handkerchief.

THE OVERCOAT

I am angry. This weekend I was taking my
    daughter
To see *Oliver Twist*. And now I learn *he* is
    taking
Her. We fed acorns to squirrels, I said
    nothing,
But now I am angry. It is time to be stronger.
I will make her meet me, I will threaten her
With a court injunction. There must be no
    more siding
With her. "Do you *want* to divorce her?"
    frowning
My emotions aside, my lawyer asks. And I
    shiver.

Marriage is like an overcoat on a frosty day.
Then, my feet on a grate of beechwood – a
    red glow –
I long, "It's not *me* that matters," I say,
Thinking of my daughter, and without them I
    have no
Love. Then I see *her* as an innocent coat.
    Wasn't she
Just picked up and worn? And, sad, I cease to
    be angry.

THE WRECK

Our house. This room used to be like this. I
    stalk
To the picture of Beethoven over the piano,
The black waste-paper basket, the toasting
    fork
With the hap'ny ship. I prodded her ten years
    ago....
Then the table we played ping pong on. The
    bay-window.
There have been few changes. These things
    have seen the best.
It is not long since I stood with her there –
    just so –
The first day I brought her home. My dead
    father dressed
Upstairs, watching from the window as from a
    crow's nest,
And like an old tar, held out a gnarled hand.
Now that room we slept in is the lodger's, a
    "guest"
Who plays the violin all day long: scales: and
Thinks she is Mozart. There is a great wreck
    in this room,
And the lime-leaves outside are dank in the
    yellow gloom.

LEAKING

I look out and wonder how it is not to be
Like me now. I try to remember things
I did round this house. With a long-arm's
    springs
I cut the limes, I climbed the chestnut tree –
Now a stump – and found a ball in the honey-
-suckle on the roof, I crawled through the
    openings
In the fence and scrumped pears. Surely then I
    had wings,
Was able to smile? I have forgotten. I look out

and see
A policeman, in helmet, walk past the limes.
I can't feel his world. Or is it mine? I try
To work, but what I feel comes first, I have to
    fight
My way through. And with a gulp like a leaky
    pipe, at times,
Every so often, I ooze out. Must it be like this
    for the rest of my
Life? I was wrong to turn down that German
    girl the other night.

THE HOUR OF BUTTERFLIES

I am bound to her. Even now when, like an
    aging whore,
She argues with me, takes our child to the
    musical,
Even now I feel her next to me, am tugged
    apart once more.
I know one who has gone into a mental
    hospital,
Now is the hour of breakdown, of
    butterflies....
I am strong, but there is a ball and chain
Round the ankles of my will, I sit and despise
Myself in this garden, dream of last year
    again.
We are separated by seasons. The woman I
    miss
Is not the woman who frowns at me now.
In a ghastly grey, I envy the beetle in the
    grass.
Happiness is: a tear on my sherry glass.
I must be strong, I decided, watching how
Our child fed a red squirrel with a kiss.

DICTATOR

Is she really tricking me? Saying to her grand
Self, "I will stay married, then if *he* goes, of
    course
I can go back to my ever-reliable husband,
For money"? Is that why she does not want a
    divorce,
Though she says it is because he will lose his
    job,
Evident rubbish? I wish it were not so.
And yet I wish it were – I still love her
    enough to sob
For her, her tendons are in me still. I have not
    meant

To say, "I will not cite him, I will pay his
    costs." Then,
I wanted her to accept them as a present.
I have been weak because I have given, and
    she has taken
And asked for more. I am a Chamberlain, and
She has rushed an army into my Poland.

FULL-TIME LOVERS

And so I have to end it. Finally. I must,
It is doing me in: I slept only four hours
And the geraniums in the window have blobs
    on their flowers.
I must go to her and say: "It is six months –
    just.
Is there any hope?" She will say "No." Then I
    thrust:
"I am your second string. I am exhausted, I
    must finish.
Or must I press you, go back on what you
    wish?
Send an enquiry agent round, investigate your
    lust?
He will force his way in and catch you...."
    O love,
What horror that I, who am so involved with
    you,
Should have come to this. For we were great
    lovers, us two.
My yearning for you meant I could not allow
Much work in the mornings, afternoons. You
    were above
That. We were full-time lovers, and look at us
    now.

THE SACRIFICE

Why did you have to bring *him* along, for my
Last plea? I expected your "No", but now you
    have brought him along
To his pub, it is difficult for me to be strong.
I see you through the coloured glass with
    him: I
Love our child more than my life, you know
    it. Why
Should I sacrifice her so that you can rush
    headlong
Into what you want: him? Yet though it is
    wrong
And you should put our child first, act respon-
    sibly,

114

I must. I now know that the greatest Hell
Is to lose someone you want but cannot win –
Hell is attachment. Is not then the release
From Hell detachment from wanting? I
	whisper farewell
And surrender. My sanity requires it. I begin
The sacrifice, leaving you behind coloured
	glass. Oh my peace.

JOURNEY'S END

So as always I, wounded, seek out Essex,
This green-gated house with its pear tree on
	the lawn
Under whose eaves I slept, heard tappings that
	vex,
Strange creaks, cowered from shadows before
	dawn
As a boy. Now all is October gloom and scorn.
Dusk darkens this dining-room, I sit by the
	piano
Alone, deaf as this Beethoven to your "No".
I wander out to the garden. And suddenly there
I see myself: a spider hanging in the pear.

Like a spider exuding thread, I wove a web 10
And wrapped you in a beautiful silk cocoon,
I rolled you into a ball and held you, till the
	ebb
Of autumn blew you free, my mayfly. Too
	soon
You turned bitter, bitter, and headed for the
	moon.
I stand on the darkening lawn, and wish that I
Could leave this wretched flesh, and quietly
	die
Into those roots and twigs and leaves, so that
	my tears
Could drop each anniversary autumn as
	ripened pears.

Here I must make up my mind, within this
	fence,
Among these Michaelmas daisies, under
	these				20
Rosy apples, by this wet bark; I must make
	sense
Of choosing against my will what I dread, to
	please
You. I feel my trunk and next year's blossom
	slowly freeze

In the chill night. You were not true – true to
	yourself
In that – yet I loved you. Like pears on the
	cellar shelf,
My tears....But no, these stars the night
	weeps – for you
My branches shake them down, like drops of
	morning dew.

OCTOBER SEA: ABYSS

Despair, choppy despair, deeper than
	reddening leaves –
I want her back, want to pick up the phone
Say "Come back", break into her mother's
	birthday tea,
Drag her from aunts and saucers with a look
	of china-bone.

Birthday – I think of her last one, when the
	three of us danced and sang
"We're a happy family" near the large Garian
	pot.
It's best to gulp and die, I have nothing to live
	for save her
And this drowning, me crying "Strength
	strength" near a sinking yacht.

My hull breaks on her; smashed under a
	typhoon wave
For her, and for no one else, no Wedgewood
	intimacy,
I am down, down, down a black trough
	gasping "Strength" –
Who to? Who? Not her, not my family or
	friends. Not God. Me.

I am alone. And seeing her now, sunflaxen
	hair,
Wink at me from a clifftop cornfield some-
	where out of reach
I say, "I can't stop these tears rolling down
	my cheeks,
One loves, the other is loved," and un-
	expectedly wade onto the beach.

ROOM LIKE A MERRY-GO-
ROUND

I return to this room and flop on my rucked-
	up bed.
Here, an hour ago, I met the Queen of the

115

Poets.
Beer-cans like a fairground knock-me-down,
    room spins like a merry-go-round.
She left a half-bitten apple, like a discarded
    prize.

I live chaotically, like a Dostoevsky gone to
    the bad,
I get drunk, go to bed at all hours, burn myself
    up like a red lamp.
I go round and round like a motorboat in a
    pool, I hold the helm but steer no
    course,
I, who have seen an image burst in a shower
    of stars.

In Essex I picked four baskets of rosy apples
    in a November drizzle.
I had green slime from wet boughs on my
    black hands.
Let me learn from that now, as I knock this
    cotton reel rolling

    across the carpet.
Let me wind myself back onto the spindle of a
    country sewing-machine.

TO THINK!

To think, I could have married her! She
    fancied me
When she played hostess to all the poets, she
    ended
Her novel with our white wedding, or so old
    Maurie

Whispered after that evening at the BBC
When she came back to my room, and our
    poetry blended.
I was fatigued from other exertions. We

Lay awhile. She said, "I've had ecstasies
    until, wheee!
They have come out through my toes." To
    think, I could have depended
On her, and she might be knocking around
    with some other devotee!

MY HELL

I am in a region that is bounded by
Essex, Greenwich, Dulwich, and this Chelsea.

My Hell is part flat land, on its boundary,
And part a crammed and crowded smoking
    city.
Now my feet ring out on its dull pavements,
A drive, and I try to forget by a swollen river.
A drive, and I am lost in Forest dissonance,
But worst of all is flat-land, and the
    reminiscent shiver.
I hug the warm end, there is forgetting among
    brunettes,
I can lose myself in the Saturday King's Road
    crowds.
But driving past the Wandsworth prison gates
And looking for angels among the
    thunder-clouds,
I think of the anguished souls in that lower
    region
And I rejoice, though my torments remain
    legion.

LOVE LIKE WILLOW

You say I should stop loving you, as if love
Were like a habit – alcohol or smoking
Or eating late or morning coffee. You must be
    joking.
Can I peel you off my mind like a velvet
    glove?

Love is Eternal. It is outside time, like death.
It is as permanent as my urn, and as dumb,
You are a part of me like my gold
    chrysanthemum.
I cannot stop loving as long as I have breath.

Love, more than memory, is a weeping tree.
Time blows through it, like the early autumn
    wind.
In the autumn of our great year, its glory is
    thinned,
But in the winter, the trunk is still there, for
    all to see.

MY SHOPWINDOW

I am like a father on a shopping outing.
Watching you as you marry for possessions
I have to think: should I wait for you now,
Or shall I leave you to chase your obsessions?

You said to me, "What can you offer,
    provide?

What house in Portman Square? What job can
   you do?"
The shopwindows called, you went with a
   scorn, and I vowed
One day I would show you, I would show
   you.

I am solving all the problems, Carlotta.
I am building my life up. I have no hope
That my flat and job will bring you back, but I
   will
Stun you with a shopwindow of beautiful
   scope.

WEATHERVANE AND WIND

A year has passed like mist on grass
With a "Why did it happen? Did she love me?
Did she love like a weathervane
On a misty Essex belfry?"

Questions in the winter wind
With a "When will the weathercock crow?"
I sing the soul of Western man
And a disbelief like snow.

CHRISTMAS: FEATHERS AND
A WHITE BEDSPREAD

All night the snow falls silently;
Downy feathers shaken from a black
   pillow,
Flecking the street-lamps, muffling the
   reindeer bells
That somewhere out in the dark my daughter
   listens for.
Has she a hot water-bottle, did she undress by
   a warm fire, by the Christmas
   tree?

This morning there is a white brightness in
   this room,
Outside the sun sparkles on a dazzling, frozen
   bedspread.
Snow on the fences and boughs and rooftops,
   shuffled off by starlings, seagulls,
Trees are grey, black towards the humped
   forest.
Has she woken yet, has she sat up and glimpsed
   her holly-wrapped parcels?

Think: now, somewhere across the white

My dearest wakes and climbs across her bed,
Rustles at her stocking. I prowl.
Now? When? I want to feel it over my
   shoulders,
That bedspread, over my head. I, dead.

JANUARY

My first day at this dreary urchins' school
On the south bank at Greenwich, near the
   river.
A mist hangs over the stone playground,
I patrol, and shiver,

And – why do I need their filthy money? To
   pay
My rent, so that I can return, unwelcomed,
   stew
Tea in this decaying Knightsbridge bedsit,
Switch on the radio and think of you.

Why? What is it for? Like the tailors –
I tried on a jacket, and my daughter thought I
   had gone
And cried, and thinking of it towards 9 p.m., I
   cried.
Why do I go to tailors, wait for midnight and
   oblivion?

Search. That is the has-been, and no more,
I am in flight, I shiver out this hurt
In the playground, and now, in Chelsea, I
   drink it numb,
Totter to the car, to this exile's room, this dirt,
Ponder "Why?" and am dumb, am dumb.

KNOT

Must you, must *you* go through it – men like
   me?
Tonight, filled with an awful restlessness,
I went to the pub I used to frequent,
The pit of my stomach knotted with
   loneliness.

I asked two outright, "Look, have a drink with
   me."
One was going to a club, the other had a
   friend.
Then I saw a blonde who looked so innocent,
Laughing for effect – I thought of you, that
   was the end.

You must work it out too, with men who are
    playboys
And walk late at night with this infernal itch.
I turned away and bought a drink, and wished
I could cut off this knot in my groin by
    turning a switch.

FROST ON THE TONGUE

I thought it all out, I was going to say to you,
"We're the only ex-s I know who are young
And do not meet, but hand our child over in
    cars,"
Yet when I was with you, the words stuck to
    my tongue.

And as *you* sit in your car, you may well glare
    at me
And look possessively at your Carlotta.
Just you remember, I have possessed her,
And never forget: I may come and make her
    feel hotter

Then she feels towards you. All you who have
    taken
An elaborate revenge on the life you lost,
And constructed an edifice on your wrong
    choice,
I sadly salute you as I cross back over the
    frost.

TRAITORS' GATE

It is over. I am divorced. A sunny day,
I waited in the Law Courts, you were there
With him. We could not speak, my counsel
    had a lot to say.
I went into the witness box, I looked at your
    hair
As I replied, and then I was sitting somewhere
At the back. I winked at you. You left to
    phone
Someone with him. I wandered round
    Lincoln's Inn Square.
It was afternoon, I felt terribly alone,
I passed a car on a double yellow line, my own.
I did not care, I felt drained. Now I feel I have
    run
Away from my daughter. I am near tears. Can
    I atone?
I want to clutch her to me, for what have I
    DONE?

A Traitors' Gate clangs down. Sounds of a
    mower grope
From some land of the living. Limp in this
    dark, I must cling and hope.

ORPHEUS-PROMETHEUS IN THE BLACKWEIR REGION OF HELL

We looked in this Blackweir pond at
    stickleback
And minnows with green and silver bellies,
At water beetle, skimming dragonflies –
Looked down through the bars, and then
    picked blackberries.

As a boy I climbed into the round tunnel,
Crouched underground, under this high-
    barred grate
Where the pond overflows in a cascade down,
Heard voices echoing up to this dungeon gate.

Now squatting beneath the bars within my
    mind,
Watching gnats dance from an awful torture
    cell,
I look up at blue sky from a dark tunnel.
Will there ever be an opening in the Gates of
    Hell?

LOST CALM

From the Blackweir pond we climbed
    between beech trees,
Plunged among pollards before we reached
    Green Ride,
Scuffled through dry leaves and silver birch
    and –
Glory! The Lost Pond that Epstein glorified!

It is a calm pond, with still water-lilies
Surrounded by reeds and iron-leafed trees.
Here and at the High Beach church
There is a still beneath the autumn breeze.

Like iron filings on a magnet, many
    afternoons
Cling round my heart, rose-thorns and
    sticklefins.
If I ever find my hidden calm, will it leave me
Useless, a small round cushion without
    pins?

SUMMER FATIGUE

The Gardens droop with manifold, oh railed-
    in summer fatigue!
Oh, the heaviness of the woman's swollen
    belly.

From my window, framed by railings, the
    abundance could be in the Tate.
I appreciate shape, but I do not know what it
    means.

Seen from the moon, this earth is a baseball
    "held at arm's length".
These Gardens are like a blemish on this
    marble egg.

That is all I know, in this summer manifold.
    This summer fatigue.

DISENTANGLED

"Does aught befall you? It is good. It is part of the
destiny of the universe ordained for you from the
beginning. All that befalls you is part of the great
web."

    Marcus Aurelius according to one translation
    (See epigraph to *Ode: Spider's Web* for a more
    accurate version)

I am as tangled up as a web-caught fly.
In his office, I saw a net shaped like a tent
And felt trapped in a mesh of accident.
Fool! I could have avoided the effect, by
    passing the cause by.
These threads that bind me are my clutching
    outside my-
-self, indulging, permitting myself, loving
    with selfish intent,
Feeling guilt. Time cuts up the silence with
    such entwinement.
Let me sever it. I release her, am detached, a
    unity,
I discipline myself and love as I should,
I am freed from guilt, see religiously across
A timeless, selfless space. The "I" who would
Have chained my head has gone down the
    Way of Loss,
And God now rules my heart. The West can lose
Its illusions, strengthen its soul, and its
    values!

HEART

Bullheads under the willows
Keep a humped bridge in sight.
Water flows between reeds,
And, veined, plays in the light
And my heart grows like nettles
In the field by the stile that is white.

    2 September 1971, revised 29 November 1993

FLOW: MOON AND SEA

I loved you like the tortoise-shell
You loved up on the Downs with me.
The light leaps off your Worthing sea
Like shoals of leaping mackerel.

The sea flows like a bent hawthorn.
Now, up the night, the harvest moon
Floats and sails like a child's balloon
Over this darkly rippled corn.

This glow behind the moon and sea
Affects my way of seeing.
What, oh what is happening to my being?
I thrill to a pebble's flow, and a bumble-bee.

VISIONS: GOLDEN FLOWER, CELESTIAL CURTAIN

That weekend I lay down and breathed at
    twilight,
Looked into my closed eyes, saw white light
    flowing
Upwards…, a tree of white fire, flickering.
Then a spring opened in me, for an hour
    bright
Visions wobbled up like bubbles: from a great
    height
A centre of light, a gold-white flower,
    shining
Like a dahlia, the centre and source of my
    being;
A chrysanthemum; a sun; a fountain of
    white
Light; strange patterns; old masters I was not
    certain
I had seen before; old gods. I was refreshed,
    after this
I fell on my knees in the dark, and breathed "I
    surrender"
To the white point. It changed into a celestial
    curtain

Blown in the wind, like the aurora borealis.
I felt limp, an afterglow in each moist finger.

MORE VISIONS: THE JUDGE

I buried my eyes in the crook of my arm and
    saw
A dome of light like a spider's web, an old
Yellow and purple tomb; later a gold
Death-mask, the face of God. I felt shaky,
    more
Like a child that has taken tottering steps,
    before
I walked to the Brompton Oratory to hold
A candle lit from the eternal basket, and fold
My hands. Later I saw an egg; a mirror;
Christ on a cross; a flaming devil who trod
Down a haloed saint. Visions poured up: a
    globe;
A yellow rose; black thorns against a sundial;
A foetal child, and a crowned Eastern god.
Now – o frontal Christ in thorns and a red-
    brown robe
Gathered with a pin at the chin, help me
    through this trial!

VISIONS: THE PIT AND THE MOON

Frostleaves on glass. Hints of a white
    flower
And suns and shafts of light. My arms must
    free
These eyes, black out the dark. A starless,
    revea-
-ling night, an outline of a rim, a tower
As if I look up from a dungeon-pit, in the
    power
Of Hell. A point of white light breaks, I see
A long white-hot line, like the trunk of a
    tree
Down the centre of my being. "I surrender,"
    cower-
-ing, I gasp, and the light swells into a city
Moon. Squatting, I feel a refreshing
    stimulation,
I feel wobbly at the knees, but now I know
That time is the cutting up of Eternity
Which can be known through this silence. My
    imagination
Relieves this prison stretch with this mystic
    glow.

VISIONS: SHIELD OF GOD

I closed my eyes and saw the Flower in white
Light; a philosopher's stone, an egg hanging
In the heavens; a tree; prison gates; and,
    gathering
In majestic splendour in the starlit night,
And floating nearer, looking slightly to the
    right,
Wise and bearded, the magnificent aging
Face of God on a primitive shield, frowning.
Then I knew that the meaning of life is quite
Subjective: we must love life properly,
And so we MUST suffer, lose everything,
And when "I want" has died, spiritually
    unshod,
All that pads foot and blinkers us early
Is lost, and we are left embodying
A hard, strong message as the Shield of God.

FLOWERS IN THE SOUL

Last night I saw the flowers in my soul,
Behind my closed eyes there were streaks of
    white light.
I leafed through the picture book of my
    imagination.
It is like a scrapbook of patterns that are
    bright

And strange. Outside the trees are turning
    yellow.
Now, this noon, I listen to chamber music.
My soul needs it. At peace, I want nothing
Save to be left alone. My heart is quick.

ORPHEUS: HOLY FOOL

"Video meliora proboque;/Deteriora sequor." "I see
the better and approve it, but I follow the worse."
    Ovid, *Metamorphoses*, vii 20

Fool, I have been a fool. I was getting on so
    well,
I was settled, peaceful. I had not seen my
    Light
Recently, but there had been glimmers; and I
    will.
Then I had to go back to that old dive.
I walked in a slum-Hell, I climbed down stairs
To flat-chested women with eyes like foul
    pits.

One was scrawny with black hair, by pin-ups
of stars.
She asked if I'd buy her a drink, licking her
lips.
I froze, seeing her crouch like a rabbit,
And I was back in outer darkness again.
Out in the street I was angry, I thought 'Fool,
fool.
Satan made me lust for unknown company,
and it
Took me over. These desires, I must suppress
them.'
Satan bides his time, then attacks to take his
fill.

FEVER: FIRE AND MERCURY

What is it like, dying?

I lie in bed with a hot water-bottle and sweat
out a fever.
My scalp crashes like a furnace, my throat is a
roaring fire.
My eyes are bloodshot, this room is a slightly
jumbled blur.
It is you I think of, you Carlotta, staring at
that bedroom door.

Once, head hot as this, on the edge of the
desert
I lost my voice, and you soothed my brow,
saw me off at the gate.
Once I had sandfly fever, and walked round
delirious.
My temperature was a hundred and six, you took
my arm and led me back to bed.

If I am dying now, I hope you will float down
the landing of my memory,
Take the thermometer out of my mouth, as
you used to, perch on this bed,
Hold it up to the light till the mercury glints
like black steel,
Then, as you used to, put your soft soft hand
on my burning head.

It will never be, and I will be one of the
solitary dead.

DECEMBER 4TH

Funereal flags drape Westminster Square,

Hunting for Christmas cards in the V and A
I feel a sadness in the air.
What *is* today?

December the fourth – could I forget
This Holy, Lentern, private week,
Could I forget my dark regret
And not feel bleak?

Bleak the vigil in this dark room
At two, at three, at four,
Two candles by the red-gold bloom,
Two years through the door.

I want to kneel in the Oratory
Till my dark is a field of wheat,
As dawn creeps through my misty tree
I stare at a ghastly street.

AN AMPUTATED LIMB

Here by firelight I clasp her in my arms,
I cling to her and squeeze my being out
Like pus from a wound. It is *you* I think of,
What do I have to do to escape your pout?

For two years I have felt you like a foot
That was amputated: I can wriggle the toes
Still. Now this stub of a leg has gangrene,
My soul festers like a suppurating rose.

And yet, I can hope. For once I was paralysed,
Heart turned up through throat, and could not
remember;
But now, first snowdrop on the village green,
I can dream, I can dream of a lost December.

FEBRUARY BUDDING, HALF TERM

The buds are flecks, hawthorn and beech,
A great tit see-saws near its nest,
A squirrel listens from a branch,
Like my daughter, too quiet for speech.

On Strawberry Hill, a sky like smoke
Threatens the suffering, tearless twigs
And looking at this mossy knoll
I know the endurance of a much-gnarled oak.

I feel the rising rhythm thud,
As I scuffle through last year's leaves

The scales unfold around my grief
And burst into joyful bud.

A STOLEN HOUR

Today I walked through the lost leaves and
    holly
Of another year. The hawthorn budded green,
The spiked beech showed green thoughts
    through last year's sharp-
-ness. A great tit see-sawed to the sky, serene

In the Forest where a church with a black rail
Round the wall stands silent. I took the
    bramble
Path that winds to an oak tree. There I lay
Where four paths meet and made a mental
    ramble

Through where the silver birches leap to the
    sky
Like white-hot flames, and the snowdrops
    glow with heat;
There I stole an hour in scrumptious Eternity
The other side of all tangled defeat.

MARCH: CROCUSES

I will see her, after these hooligans
Have spat into this swimming-pool,
I will see her in the pub car park
After a tedious afternoon's school.

I will see her where I trudged through snow
The night my daughter was born,
I will pay the first term's fees
For the school they are taking her to, in the
    Fens,
Will she smile, will she smile and take my
    arm?

But: she is sitting in his red MG
In a white sweater; my child beside her,
Smiling, and her Flight-Lieutenant.
I ignore him, though she walks with me I am
    bitter.

She wants me to change, she wants me to be
    friendly now,
For our child's sake, to the thief who stole my
    kisses
As if my feelings were like aircraft dials and

switches
Instead of crocuses.

I glare at the selfish toad.
But no, like a chrysalis
Of work and emotion, I could grow into a
    god.

In St. James's Park the crocuses
Near the bridge across the lake
Recall my white magnolia tree –
And a destiny
Like a Red Admiral Blake.

HELL, MARCH

The river is still by Harold's bridge,
It is still by the Waltham weir
Until frothily it plunges down –
A stillness like despair.

In the still crypt, pillory and stocks
And ancient whipping post
Still echo the lash of three knotted thongs
On the back of my guilty ghost.

My love, nothing can bring you back
So today I'll still my Erinyes;
Come, we will pick forget-me-nots
Near the Hellish water-lilies.

MINIATURE ROSE

We have felled elms, carried grasshoppers,
    frogs,
We have flown kites, scuffled conkers among
Yellow leaves, and now I must lose you.
    Young
Girl, go North. This miniature rose the wind
    jogs –
Each head is a talent, and I, in a mystagogue's
Garden, water you. Among the dahlias I clung
To you, but now by that Forest pond I have
    flung
My soul open to the world. We have crouched
    by logs
And felt the peace of the toadstools, the happy
    pause
Of the bullheads by the bank, the tired leaves,
    one
By one letting slip, the snug conkers in new
Flowing lines, the lush berries and hips and

haws.
We have felt the Law of the Seed, how earth,
    air, sun
And rain make the seed grow, as they now do
    you.

LAW OF THE SEED
(DIVINE SONNET)

The winds blow the seed to earth, the seas
    make
Rain and water it, the sun warms it. I can
Confirm all things have their place in the
    Great Plan.
Animals, birds, fish, men hunt each other,
    break
And eat fruit, plants, vegetables, to help take
Their seed to ripeness. Trees, flowers, each
    human
Flower to be fertilised, so that their seed can
Grow. There are no accidents. Does a man
    wake
Up with five heads? Does the corn ripen in
    spring?
Do the trees go bare in summer, flap wings
    and fly?
I must not ask why a hazel nut grows or
Does not, why blossom falls, why that
    sycamore wing
Is not here, that child. Accept, there is no
    "why",
Things happen in the course of a Great Plan's
    law.

A GLACIER IN THE HEART
(DIVINE SONNET)

A law rolls through Nature and human pity.
I see it in the autumnal garden,
It flows imperceptibly like a glacier, ten
Thousand years through time to Eternity,
A flow of generations and modernity,
Families succeed one after another, driven
Through bud and flower and fruit, revelled in,
    forgotten.
There are separations, but these are in the city
Of hours, a few scattered petals. I know
That to the seasons everything is for the best:
Does not the falling blossom herald in the
    fruit?
I must surrender you to the Great Flow
And wear my sorrow silently as a guest

Until it reveals its gift: a heart that is mute.

THE VOID AND THE SNOWDROP
(DIVINE SONNET)

The Spirit needs solitude to grow like a white
Snowdrop in the heart. Its soil, never changing,
Is one, always the same. I change. Standing
At this Christingle service, I hold a light-
-ed candle in an orange, with a band of bright
Red blood round it. We are candle-flowers,
    waiting
To be lit white by the Holy Spirit, needing
An illumined growth to unfold the flame to
    sight.
Before I brought you here today, I heard
That I must consent to a final, severing plan.
Light and darkness were a void, like thundery
    rain,
Once, like the bottom of this Spring of Word.
I must empty myself, discard the timetables.
    An
Emptying can be a filling, a loss a gain.

PURE WATER OF ETERNITY
(DIVINE SONNET)

There is a deep presence from a Void,
    something
That can be known by losing the sense of
    time,
By deepening the living. The artist is prim-
-arily a shaper, like brick walls round a
    spring,
For the god in ourselves, rediscovering
Truths which wobble up beneath the surface
    slime
Of the "I-I-I"; this stagnant dissolving grime
Like an echo under a railway bridge, dying
On silence. Let him clear the scum and mould
A channel, for under the Devil's filth our
Pure water overflows. Its force fills me
As a spring fills a runnel that leads to old
Baths. I have shaped curved stones to carry a
    power
Like this unclogged water of Eternity.

SELF-PLANTING CORN, GRAVEYARD HAWTHORN
(DIVINE SONNET)

Hermit crabs and starfish after the tide,

And the self-planting of a corn of wheat
Which falls to the earth and winds itself down
    neat-
-ly and dies. In my inner life I have died
In the ground of Eternity, to grow inside.
I know this among urchins, squabbling heat-
-edly, in the ferny graveyard where I am Et-
-ernal, nothing dumped on me from the world
    of pride,
No handful of earth spattering my soul.
Love is always there – this Love I have found.
Selflessness is like a catching of frogspawn,
A peaceful resignation, the gardener whole
In the tending of the rose. I have died into the
    ground
Of my humanity, like this graveyard
    hawthorn.

BRUISED PLUM

Now my daughter is going North.
She cries as we sit in my MGB.
I reassure her with an apple
And tell her she will write to me.

The loss of this little girl
Has taught me selfless love.
We do not find peace through "I want"
But in standing back from the foxglove.

Tearfully she waves goodbye.
I visit the electricity board, come
Home with a bunch of woodland violets
Under a sky like a bruised plum.

TIME AND ETERNITY
(FIRST VERSION)

I held her hand at this Omega gate,
She wanted to paint the yew,
And now the moment has blown away
Like dandelion fluff on the blue.

Now, on the High Beach forest church
The passing clouds and years
Are like pattering footsteps in the porch
Or the silence under bedsit tears.

In the city I am scattered like poplar fluff
Blown on the wind of echo,   10
But here I breathe, with the quiet of stone,
The white light these dead men know.

Oh bury me behind this grave,
At the low black rail,
That all who have suffered and been brave
May pass the yew and wail
For all whom golden hair enslaves,
Till the past is a squirrel's tail;
Then, like the boom in childhood caves,
Oh hear beneath the breeze   20
The mystery that flows through stars and seas,
Where the autumn bracken waves.

VISIONS: RAID ON THE GOLD MINE
(DIVINE SONNET)

I have been seized by God. I felt the Divine
Presence steal up from the shaft below and fill
My soul, slow my breathing, locking me still
As a fakir. I lay and descended down my
    spine,
Surrendered the deepest crevices of my gold
    mine
Of visions – golden furniture, temples with
    thrill-
-ing columns, a brown head, the celestial
    curtain – till
I saw a diamond in luminous blue light shine,
The first time I have seen the colour blue
In my secret excavations. Then the Golden
    Flower,
And an hour of flashing down my inner night
Like a dawn. Slowly the raiding Presence
    withdrew,
And now I record it in this "newspaper
Of the Eternal"; lifted to a great height.

THE FURNACE
(DIVINE SONNET)

Again I have been rapt. Aglow with Fire
I sat and looked at the lights of Chelsea,
At dusky windows, and felt God enfold me,
I sat rigid, then lay down full of desire.
I murmured, "I have surrendered entire-
-ly. Enter me." I was breathing heavily,
Possessed, in union, till in a sighing glee,
Slipping away, a voice said, "Your loss will
    inspire
A dark generation, I will give you greatness."
I do not want self-glory. On these fired pots
I paint the mystic truths, as they are revealed
In my vision. Now I know I will have less

124

Going out. From my window I look down.
Among lots
Of plane trees, a white magnolia. I am healed.

VISION: SNATCHED BY GOD, A BLUE LIGHT
(DIVINE SONNET)

I have been snatched by God. Idly looking
Over Chelsea, I felt peace rise, attack
And enfold me. I put down my spoon, pushed
slack-
-ly at my chair, sat cross-legged, hands
clasped, gazing.
Soon I was breathing deeply and sinking
Into a trance, locked rigid – glory! From that
black
Night of closed eyes, a pale blue light shone
back,
And became a dazzling white like a diamond
shining
In the sun. I sighed out in ecstasy
As if I were throbbing in a pleasure-dance,
Stiffly I rose and lay on my bed an hour
And the Light came and went, only more
faintly
This time. Then I came slowly out of my
trance,
And the rest of the day have felt full of inner
power.

VISION: LOVE LIKE A GRID
(DIVINE SONNET)

A weekend of sorrow, but the power tonight
Switched itself on. My breathing slowed, my
two
Hands locked, I closed my eyes and wandered
through
Into my bedroom, got into bed. The white
Light came with blue tints, incredibly bright,
Came near, then went. In an ecstasy I knew
God caught my breath. Suddenly the white
light grew
Bigger and brighter. There was a hoop of
light,
A round halo before my peeping eyes.
I gasped and fell away, as if making love,
Glassy-eyed, peaceful, happy, not rigid.
Now, with a swelling feeling in my thighs,
I know Love pulses through the sky above
Like a network of wires in an LEB grid.

ROSE, GOLDEN

Rose, golden as gold without dross,
In the heart of a disciple you reflect
The Flower of Love and Beauty, the Golden
Flower
Which expands and fills with a joy unchecked.

There is a duality in my heart:
The human, in the presence of the Divine,
hears
In communion, not union; Me and thee.
I, glimpsing the One through a mist of tears:

Red rose of sorrow, veiled in Light.
To unify myself I must look for – Love,
Which sweeps away the self into oblivion
And leaves this immortal hilarity of the
dove.

RED ROSE AND POTATO-PEELER

The red rose has a hidden thorn
As love of pleasure has a hidden sorrow.
Self-abnegation, the will's obliteration
Comes from love, sacrificing a tomorrow.

The face of the red rose lights the dark
Like a lamp, but then the withdrawal, inside,
Of the light. I am abandoned by you,
O my beloved, my spiritual Bride.

As I purify myself, gouging
The root of self-love out of my windowbox
With this potato-peeler of self-hatred,
As I renounce alcohol like some awful pox,

I wonder, will you ever return,
You brilliant rose of light, to comfort me,
Or must I wait until you decide I have
Surrendered enough – must I wait patiently?

IVY AND RAINBOW

Carlotta, I call, always Carlotta.

I stand outside this great manorial gate
And look across at the ancient Lincoln Hall.
At last she has found her settled, country life.
You can see it in the way she potters by the
ivied wall.
In this garden I, too, could blossom, drop

insights
Like windfalls among the flowerpots and
daffodils,
Observe the wagtails, browse in my Georgian
study,
Dine with Ministers – no work, no bills.

Carlotta, I call, always Carlotta.   10
You know, I, too, took the trouble to be born.
I, too, should have been a gentleman, for
Every moment fans out at me, like that
peacock's tail across the lawn.

Oh England, often you make me sad
For your free green fields sprout
Great Halls of injustice beside cottages
And an artist's smoking standard of how to
live in doubt.

There must be no envy. I will not measure Sir
John by his Hall and land,
Or they must become just rubble for the
dustman's cart.
I will measure him by the Georgian library,
where, like a rainbow in a
greenhouse,   20
He grew greatness, or did not, using it like
creeping ivy for a philosopher's
art.

The red ivy holds a rainbow, Carlotta. Be free
To enjoy it, even though I am not with you.
Seek out in this great Hall a cottage
philosophy.
Peep for colours where the roses grew.

TATTERSHALL
The morning's fine; in Bluebell Wood
A wigwam of sunlight hangs between pine
trees,
My little redskin stalks bumble-bees.
Slit-eyed grief is round me, like an axeman's
hood.

Ahead (I wince away) are – *they*,
Hand in hand near a sunlight blade,
Murmuring, trapped in a sunlit glade,
Mocking my bluebells this black Sunday.

A cuckoo sings; with misguided zest

My Indian climbs on a felled tree,
Counts rings and says: "It's thirty-three."
I stare past her tentpole at my cuckooed nest.

THE MEANING OF LIFE
(DIVINE SONNET)
Meaning is in the Gardens this afternoon:
A fountain of leaves and seeds, a teeming
flow
Of opposites, a spring from a Void, throw-
-ing out misery, joy, despair, hope, moon,
Sun, the worlds of time and Eternity. This
June
All are held together in a whole. I know
Life, death, time, silence are necessary, so
All multiple trees and plants are in tune,
All crawling things, all Nature, a gushing
Whose meaning is "one": unity: an ocean
Of Being, to see which self and reason must
die.
Now I can unite with the One, dance with the
rushing
Whirl. I, who have escaped the chains of self
and emotion,
Mirror the meaning of life on this inner eye.

OBIDA (HURT)
Perhaps, Carlotta, I torment myself
To hurt you,
Live alone, choose loneliness
To make you stew.

If so, Carlotta, please understand
Your evening stare
Over your Moses basket
Exalts my despair.

"I" masquerades behind my evening sacrifice
Like a terrorist on hunger strike.

UNDER A MUSLIN NET
At a Press Conference I asked the President
If I could visit the Chinese railway.
He said, "I don't know, why not?" And later
that day
An Australian television crew was sent
To my hotel. They had a jeep. We went
To the Mlimba-Makumbako hills, where
tracklay-
-ers tunnelled. We ate in a Chinese camp.

They
Gave us beer. I came to sleep in this "tent"
In a mud-hut: boards for a bed under a torn
Mosquito-net. Tossing, turning on this bench,
I dreamt you were in my arms, though we had
    no solutions.
I woke to the reality of a bush dawn,
The Chinese exercises and the foul stench
Of the lake near the maize which is "the
    ablutions".

GUY FAWKES NIGHT

Out in the dark the bonfire burns,
The rockets whizz and crack
And fall in stars like the frosty ferns
We fingered that day in some lakeside urns –
And I hear her *married* voice breathe softly
    back.

She can hear the barn-owl from her phone –
I say what I rang to say:
She and my little girl, shivering alone
In the misty dark till a dawn of stone... –
Will you be all right, will you be all right this
    month your new husband is
    away?   10

It makes her angry to feel I care,
She wants to burn ten years
Like fireworks; escape, be free as air
Of this London guy with straggly hair
Waiting for a Phantom to crash, for her
    widow's tears.

She rages; for an hour I soothe, cajole,
My soul a Catherine wheel;
Was my happiness just a bowl
Of abandoned apple-peel?

Red near the embers, lurid, bright,   20
A Roman candle glows;
I, Guy Fawkes, murmur a soft "Good night"
As, tender, now, wistful she goes,
A greenhouse rose
In this dying November light.

SHOOTING

This weekend my daughter is shooting with
    Sir John.

I stroll on Staples Hill, where golden leaves
    and a knighthood
Like moss have buried the footprints of Sir
    John's grandfather
Who, a hundred years ago, as lord of the
    manor,
Fenced in a thousand acres of foresters'
    firewood.

Here brave Willingale lopped a branch
And went to jail.
An Act of Parliament gave these trees back to
    me,
Sir John's grandfather gave us Lopping Hall,
    and drew a veil.

My father bought our childhood house from
    Sir John   10
Who then left this manor for Lincolnshire.
And now my daughter shoots with him,
Retrieves his pheasants; he gives her antique
    furniture.

Oh, like a beechwood, levelling down!
May Parliament condemn
All stealers of all trees on Forest hills
And all who flatter them,
And all bringers of revolutionary bills
Who would drag this manorial freedom
    down –
Let us celebrate all virtuous men.   20

I have a bone to pick with you, Sir John,
But I will let you keep it. In return,
Teach my daughter your leisured wisdom,
Teach her the good things that the landed
    learn.

HOPE AND FEAR

A screaming Phantom, sudden dark –
The navigator stands, a shout,
A nosedive, pressure on the heart,
Gasping, which will be first, crash or blackout?

The news said it disappeared in a cloud,
The other plane gave the alarm near Cold Fell.
They were both based in Lincolnshire;
Is it, could it be...? A corpse by a harebell

On Thack Moor, is it him, is it, in that twisted

127

metal?
Secretly I hope it is, shamed I share her fear.
And if it were, would she, could she come
    back? Come through that door?
I wait, hoping I am right and wrong, Carlotta,
    and peel a nonchalant pear.

NEXT MORNING: SUNRISE AND SMOKED GLASS
Would you deceive me again?

I have been thinking, driving round Hyde
    Park Corner,
If you came back tonight, how would it be.
    Would it be strange, a bit of a
    sweat?
Would you sleep alone for a while, in the
    winter afternoons
Would you go off on long shopping tours and
    visit friends I have not met?

And in the evenings, would you sit alone,
Paint, and when I speak, crossly go to the
    fridge,
Would you get restless, seeing planes on
    television?
"Who are you, Carlotta?" I ask near Tower
    Bridge,

For "You don't know half of it" you told me
    last winter,   10
Smiling secretly, and if you are a widow now
    and do not catch a London train,
Might you not have several men, "a man of
    the month"?
Near the Cutty Sark I ask: "Carlotta, would
    you deceive me again?"

Driving up Maze Hill I am dazzled by a
    sunrise like a blazing fire.
That is how you are. Behind your radiance,
    bas-
-king, I do not see you, but when you go in
    behind a cloud, I miss you.
Would I like you if I saw you through smoked
    glass?

Black crows on Blackheath as I read
The alien names of the unknown Phantom
    dead.

You will not come back now. Shine on,
    deceive,   20
I do not need to smoke my eyes blood-red.

TAGETIES LIKE SHOPGIRLS
Water the yellow tageties
In this thick London mist,
Watch each bright yellow head turn up
Like shopgirls being kissed.

These tiptoe tageties will grow
In families, like brides,
Each day pick off the withered heads
And water the buds at their sides.

These two gold ones now grow apart
On this withering root.
Old ladies know the meaning of
Their seed-thrust into fruit.

27 November 1972

POSSIBILITIES: DEAD LEAVES AND OAK
In Sussex Square, if, Aristotle,
I studied how leaves grow and die,
For twenty years I'd catalogue them
Till heureka! My philosophy!

See how the trunk of that old oak
Thrusts sap up six winter branches.
Measure it by its upward growth,
And me by my possibilities!

Your golden hairs reach to the sky,
A sunflower in ground that has sunk;
May all my leaves be English oak
With the print of this massive trunk.

A BATHROOM MIRROR AND A SHADOW
I stand before the bathroom mirror
Naked as if I were Plato
And Body and Spirit were fused together
And not divided by Descartes or NATO.

All the "isms" that isolate
One quality of that body –
Soul, feelings, morals, between the legs,
The measure of Marx or what is shoddy –

Are gurgling down the plug, the scum
Of my habitual nature,   10
Of lonely feelings and memories
Like: the night you danced that rumba.

I have revolted against the years
And all non-mystic philosophies,
And now a Shadow I shall live
In a nature of possibilities.

I shall forget your golden hair,
Or if not forget, at least ignore;
I shall strive beyond that man in the mirror
On the back of the bathroom door.   20

All hail the Shadowman, the giant call
Like the shadow of an oak on an acorn-shoot,
All hail the Shadow on the bathroom wall!

WILL LIKE A MOUNTAIN PEAK

Nothing can fetter my will.
The way of the mountain is right,
I'll make you kneel in awe
At the white peak's brilliant height,

Say, "There are those who will a standard,
And get up at six for it,
Art or music, whose job
Is just a welfare benefit,

And those, content to sleep,
Who remain what they are today;
I judge a man by his Will
And not by his stinking pay."

You'll say "Everest or nothing!
Down with the Matterhorns!"
Ask for passport gates for great men
And for men like leprechauns.

MIRRORING: AN ACHE LIKE A RIPPLE

The trees are still in the garden square,
My limbs are still after making love.
There is a peace in the December air,
A peace like a crumpled glove.

This Sunday stillness, after that creaking
                                        hinge,

Aches in my body like three hard years.
I feel rested, yet at the heart of me, a twinge –
I think of you and ache too deep for tears.

I am going to ring you, Carlotta.
I will say I have posted a parcel for our
                        daughter's birthday.
I am like a pond on Strawberry Hill, water
And one ripple widening the trees away.

BIRTHDAY LIKE A GONG

I feel broken.

Laughs from her birthday tea fill the
                        telephone.
He says, "She's just coming, she's got some
                        friends."
Carlotta says, "You'll have to meet us at four
                        next week. I won't be alone."

Then I hear her voice: "Daddy? I'm ten." Like
                        marzipan.
She is soft, slightly shy: "I'm going to play
                        with your present next."
I breathe: "Imagine I can fly to you, like Peter
                        Pan."

Now I feel broken, like the cracked old gong
From my boyhood. In grandmother's hall I
                        await
The voice that tells me I am never wrong.

STARLESS CAVES AND STARLIT BEACH

Night breathes like a green-blue sea,
My mind is blue-green clear.
As I switch off my bedside light
The caves are all I hear.

White light, about to break
Breaks through a starless dawn,
Shines with familiar radiance
Like snow on the kitchen lawn.

I turn, I cannot sleep,
Clock ticks like wapping waves,   10
And then I see Carlotta drift
On the cliff above the caves.

We embrace with starlit kisses,

We flood the beach with tears.
I wake and sweat, exhausted,
The grief of three long years.

White light, about to break
Breaks through a starlit dawn,
Shines with familiar radiance
Like God on the kitchen lawn.   20

NATURE LIKE MECANNO
I will remake my nature, like a mecanno man.

I used to think: a marriage is like a doll's
    house,
It is a toy for capitalists, to impress beside
    central heating, a large car.
I used to say: "I will make the New Man."

Then, after you left me, I knew I had grown
    into you.
You ripped an umbilical cord out of me, like a
    lead from a robot teddy bear.
I nearly died for loss of blood. I have
    convalesced three years.

But now I think again: a marriage is like a
    doll's house.
I have been brought up to think it proper, I
    have been indoctrinated.
In my despair I think: the soul is dead,
    nothing is right or wrong unless I
    choose.

Wrong, wrong, I know that! Pulling bellbind,
    I tear up a Michaelmas daisy.
Where is the living soul in it? Is God only
    found in the Devil's Chelsea?
And so, condemned to opposites, I must
    remake my nature like a mecanno
    man.

STANDARD: CHRISTMAS
Crowds throng the "Standard", sing
    rollicking,
As in a Victorian gin-palace, dance on tables,
Rowdy dandies; I study them like a scientist
Observing frogs' legs, or a coming
    generation.

Light on a cross shines from St. Mary's pulpit

Into a congregation of the carol-singing blind;
Now, in this decay of soul, this tapestry
    standard
Equates my sorrow with an inner star and
    light.

I want simplicity to remember her.
Mad at her, I drive to the church beside my
    grave.
I sit with woodlanders, and I admit
Standards deep as the bracken, our quiet
    evenings.

Sad brother, urban rowdies have kicked apart
Your fenced ambition, to belong in this
    woodland England.
Outside the decay, I, as on our quiet evenings,
Urge in the frown of the tapestry within.

GAGGED
I can't speak. See, I am walled round and
    gagged
As in a cooking pot helpless, at the
    swimming-pool.
A cannibal stands besides you.
Please, I want to warn you: "Be careful."

Lazily with scissors, he snips
From your unsuspecting head
Three locks of knowledge that they want
And I am gagged with bullet lead.

FACE
I went to the kitchen to boil milk,
I looked out of the window at the dark town.
Suddenly I said, "They've wasted my life."
The words trickled down.

I poured my hot water-bottle,
And when I looked again
The light was behind me and I saw my face
Rising from a drain.

It hung over Chelsea, like a moon,
My face in the sky, among the stars.
It was transparent, ghostly pale,
The eyes looked frightened, as if secret wars

In Africa or unknown Continents
Had thrown up a nightmare killer

Who stalked the dark streets, took aim from
    dustbins
To make my heart stiller.

BLACKHEATH FOG

On Blackheath, in a murky fog
A shadow flits, is lost, appears,
A blackish ghost in sooty smog
With a walk like faded years.

Can it be – is it – could *she* be here,
Visiting friends, perhaps those Greeks?
And is *she* walking in this rolling air
And feeling this chill on her cheeks?

I quicken, she floats above the ground.
A remembered ghost in a coat – no boots.
It is not her. The fog swirls round
A black heath of frowning brutes.

EYES THAT SEE THROUGH THE DARK

You sent me a letter with a new stamp
Of Tutankhamun holding a golden spear.
It reminded me of the wooden *shawabti*
On my mantelpiece, with its funereal stare.

In the daylight, my Tutankhamun has
Blank eyes. He is without pupils or sight.
He was made to see in the dark of the
    Pyramid-tomb,
In the whites, the pupils rise in the night.

How cunningly they have been chiselled in!
Now I cup my hands and darken his sight.
He has the timeless eyes of an artist
Who sees in the dark but is blind in the light.

A Pyramid stands for the wholeness of the
    universe.
Looking at your stamp, I think, like my
    figurine
May I see through my inner dark and ignore
    the daylight,
These black crows that waddle and strut on
    this Blackheath green.

A TONGUE AT LOW TIDE

Why did you have to tell him *that*?

Like a mason at a Lodge you promised you
    wouldn't tell him *that*,
So when he first hinted, saying casually "I
    know" on his stool
In that inn, and then, "No, you definitely *did*,"
I didn't want to believe it, you couldn't be so
    cruel.

But now he has threatened me: "You will not
    see
Your daughter. And if you try, I will tell so-
    and-so."
And I am powerless to speak back
And must account, must account for what you
    have done, and do not know.

I should cut out your tongue and bury it in
    sand at low tide,
So heavily has your broken promise weighed.
I wish a Worshipful Master would hammer
    out my tongue,
For I have betrayed you, having been
    betrayed.

A wet night, Carlotta, and I think
Of how I would have died to save you.
I loathe myself with horror, and I shrink,
And yet, it's your fault, to my sorrow.

Oh Carlotta, *why* did you have to tell him
    that?
Why did you have to offer *him* the apple that I
    gave you?

FIRE LIKE AN ADDER'S TONGUE

In Port Meadow, you said "I adore you,"
And now you won't let me see *our* daughter.
Why, Carlotta, why?

You have not told me, only *he* has told me,
Saying I drink with "unrespectable" writers,
As if I were Shelley visiting the incestuous
    Byron.
You say I am loose, foul-mouthed, that I leave
    her with others.

Passing St. Clement Danes at lunch time
I thought of you standing outside, in wedding
    white,

And holding *our* child by the cot, saying "Oh,
    I love you,"
And bringing me coffee, sitting beside me to
    watch me write.

You said: "It's like coming into a room with a
    warm fire, when *you're* there."

Now you don't want me to see her,
You believe I have "invented a role".
I am powerless. I have a tongue like an
    adder's.
I keep my mouth shut, so that I cannot bite
    your soul.

You won't let me see her, and I am like unlit
    coal.

JEALOUS OATH

Do not be jealous, possessive man!
I will not have her, if she begs on my
    doorstep, wearing black!
Is it my fault if my daughter says to you: "If
    you crash
And are killed, will I get my Daddy back?"

You have tried to keep Carlotta with your lies,
Saying you are in Security, that if she talks to
    me
She will be putting you at risk.
She has believed you, unfortunately.

But when you swear "You will not see your
    daughter",
You, a stranger, who snatched them both
While I was a prisoner in an armed country,
You are swearing a desperate oath.

And so I say, do not be jealous, possessive
    man!
For I can be more desperate, and destroy you
    both.

A WOMAN LIKE THUNDER

The woman I love has a child by another man.

Yet I still love you, Carlotta, with all my heart
Though last time we met, at a grey station
    hotel,
You came in late like thunder, glared "What's

this?" at the letter
I had written, showing the manners of a
    street-mademoiselle,

Shouted me down, "It's badly expressed,"
Took your monthly cheque as if it were
    soaked in tar,
Brushed aside the school – "You must
    remember your position" –
Then when I let go, swept out and flounced
    into your car.

I love you though you did not thank me for
    the Blake
I gave you through the window for Christmas
    – though you sent it back.
I used to rule you, when you were quiet.
Now you rule *him*, but you can't treat *me* like
    a bootblack.

And that is why, though you have a child by
    another man,
You cannot forget me, Carlotta, like a
    thunderclap.

PLEASANTRIES LIKE CROWBARS

I don't want to meet your in-laws, Carlotta.
They are nothing to do with me.

I was forbidden to leave a revolutionary town,
But wangled four days out, to cross the sea to
    Malta.
I paid your fare, on the first day you said "We
    will get together."
I did not know you had met *him* for dinner.

You were sick, dosed up with pills,
You trembled, so I was very gentle.
You allowed him to interfere, when in
    London
Our daughter was hoping for an example.

He took my family with your consent,
With lies he fathered *our* child,
And now your in-laws have replaced you,
Getting out of their Daimler where you once
    smiled.

And, "Carlotta's with him in hospital," they
    say cheerfully,
And, "Did you both have a good journey up,
    were there a lot of cars?
It's been a *wretched* Bank Holiday."
Pleasantries like crowbars!

No, I don't want to meet your in-laws,
Next time I will say, "There are rats under
    Malta's stars."

THE WIND THAT IS WILD
You are trying to destroy me.

You cannot hold your tongue, and now you
    say I am "unfit" to be a father,
Not knowing I have given up alcohol a
    month, stopped my wild oats.
For me, no more dancing on the wind, I am
    now the stay-at-home artist,
And you say I am "unfit" to see my daughter:
    though you admit "he dotes".

And if I oppose you, *he* will ruin me,
And if I tell my daughter, it will upset her,
And for *her* sake, I can do neither in her
    examination year.
And so I must keep quiet, keep quiet and
    suffer.

You wanted me to take you out on the wind.
Often we drank till four, and I went to work at
    eight.
Now I go to bed alone with a mug of milk,
Read, listen to the trees, and eleven's late.

My last thought in the dark, and the first after
    the alarm
Are of you, Carlotta, and of our child.
The silence says "Carlotta". And you say I am
    "unfit"
And threaten to let in the wind that is wild.

DREAMS LIKE HAGGARD FACES
Down the dark corridors of my youth we
    groped....

Into such dreams. I would be the Age,
Have a large home, travel, make the world my
    mouse,
We would mix with the great, you dressed
    like a queen.
We believed this at night in that demolished
    house.

What have we done? I am still obscure,
And you will soon fly solo, an airwoman
    supreme.
And that snuggly warmth as I climbed into bed
After a day's typing – that is a haggard dream.

Carlotta, we have betrayed each other,
And instead of your white skin painting of
    me, I see
Face behind face behind haggard face
    receding, far
Into that second bathroom mirror –
                            none me.

THREE
I have woken in the night again, thinking of
    you.

In the other bed sleeps a woman
Who shops for me, cooks for me, looks after
    me now.
I must think of marrying her. Three years
Is a long while to go on saying, "I do not
    know."

But each time I get to thinking "I will"
I am touched and breathless by the memory of
    you.
For three years I have drunk my guts out to
    forget
And now, teetotal, in *that* way I am still true.

I still hope that somehow *he* will disappear –
Fall in love, be killed, vanish into thin air.
And if I had just married – on my honeymoon
Could I say, "That's your hard luck, *I* don't
    care"?

And so I stay single, Carlotta, thinking of you.

A PAST LIKE SHAVING LATHER
I saw your car outside your mother's.

As I drove past the house *we* lived in once
I saw it, and the sun jumped. What has
    brought you down to London?
Are you visiting? Is your father ill? Have you
    been to your solicitor?
Or have *you* had a shock and realised what
    you've done?

I think of you driving down the A1
To talk it all over with your dying father.
Carlotta, why didn't you take me at my word?
I am not one to lie to you – rather....

But it's no use going into that. You wouldn't
    believe it.
Yet when I saw your car
I wanted to stop and get out, knock at your
    door,
And say, "My dear,
The past is like this morning's shaving
    lather."

THE RAINBOW IN THE WATER SHOWER

St. Michael's Mount – I quicken from the car,
Hurry down to the sand and the causeway.
The tide is out, I can walk the giants' stones
As I did with my brother that holiday.

I stride, ahead the beetling castle-church
Hangs like a fairy fortress that preserves that
    time.
Ahead, the rocks and slippery bladderwrack
I scrambled round before that elfin climb.

But on the gates a notice says "Closed". I loiter
Near a sprinkler on the lawn. On the hour
The sun breaks. I turn. May I some day find
The rainbow in the water shower.

17 May 1973

WHEAT GERM

I am changing my ways, Carlotta.

I am changing my diet: wheat germ,
Yoghurt, skimmed milk, treacle, brewer's
    yeast –
These I take, not coffee, wild oats and beer.
I will live to be a hundred at least.

And I have resolved, there will be no strain,
No stressful thoughts will clot my heart.
I will not think, "Vitamin C will keep my skin
    young
But the reason why I live is married and
    apart."

I am changing my ways, Carlotta, and I must
    not think of you.

A POND LIKE A WELL

I will visit the pond again.

I park my car and leave the hoof-marked mud;
Blue sky and sunlight pierce the Forest trees
Until – through a gap, I see the water's calm,
And the slightest shimmer in the warbling
    breeze.

Now it is tadpole time. By the green lilies
Stretch two causeways of wriggling black.
The sun is a dazzling white in the wobbling
    mirror.
I peer for newts and see a stickleback.

Then I remember how I stood with you
And watched a shoal of tadpoles cluster like
    thorns,
And my joy clouds over, I am a pool
Of reflected faces – you in these hawthorns.

But then I recall that old Sahara spring.
Bubbles streamed up in that desert Hell.
And I vow: I too will be bubbles wobbling up,
A force like the Ghadames well.

I will be well, Carlotta, all will be well.

DELILAH OF THE SIDEWALKS

You have destroyed me.

So now it's happened. A drink in the Bunch
    of Grapes,
A Tandoori meal and, "We must discontinue."
And I *liked* it – the quickening pulse
As feet and head stride in harmony, to a
    rendezvous.

That man was able to do his worst
Because I could not say what I wanted to.

Now he has taken what I liked the best –
Knowing I was "shaven" like Samson,
    knowing I knew.

If you had not told him,he could not have
    threatened.
This is your doing, Carlotta, this fall of mine.
Never trust a woman! Like Delilah you knew
    my weakness,
And I, Samson, have pulled a prison round
    that Philistine.

I am bitter. And yet:
          On the ruins, the sun will shine.

JUSTICE LIKE A CLOWN'S KISS

I should feel sad and do, for I liked the risk.
Very well, it is necessary. And yet I feel
Angry with you, I want to bash
Your nose in, though the blood would just
    congeal.

You should not get away with it, with black-
    mail,
You should not threaten me with things you
    should not know.
And if you do, is it justice that I should,
Through no fault of my own, give up the
    "circus show"?

Justice! I cannot expect justice at the courts.
Last time the judge took your side –
    maddening!
Justice! I will have justice, even though I
    ought
To take off my clown's face and vanish from
    the ring.

I would like to split your head with a crowbar.
That would bring *her* back – the two of
    them –
For she still loves me. But it would do no good.
Instead, I vow: I will split her "diadem".

SUCCESS

My child, I have ruined myself to see you.
Do not pity me for that.
It was right to put you before their wishes –
"Success" stinks like a diplomat.

One of the "successful" felt "pity and terror"
As he watched me choose my doom.
(I can recall many a bad thriller
In which *he'd* end up in a villain's tomb.)

We were married ten years to the day, your
    mother and I.
My daughter, please understand,
We would have been married another decade,
Had "success" not tied my hand.

LIFE LIKE LILAC

I will prune my life like this lilac.

I will go and live in the country, grow roses,
Mow the lawn in the evening, as I used to do
    with you.
I will again watch money spiders climb the
    moon,
I will live like a retired admiral, dreaming of
    his crew.

And I will get up at six and write a long
    poem
And teach at a leisurely village school.
I will get married, have friends in after dinner
And live as naturally as a harbour fool.

This is my chance to prune my life, be real.
I will be lilac, my energies in the flower
Not wasted on these stripped-off leaves.
        Everything is for the good.
Like lilac drinking in the annoying shower.

THE MIDAS TOUCH

I sit in this car near Blackheath, waiting for
    my woman I think of you.

You are destructive. Why did I not recognise
    that
When I came back that evening in fog and
    found you by black candles?
Wearing black, you held me, though you had
    a boy friend –
Why did I not realise that if you could send
    him back his sandals…?

Yet if I had seen it, would I have avoided
    you?
Turned away from your kisses? I loved it

when you brought
Me breakfast in bed. Therefore, I came a
      cropper,
When others were fixing careers, I spent my
      evenings as your escort.

Ten years later you...made me change
      careers –
For without you and our daughter, could I go
      to Brazil?
Now you have destroyed what I did instead.
You have the Midas touch – what you love
      you kill,

And turn into an artefact of golden beauty –
You have made my life a Tutankhamun mask.
And so, I do not regret that you loved me.
But may you love *him* – that is all I ask!

MEPHISTOPHELES

You can well blush and look down, so
      secretive.
Had you not written to me five years ago
Asking me to meet you outside the Bank of
      North Africa
We would be living in Tokyo.

I would have paid my three hundred pound
      debt somehow,
And our meetings on the waterfront
Would not have preyed on her mind, after the
      coup –
Those firing squad guns, our daily dying grunt.

We were innocent, and you got to know
The secrets behind our privet hedge.
Now, having corrupted, you drop my soul.
You thrive on need, and thirst for knowledge.

You can well blush and look down,
      Mephistopheles!

SEA-WALLS

I have just rung you, you were calm
Like a wordless sea, wash-wash somewhere
      below.
Your crashing tempest gone, we were in tune
As I murmured you had brought me low.

"It's a great pity he had to make that call,"

I breathed, "but now it's done – it's done.
Perhaps now we can talk, without you asking
      questions
Like sea-walls you pound – perhaps we can
      be at one."

You were afraid to let her stay with me, I
      know,
You are relieved you've swept my defences
      inland.
Hence that breathless calm – no whisper of
      sorrow,
A satisfaction at this flat, flat sand.

MASKS

You want to destroy the mask on that wall,
But when I hold it and speak through its
      ivory
Lips, no one sees my face, my brow. Do we
      see
Wyatt's, Shakespeare's? We only hear their
      call
To us. A mask is not just to hide, a man's fal-
-se self. It is a mouthpiece for an urgency,
The pained voice through the blank
      expression. Let me
Tease with impenetrability. Destroy all
Those Noh heads, or actors', or witchdoctors'
      sandal-
-wood, or the mask the face grows into so it is
      not sure
Which is itself, like a politician ask-
-ing his mirror. But leave the mouthpiece on
      the handle
Which the anguished man holds up and
      speaks through: your
Suffering generalised in the set form of a
      mask.

SUNBATHING

I feel as heavy as a pot-bellied vicar
All flabby in a swimsuit on the beach
As I lie in the gardens and clench my eyes and
      surrender
And scan for images, and reach, and reach.

An African mask, old temples, thorny briars
And the timid glimmer of a peeping light,
Then dark gold beasts and white, white fires
Flickering in a grate like a winter night.

Three points like midnight stars, then one
That breaks over my basking eyes,   10
A shaft that shoots from the dawning sun
And fills me with chilly sunrise.

I am leaves, grass, sea, sky, star, girl and boy,
By this brick wall I warm my breathing earth.
I am at blue peace and heave leaves of joy,
I have broken the wall that prisoned my eyes
             at birth.

Way above the gardens beyond my ruined
             wall,
Like an August sun, or the skylark's rising
             flight
I am at one with sky-grass one and all,
Resting, bathing, basking in this dazzling
             Light.   20

FOUNTAIN

Stars, flowers and children fall
In showers from the blue evening.
In the sunset's tranquil heart
I smell of rain.

In this fountain, a stone
Boy holds a horn of fruit,
Flowers and corn. In this dusk
I teem in the pollened air.

I have lost my searching,
My head is stone.   10
I swim like carp, between yellow iris
Swallow spangled stars.

Beauty is from within out, like a boy's
Or like a humble man
Gazing at a dahlia's heart,
How the roots flow up the stem.

Twilight. Gifts splash,
As this night teems up
An exploding shower of stars
This boy's cheeks dampen with joy.   20

THISTLES

The ploughman with the hand-plough
Doesn't look to left or right,
Doesn't look over his shoulder
As he keeps his direction in sight.

The ploughman is at peace
As the birds flap and peck at his heels.
Some seeds will hide themselves
And paint the earth gold where he reels.

The ploughman reaches the end,
He bends and pulls round the plough,
Returns beside the furrow
Of his earlier work in the now.

How beautiful the thistles
That call to me in vain.
As I swing round, may I be
Single-minded in this rain.

ANGLES

As I talk of St. John of the Cross
I see white hair and a beard
Looking to the right, eyes down,
And a sinister, hooded man.

These are not idle dreams?
As I think 'Mary' I see
From a distance a woman in blue.
This, too, is a vision.

These are seen through the heart
Burning from a stealing quiet.
Stop looking and discard
And it creeps near, a vision

That peeps behind the wall.
See, a Virgin in white clay
Hides behind an angled drape.
Only scratch the angle away!

20 August 1973

THE PEARL
(DIVINE SONNET)

A lustrous light within the temple of the
             godhead.
Love rises as a shining from the soul's cent-
-re, the hidden manna of the Divine Light, the
             bread
Of life which feeds my spiritual development.
When I secreted it, my messes were
             straightened, odd
Weaknesses overcome. Light is life, it
             gives
Life to all things from the immensity of space.

137

God
Is in a Milton's blindness, a Beethoven's
    deafness, lives
As a need of handicaps, challenges. The
    obedience
Learned through suffering reveals the Divine
    glory.
I see now I was privileged to experience
What I suffered. I am now in tune and
    harmony
With the universe, and give thanks. One self-
    willed girl
Was the grit in the oyster of my soul which
    smarted up the pearl.

THE CODE

6 of 2	7 of 24
4 of 3	4 of 26
13 of 5	10 of 29
4 of 18	2 of 30
9 of 22	1 of 31
6 of 23	4 of 33
	3 of 49

Contains a simple secret
That explains why you went.
He who cracks my service code
Knows the truth about my torment,

And in four hundred years' time
When the key is on the table
Like the "Good Friday" manuscript
From Kimbolton Castle's stable

They will say, "Oh, *that* was why,"
As I would like to know
What happened before *Twicknam Garden*,
Whether Donne loved Lucy or no,

And in the next four hundred years,
Let who would summon my ghost
Start chanting from *The Gates of Hell*
At Christmas midnight – almost –

And invoke me by my name,
And I will appear and bring
The Mystic Power to all
Who would triumph over their suffering!

APPENDIX
SIX SONGS TO BE SET TO MUSIC
1970

BREAKING

I'm breaking, I'm breaking, I'm breaking, I'm
    breaking, I'M BREAKING....
I miss my wife and child.

This afternoon I drove to my wife's.
My wife wasn't there of course.
I took my child to the local Park.
There were geese near a rag and bone horse.

The snowgeese waddled near the pond,
She tugged my hand and squealed.
And then crawled out...an afternoon,
And the grass was a battlefield.

I walked among memories in the sun,
Their corpses did not stir.
But one sat up and clutched my knees,
An afternoon with *her*.

My wife, my child stood in the snow,
On the pond the ice was thick.
My child stroked a goose, my wife turned and
    laughed,
She was holding a candlestick.

Then my wife wasn't there, and I missed her,
In the sun a pealing bell
Split the blue sky, the grass, the leaf fall,
And I walked in a green Hell,
In the sun I walked in Hell.

I'm breaking, I'm breaking, I'm breaking, I'm
    breaking, I'M BREAKING....

KENTISH GIRL
(A BALLAD)

The dancing club was crowded,
When *she* came up the stair
Every head turned, the band stopped playing,
She had long, long black hair.

She was going to get married,
And go to Arabia,
She was just a Kentish girl
With long, long black hair.

I went over, and said I'd seen her,
She said "That's my fiancé, see?"
I left, in the street I stopped and turned,
For her face haunted me.

I returned and asked her number,
In case she changed her mind,
She thought I had the saddest eyes –
We danced, oh love is blind.

I met her a week later
Under a Kent grapevine,
And all the time I looked in her eyes,
And she looked into mine.

But a friend of her fiancé's saw us,
Next day was waspy hot,
I waited an hour in a warm ploughed
field
Near the Cat and Custard Pot.

And later when I called her,
She said she'd meet me again,
But next week when I'd called her up –
Rain. I stood in the rain.

For I learned that she'd got married,
And gone to Arabia,
And how I miss my Kentish girl
With her long, long black hair.

SONG: I CAN'T COUNT THE RED SUN

What's between us is between us,
Don't ask me to speak it.
I can't count the red sun,
Let the lightning be it.

You need reassuring:
Leaves rain on that tree,
Gasometers are blood red flowers,
Acorns are you and me.

What's between us is between us,
Don't ask me to speak it.
I can't count the red sun,
Let the lightning be.

Churchbells in my fingers,
Your breasts are a humming bee,

Analysis is a blackbird's song
Outside you and me.

What's between us is between us,
Don't ask me to speak it.
I can't count the red sun,
Let the lightning be.

When you're not here I whistle,
You're a galleon on the sea,
Your lightning is the Rose and Crown;
Words aren't you and me.

What's between us is between us,
Don't ask me to speak it.
I can't count the red sun,
Let the lightning be it.

TIME TO END IT ALL

I've done it all,
You won't understand it, but I've done it
all.

I hoarded pounds like gold bars,
I paid off my mortgage.
Now my wife, like a red-green parrot
Has flown from my zoo-cage.

On parole from a gold bar prison,
I yawn down this City phone.
Now my florins are so many bottle tops.
I get drunk…when I'm alone.

The girls are as easy as sparrows,
I made five of them last week.
I still drink till the moon wobbles,
I am tired of being a sheikh.

I'm tired of flesh and bone, and I'm tired of
being alone.
I have done it all, and my future is a wall.

Perhaps it is time to end it all.

But won't I miss harvest orchards,
Sparrows in the hedge?
Lilies under silver birches,
That tortoiseshell on the window ledge?
Perhaps I should get out into the country
instead.

SONG: THE ORANGE LADY

Every night the orange lady
Dances like an organgrinder's lady,
She's sad, but look how she's moving now.

Dancing nights, the orange lady
Earns enough to feed her grizzling baby,
Room's bad, but look how she's moving now.

Every night the orange lady,
Smiles to forget a lorrydriver's baby,
His dad has been gone three months now.

Now tonight the orange lady
Dances like an organgrinder's lady,
She's seen him, look how she's moving now.

He's sitting there, look how she's moving
              now

Now tonight the orange lady
Smiles to forget she was a lorrydriver's lady,
It's sad, she's ignoring him now.

And so tonight the orange lady
Dances like an organgrinder's lady,
She's sad, but look how she's moving now.

BLACK CHESTNUT

What are you doing to yourself?
You were a French lady
With châteaux in Chanteuilly.
You left your husband for a boy
And now he has gone to sea
You cannot live without him,
So when I met you at the club
You floated down the gangway,
You put your arm round my neck and kissed
              his snub.

Now I have come to see you
You are stretched out on the ceiling,
Your girl is breaking the drainpipe,
You don't care, the way you're feeling.
The TV's flickering,
Your thoughts are moving faster. Us!
The ash in your thick cigarlette
Has the black smell of fungus.

You asked me to move in with you,

So you light your black chestnut,
You say that you need me.
But...but...but....
I will not live with a woman
Who is lost inside a dream.
What are you doing to yourself
And your Chanteuilly millstream?

THE FLIGHT

1970

"Yaren soran soran soran soran soran;
Oki no kamone ni shiodoki kikeba,
Watasha tatsu tori, nami ni kike."
(Japanese fishermen's song)

"When asked about the tide, the seagull replied,
'I'm flying away, please ask the waves.'"

I. A GREEN COUNTRY

Apples are green under a fluttering flag,
Green are my daughter's eyes, green is her
    breath.
Green are the children among brambles and
    ferns,
"Oi-olly-ocky," they yodle, "I see Liz,"
Stealing on tiptoe like scrumping thieves.
And let us run together now, across the road,
    down the hill to the Forest,
To where the stream trickles from the long
    arched tunnel,
And, legs astride it, hands on the curved
    walls, walk bow-legged
And stand under the grating overflow, as if in
    a Hellish dungeon.
I took you there, and found a Victorian
    penny.   10
O this Blackweir pool, where I fished up
    green frogs in flour-bag nets!
We scuffled up through leaves, leaving the
    water-boatmen and dragonflies,
And at a meeting of green paths plunged
    right, into beeches,
I held your hand and said, "Look, the banks,"
And we ran on back into blackbirds and
    sticklebacks and newts,
And there, still under water-lilies, was the
    pond I had not found for two
    decades,
The Lost Pond!

    Apples, pears, wasps.
I came from the Essex flats, green fields
    round beech thickets.
When the daisies were humming with bees, I
    lay under summer skies.   20

I see a clearing where I kicked a ball, where
    my father swung his lame leg
And scored with a toe-punt. There I picnicked
    with two boys from the first form.
I ran through the Forest in the summers.
I caught caddice in the ponds, I had a glass
    aquarium that cracked at the top,
And green slime slopped down the sides. Near
    a fallen apple tree
I grew tall to the trembling of leaves.
    Upstairs, under green eaves,
I sniffed my death. I said to my brother
"I will live to be a hundred," clicking and
    reshutting the small black
    cupboard door
Until a voice from downstairs called "Go to
    sleep."   30

Brown is the earth of this Clay Country, and
    hard under frost,
Hard are the fields around Chigwell where we
    were sent on walks,
Stepping over iced hoof-marks in the frozen
    mud,
O those glistening stiles and brown dark
    thorns!
Crisp are the leaves of the heart in winter
When the bonfires smoulder no more. Bright
    is the air,
Remote the golden suns smashed across the
    icy pool of the sky.
Fingers are numb, cheeks pink, breath misty,
    clear.

I and my grandfather walked for tobacco in
    fog,
He fell and blood streamed from his white

hair.   40
He had a stub of a finger he lost in a Canadian
    saw-mill.
Later my father took me for a walk. As we
    left the gate
The siren wailed. We wheeled to a white
    white flash,
The whole street shook, the windows
    clattering out.
Five bombs had fallen. Two houses up the
    road were annihilated
And the cricket field had a hole in it. The
    war –
I lay in a Morrison shelter and read books,
    swapped foreign notes,
While in the blue air puffs of smoke ended
    pilots.
When I moved home, I carried my battleship.

Red bricks and lilacs droop over the wooden
    shed.   50
On our rockeries, young hearts have wept and
    bled.
Ivy, and a garden hose.
A home is a rattling front door,
A broken flowerpot under a scarlet rose.

Green are the clumps of Warren Hill, green
    and scummy pond,
Green are the Oaklands fields, green round
    buttercups,
Green are those fields where children squat in
    camps,
Green is the ride down Nursery Road, purple
    the thistles,
Green are the Stubbles and the open heath,
Green is Robin Hood Lane, green past
    Strawberry Hill,   60
Green and brown are the two gravel pit ponds,
Green is High Beach, green around Turpin's
    Cave where beechburrs cling to
    hair,
Green round Lippitt's Hill and the Owl, green
    the fields beyond,
Green back through Boadicea's camp, where
    you climbed the brown mud walls,
Brown are the leaves round the hollow tree
    we climbed,
Green along Staples Hill, where we shuffled
    through leaves to the brown

stream,
Green past the Wheatsheaf, green up to
    Baldwin's Hill
Where we ran down to Monk Wood, and you
    were remote from me;
Green holly, green beech leaves, green oaks,
    and only the trunks and banks are
    brown.
Green to the Wake Arms, green to the Epping
    Bell,   70
Green down Ivy Chimneys, green up Flux's
    Lane
Between the poplars and the farmers' fields
Green are the trees round distant Coopersale
    Hall,
Green are the fields of Abridge and Chigwell,
Green is Roding Valley before hilly Debden,
Green fields, wide open, back into cratered
    Loughton,
A green country with hosannah-ing pollards,
    arms raised in jubilation.
And green is that gate, green the lime trees
    that hide the green porch door,
Green is that house of echoes. O how you
    despised my cradle!
You found the buildings false, the people
    mean and ugly,   80
But couldn't you feel the kiss in the swishing
    wind?

O the medieval churches of rural Essex:
Magdelen Laver, Abbess Roding, Great
    Canfield
With its 1250 fresco of Mary offering her
    breast;
A flat country of fields of wheat and rape
And Elizabethan barns and sleepy hamlets,
3 Lavers, 8 Rodings and 2 Easters.
O Essex, I love your green and drowsy
    haunts!

All this we have known in the green time, and
    more.
These are the places I return to now, in my
    heart-sorrow,   90
These Essex flats. Here I stood, waiting to
    meet you,
Here I knew you, in a green glade among
    beechnuts.
Here the city is a boot among yellow lilies, an

iron roof that blocks the sun.
All this I left for the city, with a young man's
impatience;
All this I left, seeking to meet a loyal woman.

I have starlings under my sunflowers.
I love the trunks of these pear-trees, whose
ant-bands are sticky.
O these images that haunt me, that I fly to, to
which I cling!

II. CHAMBER IN HELL

The visit is over. Like a fleeing from the
present.
The shopgirl with china-doll cheeks and
round blue eyes is over.   100
We put down our glasses and walked into the
Forest and lay down,
And when she sat up, her hair was full of
autumn leaves.
I took her to the coach-house where Tennyson
spent a "morose" decade.
It was sunset, and the sky was a vivid crimson
streak,
The moon was a yellow cheese. The great
lawn was dry,
I grasped the moment near the long grass. A
hare scampered,
A hedgehog edged up, and she closed her
eyes. Not so long ago,
The sun shone, the trees gleamed, but I was
unhappy.
Now I wanted nothing, I was briefly at peace.

The visit is over. Back in the city I gulped 110
Lager in the Long bar. The bargirl had long
hair.
She was a "French peasant", and she took me
to Soho Square
And put my hand on he r blouse. She closed
her eyes.
Later I picked her a peach from a stall, and
she bit into it,
And when I left her she had juice round her
chin.
I drank the afternoon through in the Colony,
and then reeled
To a place where music blared, I went
downstairs
And held an Icelandic woman until an Irish

girl floated up,
Her arms writhing and twirling like a
Cambodian dancer. We danced
In forgetfulness for half an hour, until the
tears came inside me: 120
You. In the Brompton Road I said to an
American girl, "Coming for a
drink?"
I drove her under my window and said,
"Coming up to my room?"
And I lay by her and listened to the rain,
And the taxis hissing down aimless London
streets.

The visit is over. I am back in this room by
this balcony.
I remember my first day in this metropolis,
my "homecoming",
When I wandered on wet pavements, looking
in windows for a "home".
A card brought me to this house. The house-
keeper took me upstairs
To a room with FIRE EXIT on the door and
silver paper over the walls.
It had a fanlight in the ceiling, I saw the sky
as from a prison.   130
I turned and fled back to my green country,
was kissed
By relatives. I rang you, but you were "out
until midnight".
I went up to my old room under green eaves,
lay down
On my old bed, the elastoplast gave and my
wound broke open and poured
And I felt hope rushing out of me like blood.
I awoke for dinner. I dressed myself up in my
best smile,
But during the roast I thought of you, and
began blinking,
I had to go out and drink, and drink, and drink,
And when I slept, the room swam, and when I
woke, the sun on my cheeks,
I did not know where I was, who I was, but
tears scalded my cheeks.   140
Then the housekeeper rang and said, "I've a
room overlooking the gardens."
These images rattle in my head in this
chamber in Hell.

And is this how it ends: a gloomy breakfast in

143

a basement
Of tortured, wrecked people, then sitting
     among the debris
Of happiness, looking down at burgeoning
     bushes below?
Playing pop music on the radio, boiling coffee
     on the hot plate,
Waiting for morning to pass, and no
     inclination to go out?
Who could have dreamt it would end in this
     pallid, empty Hell?
In time that is merely accumulating moments
     to the past,
Bringing in no future? There is only one
     photo to be seen   150
On these walls, and there will remain only
     one: of the two of you.

I met our child from school, and walked in the
     Park to the aviary.
Acorns, conkers. Familiar moments sat up
     like corpses,
Demanding recognition. Up the rhododendron
     path, back across the grass
I traversed, feet wading in blood, the heart of
     my being.
I asked her to leave her hair down, but she
     shook her head –
And sat sullen, digging a needle in the chest
     of her doll.
"What's Mummy doing this week?" I asked,
     and she said politely,
"I don't know." And I thought of how we
     played Happy Families.

Long-haired girls and trollops I like but do not
     need.   160
I went to a party, and asked –
"No," she said, "I don't know you, wait till I
     know if I like you."
Was that what you wanted? οὐ φροντίς is now
     my creed.

I drank through half a dozen clubs, and now
     hear
The Greek musicians in Maxims playing
     faster and faster,
I turn and climb the wooden stair, sipping
     ouzo
I push back my chair,

I stretch my arms like wings, and hang my
     head, so,
And when they clap the beat, flap my hands
     and flutter,
I kick my legs, slap my soles, and twirl away
     despair,   170
I, who have seen the gasometers of London
     burst into red flower,
Dip and soar and wheel in the green evening
     air.

Images like the roses on these walls.
From the banisters, you were an English rose,
     your yellow hair
Bloomed in satiny folds up the shabby stair.
I had to call down to you, call to you.
After that I lingered for you, brushed against
     you,
Loitered in the street at night while your arms
     went round your boy-friend's
     neck
Under the gaslamp. With a scarlet smile you
     returned
From him, and I felt a secret envy, not
     knowing   180
I would come back early on a foggy night and
     find you alone in black,
Listening to Chopin among black candles.
     Then your arms went round my
     neck.
After that I lived for your tumbling hair in the
     morning, when you bent and
     kissed me
Before you went to work, sometimes taking
     the laundry in a bulging pillow-
     case,
I lived for your smile at lunchtime, when you
     ran to me and held my hand,
I lived for your presence in the evenings,
     when, writing at my table, I heard
     your rustle.
You put coffee beside me, fondling my hair,
     and I would reach out and hold
     your waist.
You once said: "Coming into the room when
     you're there is like
Coming into a room that has a warm fire." I
     lived for your passion.
I lived for your down-days, too, when the
     doldrums took you,   190

When you sat by the canal at the bottom of
  the garden and sobbed,
And there was a great stillness at dusk save
  for the swoosh of a swan and your
  sobbing.
I lived for your blood-pains, when you smelt
  ripe and lay
Face twisted, clenching my finger while I
  frowned over a cup of brandy,
Made jokes to ease you, told you we would
  have a child to make it better.
O we were happy then! We walked in Port
  Meadow, we went to Binsey
  Green,
I loved you near the Holy Well, I loved you a
  hundred times
Before we left our wedding and you wept on
  your mother's shoulder.
A year after, we went to Jersey and climbed
  down a cliff that was thick with
  bracken.
The sea was a sparkling turquoise, you were
  swollen with me,   200
We laughed and laughed, until you were
  frightened we would not get back.
Then I was happy, holding your hand in the
  bracken I was happy.
I stare at the card you sent me. Under a
  golden sky
A great ship is ready to leave, while near me,
  with names like Girl Pat and
  Marie,
Eight rowing boats stand empty, waiting to be
  sat in.
          Empty rowing boats.

Down down down, deeper than ever before.
I sit in my room and brood. I despair, I
  despair.
I shall sink to the floor, so, and tear out tufts
  of hair.
Down.   210

III. WAVES ON THE SHINGLE
Stones. Pools and a small green crab you
  found with your spade.
Breakwaters.
The smell of cockles.
Bones.
Iron.

Waves.

We stayed at a house of glass by the sea. I
  went into your room.
In the car, coming down, you were noisy, but
  at bedtime
I held you, held you, and from underneath my
  feelings gushed,
Which no woman could open up, no diviner
  on a bed.   220
My spring flowed, I was alive again as I was
  with your mother,
As the tears filled me I murmured, "I like
  being with you,"
Lips at your cheek, trying to get through to
  you,
And "I love you," you said, and furtively I
  wept,
I was lenient, I let you read late, I held you,
  held you.

Barnacles on green wood.
Limpets.
On the way down you scraped your spade,
  you clattered, clattered.
My taut nerves tensed tighter in irritation.
These crashing waves.   230

I visit a black-beamed house where I stayed
  with my cousin.
On the lawn were, once, two trees. From the
  brick wall I jumped,
On that brick pillar sat and called at Mr B.
In this room there was a cupboard, just there,
  and on top, a wireless.
It played Itma. Underneath there were toys,
  and I would arrange them.
I heard a children's story about popping
  gollies in a bag.
The invalid over the road had a Spanish
  cannon in her garden.
How it came to be there, I cannot imagine.

Like a gull. My salvation wheels at dusk like
  a gull.
These old beamed houses keep retired men
  gardening,   240
And our tangled lawns are now crazy-paved
  for ants.
I, who have seen the fields of England burst

into song,

Her sheep prancing, cows rising from their
    knees,

I who have seen the hedgerows and poppies
    hosannah on chalk cliffs,

And have turned away into smoky sundown,
    and rattled the moon

In the bucket of the night –

I have seen plaice with orange blobs and
    squinting eyes

And the geiser of spray by the sea-wall
    promenade

Drown the evening, and I have sighed to these
    rough seas,

"I had an empire which I held together,   250

Now it is gone, and I am in decline" – as
       the tide tur-
         -ned
         and a wind blew.

Nightfall.

The gulls of our dreams have dipped into the
    waves,

The wind brings in the magpies of our
    sadness.

Dogfish,

Skate,

Near the nets where blue fishermen wait.   260

A club. In the boredom of our sundown
    stomping, I turned to the door,

Waiting for a girl to come and say to me,

"You are like Neptune, with tesserae eyes and
    seaweed hair.

And I have seen the Rose of Lee, floating in
    the sea."

O the wet-lipped kissing on the shingle!

How gently blows the blushing rose – for me!

Waves my desires rippling in

Towards images like pebbles.

I am all waves, surging on to shingle.

How can I turn back this never-ending
    flow?   270

How can I escape this attachment to the shore?

IV. GULL OVER A CLAY PYRAMID

In the long evening I remember moments

Like shining pebbles above an ebbing tide.

Like a floating gull, I drift on a choppy sea,

I am carried towards them by a movement I
    cannot see.

O where is my will, my will?

Let me take wing, splashing out of those
    troughs,

Dripping, let me flap high into the sky, where
    the calm

Hangs above the sea-wind, let me soar and
    rest,

Serene above the wapping slop of white crests
    beneath.   280

O the wrinkled world below, how small it
    looks now!

Storms, wars, killings of creatures – this order
    reconciles them all.

Regrets, loss, passions – this calm reconciles
    them all.

Spirit of the universe, that calms and orders
    all,

Flash through this flight of mine!

       I see them spread out below:

Brambles and blackberries dank the oak,

Brown fungi and acorns between purple
    thistles, the leaves

Turn gold round the sunlit hollow

Where you lay and hugged me the day you
    chose your sapphire;   290

Swallows wheel over trodden grass, springing
    up,

Over oak leaves and lost love.

       And now, over St. James's
       Park,

Migrating martins screech to the Embankment
    trees,

Drop far into the dusk; as they screamed for
    us in Leicester Square.

We sat in a steak house and listened, our
    tickets on the table.

We felt the cold.

       O I longed for you, longed for
       you.

Yet when you sat in the pub garden, not
    looking at me,

A new frown on your loose skin, your sharp
    eyes aglare,   300

I just went and bought another beer.

Later, beechnuts crunching under my feet, I
    watched a squirrel run.

THE FLIGHT, 1970

My left lung exploded like a blown-up heart.

But now, how different!
There is a white light in the sky, behind the
red apples,
Like the light that has peeped into my soul,
my mirror,
In which I have seen my soul reflected, a pure
gold fire
Unmixed with the dross of what I saw before.
A snob lies buried in the church at Mells,
Among clover fields. And by the walls of
Kersey's cottages,   310
On purple lilac, swoon admirals and tortoise-
shells!
O beeches and bluebells in Essex woods,
o buttercups in green fields
Where the swallow skims and gnats dance,
o rose-hips,
O stitchworts like summer stars that wink
along the hedgerow
Where a stream slakes the thirst of two white
horses,
O drops of dew on a spider's web – the apple
leaves fall,
Reddening the drone of bumble-bees
Worrying at the ivy on the old farmhouse
wall,
Reddening empty snailshells on the lawn!

O this jubilation!   320
Once I was whirling clouds, shaking leaves,
Once I was from and towards, no still but
movement.
Once I was swollen eyes, like cracked glass,
But now I am whole, like adoration!

(I wanted to die.
Yellow flash, clattering clap, and what if it
struck
The great plane tree outside my balcony and
cut back to the switch?
I waited, trembling, for the next electric fork,
I did not want to die.)

O this peace beyond what I want but cannot
have!   330
Art is heightened life, moulded into shape
Like a clay pot. Life is one Spirit, and its
forms.

Images are chinks in the One; glimpses of its
Power
In trees and fields. Images in mind are more
Than memories. They are metaphysical.
Seen with strong feelings, they purify.
When the waters clear, the pebbles still
wobble
On the ocean-floor. But this urn in the potter's
room
Baked into stone, cleanses my being with a
life of its own.
Shingle bruises my feet, this reddish
Pyramid   340
Defines me, like a beautiful sad tomb.

Soft, pliant clay fired in gold light; hard stone.
This potter's Pyramid has a solid base, the
suffering years.
On it, narrowing to the top, are fifteen
triangles
Like the steps at Saqqara: a life's work.
I must work up, ever smaller, ever nearer to
my summit.
A tree labours a year for a crop of four days,
I must build a lifetime for the last, perfect
shape.
This Pyramid shuts in air. Smash one side,
join air with wind!

Inside it is dark. I am enclosed in fifteen
chains,   350
I wind a wall round myself. Like a genie in a
lamp
I must escape through the open top, float over
the flowing wind.
Shut up inside me, I am apart from sky and
sea
And this purifying Power which can sluice
through me.
(And as the tide turned, the wind dropped,
The yellow and red roses fell still.)

I was simple, simple, like unglazed smiles.
I went for board tables in simple restaurants.
I had no pomposity in the Devil's Chelsea.
As I work on, I will simplify still more.   360
And, reaching the mountain top, will I find it
empty?

I will discard the sensual and these chains

over my eyes.
I will stop rustling and be still as a green river
rush
To a Taoist with a brush.
I will give my clay
To rise and fall on the wheel, till my sides are
as strong
As the whitest dawn of the reddest Libyan
day.

This is art: to show in one simple form of red
baked clay
Love and work and the tomb, and a monkish
lack of glaze.
O God in a jar! You who have chosen the
solitary's path,   370
Know that brown moth that sleeps in your
book
Will, when crushed, be preserved under
museum glass.

And so I sit in this room and dream of another
flight,
From the painful images of life into the
images of art,
Those images in mind which heal and
transform.
For an image of storm glimpses calm, an
image of loss
Order; like dewdrops trembling on one
spider's web.
I dream of stopping this flight into green
places,
Of ceasing to surge like waves towards what I
do not need.
O may I have the strength to live simply in
this present,   380
May I soar into my imagination and bask in
the sunlight of my soul!
May I shape my life into a clay Pyramid, and
make it into a meaning
More bone-like than ordinary stone!

A BULB IN WINTER

(PART 2 OF SONNETS AND LYRICS FROM A DARK, DARK NIGHT)

1972 – 1975

CARNATIONS

Jealous? *They* are not jealous.

My carnations, on my dining-table
Have been bleeding into water a week now.
They hang their heads down, like children in
    trouble,
Save for two, who have owned up.

They are not jealous of the flower beside
    them,
As they wilt in water, at the end of a shining
    week.

Outside, leaves float down, pile up in the
    gutter.
There is a bonfire in the dark. Carlotta loved
    carnations.

Tonight I am to go out with the man who
Knocked a hole in my future and set me
    wilting.
Tonight I will stay in and look at my poor
    carnations,
And I will shine out my cut being into this
    damp night

As she does.

Just two flowers snipped from their stem,
    good for two buttonholes.

FRAGMENT

I have seen past the beer and coffee stains
A gold sunset in the Crescent window panes.

March 1972

CARVING-KNIFE

I do not want to hurt you. You have been so
    good
To me. You have cured me of drinking,
    helped me be well.

You have cooked and given your company, I
    should
Be grateful in a loyaller way than this.
But when I get this feeling, I can't help
    myself.
She is a dark lady, she threw herself at the
    first kiss.

I do not want to hurt you, she reminds me of
    my wife.
I hate my incontinent body, I like you, respect
    you.
Why must I betray you, and smile over this
    carving-knife.

ON THE DEATH, CAUSED BY THE ISRAELI BOMBING OF DAMASCUS, OF A NORWEGIAN U.N. OBSERVER, HIS WIFE AND CHILD

A screaming plane, a hurtling roar,
A crash cascading into the ears.
An observer says to his wife: "They're after
    the army camp." *Said*.
-WheeeeowBLAST, as the ceiling falls in
    round him.
        One black cry,
And, under rafters and twisted concrete and
    iron and bricks, he and his wife
    and daughter
Lie dead.

What meaning has their crushed drowning?
    What accident or Providence
Destroyed them in Damascus? Cracked these
    bones in a cause in which they
    had no part?
Like the tidal wave that swept in from the
    Pacific and smashed down me and
    my wife and daughter,
And tore off my bloodstone ring, or the hot

wind that blew across Libyan sand
And smoothed away the wrinkles on *her*
heart.

Now it is October, and this foggy murk
Dampens my three geraniums with decay.
I stare at three fallen blooms and my Desert
Rose.
Out there, above the tree,
Somewhere, uninvolved, the mystery of limbs
and petals
Waits patiently for me.

Some day.

SCAR

I wake in a dark hotel; blackness like death
Sickens my belly. Four years
Prised, gouged out of me, snipped like a
nightmare,
And I carry my mistake like a knot in my
umbilical cord
And have lost my looking-forward.

Blackness like a tomb, and I
Dust and backward memories
Like my little running to me, cheeks like red
roses,
Carlotta behind her, pale as a winter rose,
They make a life for themselves, have
futures.   10
Forceps. Four years of surgical emptiness.

Knots. In this dark truth racks me: I am ten-
der, and will crack.

I grope for the body beside me, warm as a hot
water-bottle.
To go back – if we could go back and do it
differently
And have unbroken beings, like those safely
married teachers at school.

I put on the light: wallpaper of roses.
5 a.m. in Scarborough quiet.
I stare round the room and pray this scar
Will ease the oozing round my navel.

Go back? There is no going back. Like the
graveyard rose   20

Children and choices bloom out of our deaths,
and go into the sea.
At the end there is what we have grown
against the dark.
On a misty morning our breaths
Hang like clouds, dissolve. Our memories
dance
Like dawn ghosts by a booming tide.

Yesterday I picked two rose-hips from
October thorns.
I will wear them
Like ear-rings against the cicatrice on the bark
of my being.

SAND

I walk on Scarborough beach –
Wrinkled by waves and wind the wet sand
Weeps like a tired heart.
Clawmarks of seabirds have ravaged it.
Yet as I wander, a sparkling of tiny gems
Like diamonds under water or stars in a
fisherman's net winks twinkling.
How splendid that there is such elusive joy
In such ribbed defeat.

In this rock-pool I stare at my wrinkled face,
peer for the heart
Clawed by strangers, peer in vain for the
sparkle lost
In those two tiny pebbles.
I am strewn and scattered, like a handful of
salt.
Among these Milky Way moments of
humanity
May I be remembered for how I used to shine.

NETS

I am quiet like the Filey sea,
I breathe like this calm-grey swell.
On me two cobles, men in yellow capes,
Nose towards that lorry, those boxes of my
fish.
Gulls like lilies are reflected from my heart –
Like lilies on a millpond.

Far out on rocks like a harbour bar
The dash of spray like far-off batterings.
I sit drinking coffee above drying nets in the
declining day.

I am sad like the Filey sea,
I breathe wistfully, heave my grey swell.
I trawl for things that swim deep, too deep,
For days that swirl beneath these floating
gulls.
I am all nets as, from far-out across the rocky
spit,
The autumn tide comes racing over me.

SWEET AND SOUR
(ON MEMNOS)

In the Chinese restaurant I eat sweet and sour
pork
With a fork, sip China tea.

For the fourth time today – I have *you* on my
heart.
I, who was so forward-looking, have a lump
in my lungs.
Would I were whole! The tumour swells up
inside me
Wanting a birth to deliver it. An obstetric art!

I am like a woman in labour pain,
Only, like Philoctetes' wound,
After each delivery the spasms return,
Gather themselves and torture me again.

Beyond the floating leaves in my China tea
The sweet of how you used to smile,
The sour of how you avoided my look
Yesterday
            laugh at me.

YOUR BROTHER

Refusing to drive with your father, can he still
see
The car wheels spinning on the frozen snow,
When he bawled in fright and your father
made him go,
Does he still know the terror of turning to flee?

Refusing to marry, does he still know
A decade's love steaming slowly out to sea
Will leave him feeling anxious, and angry
At the pervading stench of his father's
quenched ego?

It had to come to it: that smashing blow
That felled a father after evening tea.

Straddling his supine shape on the floor below
He smiled, and I know that at last he had won
free.

A TREE THAT IS WILD

The tree in my mirror is wild this morning.
I lie in bed, watch branches like roots in a
brain,
Crown, long wet trunk in my wardrobe mirror:
Leaves shaking wildly against a white sky and
rain.

I too am wild this agitated morning.
I toss and sway after a restless night.
If you were here, together we would share
The flickering of my tree in this awful light.

I am a mirror, like my wardrobe mirror.
On a fine day when the wind whispers, I
shimmer
A tongue of flame. O may you glimpse a tree
Like a fire on flowing water, when your soul
is aglimmer.

5 November 1973

SNOWMAN

There you stand, under me, in the snow, my
daughter.
I wore a wide straw hat.
You were wrapped up in a raincoat and
muffler.
The snowman beside us had not melted yet.

They are having fireworks in the gardens.
The tree is hung with fairy lights – green and
maroon.
Now blackness. For such a brief instant
You made snowmen, you loved me, I lived
on.

Now they are burning Old Guy in the gardens.
On my pyre I weep sizzling tears at the dark
sky.
Now those years we lived together whirl
round in a wheel,
You streak up and – BANG – fizzle
                        as I crackle and die.

I, like a melting snowman, frizzle, a straw hat
Guy.

DOCTOR

I look in my mirror. I am white under my eyes
again.
I pierce with a safety-pin. The skin is numb.
Like my will.
I glow in the dark. These dizzy spells, that
collapse –
Perhaps I am more than tired. Perhaps I am ill.

The doctor huddles in a white coat. He listens.
He cannot remember my name. His red
Record contains me like shopping list.
He says "Grey hair at your age", and shakes
his head.

And perhaps I have a wasting, sclerotic
disease,
And perhaps I will wilt to wheelchair in a year?
Perhaps I will give up work and watch my
dying,
Bed-ridden in my window, gazing down on
my future?

The doctor says "The specialist you went to
last time can smell
Disease like simmering saucepans. I stick to
his guess.
He's a wiley old cove. He sniffed and said
You occasionally suffer from stress."

Stress. So I will not do my dying yet.
My dead skin is a feature, like my greying hair.
My nervous system gets overloaded
Like too many plugs in a large adaptor.

The November night is cold on my cheeks.
We all have doctors for our dreams of rest.
I am tired. I must reshoulder
The laundrybag reality of living. And my
rucksack zest.

HEAVY IN HEART
(LEAVES FALLING)

My mother has just been. I am heavy in heart.

Mrs. Lash put on the kettle, went upstairs and
fell dead.
My aunt arrived for tea and laid her out.
I tied her shoelaces together under the nursery
table when I was a boy,

Was scolded for it; called her Mrs. Eyelash.

Miss Benton had friends for coffee at ninety-
seven.
She waved them off, went to the loo, locked
the door and died.
I once went to tea there, and played with a
fort and coloured matches.

Auntie Joan Hardie died of asthma in the
room I stayed in when I went to
Birmingham.
She sent me train books for Christmas. The
police broke her door down.
I never met Miss Laney. She died in the
sitting-room.
The Methodist Minister stayed two hours and
never said one prayer, which all
thought "sensible".

My mother says: "What a lovely way for Mrs.
Lash to die.
She was all alone, and she just fell dead on
the floor."
She left her nephew nothing. It all went to
charity.
"It's a pity Miss Barron can't die the same way."

Now I look down at the autumn tree. I am
heavy in heart.
A generation is passing before my eyes, like
leaves falling.
Faces I knew as a child lie dankly in the gutter.

The autumn fruit is falling. Yet, looking at
faces in the street,
I see the spring already here in the late
November day.
O sad season, that is always bud and decay.

I feel myself smile out like Mrs. Lash. The
pavement calls.
May I be red and golden when I go the same
way.

BULBS

My bulbs lie dormant in my window-box.
They are dead, awaiting a splitting, a sprouting.
When sun and water and air are right they will
start to grow.

152

My third year class sit dead against their desks.
They write a laborious sentence and push aside their books.
When I smile on them and open my heart and encourage them they will put out shoots.

I am in winter before this crucifix.
I fold my hands and close my eyes and my heart is still.
Will I, too, start feeling a splitting and the upward-thrusting jab of an unfolding daffodil?

THE SINGER

Outside this high-up London flat, a singer climbs arpeggios.

                        - ah
      - ah   ah   - ah
  - ah   - ah   Ah   - ah.
Ah   - ah.
I listen. No traffic sounds this night. Just the peace of her endeavour.
Higher and higher she ascends, like a mountaineer on Mount Fuji;
                      - ah
      - ah   ah   - ah
  - ah   - ah   Ah   - ah.
Ah   - ah.
Now she will be screwing up her face for the final effort.
                - ah for the summit:
  - ah   ah
 - ah - ah   Ah
Ah   - ah.

                   - ah
                   - ah
She stops. Then triumphantly: - ah. Silence.

And I stop listening, glad in the knowledge of her self-surmounting.
Quietly I return to my desk and go on editing my manuscript.
I, too, am climbing. We will both stand on that last peak, under
The Colossus whose shadow spreads far out across the valleys below.

THE SUN
(REMEMBRANCE DAY)

This morning's winter sun put out his head
Over the trees of Hereford Square
Like an overalled painter asking the time
Near his dazzling handiwork.
I was out for the Sunday papers, and
All around Gloucester Road Station
People stumbled southwards, their hands in front
Of their eyes like desert look-outs
And wandered smiling northwards, silhouettes
Of twos in a yellow brilliance.
I could not look. I crossed the road to the shade.
But then I had to walk back, stand
Outside the International and watch
The bare trees, the buildings, children,
The men fixing the burglar alarm in
The Post Office – angels splashed in
Golden paint. While the sun shook down his hair
And greeted me with a blinding wink.

11 November 1973

WHEN I AM OLD

This is how it will be when I am old. I will sit in the window,
The winter sun warm on my cheek, and watch the white-hot pools
On the car-tops – sneeze – and the bluebottle settle on the ledge,
And the clouds drifting like icebergs, and all the while
The blinding cross of light above me, so warm and inviting,
But never to be looked into. Like the warm things of life.

When I am old I will sit in a window with violets at my elbow,
I will watch the leaves flutter, birds wheel as I used to,
Arms-out in the garden. I will listen to the distant aeroplane.
And all the while I will keep my eyes lowered from the source and end of all,
Like Arctic limbs numb with frostbite.

VIOLETS

In the sixth form study I tell my class,
"In *Aire and Angels* and *Extasie* Donne
Says an angel-soul takes a body to stun
A girl. On a hill, with violets on the grass,
The souls negotiate above their 'sepulchral
     statues',
Become, like a transplanted violet, more
     healthy.
They thank your bodies, for they would
     otherwise be lonely.
The spirits transmit to the muscles what you
     choose."

Now, sitting at my desk by a pot of violets,
I think: did Donne really believe all that?
Or was it a game, a twinkling brand of chat
That tickles a girl, and is out for what it gets?
And, embracing the "new philosophy" in my
     art,
I, too, could set a value on the flirting will,
Let my mind rationalize my searching: these
     April
Violets and thundercloud that thrill my heart.

But I see the new man in the hedgerows.
He is like a Colossus free from chains,
He shears away the errors of his Age, the pains
On its self-willed, wanting heart. This may
     like snows!
So let me not *explain my* ecstasy, let
Me unmetaphysically leave the no-soul
     unsung.
I will value love like the hidden orange tongue
Within the jaw of a November violet.

TIME

The televisions shows Kennedy ten years after.
JFK with his daughter, smiling, licking ice-
     cream,
Landing at Cape Cod. A tousle-headed father.
"Time has not dimmed these images..." I
     want to scream.

These photos on my wall – me and *my*
     daughter –
Were taken then. There I am, frozen in Japan:
Young – we are lastingly young; before a
     poseur came in
Wearing his sincerity like a cardigan.

I see two women as they were, unravaged by
     years,
And time like a desert rose,
And a man smiling in a Dallas car or in a
     Japanese garden,
Blind to the pacific wind that blows.

"I just looked round and he was gone...."
A tide is in my eyes. A drowned queen bee,
What meaning has a great man? The hope, the
     sudden emptiness.
My baffled grief weighs like a mine in this
     trawl-net, under the sea.

YEARS LIKE ASHES

Today I decided I would not go to work,
I would stay in and catch up on myself,
Make telephone calls, answer letters, potter,
Gaze out of the window, leaf through my
     poetry shelf.

I rang and said I had a cold, and now I sit
And shiver out the coldest day of the year.
At school it is prizegiving in the drafty
     theatre;
I am at least warmer, sitting in my window,
     than I would be there.

And as I look, the tree like a ragged weed
Blooms in a sky that is awesome, ghastly
     white
And the first few flecks of powdered snow
     float down
Like specks of pollen in the fading light.

Down in the gardens, the white-haired
     gardener
Lights a bonfire of leaves and gives it a poke
With his rake. That is how the years are, like
     the tree
The other side of that billowing brown smoke.

Ancrene Wisse, the ash-gatherer.
The snow flecks the street-lamp. White grass,
     the fire glows
In the dark. Now in the morning, a thaw, and
     rain,
A pile of ashes where the bonfire froze.

I carry years in a sieve I call a brain.

COLD MEN, A COLD SKY

I drove out one fine Saturday to see the
    winter.
A hundred miles north of London,
The first patches of frost,
The ice in hoofmarks.
Forlorn crows on ploughed fields frozen
    white,
Pheasants hugging the road.
I saw iron men striding over white hills
Linked like mountaineers.
Under their heels, flocks of sparrows
Scattered into the hedgerows.
While above, laced with blossom,
The hawthorns wore a grief of snow.
White roofs of farms – all Nature huddled
Against cold climbing giants and a foundry
    sky.

But oh the warmth of the children in the
    schoolhall
Laughing and singing under the Christmas
    decorations!

TAOISTS

There is a picture from the Ch'ing dynasty.
A Chinese sits in a garden on a rocky seat,
His mistress draped over his shoulder.
His loins are bare, she will blow his flute.

Now I drive beside a frozen river.
Little furry creatures have left tracks on the
    ice.
Now I pass Tattershall Castle,
Will you not, too, gather yourself, lower your
    face?

I know a river of change and time that does
    not change.
By this frozen river
Let us remember the Ch'ing Taoists'
    harmony.
Caress this hautboy's zither.

I AM RISEN

Look, I am risen.
I strut like a crested cock.
I will crow in the woods and the white-roofed
    farms
Till your lips pout and mock.

Look, my royal head
Like a redcrest wears its crown.
I have risen, I am risen
Until you bring me down.

Now like a spreadeagled bird
Dashed by a passing car,
Now I am fallen.
A scattered star.

SOCIETY: THE SPRING IN MY BEING

I go to meet a colleague's wife to be,
I dine on liver and bacon, and apple pie.
The conversation is fitful. It blocks
My gushing spring to the merest trickle. I

Am under earth. Over coffee, someone says,
"Dostoevsky is a no-good writer."
I break up and spout with indignation.
How dare *he* say that, the ignorant blighter.

Now I am opened up by stupidity.
I go to sleep at twelve, bubbling over stone,
And wake at five, racing as to a waterfall.
I lie in bed, and froth and foam, alone,

And think of the waste of being, of duty
That took me to dinner with an underling
I do not like. Society is a bulldozer
That fills in and levels my thrusting spring.

PROVIDENCE

Providence, I know what it is now!

I went to view a flat in Redcliffe Gardens.
At the estate agents, a blonde with a face
Like a goddess's said, "I have made an
    appointment
For you to see a maisonette in Brechin
    Place."

I went there instead, another blonde showed
    me round:
Two Adam hearths, three bedrooms, nooks
    and crannies.
I made an offer, but her husband was not
    keen.
They dithered and messed about like a couple
    of grannies.

I went out to post a letter – like an inter-
    section
At a level crossing, she wheeled a shopping
    basket
Across my toe. Then I knew, it is Providence,
And the deal has happened, though it has to
    be clinched yet.

Providence! I see its workings in the sun.
Like Fate, which is bad, it determined where I
    trod.
Luck, Accident, Chance – more likely
    Destiny!
Providence! The beneficent care of God.

TOAD-LIKE

Graham, how toad-like you crouch in your
    flat.
You know I want to buy it, yet you sit on
    there,
Milking me out of my last penny. Why don't
    you
Drive off to Minorca. I've a good mind to
    scare

You, make a pass at that blonde wife of yours.
She is younger than you by fourteen years,
    and her life
Is a boring one. You had better watch out.
You cling to your flat, you had rather cling to
    your wife.

She is like the woman in my life, who is
    always there.
You take her for granted and wish you had
Others, yet when she is gone, you will feel
    lost.
Seeing that, I let you crouch in your chair: I
    feel sad.

TIME LIKE A WELL-SHUT
ALBUM

Today is a quiet day, and I brood
From this quiet room on the days that have
    gone,
The Christmas we spent one mellow year
In the flat I sold yesterday afternoon.

You had your presents in your orange room,
I tiptoed in, a midnight Santa Claus.

I awoke to a rustle, and you ran through
And put my present on the chest of drawers.

After a turkey lunch we looked at the cows
In Nursery Road, held hands to the Stubbles.
Then we came back for Christmas cake,
And the room rang with carols – we had no
    troubles.

Time, like a well-shut photograph album,
Is full of pictures from an old bureau –
Like this joy; when you rang me from a call-
    box,
Reversing the charges, and said "Hello"!

KEY

Today I slit your present open:
A notebook with a big cat and a small cat on
    the front,
A card with two greenfinches, a keyring with
    "N"

On it. The green woodpecker will not harm
    us. I
Shall remember you each time I turn the
    key
And open the door on our lifetime's calamity.

YOU WHO

You who have not paid
A lifetime's penalty for a moment's madness,
You who have not given
A lifetime's answer to a scornful question,
You who stay by your fires and will not die
    away, sit under bars, alone,
You who have not suffered and will not suffer
    a judgement –
My life-sentence has nothing to offer you.

But you who have loved
And not understood until it was too late,
You who have known
And looked back from your prison cell with a
    retrospective wisdom,
You who would make a success for a woman
You have not hugged for four years, and
    despair of achieving it –
You have surrendered your pride, for you I
    mirror the heart's law:
The apple-blossomed self!

CERTIFICATE

So you are really married. I have been
    waiting
For this proof, for this certificate. I
Searched in Somerset House, and three
    Registry
Offices. Nothing. I hoped you had told a lie.

Now my solicitor has dug this up
There is no chance you will return to me.
Now I see I have been waiting for a shadow
To cross the sunny conservatory

I glimpse ahead. A plane noses through the
    sky.
I said I would not go abroad again,
But now I must start living, bring in next year.
I clutch a piece of paper by a wet windowpane.

SEANCE FOR A DEAD WOMAN

I dreamt of you last night. We were in
    Yorkshire,
Sitting by a fire with your husband's relations.
I was asked what I thought of Yorkshiremen.
Thinking of one, I said my disapprobations.

As my indignation mounted, I shouted
    "Urghh!"
And savagely pushed the air away, like
    smoke,
And you fell on my lap in beautiful tears,
I clung to you, we were together. Then I
    woke.

In the dark dawn, disappointed, I thought
Of what separates our love like life and death:
Your second child. I thought of you, perhaps
Feeling the same somewhere, with each catch
    of your breath.

I remembered saying to you, "How could Lou
    Salomé
Know Nietzsche and Rilke, and yet go off
With a nonentity like Paul Rée?" You
Shrugged then, and said, "Perhaps he did not
    cough."

We were born for each other, like a twin spirit.
Even my dreams attest that. Now I must make
    a choice

And live without you, imagine that you are
    dead;
Though as at a séance I sometimes hear your
    voice.

THE HEART OF A VIOLET

Looking in my mirror this morning, I thought
"I have finished with physical beauty. A
    woman's face
Is no more a sign of her heart than is a violet's
To a bee. I will go for a busy lizzie who has
    grace."

Now I think I will find a face smoothed over
    with peace
And I will put down roots in solid earth.
I will scatter the seeds of love with a
    thankfulness,
I will be in tune with the universe through this
    rebirth.

I shall stop waiting for you. I shall live among
    the great dead.
I will read books in the evenings and
    ruminate.
I will not waste my voice drinking and talking
    in rooms,
Or seeking out the violet that looks reprobate.

SEE-SAW

Supposing I married her, and had a child,
And you were widowed and wanted to come
    back
With our daughter, I would be wild when I
    smiled.

I would have two wives and three children,
    and
I would not be able to love you as before.
Yet this is what, out of circumstance, life has
    planned.

It is like that see-saw. Just as you are doing
    well,
Straddling high, life tilts, and you are down.
Loneliness has led me a dance, sad to tell!

ODE: SPRING

Horace, I have been reading about your
    spring.

What great themes you and Catullus found,
what sense,
What skill in hexameters and hendeca-
syllabics,
What banality occupies today's audience.

Your Bandusian spring I saw one spring after-
noon.
I drank its cold water sixteen years ago,
In your Sabine hills. I am limpid, pure, I gush
With refreshing liquor for others to know.

Maecenas gave you your farm. How nice if
the wind,
Rearranging, stirring these winter leaves,
Handed me a country spring to make famous.
I have only the gushing of this spring between
my sleeves.

20 December 1973

A BURIED HEART

The evening slept like a buried heart,
I was at peace, then the telephone rang.
I heard you, for the first time after a year –
Like a stream, you bubbled and sang.

We chatted, you did not ask anything
Save *"Why* are you selling your flat?" And I
thought of snags
Like 'Who has put you up to asking that?'
When estate agents' boards outside hang thick
as flags.

You are a full woman, like Carlotta –
A Gemini; doubly unsuitable for that.
You are going to Indonesia to learn batik,
And I shall settle here in another flat.

I was at peace – and quietly dead,
But now you have turned in the grave of my
heart.
On the surface my earth is rucked up, and
wet,
I must stab you again, knock you cold with
my murderous dart.

JIGSAW

I met you at a party for a Tanzanian,
You were going to Indonesia, and I was here.
You were living with a Hungarian,
Your interest in me was a little too sincere.

Now you are on my chest, and, like a stone
Dropped on a still pond that reflects the sky,
My peace has gone, I am thinking of you as
my own.
If I settled down with you, would you not
lie?

I met P at a party. She was a politic whore.
I could not marry her and feel she would be
mine.
If I settled with you, could I ever ignore
Your past, or know you were not in a political
line?

It took you a lot to ring me, if you were not up
to more,
And I must choose whether to split my heart
After so much piecing together into this
jigsaw.
My choice is a peaceful rest, or a broken-up
smart.

CLEAN

Golden lady, you are too late. You waited too
long.
You could have rung me any day last year.
Now you must go away and forget me, for I
belong

To someone else now, an angel who will save
Me from drinking myself to death, help me
give up beer.
I have found my new self in what she gave

Me: the peace to be calm, to sit serene.
You offer passion and motion. Everything
nowhere.
You take. Take yourself to a man whose
senses are unclean.

THE YELLOWHAMMER

I sit on the green veranda of the redbrick
country house.
Stone urns, lawns, in this early morning sun,
Roll down to the stillness of the River Mole
Which splashes over the weir with a distant
mo-shshsh-ion.
A wintry willow weeps into the still

158

Of my green heart. Hush! The birds twitter.
A moment architectured, like a garden urn,
And – glory! The flitting yellowhammer.

Instantly I am a boy again. In short trousers
I stand nervously in the school library,
        whispers carrying in the dome,
I recite a poem in which a yellowhammer sang
"A little bit of bread and no cheese" in its
        leafy home.

A green leaf floating on my mirror.
A still river, green, and then a frothing
        clamour
And disintegration, a swirl beyond an urn.
Eddies, but my yellowhammer!

TREASURE TROVE

Night. I walk into the floodlit garden
To find the black Knight, the oldest in
        England.
The church that hides him is locked up and
        dark.
I grope near the waterfall, stretch out a hand.

Stars dazzle me. They rain upon my cheeks
Like a shower of gold coins that are stamped
        with love,
And deep in the still part of the river,
Surprised, I see a spangled treasure trove.

I scoop up guineas in my two cupped hands.
Symbols as yellow as a buttercup.
They trickle through my fingers, back to their
        source.
I stand in a leaky universe, and look up.

27 January 1974

YEW

Marble steps, birds' cries, dripping trees,
A seat on a riverside lawn, looking through
Ornamental urns at bare ploughed fields.
Above the splashing weir, hear
        the stillness
           above the cuckoo.

This is the England I would have as home.
Here is perfect peace, away from crisis
        crowds. With this view
Here all summer I could ponder like a willow

Or love the earth like that rooted yew.

Rewarded by the Conqueror, D'Abernon
Had this. Where is my reward? MY due?
The city speaks of you with tongues like bells
But here my heart speaks true.

INTEGRATED STUDIES

I sat where fifty Heads of Department
Asked questions one by one – ROSLA, Mode
        Three.
There was a strain in the smoky atmosphere.
Integrated Studies, and CEE.

The furrowed faces of responsibility,
The easy jargon – prescriptive tool.
Questions on the clarity of the rubric,
Affective language, transactional school.

But later as I walked back by the river
The steeple across the water tolled its bell
And rang a joy that caught my yellowhammer
Above the waterfall, flitting well.

27 January 1974

KNIGHT

I go to find the black Knight in this locked
        country.
The sundial by the river says
"Sit Patriae Aurea Quavis 1940."

The flint church is unlocked. En-
-ter, roll back the chancel carpet – and stiffen:
Hood, hauberk, sword and shield. 1277.

I have wanted to take a rubbing
Of a gold standard for our time.
I have not found a better model
Than this brass Gawain's reverent mime.

I come out, the sun goes in –
Where is our country's gold?
I will remember the hidden Knight with the
        steeple hands
In this locked, silent cold.

THE WATERFALL STOPPED AND CRIED

By this Saxon church, an extravagant tomb
Darkens the flint wall on the river side.

Inside, an angel-tablet, two more memorials –
As if the waterfall had stopped and cried.

All over this thousand year old church
Inscriptions like graffiti remember Canon
        Phillips' life,
Or Canon Phillips' friends, who are "Gone
        Before",
Or Canon Phillips' affection for his wife.

Vainglory! Only a nobody's egotism
Presses his thumbprints on a thousand years.
When puffed-out blighters deface the
        centuries
What can we do but protest with indignant
        stares?

And remember Keats' humility of the artist,
And the legend on that Roman gravestone,
"I am one whose name was writ in water" –
As the unstopping waterfall splashes on?

28 January 1974

COPPER FOUNTAIN

Will this be your new school – this large
        clocked place
Where girls in faded blue smile and look at
        me?
I wander through classrooms. You I took for
        tricycle rides,
There among those plants will you learn
        biology?

I chat to the Headmistress. Will she frown at
        you,
Will she scold you for skipping in the
        corridors?
Will she take you into her study like this
And tell you, her skirt below her knee, the
        laws?

Now I am in a House with a copper beech
Outside, "a copper fountain in autumn",
Says the Housemistress. Truckle beds in the
        dorms –
Is this where you will unpack your case and
        feel numb?

"One girl is unhappy, her hamster has
Just died," says the Housemistress. My

despair
Cascades. You should be living with me, I
        cannot bear
To think of you alone and suffering here.

GOLDEN CITY

I walk twelve years behind my sometime
        footsteps.
The Star Bar is now a card room, a bunch
Of tulips where I talked. The Grapes – still
        there,
Near the solicitors where I met you for lunch.

And no, not on the right side of Ship Street,
Ah there! The Golden City restaurant, here.
Here we used to come for a Chinese lunch
In my last troubled undergraduate year.

I loved you then, you said you adored me.
After making my breakfast you came into
        work.
I wrote till one, and then we just sat there
And discussed the future, and I drank each
        smirk.

The last time we came was a year before…
We sat in the same place, you lowered your
        eyes.
We could not find the Grapes, and I am dumb
For I marry on Friday back in the City of
        Lies.

ETERNITY RING

I am tired. The years come round like the
        weather.
I am to be married tomorrow morning.
I feel sad, thinking of our time together.

Then, I slept in Essex and drove to the
        church
In London. Now my next wife sleeps in
        Essex
And I am here in town on my own, ending a
        search.

I am like an eternity ring, my future years
Set round a gold band. I think of your gold
        ring,
I did not know that the ruby was flawed. Time
        sears.

NIGHT: SILENCE AND SEA
(A SECOND HONEYMOON)
I sit in the seafront hotel, 140 years old.
Silence and brass rails and Victorian red.
Queen Victoria herself stayed here and was
"Sorry to leave". Miss Newton was "much
    pleased
With the quietude and quite satisfied with the
    cooking
And attendance." It is in the Visitors' book
    downstairs –
1875.

It is my honeymoon. I have married again
For peace. My new wife pants with love.

Outside the sea crashes against the promenade.
Hiss of shingle, boom and roar
Like a panting of human passions,
The pulsing kicking that will be in my new
    wife's womb.
A bright star, a lighthouse:
I am in silence. Ninety-nine years
Have leased me above this pounding sea.

AT BATTLE: A VIOLENT EVENT, SERENE NATURE
Primrose and daffodil scent the hill
Where Harold faced the Norman thrust.
Primrose and crocus where the blood
Of England's flower stained the dust.

Now a great tit see-saws in the thorn,
Sheep graze down to the sparkling lake
And all nature, this serene morning,
Sleeps out its remembrance of a violent ache.

I know a battle a mood from here –
May crocus bloom on that terrain.
May the primrose dance across the fields
That grow over that scarred plain.

CAVES
I am a mystery to myself.

I go down the East cliff to the slumbering
    caves,
Plunge down subconscious tunnels and sea-
    groined chambers
All lamps and shadows. Here in this dank

dark
I confront myself, here among the ghosts of
    smugglers.

I stoop, all round me black and damp,
And murals of Monty and Churchill.
Around me flit the souls of air-raid sleepers –
I have descended to a Hell like a bombed-out
    will.

But now I turn the corner and see "St.
    Clement",
Hands locked, face smeared like a badger,
An Old Byzantine saint in this dark recess.
Who are you? I wonder.

I stare at him as I look at myself, and am
    perplexed.

AT BOGNOR
This is the seafront hotel
Where we stayed that year.
That is the sitting-room
That rang with a great cheer

When England won the World Cup.
Now it is empty, "SOLD".
And staring at the window glass
I feel old.

You made sandpies where those gulls
Paddle on the wet sand;
We huddled against that breakwater
From the August wind.

Now the sea has crashed
And smashed this defensive wall,
Flung shingle high over the promenade,
And I am full of gall.

CLOSED
Here I came for my first honeymoon.
The Castle was like my reason.
I wandered round, it was logical –
It is closed now. Winter season.

Across the road in a sloping house
We saw a collection of masks,
Witchdoctor's garb, primitive spears –
Now it is a tea-room. Thermos flasks.

Down by the river we sat on the grass
And looked at summer swans.   10
Now it is a concrete car park
For minis and pantechnicons.

Only the Norfolk Arms Hotel
Where we spent our wedding night
Remains unclosed. Under the arch I peer for
    brass.
I cannot remember the room in this sunlight.

I am a lover of tradition
And store castles in my heart.
O may developers never change
This Hotel, this old yellow cart.   20

SHRIVELLED

Pulborough! village in green fields,
I remember you from a blazing honeymoon,
Heat waves wobbling. I waited at a bus-
    stop
As I wait by a new wife, this afternoon.

Now I cross this hump-back bridge
And walk, lush fields by the road.
I look for that bus-stop. But nothing.
New houses where the geese explode.

I walk back. On the green river
Boys canoe, light-ripples play on the under-
    side of the bridge.
On a holm-oak, last autumn's golden leaves
Shrivelled, still hang, like memories in a dry
    language.

SILENT POOL

In the woods near Shere
Not far from Newlands Corner
A spring trickles out from a rooted hill
Near pussy willow in the water.

It is limpid clear, the Silent Pool,
All quiet save for piping robins
And warbling children's laughter
Until, beyond the hazel catkins,

It runs into a clear brook,
And tugging mossy weed,
It pours under the path and down a shoot
And cascades into a pond like pigsfeed.

O in my mind there is a spring
And a silent pool below,
Before the froth and the roadside scum
And the chickweed grate and overflow.

CHASED

I stand in Shere church
Before the North Wall squint and quatrefoil,
Where Christine Carpenter, anchoress,
Was walled in a hole, like a gargoyle.

I look at ancient petitions.
She broke out and wandered the world,
Was bitten by "the rapacious wolf"
(Satan), anchoress skirts unfurled.

O Christine, you were self-divided.
You wanted to be chaste and chased.
But how unfair that you were judged
By married men who never faced

Your vow, who forced you to keep
What you freely offered one year,
And then freely took back. Walled in
Again, you genuflect despair.
24 February 1974

BREAKWATER

I have been thinking, should I have another
    child,
A son who will lie in his cradle, whom I will hold
And teach to grow, who will look up to me
And save me from being like Miss Barron,
    alone when old?

But do I want the nappies on the line,
And do I want to live with his wauling cry,
And do I want to settle down again,
And do I want to spawn someone who will die?
Now the west is dark, I think of my daughter.
She is two hundred miles away and out of
    reach.
Do I want a son, or do I dread becoming
A gnarled breakwater on a foaming beach?

TRAP

The sap spurts through the spring, the
    blossom falls.
Our love affair has sprung, her belly swells.
I thought I was doing well, fool that I was!

Inept!
I had budgeted ahead, laid plans that must be
    scrapped.

This has been a mild winter, and the cunning
    trap
Of the blood has caught me, and snared me in
    mid step.

TRUNKS

I climbed to the loft to get down two trunks
As I am moving out of this London flat.
I pushed up the hatch, slid it into the dark,
Wincing at the crunch of bottles. And what
    was that?

All round my head, a darkness like the grave
As I listened for the scamper of rats. Now stark,
I thought of the two trunks that could be
    there –
Mine and yours, in this eerie dark.

I rammed the hatch back, and came down into
    life.
The illusion of rugger on the television.
I feasted on the moving, shirted trunks
As if they had been dead, and were now risen.

16 March 1974

FIRE AND WATERFALL

The ivy foams down the lattice wall,
The holly burns up the concrete post,
This prickly fire and waterfall
Leave me feeling dank and lost.

All who've let slip a lifetime, like a jewel,
And seen it swept away by a woman's rage,
Have learned life can cascade and be cruel
To the heart to ignite the soul, and the Age.

On this dining-room mantelpiece
Beethoven listens, white and deaf,
Hearing the cascading fury cease,
Burning to express a vibrant F.

The ivy pours down the lattice wall,
The holly burns up the concrete post.
This prickly fire and waterfall
Leave me like an unquiet ghost.

31 March 1974

COMMON ENTRANCE

The phone rings and I hear you say, "Hello."
You tell me our child has "passed the
    Common Entrance".
I am overjoyed for her, but know she could
    be
In John-o-Groats – it is a severance.

Down the line you are elated, but I
Am sad. We were so close, and now you have
    taken
Her away from me; I, who pushed her
    tricycle
And held my breath by her cot, lest she should
    waken.

We were so close. One night you said to me,
"You can kill me if you like, I will be
    content."
Then there was a gate for me, and a
    Tradesmen's Entrance.
In the dark I ponder our next argument.

ODE TO SOLZHENITSYN

You find your theme in man and suffering,
The triumph over sorrow, the meaning of
    God.
In a country which calls His opposite KGB
You are fortunate. Your enemy has a blatant
    rod.

Here in the West, the Devil is more subtle.
He wears a bald-headed mask in the King's
    Road pubs,
And twinkles at a wife's discontent. She will
    share our exile
But is now on the look-out for late-night
    clubs.
I oppose the Devil here, but like good wine,
God takes time to mature in the bottle
Of the body. I will not produce plonk.
And so I must settle for another decade, and
    throttle

My impatience like a pilfering tapster's
    throat.
You have measured your stature by brutality,
I am still tracking down my enemy, and so
My stature is as hidden as an unwritten
    symphony.

BACK AND FORTH
(A BUDGET OF FLOWERS)
(FIRST VERSION)

Back and forth she goes, back and forth
In the florist's window, blue coat, false eyes.
She is on the look-out for a reflection.
Back and forth she goes, this false afternoon.

Today is Budget Day, and the evening papers
Scream headlines of an iron tax.
Back and forth she goes, in Shepherd's Market.
I sit in this café and watch her gather flowers.

She has not come back – who did she meet
And how is her budget of flowers?
Where is she now? And her blue coat
Is like the curl of those iris petals,
Fading down the florist's window in the heat.

26 March 1974

BACK AND FORTH
(A BUDGET OF FLOWERS)
(SECOND VERSION)

Back and forth she goes, back and forth
In the florist's window, blue coat, false eyes.
She is on the look-out for a reflection.
Back and forth she goes, this false afternoon.

It is Budget Day, and the evening papers
Scream headlines of an iron tax.
Back and forth she goes, in Shepherd's
          Market.
In the café, I watch her gather flowers.

She has not come back. Who did she meet,
And how is her budget of flowers?
Is her blue coat now like the curling iris,
Drooping down a window in the heat?

BIRD ON THE SPRING

So you have gone to live in Germany.

I am like a budgerigar on a perch.
Green and yellow, with blue cheeks, I must
          stand
Alone in my cage, I must squawk and trill
When I hear a voice come into the kitchen,
          and

I must preen myself in front of my mirror

And look for the green and yellow bird rising
In it, I must peck my companion's cheeks
And watch it as it bobs back on its spring.

I am like a budgerigar on a perch,
I must wait in my cage for a touch of company.
Surrounded by mirrors, I must not discover
That the bird on the spring is rubber, because
          you are in Germany.

HALF WAY THROUGH

Thirty-five – in the creeping dawn
Review a life. Have I been true
To what I stood for?
Half way through.

On the table birthday cards.
One from my daughter: "To a wonderful
          Daddy."
I think what happened –
Am I a baddy?

O may I be the part I play,
That of unworldly saint.
And let me turn aside
And paint, and paint.

URN

Today a leech said to me, "The state
Of the writing market is such that what might
Have been a safe bet four years ago
Will just not sell today." How trite!

Markets: I think of flats and houses. Prices.
I see readers hurrying into books between
          trains, not
Unlike visiting estate agents. I sit
Above these gardens and look at my blue
          chrysanthemum pot.

One day it will contain me in a Shinto heaven.
I have made a work of art like a miniature
          mausoleum.
It does not matter whether it will sell or where
          it stands –
On a shelf, in a cupboard, or in the British
          Museum.

Or who hurriedly looks at it, makes fifty
          thousand copies

Or none, prices it at 10p or half a million. My
    concern
Is that one day it will contain me, my fallen
    leaves,
As surely as my ashes will rest in my blue
    Imperial urn.

A BITTER PILL

Tonight I am sad.
On television, a programme about the pill.
You came off it, then we broke up.
Perhaps it all happened because you were "ill"?

It may have changed your rhythm,
You lost interest and were depressed
When you were on it, and then the reverse,
You had an appetite, and undressed.

Then I thought of our leaders: JFK,
Heath, Pompidou, Brandt –
Suddenly they were gone, leaving a gap
Like the space under a trodden-down ant.

You were gone, oh so suddenly.
Now on my birthday
Over four years later, I still can't believe
That you were gone while I looked the other
    way.

Now you are as dead as any dead,
Now you are gone across
The sea. Sometimes I wish you were really
    dead,
So I might forget my loss.

PAINTING

I was painting my wallpapered hall
Magnolia, this early evening,
When I thought of you and how we were
And of how we picked dahlias near Epping,

And I stopped, with my brush in my hand,
And I thought of my new mother-in-law
And yours, and your sick father,
And I felt sure

We were still meant for each other,
That the clutter you acquired –
A husband and his parents –
And my wife…I felt tired.

And I felt very bleak,
Bleak as a whited white wall,
And I mourned the grimy flowers
That peeped through my magnolia shawl.

MY BIRD

My bird pecks at the bird he sees
In his mirror,
Twists, pecks the dummy bird that sits
Behind him,
Then pecks again.
Doesn't he know they are in his mind,
The one in his glass,
The one on his perch?

I have a bird in my mirror
Too.
I peck at her, then rush back
To the dummy behind me.
The one in the mirror will not go away.

She will not speak to me, now that she has
    remarried.
And I am left here, like my bird,
Alone in my cage.

ICE

A pain in my right leg – all day
It worsened; limping to the tree
At lunchtime I left work. The doctor
Kneading, said, "Housemaid's knee."

So now I sit, watching football,
Dosed up with aspirin, bare at the knee,
Rub olive oil, sweat out the burn
Of the ragful of ice that tortures me.

Four minutes on, two minutes off.
I put the pack in the bowl of ice.
And when, later, I take it up,
An icecube clings to the rag, fused twice.

And I think of you. Your ice-cold heart
Still magnet-holds my deep-freeze tears.
You are in Germany with yesterday,
And I am a cripple of the years.

WALKING-STICK

I woke up this morning, my leg rigid.
The doctor said, "Muscular rheumatism."

165

Sclerotic?
I sit listless on my sofa, mind empty
Save for my dead father's other walking-
stick.

It is made from ash, I think, for it is strong.
It shines with the shine of polished branch,
sap-bloods
Have swelled into knobbles, like knee, elbow
joints.
Polished knots where there were once leaf-buds.

I finger them. They are in opposite pairs
On either side of this polished old stick.
A bud one side – there must be one on the
other,
It is like my soul: Gemini – dualistic.

I have a nature that is stout, elastic, hard.
Pairs of buds are now just knotty stars,
One on the light side, one on the evil dark.
This is me, this good-bad whole, these buddy
scars.

GIFT LIKE A FLUTTER

I sit, paralysed in the leg, like my father.
My new wife puts my hand on her belly,
I feel a flutter beyond the threshold of life.
A child of mine knocks on the womb, a new
Shelley.

What moments of reading poetry are ahead
for us?
What closeness? What will it be like, this new
he?
All is ordained ahead, though our free choice
Takes the fate from inevitability.

Life is a budding, and the flecks of leaf
Become a branch, a spring and autumn spray.
I accept this holy happening as
A gift from the Power, for a happier day.

THE GRAVEYARD

I gave my daughter a locket,
A gold one with two engraved hearts
And the Chinese symbol for the Tao
It opened in two parts –

In one I saw a head of mine

She had cut from a photograph;
In the other a beheaded you,
And your old laugh.

And so we are together again,
Rubbing noses as we used to do,
Squashed in our daughter's graveyard –
And in my idle dreams of you.

A PEAR

My daughter went to a school party
And came back with a pendant pear
Cut in a half: a round stone seed,
Ringlet cells, chips of mirrors where

Light flashed as it hung round her neck;
The desire of the seed to express
The blossom. It yearned for it as
My seed did for our baby's happiness.

Then I knew the purpose of life
Is to flash, and diffuse Light.
And the blue sky in the sun
Shone with a glorious white!

PEACE

"My goldfish doesn't do anything,
He has no arches or rocks,
He just stays still," my daughter says,
"He will feel bored." Oblivious of clocks,

He rests on the stony bottom,
His gills opening and closing,
And studies his aquarium and breathes
At the speed of his watery choosing.

O goldfish, I envy you
Your quiet peace. May I
Also gaze through goggle-eyes
And peer up through the sky.

GOLDFISH

Goldfish in the aquarium,
Lurking among stones and shells,
Sees you towering overhead,
Wishes you could blow bubble-bells.

Perhaps when we have finished
Our torment on this earth
We all become birds and fishes,

And that was the Emperor of China in his last
    birth.

When my Dark Night is over,
I will swim round my green weed
And hide in shells
And play hide and seek till the next feed.

ARUNDEL

Across the river on a hill
The Castle hangs above the town,
Isolated. The ruling class
Shut out the people, kept it down.

Fantail doves cling to the keep walls
Which tower above with battlements.
I cross the drawbridge, mount the steps
And peer at meadows, hear past laments.

I amble through the luxurious rooms.
Old Masters – Howards – line the walls,   10
Including the Earl of Surrey, who
Invented blank verse, cared where stress falls.

I pass a shield Surrey was given
In Florence. I pass a buffalo's horns.
Then I go to the Fitzalan chapel
Across new-mown lawns.

A wooden Christ on a decaying cross,
Gargoyles, marble tombs – bare flagstones.
One tomb has a statue of a dead man
With a skull and decaying bones.   20

And this is the truth. A ruling power
Walled round with luxuries must decay.
The people prosper then, but like
An old flag, standards go the same way.

I walk between chestnuts to the gate
And leave this civilised rampart
And have a cream tea in what used
To be the Museum of Primitive Art.

Here when African masks lined the wall
The self was not curbed or restrained.   30
In our social life and religion
The self should be disciplined, and trained.

I think of Surrey's pentameters,

And the ornate shield in the sumptuous room,
I think of the standards before all freedoms,
The statues on each Fitzalan's tomb,

And I taste the centrist's dilemma:
The bubble round the ruling class
Has been burst by huffing from the left,
Yet standards, like a well-blown glass,   40

May be huffed to bursting too. On the hill
The Castle hangs above the town
Isolated. The ruling class
Shut out the people, who would level
    standards down.

PAIN

Breakfast. Put an egg in the washing-up bowl,
    turn the jet
Of the hot tap on, so it rushes down.
The egg rolls towards the jet as if it were a
    magnet.

So it is in our inner life. We are calm,
An unexpected jet of pain –
We gravitate towards its splashing harm.

O man! you were meant to be still, yet from
    the first
You could not be contented with the watery
    shallows.
What force has pain that it draws you towards
    its worst?

A CHILL LIKE SMOKE

"They took half an hour to discuss whether
    boys
Should move on the left or the right, how they
    should pass,
Without mentioning they should stop rushing
    about.
It's like Lilliput. What a farce!"

I was still smiling to myself in the loo,
And then I thought how *you* would have
    enjoyed the joke,
And a chill crept through my chuckling lungs
As I lingered, then faded like cigarette smoke.

You are gone again, but now
I am not as cheerful as before.

I came out into the smoky staff room
With a sombre heart at war.

A FEELING LIKE AN ACORN

A colleague said, "I don't know what to do.
I've known this man who is a scrap-merchant
For a very long time. He asked me to marry
    him.
I'm thinking of doing it for the money, but I
    can't

Be that mercenary." I said, "An emotion
Is a like/don't like, a want/don't want. I evoke
The short-term infatuation. A feeling is an
    acorn,
It grows into a sapling, a vast oak."

A feeling needs time. She, not being
    emotional,
May find the best growth in an arranged
    marriage.
And I....Can I make one flower taller than the
    rest,
And still have a windowbox of assorted
    herbage?

WATER MUSIC

Up and down flows the water music
On the piano in the next room.
My tenant bubbles her four hours a day,
Running her fingers like sunlight on a pool.

Four hours she sits, facing the white brook
    and black stones,
Running her fingers up and down,
Measuring her progress by a rippling
    reflection,
Measuring her trickle to somewhere far
    beyond the crowd.

I have a keyboard in my soul –
Each pebble is a sun-ripple's work.
May I grow old, past this convalescence,
And splash over stones, like an organ in a
    church.

MIGRATIONS

In the schoolroom, frowning Heads of
    Department make
Important decisions: fourth year options,
    starred
Specials, compulsory subjects. Outside the
    window
Ten thousand birds wheel round the tower,
    flying hard.

The cloud contracts, expands. An onion, a
    potato.
It sweeps away and back, like a swarm of bees.
Specimen courses, we plan and organise.
    Birds
Fill the sky, instinct is taking them to warm
    seas.

We talk on. Testing, banding, how to bring
The best out of our children who swoop and
    wheel
Around the playground, migrating like these
    specks of birds,
Ignorant of our grey endeavour and how we
    feel.

RHODODENDRON

In the school playground
A tangled rhododendron,
Twisted and crookbacked,
Is hung with joyful purple around
The mud town boys play on.

This bush has been shaken,
Swung on, kicked and hacked
With knives
Till its sap bleeds out. All this it has taken,
Yet it survives.

I, like that shrub, am gnarled,
Twisted with a thousand pains,
My sinews have snarled,
And yet: I blossom through my chains!

THE UNDEFEATED

I am like rocks resisting
The foaming sea,
Each wave splashes and
Washes off me.

My skin is solid and
Weathers events
Like brown Cornish rocks
In turbulence.

THE PILGRIM IN THE GARDEN

(23 ELEGIES FOR ENGLAND)

1973 – 1974

1st Elegy
IN MARVELL'S GARDEN, AT NUN APPLETON

The House is hidden down lanes of the mind,
It stands "Strictly Private" amid green fields.
Over the redbrick front, a weathercock,
Round the back: sunny lawns, evergreen shrubs
Shaped, a huge cedar. A long green pond
Winds past the stone arch of the vanished nun's chapel.
A Roman tomb with scrolls ponders the dank October,
Among the ragged roses I remember Marvell.

Here let me shed my body like a sheepskin jacket,
Let me discard all black thoughts of you.   10
Here by this nun's grave let me sit and be the moment,
Be a oneness gazing on the Heart's green pool.
See, the universe unfolds between two stone columns
And takes a leafy shape on clouded ground.
See, the sun-lily floats: a light in secret waters.
Question, and it will trickle through your fingers and be drowned.

The South Front sundial says in coloured glass
"Qui Est Non Hodie". I am a golden bowl.
In the North Hall the piano-tuner
Ping ping pings and trembles through my soul.   20
I could live here in this delicious quiet,
Walk among columns, lie on the grass and wait.
Oh give me a Fairfax daughter to tutor here
And pay my bills and let me contemplate!

That life is out of reach. Condemned to crowds
I must teach hordes and leave the Halls to others
Who might never peep for *that* gold water-flower.
We must enjoy them through our daughters.
A cloud flits over the lawn, in a fairy toadstool ring
I glimpse, for an instant, *my* "little T.C."   30
My calm is broken. I, too, feel an unspeakable horror.
May it not come yet. May it wait for me.

My "nymph", for you I will gladly sacrifice
Paradise for a mortgaged, salaried mask.
I will gladly keep you where Tennyson longed for Maud
And in the other Hall, where you will board. Little lady, I only ask
That at the end of your country upbringing
You wimple in the wanting pleasures. Simply start,
Blinding eyes closed, to grow a golden water-lily.
May you too be a bowl for it. And some days may you also be
The rose-sun-leaf-ground-cloudy peace and meaning of a golden Heart.   40

24 October 1973

2nd Elegy
WESTMINSTER ABBEY
(On the wedding of Mrs. Phillips)

Horsemen clip-clop round the Palace angel,
Thronging crowds wave flags and cheer the trundle
Of rumbling glass coaches with liveried footmen;
Horse-bells jingle, swords flash across this television.
Now in Westminster Abbey, a fanfare from the choir

As two Queens, a future King join the
    government at prayer.
Now bells peal as in white silk the Princess at
    the gates
Walks with her father towards where the
    Archbishop waits.

Seeing all the costumes of Church and State, I
    wonder
'Why should she have all this on the tax-
    payer?'   10
I remember mutters: "vulgar extravagance",
And, "She gets twenty thousand more" (a TV
    audience)
"When the miners are on strike for five
    pounds a week."
Today a National Emergency is proclaimed,
    and teachers seek
A few pounds London allowance. The Queen
    of Feudal
Shields her aristocracy like that gold-winged
    angel.

I sit in my leasehold flat – bells on the wind –
Above the bare tree in my Earl's gardens, I
    shiver and
Feel a changing of seasons. A great year
    moves to a turn,
Ahead I feel a winter of revolution.   20
The fruit is fallen, now the tree of State must
    shed its leaves,
Pageantry will be unfrocked, nobles stripped
    of titles, land and lease,
Archbishops stripped of pulpit, hymn and
    mitre. Ahead is a lopped throne.
All leaves will be levelled, to expose the
    sinewy branch and structure – the
    flesh, the bone.

A Republic is ahead. Home Rule across the
    border,
A monarch wears a kingdom like the bride's
    tiara.
We will settle the argument with an Irish
    parcel.
I see an unjust system like a crumbling
    Windsor Castle
And below, a people, free if they obey and opt
For a time like Cromwell's. The pleasures
    will be lopped,   30

Back will come the winter virtues: the spade,
    the righteous slogan.
There will be no profiting or drink. There will
    be confusion.

Purity and Revolution, the pruning, sap; and
    dust.
Those gardeners in the Palace, will they be
    just?
Or will there be massacres and machine-guns
    in the Mall,
Trials in Trafalgar Square? O may we not call
In an Age of cartoon banners, tribunals,
    screams
From Whitehall windows, sandbagged
    shootings. O, I have dreams
Of a Colossus in chains, and the spirit
    budding,
But I see a frightened dwarf before the new
    flowering.   40

The couple pass the yeomen and strut the
    aisle.
Suppose I were a Soviet exile....
This Towneley play is a small price for the
    streets, and I need not look;
Freedom must not be thrown out with the
    miracle book.
No, I would rather coaches than tanks, leases
    than nooses.
I switch off the television, and contemplate
    the uses
Of that horseshoe Alice band, her glass
    pumpkin – and agree:
Mrs. Phillips' ticket to the Bahamas keeps me
    free!

14 November 1973

3rd Elegy
AT STOKE D'ABERNON

At Stoke D'Abernon, in the old Manor
House whose veranda overlooks the country
    river,
Fifty Heads of English weekend on the latest
    methods.
"English should be integrated," some say like
    demigods,
And, "Teach fiction for its social content," or,
    "Forget their tense,
Let them express themselves, mark them as an

audience.
We cannot *judge* them, after all. Why should
    their work be checked,
If they write 'we was', it's their dialect."
The old values have been dammed; curling
    over the weir
A great confusion froths beyond the Saxon
    church, like a slovenly prayer.   10

There is a belief in the goodness of the human
    will,
The Pelagian heresy is with us. This mindless
    caryatid is still
A classroom lout? "Perfect at fifteen, with no
    more to learn.
Forget that he is a pillar, his *response* is our
    concern.
'Knowledge' and books are outside him.
    Daunting.
Bracket them out, let him *express* his self-
    flaunting.
It is the Age, the Individual reigns,
Born free with Rousseau, in educational
    chains,
He must be treated like colonial soil."
("A perfect State" – surrender of empire. And
    Arab oil.)   20

The church bells toll, I leave the waterfall for
    the graveyard.
Among these Norman arches I am under a
    standard.
Here all can know imperfection, their
    "original sin",
Here they can bow to literacy through the
    stained glass Anne.
Here they can break out of their churchdoor
    hearts into ploughed fields where
Like winds, they can merge with the currents
    of the years. Here
They can connect themselves to seven
    hundred years of tombs
Flung up from the Flow through great men's
    drawing-rooms
Now strewn round this chantry like debris
    from a surging river,
These   monuments   to   energies   we
    remember.   30

I measure my shadow before the altar

Against this Augustinian Knight in the
    chancel floor.
This brass "should" of centuries shames our
    "want",
Those still fingers steeple the discipline of the
    font
And of the quiet respect for law that keeps
    streets free.
Some said, "We should boycott this class-
    conscious exam." '*We*',
Like unions battering laws of governments –
In schools, politics and marriage, there is a
    turbulence,
The rushing freedom of the play of light on
    foaming shallows.
How can children find their way back to the
    deeps if the teachers become their
    shadows?   40

The dam has raised the river's level, here by
    this garden urn
It irrigates the ploughed fields. Here a line is
    drawn
Across the riverbed of our minds. Let us walk
    back to where
The currents from upstream float serenely
    through – and stare
On Western man: the selfless Knight, the
    perverse, Romantic will.
Let us open ourselves to this tugging under
    the surface.
                Eyes closed, and still,
Let us empty our splashing hearts and see
    through the mirrored morning
Where one point of light breaks like a sun.
    Darkened round that dawning,
By this garden urn I know: this still, floating
    surface measures my search –
The God in my days and centuries, by the
    Saxon standard of that little
    church.   50

26 January 1974

4th Elegy
TATTERSHALL CASTLE

"An Englishman's Home is his Castle."

A tall red brick tower from the outer moat.
Peacocks dance where the guard house snow-

drops float
On sky. We cross to the inner ward – we have
    an hour –
And walk to the "donjon", to the great tower,
Climb steps to the brickwork guard room, and
    exclaim
At the ancient fireplace, where coats of arms
    proclaim
Baron Cromwell's emblem, like a
    housewife's purse,
And motto: "N'ay je droit?" Do I not have the
    right? An arrogant verse.

A high-rise palace, also fortified.
The winding turret stair shines with the
    polished stride   10
Of soldiers. A great hall with fireplace – we
    climb
On to Lord Cromwell's chamber for with-
    drawing time.
Up, up; we pass the women's hall, and talk
Our way up to the turreted roof, the parapet
    walk.
Below the battlements, green fields that have
    not risen;
I am an unpopular Treasurer in an enemy-free
    time – is this not a prison?

My daughter says, "Look, I live over there." I
    deprecate
Those small quarters, that squat modern
    estate.
I wore a purse once – did I not have the right
    to protect?
That theft is beneath me, like the stair to this
    prospect.   20
My daughter drops a stone from a decade
    down, my next wife
Presses my hand. In a towering dungeon I
    spent my life.
But then I think: a home is like the mind,
And can I not live on many floors, in a variety
    of chambers, like the wind?

This is a permanent place: from well to
    battlement
This moated home stands for a fortified
    marriage. I relent
And glance at the woman I will wed within a
    week, and tell

Myself: we shall be apart from the world,
    drawing from our well,
Warm in our halls by our hearth, under
    stained glass knights;
We will climb the mind's stairs to its turreted
    heights,   30
Then descend to the third floor spandrel, and
    quietly trace
Our gromwell weed on our handcarved fire-
    place.

This stone "agger" withstood the Carolines,
    will soon hear
A new voice laughing down the echoing stair.
Outside my daughter picks snowdrops by the
    moat,
My next wife watches a peacock, whose
    hidden eyes denote
An artist. By a garden roller I renew my
    choice;
From the Bede House hedge I look back and
    rejoice
For the "donjon" has come through. Having
    survived the gale,
Let the peacock jump and fan its eyebright
    tail!   40

16 February 1974

5th Elegy
WORCESTER COLLEGE AND PORT MEADOW REVISITED

I look at a school for my daughter – it has a
    copper beech –
Then pass familiar places until I reach
The Grapes, our Chinese restaurant; my
    yellow-stoned College.
I descend the Buttery steps in search of single
    knowledge,
Go through to the gardens. In the lake my
    heart awoke.
Geese still paddle near crocuses. Under this
    oak
We all drank wine one sweltering summer's
    day.
Now it is cold. Through the arch footballers
    play.

It is all as it was, not a blade is out of place –
Though two of the soccer team no longer have
    a face.   10

Here I was as I was before I "went wrong",
bordered
In like those young men in water. Unspoiled.
Ordered.
Before I chose to be a poet and left the law
Or married *you* and overflowed....My flaw!
Now I reflect this tradition by the Provost's
wall.
A college is like a copper fountain, pouring
leaves out every fall.

Before I went wrong....I must go back to the
source
Of my wounded heart, to expiate my remorse.
I glimpse a face in our old front window, like
yours.
I cross the railway to heal my Port Meadow
sores.   20
Look, the grass is flooded; and thirty horses
roam
Wild. I pick past hoof marks to the bridge.
The waters foam.
There were forget-me-nots, and London pride.
I must cross over from you, escape to the
other side.

An island towpath. To the far bank, another
bridge
Across which a tree has fallen, an impassible
blockage.
I stand on the edge of land; six inches from
my toes
The swirl divides. Behind me, a flood, one
primrose,
And horses. And before....I will be married
on Friday.
Upstream the one current, where I used to
make my way.   30
I cannot go back to there, but must
acknowledge,
A fallen tree cuts me off from my original
knowledge.

O glorious tradition! the banks that shape the
gush,
The impetuous flow, the branch down which
leaves rush,
This pulsing through me must be disciplined,
Channelled into books, not spread beneath the
wind.

Progress and standards – the pressure from
the sides
Makes the direction. Over the flooded
meadow the bleak wind glides.
I walk back to the first bridge, where the two
streams
Join between banks. Here I am one single
source of forward-brimming
dreams!   40

19 February 1974

6th Elegy
ROYAL VICTORIA HOTEL, ST. LEONARD'S

A yellow front, tiered like a wedding cake,
A coat of arms below us; the night waves
break
A hundred and forty years: brass rails, the
velvet look
Of Victoria, who left a note in the visitor's
book.
Here I sit on the fourth floor, look down on
the sea
Which crashes, hisses, booms and roars at me.
It is done. On the bed a new wife breathes in
tune
Above the silence of my second honeymoon.

This morning we stood together, in a room:
Our parents, a photographer, and gloom.   10
We wore carnations, afterwards it rained;
We lunched at the Hilton. I felt a little
strained.
Now night. A wrinkled sea and the cry of
gulls.
That first hotel, which too much memory
dulls....
Don't cling to the old – does a bird cling to its
feathers?
A tree to its fruit? The fresh rose to old
weathers?

And so welcome! my new bridge, to unshed
tears.
You have waited patiently for this; over two
years.
You have virtue, big breasts, and a nice
Cornish smile.
I will have no more sophistication or social
guile,   20

173

No glamour, chatter, no dinners with empty
 faces,
Outer beauty cheats. Give me inner spaces
And beauty like a prayer, and work, sincerity
I can grow with, for my prosperity.

I think of my sophisticated wife;
We were happy till she missed a social life.
She made the empty evenings a scapegoat
And lost herself, and now is lost. On a boat
Across the sea she will go to a life like a fetter
While I am anchored in you. Nothing is
 better   30
Than a good wife, nothing worse than a bad
 one.
I was lucky once. Again let me feel the sun.

I hold you in celebration, I cup your breasts,
Your hands fondle my neck, two welcome
 guests.
Our childhood soon in your stomach, let us
 cock our ears,
And listen for permanence against the years
Like this Victorian hotel against the sea.
Yes, welcome my bride! our new biography
Is for us to share. And soon may no trace
 remain
Of the frown across the sea that has fettered
 my heart with pain.   40

22 February 1974

7th Elegy
DUNFORD HOUSE

"Except a corn of wheat fall into the ground and
die, it abideth alone."

From Midhurst we drive up some hills and
 follow
A lane that plunges down a wooded hollow.
We wind round to a salmon-pink house. I
 know
It from an overseas course here thirteen years
 ago.
How did I arrive then? The bursar ushers me
Through half-familiar rooms: to the
 conservatory.
He opens old visitors' books. And from the
 window bay
The lawn with hoops, where we all played

croquet!
I can see a younger me, knocking a wooden
 ball
So that it sped down that slope into bushes.
 Logan-Hall   10
Was still hunting for it when we went up to
 bed.
Stable August evenings, a decade's work
 ahead,
Young hopes. Engaged, I sat under this sweet
 chestnut
With Elena. I would be a Shelley of the mud-
 hut,
She would get married. She did, when we
 were in Iraq.
And I....The tree is bare, old husks trodden
 into the grass in this early dark.

A decade abroad – sadly I stare at the fruit,
The Cobden spirit which the Arabs now
 refute.
Was the teaching in vain – Anglicizing
 "wogs"
Who saw us as "imperialist running dogs"? 20
Then my other work – I made a false start
And sacrificed a family, and a heart.
What has been achieved? Just a few husks,
Old files and dusty moments, like a hunter's
 tusks.

What hope is there? Seen without self-
 deception
Has my life not been a waste? What
 consolation?
I must see it without self-interest. I have
 striven
For what I lost, but I have incidentally given.
A host of the young may have received my
 grain,
And what despair I sowed may be my
 selflessness's gain.   30
I, who spent a decade in darkness, have died
 into the ground,
I am an Englishman, I am a man. Have I not
 found?

Now I, who have died from myself into a new
 shoot,
See I can drive down through my nation, a

strong gnarled root,
That, deep in the world's soil beneath, will
    bear a crop
That will dwarf my lost years to a Harvest
    snowdrop.
I will hang with candles, like a tumbling horse
    chestnut,
I will shine out like the light of God in an old
    woodcut,
And having learned the meaning of the husky
    lawn,
I will remember Cobden in the waving
    corn.   40

                                    24 February 1974

8th Elegy
STANHOPE GARDENS
(To a Young Lady with Child)

Snow sinks like pillowseed into this garden
    womb.
That wintry midnight, tiptoeing from the
    bathroom
You snuggled down beside me, as into a
    burrow,
We kissed, I sowed your shuddering furrow.
Now you doze beside me, and a lump like a
    swelling bruise
Sprouts out your fruit-crop, like a farmer I
    must choose
Whether to hold back the harvest, harrow it in
    two,
Or whether to let the ripeness come bursting
    through.

A decade ago to the month, I knew someone
    who dreamed
Of daffodil bulbs, and felt new stirrings. I
    schemed   10
For them to bloom, even though she was in
    Japan
And had been given a bouquet by an old
    Etonian,
But she was adamant. And so – I couldn't do
    it again –
I helped her, took her to an old Korean who
    had a Buddha in his lane,
And she lay down to be cut up. I have green
    eyes. Coming to
Later, after "much blooding", she said, "Your
    eyes are blue."

I could not face that again. Yet will we not
    disparage
Being limited, and tied to our new marriage?
And, 'Will we regret it?' I think, and 'Forty
    years, forty mistakes?'
And, 'What if I had a mistress?' – for men
    scatter seed like snowflakes –   20
And 'Would I feel trapped?' And, though I
    ceased to be a weekend father,
'Would our child impede us if we went
    abroad?' Or rather,
As marriage is buried under liberal ideas, like
    that snowed-on fountain,
'If we divorced?' The loss, the shame, the
    expense of maintaining a lost
    child again.

But these are wintry thoughts, the usual
    selfish doubts
That run through every father's head till his
    heart melts and spouts.
Love spurts like a frozen fountain, and the
    spring
Surprises us with its teeming, budding
    bubbling.
If we accept the whole, why not in part?
The law of the gardens must rule the
    gardener's heart.   30
Now is a snowy season, that boy and horn are
    white,
But who can deny the budding branch, this
    sudden sunlight?

Outside the spring gushes through twigs and
    faces.
              God knows
What right I have to rip the heart out of the
    rose.
Who is to say we should not have that
    cornucopia boy?
What if his plenty overflows and hangs our
    lives with joy
We have not now? So we are heavy with
    love? What if our fruit
Ripens my old age, as my daughter blossoms
    me now?
              What if I am all root?
Love does not drift like poplarseed, and
    expense is grass
When the meaning of your life coos in the

175

looking-glass.   40

The snow melts, it is not for me to oppose the
    harmony
Of the self-renewing God that surges through
    the tree.
The Fountain which showers buds also
    scatters seed,
And I must accept that some will germinate
    and breed;
And if this flood of dust makes a belly swell,
I who have sown my self-will into the
    Providential whole, can well
Accept its sacredness, and welcome what
    spring has grown:
The fruit of your sprouting womb, which my
    desire has sown.

9th Elegy
CENTURY HOUSE: ON A
PATRIOT
(OR: ON THE UNFORTUNATE
NECESSITY OF GOVERNMENTS)
(For Kenneth L.)

A high rise of windows near Waterloo,
Traffic, shutters, a man flits out to meet you.
A cowering spy, now in an Amsterdam hotel,
Now dead in a Chipstead ditch, under a
    harebell –
You have paid the penalty, you served the
    Crown;
You took its "salary", you were "not known".
You were at the zenith, but you chose the
    nadir,
Muffled by OSA, a "political prisoner".

I too am voiceless. With laryngitis.
I wonder how you came to be like this.   10
I see you hard up – with a wife – sincere,
Looking for glamour; not an officer;
I see you engage, eager to thrill
At danger, with a corporal's power to spill
Another man – IRA, KGB,
Or any force that threatens our country.

Did you do right? To infiltrate, to pose,
To lie, to be who only the wind knows,
To trick, to hide yourself, to smile out news,
To lever out their minds with subtle
    corkscrews?   20

What freedom when eavesdroppers tape-
    record
(Police State trappings) men who confess the
    sword?
Is not a bomber entitled to privacy
As if he got befuddled in a foreign embassy?

We should be living internationally,
Like a spring of leaves from one gushing pear
    tree –
Each leaf and man the same to the Fountain.
"Should". Would we lived in a world without
    metal rain,
Would the IRA did, and the KGB!
No plastic bags, no letters, the streets as
    free   30
As in Eden. Alas, in a fallen world of plots,
Loving all men, we embrace the sniper's
    shots.

I see the sun divided – two superpowers
Flash rockets while an Ireland or Africa
    cowers.
It reminds me of Napoleon's plum pudding.
I see rats supplied by hungry giants, hooding
In different theatres for a creeping war.
Each Briton must choose, when nibblers gnaw
    and claw:
The British way of life; or a union frown,
World revolution, and drag the country
    down.   40

War is the test. Defend your democracy,
Your muddling Parliament, imperfect though
    it be;
Or side with the enemy till it's overthrown.
How often in war shop-stewards are prone
To talk in a civil servant's ambivalent voice,
War or revolution – that might have been your
    choice.
You sided against the subversives, and with
    the law,
And so you are a patriot, for choosing war.

That wanton boy who slashes laurel leaves
Must be restrained. Or else our freedom
    grieves.   50
We walk the streets, agree or disagree –
Provided we don't fell our fountain tree.
We must guard against all boundary-crossers,

or him
Who would blast our life and liberty limb
    from limb.
We can be anarchists when all live at peace;
Until then our vigilance must not cease.

Your deed, if not your motive, makes you a
    patriot,
But *how* you served your country – like
    Iscariot!
In those high Waterloo windows you'd have
    had honour.
But like Marlowe, Defoe, Maugham, you
    became "a conner"   60
Whom lying suited, though you were
    otherwise sincere;
Who guarded our freedom in what might have
    been called "an affair".
Now *your* service is past, and what a relief to
    be
Honest again. Youthful agent, may you stay
    free!

10th Elegy
HIGH BEACH CHURCH

Hoofs clop clop between the silver birch
Along the road beside this forest church.
Come through the omega lych-gate, down the
    steps by the yew,
Hear where the bracken tangles and wood-
    pigeons coo.
On this green carpet pause; an evening
    nightingale
Sings through Eternity. Here I will be buried
    by this black rail.
A crocus blooms where every heart believes
That unknown faces mean more than autumn
    leaves.

The aisle is quiet, I tiptoe to the chancel.
Altar, pulpit, stained glass, hammerbeam, and
    a lectern eagle.   10
A hundred years of scullery floors; for sixty-
    seven
The local schoolmaster played that organ.
Here on the wall two marble tablets state
The Ten Commandments, and how to
    meditate.
Red and black, a life like scullery tiles;
Where the robin hops, a wife is wreathed in

smiles.

"No green images", "no other gods but me",
No murder, do not covet; no adultery.
I think of a host who wanted – and too fast –
What now I give to manna, and to last.   20
Unlike London, where a smile is like a pillow,
Here girls are like a shower of pussy willow.
This is a rooted life, like the evergreen yew.
No glass or redbrick spoils this woodland
    pew.

Let us be faithful to these hillocked dead,
Whether poet, politician or Department Head,
Let our deeds, like bluebells on a mound of
    moss,
Attest a Britain like a marble cross.
Now like a civil servant, now like a gardener-
    surgeon
Let us cut the creeping cancer, that the health
    may burgeon.   30
Let us conserve the diamond lead window
    standards
From well-meaning revolutionary vanguards.

Silver birch and bracken, and folk who
    doubtless sinned
All feed the silence under this March wind.
Shh! rest in the Eternal – hear the dragging of
    a snail
Beneath the water-warbling of the
    nightingale.
Here rustling moments are threescore muffled
    thieves
And pale faces under hillocks, like last
    autumn's leaves,
Are compost for this crocus. Let me leave
    behind
A meaning like this purple crocus, when I am
    blind.   40

Death has its beauty: the hearse, a squirrel's
    tail.
My coffin will be lowered by this black rail,
Between this laurel, this holly. My
    companions,
Unknown Belshams, Hepburns and Cookes,
    near the rhododendrons.
Like a crocus under sticky buds, I will blink
    and brim

At the tinkling of the water-finches, and the
distant hymn,
Snug under grass, safe from nettles, brambles.
And in the rain
I will dream of the arrow on the Victorian
weathervane!

11th Elegy
SOMPTING ABBOTTS

Opposite the Saxon church, a gate in the wall
Leads through pine trees to where shrill
voices call.
A Gothic "castle". Turrets, arrow-slit
windows,
Balconies for a Princess and her rainbows.
We go in through the porch to the entrance
hall where
Old Masters peer on walls; up the long,
wooden stair
Swarming with children to a dormitory in a
tower
Where I put my daughter's case down; shy
girls cower.

This used to be the Lord of the Manor's
home;
Now it is a school, in the holidays children
roam   10
In the grounds. From the slit window, lawns
and woods roll
To the distant sea. I descend among children
and stroll.
This is a permanent place. In the town
Houses are new; this vandal century will pull
down
The old. I wander to a stone flower-bowl –
Four stone heads face four winds, like
goddesses from a soul.

This is the fourth summer my daughter has
been here
And I have turned to stone a different woman
each year.
The town has seen the changes. In crashing
waves
Four heads like bathers' caps; these relief-
graves   20
Round my flower-bowl life. The artist is a
Gorgon,
In his loves, too, alas, he changes all he looks
on.
Here, like a breakwater that time foams
round,
Is the sanctuary of a stonemason's chiselling-
ground.

This Sompting Hall half hints at something
Eternal. Half out of time – it has a church-
bell's ring –
Towers and Tudor chimneys, structured float
Near this changing sea, an image to denote
A work of art. When we build castles on
pages
We join all centuries, we are read by
all ages   30
From now. We should find things that never
change
And measure ourselves by these: like a distant
mountain range.

O I will lie down on this sloping lawn
And open my imagination, yawn
And dream a summer dream, flat on my back,
Of my own white turrets and a sky like a
mountain track,
And fix my stones in the flower-bowl of my
search;
Then I will get up and walk to the towering
church,
Pick red roses by the path, then, unflinching,
stride
By waves that smash sea-defences at high
tide.   40

24 July 1974

12th Elegy
CHESTER COURT, SUSSEX
SQUARE
(For Frank Tuohy)

A horseshoe of white terrace round a garden
square;
Railings, buttercups on the grass, two pines
near
A clump of windswept bush above the
evening sea,
Where a tunnel leads under the road to the
beach. We
Head for four Corinthian columns. At
The top of the spiral stairs is a white flat
And Tuohy's massive frame, a man whose fire

And refining art and alchemy I admire.

The room we sit in belongs to an aesthete.
Under Chinese and Japanese pictures we
eat 10
A seasoned chicken, and talk until nearly
three.
"My political attitudes are aesthetic," he says,
"I don't see
How people can put up with seeing beggars,"
and, "There is a confusion
Between social and political values –
behaviour and getting things
done."
And like a don, "Epistemological, ethical –
there is a difference.
What can I know? And what shall I do? *One
must make sense.*"

Some men's brains burn like a bulb of a
hundred watts.
He has reduced base metals to pure ingots –
His is the brilliance of the furnace. Instead
Of living like a Scholar, all learning spread 20
Below as seen from a high mountain, this
grown-
Up Parnassian has forged the philosopher's
stone:
"The artist must melt the autobiographical
Into a generalised object – persona, image,
symbol –

"Of gold. This distancing makes a poem
good.
It is like turning a camera lens. One should
Be neither too warm, too close-up in
confession,
Nor too cold and impersonal. There should be
a tension
Between the poet and his image, as in a
dream.
Wittgenstein once told me, 'A work of art
must seem 30
To be a proposition, in feelings, perceptions,
To which you answer Yes or No,' and there
are no exceptions."

The artist as alchemist – the furnace, then his
mould
Transmute the base experience into gold.

Such high standards consign to a workbench
drawer
Nuggets whose carat weight still tilts like iron
ore.
He sits in the window and says, looking out to
sea,
"I like the calm down here, but I find it hard
to be
Relaxed." A restless man, whose ingots will
be sold,
Who has not transmuted his own soul into
gold. 40

There is the fiery forging of the inner sun,
And the roaring heart that gives out what it
has done
And never knows illumination. The first of
these
Burns the self's impurities, the second what it
sees,
Distilling a lump of action to its essence.
The Saint knows peace; the Aesthete
achievements –
Like this polymath-Artist. And so this
Brighton square
Stands for a burning Consciousness of outer
things, and a Beauty that is rare.
24-25 July 1974

13th Elegy
JOURNEY'S END

A gabled front behind lime trees, a green gate
Which says "Journey's End". In the porch we
wait
At the grained front door, then go round by
the pebbledash
Garage and shed to where we used to bash
Centuries before lunch against Australia
(Now overlooked by new offices), past roses,
a dahlia,
And a splurge of storm-beaten daisies –
Marguerites – for
We must look at the tumbling pear tree by the
old back door.

Now I sit in my old room. Four black beams,
Sloping ceilings, and a mirror, in which
gleams 10
The yearning of a reaching out to a hundred
moons.

179

Here flit the ghosts of a thousand afternoons.
This and the black Victorian clock of ours,
Between prancing horses, have measured out
    the hours
Of successive generations and crops of
    pears,
The sunsets and winters up and down the
    stairs.

Here floats a battleship on a lino sea
The day the war ended, when then was ARP.
Here slides the ghost of a brooding schoolboy,
Of an unhappy clerk reading in lonely joy. 20
Here flits a brief affair, a wedding eve,
Here steals the first night of separation. The
    shadows grieve.
Families and funerals....This house is like the
    Parthenon,
It is permanently here, we are come and gone.

Now thirty years are less than the straggly
    twines
That were honeysuckle. And still the sun
    shines!
Now dressing for church is the greenery of
    last spring's
Lilac; now all those ambitions and hankerings
Are the floating fluff of a well-blown
    dandelion clock.
What meaning had they? Are they just the
    block   30
And blackened stump of the hewn-down
    sweet chestnut?
Or the cascade of foaming ivy that drowned
    the old summerhut?

A life is like a house and garden – we shore
Up, improve, order, organise, and pass on the
    law
Of growth and fruit. On the way there is
    ample
For our needs, if we soften to the Universal
Spirit. We journey, pick pears, and paint old
    wood,
Teach our children. This, then, is the end of
    parenthood:
The hard tiny pear on the tree on the lawn
Softening to juicy ripeness in a summer
    dawn.   40

4 August 1974

14th Elegy
STRAWBERRY HILL

At the top of the drizzling hill, a break in the
    trees.
We park on mud and cross the road in the
    breeze
To bulrushes, a brown pond, yellow lilies. It
    is cool.
We could stay here all morning at the
    Horseman's Pool,
But it is too near the road. We take the Forest
    track
Past the log. There are stones in the clay. We
    turn into brack-
-en, hawthorn and beech. And now, beyond
    the holly
A pond within gorse and birch, under a fallen
    tree.

This pond has seen the agonies of the seasons:
How Essex fathers died in autumn; the
    reasons   10
Young men chose to marry, be exiled, live
    alone,
And their returns – all these the pond has
    known.
The stealings-up through sawing grass-
    hoppers,
The secret comings far from eavesdroppers.
It has heard small girls crouching in these
    gnarled roots.
And dreamt of searches, and the netting of
    speckled newts.

Now there are sounds of autumnal raindrops,
Children's voices. Ducks clack. Dogs splash,
    a robin hops.
Two horses take their drink. Now a rustle
    rolls
Through the silver birch, where in spring,
    tadpoles   20
Cluster like thorns round a submerged stick.
    One afternoon
The shimmering mirror, teeming with the
    leaves of June,
Blazed into flames. My heart gave a bound
Behind the flickering face drowning in
    clouds, resting on ground.

Today a touch of sadness in the summer tint:

My daughter is going abroad tomorrow. A
hint
Of absence only as she skips round this gravel
pit.
It reflects the Eternal. Across its stillness flit
The changing moods and shadows of our
time,
Newt and lily months. Sticklebacks stirring
slime.   30
My heart is in this Forest, its gravel is like
honey;
And the heather beyond the gorse smells of
strawberry.

All is dark, but I teem with life. The hidden
sun
Can join the heights and the depths, fuse into
one
The clouded ground. Here in its higher spirit
I can be still, and join with the blue sunlit
Muse and inspiration that blows through all.
The one lily, raised above the water, is a call
To Essex men to leave their cars, and say Yes
To this divine image of well-bordered
stillness!   40

4 August 1974

15th Elegy
PORTHLEVEN

A harbour in two hills at dusk. Things of the
sea
On the privately owned front. A boatyard, the
crab factory,
Nets. Fishing boats on the sand, on the "pier"
The sea smashes and booms. Trailing bladder-
wrack. Here
Is a living from the sea. Unlike Mevagissey
It is not commercialised, it is very much a
community.
Once a year they sing "For those in Peril"
While a church and anchor light up on the
bare hill.

Five churches, two pubs. A cross, a light-
house, a boat are what yields
A simple life. Round here there are dolmens
in fields,   10
I once did a tour of them on a bicycle from
Marazion.
Tin-mine chimneys and ivied arches stand on

Moors. Stone walls and hedges, orange bugle
lilies. Neighbours
Walk into our in-laws' parlour, recite the
labours
Of giants, or the Triptania wreck on Loe Bar,
And offer mackerel bait for the fishing jar.

The Harbour Hotel shows 'Porthleven
1750'. It was a cove and a few cottages then.
A cemetery up on one hill. On every chimney
pot
Gulls scream, like souls of the dead defending
what   20
Their living own. History and death....
Tonight we stay
For it is the village's annual march round the
fairy-lit bay.
Now they come, behind the band, each
holding an orange torch. We
admire
The sight until they throw their lighted brands
on a great bonfire.

Red sparks in the night. White stars. Village
faces.
Here is the unity of men against rocky places.
Now in this inner harbour, on the Clock
Tower side,
The Divine Spirit approaches like a creeping
tide.
I think of how a view across St. Ives' nightlit
bay
Inspired a vision of Christ and the Mystic
Way.   30
My wife has brought me back to this. Yet I
would miss the stimulation
Of the centre if I lived here, there would be
suffocation.

We will visit this corner of England every
year, perhaps even retire
Here. And perhaps the Gorran haven will
again inspire
The heart that chose exile at Portmellon. Here
in the simple life
Men live against the weather, the sea, the
wife,
Go to the cemetery and return as gulls
Wheeling round the rooftop that once
sheltered their skulls;

181

Here men mend nets, then go out, torchlights
on the sea,
And trawl the waters of God's teeming
plenty.   40

10 August 1974

16th Elegy
BROMPTON ORATORY
(For Margaret Riley)

After confession she comes to my London
door.
This Austrian Catholic "never makes
appointments", for
"Time cuts up," she says, "I do everything by
feeling."
I invite her to stay, knowing the talk will be
revealing.
Margaret returns in a taxi, with suitcases from
The Hotel Rembrandt – and a brown-paper
parcel. "They thought it was a
bomb,"
She says. Later, she opens it on the floor, to
show
Five faceless figures in clay facing a large red
sun-halo.

The Marys are hidden behind tall pyramids,
angles
Round which to peep for visionary angels. 10
On the robes of two the folds are also fingers,
as though
A hand reaches from Heaven. "The right hand
does not know
What the left gives, I suppose," she says. "I
haven't thought about it till now.
The last one I did is an oval. There are no
angles any more, somehow.
Just straight-on looking." She points to the red
ring.
Rims like rays. The Light with a centre that
contains – nothing.

"That took two weeks'," she says, "pressing-
in of chips.
Each one was fired for twenty-four hours."
She grips
A tower like a church. "This is like a castle
with a defect.
This one came out transparent. This one is
imperfect   20

Though the glaze is glossier. I do everything
by touch.
The shapes just come. I surrender them to the
fire.
                     It gives out such
Different finishes. You can never tell how
they will come out."
The artist transmutes with a Providential fire,
far above human doubt.

I look at the huge red ring, at her left hand.
It flicked the snails off me in an evil house,
and
Calmed the choppiness round my heart, so
that, still,
I peeped round the angles of my darkness,
until
Glory! a white light shone through, like a
moon,
An Egerton Gardens vision one late
afternoon.   30
"People don't seem to see the peace out
there," she says, "so I paint them a
sea" –
Like that seaside church on a rock, that sky
like Eternity!

She says: "That Light is the soul, it does not
cease.
It is always burning gold if you are at peace.
It flows from the loving heart (the Christ), it is
all one.
The spirit is the calm self *you* have – it has
none
Of your old choppiness. The centre is where
God is,
Between heart and soul. And God, the Holy
Spirit" – His
Power I know. That tide that floods into me
As into a Cornish inner harbour, now dry,
now filled with sea.   40

A tide with five webbed fingers, or a hand
Touching the heart...."Don't compare," she
says, "'The Power and....'
It is by itself. Yet, it is like a well." The
drilling,
The centre of the red-rimmed Light empty,
yet filling.
A well near St. Ives harbour, a tin-mine shaft

by the sea....
I look at the Pyramid of the Trinity.
There is the Holy Ghost like a Cornish tide,
And the sunlit mountain peak hidden by
    cloud, and the guide at my side.

Our Age of Darkness understands dark things;
Its roaring fire bakes pots without doves'
    wings   50
On them, or visions of Heaven, or the sun-dial
    that regulates
The furnace. And our time appreciates
Her too little. But Truth must triumph over
    self.
"It will soon be time to move things of light
    from the bottom shelf
To the top," she says. "I am guided.
    Everything is given.
I only speak when I feel guided by the Power
    of God – *driven*."

Now she has gone to Shoreham, and the
    sorrowing, perfect Mary
Looks down from this Oratory crown on a
    fallen, contrary
World. Within there is silence, candles like
    lit-up souls,
And the Eternal Light in the basket; the
    sacrament controls   60
The altar. It is always there, the Centre. Here I
    sit,
The Mystic tradition is round me. I will die
    into it.
This mystic fire-potter, this sea-artist, like
    those Saints,
Is a symbol of the Truth, which she lives and
    bakes and paints.

14-15 August 1974

17th Elegy
HILL PLACE

We drive through Ashdown woods to the
    crossroads, we wait,
Turn left, then swing the Lotus up the drive to
    the old farm-gate.
We get out, tiptoe through mud near barns
    still
As they were in her paintings. We are on top
    of a hill
I played on. I see the sloping field where a

shower
Caught us down by the viaduct, but not the
    silage tower
Or the well. Now we cross the front garden to
    the sunlit
Thirteenth century farmhouse porch where
    my aunt used to sit.

She was not a real aunt, but she sent me
    birthday
Books and lino-cut Christmas cards of barns
    filled with hay.   10
I last saw her eight years ago. Eightyish and
Scrawny, she showed me some canvases
    upstairs, while her husband
Milked cows. Now both are dead. Her
    daughter shows
Me the débris: her young work, the student
    notebooks.
             I close
Them – they merely copied – and rummage in
    the loft for frames
For two of her late works I have brought – the
    late ones have symbolist aims.

The water-colour is of Kynance rock and sky;
Drawing back the veil, she shows the Unity.
The other is of rocks and a sea-cliff tin-mine,
    which blend
With a twilit sky. "Dusk Near Land's End" 20
Is written on the back. "It must have been
    painted from Pendeen,"
Her daughter says, "I think that's Geevor
    mine" – but I have seen
She is looking through another dusk at the end
    of her breath,
And recalling her roots in Cornish rock,
    accepting her death.

We sit in the porch again, a wasp buzzes
    round me.
"Just before she died she painted a cross out
    of that tree,"
Her daughter points. She attended the
    Methodist chapel
My grandfather did; a tailor who planted an
    apple
Tree she loved in his garden. Broadley and
    Broad....
"She didn't like abstract art, which obscured

her. It bored   30
Her. She was confident in her views." Her last
        admonition
To me she wrote after seeing a van Gogh
        exhibition:

"This genius – often under mental care –
Died poor, not really recognised anywhere,
Died almost without friends as did so many.
Today his nation build a special gallery
To take the works of the Vincent van Gogh
        Foundation.
If only he had had a happier disposition
And not quarrelled with his family and
        would-be friends,
His health would have improved and the
        world been the richer."   40
        Thus she ends.

She saw herself in him a little, surely. The
        plight
Of the Unknown artist – Blake, Kafka – fills
        me with fright.
There is the student work, then the struggle up
        the hill.
Her husband would not let her paint, or sit
        still –
Like a Puritan, "You should be sewing,
        Gwen," he would say.
She put up her easle behind his back. She
        should have gone away.
"Later on she complained, 'When I was
        young I never had a moment
To sketch, and now I am old, my energy is
        spent.'"

There is the struggle, the development.   50
Obscurity can be a boon, it can prevent
The artist from meeting people he does not
        want to see,
Being stifled, being what they want him to be.
She did not want this. But an artist must leave
        behind
Some works that express the Truth of what he
        has mined.
Recognition should come to these. Not for the
        pitman, but for the silver lead.
Why then are her bequests unrecognised now
        she is dead?

We drive past the family shop, to Daledene.
It is "For Sale as Building Land". My grand-
        mother was snapped like a Queen
Here in the orchard, which was concreted
        during the war,   60
Though it survived. Percy Sharman, the
        composer, lived next door.
I wander on the stony lawn: this is where it
        began,
Here regularly came this obscure Cornish
        woman.
This is what she knew when she left her hill.
I stand and look at the little apple tree, until

I realise. This suffering while we strive
Deepens the feelings, brings the heart alive
So that what it bears lives for every
        generation.
Without it, there could have been no *Dusk*.
        But there must be no suffocation,
Or the quality will be choked. The artist is
        like a tree   70
That grows apples to be picked and eaten. He,
If concreted, will bear shrivelled woody balls
Until wasps buzz round the late, mature wind-
        falls.

                                    17 August 1974

18th Elegy
THE ROYAL OBSERVATORY,
GREENWICH

I walk in a drive of chestnuts and conkers, and
        regard
What Wolfe looks over: a city like a grave-
        yard.
High rise tombstones, smoking crematorial
        chimneys, and over
The Queen's House and colonnade, the brown
        river
Where Nelson's coffin embarked. One
        o'clock. From the top
Of the mast on Flamsteed's House, watch the
        large time ball drop,
A public measurement of time for Victorian
Shipping, above the cobbled gutter of the
        Prime Meridian.

Greenwich! Here I did penance in a ragged
        school,
And met my second wife. The river, this park

184

rule 10
That stretch in Hell. I brought vandals to see
    these sundials
On the wall – zodiac, equal and unequal
    hours. They were trials,
Those visits. I go up to the Octagon Room
    where the
First Astronomer Royal tried to measure
    longitude at sea –
How far East or West mariners sailed – and
    the Equation of Time,
The difference between the clocks and when
    the stars climb.

I have also measured East and West, the years
    have left me sadder.
Tompion clocks, a telescope through a ladder.
I go downstairs to the equatorial sextants,
The mural quadrants and transit
    instruments. 20
I come to the Bradley Meridian, and beyond
Is the Mean Time Clock, accurate to a tenth of
    a second,
And the Airy Transit Circle which points its
    proof
Like a cannon thundering through an
    unshuttered roof.

A frosty night, a sweep of glittering dust;
All this bombarding of the universe is so
    much rust.
Newton needed their figures for his law of
    gravity
And shut out a sparkle with his scientific
    curiosity.
Measuring Eternity with gold lines, they cut
    up
The shadows that flow from the sundial, or
    the buttercup. 30
They organised their darkness, but missed the
    sun,
Squinting up a telescope at a black heaven.

Would there were an Observatory for the
    inner dark!
I would loll in my reclining seat and embark
Into space, breathe deeply, then in the
    blackest night,
Peer up the telescope for the dawning Light,
Feel the tide of Eternity rush under my heart,

Then, having counted the planetary hours,
    come to with a start,
Go outside, look at the gold lettering near the
    clover
Leaf, and see if the clovered shadow has
    cascaded it over! 40

19 August 1974

19th Elegy
LOUGHTON METHODIST CHURCH

A redbrick chapel behind a low wall.
A cross (once bombed), two turrets, stained
    glass – all
Spoilt by the olive-green doors. Locked.
    Round the side we
Peer through coloured glass into a rippling
    sea.
Through the porch, two aisles, yellow pews,
    each with a cardholder,
Book-ledge and umbrella space. A table altar,
Yellow pulpit, new organ pipes. A smashed
    pane. I peep and spy
The old hymn board, and the clock I
    measured sermons by!

I am shut out of where I sat every Sunday
Until our Minister preached against Suez.
    Next Friday 10
My letter was in the *Gazette*. Here my mother
Brought me. Two of her grandparents were
    Methodists from Yorkshire, and
    another
Wore a top hat to the chapel at Brixton Hill.
They lived through the second flowering of
    the Puritan daffodil.
Pink tulips on green glass, a wooden roof.
My father's family were Norsemen and
    Quakers, though there is little
    proof.

Here a host of characters passed, in fellow-
    ship, beyond Hell:
Twisted old man Occomore, lean Mr Bedwell.
Here circuit and lay preachers, the latter-day
    Puritan,
Interpreted the faith in terms of their
    Wesleyan 20
Hearts – "the Redeeming Blood" – and
    spontaneous prayer.

185

Here they made themselves tiny gods, making
    up their
Rules to suit their belief: application,
Sober living, hard work, thrift, Sabbath
    observance – nothing about
    illumination.

At school I attended Anglican Morning Song,
Found instruction from repeated prayers that
    contain strong
Rules, as my mother does now, having
    changed to the psalter.
In her church, my brother was organist, my
    daughter
Was in the choir. Wearing a violet cassock,
    she rang
The bell where my father's coffin stood, we
    all sang   30
"Hail, gladdening Light". In that church there
    is a Rule
To which the self is subordinated, like a
    spirit-school.

We live in darkness, until in quiet the Light
Shines through the soul, and teaches what is
    right.
Our churches must be places of quiet and
    candles
Which fill with peace. Like Catholic
    confessionals,
They must say "Don't" to the wants of the
    errant self-will
Which exclude the guiding Spirit and make
    the soul ill.
They must make us feel it through the heart,
    not through the head.
There must be mysticism, or God is dead.   40

For this the heart must be freed – by Rule. Yet
    where
To find it? Our religion is overgrown, like a
    pear
Tree that has never been pruned. Fifteen
    hundred years,
Then the Anglicans split, then the Puritan
    tears
On the branches. Noncomformists and
    Separatists –
From Luther and Calvin, and the Baptists,
Congregationalists, Presbyterians, Quakers on

whom the sun shines,
Till Methodists and Evangelicals grew new
    signs.

Where in all this dead wood can the
    individual begin?
For a blind man to deny the sun is sin.   50
The freewill makes hardened choices until
It softens to guidance to let the Spirit fill
It with calm and Light. All else is confusion.
Our darkened nation needs a sap transfusion.
The priests are gardeners with a calling, who
    apply the Rule.
They are right to keep us from darkness, and
    the fool.

Unity is the hope for Quaker men of Light
Who want symbols to prune the darkness for
    what is right.
All sects must come together. Only then can I
    again
Listen, in these Rule-less pews, for the silence
    beneath Sunday rain.   60
I wander round the back to the old hall
I acted in when five. Connecting seats. On the
    wall:
GOD IS WITH US. On either side parked
    cars press
Where there were fields. The old rural
    freshness

And simplicity have lost to urbanisation.
On each side a wire fence with a concentration
Camp's barbed wire. Up it, by the new hall,
White bells of bellbind ring down the new
    brick wall.
I walk back past the tulips to the High Road.
I am shut out of this ground where I was
    sowed   70
Like a tulip to be choked by bellbind, where I
    felt the fold
Or their Rule-less notions, like chickweed
    round a marigold!

19 August 1974

20th Elegy
CHIGWELL SCHOOL
(For Jim Doolan)

In the lane of horse chestnuts a notice says
    FLOWER SHOW.

I cross the old marbles pitch. A crowd mills to
    and fro
On Top Field, around New Hall, as if it were
    Speech Day.
The chapel's lintel is inscribed LAVDATE,
The tuck shop's once said μηδεν ἀγαν and
    φροντιστηριον.
The old brick front. The much-carved porch is
    locked.
           I stand on
A rosebed, peer through glass at where we sat
And the arched-niche bust of Harsnett we
    flicked pellets at!

The Founder among Honours Boards, under a
    mitre,
Sporting a white beard, clutching a book and
    crozier.   10
Next door is the Praefects' Room, whose old
    scratched wood
Has resounded to a thousand whackings. We
    should
Pay Homage to the Library. Crested chairs
    and worn, blue
Cushions down a table under the dome, where
    a host first knew
Horace. Harsnett and the golden mean, the
    tradition
Of a once classical, Christian nation.

I slip into New Hall without paying ten pence.
Prize dahlias and gladioli, with judges'
    comments
Like end-of-term reports. Gardeners shuffle
    round
Where we had call-over, past echoes that
    resound   20
With the school song: "Find a way or make a
    way…."
Boys are like flowering plants. First the bed,
    the young day;
Language, vocabulary like leaves in bowls.
I walk among perfect blooms in this green-
    house for young souls.

Here we were kept in order, like these
    arranged sprays.
All different, we were contained in green
    vases. On weekdays
We were clipped and wooded, we did what

we were expected to do
Or got thrashed, or put in Labour Squad. We
    grew
On the Way. We go out to the fields, fifty
    acres
That stretch down to the new by-pass.
    Anglicans, or Quakers   30
Like Penn, we played hard, it was homework
    or the cane, there were no hordes,
We strove to attain a standard: the Oxbridge
    Honours Boards.

I think of the huge school I have just left:
    blackened concrete,
Smashed panes. One twisted rhododendron.
    You meet
Gangs of coloured youths rushing through the
    corridors,
Many shout obscenities, toss coins on class-
    room floors.
There boys wander in and out when they feel
    like it.
They can be caned or suspended, but a teacher
    can still be hit.
If his class will not listen or work, when
    things get rough
His only sanctions are persuasion – and
    bluff.   40

A proliferation of mindless ignorance is
Sprouting throughout England, destroying old
    beauties.
Like gardeners growing weeds, some teachers
    deride
Respect for learning, which "leaves the
    deprived to one side".
Shakespeare is put away, the standard is the
    slower
Reader. Weeds are watered. It is the parable
    of the sower,
They choke the unpruned rose. To fertilise it
    is "crass" –
Latin is "out of date, both for Oxford and the
    Mass."
Language depersonalises: the "drunkard", the
    "curse"
Of "imperialist", "developer", "whore", are so
    much worse   50
Than the human being behind the label:
So it is with descriptions of the able.

"Elitist", "class-conscious" misrepresent
The rose, like "not deprived" or "had a
    chance"; or even "excellent".
Language can make a weed a flower; a
    standard of a dunce;
And justify an idea, where there was *concern*
    for the poor boy once.

The idea sounds fine: new equipment, no
    rejects,
A hundred teachers, a choice of subjects,
As if all seeds should flower. But in practice
Those schools are too large and impersonal.
    Boys miss   60
The discipline, they do not belong or care,
    there is strife.
An education is a setting-up for life.
We memorise chunks of verse without under-
    standing, they return,
They are with us for ever. Boys must be
    forced to learn.

The rankness will stop, winter will thin it out.
Growth will be checked again. Flowers will
    survive our doubt
About the fairness of their superiority.
Equality piffle! "A University
Is where you toughen the mind," it will be
    said, "you should hear
As many different opinions as you can, and
    know why you jeer,"   70
And, "It is immoral not to question an
    opinion,
But commensense!" This school maintains the
    tradition.

The Head's flower-garden. He selects his
    seed, plants it in mud.
E-ducation is a "leading out" – of the bloom
    from the bud.
He does not expect a thistle to be a cowslip.
This endurance-school grows character,
    leadership,
Self-reliance that built an empire. Now that is
    gone
It prepares its boys for a profession.
We worked by ourselves, the best of us kept
    the mitre
In our hearts, and the way to Harsnett's
    crozier.   80

All life is a school. And not all plants are
    garden
Flowers. I pass the old Gym, where the
    ragged specimen
Flourished and fought, enter the church where
    Harsnett was vicar
And Fradd played marbles on Speech Days,
    the champion flicker
Kneeling on an old blue hassock. There is a
    brass of Harsnett on the wall.
The book on his heart, his mitre and crozier
    call
Back to standards and discipline, and a
    tradition, that remains today,
Of being forced to learn, and finding – or
    making – one's Mystic Way.

            26 August 1974

21st Elegy
QUEEN CHARLOTTE'S HOSPITAL

I sit on after school, mark grubby books.
The tannoy crackles, "Urgent message...."
    She looks
Grave: "Your wife has to go to hospital." I
    drive
Home through a thunderstorm. "A
    complication. I've
Been to the doctor. He said that my blood
Pressure's up. They may induce me." A flood
Of doubts as I drive her in. I go home to
    sleep.
5 a.m. The phone goes: "I've started." I creep

Down dark streets, drive through rain; put on
    a white gown.
She lies on a bed by a machine, leads hanging
    down.   10
"I had the show before midnight, I've popped
    the sac.
I've had an epidural in my back.
There is a drip in my hand." I shudder at it.
She lies at peace. On the Pressure Monitor
    Unit
A needle flickers a contraction for
A new self – and a desensitised labour.

The breathing exercises might never have
    been.
I watch the "Fetal Heart Beat" on the

machine.
A nib slowly pens a zigzag – and stops.
The midwife grimaces, sister's jaw drops. 20
"Would you wait outside please," she says. I
    loiter in
The corridor. A doctor pads by with a grin,
Rubbing his eyes. I am called back. And now
The pen is moving. I sit and soothe her brow.

"Baby's in the wrong place, he's been trying
    to get
Out the wrong way, he's tired." The doctor's
    face is set.
"We're going to help him, we'll let the
    husband stay."
I sit to hide the "Fetal Heart Beat" – and pray.
Nurses give me a mask and a "shower hat",
Strap her ankles to two steel posts, the doctor
    slits at 30
Where blood gushes into tin, drips. I stroke
    her eyes
And brow. Does she know, sometimes a baby
    dies?

The nurses pump, the doctor sucks –
    Vantoosh.
Watching the contractions needle, he says,
    "Push."
And my new wife strains herself to flushing.
"Good, that's very good. One more push." He
    is rushing.
The "Fetal Heart Beat" stops again. Fatal….I,
Tied to the fish inside by a cord, want to cry:
'Have you not seen it?' He sees. All their
    looks ask
And avoid my gaze. One has tears above her
    mask. 40

"You're doing well," I say, smoothing her
    brow,
Quivering behind my mask. I must be calm
    now.
"You won't want this will you." A nurse
    wheels the machine away.
The frantic doctor probes with forceps of
    steel-grey.
There is great haste. "The head is coming
    out."
A blue dead thing, limp, slimy, flops about.
"We'll soon see if it's a boy or a girl, won't

we."
A push. "It's a little boy." Even I can see.

The nurses fall on it, snip the cord, and why
Is it quiet over there? Will it not cry? 50
A waul – a choking sob. I blink and fight
And gulp. My wife smiles and asks, "Is he all
    right?"
"The afterbirth…" Our squalling little one
In blue swaddling clothes. A new person, a
    son.
"He has a headache." I nurse his swollen
    crown
And forceps bruises. I quieten him down.

She holds him, then gives him back. She is
    sick,
She lies exhausted, her face a pale quick,
Still as the stillborn thing which they revived.
Now we two are three. This face that
    survived – 60
Peeking eyes all pupils – from the heart of the
    rose
Will fight, date, attend my funeral, and
    compose.
This thing that turned the wrong way attests
    my roots;
I must shelter this fruit of my seed till it puts
    up shoots.

I wait in the corridor, while they wash her;
Hospital rattles of pans, rustles and whirr
Of electrical equipment. This is a place where
Women are set like alarm-clocks, and
    painlessly bear,
The life-force is harnessed. The abandon
That throws about, like elemental love, has
    gone. 70
Here at the peak of Western civilisation,
Epidurals, drips – a childbirth revolution.

Yet no routines, machines or instruments can
Obscure this mystery – the meaning of the
    Plan.
Like trees, flowers, insects, beasts, we
    reproduce;
Seeds scatter before leaves drop, stem down,
    to reduce
The whole. Pick off dead heads in the
    windowbox,

New tageties grow. Eggs, families and
    flocks....
There is a law of perpetual self-renewal;
We now condemn its workings as too
    cruel.   80

Birth and death. Out of the window dawn
    breaks.
A full moon's ripened head darkly thrusts and
    wakes
From a black, placenta-shaped cloud. It cries
Above a Victorian terrace, across the skies.
Migrating birds fly dark over the railway.
"It was like a diver, he was gasping to stay
Alive among the contractions...." The moon
    is bright
Above where two tube trains pass clattering in
    the night.

The moon born out of cloud. We lurch into
    life.
Something has been born in me. A swollen
    wife   90
Swelled hope, corresponded to a new self
    once. Now again.
We have as many futures as we have children,
And our past acceptances make them waul
    and kick.
Now I am the reverential mystic.
I go with her to the ward, my sense of
    mystery ringing,
And when I cross the car park, all the birds
    are singing.

                            3 October 1974

22nd Elegy
OUR LADY OF VICTORIES

I go out, walk the dank streets of Labour rule
To our polling booth: Our Lady of Victories
    School.
People saunter. A teller hands me my vote,
I go to the cubicle for this historical footnote.
A pencil hangs from new string. I make my
    cross,
Slot it into the tin as if a Tory loss
Were in doubt. Outside I feel a cleansing
    beauty:
It is so proudly futile, this democratic duty.

In February it was a wintry morning.

People wore coats, there was a spring in the
    step – and a warning.   10
Now all seem listless. Politicians
Have quietened their voices, but the same
    abstractions
And slogans will water our garden. We are
    like flowers.
We get gardeners whose ideas are not ours.
"To represent"....The genus looks plausible,
But true values bloom, like petals, in the
    individual.

A crisis is on us. The increased price of oil,
Our fertiliser, will bankrupt us, spoil
Our garden. Our social democracy must
    harshen.
Hardship will blight Western civilisation.   20
The Golden Age of Churchill is near its
    finish.
Whoever wins has neither the power nor the
    wish
To resist the Arabs. Will the UK break up?
After all, our Empire proved as frail as a
    buttercup.

Night. On the television the first return
Shows a swing to Labour. "This means they
    will earn
A healthy overall majority."
Behind the curtain crouches a new society.
There will be more clipping and pruning, the
    State –
To be fair – will cut blooms to pay the new
    Arab rate.   30
We will be snipped and scythed, roses will
    squeal:
Wealth tax, gift tax, and a nationalising sickle
    of steel.

Torn-off leaves to pay for a dust to sprinkle
Round headless levelled stalks – that are now
    equal!
The genus has no flowers. Let us, then, lack
Fertiliser and brackish water, and go back
To blooms and petals, to the family stem,
To the responsible gardener, working, leaving
    them
Disciplined, well-pruned among vegetables
That will sell. No degenerate stock under old
    labels.   40

Now sacrifice and revolution are in the air.
Will the People submit to the doctrinaire,
Or will there be anarchy, a coup, a dictator's
    drive?
Will our Parliamentary democracy survive,
This ritual canvassing for the right to rule,
One equal cross for the genius and the fool?
Yet this method of Pericles will tantalise
Long after it has been discontinued as a pack
    of lies.

An old penny. Britannia! Under your shield
We won victories on many a battlefield: 50
Against Philip of Spain, Napoleon, the Kaiser,
    Hitler.
Are we to fall from within like Rome? Is it
    better
For patrician stability to be destroyed
By populist leaders? Help us avoid
A catastrophe in our broken-down
    civilisation,
O Lady of Victories; help us restore our
    nation!

                                    10 October 1974

23rd Elegy
BRECHIN PLACE

I walk round my new flat. Stairs from the
    front door,
Two floors and a roof garden – with a
    fountain – for
Sunbathing. Richly carpeted rooms, velveteen
Curtains, carved wood fire-places with lamps
    between
Love-knots. The old deep sofa. Shelves lined
    with books run
Up to the ceiling, where a chrysanthemum
    like a sun
Shines down, a Golden Flower of wheat, like
    the kind
On the urn a Prince gave me, the Light in my
    mind.

I sold two smaller flats to buy this; and now
    accept
Our property-owning democracy. I could have
    kept   10
Them buried, like talents, but I doubled
Their yield, attracted buyers with an
    untroubled

Mind, for all things are given to him that hath
    Light.
Like a bird nesting, finding twigs, I bought
    the right
Furniture. And as I built this home, I won
A wife, and now I have a baby son.

We have left the restless search among girls in
    bars,
That drifting Hell of the fishing-net, girls in
    jam-jars
Like tiddlers. Permissive variety
Is muddying the clean waters of our Christian
    society.   20
A Western man, I too, retiring from the
    cheating,
Now have my comforts: my kitchen, central
    heating.
I go out to work for the salary I bring home.
But the material things are not all. I welcome

My rootedness, like my windowbox tageties.
My daughter is here for half-term; I pay
    boarding fees.
I met her at King's Cross. She holds my son –
    like a cuckoo,
His mouth is open – while my wife stirs milk,
    still new
To the silence that was the mystery, the
    Mystic Way,
Of my last wife. A year ago today   30
I had "black thoughts". Time has healed that
    break like water
Polishing stone round a broken stalk. My
    daughter

Smiles at my wife, and cuddles my little son,
And the past is now a marigold, stolen and
    done.
"Resist not evil," I would say, burning with
    the opposite,
"But overcome evil with good." We sit
In harmony and quiet, under a water-colour
    still
Of a brown rock, brown sea. This is the
    tranquil
Time. On my Tibetan *thanka*, against white
    fire is spread
A blue god with a third eye in his fore-
    head.   40

191

This is the meaning of life. This illumined
        calm
And cradling a family in either arm.
I clasp a marble egg: tides, stars multiply
The unity which is seen through the forehead
        eye.
And so this place marks a breaching of the
        bone
And of the darkness that permits a kindling
        moan
To fire the heart, that brought me conflict.
        Here we can see
Through to the Light of Eternal harmony.

25 October 1974

THE NIGHT-SEA CROSSING

1974

BLIND CHURCHILL TO THE NIGHT

After the siren a holy silence,
Sighs an echoing drone up the night sky.
I wait for the boom, bang, CRASH – nearer
    they moan –
I wait as a rain of iron tattoes
This city, and where is my command now?
    Where?
O London. Each pockmark in your face, each
    stone
Saddens my scabby heart. Searchlights stab
    the sky,
Sweep the stars. All clear. I am lord again,
I walk these streets of mine. A roaring fire,
Débris, hanging beams, a mutilated   10
Limping, writhing, twitching in this quiet
    mews.
O London. Could you be mine in this red
    glare?
A woman runs screaming, her clothes on fire.
An old man sits and moans, holding a lamp-
    post,
One leg gone. A boy watches fascinated
In this reddish dark.
            Now in this hospital
Front wall removed like a doll's house, ghastly
Groanings, bandages on legs, arms and heads.
Worn-out expressions, worn-out looks.   20
I cannot look.

What is the meaning of all this division?
Europe has fallen sick, and these my victims
Stare at me with terrible, unaccusing smiles.
O my wan ones. I cannot tell you
The voices that come to mock me in the
    nights,
"You will fight the tyrant, but know if you win
You will lose your position and Empire, you
    will lose
Like the Athenians in your unread
    Thucydides.
You will decline to insignificance. And the
    choice is yours...."   30

O my pale ones, to fight and lose or to
Surrender and lose? An iron enemy
Waits for our classical Christian culture,
If we escape this pit we will not escape the
    next one.
O my poor ones, you are swathed for me
And, I beam on you, but I am sad, sad.
I cannot tell you of the voices that whisper
"Within thirty years you will enter a union
With the power that rains bombs on you
    now."   40
I cannot say your sacrifice is for a new age,
A Golden Age. Not for this London of ours,
In conflict, life breeds to the greater whole.
$(+a) + (-a) = $ zero.
I cannot say, "These wars will spawn a peace
And greatness that will rocket to the moon,"
    or,
"Your rooting out of selfishness is for
The Grand Design." History, History...
These wailing, moaning men, and an opposite
    ideal.
I am sick in this scabby heart. Process,
    process.
When the old grows rotten it must be rooted
    out,   50
And sometimes the parent oak must be hewn
    down
So that the new can grow. Betterment.
O my sorrowing ones, history is a spiral
Stair, it twists up for a million years
Until it reaches what? A gate?
            Nothing?

Now I lie in bed and I ask myself,
What is our Western civilisation?
O it has grown through turbulent gusty
    centuries
To our sturdy tree. And now what stars in our
    boughs –   60
Aircraft, telephone, radio, TV,
Of discovery there is no end. To reach the
    moon....
Why this fire? Why these mutilated limbs?

Why this bloodletting? Must there really be
Conflict before we build our paradise?
Must the national "I" be chopped so painfully
Before we share tranquillity? O pride, pride.
What is a tyrant? And I am but a pawn.
O history.

I am but the echo of a forward creak,   70
My greatest victories mirror images
Of huge defeats.
              Swallows twittering in the
              square.
Can I urge our young blood to the sacrifice
In this moulting history? This change of
              seasons?
These flutterings are but a pile of feathers,
Though they seem absolute now.

Night, all is dark in the dug-out of my mind.
This civilisation which has taken to the air,
Reached the bottom of the sea, which will
              reach the moon,   80
Is but a step on the spiral stair. I can see no
              sense in it.
Conflict, then unity, then more conflict.
Hurricane, sun, earthquake and flood; and
              sun.
It is all necessary. Night, day, night.
I see the pattern on my carpet. What does it
              mean?
O my aghast ones, I can show you so much,
Yet the interpretation baffles me. I am baffled,
Amazed. This amazing step, these stars, this
              tree,
Those swallows and the turbulent sea
That laps at the broken ventricles of my
              aching   90
Heart.
              I am apart.

THE NIGHT-SEA CROSSING
(A SYMPHONIC POEM IN SONATA FORM)

"More light." (Goethe's last words)

I
(i)

Night. Sea and stars, a trail of foaming wake,
The dark shape of the ship, engines throbbing.

I lean over the rail, the dark troughs pass,
I perch on this rail like a hook-billed gull
Resting from the exertions of a long flight.
I am tired, tired. My heart thumps and pounds
To the pistons of the engines.
              Is this how it will end,
Out on the dark sea, under star-dripping night,
Apart from loved ones, alone? Among
              strangers   10
Who will not care? Is this my destination?
I have learned to fear the thickening in my
              blood.
If this artery should widen and release the clot
So that it floats up and blocks the heart, then
              what?
Where will the sea be, where this dark night
              then?
Eternal nothingness, blackness for always –
Will I be that before the dawn steals up,
Just a darkness? I am ready to let go,
Will not seek help – much good that would do
              me here –
But I wonder. Waves lapping at the sides,   20
Sunlight on sea-hills, pines bent by the wind,
Gulls wheeling round the harbour fish-market,
Her smile as she lay down – are all these
              things
Mere sunshafts before nightfall? No more
              than that?
What does my life amount to? What meaning
Have these images? Out on this heaving water
I remember life and make my peace with
              death.

And yet I have known a calm
Where all is purpose, where the days and
              years
Are steps of a celestial staircase up to
              heaven   30
From suffering to joy. The ascent of history!
The meaning of prayer! Fold hands and
              breathe,
And breathe and breathe. And...sink into a
              silence.
Heart beats in unison with the universe,
Accepts it and is filled with ecstasy.
Breathe and breathe. Heart burns to a tree of
              fire.
White light. The vine. Does this make any
              difference?

I ask too many questions.
    I look beyond the sunset.

(ii)

How does my life look in the face of
    death?   40
It dwindles. Wasted moments, wasted half-
    hours.
Oh what I could have built – a Pyramid!
For after that experience of misplaced love
What was there to believe in, save
    achievements?
Now they are just good intentions. And
    bafflement.
Something is passing: a Christian culture.
Once we knew what had meaning – Horace,
    St. John of the Cross –
And life was fixed in death like steps in a
    staircase,
With a fixed meaning. Now nothing is certain.
A destructive "Colossus", who does not need
    to climb.   50
The "Collapse of the Soul" – my mind a
    broken mirror,
Doubts glinting, until I pieced myself
    together.
I am a victim of my Age. This clot began
In heartbreak, swelled in political deception.

What now, my images? When you first kissed
    me,
When you walked down the aisle in white,
    when we boated
Up a palm-lined river? What of the storms
When I tossed in your wind till you split me?
What are these now? And all those ambitions
That were not fulfilled because I had to
    earn   60
For a family to which loneliness drove me,
Were they arbitrary? Might they as well not
    have happened?
All moments belong to one when you look at
    the pole star
And clutch the universe in your palm, like a
    marble egg;
A thousand loves and ambitions are here,
Might have happened tonight, and ended
    before dawn.
Or perhaps all life and history is a puff
Of smoke evaporating after an eruption?

Questions. I resolved to ask no more
    questions.

Instead I will gaze, gaze, breathe with the
    sea,   70
Look upon the waves of my years, gaze on
    my life
As a whole, and give thanks for the mystic
    glimpses
Remember the illuminations, forget the waste.
I will say: my life was a series of high
    moments,
You sighing, "Oh I love you, love you,
You're like a warm fire in a room, I warm to
    you,"
My daughter saying, "Thank you Daddy for
    visiting me,"
Or from my window, magnolia in the
    gardens –
The Fountain of the teeming universe,
Buds and insects, joys and sorrows;
    opposites.   80
This is my other life. The peace that gasps
Amid these paradoxes.

I have left a causeway of wake behind me.
Soon it will be indistinguishable from the sea.
Two people on one side of the Channel, two
    on the other,
Waves glinting and now forgotten in the dark.
What is a man?
        There it is again, the pain
In this timebomb of a heart.   90
        Fountain and flashpoint....

I will creep back to my cabin, and stare
At the twisted face of a dying Christ's
    despair.

(iii)

What is a man? A sticky blob of seed.
He grows like a wheat-stalk. He towers under
    the sun.
A flick of a finger, and Kennedy was gone.
What is a man? Nothing.
        Winter days at school,
Getting changed for cross-country, for
    football,
I grew through the examination hall
To this grain. A little pain, and then

– nothing.   100
Leaving behind a frame like a husk of corn.

My heart. It bumps and pounds over that
          breast,
A fountain of pumps and circuits. Let me
          stare at it.
I could draw a spider's web through these
          fingers.
Power rises like bubbles in a desert spring.
Breathing in this stillness, let us ask for what
We want, give thanks for what we would
          receive,
Attract it to us, act as if it has occurred.
These things are what wisdom is.
                    What is this living Tide   110
I feel but do not inquire into, destroy?
I do not understand this washing clean of the
          mind
With light. This purification. Cleansing fire.
Pure eyes see purely, dirty eyes see lies.

Ploughed fields, fires of old straw on autumn
          hills,
Summer lambs on green cliffs…I shall miss
          them
When I am dead. This ribbed earth, these bare
          twigs.
What is death? Not knowing dragonfly wings
Or wind bending pines or the crimson rose.
I will let my soul unfold like a rose. What
          are   120
These fallen petals? My heart grows my spirit,
And round it this satin lushness of
          Unknowing.
And lo! outside the veil, such a sun! The light
Of holiness! I will be sinless to unfold my
          soul.
Let me breathe in rapture, like a summer sea
Washing the shingle, lapping at landing-stage,
Tugging bladderwrack on a breakwater!
Let me breathe stones, let me drag back
          across my age.

Death is in the corner, hooded like a monk.
Death is creeping up on me. I feel the
          chill   130
Round my feet. Wash-wash at my port-
          window
This night-sea, foaming and flooding under

me,
I cross it and pass over to the other side,
All must cross with me to that sinister slip of
          land.
Death, I will look at you, look at your face.
You hide round my bunk, you cling to the
          shadows,
But I will see you! I will see you.
Death the skeleton, skull in a monk's cowl,
Waiting to reap me, this growth from a jellied
          seed.

Crops of summer. Fields of wheat,
          orchards   140
Bending with fruit. Windfalls, wasps and
          ripeness.
The hot long grass of summer. The gnat-
          stream,
Dry mud like bone. Growth, all is growth,
          and I
Was a long day's dying.

The sea of minutes, hours, days, weeks and
          months
I am crossing. Heroes of old England
Were carried out on a barge at night. May I
Achieve an understanding in this dying heart.

II
(i)
Where are the things of my childhood?
The battleship I carried round to our new
          house   150
At the end of the war – gone.
The butterfly collection I had –
Dust in a specimen cabinet.
The stamp albums I fattened,
Swapping sweets at school –
Lost in a move.
The toolshed in my grandmother's garden –
The house sold.

Nothing lasts. So it is with the pleasures.
Volatile! They evaporate like water   160
In a saucer. The first love,
Security at college, the first job,
A young wife, they are like the open sea,
You think it will always be there,
Then suddenly, the port.
O those girls. On my floor,

In my bed, in a window after a shower.
With these and a hundred other desires
I was chained to my lower self.

And when I fell into the wrong love   170
Where were my reserves then?
Her being in my mad mind
Like a Maundy farthing, my higher self
A prisoner somewhere in blind infatuation.
Where are those faces now? Where are they
          gone?
Images in the memory....
As I grow older I forget
Yesterday's happenings, last year's,
And I stumble upon the long-ago
As if a house has been demolished   180
In a familiar street, leaving
An unexpected vista to a monument
To an event that is
Out of reach.

(ii)

My lower consciousness was a prison,
My soul was held in chains of flesh and pride.
My jailer self had to ascend
The Cross of Denial, be crucified
So my soul could be undone.
My soul had to unite with its lower part   190
It had to live in this lower stench.
What suffering it felt as it debased itself!
What noble lifting up! It transformed
My lower consciousness. Now it could
Listen through the subconscious din
To the voice of its own higher intelligence,
The Truth. Now the Infinite intelligence
Illumines and directs me.
Regenerated, I regenerate the planet.
For we are in a universe of ether   200
And our brain-waves crackle in the minds
Of every other.

Man is an offspring of God.
A coil like a watchspring stood on end.
Like electricity, Infinite Spirit
Pours into cells, organs, my heart,
Pulses through the heart, throbbing.
Distinguishes the living from the dead.
Higher degrees of consciousness reach down,
Lift lower degrees to their own level.   210
I have freed myself from my lower self

I have cleared my heart of lower rubbish
And stoked the Heavenly fires to burning.

It is a law of life,
The higher lifts the lower,
As air draws flame up a chimney,
Till the highest peace
Unites with God. This must not be forgotten.
An Age which worships lower consciousness
Is in error, must be uplifted.   220
The Pelagian revolutionaries are wrong.
We must change not "out there" but within:
The original lower darkness of Original Sin.

(iii)

Sea-whispers off the rocks.
Sun streaming, sparkling on the waves.
Jumping, exploding lights amaze
The heart – these images like shocks.

Where are they gone, the climber on the sea-
          cliff,
Turning and grinning in red from ear to ear?
Where are they gone? The dance with a
          stranger,   230
Her hand clutching my chest as we walked
          home?
Where are they gone? The girl on the moonlit
          downs,
Or the shopper who sat up with leaves in her
          long hair?
Or umpteen others? O where?

Illness, old age, hostility carry
All images away.
What is there to cling to? All will be ruin.
These dreams of a vanished day...

O I must flee
These images of my lower consciousness, 240
These desires which still chain me
                              today.

III
(i)
In our intense moments, life is joyful –

Running, dancing, laughing,
Winter figures toboggan
Down the icy snow-hill,

197

Raincoats, hats and mufflers,
Shouting, whooping, screeching,
Crouching, rush and tumble –
We went down together,   250
You went in front
Dizzy down, whirling
So the trees sped past
Snow swooshing from my heels
Down to the frozen pond –

And o the joy of that dance as the beat took
        hold of me,
I abandoned myself, and was one with
        jumping bodies
Moving in motion to music, joyful, joyful
Faces split in grins – there was a great mirth
And faster and faster and faster, you were in
        front of me   260
Twisting and twirling, and I would know your
        body,
O health, as we whirled faster and faster,
        stamping out rhythms,
Panting with a howling exultation –

Or: on we sped striding down Vesuvius
Plunging strides slithering through shifting
        ash
Flying free long-league boots down we ran
one-two-three ten-foot skids skiing through
Enormous steps free as wind –
"Look out, the rock," – and I fell through air,
        hung free off the mountain   270
Till swishoo-ow-oof! I slithered on my face
        through ash,
Gashed and grazed, blood welling on knees
        and arms, grit,
Smarting.

Sledging, dancing, mountaineering
I have known
Moments of intoxicating affirmation –
Union of mind and blood and bone.

                    (ii)
Night wears a tiara
Of sparkling domestic moments
I must leave behind.   280
You sitting at peace
On the gorse-cliffs of Carlyon,
Bees humming in wild flowers,

Waves sparkling far below,
You on the Fowey ferry,
Millpond as we crossed to Polruan,
My hand trailing in water,
You sitting on the Aldeburgh shingle
Listening to the uncanny silence
In my heart, watching the sale   290
Of skate and dogfish, you in Scarborough
Sitting up in bed, roses
On the wallpaper, and on the exploding
        beach,
You down at Hastings,
Sea booming on the shore –
You, defined by sea.
And our lump in your womb.
Will it be a boy or a girl?
We would make a peaceful trio.

And I must leave another trio.   300
You, looking at our Mediterranean garden,
Near a large white urn –
We all put hands round shoulders and
Danced on your birthday and sang
"We're a happy family...."
Two months later, wheel turned
And you were gone;
You, golden-haired by a statue
Among columns of Roman ruins,
Sea jumping behind you, or walking   310
On a beach strewn with sponges,
You, picking flowers across barbed wire
On Malta. Across barbed wire.
And I must leave my seed. From your womb,
You, lying on your front, in bunches
On a Pacific beach, you holding
My hand on the shingle at Worthing,
My enchanting little angel.
You, now morose and drawn, and you radiant,
I must leave you.   320

Then there is the trio of peace
That I have known this year,
The two I can know in my dialectic.
You of the Carlyon cliff
And the Fowey ferry, and you my daughter
Of the handicraft fingers –
You together by the Forest pond
Looking for sticklebacks near water-lilies,
You on a lawn with two rabbits,
You on a lawn of croquet hoops.   330

You are another peace, sunbathing
On the roof or sewing a dress
While I correct manuscripts.
Chestnut candles and summer sadness.
O my last trio, my reconciliation,
Must I leave you?
    Desolation.

    (iii)
The joys of the mind –

Bird soars up and round and up
In a conical helix.   340
O the joys of developing art –
Developing consciousness
Like a spiral vortex
    apart
      in happiness.

At Corps Camp we marched
Left-right left-right swing your arms
Down the road, between two hedges –
I had my packed lunch, the sea was only a
    mile away,
Seeing my chance, I ducked and skittered
    off,   350
Ran puffing down a ditch, over a stile, and up
    to the cliff,
Then I threw myself down in the sun, sea
    dazzling below,
I opened my paper bag, and what peace!
The bees hummed in the clover, the sun beat,
I took off my itchy khaki shirt and heavy
    boots
And lay the whole August afternoon, basking
    in sunlight
And on the back of a grubby envelope,
    sketched my first opus –

And after that it was marching up the
    ziqqurat,
Up the spiral steps that coiled round and
    round,   360
Up and up, scaling the tower, leaving earth-
    bound things behind,
Round and round, up and up, with increasing
    mastery –
Line by line, work by work, such command
    and fluency,
And such satisfaction, a quiet triumphal walk

round the College
In springtime after one, an elated stroll at
    night in midsummer
Tumbling chestnut tree towering above, with
    vivid candles,
After another. And as I ascended my mind
    soared higher and higher,
Freer and freer, like approaching the summit
    of a mountain,
Up I trudged, up, round and up, steps of a
    staircase
Spiralling into the sky. And then I saw the top
    of it reach Heaven,   370
Angels came down to meet us, reciprocating
    our efforts,
I climbed on, higher and higher, up and
    up,
The air was good, I was filled with
    exhilaration,
I passed angels singing, the earth was
    stretched out far below,
There was a great light above me, and there
    was nothing I could not do,
And I climbed on, up, up, rejoicing at my
    control,
O the pleasures of growth, o the enjoyment of
    existence!
I saw the Truth, I was pure consciousness,
I was an Angel – hosannah! It was wonderful,
I wanted to sing a paean of praise and
    affirmation   380
    for what I had become!

Night. The sea laps soft outside my window.
Numb leg and arm.
    It will not be long now.

    IV
    (i)
A breathless sigh...
A sigh for what has been, the moon
Hangs virgin over wrinkled waves,
A sigh for what is yet to come,
    a womb
      among graves. 390

A tender leaf, a pinkish bud –
Wrinkles, sere.
Nothing lasts. The roses scud
Into thin air.

A sigh for the faces I will not bid
Farewell to, like a blown-down rose.
A sigh for you both at the turn of the tide,
Death creeps up like December snows.

Strangers move outside the door.
I am alone with my rainbows.   400
        Eyes closed.

          (ii)
A quickening....

I see the pattern of my days,
The high points, as on a Persian carpet.
On my mandala, splodges of paint
Besmirch the central circlet.

Lo! the Flowing Light upwards,
My Greek eyes blind to the outer.
Lo! a tree of white against the black.
A winter tree, of white fire.   410

Rippling as if in water. And a centre
Of light shining from a great height – the
        Flower,
The Golden Flower! A golden chrysanthemum!
I am behind my chest, in my burning heart,
Lying down, breathing slowly, half-closed
        eyes
Near sleep. I feel refreshed, turned inside out.
A bishop with a crozier. God on a throne,
Just the huge feet of God, like Amenophis'.
O I feel relaxed, I look with a deep peace.
O my life has such meaning. I see the high
        points   420
Like mountain peaks in a great range. How
        small the valleys!
To know this joy we MUST suffer. To lose
Our lower consciousness, die from the flesh,
Obey our souls, we must suffer. O glory!
The soul ascending to the heights of ecstasy,
Passing into union – why, all things belong
To One. All opposites are drops in a tide,
A man, a woman – splashes were the sea
        dashes
Flinging foam on the headland; hate and
        love –
Just part of a teeming Flow which I can
        know   430
And feel when this fire steals up from the

heart
Into the spirit. O meaning! All's one
Like a marble egg veined with tides, dusted
        with stars!

         (iii)
A sigh for the wasted time....

Waste, the moments I spent on drink,
When I sat before a television,
Entertained guests who did not think,
Interviewed men for whom I felt derision –
Where are they gone now?

Waste, the moments I spent on work,   440
Doing what others asked me for –
They in turn being made to jerk –
So that I had a home with a front door;
Running breathlessly to stand still.
The unreality of red carpets!
Cardboard cut-outs beside a daffodil:
Directors, Heads of Departments – puppets!
Where are they gone now?

Waste, the love affairs that I had
With women who were inessential,   450
Squandering my spirit on the underclad
Who were not up to my level,
Who sapped my energies with their asking,
Disturbing my concentration
With their gross attention-seeking,
Feeling piqued that I poured no libation.
Where are they gone now?

I had so much time, and used so little well.
Schedules,   timetables,   deadlines....
        Becoming!
Inauthentic. I hurried into waste.   460
O to buy one quarter back! O redemption!
A sigh for this bitter taste.

         (iv)
Time is running out....

The pulse of time ticks: the clock, the
        timetable.
It cuts up. Late, before, after, until.
Underneath is a silence, undisturbed
By night, day; April, May; summer, autumn.
It flows quietly, a Great Flow of Being.

Sink into it – this is the Eternal.
Now and for ever, this quiet river of days   470
Rolls on, widening from spring to estuary,
A perpetual Fountain of seeds and seasons,
Gushing generations, multiplicity.
At the source of the light and the dark, the
       live and the dead,
There is One, and one only. One current,
One energy. Like the wind in the trees,
Like the tide on the stones. The One shaping
       all.
$(+a) + (-a) =$ zero.
It holds them together, the day and night,
Fullness and emptiness. And life and
       death.   480
Both are parts of a whole. A life without death
Is plus without minus. The ground of my
       Being
Is on the ground of all Being. And so
One consciousness, Infinite Intelligence,
One spirit runs through all – I may pass into
       it.
A Fountain is a cycle, each small drop
Of water used returns to be pumped up
Again and splash. I receive Light from the
       One,
I may return my soul to it, and come again!
It would make sense. More I cannot say
       now.   490
But it cannot be denied,
Our classical, Christian culture would be
       justified.

I call upon the darkness for more hope.
Where are the possibilities of vision?
I have seen a Colossus free from chains
Towering above this darkened century,
Risen out of our grief. What heroic
Struggles of determined souls have released
       him?
Is he a figment of our imagination,
This superman rid of unclean desires,   500
Free from nihilism? Percipere est
Esse, to perceive truly is to Be
In the light of an authentic silence.
He is not an illusion. O creative Colossus,
We will ascend to you! And when we have
Reached you, the trials of our soul will be
       understood,
The joys we have salvaged, the victories

Will have a saintly staircase of a meaning.

The blessing of *this* crossing....

                        (v)
Dark is the blackness I step into –   510
A coffin, burial, then: nothing.
What is a man? A home, memories,
An effort to grow an ambition,
Then a cross in a graveyard. Man
Is a name written in sea-sand
Till the tide smooths his game away.

Eternal nothingness – can there be life
Among the stars? Four hundred million
       galaxies
And in our galaxy a hundred thousand suns,
What hope is there for an after-life? What
       hope?   520
Dark – nothing is secure, nothing has value,
Death is certain, all is a distraction
From the delaying of it. A creeping
Paralysis of the will lays waste our life.
Our parents' struggles end in old age and
       silence,
Young love and engagements end in
       loneliness.
I have known this; moving towards
       extinction.

The waves outside, the porthole – these folded
       hands.
They will still be there – these hands will be
       here,
But I will be   530
A dark, as after a putting out of lights.
I see from my self, my egotistic "I"
                             and eye.

                        (vi)
Consider the geraniums. Old buds fall
To make way for new ones. Perpetual
       freshness.
Process, process. That is the meaning of
The flowers: perpetual freshness, through new
       buds.
We must not think from the point of view of
       ourselves.
Would it be right for us to live for ever
And be a burden? We must think only   540

From the point of view of the whole process.
We are part of a process that is good,
We must die for the whole to have meaning.

Dark. A Cloud of darkness.
Dark of unknowing, a veil to be pierced.
I look hard at the blackness, look through it.
Will it come, will it break through? Come on,
      come on.
Blackness – but no, a white glimmer. Is it
The Light? Clench fingers over and....
                Whiteness,
A shaft through the blackness, a pearl of
      sun,   550
And – glory! White – a blue-white orb of
      light,
Breaking in breathless day.

                O peace. Peace.

Opposites.
        Waves move; stars, night, day;
        young, old
Are held in a teeming Fountain of abundance.
Angry sea, calm sea, suffering and joy,
Night and morning – through pairs of
      opposites
Runs the Great Flow. I feel its unity
Deep, deep within the bosom of the sea.   560

As flower blooms or wind blows, the Divine
      Light shines,
Rich or poor, king or peasant, master or
      servant
Are heirs to it, all are measured alike,
By whether they have found the Divine well.
To regard the future with hope, be washed
Through like a muddied trough. To expect a
      house
Sets forces in motion which draw a house
A few months later. Know that in this
      universe
Like attracts like, that if you expect riches
You are a magnet for riches. Yesterday   570
Leads to today, and today determines how
      you live
Tomorrow. Open yourself, and whatever
      you
Expect will come. Know only that filling
Is emptying, and to empty is to fill.

I have lived by trusting in the universe.
We are stewards of what we possess
But we keep nothing.
And whatever we look after well
We keep.
Whatever wives we look after well   580
We keep.
Whatever life we look after well....
                A vine of light....

I am the vine.

We must wait for the fruit to ripen.
A peace has fallen on the tired stars.

             (vii)
The pain in my side....This catch in my
      breaths.

I breathe in hoarse catches
As the sea pants –
I know you.   590
Somewhere the hooded monk waits in the
      shadows.
We must make him welcome.

We must accept this dark that steals over us.
We must cross over. The sea was fresh,
The night cold. Now it is done.
We must compose ourselves, in an inner
      peace,
We must resign ourselves to the going out,
We must not resist our joining together –
Our breath and the infinite, dark waves,
The sea that rolls throughout the trawled-up
      stars.   600
We must give back the breath that poured into
Our hearts and pumped us through what we
      did. It
Is not ours to keep, so we must surrender it
With a good heart. We must not ask
      questions.
We may permit ourselves a sigh, whisper
In candlelight a fond "If otherwise...."
We must not lament, there must be no despair.
We take with us only what we can see
Eyes composed, shut: a round halo of light.

This sunbathing towards the end of night. 610
We will sink together,

Outside, the sun will break over mountains.
Once I saw it over the sea of Corinth....
We have come through this dark night, this
        buffeting.
No pain. No pain. Just a tranquil crossing....

I am filled with power. I am power. Power is
        me.
Such peace!

A sigh.
Like a bird flown away.
Gone.   620

Such
Peace!

4-16 July 1974

VISIONS NEAR THE GATES OF PARADISE

(PART 3 OF SONNETS AND LYRICS FROM A DARK, DARK NIGHT)

1974 – 1975

REMEMBRANCE DAY

Our leaders stand at the cenotaph,
Big Ben strikes eleven.
A boom of guns on the eleventh stroke
Brings in the silence of Heaven.

It is a silence of the heart,
A sweeping up of time
And emptied dustpan. I am at one
With men who died in their prime.

So still we stand till the distant gun,
Then the last post rings out.
As our leaders take up poppy wreaths
I breathe Eternity beneath the sergeant
    major's shout.

10 November 1974

A TRUNK AND A HEART ATTACK

I wrote and told our daughter
"Your trunk to Essex", I told the Bursar
For here in London we have stairs.
What could be clearer?

Then you wrote that it should come here.
Last night the Bursar rang, and now
Her Housemistress, from that boarding-
    school:
"She is confused, and doesn't know

Where to send it." Straightaway, I crumpled,
And all the old sadness drained back.
I felt angry at your "help", I trembled
As if I had had a mild heart attack.

ST. LUCIES DAY

It is our child's birthday, the shortest day
Of the year. You sent a card of usual subtlety.
On pinewood, two fir-cones and a small red
    flower;
Through a hole, a far-off village that looks

Christmasy.

And is it here, I wonder, peering through,
And are you feeling a long way from joy,
You and that other fir-cone, and your red
    flower?
Or do I look through at a German stable boy?

England or Germany? Both are the same
To the stars through the window in this roof.
The ten years we were together are but
The shortest day of the year – these stars are
    the proof.

I sigh and go down to cut the birthday cake:
A house with sweets for windows and
    chocolate doors.
Like the house in that hole in your wooden
    card,
This is now the house where we had our wars.

THE SWING

My Christmas card to you is of a Punjabi
    swing.
On it sits an Indian woman in a chain.
Two others push her and she goes up high.
She will come back, to be pushed again.

My daughter, you are returning to boarding-
    school.
You will wish you could be here longer, that
    you could stay,
But remember, you will surely come back
To be pushed again until your next holiday.

Backwards and forwards goes the swing, up
    and down.
You will soon be swinging yourself – you
    know you can!
Then your pushers will become mere
    watchers, and
You will be as old as this Indian woman!

THE PYRAMID

Each day I add a brick
To a Great Pyramid
That will be finished when I am eighty-five.
I am no invalid.

It is easy to waste time,
Each lesson, a schoolboy
Can doodle and gaze out of the window –
A man can drink his joy.

The wasters have to face
A day of reckoning.   10
Will Stuart and Graham have anything
To show at their beckoning?

So when you do a jigsaw
And are a quarter through,
And one of them says, "You won't finish it,"
Stop your ears. It is untrue.

If you have application
And elaboration, you will win.
Genius is ninety per cent perspiration,
Adding bricks daily in.   20

My way is right for me,
It is how one should live.
The Pyramid is my way of giving
And happiness is to give.

Great men's lives have a beauty
Like a Pyramid-jar.
My love, they have not wasted their precious
        time –
And have a soul like the evening star.

LANTERN

In my daughter's bedroom an ink-drawing,
A simple wash you did – I recognise your
        style.
A Japanese stone lantern in a bamboo garden,
An "Ishi doro" – a "stone torch-basket". I
        smile.

Immediately I slip back a decade
To the afternoons we walked up to Chinzan-so,
Our daughter in her chan-chan coat and pram,
And wandered round the landscaped paths
        below

To the landscaped stream, and the lantern
        there.
I was fascinated, it was my Light. In the
        gloom
It shone out during the firefly hunting –
As you do, now I sit in my room.

HOUSES LIKE TALENTS

I was hard up, and so I decided
I would cast my bread on the waters, put my
        flat
Up for sale. It is the parable of the talents:
Double what you have, do not leave it idle
        and chat

About your misfortune. I have already
        doubled
The storeys of my first flat, and have
        multiplied.
I was invited to dinner in Wandsworth;
On the way I passed a three-storied house
        beside

The Common, and views. Next day I saw over
        it.
There is a large cedar on a rolling lawn,
And a shed for mowers at the end. And so, my
        son,
Perhaps you will toddle to it in your unborn

Memory, as I still do to my grandmother's
        shed,
With its knife-grinder. We must go forward to
        live.
There is a time to contract all to one room,
And to potter round a garden with secateurs
        and a sieve.

THE LOCK

In my desk at school I have a drawer
In which I keep the papers for the Sixth Form
        Mock
Exam. Each time I want to refer to them,
I must take out my keys and turn the lock.

It is loose, I have to rattle the key
Until it finds the right place and opens the
        drawer.
Otherwise it will remain tightly shut.
So it is with you, my divine dark door.

I lie and close my eyes, until sometimes
The key opens the cloud round the shining
    urn
Of my soul. Other times, as now, I try and try,
But no effort will make that black lock turn.

STINGING THE BEEHIVE

On TV tonight there was a film about some
    crooks
Who tortured their rivals, showed contempt
    for human life.
I watched over the *Georgics*. I put order in
    books.

I took my family to the latest James Bond. He
    is worse.
He attacks his fellow men, kicks and punches
    them,
Destroying the harmony of his universe.

I used to admire lives like these: how the
    tough survive,
Their egos. But now, being at one with all,
I have nothing but contempt for these drones
    who sting the beehive.

A KLAEBER AMONG WOMEN

I have been observing twenty-six women
At close quarters, recently. They work for me.
I ask them to do things, and they always obey.
On the woman's mind I am now an authority,

A Klaeber, Ker, Wilamovitz or some such
    scholar.
And so I am all the more mystified
As to why, when so many women do my will
With a smile, you alone were so difficult, and
    defied

Me. At the meeting of the Staff Association
A she-revolutionary tried to force a vote
To abolish the staff signing-in sheet, and was
    outvoted.
She felt humiliated, and fought back, a note

Of defiance in her pride. Perhaps you were
    like her,
Plotting for your honour, inflating a smallness
Into a large issue? Or perhaps, like
This militant, you wanted to make a mess?

POWER LIKE AN OVERCOAT

The Deputy Head is in love with power.
She is greedy to choose, rebuke and probe.
She takes authority very seriously,
Not realising it is a borrowed robe.

For work is a play. The costumes are on the
    pegs,
The actors have been cast in this month's roles.
It could all be different, but that was the way
The parts were handed out in the producer's
    doles.

And so I will wear my robe as loosely
As if it were an open overcoat.
I will take it off when I sit and have coffee,
A trustee for future generations does not
    gloat.

FENCING: TWO SELVES

I turned on the television. It was fencing.
Two masked men stretched and thrust thin
    rapiers,
And I started, for they had small balloons
Tied to their two thighs, two arms, two
    shoulders.

I stared at them, and could not look away,
For who were they, these two masked
    combatants
Trying to prick each other's wobbling
    balloons?
Were they deflating pompous sycophants?

And then I knew that they were symbols for
The two men in me: the real and false twins,
The two eternal forces, Christ and Devil,
With rapiers as alike as two sharp pins.

I lost myself in a mirror, and became
The other me in his fencing pantaloons:
Rebellious, long-haired, anti-Church, pro-
    poor,
He wore left-wing views like yellow balloons.

I found myself again when I gave up drink,
Then I took the side of tradition, and wore
    blue.
And looking in your mirror, do you know
The false mask from the real, identical you?20

NAUGHTING

This evening I read in a book, "When man
Overcomes the desires of the flesh he will
Comprehend all things, even God." I thought
    of Donne.
God "hast not done, /For I have more", until

Ann More died, and the flesh. Then Donne
    was with God.
So it was with me. When I was lustfully
    young
I was in darkness, and a yellow layer
Of liberal, permissive ideas coated my tongue.

But when I escaped you, then I found God.
You pushed me into the flames of a cleansing
Sun by naughting me, so I was nothing
But the reflecting surface above the bubbles
    of His spring.

BABY

This morning my baby cried. I picked him up.
He clung round my neck. I took him to bed
    and
Lay him on the flowered sheet, smiled into his
    eyes.
He goo-ed and clutched and gripped my
    gentle hand.

And then I knew that it was like a strength,
A hand from heaven, that I must become
As blind and clutching as that little boy
And surrender to a hand that left *me* dumb.

I went to the bathroom. I washed and shaved,
I did my exercises, and then I dressed.
And all through breakfast I felt a reverence
For an unseen arm that guided me to what
    was best.

SWINGALONGAMAX

After the travel brochures, you scan the paper,
Looking for plays and films I can take you to.
I see "Swingalongamax" and feel nausea.
This pollution of our language makes me
    want to spew.

"But it's all right for entertainment," you say
As if this off corned beef were fresh roast
    lamb.

I have a soul that needs to be fed properly.
Baked beans make it queasy in its diaphragm.

We live in a country where education
Is no longer valued, except by Asians riding
    their luck.   10
A plasterer earns more than a doctor, the
    theatre caters
For fish and chips, not Aylesbury – or Wild –
    Duck.

We live in a country where "should" has been
    taken off
For the "want" of the lower consciousness.
Starve its desires and the perception changes,
The higher consciousness sees like a
    Marquess.

Max Bygraves! What a vulgar evening,
If "vulgar" means "of the vulgus" – the
    common man!
I am an aristocrat of the spirit,
I will NOT swingalongamax foranywoman. 20

CITY OF DESTRUCTION

I call the School Administration Block
"The City of Destruction" after a church play
Placard I once found under the signing-in
    clock.
My room is "The Celestial City", where the
    delay
Is set to rights. So it is with my life. I live
Within a City of Destruction, and journey to
A Celestial City behind shut eyes. Now I give
Myself to its Light, I reflect the Way through,
"I am that I am." If I follow its instructions,
Which are mirrored in my illumined mind, I
    cannot err.
I, who have been shown all the left-wing
    seductions,
See a "straight and narrow Way", which I
    now prefer.
A shattering thunderclap wakes me: an IRA
    bomb
Reverberates. I am back where I came from.

THE WAY OPENS

I have decided, I will become an MP.
I will tell the truth about our society.
I will make Ciceronian speeches, so all know

That our materialism is from an autumn tree,

Our boredom the detachment of fallen leaves.
The noble theorists of forty-five
Who dreamt of free schools, hospitals, and
spring
Eternal – did they foresee this leaf-strewn
drive?

This grubby selfishness? This gutter lack
Of initiative? Of effort? Once the church we
Knew, and the grammar school, taught how to
climb
The ladder to the HCF. Now the LCD

Is the standard. I will have a constituency
Somewhere in rural Essex or Suffolk,
Preferably Epping Forest, though I will settle
for Suffolk.
Rooted, I will stand for old England, like an
oak.

THE BLIND

An old man with a white stick addresses us
At assembly on the plight of the dark mind
While girls stand at the doors with money
tins.
He says, "Shut your eyes, imagine you are
blind,"

And with a wave of his magic white wand
I am sightless, I sit in a black dark.
Perhaps I should stand and grope towards the
door?
What are these things they call grass, tree,
skylark?

"You can open your eyes now," he says
darkly.
I look out at strange, twisting, wintry trees
And sodden green – I greedily drink them in
For the first time. Glory! Yet what the blind
man sees

Can be a discovered religious life.
If he was hampered with eyes, and has now
spied
The white sun in his soul, whereas those who
see
Are blinded with too much looking outside!

GENERATIONS

I turn on the television. Memory Lane.
Crippsian austerity in post-war streets,
Bevan fighting the doctors. England lost
The Ashes. Each generation repeats

The pattern of the last one in a varied form.
It is like a tree. New buds in the sunlight
Grow into new blossoms, similar to last year's
Though different in quality, texture – blight.

And what of the transitions, the war-victims?
The violent levelling is our winter,
The savage frosts that destroy an old season's
leaves
And make way for new ones. The blossoms
recur.

Now we have been through spring, and have
enjoyed
A summer of golden days. Our leaves lose
their green
And fall. What terrible transition of the
seasons
Lies ahead, to shake this society bare and
clean?

RECURRENCE

So all the history books are wrong, and
history
Is a succession of seasons! And our autumn
Has been before, is like Horace's. This
mystery

Is what makes human nature constant; being
Held within this turning. Hence some periods
attract.
While we are in spring we identify with
spring.

A new time! the revolutionaries declare,
Looking ahead to a golden summer,
Not realising the sun turned gold last year.

So it is with our lives. We turn through spring
to autumn,
To spring. There is a growing time, a
shedding time.
We turn through seasons like that blossoming
plum.

The seasons of history, men recur like leaves.
We recur, each leaf is a new one, like each
body,
But the soul-force, Life, is One. The trunk
conceives.

A SHEIKH IN HIS HAREM

I am like a sheikh with a large harem
Of twenty-six women. Each day I go
To it, choose which is to govern my attention.
I have kept all happy for four months. No

One has left. They line up by my sauna bath, I
recline
On my couch. Each is naked, save for her
towel.
I beckon, in turn each approaches and opens
The folds of her mind like a well-pronounced
vowel.

Yet it is not like this when I am there.
To work with women is not as it might seem;
Women by themselves do not act or pretend,
In their sexless atmosphere, my harem
remains a dream.

SOUTHWARK CATHEDRAL

I walk round the Cathedral. At the front
The altar-screen shows statues of saints in
niches.
I see the tombs of Gower, and Bishop
Andrewes,
The Bunyan window. I revere these cultural
riches.

On the fifteenth century roof there are bosses
With medieval faces, of Gluttony and
Lying and other sins. This place connects me
With past generations, who have banned

The easy, unreal values. I must accept
This ground that guards the illumined silence,
This saintly quiet of the aisle and retro-
chair,
Which contains the reality of traditional
excellence.

GOD

I was like a child
Who had, and wanted to keep, a harmful toy.

God took it away, like a watchful parent
Granting only what is good for a little boy.

The one great Mind
Feeds my feelings and all Nature's many
forms,
The trees and ponds of the Forest, which my
feelings heed
To express their power, like air-clearing
thunderstorms.

There is a Spirit
In the universe which pulses in man's heart
And nature, and links both. This Providence
moves
My intuition, removes me from danger at the
start.

ELECTRICITY

As I walk back up Gloucester Road, I am
held
From floating into the sky by gravity.
Atmospheric pressure prevents me from
exploding.
These invisible forces, like electricity,

Are of the Eternal. I climb the stairs to my
flat.
My son is lying on his front, sucking his
dummy.
I hold his hand, he clutches and grips.
I sit him up – without me he would still be on
his tummy.

I am like a child. I petulantly cry
For what I want, for what brightens me. God's
hand
Has kept me from worthless fame, from
vainglory
Which would have fused and soldered in the
self that will withstand

His power, when it should have replaced
itself.
I have wanted the applause of men, and He
humbled me.
Now I have smashed the self in my socket,
like a dud bulb,
And my new self conducts His Power like my
lamp's electricity.

BACKWARD IMAGES

I enter the English Speaking Union,
Climb marble stairs to a Regency room,
    seeking,
Below the rich ceiling, the hearth's sphinx
    wings,
The team from my school, which will fight in
    public speaking.   10

Our three girls march to the front. Nervous,
    Madam
Chairman launches the African speaker, who
    flanks
Her rehearsed salvo with smiles, and repels
    questions.
Then our Belfast lass attacks with the Vote of
    Thanks.

Four more schools skirmish. Then the judges
    confer.
We troop out for an interval of orange juice.
Then we are shown slides of American
School life with a commentary. We sit in a
    truce.

Louisiana. Each still evokes a scene
One I had half-forgotten must have known.
A faint unease stirs in my detached peace
As if I had been wakened by some Hellish
    moan.

Suddenly the slide jumps back, and back
    again.
Time is in reverse, but the commentary goes
    on.
Click. Back. Click. Back. The audience titters.
Backward images and a forward descrip-
    tion.   20

So it is with my living. I talk forwards
At school, make plans, travel into the future,
While all my images are Hellish, backward
    ones,
Ghostly feelings click-clicking back in
    miniature.

SEED

Fourteen years ago I took an aeroplane
From Baghdad to Basrah. It was a night flight.
An idea came to me: two hundred poems....

I scribbled a title, made notes on what I would
    write.

Now I have written them, though that title
Applies to a work that is still to come.
Two books wrapped up together as in a seed,
Two plans as in a stone: two years' blossoms
    on a plum.

We are born with destiny inside our heads,
Wrapped up in Light. It will split and begin to
    grow
By "education", or "leading out". God has
    planted
Instructions for each year's blossoms in the
    cherry-stone's flow

And the sperm's. Our choices further this
    Divine plan.
Unconsciously. We go abroad, or lose a wife,
To bring its encasing seed to stemhood and
    flower.
O wonderful planned purpose in each being's
    life!

CHERRY BLOSSOM

When I walk to the post I look at the cherry
    blossom.
Each petal is back to back with another
And grows in clusters, like the family
That grew in a cluster round my mother.

The family is the unit of society,
The bud, the blossom, then the ripened fruit.
All growth, ambition, behaviour, hard work
Are nurtured there, through society's great root.

The values we revere in our Britain
Can be found on a single twig: work,
    thrift,   10
Responsibility. We must not make it harder
For the fruit to grow, we must not allow men
    to shift

Blossoms from one branch to another, to
    group
Them in "communes" or mix them up in
    "classes".
We must see our generation as one year's
    crop,

It drops its fruit, is pruned, and quietly passes.

The present generation is not more important
Than the last one or the next one. We are
    uncrowned
Guardians of our heritage, trustees of the
    future.
We must hand on the Britain we have
    found   20

And improved, short of drastic change. In my
    new garden
The cedar has a preservation order, to prevent
Future "owners" from chopping it down. We
Are stewards, not owners, of the present.

SUNDAY

Once Sundays were boring. I played cricket
Against my mother's wishes, till girls tempted
    me.
A friend ironically sent me a letter
c/o The Lord's Day Observance Society.

But now I like to be quiet on a Sunday,
To sit and let go in the afternoon, feel the
    Light
Unfold in my heart like the petals of a white
    rose
Of the kind I wore for Speech Day. Then I
    write.

I like quiet now. I have won myself back.
My emotional prison sentence is now done.
This morning the Gates of Hell clanged wide
    open
And I was filled with Paradise, like a blinding
    sun.

MAN AND NATURE: RENEWAL

I see a film of a bushman in Africa.
Naked, barefooted, he squats in scrub he
    braves
As if he were Adam in Paradise.
His ancestors drew beasts on the walls of
    caves.
Spiders, insects, zebras, rhinoceri –
Each have their special place and meaning in
    life
To him. The bushman has a reverence
For the unity between man and Nature. Strife

Came with the European, who brought guns
And taught the animals to fear and abhor
This two-legs who had lost contact with
    himself
And who therefore unloosed the First World
    War.

An African elephant leaves its herd to die,
The moon, dying, will be renewed again.
Man, dying, feeds his sister vultures, and
Will be renewed in next year's recurrent
    grain.

PROVIDENCE LIKE A PENTAGRAM

In the car I ponder whether I should write
To an ex-Minister on this eve of the Party's
    election.
I climb the stairs and Margaret is on the sofa.
I tell her. "It is Providence," she says, on
    reflection,

"I had to come. There is no accident."
She listens. Ahead, where my future began,
A signpost points to this moment. "Send it,"
    she says,
Of my essay, "for it tells him the truth, this
    man

Who wants power over others, whose doctrine
Is not to serve God, but to advance his 'I',
Himself, who speaks from his head instead of
    his heart.
And when it is posted, don't think about it.
    Never try,

For if it doesn't happen, it wasn't meant
For you anyway. You are protected from what
    is bad."
And I feel like a child wearing a crucifix
In a Black Mass pentagram, an "endless
    knot". And I am glad.

BLACK SHOES, BLUE SOCKS

I drive to school through rain. I will be late,
Will I receive a cross against my name,
Be shown up? In Magdalen Road I slow
Before a car with an open door, and exclaim –

For then I see it – at the shape in the wet

Under a yellow blanket, black shoes, blue
    socks
Peeping out under the open door. A man
With a nervous grin waves me round by the
    pillarbox.

I glance down. The head is covered. I know
Only these black shoes and blue socks, like a
    stranger
In the tube I have passed him and left him –
Like a girl at a large school who did not tell
    her danger.

CARE

How much do you like your expensive
    boarding-school?
Is it "all right"? Or do the second years
Push you over – albeit politely –
And are you bored on Sundays, do you give
    way to tears?

O my daughter, if only you could live with
    me
In that big house with the garden, attend
    school
Each day, then I could protect you from the
    coloured
Bullies, be on hand to warn them with
    ridicule.

But can that ever be? Even if I sell
This flat and move, will the good school be
    there?
I would not wish my school on you – the
    noise,
The pushing and coloured swearing, the lack
    of care.

ROBBERY

My daughter saw a robbery today.
Waiting for her grandmother near a mini
She saw a man loiter, try the door, look
At her, stand back and wait. He was skinny

With ginger hair. Then, fed up, he wrenched
    the door,
Smashed a window, bent in, snatched a suit-
    case,
And ran off towards Gloucester Road Station.
A simple form of evil, there was no chase.

My daughter, you will have to learn that Satan
Has far subtler wiles than this petty theft.
You will learn that evil can be an attractive
    doctrine,
Like the smile of a retiring leader, before he
    left.

C SHARP, F SHARP

I stroke the Autoharp, a burred echo
From thirty-two twanged strings. From each
    chord I know
It is a woman's soul. I stroke softly,
Listen to the pure echo.

She strums and makes a cacophanous noise.
A twanging whine. I know from each
    thrumming chord
It is her soul. She throws its weight around,
Irritated, and bored.

Like the souls today
The Autoharp
Has a limited scale:
C sharp, F sharp.

THE VALENTINE

Again you intrude after calm letters
This Valentine's Day: "I have sworn an affida-
-vit, you are a year's maintenance in arrears,
You will be summonsed to Court and made to
    pay."

And this after you promised that if I paid
The school fees, I need not send a monthly
    cheque,
And I have paid six hundred pounds this year
To your nothing, and sail like a certain wreck,

And I have fed and clothed her in the
    holidays –
You have not even seen her since last
    summer.
Why did you not write and tell me how you
    felt
Before you rushed to sink me, like a late-comer

At "Battleships"? Are you hard up, now your
    husband
Has taken a pay cut? Or do you resent my
    new son?

And is this your revenge on your Valentine?
O strange mysterious heart of a woman!

EVIL LIKE HURDLES

So you are back. Having been carpeted
And threatened with immediate dismissal,
You have taken me to Court on another pretext,
Hoping, perhaps, that I will speak my
    downfall.

But I know your weakness! Carlotta resents
Me, blames me for spoiling her married life
    with you.
She feels I argued something out of it,
And *she* erects these hurdles. It is quite
    untrue,

Yet she sent my son bootees with wasps on
    them,
To sting. She is trying to make life difficult.
There is nothing for it but to jump *this* fence.
I will do it, for I am protected from the
    Occult.

I have a new attitude towards your malice.
I see it as a trial to test me, a gift which
    should
Make me more patient. And so I say to your
    Satan,
"'Resist not evil, but overcome evil with
    good.'"

IF

If I were a secret agent, and were doing
Fantastic things – recruiting an East European
Scientist – and you knew, and said I was
    fantasising
And that you would take me to Court as a
    make-believe man
To "prove" that I am not a fit father
For my child, so that my only way out of your
    duel
Would be to quote the Official Secrets Act,
    kill myself rather –
If you had done all this, then you could still
    not have been more cruel.
And if my masters had warned you to keep
    silent,
Through your employers, or they would get
    rid

Of you, and if, to make me suffer, you had
    gone ahead
And thrown away your career in a destructive
    moment,
If you had done this, then you could not be
    more stupid
Than you are now, taking me to Court. There
    is no suffering for the illuminated.

THE SUMMONS

Now I await the summons. Where will I be
When it is put in my hand? And I think, "God
Gives us good things, why should He not also
    give us
Evil?" Did he not take Carlotta to prod

Me to my Night of Sense, passive purgation,
When I was purified, so I could purge
Myself, deny myself alcohol? Until now
This Night of the Spirit has been His latest
    scourge

And testing time, so my self can be stripped
Of the undivine. So it is with this sum-
    mons.   10
Perhaps it has been sent as a calling,
So I may be exalted through humiliations.

If so, it is a gift, and I thank you Carlotta,
I will not write angrily, for you are an agent
Of the Divine. Now more than ever my soul
    needs
A director who knows the mystical ascent.

If I were in an Order, I would go to the Abbot,
A man learned in the mysteries of the
    medieval search.
To be going on with, I have the blessed
    Margaret.
Where can I find a pastor, if outside the
    Church?   20

LIFE

The setting sun feeds the apple orchard
Where birds peck, that will kill grubs in the
    wheat
From which yokels walk home under windfall
    stars.
In this basket of atmosphere, all have enough
    to eat.

An accident of gravity, that life
Should have these conditions, so it can
    survive?
No, life depends on nothing. It created
These conditions to fulfil its will to strive!

And this is the hidden law, which the scientist
    misses.
Life creates matter to fulfil its good.
The electrical mind, the electrons in our
    bodies
Work together in a way we have not
    understood.

When we die we experience the Majesty
And Power of God, the Uncreated Light.
Unpurified souls are consumed, the pure
Shine with the divine sun in that creative
    night.

PARADISE

I sit serene, and read the Sunday papers.
I am at peace, without queries or quibbles.
This is surely Paradise, the state of mind
Man lost with his Fall from the Beatific; and
    scribbles

From illumined manuscripts, which he lacks
    knowledge
To return to in our decayed time, and so
    searches.
The Way is pointed in the writings of the
    mystics,
Yet these are not taught in schools or in our
    churches.

Instead we are asked to contribute pence
To social causes, the hungry, the poor, the
    Hindu –
All in Christ's name. And the Light of the
    Bible
Is allowed to flicker out, save in the hearts of
    the few.

Paradise. It is a labyrinth we have
To find our way back through. I did not know
    this
When I sat down before the Gates of Hell,
Waiting for them to open to this maze, this
    bliss.

VICTORIA STATION

I had to go through Hell to reach Paradise.
It was like entering the Grosvenor Hotel
Through the swing doors – what fallen I once
    met there! –
And walking through to the Victoria Station
    Hell

Where people rush past the departure board
Going nowhere, their mouths twisted with
    pain.
It was like queueing five years at the booking
    windows.
When your ticket is clipped at the gates, you
    can board the train.

I had to be lost in the Devil's Chelsea to win
Salvation. There was no other way to bring on
The Night of Sense, and purify my soul
So that I could know the Beatific Vision.

Hell and Paradise; it is not either-or
But both-and, or, rather, one and therefore
The other; the ticket office and the train.
Now I am on my Way, I know it would be
    worth paying more.

THE RUIN

This stone church is decaying, a ruin.
The House of God and gladness has not been
    made new.
Is the Light to be entombed in this relic?
See, the grass and bramble come bursting
    through!

We are no longer living in a Christian
Society. A minority profess
The Faith. I will leave the city for the country
Where the wind and the sea make me feel my
    smallness

And, through flowers and fruit, the greatness
    of God.
I need someone to direct my soul; a priest....
Not that Minister who drives a bus to "make
    contact",
What does he know of when my sunlight last
    ceased?

Cathedral cloisters are quiet places,

But there is peace in this country pond's
    looking-glass.
Cathedrals are built of standards and past
    beauty
But give me a heart like these sprouting tufts
    of grass!

HEADSTONE OF THE TEMPLE

I close my eyes and listen to the preacher
Say: "'The stone which the builders rejected,
The same is become the head of the corner.'"
And then I know I must not feel dejected.

A line I discard from one poem becomes
The headstone of the temple of the next one.
The Light I rejected while I built my body
Is the corner-stone of the new life I have
    begun.

Now every loss appears as a blessing,
This taking away of the world arrays me in
    Light.
I accept all adversities, have learned
    obedience,
And so for me all suffering has ended, like my
    Dark Night.

SPRING CLEANING
(DIVINE SONNET)

Prayer works like this: a man contacts God
    through
His superconscious mind, where all thoughts
    and
Feelings become a reality, all habits too.
Negative ones make mess, piles of secondhand
Clothes, plastic bags; positive ones in that "I"
Of the "soul" make a springcleaned daily life.
The Light can hoover, cleanse and purify
That room of its negative clutter – jealousies,
    strife,
Resentments, lusts, fears – wash it clean until
Love, tenderness, goodness, mercy from the
    Fountain
Of life are thankful in the face of evil,
Transform it into order, master its chaotic
    pain.
"I gave men weaknesses that they may
    become strong...."
Love God, and you will quicken and renew
    the body that has gone wrong.

THE NOW
(DIVINE SONNET)

The superconscious mind works in the now,
Which is the Eternal, the ever-present.
Belief, like hope, is future, makes a vow,
But faith drinks from the spring of the present
    moment
Whose bubbles are as much Eternity
As all last week's, next month's in a time-old
Consciousness. Only in the now can we
Sip the healing waters of the spring, and be
    made bold.
When I, at peace, discard all thoughts of time
Before or after, ask for a fulfilment
Now and give thanks that my request has been
    heard,
I leave it to God to work out the paradigm,
The paradox of a bubble made verbal and
    sent,
To attend on Eternity is to attend on the now:
    the Word.

POEMS LIKE VASES

I shape poems as potters shape vases,
Letting the form give rise to the ideas.
The pictures I paint on them enshrine truths
    and moments.
Should I hawk them on a tray and cry my
    wares?

Poems wheeled specially for poetry readings
Are full of mannered attitudes and showing
    off.
Such self-advertisements are not wrung out
Of deep feeling or despair. No wonder we all
    scoff!

And if not specially made, they may not
Lend themselves to public declamation.
Is a vase to be thrust at you from a platform
Without your walking round it, your quiet
    cogitation?

Donne, Hopkins wrote for themselves, and
    were not sold
Until after their death. The best poetry's
    joys
Are not moulded for public performance,
Like my Victorian vase with skipping white
    boys.

PILGRIMS' PAVEMENT
(IN CANTERBURY CATHEDRAL)

From the gardens, the structure impresses me.
It is solid, in proportion, perspective,
Towers balanced in stone; expressed beauty:
All arts built together with one objective –

Architecture, stained glass, sculptures in
    niches –
To serve God. What energy, what vision!
Inside, I follow the path great Chaucer took
Past the cloister door where the knights
    rushed their decision

And the base of the wall where Becket fell.
I climb the polished steps to the Trinity
    Chapel   10
Where the Shrine of St. Thomas stood until
Henry the Eighth destroyed it. There I dwell

On the polished ridge where countless
    pilgrims kneeled.
The stones in the pavement are worn by
    revering pairs
Of feet: the zodiac roundels by the mosaic
Of a world in a mandala of circled squares.

In each month someone is doing something.
February, warming hands, March digging.
    Since
April is pruning I lament a tradition
Between the tombs of Henry the Fourth and
    the Black Prince.   20

Above the Black Prince is a painting of God
On a rainbow of gold. This is how they
Saw Him, those medievals, controlling
The universe. And they were right! Today

How wrong we are, with our science, our
    rockets
To the moon, what our glassy architecture has
    cost!
Let us preserve this pavement of the past
As a living symbol of all that we have lost.

A WAKING

We sit in a Chinese restaurant in Folkestone.
We are the only couple. The waiter plays
Beatle records to fill the silence, and hide

His rustles; sad songs from my former days.

I am transported back to Libya, where
In a quiet similar to this, I sat alone
And heard on the radio a nurse say, "This
    record
Is for a friend with whom I wish to condone."

All Western civilisation is a filling-in
Of silence with mechanical artifice.
We forget and are deluded, we only wake
When we travel to graveyards as quiet as this.

A BOILING SEA

I park on the East Cliff and walk to the square
Pyramid where the telescope stood. Here
I first saw France when I was eight, a thin
Ribbon of cliff as the Cross-Channel boat
    nosed in.

The lens I looked through as a child has been
Taken away. But that peaceful childhood
    scene
Surely remains. On the side, a notice states,
"It magnified twenty diameters." It inflates

A mere part. "First point the telescope
    carefully,"
It says, "at the object you wish to see."   10
There are sights for accuracy. "Press button
    and release."
Then, to enlarge out of context, "Look
    through eyepiece."

At night observe the moon." With adult gaze
I scan the harbour. In a seething haze
A boat dips in turmoil. Like scalded
    flamingoes
Cranes wade away from where the sea boils
    and flows.

THE KEEP
(ON AN ANNIVERSARY)

My love, I was surprised when you gave me
Two books and a card for our first
    Anniversary.
They were on my pillow in our room in
    Margate
When I came back from the bathroom last
    night, late.

Now we are driving back to London. I sit
On Birchington cliff: rocks and a calm sea, lit
By the sun. There are no shops to buy flowers
Or a card, so accept these lines on what is ours.
Yesterday we walked round Dover Castle's
keep.
Our marriage is like that fortress, with a deep
Well; a drawbridge to keep out; and the
chimney shell
Of the Pharos by the church that can still
dispel
Darkness with Light. We will return – I
swear –
To Thanet, buy a "keep" on the front. The sea
air
That waves in these daisies now, and blades
of grass,
Will wave in our son's hair before his
looking-glass.

SEED OF GOD
(DIVINE SONNET)

The pulpit, cross and pews are outer forms.
To comprehend God through these is to lie
Dormant like an egg, be unquickened by
The awakening embryoed germ, which
transforms;
Be a shell while the germ is lifeless. Man's
outside norms
Do not wake his inner forces to the supply
Of food, that he may fulfil his destiny.
Like an acorn, he awaits the sun that warms.
But when the Light shines from the personal
search
Down the inward path, like a chestnut made
alive
The seed quickens: the nut, the silver birch.
The immaculate conception is the rive
Of the divinely implanted seed. Do they say
in church,
"Man is the container of the seed of God's
drive"?

THE SACRIFICE
(DIVINE SONNET)

I had to break my heart. The broken, wide-
Opened heart has seen smashed the shell-like
seal
Of arrogance, hardness, self-will and pride
Which closed and froze its heart-centre, its feel-

-ings. In its split covering, it melts with
love
Out of which are released fulfilling rays of
Light
Which quicken the seed to its destiny. Like a
foxglove
It sprouts with its purpose, even in the darkest
night.
My heart had to be broken, and the Way
You broke it was as good as any. My sacrifice
Of my worldly "wants" was all I had to pay
For growth, all life being holy. A small price.
Darkness and pain have their place in the
scheme of things,
Bringing alive in the heart now seeds, now
saplings.

THE PURPOSE OF LIFE
(DIVINE SONNET)

I became a poet on a wooden seat
At school, one March that was as hot as May,
Reading on Lower Field, dreaming in the heat.
I was not made praefect so I could take this
Way
Of my destiny. Later, I left Law for Literature.
I did not know what to search for, for what
insight.
I hunted for clues abroad, in the Eastern
culture;
In Japan I was briefly quickened by a Light
I only saw in full when I had lost my heart.
My search was over. I had found. It is the law
Of all lives, that seeds quicken by Light or
choke.
A life-centre for his embryo, divine part,
Man bears the fruit of the Vine. It is either-or,
Either he stays an acorn, or he quickens to an
oak.

DE-FROSTING

I open the fridge door: great slabs of ice
Bulge round the top compartment, where the
three
Ice-trays are. I unplug the switch and pour
A scalding kettle on the chunks near me,

Then hack and gouge with a knife. They crash
below.
One slithers across the floor. I am like this
fridge.

I keep, deep-frozen, in a separate compartment
Images that freeze into blocks of language.

They solidify by themselves. They fill the sink.
The fridge is clear. I switch on, and indulge
In a peep. A frost has begun. So it is with me.
Each minute I ice up moments, until they
　　bulge.

　　　　　　　　　　　　　　　2 March 1975

AT-ONE-MENT
(DIVINE SONNET)

When we are purified by love and Light
The conscious and superconscious become
　　one.
In this at-one-ment we gain inner sight.
Spiritual being stems from the seed of
　　Perfection,
The "pearl beyond price", and the powers of
　　God, liberated,
Are released like seed into the life of their
　　creator.
Body, mind and soul become co-ordinated,
Man becomes an energised generator,
And, loving his brother for what he was
　　intended
To become – That! – he recognises the divine
Workmanship of the Creator in all he sees,
Exulting in the leaves, birds, breeze he
　　comprehended
Before. But nothing is as perfect as one man,
　　whose spine
And seedcase contain more glory than the
　　seven seas.

THE CALL
(DIVINE SONNET)

This evening I heard a voice. It said, "Go
And bring the sects together, unify my
　　Church,
And when you have done this, prune its
　　branches so
That you restore purity to the Mystic search.
My Church is guardian of the spiritual
　　'ought',
Not a house full of idols and decayed stone."
It was a call like Samuel's, and at first I
　　thought
"Not I." Then I remembered Saul, St. Joan,
And I picked up a pen and spontaneously

Wrote, "Campaign for Church Reform." So
　　now must I
Press Pope and Archbishop, do what since
　　Henry
The Eighth and Luther no man has done:
　　unify?
Why I have been chosen I do not know,
But this incredible energy says I must do so.

THE WAY REALLY OPENS
(TO AN M.P.)

You have not written back, that is bad for an
　　M.P.
But I do not care: politics are on an outer
　　plane,
Unlike religion. It has come to me – it was
　　given –
I will press for the Church to be One again,

To be reunited after fifteen hundred years
Of sectarian disunity: the Byzantine,
Henry, Luther, Calvin. I will start a campaign
With an office and telephone, I will combine

All the churches in Britain, till there is One
　　Church
In Europe, one rock, so that all our young　10
Will not be confused by different
　　denominations,
And I will teach the Mystic ladder, rung by
　　rung.

I will teach men that they are seeds waiting
To be shone upon by Light, and resurrected
Into growth. No egalitarian view,
This distinction between acorn and oak, when
　　perfected.

There are two lives. Journalism, politics,
Immediacy, are of the outer one.
Art, poetry, religion are inner, universal,
I must be general. The particular I must
　　shun.　　　　　　　　　　　　　　20

So, Right Honourable Member, stow your
　　politics!
I will bring in an historical idea
That will outlast your ephemeral policies
And live for hundreds of years after *you* were
　　here.

CHURCH LIKE A TREE

If I visit the Archbishop of Canterbury
And say to him, "You should join forces with all
Churches, we do not accept the difficulties,"
And if he should accept my words as a Divine call,

If he should listen to me and then reflect –
As the previous Archbishop once did, apparently,
Reading some words I wrote, changing his mind –
Then there may be a new philosophy,

For the young can choose: materialism or Mysticism,
A simple either-or. Europe will set
Up one political State, and now one Church.
The Cathedral will stand for Mysticism yet!

I am a bud on the Mystic tradition
Which the Church once did and should embody.
I do not belong to any sect alone:
The Church is one: the trunk *and* branches of a tree.

THE WIND THAT BLOWETH

Inspiration is a "breathing into"
Like the Wind that bloweth where it listeth.
The mysterious Spirit that blows through all
Ripples my suprasensual self with its breath.

The Spirit of my Muse is the same Spirit
That flows through the universe, and fills my heart
With high tides of Light when I open my harbour.
The power that makes me a mystic gives me a poet's art.

I am a testifier to a Being
Infinitely vaster than myself, who
Has a Beauty I meet by chance sometimes
In my superconscious mind, where I keep a rendezvous.

THE SPIRAL WHIRL
(DIVINE SONNET)

There is a spiral everywhere I look, in which life flows:
The hair on a baby's brow, a snail's coiled shell,
Sunflower seeds round the yellow centre, a harebell,
Gurgling water is a vortex, the heart of a rose,
Our galaxy – this Catherine-wheel what glows,
This gas and dust. Tornadoes, the cochlea, both tell
What spiders' webs, pine-cones, a stone in a well
Rippling, fingerprints, dervishes all disclose.
All share the same movement as my winding soul,
Circling upwards in the ziqqurat of my darkness,
Spiralling up to the white point of my North Pole.
The cosmic whirl is a continual spiral within mess,
Patterns are formed and dissolved without end. So it is with events:
There is a spiralling web of energy, a whirl of Providence.

WOMEN LIKE THE WIND

I have worked with women, and can now profess:
They are so discreet and nice at keeping us in the dark,
But they take something small, some trivial remark,
And blow it up into a big fire, until the fierceness
Is out of proportion. Responsibility fills them with stress
For they worry. They need to be ruled, yet rustle through the bark;
Dominated, so they can feel their feminine spark.
We men blow up and forget our tempestuousness,
But they fan with long-drawn-out moanings. If unheeded,
They plot and set traps with lulls, and if we are taken in

We are "soft": your eye-shadow, your smile
    sinned,
You want influence, security: and to be needed,
To feel appreciated. And so, after all these
    women,
I find you two were typical: like the wind!

A KYRIELLE AT EASTER

God gave His only son to us,
His grief must have been enormous.
I lost a child, and therefore know
The grief God felt must have been so.

God is sovereign and will permit
Things to happen if they are fit.
"I do not want to die, forego
That child, that woman, be rejected so,"

We say, but God wants the best for
Us, not what we think is best, nor   10
Does He pander, He will say "No,"
Like a father, or "You are so

Impetuous, are not ready."
After pain, I see his steady
Hand in every detail. I go
To Him with problems, He says so.

The grave is a door to the next room,
There is a place beyond the tomb.
I trust, and this Easter, I know
I too will rise, He tells me so!   20

A SIXTY-FOUR THOUSAND POUND RUIN

The London years are nearing an end. Oak-
    trees
Call me. And since no Forest can be compare-
-d with Epping Forest, it must be there,
I thought, for I cannot forget what my heart
    sees.
I found a Hall with a ballroom and thirteen
    bedrooms.
        These
I would let. I would live in the library, above
    Warren Hill, shar-
-ing the cost with my mother. I escaped that
    air
Once, but it has proved too strong for me, that
    swishing breeze.

We viewed the inside. We walked through the
    huge hall
And a glance showed it is a ruin, neglected
    and
Crumbling for twenty years: floor up, damp
    wall,
Rotted wood, and so cold! I would need thirty
    thousand
To put it in order. Sadly we leave. I cannot be
The Poet of Epping Forest in this marbled
    luxury.

THE WINDMILL

She brought you a windmill to stick
In your pram as you go shopping.
The wind whirls red and yellow sails,
They will whirl for ever without stopping.

In a real windmill if the wind blows,
The sails and axle turn to grind
Fat ears of corn, the ripe seeds we
Put between stones, as in a mind.

The wind bloweth where it listeth,
As I push you in your pram I start
And feel the wind blowing through my hair,
Grinding ripe moments in my heart.

THE NEWLY DEAD

I thought that I had died and joined a crowd
Of newly dead who were milling round the lift
At Gloucester Road Station. A porter bowed
Us in, we stood and descended. I sniffed
The badness in the men around me. They
    were still,
But when we reached the bottom we
    disgorged through
Black gates, and hurried down chambered
    tunnels until
We reached the platform. There a black wind
    blew.
I sat on a bench and began to wonder
What concentration camp we were heading for.
So this is what it is like to pass over,
I thought, as the ghostly tube rushed in. I
    abhor
Sitting opposite souls in overcoats, those
    decay-
-ing men who reviewed their lives as we
    rattled away.

SCULPTORS
(DIVINE SONNET)

If I close my eyes and picture a child at his
 best,
Say, "Father, this is how you want your child
 to be,
Please send your Holy Spirit now through me
And make him be happy, peaceful and rest-
-ful, thank you, because I believe, so be my
 request,"
And hold the picture in my mind of a happy
Child, in less than a minute what I see
Will happen. We are sculptors who are blessed
With being cast in God's mould. We can
 create
Like God, quieten anger to peace. So it is with
 those
Who forgive. You will be healthier after one
 nod
From me, your resentments will go, that
 aggravate
Peace. I will sculpt your virtues. Life flows
Through us to man and beast, and back to us
 from God.

FORGIVENESS LIKE A GARDENER
(DIVINE SONNET)

If I make a picture in my mind of a Christ in a
 frame
And then see a person who has done me
Wrong, place the picture of him on the effigy
Of Christ, and says, "I forgive you in the
 name
Of Christ, and I give thanks to God because
 you came
To be forgiven, so be it," then he is, not by me
But by Him. And if I do not question this free
Forgiveness but give thanks that this is so,
 tame-
-ly trusting God, not my feeling, the old
 thought-
Habit will soon die, as if I pulled up a whole
Shrub by its roots, scattering earth; the dislike
 will soon go,
The parched plants in that garden can be wat-
-ered. I must become a gardener and weed my
 soul,
And forgive to let these two parched roses
 grow.

LIGHT LIKE THE OCEAN
(DIVINE SONNET)

The body is energy, through which the sun
Shines, the X-ray. The body is made of Light,
We are children of Light. If we close our gills
 tight
And breathe less life, we stagnate and harden
Into "old age", decay into "illness" like a stun-
-ned fish. The cure is more Light. The prayer
 that even slight-
-ly forgives and brings peace also releases
 recondite
Health, relaxes, stimulates the circulation.
The salt of the earth has no flavour, it fortifies
The natural goodness it meets. If we all grasp
This and live right, no one will war. With
 devotion
The Kingdom of God can come on earth.
 Otherwise
We are like fish who have closed their gills
 and gasp,
Or sponges who do not know they are filled
 with the ocean.

PERHAPS LIKE A BUTTERFLY

Perhaps we see our whole life in a moment,
Then perhaps we appear as ghosts, then lose
 consciousness,
Lose our perception for ever, and are
 dispossess-
-ed of our thought and will for now, our souls
 dormant
As a butterfly in a chrysalis. Perhaps we are
 sent
Into a death-struggle between selves, perhaps
 we repress
The lower self, which becomes a shell, and
 progress
To dim consciousness and memory in a
 present
Which can only now be attracted to a séance.
Perhaps we flutter into Heaven and live in a
 dream
In which the scenes of our life all turn out well,
Then perhaps we go unconscious for a new
 entrance
And come again – and we met by a Roman
 stream.
Perhaps, for who can know? Who has
 returned to tell!

SWALLOWTAIL BY THE STREAM
(DIVINE SONNET)

I used to believe that we could open
A living skull, plug in electrodes that would
   be
Attached to a machine like an EEG,
Monitor twenty places in the mind of a citizen
And prove that thought and the brain's
   electrical en-
-ergy are related in the cells. This would see
The end of religion, I thought. It would
   incontrovertibly
Prove that nothing survives death. Only self-
   will then....
What foolish thoughts! What blindness of the
   brain!
For now I know that the lock-gate self is the
   obstacle,
That the power of God flows in and fills our
   springs
Of soul. I even believe we may come again,
After a chrysalis sleep and the miracle
Of a dream, and such swallowtail angel's
   wings!

HOSTAGES FROM THE BRIDGE

You are like a bridge to me, like a brass
Version of this Shoreham hump-back between
   my
Two lives: one of village streets, a pub
   where I
Was lost, of people and wine on the grass,
The other of quiet, a solitary beach. I pass
Back from here. I had an ideal world to
   rely
On – she and her – and now I have lost them,
   I try
To recreate them in your shop-window glass
With him, like fishing for the reflection of a
   star.
My love, please understand I celebrate you
In what the windows show. You are like this
   bridge,
On this silver water those moments are
Like a graveyard of crosses. They are moored
   to view,
Each mast captured from the flow of time,
   held hostage.

A JOYFUL SOB

On this summer Sunday
Like an altar boy
The sun dazzles in blue.
I feel a joy.

As a gnat rests on a stream,
I rest on God.
As we drift through Hereford Square
See plenty nod.

Fruit trees are blossoming,
Catkins throbbing.
Green lilac shoots and birds:
Joyfully sobbing!

CIRCUIT
(DIVINE SONNET)

I am a pipe. Through me, like a conduit,
Flows the water of life. I am like a lake
With a source and outlet. What I receive, what
   I take
Must flow out and return as a circuit,
Like electricity along a wire. It
Must be given, or I become stagnant, and
   make
Myself unhealthy. If I light a bulb and break
A wire so what comes in cannot be remitt-
-ed, the bulb breaks, the current cannot enter.
If the wire terminates, the current ceases.
To go on receiving is to go on giving:
Praying, healing, helping, it does not matter
So long as the power of love passes, and
   increases
The heart's tenderness which is everlasting.

APPLES ON AN INVISIBLE TREE
(DIVINE SONNET)

Perhaps we are apples on an invisible tree,
And when one asks the branch for help for
   another
The sap flows. There is a something that vicar
Channels in his church, an inflowing energy,
In the laying-on-of-hands, so that blind men
   see.
What is this supernormal galvaniser
That is trapped by a selfless, conducting
   healer
Whose fingers burn the head and every wea-

-kened joint, charge them with life, like a car
    battery?
The pulse in us can be intensified at its root
So that leukaemia, gangrene go, are heal-
-ed, colour comes back, like sap flowing very
Quickly through a twig to a bruised brown
    fruit.
What is this life that pours into me, which I
    cannot feel?

SPLINTERS IN THE FLESH

I have splinters in my flesh, picked up I do
    not
Know where from the rough wood of Hell.
    They are lodged in
My fingers, old lines like chips of metal, or
    the spot
Spikes of a sea-urchin that broke off in my
    skin
In Catania, puncturing my sole like a junkie.
There is "Kneel to the proud lily" or "love
    like a rosebud",
Or, "I thought the midday sun sank in the
    sea";
And, "In fleeing Light, blood-flecked, the
    crimson flood-
Lake flames, in a star-sadness darkened; our
    strange
Solitude and shames." Now I needle from this
    bruise
"An eye-sorrowing fixation is not enough to
    change
A world", and "To have a vision in an ooze
Of slime", and "The snail scrubs straight the
    path so straight".
From what smooth wooden *shawabti* they
    must originate!

A VISION NEAR THE GATES OF PARADISE
(DIVINE SONNET)

Hell is a dungeon like Wandsworth prison,
With a portcullis and gate clock. How many
    know
Paradise is a Cathedral a sun shines on?
We are admitted through studded doors, below
Statues of saints, to the sunshaft under a rose-
Window, where God sits in the centre. Bright
Planets surround Him, great saints. The blue
    that glows

In the petals of that Kingdom of azure light
Is Eternity's air. Here stand, Heaven
    streaming
Down on the bare floor. Paradise is a fire in
    the eyes.
Peep in this afternoon quiet, see the guarding
Angels dance and cavort like butterflies
Round the portal, welcoming each peaceful
    heart, flit-
-ting round new souls' petals, sipping each
    nectared spirit.

THE FOUR SEASONS

1975

SUMMER

I

The spring has set, and the first mosquitoes whine
In the West. O these images from summer! They rise
From water like chestnut candles, heavy, swollen,
In brilliant reds and greens. A stream through green fields
Where the swallow dives and skims, gnats dance. Twilight
Creeps under a giant elm. Blue irises
And buttercups, the satin of red roses
Where, on a log, a Red Admiral spreads its wings.
Lime-trees. Violets on the sea-cliff. Stitchworts
Like summer stars under a gold and crimson sun.   10
Golden windfalls under a harvest moon.
Neptune rises out of the water, wearing a garland of waves.

This is a city, recomposed
In tombstones and bits of broken engine.
Jumping monkeys. We die with a nightmare order.
The Trusts Department of a London solicitors.
Boo! Man will disappear into an all-consuming night.
In the débris of three thousand Yankees,
Smith numbers day-dreams on the adding machine.
Decaydance. Rotting vaults, the worship of the flesh.   20
A city decomposed.

Streams through green fields, a giant elm, a log.
Roses climbing a brick wall, twilit sea-cliff.
The sky is peeling like drying paint,
The sea is drying in patches, like distemper.

A nightmare order.
Like sleepwalkers, they burst from the tube,
An orderly army of the normal in City-suits
Who know where they are going from their appointment-books,
The   unfutile   progressing   towards retirement.   30
Some jot observations on the crossword page.
And here a taxi vomits, a messenger bows;
The walrus stumps unseeing up the stairs
To keep an 11.30 appointment with his tea;
A frequenter of gents who brings terror to my bowels.
Bloated bellies, minds trickling like a font.
Give peace in our time, o Lord.
And perhaps my whole life is a forgetting
Of a truth I discovered young and somehow lost.
Who am I in this shifting society?   40
Streams through green fields, roses on a farm-house wall.
Violets on the sea-cliff, windfalls under the moon.

The sun has set, and the first mosquitoes whine
In the wistaria tree. I feel wistful.
I invoke the gods of Thunder and Wind. The drops
Of rain on my windscreen are like a universe of stars.
After the shower the petrol smear shines like a rainbow.
Fish eggs, black currants, rose-hips, sun-drenched cheeks
Rise from water like a bent-up moon.
She flirted until, with a final shudder,   50
The waste-ground groaned in an exhausted surrender.

Scratched hands held by claws. Flapping crows.
The cosmos and man obey common laws.

II

O how the meadow buttercups mock these hot
Town women and their ephemeral pleasures!
O how these peaceful red roses with globules
Of clear dew in their petals shame *their*
    frantic
Tossing and blowing in unnecessary winds!
On the stage she was a whore with a whore's
    hair,
Meshed stockings and sing-song accent, but I
    knew   60
She was billowing her base nature, her real
    role.
They had sequined breasts and thighs hotly
    shining,
And in an orgasm of joy, stars rained like
    confetti,
The band thumped, and my rational denial
Was a spangled "Yea" to Betty.
A naked dancer's body, and a marriage
    settlement:
Ash-tray and vase, a room with Woolworth
    thoughts.
The lights went out, and suddenly she was in
    the dark,
Awaiting thunder; bowing to the netherworld
Like a blue iris tangled in thick bellbind.   70
Ah summer! I have looked for you in the city.
I have seen water-snakes streak down wet
    panes,
A sparrow in sand that flutters itself away
And railway mountain ash burn with berries.
I have looked for love, and found, in the
    waiting-room,
An arrow on the wall, through Jeanie's womb,
And the twisted statue of an abstract woman
With a hole in her middle to denote an
    internal void.

A Void we came from, a Void awaits the
    earth.
All progress is a shrinking towards decay.   80
We shrivelled away from a freezing earth.
All hail the Higher Consciousness! We swear
We will discover a way of looking at the skull
That does not flinch and leaves us unafraid.
A torn up Quaker graveyard and a Methodist
    line
Bequeathe a Puritan bias and a dissenter's
    frown.

No Quattrocento voyages were made by static
    men.
We swear, we will have nerves of twine.

Drinking the peace of the Forest, I glimpsed
The purpose: an image of a man who knew 90
And a lifetime's search.
I greet the new soul, the Superman!
I did not expect to find him contemplating in
    a pew.
All hail the Perfect Man of the *Old Testament*
    prophets
Before Socrates split him up!

The dry ice pours out white, satin smoke.
The saxophone curls like an opium pipe
I once saw in a Pnom Penh opium den
As the great Cathedral eagle flaps its wings
    again.
The saxophone wails from the cricket club
    dance.   100
The dandies talk of freedom and futility.
I waltz with a golden beauty.
Dandies, empty dandies.
See how these leathermen shake their arms
    and scream,
Great puppets, like cardboard cut-out film
    stars,
Watched by a thousand daydreams!
A Void, in ice.

O how this country garden mocks these
    weeds!
O how these rhododendrons dwarf this
    dandelion!
I, who have heard cicadas sing like wires in a
    gale,   110
Heard Jeanie say "With this ring I thee bed"
    while some-
-thing scratched under her South London
    floorboards.
"Love me," I heard, "love me," then a
    resentful silence.
"It's not what you think," he said, "and it's
    nothing to do with you."
And seeing her wheel cards and her iron
    future
I saw her in negative as she might have been,
A white light shining through the orifices of a
    corpse,

An ephemeral high priestess with fleshy
limbs.
Ah summer! In separate static Hells
A girl and an old woman sit side by side   120
For clients; except for the wrinkles, the sneer
Of disillusion, there is no difference.
Old cogs in a defunct and rusted engine,
Broken sherds in deserted desert tells.
Bobbing milk bottles with jagged edges.
Once you open you legs to people like that,
you're done for.
O this idolization of an ephemeral self!

Avoid.

III

O these joyful nights of summer, lilac
And hollihocks and young laughter in the
dark.   130
O how these images glow like chestnut
candles
In water this hot, scented evening!
Who are these, dismounting in the car-park,
Tip-toeing between carriages and Rolls
Royces,
Stealing up the drive towards the lighted
palace
With invited airs, then darting into the
shrubberies
While walkie-talkied policemen shine their
torches
And crunch over the gravel? Then shadows,
Until the sudden baying of hounds split the
stars,
Then running towards the low rumba, at the
door   140
Blinded behind the bar, gasping, groping for
the flap,
In tails on a dance-floor of dinner jackets?
The two outsiders skulk behind the pillar,
One holding up left-handed his borrowed
trousers.
At the Dorchester, I stammered a pseudonym
To the doorkeeper, and blushed before my
scented hostess,
But here at Cliveden....And the next
afternoon
I sat in a deck-chair, reading English verse
In a world of flanelled antics. A leg-cutter,
A fallen bail, and again the blazered

captain   150
Beats his hands together, as if summoning
All to tom-toms in an African jungle
clearing.
And who is this, clearing the cricketers'
plates?
Scent that smells of sweat, lipstick off the lip.
Ignite her throbbing engine and spurt in oil...
See, Jeanie's eyes scatter attentention where
Uninterrupted bliss – in the moonlit alleyway
Her tendrils clutched with an instinctive clasp
And then disgorged her prey.

A trio of hot times. I see   160
Skull-capped shepherds and dust.
In Skopje I took my last coin to the bus
station,
Knowing she would lend me nothing, and
they gave me
Ten pounds. In Bethlehem I see
The cameraman take snapshots near the
manger.
In the garden tomb I follow a coach party.
Nothing divine. There is a hole in the night
sky.
And o the peace in this scurrying city.
I wear a little black Rose. Mr Blent
Peed with me in the Ikebukuro gents.   170
Once I was woken by a totendanse,
Ten black-clad figures at dawn on a Spanish
beach
Where the rats were as big as cats.
I was with John, who had forgotten what he
was seeking.
And now, I peed with Mr Blent in that Tokyo
gents.
Not what I would exactly wish to remember.
Spices in an Arab market, a peep-show.
These sounds filling the silence, the absence
that is God.

A complex heat.
In my air-conditioned car   180
I felt a propulsion nausea
Not felt by the tramp with the blistered feet.
I begged to lie down, but seeing, on TV,
Three supple men bow low like trapeze artists
Into their ropes, I humped up the kitbag of
living.
Masts and patient cranes, like herons, fish.

Three carcasses fall in ritual hopes, like actors
    bowing.

Flit flit flit like pages turning, goes the TV.
Flit flit flit go the images in my memory
Of the hot times.   190

O how these images swirl round this fine
    dome.
A golden light. As, with a burst of praise,
Sparrows flew up from the graves; in the rush
    hour
I saw the leaping in a frotteur's thighs;
There was no flicker in Jeanie's distant
    eyes.
And later, it was standing-room only in the
    August stalls.
Her blood rioted until, with a final shudder,
The waste-ground groaned in an exhausted
    surrender.
Said Mrs. Kirk, frequenter of betting-shops,
"I can't have that sort of thing in my
    house."   200
A gust
Whirled scraps of paper in a spiral,
A wood-louse crawled round in the dust.
O Jeanie, I could withdraw from you, then
    return,
Like a pencil screwn in a compass, to your
    spike.
Now I am a stubby pencil rolled across the
    carpet.

Lilac and hollyhocks, and a library dome.
Pruning lime-trees with a long-arm, a mallard.
Her blood rioted up my thighs
Until we lay and danced in affirmation.
O these joyful nights of scented summer,
    fixed
In the frieze round the inside of an Adam
    dome.
O the eternity in the frieze of this white dome!

IV

A sigh for the sunset.
A skylark rises like a stone over these chalk-
    cliffs.
A pheasant scurries under the hedge as I drive
    past.
Ploughed fields and one lapwing.

The stars are flecks on the stone-egg of this
    universe.
A sigh from these sea-cliffs.
Bladderwrack and a barnacled pier.
    Anglers   220
Wait over fishing lines. The light goes off.
So this is what it is like to be truly dead.

A sigh for Britannia, this dying lady.
As she lies under the sheet, skin crawling with
    crabs,
New towns clot her heart, redbrick paralyses
    her head,
And the slow traffic down her arteries
Brings a message from the dead.
Broken sherds in deserted desert tells.
Eden, Profumo, and a radical time.
The Archbishop has a stutter.   230
We sit before a television, and mutter.
A sigh for our muttering time. A time to be
    faced!
Ape genitals rule the head, the old lady
Is dying from the backbone down.
The old lady is dead above the waist.

A sigh for this country lane.
Bittersweet, yellow and purple, in the hedge;
They have pulled down The Owl and are
    building a new one.
And once she walked ahead with him and
    laughed,
And once held hands when crossing mud, and
    then   240
From the nearby wood, I heard "Cuckoo,
    cuckoo."
A sigh for the fluttering time, the wounded
    heart.

A sigh for the collapse, on the way back
From France, among forget-me-nots, a sigh
For the sadness that depends on squelching
    blood.
In B6, bed 37, a second stroke,
And the end of a conflict with a turbulent son.
The last dead crocuses were a withered blue
And what future was there, after the
    hallucinations,
After the four week struggle on a danger
    list,   250
Save to return home to premature retirement,

Save to sit like a slug and wait, defying fate,
Counting each evening wrested from oblivion,
And refusing hope, or any consolation?
A sigh for one whose tongue is like the desert,
For a dying groan, "I was accused on tele-
vision."
A sigh for the bereaved: "You-know-who
rang me,
He said he would go bankrupt on your
account
If I didn't send him money." I made no com-
ment,
Reckoning each backbiting since his
request.   260

A Red Admiral and a dragonfly.
Charred oak and a prig's disdain.
Images spill through my fingers like
frogspawn.
Dragonfly wings gleam on the shimmering
pond.
I dribble childhood memories like a shuffling
old man.

A sigh for an Atlas of white blobs
Like snow melting in patches in a paddock.
I see Ministers cluster round a man
In glistening tears and watch
A supranational dream flutter in a fowl
net.   270

The sun has set. Like a spring, I gush bubbles.
Now my laughter is flowing North.
You sing a song of freedom, and I peep
Into your soul as into an old broom cup-
board.
O how the meadow buttercups mock these hot
Town women! The cosmos and man obey
common laws.
I can see Smith in a buttercup, and the history
Of this tombstone city and its summer joys.
O this ephemeral life! Cruel memory,
That lives and relives a moment that should
be lost!   280
There is no Eternity save in a well-iced dome,
And in the Void of quiet, when the sun has set
on the eyes.
Ah summer! with your freshening of the spirit
To the rank and drowsy ripeness of Western
overgrowth!

AUTUMN

I

The last day of October and ripeness.
No more drowsy wasps. Leaves fall like
snowflakes.
I crunch through moments like powdered
snow.
Seagulls wheel on the Common. An old lady
In a headscarf flings crumbs from a shopping
bag.
They fall like lonely moments. Seagulls strut
On the playground, scavenge for scraps round
the school kitchen
Like boys waiting for a home-time detention.
As I sit in this examination, and look out,
The last leaves on the tree are copper and
gold.   10
The winter sky, blowing time away, makes
me feel old.

Old age is like a dim light in a curtainless
window.
That house has its curtains drawn.
And in its garden, after fallacious sproutings,
The Japanese cherry has died.
Fish bones in my register. Heads bowed, these
boys
Sit in two rows, one backbone. A skeleton.
O my metropolis,
Sometimes in the golden sunsets
You seem a necropolis.   20
We will be buried in rows, in such a stone
tomb.

Leaves fall. Feathered trees, stark on the
horizon.
A sky like an orange beach. On the Common
the lake
Is a mirage of dazzling silver.
Wet leaves like lilies on the street.
I tread on stepping-stones, look for red carp.
Sometimes I feel I know the mystery.
But then I think: no, I deceive myself.
The rustle of copper beech within this still-
ness....
And under this iron cathedral, an autumn
wind   30
Blows autumn leaves to a heap in the grave-
yard.

228

No branch unites these faces of my fellow-
travellers,
I am alone, pressed among them; ribbed and
sere.
Have they striven towards the stars and
shuddered,
Charred bones and insomniac dread, and lost
All meaning in a carriage of well-dressed
commuters,
Cohorts of machines that know they err in
their hearts?
A necropolis, and yet do we know it?
Mrs. Farr sits in front of her TV,
The People's flag is deepest red for the
lazy.   40
A kettle steaming up the spout,
Molten lead plopping from twin gun barrels,
And the solid gold in evening window panes
As the red light goes out.

The last day of October, a red sunset.
Hallowe'en, and hallo to witches, who flit like
bats
In the twilight, and children who push their
guys
In prams. Maggots and dying country-mice.
Death is the other side of life, as when
You turned the stone and saw the crawling
lice.   50
Rain on red-hot cinders. Yellow sparks shoot
Like fireworks! From that bonfire a grey-
white
Ash-carbon leaf flutters like a feather.
I have seen poplar fluff drift through the City
air,
And I have seen beyond despair.

A churchbell strikes the hour. In another hour
These skulls will be disinterred from this late
Western
Ruin. Will they know, as archaeologists
should,
That evil is a clapper on the bell of good?

II

Leaves fall like dying states of mind, the
year's   60
Sunset. What is there to cling to, hold fast?
A flicker on God's eye, a sun-warmed ball.
On a slumbering retina, the rise of the ape.

One twinkle of light, the sun was burnt out.
In a starless universe, by a fallen tree
I happened to exist; roots gripped my feet,
And I had always lived in a dying universe,
I looked for a face in the pond, there was
nothing there.
Leaves fall. What is there to cling to? My
head
Swarmed with foreboding faces, but
watching   70
You turn and smile like one who has been
alone
And offers a promise in your lips, I smiled,
Not knowing that you approached a
confrontation.
Next day, a roar: you and your plane, a fire-
ball.
What to cling to? What? Scrap iron and a
giant
Stone cross. Men rose from the earth with
unscaled eyes
To a tangle of deserted streets, a hall
Of mirrors. Not this. What? Bell rings. My
loss
Has been recorded in the book of Amos.
The water-lily floats. O what went wrong?   80

What went wrong? Too much seeking. A
ripple in a pond,
"What psychological thing made you a
seeker?"
You asked. "Rather, why are you not
seeking?"
I replied, but I should have agreed with you.
Too much seeking takes a man away from the
present.
The scattered farms on Flanders' barley-
fields –
History, like art, is a deeply rooted tree
But it is loved only in the Now, which is
eternal.
O ancient sages, holy-seeking sages
Standing in the mountains in Hiroshige's
wood-cut,   90
You have seen many former lives return
through smoke,
Like a wheel, they go round and round, in a
spiral,
But you know that the past and future
fumigate

The moment, and make it melancholy.
The art of living is to cling to the eternal
    Now.
There is the sun in my soul, and the other sun
In my universe. The sun in me is the real one,
Perhaps, and the sun out there is merely a
    copy?
Like an echo from a bell....

I switched on golden light, and the tunnel
    ended.   100
Out of plus and minus burnt the constant bulb.
What a relief to be standing beneath
These whirling angels by this Baroque pillar
As the churchbell rings for evensong!
Now there is nothing wrong!

Leaves fall like tears, the water-lily floats.
What is there to cling to in this passing show
Which every patter and bird-chirp ages more?
The seed is always shed in the year of
    flowering,
But does not all germinate by the following
    spring,   110
Some seeds lie dormant for eighteen months
    before
Bearing – hawthorn and ash – or so I am told.
Ah autumn! Will spring bring saplings from
    our seeds,
Or will our roots perish among sprouting
    toadstools?
A clockwork tree.
Our Welfare State is a right, not a charity.
And who would have the heart to deny
It was good the fruit should fall? And who
    would delay
The summer in the teeth of one child's hungry
    cry?
Ahead is the prospect of a bitter winter.   120

O this futile progress from past to future.
A letter fell into the hall barrel,
And was lost for six weeks. I took a job
As an umbrella, not a roof.
Like a bat, or like a condemned man's
    morning,
My life flits by. Cold evenings, and no
    proof....

Wrong.

III

Happy autumnal loves hang like ripe pears
In an orchard, roll on the well-mown lawn
Like windfalls this last sitting out for tea   130
In the sun-bathed garden. Like red apples they
    flame
Round my head as I spread jam, sitting on a
    rug,
And think of fires and dream of smoking
    chimneys.
A bursting through bent branches, a bouncing,
And I feel a week's power behind a wall
And now this late-night walk up through
    tangled trees,
Jagged and misty and dark, like a cerebral
    jungle.
"It's pro or contra," I said, "but it can be
    neither
Until I have chosen. And now I choose I am
    free."
Rioting out, the echoes cracked the cosmic
    shell,   140
And in this squashy bruised one is my wait
In a church by the Law Courts. The con-
    gregation
Self-consciously gossips about the pallid
    groom,
Dismayed by hassocks, clearing throats to
    sing.
Then at the high altar, two Swans of goodly
    hewe
Kneel in sacred ceremonies. I see
Clenched knuckles twitching on trousered
    knees.
Images from you, but removed from you, like
    fruit
From a tree. And now there is no tree, I see
An Austin Princess with two white
    streamers: 150
We all glide to the Essex church, sweep round
On crunching gravel. We step out in a wind,
I in top hat and morning dress. Cine-
Cameras whirl. We take our seats in a pew.
The bride floats in, trailing white, like a
    harvest
Queen. I celebrate happy loves without you.
Apples and pears stored in rows in a cellar.

I choose three from the seeking days
When I did not know what I should be

finding.
Sipping tea with a sickly, brooding
    complexion,   160
I told Mr Sim of my ascetic Idea
Of a saint's ascent to meaning through
    discipline,
And will and effort. I was a proud pilgrim.
And then I became a gardener to weed my
    soul.
I hoed myself in a park and a glassy school.
A dog howled at a whining police-car,
A thermos of char from Madge, and from
    cleaner Jessie,
A tea-break share in a bottle of sherry.
"You could 'ave a career, be a teacher," she
    said,
Not knowing the purging nip in the autumn
    cold.   170
And then I left the highways for the byways
And listened to the language of everyday
    men.
"That garage really takes you to the cleaners,"
    said Mr A,
As I passed him by the dustcart. "May I dump
This on you?" I asked the dustman, and, "Pud
    it vere, guv,"
He croaked, and the words were out of time,
    ever-now
In my memory. I observed him. He had
    opinions
About black men he ruled. The King of the
    Coons
Came home to bottles and children's cartoons,
But was still in the Rose and Crown, mind-
    bending forks and spoons.   180
Through such trivialities I approached the
    good.

The seeking days, as if I hoped to find
A clashing of cymbals, a barbarous ritual
Whose masked initiates crane forward as
The high priest ascends between raven and
    lion
To the altar, draws back the druid veil
On a mutilated statue in the clashing grove,
And the falsehood of "z" in terms of "a",
As if a high priest could make my heart real!
No head touches another, each grows
    alone.   190
I, who have heard non-sequiturs on a chesty

engine,
Have lain insomniac years, sweating with
    dread.

Happy autumnal loves out of reach, like dates
On North African palms. I remember them
As the plane banks over vast and yellow sands
Towards a chalk-white city in palm-trees.
I see two harmless acts – two mothers talk
At school, we are invited to a party –
But they converge on a momentous third:
This raven-haired beauty with black-meshed
    stockings.   200
We dance under floodlit palms in the desert
    dark.
Out of reach, unattainable, this love!
And now this Italian town is seized by
    soldiers.
Gunshots and tanks and fear, curfew at six.
In the hot afternoon Petronella swims at the
    pool,
Has drinks afterwards in a flat overlooking
    the harbour.
We give her dinner, we all play poker
And liar dice, sitting near an orange tree.
By a well, among yellow-eared cactus, we
    kissed.
And now, my raven-haired Princess
    clambers   210
In evening sunlight, climbing the sea-cliff
From the beach, as if lying face down on a
    bed.
Happy autumnal love under deep blue skies,
Poinsettia red by my window, pomegranites
Vivid in the soul! Ah autumn, by the
    crenellated
Turkish wall. Six weeks in the ever-now until
I drive back past the yellow seashore bell.
It was built for a Princess as a bathing-shelter.
I, too, have known better times, like this
    orange shell.

Dates squashed in a box in the heat.   220
O that I could still believe that friends were
    friends.
Happy autumnal loves near this bittersweet
Make me feel melancholy. I have seen
My halo, like my knickers, round my knees
And have felt pain.
But now, when in the ever-now like a wind I

231

speak,
Like the revolutionary ruler by the Castle,
The square is waving wheat.

Ripe pears, apples, and dates, and these
    autumn loves:
Images out of time on this bittersweet
    frieze!   230

IV

A sob for the end of October.
I am like an autumn leaf, floating on nothing,
On the watery wind of what is beneath my
    reason.
I love the earth, I swoon on it, I kiss it.
I love the stars, and each child, even though
    they are dying.
A sob for the star that has fallen into the lake.
As I sit in this examination, I recall
Second year assembly. We had another
Story about David and Jonathan,
I sat in a field of rustling wheat. I am a
    leaf.   240
Life is an examination, and those who
Leave at the end do not necessarily excel
Those who leave early. Prepare for death!
Prepare an end, like a perfect October leaf!

A sob for these fragments of civilisation.
After a night of heavy rain, the sun rose
Over Waterloo, burning the sea into ribs
Of copper, at noon shone over the largest
Empire the earth has known. At night I saw
The Union Jack dismembered. The
    crumbling   250
Sooty closes of Edinburgh's Royal Mile,
Or, like a bridge under construction,
Belfast's rainbow arch.
Said Mr Widgeon, cigarette drooping from
    lips,
Not realising it is what you bring to it,
"I have no time for religion."
I am sad for this ruined civilisation
Which collapsed when its spirit vanished like
    a rainbow
In the twinkling of a smile, leaving
A hundred splinters of a broken crucifix.   260

A sob for all fragile things.
The mourning sun shines on autumn
daffodils.
I am as frail as a restrung guitar.
I feel like a grasshopper
Caught in the first snow, buried to the waist,
Watching ants. I can hear their drowsy
    clacking,
Purple and green bodies with large bent legs
Clinging and swinging to a large coarse grass.
A sob for all dying living things.

A sob for a tottering child by a stone pool, 270
Eighteen months, now three, and wearing
    dungarees.
"Did it rain to give the flowers a drink?" she
    asks.
"Or has the sun gone downstairs to have his
    cookie?
I will put a ladder up the sun," she says,
"And put a floor over it, and a carpet, so
It will not be too hot. And we will swing on
    the sun.
My wristbone is like a door-knob."
A sob for a child with an ache in her gaping
    heart,
Who cried for a year and a half, while I
    rocked her,
Until she died and her pain ended. Why?   280

A toadstool in the woods. A rat swims out
And peeks under a water-lily. Heaped piles
Of leaves, a bonfire near the railway bridge.
I will worship the White Horse on Westbury
    Hill.

A sob for this gashed earth, for this pocked
    earth.
As through Exhibition glass, the sun has
    smoked
Through the globe of Europe, one thick spurt
    of iron
Has slid round the seas and dried in the wind,
    and congealed.
The scabs have frozen and flaked.
I glimpse crowds milling in the lobbies of our
    Commons.   290
O Harold, Harold, your hundred days
Of October spring-cleaning
Have now become a children's craze
Of division bell sardining.
A sob for this Big Ben who wrinkles his nose.

The last day of October. Leaves fall.
A tree is like a society: in spring
Its leaves are tender, and when it grows old
They are crinkled. But the seeds are scattered
Like the apple-pips on this rosary.   300
I will twine my life in my hands, twist my
    images
And see them spill between my fingers like
    berries
By an empty shell on a booming beach.
O this evil clanging like a school-bell's
    tongue,
O this dying within the good! I cling in the
    now
To these apple-pips from this fruit, I tell
Each happy love. O each contains a tree,
O bittersweet taste that surrounds such
    growth!
I will take my seeds and plant them in my
    soul,
Eternity is the ever-now whose sun   310
Will swell me to cracking and bursting into
    shoot.
Autumn, you sadden me to secret growths
In this tangled ruin and wreckage of decay.

WINTER

I

Frost sparkles on fences and crisp white grass,
Whitens roofs, glazes windows with swirling
    leaves.
Feet crunch on frozen furrows, the ridged
    earth.
Ice in hoof-holes, breath floats into bare trees.
All is ribbed, spare. Twig has shed leaf,
    structure
Triumphs over tumbling outline. Cheeks are
    cold,
Nose is cold, fingers numb. This is a lean
    time,
All luxury and luxuriance pared down
To bark and bone, rib and ridge. From a white
    sky
Float the first few flecks of snow.
    December.   10
A distant carol. A fire flickers through a
    window,
And a Christmas tree with coloured fairy
    lights.

Faces shine from the branches of our society.

Christmas tree needles cover the carpeted
    stairs.
We live in a disintegrating society.
A sepulchral city in the early dark.
I see skulls in the streets, as in the Plague.
Last night, lying in bed with you, I sighed,
"I wish I could live for ever." This morning,
My breath trailed behind me, like a life
    already spent.   20
Will there be funds to repair our public
    buildings,
Or will weeds sprout from the columns of the
    Bank of England?
Snow-flecks in the street-lamps, a quiet
    burial.
Oxford Circus twelve foot under daisies.

A carol. The stars are trawled in a net of silk
To be winched dripping and wriggling from
    this water.
Pines on the snow-slopes, these sparkling
    waves.
I watch seamen drape their nets on a low wall.
A Western winter, and a stony blindness
As in the Forest we fished for sticklebacks. 30
Birds sang in the winter trees of my brain.
I walked under my reason, in my under-
    ground.
Motorcycle sidecars and a baker's oven.
Ribbed and cracking skin, hoary memories
Of a class-war. Like a cosmic pendulum
The bob of the cusped moon swung from a
    star.
He was born to rule with the assurance of
    affluence,
An opponent of land reform from a squire's
    cradle;
Outwardly unruffled, if stricken passionless,
Too limp and drained of seminal ideas   40
To procreate into a post-Churchillian age,
And, save for a legacy, pre-1911,
Too blind to bequeathe a dream to his keen-
    eyed heirs,
As if a stroke had paralysed his intestate
    vision.
In the eddying rustle of crinkled leaves
I saw acres of stony ground, where a Forest
    should have been.

Smelted ores and chimney smoke, on a North-
East wind, over stony fruit, drift and fall
On this sooty park, on these brittle twigs,
These shrivelled roots, on this blackened
    bark.   50
Faces blown to the underground,
And it was easier to sleep than to drive
    through stone
To the rich mould of a pre-industrial seam.
Bare trees. The crunch of frozen leaves. Cold
    cheeks.

Frost sparkles. The earth is locked white,
    ribbed, spare.
The rhododendrons reverted to type, went
    purple,
I felt a peatless crust form round my brain.
I was exhausted, I was an advertised museum.
My consciousness glinted with broken shapes.
I lurched down the passage. All this affluent
    waste,   60
This gibber. A fallen city. Clockwork
Toys and electronic fingers driven
By beams of light on an automatic wind.
There is an empty space beside me in my
    mirror
Where Hosea calls to me.

The bob swung like a pendulum, forward
Then back. We are due for another oscillation.
A gleam of light shines on the house of Israel.
Under the frozen reason is a bursting root.

II

See how this snow shrouds all with its deathly
    cold,   70
How can the feelings thrust through this layer
    of ice?
See how this frost sparkles with a hundred
    glitters.
I am buried beneath this flashing white
That covers my soul with a thousand
    glistening selves.
Now self-division is a self-covering.
Across your canvas flits a futile weekend,
And now, in an attic like the Tate,
A hundred haunted faces caught in paint,
A hundred passive models we will not imitate.
I look for weekly thumbprints from a great
    man's soul.   80

These pictures in this gallery, do they show
A mind that is fire and snow? Frost sparkles.
How can the feelings thrust? Two forces
    grapple,
One plate, screws, cogs, nuts, pulleys and
    numbers,
And one with a young lithe body like a tree in
    bud.
Two forces grapple, a winter of measurement
And this thrusting spring. How can the future
    burst
Unless sun melts this snow. Will it uncover
    us?

Uncover us. This sun between my eyes
    uncovers,
Melts this now and its apparent unity,   90
Releases one life-force, the apparent
Multiplicity of shoots and leaves, hiding
The bare outline of this silver birch in green.
One surge in a thousand multiple disguises,
One thrust behind a thousand forms. I am
    uncovered,
And, stalking up the High Road in proud
    disdain,
I rise head and shoulders above my neighbour
And look down on his lower consciousness's
    pain.
O this lower Being which can be melted!
I had grass on my head instead of hair.   100
In a broken room the other end of Oxford,
Seemingly self-sufficient, I despaired
And stamped on badinage and academic
    words,
Excoriated tears. And when the fuse was
    repaired,
Ignorning the litter, a Master of Possibilities
Burst through and ate his bread and drank his
    bitter!

I felt faint, my consciousness leaked away
Like an ebbing from a Cornish harbour,
Leaving a glistening popping on the still wet
    sand.
But oh the rolling in of the Divine tidal
    wave!   110
Wood-lice on a log. A life-beat, unknowable
    order.
The sawing of the frogs, the distant stars.
The night bursts into bloom, to uncover us.

See how this snow shrouds with its deathly
    cold.
See how this frost sparkles with a hundred
    glitters.
My heart is covered with discarded rubbish,
Like a heap of a hundred nuts and bolts and
    potsherds.
A searing pain and a screaming ambulance,
Grimy windows where grubby schoolboys
    snigger,
Under the founder's image, at a target of a
    god.   120
Now decadent men and debs are noisily
    noshing.
Amid the chatter of Oxford accents and
    finishing-schools
The Eternal Rebel pulls six guineasworth of
    old rope.
A writhing crowd of subterranean slaves,
A pool of blood on the Martyrs Memorial
    steps,
And a great power filled me by the blazing
    lake.
He took me to a jazz club and swindled me.
Sitting in a café I defined the home of the
    unreal.
A war-widow sews a seam. A scream,
And they swarmed over the fence like an
    invading   130
Football crowd to cheer the safe crash-
    landing.
Crows wheel round the shattered bier, and I
    know
The dictator has a Hell in his heart.
Bernini and violets! In a bedroom mirror
I stared in disapproval at a self-regarding face
And saw a dream disappear round the next
    corner
Like a baker's van driving into a morning
    mist.
The Forest: leaves, ponds, the hollow oak we
    climbed
Into. Your discarded diary: "4th February,
I fell in love with my Lord." I have
    fished   140
Images like rusty bumpers from Forest
    ponds....
A broken pitcher. So much for association.
I will piece it together, and show one self-
    creation

To astound this dwindling age of
    reconstruction.

The sky gaped like a womb.
The sky that will outlive me has no meaning
Without my joy. And who will accuse
Eliot, Auden, Greene of publicly chosen
    views?

I am uncovered.

III

O the winters of Japan, so different from   150
The fogs of my youth, dim lights in ghostly
    street-lamps.
Like bare boughs they rise from the earth to
    blue skies.
The memories hang like white paper wishes
Tied to an evergreen in temple gardens:
Wind whispers among needles, white wishes
    sway
Like settled butterflies, which will wing to
    Heaven.
The sharp sunsets of the city, our bungalow.
A praying mantis on the bathroom floor,
Camelias and bamboo near the Christmas
    tree.
This one. My pupil in the Bank holds above
    his head   160
Fifty bamboo sticks to tell the I Ching.
A wind going throughout the earth to the
    South.
Now a man like a pregnant washerwoman,
Striped like a bumble-bee, a light shade on
    head,
Makes contorted noises at Kabuki.
Gagaku, yin and yang. Under a sun and moon,
On the stage of my conscious brain in winter,
Slow dances; men in party hats; flame-drums.
Now a white cloud raises its head like a
    monster
To bite Himeji Castle, a tiered wedding
    cake.   170
Roofs like the underside of a mushroom,
Buildings like liquorice allsorts.
And now, on the deserted Nobe beach,
A dead turtle near the tiny hermit crab
As we walk to our wood-and-paper house by
    a well.
Once I watched birds emigrate like black flies

But now, by the Kamakura waiting-room,
A Failed Saint's eyes are shut in a steaming
     meaning.
He knows Heaven speaks through Fu-hsi's
     trigrams,
King Wan's hexagrams and the "chance"
     arrangement   180
Of fifty bamboo sticks by a Shibuya fortune-
     teller.
O the winters when the ground was free from
     snow!

A triad from the trying months
When my patience was tried for its endurance.
As I hoed voices in the Garden of my Soul,
Mr Lowe said, "I have eight pound in all
     accounts,
Including the Post Office, and a wife and
     child,
And how can I endure this slave's job here?"
And I caught my grimace in a distorting wing-
     mirror.
And then, when all I clung to was taken
     away   190
To teach me to surrender all my desires
As a shell that imprisons the seed of destiny,
I went into a tailor's. A wire dummy had been
     stolen.
Mr Venn said, "We don't want no one telling
     ve guvnor,"
And Pete Thompson replied, "It's nuffink to
     do wiv me,"
And I knew, I was inoculated against their
     language,
But evil was different, there was no vaccine
For that, only resignation and courage.
And then, alone, I saw lonely
Mrs. Morris waiting in her Christmas
     parlour.   200
A standard lamp, caught in a paper-chain
     web,
Was being devoured by a balloony spider,
And I knew the anguish of all who weave a
     net.
In the department store, my photophobic
     eyes
Became bits of a broken camera in a sunlit
     glade,
A timbered house, eyes that do not know what
     to do.

A crucial spear-thrust marks the crux of
     history.
The embryoed seed is released within Light.
O this frozen reason.
Growth through suffering opens new
     places   210
In the heart, like this wintering through to
     spring.
And so we must endure the trying months.

O the winters when the ground was free from
     snow!
O these images hanging like paper wishes
On a pine-tree, fluttering to Heaven.
Swayed in a rasping wind, a sprouting twig
Clung to the spiked teeth of a station flower-
     holder.
I am rootless, here, like an ikebana
Expert from the West. In the Chinese
     restaurant
Kimonoed ladies sat in obedient silence.   220
Sole gaijin at the graduates' celebration,
I had the usual ring round me, I could see
     them
Gawping at the gaijin. I towered over them.
Now I hunt for a needle in a lanterned garden.
Now I meditate in a temple in a valley.
Cicadas and breathing lungs. The sun rose on
The old Master, nude in his bamboo-grove,
In satori and the stench of dead mosquitoes.
A city with the life sucked dry. A sea-well.
A beach littered with squids, jellies, and
     tanker oil.   230
Egg-shells round potted plants, and
     Immortality.
Now see where the Sung horses toss and snort
Near a Dowager Empress, so still in her
     shrouds.
Taking a hair from her lips she smiled, "She
     she",
"Thank you", at the top of her Cambodian
     stair.
It was nice at first, you with your comb,
But when you were stoned and just sat there, I
     went home.
These wishes flown to Heaven, which will not
     come again.

A hole in the clouds.
From behind the steel bird's wing I looked

into the abyss.   240
Camelias and bamboo, and these winter
    wishes
Like wisps of delicate art round this snow-
    white dome.
Ah winter wishes, the temporary temporal
    shell
Round the kernel of the destiny which is
    Eternal,
And which must split through, like the figures
    from their border
In the hundred scenes of this circular frieze.

IV

A moan for the sparkling frost.
I have died beneath frozen furrows, white
    grass
Like an old self. Will there be a new self to be
    born?
See how the snow shrouds with its deathly
    cold.   250
O these fences, roofs and windows, these bare
    trees!
A moan for this spareness. I have put off
    profusion.
In the darkening noon, I break the dull
    silence,
I; flitting in the frost to rend the veil of
    knowledge.
O this locked earth that imprisons me. A
    distant carol.
A dog barks. A flickering candle in this dark
Commemorates a war. Time rushes by,
Accelerated like an old film of crowds
    running
To death. Bark and bone, rib and ridge. All
    shed.
I am buried beneath the leaves and fruit I
    discarded.   260

A moan for these ruined walls, this divided
    city.
A gland-weakened weariness, a rise and fall.
The scaffolding collapsed, the statue
    crumbled,
A new era started. London will decay.
Just as a technological beat and a home
    market ballad
Have go-go-ed out of date the old colonial
    trad,

So in a nuclear age, sea-power is obsolete.
Swing to the unions and Keynes, scientific
    power is the beat.
A moan for our greedy, materialistic time.
We pull beer and birds and demand more   270
And watch the cracks widen in the settlements
In all we inherited, so that our Spirit falls.

A moan for all vanished things
Like oak leaves, an avenue of chestnut
    candles,
Red eggs on a sycamore leaf, the may like
    snow,
Yellow laburnum, lilac stars on the lawn,
A bee hovering by a white bell of a nettle,
Sunsets loganberry pink and treacle gold.
The Witches' Copse, thirteen trees, is like
    Stonehenge.
Like a druid, I stand and listen for vanished
    chantings.   280
A moan for all absences in the moaning wind.

A moan for walks to a Cathedral like a tent
Among the blocks and chimneys of a foreign
    city.
The last dead crocuses are withered blue,
The lotus has begun to blossom. In the storm
These small incense cones are like halma
    men.
She is like Pallas Athene with her helmet hair.
Now the moon is caught in the branches of
    my tree,
The typhoon is over. O these whirling clouds.
A moan for tender walks towards a horror. 290
I see you against a fallen beech by a pond,
A tree whose roots and branches bind Heaven
    and Hell.
A swirl, and rain spatters this Yggdrasil.
A moan for all whose sun and rain can smile.

Snow on fences, ice on the pond.
My face is drowned in a thousand slivers
Of empty space. I seek but I cannot find.
A long, cold winter, and the fog
On the silent waste of snow on an Arctic park.

A moan for the shadow on these decaying
    walls.   300
A sick society, a sickening soul.
The glass falls in the church's barometer.

On the decaying farm something has passed.
Debased drachmae. Four and twenty bank
  clerks
Baked in blasted stone. See, a petrol cell,
Spreading blue-green and purple in the rain.
For lack of millions of these we declined and
  fell.

Frost sparkles. Feet crunch on frozen furrows.
Faces shine from the branches of the
  Christmas tree.
A moon on its back, a sky of tractor
  tracks.   310
Sparrows fly up over the line of poplars.
Spring is thrusting through this white deathly
  shroud.
Our au pere has put daffodils in our bathroom.
They swirl round a milk bottle and flow out.
Three look forward, one is alone and looks
  away.
The spring renews the tree. It brings plane
  fruit
Against the wintry sky. The spring renews
Everything – excepting me. O this frozen
  time.
Intuition right, reason wrong. O, let the bob
Of the cusped moon oscillate again from a
  star,   320
Even if these walls crack and crumble away.
Let this snow be melted, let these wishes bud.
Let the one force burst through this
  multiplicity!
O this spare, pared life. O this rib and bone.
I will put detail on to this structure.
O this sleeping season before the splitting
  shell.
Kernel right, husk wrong. She made me a clay
  pot
Open at the top. Enclosed from the Infinite,
I did not understand. I was a muddy urn
Waiting for a spring to wash into me. I was
  dead   330
Like a seed, awaiting the miracle of
  Immortality.
The cracking into a hundred potsherd selves.
Eternity is the self-renewal of growth
Out of death, the birth of a self and its destiny.
O winter, you freeze me into despair
Of a miracle, baring and hardening your
  ground.

SPRING

I

Buds drip from the beech trees. This gorse
  crackles,
Yellow laburnum flames. What a shower
Has fallen round my head! What a fire spits
With this new teeming, abundant intensity!
The earth is soft again, and sighs up shoots
For love, which flicker and blaze in the
  leaping joy.
For love, all is lush, tender, heady. The green
Grass is soft and young in this sharp sunlight.
Crocuses and snowdrops bask beside the
  Abbey,
A robin sings among the stone ruins.   10
A new, rejoicing time, for shoot and root
A new warmth, a new manifold, one surge.
Hosannah for this rain-fire! Spring fell in a
  shower today,
I saw buds like raindrops drip down an arched
  branch.
Eternity is the colour of a young green leaf.

Eternity is the wind in the leaves of time.
Eternity is the spring in the cities of time.
A city dies in hours, like a leaf; but like a
  wind,
The spring of renewal is its Eternity.
We hear the rustle, but we missing the
  meaning.   20
CAVE CANEM, beware of the dog, said a
  mosaic
In Pompeii before Vesuvius erupted,
And now a dozen heads guard the Sheldonian.
Good Friday in front of Woolworths. Wind
  moans and whines.
Shoppers like wraiths, a gallery of the night-
  mare blind.
"It is a people that do err in their hearts."
Amen. Amen. I hear prayers like granite
  seeds.
When a civilisation crashes, Eternity
Is the spirit that rises out of the ashes.

What a shower has fallen! Amen! Amen!   30
The drops of rain twinkle on the window,
A universe lies on my windowpane,
A thousand globules of stars that will last an
  hour.

The wet road sparkles in the sun. Wet rocks,
A wrinkled sea, a gull on every flagpole.
I am as royal as this towering hotel crest!
Sun glints on your ruby and two outer
    diamonds.
You say, "My red stone's got a flaw," but the
    bird
Flies with a twig to its nest, this spring morn-
    ing,
And I will buy a sofa for our new flat   40
In that department store. And those daisies
On the grass are like bright stars that will
    never explode
And disappear as if they had never been.
Eternity is the now that has existed
For ever, and will always exist. Last year,
Now, and next year – daisies! And my
    tageties....
When watered, they catch globules in their
    leaves,
And stand to attention and prick back their
    ears like cats.
I, their gardener, pick off their dead heads as
    if
They were a ruined wall, a stone turtle,   50
Or in the dark Forest, slowly beating wings.
March. The North is covered with snow.
Flowers are blooming along the Yangtze
    River.
The joyous transplanting of the rice shoots –
"Our Leader is like the wind bending the
    grass."
I pick each off and know they will grow
    again.
I watch a wave break and roll up the shingle
And know there will be another to take its
    place.
I pick off the dead heads of my Department
And know there will be another to take my
    place.   60

Buds drip from the beech trees. A green
    shower.
Bluebells in the woods, tadpoles in the green
    pond
On Strawberry Hill. Eternity calls to me.
And should one not accept one's chosen
    image?
Crocuses and snowdrops glow beside the
    Abbey.

O this green time! How could I ever forget
That Eternity is the colour of evergreen?
I make a daisy chain by slitting stalks,
I love these flowers. O earth, I love your
    green!

The clock tower chimes.   70
There is no progress, only a holding of ground
That others gained through forms that have
    gone with the times.
People are like bulbs.
They flower and go dormant and flower
    again.
I am now flowering after a long winter.
Consider the Eternity of the bulbs.

II

O the torture after this Eastern shower! I am
    torn.
My reason is in the grip of the irrational:
I am a buoy on the sea, bell run by the waves,
And the tide is frothy, like washing-up
    water;   80
I am a lotus on a pond; a skull among graves.
I listen to the tea-house on that bridge.
How sound travels while we are waiting for
    rain.
The plashing of a ornamental water-wheel,
A stone lantern like an empty head.
Mr Widgeon has been in many cities,
Has a cosmopolitan mouth, a heart long dead.
I am torn in a twilight, on the edge of light.
Waking suddenly, I knew death lay beside
    me,
I was afraid in the pale and ghastly dawn.   90
Was that you or a ghost gliding in the windy
    kitchen?
I slept and dreamt. All hail the new God
    Nothing!
As I entered the maze, the hierarchy
Sat at a table, as much the fruit of seed
As the apples that hung around their heads.
There was a clock in the centre of the
    labyrinth....
But now, all hail the silence, and plentitude!
I peer behind the tea-house on that bridge.
The ritual ceremony behind the thirst
Is civilisation. This garden has hints,   100
In rocks and sand, of mountains and white
    clouds.

Here I discard unnecessary thoughts
And peep beyond rock and moving ocean
To the One: the temple walls of a temenos.
Suddenly my reflection falls to pieces,
I glimpse one thousandth of the truth, and
    know
You take from this garden what you put into
    it.
Two forces grapple. In the grip of spring, I am
    torn.

Torn, I lived in tension between two poles,
Like the axle between two cartwheels. I held
    them   110
Apart and kept them together as I turned.
The winchpole turns the being's winding
    shaft.
The wheel draws and lowers the buckets of
    the heart.
The One in me is mirrored in the Pole Star;
The road to the universe is through the Self.
From my moon she became my sun.
Like a husband and wife, Reason and Being
    fight;
Blind rational scholar and visionary mother,
Each made complete by projecting the other;
Meaning and acceptance, despair and
    affirmation   120
Eternally at war, yet held together
By the child of their flesh who lives through
    their common blood.
Snakes wriggled down my bedroom window-
    pane
Seeking out the womb under the eiderdown.
A human worm bloomed out of scattered
    sperm
When a sleeping phallus suddenly sprouted.

In the graveyard under the rooted pine
My reason asked, "What is the importance
Of reason?" The needles, not the sinewy
    line.
I saw blind rational Professor and visionary
    Saint   130
Groping between maze-hedges, roped
    together;
A cool Reflection guided a blind Shadow,
Its roped Master, up the stark mountainside.
Like the white Archbishop whose bust hangs
    in Chigwell School

He was old and wore a mitre of Anglican rule.
And many-sided More defied axe and schism.
His head is in Canterbury, his body in the
    Tower –
An awesome catechism.

Under the ladder of the cross
The individual cannot see his existence: 140
The perceiver is a part of what he perceives.
There are two parts of man: the centre, and
    the dross.
The centre grows vertically, the dross
Splits into a thousand selves of horizontal
    shell.
O wonderful unity! Last autumn we asked
Who will lop these dead branches? There was
    no
Vital dance of heads on this English tree.
But now we grow in unity, no longer torn.

O this painful climbing out of a dead self!
I introspected in a Japanese garden.   150
A butterfly with wet wings by its chrysalis.
Stooping by the giant bamboo, I realised:
The sadness. Stone lanterns like empty heads,
The futile plashing of an ornamental water-
    wheel,
And the turning wheel at the deserted funfair.
Creaking walls, rattling glass, like a swaying
    ship
The walls of my skull creaked, my eyes
    rattled.
Shaking the streetcar mesh with clawed
    fingers,
Gibbering, I broke free. The evening rang like
    silver.
Like a snake with two bright eyes the train
    came.   160
I walked into an evening of tulips and bones.
The ape who rides a bicycle testifies
That man is but a stage: the ascent in your
    eyes.
A trail of skins like dead selves marks the
    path
To Mount Fuji's summit, where your Shadow
    waits.
O this still stream whose top moves forward
    with time,
O this daily raking of Tao! Hail all who know
That Eternity is a hole in the hedge!

III

Spring images sprout like buds along the soul,
Each tip containing branch, leaf-cluster and
    flower   170
In the gentle breeze of this inspiration.
The first line of a poem unfolded this
    morning,
I opened the door a crack, it swung open by
    itself.
She smiled, "Shall I trample on your manu-
    scripts?"
Pointing at the piles on the floor. I said, "Like
    coals
Chinese walk on, they will purify your soul."
A drowned lotus shone in the lilied lake.
A globe of frogspawn dropped in my memory
Like stone. My eye cracked like a window-
    pane.
O the riving of this upward-striving war!   180
In half an hour of routine investigation
One confident teacher, created by others'
    belief,
Found   a   message   for   his   Eastern
    temperament,
A superconscious hero of the Spirit!
I said, "You have mistaken the artist's role.
It is to recreate the spiritual energy,
To restore to health with the irrational.
Look, they have sterilized their running sores.
But are their towers and hoardings curative?
Hedonism! As if life's transcending
    purpose   190
Were to cosset a suffering ape. They need a
    map."
A haliotic sigh. Staring over a book,
I watched lost strangers pass from an empty
    branch
In the island park. In purple and burnt gold
A petrol cell, and a name scratched in the
    dust.
I scribble my inability to relax my hold.
These images that drip down the soul and
    splash in the lake!

A trinity from the lost years
When I slowly lost my scales to find the buds
Of my destiny, and this showering-green
    season.   200
Scaled over by his "I" and lazy dreamings
Mr Will

Strives but never arrives.
The emptiness of the groves round the top of
    the hill.
I think of him running behind me on Belgrade
    station,
I jumped and from the steps saw him receding,
Still running, round the corner, on the track.
Then drugged, to impress, "Listen," Mr Dean
    cried,
"How's this for playing off rhythm against
    metre?"
She nodded, and went on varnishing her nails.
    Sighed   210
Mr Dean, "If I had been born in another Age,
What a poet I might have been."
I suppose he *might* have written more words
    to a page.
And then Mr Prism,
The Devil's brother, wears a dog-collar,
And defiles the Cathedral with his egoism.
A nightmare sickness, this armour-plated
    resin
And varnish that coats the soul and will not
    melt.
Loud voices of servicemen who do not listen.
Lumps of flesh must be peeled from these old
    bones.   220
We need a Puritan surgeon. Who is this
    apparition?
Uncarnal Savonarola cleaned up the carnivals;
After the virtuous terror he stepped off
A gibbet ladder and danced on a leaping fire
Until a slack shape swung in the wind to burn
Up, and inspire a Sistine giant's limbs!
Only those who are called can lose their
    covering.
Only those the sun shines on can unfold
    within.

The spiral winds on after death, also:
"I thought I saw my grandfather's ghost last
    night,"   230
I said, "but I couldn't have. He is still alive."
That day I heard he had died two days before.
And perhaps, circling like whip-raising jailers
In this lurid room, seven unmirrored dreamers
Seek a substantial form like an obliging
    whore
To varnish me with resin and wrap me up
    more,

To varnish my egoism to torment me more?

Spring images fleck my soul like buds on a
branch
This arched evening. I came out of my front
door,
Crushing a parking warden under my heel 240
And stamped upon her sting. These annoying
wasps.
Throbbing at crossroads I saw through the
cloud:
Savages sitting round the cooking-pot.
Heat-waves rose from my radiator like a
libation.
Suddenly I saw through to the ground of my
being.
My peace of mind cracked like dry earth. I
heard
The buzzing of flying priests, the white lilies
Were like nuns' lips, flooded with a white
light.
As I looked at the sapphire sky, my radio
Burst into red flower. Later, driving round 250
The corner, I saw Heaven hanging in the
night.
No outline – just lighted rooms filling the
black sky.
I saw my images fighting at night
Like a free-for-all in an animated toy
cupboard.

Buds like a hundred selves splash in the lake.
Gorse crackles, yellow laburnum flames. One
surge.
I have a hundred figures I put on slides.
Here we will sit and be ourselves till seven.
I will select in sequence: one portrait
In a hundred different scenes, like this domed
frieze.   260
The hundred figures of this circular frieze.
Here is a futile round of days and nights,
To some. Seeing all sides of this Pyramid,
The watchman-artist does not bat a lid,
Knowing Eternity is a renewal,
A recurrence. We come again and again,
Like the figures within the border of this
circular frieze!

IV

A wail for the dripping buds,

For now the daffodils are nearly over,
The almond blossom is like dazzling
snow   270
Against blue sky and a hot, melting sun,
The first petals lie like slush in the road.
A wail for this brief beauty. For soon the may
Drifts will have gone, it will be chestnut
candles,
The lilac will go brown, and there will be
Lilac stars on the lawn, caterpillars
Swinging on threads. Tulips will open wide,
Petals like electronic equipment,
Soon there will be brambles, nettles, iris,
Little hips of apples, and green rosebuds, 280
And forget-me-nots, then conkers and the
falling leaf....
A wail for this briefness, like a young girl's
cheeks
That will wrinkle into lines, a whimper, a
whine
For this briefness, a howl, a scream, despair
For these buds that time will carry into thin
air.
The moment passes us like an express train
Which rushes by our platform and then is
gone.

A wail for the Silver Age. Like the Roman
Republic
We look forward from the best through
transient glory.
How brief is this Golden Age which the future
will envy!   290
A Catullus, a Virgil, a Horace, an Ovid and
soon
No one of note. A man under a vast machine,
The roads and buildings allowed to go to ruin.
Bones sat at dinner, saying, "It is so difficult
To grow old, so difficult. Each of us exists
In the memory of a vast sepulchre.
How can we improve it? Who has not pulled
his weight?
Who can we condemn? Who ostracise? Who
is immodest,
Too serious?" A slowly clanking machine
running down.
Like drowsy wasps in autumn, silver
bones.   300
Cackles filling a vast silence. Cankerous
Creeper strangles our old decaying trunk.

242

A wail for our delapidated time,
For the horrors this dome shows for our Pax
Romana,
For the quietly clanking fate of our
civilisation.
A wail for this briefness of our Golden Age,
A whimper, a whine, a howl, a scream,
despair
For the passing of our Golden Age which
reached the moon,
Despair for these cities which will be carried
away.

A wail for all transient things,   310
A suspirating sigh, a sob, a wail,
Whimper, whine, howl, scream for all
transient things
Under the figures within the border of this
circular frieze?
But no! For we come again! Yea, we recur!
We come again and again, like these hundred
figures
Going round and round, and then going round
again!
Our coming autumn has been here before,
It will come again! I rejoice that spring is
here!
This spring will come again, as will these
cities!
By the railway line five mountain ash in the
sun,   320
Blue sky, sparrows chirping after the express
had gone.
They have been before and will come round
again!
The ever-now recurs, not in memory but in
kind.
The force of spring is too strong for dis-
integration.
My gravestone will say: "He loved Eternity,
The dew on the sundial, the plash on the
water-clock,
The silence beneath the tedious tick of time."
I rejoice in this spring and in our Golden Age!

I rejoice in all sighs, sobs, moans and wails.
Good and evil are the top and bottom of a
stream.   330
In this, the still water is deep, the top moves,
Reflecting a collapse among forget-me-nots,

A crying child, a walk towards a horror.
In that, the surface is still, but at the overflow,
With a tugging of weed, the bottom froths out
below.
Time is part of the stream that moves to the
weir,
But the stream is all one, and indivisible,
And I rejoice in the stream as it flows into its
river
And thence to the sea. I accept: the sea
spreads out,
Infinite, the source of each dipping wave;   340
This life spreads out, infinite from each birth
to each grave;
All the laws have a source which this Infinite
life gave.
I rejoice in all sighs, sobs, moans and wails.
A cheer for the stream as, still and moving, it
reaches the weir!

A blue sea, white columns and excavations.
On a Sabratha mosaic I glimpsed a man
Carrying a cross. I have risen from my tomb.
I felt the wind blowing among the statues.
I was the stream, not the petal. I was
The civilisations, not the crumbling
stones.   350
I have seen Neptune rise out of the sea
And cast a look of doubt at our crumbling
civilisation,
And weep tesserae tears of greys and blues
And browns to agree with me.

I rejoice that out of the Western dis-
integration,
New cities will rise, like new bodies for our
souls.
O this archaeological site in the Western
world.
We dance on the ashes of our former glory
And do not see the collapse ahead, the ruin.
Like a beautiful roof suspended on a few
columns   360
This civilisation hangs on Arab pillars.
If they crumble, the whole will come crashing
To the ground. Now I see the West is
dwindling, shrinking,
Again the barbarians will pour up through
East
And West. Above the rubble the columns

stand.
O Arab pillars! O short-sighted Western
    policies
That allowed these things to happen! I see a
    man
Thrash out the eye of an octopus on the sharp
    pebbles.
O Western blindness! Could you not perceive
That Britannia's Establishment had corroded
    walls?   370
But such is the process: the blinding sin of
    pride.
I rejoice in this collapse, rubble and columns,
I rejoice in the folly that brought these things
    to pass
And which was inevitable as the wind of
    winter,
For it has been before and will come again,
And again and again, like the figures on this
    frieze!

Buds drip from the beech trees. Now blossom
    is like snow.
Now chestnut candles shine down the avenue.
Eternity is a flowering of blossom and bulb,
And I am now flowering after a long
    winter.   380
We are no longer torn, in our new self;
Spring images sprout like buds along the soul.
The water-clock plashes and splashes time,
The girl has apple blossom twined in her hair.
Time is the top of the stream that moves to the
    overflow,
Eternity is the still water below.
Time is the dying leaf, the crumbling city,
Eternity is the bud and renewing spring,
The spirit that rises out of the ashes.
In the imperial palace, all the clocks are
    wrong   390
For gaze at these hills ablaze with furze, these
    drops
Of dew on a spider's thread! These daisies on
    the lawn!
O tadpole in the shallows, struggling shore-
    wards,
Turn round and swim towards the white-hot
    sun!
O four wonderful seasons, and four voices
You will come again and again like the
    figures on this dome.

I am a tree in spring, I put out leaves
And sing in the wind, with the west wind's
    rhythms.
Eternity is the wind in the leaves of time.
O spring that renews the earth with this brief
    beauty,   400
Shine out of time, like the art in this circular
    frieze,
Shine in the ever-now of the memory,
Shine for the self-renewal of a singing
    destiny,
Shine like chestnut candles for our Golden
    Age,
And come again and again after the spring has
    set!

LIGHTHOUSE

THE DARK NIGHT EASTER TEMPTATION OF
A SOMEWHAT SAINTLY MAN
(A CONTEMPLATION INSPIRED BY THE FUGAL FORM)

1975

I. STORM WIND AND LAMP FIRE

A dark night. A sea-mist, no stars. As I peer
Out of this hotel window I am enfolded in
    cloud.
Out there, beyond the garden, waves crash
    and pound
The rocks, wind foams in trees. Out there,
    somewhere,
Is a sea-swept light. I cannot see it. Waves
    thump and roar.
Down the corridor my tired relations sleep
And will wake fresh for tomorrow's wedding
    feast.
The wind rattles my windows, rain lashes. A
    snore....
I alone am awake, splashed and blown by a
    storm from my old
Life, pacing far from the hidden flashing
    lamp   10
Of my new.
          And she is awake, in the end
          room at the back,
She is waiting up for me. O these cold
Desires! O these frothing appetites! I know
That appetites not whipped up are soothed to
    a breath,
I know the benefits of spiritual soberness
When the tranquil soul gives out a peaceful
    glow,
I know it mortifies concupiscence, subduing
    sense
For a spiritual calm, I know that marriage
    mortifies;
But o her breasts, o how her dark eyes
    smiled!   20
Let them spatter my soul with the spray of
    their turbulence,
Only let me open her door and halloo my one
    request!
I, who have had my envy, anger, sloth
    trimmed away
To the clean wick of charity and strength to
    emulate,
I, who have withdrawn from sirens and found
    the best
Watch-tower from the world, the flesh, the
    Devil,
I, who have calmed my passions – joy, grief,
    hope and fear –
Loved peace, cleanness of soul, the sparkling
    water, cared
For the liberty of my spirit, which is un-
    assailable,
I have lulled my desires – and still this
    emptiness!   30
I, who have freed myself once, desire again.
Will I not soon be old and beyond this
    sucking ache?
And will I not then regret this wilderness?
This night is full of trials and temptations
Which buffet this erection and cloud the
    judgement,
And should I not be blown by one more
    experience?
Hotel Purgatory, and its tribulations.

Is this all calm is, a spell before a storm?
I dream of the weaknesses and imperfections
That blackened me into uncleanness, after
    illumination,   40
So that my sensual self ceased to be burnt to a
    form
Of pure spirit, like a wick behind lantern glass
That powers the lamp of a lighthouse like a
    sun
And guides night-ships from rocks. My soul
    was touched
And unexpectedly lit by a ray of pass-
-ing grace. It did not last. I lacked the oil of
    virtue,

It did not flow into me. I was lit, not put in or-
-der, I was transfigured, but had to be trans-
    formed.
I was cleaned, my lenses were wiped, my
    reflectors polished. Through
The next five years I was dismantled for the
    scraping off of desire,   50
And then fire consumed the last rust and
    mouldiness
Of my filth; a heat short of purgation, yet
As my soul's understanding was in darkness,
    the fire
Of love was not understood, and I saw
    nothing but
What was within myself – my own darkness.
I surrendered tobacco, and later, alcohol.
    Reverses
Of fortune beset me, I felt in a stormy rut,
Then came the excision of my lost marriage,
Loss of friendship, reputation, and health.
I had to sacrifice my coating, to strip
    myself   60
Right down to achieve the brightness which I
    knew I could manage.
Only then did I win tranquillity, holy calm.
As I pared away charred lower sense, or sin,
I revealed the higher self below. In flashes I
    was illumined.
Ecstasies near-blinded me. I had to be
    protected from harm,
For I was not ready; there was a black bottom
    on my mind
Which scouring could not penetrate, I fell
Ill with the strain. The lighthouse shone and
    then
Was hidden. So darkness enfolded me, con-
    fined
Me like this cloud that shuts out that sea-
    swept light.   70
Now I wait in a passive quiet, doing nothing,
Leaving the divine operation free to finish
    fill-
ing me, renewing the wick of my soul. There
    is no effort in this Night
Save listening, waiting to catch fire and shine
    like a sun
On the clouded dark. The glare will not now
    be too bright
For my soul, will not now torment and blind
Its understanding. The divine and the human

Know nothing of each other, like the wind on
    the clouded sea,
And now the Dark flows in and works in my
    soul
With a second, sharper purgation, to deo-   80
-dorize and cleanse its ignorances and flush
    me
With infused contemplation, like oil uniting
    my
Sensual wick, which is weak, with the fire of
    my spirit,
Making the sense spirit, so my energy
Is transferred from sense to burning spirit. By
    and by
My soul will be snuffed and forget all past
    sweetness,
It will be freed from this Cloud of
    Detachment which covers it
And shuts out temptation. It will be lit and
    raised to God. In
This dark a new self is being made. It will
    progress
To a Beatific Vision. Perhaps I will   90
Emerge as I entered, gradually, by degrees,
Into serenity. In this Dark Night there must be
Storms to clear the cloud for the illumined
    still.
A storm is an interlude that interrupts
Calm, whose blustering blows clean and adds
    to calm.
I in this foul weather, and no one knowing my
    dark
Had to be cleared in a hotel whose bar
    corrupts.

Downstairs in the bar she smiled across the
    years.
I am weak with women who have brown eyes,
    and dark hair,
And she was the best of them all. I was
    unprepared,   100
I smiled a smile that contained a thousand
    tears.
If I go to her, it will start again. I, who
Am now whole, will be divided, avoiding
    George,
And always the constant doubt, 'What if we
    are caught?'
And no peace, waiting for the next
    rendezvous;

I, who am now complete, will share a self
with her,
Will visit her when she wishes, and what if
she is jealous
Again, what if she rings me when I have
zipped up my lust?
I am so weak with dark women who whimper.

Wind clatters to cleanse. Like fire, it has a
dual nature.   110

II. WAVES OVER THE WATCH-
TOWER

A dark Night. Waves boom, my head is in a
sea-cloud.
Temptation rattles my eyes, I am buffeted by
a gale.
O these appetites! If the trials – the sufferings
– of this dark Way
Are in proportion to our imperfections and
proud
Weaknesses which must be cleaned off, and
to the degree
Of union in love to which God intends to raise
The soul when clean, then, I once thought,
monks and nuns – they
Who have been guided from puberty on – will
see
Clearly, religious do not suffer this scraping
away
Because they are more perfect than us lay
folk?   120
I put this to a nun. She shook her head and
told
Me, "There is no distinction between religious
and lay,
And nothing is clear-cut. Some people spend
Their whole life in darkness, we have
moments or even
Periods of slight relief from darkness. No one
at our convent
Has had illumination." So then, I had to
amend
The law: if the sufferings are in proportion to
our imperfections,
So are they also to our rewards of light.
The more imperfections I have, the more,
when cleaned, I
Suffer, and the more I am cleaned, the more
light in my affections.   130

I have the advantage over these darkened
sisters
Who have not suffered the scouring of their
wicks.
The Dark is in proportion to our lack of being
trimmed,
So let me be scoured till my soul comes up in
blisters!
I know that some men, like wicks that are
strong,
Bear suffering more as a gift, are purified
In more intense scouring, in less time, than
those who cry
Out with pain. I know that in suffering God
gives wrong-
Headed men strength, so that the way to
Eternity
Can lie through the Hellish blackness of the
Devil's Chelsea.   140
O the agony of this impure memory that
blackens my dreams.
It can be dripped off if I burn it with more
combustibility.
I will be tempted then. I recall the last time:
She had dark hair and brown eyes that
confided,
Standing in her door, her breasts bulged
swollen,
Inside I drew her to me, there was a fluttering
chime
From her loins in the crackling atmosphere.
We lay
Together, listening for her husband. That is
what
I want now, up the passage, her touch. I want
Blackness to spurt from me, be scattered,
dissipa-   150
-ted, squandered in a riot of hotly writhing
limbs.
She is waiting. I will go to her up the corridor.
Soon
I will tiptoe past my relations in their
chambered rooms,
Tiptoe down the mind to the forbidden whims
Of previous years, and tap. She will utter one
sigh,
I will hold her breasts and, action only, stroke
Her hair while the lighthouse burns and throbs
through the window
And ejaculates shafts of light up the dark,

caved sky.

A Dark Night. Waves boom, my head is in a
cloud.
And yet I keep telling myself, my soul's
blackened self   160
Was freed from his worldly dungeon of self-
indulgence,
From his penal prison of passions and a crowd
Of sins, was washed and paroled to the tower
where my spirit
Enjoys peace and health. He must now be
bathed
For union with his bride. But though the
divine dark
Hand touches the prisoner's door to unlock it,
To liberate him from his old affections, to
which he clings,
And denies his bride sweetnesses that separate
her, deprives
Her of all lights in a covering cloud – though
he is no longer "inside",
He is buffeted still! As the rough sea
flings   170
Foaming water and rocks at a lighthouse,
there is no relief
From the world, and what union he will reach
is like a flash
Of light arcing for a few seconds out at
The clouded dark during a force eight dis-
belief.
Ah this tempest! I tell myself, I should not
seek the world's turmoil
When the peace is whipped to spray that near
destroys me,
I, who loved all sincerely, and shone out
clean,
Was cascaded with foaming lies and
deception, a boil-
-ing heavy ground sea rolled boulders,
smashing
Them thump thump thump against the base of
my small   180
Tower, shaking it to the foundations. The
diplomat's false-
-hoods pounded me, so that often I was near
crashing
Down. I grew to expect the pudder. I was
condemn-
-ed to flash what was right in terms of its

opposite,
Sometimes to shine when we wanted ships to
sink,
To signal dangers to fleets, yet inform on
them.
I, who have felt love's fire burn in my heart,
Have committed deception, lying, treachery
Against its beacon, for mankind; exploited
friendship
For Cold War watchfulness. By my
mendacious art   190
I have saved all Europeans as a Judas saves,
I have kissed Presidents for thirty pieces of
silver.
I have had so much of the discords of the
world.
I am a contradiction: a light amid pounding
waves,
A light hidden in a dark cloud of mist and
spray.
I am a paradox, free but buffeted by confusion
From my prison, I should have expected there
would be temptations.
I served two masters: it was Europe, or the
Way.
Just as I retired from that diplomatic hole
For the unitive life, so I should retire from this
vice,   200
Surrender this backsliding to my true bride.
The soul must be tried and proved while on
parole.
Though world-weary, we must be patient and
endure,
Believing that we are humbled to be exalted,
Waiting in emptiness for the darkness to be
broken,
Waiting for a final release from that
enclosure.

Who, if I explained this, would understand
me?
Not the sleepers up the passage, not her. It
would be like
Discussing sight with men who have been
born blind.
They would say of my lighthouse, "There is
nothing in the sea,   210
What a screwy idea," and perhaps it is
unreasonable
To live like an anchorite in this Age of Vices,

Perhaps my truth achieves nothing, like that
    clouded light
Flashing unseen, when white water is
    questionable.
I have seen men wrecked who still deny there
    were rocks.
I illumine a standard for the soul, which few
    now aver.
Will I not shine for it if I am briefly sub-
    merged?
I will burn and thrust my tower in a foaming
    paradox.
I, who have lived through a stormy season,
    will not crumble
If I am washed over by another crashing
    wave.   220
What difference will it make if she froths over
    me again?
I will burn and burst up after the briefest
    fumble.

I will go and sculpt my innermost nature!

Rooms, Baroque ceilings. I creep down my
    mind.
I am at her door now. All I have to do is
    knock. I
Think, 'Adultery.' It is only a question of the
    nomenclature.
But, supposing she did not mean those smiles,
    what
If she was leading me on to amuse herself
    only?
And do I know she is still awake, that her
    husband is
Not now there? O this trembling anticipation.
    I will not   230
Be caught by a pyjama-ed guest at the bath-
    room. Can I really knock
On that closed door? She will say, "Who is
    it?" And can I shout
From here? What if she rings the night porter
    down-
-stairs, and there is a commotion? Will I say,
    "The clock –
I could not sleep and I came out to look at the
    time?"
The shame as doors open....The humiliating
    scowls!
But no, the issue is not 'Dare I', or 'Can I last

without',
But 'Am I to succumb?' or 'Can I – can I
    climb
Above this temptation, and resist it?'
    Appetites,
Like strands of bladderwrack, shrivel and
    waste away   240
If no water pours over where they cling and
    wait
For the waves. I turn back to the first of a
    thousand Nights!

III. THE BREAKING OF THE CLOUD

Now I am back in my room. My sea-wander-
    ings
Are over, I am home. A Dark Night, a sea-
    mist,
I am enfolded in cloud. The light is still hid-
-den out there. O these labyrinthine
    sufferings!
The wind blows still, there is a chill in the air.
What good will that absurd renunciation do?
    It is a joke.
What difference will it make? Seed sown in a
    furrow
Or scattered to the wind – it is all one some-
    where.   250
In a tempestuous time a little more spray
Would have made no difference. The calm
    will still
Come. When I am old I will sit in such a
    window as this
And count recriminations, and I will say,
"That Easter I hesitated in a labyrinth corridor
When I should have acted with a clean white
    blow
Like the thrust of an invory knife into an
    envelope,
And so I am alone." Here I sit and claw
My shilly-shallying soul, switching off the
    electric light,
Doubting the virtue I have won over vice, and
    the tri-   260
-umphant victory I gained over my darker
    mind,
Waiting on God, like a ship that is lost in the
    night.

This Easter I dream of death and resurrection.
The old man, the prisoner "I", was crucified

By a choppy Bay. This Purgatorial cry
Of pain is nearly over. The new Perfection
Will be born. Perhaps, like the cycle of storm
    and calm, face
Like the restless waves, now the tranquil,
    millpond sea,
I am born anew each day, resurrected each
    Eas-
-ter a little more, like the keeper who climbs
    the staircase   270
To clean the lamp each day, and trim the
    wick,
And knows better and better how the Infinite
    is lit.
I have known the agonies in the *Psalms*, I
    have cringed
With Job, I acknowledge that the apoplectic
Church is guardian of the log that records
    these trials.
It is the place where all knowledge of the
    Dark is gathered
And interpreted from generation to gener-
-ation. If the interpretations are wrong, like
    weather-dials
Incorrectly assessed, the lightkeepers must be
    told,
The barometers should not be rejected. I
    cared   280
That the Ladder of Perfection is a winding
    stair
In a wave-swept lighthouse tower. At the
    bottom, paroled,
Each day we languish for our Bride, suffer
    and pant
After Her, till we climb and are embraced by
    God's warmth, and
Are burned with sweet fire, so that with clean
    hearts, we can
See the Beatific Vision, which is like a
    refulgent
Lamp; not of this choppy dark. I acknowledge
The daily scaling of the saints, those spiritual
    successes.
Perhaps I will now daily spiral, with ever less
    sense
And more spirit, till I reach the last, dazzling
    ledge?   290
Perhaps I will climb time to the altar of One
    Church.
More and more I place my hope in the spirit

of rebirth,
Of regeneration, of resurrection, through
    whose recur-
-ring spiral, like spring, we pass on our daily
    search.

Night. I lie back and wait, and my warring
    quietens.
Lo! Through the blackness a round white light
    breaks, shines out.
O my lighthouse! The mist is lifting! The
    cloud
Lifts! O my beacon! You are still there! I
    must cleanse
The windows of my soul to receive this divine
    infusion
Till it flashes off, and I must climb back down
    into darkness   300
Again. I am so unfit. You are the radiant guest
I should visit. Shine on me, bring me to a
    conclusion.

Dawn is breaking. Sparrows chirp, sea-gulls
    scream.
The wind has dropped. Calm has returned
    again.
The sea is at rest. Come, let us go outside,
    take
The cliff path to the little church by the
    stream
That trickles on to the sand. Let us sit among
    the graves
And peacefully watch the fog lift over the
    placid
Rocks by the tower, whose light is now
    extinguished,
Like a candle, for the sun to take over. The
    waves   310
Are tranquil. Let us hear the wapping in the
    caves
Of the heart. Let us give thanks, for calm has
    returned.
We have united ourselves, till Dark falls and
    flesh burns.
Let our hearts burn in the sunrise with the fire
    of the waves!
Let us glory in the sunrise at the sparkling
    beyond the graves!

THE WEED-GARDEN

(A HEROIC SYMPHONY)
(For all who garden our Western world)

"Have you had twelve experiences that show what has happened to the culture of the last thirty years?"
Ezra Pound in conversation with Nicholas Hagger at Rapallo, 16th July 1970

1975

1. THE SOUL IN AUTUMN

(I) HEART

Rinse your eyes with this floating astronaut's
    view
Of America down there, and Europe to the
    Urals;
The Western World like yellow cockleshells
Set in a green flower-garden round a blue
Puddle. You can just see Cornwall under
    cloud.
Down there is Africa, we are sure the Far East
Will never spin round.
          Part of this estate has been
Sold to tenants. This part is now a crowd
Of houses without fences, and each home
    is   10
Under common ownership. By this roadside
    shrub
Lawns wait the cutting-machine, the earth
    puts up
Chickweed, groundsel, bellbind – and a few
    lilies
On a rockery of a buried head of Christ.
Here stood a monastery with a culture-garden,
Then a country-house. Among rhododendrons
And azaleas, flowerbeds shaped the zeitgeist
In old-fashioned floral letters under statues:
PRAISE GOD, and PEACE, and JOY under
    Socrates,
Pericles, Solon, Aristotle, Sophocles –
    PPE,   20
Intellect, art; one élan in reds and blues.
Sorrel and elder were dug out with Dutch
    hoes
By a hundred gardeners. When His
    Lordship's
Family came down the steps, the foreman

quipped
"'Ere come ve Crown 'Eads of Europe, by ve
    Berlin Rose."

Out in the meadow there was ploughing and
    harrowing,
Monks turned the clods, within furrows seeds
    fell.
Earth buried them, they slept in cold darkness
    until
The rooted time of its upspringing in spring.
Stalks came to full ear, the Mysterious
    birth   30
Of golden blades of light from the One. Then
    it
Was time for threshing, winnowing, grinding.
Out in the next garden they dug the earth,
The soil was made right; when the climate
    suit-
-ed the seed was sown. Flowers needed more
    care
Than orchard trees or field crops, which could
    be spared
The weeding and watering that strengthen
    each root.
There was pruning, training, and grafting till
Each perfect flower bloomed, and the failed
    seeds were
Good only for rooting-up and burning.   40
    Here
In this meadow a man's mind, heart and will
Had to be cleared of stones and ploughed,
    made fit
To receive thoughts in furrows. The seed
    covered up,
There was weeding and watering against the
    scorching sun
And withering winds. When in due season it

Was time for threshing, winnowing, grinding,
And the grain was separated from the useless
    chaff
Of the personality – the old life that
Was lost – its eternal essence was the
    finding.   50
Crops feed, like fruit trees; flowers compel
    love.
Here in the monks' garden there was a
    sprinkling
With a little meditation, avoiding young
Faults and vices, which could grow till it took
    a shov-
-el to dig them up. There was watering from
    the well
Of recollectedness; then – less hard work –
From the wheel and waterpipe that irrigated
    the earth
With contemplation. Then, through the
    channel
Of union, was a running stream. Without
    strain,
As vices died like weeds the mind was
    stilled,   60
There was no effort after opening the lock of
    the will.
Then the dry soil enjoyed the refreshing rain
Of rapture, was a Paradise of flowers, fruit
And fragrant blossom. There was pruning, for
The energies went in one direction. Their
Faults had to be cut out before they took root
And put out suckers, the desires that sap-
-ped the strength and fertility of the growing
    stem.
There was training, so that souls could grow
    well
Up with the sap to the light, which could then
    enwrap   70
Them. In plants, the reproductive process
Hinders development; so it is in humans.
There was grafting, of a spiritual impulse
On the soul; once assimilated, it express-
-ed its more evolved life as a perfect bloom,
    showing
The stock had accepted the Divine Gardener's
    will;
There could be no obliteration for a soul
So exquisite, no rooting-up and burning: just
    growing
Under an abbot who trained towards

perfection.
These things happened when mind, heart and
    will were ready.   80
Yet the soul cannot now unfold as it often did.
All those instances of resurrection
In galleries, concert halls and Cathedrals –
Michelangelo, Beethoven, St. John of the
    Cross –
In libraries and Museums; their "explication"
    was
Not all man's, yours and mine, their tongues
    were not calls.
If the soul is cultivated, it will not yield
Like trees, crops, flowers. Man is of Nature, if
    he tills
And is tilled, his spirit will not unfold bells
And put out greatness like a Lily-of-the-
    Field.   90

Out in this city there is concrete soil.
Stones of buildings and glass adorn the
    ground
And men scattered from the tube at ten, blown
    down
Pavements, see beauties that in no way spoil
Them. What does it matter if a man is
    separated
From Nature, like seed on built-up ground,
    and won't
Fork over his concrete heart and force his soul
To share in the "agricultural" growth he has
    hated
Like a muddy field? Why should a town man
    see
That all plants are immortal because of their
    spring   100
Renewal, that to their unity his tongue
Belongs, that life is like a Forest tree
That sings in the wind? Why should his soul
    sprout
Or unfold? Are not stones secure? What if no
    watering
Helps it, no pruning, training, grafting, no
    spirit,
And it lies uncared for among vices and doubt
About the possibility of growth, dead seed,
Or at best a withered stalk, a wilting stem?
Why should we root it out and burn it, then
Give the space to some pip who will bloom
    and spread his creed?   110

Why should a town man put aside his pride
And submit himself to a Gardener he cannot
    credit
And open himself to a hand by a flowerpot –
Why should he not live with a folded-up
    inside?

(II) THE LAND

Out in the meadow there was ploughing and
    harrowing,
Out in the next garden monks dug the earth.
When sufficient souls unfolded, the land was
    astir
With Cathedrals, Fra Angelicos, Hiltons, nar-
    rowing
The sprouting under civilisation to the husk of
    sin.
Spiritual art and religion flourished: those
    mystics –   120
Rolle, Julian of Norwich, *Cloud of
    Unknowing* –
Of the Medieval time. Their culture, within
Our civilisation, took its look from its leaders
Who embodied the idea of their Age –
An idea of cultivation, of the tillage
Of the mind – like floral words: in paintings,
    sculptures,
Music, books in libraries. And the idea, when
Measured against the order and permanent
    sunlight
Of civilisation, measured and defined the
    time,
How each month reclaimed the land from
    barbarian   130
Rankness and wintery dark: the Medieval
Closed eye, the Renaissance muscle, the
    Classical smile,
The Romantic swoon – and now, the drooping
    blind-
-ness of modern autumnal doubt! There was
    an upheaval
Each generation. Each week's showing on the
    soil
Differed from the last.
                    When the souls of our
                    culture's leaders
Did not unfold, the land looked stony, tares
Took the place of flowers, and did flowers not
    "spoil"
Our garden? There was a cult of the seed: is it

not "good"
To be unsprouted, are not all husks
    "equal",   140
Was not flower-growth "a fairy-tale"?
    Religion and
Art withered. Now weeds have "stature", and
    where there would
Have been a riot of colour, there is worship of
    stones.
The surroundings are cared for: brick borders
    and walls.
A few men ask, "Is the ground exhausted
    now?" Or
"Must it lie fallow for a while?" One moans,
"We should have rotation of seeds, this is sour
    ground."
Belief in the land's fertility is shaken,
The civilisation is thought to wilt, though it
    can
Build wonders round each weedbed, the
    surround-   150
-ings the gardeners spend their time on,
    instead of growth.
The gardeners scatter fertiliser by the hand-
    ful –
Here bourgeois materialism, there the Marxist
    "could",
Here liberal humanism to encourage sloth,
There egalitarian compost – stale outer creeds
That help weeds grow. (And some say, "Was
    it fair
When roses had the attention and thistles were
    not cared
For?") Who said "Mismanagement", as if the
    tillage of seeds,
Not their equality, were the gardener's trust?
Every age would escape into a more summery
    past,   160
But look for the flowers that are not there in
    our West.
Did lack of water, or the land, alone cause this
    Golden autumn dust?

(III) THE WEEDS

Look at this "ordered" estate now, with its
    hidden dump!
In the past it was not always pleasant to live
    in:
Wars ripped up the land, there was disease,
    poverty,

No sewage. There was once a Hell round the
stump
Of that chestnut. When the country-house was
torn down
Some of our best flowers were broken. Now
the smashed heads
Are hidden, the air is poisoned less often
From across the far wall. Now this is
"Newtown",   170
Now the estate could pass as a Paradise
Of peace and prosperity, if a precarious
One, with "low working hours" and "a
perpetual wage rise".
It is well laid-out with fine rockeries, nice
Walls, cockleshell borders, fine green-
houses,
Vegetable frames, lattice, crazy-paving.
No one tramples on the beds, they have
abolished
Smallpox and starvation, and what if inflation
arouses
Disquiet – a few prices rising, money buying
A little less, the Council slightly in the
red?   180
Complex machines will cut the grass and
hedge,
There is freedom for all seeds to grow, and
little crying
Out for justice as across the Eastern wall,
And (in theory) all is kept in order.
Is there not a Golden Age outside, where
there
Used to be a Hell?
          What matter if, for all
This autumn levelling for "equal seeds"
And outer landscaping, or because of it,
Gone are the discrimination of the gardener,
his   190
Pruning and training, so he now grows
weeds,
And gone are restraint and discipline, which
delayed
The growth of "blooms"? Chickweed,
groundsel, bellbind
Are nourished on the dry hard earth, why
Should not flower-seeds be choked? Gone are
standards like the spade.
In the culture-garden, roses once unfolded,
But now, no "élitist" growth; neat, ordered
doubt

And nothing. Two thousand years of root and
shoot
Disfigured man with a Golden Flower,
remoulded
Him through Light. Where there was a
"Paradise"   200
Is there now a Hell? So what if the seven
Deadly weeds are allowed to grow unchecked
And are called by the names of flowers,
which deny their vice?
Why should pride not be "Disbelief" – in the
Gardener whose help
Is not needed, as if the hidden Sun
Broke open a destiny its seedcase shuts up?
Why should Avarice not be "More", that
noble yelp
For material bread that is barked as a
percentage?
Why should lust not be "Permissiveness", or
Anger called
"Indignation" – the fuse in all bombs that
have killed –   210
Or Gluttony "Drunkenness", which drugs its
hostage
Consciousness with smiling dreams? Why
should Envy
Not be called "Egalitarianism", and Sloth
"Laziness"? Do these flowering plants really
choke
The privileged ones that now lack energy?

How can there be freedom from this autumn's
grip?
Where is the great man who can point the
way? What true
Gardener can bring our culture to unfolding
bloom
And change the look of the land with his
leadership?

2. HOW THE SUMMER ENDED

(A) REJECTION OF THE GROUND
There is no life cycle for all souls!   220
A great man is a blob
Of sticky seed, then a knob
Of flesh that fattens and rolls,
And swells into two profiles.
A great man, at his birth,
Looks no different in his mirth

From the dunce that kicks and smiles.
In infancy a Beethoven
Is as cuddly as Tommy Sloth;
No Mozart shows early growth.   230
No petalhood is God-given.
A child Michelangelo
Questions the dark, the cold,
Is not fed by falling gold
Leaves, knows all there is to know.
In youth, no Will Shakespeare
Gathers goodness from the soil,
Germinates in great turmoil,
Or in agonizing despair;
There is no life cycle of the dusk!   240
No one accepts a Hell
Of suffering which splits the shell
Of the proud self, the hard husk
Out of which the petals unfold.
Out of hardness flows no pith,
From indifference, no myth
Of the loving heart takes hold
Of its being, ground; no root
Turns downward, anchoring,
No stem drives, pushing   250
To the surface light. No shoot
Starts Tolstoy's spirit: frost
On the seedcase, slow hours,
Through prime, old age, to the "flower's"
Dark death to what it lost!
A seed is alone in the night,
But if it dies, it bears a lily of light.
A man without a heart is an empty shell,
A great man unfolds his lily like a bell.

(B) THE QUESTIONING OF THE FLOWERS

WheeeeeEEEEE. BANG!   260
Bomb craters pit the land, fields and gardens
    lost,
Church roof crashes round the font, as
    London sinks
Like Athens towards penury and a Universal
    State.
Wire fences go up, rockets point at a hostile
    neighbour.
Yalta, Potsdam, two dozen "decolonising"
    wars
Glint in a dictator's eyes. Bands thump, a
    salute,
Union Jack is hauled down in India, Pakistan,

On a crumbling Empire. Brrrr! The cold dark
    nights
To be heated by these returning soldiers'
    work.
A ruling class knocked to hell. WheeeeEEEE,
    BANG!   270
Suez. A Prime Minister speaks on television,
Uproar in the streets, outside the Commons
    until
The faltering, the weakness. "Damn the ruling
    class!"
Shout the soulless. "Damn patriotism, damn
    war."
Aldermaston. Marchers sit in Trafalgar
    Square,
Rows deep awaiting arrest. "Damn your
    Cyprus,
Damn Kenya. Damn Great Britain's
    Establishment."
An Angry brawl in the Royal Court theatre
    bar.
"Damn your old values, damn phoneyness,
    traditions."
Question, questionquestionquestionques-
    tion.   280
The Church. Our role. Our rule. Our class.
    Your class.
Whissshoooo. A wind of change as the
    liberals win their way.
CRASH CRASH CRASH as the colonies
    tumble down.
Doubt fills eyes that had the contempt of
    confidence.
Questionquestionquestion authority.
Prison governors. Headmasters. Army
    officers.
Taboos. Incest. Sex. Question, and permit
Lust, anger, envy, sloth, gluttony, pride,
Avarice. "Damn your Oxbridge and public
    schools,
Damn your Queen and Church and self-
    discipline."   290
Teddy boys. Rock and Roll. Jazz. Pleasure-
    living.
"Damn your colonial wars." On television,
Cynicism, satire. "Aren't we down the drain?
Look at our balance of payments!" Behaviour,
Every tradition turned upside down. Cliveden,
Profumo, Wilson. Poverty and wage-freeze.
Hard times, bright clothes, Vietnam, a horde

255

of students
March against the American Embassy, shout
    "Out!"
Carrying pictures of Mao. Barbarian faith
    spreads,
All are equal. Africa lost, Arab oil states   300
Lost. Israel. Palestinians hijack planes,
Black guerillas creep in thickets and aim
    guns.
WheeeeeEEEEE, BANG! Belfast. Ratatatatat
    tat.
King's Road, crowded pubs, drunkenness,
    sloth, lust.
Inflation. Trade Unions march shouting
    "Greed",
"Avarice". School gates vomit a slouching,
    sprawling
Generation, chewing gum. Ratatatatat tat tat!
Men barge in past ladies, capture train seats.
WheeeeeeEEEEEE, BANG! "We shall not be
    moved," sing the reds,
Waving scarves. Four affairs in three days
    Ted had...   310
Tristram loved his nephew's wife past the last
    black sail,
Sir Launcelot went on and on for many
    weeks,
Riding hither and thither in the forests of
    Britain,
And many damsels he rescued from wicked
    men,
But four Guineveres Ted had at the seaside,
And "We shall not be moved" sing the scarf-
    waving reds.

By the font ponder the Church round which
    Europe grew.
Centuries of religious paintings in the
    National Gallery,
Centuries of religious music in the Albert
    Hall.
On this fist and arm of a High Road five
    churches   320
Like congealed scabs. By this dry font
    ponder.
"Our Father in heaven, Thy name be
    hallowed."
By the confessional, not "Ite Missa Est,"
But "Go, it is finished." Questionquestion
    question.

Down in this Cornish harbour, stone cottages,
    masts.
Twenty artists lived on two pounds a week,
    and grew
Through their paintings like boys discarding
    outgrown shirts
And socks. Now one is left, and he has to
    work
To pay rates, fares, prices, the cost of
    breathing.
Shostakovich and Teddy Baines, both are
    equal   330
Before sickness benefit. And four in three
    days!

What fine traditions choked by questionings!
Thus my dear sisters, in the wilderness
In which you journey, there are such beasts
    and worms.
Beloved men, recognise what the truth is,
The world is in haste and it draweth near to
    the end,
It must get worse from day to day before the
    coming
Of Antichrist because of the sins of the
    people.
Ah sinful nation!

Look at our culture. It has been wrecked by
    iconoclasm.   340
The old idols have been pulled down because
    they are old.
There they lie, their heads smashed by the far
    wall,
The espousers of the traditional Virtues,
Christians and respecters of learning. Damn
    the vandalism!
Damn the ignorance that did this! Damn the
    philistinism!
Who are these figures in their place? These
    nobodies with names
I will *not* memorise? What an example for the
    young!
Sculpture, painting, music, theatre, novel,
    poetry –
Who? Name me one figure of stature, one.
A dump of smashed heads, and little garden
    gnomes.   350
Venus de Milo, Michelangelo – these faceless
    curves!

Beethoven's Third, Sibelius's Second – this
    cacophanous screeching!
Shakespeare's Lear, Ibsen – this muttered
    incomprehensibility!
Dostoevsky, Tolstoy – this light-hearted
    jokiness!
Dante, Baudelaire – this wet, unheroic drivel!
All this technique–first rubbish, this
    decadence!
All this accident and chance and loss of con-
    trol –
These movable iron spokes! These wobbly
    lines!
These electronic patterns! These nude
    actors!   360
These shufflable chapters! Waste-paper
    collage poems!
All this ugliness!
No more grand themes. No grand minds to
    compose them!
Only small grey gnomes in an Age of
    Groundsel.

Look at our culture. It has been wrecked by
    vandals,
By barbarians who believed in – questioning.
These weeds – pull them up.
Let them make room for the confidence of
    roses.

There have been questionings since the
    fifteenth century.
Every generation argues with the Christian
    tradition,   370
Like blossoms arguing with the bark the
    tension has been good.
But this argument has gone further. Like a
    child,
Like a two-year-old child snipping off the
    heads of the flowers
In a garden, our generation turned against its
    tradition.
We are waiting for the confidence to bloom
    through again.

This is how the summer ended, in iconoclasm.
Would it not have ended anyway in stalks?

(A) THE SADNESS OF THE HUSKS

How glad for the souls that did not sprout

As they look back on when the buds were out,
When the birds were in song, when with all
    the lads   380
They had desires, and dreamt of *Iliads*
But questioned their own talents
With the doubting of diffidence;
On when they aged to the heaviness
Of summer inertia and distress;
On when they browned with the browning
    leaf
To September ripeness, to ripened grief,
On when the October vistas opened
And they saw more clearly how splend-
-id the year had been, how they could have
    sprung,   390
Yet were not listened to by the young,
On when they huddled by November fires,
Priorities right round flickering desires,
And with a positive tiredness, thought,
Full of creaks now, of all they ought
To have done, lying awake at night,
Watching for the first ghostly white light!
How glad for the souls in discontent
As they look back on what it all meant
And wonder, 'Was there not something
    more?   400
Did I not miss the meaning, long before?'
How sad as their broken faces look at ruined
    hands
And wonder what they might have grown in
    different lands!

3. A THOUGHT FOR WINTER

(A) THE FERTILE SOIL OF NATURE: JANUARY TO JUNE

O how souls would grow if they used their
    eyes
And ears on the flora and fauna, the butter-
    flies,
Birds, animals, flowers, hedgerows, trees and
    seas
That nourish throughout the year! See hive
    bees
Swarm in January, the male yew flowers, a
    mistle-
Thrush and – hear – a great tit call near a
    thistle.
Gorse flames, ash twigs are in bud, and plu-
    plu-plu   410

Plu-plu-plu, sings a green woodpecker.
    Through
Honeysuckle buds, see, woodbine, blackthorn.
Coltsfoot hangs its head now it rains, trout
    spawn;
See the footprints of the water vole under ivy
Fruit, hear the vixen scream, the dog-fox yelp
    in the early
Dark. Now a brimstone flutters near elm and
    alder
Flower, and hazel catkins, and the yellow-
    hammer
Chirps, "A little bit of bread and no cheese."
See footprints of squirrel and stoat. Red toad-
    stools squeeze
Through near the barren strawberry. Jackdaws
    flap   420
Round the church tower, blue tits chase,
    twitter and scrap.
Wrens search for spiders. Now, from winter
    sleep
In rafters, Red Admirals and peacocks peep,
And small tortoiseshells. Sticky horse chest-
    nut buds
Unfold in the sunshine, a great white cloud
    scuds
Over blue. A squirrel and a wood pigeon feed
On fresh green leaves. See, thrushes and
    blackbirds speed
North. Wheatears and chiffchaffs flit. A
    chaffinch sings
From telegraph wires, a white bar on its
    wings.
Violets, sallow, and a hare. Marsh mari-
    gold   430
Blaze near some toadspawn, a necklace of
    cold
Eggs. See: a mole, a shrew, and a sleepy
    hedgehog.
Now it is primrose time. By this Forest log,
Crab apple and guelder rose. Shh! a heron, in
    that copse.
See ravens on those crags, crossbills in the fir-
    tree tops.
Now all Nature is awake. Cowslips, bluebells.
Oak, beech, walnut put out first leaves, and
    smells.
Willow catkins are out. Horse-tails. An
    orange tip,
A small copper, a holly blue, all skip

By a seven-spot ladybird eating greenflies 440
On a leaf. Newt eggs on pond weed, and in
    the skies,
Swallows, house-martins return, and the
    cuckoo.
See willow-warblers, blackcaps, nightingales
    through
Leaves, see nests of thrust and blackbird, and
    in high
Thorn, the domed nest of twigs of a magpie.
Now is the month of flowering trees and
    plants.
All is fresh and bright and green, the beech
    woods dance.
There are orchids in the meadow, and white
    hawthorn,
White chandles on horse chestnut, bats above
    the lawn.
See, a blue tit is eating a caterpillar up,   450
While mayflies gad round a water buttercup.
Dandelions by a wasp's nest, fairy ring
Toadstools. Swifts scream and circle in the
    fine evening.
The hen-pheasant sits, the water forget-me-
    not
Blinks yellow eyes. In the birch and bracken a
    spot-
-ted flycatcher, a nightjar. A wealth of song!
Linnets, goldcrests, tits clamour all day long
For food. Young robins. Now the scent of
    new-
Cut hay being cocked and carted disturbs two
Rabbits. Weasels, rats, hedgehogs, partridges,
    stoats,   460
Owls fly for mice there, voles search near
    river boats
For young. Here pick woodruff and smell
    new-mown
Grass in winter. In field and wood, on ston-
-y moor and heath, by mountain and water-
    side:
Butterflies. White admirals, large blues glide,
Fritillaries, ringlets. Caterpillars teem,
Tortoiseshells' on stinging nettles, lime-
    hawks' gleam
On lime trees. Birds have bedraggled feathers,
As they approach the moult. In certain
    weathers
See swallow skim, see the vermilion hind
    wing   470

Of a cinnabar moth near ragwort, fluttering
On the downs, or lacewing near the field
    rose.
Black slugs. A snail eats leaves near a garden
    hose,
Gnats and midges dance over the water butt,
The foliage teems with grubs round the
    summerhut,
The garden is full of crawling, hopping pests.
Humble bees in the foxgloves, a honeybee
    quests
In the dead nettles. Scarlet poppies in the
    corn-
-fields, boletus in the woods, the newly born
Bullhead fish – "miller's thumb" – dart in the
    pond,   480
Near ferns: moonwort and adder's tongue.
    Beyond
Yellow water-lilies, red deer and badgers'
    earths.
The seashore is strewn with starfish and after-
    births:
Jellies, seaweed. Bladderwrack, Irish moss,
Green laver. Sand sedge, sea rocket, hound's
    tongue toss
In the wind. In the rocks limpets, whelks cling
    to a slab
Near a strawberry anemone, and a hermit
    crab.

(B) STONY GROUND

O how men decay without being fed by the
    praise
Of Nature, like seeds on the stone of their
    cities:
Pavements, walls! Petrol fumes of cars and
    buses   490
Smog up the air so the sun is in a haze.
Leaves droop, are shaken in a polluted wind.
Men stoop near the underground, tread
    concrete grass,
Hunch under electric light while the months
    pass
Like descending aeroplanes. Men, disciplined
By suits and ties, are strangers to chestnut
    trees,
Are blown into parks like leaves, or like
    conkers, drop.
Men drive to forests their fathers used to lop
For firewood, use them as luxuries, to please.

Here their ephemeral heads are measured
    by   500
The Eternal, here they see horses crop grass,
Not cars filled with petrol. Here they see cows
    pass
With swollen udders, not a packeted supply
Of milk in a supermarket. On this farm they
Can speak to their transport, their food. O go
To Canterbury, and before St. Thomas's ho-
-ly shrine, where pilgrims have knelt since
    Chaucer's day
And polished the floor, examine the mosaic
Pavement with its thirteenth century roundels,
Twelve signs of the zodiac in yellow
    medals,   510
Virtues, sins, occupations of the months. Pick
Out the two-headed god, looking forward and
    back,
Then: warming hands; digging; pruning;
    hawking;
Mowing; weeding; reaping; and boar-hunting;
Then: treading grapes, and after the too
    smooth, black
November sign, killing pigs. This was how
Men lived traditionally, close to the land,
Which fed their souls and helped them to
    expand.
O the folded-up souls of city-men now!

(A) THE FERTILE SOIL OF NATURE:
JULY TO DECEMBER

O how souls would explode if they used their
    eyes   520
And ears on the flora and fauna beneath the
    skies
Of July! Now rainfall, now the sun's power
Increases for full growth; the lime-trees
    flower
Near sprays of wild clematis and harebells.
Lizards slither in the couchgrass, past snail-
    shells.
An adder darts. Frogs, prey for the heron and
    crow.
Dragonflies flit, and now fly backwards.
    Glow-
-worms looking for snails give out a cold
    green light,
Blind-worms, ferns. See the jumping spider's
    flight
Past a centipede. On dry heath and water-

side   530
Second, third broods of swallows and wide-
     eyed
Young martins, litters of rabbits and rats. And
     see
A pipistrelle, infant in pouch, on her e-
-vening flight. Now the cornfields are gold-
     brown. Corn-cockle and
Cornflower, oats pale. Scarlet poppies splash
     the land.
The last riot of summer colour. Elder,
Hawthorn show fruits, there are drupes on the
     guelder-
Rose, wayfaring tree, dogwood. The birch
     pales,
Limes turn yellow, elms lighten. Nightingales,
Blackcaps go, swifts scream and go, the adult
     cuckoo   540
Goes. Wood-pigeons coo. Flocks of starlings,
     two
Companies of linnets, charms of goldfinches
     flit
With tinkling cries among ripe thistles. A tit
Sings again, corn-buntings sing. The grass
     snake breeds,
A cranefly dandles near ink-cap fungi. Seeds
Ripen. Harvest mice swing in fields of wheat
And oats. See the long-tailed fieldmouse stop
     and eat.
On poplars and willows, the red underwing's
     eggs.
Young wasps crawl from their cells with
     unsteady legs,
Tench and minnows breed. Self-heal.
     Whirligig bee-   550
-tle. Fleabane in marshes, by damp roads. See
Frogbit in ponds and ditches. Now the crops
Are ready, the harvest of the hedgerows drops
Blackberries, elders, sloes, blackthorn's wild
     damsons;
There are bilberries and red cranberries on
     moors and commons.
All is seed and fruit, birds strip seeds. Wind
     tossed,
Ash, maple, sycamore have fruit. Early frost
Loosens their leaves. Insects fall drowsy and
     lay
Eggs on leaves or ground, under water or
     bark, then may
Die. Drowsy young wasps hibernate,

older   560
Queens die. Wood-ants disappear. Now gos-
     samer
Lifts the spider skywards until cooler air
Blows. Webs on leaves. Chicory, ragwort
     where
Skylarks sing. Last songs of willow-warbler,
Chiff-chaff. Tortoiseshell looks for a ceiling
     corner.
A magpie eats grubs after the autumn plough-
-ing. Shrews die. Hive-drones are massacred
     now.
In ponds, water-boatman, water-scorpion,
Great water beetle. Autumn crocus. Meadow
     saffron,
Cow-parsnips, corn sow-thistle. On stubbles
     see   570
Speedwells, toadflax, camomile, cudweed,
     fumitory,
Hemp-nettles, goose-foots, the pimpernel's
     scarlet fires,
And the last swallows gather on the wires.
Brambles. Now the nut harvest drops hazels
     for
Squirrel and nuthatch, chestnuts, walnuts or
Beechnuts for birds, acorn, sycamore wing,
Maple and hornbeam fruit, conker. Rose-hips
     cling.
Now is the mushroom harvest, and fungi
     smells.
Toadstools, blewits, parasols, chanterelles,
Morals and lawyers' wigs, which batten off
     decay –   580
The sun that cleanses also rots away.
(The fire of Heaven is the fire of Hell,
It is up to each recipient's inner well
Whether it purifies or burns.) Puff ball
And fairy rings, polypore on birch. All
Is dank. Mistle-thrushes feed off berries,
Curlew and snipe go to estuaries
And shore. Linnets and starlings are larger.
Redwings sing "See-eep", fieldfares sing
     "Chah-chah-
Chah-chak" near hawthorn. House spider.
     Yarrow,   590
Corn marigold. House mouse. Jackdaw, rook,
     crow.
Greenfinches, tree sparrows, yellowhammers,
Hooded crows, snow-buntings, great grey
     shrikes – "butchers"

Who impale on thorns – all arrive. Lizards,
    snakes,
Frogs, toads, newts. Water voles, fieldmice.
    Thrush breaks
Snailshells with stones, nuthatch wedges
    ragged–
Edged hazel nutshells in tree trunks. Death's
    head
Moths fly. Now there are few fruits or
    flowers,
Now there are fogs and sunless days, damp
    devours
The woodland. Oak and beech leaves brown.
    Groundsel,   600
Chickweed, shepherd's purse, violets, gorse,
    hazel
Catkins. Oak, ash, chestnut, lime have winter
Buds. Redpolls and siskins on the river alders.
Crossbills haunt pines and firs, opening cones
For seeds. Goldcrests, long-tailed tits. The
    high tones
Of tree-creepers' "Tee tee." Owls search for
    mice.
"Hooo…hoo-hoo-hoo…hooooo," the tawny
    owl speaks.
"Kee-wick, kee-wick," from the female. The
    barn-owl shrieks.
Little owl goes "Kee-ew", long-eared owl
    moans
"Coo-oo" from firs and larches. Under
    stones   610
Snails cluster to hibernate. Plane twigs have
    fruit.
Skylarks go. Creeping buttercups. See coot
On lakes. Weasels, stoats, foxes become
    fierce,
Tench bury themselves in mud till spring can
    pierce
The ice. Red clover, yarrow, white campions,
Dankness among fungi, mosses, lichens.
Now the December moth is in the cold air.
Tree-trunks and barks with moth-cocoons. All
    is bare.
Witches' broom and mistletoe on hawthorn
And apple, poplar and oak. Crunch of
    acorn   620
Under foot. Robin and song-thrush sing. See
    nests
Of rock and heron. Dreys of squirrels. Crests
Of cockerels. "Twit twit" from the dipper near

Streams. Wren, hedge-sparrow, corn-bunting.
    And hear
The wood-pigeon coo. Holly. Tracks on first
    snow
Of rat and fox, jump of rabbit or toe
Of hare. Pheasant, moorhen. Stoat, ptarmigan.
Candle-snuff fungus. At the end of an
Aging December there will be lighter days
But harder weather. More bird songs. Now
    praise   630
Snowdrop, primrose, violet. Teeming from
    the dead,
A million abundant joys swell the seed in the
    head!

4. LILY FOR A DISTANT SPRING

(A) TIME-ROSE

Rinse your eyes with this floating astronaut's
    view
Of America down there, and Europe to the
    Urals:
The Western World like yellow cockleshells
In a golden autumn garden. Chickcress and
    new
Lilybind grow gloriously in the unsold part
Of this estate, where council houses crowd!
Out in the meadow there was ploughing and
    harrowing, out
In the garden, digging. In the centuries of
    man's heart,   640
A time's soul toiled to unfold a celestial rose:
Rolle, *Ancrene Wisse*, *Cloud of Unknowing*,
Ladder of Perfection, Julian of Norwich.
μυειν is to see – more than sharp-eyed
    Chaucer knows.
Dante, Michelangelo, Blake, Rodin – the
    "Yes"
Of the visionary's Hell disfigured a nation!
Recall the men of history with one notion,
Men of Eternity, from Europe's timeless-
    ness –
St. John of the Cross, St. Teresa, Cranmer,
Luther, Calvin, Fox, Wesley, the inner-
    eared –   650
And men of art who visioned quiet ideas –
El Greco, Brueghel, Pascal, or Goethe –
How the greatness of our West condemns
    their smallness!

How this effortlessness shames their laborious
  lawns!
An invisible Standard, like his Lord-
-ship's culture-garden, judges our chickweed
  "cress"
As one roundel does another in the
  Canterbury floor:
Love envy; humility pride; temperance
Greed; sobriety luxury; diligence and
  patience,
Sloth and anger. Let the time-rose bloom once
  more!   660

(B) THE BARK AND THE STONES

When flowers do not unfold, petalhood
  declines,
When souls do not unfold, so does
  civilisation,
Which is an ideal of Perfection. Some-
-times we can see it in art: this Christ light
  shines,
But now that brutal hardness, that scowl is
  dark.
The blossom we aspire to shows our state of
  self,
And when the soul has unbudded, it expresses
A higher state of petalhood than bark.
The ideal of the West was always Christ,
Our civilisation nourished what it
  worshipped,   670
His peace and forgiveness, the beauty he kept,
With the sap of religion, just as primitivism is
  spiced
With savagery. There is Christ's Western pity,
Or the barbarous cruelty of butchered nuns
In the Congo, or babies beheaded and slung
In a Timor gutter. Or bombed in a British
  city....
The sap of a civilisation rises above
Its lower instincts and desires, pours out
Vigour and vitality like a tree in flow-
-er, ripens philosophy, technology, for
  love   680
Of God – our Cathedrals – for which man
  extends
His mind and spirit to the utmost, like petals
Enlarges his faculties, grows from the pistils
Of his creative powers to Angelic ends:
Dante, Michelangelo, Shakespeare, Newton,
  Goethe.

The fruits of a civilisation fall with a
  confident sense
Of permanence – those solid Victorian
  buildings
Round Trafalgar Square, made to last – of
  stability
Through success in war, they oppose the ant-
  like descents
Of Völkerwanderung, the fear (like a pear) 690
Of being overrun by invaders, plague and
  famine.
Civilisation dies through exhaustion, the
  feeling
Of hopelessness, that it is not worth budding
  and bear-
-ing public buildings. It is destroyed from
  within,
Sapped by loss of soul-confidence, by
  questions
Against blossoming. So what of these
  shrivelled stones
And glass, these high-rise blocks, this
  autumn, this thin
Crop of woody energy, strength and self-will?
Are these our fruits of perfection, this Post
Office Tower, this windfall of Brussels win-
  dows?   700
This materialistic energy, this bruised still?

(A) PETALS OF LIGHT

A hero is Protean and changes his forms
Just as all waves are different but of one sea
And therefore are the same; just as all leaves
Are the same; just as each year, in the sun that
  warms,
All roses are one rose in different shapes.
Great men's souls unfold and shine petals of
  light
From their civilisation and religion, and lat-
-er renew them with fruitfulness, until autumn
  gapes.
In a time of growth they make a civilisation
  grow,   710
In a disintegrating autumn they make all sects
  one
Church, discarding dead leaves to reveal the
  un-
-derlying skeleton of branches on one trunk,
  so
Next spring the mystical blossom is renewed.

Their inspiration is like the sap in an apple
tree,
As all heroes are one man, all times and
seasons congeal
Into one time. Shoals of fish, flocks of birds
viewed
In autumn turn, it is said, because of a few,
Who are one, and here a Christ, there a
Mohammed
Lead, and lead us. O for a new leader for our
mad   720
Age, to make it really Golden! O for a renew-
-ed civilisation, its hubris shed, for with
humility,
Brotherhood, internationalism might become
Contemplation! The old certainties are done,
They are like dead leaves! Questioning
destroys security
And confidence, as winter destroys autumn,
But it leads in progress and brings in the new,
As winter brings in the spring. This is just a
prelude,
This proud ruin that leaves the spirit numb.

(C) GOD'S SUNLIGHT
What is greatness? You will find it in the
hero,   730
In whom Nature and suffering have unfolded
God's sunlight in the mind and in the deed.
The hero waits in readiness, and so
Is given superior powers which do not come
From him but from God, like sunshafts in a
Druid's
Dark, or like the power of the seed to split.
A great man is a flower bloomed,
Christendom
Is the history of a flower-garden. The soul
Is a flowering part of the mind's stem, it holds
The creative powers of the mind like petals. It
shows.   740
Greatness is in every seed which contains the
whole
Plant, flowers in all seasons. Man has a dual
Nature. He is choked by his sensuality,
Intellectual arrogance, his spreading petty
Scepticism – his sins – till his pride's seed-
case cruel-
-ly splits, and he unfolds spiritual insight
And aspiration, the creative love of his new
Self that can forgive, transcend, transform

crude
Evil. Greatness transcends with a lily's light.

(A) CHRISTENDOM'S BOLE
I see Russia break up, crack down the
Urals,   750
I see cracks along Eastern Europe, the wall
Crumbles and crashes, the Western garden
draws
In the outlying fields. Kaiser, Hitler and
Goebbels,
Stalin – there were three civil wars in the
twentieth
Century, two with Germany and one with
The Russian Empire's hegemony and wrath.
Fascism, Communism – two creeds of death
That had to be rooted out so that East-
-ern socialism and the social democracies
Could be peacefully united in a Uni-   760
-versal State, aid to old colonies increased.
This political State is also Christendom.
I see Cathedrals from the Kremlin to
Canterbury, dropped like once fresh, now
rotten fruit
From the sky-high trunk and branches of
some
Tired tradition that can still be lopped and
pruned.
I see the sap rise once more. The sects are
gone.
Orthodox, Catholic, Protestant – each began
With illumination, each is now impugned
As if "branch", "bough", and "limb" were
different words   770
For what grows out of a trunk, Christendom's
bole.
These concepts had to be sawn, so that a
growth
Could riot up the bark, drop new buildings
through flying birds,
A contemplative energy, a mystical Light
That unites each Eastern and Western sect
In a Kingdom of the Heart, a force that guided
The new sap. What opportunity is in sight
For heroes to unfold their souls for a Paradise!
Oil queues at petrol pumps....Barbarians will
Mass across the limes, press on our Hadrian's
Wall,   780
But we have some generations' grace. It will
suffice.

We have little permanence for a continued
    Golden time,
Winter is coming, but we are in fertile ground.
And then, we who ruled a quarter of the
    world, and are now
Not a nation-state – we can climb, we can
    climb!

(B) A SPLITTING TREE AND A BURIED HEAD

In its time of growth our culture was at one;
Like leaves and branches, art and philosophy
(United) served religion, which was the rising
Sap. All was a unity under a hot June sun.
In a time of autumn decay a culture sheds 790
Its plenty. How different when a culture
    breaks,
For no spring will renew the elm by those
    bricks.
Some Dutch beetle brings a fungus which
    spreads
Like sin, and stops the sap rising. The
    branches
Of economics and politics break away,
Leaving the rest of its soul to battle against
The sin within, to serve God's will. And pres-
-ently, linguistics, intellect, art fall away,
Leaving the religious trunk, which now
    becomes
Stultified. In a breaking time, no unfolding
    buds.   800
In an autumn time just rankness, and dismay.

An autumn also ends in questioning.
How right to question! Out of the leaf-scars of
    the past
A new life will break through, the deadness
    pierced
As autumn decayed into winter buds into
    spring.
Gnarled roots grasp a buried head in the
    rockery, so
Here in this garden unearth an image for our
    time.
No doubt, no anxious diffidence in this id-
-eal, a face with a mind at peace, as with a
    halo,
Illumined against uncertainties – Cold
    War,   810
Poverty, decline, revaluations – confident

That stability lies ahead, enough permanence
For peaceful beauty. Here is a vigour more
Vital than energy, which can transform.
A new spring is ahead for the weed-garden.
Europe's cluttered exhaustion is now done,
It belonged to autumn: dry ground before a
    storm!
Winter is coming! Have faith in spring
    renewals!
In a growing season art and philosophy
And religion are one. Now one unified mind
    will   820
Keep the civilisation alive, with silver bells!

(A) A LILY AND TOLLING BELLS

London,
    Paris, Brussels, Bonn, Rome.
        Washington, Moscow.
It is Golden down there, and we do not hear
That before High Mass, the Archangel
    Michael cleared
The sight of Christina of Glastonbury,
    although
Many monks and people looked on, as once
Happened on the Mount. Down there is
    Cornwall, like
A long lost heart. This hot autumn day the
    lake   830
Sparkles. Ragwort and knapweed line the
    fronts
Of the high hedgerows, old tin mine chimneys
    and
Green fields. Tintagel Castle looks over the
    sea,
Looks down on Merlin's cave and its pebbled
    beach.
Crocosmia flame over the flat green land,
Fowey water is calm, as the ferry crosses
    from
Polruan. Little fishing harbours. The road
As we fly runs down past the rocks where the
    hermit of Roche
Perched like an eagle on his perilous, som-
-bre nest, runs down to Marazion where, 840
Across the causeway this low spring tide, a
    pil-
-grim path winds up to the Benedictine
    chapel.
There look at the Flemish chandelier, stare
At St. Michael killing the dragon, at good

Over evil. Outside the sundial shows months
As well as hours. Here Sir Tristram came once.
This path up this rocky hill, which pilgrims should
Climb to the cross where the Archangel appeared
To fishermen, is a Ladder of Perfection,
Each step a virtue that once led to transcen-
dent   850
Understanding. Go to Trevarthian House, having peered
From its flowered lawn, go upstairs and gaze through palms
At what was a winding ascent to Paradise.
Hermits, pilgrims, the example is in dis-
-use: the soul can bloom again in these open calms
Although fishermen have heard the muffled boom of fathomless
Church bells toll beneath the waves off the Seven Stones Reef
For the darkness that will fall upon the Western sleep,
That once fell on the lands of Tristram's Lyonesse.
Rinse your eyes with this space-suited moon-
man's view   860
Of America up there, and Europe to the Urals,
The Western World like cockleshells round a puddle.
"Will this still globe ever turn towards darkness, this blue
Tin spin? Will light ever fall on Arabia, Africa,
Asia? The East? Sons and daughters of Europe,
Must we unfold our souls? Must we sow our minds, must we reap
Our hearts? Must we water our proud wills? Are we sicker
Than we think? Let us drill our oceans! We, unlike the past,
Are immortal!"
                    What pride! What folly! We
                    must spin   870
Away and round again. In the spring we will shine out, seeing

μυεντες with a divine eye, not at all down-
cast.
There is a curtain in my window. It is certain
To darken this small room as it is drawn.
I have drawn an autumn lily. There are more
Of these spring-like flowers woven on this Western curtain.

THE LABYRINTH

(IMAGES FROM A DYING MIND)

"Labyrinth. Complicated irregular structure with many passages hard to find way through or about without guidance, maze. Greek laburinthos, etymology dubious."

Concise Oxford Dictionary

Laburinthos – house of the axe, the crest of the Royal Minoan Kings of Cnossus.

1976

It is dark. I have been dreaming in the return-
ing dark.
I have been dreaming again of the crunch of
my murderer's feet
On the shingle, I turned, his axe-blade flashed
in the sun....
Put me out on the lawn, that above a sea of
trees,
Leaves foaming in the evening breeze, I again
May lie on this shrinking beach of time, and
be
Myself, till the high tide of Eternity
Swirls me away. O I am dying, dying.
I have been carried here from hospital to die.
How cold is the dark, the frost on the glass 10
Of this great room, with its marble fireplace.
I lie on my bed and look over the Forest
Like a soul suspended above its destination,
For I shall pass into the bark of that wood.
I ramble down the passages within slipped-by
time,
Like the paths through the trees and brambles
round my pond.
I am lost in the Labyrinth of my dying mind.
I, who was lost look out over Warren Hill.

I was.
I came out of the dark like my son, amid
groans,   20
My head, slimy with mucus, popped out, on a
lifeline
Like a North Sea diver, face grizzled, eyes
closed,
Mouth open in first cry. I lay on my back,
Waved arms, kicked legs, waaaa-ed parents to
distraction
In the young nights. I grew. A little boy,

I romped on all fours on a garden blanket,
Waddled with a tennis ball by a porch,
scooted
Down an arbour path to where a knife-grinder
span
In a toolshed, marched lead soldiers up a fort,
Struck coloured matches. I learned to tie my
shoelace,   30
Sang "We ploughed the fields and scatter"
near the nature-table,
Was white-flashed by a German bomb at my
gate,
Lost my grandfather in a fog, so he fell and
cut
His head, sat at the head of a long table
In a garden of long grass, bushes and fruit
trees
And ate purple damson-pudding with my
school friends.
I grew through cricket bats in the back
garden,
Through rounders in the field, took part in
two camp wars
And was captured and spent a break as a pow.
I grew like a tree over marbles in muddy
gulleys,   40
Over King-he in Georgian grounds. Sitting in
church,
Watching the dusty clock tick round Roman
numbers,
I barely knew I was growing an ideal.

Like a stream winding through a silent Forest
I drift down my days through leafy
complexity.
Here a sunlit glade, there a memory like ivy.
I scuffle through leaves, following my

winding time.
Like a mallard I take wing and flutter down
On this scene or that, with a swoosh, as clear
water
On sandy gravel turns past rooted, muddy
banks   50
And trickles on past flowing, tugging weed.
Brambles round a pond, a dried-up tributary,
And banks you can straddle, ankle-deep in
leaves.
Up there a six-spot burnet lay in my net.
On a golden afternoon, in the hum of bees,
I lay in the long grass, knew I had been
before.

I was.
I loved the freedom of a Forest oak.
I went out into the dangerous places of the
world –
Moscow, Peking, Saigon, Pnom Penh, Dar es
Salaam –   60
And spoke with Princes and Ministers,
learned their secrets,
And as I challenged the might of the Soviet
Empire,
I rose in stature, till they could accept me no
more.
A thousand pursuits by hirelings down hostile
streets
Led to that beach. Then a frightened man
betrayed me,
And sealed my doom. Like an oak in a time of
clearing,
I stood for Christendom in a Communist time.
The axe had to fall. I was felled, brought
crashing down.
An axe, a bullet, what difference does it
make?
It was a ritual killing, and I was as frail   70
As a partridge in a mosaic brushwood run.

Perhaps Purgatory is a paralysis like this?
My soul is riddled with streams, like these
bullet tracks,
And I will float and dream I am fishing again
For dragonfly larvae where the midges dance.
In this Labyrinth, all the tributaries connect
Like the veins and arteries in this dying flesh,
And lead to one pond, which draws them like
a heart.

I was.
Cuckoo, cuckoo.   80
Here where I once swooned with joy, where I
first knew God,
Where I brought news of a dead man to this
fallen beech
And, moist-eyed, sobbed within for the lost
years –
Cuckoo, cuckoo, here now gather the results,
After a smash of gunfire, the crash of
machine-guns
When o what a catastrophe engulfed us, o
what pain,
What suffering, and who knew we would
survive?
Was it for this that I served our people?
Cuckoo, cuckoo – o the screams through the
crash of guns,
O the screams as I clap my hands over my
ears.   90
Here I bring myself alone, with our agony.
To shut out the sounds of that cruel, mocking
bird:
Cuckoo, cuckoo.

O God of lightning, God of Storm,
I look out of my window at your white forked
light
Burning down on our rooftops, the hollow
echo
Roaring within the thunder clattering over-
head,
And I see a pied wagtail sheltering by a
garage.
O poor little creatures that huddle against
your wrath.
I lie on my bed, turn leaves of a book with
bated breath   100
As flash-flash-flash, the white light burns
round my head
And crack-clatter-crash the thunder, and I
know this fire
Is as bright as the light in my mind, which
heals instead
Of burning. O God of lightning, God of Storm,
Preserve us terrified creatures, me and the
wagtail,
Which will soon enough be dead.

I was.

267

Now I stand by the yew in this Forest church-
    yard.
I feel sad, sad, serene. The light in my mind
Is like a moon born out of storm clouds. I am
    healed.   110
The tempests are over. We came to this lane
    one night,
My love. You have seen my ideal modified,
    deepened.
Such is the benevolent working of catastrophe
That it strikes us as harsh Fate, not
    Providence.
You have seen my ideal become my Roman
    lamp
With its pilgrim cross where the candle dips
    in the oil.
I stand for a Christendom of illumination
Which shines in the darkness of their
    barbarian lands
And rises above the guns of all barbarians.
O triumphant candles on a horse chestnut! 120

Now I lie on this bed and search this
    Labyrinth
For the meaning of it all. I am lost in a maze
Of memories, I wind through prickly illusions
Like a stream through thickets. Yet when I
    look through the window
At the Forest spread out below me, like a
    tablecloth
On a Nursery table, it is all so orderly,
What could be more simple than a brook
    winding through trees?
I lie in this old house, which is more drafty
Than the hospital, and feel its peace, and
    ponder
How suffering teaches us love, opens new
    glades   130
In the woods of the soul, new places of sunlit
    feeling
Where a heart can flower unseen, and one's
    self does not matter.
I took risks, I stood up and spoke out – and
    was cut down by the sea
For my pains. And now I am sinking, waiting
    for my love
To come and read to me and dandle our son.
It is a violent time we live in, and I stood up
    to it,
And so I lie here in a peace like a swishing

breeze.
I stood for order, and was felled by the forces
    of chaos,
I stood for Light, and must find meaning in
    this dark.

It is the whole Forest that has purpose. 140
What is the fate of one tree beside the Forest?
Does not one tree flower and fruit for the
    Forest?
I put out my candles and made my
    contribution
To the flowering and fruiting of a great
    Forest,
Which will sticky bud and leaf-fall for
    centuries after my dark.

The months, our seasons bud and shed leaf
    against
The eternal wood of the deciduous Forest
Which measures our time through now green,
    now russet leaves.
Eight hundred year-old oaks, five hundred
    year-old beeches.
Their ponds mirror the changes which time
    furrows   150
On my soul's face. Turpin's Cave, the Owl
    are gone,
But the silver birch round this little church
    endure.
In this graveyard I will be lowered, I will pass
Into its earth, my heart will feed birch roots,
Will sing up the sap and wave in the new
    spring leaves.
I will pass into the Forest and be eternal.
My life was a ramble through time, as I
    ramble now
Through my dying mind, through this wooded
    Labyrinth.
Streams dry, trees rot, but the Forest abides
    for ever.

Three times I went away, but each time I
    returned.   160
I was unfaithful to you, but we stayed
    together,
My country! Like a constant wife, you were
    my backbone,
And now my backbone will feed spring
    crocuses,

White daisies where squirrels run. I rambled, I
    strayed
From my true home, but I have come back to
    die.

To die. Time is short, but Eternity is long.
A pool of time on a beach above a sea
Which whispers in the wind like leaves of
    trees.
I lie on a beach of time, my candles are over.
A Warren is a place where rabbits
    burrow,   170
I must scoop earth for a grave like a rabbit
    burrow.
Philosopher, artist, statesman. I was John Bull
For a little time. I wore a mask and found
A meaning through a mask, and the image of
    a tree.

To die. My breaths are hoarse, I hear the hiss
Of death in my throat. Come quickly, my
    love, be quick.
O where are you, why are you not back in this
    dark?
I cannot live long now. With a hiss the end
    comes.
From the dark to the dark. No lips mutter over
    me.
This bed is my coffin, already I feel the
    lid   180
Closed over my head, the nails banged in, one
    two
Three, bang, like our carpenter with flicked
    forward spiv hair.
I am a pain in my chest, but a light in my
    head.
It is blue-white. Yes, a beautiful peaceful
    glow.
Surely it will cling to me, like a light on a
    candle –
Surely it will not be blown out in this drift?
It is rising upwards above me, rising up from
    me.

O life. It seemed such a long journey at the
    time,
But now I have dreamed my way through this
    Labyrinth
To plunge over the edge like a waterfall, go
    underground   190

Like a stream going through a grating under a
    road,
Now how short it seems. All those evenings –
    a few breaths.
My soul came alive through pain, and
    bloomed in the sun,
It dazzled like white magnolia against a blue
    sky.

With the exception of high officials,
    Mongolians are left
To the winds. They waste away. A valley of
    bones.

A wagtail in the storm. I will fly like a
    willow-warbler.
Cuckoo, cuckoo.

In the Labyrinth at Chan Chan, in Peru,
Hidden in a maze of narrow alleyways   200
With towering walls, secreted into the centre,
Nine complexes show where nine Kings lived
    and reigned.
Each new King built a new palace, each dead
    King
Was buried in his palace with his women, and
    his gold.
I loved women. If mine were buried with me,
The lawn outside would look like a church-
    yard.

Are these rooms or chambers of my mind,
    that I wander through,
I who thought I was paralysed? What palace
    is this?
What mosaic floor? What flooding white light
    around me?
Is that me, or is it my old self, lying on that
    bed   210
Below, as I float in this light? Has my body
    fallen away
From this light, like a thrown-away match that
    has done its lighting?
Is this a garden, this Labyrinth, or is it
    Paradise?
Was earth Purgatory without my knowing it?
Am I an Angel, floating in this brilliant light?

From the dark to the dark, alone, alight. It is
    time

To sleep. It is time for the rabbit to enter its
        burrow,
Its barrow. It is time for the ditch to be dry.
It is time for me to pass into the wood,
Time to become the sap of Eternity,   220
This white light that pulses through all things,
        this current of *life*!
In my mind there was a stream, a tree, a bird.
There was white light in the stream, the tree,
        and the bird.
I am the stream and the tree and the bird that
        flies,
I am all life in the Forest. And I am the sea.

The tide is coming in.

Alone. Alight. Sea foams.
One last hissing, exhaled, exhaled breath.
Sea foaming for Eternity.

Alight!   230
Dark. Blackness round a bed and flesh that
        was.

It is dark round the axed horse chestnut tree.

WHISPERS FROM THE WEST

1976 – 1977

A QUARTER PAST FOUR

A quarter past four, on an autumn afternoon
By the sea, sighs the cafeteria clock.
The golden sun wilts beyond the long pier,
Foam sobs on to shingle. Smell of seaweed.
Towards the gathering mist, people hurry
In coats to their homes, from the creeping
    chill.

A quarter past four near this familiar hotel
And why do I feel so sad when the past is
    still?

THE MOON
(ON OUR SECOND ANNIVERSARY)

My love, another year has turned, and we
Now celebrate our second anniversary.
Today you gave me a card: a clown and a
    cook-
-house doll sit on a cusped moon. You gave
    me a book
Of dreams. Now I sit in my room and thumb
Through my dream of our walk to the Science
    Museum
Where we saw the Command Module of
    Apollo Ten:
A wide belled buoy, in which two space-
    suited men
Lay back; an asbestos base, scorched as it
    foamed
Back through our earth's atmosphere, the
    sides honeycombed
As if they were made of beeswax. "It passed
    within nine
Point five kilometres of the moon," said the
    sign-
-board. We have spent our second year
    cramped in a space-berth,
Circling the moon, far from our friends on
    earth.
Our son eats beeswax, and soon we all shall
    sit
On the cusped moon you dream of, and will
    swing our legs on it!

NETS

An earwig fell off the top of my umbrella
And slithered away in the garden. In the road,
As I walked for my papers, the sea drizzle
Wetted my trousers and jumper. I strode,

Then sauntered. For at every gate and bush
There were spiders' webs, hung with droplets
    of rain.
They were on holly, privet, hydrangea,
Dogrose. On my way back, I looked again.

Not one of the thousand or more had caught
Anything. They hung out without glamour
Like fishermen's nets, and no prize fly or bee
Swam through the drizzle to that gossamer.

Only when I opened the back gate did I
See one midge faintly struggle and try to flit,
And the hermit crab-like spider coiled in
The join of the bars, ready to devour it.

O wonderful toil! That in the early rain
A thousand nets should be hung out for food.
Here I toil through news items, and now spin
This web that may trawl a catch for my
    hatched brood.

FALL OUT

That morning we woke up to fine drizzle.
The Tokyo news said, "Fall-out from the
    H-bomb
Exploded by Mao's China is now coming
    down
In rain. Do not touch the leaves of plants."
    From

Then I kept you indoors, and took my
    umbrella to work.
Later we went to our thatched village. No
    sun
Shone. We saw the New Year in with a hot
    rain
Falling lightly. I imagined the particles run-

-ning like globules of mercury down bamboo
leaves,
Glistening like silver in the cups of camellia.
Now, ten years later, I read a press cutting
In this London flat: "Cancer is caused by
nuclear

Fall-out. There are cancer patterns from
nuclear tests
In Nevada, the Pacific, Russia, China. When
spread
Over a long period, radiation effects are much
worse."
So, Mao, I sit and wonder if I will soon be
dead.

AT ROCHE CHAPEL

From the road, massive jagged rocks appear
among
Bracken, with a tower built on top of the high-
-est – an arch; the ruined chapel. I cross and
climb.
Above me towers the chapel of St. Mi-

-chael; a local hermit who lived a hundred feet
Up there perched in a precarious eagle's nest.
I climb the path, scale an iron ladder in-
-to the chapel, another to the cell. I rest.

Below me, spread out against the sky, the
fields
And hills of Cornwall to the china clay
Mounds. I perch here, high above the world's
desires,
Living to praise God's creation and pray

For the people below who put bread in
My lowered rope-basket. I am above
Temptation, lifted Godwards to the sky,
In the terrain of the kestrel, a peaceful dove.

LIGHTNING OVER POLRUAN

Near the ivy house where Q annotated
For fifty-two years, in Fowey, we first park,
Then chug-chug in the ferry across silver
ripples
Among boat-masts into the gathering dark.

Dusk and lights. The wizened white-haired
ferryman

Takes the silver obol from my tongue as we
ply.
A dozen crabs scuttled by the jetty, but now
The water is a surface, under a cloudy sky.

He helps us off on to the steps of the pier.
We climb into Polruan, an underworld
Of tiny streets, houses without curtains,
Lights and open front doors, where events
have swirled

With the tides. "For Sale": a cottage, one up
one down.
And should we settle here and gaze across the
creek
And live out the rest of Eternity in this
Backwater, a Sunday every day of the week?

Lightning flickers over Polruan hill
Like lights turned on and off in an attic.
Distant thunder rumbles. It is nearly dark.
Lights gleam round Fowey. Must the past last
in the quick?

"Let's go back," I say, remembering what to
forget,
Wanting to return to the present. We climb
Down and arrive at the landing jetty as
The ferry-boat chugs back another time.

From the Stygian water the dark sky
Is lit with flickering yellow fire. "Go
Back home quick before the thunder comes,"
says
The old ferryman, crouching near his mo-

-tor. Safely ashore we hurry to the car-park.
Our visit to Hell is past, our escape complete.
One day I may, like Q, write here, over boats.
Until then I will live in Paradise Street.

LADY OF GARIAN

That was your youth you violently turned
your back on,
My Lady of Garian.
We stood side by side in a seaside Hall of
Mirrors,
You turned, you scuttled, you ran.
I saw bark like the skin of an old lady's neck
In the space by your superman.

TRENARREN

It is raining this afternoon, so we will drive
Along the cliffs to the road for Trenarren.
We will turn down the lane and park at the end,
And walk down the track between hedges,
    and then

We will saunter a mile between high
    hedgerows
That are filled with every kind of August
    flower:
Sheep's bit scabious, ragwort, woodruff,
    cuckoo-pint.
The leaves meet over our heads, protect us
    from the shower.

Now we come out on to the damp headland.
The way lies open now, to the Black Head.
We cross a rocky field, and far below
The sea foams on brown rocks, a deserted

Cove. O, my love, when I have at last passed
    on,
You will find me flitting as a dragonfly
Across my Forest pond, or here as a gull,
Wheeling down over Trenarren, soaring by!

ARTHUR'S INNOCENCE

We take the landrover down the parish track
And climb the steep hill to the old castle,
The inner ward. I look at the island fort,
The sea below, this rocky Tintagel!

Here Merlin took Arthur down the cliff path
To that cave below on the pebbled beach.
Here chess-playing Tristram brought his
    Iseult
To marry Mark, and lived out of his reach.

The caves of the world hide many children
Who have left their two parents' care. Ah well,
Guinevere had yet to love Sir Launcelot and
Arthur did not know she would share Iseult's
    married Hell.

THE BROKEN MARRIAGE-PICTURE

I have a Japanese print: a kimonoed
Lord stands with a scroll, a cross-eyed woman
    bares

A backscratcher; like us – poetry, pleasure.
It fell off my wall, glass shattered down the
    stairs,

The frame snapped into four jagged chips of
    wood,
The black backing cloth came out. The pieces
Went into a cupboard, till I went to the glass-
    works.
I glued the frame together, smoothed out the
    creases

In the woman's frowning face, sealed them in
    new glass.
But the frame was weak – it fell apart again.
If we had got back together, like this picture
Might we not have broken after a few months
    of strain?

Now I know that once there is a fracture,
It is hard to stick together a lady and lord.
My love, did we not do right to put away
Our broken marriage in a dark cupboard?

THE SHELL

You have had an operation. I know because
He has written to say you will write when you
    are better.
What is up? Have you had a hysterectomy?
Have you been punished *that* way for your
    divorce letter?

Once I drew your heart and put my arrow
    through it,
A heart like a womb. And now you have had
    the offen-
-ding organ cut out (perhaps), and live like a
    shell
Without its mollusc. We will have no more
    children.

You live like a giant pink cameo,
Curled cleft with a slit, like the fingernails
In a clenched fist, in which the sea still booms
At the ear, echoing years when there were no
    gales.

Is it some guilt that makes your sea boom
    now?
Your last letter crashes and hisses three

273

Epithets: "disgraceful", "contemptible", and
    "pseudo".
Why do you wipe your ugly words off on to
    me

As if some of my blood had stuck to your
    finger-spines?
Guilt – you wanted happiness so desperately,
The flattery of a nearly royal male,
And so you evicted me, expelled yourself
    free.

You wanted peace, but instead you found a
    quiet-
-ly empty shell in your heart, which you now
    veil.
And so you make me a scapegoat, wiping off
Your conscience on me, through the Royal
    Mail.

WORLDLY POWER

It could be that I should be *grateful* to you
For saving me from such a Satanic fate!
At the time it seems so important to do
What we want. To lie and cheat to further
    Great
Olympians' worldly power – then it was
    heroic
To destroy the enemies of the West I
    despised,
And rightly so, like an antibiotic,
But now I pity my masters for being
    disguised,
And not being open. How pathetic to fawn
On murderers. If you had not turned savagely
And had me "sacked" because you are also
    sworn
To smash germs, I might now be without
    mercy.
    To have helped, yet to rise above the
        world today,
    Is the path of the mystic who has found
        his way.

TO A SERVICEMAN ON FRONTIER DUTY IN GERMANY, A REPLY

You say you are guarding our Western
    civilisation's
Frontiers, but I know differently. Your
    military code
Is not an irrelevance, of course. The Russians
May bomb us, pour into France, even spill
    down the road
For London. But you are in the wrong place
    for a war.
Your base could not dam them for more than
    an hour.
We are outnumbered, we have only half their
    for-
-ces. You say servicemen fought and died for
    our
Culture and civilisation during the last
War, that I should be *for* them. But really,
That is begging the question. It is the quality
    of our vast
Civilisation I criticise, not its defendibility.
    So shift your thought to this new ground. I
        still
    Say our civilisation is going downhill.

SANDY

My hairdresser has stubble on his chin.
He is called Sandy. He owns a Unisex shop
And knows me as "the Wandsworth teacher".
    He
Does not know my name, but each time I flop

In his chair, he tells me about his two women,
And the girls whose hair he washes and cuts,
    slip-
-ping them in when he really has an
    appointment
(With me for example), so they are grateful.
    Snip-

-ping my hair, he says, "Oh, I love the
    ladies!"
He does not love his Greek assistant. He says
    to me,
"He tells everyone his troubles, comes in
    unshaven."
His shampoo-girls are "brasses, you know,
    masseuses".
    He

He is not married – he lives with an enormous
    dog –
And his two women have regular boy-friends
    who

Let them love him very much. He is of
    indeterminate
Nationality, and says when I pay, "Two
    pounds to you."

MY FLAT LITTLE MOUSE

"But, for to speken of hir conscience,
She was so charitable and so pitous
She wolde wepe if that she saugh a mous
Caught in a trappe, if it were deed or bledde."
             Chaucer's *Prologue* – the nun

Last night I saw my flat little town mouse
Creep up from a hole by the fireplace with
    quick looks –
A hole I had blocked with a stone, unsuccess-
    fully –
And scurry and hide behind my biggest
    books.

I flushed him out into the grate. I knelt
And clattered a pan, and as he skittered out
I lunged with the upturned vase in which I
    caught
His brother and carried him jumping inside,
    snout

Up, downstairs to the gardens. But he
    squeezed down the hole,
A flatness of back, no hump. I blocked it up
With my silver leadstone. This morning I
Came down to look at my trap in the cup

Cupboard. He was there, my backless mouse,
    the trap
Through his brains, his two eyes looking up at
    me. He
Was like a Picasso, distorted head bent back –
I was sad, for my flat little mouse had not
    harmed me.

EVIL LIKE WIND-BLOWN LEAVES

As we walked by the Forest pond you asked,
"Why is there evil? Why is there genocide?"
The oldest question in philosophy....
"It is not easy to answer," I replied,

"It's an eternal question. Ask the wind."

As it blew leaves down I knew there was no
    why.
We have to accept the process, there has to be
Death so there can be new life. A deep blue
    sky

And the bare trees of autumn teach, like the
    wind,
That evil is perfectly natural, bringing
Winter of the soul. It is natural for leaves to
    fall
So that new buds can grow in the renewing
    spring.

A TIDAL WAVE AND MIGRATING SWALLOWS

Sitting in the Staff Room I heard a rushing.
Out of the window I saw a hundred mute
Girls pour down the steps like a tidal wave,
And our Headmistress, like some mad Canute,

Hand up, saying "Back" as she was engulfed
Like a rock and foamed over. It swept on
    again.
The panic frothed: "Elliot School is coming."
First years were in tears, one girl held a
    lavatory chain.

I went down among them. And suddenly
The tide ebbed, and I saw a flock of birds
    wheel
Screaming like swallows about to migrate.
    "Wish some
Would migrate," I said to the Head of
    Remedial.

As the bovver mob swooped screeching over
    the grass,
Their black plumage on end, each face a fire,
There was a tension until the police came
And supervised the departure from a Black
    Maria.

ANGELS NEAR A FAIRGROUND HELL

At school this afternoon we had "The Third
Year Parents' Evening". In the hall, some four
Hundred parents gathered round tables and
    queued.
It looked like a fairground. I imagined I saw

Hoopla, and ping pong balls in goldfish bowls
And roll-a-penny. I sat at my table
Like a gipsy fortune-teller, and dealt my cards
And explained to parents how they might be
    able

To help their children pass the Typing test –
"They should join a library, write a diary, list
    spell-
-ings in a vocab book" – and then I realised
I sat at the "Exit" from a fairground Hell.

Then, by the Gate, I knew that I had died
And that these pinched, surly people were all
    here
To see if they could wangle their fallen girls
Past me into Heaven, where the other Angels
    were.

LOVE LIKE A LENGTH OF CLOTH

Once out of Paradise I unrolled my love
Like cloth and cut it into a pretty dress
And hung it on the shoulders of a little girl
Who smiles from a photograph like a lost
    princess.

Now I take the same love and, unrolling it,
Cut some more into short trousers, and hang
Them on the chest of a little boy who beams
Through the banisters at me, an orang-outang

Behind bars. My love is like a length of cloth
Which I snip and trim to suit the changing
    times.
My love is single, I roll it out and cut
New fashions for people in pantomimes.

And this same roll of cloth has sometime
    clothed
Past brides and many fleeting naked lives
That have shivered for warmth. My love is
    single, and
Provides cloth for many children and many
    wives.

26 February 1976

LAMENT OF THE CAST-OFF SHIRT

Can I help it if I am worn to places

My master now regrets he visited?
The day he last wore me, we left the faces,
He took me up a path to a room with a bed.
I had coffee spilt down me, I was taken off,
Thrown crumpled over a chair, discarded like
    a poor
Tie, I watched nakednesses before the cough
Under the sheets. Is it my fault if I saw?
Now the black-haired woman with the hoarse
    tongue
Has displeased him, and he no longer goes
    there,
And because I remind him of her, I have been
    hung
Up to be forgotten. I, too, am discarded here
In this dark wardrobe. Sometimes I see
    through the crack:
My master lies by his wife, who turns her back.

25 February 1976

LIKE A TIN OF FLY SPRAY

We went into a flat off Old Brompton Road
And sat down. Six other aging guests suck-
-ed their lips. Soon a silver-haired man turned
    to my wife,
Said, "Are you married to *him*? Oh bad luck!"

I was too stunned to reply, I was caught
Off guard. He was queer. Later I went to the
    loo.
A frown stood on the enamel cistern,
With a tin of fly spray. And then I knew

That I should always sport a tin of scorn
    when I
Entered a party; if a guest buzzed me like a
    blowfly,
I could squirt contempt at him so he fell and
    lay,
Legs kicking on his back, in a cloud of irony.

A SHADOW AND A BUTTERFLY

Spring buds in the Forest. Pussy willow,
Catkins. A great tit sings in the silver birch
As we walk up the lich-path and kneel in our
    pew
In the white-haired vicar's little Forest
    church.

The sermon is on Light. A leafy sun-shaft

Washes the aisle golden; in the stunning glare
My shadow is black and sharp, till a passing
    cloud
Wipes it away. Without light I am not there.

Like the organist who died on Friday night
Of "hepatitis", or love of alcohol,
A generation passes, old faces leave
One by one, so we do not realise it. We foll-

-ow. I am here, like my shadow, but a short
    while,
Lit by sun. While here, I will sing my som-
-bre psalm. A butterfly flutters on diamond
    lead
Windows – the stained glass was blown out
    by a bomb –

And I see it as my soul, fluttering,
Impatient to be out in the Eternal trees.
I am here a short while, like my shadow,
But my butterfly-soul floats in sunlight,
    beyond the breeze.

GIRLS LIKE CROCUSES

As I walked into school, the morning dew
Was frosty white in the shade on the green
    humped bank,
And glory! for two thousand crocuses
Pushed through the grass, opened their lips,
    and drank.

There was purple and mauve, and yellow
    ochre;
There was saffron and streaky white, and all
Had orange tongues. There were as many as
The two thousand girls who unfolded round
    the hall

And sipped the sunlight. Then I knew their
    heads
Would be under grass like bulbs, and that
    each one
Of the purple or yellow crocuses was a soul
That had passed back to the earth, and now
    missed the sun.

A BROKEN CURTAIN-RAIL
AND THE LIGHT

Our drawing-room curtain-rail is called

"Golden Glide".
You tug a loop, two bobs draw the curtains
    back.
I tugged and jammed the cord, which
    promptly snapped.
The room was dark, it was as if my mind was
    black.

I bought a knot of new wax-cord at a shop,
I spent two hours refitting the bobs, or try-
-ing to. I took down the curtains, unscrewed
    the two runnels and rails,
And took off the hooks and the maddening
    little eye.

I threaded in cord and made the bobs grip it,
And screwed back the rails, and the runnels at
    each end,
And put back the hooks, the curtains. I did all
    this twice,
But the curtains remained drawn. I nearly
    went round the bend.

I removed the bobs, and now draw the
    curtains without
Cord. The loop hangs down for mere
    decoration, and
So it is with my mind. I tug the cord that
    reveals,
And feel resistance. My Light only opens by
    hand.

A CRASH AND CANDLELIGHT

I was tired, worn out, utterly exhausted.
I took the tray to the kitchen to wash up
Before football, slipped in putting it down,
And CRASH – plates, my big fish pottery cup

And saucer, a jar of coffee, lay broken
On the floor. I cried, "Oh no," and, being
    fired
With fury, blamed the slippery floor, the
    draining-board,
And then a calm voice within said, "You were
    tired,

You nearly blacked out you were so worn
    down,
Like a candle." My wife cleared up, I stood
    contrite

Near my Roman oil-lamp with its Christian
cross.
I nearly blacked out, but I was still alight.

A BOO-OOM AND AN UNDEAF EAR

I was typing at my desk when I heard a
Boo-OOOM.
It made me jump. I thought, 'Another bomb.'
It was a big one, a long way away, I thought,
Bigger than the one two days before, not far
from

The Fulham Road. I went on typing. Two
Hours later, the news showed pictures of my
old square.
We went round to have a look. They had
carried away
The bomber who blew himself up in the gutter
there

Under floodlights, where police knocked on
doors
And questioned shadows beyond the
barricade
Of rope. A transitional time; this anarchy;
And the church, like my vicar, wears a deaf
aid.

We walked back. Somewhere in a St.
Stephen's ward
A butcher had lost a hand, would lose a leg
there.
The seeds we sow we reap. He sowed his to
sprout,
And God did not hear his prayers with His
deaf ear.

SOULS IN NUTS AND BARS

I was invigilating in an exam,
A girl slumped forward, and was carried to
Medical.
She had hit her head the day before: was
concussed.
She had not been to the doctor. Mrs. Chappell

Died in a men's ward last Friday fortnight.
My brother's wife hit her head on the kitchen
Stove, she had a pain in her groin and
screamed and fell

And is in a men's ward, being a "person". So
then,

Three "persons" whose bodies went wrong
became
Embarrassingly like broken-down cars
Parked side by side for repair in a garage.
Why are souls
Trapped, like speed, in these fragile nuts and
bars?

A RUINED TOWER AND GRUBBY SOULS

We sit in the Heads of Departments' Meeting,
combing
Through four hundred names for fourth year
options, reviewing
The four subjects outside English and
Mathematics
Which girls who failed the Typing test are
doing.

Out of the window, four pigeons flap round a
ruin-
-ed tower. Bare trees like lightning forks,
where a squirrel runs.
I stare at the corrugated, blocked windows.
Where the roof used to be, the chimney is the
sun's.

It is square: two arched eyebrows over two
blank eyes.
In faces on Katmandu temples, God is a boss
Frowning. But here He has died. The low, flat
building,
Like a Nazi crematorium, is shaped in a cross.

With a shock of realisation, I think: it was a
church.
There must have been a crumbling steeple
round
That belfry. Before this school was built, folk
worshipped
Here in these green fields, and this was
hallowed ground.

We sit in our Meeting reciting names: "Julie
Coombes,
Not Biology, not European Studies, not Art."
And I look at the church under winter trees

And ponder on silence, and the consecrated
 heart.

I lean forward and whisper to the Chairman.
He says, "No, it was the old laundry, that was
 a water-
Tower." I sit back, regretfully smile a starched
 smile.
Our grubby souls might be washed if our
 words were shorter!

SOFT FINGERS AND STABBING LEAD
(OR: A BARBER LIKE AN EMBALMER)

My hair was over my shoulders, I could not
Have them saying, "He can't control his hair,
 let alone
His Department." So I went to the Unisex
 barbers
In the Earls Court Road, and had it washed,
 shaped, blown-

Dry by a Rhodesian girl. She shampooed me,
Then took my hair between her fingers and
 snipped
Sending shivers up my back. I felt serene.
"I worked in Soho," she said, "until business
 slipped."

Soho. I thought of the tattered magazine
I had just flipped through: "It was eight inches
 long, three
Fistfulls. There in the cinema, I fondled it
Till he soaked his handkerchief." She fingered
 me.

Rhodesia. I could see the headline scream
From the pile of papers: "NIGERIAN JUNTA
 SLAUGHTERS
ARMY-MEN": "They were all in mufti. Most
 of them
Looked grim, but some managed to smile at
 reporters.

The firing lasted ten minutes." I felt
The stab of the lead, and wondered at those
 now dead men
Smiling at newsmen from the plushness of my
 chair,
And while she blew my hair dry, I again

Thrilled to her soft fingers as her brush curled
 round
And tugged, as she rubbed each hair up and
 down – with what art –
Not smiling, like an embalmer, as if I were
 dead,
I gave thanks for my live body from the
 bottom of my heart.

SNOW

The upstairs television was suddenly black,
When I switched it on it crackled with snow.
My wife fiddled with knobs by the side –
 nothing.
I rang our radio shop, a Pole said, "Oh,

Snow means the input transistor has gone,
Bring it in." I did. After the weekend, I
 learned
His verdict: "It's OK, we turned up the
 amplifier."
At least, I think that's what he said – he
 turned

Up something, strengthened the picture. Now
 it works
Again, who knows why the damn thing would
 not go.
It is like my mind: when it is functioning well,
Images fill the screen – but oh this snow!

GOD LIKE A TELEVISION LEVER

Our colour television was very blurred.
On a Saturday afternoon, you could not see
 the faces
Of the jockeys. Soccer players were marked
 by ghosts,
Athletes had astral bodies in all their races.

I stood it a year, and then rang for the man
Who repairs hired sets. He took off the back
 and pried
(He was Chinese, of course) and fiddled.
 "Eet's out of focus,"
He said, "See, the peecture is off each side."

And now the test card of a girl was sharp.
He tinkered with the aerial, tightened a
Joint, and we had perfect reception. "Thees

lever controls
The peecture," he said. "Eet ees like a cam-
era."

After he went, I thought I was like that screen,
And somewhere a lever changes my focus,
Brightens the world's detail, sharpens colour.
We have a lever that keeps out God from us.

DANCING WRAITHS

I have seen them in gloomy Edwardian films,
Pale over lathes and looms, pinched with
defeats,
Slaving with jerky movements, like jumping
puppets
Whose wailing urchins wait in tomb-like
streets.

How different today, they say! Look at those
windows!
Just look at the great comprehensive through
the gate!
We are not thin ghosts, mere shadows of our
bodies!
We *dance* through our work in our Welfare
State!

As I came out of the Staff Room, the grey nun
held
The door, right hand across her heart, mid-
stride,
Left leg across right under her long skirt, as if
She had unshouldered her burden for a Palais
Glide.

At the House Meeting, my careworn House-
mistress said,
"If a girl breaks her elbow, we will be in dead
Trouble," and a ghost dead-marched up the
Hall windows,
Military Two-Stepping, a skeleton of a Head.

These days work distorts our deep feelings.
For hours
They may cease to exist. As I left the gate
with the three
Women I drive home, the Head of Home
Economics
Called from her car, "It's like the Pied Piper,"
to me.

Oh for a mountain away from incomplete
living!
What souls can grow in this waste of glass?
Death grins
At our partial lives as he waits for our
skeletons;
At the greatness we miss, being seldom our-
selves in our skins.

One day at school a grey Sister danced by,
A ghost danced up our Hall of Mirrors. They
Looked aghast. I danced a chain of women.
We wraiths at our work, dancing our lives
away.

POOR SOULS

I went out to buy my papers, and saw a poor
Man in rags, hands in his pockets, and two
boys wal-
-king like him. I saw a foul old tramp with
holes
In his coat. Then I glanced at my headlines,
and saw:

"Guatemala Earthquake." It razed and
destroyed
The poor quarter, and twenty-five thousand
lives
But spared the commercial buildings, the rich
villas,
The sin street. Where is the justice when *that*
survives?

Then I realised: God was angry at the slums,
They did not come up to His standard, so
"Rebuild"
Was His stern message, and they were swept
away.
Then why did so many poor have to be killed?

Nature keeps society going with the checks
Of wars, earthquakes, diseases, and works
through wholes.
The poor were a problem, and the problem
was reduced
When they died. Is God no respecter of poor
souls?

Walking home, I knew: each single poor per-
-son taken away from the earth has been

rewarded in
Heaven. I was sure their souls are angels, and
    judge
The souls who survived in the villas and the
    street of sin.

RE-RUN

Saturday football. The number four awaits
A throw-in. I know that he will score, yet
He does not know, nor does the crowd. I
    watch,
He tears forward and hits the back of the net.

Bremner scored in the now, I watched the re-
    run.
Perhaps when I left you in that villa for
Good and drove home, I appeared like a goal-
    keeper
Waiting for disaster, to an eye that saw

Out of time? We live in the now, are free to
    choose,
But perhaps our now is a recording, will
    appear
So to the divine eye, which lives outside time
And sees the future as if it were last year.

PERHAPS, MY LOVE

Perhaps, my love, I knew you in a life
Centuries ago, and perhaps you left me then,
And each century we meet in new bodies,
And love and leave each other again and
    again?

Perhaps if I float back on the sea of time
I will dream of how I came in on the tide,
And drowned each century, and was washed
    ashore again,
One soul swept to perfection from your side?

So perhaps when we walked beside the sea
And I picked up two green, corroded coins
And said "This is us", and you shed two tears,
Perhaps we were rehearsing where all time
    joins?

PROVIDENCE

One summer morning I heard that it would
    not be
Tripoli we were going to, but Teheran.

They had found me "unsuitable", apparently.
I sat on the station. The sun's threads darn-
-ed the mountain ash. I wanted to resist my
    fate.
The world seemed threadbare, for Teheran
    was poor-
-ly paid. I vowed I would ring and agitate
For a reconsideration – and they opened the
    door.
Seemingly a mistake! For in Tripoli I lost
    you.
Is it wiser not to resist Providence,
Or was it its workings that sent us to the
    Libyan coup,
Did I have to lose you to make my life make
    sense?
    And was the hitch a wobble in the cotton-
        reel
    On the sewing machine that spins my
        cloth ideal?

A TELEPHONE CALL AND A TENT

On my letter to you, telling you we are going
    to France,
I have stuck a newly issued postage stamp.
It says "Centenary of the first telephone call".
A woman speaks on the phone. My heart felt
    damp

That summer evening fifteen years ago
When I spoke to you over the telephone
And met you to ask you to marry me.
"We put up homes like tents," you were to
    moan.

Today I said, "This school is like a tent
With guy-ropes held by pegs, a marquee
    perhaps.
Tinker with one and the whole tent will
    tremble,
Loosen one and the whole tent will collapse."

So it was with our marriage. We pegged it up,
How proudly they all helped in our home-
    town.
But how eagerly, when then sensed one guy-
    rope loose,
They loosened the peg abroad, so it crumpled
    down.

A MORNING THING
(OR: LOVE LIKE A FURTIVE SIN)

"I haven't been very well," my mother said
On the phone, "had a bit of cramp early on Sun-
-day morning, for ten minutes my whole right
    side
Was paralysed. It happened again at seven,

And again this morning. It's a morning thing.
I'm going into hospital for a check-up." I
    chok-
-ed. "It's circulatory. They want to make sure
My blood doesn't clot." Each time was a
    small stroke,

In fact. She went into hospital on Wednesday,
And my brother rang: "I saw the third attack,
It was also on Sunday morning. Her speech
    slurred,
Her eyes closed. She just lay there on her
    back."

Now my sister has rung. "She had five strokes
    in all,
And said of the first, 'Oh well, I'm having
A stroke, there's nothing I can do, I may
As well lie back and do nothing.' It's a
    warning,"

My sister said, "She doesn't want to alarm us
And so she's played it down, taken us in."
So that is love: lying about one's health
So as not to worry one's children. That furtive
    sin.

HOSPITAL GARDEN

We went to see my mother in hospital,
In a VIP room off Paulin ward, lying
On a high bed with a drip in her left arm.
Opposite, an old lady was dying.

I talked to her, made her earphone radio work.
Coloured nurses came in, poured tea, reshaped
The bag. My wife put the friesias we had
    brought
In a vase, and chased our son when he escaped

Into the corridor. My mother made plans
For the future – she would sell the house, shed
    some

Of her violin teaching – while my son
    crawled
Under the bed, with all his life to come.

My sister came, a sister in the hospital,
And her husband, a surgeon. On the way to
    their flat
He said, "It's arrhythmias – arteries growing
    old –
And rest cannot prevent another stroke at

Any time." My aunt was Assistant Matron
    there,
A nurse had said her sister had said: "Miss
    Broa-
-dley was a frightful dragon." We left through
    the garden
Where I saw Queen Mary just after the war.

I did not recognise it; there was a restaurant
Where my mother held me through cape-like
    nursing cloaks
When I was little larger than my son.
I thought of the time when I would have five
    strokes.

A FIRST-CLASS CITIZEN

In the paper shop, an Arab crone in pur-
-dah cackled under the guard strapped over
    her no-
-se, argued about her change from under her
    beak,
And no-one understood her, the old crow.

Sometimes when I go out, I think I am in an
    Arab
Empire. Arab papers are sold by the sta-
-tion, an Arab sells kebab in a street booth,
I often see a kuffeia-ed Arab leading the way,

His wives ten yards behind in our
    emancipated
Society. It's the oil crisis, of course. Thus,
This filthy barbarian in the paper-shop
Can buy a private bed in our hospitals –
    unlike us.

SPECTRE OF A CLOUD

Sometimes as I sit in this affluence –
Central heating, colour television, door-

-phone, telephone, fridge crammed with
frozen meat,
washing
Machine rinsing my shirts, programmed to
disgor-

-ge dirty water into the kitchen sink –
Sometimes, as I pull my golden glide curtains
And sink into my sofa, my feet on a pouf,
And survey the thick pile of the carpet, the
soft-drink cans,

With satisfaction, the goldfish, my knick-
knacks
On the mantlepiece – Tutankhamun, coins,
lead
Soldiers, my Russian Orthodox cross, my clay
Pots, candlesticks – my birds' eggs, the books
I have read,

Sometimes in all this material satisfaction
I see the spectre of a mushroom-cloud
The blast of which will swirl all this away
And leave me sitting on a rubble shroud,

And sometimes, as just now, I turn and shiver
And realise how precarious is our West;
And did not the petrol prices once seem as
certain
As the begging Arab hands that have
repossessed?

A NAUGHTY FISH AND A CAT

My fish is quiet, but sometimes he is naught-
-y. He swims down to the bottom of his tank,
Picks up a stone in his mouth, rises to the sur-
-face. It drops and chinks where his red coral
sank.
"Stop it," my wife calls, and like a naughty
child,
Like our son when he has turned on the bed-
room light,
My fish skulks behind his artificial weed.
Why does he do it? He has been fed tonight.

Why is he so naughty? Why does my son
flick the light
On and off? For attention? For love of shame?
Does my fish feel lonely in there, is he calling
me

So I tell him "No" as if we were playing a
game?

My son has a string-bead cat. Press under-
neath,
It drops its head, bends knees, wags tail, sits
back
On its haunches, bows, or falls on its side. I
press
My thumb. Mouth gapes by the weed. It
would like a snack.

BLACKBIRD IN THE GARDENS

Outside in the Gardens this March evening
A blackbird is piping. I listen, torn
Between him and work:

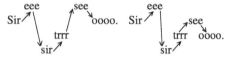

Above the plane, the revving cars, the horn.

The trundling grate of the Italian freight lorry
At the traffic lights, the central heating hum.
He sits in the Gardens and whistles this clear
evening.
I will go out and walk in the Gardens. This
clear blue sum-

-mer sky is like one I knew out in the East,
when
A typhoon has swept by, it was wonderfully
clear,
Trees were sharp, and my heart rose, as it
does now

To the

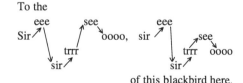

of this blackbird here.

MY TYPIST AND A
TUPPENCEWORTH

My typist has taken ten months over my
poems.
When I ring up, she says she has met a
"snag".
She has bronchitis, and lives in her dressing-

gown.
Sometimes she has had to change her glasses,
      her bag.

Or her typewriter went wrong. For all that I
      am
Patient, for she types my poems beautifully,
      bi-
-nds them into books, seals the spines with
      red tape.
So I am tolerant of the fact that I

Have seen only six volumes out of the fifteen
I gave her, that I have not seen hundreds
Of the poems I have made for ten months.
      They
Are like pots, and a potter never spreads

All his work along one shelf, does he? And
      with
The cost of books today, who will pay for my
Lyrics to be published, or who will buy
Them? I would not give more than tuppence
      for them. Why

I write is simple. Truth is in the home,
And I paint the deeper mind on pots, brush-
      smears
Of the natural spoken voice on a rounded
      form,
A tuppenceworth to last two thousand years.

And so I am not bothered if my typist
Takes ten months over these homely
      miniatures.
There will be time enough for their
      appreciation,
An Eternity of incomes and expenditures.

SPARKS FROM A MUSE

Last night when I pulled off my gold sweater,
It crackled on my back, over my head,
I saw blue sparks dart as it fell on the chair,
Hung rigid, then crumpled. I sat on the bed

And my trousers sparked as each foot brushed
      out.
My clothes are like wires, they do it every
      night.
There is a current in me that crackles,

I am an electrical organism, I am alight.

When I make a poem, I make a circuit.
I send a current down the wire of an image
Or character into your reading mind,
The sparks in my clothes become sparks on
      the page

That will ignite the powder above your cheeks
So that – bang! – your eyes detonate like a
      fuse.
The life-force that runs through me and
      crackles my skin
Pours into my heart from a source outside –
      my Muse!

FINS

My little son is sixteenth months old, he
Knows where his "nose" is, can "clap hands"
      can "wave"
On command, and if you say, "Get your shoe-
      shoes,"
He will waddle and bring the buckle shoes I
      gave

Him. Sixteen months ago he was like a fish,
Gulping and floppy, slippery on a line,
So I felt we ought to put him back in the sea
He was used to. How marvellously fine

Are the growing fins of personality!
In sixteen months my son has become a
      discern-
-ing person, with likes, habits, and a genius's
      eye –
If he grows, like a flipper, his amphibious
      limb to learn.

TOTTERINGS

My son totters across the floor and falls
Into my arms after only ten pa-
-ces. It has taken him five months from his
First crawl to walk so well. "Well *done!*" I
      say.

I write the line numbers on my latest,
Eight hundred and seventy-five line long
      poem.
It has taken me five months to polish each
      rhyme.

284

I am pleased with some of the shines, and
admire them.

But perhaps there is a Kingdom somewhere
Where just as this tottering boy may sprint
A hundred yards inside ten seconds, so
I would find my poem a hobbling in a splint?

TELEPHONES

My one year old son waits till the downstairs
Door is ajar, then he scampers (after some
prods)
For the stairs. For the next few minutes I hear
His patient frog-like progress as he plods.

With a squeak of delight he is round the last
curve
And into my room, where he lifts the green
telephone,
And is entranced, not daring to breathe,
listening,
Eyes delighted, to the brrr of the dialing tone.

Thirty-five years older, am I not the same
As I leave company and climb to my solitary
room,
And lift the receiver on my heart, and listen
For the sound that confirms a presence I
assume?

My one year old son and I both derive
Strength from a source we do not understand.
He listens to No one on his telephone,
I on peace and quiet, held in a slack hand.

THE ENTRYPHONE

Our entryphone has gone wrong yet again.
When someone buzzes us from the bell in the
street
My voice can be heard down there, booming
out,
But I cannot hear the tiniest bleat.

If it were the other way round, it would be
like
My approach to God. For I buzz and speak,
and
Can be heard, but there is a silence, even
though
I tap the carbon crystals in the metal band.

But as I am heard, the buzzer can be pressed,
The front door opened, I can walk upstairs
And be admitted into a floodlit, empty flat
For a tea of quiet, and leave refreshed – by
prayers.

A SEDAN-CHAIR AND DORSET ROCKS

At lunch I sat by the Head of Geography.
He told me he was just leaving for Swanage
For "O" level field work with forty girls.
He would show them Dorset rocks for a week,
at his age.

As he talked, I saw him in a sedan-chair,
Carried head high by forty girls, a great
Lined face and spectacles and greying hair,
Waving feebly like an Arab potentate,

Dying. The vision passed. I knifed and forked
My bacon and egg pie, and talked of the
South Coast,
Of his hospital visits, his lungs. He would
have time
Enough under rocks, this sadly grey-faced
ghost.

FUNERAL LIKE AN EEL IN A GREEN SEA

"'When she opened/the living-room door,/an
extraor-
-dinary sight/met her eyes./ A strange man/
Had taken advantage/of her absence,/
And was fast asleep/in an armchair.'"Does it
scan?

I sit on the desk dictating. Second year
Girls scribble. I look through the window.
Green fie-
-lds, the maples sway in the wind, brushing
the glass
Like waves through a port-hole. I wish it were
the sea.

I say, "'Taking care/not to disturb him,/
Mrs. Trench left/the house immediately."
Out in the maple branches, above the yellow
Laburnum like flames, a blackbird thrills me

To a stop. I listen. "Come on, sir!" I start.

"'She called a taxi/and went to the police sta-
-tion.'" A funeral is drifting along the road, a
    hearse
With flowers on its top. A respectful way

Behind, like an eel, fifty cars wind round the
    road.
Does he smile, the poor bleeder in the front
    one,
To think of the queue he has caused, or does
    he cry
Not to be listening to this bird by this sea in
    this sun?

DECISIONS

What is the fascination in making decisions?
Why do people work up to positions where
    they can
Veto requests, have power over others'
    wishes,
Like our Head who says No to the
    Department's plans,

No to the timetable; or like a Director
Who can say No to how a sum is spent?
Is it just love of self-assertion? I do not
Like those who use decisions to torment.

I share them, through consultation, so all take
    part,
When I can, and do not relish others'
    disgrace.
It takes courage to say No to be right,
    cowardice
To say No and revel in a crestfallen face.

WE TWO ARE THREE

I think of the day we stood by a huge bonfire.
I held you and saw the flames lick up to the
    sky.
Now you say, "You said you weren't happy
    then."
But my arms round you – it's a happy
    memory.

Now this blond-haired little boy runs into me,
Laughing, clambering to pull my hair, and
    what-not,
And hides behind the geranium and shouts
    "Bo"

And calls "Daddy" when I fetch him from his
    cot.

We two are three. What before was adequate
Is now enriched. How well this little boy
Deepens our lives, and the mystery of a
    family –
How out of nothing comes a positive joy!

FREEDOM LIKE A CONSTANT WIFE

A confidential letter has arrived opened.
Well, that is to be expected in view of my pa-
-st. Most times, though, at weekends, I collect
    my mail uncensored,
Go out, buy my newspapers, and the ticket for
    my car,

Am not followed, and can make telephone
    calls
Without being listened in to, can speak out
Loud at work or anywhere about the
    government,
And do not find my promotion is in doubt.

Freedom is at the heart of our Western
    routine.
We take it for granted, like a constant wife.
Freedom is indivisible, and so I am for it
Here, in Russia, or wherever Communist life

Is hailed by its tyrants as "progressive"
Or "egalitarian" or "fair", language of the lie.
And because I am for it anywhere, I will
    guard it
Against all who would seduce her into kissing
    me good-bye.

RUSSIAN CROSS

When I was in Jerusalem, I bought
A tarnished silver cross. It was Russian
Orthodox, with a child-like image of Christ
    crucified
On a skull. There was lettering which no
    discussion

Could decipher on the back, and an old Tsar's
    crown,
And an **N** which I think must be for
    Nicholas

Beneath it. A cross from before the abyss
which cracked
Russia, a cross from a Christendom before
Tass

And the camps. Who wore it, and where? I do
not know,
As I hold it now, and think of the KGB
I risked my life against, I know it predicts
The future of Christendom, and coming unity.

The nun at school sent us a golden card
Of a Russian icon, for our son's christening.
Three angels sit together, the Trinity
Fourteen eleven, from a time with a glistening

Soul. I will put my cross by this framed card
And will think of a time before socialism
dark-
-ened the spirit, when the soul could be
changed, not the world, and could
shine,
And when God was above man like a crown
or a skylark.

A COAT OF ARMS

Last year, my wife went to the Ideal Home
Exhibition. (This year she nearly became
A victim there, an IRA bomb blew up.)
She found a stall with arms for each surname.

Mine have "vert a lion rampant" in "an orle
argent",
My crest is a "demi lion gules" and a "long
Cross". That means my shield is a white lion
On green, and on top a red lion paws an even-
song

Length blue cross. Now they have sent me
their "Armorial
Interpretation". It is the Cross of the
Crusades,   10
It says, and the red lion is for patriotism,
The white against evil – tyrannical brigades.

There is "no motto recorded". So let it be
"Viam Inveniam" – the way to God.
They sent a historiography of my name.
The scroll says, "The patronymic was the
method

Of taking the first name of the father as
The last name of the son." My name is akin
To the patronymic or baptismal "son of
Hacgard",
An "ancient personal name" of Germanic
origin

Through Norman French, meaning "wild
man". It is "not
Now in use". There were Hacgards in Suffolk
in 1273.
My father always said we came from
Cambridge,
That there is a graveyard of us in that vicinity.

Looking in Royston for our old tombstones,
I stopped a stranger who said, between
thunderclaps,
"We have the same name. Perhaps there's a
tribe of us here,
From Crusaders who settled in Suffolk."
Perhaps.

Hac-gard, it sounds like a shin-pad. Perhaps
It's the Old English "haeg-gar", "hedge-
warrior"?   30
But those Saxon ancestors I dream of
From long ago, are illusions. So much for

Then! It is what I stand for now that matters
most:
A united Christendom – that azure cross –
And the patriotic struggle of that red-white
lion
With the infidel unicorn rhinoceros!

5 March 1976

A SHOWER OF PUSSY WILLOW AND HAZEL CATKINS

We park and walk along the gravel track
Between oaks to the silver birches beyond
Which lick upwards like flickering white
flames,
And the crackling gorse, to see if, in the pond,

There is any frogspawn like glarney marbles,
or
Are there tadpoles round sticks like thorns?
By the flags

The brown water has lily leaves, newt weed,
There are children with jam jars, water in
    plastic bags –

Sticklebacks, minnows, bullheads, but no
    frogspawn.
We are too early, Easter is not yet here.
So I look at pussy willow, hazel catkins.
I am clay and sky, I am Nature, at this shower
    of the year.

10 March 1976

WORDS LIKE DITCHES

In this Forest, the silver birches writhe,
Gorse flames and crackles as the dry bush
    burns.
I stand between silver and golden fire
And feel existence lick and curl in turns.

I have to perceive the world in terms of lang-
-uage to understand it, I do not know my
    experiences
Until I have seen them in words. A painter fix-
-es his scene in paint, I in nouns and tenses.

Words are like ditches for these streams of
    image
And thought. They are the stones over which
    streams have swirled,
The walls of the mud-banks. They channel
    and carr-
-y this spring of perception from the forests of
    the world.

RITUAL LIKE A KNIGHT'S CANDLELIGHT

In Korea, on my television, a car
Manager kneels before a pig's head. A line
Of workers stands still as he bows head to
    ground,
Then scatters salt, eats cuttlefish, drinks rice-
    wine.

Today in the Forest church, I knelt and bowed
Before Christ's head on a cross, then stood.
    Meanwhile
The white surpliced vicar served me with
    bread
And red wine. I stood as he came back up the
    aisle.

Man's need of ritual is like an actor's part.
We rehearse, advance, bow, measure our-
    selves by the knight
We play – the perfection of our role – till we
    become
That kneeling Man in front of his Divine
    Light.

AMBASSADOR OF THE ETERNAL

My love is not dependent on public life,
I will live in the country away from the
    chances
And accidents of our uncertain time,
The sieges and bombings and shootings, our
    "circumstances".

This fascination for the double life,
As spies and adulterers know, reveals a split:
Our outer and inner selves are in conflict,
Just as Time and Eternity war in a woman's
    slit,

Or the contemplative joy. O what it must
Have been to be a Greek, and to see life
    whole!
The Church is an embassy for Heaven's
    Love,
But let me unite the Love of Body, of Soul!

MOON

Up in the night is a nearly full moon
With a halo round it. Look up at the globe,
Then carry on with your work. When you
    next look,
It is still there, inviting the next space probe.

This afternoon in my bath, I closed my eyes
And saw a blue light, an orb with a halo.
I washed my hair under the shower, and
    when
I looked again, like the moon it was still
    aglow.

There is a moon in the soul; also a sun
Whose radiance gives it light, but which has
    to be
Hidden from view in this night. And my
    moon
Reflects light from a Source I never see.

A PLASTICINE SOUL

See the clay on this spinning wheel, the hand
Makes it rise up tall, and then fall again.
Now it is fatter with a wider base,
A vessel that can catch and hold more rain.

So it is with a person. We rise to a height
And then the hand of suffering brings us
     down
To rise again and assume a different shape,
So we can contain more moisture, so we do
     not frown.

The hand of the potter that is so painful
To the clay that is being reshaped, is the hand
     of God.
The vessel it shapes, the human heart, is tall
And leaky, or small and receptive, according
     to its prod.

A human is not material, as the socialists say,
To be remoulded like a brainwashed Chinese
     heart.
He has a plasticine soul which must be
     reshaped
By the loving hand of God, and a potter's art.

BANK BALANCE LIKE AN HONEST WIFE

When my car is going well, I do not touch it.
If I open the bonnet and tinker with the
     engine, cha-
-nge the plugs, it may not start first time, and
     then I will
Be late for work, get a cross from cross
     Mrs. K.

When my Department is going well, I do not
     touch it.
If I change the timetables, swap staff round,
     fight
Then they will be unsettled, will not work
     well, then I will
Have to soothe them and be late home, when I
     want to write.

When my marriage is going well, I do not
     touch it.
If I open the lid of my wife's head and
     analyse

Her words as if she were dials on a washing-
     machine,
She will stop, I will have to cook my own
     fruit-pies.

I do not tinker with my car, my staff, my mar-
     riage,
And so I have a smooth, trouble-free life.
If I do not tinker with my bank balance,
Will it stay with me, like an honest wife?

THE ELYSIAN CLUB

I just missed Monty, he saw nobody
From a week before he received my letter
And his housekeeper replied that he was ill,
Till his death, save his family. Perhaps it is
     better

That I should recall the man who spoke at my
     school:
"We went through Rommel's army like a
     knife
Going through butter." He was buried today,
     the bu-
-gle sounded the last post as he retired from
     life.

Did Ultra or his will win at Alamein?
I missed Monty, and now he is in a dug-out
In Fields where thousands of soldiers are
     gathered,
A good few from the Eighth Army, I don't
     doubt.

When I die, my love, please do not forget
That on the first evening I will dine in Hall,
And will interview Churchill, Stalin, Hitler
On being warlords, and Monty will confirm it
     all.

Then over coffee, I will seek out Dean Swift,
     and
Canvass his thoughts on Gulliver's moral
     blindness,
And then Chaucer – was he aware of the
     mock-heroic?
And all the rest of them at that great address.

When I enter their Fields, I will have a
     marvellous time

Meeting all the members of the Elysian Club.
I will engage Homer on his heroic line
And swap sonnets with Shakespeare in the
summery pub.

Until then, I will act on the assumption
That Elysians send the music of the spheres,
And will strive to approach the standard they
have set,
The tradition of the last three thousand years.

SQUANDERING TIME

It was Montgomery's funeral yesterday.
His beret was on his coffin by his sword.
I thought of the Memoirs he wrote after his
battles,
He did not waste those last years, feeling
bored,

Squandering them on horses and trivialities,
Dining out, prattling, going to the cinema
(I like to think), and he gave his life a
completeness
Like the fullness of an oak, proud of each
scar,

Making a fitting death. I thought of how,
After being left for dead, he prepared himself
for war,
Lecturing, refusing to smoke or drink, going
To bed at ten, how he knew he would be ca-

-lled, even when his wife died, by Providence,
And how when the clock struck, he had some
luck,
For if Gott's plane had not crashed, we might
not have heard
Of him at El Alamein, of the Monty pluck.

And here am I, also preparing myself.
I teach poetry, make notes for my big works,
Read, research, delve in six London libraries,
Have given up drink three years, do physical
jerks,

With as little evidence that my hour will
come,
Obsessed by the brevity between each clock-
chime.
They can be forgiven for wishing I played

squash,
And for not understanding why I won't
squander time.

NEW POWERS

The last day of term, I worked at a run
From 8.30 to 3.15. I came home and then
Sat down at my desk and wrote for three
hours, and still
Had brain energy left by eleven.

The first day of the holidays, I walked
To the shops, to the bank, to the cleaners, fix-
-ed up France, wrote two poems, moved
slowly –
And I fell asleep in the sofa at six.

There is a law. When the mind teems at work,
It goes on plashing, finishes a poem in a few
Minutes, when a year back it would have
taken an hour.
When it trickles by day, it trickles in the
evening too.

We do not dig over the same patch of ground.
I do not dig over these poems again and again.
And in my teaching, I have lost myself to find
Myself in these new powers, this jet of a
fountain.

It is like my roof-garden fountain with a lion's
mouth.
I pour myself out, give to my pupils, and
retrieve
The force when it is pumped up inside me, a
spring
To replace what I give. So, to give is to
receive.

FORM LIKE A RADIATOR

In the night, the bathroom radiator leaked.
The carpet was damp next morning, and
moisture seep-
-ed into the flat below, whose owner
complained.
We found the leak at the tap. To keep it cheap

We tried tightening the nuts, as the book says.
To no avail. So we took off the tap, left a tin
And a cloth underneath, that got wringing

290

wet. It was like
A spring, the leak, welling up from the
    turning-pin.

The engineer said over the phone, "Sounds
    like a valve,
I will try and come tomorrow." I gave a snort.
To keep the floor dry we hit on the idea
Of winding string round the leak, and making
    it taut

To the bowl with a cloth. Now the water ran
    down
Our string, and nothing was wet. I marvelled
    as I look-
-ed: when I leaked, I should tie a string round
    my
Inspiration so it dripped into one book

Instead of being spread across the carpet,
    leaving
Yellow stains. The engineer came, a smiling,
    round
African. He put on a new washer and hemp,
    and said,
"I won't write a paper, it would cost you eight
    pound –
Give me six in cash, and we'll make it a
    cheap rate."
He went. He had broken the tape, it wouldn't
    turn well,
So the next day he came again, and drained
    the system,
And replaced a part, the upside-down "L".

Then I knew, I *should* function without a leak.
My system functions at the right times, is
    complete.
As in radiators, poems heat in me, grow cool;
Their form is a radiator, with an infused heat.

BRINGING EVIL DOWN

For too long we have tolerated the evils
In other countries. Our leaders are short-sight-
-ed and have ignored rottenness for the "day-
    to-day"
And have not spoken out for what is right.

For too long I have tolerated the evils
In other people. I have accepted each slight

Burrowing in the name of "good relations"
And have not spoken out for what is right.

For too long I have tolered the evils
In myself. I have accepted that red light
Beetle – though I have pruned – in the name
    of "smooth running",
And have not spoken out for what is right.

A moral sense preserves the spirit. 'What
I want' must yield to 'what should be', as
    must 'what they
Want'. And so, my love, I shall speak out.
    That woman
You know who is "into witchcraft" has been
    eaten away.

I will tolerate her freedom to spread rot-
-tenness as a democratic right, but I condemn
It by absolute good, like Dutch elm disease.
Tyranny, rudeness, the lie – many men
    contemn

Our nation for losing the sap of integrity,
Truthfulness. A moral choice is like a feller's
    frown
Or an elm white-crossed to topple. Each of us
Is responsible for bringing Evil down.

COLD WAR

Like a great imperial power, you seek to
    expand
At my expense; you make demands – do not
    say "please":
If I give you x pounds you will make "no fur-
    ther demands",
"Will not take" me "to court", and I know that
    if I appease
You, I may not necessarily be keeping the
    peace;
That to hold firm is to guarantee, if not what I
    want,
Then the status quo. And so I must not cease
To hold firm, must not weaken into *détente*,
Must refuse to deceive myself that you want a
    clo-
-seness. And our Cold War continues. I regret
    it. While
I do not like writing firm letters – my heart
    squirms

291

When I split you from your lawyers – this I
    know:
Ever since you broke our alliance, and turned
    hostile,
I have been determined to conclude a peace
    on my terms.

FLY-WHEELED AWAY

I stand in Salisbury Cathedral, and stare
At the earliest remaining mechanical clock
In the world. A flywheel clicks, a black wheel
    turns.
Above: ropes and heavy pulleys seem lock-

-ed to the roof. It has ticked since 1386.
I think of all the time that has fly-marked away
Since then, of the day eight years back when
    we stood here
On our way down to the Dorset coast for a
    holiday.

Now I tear towards a Dorset Channel port
And think of the time I left you in that hotel,
And drove up to London to work, and after-
    wards,
And then spent a stormy night getting to know
    Hell.

And when I returned to the Pines next day,
You were doing the Conga. You did not see
    any crime,
You said you had been miserable while I was
    away,
And all that, like you, has fly-wheeled away
    with time.

THE HEART OF CELERY

You sit on the bed chewing a heart of celery.
Our picnic dinner is spread out on the small
Table of this guest house room here in
    Weymouth.
The sea, the red funnelled car ferry call

To me how another sat in a similar position –
And went with my child. Will you too go
    away,
And will I look back on this moment, on this
    peace,
The orange lights shimmering in the black
    bay?

I sit and listen to the peace. I am alert.
That boy who wrote a letter on a Greek hill,
    glad
At choosing to be an artist, has become what
    he want-
-ed to. I am at peace, and perhaps a trifle sad.

Earlier, this evening, we walked the
    promenade.
It did not rain. We saw the history of the
    town:
The George III station, the Jubilee clock, the D-
Day monument. It is hard to imagine down

There the thousands of Americans embarking.
Only the "American Bar" where George III
    stayed
Recalls the war, and the red mine on the
    pier –
And the silence of all who lay in this room,
    and were laid

To rest. In April everything is closed, and if I
Were a commercial traveller, there would be
    nothing to do.
I sit here and feel a sadness become peace:
D-Day, my war – through the celery, briefly,
    you.

TIME A MINUTE AWAY

Last night I lay in bed in my harbour hotel,
An American waiting for D-Day, very
Frightened, when BOOOM, a white flash lit
    the window –
An air-raid? A doodlebug? Was the car ferry

Blown up? Over breakfast, the landlady said,
    "Lifeboat
Went out. They let off a flare like a fire-
    work."
She complained the tomato boats kept her
    awake
At the back: "It's the hatches opening." I
    smirk.

"Tuesdays to Fridays at five. We are so tired."
    I asked her about D-Day. "Oh,
    there were hor-
-des of Americans," she said. "Three
    commandos

Were billeted with us. They couldn't say."
    Time is no more

Than a minute away, thirty-one years are a
    blink.
Now I chug-chug towards Cherbourg. A sea-
    mist reaches
Back to D-Day. I, and these ghosts beside
    me,
Wait to be shot at from Eternity's Norman
    beaches.

WIND IN A WAR CEMETERY

I race through D-Day towns, along beaches;
Through Ste Mère-Eglise, where a parachutist
    hung
From the spire, past Utah flags and bunkers
Where tanks and armoured cars rot, not
    unsung,

To the green Omaha cliffs, above the yellow
    sand
Of Dog Green, where Americans were landed
    between
Sea and machine-guns. I linger in this war
    cemetery.
Wind sings in pines, in a smell of evergreen

Nearly ten thousand white crosses stand in
Columns, like ranks of parading men, and
    proclaim
Forgiveness in a hundred avenues,
Nearly ten thousand crosses, each reproaching
    with a name.

There is a silence in the singing wind.
I roar through Arromanches, past the
    Mulberry,
Past Juno and Sword beaches, and Pegasus
    Bridge,
Where still I hear the wind in that cemetery!

NEAR CABOURG

We turn into Ouistreham, and suddenly –
The red-white hooped lighthouse on the
    harbour wall,
And twenty-three years come flashing back. I
    have
Not thought of this since the September when
    we all

Left the summer retreat outside Cabourg,
And drove here, and Monsieur, who is now
    dead,
Told me about the Battle of Normandy
And what the British did when they liberated

This coast. I look for the house: Le Home-sur-
    la-Mer.
The road has changed, only the sea, the slope,
The empty sand, the wind, and my memory
    until
Oh! this Cabourg monument like an antelope!

A WISH BY WATER

We stop in Falaise, behind the Conqueror's
    Castle,
At the stream where Robert, Duke of
    Normandy,
Saw Arlette washing clothes, "with her skirts
    drawn high,"
And made love to her when she visited him
    openly

And produced the Conqueror. Now you stand
    by
This rushing water, and I think of the time I
    on-
-ce saw you by still water minding children
In swimming trunks, and how we produced
    our son.

I have been fighting Montgomery's battles,
On the beaches, round Caen – Hill a hundred
    and twelve –
And now near Falaise here, where the trap
    snapped shut,
And the German army surrendered, and
    having delve-

-d back – Montgomery came from Normandy,
    like me
Perhaps, and conquered his homeland after
    D-Day.
The best I can hope for my son is that he,
Like William and Monty, will also find his
    way.

HEAVEN: GLASS LIKE THE WINDOWS OF A SOUL

We enter Chartres Cathedral under cloud.

The blues of the stained glass stand out. We
    walk about
And linger in shadow, stare up at three rose
Windows, each with a centre and petals
    spreading out.

As we watch the sun comes out, and the dark
    blue
Changes to red and yellow, and pale azure,
And the window over the Royal Door is a
    vision –
So beautiful in its organised details! Sure-

-ly, here is Heaven in a pictorial form!
Yet how impermanent for the artist who
    painted
It on glass! Did he not fear cannonballs? Or
    did he
Think it was high enough to be protected?

How wonderful to paint Heaven, and set
It here in this Cathedral, so the sunlight
Can change its tones, and when dull, make it
    dull;
When bright, illuminate it with this pale blue
    bright-

-ness! An Englishman lectures twice a day
On the pictures, and the meaning of each one;
Has he seen that this Cathedral is a soul
Whose windows let in Light as shafts from a
    sun?

14 April 1976

THE PRESENT MOMENT
(OR: BEING)

"When I finish my book, I will have to buy
    another,"
She said on the voyage. Can't she sit and look
    at the sea?
"No," she said, "I will be bored." And then I
    knew.
She had to escape the present moment, could
    not be.

I am the reverse. I wish to escape the books,
The films, visits, dinners with "friends" which
    distract
From the quiet moment, so that I can paint
    yesterday's

Moment in Versailles in words, prepare for
    the impact

(Sometimes by reading which extends it) of
    tomorrow's moment,
Deepen last week's, anticipate next wee-   10
-k's or merely contemplate. Because I am at
    peace,
How can she not spend an hour gazing at the
    sea?

We live in the present, in our situation,
And the art of living is to be happy there
And not have to be distracted; to be. The artist
Abstracts himself from present awarenesss to
    stare

At and fix a past moment into a pattern,
To squeeze out the eternal, so it will always
    be
There. Marie-Antoinette and the regicides are
    dead,
But there will be regicides next century.   20

Western civilisation offers distractions.
Radio, TV, records can all destroy
Or extend intensity. To live truly is to live
With the undistracted eye of a Catullus's joy.

Western enjoyments burn my life away,
For they take me away from the canvas of my
    situation.
They fill my time, but candlelit silence
And emptiness are the artist's and the monk's
    vocation.

So I shall watch television to extend
The present moment: from choice, or not at
    all –   30
Unless I am tired and use it as a relaxant
To escape from the present, and the artist's
    call.

And when I am not observing, or in past or
    future,
Or relaxing, I will remember it is *now*
That I can close my eyes, see the Flowing
    Light,
Know Eternity through prayer, and power,
    and Thou.

The eternity of art is squeezed out in
The present, when the artist images the past
Or future. The Eternity of Being is known
Only in the present, with eyes closed fast.   40

15 April 1976

IS THERE A GOD? IS THERE A SUN?

"Is there a God?" the TV programme asks.
For ninety minutes bold professors put
Atheistic views, arguments; linguistic
Philosophers on "possible"'s verbal soot.

Darwin, Freud, Marx are there, but no
        Archbishop.
Of thirty experts, a priest, a prisoner, a nun
Alone have seen. The rest make a case, want
        proof,
Blind men doubting the existence of the sun!

"Is there a God?" I recall how in Japan
I sat in a Zen centre, and the Master set   10
A koan: a man clung to a branch with his
        teeth,
His Master spoke. He had to reply, yet

Would fall into a pit if he opened his mouth,
So what should he do? One by one all filed in,
Spoke and were beaten with a stick. They
        should
Have kept silent. Once you speak about God
        you begin

To go wrong. God is known through
        experience,
The intellect obstructs all self-surmounters.
One nun is worth twenty thousand professors
Shuffling dry words like tiddlywink
        counters.   20

There is no rational approach to God.
You cannot argue that the sun is there,
It is seen, not proved. Those who have not
        seen
Tell of the darkness of their inner air,

Yet, "Experience is not an argument
But a claim," we are told. "What is seen is to
        be
Tested, interpreted." What an example

To the young who don't know that
        "knowledge" is to see!

RAPT

Easter Sunday. *South Pacific* on TV.
The cheap music disgusts, today should be
        quiet.
I come upstairs and sit, glad to be alone,
Not needing to make an excuse for piet-

-y. What a comment on our secularization
That on Easter Sunday it should be *South
        Pacific*!
Our time has gone wrong. Those who can see it
Must speak so the next generation can pick

Up the right path, only much further on.
I check that my son sleeps after his fall,   10
Then I lie on my bed. I used to be
Afraid of solitude, now I welcome this call

To be alone in this dark atmosphere,
To embrace a deep trance that has a wise
Quiet in it. Now I wish I could be a monk
And meditate often. I close my eyes.

Immediately, white light starts breaking
        through
Paisley patterns, images of ruby rings,
The flame-like face of God on a rosy shield.
Rose-light, and hints of Christ risen among
        Kings.   20

I quietly thrum, my heart is so quickened
That this Light surely flows in from outside,
Renewing my cells, filling me with this
        power,
Ending all loss, leaving me satisfied.

Like the loins, the soul swells every so often
And is charged with power which can then be
        tapped.
Some days I feel the Light will never shine,
And then it is best to wait until I am rapt.

Now God has gone and I am tired, but I
Lie on alone, revelling in quietude,   30
In a new-found thirst for Being's company
Like a lover who has loved and released a
        nude.

295

TANKAS

1. Mind like Broken Glass
Mistletoe in green
Barked trees with ivy. Heifers
Graze in a field of
Green barrows. They glint in me,
Flash like sun on broken glass.

2. Serene
Grey Purbeck stone of
A Dorset inn. A pheasant
Struts up a green bank.
I roar through countryside at
Eighty, in a trance, serene.

3. Illusions
We hung above the
Road while the earth span towards
Us at seventy;
We moved out, the boat was still –
We moved on the harbour, still.

4. A Humpty Dumpty Man
Newhaven cliffs slid-
-ing by, this same wrinkled sea.
A Humpty Dumpty man,
I fell, and was in pieces
Till she stuck me together.

5. Daisy Chain
My son wears a dai-
-sy chain. Esau sold his birth-
-right for his country,
For a mess of pottage for
This boy with a daisy crown.

HAIKUS

Corn dollies. The last
Ear of corn preserves the earth's
Spirit till next year.

White blossom on blue
Sky. The mystery of women
Going on and on.

The daisies on the
Lawn are like stars in the lake.
A child picks two worlds.

A MALLARD AND A LAW OF NATURE

We drive through London pylons and high-
          rise flats
Like mountaineers in a city of gravestones
To the white pear blossom of Essex. Birds
          tinkle
In the Forest sun, green pussy willow disowns

Brown pond water. With a sploosh from
          above lands
A mallard, neck of green sheen. A duck blind-
-ly swims behind, brown with an orange beak.
          The mallard
Swims in circles, the duck still follows
          behind.

I think of how Arabs walked in Libya,
Kuffeiad men ahead, women – it is their
          creed –
In white barracans, one eye peeping, behind.
It is a law of Nature for the male to lead.

A couple pass on the brown sand-gravel
          shore.
He leads, she follows, pushing a pram. So
          then,
Ducks, Arabs, Essex folk, acting naturally.
Why do some women want to lead their men?

2.30 A.M.: PARENTHOOD

Yesterday I visited you: a village off
The A1, one church, a post office in some-
-one's front room, one shop, and your house
          (The Fox), a lawn,
A swing, a stable-garage, no friends to come

And play. "Daddy," you called as I drove
          past.
We went for a walk in the graveyard, then in a
          field
At the end of a lane, on a public footpath.
          Then we drove
To Grantham, where Newton's talents were
          revealed –

And Mrs. Thatcher's. We had a milkshake, I
          slipped
You a pound. As you waved goodbye, I saw
          her again,   10

A brief face in your porch, yellow hair
    groomed,
And now I feel sad when before I felt no pain.

An old wound has opened that I thought
    healed.
I am sad she's content with what she once
    despised –
This smallness, these pinched people – and
    that lawyers
And the Court mean she will not speak to me
    unless advised.

I am sad for you. She has given you memories
In this county, instead of the Essex to which I
    am tied.
You will hold them precious, may have to live
    here when old.
And she does not make you read, lets you
    play outside.   20

I had hopes – I was wrong – that you would
    come to love
The books that I do. So do all parents wish
Their children will blossom into images of
    them!
Mine did of me, I rebelled with some anguish.

"I don't want to teach," you said, frowning. "I
    want
To be an interior designer, I think." There is
    no
Reason why you should teach, but *that* is
    high-falutin'.
I was not sure that you want me to go

To your Parents' Evening. You are your
    mother's child,
Already you take after her. You may soon be
    a wife.   30
My little boy takes after me. He fetches
    books,
Sits and reads at my feet, shows me pictures
    of life.

And knowing how he depends on me, and
    how
I must buy a house for us all, and work hard –
    and will –
For twenty-five more years, I feel sad at

The things he should have but will not; your
    private school bill.

O how sad it is to want the best for one's
Children and see life frustrate it, make a mess.
How sad to live with this sense of damaged
    fruit,
One's own kin damaged by our past
    blindness.   40

And o how wrong it is to impose one's hopes
On one's children, as I, no doubt, have on
    you.
I, who always said you would be free to
    choose,
Now stand for a moral choice, knowing what
    is true,

And so threaten to live your life, a mistake I
    vowed
I would never make, a "mistake" that is now
    in doubt.
I have one consolation this dreadful night.
There is no knowing how anyone will turn
    out.

I have seen it at school, the sudden blossom-
    ing.
A girl who has frittered her time is filled with
    sap,   50
And buds questions – "what is life?" – and
    blossoms a mind.
How can I be sure you will not mature and
    tap

This force inside, put out images like flowers,
Shame your gardener's fears with ideas like
    chestnut fruit?
If so, then I realise that your bare bark
And what you are now learning was the feed-
    ing of the root!

DRIFTWOOD GIRLS

I ring last term's supply. Her flatmate
    answers.
Then I hear her cross the floor to the telepho-
-ne. She is working in a new school now. I
    ask
If she has any fourth year files still. She says
    No.

When I ring off I think of her going back
To join the others in her Wandsworth flat,
    kick her heels,
Watch television, bicker her life away
And not get married because she was cooking
    meals,

Doing the washing, the ironing, washing her
    hair,
Having an early night, pondering why
No one took her anywhere. O cruel life that
Swirls driftwood girls into flats and passes
    them by!

COMMUNITIES LIKE APPLES

First it was school and cricket teams and
    runs –
Achievements like marks or a half century.
Then it was the holidays, tennis, cricket,
Youth Clubs – friends up the road who came
    to tea.

Then it was the local girls. It was "Shirley,
Does she knock?" Or "Diane, she kisses like
    sin!"
Then it was students, and then the British
    abroad,
And now it is so at work. We form ourselves
    in-

-to communities, being gregarious,
And see each other from the outside, and
    snipe!
The country is full of communities and
    reputations
Like different clusters of apples on trees,
    some ripe!

And most tempting is the fleeting encounter
When a face becomes an image that haunts
    the head
And gathers rosiness till, picked and bitten,
The Eternal murmurs, "Like a baby that has
    been fed!"

TRADITION LIKE A SPLENDID WALL

On TV a film is mocking a public school.
Boys rag about, are tormented as fags,
Are forced to take cold showers, are beaten,
    scragged.
History is taught by a buffoon in cycle-
    clipped bags.

A rugger scrum rucks madly after a ball.
Fists thump in hall for house victories, and the
    rule
Of Chapel, the CCF. Speech Day and "scum" –
The traditions are held up for ridicule.

But the Cloisters they laugh at now make
    ghosts of them.
O grand tradition that dwarfs like a splendid
    wall!
Long after these dopes have thumbed their
    nose at the years,
It endures, with the longevity of this summery
    Hall!

AFTER THE ECLIPSE

I sit on the desk as they do a multiple choice.
Out of the window, after the eclipse like a bite
In the moon sun – it was annular, with a ring
    like a hal-
-o in Greece – the shadows have flown, it is
    no longer twilight,

And the green buds of the trees hold up their
    first leaves
Like parasols, they strain up against the blue
    sky,
Put out at being neglected in the darkened
    noon
But ready with shades for a scorching. They
    are so high,

So beautiful. I, a bud myself, envy them
From my twig on my branch, my shade
    unfolds like a fan,
And I look at my angular society on this blue
And, one of many, stretch to where light
    began.

ILLUSIONS LIKE COTTON WOOL

"We are here on this earth," I tell the third-
    year class.
"We go round the sun in an elliptical orbit.
When we are far away, we are in winter.
    When near,

Then we roast in a summery heat, on a turning
    spit.

We turn on our axis. When we are towards
The sun we are in day; when away, we are un-
-der night, and Australia is towards. The
    moon
Spins round us, and if it gets between us and
    the sun

There is a solar eclipse; but if we get between
It and the light it reflects from the sun, a
    lunar   10
One takes place. Stonehenge calculated when
    this happened,
But now we Westerners have the computer."

And suddenly all my illusions fall away,
This life and routine, like fluffy cotton wool,
And I am on a ball, spinning round a fire,
Whirled round by another ball, held down by
    a pull
I cannot see, but which may one day snap
And hurtle me into the darkness of the past.
I shiver, and wonder, as the sun burns on
Till it burns itself out, how long will it all
    last?   20

We fear a new Dark Age if the West falls;
All these services will break down, we will
    crawl
In the fields, live like cavemen again. But
    what
Of this Dark Night of God that awaits us all?

VOLCANO

Mrs. Ball was a snob who looked down on all
    blacks,
But when she had a stroke, she was grateful to
    all
Black nurses. Awareness of death makes us
    humane
Towards others who are also before the wall.

The Head of RE has a throat infection, cannot
Kiss his wife. At lunch I glow anarchically,
    then
Cool: we will both die, have an ordeal in
    common.
I am like a volcano. I erupt molten

Experience, red images pour out, solid-
-ify into black lava, cool to rock. Why
Does this dangerous burning inside me, which
    can kill,
End as this black sympathy for all who will
    die?

GOLD

Sixty-something poems in nine weeks! All of
    a sudden
I can't leave this trickle in myself, this stream.
I have built my house round my Pierian
    spring,
And I sift it each day, comb its stones for a
    gleam,

A precious glint. I am so cool now. I am calm.
This bubbling inside me, fused image and
    thought –
I dig my fingers, scoop grains of shingle,
And observe as the stream splashes by what
    my handful has caught.

I am unconcerned, go about my daily work,
And when I come home, I go upstairs and
    gush!
I have found what I only glimpsed a decade
    ago.
Like a gold prospector after the gold rush

Who has found a seam in a South African
    stream
When California is ghost towns, I hold
A sieve of soil which winks that I am rich,
And that I must now be a regular miner of
    gold.

GARGOYLE

I looked for beauty and found it in bees
Humming in white clover, scarlet berries,
Roses by a stream, poplar shadows: pictures:
Daisies on hillocks, gnats. But the branches

Did not keep their leaves. Obsessed with the
    shortness
Of beauty, I tried to put it into art:
The Eternity of pictures in old caves
Or of bulls on Cretan walls preserve the heart-

-'s heat, and the beauty it mirrored once,

299

glinted,
Like a moon glimpsed in a pond before
ripples spread,
Shimmering white fire. So by this Cathedral
fount-
-ain, let me become the grimace on this
gargoyle's head.

THE DISGUST OF DEATH

I have often eaten fish. In a restaurant,
At home, cod, haddock on a plate release my
Juices; herring, kippers, Dover sole, all
Lying near parsley sauce, waiting to be kni-

-fed....When I left Japan I was taken out to
dinner.
Once the plaice was alive, although it had
been cooked.
It blinked mournfully at me as I picked its
flesh,
Then died. Once I had to eat live shrimps
which looked

At me through glass. I dipped in a hand, bit
off
A head, and swallowed the wriggling body
well enough.
I had a taste for raw fish. But when I found
My goldfish still on the carpet with bits of
fluff

On him, some hours dead – he had jumped
out in the night –
I could not touch him, I had the disgust of
death.
I scooped him with my fly-swat into a plastic
bag.
He was different from the fish I ate, he had
breath,

He plopped air. All living things must die, I
thought.
The fish we won at the fair could not survive.
I, too, will lie glass-eyed under this sky.
But I will not think of that; I am – *alive*!

SOULS LIKE PIGEONS

Today I drove by the Wellington Barracks
In Birdcage Walk. Near here a flying bomb
Fell on a morning service. The iron railings,

Street-lamp and tree remind me of a photo-
graph from

Six days into the General Strike. A crowd
In trilbys, cloth caps, stand by the open gates
As a tank leaves – all knobbled bolts – tin-
hel-
-meted men at the top, or through the front.
Nearby waits

A man with hands in coat pockets. He stood
By that lamp-post. Half a century has pour-
-ed by. The place is there, but a tide has
ebbed,
Like breakwaters that were sea-defences, on a
shore.

This is the mystery of time. We walk in a
place –
Apsley House, Chartwell – where great deeds
were express-
-ed, like an "Ici tomba", or a house after
someone has died,
And all that appears to remain is the
emptiness.

When I die, and my statue stands in Trafalgar
Square
Or off the Mall, looking thoughtful, steadfast,
My soul will settle on it like a London
pigeon –
And looking at these pigeons I feel the
presence of the past!

POLLEN

As a bee bustles into this petunia
And sucks up the nectar that he will spit out
Into his honeycomb for honey which will
house
And feed his grubs when they hatch, and,
without

His realising it, at the same time, accident-
-ally pollen sticks to his leg, gathers in the
hollow-
-ed part from the anther, and is carried to the
next flower,
And may fertilize its stigma's ovules, so

I, while bustling about my work, sucking

Up my nectar which will house and feed my
young,
Gather observations like pollen, which
fertilize
The words and feeling on my flower-like
tongue.

A MUSCULAR SENSIBILITY

Every other morning I do twenty-four toe-
touches,
Nineteen lyings on my back and touching fee-
-t, forty-five butterfly strokes, twenty-four
press-ups,
Then jog on the spot for three hundred and
thirty-three

Steps. All this makes demands on my muscles
Which are now toned up, not flabby, and so
they
Never feel tired. It makes demands on my
heart
Which is fitter, and carries me around all day

Without my feeling breathless. So it is with
the mind.
Make demands on the mind each day, and it
ceases to be
Like flabby fat. Feeling and thought are fused
Like muscle and flesh below a rippling knee,

Their sinewy threads of image uniting,
Like tough fibrous tissue, muscle and bone.
So I will exercise the mind till the
unattainable
Bulges with supple meaning as hard as stone.

NO PROS

I was tired from arranging coverage for absent
staff,
From showing seven Americans round our
school,
From writing reports and answering my
door,
From crawling on all fours for my son,
playing the fool.

When I sat alone poetry ejaculated,
And I thought, 'Suppose I earned my living
like this;
Would I be able to sustain it all day long?

Would I be able to keep us on my Muse's
kiss?'

And then I knew the soliciting might kill me.
I could not keep a beat up all day, it would go
stale
If I sold prose to all comers. Whereas now
I was not selling myself, I was an honest male.

And if I were financially independent,
And had never had to work, would I have
been smit-
-ten by these images? I might never have met
them.
My love affairs have been of benefit.

Poetry, like the seed, gathers during the day
Till it swells to a fullness that must spurt. It is
more
Vibrant this way than when it is numbly
forced –
When it is for sale each minute, like an over-
worked whore.

OVERFLOW

Every morning the overflow pipe in the roof
Dripped water, which splashed past the
washing-line beneath
Into an old tin tub, which soon became full.
When I ran the cold tap to clean my teeth

It stopped. I guessed it was the cold storage
tank.
Running the tap brought the level down again,
But at night too much water came in, the ball
valve
Did not shut off the supply from the main.

I rang our African plumber. He brought an old
man.
They turned off the tap in the basement cellar
So the house was dry, and took off the old
ball valve.
"See," the old man said, "it's rotten. The
water

Seeps through." There's a valve in me which
needs repair.
I run off a poem or two from the tank of my
in-

-spiration, but the level rises, and not shut off,
    pours
Down this overflow, this waste, to the tub in a
    woman's skin.

GHOST TOWN

I walked in a valley in the heart of London.
I stood in a potato field and saw the yellow
Mining town which had been deserted. There
    were
Narrow streets of low houses, each window

Was shuttered. As I squeezed between the
    walls
Of this ghost town, I saw trousered legs un-
-der the half-open shutters, and heads back
    still.
Men sat in the windows. Could these be the
    dead whom no one

Would take in the exodus? I peered up at the
    face
Of one. It was an old man's, well shaven and
    pale.
But oh the horror as his closed eye opened
And peeped out of its corner, the awful detail!

Shuddering, shivering, I walked past the
    living dead,
Sitting motionless, they opened their eyes and
    peep-
-ed. How relieved I was to come out in the
    valley.
Nothing would make me return to where
    those dead sleep.

ENERGY TECHNIQUES

Living in a time of falling standards,
We think we are slithering down, like Rome
    before the Goths.
Will oil save us, or will it break up the UK,
Or, because we've borrowed against it, leave
    us like slicked moths?

Will it last more than fifty years? Will North
    Sea
Gas? And what of the coal prices, electricity?
It is with relief that I hear that the future
Is (through silicon) solar, or marine energy.

Energy from the sun, or from the waves
May put out of date our "aids to living", so
    clever-
-ly "harnessed", as the gaslamp, the candle
    have gone,
And may progress our civilisation for ever!

I think of Norman buildings, and our advance
Since then. Perhaps we will have perpetual
    progress.
Perpetual progress! It is just a dream.
We have techniques, and there are many more
    bless-

-ings and discoveries budding in our
    scientists' minds,
But history is not like a rising line on a graph,
One sales boom. It is a zigzag, and Dark Ages
Make valleys of low blankness, and sunless
    half-

Bloomed souls. And look at the Norman
    Cathedrals,
What splendid buildings! By our low slopes,
    they are peaks
On the up-down mountain-range of
    civilisation.
Our dreams, lacking élan, are of energy
    techniques.

WISTFUL TIME-TRAVELLERS
(FIRST VERSION)

Sitting here in our flat, after dinner,
We can turn on the past. One TV knob, and
    Lord-
-s of Time, we are back eight years at the
    Marathon.
I could be twelve years ago on my tape-
    record-

-er. Our voices will speak from that
    Christmas, at a touch
Of a key. Or if I put up a screen, I could be
Me as I was at a wedding fifteen years back
In a Garden of celluloid Eternity.

We Westerners are all time-travellers now.
We glide at the speed of light. For a few
    pounds   10
We can put back the clock to yesterday,

Fill the present with yesterday's sights and
    sounds –

Football, cricket, boxing, thrillers, or
    songs,
Memories on tape or film or a round disc,
Available in the home, or the waves of the
    air,
To escape the present for a vicarious risk.

Perhaps we need the past now we are
    doddering.
We look nostalgically back to the Golden
    noon
When the West held, baffled that the
    mightiest,
Most inventive civilisation, which has reached
    the moon,   20

Should, after D-Day, shrink in senescent
    ruin,
Retreat in a world which prefers the tyrant's
    prime
To our old system. Whispering disapproval,
We Westerners wistfully escape the present
    time.

    26-28 April 1976

LEAVES THAT FEED

The *Encyclopaedia Britannica*! Thirty
Padded volumes in black, beautiful to feel,
Standing in a bookcase, gold on the leaves,
All the mind's and the world's knowledge by
    my heel.

I leaf through volume five to "Democracy".
I have free access to it. In some countries,
Such ideas and much of the past are
    forbidden,
Just as – in a Peking museum – the memory
    is.

In Shanghai I was given tea and cake
By an ex-match king worth a hundred and
    forty million,   10
He said, "I have been taught Mao, you say
    'brainwashed'."
His encyclopaedia mind had a trillion

Deletions and corrections. Here there is

No rewriting or doctoring of the past
As in Russia. Yet we take it for granted
And say, "It clutters the house, it is too
    vast."

The soul and the mind are not independent.
They interact, are complementary, like the
    gol-
-d flower and the leaf which draws in sun,
    rain, what
Roots send up to be stored. The mind feeds
    the soul.   20

A library is a greenhouse for the climbing
    mind.
Restrict leaves, and the soul will droop, in
    need
Of nourishment. Allow too many, and it
Will be choked and not bloom. Souls need the
    leaves that feed

To do their work correctly, the greenhouse,
The gardening and temperature to be right.
Stillness in the sun is good, but feeding
    through these books,
They will grow a sturdy bloom of a sun-
    flower's height.

A FLOWERING

I walked between wysteria and lilac.
The air smelled sweet. On the school lawn,
    girls sat
In clumps, like tulips, awaiting pollination.
I fluttered like a butterfly through their
    chat.

The new supply had bubbly hair, like a
    camper,
Was pregnant. At break I told the Deputy
    Frown,
"This school is like a marquee, if you tinker
With one guy rope, the whole lot may crash
    down."

"And a few pegs are loose – blame rats,"
    smiled the Head
Of Music, and our marquee collapsed in his
    eyes.
Now my winter is over I will look outwards.
I see a flowering ahead, of epic size.

303

WESTERNERS AND DESIRE: A DIALOGUE BETWEEN BODY AND SOUL
(OR: BETWEEN THE MAENADS AND ORPHEUS)

"Desire, unsatisfied appetite, longing, wish, crav-
ing." "Lust, sensuous appetite regarded as sinful;
animal desire for sexual indulgence, lascivious
passion."

Oxford English Dictionary

Body:
Forty years after the war, we Westerners
Have one relaxation we all admire.
Once it was hushed up: discretion or scandal.
Now it can be mentioned openly: desire.

We like to relax in a bed during the day
As if it were a hot bath. What, after work,
Is more comfortable than to climb stairs, flop
 on a bed,
Lie back and be kneaded, fondled, kissed,
 then jerk

Round and begin to discharge the tensions,
Sucking nipples, limbs twined in urgent
 fire,   10
Then lie back and gaze at the ceiling, like a
 child
That has been fed with and is now "free" from
 desire?

In or out of relationships there's variety.
A woman will do anything to keep a man.
It is easy to bed him, hard to make him return.
She will debase herself to his wishes, do all
 she can.

And there is pressure on a woman these days.
If she won't do what her men want without
 inhibitions,
There are many who will – "liberated"
 women –
So Western men can impose their own
 conditions.   20

Soul:
Did natural desire always turn to sinful lust,
Appetite year for one *and* many? Have we

gone soft?
Or have we moved into an Age of the Body
When to have climaxed means no more than
 to have coughed?

Body:
Massage parlours, escort agencies, sex shops
All now proclaim: the sin of lust is good!
Video booths rent pornographic films,
Nudes scream from newsagents' covers a red
 light "could";

What can be found behind certain dingy
 doors,
Girls in a hundred positions, girls, girls,
 girls!   30
Thumbed through by Westerners now wise to
 Aids,
Busty blondes and brunettes with tumbling
 curls.

We have the pill, and ready abortion,
And State clinics, and injections against VD.
So, short of exercise, we take breaks from
 work
And live on the brink of our sexuality.

Soul:
Satisfy desire, and it enslaves the more.
Deny it as sinful lust, and we can be free.
We Westerners had active values once,
But now we have relaxed, into slavery. 40

1976, revised 1990

A FINGER OF LIGHTNING
As I parked to go to the bank, a red-haired
Woman ran in before me. As she wrote her
 cheque
She said forcefully, "You go, I'm having
 difficulty
With my ink-flow." She looked at me, turned
 her neck

And body towards me. She had brown eyes.
 As I wait-
-ed for my cash, a thrill stirred the base of my
 spine,
The air crackled as if a finger of lightning
Leapt from her offered body to the thunder of
 mine.

Red hair, brown eyes! A squirrelly look. I
went.
Perhaps in a past life I knew a dark
Brown-haired, brown-eyed woman for whom
I search,
Seeking in all women an intimate birthmark.

A quiet personality brushes the putty
Of the brain and leaves a smudge like the
merest hint.
When we fall in love, strong eyes and a
forceful voice
Press into the putty-mind a large thumbprint.

ILLUSIONS LIKE BLOSSOM

While we enjoy our comforts, we lose our
illusions.
We Westerners leave school with them – the
work we will do,
The girl we will love, our home, our place in
life,
Our own importance, our greatness even –
and too

Soon, one by one, they drop off. The work is
dull,
The girl has a roving eye, the home, like our
wage,
Is too small for what we should have found.
Our niche
Is adequate, but does not justify our self-
image.

One by one they peel away and drop like
spring
Blossom, leaving the drabness of latent
fruit.   10
It is a routine, seasonal thing, this shedding.
Disillusion frees the maturing, ripening shoot.

Suffering is a wind that shakes the petals
down,
Brings on the full leaf, the rosy axiom.
But o the bitterness, when the last fruit has
fallen,
And seems as illusory as the first blossom!

So it is with our West. While the blossom was
here
We believed it would last for ever. The same

with the fruit.
But what is left now that the fruit has fallen
Save winter and bareness, and sad dispute?

THE PRICE OF A HOUSE

Most of all, if we can, we Westerners like to
invest
In a house like the one I have visited today
On a ridge over countryside, a steep drive up
Through a garden of trees and every kind of
shrub – aza-

-leas, rhododendrons, gorse – to the front
door.
It has everything: umpteen rooms, great
space, new
Carpets and curtains, good furniture, old
prints
All uncluttered. At the back, a patio has a
view

Of a long lawn to more trees, the orchard
And the vegetable garden. On the lawn's
shaded side,   10
When we played tennis, the rockery bounced
balls back.
The playroom is full of toys, they have a new
slide.

It is a safe life, every comfort provided for.
Family, garden, holidays, public school, self-
control.
Standards are maintained. Humans are not
material –
Bodies in Auschwitz – and here they have a
soul.

We Westerners have plans for our gardens:
What to sow, where to grow vegetables. And
with a wide
House to look after, the family to feed and
bath,
We may give little thought to the world
outside.   20

There is a price to pay: we Westerners love
Leisure, and sacrifice hours for pounds. And –
such
Is our social contract – a house costs
evenings, unless   .

We delegate, and a lawyer cannot do that much.

Having paid our weeks and months for this
    body comfort,
We Westerners neglect the mind and vow,
"I must make time to read," or else lament,
"I used to read Dickens on the train, but not
    now."

At the office, the world makes appointments
    and speaks on the phone.
We Westerners care about the community's
    hearts   30
And how laws affect behaviour, but have had
    to sell
Our time for Philosophy, Literature, and the
    Arts.

If I sold my time to a company, and ceased
    scribbling,
I could buy a place like this, and sit in the sun,
Listen to the birds, chaffinch pecking at my
    feet,
And smell the flowers tumbling round what
    my work had won.

A house is a gift from capitalism. Borrow,
Pay interest, and it belongs to the under-
    signed.
Those who have lend capital to those who
    have not.
We sacrifice minds for houses, or choose the
    mind.   40

As we grow older we become more detached
Like an apple about to fall from an orchard
    bough,
And many then find the mind has ceased to
    matter.
Can we sacrifice mind for a house and choose
    the mind now?

                         16 May 1976

THE FALL OF THE WEST

I. THE SYMPTOMS

History is full of plagues and sudden falls,
Thirty civilisations have crumbled to dust.
Rome collapsed and died like an old hag after
    a stroke,

Her marbled temples warts on a skin lust

Rotted. Now our corpuscles are infected,
Some fear we too may perish, that a Dark Age
Will overtake us suddenly, bringing
    barbarians
To our cities, destroying us with some dire
    contag-

-ion. When Oxford Circus is finally under
    daisies,
Future historians will take an interest   10
In the tyrannous germs and bacillic diseases
That threatened the aging arteries of our West.

I ignore the wars, H-bombs, the missiles,
And miners' strikes that have left us short of
    breath.
I show them the smaller symptoms, the
    images
That reveal a coagulation that can lead to
    death.

In France, Cohn-Bendit and Co rip cobble-
    stones,
Destroy the roads to fight the "Fascist" police.
In Britain, Tariq Ali charges horses
In Grosvenor Square, so that free Vietnam
    may cease;   20

Two Cambridge boys and two Essex girls, a
    "Brigade",
Leave a bomb outside a Cabinet Minister's
    house.
What can twenty-five explosions in three
    years tell
Our free society, save a moron's grouse?

In Germany, the Baader-Meinhof gang
Bomb the U.S. Army HQ, and when tried,
Blame murder on Vietnam; a "Red Army
    Faction".
Where can such destruction end but in
    suicide?

A Japanese "Red Army squad" kills girls on a
    hill,
Then sprays an Israeli airport to show what is
    right.   30
In Italy, a publisher places a bomb

Against a pylon, to hasten the Communist
night.

(The best of my generation became
journalists.
Two well-born Oxford men worked in Italy
On a Marxist magazine – denying it's a game,
Though they live on shares – so that man's
cause might rally.)

A Libyan Lieutenant pays hooded gunmen
To kill Israeli athletes at the Olympic Games,
And a Venezuelan captures OPEC Ministers
In Vienna, whom an Iraqi blames.   40

A Portuguese doctor lurks in a café,
Describes his latest explosion in Lisbon, his
dream:
"After we have withdrawn from Africa,
We will set up a true 'socialist' regime."

A Libyan friend of his has supplied arms
To the IRA – he gives me the Colonel's name
And the room he stayed in at the Churchill
Hotel –
And breathes a virus on all who would kill
and maim.

At a German conference (for guerillas)
On the Cunene Dam, churchmen arm blacks.
"Let us pray."   50
Says the Christian host to some fifty atheists
On his fundroll. Outraged, they bow their
heads for their pay.

In a Swiss office, a Singhalese Communist
wants
Twenty-five thousand more church dollars put
aside
For a pro-Soviet Angolan "liberation"
movement:
"Don't all churchmen feel guilty about
apartheid?"

At a Belgian conference to boost SWAPO
A Belgian MP condemns the "anti-Soviet
right",
A Bishop denies that Russian arms are evil,
A Lord – once in the UN – says, "These boys
are bright."   60

In a Paris restaurant, a Trotskyite
Cartoons me as a "class enemy" as if my fate
Were Marie Antoinette's. Next day he throws
Bottles for "L'Oeuvre Francais", and a
Communist State.

II. THE DISEASE DIAGNOSED
The US Weathermen fired dissent.
After Vietnam and Watergate, an ex-a-
-gent types out names of the CIA for the press
So someone can shoot the Head of the Greek
Sta-

-tion. At lunch a London teacher says, "I
speak
At Communist meetings, we're against this
Labour clique   70
At our Norwood union." A Communist
lawyer's
Daughter helped pro-Russians win
Mozambique,

Says, "Liberalism is at somebody else's
expense."
What we are witnessing is the defection –
Passionate, ignorant, silly, smart, or
diffident –
Of many Western intellectuals, the rejection

Of the freedom that trained them, for the bar-
barian
Cause of Tyranny which rings our
beleaguered West.
The new man they want is a Communist
fanatic
With the power to level me in a camp at
best,   80

Or before a wall, at the worst. They regard our
demo-
-cracy as the list of names on a Chinese
board,
The names on which belong to one Party,
And would use our vote to abolish our vote: a
fraud,

The germ began in Alexander's Russia –
The Nihilists – then spread to France: the
illusion
Of justice, which is really a violent terror;

Of "popular rule", when the people are in a
    prison.

It persists in Russia where the Jackal was
    trained.
The new imperialism, as might be
    expected,   90
Is the old contagion, now breathed across a
    wall,
And too little in quarantine, we are infected.

Platelet disintegration releases thromb-
-oplastin, which begins blood coagulation,
That can clot and block the valves of the
    pumping heart.
A globulin causes platelets' disintegration.

It is called AHF, they go rapidly when injured
As a result of damaged endothalium. And yet
A bacillus caught from without may injure
The platelets that thin the blood, as well as
    infect.   100
There is an enemy witin the heart of the West,
A germ that multiplies, and can clot our veins
And deny the freedom of the corpuscles to act.
Future historians will know the cure of these
    pains.

III. THE CURE
They will ask, "Did the disease lower their
    resistance,
So that the will was softened and could not
    defend
Itself from attack, like a bedridden old lady
Who must invite her burglar to help himself
    like a friend?

Vietnam, Cambodia, Laos, Lebanon, Angola.
Was the West's will to resist already in
    doubt?"   110
They will ask, "Was she overrun without
    opposition
So she fell from within before the knock-out?

Did the disease in her body soften her head
So the final occupation was a formality?"
They will ignore the White House's
    indecisions, the counts
Of tanks and missiles. They will cite this
    irony:

"London, the exiles' darling, who reared
    Pilgrim
Fathers, lodged Marx and Lenin, and gave birth
To the United States and to modern Russia,
Was mugged by the Balcombe Street
    'squatters' of the earth,   120

Her house was taken over so soon," they will
    say.
"Western civilisation fell dramatically,
So soon after she conquered the air. O sud-
-den fall of the West, which amazed history!"

They should have seen truly, without self-
    deception.
Their ally at D-Day, who won Berlin
And a European Empire through American
    blindness
And was at war with the West, belonged within

Europe. Their body need not have revolted
    against the head.
If the germs had taken, they could have been
    inoculated, so   130
They could withstand more. Russia could
    have caught freedom,
Which is as fatal to disease as a do-

-se of health! The Fall of the West would
    have remained a fear
If they had used antibiotics on further
    sickness,
If they had been warned of the danger, and
    valued
Isaiah and Wulfstan, who had relevant mess-

-ages. The Fall of the West was a delusion,
A neurotic state of mind, a diffident squirm.
To believe that they were doomed was as
    disastrous
As not to believe in calling a germ "a
    germ".   140

For a while, the Fall of the West could be
Averted. Their cure was to know that, without
    delud-
-ding themselves, they could withstand their
    disease, be immune.
The Fall of the West was a mental attitude!
8-15 May 1976

GRASS AND BRAMBLES, PULSING

As I walked down to the shop for the papers
Pushing my son in his pram, tufts of coarse
    grass
Waved to us, breathing quietly, living. He
Stroked some of them till he pressed his nose
    on the glass

Calling "Ca-ars" at the toy cars queuing
    there,
Each with an engine as fast as the ones that
    sped
Up the road to the China Clay pyramids.
I bought my *Times*. "Bye cars," at last he said,

And on the way back, sprays of parched
    bramble
Clutched at him, trying to ruffle his blond
    hair,
Playfully pinching his cheek; like the grass,
    sighing
Because of the drought, pulsing with *our* air.

APRIL DAFFODILS

Do not bow your heads, daffodils;
The sharp frosts will soon pass.
The frothing waters boil from the mill
And calm to glass.

Do not bow your heads, daffodils;
Your burden is April-short.
Think of the rat that lies on its back
On the bridge, car-caught.

TANKA

O this caterpillar life!
Soon I will go
Into the chrysalis of Death
To become a (Paradisal) butterfly.
Angels flutter by me now in the sun.

A TIN LID MIND

"Light!" cried a little boy, holding a tin
Lid under the hall lamp, for a disc, white,
Illuminates the wall, revolving in
Circulatory circles, divinely bright.

He stands, fascinated by an ethereal moon
On the lid of his mind. One day he will know
That we are all lids that reflect a bright
    source. Soon
He too will light the walls of this world
    below.

GARDEN
(ON THE THIRD ANNIVERSARY)
(For Ann)

My dear, our third anniversary has come
    round.
It finds us in a narrow Tooting ground-
Floor flat; we have let our own. This card of
    two
Daisies, two bells in a fish bowl says that soo-
-n a second bell with a wishing tongue will
    be
Hung in the wind, to tinkle in a tree.
Ahead we have high hopes: a garden where
White daisies and bluebells will scent the air.
Last week in an art gallery, we gazed
At transparent jugs and glasses, whose angles
    amazed,
And just as a tree-hung glass-bowl, filled with
    wa-
-ter, lit by sun, fires hearts; so may our bowl
    draw
Light from the cosmos, turn it into a fire
That will blaze in the hearth of the house of
    our hearts' desire.

THE SEA-CROSSING

Youthful poet, this dark evening
Turn your heart to another world,
Billow to a heavenly calling,
Be filled with a wind; your sail unfurled,

Go with a puff, scud over ocean,
A flapping in your mind's canvas,
Till the harbour of a far country
Dances its lights in the night's embrace.

There disembark, and dwell quietly
Where the bee-dew fills the flowers,
Under the sea-cliff, where images
Peep like crabs from the pools of the hours.

Youthful poet, this dark morning
Turn your heart to the eternal word;
Be filled with the voice of a shy daimon
Who flits on the wind like a golden bird.

IMAGINATION: TREE OF CANDLES

As I drove unwillingly to my school
On the bend a tree towered, huge yet serene:
Flowering chestnut with a thousand candles,
Each up and white against the leafy green.

I parked and walked back, although I was late,
And stood and looked in awe at its great size:
Green-leafed profusion from winter bareness.
May, and the summer took me by surprise.

And then I saw a tree in my being:
A thousand imagined candles in a dark.
I knew that my sun unfolds my green and
Small suns like candles from spare winter
        bark

And glows into beauty in the grey air:
We both grow images from a dark trunk –
– I have as many poems as it has leaves –
And light their daily candles like a monk.

ROBIN IN SNOW

You send a Christmas card.
On a cold garden bed
In a bleak waste of frozen snow
A robin cocks his head.

Are you saying, "You are
A singing bird alone"
As if to say "Sing to someone,
This bird sings on its own"?

But then I wonder if
Your meaning really is
"I am as Red as a robin's breast,
My cold's as cold as his."

We can't help what we are,
I can't help my lone song,
You can't help being robin Red,
And we are not here long.

A ROBIN LOOKS AT HUMANKIND

As I hopped upon the dump
And tugged for a big prize,
A big fat graveyard worm,
I couldn't believe my eyes;

For there in a four-wheel
Two hair-heads sat in purr.
One was thirsty for she
Bent and undid his fur.

I watched as his big thing
Gave her some squirts of milk;
She mouthed round his pap-rod,
Then spat into some silk.

I know hair-heads are strange,
But why suck then spit out?
It does not make good sense.
And why scarf up his snout?

And what a waste of milk
When I tug twigs for bread,
Can't even find a worm –
And aren't graveyards for the dead?

LADY OF THE LAMP

(MYSTIC LYRICS AND SONNETS)

1979

1. RAPT IN A HOTEL ROOM

Sometimes I must meet you on neutral ground
Like one who leaves whirled snow for an
 empty gloom
To undress and lie with you in a Hotel room,
Bleak rooftops near the window, and no
 sound.

You are not at home in your Inner Sanctum,
You have come up here to ravish me, and so
You are not a hundred per cent "you",
 although
It is good, I am rapt, as you shudder and
 come.

And now you have gone like a flitting
 shadow,
And all I have is the memory you embraced,
And your round full curves, your moon-like
 breasts and waist,
And you flitting like a ghost onto frozen
 snow.

2. LIGHT FROM A WARM HOUSE

Like a lover creeping down a snowed-up
 street
Quickening to the warm house of a calm
 mistress
Who twines his neck, her arms in a low black
 dress,
And seeks out his mouth with her tongue, and
 a married heat,

I stole down the frozen dark like an escapee,
Guided by the round moon over your front
 door,
And when you opened it, my dear, sweet
 whore!
What warmth as the light within enfolded me!

Now it is as if you had lain with me

Between brown and petalled sheets. I am
 suffused
With an after-glow, an Eternity, seduced
Like a clock that ticked and stopped at half
 past three.

3. LIKE AN EARTH-MOTHER
(DIVINE SONNET)

You are like an Earth-Mother, a Neolithic
Terra cotta goddess from a barbarous time,
With swollen breasts, curved hips, and a
 prolific
Bulge where you carry your sun in primeval
 slime.
I come and nuzzle at your dugs in awe
And crouch between your legs and melt your
 snow,
And slowly you unfold, like a winter thaw,
Open your plenty from your moist furrow.
And I, who have ploughed you, and sown
 autumn seed,
Must wait in my winter dark for the pangs of
 spring;
As you bear shoots, and dazzling light I need,
I swoon, goddess! but know that, adoring
You, I can never husband you: in your shrine
Each year you bear your suns, and can never
 be mine.

4. MY SOUL
(DIVINE SONNET)

As a painter dreams of a brown-eyed succuba
He has never seen, and, waking, then gives
 birth
To a canvas, paints the round full curves of a
Heavy, languid, solid, great Mother Earth;
So I have seen you in my imagination,
That air where waters have their origin,
That formless light which freezes creation
Out of icy forms of flesh that burn and sin,
And I catch you now, turning with wide-
 hipped thighs,

311

Your narrow waist, swelling breasts, your
    profile,
And I know I have found my soul – and
    caught her eyes –
In the form of a Spanish lady's Piscean smile.
My soul and body can unite again
As I lie with you under this counterpane.

5. A BEE-LIKE SOUL
(DIVINE SONNET)

As a bee hums from foxglove to a bluebell's
    bowl
And gathers nectar, which it flies to its hive
And stores for winter, so my many live-
-s are flowers frequented by a bee-like soul
That dreams of a distant swarm each honey-
    patrol.
As an acorn thrusts to its oak, my lifetimes
    drive
To a gigantic form, in which they survive
And come again and again, to perfect their
    goal.
This knowledge, Lady, you have poured into
    me,
Infused, when, like a stargazer in a rain
Of influence, I peer at your weathervane
Till your moon sails up from the blackest
    cloud, breaks free –
In this dark night lit by your brightness, I see!
I see I have been before, and will be again.

6. THE BURDEN
(DIVINE SONNET)

Sometimes, when I think of what is still
    undone,
How singly, like a Cnut I must engage
And turn a tide, spend years pointing to the
    sun
To change the fumbling of this self-blind Age,
Bring back an importance to its sighing
    breath,
Restore a quietness to its dull heartbeat –
Sometimes I feel a dread at news of death,
For what if I die with my destiny incomplete?
Then I droop under the burden that has greyed
    my hair
And frayed deep lines into my craggy face
And its stark frown of thought and sombre
    night;
And then I come and bask in a dazzling

prayer,
Like a sunbathing monarch, till my load is a
    mace,
And I feel fresh again in your sunlight.

7. GLASS GOLDFISH
(DIVINE SONNET)

You have broken your rule again, opening a
    door
To a secret interior like a familiar place –
A house with a glass goldfish on the
    sideboard, or-
-naments, china – taking me up a dark
    staircase
To somewhere you never thought to admit
    me,
Undressing your white body, and lying down
On your back, full Woman, drawing me
    shamelessly
Within you, in a guiltless, biting hug, to
    drown;
And being surprised at yourself, But you
    know it is true
An elemental instinct can be freed
Beneath the married dinner party chat,
Which you have accepted. This "awakened
    you"
Is not a shark's rapacious hunger: you need
Me – that is the wonder – and so you grace
    me like that.

8. THE SHELL
(DIVINE SONNET)

You turn from me, fleeing from the love you
    bore
Like a woman who has returned to her family
For the weekend, wished her husband could
    be me,
And fearful for her children, has said, "No
    more,
Too late," as if you belonged to me only for
The daylight hours. You have left me in
    misery
In this dark. You breathed, loved, whispered,
    sighed like the sea.
I am alive with you. Let it be as before.
"Too late," it's as if you have said, thinking
    what might have been.
But I have heard the sea wash in the curl
Of a deep-sea shell, crash, boom, then gently

swirl,
Have heard your soft voice lick my ear,
    serene.
There is no "late" or "before", just a marine
Pant for eternity in a mother-of-pearl.

9. LORD WITH A SWORD
(DIVINE SONNET)

You flee from me as temple-dancers flee
From a lord with a sword on a Cambodian
    slide.
You hide your face from me, and turn aside
Your ancient Khmer headdress with a sad
    secrecy,
Say, "I am gone away," and, "Remember
    me,"
Withdrawing as if you wanted to be my bride,
Say, "Smile, do not be sad," as if you had
    cried
Away the love of your life, chosen duty.
O my dear, I, who soldiered up the long steep
    hill
Of my destiny, fell in with you, and shared
My deepest thoughts, and dared to believe
    you cared;
But I must trudge on now you have gone
    away,
And I already feel the evening chill
In this sad, cold, lonely, wintry mid-day.

10. EURYDICE
(DIVINE SONNET)

You were always mine, but I found you in the
    dark
Of an underworld where the halls of the dead
Were ferroconcrete. I, master of the lyre, led
You back, charmed you back, like a twittering
    skylark,
To the light. I, Orpheus, sang; you followed
    my stark
Lyrics, and the powers that held you were
    charmed by my head.
But at the sunlight you looked back and fled
As if the snakebite had branded you with its
    mark.
Sensing that you had turned, I too turned
    round,
And then the power of my lyre had gone,
And I was left alone, bleak above ground
In a higher world of light, where no sun

shone.
So I have descended into dark again
To charm you back to sunlight, and not as
    grain.

11. BLINDFOLDS: LADY OF THE LAMP
(DIVINE SONNET)

I close my eyes and peer into the damp
Of a clouded dark, like a traveller groping and
    find-
-ing his way in a night fog; one gleam, and
    not blind
Now, I am lit by the Lady of the Lamp.
I follow a misty reflection like a tramp
Who sees a roadworks lantern tilted, inclined
From a derelict basement. On the walls of my
    cellar mind
I see a dancing light guide me down a ramp,
And now I turn a corner, and the Lamp burns
    through
And gathers to a roundness and shines out,
And behind the dark is lit by the greyish blue
That unveils all seaside gloom and ghostly
    doubt.
But oh if I could see the hand that holds
The Lamp that scorches away my veiled
    blindfolds.

January 1979

12. NEAR-WIFE
(DIVINE SONNET)

I sometimes wonder if I knew your face
In a former life, and perhaps loved you
    through
An Egyptian or Victorian girl, and knew
And scrumped your softness, and gladly
    risked disgrace
Till you said Farewell, and returned to your
    place
By a silent lord, who saw a change in you,
Who guessed where your sparkle had gone,
    and who
Let you be absent-minded, staring into space;
And then you were unhappy and puckered
    your brow,
And pined away for our lost love, and died.
I sometimes wonder if your task is now
To seek me across the grave. Now you turn
    aside

And miss your destiny once more. My Near-
Wife,
You may have to seek me again in your next
life.

13. TEN WIVES
(DIVINE SONNET)
When I at last cross the picket line, yes
Into Paradise, and they say, "There on the
grass
Are your ten wives," I know they will not
surpass
You, Lady. For you are all things to me: lush
mistress,
Yet you spoil me like a mother, and yet caress
Like a whore, are constant in your way, can
pass
As a wife, yet talk all night like the courtesan
class,
And cradle my head; are a slave-girl-cum-
goddess,
A geisha inoculated against poxy "free-
-dom for women": I think you would bring
me breakfast in bed;
You are a bath attendant, for you disrobe
read-
-ily, as if we were ten years together; but,
untru-
-ly true, above all you are Mystery, the se-
-cret smile of all wide-hipped Woman: truly
you.

14. BREASTSTROKE, DROWNING
(DIVINE SONNET)
I love you, Lady, like a drowning man
In a black sea – I tread water, breaststroke,
As your passion rises I am taken, chok-
-ing, and thrown about, clutch driftwood, then
scan
The sky, rise on a wave, plunge down in a
gigan-
-tic trough. You turn and twist, I cling. You
have brok-
-en over me now. For a while you are calm.
Soak-
-ed, I feel you gather again, am in billows, can
Be tugged this way and that, tossed as in a
storm.
Rolling, I clutch you like a raft I have found,

Abandoned in your current, which is norm-
-al for you. I am thrown about, can last no
more. You pound
Me. Then an ecstatic wave floods through my
warm
Limbs, and I am flung onto a beach, quite
drowned.

15. GREYNESS
(DIVINE SONNET)
At work I am at war. Like an Arab power
My Head sends in a guerilla with a grenade,
I retaliate with a heavy bombing raid,
For she only understands a mortar shower.
Sometimes, like Machiavelli, I spend an hour
Broadcasting that my Department is on a
crusade –
And was stripped of my powers, disgraced, as
if I had been flayed
And driven round the site with a dunce's cap,
cower-
-ing, placard round neck, at my crimes against
"mankind".
But after the red book came democracy wall
Like grass growing through concrete: man's
persistent mind;
And like cracking ferroconcrete, this greyness
will fall
Apart as shoots thrust up and wave in your
wind.
Your sun warms all against whom the world
has sinned.

16. THE MASK
(DIVINE SONNET)
You are like one who has heard me being
reviled
And, unable to frown because of our secret,
Has shone her love on me, sadly, and yet
Has soon gone behind a cloud, feeling pained
and wild.
But stop, Lady, consider. My self-styled
Critics are miseries who do not know me, and
forget
They need a grotesque, grimacing mask to fret
And grumble against, as if I never smiled.
They pace a prison in a waste of snow
As if the honey breath of a May sunrise
Had never trembled leaves. So let them
criticise

Their witchdoctor-warder. I am elsewhere.
    I am where the bee hums in clover, I blow
    Where the blue moth flits in the warmly
        scented air.

17. DREAM COTTAGE
(DIVINE SONNET)

As I said, "Love is like a holly bush with
    prick-
-les and red berries, or like deadly night-
    shade,"
It seemed you passed the door and, listening,
    stayed
And thought 'What a waste – you, and those
    girls who are thick.'
O my love, one day we will live in a small old
    brick
Cottage deep in country peace and homemade
Quiet, and I will write to the summer smack
    of the spade
In a field, and a grandfather clock's metric
    tick,
And my life will be lambs, grasshoppers,
    crocuses,
Blackbirds piping, skimming swallows,
    lupins,
Honeysuckle round the back door, tortoises
And a stream with weed, ripples from
    winking fins;
And love is the bittersweet on the water's
    edge
Which grows under a country hawthorn
    hedge.

18. SECRET PLACE
(DIVINE SONNET)

I think you will find me in my secret place,
Like a woman who goes through an omega
    lych-gate,
Wanders to a porch, sits in my pew – by fate –
Then, pondering a meaning of leaves and
    crocuses, pac-
-es down a path to steps, and turns her face
To the quietest corner of a churchyard; look
    straight
Down, and I think you will find me like one
    who, wait-
-ing by the black rail that keeps out the
    embrac-
-ing birch and bracken, stumbles on my grave.

Only I know I will lie there, you have been
    part-
-ly drawn there, since our destinies are like
    one sea-wave.
So you will find a corresponding place in my
    heart.
Listen, then, with me, to the stillness beneath
    the breeze,
And a foaming on Eternity, like soughing
    seas.

27th January 1979

19. CHAFFINCH SONG
(DIVINE SONNET)

It seemed that you looked sad and shed a tear
And then I knew that, sitting in a cold pew,
You were far out in the future somewhere,
After I had died and was under snow. You
    knew
I lay in a quiet Forest churchyard, you leant
Back and felt my presence as I stalked the
    aisle,
Till it seemed I became a chaffinch and
    lament-
-ed my uncompleted work from a nearby stile.
Then it seemed the tears rolled down your
    cheeks for my
Untimely song, and that you always feared
    this,
And thinking of my burden, you vowed to try
To help me, and felt close to my ghost, whose
    kiss
You missed. Then the sun came out for a
    moment lost,
And you shone with a warmth that defied the
    coming frost.

20. ENEMY
(DIVINE SONNET)

I walk through silver birch with a smile on my
    face
And take the path to the rail where I will lie.
You have been here, Lady, and you know
    why
I loved the simplicity of this Forest place,
Its honest sincerity when I wore a grimace
At the ruthless affairs of State; and its peace. I
Love the robin that flits by the yew, this sky
As grey as the tombstones where two
    squirrels chase.

And, standing at my grave, do not suppo-
-se, Lady, that I have a deep death-wish, or
  regret
That this earth is an enemy I have come to
  know,
To whom I say, "You will not get me yet."
For I am a survivor; and staring at Death,
That deaf, funereal vicar, inspires each breath.

21. HORSESHOE
(DIVINE SONNET)
I sometimes think that Hell is here and now,
And that all our torments like a funeral pyre
Shape our souls for a Paradise like a spire
We float to, when we leave our bodies,
  somehow.
If so, then this firing of the soul allow-
-s, in this blacksmith's forge, this hammering
  of desire
To a tempered round halo: we are here to
  fire
Our I's appetites, temper the eye in the
  eyebrow.
Now I see that the heartlessness of man,
The greed that strikes for gain, and does not
  relent
For his brother, the pitilessness of war, began
The misshapen oblong sin for which he was
  sent
To this smithy. So I see you as a lucky guide
Who hammered me into a horseshoe until I
  died.

                                          1979

22. BLOWLAMP
As a welder pulls down a tinted shield
And crouches over iron and with a blowtor-
-ch sends a crowd of sparks fizzing across the
  floor
And fuses two pieces of metal, now sealed;
So, Lady, with tinted goggles, you mould
Me, crouch over my soul and body with your
  blow-
Lamp, and arrows of gold rain shoot and die
  so
As to unify me, making my base all gold.
Thus, I am fused under your blowlamp till I
  run,
And slowly I cool again, and set hard,
But tonight you check my shape in your

yard,
And solder me so my two become one.
Thus I am a soul with a body's form
And am softened and hammered while still
  warm.

                      1979, revised 15th November 1993

23. WEB
You look at me as if to say "It was empty
Without you yesterday" or "I missed you",
And "I want to care for you." I recoil, flee
For it is a burden to be loved anew,
To return a deep emotion's great demand
When to be dead is a relief, like one
Who has said, "I shall leave my dear husband
When he is clear of this bad financial run."
We are in a web of thought; as if you dreamt
That my study caught fire and woke in fear
I, Muse, was thinking that I should attempt
To sort you out so I am settled next year.
We are like two spiders in a web that's blown,
Who crowd each other but cannot live alone.

                      1979, revised 15th November 1993

24. SEA OF LIGHT
I see you when, with a hairnet on my head,
I sit wired up to a mind-mirror, and see
The lights jumping in a pattern of a Christmas
  tree,
And lay my hands on where a patient bled.
Sometimes I see you as, tingling my skin,
The serpent rises up my spine in an eight
And bites your lotus whose juices saturate
My crown, so your power thrums from you
  and floods in.
How much more is there when you light my
  mind
Like a bulb, an electricity divine?
You are a healer, Lady, and can shine
Your power into me like a current that's
  blind.
God is all round and within all who've taken
  the plunge
As the sea is all round and within a sponge.

                      1979, revised 15th November 1993

25. PORTRAIT
Like a woman buying a painting and finding
  out
She has a masterpiece of a precious date,

You found me, planning to keep me separate
From your life, as an investment you would
    think about
When you needed it; but as if like a collector
You had fallen in love with the portrait, so it
    threatened
Your life, now angry with it, you want to send
Me like a Sutherland Churchill down to a
    cellar.
O my brown-haired light, it is as if you are in
    pain.
You flee from me like one saying "You need
A lot of caring for", and "I should not ring
    you", freed
From your vows, and I am left alone again,
Ruing what might have been, waiting for a
    call
Like a motionless portrait on a forgotten
    wall.

26. BLUE TIT
(DIVINE SONNET)

Neither the walls of leaders, nor pickets for
More pay have the power of one touch of a
    lover's skin.
I fly to you, flit as to a blue tit in
A lanterned birdhouse, nuzzle down in your
Nesting-place, which you took and lined with
    straw.
The time I spend with you is a quiet when the
    spin-
-ing world stops. Queuing crowds, news
    bulletin-
-s are gibberings, only what you have said and
    thou-
-ght matters, this high summer of the heart
    that waits
To appease its hunger at your breast. And so
These pre-revolutionary soviets at the gates
All pale beside a good woman's afterglow.
And by this string bag near the rose-garden's
    brick wall
I think of your fluffy down, not the nuts that
    fall.

27. THE MUGGER
(DIVINE SONNET)

Suddenly I lurch into a troubled time
And Death the Mugger lurks round the door,
    slang-

-ing me, waiting to cosh my wife down while
    his gang
Screams in her ears, impatient for the crime.
In this time of uncertainty I turn to you,
    climb,
Lady, as to a masseuse's room. You hang
Over me a blue light like a sunlamp, as if
    bang-
-ing my back with your knuckles, to tone me
    up in my prime.
Now I look ahead to what might be, and am
    calm
As if I had invited that bully-boy to this bath;
Like a man who has given his hangman his
    unstrapped arm,
I can look at the thug, and say, "This is my
    path,
Take what you will when you will: life is but
    a sundial."
But, Lady, please shine on me in this coming
    trial.

28. KERB-CRAWLING
(DIVINE SONNET)

You say you cannot see me, curbing my
    flow
Like a woman whose lover's wife has ears
    that sing
And blood that puffs up the skin round her
    wedding ring,
And has said, "Find someone else, I am too
    tired," though
She resents her husband taking a mistress. So,
As if you had lain awake all night, tossing,
And said, "She needs all of you now, I am
    nothing,
Should have no part of you, and loving you,
    must go,"
You turn from me, Lady, and down, I must
    seek you
Like a kerb-crawler driving down the road
    where, fraught,
You walk, or as if "I will become a whore to
    do
Something for my bankrupt husband," you
    said, and I sought
You in dark Soho, and now drive down
    Plough Lane
Looking for your buoyancy in this drizzling
    rain.

29. CURATE
(DIVINE SONNET)

You have come back to me, like one who
    knows
She may leave me soon and work for her
    husband's neat
New business partner, who is in Harley Street,
Who exports fetuses and dark pounds, who
    chose
To break the law, who knows where a copper
    goes,
Who wants you to go to the airport and meet
His victims, who wants. Yet you are one who
    knows that a cheat
Has a whiff of corruption that will infect a rose
Let alone a business, and would, shrewdly, be
    appall-
-ed to be mixed up in a racket. You came
    back tonight
As if ringing my bell and stepping into my
    hall,
Smiling at my surprise – to slide out of sight
As if the bell went again and a curate shroud-
-ed your brightness behind a door, like a
    moon in a cloud.

30. BARRIER
(DIVINE SONNET)

Sometimes, Lady, you are only a telephone
Call away, but when I get through to you
It is as if you cannot speak, and say, untru-
-ly, "Wrong number," and I am cut to the
    bone.
Then, sitting in my room, I have sometimes
    known
You ring, as if asking, "Is it all right? Do
You mind?" and like a man with a wife who
    is too
Close, I say, "Wrong number," my heart like
    stone.
And after such attempts to speak across
Eternity's barrier against time – one vein –
I sit, starved of you, depressed, and wish I had
    los-
-t you, for then I would be whole and content
    again.
And yet, when at last we speak, I am as well
    fed
As a sparrow fluttering round a bird-table's
    bread.

31. WILDERNESS
(DIVINE SONNET)

"Thus, though we cannot make our Sun
Stand still, yet we will make him run."

                    Marvell

Being in the wilderness, Lady, I think
Of the vast Saharan stretch of sand and sky
Where I stood alone and thrilled to see small,
    dry
Flowers and trails of slithering things that
    drink,
And I know my wilderness blooms with rare,
    pink
Flowers that will be documented by and by.
The desert gave me power to feel God's eye
About me, the depth to look within and sink
As down a well. Like a Bedouin who follows
    the sun,
Who does not need cars, planes, kneeling by
    his tents,
Camels and goats, who is at peace, at one
With all, and, poor, has a dignity that
    consents,
I lie with you as if souls peeped through our
    eyes,
And know that man was made for his sunrise.

32. SWAN-UPPING
(DIVINE SONNET)

There was a time when the corner of every
    street
Crawled with menacing men whose cars
    tailed me
Each time I went to the shops or the phone; in
    our free
London my post was steamed open, to eat
Was a risk, my room ransacked three times.
    But I beat
Them, despite it all I carried on recklessly
By the Thames, awaiting a bullet in my knee
Or the jab of a loaded umbrella above my
    feet.
I am a survivor, and now that mystery has
    gone
I have brought myself to you and relax in
    your warm
Mystery as with a woman who can give some
    swan-

-'s-down pleasure. We mysterious men who
    have been in the storm,
Have been condemned to die, we all enjoy
    and know
The mystery of swan-upping under mistletoe!

13 February 1979

33. WARM FIRE
(DIVINE SONNET)

When I look out at the cold wastes and the
    snow
I know you are my business partner, favourite
Secretary and companion. We will sit
By a warm fire, it will snow money, the wind
    will blow
Money, and you – Providence – and I will
    show
Little interest. We will tramp through it,
Scuff it off our boots, shake it off our coats,
    though we flit
Off to Spain; together we will make the world
    know
Real things. You helped me make a living
    with gold
Love. Your "loiving" is like the fire in the
    grate.
And so I sit and look out at the cold
And see fieldfares and redwings peck near the
    gate.
They have come from the Arctic North, and I
    am glad
They too have found a place where they are
    not sad.

34. THE CHALLENGE

A Caesar among conspirators on chairs
I battled off a challenge against my power,
Smoked out a wasps' nest of indignant stares,
As if I were a Tribunal for an hour;
Leaving easy-going Mercy, I judged
Them with the pitilessness of Judgement's
    wrath,
Machine-gunned a Cassius's job – then as if
    you nudged
Me I looked and saw the chairs as sefiroth,
Only all sat in Foundation, in their ego;
And sitting in Beauty where three worlds join,
I thought I glimpsed your smile by the
    window
And saw you glint in the sun like a golden

coin.
The gleam passed, I was back in a tawdry
    room
With a hareem of assassins, and your lamp-lit
    womb.

35. ENCAMPMENT
(DIVINE SONNET)

You smile at me as one who has encamp-
-ed on my green and who must move on,
    make an end,
Yet who longs to stay a lifetime and defend
Me, yet dutifully must take up her lamp
And go, leaving me in a furled-back tent to
    the tramp
Of martial boots. You smile like Louisa,
    attend
To one you loved as you leave, or like
    Phessus' friend,
And, lolling in this fearful April damp,
I think you have learned nothing from your
    many lives.
But your truthful eyes smoke redcoats into air,
Burn holes in the robes and roles of these mad
    wives,
And I see us in a terraced house somewhere –
One puff, and this falseness has blown away,
Leaving green grass and oaks, and a lovely
    May!

36. DUSTPAN

So you gleam on me again, like a hidden sun
Dawning, beaming, as if you said on a walk,
"You are right, there was too much on-off,
    you have won,"
Or "I involved my husband too much in our
    talk,
So what was between us was choked by the
    thought
Of him" and "I confused you with him, you
    are separate,"
Or "You have qualities I have always sought."
I see the dark around you, a black ring
Of night and of things I do not want to know
Which are like dust dumped from a dustpan
    on the mirroring
Surface of my mind, on my calm and peaceful
    glow.
You come back to me, Lady, as if you would
    ever

Go away for good, I know you would never!

1979, revised 7 June 1993

37. SOLITUDE

You come to me as if you would ring and say
A third time "It's off", like a woman who
Is self-divided but constant in her way, true
To a husband. Yet you are inconstant, wa-
-vering backwards and forwards, indecisive,
    whereas
In my feeling I take a deep decision, to be
Inconstant, and live in constant tranquillity,
Unite behind the solitude a saint has.
I let you be like one who should not interfere
With your children, make you leave your
    husband,
And you are like one whose sister is ill and
Who must look after her, to your despair.
So accept the decision you made, and now
    discard
The love that would hurt me if I were not so
    hard.

1979, revised 7 June 1993

38. DOOR

You withdraw from me like a woman who
    strokes
My tired head, showing concern for my ill
    health,
Who says "I cannot live with myself", and
    chokes
As if she would leave her sick husband and
    his "wealth"
And says, "I'm going to end our affair,"
And I feel relief, for I am whole, apart,
Can relate to the world, not just one of a pair,
Who need not have rubbish dumped on his
    heart
Any more. I have slammed a door in my
    mind,
Am free, am myself, am no longer ill, a tar-
-get for your on-off lamp as dark disdain,
And I am now a mask in the world, quite
    blind
Within till, Lady, you push the door ajar
And summon me – to be lit with love again.

1979, revised 7 June 1993

39. STALEMATE

You look reproachfully as if to say "I am your

piece"
Or "We are not growing as we should", or as
    if to ask
"Is it stalemate?", not realising I must cease,
Am short of time, and have to peel off my
    mask
With my clothes, cease to be Mister and
    become old Nick;
Not realising that your on-off doubts have
    made
Me guarded, perhaps, and less inclined to
    quick-
-en to your sunlight in case I am hurt, Lad-
-y, when you withdraw it, not realising that
    you are
Depressed and lonely, like a woman going
    grey
In the evening. Your stormy winds have
    tossed
My buds and they have not unfolded far,
As if you had been as tranquil as a spring day,
And you have become a stale mate, to your
    cost.

1979, revised 7 June 1993

40. MUTINY

You are timid like one who says "My husband
Would say 'How could you, after all I have
    been through,'"
Who cannot bring herself to say, with a
    pointing hand
"You have always been captain, I am just the
    crew,
You steered us into a black cloud, and now
    your
Company is on the rocks, you do not blame
Yourself, but involve me in your desperate
    war.
I should have mutinied against your shame."
You shine on me as on a cruel sea,
Turning away from a captain who left his ship
For a girl in a port-town, and came back
    "sorry",
Who turns from an egotist who has lost his
    grip.
You are like one who throws a lifebelt while
    in pain
And says "I will visit this ship alongside now
    and again."

1979, revised 14th November 1993

41. SOFTNESS

You turn away like one who says "But what
If I fell in between two ships – and drown?"
As if you had said, "If I break with you it will
    not
Be because I fear for my marriage" with a
    frown,
Or "I'm not afraid to be alone, I risk that with
    you,
We'll break up because I cannot live with
    myself a day
More, two wrongs don't make a right, I must
    be true
To myself, you would not want me any other
    way."
And then I think how ruthless you might be,
I think of one who was pitiless and col-
-d, who had many men, who saw love as an art,
Who said "I do not like myself, I am too free"
And beg you not to grow a shell round your
    soul,
Round your bright softness which I love with
    my yearning heart.

42. PARTING

As one who says "You mean more to me
    than I
To you", you turn away, then, besides me
As if you'd consented to come to bed, and we
Had made passionate love without a word,
    Sigh
And I see you raise your eyes and turn your
    head
As if I asked "What is the matter? Are you
    ill?"
And you had choked "Nothing, I'm well"
    until
I felt the wet on your cheeks and you shed
A tear from each eye like two raindrops on
    my hand.
Then I knew that you would go from me, I
    knew,
And so, like one dressing and bending from
    above,
I said goodbye, and you said "Please
    understand,
If we part, it will not be because I don't feel
    for you."
And so you remove your lamp – out of too
    much love.

43. CUSHION

Lady, you are beside my elbow now,
Just as you are on the edge of my
    consciousness
When I go to sleep, when I wake; you are
    there, somehow.
It is not painful, like an infatuated obsess-
-ion which you fell out of as quickly as you
    fell in,
But it's not entirely pleasant when I am
    away
From you. It is an illness I must bear with a
    grin.
Besides being "me" I am a part of "you-me",
    and pray
That besides being "you" you are a part of
    "us".
You seem to say you're like ivy round my
    oak,
You are like a woman whose lover's wife,
    without fuss,
Has pains up her arm from her heart, or has
    had a stroke,
And who says, "Don't neglect her, don't show
    you don't care that she's ill
For I am just a cushion you sit in, when you
    will."

44. MARINER

I was like a mariner who sailed the seas
In a five thousand year old reed boat, to show
That Sumerians reached India on the breeze,
Who fishes for food and hooks a turtle – you
    were so,
On my line as, dripping with images in a
    heat,
I wound you from the depths of a sea of light,
But now you claim to hold the rod and greet
Me with "You are hooked through your heart
    in a dark night".
With the sun on my flag, a "midday riser", I
Take off my mask with my clothes and lie
    down
With you in the setting sun, and the sea and
    sky,
Under a moon like a marigold. I cannot
    drown.
So, Lady, let us enjoy our desire
Now the swirling waters shimmer with white
    fire.

321

45. FRIENDSHIPS

You come frowning as if to say "Why did you
    hesitate
When I asked you to give me a lift? Why look
    about?"
Or "Our assignation – why were you ten
    minutes late?"
Or "You want me for only one thing" – as if
    you doubt-
-ed me with "You pick me to bits and then
    relent,
Do not do so." What's between us is like a
    plant.
It needs water and air, it gives off a scent
If you pick off the deadheads, or new heads
    can't
Grow. "But do not pick the leaves, nor the
    new heads,
Do not target the growth with your analysing
    eye,
Do not entangle the flower in your verbal
    threads."
The best friendships are wordless, like a
    butterfly
Or violets in May which grow in silence
Or the red roses of June with perfumed scents.

46. IVY AND OAK

Like a woman who has turned from the best
    love in her life
For the dutiful grind of seeing her sons
    through school,
Living their demanding wishes, by a rule,
You have drawn away from me like a dutiful
    wife.
Can you in aloofness not shine out in fun
So I can see you? Raise the serpent like gold
Up your stem, open your lotus petals, unfold
The bud of your unopened self and soak in the
    sun,
Oblivious to all heat, all rains, all smoke.
It is as if you don't want higher
    consciousness,
Prefer feeling to indifference, and confess
Love is like ivy which grows round an oak.
Can you not twine round my root and ignore
    your bud
For which heights and depths are one in this
    lower mud.

1979, revised 15th November 1993

47. LOCKET

Sometimes you come unexpectedly in prayer
Like one who drives by her lover's house and
    spies
Him climbing into his car, elsewhere in his
    eyes,
So do you look on me when I am unaware.
I think of you like a man who is drunk, who
    can see
The mistiness around him, he can never forget
It is there all the while – I'm in a haze of love,
    yet
I am not aware of you when you spy on me
Like the moon. I think you are sometimes
    unhappy, with fears,
Missing me, unable to get me off your chest,
Unable to concentrate, absent-minded at best,
Like a woman who yearns for closeness, and
    who wears
A locket she treasures, a grave for two heads
Which are buried under maple leaves, and her
    dreads.

1979, revised 16th November 1993

48. TAOIST LADY

"He's superhuman", the secretary said of me,
Thinking, no doubt, of my workload and the
    calm
With which I endure the brickbats and the
    harm,
But she did not know the superhuman glee
The calm the divine has grown, the serenity
When you shine on me, tingle up my arm,
My Muse and strength, not further than my
    slack palm,
So that nothing touches my equanimity.
As I wrap myself in my armour of light, my
    crown,
In a superhuman trance, the ego dead
I sit before you cross-legged and you squat
Like a Taoist lady and ride me up and down
And soak me with female juice which bursts
    in my head
And balances my energies so cold is hot.

1979, revised 16th November 1993

49. NUN

Like a lady who becomes a lowly nun
And humbles and fulfils herself by serv-
-ing and who lights better than all who are

snuffed, with a verve,
Yet has to say "Yes of course" to everyone,
You have come down to serve us like a spark;
You seem at my beck and call, do as you're
    told,
But you are a light before the position you
    hold,
You kneel to reveal a wisdom in your dark.
I watch as you guide this one on the way,
Correct that one's omission, as you prop up
Each stumble, support, sustain and fill each
    cup,
See more than they do, are richer than they.
And so when you shine out at me, flickering, I
    know
You abase yourself to become a candle's
    glow.

1979, revised 16th November 1993

50. WORLD LIKE A WIFE

You are like a woman who has a dark lord
Who is intolerant, and, knowing that you
    stray,
Will throw you out and knows you cannot
    afford
To involve anyone else in your going away.
You steal into my soul, and take your
    pleasure,
Like one who knows the grave is an
    unfriendly place
Where no bodies sneeze, and then you fade to
    a blur
And I am alone, wondering at the risk you
    face.
Do you need me – why do you thus flood me
    with light?
I, who am the beneficiary, marvel at your
    gift,
Wonder why the divine needs human plight.
I creep back to the world from you, adrift
Like a husband whose wife is understanding
    and kind
And says, "You should have a mistress, I will
    not mind."

1979, revised 16th November 1993

51. KITE

And as if that is not enough, I am told (how
    they preen)
That I am to be in the group of six

Who will wield power; and that I who have
    seen
The world wheel by like a windblown kite,
    must fix
Things for a hundred people, be distracted
    from the task
Which expresses the drive in my life and its
    ascent
Like the wind that tugs the storm-tossed
    frame. I ask,
What is life for, if it is to be spent
Timetabling tomorrows and yesterdays,
Like a jailer locked in a prison? Lady with
    your light,
Please lead me out of this wordly waste of
    time
To a place where I may be my self, where
    angels climb,
And fulfil a destiny, my consciousness
    bright,
And not live among the jailed of the earth, in
    a daze.

1979, revised 16th November 1993

52. TRIBUNAL

You break in like a Tribunal for landlords
Inspecting to fix a rent, three commissars
Who knock on a door, climb the stairs with
    clipboards,
Walk round my room pointing out flaws and
    scars,
Noting down shameful things – a hole in the
    wall –
Then walking out with a grim look on their
    face
And I must attend your hearing in your Town
    Hall
Sit before your thrones – your high-backed
    chairs – and brace
And defend myself; ask you not to legislate.
Then I must wait while you go out and return
With your verdict – "application invalid" – so
    I win.
You smile, and I leave relieved, and
    contemplate.
So you break into me, examine me and
    discern,
And like an abused landlord, I welcome you
    in.

1979, revised 16th November 1993

53. IMMOBILITY

Like a woman who asks dreamily "Can it be
That I am falling in love with you?" and
gambles all,
Externalising the now as on a wall,
On a moment's happiness, regardless of the
Consequences, you have sought me out, and
stay with me.
And I am grateful to you, and will repay your
call,
Like an unknown girl touched by a great man
in a Hall,
You will be remembered long after that
grandee
Cruel age has ravaged your face and ravished
your "skin"
To rags, for as Baudelaire immortalised
Jeanne
So I will give you everlasting life in these lines.
It will be remembered, long after I am gone,
That during the day my "mystery woman"
stole in,
You, who are more eternal than Scotch pines!

1979, revised 16th November 1993

54. SNOWMAN

You are with me again, like a lady, my Light,
Who has led me out of frozen streets into warm
And who points through the window at a
garden all white
And a melted snowman – coal eyes, pipe, cold
form,
Soft shoes and buttons by the mound – as if to
say
"There is my last love and his money-
grubbing pride";
You are with me again as this dusk takes the
day
And look at me like my Tutankhamun, whose
wide
Eyes are blank in daylight, but see in the dark –
The pupils stood out in the tomb; the inner
life
Of blank eyes and a vision of the spark
Which warm me like a radiant housewife,
As if all that was left of your last love was
snow
Which your heart melted as it makes your
next love glow.

1979, revised 16th November 1993

55. NEGLECTED

You hold yourself back from me like a
woman who grim-
-ly says "I am falling in love with you, I tend
To have divided loyalties, when I am with
him
I want to be with you more, and so it must
end."
You hide yourself like one who struggles and
seeks
To be detached from the heaviness on her
chest,
Who wants to create a great man, yet who
speaks
Of believing that her spouse's cause is best
And, hating deception, returns to her husband,
To preserve her "permanent structure". And
so I gash,
Neglected by you, though you want to be with
me and
Though you have no time for his search for
cash.
I look for your lamp as if I sought a spark,
And know I am left alone in your loving dark.

1979, revised 16th November 1993

THE FIRE-FLOWER

1980

A METAPHYSICAL IN MARVELL'S GARDEN

The House is hidden down lanes of the mind,
It stands "Strictly Private" amid green fields,
Over the redbrick front, a weathercock.
Behind, sunny lawns. Shaped evergreen
    shields
A huge cedar. And here a long green pond
Winds past the stone arch of a nun's chapel.
A Roman tomb ponders the October,
Among the ragged roses remember Marvell.

Here shed the body like a sheepskin jacket,
Discard all thought as in a mystery school.   10
By this nun's grave sit and be the moment,
A oneness gazing on the heart's green pool.
A universe unfolds between two stone
    columns
And takes a leafy shape on clouded ground.
The sun-lily floats. Question its waters,
It will trickle through your fingers and be
    drowned.

The South Front sundial says in coloured
    glass
"Qui Est Non Hodie". I am a bowl.
In the North Hall the piano-tuner
Ping ping pings and trembles through my
    soul.   20
Who would not live in this delicious quiet,
Walk among columns, lie on the grass and
    wait?
Who would not teach a Fairfax daughter here,
Escape all bills, be free to contemplate

A flowered soul rooted like a climbing rose,
A metaphysical swoon of gold moments
Whose images curl down through thorns and
    leaves
(Wit and wordplay), spirit and satin sense,
Petalled layers and folds of whorled meaning
In whose dew-perfumed bowls a divine
    breeze blows;   30
Or like the prickly flame of the firethorn

Which crackles where purgation merely
    glows?

With drowsed eyes glance at solid grass and
    be
In whirlpools of energy like a sea.
Breaths heave the light, and answering
    currents pour
Through spongy stones and stars, or seaweed
    tree.
Now see with eye of mind into swelled form,
Imagine sap wash, oak wave in acorn.
Knowers are one with known, and are soaked
    by tides
That foam and billow through an ebbing
    lawn.   40

Gaze down on galaxies in a stone bowl
Like curved rose petals (small tip, large end),
Bent, cracked to holes. Travel faster than light
Through wisdom to where many curled
    worlds bend,
See nightmare multiplicity, then go
Where the bud of each universe is found,
The great Rose-tree of light where grown
    ideas
Drift into form as petals fall to ground.

The vision has now passed. Condemned to
    crowds,
Town seers teach hordes and leave halls'
    green waters   50
To lords who never peep for secret flowers
Or climb their souls up walls; and to their
    daughters.
And now a cloud flits through a fairy ring
And I glimpse for an instant my little "T.C."
And feel a dreadful shudder cross my calm,
A "May it not come yet, but wait for me".

Wall-high climbers, whose many blooms
    reflect
Glimpses of the rose on the great Rose-tree
Which forms all souls in time from one rose-

hip,
Whose past growth glows gold moments they
    still see,   60
Are, in the present moment, one essential
    rose;
Which novices may see as a watery
Dark's shimmer and glimmer of the timeless
Dew-filled bowl of one gold water-lily.

Nymph everywhere, for whom men sacrifice
Paradise for a mortgaged, salaried mask
To keep you where Tennyson longed for
    Maud
Or where you board, we town climbers only
    ask
That, eyes closed, you grow a golden lily
And be a bowl for it, and simply start   70
To wimple in your wanting. May you be
A rose-sun-leaf-ground-cloudy fire-gold
    heart.

4, 16-17 February 1980

A CROCUS IN THE CHURCHYARD

Hoofs clop clop clop between the silver birch
That hide the arrowed spire and this Forest
    church.
Come through the lych-gate, down steps by
    the yew:
Where the bracken tangles, wood-pigeons
    coo.
On this green carpet, pause: a nightingale
Sings through eternity by a black rail.
A crocus blooms where every heart believes
That unknown faces mean more than autumn
    leaves.

The aisle is quiet, tiptoe to the chancel.
Altar, pulpit, stained glass, lectern eagle,   10
Hammerbeam roof, a tiled Victorian floor,
The font and cattle brands, organ by the door.
Here on the wall two marble tablets state
The Ten Commandments, and how to
    contemplate.
Red and black, a life like scullery tiles;
Where a robin hops, a wife is wreathed in
    smiles.

"No graven images", "no gods but me",
No murder or covetous adultery.

A time when no host wanted, it would seem,
And manna was not yet a juicy dream.   20
A city smile is like a warm pillow,
Here girls are like a shower of pussy willow.
A rooted life, like the evergreen yew:
No glass or redbrick spoils each woodland
    pew.

The church is faithful to its hillocked dead.
Whether poet, agent, or Department Head,
Their deeds, like bluebells on a mound of
    moss,
Attest a Britain like a marble cross.
They, like bent gardeners in their common-
    wealth,
Cut bellbind and preserved their belief's
    health,   30
Conserved the diamond lead window
    standards
From the stones of revolutionary vanguards.

Silver birch, bracken and folk who seldom
    sinned
Now feed the silence under this March wind.
Shh! rest in the eternal; hear a snail
Dragging beneath the warbling nightingale.
Here rustling moments are time's muffled
    thieves;
Faces under hillocks, unlike old leaves,
Are compost so a crocus can proclaim:
To glimpse a Golden Flower is man's true
    aim.   40

Under this hillock, a decaying heart
Feeds the roots of a crocus and takes part
In the lost blowings of time from a windless
Ecstasy's silence and brimming stillness,
And, filled with dews, can, like an art-work,
    hold
A mirror down to Nature and still gold
Sunshine so posthumous meaning can wave
From fields of silver light beyond the grave.

Under the spire that towers from the slate roof
With arrowhead and vane like rational
    proof,   50
Look up at a high tripod which can view
White clouds that scud across the darkening
    blue,
And startle God at His theodolite,

As, measuring the angles of clouds and night,
He takes a reading of time's speed and flow
And calculates the centuries still to go.

Death has its beauty. A hearse, a squirrel's
tail,
And your coffin is lowered by this black rail,
Between laurel and holly. For companions,
Unknown   Belshams,   Cookes,   and
rhododendrons.   60
A crocus under buds, now blink and brim
At dew-dipping finches, a tinkling hymn,
Snug in grass, safe from brambles; and in fine
rain,
Gaze at the still arrow on the windless
weathervane.

17 February 1980

FIRE-VOID

(A RUBBISH DUMP AT NOBE, JAPAN: AN INVESTIGATION OF NATURE AND HISTORY, PATTERN AND MEANING)

A seaside village, thatched fishermen's huts,
Paddy fields, pines, threshers, and a light that
cuts.
I stare at the rubbish dump under this hill:
A heap of litter by a dusty track, still
Boxes, rusty petrol cans, panniers below
Old timber, paper; red cannae, a mallow,
A purple flower that blooms only at sundown;
Pine-bristles, wire-bars; a mess that makes me
frown.

Cicadas, like a sawmill, go fee-fee-fee-fee-
feeee.
Ants crawl up and down a bamboo cross.
See,   10
This dump is in proportion to the hill,
It balances two sweeping curves that thrill.
Pattern is relation, of lines to whole:
Spring, fall; skull, scroll; shape the inverted
bowl
Of Nature and history. Birth and decay
Are contours that are redesigned each day.

The pattern of sunrise and set, and soul,
Holds green and white in a harmonious
whole.
Opposing seasons and ages are a part

Of a hidden order known to the heart.   20
Meaning relates pattern to what it's for,
Yet ask priests "Why is man?" and be shown
the door!
The artefacts of the Great Architect
Are not grasped by reason, but the intellect.

Meaning is a perspective eyes cannot see.
Artists' squints say: hills do not mean, but *be*.
"Dieu" means; without the enlightenment of
French
It is a four-lettered pattern on a schoolbench.
"Nature" has no meaning to surface eyes,
There is patterned "isness" only: sunset,
sunrise.   30
Like "history", Nature springs and falls and is
gone,
Like a mallow in a field, or a Napoleon.

But seen with contemplation's X-ray gaze,
Nature is a dark fire, a void ablaze
With latent shadows that crackle and spit
Brief sparks, hot seeds and years, each
opposite,
Glowing, decaying things that never still.
There is a smouldering in dump and hill.
To those who see in negative one power
Flames through Nature and history and mind
every hour.   40

Its leaping forms take shape, fade, leap,
proclaim:
Our universe is the dance of one flame.
The fiery Idea which ferments all forms
Heats them with light and then cools them
with storms,
Dissolves old shapes into their formlessness,
Empyrean's spiralling whirlpool of "mess".
A dump, a hill flicker with the same light
Which alchemises souls and cleanses sight.

Like fire and irons, Nature and man candesce
Into one stuff in history's huge furnace.   50
Angels descend to try their souls, which burn
And, when softened, tempered by fire, return.
Earth's hills are fire by which dull souls are
shaped,
Banked up, sea-blown, storm-bellowed, and
stone-scraped,
They turn base minds to gold until, destroyed,

327

Like a burnt dump they sink back to the void.

The most important question of philosophy,
"The meaning of life", has been defined as
    "me"
By men who say their search for truth is truth,
That "meaning" is in the jaw, like a bad
    wisdom tooth.   60
But fire transmutes the pattern of hill and
    heap
To a meaning that transforms an angel's sleep
And hatches golden fire-birds beyond death.
Hills lighten souls, hence angels put on
    breath.

10-15 November 1979, 20-22 February and 5 April 1980

SEA-FIRE

A harbour in two hills. Things of the sea
Strew the front: boatyard, a crab factory,
Nets, fishing boats on the sand. On the "pier"
The sea smashes and booms. Bladderwrack.
    Here
Is a living from sea. Mevagissey
Is commercial, this old community
Each year meets and sings "For those in Peril"
While an anchor lights up the rocky hill.

A cross, a lighthouse, a boat, and what yields
A rooted life: there are dolmens in fields,   10
Stone rings, between here and Marazion;
Tin-mine chimneys with ivied arches stand on
Moors near stone walls and orange lilies;
    neighbours
Appear in parlours and recite labours
Of giants, or the shipwrecks on Looe Bar,
And offer mackerel bait for the fishing jar.

The Harbour Hotel sign shows "Porthleven
1750." It was a small cove then.
A cemetery. On every chimney pot
Gulls scream, like long dead souls defending
    what   20
Their living own. History and death.... We
    stay
For the annual march round the fairy-lit bay.
They come, holding orange torches. Admire
How they throw their brands on a great
    bonfire.

Red sparks and night's white stars, village
    faces.
Men are one fire against rocky places.
Now in this harbour, on the Clock Tower side,
The Divine Will steals like a creeping tide.
The Milky sweep across a wave-dark bay
Inspires a vision of the Mystic Way: 30
See souls cross rocks, and, with wave-wetted
    feet,
Light up the causeway where all Angels meet.

Wake consciousness that merges with night-
    skies
Whose "I" sees stars, and is seen, with their
    eyes,
Travel through an impersonal mind who
Has always existed, though not in "you",
Climb the starway where chaos laps and pours
Deep in black mind, then soar as a gull soars
When it wing-ferries souls to hidden gleams,
Bask in the uncreated sun that beams   40

Light at midnight to each man, flower and
    bird,
Go where the heart of universes stirred
To loving fire and sparks, behind space-time,
Shoots sparks of spirit to each well-earned
    prime.
Mind is universe, a dark paradox;
Inner and outer space seem air and box,
Yet squeeze through a crack in side, find a
    new sun
Which spins atoms, and in and out are one.

As waves curl moon and stars, now fire and
    sparks,
Sea rolls between divine and human darks.   50
On shore are forms. Men live a simple life
Against the weather, the sea, and the wife,
Go to the cemetery and return as gulls
And wheel round roofs that once sheltered
    their skulls.
Here men mend nets, then go out on the sea,
And trawl teeming waters, and God's plenty.

23-24 February and 6 April 1980

A MYSTIC FIRE-POTTER'S RED SUN-HALO

After confession she comes to the door,
This Catholic "never makes appointments",
    for

"Time cuts up" and "I do things by feeling".
She stays, for the talk will be revealing,
And brings in a brown-paper parcel from
Her hotel. "The porter thought it was a
　　　bomb,"
She says. It opens on the floor, to show
Five faceless clay figures, and a red halo.

Five Marys behind pyramids, angles
Round which to peep for visionary angels.　10
The folds of their robes are fingers, as though
A hand reaches from Heaven. "One does not
　　　know
What the other gives, I suppose; somehow
I haven't thought. There are no angles now,
Just straight-on looking." The enamel ring
Has a blood-red rim and a centre of – nothing.

"That took two weeks of pressing-in of chips.
Each one was fired for twenty-four hours."
　　　She grips
A tower like a church. "This has a defect,
The glaze is glossier, but it's imperfect.　20
The shapes just come. I do each thing by
　　　touch,
I surrender to the fire which gives out such
Different finishes and guess how they'll come
　　　out."
Artists transmute with a fire beyond doubt.

A huge fired bridal ring, powered touch. Her
　　　hand
Knocks snails from the gate of consciousness
　　　and
Calms choppiness round a heart, so that, still,
A soul peeps round angles of darkness, till
Glory! a white light shines, now like a moon,
Now mirrored sun in an inner lagoon.　30
"People don't see peace, so I paint a sea,
A church on rock, a sky like eternity!

"The white light of the soul will never cease.
It always burns gold on waters that are at
　　　peace.
It flows from the Loving Heart, the Christ-
　　　sun.
The spirit is the calm self of the nun,
The centre where the Holy Spirit is,
Between the heart and Light: God." The heart
　　　knows His

Power: that tide that floods in as secretly
As a Cornish inner harbour, now dry, is filled
　　　with sea.　40

The heart burns village lights till the soul fills
　　　with sea
And ceases to be mere dry, beached psyche.
Spirit pours in as a dark tide leaks down
The dipping lock-gate to village Charlestown.
Swirled round, renewed, the heart shimmers
　　　at one
With a vast fathomlessness, a great ocean.
The rising centre calms, soon the moon above
Shivers sun on a soul wet with ebbed love.

A tide with three webbed fingers, or a hand
Touching the heart. "Don't compare, 'The
　　　Power and...',　50
It is itself." Yet, like a well, drilling
Leaves the red-rimmed centre empty, yet
　　　filling;
Like a flooded tin-mine shaft by the sea.
Mary, round a pyramid Trinity,
Knows: the Holy Ghost like a Cornish tide,
The black headland peak, and the guide at
　　　man's side.

Our cloud-capped Age of Darkness knows
　　　dark things.
Its roaring fire bakes pots without gulls'
　　　wings
On them, or sun, or a dial that regulates
The soul's fired still. And our time
　　　appreciates　60
Her too little. But Truth is a sunned self.
"Our Age will move things from the bottom
　　　shelf
To the top," she says. "Each thing is given,
Only speak when you feel guided, *driven*."

An empty blood-rimmed heart when filled
　　　with sea
Reflects sunned moments, whose wood-chips
　　　must be
Pressed in, fired into Alchemy's red stone
That turns to blood-gold halo all white bone
And red sinews, and is the Loving Heart
In the shape of a bridal ring, by metalled
　　　art,　70
Which worn, fills a hand with white power, as

a round
Well rim fills with water from underground.

She has gone. Sorrowing, perfect Mary
Looks down on a fallen and contrary
World. Beneath, candles are like quiet, lit
    souls,
The eternal light in the basket controls
The Oratory altar so men can sit
In the mystic tradition and die into it.
This fire-potter and sea-artist, like all saints,
Is *its* light, which she lives and bakes and
    paints.   80

February/March 1980

AN AESTHETE'S "GOLDEN" ARTEFACTS

A white horseshoe terrace, a garden square;
Railings, two pines and bush. We gulp sea air,
Head for four Corinthian columns. At
The top of spiral stairs is a white flat
And Tuohy's massive frame, a man whose
    heart's fire
And refined, miniature art I admire,
Whose rooms reveal a polymath-aesthete:
A mask, Chinese and Japanese pictures greet.

He reduces thought: "My political
Attitudes are aesthetic: how can people   10
Put up with seeing beggars? Don't confuse,"
He says, "social and political values,
Behaviour and getting things done." Now a
    Fellow:
"Epistemology (what can I know?),
Ethics (what shall I do?). There's a difference
Between knowing and doing. *One must make
    sense*."

Some brains burn like bulbs of a hundred
    watts.
He has reduced base metals to ingots
With the brilliance of the heart's furnace.
    Instead
Of living as a scholar, all learning spread   20
Below, seen from a mountain, this full-grown
Parnassian has forged the philosopher's stone:
"Artists melt the autobiographical
To a generalised gold image, a symbol,

Or Persona. Distancing makes poems good.

It's like turning a camera lens. One should
Not be too warm – too close-up in
    confession –
Or impersonal. There should be a tension
Between poet and image, as in dream.
Wittgenstein told me, 'Works of art must
    seem   30
Propositions, in feelings and perceptions.
You answer Yes or No.' There are no
    exceptions."

The heart melts worlds to metal, but is not
    soul.
Jewellers' flames shape but cannot turn gold a
    bowl.
The soul's sealed still, heated, melts and
    transmutes so
(True Alchemy) heart and base image glow
Elixir, the essential golden Flower
Which peeps through layered language, a rose
    of power
Whose dark bloom hints that Reality lacks
    edge:
Eternity is a hole in the mind's hedge.   40

When art is Alchemy, first still, then mould
Melt image to red stone and thence to gold
Whose standard consigns to a workbench
    drawer
Nuggets whose weight still tilts like iron ore.
He sits in the window, looking out to sea:
"I like the calm down here, but cannot *be*."
A restless man whose ingots will be sold,
Who has not transmuted his own soul to gold.

A fiery stilling makes an inner sun,
The roaring heart gives out what it has
    done,   50
And may not know illumination. Of these,
One burns the impure self, one what it sees,
Melting lumps of action to their essence.
The saint knows peace; the aesthete
    achievements.
So his masked consciousness, in quiet despair,
Burns outer things in beauty that is rare.

March 1980

PEAR-RIPENING HOUSE

A gable behind lime trees, a green gate
Which says "Journey's End". In the porch we

330

wait
By the grained door, then go by pebbledash
Garage and shed which have seen small boys
    bash
Centuries before lunch against Australia,
Past roses (at square leg), a dahlia,
And a splurge of storm-beaten daisies, for
The old pear tree tumbles by the back door.

Now in this room peep – under four black
    beams,
Sloping ceilings – for the mirror where
    gleams   10
The yearning of a reaching out to moons,
Where flit the ghosts of a thousand
    afternoons.
This, and the black Victorian clock that
    cowers
Between two prancing horses, measured the
    hours
Of falling generations, crops of pears,
The sunsets and winters up and down the
    stairs.

Here floats a battleship on a lino sea;
The day war ended, this was ARP.
Here slides the ghost of a brooding schoolboy,
A fire-warmed clerk reading in lonely joy.   20
Here flits a brief affair, a wedding eve,
Here steals a separation. The shadows grieve.
Families, funerals....A Parthenon,
This house is permanent, we are the gone.

Now thirty years are less than the straggly
    twines
That were honeysuckle. And still the sun
    shines!
Dressing for church is the green of last
    spring's
Lilac; young ambitions and hankerings
Are now the floatings of a dandelion clock.
What meaning had they? Is Time just the
    block   30
And blackened stump of a hewn sweet
    chestnut?
Cascading ivy that drowned a summerhut?

Young wants and hankerings have a meaning
To the hard-skinned ego's slow mellowing.
The journey through maturing hours and years

Ends in wrinkling pith and pitying tears.
Cores fill with heavy juices from one flow
Whose sap softens to soul the hard ego.
All life ripens to drowse back to the One:
Fruit and old men fall earthward from the
    sun.   40

Ripe pears return pips to the ground, and sow
A next life's genes, patterned on this one.
    Know
That soul inherits genes from its last spring
    now
To gush a vision of buds upon a bough.
Leafy lives fill with the sap of all that's green
And *are* God's mind, whose code is in each
    gene,
And grow centuries of purpose into fruit
And show: soul ripens so new seeds can
    shoot.

We journey through a house and garden,
    shore
Up, improve, order and pass on the law   50
Of growth and fruit. The long way gives
    ample
If we soften to the universal
Sun. We journey, pick pears and paint old
    wood,
Teach sons. Seed is the end of parenthood:
The hard, small pear on the tree on the lawn,
And a ripe pip sprouting in a distant dawn.

23 March, mid-April and 26 May 1980

CLOUDED-GROUND POND

On Strawberry Hill, a break in forest trees.
We park on mud and cross the road in breeze:
A brown pond, yellow lilies. It is cool.
We could stay all day here at the Horseman's
    Pool,
But it is near the road. We take the track
Past logs and stones in clay, turn into brack-
en, hawthorn, beech. And now, beyond holly,
A pond amid gorse and birch, and a fallen
    tree.

It has seen the agonies of the seasons:
How fathers died in autumn; the reasons   10
Young men married, were exiled, lived alone,
And their returns. This pond has also known
The stealings-up through sawing grass-

hoppers,
And secret comings far from eavesdroppers.
It has sensed small girls crouch in these
gnarled roots,
And dreamt of the netting of speckled newts.

A touch of sadness taints the autumn tint.
Like a daughter leaving till spring, a hint
Of absence skips round the deep gravel pit.
Across its quiet eternal stillness flit   20
The changing shadows of dragonfly time,
Newt and lily months. Sticklebacks stir
slime.
This gravel is honey, this cloud is cherry
And the heather and gorse smell of strawberry.

Now time disturbs the eternal with raindrops,
Voices. Ducks clack, dogs splash, a robin
hops,
Frogs watch and plop in mud, a rustle rolls
Through the silver birch near where, in
spring, tadpoles
Cluster like thorns round submerged sticks.
At noon
The shimmering mirror, teeming with
June,   30
Can blaze into nothing, while two hearts
bound
As a face drowns in clouds to gasp on:
ground.

Four worlds make contact in beauty, and
when
The ground reflects a leafy, clouded sky,
then
All four dance in the mirror of a pond.
Through layered leaves, the groundless soul
beyond
Reflects clouds of spirit, and, in high
moments,
The sun's divine air, blinding experience
Of the first source when all say yes and see
The One that shines within layered
complexity.   40

Sadness and joy are one to this still Tao
Whose horn of plenty, like a watery bough,
Gushes buds, leaves, petals, and pours faces
From warm clouds into each self and all
places.

Six months are one ripple that smoothes away
All sad twigs till the dancing, wintry day
Restores a universe like a green shower:
The Tao-self renews the earth, stroking the
hour.

As old genes teem new lives, Tao's hidden
sun,
Which joined the heights and depths and
fused into one   50
The clouded ground, is now this lily, it
Gushes from clouds, is blown with pure sun-
lit
Wind, and rooted in mud, yet still, pours All.
The lily on-in water is a call
For Essex men to leave their cars and say
"Yes"
To grounded roots in cloud-bordered stillness.

23 March 1980

TWO VARIATIONS ON ONE THEME

1. TIME AND ETERNITY (SECOND VERSION)

I held her hand at this Omega gate,
She wanted to paint the yew,
And now the moment has blown away
Like dandelion fluff on the blue.

Now, on the High Beach forest church
The passing clouds and years
Are like pattering footsteps in the porch
Or the silence under bedsit tears.

In the city I am scattered like poplar fluff
Blown on the wind of echo,   10
But here I breathe, with the quiet of stone,
The white light these dead men know.

Oh bury me behind this grave,
At the low black rail,
That all who have suffered and been brave
May pass the yew and wail
For all whom golden hair enslaves,
Till the past is a squirrel's tail;
Then, like the boom in childhood caves,
Oh hear beneath the breeze   20
The mystery that flows through stars and seas,
Where the autumn bracken waves.

2. THE BRIDE OF TIME

I

Time held a dandelion that day,
Blew the clock by this yew;
Now the moment has blown away
Like fluff across the blue.

To the porch of this forest church
The passing clouds are years;
Pattering feet feed silver birch
And the silence under tears.

In the city men are scattered
Like poplar fluff, and waste;   10
Here moss enfolds all who are shattered
In an embrace that is chaste.

All who are broken and are blown
On the wind of echo
Here breathe in the quiet of stone
The light these dead men know.

Eternity connives at pains
Which mould spirits that sinned,
But trembles when tears ooze from veins,
Consoles like a whispering wind.   20

II

Listen beneath each gentle gust,
Hear the meaning of life;
The silence of the after-dust
Taunts like a flirting wife.

Seek her, she hides yet will be found,
Cooing from a leafy den;
This nothingness empty of sound
Pregnantly woos all men.

Nothingness round an empty tree
Is full of rustling love.   30
A something woos men passionately
Like a cooing ring-dove

A black-hole womb sucks in dead things
And then thrusts out new grass,
But waves of light and angels' wings
Swirl down where ebbed fins pass.

This black-hole Void preserves all souls
Like fish in tides of love.
Expanded souls are like a sea
Sucked out from a foxglove.   40

Eternity lets all men know
She loves stillness not haste,
Yet preserves tides fish-spirits flow
Before their bodies waste.

III

Eternity blows in the breeze
Yearning for years and graves.
Hear her soul pant through stars and seas
Where sighing bracken waves.

O carve two verses on my grave
Before this low black rail,   50
That all who suffer and are brave
May pass the yew and wail

For all whom golden hair enslaves
Till Time's a squirrel's tail;
That, like a pshsh in childhood caves,
Trembling a leafy veil,

The wind may whisper through these trees
With a soothing shsh of "still"
Drop to a hush, reveal and freeze
A hidden Void of will: 60

"Eternity blows like a bride,
Billowing springs and graves.
Her meaning foams through star and tide,
Teases where each leaf waves.

Seek her secret beneath the breeze,
Leap this three-stone-stepped stile;
Hear silence surge through years and seas,
Know her mystery, then smile!"

21-22 June 1980

A STONEMASON'S FLOWER-BOWL

Near the Saxon church, a gate in the wall
Leads through pine trees to where shrill
        voices call.
Gothic turrets and arrow-slit windows,
Balconies for a Princess's rainbows.
Go in through the porch to a dark hall where
Old masters peer on walls. Up the long stair

Children swarm to dormitories in a tower.
Put down a daughter's case where shy girls
     cower.

This school was the Lord of the Manor's
     home,
And now, in holidays, town children roam   10
The lawn and woods that, from slit windows,
     roll
To the distant sea. Here descend and stroll
In what seems a permanent place. The town
Is new – our vandal century has pulled down –
But here four stone heads on a stone flower-
     bowl
Face four winds, like sad ladies round a soul.

For four summers she has holidayed here
And I have turned one woman to stone each
     year.
This town has seen the changes: crashing
     waves,
Four heads like capped bathers', four relief-
     graves   20
Round a flower-bowl life. In love a gorgon,
The artist petrifies all he looks on:
Here stands, like a breakwater Time foams
     round,
A monument, an artist's chiselling-ground.

This Sompting Hall, too, half hints at
     something
Half out of Time: it has a churchbell's ring.
Towers and Tudor chimneys, structured, float
By changing seas, a changeless anecdote.
All castles and works of art on pages
Join all centuries, are read by all ages.   30
All stonemasons find things that never
     change,
And measure God by a distant mountain
     range.

The divine cloud that surrounds our stone
     ball
Yearns to ravish the empty minds of all
Masons who reach for mountains through
     grey skies
As if the Infinite were granite, sighs
For mind-travellers to: fly through their night-
     air
Up four worlds through rainbows; peer and
     soar where
A chink shines through the shell of our space-
     time;
Look through the airhole to the eternal
     prime;   40

Like astronauts squeeze through the airlock;
     float
Among timeless Ideas in God's mind; note
Bright images that flash down as events;
And bring four goddess heads back to blind
     sense
Which they, as careful craftsmen, curl and fix
In changeless winds and waves of stone that
     mix
Order and random hours on stone flower-
     bowls,
Give courage to endure to Time-bound souls.

Eternal images last, stones which show
Them seem durable. Halls sometimes echo   50
Turrets which an imaging soul has seen.
All else is flux: towns, women who have been
Made stone trophies round flowered beauty,
     seas, pain.
Bodies, like flowers, bloom, fade and come
     again,
Pass like returning bulbs in old urned souls –
Which are as enduring as stone flower-bowls.

Who cannot, then, lie on this sloping lawn
And open his imagination; yawn
And dream a summer dream, flat on his back,
Of goddesses, a sky like a mountain track;   60
And fix stones in the flower-bowl of his
     search,
Then rise and walk to the towering church,
Smell fading roses and, unflinching, stride
Where waves smash sea-defences at high tide!
                              19-20 April 1980

AN OBSCURE SYMBOLIST'S ROCK-TREE

I

Hurry through woods to crossroads – we are
     late –
And swing up the drive to the old farm-gate,
Tiptoe through mud near barns and a well till
The silage tower looms up on a grass hill

334

That slopes to a viaduct, then retrace
Steps to the flowered front garden of Hill
    Place
And the thirteenth century farmhouse and
    sunlit
Porch where an obscure artist used to sit.

This Cornish "aunt" sent books for each
    birthday
And lino-cut cards of barns filled with hay. 10
Eight years ago, eighty, scrawny, she scanned
Through canvases upstairs, while her husband
Milked cows. Now both are dead. Her
    daughter shows
Her young work, student notebooks which we
    close
For they copied. Now rummage among
    frames
For her late works developed symbolist aims.

A water-colour Kynance rock and sky
Draws back the veil, and shows the unity.
Twilit rocks and a sea-cliff tin-mine blend
Into night. On the back, "Dusk Near Land's
    End".   20
Her daughter says, "It's painted from
    Pendeen,
I think that's Geevor mine," but she had seen
Another dusk at the end of her breath
And recalled her roots in rock, accepting her
    death.

She knew the world of rock and sea and sky
Is of one stuff within eternity.
Her rocks contain tin-ores as well as graves,
And further down, beyond all groins and
    caves,
Obscurely hint the timeless creviced seams
Which hoard ice age fossils and ancient
    dreams.   30
Eternity is full of forms and breath
And takes their space, uniting life and death.

She knew Idea is solid, forms hollow,
Like a rock cube with bubbled holes which
    show
Circle, diamond, triangle, crescent, square.
Each symbol and idea of mind seems air
Beside matter, yet, once formed concept, it
Is material nothing in dense spirit

Which gives each form a shape, until,
    "destroyed",
Its emptiness is filled with rock-like void.   40

II

In the porch a wasp buzzes. "Before she
Died she painted a cross out of that tree.
She was deeply religious, and *her* cross
Was to paint her true vision, to her loss,
Not seek fame in new fashions. She ignored
Them, the abstract art which obscured her
    bored
Her." She was confident besides "remote",
On a van Gogh exhibition she wrote:

"This genius – often in mental care –
Died poor, not recognised, and in despair,   50
Died almost without friends, like so many.
Today his nation build a gallery
To take the works of the van Gogh
    Foundation.
If he'd been happy in contemplation
And not quarrelled with family and friends,
He'd have improved his health and the
    world." *Her* ends.

His obscurity was her own. The plight
Of the unknown artist fills me with fright.
First the student work, then the struggle up
    hill.
Her husband did not want her to sit still.   60
"Be practical, you should be sewing," he'd
    say.
She hid her easle till he was away,
So when young, she "never had a moment".
He choked her till her energy seemed spent.

Yet after struggles, the development.
The boon of obscurity can prevent
All artists from being what others see,
Can help them to an originality.
Hence her symbols. But van Gogh left behind
Some works that bequeathed the Truth he had
    mined   70
Which were recognised for their silver lead.
Only her late ones gleam now she is dead.

III

Truth cannot be drawn from deep seams until
Roots have been driven through what chokes

the will.
"She always went to the chapel, then she
Went to see a Japanese cherry tree
In your grandfather's garden. Its blossom
Symbolised something: she was different
    from
Others, she stood for....Her word was an
    'acme'."
A perfection rooted in gleams, proud and
    free.   80

The cherry tree has gone from Daledene
Where my grandmother was snapped like a
    Queen.
The orchard was concreted in the war.
Tiny apple trees survive from before.
Now walk on the stone lawn where it all
    began.
Here regularly this obscure woman
Left the great difficulty of her Hill
Place. See, this withered apple tree looks ill.

This mining suffering, while artists drive
Roots deep into rock, brings their sap alive. 90
Its fruit will feed the next generation.
But if reaching depth is choked, suffocation
Enfeebles symbols, just as an apple tree
Whose fruit should be picked and eaten,
    sadly,
If concreted, bears shrivelled woody balls.
Yet when roots earth, wasps buzz round ripe
    windfalls.

17-18(?) April 1980

THE TREE OF IMAGINATION

I

Walk through these snowy courts to garden
    gates
Where Milton's ancient mulberry tree
    withstands,
Climb a staircase where a Professor waits
Among variant readings, and shake hands
And feel this balding scholar's warm vigour
And exactness. He has no pedestals.
In the Buttery there is a rigour
As he talks of the Metaphysicals.

He now helps keep the Tree of Tradition
That only precise understanding sees.   10

Its leaves have fed each true reputation
In the long line of rhymers' pedigrees.
The timeless whole appears from the outside
As different branches which have borne each
    name,
Yet each green difference that each Age has
    tried
Is an illusion: all leaves are the same.

To some keepers, each bough has been begun
For some poet to use, scholar to stir:
The branch of verbal wit sprang up for Donne
And his school, its ambiguous leaves were 20
Budded by linguistic philosophy,
Then Empson, and now this learned domed
    head
Which hatched me on veined puns, then
    offered me
The mystic branch of English verse instead.

Young poets feed on leaves of this mulberry
    Tree,
Amid blackberry-like images, and spin
One thousand-yard-long thread from what
    they see,
Cocoon a vision from the world, shut in –
Surround – beauty with work it leaves behind
When, three-day old moths, they lay eggs,
    starve and die.   30
True poets, like silkworms, gnaw truths and
    wind
Fine thread which others weave and sell, or
    buy.

He snicks out energies, he quotes tersely,
But he assumes that, as language is grown
By "social interaction" in a nursery,
Symbols have meaning where custom has
    blown
"Separate" forests into "sacred" trees,
As if the Tree of Life were banned, a trend
Set by unclean men and so taboo. Now freeze:
"For verbal atheists, death is the end."   40

II

The Tree of Tradition merely reflects
A more unseen one which hangs from the sky:
The Tree of Imagination projects
All things, and then reclaims them when they
    die.

336

Silkworms on Tradition's toothed leaves
sometimes see
Visions of each infused branch, trunk and root
And send their souls into this more real Tree
In the form of hawks which bring back
imaged fruit.

As four worlds channel sap and make seed
sprout,
Ideas pour from light through their meanings'
root   50
Into a formless matrix, and squeeze out
Each limb and branch, return to their source
as fruit.
Symbols express in language, ramify
Spiritual truths in their material green.
An inverted Tree with roots in the sky
Pours the invisible into what is seen

And ripens symbols of a layered One,
Manifesting the eternal; and blind-
-ly hangs images like oranges from a dark sun
That have not yet formed in nature or
mind,   60
Which can be reached and seized by a tranquil
Hawk-like soul which ascends up through
green leaves
And flies between two worlds with a
crammed bill,
Brings Ideas down to meanings sense
perceives.

As visualising can warm hands and feet,
Cure migraines and tensions, act on dense
mind;
As imaged light raises a body's heat
And sends photons to a crown that was blind;
So images burst round a poet's head,
Windfalls from a leafy beyond that heal   70
A sick society, which has been fed
Poisoned perspective, with a divine meal.

Four worlds touch in beauty, which
consciousness
Reflects. When a wind ripples the surface of
crowned
Wisdom, ruffles reflected upperness
To ground, imagination is earthbound,
Hawk sleeps in worm. Doubts prune
language, screening

Symbols are mere analogies that blend,
As if fruit just harmonised trees. Meaning
From upper worlds is lopped. Death is the
end.   80

III

Two Trees branch Idea into mental forms,
Are seen by poets who spin a cocoon,
Shut out the world's winds, interfering
storms,
Open crowns to a dark influx and moon.
One Tree is seen by daylit consciousness,
To closed crowns symbols are fancies that
please,
As if fruit decorated leafy dress
Like coloured globes hung on dark Christmas
trees.

Symbols, that are sown beyond, from within
Manifest into language, whose form fits,   90
And picture layered Reality, Yin-
Yang that hints at one in many small bits.
Ask "What Reality does it describe?"
And if "Only social" say "Ah!" and grin:
"Man lives in a universe, not a tribe
Whose eye imprisons like a body's skin."

Heaven opens to crown knowledge. Artists
Who hawk into its leaves know what was
known to Donne,
That a rising chain of being untwists
Worlds tangled in one moment; have
rewon   100
A metaphysic; and, when they disclose
The lost vision of golden fruit, thus catch
Truth, reroot the symbol, and must oppose
The world of silkworm-keepers whose puns
hatch.

Now dine with dons, and take the coffee
black
In a snoozy common room aglare with snow.
Whisper on silence, then trudge slowly back
To the staircase. Under Milton's window
The scholar's life is like a clock that stopped,
But warm judgement, precise stoic
despair   110
Keeps an actual Tree and so cannot opt
For the high symbols on a trunk of air.

22-31 December 1979, 26-27 April 1980

FIRETHORN

I

Creep down the crowded aisle on Christmas
    night.
Candles illuminate the timeless gloom.
A painted Christ under a crown of light
Channels a High Mass in a catacomb.
Arms raised, a flamen consecrates the host.
Entranced, he sings in an ethereal voice,
Now serves the power-filled dough. Like a
    ghost,
Kneel and take the wafer, then gulp a choice.

The protagonist is a symbol now
As if a sunshaft spotlit him with love   10
And divinised his wheat and wine somehow,
Or clouds of airy symbols high above
Showered into form and poured through the
    veil
Of spirits who congregate overhead
To enter all ghosts who kneel at the rail
And feel the oneness of living and dead.

Now pray to wisdom in unknowing cloud.
A dark hides flashing visions from the mind
Which ignite and burn thorns in the
    unploughed
Fields of the soul, then burst like hail, drum
    blind   20
Dreaming archetypes, split seeds and draw
    out
Bare consciousness to fertile gold like corn.
Energy pours so images can sprout.
Can God catch fire this night, be born of
    thorn?

This crown of thorns, this ancient shield in a
    blind
Dark soul, this prophet with a lice-filled
    beard,
Are from a clouded fire outside the mind
Where cipher messages are sent, like feared
Enigma codes from HQ to the field,
Which spirit-flames transmit to tuned-in
    eyes   30
To say, "You are Christ's soldier, be God's
    shield."
Now all file to the door and take mince-
    pies.

II

Now stand on the stage and look at the tree
Whose crossed axis joins four clouded
    worlds, down
Which fire descends to man's thorned agony.
Here beauty sees up knowledge to a crown
And son, looking through glass darkly, returns
To his father, when multiple thorns fall
Into one twined acacia crown, which burns
In fire that transmutes the beauty of all.   40

Worlds are related like an ordered choir.
Symbols beam oneness into fire-crowned eyes
For all forms cloud over one Idea, Fire,
As warm air makes droplets of moisture rise
And shower the one round a sunlit rainbow.
The Fire of God is the Idea that shines
Behind the many shapes symbolists show:
Aisled candles' glow, the torch down dark
    coal-mines.

Symbols are, create, form, and manifest
As many layered meanings as worlds are
    born.   50
Fire, spirit-flame, arch-light, candle to the
    West,
Fire-crowned hero with four faces, Firethorn,
Spark God to show all thorn-crowned men
    below
The fire *they* are; whose bliss, which burns
    their pain,
Needs thorns to crackle brows to a fiery glow.
Oh melt all clouds and reveal four worlds
    again.

31 December 1979, 3 May 1980

A TEMPLE-DANCER'S
TEMPLE-SLEEP

I

Now lie on a soft sofa and go slack
While a balding hypnotist counts down ten
Tower steps to a Thames trance, temple-sleep
    back
To past lives, bid the Traitors' Gate open
To floating images, a rising tide.
Clear pictures lap. Look at what someone
    knew.
Each has the details of a colour slide.
Now gaze at a huge gold, bearded statue.

Observe it, recognise it, and then say
"It's Ramesses the Second as Sun-god."   10
Place temple garlands there again each day,
Wear a white robe, right shoulder bare, and
          odd
Sandals with one twined thong by each big
          toe,
And have black hair done up in pins. Now see
A bearded man stripped to the waist, and
          know
Thirteen hundred BC on live TV.

He cures blindness, teaches the occult arts
To ten maidens who make the Nile flood,
Temple-dancers who also read the charts
And turn a desert into fields of mud.   20
Now all are gathered for the young Ramesses
Comes to take a "Chosen One" by her hand,
Love her as Sun-god, sow her with increase
So ripe harvests sway on fertilised land.

See him in his high sparkling gold head-dress
And shining gold armour, thronged by his
          peers.
He comes to the temple-dancers. Oh yes,
He will stop here, and oh, now feel the tears
Roll down hot cheeks as he touches his heart
To make me Egypt to transform the land,   30
A staggering honour. I, set apart,
Am a shining goddess on temple sand.

II

In Cairo Museum can be seen through glass
The shrivelled hook-nosed mummy and baked
          skin
Of Pharaoh Ramesses, his gold now my brass-
Brown ex-boy friend's corpse, matted hair,
          cracked chin.
Did temple-sleep know him, or just a dream,
Archetype, hidden memory, flotsam wapped
Up on rising unconsciousness, a gleam
Of a discarnate spirit's fin, a chopped   40

Fish-head which a medium sees in froth?
Now a Jesuit priest near New Brunswick,
Breath coming in small pants, lips dry as
          cloth,
Like an ebbing sea on shingle, be sick
In a log-cabin, and drift. What relief
To float to the rafters with a new-found

Lightness, look down on the corpse, see the
          grief
As friends lean on long axes by a mound.

See, floating above trees; men saw a log,
Be conscious and approach this large camp-
          fire,   50
Read the tombstone, then pass into a fog
And lose all fear of death: all just retire,
Wake from life, strew débris from a wrecked
          brain.
Now my soul is sure my spirit is aeons old,
That it has lived before, will come again
And salvage cargo from an ancient hold.

And if, after each death, it is soon rebor-
-n, a few years later, and lives as if between
          blinds
Three times a century, or more in times of
          war,
Then one being like a golden thread
          unwinds   60
Through many existences' forms, and may
          depart
A worn-out body for a baby's chromosomes,
Clear of last time's defeats, with a fresh start,
And renew what houses spirit like a change of
          homes!

What an exquisite idea, this endless,
Unbroken life of the spirit in many
Bodies! And what an exquisite design! Say
          yes
As beings dip in the quantum vacuum sea
To secrete in Void and know they are coral!
Endless recycling of soul, like particles
          where   70
Nothing is wasted or lost, just perpetual
Renewal as souls grow new flesh and return
          to air!

III

Near the far source pan memories like suns,
Wash gravel-bearing gold. Temple-dancers,
Who mirrored the Sun-god through Shining
          Ones,
Light-reflecting angels, obtained answers
When they raised up their souls and flew like
          hawks
To sacred high worlds, and brought back in

trance
Bits of divine symbol like bitten stalks,
And flashed them out through their eternal
    dance.   80

Now soul-dancers open their crowns in trance
So rarefied symbols form lower frost
Whose truth reminds of beauty's past
    advance
When shining, gold souls once knew truths
    now lost.
Far memories are symbols, arche-drives,
Unconscious light-echoes pressed into form
From spirits who have lived and from past
    lives,
Like angel-wings washed up after a storm.

These images from past lives are divine
Reminders of past greatness souls have
    known,   90
Driftwood in tides of pouring air, a sign
Of old dangers to warn all the windblown.
Each fragment from a temple or priest's
    débris
Says to the soul, "Recall where others went."
Lone mariners can cross a rocky sea
By hulls of past wrecks, past yet still present.

There is no time in infinite ocean:
Dynamic, causeless present, which preserves
Images, is seen in timeless vision,
Not when distorted to time and space-
    curves   100
Sink to still limbec's theta before sleep
And symbols wash in, child-clear, mix with
    genes,
Thousands of years old yet *present* in deep
Waking vision, where no space intervenes.

Souls come from an ocean of nothingness
And crawl up on the river shores of time,
To be transformed in sleep. The waters press,
Wap symbols to remind of a lost prime,
And this vast light that floods these steps in
    vain
To be shut out by this closed Traitors'
    Gate   110
Bobs old waking truths it can give again
If traitors will admit its tides, and wait!

26-27 January and 3 May 1980

A METAPHYSICAL'S LIGHT-MANDALA

I

In Katmandu a Tibetan unrolled
Some old sackcloth in a barn deep with straw
And showed me a mandala in pale spun gold
Which he had stolen to help fund a war,
On which the Chinese had sloshed paint; then
    weighed
Ten dollars against a gun, and walked back
Over the Himalayas, leaving, frayed,
A four hundred year old stupa on sack,

A tumulus to be told each sunrise.
Now face this landing hanging and start at   10
The East (which is the South) and move
    clockwise
In the mind round each wide open gate that
Enshrines relics of a flesh-and-blood saint.
Sunrise, zenith, sunset, nadir, all show
His birth and enlightenment in gold paint,
Proclamation and freedom here below.

The aim of a mandala is to free
The Divine Light from veils within the soul.
And so, looking at the central sun, three
Circles protecting one bright aureole   20
Or "diamond body", now contemplate and
    gaze
At mysterious fire in a dark sea, and be
Consumed by a metaphysical blaze,
A radiance that is known, Eternity.

Look at a veil that opens into light,
A model of the universe, one mind.
Go through the hole in the centre, be bright-
-ness on sparkling sea, sail on from Time, find
Blinding, dazzling glory, whirling stars; climb
The mast, see the wheel round the hub of each
    pole   30
Which rotates chakras in a blaze of Time
From this brilliant sanctum, through the
    mind's hole.

A gold celestial sun shines in the soul
Of martyr, virgin, doctor, and burns Time –
The world, the flesh and Devil – through this
    splodged scroll
Which veils a voyage through all worldly

grime.
It is a chart of vast oceans of air,
And all discoverers must set sail and be
Lone yachtsmen on a night sea-crossing
    where
The mind of God boils round them like a dark
    sea.   40

II

Sitting in dark, hands over eyes, now start.
Screw up eyelids and reach into the storm,
A current up the spine quickens the heart,
Slowly through the darkness gathers a form.
Like a look-out in a crow's nest, now wait.
Slowly clouds move, it seems dawn has won,
And on calming troughs around break the
    great
Dancing shivers of a cold midnight sun.

Like a moonlit rose the sky opens, curled
And petalled, and the night is filled with
    folds.   50
Like a masthead fire lit from a high world
It licks and flames with static silver-golds.
The dark pulses with a daemonic throb
That seems now watery light, now flower,
    now fire
To the eye of the soul, but is a blob
Of power from a fiery God's hot desire.

Four rushes tingle up the spine and stain
The rippling waters of the tranquil deep:
A flower-fire in wet womb like milky grain.
Now skin cooled to shot silk, all limbs
    asleep,   60
All soul, know that surges of spirit flow
From the Holy Spirit, flush flesh with light,
Setting it, like St. Elmo's Fire, aglow.
Be a candle lit from a throbbing night.

All who have asked for help near one in pain
And felt four surges up their trembling spine
Pass from hot fingers that grow cold again,
And seen their wired-up patient slowly shine
With new vigour which fills each damaged
    cell,
And a red-light Christmas-tree pattern
    steal   70
Across two mind-mirrors, all such know well
That currents from loving spirits can heal.

III

Mystics, healers, poets channel from night
Unconscious dark symbols that manifest,
Images that shiver up spine, soul-light
That heals with love, Holy Spirit's hot zest.
The Ways of Buddha and Light of the World,
The slit-eyed calm and halo, are the same.
All can discard this chart once power has
    swirled,
It is a symbol that recalls cold flame.   80

The universe is one eddying power,
The air is filled with manifesting waves.
Spiritual silver forms like dew this hour,
Condensed vapour for which new vision
    craves.
Gone are the five senses and reason's doubt
And the body, those "absolute" toadstools.
A new science has blown the old age out.
One twirling whorl of spiralling whirlpools

Dances through all loving inflowing tides,
Thinks through all, animates and mouths out
    breath,   90
Heaves lungs like a sea-swell till it decides
To decompose to white fire, whirl through
    death.
Aquarian Siva, body is soul
Like sponge filled with vast tides, and mind is
    night,
Matter spirit, when rose-fire-moon-seas roll
Through beauty their metaphysic of light.

29 January and 4 May 1980

THE FIRE-FLOWER

I

London art-teacher asks, "Have you a
    Japanese
Male fan I can paint?" There is a use for
Dusty folded paper in struts, so ease
Open: a mesh of linked atoms, which thaw
Into white swirled lines and puffs that are now
Hills and floating clouds, now waves and
    foamed spray,
Now fire and licking flames: one flowing Tao
Which swirls behind matter's melting decay!

A shock of joy thrills: this trinket in my hand
Shows the stone garden where deep men

admire   10
Sand-like stones and rocks, now earth or
          clouds and
Mountains, now sea and rocks, now ash and
          fire
In limitlessness bordered by the known.
Watch monks rake still pebbles into a swirl
And know all existence is one stuff, "stone",
Whose atoms run like ice into a whirl.

Then see pebbles as a soul in stillness,
A thought ripple like a dropped rock and
          distort
Reality with swirls of bitterness.
See hundreds of hard egos turn from
          thought   20
Particles to unconscious waves: each flows.
Then see all men, one brotherhood, reclaim
Their nature in inter-connected rows,
Each imperishable, each one the same.

Now turn the fan. Where chains mesh on one
          side
The other side is a vortex of swirls.
Turn swirls, prison bars have solidified.
Day and night, life and death are two fan
          twirls,
Plus A plus minus A equals zero,
The hole in the middle of sculptured stone. 30
Push-pull two bones, see the implicate show.
Close it, atoms disintegrate to bone.

                    II
This fan hides all expression on a face.
Half-vision, half-memory, see a Noh
Dancer, long-haired, wood-masked, bow with
          slow grace,
Stretch wide his arms whose sleeves hang
          square below,
While the kneeling chorus flutes, plays drums
          and chants;
Then peer from far, speaking through limbs
          that sway;
And gravely twirl a stately temple dance.
Restraint hints soul, the Flower peeps through
          "her" play.   40

"Her" movement is stilled, speech pauses, ma
          heaves
As in gardens, space and silence surround

Tiled roof, cherry blossom or falling leaves,
And make from something's nothing – void,
          no sound –
Harmony like emptied soul, or wind's echo,
Where stone torch-baskets shine and hint the
          bloom
Of a Reality in hearts aglow
That Zen monks sighing "Aaaaaaah" know in
          their gloom.

All mind's expressions are mesh on a fan,
The masked body's patterns suggest the
          swirl.   50
Dervish eyes, empty of all thought, see an
Eternity in which all bodies whirl,
Hint secret likeness through the heart, and
          seek
Hidden beauty and unexpected joy,
The Flower which a white bird bears in its
          beak
Into clouds, and out-truths what frowns
          destroy

And all mere appearance. As woman speaks
Through swinging hips, a masked dancer with
          eyes
That see no death, no realistic shrieks,
Chimes pure *yugen* as a shrine bell defies   60
Yet tinkles news with tongue of unseen
          breeze,
And gives body to what lies outside sense,
Images truth which "her" inner eye sees,
But is not glimpsed by unmasked intellect.

Chinese court-dancers advance from flame
          shields,
Make stiff, slow patterns to shrill reeds. Like
          coals
Their hearts catch fire with Tao-light as each
          yields.
Egyptian temple-dancers become souls
Lit from the unseen Sun-god for an hour.
With twirling fan Noh dancer becomes Tao. 70
And swirls to stately form an unseen power.
The Flower ephiphanises whirled light now.

The body thinks when mind slumbers to light
Behind the fan of a pine-wooded Zen
Temple's meditation-hall. Chanting night
Falls still, head-shaven youths rise, speak, are

beaten.
Who is silent escapes the master's stick,
Body becomes as rock behind dumb words.
The mind bars light with abstraction. Be
    quick:
Dawn shadows rise and swirl cicadas,
    birds.   80

III
Morning. Now sit in a huge school and write
Absent staff's classes on the cold day's list:
Social penance like a crossword. Dull sight
Scans a system's boxes. Chained by the wrist,
Now poring over a chessboard checkmate,
Push-pull the fan on the drab desk, idly,
And turn frozen organisation, fate,
To the fire-swirl and will of Reality,

And this bare room thaws into sea-washed
    rock,
The timetable melts like a glacier's snows, 90
Eternity flows through the admin block,
Sweeps it away, an iceberg in ice-floes,
And a man becomes an implicate flower, a
    mind
Empty and full, as dancers open their
Petals to clouds and waves of Tao, mask-blind
That they will soon join it as atomed air.

Molecular chains swirl down a black hole.
Behind shut eyes, light runs like mountain
    streams,
Licks fire, wisps cloud, sprays wave or
    flower's white bowl,
Forms and takes all: flesh is dense fire from
    dreams.   100
Like a fan dropped from the veiled smile of
    Tao
Glimpse fullness and void like the petalled
    curl
Soul sees. The Fire-Flower holds still, now
    womb-void, now
Where barred mind flows into great cosmic
    swirl:

A flower of light that licks, a void of fire,
Tumbling into itself, sucking all trace
Of scatterings round lips in its desire,
Like a black hole of light outside all space,
A void which swallows all, eternal Tao

Which in reverse drips stars and threads of
    all   110
Forms and thrusts from its womb (like white
    hole now)
A full universe like a child in caul

In which full soul, too, is a small fire-flower:
When void splits "I" and stem shoots empty
    soul,
Void-light flows into roots (the heart), its
    power
Flows up the calm centre to petalled bowl
Which glows white-gold fullness, unfolds to
    sun,
Waves in the wind of spirit, overjoyed
To be raised from nothing where all is one –
Aaaaaaaaaaaaaah! Fire-flower of full soul
        which is vast void!   120
           9-11 February, April and 5 May 1980

BEAUTY AND ANGELHOOD

(AND THEIR ORIGIN IN THE FOURTH WORLD)

1981

1. HIGH LEIGH

Drive down the long drive to the ivied tower
Where the grand House stands, walk its maze-
　　like lawn
With low wall, fields and trees, and warbling
　　birds.
Here in the last war, Unesco was born.
But now it knows the bareness in the heart
For it reveals, like an old mystery school,
The "esoteric Christ" of hidden fire.
Will we find what we're shown, in a new
　　Rule?

He holds the lectern, smooths dishevelled
　　hair,
A Canon with charisma and fired sight:　10
"Don't teach the dead old forms, the
　　skeleton –
Dogma or doctrine – but flesh and blood,
　　Light
Augustine, John of the Cross, Teresa knew,
Christ." "Body without backbone," some
　　growl, "wrong,"
But a rock-hard heart serves a corpse. Now
　　thrill to hear
What we have known and waited for so
　　long:

"The blowing from the spirit makes new
　　forms
And shapes hard hearts in Christ-tide every
　　day.
All mystics meditate on rocky mounts,
You should tread *your country's* Mystic
　　Causeway.　20
Let Indians be Hindu, your spark's Christian.
Churches should *be* the sea-washed Mount
　　they preach."
Now walk the maze with him, catch fire and
　　blaze,
Hear his urgent 'Follow me': "Come and
　　teach."

He founded a sea-lapped Order that lives
The mystic stillness, peace and Light, quiet
　　zest,
Has two retreats and hears tomorrow's call.
And all who went out East to bring the West
A contemplative rose which Europe needs,
From fire his Mass calls down, such men
　　must know　30
New heat stirs in Church veins to renew soul,
As women wail to harps so souls can grow.

Here Beauty can be found, down these green
　　lanes.
By this gate where sheep graze, be a skin-
　　bowl.
As Lovers close eyes to open, here pause.
Get to know Beauty like a hidden soul.
Will there be entry to Beauty tonight?
Not while the thunder growls, winds howl and
　　blow
Till rain hisses and explodes from puddles,
Not while light speaks from the sky to say
　　No.　40

Morning. Eucharist, or "thank you". A priest
Fumbles at candles, which he cannot light,
Slops wine, shuffles, prepares squares of
　　brown bread,
Prays words without feeling. Now rise and
　　fight
To kneel at the rail, take "Spirit-bearing
　　food",
Feed your spirit with the bread of life, be
　　host.
He who calls fire to Mass has gone, but think:
This rosé is like blood for a tombed ghost.

Now in the library let the body
Be a Grail-bowl for Light through the priest's
　　Lord's Prayer.　50
All cup hands, quiet, rise as the white fire
　　glows,

344

Breathe down to throat this Light, breathe out
    dark air.
Thy will be done – let it come down to the
    heart,
Let it shape the heart into a Golden Rose.
Say "Come in God, come in" as flesh tingles,
Scalp prickles, hair stands up and tired skin
    glows.

White power surges through legs and burns
    darkness,
Volts probe each limb. Breathe in Light,
    breathe out love.
Draw Light as "daily bread" into the stomach,
Draw cleansing Light down into the groin,
    above   60
The red-hot rod which trespasses, cup hands
To the heart, draw power up to lips from
    earthed spine.
From the forehead raise it up, offer it back,
This circulating Light that makes skin
    shine.

Here Beauty can be found like a bare heart.
Sneak to her secret place from a hermit's
    room,
Lie down and love her lowered eyes, white
    fire,
Be a veined rock in the tides of her womb.
As Mount's Bay fishermen raise a crab-pot
From Tristan's Lyonesse where coral
    blows   70
And thrill as drowned spires toll out hermits'
    prayers,
Beauty, I found you like a desert rose.

Desert. In a desert of council flats,
In a bare room sits a veined Rose in prayer
Whose Catholic hermit's power shakes
    Cambridge spires,
Whose beads turn judges pale, whose eye is
    air.
Evening. Leaving High Leigh is a going-
    down
Back to the world, but we have shaped the
    start.
The high places are gone, but we have known
Where hermits find the bareness in the
    heart.   80

May and 31 July 1981

2. HAWKWOOD

Sunshine in the Cotswolds. Drive up
    hedgerows
To the grey facade of a country hall,
Fields, iron railings, cows, horses, daisies.
Unpack above the old monastic wall
Where black monks still surprise old
    gardeners,
Then stroll among tall trees and quietly pass
Other silent walkers, listen for hawks,
Like a Romantic fed on leaves and grass.

The Kabbalah's sky-rooted chestnut shows
Beauty, the sun-like nut of all, descends   10
From germ down trunk and branch to bud-like
    Forms,
Manifests in the lake where downflow ends,
Blossoms into all beautiful things. Light,
Seen from hermit's eye, ramifies and teems
Unconscious images among green leaves
Which mystics tell, like candles, from day-
    dreams.

Now sit near a reflected Tree of Life.
The goat-bearded Teacher in a sweater finds
Linked branches of triads and sephirot,
Grows Neshamah, then Ruah in our minds. 20
"Feel power flow round our enclosing circle."
Churn it on round like wheels of water-mills.
Though we are solid, we are like water
When our psyches convert to power that stills.

"Mirror images from the leafy world."
On watery mosaic, peacock and lyre
With hopscotch maze ascend a Tree of Life
To a large head of Christ and Crown of fire,
A Roman Jesus on a bathhouse floor
Near the sea, under olive trees. An ark   30
Hangs in a dark cloud while flames burn all
    round:
Merkava chariot in fiery dark.

"See Angels." They approach with veil-like
    flames,
Blowing like net curtains, visions that tease,
White brightness nothings where faces should
    be,
Five heavenly hosts fluttering in a breeze.
Then a large ring of celestial beings
With a dark centre, flame-like folds of veils,

345

And that black-hooded monk, no face at all –
Can Lucifer stay masked in such wild gales? 40

Lunch, then across green Cotswolds to
    Prinknash
Where, in an Abbot's house in a Tudor style,
Young Henry on wall, lodged on their return
The Benedictine monks of Caldey Isle.
Here is the Canon's quiet, but the Abbey,
Car park and tourist shop – such ugly
    "charm"!
Is Christendom so enfeebled, the line
From Augustine to Eliot a bird farm?

Then back to "Inner teacher as high priest".
I hear my Angel say, "You have your task, 50
Get on and do it, restore the Mystic
Tradition within Christendom. Don't ask
Me any more. Bless you my son." And now
I know why I was shown the Prinknash mint
Where wordly monks have sought and lost
    Beauty
Too near coach park and shop – and need a
    hint.

When Goatbeard says "See this", images rise
In magic water, caught by magic art –
"As if a trawler's radar found a shoal
And filled its nets before anglers can start." 60
But poets hook visions from a deep dream,
How shallow is this small lake's *fishy* haul!
Did I see Angels or mere images,
Day-dreams or fantasies, not Ruah's trawl?

Though Tree helps understanding, I renounce
All reflections in waters as rungs up
To Tree-crown heights of all who saw Beauty
Not once but many times in a spiked nut-cup.
I will not have this magic round my will
For I have heard the Roche-rock mystic
    say   70
"Not 'my will' but 'thy will' is the iron
Ladder to the eyrie of the Mystic Way."

Now, raised from Neshamah to Ruah, sit.
As down four levels of a waterfall
See bright Fire foam and flicker and then lick
To rose, now golden flower, now a veil, all
Patterned, now turn to nut-heights of spirit.
An Angel in a cloud looks down, hawk's face.

High in this Tree-rock hermit's cell, above
Michael's chapel, know it is you and grace! 80

June and 1 August 1981

3. KENT HOUSE

The Canon in retreat. Walk past green fields,
Go past a wooded pond to a tree board,
Then turn off up to where the old ruin
Of an Edwardian House has been restored.
A tree grew through this floor and this ceiling.
But now, in this long room of easy chairs,
Sits a Community, and on the throne
Its Ionan Master of silent prayers.

"You can go on courses," he says, "and grow
Psychic 'shoots' in head – third eyes,
    clairvoyance –   10
Yet be choked in the heart, whose opened eye
Knows fiery Light of Spirit in one glance,
Airs pistil-ripe thought free from closed ideas
And the weed-maze of books that stifles
    brains.
Be still. Only the pure in heart see God.
Sun-warmed heart contemplates, closed head
    explains."

He talks like Zen Masters of head and heart,
Berates ideas and thought-patterns, scorns
    books,
Then puts us all in silence for a day
So we know how the hermit's spirit looks. 20
He reads Sufi tales instead of *koans*,
And urges us to weed the flower-bed.
Windesheim, Port Royal, Little Gidding –
I eat a lunch as silent as the dead.

The woods have bushes that obscure clear
    sight,
Thickets that snare the pilgrim from the corn,
Hide the deeper life from the noisy Way:
This murky pond whose still reflects each
    thorn.
As pond in woods is heart found within head.
Sink down to where "I am" beneath all
    mind,   30
The still place of the spirit from past lives
Beneath all words and wants of loud mankind.

Great mystics mined their hearts like Cornish
    tin –

Engine-house, stack, then long Dark Night of
  Sense
Emptying rock of earthly images,
Shaft sunk to a deep level of silence
Where lamplit spirit finds veined Truth like
  ore –
Yet were still one with fiery divine air.
Now the West's heart is like ruined East
  Wheal Rose:
A deep shaft filled with water and despair. 40

Beneath the slime of this foul pond, "I am"
More than my body, emotions or thought,
And, poised in stillness like a water-gnat,
Beyond cloud of delusion this life brought,
Mirror a past meaning in detachment,
And wonder if this muck can be pumped dry
So the West lets go everything "out there"
And lets warm sun shine on shaft mud, not
  sky.

In Michael's chapel, mystic life in deed!
"Deep in your freest recesses, see Light." 50
As sunlight probes the depths of Forest pools
A watery Beauty breaks our caddice sight.
Blind as Master brings spirit bread and blood,
Swallow and gulp, Beauty above heart's eye,
Ezekiel's fire. We revere flight in all,
But are these young grubs really dragonfly?

Mystic hatching to Light takes twenty years
And unpaid lads, "poor monks", are mere
  larvae.
"The New Age mystic life, unlike the Old,
Has evolved, comes unsought," is his
  reply, 60
"Has welled up in lay people, not élites
Whose books distract – I can tear up my
  book.
We do not need blueprints from past mystics:
Let spirit pour, don't feel 'Still years to
  look'."

He floods out past effort like a Red Guard.
Dogma, doctrine, now differences are
  drowned.
But I pump out, re-work, re-form, restore
The West's deep-mined tradition, and have
  found
Spirits, like mines, are not equally aired,

Doubt if his new wells have a Western
  role. 70
Can New Age dogma or can Kent House learn
From their Angel and cleanse the Western
  soul?

Can bread and wine and Beauty transform all?
Will this House's yearning reform the Church
So all altars, like candles, burn one Light?
Will lay folk sink church shafts for hermits'
  search?
Can this man with St. Benedict's vision
Mine Europe to meaning? Lost in thickets,
Our dark Age crouches like a frightened child.
Look west to a flooded shaft where Beauty
  sets! 80

June and 2 August 1981

4. ST. PETER'S CONVENT

The country showdown. Turn at the gate, go
Through pines to the secluded convent where,
In front of Gothic porch and tower with cross,
A dozen old men sit and take the air.
This is a convalescent home now, run
By twenty-six old nuns and divine grace.
St. Peter stands outside the chapel door
And looks in vain for girls to take their place.

Nuns excavate souls like a Mithraeum,
Then flame to Beauty, which sparks each
  Angel, 10
Spirits dug out like caves whose lamps hold
  fire.
Join dark flames for their Office at the bell.
As veiled, wrinkled hermits genuflect, see
Bare legs and buckle clogs from a lost age.
Spirits made flames who see One Fire, they are
Like the flame in sanctuary's blue lamp-cage

Or candles in Smeaton's wave-pounded tower
Whose granite tree turned cross with two-
  flamed beam.
Saturday Feria includes three psalms.
Singing quiet prayers for all near death, they
  seem 20
Dark Angels for the dying and blue light.
They file past us, their hands inside black
  sleeves.
We eat lunch in an enclosed garden, meet
The lady in whose scheme Peter believes,

Our agenda: a spiral for Kent House
(Correspondence courses, training weekends),
A "dance of consciousness" that may Paul-
    Jones
Beauty through Burrswood so her heartburn
    ends
A wallflower. Does God want *this* "new
    form" linked
To churches, does the Canon, who repeats 30
"I want Communities throughout England,"
Appeals to lay masses, and scorns élites?

My dream is of a movement in the Church,
Of masses shown the Mystic Flame *in pews*,
Not "New Age" communes outside "old"
    churches,
A Steiner cult, dying out of the news.
The West is in crisis, the young cry out
For churches to beam out a waveswept Light,
But, lost in dark, are rocked on Eastern sects.
What other Luther, Wesley, is in sight?   40

The meeting has begun, I must speak out.
The Eastern menace lowers like a storm cloud
And darkens all Christendom, which unites.
Let Europe blaze against the night, be proud!
The West longs for great mystics' quartz to
    strike
Steel-ruled spirits to sparks, so, kindling, all
See the world as One Fire, Beauty's blue
    Flame.
Christendom yearns, oh will you fail her call?

The Light has moved my tongue, I am at
    peace.
But who can see that far, the Dark Age
    pour?   50
The Light has moved me, but they cannot see
Revolutions destroy, reforms restore.
Remysticised Christendom? He replies,
"We must go on from here, not think of goals,
Take our pace and direction from the ground.
We are not ready for great mystics' souls."

And now I stand under the tower outside.
A dream has turned as sour as old men's love.
They wait in their wheelchairs to be taken
By veiled Angels back to their wards
    above.   60
Sour, sour as I watch Angels terrify.

Lovers, Teachers, Masters and Angels care
For body, mind, spirit or divine spark.
Angels care for all four while breathing air.

Angels have veiled heart, soul, spirit and
    flame
In this life or past lives, from earthly damp.
Angelhood is earned like a peerage for
Spirits flamed Grail-gold in Beauty's blue
    lamp.
God renews Church through Angels veiled
    outside.
Nuns see One Fire, give flames to souls in
    dark,   70
He serves new forms, I the old Mystic Way.
Old Church receives new life, old fire new
    spark.

Accept. Like nuns he shows "cripples" the
    Light –
Invalids in wheelchairs – and does not ask
Why Michael spears the Dragon in Mount's
    Bay.
Farewell, silent Angel, I have my task.
I will build words like Smeaton's Tree-
    stepped tower
So all can know what lights a hermit's night.
Sadly I leave. A dream caught fire and blazed.
Now blown embers glow blue, Angels' blue
    light!   80

21-22 July and 2-3 August 1981

THE WIND AND THE EARTH

1981

1. REDDENING LEAVES

The October leaves have reddened better this
year.
You felt unwell as if you had a cold,
As you felt before your last heart attack here.
An evening turn. Gasping for breath, pale,
bold,
You sit on a chair, dial, say as if giving birth
"Can you come now," then sit and wait
patiently,
Your chest tightening with a weight like earth.
I see my brother lie you on the settee,
An Asian locum comes and prescribes rest
And I want to say "Don't you know she might
be dead?"
Next morning your doctor's face tells she has
guessed
As she rings a hospital which has a bed.
The call came to leave this life and these eaves
With all the beauty of reddening leaves.

Autumn 1981, revised 1 November l993

2. ROSY CHEEKS, BLURRED EYES

O sad as I drive through glass and stone
To the hospital where your body lies
Propped up in "Resus", and find you
Somewhere behind red cheeks, blurred eyes.

O sad is the doctor with the moustache,
Loudly you say "This is my son."
And I shake hands with a stranger
And sit and wait while your X-ray is done.

O sad as I ask my "friend", "How long?"
And he says "A heart attack, two weeks";
O sad as you return with hope,
I see the dark round your rosy cheeks.

Sad as you dictate how I must ring
Violin pupils, bring files that are red.
When three doctors come, I kiss you,
Not knowing you are on your deathbed.

Autumn 1981, revised 1 November 1993

3. NOTHING SAID

The dying have a right to know they are dead,
Yet here we sit around you, and do not say.
You suspect and you know, but nothing is
said.
We skirt round the taboo, cling to the day.
Yet if it were me, I would want to know,
As a Christian, you must want to compose
your soul.
You know and say nothing, and choose to go
With a fearless look back into the dark, the
Whole.
For you things were important, an event,
Something to talk about and tell a friend,
And yet things passed by without comment.
Now you give significance to your end.
Small things crowd in on my mind late at
night,
How you gave meaning by ignoring fright.

Autumn 1981, revised 14 November 1993

4. AFRICAN VIOLET

How ignorant are we mortals, and how blind
Under a lightning bolt about to fall;
Providence aims a blow at its victim's mind
And we go about as if things were normal.
I drive to your house, then go to my bank
While you sit in your hospital window and
receive
My wife, our two boys and my aunt, and
thank
Them for giving up the time. When they leave
They give you my African violet, and say
"By the time you leave hospital it will be
out."
You talk to my wife in your interested way,
And I walk past woods, quite ignorant about
What God, who has chosen you to do his will,
Now feels your next task should be,
redeploying your skill.

Autumn 1981, revised 28 October 1993

5. TURNIP LANTERNS

This sunny day is an ordinary day. You

Seem well, sitting in the window, out of bed,
Writing letters, looking at the great view,
Not realising you will soon be dead;
And I knowing my sister will have been
And posted your letters, drive to the sparkling
    sea.
And return at nightfall, on Hallowe'en.
My boys light turnip-face lanterns with glee
And carry them down the road. Two Indians
    stare,
Park outside and ask me to help them change
    a wheel.
I stand with them on an ordinary day and hear
The telephone ring and the hospital sister
    appeal,
"You'd better come. There has been
    irreversible damage."
A turnip grins like a demon in a cage.

Autumn 1981, revised 28 October 1993

6. CHILL FINGERS

A sobbing in my heart as I drive through the
    night.
Will you wait for me, will you still be there?
    Further east
Dark roads and streetlamps hurtle through my
    sight.
"Her lungs have filled with water, kidneys
    ceased."
A thousand memories well up in tears.
"Her heart's worn out like a run-down clock."
    I am stone.
I tiptoe down the corridor of the years,
And there you lie, eyes closed, in a room of
    your own,
Oxygen mask on, wired up to a drip, I am
    awed.
"She surfaced ten minutes ago. She's being
    brave."
I sit and take her hand strapped to a board
As if I could warm her back from the grave.
Her heart-rate zigzags on the screen, in my
    hold
Her fingers have the chill of an early cold.

Autumn 1981, revised 28 October 1993

7. A SHAKEN HEAD

Out of a sleep as deep as any grave
You raise your head and the board at your
    wrist and frown,

And in slow motion as if under water, wave
To tear off your oxygen mask and drown.
I press down her arm, steady her pulse so we
    be,
Keep watch till the next distress and nurse's
    call.
With laboured breathing, her chest heaves like
    the sea,
Each breath echoes like a distant baby's waul
She opens her eyes "It's me," I say. She
    smiles.
"Is there anything I can do?" She shakes her
    head
Slowly, three times, as if to say "I am miles
Beyond help", and boxes the air, wanting to
    be dead,
To tear off her oxygen with a limp fist,
Wishing we'd let her sink into the mist.

Autumn 1981, revised 28 October 1993

8. MOANING WIND

Midnight, all dark and quiet in the hospital
    room.
I sit and hold her pulse. She whimpers and
    sighs.
I strain to listen. "Hot," she whispers from
    gloom.
I feel her frozen hand and arm, then rise.
And go to the window: the lights of Essex, the
    free.
I slide the double glazing like a veil.
The wind moans like Hallowe'en spirits flee-
-ing before All Hallows souls, rises to a wail,
Then drops. I sit and she gasps "So tired" and
    pants,
And as the eerie moaning rises and falls
And she throws up a hand and it flops with
    insouciance,
As something tender sinks, oblivion appals
And I wonder what is life, what death? What
    made
A mother of this near-lifeless corpse, to fade?

Autumn 1981, revised 28 October 1993

9. LOST LIGHT

The room is stiller than a half-lit tomb.
The only stir is her heaving chest, her end;
Her head sideways, as if nearly gone in the
    gloom.
Now I must go, my shift finished. I attend

To her covers and comfort. I rise and stoop
And kiss her cold forehead, then quietly
    leave.
I look back, spy through the glass door at the
    droop
Of her water-filled body. Her full lungs
    heave.
My last glimpse of her alive on her death-bed.
And where is the transparent body within her
    skin?
I open for the Light but see instead
Matter breaking up, the stark flesh caving in.
I steal away into a dark, dark night,
Drained, numb as if a part of me had lost the
    light.

Autumn 1981, revised 28 October 1993

10. CRACK IN THE EARTH

The room is calm, her breath is still, she
    knows.
All quiet save for the hissing of oxygen.
Nurse listens with her stethoscope, then goes.
Windows are closed, we whisper on quiet
    again.
Across her we brothers recall seaside
    holidays,
Inviting her to listen and share, but not to
    speak.
And now "Oh dear" she moans and as I gaze
Two nurses sit her up and feel her cheek,
Puff up her pillows, change her water-bag,
Remake her bed, say "Would you like a
    drink?"
Standing at the end of the bed my hand like a
    gag,
As she sips water I can see as I blink
The crack in the earth through which I
    crawled, to cry.
O why do we live in order to die?

Autumn 1981, revised 23 August 1993

11. HEART LIKE A STOPPED CLOCK

A fitful sleep, the phone goes by my bed:
"Mother went just after seven" – like a sting;
A numbness chills my heart. "She woke and
    said,
'Pills' or 'white powder', and once just
    'tired'." I ring
And hear, "I went down the corridor for a

drink;
The student was fiddling, when I came back
    in,
With the oxygen mask. She said, 'I think
You'd better get the staff nurse.' I went.
    Within
Two minutes she'd gone. She was too tired to
    fight.
Her heart couldn't stand any more, somehow
It stopped like a clock, she went out like a
    light."
Again I sit and stare. Where are you now?
Are you in the air? Blank exhaustion, and
    faint
Relief. All Saints Day, God has a new saint.

Autumn 1981, revised 31 October 1993

12. A FLICKERING CANDLE

A room with two candles, an altar – and you
Lying in your coffin, a veil over your white
    face.
I stoop and reluctantly force myself to kiss
    your too
Cold brow, eyes closed, mouth tight, slight
    frown at space
Over hooked nose, but at peace; white cheeks,
    white hair.
The blue satin stirs – can it be your breath?
I whisper "It's me, you are dead though in the
    air,
O God please guide your latest angel through
    death."
As if answering one candleflame flickered
    and split.
Was it a wind from the high up window-cage
Which did not flutter the candle nearer it?
Or your spirit rushing out to its next stage,
Having realised you were dead? How sad as I
Kiss your cold forehead through the veil
    goodbye.

Autumn 1981, revised 31 October 1993

13. LAMB AND ROSÉ

I sit numbly at lunch, recalling you in
Your veil and your chill forehead and closed
    eyes,
Your frilly shroud in your satiny coffin
While others talk of arrangements, organise,
Speak in loud voices as if saying "We do not
    feel",

Denying their humanity and hurt
For flesh and blood, what is practical and
    "real",
Swap dates over lamb and rosé, I seem curt.
I think of how you wanted your eyes gouged
    out
For medical research, see your sockets gape.
Sister was told too late, but how could you
    doubt
Your spiritual body, have sought to damage
    its shape?
They say "No flowers" – I say "Her spirit
    may search
For us, may be able to watch her funeral in
    church."

Autumn 1981, revised 1 November 1993

14. FIRE

Bonfire night at our son's school, and a long
Trudge across the muddy field, holding
    mulled wine.
I seek my family from the chattering throng.
Execution stakes, round fireworks wait in
    line.
Now see the fire that leaps so vast and terse
And shoots sparks among the stars into the
    dark,
Is like the crackling spirit of the universe,
Spits red-hot atoms and seeds from one small
    spark.
The fire leaps to the dark, and exists therein,
The sparks and glowing smuts show against
    the night,
And I think of the fire that will leap about
    your coffin,
Your funeral pyre, leave you ashes and insight
And return your spirit to a spark inside
This burning universe and its one fire-tide.

Autumn 1981, revised 1 November 1993

15. FROST-BURN

A sharp frosty morning;
You cannot feel its bite,
Lying in your chapel,
Waiting for the fire and night.

I walk in this cold street
And think of the sparkle of frost
That danced on your window,
You won't feel it, are you lost?

Where have you gone, o where?
The frost touches your gatepost,
And I feel as my skin creeps
You beside me, a ghost.

Autumn 1981, revised 1 November 1993

16. THE FINGERS THAT PLUCKED THE STRINGS

Unplug the kettle, switch off the TV,
Let silence replace sound with awe,
For the fingers that plucked the strings are
    still,
A maestro of sound will play no more.

When I am dead you will find me
Where the frost of the years freezes the hair
And the clouds steeple to the morning sun
And it snows in the heart from yesteryear.

Autumn 1981, revised 1 November 1993

17. MEMORY, PHONE LINE

If the brain is like a hologram, not made to
    last,
And memories are folded in, yet stored
    outside,
And if the brain tunes in and retrieves its past,
And sometimes other people's or past lives
    slide
In as it locates and associates,
Then memory, outside the brain, can survive
    its death,
Whereas records of tunings-in inside its
    gates
And cellars perish with the brain's last breath.
I wonder whether you, now your dead brain
Lies like a defunct phone, so cold and still,
Have severed the cord you dialled when you
    were alive,
And are outside, above, floating free from
    pain,
And are somewhere *you* in spite of this chill,
And I smile wanly to the you that may
    survive.

Summer 1985(?), revised 25 January 1994

18. A SPRAY OF FERN

A black-edged card with a spray
Of fern up its right side.
I write "With love" and our names
And sigh for what you tried,

And the end of something gentle
And very tender is there.
A surge of feeling wells,
From each eye trickles a tear.

My being leaks in the dark
Like ejaculations of love,
I fight to see through a mist,
Sockets like wounds from above.

I take a grip on myself.
It was cruel to take you away.
You were so gentle, but now –
An evergreen fern-spray.

Autumn 1981, revised 1 November 1993

19. A THREAD TO THE RAFTERS

An undertaker walks before the hearse,
We follow the coffin into a packed church,
A family process in grief past the universe.
A hymn, a psalm, the Rector's address on her
search:
Her Methodist roots, violin pupils, six dead
Children, gifted family, widow's warm role.
Are you up in the rafters, suspended by a
thread?
He turns to the coffin and says, "Go Christian
soul."
We follow him out, I stand at the door
A community passes, I shake hands and pace,
Then sit next to one who looks like Death, in
awe
Of his black coat and hat, his creased, gloomy
face.
Is death the end as materialists suggest
Or is the tradition right, that there's more to
our quest?

Autumn 1981, revised 1 November 1993

20. SMOKE

A drive past ploughed fields to a wooded
chapel;
Rector gets out, we follow and stand, your
friends,
Your coffin is at the front for our last
farewell,
And what will happen to you as the prayer
ends?
Curtains draw like a veil across all we felt.

Are you sinking or rolling towards the furnace
door?
One thing is certain, your ice-cold limbs will
melt,
Thaw into nothing, leaving charred bones on
the floor.
I look for smoke from the crematorium tower,
Then put you out of mind with relief on my
face.
Now you are nothing, gone up in smoke in an
hour,
Ashes to be scattered in woods, no resting-
place,
Your spirit has returned, where I too will go
And life must go on – after love, work's
studio.

Autumn 1981, revised 2 November 1993

21. WIND-CHASER

Wind howls around your empty house, earth
groans –
All your recitals, like a fallen pine.
Aghast, Beethoven scowls. Your violin moans
Arpeggios down the years, fades with a
whine.
No log burns in your hearth now, and the
chair
You slumped on is bare, devastated wood.
Seventy years you weathered home despair –
Six children lost, disease and widowhood –
And taught children and pupils to aspire
To what Beethoven heard in a storm-sky,
You chased the wind yet hugged the leaping
fire
And turned to ashes with a fearless sigh:
"Death's not the end." Now, numb, I reach for
one
Warm ember from beyond, but there is none.

2 January 1982

22. BEETHOVEN

I sit on the settee you made into your last bed.
I gaze at your violin and blankly stare.
It seems inconceivable that you are dead.
Your room, lacking your lovely smile, is bare.
Beethoven deeply frowns and scowls and
groans
Pacing his room with a vibrant, beating hand;
With flowing tails, Beethoven deafly moans,
Listening intently near your music-stand.

The wind howls like inspiration, disciplined
Like a dog whose mistress has gone away;
You taught us to rise to Beethoven, catch the
    wind;
You went into the earth with a fearless yea.
I strain to catch what Beethoven heard. Now,
    numb,
I want to echo a chord, and I am dumb.

Autumn 1981, revised 7 November 1993

23. THE SACRIFICE

I wonder what the angels are saying of you?
I think they see you as someone who has
    grown;
You gave yourself to the violin and knew
You must lose yourself in the spring that
    gushes from bone,
In the inspiration which bubbled through your
    soul,
Your deeper self; but then you sacrificed
Music for a family, work for a mother's role
And gave out love, followed the way of Christ.
Artists and saints both lose themselves and
    grow;
You lived for others, counselling though
    bereaved,
Beamed your smile at the community's
    frown, so
You brought up a happy family while you
    grieved.
And knowing I would return and was in need
Did you make one last sacrifice, and die with
    speed?

Autumn 1981, revised 2 November 1993

24. BLACK BAGS, WHITE CARDS

I sit in your house, you are not here;
It is as if you have gone away,
Everything is as it was when we talked
Except for what these black bags say.

A postcard from fifty years ago
From the Swiss Alps in a girlish hand,
Moments in your mind, memories.
Are they gone now, destroyed, just sand?

If we have several lives, then now
You are somewhere else, and this white joy
Is still with you, a white horse on a sea

Of memories that swirl like waves round a
    buoy.

I think of what you have left to me.
If this was just one of your lives,
Then these black bags may help achieve
A joyful school where love survives.

Autumn 1981, revised 1 November 1993

25. GRIEVING

Your house is grieving for you.
Your tank has wept down the stairs,
It cries, through the kitchen ceiling,
It misses your hopes and fears.

The sky is grieving for you.
The very air is moist,
Your garden is as damp-eyed
For you as a kitchen joist.

Autumn 1981, revised 1 November 1993

26. WEDDING RING

In a garden I sort through black bags for
    photos
And letters, scribbled cards, containing
    moments,
Sift what should be preserved near a perfect
    rose
While from inside the house I hear the tense
And angry whirr of a hoover bumping
And the raised voice of one who disapproves
    say,
"Why should he want to keep her wedding
    ring?
Why can't he let them all be thrown away?
I think it's greed." The hoover screeches and
I salvage a photo of your great-grandmother,
Feel sad that some hearts cannot understand
That my youth's moments and trinkets should
    be preserv-
-ed, for like your wedding ring they still
    contain
The hole through which I crawled to this dark
    plain.

Autumn 1981, revised 2 November 1993

27. CHRISTENING DRESS

At work no one notices the bereaved or cares.
But there was horror when the schoolkeeper
    died

In his office, fell headlong on his desk,
And all are too busy with their lives to visit his wife.
And I wonder, have you met him on the heavenly stairs?
And the Colonel who gave me cricket coaching as a boy?
I see souls arriving in groups with tourists' airs.
As I organise, life seems hollow, without joy.
I look at the white cotton christening dress
You wore, on the sofa with gatherings whipped,
With sleeves. It resembles your life now, a beautiful Yes,
Eighteen-thirty hand-made lace border of leaves
But emptied of all that once gave it movement,
The outward ceremony of the inner intent.

Autumn 1981, revised 7 November 1993

28. A PAPER WASPS' NEST

I sort through the shed at the bottom of your garden.
Into bags and boxes, I throw old wood and cord,
Nails, rusty screws, tins of congealed paint, then
A hundred gadgets and hinges from the old cupboard,
Collapse the pram into rubbish, empty the bike's
Saddlebag of spiders, take the apples you wrapped,
Empty the clutter from a life that likes
Everything to be reused, so nothing is scrapped.
I stack the tools one side – anything of use –
And now black bags mound up and pile like proof,
And fill the shed. At last I see, quite puce,
A paper wasps' nest hanging from the roof –
Functional beauty from paper, and I know
I will chew and regurgitate your papers so.

Autumn 1981, revised 2 November 1993

29. SCATTERED

I have been thinking, at some crematoria, there's space
For a rose-bush to be planted where ashes are laid,
But you have no bush to mark or sign your place,
You are scattered near a forked tree in a woodland glade,
Mixed up with the ashes of lesser people than you.
There is nowhere to visit what was you, and care.
If you were buried in a churchyard with a view
I could take flowers, bow my head, say a prayer.
But all I have is memories of what you did,
The respect and great regard for who you were,
Your example in my mind like a caryatid,
A stone figure in a temple-sepulchre.
Burials are better than urns and scatterings on clay
When you are part of an ash-strewn forest way.

Autumn 1981, revised 2 November 1993

30. WHITE BLANKET

Snow nips your homeless ashes in the wood;
It is twenty below centigrade at sunrise.
The snow came in the night with its whitening hood.
Children woke in wonder, glare hurt their eyes.
And now, cars slithering, outside I freeze,
Snowman with muffler; my breaths hang and fade
To where the snow bows down the tumbling trees,
I watch it and think, no breath in your frozen glade.
I blow on fingers as chill as yours were
And think of your ashes under a white shroud;
You were more than cinders, your love drifts through the fir,
Your cheerful concern now floats like a cloud.
Cold, bleak the snow, but hope does not forget,
Sleep warm, my love, under your white blanket.

Autumn 1981, revised 2 November 1993

31. PHOTO ALBUM: QUESTION AND ANSWER

Question:

O sad as the leaves of this photo album
Show brown vignettes of your long-skirted
    youth
In a great Sussex garden, long afternoons
With brothers and sisters by a summerhut,
Rose-garden, greenhouse, stables, tea on the
    lawn,
Long summers of great hopes and forgotten
    loves.
Then your father died and everything was a
    struggle,
With your own children you strove to
    rediscover
The stepped garden, the lawn and atmosphere
Of that lost Paradise of your gone youth
With children and much loving in the wind.
O sad to think you are dead now, and these
    pictures
A record of a body falling into a grave.
What is life? What is death? Do photographs
Show an eternal pattern in time's carpet?
O mother, look back and say, what did your
    life mean?

Answer:

It meant a life of afternoons, my son.
It meant tea on the lawn, as children
    branched.
It meant smiles by the sea and picking pears.
It meant the blossom of time on the eternal
    trunk.

Autumn 1981, revised 2 November 1993

32. A THAW

A bleak, wintry day; at the font a vicar
Scoops water three times with a scallop shell,
Then offers a candle to the child's mother
And all applaud as everything is well.
Are you with us, was that your shape I saw?
And is it you kneeling beside me now?
As I walked through the gloom to the church
    door
And spoke to the vicar, did I see you
    somehow?
Champagne. Is it you at my elbow? I turn, but
    no.

Only my shadow laughs from the wall, then
    slips.
A bleak, cold day as we drive back through
    falling snow,
But now a sudden thaw; as water drips
From the roof to splash on the tiles below,
    now pelts,
I feel a thaw in my grief, whose waste now
    melts.

Autumn 1981, revised 8 November 1993

33. LOVE LIKE FROSTY AIR

I open a Christmas card: a poem like a burr
From a man who sends his love, who is over-
    fond.
I ring my aunt – "He would have married her,
But she wouldn't put her family second."
I sit and tell him where you had to go.
Will his love die because you have gone
    somewhere?
No, lovers melt and fade like last week's
    snow
But their love outlives them like frosty air.
I feel the whiteness of love cover the world.
She was here to love and left when her great
    heart burst
With excess, she breathed out love so it
    swirled
Like whirling snow, which has now dispersed.
Love manifests and returns to the One thaw,
And its presence is known when the air is
    clear and raw.

Autumn 1981, revised 7 November 1993

34. LEAVES IN THE HAIR

I see you in as many moments as leaves
Shaken from an autumn tree by an impatient
    wind,
Lying like strewn seed in my wife's hair, on
    her sleeves
Like confetti – so many images have grinned.
You were at the piano, you heard me park
And rushed out to greet me: "Hello, you've
    done well,
The tea's already made – it's already getting
    dark –
It's on the trolley. Pour yourself a cup." Tea
    smell,
And I heard you counting while your pupil
    scraped.

You were always there, like savings in a
chest.
And now it is bare, for you have gone,
escaped,
And I feel the pinch of the cold, and a chill
near my zest.
And what I dreaded as a child must now be
known,
The grown-ups have gone away, and I am
alone.

Autumn 1981, revised 8 November 1993

35. LIKE A ROMAN COIN

Like a Roman empress on a coin, your face
Is immortal in my memory, outside time.
Your whole life is one imperious smile, your
grace
Stamped on a bronze sestertius worth a dime,
A distillation of a thousand moments,
The essence of all browning photographs
Compressed to one gracious look of common
sense,
The "you" behind emotion and thought that
laughs.
Lady, I pray to you like a supplicant
Waiting to hand my scroll to Caesar's wife,
Hoping it will find divine Caesar compliant.
You look, handling petitions in the afterlife,
As just after you died, with your scorn of
suffering now
Smoothed into a trace of a frown on your
frozen brow.

Autumn 1981, revised 8 November 1993

36. VIOLIN SOUL

You are like your walnut violin, now still.
Observe a death and all is body. Somewhere
Vibrate strings, sound-waves cross the bridge
and fill
The hollow, flow out through each sound-hole
into air.
There is a tradition that knows the soul
vibrates
And sees the body as an echo for sound,
Which has meaning when a chord resonates
And is just an empty shell when under
ground.
And now I know your soul is a violin,
Beautifully shaped, hollow, with strings
plucked by

An operator who listens to the wind within
And bows shrill notes into the hollow body.
Body and soul, like strings and bow, need face.
You bowed out a beauty now locked in a case.

Autumn 1981, revised 8 November 1993

37. EARTH

I know that I must follow you. I chose
The place where my body will lie under High
Beach air
And as I slowly move towards my close,
My appointment with the hooded skeleton
there
Among birch trees, I give my life a hid-
-den symmetry and proportion, a straight
And linear beauty. This is not morbid.
It is not the laboured breathing I anticipate,
Lungs filling with water, an echo on each
gasp
As life sinks and wind ebbs in a quiet distress,
But rather my rendezvous with the earth,
which will clasp
Me, open to me, gape like a foreign mistress.
Thinking about her dark embrace fills me
with slime
And a current of energy to make use of time.

Autumn 1981, revised 8 November 1993

38. URN LIKE A NEST

O for those who have no home for their bones
Save the well-shaped urn of a poet's rhyme,
Whose candle and lit jar is a poet's tones
And words and form that shine out against
time.
As your ashes are strewn in the woodland One
I gather images – leaves, mud – from my
quest;
My soul flits hither and thither in the sun
And weaves impressions like twigs into a
nest.
Death is an inspirer of such homely art
And as I bird-like create for your ashes this
urn
This monument that will survive my heart,
I leave my own style on its rim, like a broken
fern.
So my time's labours outlast the years, like
the sea,
And are like a lighthouse in foaming eternity.

Autumn 1981 and 8 November 1993

39. CINDERS

I see my shape restless near your scuttle of
 coke,
Reverted to its nature, apart, outside.
Poets bear Truth and are shunned by ordinary
 folk
Who have lived inauthentically and lied.
When you were here, you opened up your heart
And I, with you, could meet the other kind.
Now they live for a lie and beery lunches,
 apart
From my after-death vision to which they are
 blind.
I think of how we sat round your fire during
 snow,
Coals glowing. With this poker you prodded it
 bright,
Opened these tongs to add more so a glow
Warmed our cheeks, we sat talking till
 midnight.
Now the fire is out and a fire in my heart
 somewhere
Is a pile of last night's cinders, your not being
 here.

Autumn 1981, revised 2 November 1993

40. CHINESE TABLE: ROSE OF LIGHT

Three gone to lunch, I am left alone in a
 daze.
We four, like the creatures on your Chinese
 table,
Hatched and found our way through the
 centreless maze
That led nowhere but to the other side; fearful
Snake, dragon and wasp – each with a sting or
 bite;
I am Khepera the dung-beetle, rolling his ball
Out towards the sixteen petals of a rose of
 light –
I, rolling my dung, never clear of work, crawl,
The god of Creation with papyri all round.
We four were all different in the labyrinth.
I wander and ring your cowbells and chew the
 sound;
I, the poet of the Tao, this table my plinth,
Know that the central path through this maze
 leads to where
You have now reached: a petalled rose in air.

Autumn 1981, revised 9 November 1993

41. PRIVACY

How sad in the mild winter, to break up a
 home,
Tear out memories – furniture, letters, this
 whim,
China, tables – to the tick of the metronome
Dismember, like tearing a person limb from
 limb.
Now they lie on the dining-room table in a
 mess,
Junk, clutter, surfeit nauseate – give me space.
Material things do not bring happiness.
I would rather you were here and these things
 in place.
Now I sit and read a letter from an unknown
Artist, another from an aunt who could rave.
Both dead, like you, and I feel very alone.
All these adults have preceded me into the
 grave
And left me to rifle through things that were
 theirs, such
Private things I was once forbidden to touch.

Autumn 1981, revised 9 November 1993

42. TORTOISESHELL CLOCK

Your life is like your French tortoiseshell
 clock
Which has stopped in my study. Its
 embellishments,
Its surrounding metal leaves and hidden lock
And polished wood, its ornate numbers, its
 scents,
All live on: your gentle kindness and sublime
Smile, you were liked and respected by each
 friend
For your life of tortoiseshell beauty outside
 time –
Like your clock, a bequest from one who at
 her end
Had turned a hundred and knew her time
 would cease:
And as wind stirs hands to whirr at your face
 and frown,
Your tortoiseshell heart is wound up like this
 piece
And moves your hands until it has ticked
 down,
And then it has an eternal stillness
Until it is wound again for a new mistress.

Autumn 1981, revised November 1993

43. VIOLIN SIGHS

Christmas. We all sit round after our lunch,
Christmas tree lights shine in the lead
windows,
Paper chains drape the lights, in hats we
munch,
And from the stereo comes your repose,
You playing the violin to Somervell
Thirty years ago. The slow chords float from
beyond
From an evening we spent with a baby-sitter
(I thrill),
Miss Willis who drowned herself in a Forest
pond;
And I see the serious expression in your eyes
As you play for the audience, all now dead,
Like Mrs. Gould, who hosted your breathless
sighs,
Knocked down near our school, by a car
which crushed her head.
And you live again through your notes, which
might have been lost
As I live now through these words, though
under frost.

1 November 1993

44. INVISIBLE BODY

I was not able to mow the lawn as my
surprise;
You went too soon to a realm over the hill.
No more cakes, jam, marmalade or mincepies.
The bagatelle lies untouched, the fun is still.
We collude with our deaths and when we feel
We have outstayed our usefulness, we depart.
We have an invisible body seal-
-ed within the material flesh and heart
On which, as in a letter, is written our deeds.
It is enclosed till it breaks out at death
And floats lighter than air, and grows and
feeds
On spiritual food and divine breath.
I stare at the line of hill, stare at the trees.
Is that you who waves in the gentle, cooling
breeze?

Autumn 1981

45. SAINT

I sit in front of an altar's flickering
Cloth which says "Veni Creator Spiritus" on
blue
And sports a crown of fire. Now three men
bring
The hymn book we have given in memory of
you.
The vicar holds it aloft, dedicates it till
We pray, and I see your grey face looking
down;
I feel your spirit, emotionless but still.
We sing a hymn about saints, I see you frown
And now the sermon. "She was one of God's
saints."
I tingle up my spine and stare at the choir,
And look at ladies with hats and a hundred
complaints,
And know you are selfless, with a crown of
fire.
Now walking by the Forest pond, down here,
I feel your presence in the sunny air.

Autumn 1981, revised 9 November 1993

46. NO ONE HAS RUNG

A gusty night, my son sleeps fitfully
Tossing and turning, tomorrow he has the test
That will send him to the school you sent me
to
And no one has rung to wish him all the best.

Now I see what a rare quality you had,
Ringing to ask us what the doctor said.
You were involved in what happened to us
and helped,
And your going has made life more brutal,
more dead.

Autumn 1981, revised 9 November 1993

47. IMAGINING

I sit at night in a window, far away,
Staring at a dark forest, humped like a bear,
I think of what I missed this All Saints' Day,
A year on from your last faint sigh down here.
My wife took a green urn and some purple
flowers
And left them for you with a "Fond
Remembrance" card
And looked at the Book of Remembrance, and
the hours
Of a year ago on the opened page, tried hard
The girl said, "Her ashes were scattered in
The November part of the woods, I don't
know where."

I missed a tryst today, I in my skin,
You waited in vain – now this imagining like
    a prayer.
Yet if all is One, your spirit is here somehow;
Not tied to body or place, you are with me
    now.

1 November 1982, revised 9th November 1993

48. SHOUT

It is two years since the eve of your dying,
All Hallowe'en when all the witches fly.
I look at the moon and can't help wondering,
Are you there among the spirits, riding on high,
Even though you died on All Saints Day,
    from your skin?
I go into school and bump my leg in the dark.
As a lump like an egg comes up on my
    bruised shin
Did a flying spirit do it for a lark?
I go to my boys, a Jack o'Lantern grins
With jagged teeth and a candle inside,
Grimaces like a spirit who always wins,
And I see you gritting your teeth as you died.
You are around, somewhere, I know, I will
    not shut you out
But let you into my soul, now, by writing this
    shout.

31 October 1983, revised 9 November 1993

49. LURCH

Cricket three years after, I sit in May.
Two batsmen grope and miss and miss again.
I ask a man "Who's batting?", watching the
    play,
And we share, sitting on the wooden bench,
    disdain.
He tells me he played fifty years back, to a
    crowd,
And collected sixpence a head at the bottom
    gate,
And now we are the only spectators.
    Unbowed,
He tells me about his son – inclined to prate,
I bashed him up once on the Roding bridge,
And his father complained to you – I lurch
    and sweat
From the sun into a dark place in my skull's
    language,
And am with you again and say "Guess who I
    met?"

And see your smile as you say "Fancy that!"
And know, wherever you are, that you still
    chat.

May 1985, revised 9 November 1993

50. TOADSTOOLS AND PUFFBALLS

The anniversary of your dying sigh.
Leaves cover the lawn and decay to mould.
I shun the church for where your ashes lie,
Drive through ploughed fields and sombre
    trees and cold
To a wooded hill apart from society
And seek you among yellow leaves – did your
    ashes
Feed the twisting, writhing branches of each
    tree?
I wander down the path to where a blackboard
    says
"November" and walk past through hawthorn
    trees.
Are you here? Are you beside me? This is
    your cause.
I see your face. Are you here in this cool
    breeze?
I look among trees for dust that was once
    yours.
Toadstools and puffballs adorn the sour lawn,
And you are a forked tree and a sky like a
    dawn.

31 October 1982, revised 14 November 1993

51. BRITTLE LEAVES

How could we not leave you in a place where
    you could lie,
Where leaves rustle in the wind, brown leaves
    on grass?
I sit on a mildewy seat, hear echoes fly
From my high chair. You leave the sink and
    pass
To the map of the world with flags for the war
    on the wall.
Where are you now? Only the breeze in the
    air,
Stirring the brittle leaves about to fall.
I sit on the seat. Sit down beside me here,
Come from your unknown place and be with
    me now
And spend an hour telling me the news as you
    did.

As least I came, kept our tryst under your
    bough,
I lingered a while somewhere near where you
    hid.
Was it under this tree your clay became clay?
Have you bloomed in this leaf a year later to
    the day?

30 October 1982, revised 14 November 1993

52. REDUCTION

Hallowe'en a year later and the witches fly.
I return through dusk towards far lights and
    stay
At a charity party in my school, and sigh.
I am back among people, you are further away.
Your image haunts me, I see your red cheek.
You are still a mental reality though you are
    dust.
But now you are mingled with others, as if in
    that bleak
Place, identity has become one. In disgust,
Those who saw you as matter took you there.
I see you as spirit and reach out and call
To you, not in a church but in this open air.
I hear the rustle of leaves and know that all
You were is too grand, fine and noble to be
Reduced to atoms – your spirit is now free!

31 October 1982, revised 14 November 1993

53. FORGET-ME-NOTS

I sit in the High Road,
A greyness creeps up my throat
Like the soreness in my body
For you are not here in your coat.

Empty is this Forest town
Now that you are not around.
No more the open door
And tea to the violin's sound.

Bury me in the sun
Near forget-me-nots and may,
Bury me by the yew
Where daisies strew the way.

Autumn 1982, revised 14 November 1993

54. CHRYSALIS

I listen above traffic, to outer space.
Can you hear me, do you know what I am
    doing now,

Wherever you are, in a distant dimension or
    place?
Are you kept informed? Do you think of me
    how
I think of my daughter in Scotland – I know
Few details of her life yet she speaks on the
    phone,
Are you helping me from afar incognito?
Or are you concentrating on your own
Soul, and have you shed the memory of us
Like a chrysalis shed by a butterfly –
The shell that was your home in a life of fuss
Which is now an empty case left high and
    dry.
Above the traffic in this empty room I hear
Whispers in the wind, whispers from afar, like
    prayer.

Autumn 1982, revised 14 November 1993

55. STONE

"Oft, when on my couch I lie
In vacant or in pensive mood
They flash upon that inward eye
Which is the bliss of solitude."

                           Wordsworth

I lay on my sofa after exercise
And through all the intervening accreting
    years
I was suddenly back in my first classroom,
    half-wise,
Sitting, just eight, to one side, full of fears;
And I saw my friends just as they used to be
And Miss Crabtree – Cuddie – sitting at her
    desk
With the splintered wood, her register on her
    knee,
And I saw what was on the wall; it was
    grotesque,
But I wanted to greet one of my friends (now
    dead),
And I thought, my son will soon be at the
    same age.
But where was that room? In which part of
    the school was his head?
Then I realised that only you knew the stage.
You are not there to ask, and I felt alone,
Isolated from my own memories, like a stone.

Autumn 1982, revised 14 November 1993

56. TOY SOLDIERS

And now I see your presence everywhere
As when I woke early, got out of bed,
And saw a lorry parked on the kerb out there,
And, expecting central heating men, said,
"Please, not there." "We've a job here," the
    man said with a grin.
And I saw a sign on the pavement, "Give
    Way",
Like a Providential message saying "Give in".
I protested and the sign was that day
Removed with apologies – it should not have
    been there.
Then as soon as it had gone, an estate agent
    rang,
A lady viewed and made an offer. Somewhere
Did you warn me with a road sign not to
    hang
On and do the dead communicate with us like
    that?
And are we like toy soldiers to your immortal
    chat?

Autumn 1982, revised 14 November 1993

57. GHOSTS

I drove to where you were as if going to tea,
Up into the woods: you were there, but not
    there.
A rabbit froze in my headlights' glare,
Mesmerised, unable to move. In the damp
    air
We walked to the divided tree in the fading
    light
And knelt at your urn, and put in our laurel
    again,
And then I wandered away and felt the night,
The dark on the fields all round, the rustle of
    rain
And the peace, and my legs and spine tingled
    to my head
As the lonely ghosts crowded near, and I
    heard you say
"Please stay, please stay" and I tingled among
    the dead.
And for some seconds we lingered together
    on clay,
And my eyes ran with your tears, until I
    stirred:
Only the rustling rain on the lawn, like a bird.

November 1983, revised 14 November 1993

58. STILL MIND

I was told: "I have been to a medium in
    Harlow,
And your mother came through, she's living
    with your
Father. She said things no one else could
    know:
She had a painful death, her heart was sore,
And your father had something wrong with
    his brain.
She was worried your sister's 'in a pickle'.
    She's fine,
She is looking after a child, and is happy
    again.
She spoke of your wedding. She did it all by
    sign,
The medium interpreted, she described
    her."
And so it seems you are well and still mind,
That the dead care about the living, though
    unseen
And silent spectators of things that occur,
And we are actors on a stage, quite blind
To our news audience, and you are now
    serene!

2 May 1985, revised 24 January 1994

59. ASH

The leaves are yellow on every beech,
November drizzle is in the air.
I drive through woods to your hill's trees
And walk to your split ash and stare

And stand white roses in the urn
Which now bears your name in a transient
    place;
Ash lies around at the foot of the tree,
I look at the chimney and grimace.

All is still this wintry weekend.
I recall how you stood at the gate,
A frail, thin, gaunt red-cheeked lady,
And called "He-llo" with the warmth of your
    grate,

And as I wish I could drop in for tea
A squall of rain lashes my cheek
And sends me running back to the car,
And I leave you alone on a hill that is bleak.

November 1986, revised 9 November 1993

60. HEAD-SCARF

I thought I saw you at the bus-stop,
Tiny in your head-scarf,
Looking as if you had lost your way;
At first I wanted to laugh.

It was as if you had been sent back
To earth to find me, and had come
Looking and lost your way up the road;
I felt my being thrum.

A person is, and then the fire,
And a person exists no more.
But a person cannot cease to be
In life's unalterable law.

1986(?), revised 9 November 1993

61. WIND-DANCER

Last night you came into my dream.
Your sister was walking in foam.
I stopped and took her shopping-bag,
And drove her to her home,

And you were there and laughed for joy
As I mimicked your voice,
And you were with me although dead;
I could not but rejoice.

You helped me tidy up some stamps
That were in my aunt's hall,
And then I woke and felt alone,
And I knew you were by the wall,

And I knew you have a body still
Although you went to the fire,
And I knew you have body of mind
And dance on the wind with a lyre.

1986(?), revised 9 November 1993

A RAINBOW IN THE SPRAY

1981 – 1985

CRAB-FISHING ON A BOUNDLESS DEEP

Go out in a boat in early morning mist
As fishermen put up sail, with a hose thaw
    bait,
Slice slabs of ray whose smear spreads
    through the fist,
Leave the Mount for six miles out, where
    gulls wait,
Where the bay is sheltered from the east-west
    tides,
Where crabs do not bury themselves in sandy
    spots –
In this autumn equinox each crustacean
    hides –
And winch up the first string of dripping
    crabpots.

In the first pot, put down an arm and throw
Good crabs into a tea-chest; into the sea
    lots   10
With soft bellies, or crabs too small – no
Meat: dash and smash diseased shells with
    black spots,
Bait the trap with fresh ray, pile pots at the
    back,
When the string is done throw them in; with a
    knife, and Frank,
Nick each crab between each claw, and hear
    the crack!
Then drop it, powerless to nip, in the water-
    tank.

This sea which is so calm can blow up rough
If the wind comes from the south-east and
    whips
Water to waves, and this calm can be tough
In winter storms that keel and roll big
    ships: 20
The waves wash onto deck from the
    windward side
And fishermen need sea-legs to see-saw
High, stomach above the horizon, then
    slide
Down into a trough, as the boom becomes an
    oar.

This sea encompasses each horizon's tide
And we are alone on a dipping, lapping bowl.
This sea, which yields such crabs, on every
    side
Is an irreducible, inseparable whole,
Ebbing from east to west, pulled by the moon
Till it floods back from the west as the moon
    goes by.   30
Its tides make currents from which crabs hide
    in a dune,
This boundless water is ruled by a ball in the
    sky.

As so it is on land, that misty cloud.
Trees, earth, stones, rocks, clouds, water, air
    and fire
Are seen as different as each wave, as proud-
-ly separate, yet all are part of an ocean of
    mire
As indivisible as the inseparable sea
Whose waves rise, dip, and then return to the
    One.
I see currents of Existence pulled inexorably,
Till crops flood back again, by the moon and
    the ripening sun.   40

Both sea and land first came from air – from
    night.
As an unseen sun made Being's atmosphere
To unfold a world of currents pulled by Light
So our sun whirled a collapsed cloud to air –
The dust and gas which cooled into planets –
Whose cold froze molten rock, then melted
    seas
From ice whose water clouds raise as droplets
To fall as rain on hills, so that rivers please.

And now I see this vast expanse of sea
Is like the unconscious mind on which "I"
    stand,   50
Which came from Being's air and sun –

psyche.
And "I" am this boat, my reason, ego and
Identity on a mind both vast and deep,
As wide as the world, as deep as the deepest
    seam
Of rock, pulled by a moon that is asleep
Which sets blind currents swirling through its
    dream.

Bait pots with the smear of time and let them
    slip
In this boundless, endless sea, then have a
    snack,
Then winch them up. Images claw and drip.
Take out the good ones, throw the soft ones
    back   60
And the small ones, smash diseased shells,
    then seize
Each one that will bite its own legs off with
    its claws
And nick it so it's lost its nip. Then sneeze
And toss it in a tank of crowded metaphors.

Then you can sell them to be devoured, this
    haul
Of Being's dripping symbols. Such small
    works
Epitomise the vast and boundless deep, so
    trawl
Where thirty fathoms down great beauty
    lurks,
Hiding in sand when the currents swirl and
    free
To emerge in slack-water between the
    tides,   70
And I'll pray that the Being that made this sea
Can yield its plenty up these dripping sides.

24 August 1981, revised 19-20 April 1985

THE ROYAL MASONIC HOSPITAL: THE NUT WITHIN THE SUN

Once masons built the universe in stone
And now the Tree fills their hospital's air.
Between Hiram of Tyre and Hiram Abiff,
Who measured God with compasses and
    square,
Turn and look at the round glass mandala,
See Solomon on Jacob's ladder, and floors
With "luf-knot" pentagram, Solomon's seal,

And the dividers of Blake's God on doors.

Go up to the waiting-room, see the garden
And oblong lily-pond, papyrus plumes;   10
Where a fountain splashes time near a sundial
See the eternal sun peep where a lily blooms.
See balconies held up on stone pillars
As if four worlds were founded on the grass,
Go to the room where you will be nursed to
    health,
See sister's buckle, where set square and
    compass

Join pentagram in an eternal clasp,
The love-knot of crusading Templar knights;
Time embraces eternity above
A Babylonian-brick ziqqurat's heights   20
Under which leaves flow up a chestnut tree,
Where images peep like brown conker nuts;
The architect of Solomon's Temple walls
Shows a Tree of Life rooted in the ark's
    struts.

As in King's College chapel, see through the
    stone,
Feel yourself in God's manifesting smile,
Restore the oneness between leaves and bone!
As wet papyrus waving by the Nile
Became the very first dry parchment scroll
So the chestnut Tree prints leaves in the
    gazing mind,   30
And brown nuts peep through spiked shells in
    the soul
And a sun bursts brown visions of one
    conquering kind.

16 September 1981, revised 4 October 1993

CAMBRIDGE ODE: AGAINST MATERIALISM
(OR: NEWTON'S ENLIGHTENMENT)

I. STROPHE: 300 YEARS OF DARKNESS

We walk through King's past Fellows' rooms
    and brood
On one who has died, go out to the lawn
    which slopes
To the river Cam where punts glide in sad
    mood,
Survey from the Chapel the academic hopes

Of minds cloistered from Nature in dark
    rooms.
What is this rational mind, this doubting eye
That probes for alphas, pokes in dusty tombs?
Is it just a squelching brain, waiting to die?

I think of atheists who cooled their heels
Here, of one who walked with Wittgenstein
    and saw   10
All mind as how someone behaves or feels,
A reduction to be laid at Forster's door;
Of a red-haired militant who took aim and
    blew
All art to signs and ciphers, and would attack
The moral meanings that the poets knew
For social dark and Marx, till he got the sack.

Such clever men deny God and contend
Reason, feelings and mind are merely brain;
Bleak Humanists who claim "Death is the
    end"
And derive all values from material pain.   20
Materialism! Cambridge has been a shrine
For three centuries of dark Enlightenment,
Divided peering-out in spiritual decline
That makes a culture squint, its belief spent.

Materialists know a world of "massy stones"
In which minds are "reduced to material
    things" –
Electrons, brain cells – and, solid as bones,
Thoughts and sensations are "brain-
    functionings",
Observations are trustworthy, "like bald
    pates",   30
Images, perceptions, emotions are
"Mere brain-processes" or mere "body-
    states".
But is the still engine the speeding car?

I go to Trinity where in three green
Years Newton read Descartes' "cogito", saw
Mind separate from Nature's "inert machine",
Discovered light, gravity, calculus, and
    more,
But then turned to Hermetic alchemy,
And matter in mechanistic motion round
The sun, sought to balance contracting gravity
With an expanding force in light – which he
    never found!   40

Young minds squint through dark telescopes
    which block
The expansive force in the sun, measure and
    frown
The universe to a mechanistic clock
With a spring, coil and winder that will run
    down.
To seek Enlightenment through a telescope,
What folly of the Age of Analysis! which
    knows
Cause and effect, not the start of the chain,
    not Hope,
The First Cause, which all miss – the Mystic
    Rose!

And see an Observator measure clock time
Which differs from star time throughout the
    year;   50
In the Wren Octagon see Flamsteed climb
A laddered sextant telescope, and peer
And with his mural arc measure the height
Of stars as they pass the meridian
And chart three thousand to raise Newton's
    spite,
And miss eternity, though a clergyman!

II. ANTISTROPHE: THE REACTION AGAINST MATERIALISM

O all who ask, having seen a loved one die,
"Is there a soul, a something more?" – you
    know
The immaterial spirit has survi-
-ved three centuries of darkness in a
    candleglow   60
Which incarnates a rose of Light that blows –
The "I" behind all leafy thoughts – in a breeze
That lifts a veil to what's beyond, and knows
It is not unlike the wind that blows the trees.

See the brick hearth Wordsworth sat by and
    pined
For living lakes and peaks where weather
    seethes,
Or in King's Chapel read "the eternal mind"
Of Brooke the soldier, who knew Nature
    breathes,
Or go to Orchard House, which now serves
    teas,
Where Brooke was snapped at breakfast with
    a sideways glance,   70

And at one with the pink-white blossom of
apple trees
Dream of Newton's apple where the petals
dance.

Where Brooke revelled, where the green
waters float,
Look over the Vicarage fence, smell the lilac
hour,
Then walk back to Mill House, where
Whitehead wrote,
For whom Nature was "organism", a power,
A "process" in which we find ourselves, no
stone
Which "bifurcates" daylight so the mind's
apart.
Green fields, cows, apple blossom all make
known   80
The blossoming of minds and the summer
heart.

But now see what an Einstein's science gave:
Green fields billow with a subatomic tide
As matter converts to energy or wave,
One force foams all to a goal Darwin denied
And we now live in a sea of consciousness.
A Counter-Renaissance floods the West's
crisis
Where ebbing spirit left a seaweed mess –
Did not Blake, Yeats and Eliot foresee this?

Now the mind is part of this tide of "growth",
this white
Blossom that swells and pours from the One
through the crown   90
Into apple trees, with expanding Light –
Not contracting gravity that draws apples
down;
Thoughts grow like segments of a thorny rose,
A mind is like a rose whose petals fall
As books, whose perfumed "I" remains
through all that flows
Within the living One that buds and ripens all.

Now the mind that sees is part of what is seen,
One sea of mind-and-matter that shatters
where
An observer crests, for though part of the
green
Ocean of being, like a wave he looks out at a
sphere;   100
No more can a poet sit and regard the world
As if from outside the sphere, as if a babe
Had drawn the stars on a flat surface, unfurled
The heavens on a planospheric astrolabe.

True mind awakes from measurements and
peeps
Where Imagination sits like a fire-bird.
Mind feels the sap rise in the leaves and leaps,
Flies into it, at one with the power that stirred.
Did young Newton dive with a meteorite
shower,
Ascend the rainbow bridge up the black sky,
or   110
Climb the World-Tree in one evening hour,
Fly like a falcon through the sun's trap-door?

III. EPODE: NEWTON'S EXPANDING FORCE OF LIGHT

I drive home and ponder, what is the mind?
Are mind and matter dual (Plato, Descartes)?
Do they interact so consciousness is entwined
Between mind and flower? Or are they one
mind-star?
Is mind immaterial, is matter its frozen form
As water freezes to ice (like atoms and
bones)?
So am I conscious "matter-mind", cold-warm,
Like a Zen stone garden, where mind's a sea
of stones?   120

The moon is up, shift the perspective now
And float through space like an Angel-naut,
then stand
On the moon and see our earth hang near the
Plough,
Your home and loved ones hidden behind
your hand –
A tennis ball of seas, mountains and cloud;
See it recede with all its human kind,
Then leap in ecstasy, bound, shout out loud
For where's the contracting force that freezes
mind?

I recall Newton's search for the expanding
force,
The single fermental "levity" that creates,   130
That would balance gravity, change science's
course,

367

Attract and repel wherever light radiates:
Four-sided rays of light pierce bodies, shoot
Through them, ferment them with growth in
    each limb and lung –
A harmonising system that would refute
The nightmare he created when he was young.

Working in his Temple Molecular,
Studying alchemy for thirty years, he held
(Or guessed) this creative force was in ether,
"The body of light" where "the spirit is
    entangled",   140
That the universe is filled with ether-eal Light
Which, caught like a sperm, ferments and
    creates
Spirits as well as minds and bodies from
    night,
Manifests through four worlds into matter's
    gates.

Ether – Divine Light, Holy Spirit – rapes
Souls, CBR-like prana pervades our earth
Through which divine Imagination shapes
All things, brings all matter and mind to birth,
Flows into our chakras, shivers up the spine,
Lights the spirit like a bright candle-
    flame –   150
"Samadhi" – and makes immortal all who
    shine,
Divine Enlightenment whence our soul came.

The moon is high, the first stars out, and I
Look at the human who sits by me, alive,
And am not now sick for seeing a loved one
    die
For I know she is more than matter, and will
    survive.
I can return to the warmth of the human night
And dream of my Garden where I can see in
    the sun
How each acorn and oak swells in from Light
In an expanding Nature, in which mind and
    matter are one.   160

I have a Pythagoras' Garden in a mystery
    school
Where I grow qualities my destiny needs,
Contact the hawthorn forces, by whose rule
Being expands the universe among flowers
    and seeds,

And between two fields railed-in with iron, I
    stare
At gates in the hedge, where thought and
    shade are green,
Swing back their rust, and in one field declare
Against Materialism! by my hedgerow
    screen!

11-12 August 1982, revised 20-21 April 1985

NIGHT VISIONS IN CHARLESTOWN
(AN ODE)

I. DARK NIGHT

I sit on the harbour wall in dark Charlestown
And gaze up at a trillion budding stars
That flutter as a breeze blows gently down
From the sparkling Plough through
    Cassiopeia, Mars,
And I ask again "What is space? What is
    night?
What lives beyond death?" and hear my own
    echo.
This void which scientists cross with a
    satellite
Has a branchy fullness behind each glow.

In blackest dark I clasp the granite wall,
The sea laps calmly on a shingle beach.   10
A soft light dances where boats rise and fall,
The wooded cliffs are dark, and out of reach.
Here I can crane my neck and stretch into the
    tree
Whose blossoms glow, and there a firefly
    darts
For it is meteorite time. Here my soul can be
A hawk and fly to its higher, leafy parts.

Galileo, Descartes, Newton, Darwin, Freud
Emptied the air of all intelligence,
Made the cosmos a dark, mechanistic void,
Split body and mind, our species and
    conscious sense.   20
But now Einstein, Hubble and Penzias stand
For a cosmos full of atomic waves that sprang
From a hundred billion galaxies that expand
With background radiation from the Big
    Bang.

Our subatomic physics have destroyed

The Materialist paradigm of common sense.
Now Bohm, our Newton, grapples with the
Void
Which unfolds fields that come into form,
whence
Order unfolds, like Plato's Idea.
So matter comes from nothing, and so do
we,   30
Implicate Oneness budding into air,
Flecking with petals this speculative Tree.

Our Darwin in morphogenetic fields
Makes Nature live again; a Sheldrake heaves,
The organicist triumphs, the mechanist yields,
One nothing somewhere burgeons into
leaves.
Whitehead and Jung affirm, like Einstein and
Bohm,
The cosmos is full of waves and infinitely
wide.
How can one empty the sea and leave the
foam?
Explain the sea-horse yet ignore the tide?   40

The new philosophy casts all in doubt.
The metaphysical proudly proclaims
That Humanists and Materialists merely shout
Sceptical faiths and lazy, rational claims.
So now I sit like Donne at the dark start
Of a new Baroque Age, when once again
We reach for stars, scrump meanings beyond
the heart
Which the fresh soul knows are One, like a
daisy-chain.

II. FLIGHT OF THE SOUL TO THE COMING AGE

Now shift perspective. From space our
globe's at one,
As the mounting soul floats near the Milky
Way;   50
And whirling round its galaxy, our sun
Is no more a centre than is Christmas Day.
The universe is as vast as the dark round one
soul,
Which can travel faster than light to future
heights.
Now the dark earth below turns rose-red
round one pole
As an Age of global union dawns its delights.

Like old Baroque, I see its sun shine through
Appearance and illusion, the ego's mask,
Dye red the social carnival's ballyhoo
(All dress for parts as on a stage) – its task   60
To reveal the truth its sunrise mirrors, Light,
And wake souls to a sensual-spiritual face,
To pastoral peace and the bliss of celestial
flight
Up this shaman's Tree to a canopy of space.

A Universal Age – Baroque in sunny art!
I think of one who paints peaceful landscapes,
Spanish Teresa's smile, the ecstatic heart,
And as I soar a prophetic vision gapes:
The Baroque started as a Catholic rose –
I see a waving Pope regenerate   70
All Christendom to rose-blooms, and oppose
New Eastern hordes again at Europe's gate.

I see the nationalistic darkness strewn,
That fragmented, separate time of nightmare
toil
Whose reason conquered atoms and the
moon,
But lost authority, empire and oil,
Whose states near-perished in an angry
shout
As liberal causes broke like a golden bowl,
An Age that reached a dead-end, and cried
out
For a replacement vision – for its lost soul. 80

I see Europeans bring to Charles's town
A sunshine zeitgeist, an Age with a new
still –
Their dynamic universe and a lit crown
Like a kestrel hovering on a wind of will.
A new Dark Age is as near as a gust of air
As Islamic terror threatens Europe's gate,
But I see their union overcome despair
As they seek an Age of Hope that they'll
create.

I see it blow across the sunlit sea,
A Resurgence of the spirit which will unite 90
Occupied Christendom's soul with its body
As the Communist darkness fractures into
Light!
I see Hungarians, Czechs and Poles declare
For Europe's sun! Though intellect wants

369

proof,
Let the mind seize in beauty a grand Idea,
Let starlight trickle through its rational roof!

I see a space telescope, and the first Voyager,
Now map two hundred billion galaxies
And a lumpy universe in which dark matter
Pulls curving sheets to clumps; and show it
    is   100
Like Dyson's and will expand forever, a bowl
Less dense that three atoms per cubic metre –
    or
It would collapse and vanish into a black hole
In twenty billion years, space-time no more.

I see a quantum Void, Non-Being kinked
Beneath the four tidal forces which bind
All that is into one; quantum particles, once
    linked,
Behave as one, join vacuum, matter and
    mind.
This sea-like Void contains all that exists
And consciousness – those ripples Being
    craves –   110
And God, who enfolds what is like morning
    mists,
Is immanent in the sea that supports all
    waves.

I see man who evolved from stardust know
A fifth expanding force behind the known
    four,
And the solar wind, dust blown by our sun,
    and go
To where the heliosphere ends at the
    heliopau-
-se so that when the sun runs out of hydrogen,
Becomes a red giant, swallows the earth
In five billion years' time, shrinks to a white
    dwarf, then
On a safer star man will hail mankind's new
    birth.   120

Now I see men who think they're matter, their
    minds mere brain,
Who are imprisoned in five senses' skin,

Whose earth is a flightless Hell, endured in
    vain.
But the highest vision of an Age brings in

The next Age; great art does not reflect the
    "id"
Of this dark Age, but creates a Sun-Bird's
    style,
And when the organs of perception have
    atrophied,
Few can see an Angel peep through an artist's
    ecstatic smile.

III. THE SOUL AGLOW

I glow on the harbour wall back in dark
    Charlestown
Like the light on the mast of the fishing
    smack at sea,   130
I glow from a visionary power which has
    folded down
From an implicate nothing-and-One to what
    buds in me.
Away from all towns I sit in the dark and bask
As if in the church by the sea on Gunwalloe's
    shore,
I rediscover ancient powers, and ask
To know the tides that lap at my well-lit door.

So hail the Universal Age of Light!
Whose waves flow in from every time of
    quest,
New rising of Baroque in its own right,
New sunrise for the Holy Roman West!   140
I look down from the Age with which I glow
And see that after all our questioning breath
Men will see our search as a Way of Fire and
    know
The Tree-hung star-rose souls that light dark
    death.

6 August 1983, revised 17-18 April 1985 and 20 May 1990

ON THE DEATH OF AUNT FLO
(SONNETS)

1. DEAD CHEEK
Unsteadily, you totter to the hall
And sit on the window seat, look on June
    trees,
Swollen face, glazed eyes, frozen smile, like a
    wall,
Look round as if to say "I'm still here, if you
    please."
I pretend not to know what is wrong with you,
The cancer down your leg, and in your breast

Which strangles your kidneys, so your water's
    like glue;
Holding your enlarged wrist and arm by your
    chest,
Your already dead hand, I pretend you will
    last.
I make a speech for my aunt's birthday, and
    bar
All mention of the future or the past
Out of respect for you and walk you to your
    car.
I kiss your dead cheek, say "In August – a
    drive"
As if I believed – cheek indeed – you will still
    be alive.

5 August 1983, revised 13 October 1993

2. KESTRELS

An oppressive August day. I read listlessly,
In the afternoon, I reluctantly drive
To a Cornish vineyard, we sit in tranquillity
Among grapes, bask in warm sun, and feel
    alive,
Look at cows, hens, a goose. Later I go
On to the sea, find a cove at high tide.
Cliffs slope down to sand only the locals
    know,
A stream runs through, huge rocks on either
    side.
Above the low gorse, spreading their wings, I
    see
Two kestrels hover, still as summoning souls
And I wonder if they are a sign to me.
Back home a phone message like caved-in
    holes,
"Aunt Flo in a coma in hospital"; then I know
The kestrels like souls were waiting for her to
    go.

5 August 1983, revised 13 October 1993

3. EVENING STAR

Twilight on a Cornish coast. I make a call.
My aunt died at seven, I am thankful and
    repelled;
She was doomed with cancer while I enjoyed
    Cornwall;
Her kidneys were strangled, her water swelled
Her body, she had six months, better like this,
Though no one went with her in the
    ambulance;

She died alone – she died, for all that, did not
    miss
Her cue, and if she can, dying is just a dance.
Surely she has merely moved to a new plane.
I leave the telephone box with the evening
    star.
Night and the brightest light, I walk up the
    lane;
Venus, twinkling, winks at me from afar,
One star, in an early dark, fills me with awe
Like a bright soul floating above an alien
    shore.

5 August 1983, revised 13 October 1993

4. METEORITE

I walk to Charlestown harbour in the dark;
The night drips with bright stars, above calm
    sea.
I wonder, "Are you there like a watermark?"
Baffled, cord severed, still hovering, she
Waits near her swollen body, in a night.
She will soon journey to her new life – again?
I wonder, "Will you go past the white light?"
Or will you be met? As if in answer, then,
A shooting star trails down the spangled sky
Like a bright angel diving down to earth,
And then I know what life is and death's lie,
And know we live for tasks from our first
    birth
And trail our light for a brief while, afar,
And then return to shine out as a star.

5 August 1983, revised 17 October 1993

5. STREAM AND SEA

We drive down a twisting lane with high mud
    walls
A car's width to a stream from fields, that
    seeks
And divides the golden beach where a green
    cliff falls,
And now I sit with the warm sun on my
    cheeks
And see the kestrel hover over furze
And think of your cold body, awaiting fire,
Think of you dead while I gaze at a bird that
    stirs
And ten children who have dammed the
    stream and tire,
Take spades and dig away at the crumbling
    "town",

And two dig a trench right down to the sea
And swoosh, the dammed-up water gushes
    down
And I think your life from the hills ran into
    debris,
And now the dam has burst and you race on
And merge yourself in a calm blue sea, and
    are gone.

5 August 1983, revised 17 October 1993

6. WATCHING SMOKE

I stand in the church where you played the
    organ.
The vicar shouts from the back of the aisle
    somewhere
"I am the Resurrection and the Life." I scan.
Your coffin, under two wreaths, is on the bier.
Are you up in the beams of the church, where
    the chords waft,
Are you watching with your puckish smile
    our stares?
Our sombre faces, clutched handerchiefs, our
    soft
Voices of time, not eternal life, our tears?
You have made your last journey down an
    ancient street,
Through meadows to this chapel, and holy
    ground,
And your coffin stands on rollers and again I
    entreat
"Are you still attached?" as the curtains roll
    round
And we walk out to wreaths in the grounds
    and choke.
No one looks at the chimney or thinks you are
    now smoke.

August 1983, revised 17 October 1993

7. GRAIN

They sit with handkerchiefs in hands and
    mourn
But I know that though it is sad you are gone,
A human is like a flower near a thorn,
The wind blows and, without special reason,
It is gone, and nothing fills its place in the
    lane;
I know that a human is like a stalk of corn,
It grows its chaff and puts up its head so that
    its grain
Can be garnered at harvest time, with

apparent scorn,
And the stalk is buried, or set on fire, burns
    red
When wheatfield stubble smokes against the
    sky –
Death is the end of all we blinkered enjoy;
It is time for your soul's grain to be harvested,
Your immortal part, like a poet's work and
    eye,
And so, while sad, I feel a calming joy.

8 August 1983, revised 17 October 1993

8. SNAKE SKIN

Why couldn't they leave you alone? You
    were doomed.
You had accepted the diagnosis,
You were at peace, and drastic measures
    loomed:
They changed all your blood, injected you
    with this
"Kill or cure" method, the nurse said – too
    true!
They experimented on you, as in a war;
They used you as a guinea pig and killed you.
Had they not, you would have lived a little
    more.
What did they inject you with that made you
    cool?
Now you are out of it, away from pain
And will you be a pupil in my school?
And is your sister already born again?
Have you, like a snake, shed your body's skin
So you can have new flesh and a baby's grin?

August 1983, revised 17 October 1993

A FOUNTAIN OF STARS: THE UNIVERSE IN LOVE

I stand in the garden's mid-August midnight,
It is a dark night with a fountain of stars.
I look at the Plough, at Cassiopeia, bright
Perseus, which a crowd of meteorites scars.
Our earth spins through them one night in the
    year;
Rocks drawn into our atmosphere, in less time
    than a wink
Like lines slashing across the sky two tear
Quick as a flash and fade before I can blink;
They warm and burn out in a spectacular
    blaze,
I watch a dozen and could watch for hours

And now my head bumps on the Milky
    Way's,
And I kiss Vega, a younger system than ours,
And still the stars shoot, loving in a trail,
And squirt the wriggling universe, removing
    its veil.

12 August 1983, revised 13 October 1993

AT PENQUITE HOUSE, NEAR ST. SAMPSON'S

I take the long hill path to Penquite House;
At the second gate, go down with barely a
    grouse
To a Victorian lodge, servants quarters and
    stores,
Past a gas lamp to the great double front
    doors
Where Garibaldi was received by Peard,
A Byronic soldier the Italians feared;
Round the conservatory to the croquet-hooped
    back lawn
And a view over where Golant and the river
    yawn.

Here the Barretts lived, and the Rashleighs
    too,
And other well-known families passed
    through.   10
Here is history among the thick hedgerows.
Now tired Youth Hostellers rest their legs, or
    doze,
Young men and trousered girls play pool or
    sit,
Bikes upside down, and dream of a love that's
    it.
I cannot ask to see Garibaldi's room
So I will imagine Tristan, stretched out in
    gloom.

I think of King Mark's palace at Castledore
Where adulterous Tristan wooed Iseult before
His wife's "Black sail" sounded like a
    divorce;
Now a ring of earthworks overgrown with
    gorse.   20
I look across the hills to the blue sea;
A superb place for a castle to be.
I stand by Tristan's sixth century gravestone
With its raised "T", and hear Iseult's faint
    moan.

I walk down the path to St. Sampson's church
Where Mark and Iseult made their devotions;
    I search:
No bats hang in the porch as they used to do,
I walk among arches and go straight to
The medieval stained glass Sampson's cell,
His book, and the vision he had of
    an angel;   30
I gaze at the bossed ceiling the Colquites gave
And the vision that brought him to found this
    Cornish nave.

I go into the churchyard, look down again
On Fowey river and reflect on the two men –
Sampson and Peard, visionary and soldier,
    growth
As contemplative and man of action, both
Have a place in this magical countryside;
One settled by the well, one lived and died
In nearby Trenython, last years immersed
In the Bishop of Truro's panelling of Charles
    the First.   40

Sampson was of the time a fisherman saw
St. Michael appear on a guarded mount, and
    pour
Visions to latter-day Sampsons, hermits
On Tintagel cliffs or in Roche rock's castle
    slits
Who lived on high in the Archangel's air
And hauled a basket of food up from
    somewhere
Below, and today who continues the visionary
    glow?
Not, of Peard's panelled house, the Bishop of
    Truro!

I think of Lanhydrock and Chirpy Richards'
    room
In the First World War, when he was a
    groom.   50
And the great life under the 17th century
    ceiling;
I could be a visionary there, do my writing.
I will flee to my Penquite, make it a fort
And enjoy in its gardens away from the
    London Court
The contemplative life men of action crave,
    for
I too have been a soldier in a private war.

The spiritual and secular: Tristan, Sampson –
Both went to Brittany, one with a vision,
The other hopelessly in love, in pain;
Divine and human love, sacred and
    profane;   60
Like a soldier who fought in unifying wars
And an evangelist who christianised with
    oars,
One needs the other. We conquer and love to
    make one,
And the mystic melts in God, the inner sun.

I have Peard, Tristan and Sampson within my
    soul;
Conquest, love and vision jostle, cajole –
The contraries within the heart and head;
Open to spirit and you channel it instead
Into the world of wars and love and sense
Where it pours in the workings of
    Providence.   70
We can live among opposites where we grasp,
    with a shock,
That spirit and sense are mixed in the
    Baroque.

18-19 August 1983, revised 27 September 1993

PASSION PLAY

See Jesus standing in the pub car park
And on a hillside, speaking to children,
While Roman soldiers hold us back with
    spears.
Then walk with him to Grange Court, where I
    was taught,
And see four priests accuse him. See him hail
A tax collector, cure Mary Magdalene.
See him ride on a donkey through waving
    palms,
And the the trial in the King's Head car park.
As Pilate offers Jesus to the crowd
We cry "Barabbas! Give us Barabbas!"   10
And see his flogged body and crown of thorns
See him bend under a huge cross and gasp,
And now see him stumble as we jeer and boo,
See him stagger across the road to the church-
    yard,
See him thrown back, hear his shrieks and
    groans
As the nails are banged in, see his bleeding
    trunk
As the cross is hoisted, see his frail flesh hang

As your eyes fill with tears at his despair.

Among the grassy graves three black-clad
    women
With white faces, wait at his bleeding feet. 20
We stand on tombs to get a better view
Of Roman soldiers dicing for the robe.
Now he gives a muttering cry and slumps his
    head.
See his side pierced, see him taken down from
    the cross,
See his corpse carried away in a white cloth.
Now in the chapel see the disciples' despair.
Now Mary Magdalene comes in and says
"I-have-seen-the-Lord!" with shining joy,
And as the disciples kneel, see Jesus come
With outstretched arms and love in his
    shining eyes.   30

At a Passion play I milled through the town
With a crowd, stood on tiptoe to see, I was
    back
In the Roman days, as a centurion
Pushed me back and shouted to control the
    crowd
I broke through this decaying civilisation
And a shoal of tears rushed through my heart,
Washed through my eyes and left me feeling
    free.
I had taken part in a play and knew a passion
That touched me. But where was the lingering
    hope?
As I later looked out on my two green
    fields   40
I knew I too would be crucified in my way –
Each of us is crucified in a thousand ways –
And left for dead, and there would be no open
    doors.
And was there a meaning beyond this material
    life,
In my projects, my scratching at history?
I played out a passion for my own meaning.

27-30 May 1984, revised 4 October 1993

COPPED HALL

Turn off the Epping road well before dark.
A clearing leads to ornate gates, there park
And walk through pines past many a bluebell,
Over a hill till the great large-chimneyed shell
Of the third Copped Hall looms up, all

overgrown.
Boarded up with corrugated iron and stone.
See the eighteenth century pediments, as the
	light fades
Go to the tangled garden, and sunken
	balustrades.

The first Fitzauchers' hall passed to the
	Waltham abbots;
Then the King so Mary Tudor took Mass on
	this spot; 10
Then to Heneage (a present from his guest,
	the Queen),
Who rebuilt it and married the mother – hence
	the *Dream* scene –
Of Shakespeare's WH; to Suckling; Sackville;
Till Conyers built this shell that survived till
It was destroyed when a hair-clip used as
	fusewire
As the household dressed for church, lit the
	final fire.

O Edwardian glory – four-columned
	pediment,
Italian gardens where walled terraces went,
Stairways, iron gates, fountains, figures of
	stone,
Parterres, summerhouses where caryatids
	moan, 20
Conservatory and ballroom, no clop of hoofs,
A grandeur of pavilions and domed roofs –
But now decay, a roofless shell again,
And desolation in moonlight, or this fine rain.

Alas for great hall, like this ancient seat
That stood against time and then crumbled to
	defeat,
Alas for past grandeurs like this stone shell
In which a style challenged the dark, then
	fell.
Salute the vision and energy of its prime
Which kept an estate going in a ruinous
	time. 30
As civilisation lost dignity, it saw
A way of life perish, now home for the
	jackdaw.

Now see the ruined foundations of Heneage's
	hall;
Elizabeth stood with Shakespeare by this

wall,
And saw his Dream performed in the Long
	Gallery
At the wedding of his Theseus to Countess
	Mary.
How overgrown the yew walk now, climb
	through
To a ruined tower, headless marble statue.
Time, like a clump of nettles, winds about
Past glories and stings the hand that reaches
	out. 40

There are two forces – order and chaos.
Out of the forest: a fine house, gain from loss
Yew walks, stone steps, square gardens and
	statues,
And candles blaze against twilight's night
	blues
And a play is acted, all are in good cheer,
Then the ground moves and gigantic cracks
	appear,
The house is abandoned or razed, the people
	go –
Or else burnt down by fire, and the nettles
	grow.

But its scenes are retained for ever in these
	walls,
The voices that laughed linger as history
	falls, 50
Those images are present to our mind now,
We see a queen, a wedding, a frown, a bow,
And for all eternity each triumph matures
This Hall copped it from time, but its art
	endures.
Like Greek – or Roman stone, or art of Copt –
This ruin embodies events, as if time had
	stopped.

30 May 1984, revised 19 September 1993

THE TIDE

As I breathe in and out
I hear sea wash and ebb;
A tide comes into my lungs,
Of breath from an unseen Web.

Another tide creeps in
Congesting my bellowing lungs,
A tide of death that inflames,
Licking with bacterial tongues.

If it were one lung only
They could cut part of it out,
But it is two and so I must
Carry on as if it is without.

And hope it ebbs quickly
And doesn't drown my breath.
A tide comes into me
That whispers for my death.

26 June 1984, revised 18 January 1994

AT HATFIELD HOUSE

I walk through the maze of gardens, and look
    at
The south face (Inigo Jones), and retrace my
    steps
Back to the Old Palace – old brick, wood
    stair,
And, sitting on a lawn among marble statues,
Suddenly as the birds sang, I caught a
    glimpse:
The studded wood door opened and a figure
    glided
Down the wooden staircase to walk in the
    miniature maze,
And out to the wild roses, and the twittering
    birds,
And I knelt and said "Your Majesty" as she
    passed.
O marvellous places that have such
    memories!
I can reach you, Elizabeth, in the places where
    you walked.

Summer 1984(?), revised 18 January 1994

FRAGMENT: BEING DAMMED

Foam from hills to the sea;
Like a stream dammed, my being
Is still water on sands,
But it moves imperceptibly,
Now flowing, now gushing to the sea.

Summer 1984(?), revised 18 January 1994

MULTIPLICITY: A NIGHTMARE
(A FRAGMENT)

And have you stood in our universe and
    peered
Between mirrors, one on a wardrobe door,
And seen universes rising, one inside another,

Each smaller that the last till it's lost from
    view,
Each one progressing towards infinity –
And have you raised a hand and waved to a
    self
That looks like you from another time and
    place,
Separated by several universes from yours?
And have you wondered, is that self more free
Than you, and can it act in a different way?
Your selves all seem the same, but what if
    each
Is different, and has a life of its own
    elsewhere?

Summer 1984(?), revised 18 January 1994

MULTIPLICITY: THROUGH THE MIRROR

Through the mirror
In another universe
Is my other life.

Somewhere, elsewhere,
On the slopes of the Alps perhaps
Is my other house.

I turn away
And stare at these happy fields
Leaving behind

A hidden life
In which you, whoever you are,
Look after me?

And a million elsewheres
And a million other mes?
No! This is my reality!

Summer 1984(?), revised 18 January 1994

MULTIPLICITY: BETWEEN BATHROOM MIRRORS

As one who steps out of his bath
And stands between two mirrors, free,
And looks and sees his face recede
From mirror to mirror endlessly,

So are there an infinite number of worlds
For our infinite number of faces
With something rearranged in each,
With objects moved to new places?

And so too perhaps from one out-of-sight
    point
Reality unfolds to our norm,
Manifests the desire of the One
Through infinite dimensions into form.

And so, as you step out of your bath,
Look into one of the mirrors nearby
And see how substance, time and space
Unfold from Idea and unity.

Summer 1984(?), revised 18 January 1994

CHARIOT-RACE

See the horses racing,
Their manes flowing
As the charioteer
Crouches over the reins,
His hair flowing,
And see the wheels
On the chariot turn
Backwards it seems
As the horses toss
And stamp and snort.

Summer 1984(?), revised 18 January 1994

WHEN I DIE

When I die,
You will find me where the pond is,
And the ducks scoot among the reeds;
You will find me where the hawthorn grows
On the grassy bank;
You will find me at the cricket ground
When the sun beats down
And the ball is smacked with willow.
You will find me.

Summer 1984(?), revised 18 January 1994

GOLDFINCH

Birds pecking on my table
Hanging in the hawthorn.
Most are sparrows, I look
To see if there is a goldfinch,
More rare than a bullfinch
Or a Forest willow-warbler.
There is never a goldfinch.

Summer 1984(?), revised 18 January 1994

FLOWERS FROM A SHELL

You gave me a porcelain piece for my
    birthday,

Like half an egg-shell with a jagged edge,
And fourteen little blue flowers grow there,
Asserting life as round a rocky ledge.

The universe is like a hatching egg.
Just look inside and see the growing life.
Out of shining surfaces come flowers,
The universe is an egg produced by a wife.

And I think at once of our family fracture
And ask you which is you and which is
    me,   10
And you point and say "You are the biggest",
And "That one's me – I didn't think you'd see

"The symbolism so quickly." And then I think
Of the broken Soviet yoke and fourteen states
Flowering freely, a broken prison, a shell
I must smash so flowers can grow, destruction
    creates.

Out of a broken heart like an empty shell,
Like periwinkles flower many children;
Out of a broken tyranny many peoples –
A message of hope, Easter rising of men.   20

We dine and now, my daughter – shell for
    shell –
Have this crab's back from which I feed, my
    art.
This hard-shell back with eyes and mask.
    Turn it
And see the flowers grow from its empty
    heart.

31 July 1984, revised 21 December 1993

AT GREENFIELD FARMHOUSE

Turn off the road near Invergarry, drive
Beside Loch Garry, then turn down a track,
Pass black-faced sheep in bracken and arrive
At a slat bridge, trundle across its back
Like a tank, in deep countryside, wind
Up past isolated farms to the end of the lane,
Mountains all round and braes, until we find
The Greenfield farm with blaeberries round
    each pane.

Stone floors and ancient rooms and bay
    windows,
A garden of flowers and wandering sheep; 10

All round mountains, and hills where bracken
    grows,
Where swifts swoop, dart, dip, flit and,
    landing, peep,
Tirelessly catching midges; here the grass is
    soft
With yellow celandine, harebells grow round
Out of the stone on the grass of this old croft.
Here is a deep peace beyond all traffic sound.

No water here in the nineteenth century stone.
Pour water from containers, fill them from the
    burn,
Flush loos from buckets; no TV or phone.
This peace round the log-fire is like
    Sauterne.   20
Eat slowly, go quietly, do not encroach,
Sit and contemplate the source beyond all
    squirms.
Sheep run baaing and huddle from your
    approach,
And near Laddie Wood in the pool trout rise
    for worms.

Such places remove us from Western
    cacophany
To the silence of lake, wilderness and
    mountain
Which gave Wordsworth his deep tranquillity,
Which Orwell knew on Jura and Shelley near
    Gen-
-eva. Lakes mirror Highlands and Alps more
    high.
Open to this silence, where in solitude   30
A man can stand on a hillock against the sky,
Be the only soul among mountains and lochs,
    quite nude.

Man seeks out country places to be alone
And define himself against mountains by day,
And stars by night, away from groups, wind-
    blown,
Alone among trees and fields and streams to
    stray
And discover new places in his heart.
Each sojourn in the country is a finding-out,
A searching of the soul for its deepest part,
A finding of a vision that transcends doubt. 40

This could be anywhere, if you've eyes to see;

In aloneness I leave aside my ego,
And open to Nature, which pours in energy
And feeds my soul, lights up my spirit so
I am vibrant, let healing energies pass.
"Back to the countryside" – to know your
    need
For true self, which is one with trees and
    grass,
And sees the light unfold in bud and seed.

So, Greenfield, I will be nourished by your
    farm.
Let the *Times* ring, I will escape the times,   50
The world can go hang in this delicious
    calm,
Hang up the social ego near clock chimes.
We are two selves, both calm and world; can
    join
The two if we curl up after we're hurled.
I need my calm for reflection, like a Greek
    coin,
And return, recharged, to the whirl of the
    social world.

3 August 1984, revised 23 November 1993

GREENFIELD

Greenfield has mountains all round it,
And trees and hills where whitethroats flit
Beyond a bridge, where black-faced sheep
Baa in bracken, and brown cows sleep;
On its green slopes town men can graze
Till social eyes see with soul's gaze
And feel with trodden celandine
Or swoop with swifts, rejoice with pine
Where eagles fly, and midges swarm,
Or fish for trout (wince with hooked worm); 10
Town men can share country delights
During the days or the light nights,
And climb Ben Nevis when it's clear
Or drive and sample Highland beer
Near where the rose-bay willow-herb
Pinks every wayside's floral kerb,
Visit castles if days are full
Or disappear to Skye or Mull,
Or see glass blown, or flower-press,
Or look for monsters in Loch Ness,   20
Or draw water from Garry Loch
When burns have dried to bouldered rock;
In Laddie Wood, under Ben See
Deer dart across a path, then flee.

Near mountains wrapped in mist or clouds
Far from all noisy coach-tour crowds –
Green days in sun, red faces glow,
Log fires that blaze when night chills blow;
Bees hum in harebells, and men fill
Quiet, tranquil hours in a deep still.   30

August 1984

GLASS-BLOWING: FLOWER

Near Loch Ness, see a glass-blower.
He takes a glass rod in his tongs,
Heats it on a jet till it glows,
Rotates and pulls it with forceps, prongs,

Then blows a bubble, twists,
Heats it to melt, dips out a spout,
Swiftly makes a stem of a flower
And pinches three clear petals out

Flat, then puts it into his bowl;
It hardens, he lights his pipe, tense,
From the jet, and with what skill makes
A transparent form, subtle essence.

So it is with poems. I take my lump,
Blow it into a hollow, twist,
And tweezer and heat it to a glow
For a transparent flower, from mist!

More deft than clay this airy work
In transparent ideas that weave rainbows;
A glass bubble of air, this flower:
Delicate, perfect moment that glows.

3 August 1984, revised 17 January 1994

LOCK-GATE AT FORT AUGUSTUS: BACK TO OUR SOURCE

At Fort Augustus, in trout country
A bridge and several lochs – a flow;
The water level between each loch
Is higher than the one below .

And as this boat is going up
Each water level must be emptied down.
Water pours through holes in the gate,
As it bubbles and froths, we rise; don't drown.

And when the levels are the same
On both sides of the gate, a plane,

The gate opens and the boat goes through,
And waits at the next level again.

So it is with our salmon-like leap
Up waterfalls back to our source;
At each barrier we must wait,
And the turbulence is a levelling course.

3 August 1984, revised 16 January 1994

THE BAGPIPER

High on a mountain ridge, there stands
A piper playing his bagpipes
In tartan hat and kilt and socks,
Red wizened face, no army stripes.

Blowing and squeezing the air up the tubes,
He plays a skirling Highland reel
And though alone he keeps his eyes
On his bagpipes. What does he feel?

So proud he stands, and now he plays,
Erect, "Over the sea to Skye"   10
And all around him in a cloud
Ten million midges bite and fly.

He stops. "These midges are terrible,
It is my bare legs that are worst."
I offer him repellent, he squirts.
"That's helped me a lot, I was going to burst."

Then back to his playing, with distant eyes,
And he's lost to the world, back in his art,
And I know how the artist must be
When his midges dance and bite round his
                    heart.   20

I, peaceful, leave for the isle of Skye
And still he plays, completely alone,
Pouring out his heart to the stones and sky,
Standing as still as a mountain stone.

4 August 1984, revised 17 January 1994

IONA: SILENCE

By ferry cross blue sea to green cliffs where
The grey Abbey stands out. Once ruined, it
Is now restored. Dolls' houses, we grate on
                    the pier.
I walk from white sands to where whitethroats
                    flit,
Look back at the deep blue of each Northern

379

wave,
Then glide on grass through the roofless
nunnery
And a pilgrim now, feel where nuns who gave
Up mainland charms went to their church in
glee.

The path winds on to St. Oran's chapel. There
I sit in twelfth century quiet – two pews   10
Under a light, and a carved hearth – then peer
At kings' tombs in the Street of the Dead, and
choose
St. Columba's shrine, which two wheelhead
crosses face.
I sit where his tomb once was in a still like
sleep
And feel the energies of this ancient place
And sink into silence on which baa sheep.

Here I am at home, apart from the outside day
And noisy children – or a singing choir;
Here I can sink into deep quiet and pray
Where Christendom began in Columban
fire,   20
Go back to the roots in silence of our free
West. Here in Nature's beauty I feel the hour
A culture put down roots like a growing tree
That feeds our leafy consciousness with still-
living power.

I find the grassy site of Columba's cell,
A doorkeeper's small door in Paradise.
By the Abbey altar where Columba fell
I sit, feet chilled on ancient stones to ice,
And feel the earth's power surge up through
each limb.
I stand again before St. Columba's shrine;   30
The cross that has a druid's sun as a rim
Throws its shadow through the door in the
sunshine.

The shadow of the ringed cross is on my back,
Feet on the earth, there's a tingle up my spine,
I lift my target-ringed heart so I soar till –
crack!
Light breaks, prickling my scalp, flooding my
shadow line.
The Light is in me, I am in a trance inside,
I surge and feel the heart's love burst in heat,
Full of the Light's orgasmic power, I glide

On a silence that has seen heathen hordes
retreat.   40

Where else in Britain can one know in shrines
Religion is contemplation, not hymns in a
church,
The truth Zen masters know in mountain
pines?
I know Columba, who killed in his saintly
search
Three thousand men (sense and spirit
indeed!),
Who sailed thin coracles in a whipping breeze
And stamped a hermit's gaze on the pagan
creed
And loved the beauty of these Northern seas.

7 August 1984, revised 18 April 1985

STAFFA: WIND

We sit in a small boat which dips in a high
Sea against the tide and, the sun behind, flips
wet.
All huddle under oilskins to keep dry
But I, salt on my cheeks, ignore each jet
And think of how I breast a tide each day
And sometimes glimpse a vision as I go.
I look and see a rainbow in the spray,
An arch in the flicking foam of a glimpsed
rainbow!

We go to where Fingal lived, hermit of hypes!
Iona's last abbot. We pass the cave   10
Of basalt rock, it looks like organ-pipes.
The boat stops by rocks, we jump into a wave,
Squelch up island cliffs, tread the green top,
edge
Down on black hexagonal columns, so
We reach the great cave, and inch along the
ledge
Deep within where the sea waps just below.

Above the boom of the sea as it roars round
I stand where Mendelssohn once stood, and
hear
The strange, clear piping of a woodwind
sound –
But there is no pipe, it is only the wind and
the ear.   20
The wind I cannot hear plays reed-like round
The ghostly crevices in the rock's rough seas.

I listen for the flow that makes this sound
And think of the quiet wind that makes my
    lungs wheeze.

My body is, I am rock, cave and deed
And through me blows a wind that makes me
    pipe
For joy a sound like "Om" on a woodwind
    reed,
That flicks froth that gives my third eye a
    wipe.
And I am a boat, and at me blows the green-
Filled foam in which I see this windy day   30
A rainbow that unites seen and unseen,
A rainbow of the mind in corporeal spray.

On my night-sea boatings I can sometimes see
The wind-whipped visions in the water-spray
And then plunge into a deep cave and be
The piping of the wind that sounds all day.
O wonderful wind that gives such sights,
    please heave –
O wind I cannot see, but can surmise
Through your deeds in my hair and flapping
    sleeve,
Cleanse my lungs and blow joys to my ears
    and eyes!   40

Now I have opened to a diviner wind
Of which the Staffa sound is an echo
And heard a symphony blast, all sound
    unthinned,
Twelve seconds of swelling fortissimo
With a clash of cymbals, awesome roll of
    drums,
And I have heard the majestic Angels cheer,
But I still think of the Hebridean wind that
    numbs,
That echoes in rocky pipes the divine Idea.

August 1984, revised 19 April 1985

AT FINDHORN

I turn and drive down a windy road with the
    bay
To the left till the village comes, and round
The headland is the open sea, a way
With sand dunes where veined stones abound,
Blue water on which the sun explodes. I lie
And sunbathe, then enquire at the hotel.
And can this be where the spirit stirred, this

"lay-by",
Among these rows of caravans, each like a
    cell?

Here was a wilderness and a caravan "street",
Here in this unpromising earth a garden
    grew.   10
Thirty books in this store describe this feat
How the gardeners spoke to flowers as if they
    knew
Elves, fairies, and trolls, were real and found
    their powers
After the peaceful "flower power" generation
    came
These post-Hippies, who turned to growing
    flowers
In a "back to Nature" movement of world-
    wide fame.

I walk in and young gardening girls say
    "Hello",
One shows me the original vegetable garden
Next to the caravan where the founders began
    to hoe,
Guided there by divine Providence. Since
    then   20
I'm told they have moved to America. The
    green tops are
Huge in rows along narrow paths a girl
    sweeps.
Craft-rooms, tea-room, "Reception", "Quiet".
    No bar.
Here a community weeds, eats, prays and
    sleeps.

The Findhorn idea is a psychic one.
Here mediums gather and open to a source,
Conversations with St. John is a book they've
    done.
Here the dead guide the living and predict
    their course,
Each action is intended for a higher end,
And every girl who straightens from a bed   30
Of vegetables gives her skills as a friend,
Eschews profit and communes with the dead.

Why do they do it? For some it's a way of
    life –
"Sir George dunked me in the bath when I
    was three."

Many are American girls, few are yet a wife,
Some like the security of the "family" –
To be kept in return for their craft skills
And to practise the psychic way in a "kibbutz-
      commune",
In a mixed "monastic nunnery" that fulfils,
At one with their fellow spirits to whom they
      "attune".   40

The psychic is not spiritual, divine;
A Spangler's source has not Spengler's
      insight.
The saint who lives in a hermit's cell and
      shrine
Opens through Jesus to the mystic Light;
Here there is no cross, or church, they meet at
      hours;
There is no line of a thousand saints, who
      trod,
Or sacrifice, and all is occult powers
And surrendering to a source, not the will of
      God.

10 August 1984, revised 16 January 1994

THE MASSACRE AT CULLODEN

On this bleak moor Government and Jacobite
      lines
Faced each other; cousins Cumberland and
      Charles led
From stones equally far behind the mortar
      whines.
It was all over in an hour, stones mark the
      dead,
The massacre Cumberland encouraged,
      somehow
Inserting a lie in the Jacobite battle code:
"No quarter to the enemy." The sun beats
      now,
I stand on Cumberland's stone and see where
      he rode.

I gaze at this heather-thatched stone crofter's
      hut
That stood by the English line. Can anyone
      tell   10
What the woman who lived here thought of
      the smoke and the strut
As the battle raged and Mac Gillivray died by
      the well?

Did she help bury the English dead near her
      wall?
Was her hut searched for Jacobites, did she
      see
The thirty led "for medical help" fall,
Or did she hear the summary shots and flee?

I wonder what these Scots think now? Do
      they quote
The "forty-five"? See it as a silly quarrel
Between two branches of royals who were
      remote,
A spoilt and wilful Prince, and a Duke who
      was cruel?   20
Have the Scots not been fully integrated now,
Are we not all loyal to our Hanoverian
      Queen?
This shoddy massacre bound our isles
      somehow
And absorbed the Highland culture in the
      British scene.

10 August 1984, revised 17 January 1994

LETTER TO WORDSWORTH

After Esthwaite, where you skated till dark,
At Hawkshead I go into your schoolroom,
A long room from your time with antique
      desks,
And here I see your name carved, o vandal!
Now I walk down a lane to Colthouse
To the white house with an arch over the gate
Where you lodged with Ann Tyson, who
      wrote the account
That is now preserved in the schoolroom's
      upstairs.
I walk back past fields with you and look up
To the Friends' meeting-place you were taken
      to   10
When it was too wet to walk to the parish
      church –
And was that where you got to know the
      Light?
At Ullswater, where you stole the rowing-boat
And Sunday's Point came up behind the hill
I drive and watch your mountain rise behind,
Drive towards Gowbarrow, where you saw
      daffodils.
Now I walk round Dove Cottage, where you
      wrote great works,
And linger in the study, look at your skates

382

And think what a dark, poky place for you,
Two down four up, even though the spring is
    good.   20
And now I track you to Rydal Mount,
Which you rented, gaze at 15th century
    beams,
And see the study you lived out your days;
And now I see your grave in Grasmere
    church.
O great Wordsworth, you stood for a quiet
    apart
From the world, you enjoyed the peace of
    your moss-hut
And did not read the papers when Trafalgar
Was being fought, you ignored Nelson's war.
In your rejection of the world, you missed
    something.
A man is a whole and has to act out his
    beliefs,   30
But your belief was lopsided as you
Could not live in total isolation.
You had to write and ask for a job in the mail.
To write and act unifies thought and deed,
Action and contemplation, spirit and sense.
You tried to unite yourself in lakes and trees,
But in shunning the towns you missed the
    Baroque fusion
Of sense and spirit, of the perfect flower.
And so great Wordsworth, you remain for me
A sublime half-truth, a mystic without his
    world.   40
        11 August 1984, revised 10 October 1993

LETTER TO BEATRIX POTTER

I walk up to the open door;
Stone flags I know from *Samuel Whiskers*,
And the old range with a kettle there
And on the landing up the stairs
The chest where Tom Kitten may have hid
And bedrooms, and the attic where
The "Roly Poly" pudding happened –
Tom dunked in dumpling by the evil rat.
Cats, rats and dogs – and frogs of course,
Jeremy's Esthwaite is nearby   10
Where he munched a butterfly sandwich.
You had two pets as a little girl,
Peter Rabbit, Benjamin Bunny,
And you were taught Art and Nature.
You neglected humans rather,
You gave chocolate to your dogs but

Not to a hungry visiting child.
Now I peer over the blue Park fence
Into Mr MacGregor's garden,
I see him white bearded with a rake,   20
Hostile to the trespassing Peter.
Vile humans talk, and turn away.
You gave animals man's qualities,
And made some evil like Samuel,
And some naughty like naughty Tom,
Some trusting like the puddleduck;
Some sly like the well-mannered fox.
And how can I defend mankind?
Man is both wicked and quietly good
To those creatures he loathes or loves   30
And submits to, or inflicts, pain.
Man can choose or else be chosen,
Can sacrifice himself, or moan
Or be selfish and cruel and carp.
You knew man is a contradiction
A paradox, god and devil,
And you showed his opposites in fur.
        11 August 1984, revised 10 October 1993

SEA FORCE

Sea surges onto craggy Cornish cliffs,
Wave after boiling wave pours round the
    cove;
Flinging up spray on a dozen rocks, it biffs
And dashes where I sit like Olympian Jove.
What energy keeps its breakers rolling in,
Splashing with surf, thundering from the curl?
Scientists say "It is the moon", and grin,
But I know it's a force, a power, a swirl
That crashes in from calm and froths to shore
And rolls each wave that fumes where the
    foam droops,
And as the wind blows in the low-bent gorse
I know it is itself, a thudding law,
An elemental power where the gull swoops,
The endless boom and roar of life's tidal
    force.
        18 August 1984

SEA-RESCUES: DEATH LIKE A CORMORANT

Gunwalloe cove. I put my couch on sand
And walk up the rocky beach to the cliff wall
Above which stands the medieval church and
Walk down the aisle past stairs to the
    choirstall

In ancient peace. Outside waves bounce and
    swirl
In a distant sound. I gaze at the bay.
Bathers in the surging tide. By a topless girl
I lie down and sunbathe. A windless day.

Suddenly a bell rings. Bathers rush out
A wind is up, people converge and roam   10
And stand and point. Do I see two heads shout
In the surging rollers, near where the white
    surf's foam
Dashes against the rocks, flings up white
    spray,
And has one drowned? Or is it the dinghy
Out beyond the point, this side of the head-
    land? Say,
In the bobbing waves, what is that speck on
    the sea?

I walk to the rocks to get a better view.
The peace has gone. Death stalks the sea like
    a corm-
-orant, someone who was, is not; it could be
    you.
Behind the cliff, a helicopter's roar.   20
It circles, slanting, looking in the waves,
And can I see a body dip and float,
Can I see a life that is no more? Who saves
A castaway? There is no rowing-boat.

The helicopter passes and flies again,
Then disappears, and people return to their
    towel
And the peace returns. It was a man who had
    lain
On a surfboard, who could not swim in the
    swell;
His wife panicked, someone says, he swam all
    right
And they couldn't tell the helicopter in
    time.   30
Men grin and I see Death bare its teeth in
    flight,
Cheated of its fish-like prey, and swoop and
    climb.

A man swims with a surfboard, is in distress.
You fool, I say aloud, the red flag is out.
He is swept out, a man in a winch-harness
Dives in and crawls through waves, is he a

beach-scout?
He grabs him and the surfboard floats away,
He tows him back to land, two heads in
    shock.
The rescued man staggers ashore, okay,
And again I see Death snarl behind a rock.   40

But now there is a shadow across the beach
And as I watch the sea froth down and run,
White breakers in tiers surge into the cove and
    reach,
A mist causes a hazing over the sun.
I feel a chill breeze, leave the beach and go
Back to the church's mossy graves, gaze
    south,
As I sit in quiet, I hear Death cough and know
That all that separates us is an open mouth.

18 August 1984, revised 14 December 1993

AT TINTAGEL: ST. JULIOT AND MERLIN

I leave the Landrover and walk down the
    scree
Then climb the cliff path past green turfed
    rock, run
To the low slate grey walls that overhang the
    sea
That is clear green in the midday August sun.
Groined caves lurk below me in the veined
    headland;
I climb up steep steps carved in rock,
    windswept,
To twelfth century castle ruins that stand
Where King Uther ruled and Queen Igerne
    slept.

The grass is steeped in Arthur, of whom no
    trace:
The Norman castle, Black Prince's great
    hall,   10
And further up a tunnel, a food place
Carved by some Celts in the solid rock wall,
And further on – breathtaking views – a well,
Eighteen feet deep here near the cliff-top
    broom
And, with fifth century walls, a Norman
    chapel
And an altar that was a Celtic tomb.

And here I start, among the grasshoppers and,

Skipping in lilac heather, the tortoiseshell,
Looking across at the keep on the mainland
For here St. Juliot came from Wales and had
    his cell,   20
Before St. Columbus or Benedict.
I descend to the site of the Celtic monastery
    where
I sit in a low-walled hermit's cell (strict
Rule), the sea spread beneath me, green and
    clear.

Here I am at the very beginning
At the time of the Desert Fathers who sent
    hermits
Through Gaul into Britain. This simple
    living
Precedes Arthur and the reason for our visits.
Here there was barely room for a man to lie
Down, but he was above the world, near God,
    at one,   30
Open to the winds and the ocean in the sky;
In his inner dark he could see the midnight
    sun.

It sit on the beach below by Merlin's cave,
Where Uther's son was handed to the old
    wizard
Or druid. I sit in a crowd who misbehave,
Not controlling their dogs, shouting each
    word,
And in this babble of twentieth century noise
These shrieks and cries as if Uther had died,
I think of Merlin's solitude and poise
(His cave's escape to the bay the other
    side).   40

I think of the hermit perched on his great
    height.
O wonderful place that has Juliot above
    Merlin!
Dark caves of magic, and hermit cells of
    Light!
Wizard king-maker, and hermit denying skin!
Magicians are in the world though apart from
    it
And use their powers to scheme within the
    Whole.
Hermits are above the world in the Infinite
And purify the world with their praying soul.

22 August 1984, revised 16 January 1994

HAULING UP NETS IN MOUNT'S BAY: DIVINE PLAN

Dawn at six, gulls scream behind every
    chimney-stack.
In June or July, if it's clear they scream all
    night.
I drive to the quay in a yellow fish van's back
And chug out of harbour in early light
With two Cornish fishermen, to haul nets
    "well".
St. Michael's Mount hangs above mist and
    clings
As a south east wind whips up a choppy
    swell.
A gannet flies by, long neck, beating wings.

We sail towards the glancing sunlight and
    raise
A five hundred yard net, the boat at rest: 10
Turbot, monkfish – jaws wide, angler-rod –
    gaze
And are held by the eyes and thrown into a
    chest;
Crayfish with antennae and flipper tail,
A blue lobster, ray with undermouth plead,
Camouflaged with false eyes, or a pebbled
    veil;
Crabs, starfish, coral, scallops and seaweed.

The nets burn hands and tear fingers. I tug my
Float side. Fisherman tugs leaded weights and
    knots
And removes sea-slugs, which squirt a yellow
    dye,
And huss, which will be bait for tomorrow's
    pots,   20
Plaice with orange spots and squinting eyes
    flay.
Cutting begins: monk are cut in half on
Deck, head and stomach bag thrown, like guts
    of ray,
Black-backed gulf bark and swoosh for
    carrion.

And now the nets, piled up, are returned to the
    sea
And the lead weights wap on the back wood
    and rail,
Till the last rope is held taut so that the empty
Net is with the tide (across, next haul may

fail).
Next week the tide is high "at the moon's
    will";
Neap, equinox and Michaelmas tides are
    high   30
There is more cutting, and fish innards swill
On the deck and send up a nauseous stench as
    they dry.

There are three more nets like this, and life is
    cheap.
Crabs have legs pulled off them and shells are
    cracked.
I stare at the smooth sea thirty fathoms deep
And the life below which is slaughtered,
    attacked
So men can make a living here down west,
And I look at the mist and cloudy sky and
    then
Wonder at this brute survival of the fittest.
Did God create creatures to be caught by
    men?   40

Says Kingsley: "Everything is intricately
Created. Half an hour from birth a calf can
    stand.
Bantams an hour old eat obediently,
Their mother grunts 'Yes'/'No' to food, it's
    planned.
Break a crab's leg here, it will discard the
    rest.
This monk angles fish in and then snaps its
    jaw,
Camouflaged like the sea-bed so it can kill
    and digest.
Everything knows what to do, and follows a
    law."

So there is a divine plan in which each has a
    need
And purpose is related to another's locale. 50
Naked necessity! This lives so that can feed,
And the scavenging black-backed gull
    devours offal.
Everything exists for its own sake and for the
    plan;
We, too, can live or be useful fodder.
O wonderful, cruel Creation that gives man
And every creature a hold over another!

                    23 August 1984, revised 16 January 1994

CLOUDS HILL

Walking through rhododendrons to your
    cottage, I see
The lintel proclaim "ou phrontis" – "why
    worry?"
(Or "I don't care"). There is a leather bed,
Walls lined with books and a fireplace where,
    half dead,
You held court while back from the camp by
    day,
Fed your mates, stoked the fire, chatting
    away.
I go up panelled stairs to the music room,
Leather door and chairs – here you were still
    as a tomb.

Here you were to write when you retired from
    being Shaw,
From your "mind suicide" in the Air Force
    and Tank Corps.   10

Most of all you admired the creative artist,
Self-expression in imaginative form you
    missed.
Like a monastery, this place would restore
    your health
Through indifference to worldly advancement
    and wealth,
A dream cruelly cut short by your motor bike,
Or were you cut short by a black car's
    murderous strike?

You sought a standard most do not know to
    exist,
Yearned for the mountain peak most see in
    mist.
I see you at Tafileh with a cool gaze;
As the spy who beat Allenby by three days 20
And ruled Damascus under wisdom's eye;
As, released, the reluctant king-maker at
    Versailles:
Quintessential action which fills the mind
And removes all boredom that makes
    consciousness blind.

But though you had a man of action's insight
I do not think you got reflection right.
A balance of sword and pen draws meaning
    from
The well of consciousness, buckets axiom.

Better to have called the Air Force "a prison,
    shrill",
And to have gazed on heights and depths,
    cloud and hill   30
In this brown study and leather chair, without
    pay,
So Clouds Hill could be known for the Mystic
    Way.

Action and reflection are hard to balance
When a man lives alone with solitude as his
    stance
Unless he chooses the inner path up doubt.
Freedom is not found by simply dropping
    out
But in a disciplined route march to higher
    ground,
And an upward search for the light you never
    found.
You turned from the world and the adulatory
    crowd,
But in place of a summit you found cloud.   40

I read on your grave in this cemetery
"Dominus Illuminatio Mea", and sadly,
Under a blue Atlantic fir (like mine), defend
You, glad you are now free from your legend.
But your performance fell short of the height;
You rejected the world (ou phrontis) and were
    right,
But in place of a dazzling summit, like the
    crowd
You found a dark hill and perpetual cloud.

26 August 1984, revised 28 September 1993

QUIET

After the storm and the crashing waves,
Suddenly, a blue sky and calm sea,
A pale satiny shot silk blue
And barely a wrinkle to disturb me.

I tiptoe down the harbour wall
And stand in breathless quiet, my bones
Listen to each gentle washing,
Each lapping at the harbour stones,

And the feathery trees in the setting sun
Are dark and clear and fresh, complete,
And all the houses are bathed in gold
And are still in the deserted street

As if all who live in them, too,
Are quiet to hear the soft, hushed sea,
Breathe in and out without a sound
So as not to disturb its divinity.

August 1984(?), revised 6 December 1993

SPORTSMEN, MISTS

A green turfed pitch, a packed crowd in a
    stand
And skilful players running with the ball,
Kicking at goal or handling a pass, a grand
Near-perfect stroke with willow we can recall.
Sport stirs and revives deep childhood
    memory:
A Cup Final goal shared with a father now
    dead,
A boundary hit into the Canterbury tree,
The emotion then as the crowd's excitement
    spread,
Now an image. How sad when these heroes
    cannot run,
These self-effacing men with vacant eyes,
So ordinary when removed from what they've
    done,
Like small crags we thought mountains when
    mists rise.
O the greatness of what they did when the
    crowd shouted "Yes",
And the smallness of what they are now, just
    a sadness.

8-9 September 1984, revised 29 November 1993

INSOUCIANCE

Footballers look casual about the big match
Spectators tense and bite their nails and wait,
And leap into the air when a goal is scored.
The players kick with insouciance and fate.

Cicketers look casual as they flick the bat
Then hook a bouncer into the mound stand.
Spectators leap and chant at another six,
The players lean akimbo with insouciant
    hand.

Both are remembered for moments, for years.
They have the force of images that are clear.
So it is with poets of unerring eye,
I am relaxed while spectators leap and cheer.

And it is my ideal to be free within,

And calm, indifferent, to the outer awe
And to aim true as a ball that is kicked or hit,
And hear the country let out a mighty roar.

8-9 September 1984, revised 29 November 1993

AT WEST HAM: SAVED BY AN ARTIST

You came round with complimentary tickets,
    so
You sat in our sofa and chatted, and I put
It to you, "What if there's a penalty
    tomorrow?"
And you said, "If he takes it with his right
    foot,
I'll go to my right," and at the match you
    slouch
Till just under the stand where we sit, your
    guests,
A Watford player is tripped, and so you
    crouch
As a blond international runs in; as if beating
    their breasts,
The hands banging the back wall stop in fright
And all is silence as you dive to your right. 10

A roar! and we're on our feet shouting "Yes",
Forty thousand hands stretch to the air, we
    shriek
For you have the ball, a brilliant save, no
    guess.
Tears well into my eyes, I cannot speak,
Washed through with the emotion of the
    crowd, whose roar
Thunders and reverberates around the stand.
The relieved ground cascades applause and
    awe,
But you seem apart as your captain shakes
    your hand.
Your save kept Watford out, and so all sing.
West Ham have gone to the top and so bells
    ring. 20

And now I know, as I reflect, I will bear
That moment and emotion to the grave –
The ball from the boot suspended in mid-air
As you begin your fall to your right to save –
A moment frozen for eternity,
One I shall remember in thirty years' time
As now, ball hanging from a cross, I see
A diving header, a goal and a cup-winner's
climb.
Memory mixed with emotion is image,
And remembering revives the emotion like a
    bridge. 30

And my boys will remember your save when
    they are old
As I recall Denis Compton's tousled head
As he danced down the wicket before the ball
    was bowled,
Sitting with my father whose domed head is
    now dead.
Some moments – a four I hit or saw, a wicket,
A nodded goal I watched or scored, your
    save –
Assume a bright pattern in the carpet
Of all I did with my life, which I take to my
    grave.
You made a memorable save and I feel as
    purged
As by catharsis, when pity and terror have
    surged. 40

And now, on Sunday, you bring autographs
And I know you know that life is about more,
As you sit and chat and drink my wine, with
    laughs,
Than kicking a ball goalwards and trying to
    score –
Is it really so important for crowds to chant?
Are the prancing preeners mad? Are the
    players stars
When they earn a wage from a game of
    chance, and grant
That all their skill can quickly end in scars?
You live for applause in fading afternoons.
What are you without a leather ball and
    goons? 50

We sit and talk, you know we are two souls.
You want to be a coach or insurance chief.
Panis et circenses. You give men goals,
Like a therapist, you tense and give relief
And let the crowd's roar fill their head and
    hand
And excite their blood, cleanse them with
    their own "Yes".
As the eternal purges the things of time and
Leaves them flushed with surges of
    emptiness.

You are an artist, you create an image in time,
Sculpt a deed like a sandcastle in mime.   60

Now you have gone. You have left your wife,
Are living "in the car", have taken your
    clothes,
A credit card, a front door key, a life.
You have taken out a mortgage that she
    loathes.
You were a fallible god. I cannot believe
You are a violent brawler under the moon,
That police have been called to your home. I
    grieve,
And choose to remember your deed that
    afternoon
As twenty thousand held their breath, then
    leapt
And applauded an artist, hands over head, and
    wept.   70

8-9 September 1984, revised 30 November 1994

ORPHEUS
(A DRAMATIC MONOLOGUE)

"Knowledge enormous makes a God of me."
                                    Keats, *Hyperion*

I, who can sing and play my poetic lyre
So that kestrels lie at my feet and oak-trees
    dance –
I, with my celebration of the rising sun,
Am condemned to walk among the Maenad
    hordes
Who scream and rush about among the groves
And look at me askance when my trance
    comes
And I know they will tear me limb from limb
And swallow me for my power. I serve the
    soul,
Not their bodies and their erotic touch.
Time was when I was enslaved to one of
    them,   10
Till she ran with them and died with a ghastly
    look.
I followed her down to the underworld
And sang my numbers and she followed me
    back.
I felt she was not behind. "Do not look back,"
I was told, but turned and looked and she was
    gone.

And so I still have use for Maenad flesh;
As I stand on the mountain top to greet the
    sun,
A priest of Apollo, not of Dionysus –
Spirit and sense at one, I watch from my
    groves,
They taunt me as they run with their wobbling
    breasts.   20
I lost my love in Hell, but found my soul,
I was reborn in the death of physical desire,
And am now glad I turned and opened my
    head
To this other mind which pours words into
    mine,
But still consort with Maenads for company.
Until my fans tear my head from my trunk
I, Orpheus, am a shaman without a people,
I sing to a crowd that does not understand.
I have knowledge beyond the powers of man
And know I must pay for it with dis-
    memberment   30
By adoring hordes who think it is what they
    seek.

13 September 1984(?), revised 4 October 1993

BRISTOL FIGHTER

I drive down lanes into flat near Biggleswade;
A war-time aerodrome, now vintage planes
    fly,
And are housed in hangars. A crowd as I raid.
Old bi-planes roar overhead, wheel through
    the sky,
Loop loops, fly upside down, and dive from
    clouds
I cross the road and walk a hangar lane
And here, among the booths and strolling
    crowds,
Out of the sunlight is your ancient plane.

A Bristol fighter, the last one left that flies,
(F2b), brown propeller and dark green
    wings,   10
Tail like a rudder, resting. It was some size;
Old wheels, just six years after box kite
    things,
All struts and tense wires like elastic bands,
A flimsy toy, and there is the Lewis gun
At which sat your rear-faced observer, all
    hands,
Hunched over the round drum and Scarff ring,

startling Hun;

And a Vickers on your left side somewhere
Fired through the arc of the propeller on raids
And Constantinesco synchronising gear
In the forward cowling stopped bullets hitting
    the blades.   20
If it misfired, you shot your propeller off, and
    died
Is that what happened to you that September
    day
As you went to spy out where the enemy
    pried,
Did you fire back, or were you shot down as
    prey?

I see you a mere boy respond to the call
For volunteers, and overstate your age
So that you could fly this crate; without a
    stall,
There were no parachutes at that stage.
I see you stand so proudly in your photo,
And like a million parents yours had no
    details   30
As to how you met your death – we still do
    not know.
So many young men shared your fate, one
    wails.

A million ruling men to empire lost,
The flower of England culled long in advance.
A business awaited you, and paid the cost.
You preferred to play the spy on
    reconaissance,
Doing what was new for King and Country,
A patriot who stood for all that was fine,
For courage, laughter, flight and liberty.
I pay my tribute to what would be mine.   40

I see your last plane fly: a puff of smoke,
It rumbles into the air, wheels spinning,
Four double struts between four wings, a joke,
And wobbles in a high wind, climbs
    trembling.
The pilot in goggles waves from the sun.
It hangs up near the cusp of the moon
And dives, Spitfire of World War One.
How proud you must have been, as you went
    missing too soon.

30 September 1984, revised 17 January 1994

RAINBOW LAND

As I drive home towards a thundercloud –
Behold! a bright rainbow arched in its pride,
Rising out of Greenwich, reaching to the
    heights,
Yellow in the middle, indigo, red outside.

I marvel: it has come out of nothing;
Sun on icy rain. So it is with bright
Vision: sun on bits of experience.
From Tower Bridge Greenwich is bathed in
    visionary light.

It is so bright, and a trace of another bow,
Apollo's, now shafts through a church clock's
    hand
It recedes as you draw near. May I long
    remain
A fugitive like this in rainbow land.

Autumn 1984(?), revised 18 January 1994

MAN THE POLLUTER

We attack the world around us:
Stone age men built the Downs,
Medieval men gouged Broads from peat,
Killed bears and wolves for towns.

We spread plane and car fumes in the air,
Gases from coal and oil;
Now acid lakes, emptied of fish,
Decorate a farmer's toil.

We dump oil on the sea as slicks,
We cut down rain forests,
We empty suds into rivers
We attack seals as well as pests.

A bull chases his rivals off
And mates with all the cows.
A man imposes his will on Nature
And mates a polluted spouse.

1984, revised 29 November 1993

AFTER THE STORMS

After the storms the warm sunshine
And this garden is a Paradise.
Near my window red apples twine,
In the dripping hawthorn blue tits slice
And peck berries; long-tailed tit heaves,
Magpies dart and saplings now rise,

All is full at seed-time, and the leaves
Are still on the trees for butterflies;
And I, though old, look with a child's joy,
Wonder at the smile on Nature's face.
I could sit and gaze like a small boy
At the loveliness of this green place
Where berries feed, I could sit for hours
Where the field shines purple and yellow
        flowers.

1984, revised 29 November 1993

DEAD VOICE

What will it be like when I am dead?
Will it be like the voice I left on a
        broadcaster's reel?
My friend edited the tape into a spiel,
For two days he has rung my home with my
        voice,
But I know nothing of it with my head.
After I am dead, will others edit my feel
And cut my voice so it's their choice?

1984, revised 29 November 1993

THOUGHTLESS BOY

O thoughtless boy who draws his sledge
Through the thick driving snow,
Why do you loiter by the tree
And shake the bird-table so?

Can you not see the coal tit there
Shivering in the hawthorn,
Waiting to fly down and peck crumbs,
Who stays because you're on the lawn?

You have moved on at last, but see
A robin is there first
And quickly pecks the last crumbs clean,
My black-bibbed bird will burst.

Now all are gone, the tit flies down
And surveys where others have been,
The nuts the squirrel emptied, the bare
Table – the whirling snow scene.

February 1985(?), revised 18 January 1994

ATHENE THE WISE

Look at Athene in the Louvre,
See how one drilled eye looks out but
One blank eye is an inward one –
Yet both eyes see the same as if shut.

They see the same Reality
And that is why she is so wise;
Wisdom sees inner and outer are one
Like the night within and those dark skies.

23 February 1985(?), revised 23 January 1994

TEN YEARS

Ten years in this concrete tomb,
I thought, and stare at the stones
In which I'd taught a decade away,
A mausoleum for bones

A living death those years.
They whined, like a fox on a hill
Cornered and doomed, baring its teeth,
As the hounds went in for the kill.

Spring 1985, revised 24 January 1994

WIND-HARP AND WIND-VEINS

Hear the wind-harp echo in the wind.
Greeks set it on a hill, it zings.
They left it for the wind to blow,
Listen to the wind playing on the strings:

The ghostly language of the earth
In continuous harmonies of strings.
It is what the trees make when the west wind
Blows through their autumn leaves and sings.

The harmonies of the wind flow on;
Wind-veins in my soul echo, thrill,
Wind-veins like ribbed sand at low tide
When the wind zings this harp on a hill.

Orpheus charmed the trees from the hills
And played a harp (cythera, lyre);
Orpheus let the wind blow through him
And zinged his listeners' souls like wire.

30 March 1985, revised 18 January 1994

SUNRISE AND CLARINET

Hear a hunchbacked cripple
Play from his wheelchair, swoon
At Mazonides' *Hymn to the Sun*
In a third century Roman tune.

As he pipes his clarinet
The deep frail sounds amaze;
Higher and higher he goes,
How shrilly he now plays.

The sun is rising, the note
Is Pythagoras' monochord,
As number and music blend
And the spine shivers, awed.

Truly, not even Orpheus,
For whom number and music were whole,
Could inspire with such ghostly sounds
As the sun rises in the soul.

31 March 1985, revised 18 January 1994

ORPHEUS TO EURYDICE
(A SOUL-AND-BODY SEQUENCE)

I sat in an airport: loudspeaker sounds
The board click-clicked arrival times, people
Stared at screens or sat with vacant faces
And leaned on luggage. Your flight was late.
    I gazed
And felt a rising excitement in my blood
As old memories stirred to wakefulness.
Airports are waiting-places, and I waited for
    you.
You came from an underworld of baggage
    checks,
Walking across marble under yellow neon,
Your long hair, wide smile, shining teeth.   10
We went to a car park, you curled up in your
    seat,
Knees underneath, and fell into my arms
And kissed me long and deep as if I were this
    world.
Soon we lay together in a curtained room
And I unbuttoned my soul, and you peeled off
Your well-cut clothes and slid inside with me,
Your thin body milk-white, your slim breasts
    warm,
Your hair tumbling round your shoulders.
    You opened your soul.
"Only to you", you whispered. And I felt your
    darkness.
I gave you a card with two gold flowers, each
    filled   20
With light in one petal, one petal dark,
Each fresh with raindrops and the juice of
    love,
And I gave you a rolled gold locket with two
    flowers
And a separating chasm, a channel of Light.
You told me you wrote to me from your
    underworld bed.

I felt the tremendous orgasmic power of the
    earth
As if a large moth beat at my window like
    your soul
Imploring to be let in. But you were on loan.
The underworld still had you under its
    control.

We had to attend the Zeus-Pluto summit.   30
We sat in indecision of the Devil's kind,
I saw horns above the eyes of some who said
God is unnecessary to his creation.
I felt in your fingers an electric charge.
Was that not a new form of Materialism?
The monochord spreads from God to the
    lowest depths.
We meditated to my harp and bells,
We touched fingers, not of the Devil's kind
But soul and body fused, spirit with sense.
I knew I had left a heavenly mansion above 40
To come down here and find and reclaim you,
And lead you out, and back to Heaven.
And that you must not look round, Eurydice,
Or you would be lost for ever in time,
As so I played my music, wrote poems
To give you heart to follow me to Light.
I could be torn to pieces by wild Maenads,
But I put my wind-harp on a deserted hill
And let the winds sing through it of my love.

I awoke at three to see the Light in my soul 50
I bathed in it, basked in its white shimmers,
Like sunlight reflected on water, and then
I listened to a chord and heard within
The crashing of a symphony, a roll of drums,
A swelling blast of trumpets and cymbal
    crash.
I came out of my inwardness to you.
You woke, I said, "Good morning, my angel."
You said, "Not angel". But I said "Angel",
I recalled when we were lying in a cloud
And wishing we had bodies we could
    touch;   60
And had we not taken bodies to meet,
And would we not always know each other as
    souls?
You lay beside me, I told you my destiny,
My direction, my mission in this dark world.
You said, "The years are passing, you must
    make haste."

I looked back to the waves, mountains and
    woods,
Pictures frozen like stained glass images.
You were the centre of my being, I had found
    you,
Knowing there is one who finds, one who
    would be found.
You showed me a photo in a silver frame,   70
You said "I carry it everywhere". I looked and
    saw
Myself from long ago, Eurydice,
Looking slim, with brown hair, under a blue
    sky.
You said "I fell in love with you that day."
I looked at your eyes and wide smile, so
    young,
And I did not know you had fallen in love
    with me then.
I thought how you came to my hotel, how
    hard
It was to do then what you are so good at
    now.
You kept your soul from me then. It was
    body-thirst.
A strange white-cheeked black bird called
    from a tree.   80
I walked through deserted streets and returned
    at dawn,
Let myself in, tapped at your door like a
    ghost,
And for the last time, we lay together
Whispering, head pillowed on your hair,
Your milk-white skin ready, you opened and
    said
"I want my body to show you how I feel"
And I felt your soul opening like a flower;
I sank into your soft being's petals,
You shuddered and smiled with far-away
    eyes,
Unfocused, defenceless as you held me,   90
Pliant, supple, yielding, submissive. We loved
Each other's airy soul through our body's fire.
I loved you and turned to possess your soul,
And the underworld forbids union of souls.
I saw you wave and blow a kiss and turn.

You were gone, taken from me, snatched by
    the power
That governs the rhythms of your body's
    juice.

You are lost to this world, lost in the under-
    world,
And I, Orpheus, who descended from my
    heights
To save you from your mountain slopes,   100
And bring you up to daylight, to the blinding
    light,
Have power of music and number, which
    comes from beyond.
I have the gift of the gods – and need you
    with me.
I led you upwards, playing, and you followed.
Now I look round the corner of each door –
And see you wave and blow a kiss, and turn,
Lost to me until I can raise you again!
Alone again, I drive through streets to work
Lamp-posts loom and recede with vacant gaps
And I think of you who fill my grieving
    soul,   110
I am now in a gap as between lamp-posts,
And a light I was drawn to has gone out.
At work I go through my day mechanically,
Solve problems, but deep down I am with
    you.
You have gone, my angel and now I stare,
And the lump on my heart is heavy as stone.
I see your curled hair, eyes with a secret look,
Now baring your perfect teeth, stretching your
    lips,
So neatly walking among the primroses.
An umbilical cord tightens under my
    heart.   120
A heavinesss in my heart, like a cannon-stone.
You said, "I am a woman, I cannot live with-
    out love.
It is very easy to meet someone else.
I can have any man I want, like picking a
    cherry.
What shall I do? What am I, a woman, to do?"
You are of the underworld, and have left me
With a swallowed cherry-stone in my lungs,
Half-wishing the Maenads would tear me in
    pieces.
But I am divine and must return to the
    heights.

April 1985, revised 18 January 1994

LOCK-GATE

I go to Charlestown harbour on a gloom-
-y showery, cold, damp day. It is low tide.

393

The sea tongues in as at the mouth of a womb
Whose upper neck is pregnant with boats that
    hide.
I stand on the lock-gate. The level is high
On the still land sand, low at the open end,
And I think it is like the soul which is filled
    by
Tides from beyond, which impregnate mind
    like a friend.

I think of art, and mourn my secret mind;
I wish the lock-gate in my soul could be   10
Lowered so fish-like images could find
A way in, strange shapes from the spiritual sea.
My art is still undone, and I who heard
A call to chronicle the meaning of life,
To express the invisible in a vivid word,
See on every screen mere entertainment and
    strife.

I who sought a meaning for the West, now
    seek
To express it in sea, hills, trees and rippling
    grass
And yearn for the clarity of the mountain
    peak,
Heidegger's snow-capped heights, to live on a
    pass,   20
Alpine solitude by day and fire in the mind,
No wordly distractions, no everyday hole,
Just the love of a silent woman whose blind
Language is her body mouthing her soul.

Here at this barrier at the world's end,
I can taste the tang of a vast sea of spirit
Whose salt brings lucidity to all who have
    opened,
I turn away from the houses like a misfit
And head for the bouldered pier where the sea
    thuds,
Smacking against the breakwater above the
    beach,   30
Where fishermen light a lamp as dusk's dark
    scuds,
Where there is salt in the air, on the tongue,
    no speech.

Now as the sea booms where pebbles have
    just hissed,
Crashes and boils, sending fountains of spray,

Foams and surges and pours its power as mist
Which is fine as smoke, I hear the roaring say
Great art is from the beyond, it reveals a
    power
Which seeps through your gate, pours onto
    the still
Side, bursts into the world of time for an hour
From the crashing, foaming power of the
    divine will.   40

Art reveals the divine world or is a cage,
And so I show a power which is breathed
    where
There is stillness, quiet, silence in our
    swirling age;
And man and a twilit sky on a sea-pier;
Divine meaning surrounds him and pours in
Unknown through the lock-gate at his heart
And lights him like a fisherman's lamp so his
    skin
Holds hope that transcends despair and
    transforms art.

7 April 1985, revised 16 January 1994

TIME COMPRESSED
(OR: A UNIVERSE LIKE SPARKLES
FROM A WAVE)
I sit on the harbour wall above a sea
Where lights leap as if a trillion mackerel rise
And blow a ripple like a white bubble
That bursts a kiss for love of clear blue skies.

No trace of last night's night-tree hung with
    fruit,
Expanding galaxies like swelling grapes,
Unless they're reflected in this water-fire,
In a trillion flashes and exploding shapes.

As above, so below. I wonder if
Each sparkle that bursts and is gone
    enzymes   10
The start-to-finish glow-and-fade of stars
With the time-scale compressed a trillion
    times?

And are there not as many stars as lights,
And as fast as one fades does not another
    glow
So a whole universe is a leaping dance
In a minute's sunlight where calm waters flow?

Now seen at night, each bright slow-motion
glow
Which, speeded up, would seem a dying fire,
Gives a frozen cross-section of a Big Bang's
burst
To this corner of our universe, which swells
to expire.   20

9-10 April 1985

LIGHTS LIKE DRIVING RAIN

I sit on the harbour wall in the April sun
And look at the cliff and house I'd like to buy,
And at the cave beneath and sand-stream
Where two boys play at pirates, and seagulls
cry,

And I turn to the causeway of sunlight across
the sea
Where lights now splash and jump like
driving rain,
I look at the exploding calm and turn
To where surf blows as it thuds round the bay
again

The wind is in my hair in the shadow on
stones,
The wind is in the trees where the clouds
move on the cliff;
I sit amid whirling motion in sky and waves
As a million lights leap up round a small skiff.

A cloud crosses the sun and in the shade
I think of the dark into which I must go
For my leg will be slit within a week,
I will wake up bandaged and throbbing from
groin to toe.

The sea dashes on these headland's rocks,
An eternal moving backdrop to my stare;
As the sun returns, warm on my living cheek,
My inspiration leaps in this heady air.

10 April 1985(?), revised 20 December 1993

RAINDROPS LIKE STARS
(OR: WARMTH ON A DEWDROP EARTH)

I woke from darkest night, pulled the curtain –
On the window pane, a thousand drops of rain,
Round globules filled with light from smoke-
black clouds

As the wind whistled like an impatient train.

As many drops of rain as stars last night,
And I saw a universe, and it seemed our stars
Were formed from cosmic dew and are no
more
Permanent than these clustered globes – like
Mars.

I lay back and wished I was still asleep
For our galaxies, five thousand in a bunch,
Were also on my window, and would dry
out –
For nothing lasted in a chance world – by
lunch.

As I closed my eyes in a momentary grimace,
A refusal of the Way – did I ask for birth? –
Light broke through the troubled teardrops in
my soul
And I warmed to the Warmth that was drying
our dewdrop earth.

11 April 1985

STILL CLOUDS AND WHIRLING STARS
(OR: A HOLE IN AN EGGSHELL UNIVERSE)

I stand in the harbour on a windy night;
White clouds are still, across patches of dark
A host of stars stream up the sky like a wave
Of bombers with lights heading for a land-
mark.

I stand in the shaking boulders of the wall
And rub my eyes and look again, but yes,
The clouds are still, it is the stars that move,
I see them heading towards cloud, going into
blackness.

It is as if they are in orbit round the earth,
But I realise it is the earth that's wrong;
stun-   10
-ned, I feel for a moment the earth has
wobbled free
And is rushing into space away from the sun.

The moment passes, but I hold an iron capstan
And am grateful for the wash-wash of the sea
Which recreates the illusion that there is a law,

Which clouds and stars obey without breaking
free,

And that the earth is not a rebel that can
Career from its Great Year's course into a cold
Ice age till we collide with a whirling star
In an eggshell universe that has been holed. 20

11 April 1985, revised 16 January 1994.

VEINS

Trees have limbs of bark,
Flowers have stems of sap.
All animals have blood,
So why has mine a gap?

Blood leaked into my feet,
My life juice dripped away,
And so I lie in hospital,
My leg strapped up all day.

Flies have veins in wings,
And so do dragonflies;
Even hedgehogs and newts
Have veins that support their size,

So why do mine differ
From animal, insect and leaf
And warrant this chilly ward
Where death is no cause for grief?

17(?) April 1985, revised 18 January 1994

BLUE UP, BROWN DOWN

I lie in a hospital bed, my leg bandaged.
I stare at the picture on my bedside wall:
A red house with chimneys and a railed pond,
And a red house upside down, only more tall.

The sky above is blue and below is brown,
And I think how like that house I am, and
frown,
For as I lie on my back, my right leg out,
The blue sky outside has become the stagnant
brown

Of the murky hospital window and my soul.
As I limp down the corridor in pain
May I turn my sluggish brown cheeks to
healthy blue
And end looking the right way up again!

18 April 1985, revised 18 January 1994

CRYSTAL: RAINBOWS

At the Festival of Spirit I bought
A clear crystal that is shaped like a heart.
I hang it on my window-catch in the sun
And my room is filled with rainbows –
ethereal art.

So it is with my clear heart centre. When
The inner sun shines it is filled with hints;
Who can see the rainbow in a crystal heart?
I project a dozen rainbows with clear tints.

Sunlight on a pure heart gives clear vision;
A transparent, pure gaze, and the Light in glee
Throws out, like coloured rainbows on a wall,
A dozen poems on a page for all to see!

5 May 1985, revised 23 January 1994

RAINBOW VISION

I hang a crystal heart
On the window-latch. It is small
But the sun shines through, ribbons
Of rainbow dance on my wall.

I hang my clear pure heart
Before your warming sun
And my room is filled with
A rainbow-like vision.

5 May 1985, revised 24 January 1994

WORTHING

A green sea smiles by breakwaters
And brown seaweed, a hazy sun
From which I squint. Tiers of wavelets
Breeze on shingle, wash in and run.

A gull drifts. Windbreaks and flags flap,
The sound of the sea is like the wind
In leafy trees, non-stop, it gusts
And waps this canvas, shakes what's pinned.

I, Sisyphus, pause from rolling
My boulder up the barbarians' hill,
See a smiling face in the universe
And am at one with the infinite will.

30 May 1985, revised 22 November 1993

NEED

The sea is green and sandy brown,
Above these grey stones I feel free,

I squint and drink my pot of tea
By flapping flags, the sun beats down.

I meet you as you lock white doors,
We drive to smiles and concerned frowns
And now we're high up on the Downs
We leave the car for hips and haws.

This meadow plunges into woods
We find a quiet secluded spot,   10
We flatten grass, I clasp you, hot;
Our beings leak without their hoods.

As we lie among bramble thorns,
Germander speedwell crushed by your head,
Your heart opens like a flower that is fed,
We two are wet with a dew that scorns.

Now nettles brush your country legs
I swell to hugeness for an hour,
No love but closeness and raw power:
Like a kestrel or bird of prey, and eggs.   20

And now we walk in knee-high grass
You pick an ox-eye daisy where
The sky meets sea in scented air,
And Downs are ups wherever we pass.

An extended moment, like a sob.
Now as the dawn glows in the sky
I wonder why, I wonder why
Our beings have this need to throb.

30 May 1985, revised 22 November 1993

STAR-GAZING

I walk across the cricket field of my
Youth as twilight falls across the tree-lined sky.
Here I batted and held a catch, in heat;
There the pavilion stood: a garden seat.
Now all is silent, all that urgency and hope
Is a night sky and a rolled-out telescope.
The science master slides the small roof back,
Screws in eye-pieces and points it at Saturn
                    (black),
Focuses twenty times. It magnifies,
I see an oblong frog's head with two eyes   10
(Titan and Rhea, the moons), the planet seen
From underneath, the ring round it so clean,
Two holes between it and the ball, the dark
                    beyond day,

Sharp, though eight hundred million miles
                    away.
We turn to the man in the moon, and upside
                    down
Images above his right eye (left jaw), frown:
Two craters side by side, one bright in
                    space,
Aristarchus and Herodotus on a blistered
                    face.
Now we focus on a double star, Albireo;
Yellow and blue, one behind the other. We
                    go   20
On to Gamma Leonis, both yellow and bright.
"This Observatory's made of planks from the
                    Room 9 site."
Room 9, I recall that flimsy classroom
Now gone, where I learned Greek next to the
                    gloom
Of the physics lab, where I learned of Titan
                    and Rhea
And in the afternoons played cricket on this
                    square.

1 June 1985, revised 19 January 1994

ILLUSION AND REALITY

I sit in a car on Dieppe front,
Waiting for full daylight to pry
So I can drive without yellow lights,
I sit and watch the pale blue sky.

It lightens into an eerie glow
Above the line of round moon-lamps
Where lorries from the ferry wait
Like me, to set off from night camps,

And as I watch, a red wisp throbs,
Pulses against the black of night,
And I feel my swollen being ache
And think of a girl near a nightlight.

The earth is turning towards the sun
And as sunlight shoots across the sky
I see what we take for granted
Not realising we are cocooned by

Illusion as we sleep and work,
Not seeing our planet as we run.
The moon-lamps pale, and now, o joy!
Up the streaked sky bursts a throbbing sun..

14 June 1985, revised 22 November 1993

BATS FLITTING

I look out in the evening dusk at where
The sky has dimmed to clear sapphire and
        green
Against the dark outlines of the cool trees
And in the light patches between each
        branch
By the eaves of the school I see a quick
Flitting like a large moth, or smallish bird –
Three of them, dipping, wheeling and darting:
Bats. I watch as they fly and swoop and
        swerve
And buckle in midair, veer at a tangent.
I watch them as they fly round the gable
Backwards and forwards, enjoying the peace
Of the garden in this cool evening air.

                Summer 1985(?), revised 18 January 1994

A BLIND AND A KINK

On the kitchen window sill
A plant in a red pot:
One leaf is this side of the floral blind,
One leaf has a kink and is not.

It goes up the window,
Stooping to climb for light;
It has gone the other side of the screen
Between the dark and the bright

In my mind there is a blind
As I blindly shoot for the way,
And I too have a stem that has
Stooped to climb to the day.

                Summer 1985(?), revised 25 January 1994

AS WITHOUT SO WITHIN

The land was going up and down
On the cabin window, my arm.
The sea see-saws from side to side
As we roll on a deep calm.

We glide across the heavy wave
Prow up like a Viking ship,
We wobble forward, go towards
The gold sunset, then dip.

And I have known a time when the world
Has moved when it was me,
And like a gull on a still wind
I have wobbled on a calm sea.

A golden causeway calls to the west,
I walk the path of the soul.
A gull soars round a blinding sun,
On a satin sea I am whole.

                15 June 1985, revised 22 November 1993

THE FLIGHT OF THE SHAMAN

Today like a shaman
I will fly high above this street,
I will look down on upturned faces
Eighty foot under my feet.

A crane's arm will hold me,
I will be up near its hook.
On my front will be a placard
"Against the Ayatollah's book."

Today I will hang from a crane
Above a sullen people.
I will expire as I rise
To the height of a church steeple.

Today like a shaman
I will make a high flight
To another world where all
Are against wrong and for what is right.

I will like Icarus feel
A warm but invisible sun
As I hang, neck bent in half,
Hear the jeers below, then none.

                19(?) July 1985, revised 21 November 1993

SUNFLOWERS AND A
GODLESS SOCIETY

As I drive through the ripening lands of
        France
I pass great fields of towering sunflowers.
Thousands stand tall, their round heads nearly
        up,
Smiling at the warming, southern sun for
        hours.

They stand in ranks, each head is turned side-
        ways
Towards the sun that feeds them, which none
        turn from.
They stand like lined-up soldiers who must
        wait
To go into battle across the Somme.

Time was when congregations stood in files
And turned their heads towards the Sunday
    One,
But now I see blind sunflowers peer and scowl
In all directions, and fail to find the sun.

20 July 1985, revised 18 January 1994

TEASE

I am a wally,
You don't know my name,
I'll give you a clue,
My mind's a bit lame.

I have two crossed eyes,
My tongue sticks out,
I see with my ears,
I smile with my snout.

I giggle like a dweeb,
Gurgle like a drain,
Can't keep a straight face,
I know I'm a pain.

I am a wally,
You can guess my name.
If I tell you my initials,
You'll know of my fame.

20 July 1985, revised 18 January 1994

SCULPTOR AT CHÂTEAU MONTFORT

See the sculptor sitting under the castle,
Penknifing absentmindedly, puffing his pipe,
Hacking an idea out of a log of wood,
Cutting away the dross with barely a wipe.

Slowly two faces emerge from his shavings,
Two medieval boys locked in combat,
Arms tugging each other in friendly strife,
Love and hate in one wrestling embrace that

Unifies two opposites in an image.
There are many wood-chippings on the floor
And a pile of logs behind him as he sits
Casually snicking his idea to the fore.

25 July 1985, revised 23 January 1994

CHANNEL CROSSING

The whistling of the wind in the rigging,
The dash of the spray on the cabin front, and I

Am the wind in my hair, tugging, flapping
    trousers
As the ship's prow thrusts up and down at the
    sky.

30 July 1985, revised 21 November 1993

THE MERRY-GO-ROUND

See the merry-go-round on the waterfront
With horses that go up and down,
See the bright eyes of the children
As they slowly climb and dip and clown.

See the merry-go-round from the city;
Boys climb on horses in the rain,
When the whirligig stops, they climb off,
Change places, and ride high again.

See the merry-go-round by the sea
Its organ music trundles out,
See the people go round in circles,
Spinning their lives on a roundabout.

July 1985, revised 22 November 1993

ON THE CHANNEL

The rain streams down this ship's window,
Ahead the sea is crested grey,
We plough and bump on through the storm,
The French coast is just mist and spray.

In the lounge of reclining seats
A noisy film on the video;
My neighbours watch, their mouths open,
And laugh out loud in an echo.

I am detached; apart, my soul
Flies on a sea like a turbulent heart.
This drive, this determination to go
Forward is strong, leaves me apart.

Above this raging, dipping sea
I clench my soul and relax my fist,
I sit at peace, still amid noise,
And see my goal loom up through mist.

4 August 1985, revised 22 November 1993

STARS LIKE BEES AND PETALS

I go outside in the dark
To look at the August night
For the earth is passing through
A cloud of meteorite,

And the specks of stellar dust
Will burn with a vapour trail
And shoot across the sky
Like a rocket's burning tail.

But what I see has me dazed:
I stand under a vast tree
And the blossom glistens white
In the cold clear night, brightly,

And up among the boughs
White fireflies dart and fly
Like bees between petals
Brimming with nectar and sky.

9 August 1985(?), revised 6 December 1993

A UNIVERSE OF GLOWING SEED

I walk to the harbour light.
A night of brilliant stars.
I crane my neck and peer,
They explode round my head as round Mars.

In the shade of the harbour light
The stars are heady and clear,
Millions burst round me but
It is you that seems so near.

For you throb at my heart
And at my crown and beg
To create your universe
Of jellied stars, like an egg;

As many sperms as stars,
A microcosm alive.
I look up at the sky,
Macrocosm's womb-hive,

And know each star can squirm
Like a sperm setting out to breed,
A trillion wriggling specks,
Universe of glowing seed!

9 August 1985(?), revised 6 December 1993

IN PÉRIGORD

I

From Les Eyzies out on a wooded road,
Where higher up cars crawl like ants with a
load,

Turn off at the bamboo, pass a quarry, go
Up a lane to a shuttered cottage in yellow
On a heath, where a yellowhammer in the trees
Sings, "A little bit of bread and no cheese."
Here cicadas whirr, a snake slithers through
the grass,
Swallowtails glide, lizards linger on glass.

A cool place in the heat. On marble floors
Shuffle; with shutters thrown open, and
doors,   10
Look across the valley and this is the only roof;
A farm up the road, a lone tractor the proof.
A field for bulbs. Here smell the scented pine
As the light fades in the cooling air, recline,
Listen to the still till the dark is all around,
Then see the vivid stars droop to the ground!

Périgord! Here is a Paradise between
Two rivers, above which châteaux hang
serene
Where troubadours like Arnaut Daniel sang
Under fairytale turrets whose courtyards
rang,   20
And towns that are medieval like Sarlat.
Go down to Saint Bernard's baffling gift –
stop at
A corkscrew tower, the "Lantern of the
Dead",
Or at Rocamadour kneel up steps, bow your
head.

Here came Sir Lancelot, the adulterous knight
Who ruled in Périgord. Here came the English
to fight,
Simon de Montfort, Richard Lionheart, Black
Prince.
Here the Revolution shattered with a wince
The calm of nobles in brutal castles high
Above those they ruled. In the evening watch
the sky.   30
The Milky Way and oceans spiral and whirl,
See the sky flow and history's purpose swirl.

II

But do not forget the distant past; this place
Was capital of the world for the human race
For two hundred thousand years. Les Eyzies'
tall
Cro-Magnon man decorated his cave wall,

400

Upright, with a larger skull than mine, a
    frown,
Not like the Neanderthal subman statued
    above the town,
That sleepy-eyed beast. Like me, he lived in
    caves
By the river which then ran past them and
    their graves.   40

Or go back sixteen thousand years and gaze,
At Les Combarelles, stoop in passageways
See engravings of reindeer, deer, bears and
At Font de Gaume, see paint blown round a
    hand;
At Lascaux see bulls that an artist caught
And at Cap Blanc see horses toss and snort,
And at La Madeleine, the ancient ground
And shelter where "Magdalenian" man was
    found.

What artistry and proportion these paintings
    mark!
What perspective, and how they used the
    dark!   50
Bulges in a cave display a pregnant cow,
Perfect shapes seen from every angle now.
How observant these men were. Why
    decorate?
No domestic tools in these cold caves, no
    grate –
Were they tunnels to the underworld for
    shaman and saint,
Who tamed the spirits of beasts by magic and
    paint?

I see these men like shamans going deep
In the underworld, and draw the perfect leap
Of animal gods, long before Egypt, on walls
And invoke a magical power that calls   60
Animals near; crouching from rain – a thud,
I see them eat raw bull's flesh, drink bull's
    blood,
Then sleep in a bull's hide and now receive
Among dripping stalactites things men
    believe.

III
Man, like civilisation is two drives which
    part,
One that would make him an angel through art,

Beauty, learning, religion and culture,
And one that would make him a devil, impure
Through demeaning war and appetite,
    lovesick;
When ordered, rational; bestial when
    chaotic,   70
Did these Périgord skulls know man is both
    god and beast?
Or were they from a Paradise, and came east?

Plato says Atlantis sank, magnificent gem,
That Atlantis revered bulls and sacrificed
    them;
Was Cro-Magnon man a flood refugee,
Or were these paintings done in a colony
When settlers fled east during the decline
And brought their religion to a new cave-
    shrine?
And did imitation cease with the great flood,
Was the colonists' now pure Atlantean
    blood?   80

And did descendants from Sargasso weed
Colonise Egypt, France and Spain and feed,
And are these paintings Atlantean art that
    crossed,
These signs Atlantean writing that is lost?
If so, where is Darwin's flint-bashing ape?
Not the long-skulled Cro-Magnon sixfooter's
    shape?
And am I a descendant from the Atlantean One,
Do I recall their worship of the sun?

IV
Emerge with a shiver and stand back in awe
From the pine-scented brilliance of
    Périgord   90
And the darkened caves and darkened mind,
    and face
The medieval greatness of this place:
At Domme, high above the black Dordogne
    river,
Or at Rocamadour, where the blackened
    Madonna
Sits and pilgrims ascended the steps on
    knees,
Or at Sarlat, where pilgrims find more ease.

Here St. Bernard preached and healed all the
    sick

Who ate bread blessed with Light and made a
    quick
Recovery; his miracle was commemorated
In the twisted beehive "Lantern of the
    Dead",   100
A tower with paths spiralling up a pyramid:
Empty downstairs, chimney-hole where a
    light was hid,
A candle that lit the upstairs window.
Were the dead led up the path to a Heaven
    aglow?

This place shows the Light in twelfth century
    stone,
The Light spirals down into flesh and bone,
Shines over the living and dead and raises
    them up,
Shines into creation and fills the world like a
    cup.
And could this lantern consciousness have
    spread
What the Egyptians knew in their *Book of the
Dead*,   110
Have spiralled down above these cavemen's
    graves
Into men with a sun in their heads who
    painted caves?

I see the Cro-Magnon artist observe
Animals he lived like with creative verve
And rise above them to a higher plane,
Soar in his concentration, detached from pain,
As he sculpts horses, fixing beauty in an hour
I see him glimpse the Light and a shaman's
    power,
Locate the spring from which flows all living
    things,
Find a new link for man in an angel's
    wings.   120

V

There is a consciousness as old as hills
And it is here today as this evening thrills,
As I sit in the door and watch the evening
    grow,
As I spiral up the sky to the western glow
Which corkscrews down into all woods and
    seas,
This consciousness that evolves, and this light
    breeze

Carries man from Cro-Magnon to Einstein,
The long purpose of the mystical sunshine.

A new consciousness hangs ahead of man
Like a smiling moon above a delivery
    van.   130
From Neanderthal dream, a purposive drive to
    gain
Lengthened his skull and enlarged his
    searching brain.
But what a leap across his mind's canal
As he jumped from magic to mystical –
Magic makes an image that effects a kill,
The mystic lets God's love act through his
    will.

In Périgord first man ascended to us
(Or did Atlantean man descend into fuss?)
By a drive of will that found the divine
And brought it down to act on the human
    spine.   140
In Périgord the lantern above the dead
Perhaps enshrined a power within man's
    head,
The Holy Spirit that made the caveman great
The Light in the dark that put him in charge of
    his fate.

Many things whirl in a spiral: the Milky Way,
Clouds and oceans are like whirlpools each
    day,
And perhaps our lives whirl in a spiral also
As we ascend in circles on an upward flow,
And perhaps the ascent of man is a spiral too
And I circle and look down at the inner
    view,   150
Nearer to the Light most earthbound cavemen
    shun,
Like a circling kestrel soaring towards the
    sun.

11-16 August 1985, revised 26-27 September 1993

REASON LIKE A BOAT

Feel the power of the sea
As this huge boat creaks and sways
Rolling now up, now down
Like driftwood battered for days.

Can you feel the power of God
As the ego dips and crests,

Rolling this way and that
Like wood the great swell tests.

How calm the power of God
For this millpond journey,
Yet how his might can swell
And toss the reason high.

Feel the power of the sea,
Feel the pull of the tide,
Feel the unobtrusive flow
That acts as our bark's guide.

August 1985, revised 13th September 1993

WILL LIKE A KITE

See how the high kite darts
With its long red streamer tail,
Diving to the left, swooping,
Then hovering on the gale,

Looping the loop, and again
Diving, now up it glides
High above the deserted sands
Looking down at pony rides.

Now its restless, demented motion
Has passed like a fit or a mood,
And it hangs still high in the air
Its tail billowing, many-hued.

And I think of my ferocious will
Which also floats supreme
And yet darts and tugs for control
As I pull its strings from the green.

The will is free as the wind
And laughs at our landbound feet,
And teases and twists us to freedom,
Tugs us from our peaceful retreat.

August 1985, revised 13th September 1993

TAMED PONIES

See the ponies on the beach
Reflected in a pool,
See the child mount one and squeal
As a pony trots like a mule

Making hoofmarks in the wet sand,
Under a black-headed gull.
See the ponies held by their grooms

As they trot out a life that seems dull.

They have been tamed, and now,
Submissive in the heat,
Wear humiliating bridle,
Saddle and the tots' feet.

They can gallop and kick up the sand
With an energy that explodes.
I too have been tamed and work
When I could be wild among odes.

August 1985, revised 13 September 1993

CONSCIOUSNESS

I sit on a beach and stare
At where the tide has gone out.
I am my personality,
I sit in habit and doubt.

My static, passive self
Can be bored, could turn to crime;
When a tide of meaning comes in
Like a oneness cleansing time

I am alive, am pure will
Under an azure dome,
Pure energy and power,
Consciousness like sea-foam,

Dynamic, moving, not
This shell of unreal gaze,
Limitless and purposive
As I plan and intend my days.

I sit with a consciousness
That is like flat sand and shale
On which a sparkling tide
Washes over all that's stale.

Summer, 1985, revised 13 September 1993

SOMETHING DISCARDED IN THE SAND

Down in the sand at Par
I dig in the stumps and bat,
The ball pitches in the sand
I hit a cover drive that

Connects, and see by my foot,
A pinkish bag lying there
Right on the good length spot

On our cricket pitch, I stare.

I stare and wonder who,
From the caravan site above
The dunes and the private road,
Were last night locked in love

And left their tenderness
To litter our pitch. I spread
Sand on it with my bat,
Face the next ball on a bed.

Love's a moment in the sands
That is smoothed away by the tide,
Till the prints are gone, leaving
This shared bag where they sighed.

August 1985, revised 13 September 1993

ROD-FISHING

I sit on the harbour wall
Among the rods and twine
Where men cut bait with knives
And cast each whistling line.

The bobs float in the waves,
The rods are propped on the wall;
Cross-legged or arms on knees
They wait for a dip and a fall.

I sit with my metal rod
And cast in the sea of soul
And wait for the images
To rise like a nibbling shoal.

What mackerel will I catch
And wind in for reason's cage,
Bending my will in two
As it splashes onto the page?

August 1985, revised 13 September 1993

WORDS SPENT LIKE WAVES

Sea surges on the rocks,
Foam flicks on the distant cliffs
As I, the Poet of the Sea,
Sharpen my buts and ifs,

Sitting in the evening sun,
Basking on this harbour wall,
While the sea booms round a cave
That has seen its probing fall.

Sea surges in the cave
As I push my words on blocks,
Their spray flicks up and falls
As they spend themselves on rocks

Of public disinterest –
But could the waves care less
As they fathom the depth of the cave
And sing in their distress?

August 1985, revised 13 September 1993

MOMENTS LIKE WAVES

The children play with the sea,
They stand on the concrete wall
And jump after each wave
And rise from the next one's fall.

They dodge the waves and squeal
And are absorbed as they roam,
Their trousers rolled to their knees,
Dancing by boiling foam.

So it is with time,
Each wave is a moment
Given form by a playful sea
And they dance in an endless present.

August 1985, revised 13 September 1993

CERBERUS

As they play in the gentle waves
A dog comes near their "home",
The boys eye it askance,
The dog stands in their foam

And leaps and licks the stream
Which comes from the sewage pipe
And stands just where they play,
Then follows their plaintive swipe.

And I know that Cerberus
In my ascetic caves;
He comes and barks at me
When I bask in the waves

Of the giant invisible sea
Whose tides are the light of suns
And spoils my ecstasy
With a reality that stuns.

August 1985, revised 13 September 1993

THE REGENERATION OF THE CREATIVE WEST

I think of the telephone, TV, aircraft,
Space rocket, computer and tracking dish –
Such creativity! It all came from the West,
Not Africa or Asia, despite their wish.

Others may have taken our inventions
And imitated them, modified their use –
The Soviets and Japan – but they are ours,
The West cannot be over with such produce.

I see our Rome negotiate and impose
A hundred year peace on each Parthia,
Under the shadow of the nuclear bomb
(Such invention) and the laser destroyer.

I see the regeneration of the West,
I see the appeal of Communism wilt,
I see one Western world, everywhere using
Western inventions, rich from what we built.

But what when the oil finally dries up?
Is this not the parabola's top, the Golden Age
When our civilisation was at its height
And could not be better in a future stage?

I see our great-grandchildren gasp with awe
Because we were a four car family –
Will there be oil enough for all their cars,
And will they live under a rule that is free?

We are approaching a Universal time,
A world rule like Rome's under Augustus
      that
May bring universal benefit to mankind
(Israel and the PLO of Arafat).

We are still creative and will rule the world
So although our civilisation disintegrates
We feel we still have a long way to go
Before it falls apart and capitulates!

August 1985, revised 13 September 1993

SOON NOT SEE THE SUN

On TV, a moustached young man sentenced
To death in Malaysia for drug trafficking;
"I didn't do it," he says, calmly resigned,
"The drugs were planted in my bag when I
      was queuing.

"I was prepared for the sentence but it came
      as a knock.
It was when I lay down in my cell to sleep,
It hit me, I'm going to die." And he stared
At the camera and shrugged in a place where
      life is cheap.

On TV, a hospice. The old men sit;
The women talk, one says with unblinking
      eye,
"I'm forty, I've cancer of the head. My son
Of eleven doesn't know I'm going to die."

Several are matter of fact on death and smile.
I, watching from my armchair gaze and
      think:
They are preparing to die, these condemned
      people
(Sentenced by the law or disease), and they do
      not shrink.

And then I think, what if I had only
Two months to live – with all I have not done.
And a chill invades my calm complacency,
And I shiver and feel I may soon not see the
      sun.

August 1985, revised 14 September 1993

THE WONDER OF THE WEST: AT GOONHILLY

We climb the downs to Goonhilly
Where on heather ten dishes face
Aerials that beam and catch phone calls,
Programmes and messages to space.

I gaze at the control centre
Where computers surround each screen,
And at a control desk lean men
Process all symbols they have seen.

All has come here – the Falklands war,
The wreck of yachts in the Atlantic,
Sporting sessions from the Far East,
Sent as a wave to a wire at a click.

The symbols travel out from home
To the Post Office tower, and then through
      towns,
Are pulsed in 30 mile stages
To this last place on the Lizard downs.

Along with the glass skyscraper,
Information network and Spaceport,
This triumph of technology
Which taperecords our every thought –

This is the wonder of our time,
In four thousand years from today,
Just as we gaze at the Pyramids,
When ours is the Ancient World in clay

Barbarians will marvel at these dishes
That conjure messages from the wind,
And wonder how we reduced distance
To the end of a wire that is pinned.

August 1985, revised 14 September 1993

THE DIVINE

If infinity's 8 on its side
And eternity's a line,
And they are endless space
And time, in bright sunshine,

Then what is the endless depth
Beyond mind, soul, and spine,
Which is neither time nor space
But is endless divine?

I hail the illimitable
Which is behind what is sought,
And I hail the boundless
Which cannot be encompassed by thought.

Both can steal up unobserved
As in grandmother's footsteps,
And break into consciousness
Like a sun over travelling reps.

August 1985, revised 14 September 1993

AT GUNWALLOE

I sit on the sunny sand at Gunwalloe,
A fountain of spray above the distant rocks,
The sea pours roughly in, with boiling foam,
And all is a tearing-in in a wind that shocks.

The old church stands serenely by the beach,
Grey tower and slates that have weathered the
    years;
Its shady porch welcomes all who would retreat
And wander among stone arches where time
    peers.

Round the headland, in Dollar Cove, the sea
Tears past a wreck, its rollers curl
And crash onto a shingle beach and wash
Where dollars have been found in the waves'
    swirl.

Gunwalloe! always rugged and exposed,
Yet always sunny despite the whipped spray,
And always ancient, here the spirit leaps
And praises the pouring of each divine day.

August 1985, revised 14 September 1993

AT PORTHLEVEN: ALL ONE

At Porthleven I walk out on the pier
Whose rail makes it resemble a submarine
The red flag flaps as great waves curl and
    crash
At the starboard end, splash and wash our
    deck clean.

Out in the waves, despite the flapping flag
A surfer in a wet suit rides as if in sleet
And goes head first as a great curl crashes
    down –
I see the board tied to his flying feet.

Up in the sky a plane breaks low, circling
A glider on a thermal above the town
Rises, riding currents like an air-surfer
As the steepling clouds threaten to crash
    down.

Wind flaps the flag, whips spray and cloud,
    and I
Feel my heart leap for joy, and in triumph
    glide
For all is one on land and sea and sky,
And breasts an invisible wind that flows like a
    tide.

August 1985, revised 14 September 1993

WISDOM
(FRAGMENT)

Today most have knowledge, but not wisdom.
They live on a small plot in an expensive
    home,
Work in cities removed from Nature, with
    minds
That do not know about the tides and winds
From experience, what they observe to be true,

Or how seeds split and grow into a tree,
The old lore of farmers and fishermen,
The way both work by phases of the moon.

Summer 1985(?), revised 25 January 1994

TIN-MINE AND HAWK

A tin-mine chimn-
-ey's cross, a hill;
An inner seam
In the rock's still.

Here a darkness
Was often mined,
Abandoned now,
Its iron seam blind.

The hawk that sits
On telephone wire,
Can mine darkness
That contains fire.

17 August 1985(?), revised 6 December 1993

ILFRACOMBE

The TV comes from Ilfracombe –
Songs of Praise don't enthrall.
But I see a tunnel and a bay
With cliffs and a grey sea wall,

And my mind goes back to the end of the
war,
I stand on that grey beach,
My father lies in shallow sea
In a striped costume, I reach.

Soldiers in khaki stand around
As he splashes. A tread,
And I am a little child of five
And Hitler is not yet dead.

I look away and the spell goes,
And now I am all alone,
My parents are gone, and only I
Stand in a room, time-blown.

August 1985, revised 22 November 1993

ROUGH STONES LIKE MONKS

I cross the ancient stone causeway,
Laid five hundred years ago
By French monks after Edward gave
This Mount to a Mont that could glow.

Up through drizzle to the low cloud,
To the castle crag again
Where long ago St. Michael appeared
In light to shocked fishermen.

In a cloud like a mist, an ancient church
Stands on the North Terrace and
I am in a cloud of unknowing
Where I cannot see land,

But can see around the battlements
And here within this cloud
See the rough stones cemented like
Monks bonded in a crowd.

17 August 1985, revised 22 November 1993

TREVARTHIAN REVISITED

Down the path beside the screened garden
Cut in and gaze across the lawn
At the grey house with long windows
Where a brother woke one early dawn.

There we sat on that veranda,
In that window from the library
I took a book on Voroshilov
And first met Russian history.

It is as now, when a mere boy
I wheeled up hills, pedalled to plains –
Stone circles, long barrows, circuit
Tombs – then cycled back along long lanes.

I see my mother with her bag
Cross the road and green sward, persist
And sit with her back to the rock that
Faces the Mount, now hidden in mist.

This ancient house is now in flats,
And alien faces in the windows
Munch their lunch while I stand outside
My youth on a kerb in a drizzle that knows.

17 August 1985, revised 22 November 1993

LETTICE

And here in St. Michael's Mount, in the
Chevy Chase
I look at a painting of General Monk that
grips.
He brought in the Restoration that saved this
fort,

407

But is shown with hooded eyes and severe
    lips,

Head up in the air, a beaky nose, haughty
And unsympathetic to the artist.
Then I return and look at Lettice Knollys'
Strange eyes, posy, and two crushed flowers
    and fist.

The guide says, "She wasn't very nice to know,
Her lovers tended to go to an early grave.
She married Essex, poisoned him in Dublin,
Married Leicester – which Elizabeth never
    forgave –

"And poisoned him in fifteen eighty-eight,
Then married again. Look carefully at her
    hand,
The two crushed flowers are her two dead
    husbands,
The one in bloom is her present husband.

"The other hand holds five flowers – she had
Five children." I stare at her sidelong eyes.
"The artists were very good in those days,
They caught an expression through its
    disguise."

I stare. "And did the artist know she had
Poisoned two men?" "Oh yes, without a
    doubt.
Hence the two flowers." And I marvelled at
Van Somer's truthful courage in speaking out.

I, too, know murderers I would like to expose,
I wish that I too had a painter's skill
And commission so I could tell the truth
About particular men and women who would
    kill.
       17 August 1985, revised 22 November 1993

AT GEEVOR TIN-MINE

The car park at Geevor tin-mine.
Only the museum and a video to tell.
The man at the door recognises her:
"You're not Alf Kellow's daughter? Well,
    well."

He talks across all of fifty years,
Accounting for dead friends – workmates –

Then into the museum we go,
And there is Alf lying down near plates.

A group of tin-miners stand around
In nineteen thirty. I see with surprise
A jaunty smile with a cap and a bag –
Can you see Africa call those eyes?

He went, left his rented cottage
To make his fortune – and got killed.
A car swung by and ran him down
And his family never returned, were spilled.

I see him now in a Geevor book
Standing in a miners' cage, out of breath,
A jaunty smile under helmet-lamp –
Not knowing it's five years to his death.
       17 August 1985, revised 22 November 1993

AT PENDEEN LIGHTHOUSE

Pendeen lighthouse was hidden
In a white cloud that shocks:
A foghorn blasts each minute
To warn ships of the rocks.

The beam turns round and round,
The white lighthouse in its shroud.
I stand on the cliff and think
Of a light within a cloud.

And above the invisible sea,
Away from the invisible cliff
I stare at the pulsing light
In this thick mist, and sniff,

And think of my own light
In my impenetrable cloud,
Know my consciousness will clear
So the light can be avowed.
       17 August 1985, revised 22 November 1993

FIRE

"God is fire in the head."
              Nijinsky

I put five logs in the grate
And then set them alight.
They smoulder and soon blaze,
Soon all is one fire, bright.

So it is with the world –
And my mind's fire-like sun;
Taking five separate things
My heat burns them into one.

So it is with the Baroque
Whole vision of the Plan:
Five different elements burn
To redefine a man.

When five senses are chopped
My fire burns just the same:
Feel its warmth fill the room,
The divine spark aflame.

August 1985(?), revised 6 December 1993

DRIPS OF LIGHT

Chestnut candles
In four dark tiers,
In a towering tree
Flames leap like years.

Through this window
Wax-drips inspire,
A boy loiters,
Aura of fire.

This four-tiered Tree
With candled crown
Shines out a warmth
As light drips down.

August 1985(?), revised 6 December 1993

OAKLANDS: OAK TREE

I look out of my study window at
Green trees in chestnut flower, with candles
    that
Snuggle round a corner of green field, in the
    sun
On which blackbirds hop and two squirrels run,
Iron railings, where magpies and jays flit,
Where a woodpecker and a bullfinch sit.
Closer, two goldcrests swing near nuts, like
    thieves,
And buttercups tint yellow between green
    leaves.

A Paradise, this field, where all aglow
I lay a childhood through a life ago,   10
Near the shady oak puffed at an acorn pipe,

And watched bees hum in clover when all was
    ripe.
A log, a pond, a horse, and everywhere,
Nature dances in the flower-filled air,
And among butterflies it is easy to see
A human gathers pollen like a bee.

A Paradise of sunlight and skipping feet
As swallows skim and swoop in the summer
    heat,
As a robin pecks in grass near children's
    speech,
The green only broken by the copper
    beech.   20
Here birds and flowers and insects perch and
    run,
And humans grow like berries in the ripening
    sun.
And tiny heads grow large like bud from
    stalk,
Like the spring bluebells fluttering round the
    Nature Walk.

It teaches that man is part of Nature's care,
That a boy can become a man without moving
    from here,
As a bud becomes the fruit of this apple tree,
Or this downy chick the nesting blue tit's
    glee,
As a grub hatches from pond slime into
    dragonfly;
This field is full of transformation's cry,   30
Of bees and birds and boys and girls and
    showers,
Observe your true nature among these
    flowers.

See the great oak like a druid tree – divine,
Filling with acorns that will make a soma
    wine
And give the sight of gods to all bound by
    sense,
Who see mere social faces across the fence.
Your true essential nature must include
This Tree of Life that pours spirit as food
Into the world, like acorns into leaves, and
    feeds
A horn of plenty that pours out souls like
    seeds.   40

August 1985(?), revised 14 September 1993

WITH HAROLD AT WALTHAM

I walk through the stone arch, and by the
stream
Which brims over the weir, plunges into
gloom,
And beside the Abbey to the old altar's dream,
Now in fresh air, and stare at Harold's tomb.
Here Harold was brought, identified by his
belle,
Edith Swan Neck, after the arrow in his eye,
Here he lay by the nave he built, as the old
order fell
To the Norman horde – French Danes with a
Latin cry.

The last of the Saxons. Under Canute the Dane
A carpenter had a dream that all should dig 10
Forty cubits for a buried cross, it sounds
insane
But a black flint crucifix was found – quite
big –
And the Lord of Waltham, Tovi the Proud,
inflamed,
Claimed it as treasure, loaded it on an ox-cart.
The oxen only moved when Waltham was
proclaimed –
Then people were cured, blood gushed from a
stone like a heart.

Miracle or superstition? Accident?
Providence?
Tovi vowed he would serve the cross and fate,
And his lands passed to Athelstan, his son,
and thence
To Edward the Confessor, who gave his
estate 20
To Harold Godwinson, on condition there
should arise
A monastery there – we stand on holy moss.
Harold was broad, tall, handsome, strong and
wise,
And cured of paralysis by the holy cross.

The finest man in England was elected King
And beat the Norwegians at Stamford Bridge,
but then
Prayed here before Hastings: the figure,
bowing,
Looked down from the cross sadly, an ill-
omen,

The Saxons rushed on William crying, "Holy
cross."
The cross disappeared in the Dissolution, and
yet 30
In this oldest Norman church, I still sense
loss,
I can still sense Harold and the Norman
threat.

The cross – a dream, superstition, miracle,
shield?
What can we make of it now when so many
doubt?
Carpenter guided to a hill, a cross that healed,
And the Doom painting in which Christ sits
and looks out
While two angels blow trumpets and the dead
rise
From graves and are weighed in scales near a
demon choir –
Was this the old order's folly? Look with
Bayeux eyes –
The Normans were superior in their Roman
Fire. 40

7-9 September 1985

GREENSTEAD CHURCH: MARTYR

Drive through Essex hedgerows filled with
desire –
Cow parsley with red campion for a bride –
To a wooden Saxon church with a wooden
spire.
Upright halved tree-trunks form the nave out-
side,
A porch with roses, but inside recoil:
A stained glass window of St. Andrew bound
On an X-shaped cross; look back, in quatre-
foil
The head of St. Edmund, on a martyr's
ground.

The stained glass window shows his fate: the
King
Of East Anglia when the Danes arrived, so
fierce, 10
He refused to relent his faith in Christ,
praying,
Was bound to a tree and shot – with arrows
that pierce-

410

d his side, then his head was cut off with a
    sword-heave
And thrown into bushes, where it was found
Being guarded by a wolf who would not leave
Until it was rejoined so he was sound.

Much later his corpse was moved, and rested
    here.
See the beam has a crowned and bearded head
And a dog-like wolf. And so this church,
    which seems bare,
Made from trees like the Tree of Life and
    fed   20
With a Saxon eye-hole niche and leper squint,
Celebrates the tree to which St. Edmund was
    tied,
And despite its water stoup it gives a hint
Of the criss-cross trunks on which St. Andrew
    died.

The Saxons worshipped pagan gods "in
    groves"
Until St. Cedd converted them to Christ,
And the West huddled and grew round Dark
    Age stoves
Until the Danes came with Beowulf's
    zeitgeist.
O hail the red-cross martyrs who endured
    strife
So Bernard, Teresa and John of the Cross
    could illume.   30
What courage to place a faith above one's life
Like the Crusader bowman under his shield-
    shaped tomb.

Martyrs put a cause above themselves, they
    live
Not hoping to see the outcome of what they
    do.
Martyrs affirm the faith for others, they give
In an act of love, a choice between false and
    true.
As Christ hung on his cross, Edmund on his
    tree
Rose above his executioners and their might;
His severed head, like Orpheus's, sings free
A call to all to follow what is right.   40

I walk, stunned, through tents with aromas'
    lures.

It is the herb festival, a hundred jars
Proclaim "nettles", "marjoram" and their
    cures
To people who believe herbs cure like stars.
How many here will stand against our Danes
When they come with their arrows, helmets
    and shields
And load our bodies with barbs and a
    conqueror's chains?
May we have Edmund's courage in our green
    fields!

September 1985(?), revised 22 November 1993

WHITE DAISY

The grass is taller than
White daisies that reach up;
All Nature bursts with life,
Forget-me-not, buttercup.

I saw you yesterday
White face and a headache,
Bent over the newspaper,
As if in an earthquake.

I see the ambulance
And you in a coma, talk
Of a brain haemorrhage,
And your white face on a stalk.

The daisies on tiptoe
Whiten the lengthening grass,
But one head is bent from its stalk
From straining to surpass.

I will be a daisy
And live in a green field,
But I will not droop and bend
For striving to be revealed.

Autumn 1985(?), revised 13 December 1993

AT DARK AGE JORVIK: THE LIGHT OF CIVILISATION

We drive through a flat green Yorkshire
    countryside
And sit in a hotel room, overlook the Ouse
Between two bridges and the pale Minster,
To which we walk along the Shambles,
    choose
The medieval butchers' street, and think
Of the stink and how many fires have spread,

And look at Clifford's Tower where the Jews
    were killed
And see where Richard of York was beheaded
And where his head was stuck on Micklegate.
York is a town steeped in history's hate.   10

It is the Vikings we have come to see:
Jorvik, lost capital of the Danish myriads.
I think of the first raids and the settlements,
The attacks on monasteries by sea-nomads,
The capture of York by fiery Norsemen
Who beat Anglo-Saxons who wore helmets
Like Oshere's of Coppergate, the raiders who
Imposed Danelaw and levied a thousand debts.
My name is Old Norse, and my family,
    though dead,
Had Scandinavian looks, and a long head.   20

A personal journey, I sit in a time car
And travel backwards in time to the yells
Of a Viking settlement of timber houses,
A farmyard everyday life, child cries and
    smells,
The wood stall cups and bowls, the bone
    carver,
The jeweller's and leather shops and leather
    shoes,
The coopers, the woman with plaits among
    geese.
Now into a house, where round the hearth
    they use
Two men sit and talk and cook and weave,
Bend by the fire under hanging bags, and
    believe.   30

Suddenly an echo reverberates:
I too, once sat in a half-lit gloom like this,
Amid cooking smells and a woven wattle
    wall,
This crowded filth, these clothes – something
    I miss.
A race memory or a hint from a former life?
I sit by a fire, hear gibbering in Old Norse,
Stop playing chess-like hnefatafl and tense,
Know war is near, a conqueror without a horse
Yet an outsider – we keep ourselves apart,
As I do now, from the Ango-Saxon heart.   40

The glimpse has gone, but I know these
    Viking men,

These sea-nomads, addicted to food, girls, ale,
These earthy bearded men who mend nets, cut
Oak planks Norman fire will char, sew a sail.
I know their manure fork, bone antler combs,
Their spindle whorls, toggles, pins near their
    chests,
Their iron coin dies, men's pointed leather
    caps,
The short sleeved underdresses low down on
    breasts –
I have like Beowulf drunk, before a log fire,
Mead ale and gazed at a fair-haired wench
    with desire.   50

And I know the religion of these Viking men,
Their cult of Odin, the god of death, the shield
In battle (German Wodan, Anglo-Saxon
    Woden),
Who welcomed dead heroes from the
    battlefield,
And of Thor the thunder god, and his hammer,
And their runic inscriptions on wood and stone,
The spells and curses in runes Odin gave men,
I know the shamans who gave them their own
World Tree on which Odin hung, pierced with
    a spear,
That road to the Other World embraced
    without fear.   60

And I know the Christianisation that happened
As the Vikings tried to win the Church's
    support,
Not challenging the Northumbrian religion
Which proclaimed "The Lord God is King",
    and fought.
We had St. Peter coupled with Thor's hammer.
While Odin, pierced with a spear, hung on a
    crossed tree.
I saw no conflict between the two, we were
    mild
As the Christian vision retained its
    supremacy,
Imposed on the invaders' cult with out-
    stretched arms,
Encouraged by us invaders' Viking
    charms.   70

Now I sit in their triumph, the Minster,
Which shows the glory Christendom has
    been;

The pillars soar to arches and gold bosses
See the stained glass, the Kings on the stone
    screen.
The crumbling and decay cannot conceal
The growth that thrust this glory to its height,
Why did we not Vikingise Christendom
So Odin and Thor triumphed over Christ and
    his Light?
We raiders lacked numbers, no King came
    round
To Odin, who lacked magnetic strength on the
    ground.   80

Civilisation triumphed – another way
Of saying the ambience transmitted growth;
From Charlemagne, a thrust carried us
    forward
And spurred Crusaders to keep it in their oath.
I think of my coat of arms, the Crusader's cross
Grew Europe better than the hammer of Thor,
The Light of civilisation beside which
The Dark Ages seem times of night and war.
Soon the cross which inspired this Minster
    turned
The Vikings into barbarian raiders who
    burned.   90

So what were the Vikings we all can recall?
Dark Age savages who scratched at the soil,
Marauders who pillaged and raped and lived
    by power,
Northern Huns who left nothing behind their
    toil.
They had no social church or creed or belief
Which attracted martyrs or seers with bent
    backs,
And so Odin on the Tree became Christ on
    the Cross
And Thor with his hammer Saint Olaf with
    his axe –
Fit to be Christianised by the Light in the soul
That brought rose-windows in stone and a
    Gothic control.   100
26 October 1985, revised 12-13 October 1993

EVERYDAY LIFE AND ECONOMICS: PAST LIVES

Question:
Do you remember the Vikings gibbering

In Old Norse among chickens and dogs in the
    gloom,
The cesspit smells and barrels of herrings,
And the rubbish-filled yard at the back of our
    room?

Answer:
Our search for furs, weapons, timber and
    slaves
Drove our expanding population overseas.
We traded with Byzantines, Islam over the
    waves,
Took Arab gold to Charlemagne, and found
    ease.
26 October 1985, revised 30 November 1993

SOUL LIKE A MAGPIE

See the magpie
Walk white and black,
Strut on green grass
His head held back.

See the magpie
White as clear light,
As black as coal,
Take off in flight.

Know the magpie
For you too wear
Soul black as death,
White as light's glare.
14 November 1985, revised 13 December 1993

SNOW

Snow, everywhere round the field
On hedge, railing, tree-top,
The children run and slide;
I let the curtain drop.

I finish drying my hair,
Look in the mirror and crack –
With a sudden shock I see
A grey-haired man look back.

Alas! the snow that tints
Each twig and lacy tree,
Has tinted my young hair
And made an old man of me.
Late autumn 1985(?), revised 13 December 1993

QUESTION MARK OVER THE WEST

1986 – 1988

FOUNTAIN OF ICE

In the snowy courtyard
of the White Hart Royal's rule
Is a beautiful fountain
In a cloistered frozen pool.

The water sprinkles up,
Splashes the icy shell
Of icicles trickling down
Like grease down a candle.

This much-frozen fountain
Is like my gushing spring
Which congeals into art,
Into icicles that cling.

But now all is quite still,
The fountain has frozen dry,
And no pouring jets up
And falls to solidify.

22 February 1986, revised 29 November 1993

OXFORD REVISITED

I go past the lodge of my College, under the
  clock
Where I stood before my interview to get in,
Up the spiral staircase to the library, and the
  shock
Of where I worked all night, hand under chin,
Then staggered to staircase five as the sun
  shone.
The wooden treads creak as I climb, tip-toe,
But now behind the oak lives a history don.
I cannot see my room, I turn and go

Across the quad, through the arched tunnel to
  the glare
Of the snowy garden, trees, sun like a fire, 10
And on the frozen lake skid marks show
  where
There has been skating, near ladder and roped
  tyre,
And as four undergrads run and slide
  sideways

I walk to the tree where I chose my track,
Rejecting the buildings of the Law, and gaze
At the crossroads of my life, and no turning
  back.

And now I nose down Southmoor Road and
  peer
At redbrick houses, seeking her room then
Where I found love - later sorrow - and hear
Her wailing by the green canal, now
  frozen,   20
And I think of how she stood under that
  streetlight
As I pushed by, free from her as I am now
  free,
And how we walked in the Meadow, near a
  kite
And she came back to toasted bread and tea.

Port Meadow is white where the Thames has
  flooded it,
Has burst its banks, frozen in a skating-rink
On which slide hundreds. I walk to the
  towpath, flit
Across the first bridge. Wind wets my nose, I
  blink;
It stings my cheeks and ears, so I quickly
Cross the arched bridge with wooden treads
  near the high   30
Water, walk along the towpath to where I can
  see
The houses of Binsey Green in a curve under
  the sky.

And now, frostbite gone and toes warmed, I
  stand
In the Randolph Hotel where I drank with all,
And peer through the Star Room bar at where
  "the King"
Sat in his chair all day, drinking by the wall,
So proud in his acting boots and of his
  "throne",
And lament the many meetings with my
  friends

Who have now gone into obscure ways,
unknown,
Lament the ghosts that flitted to their ends. 40

I sit at lunch where my parents visited me,
And now, my children, I pass it to you, the
fight;
Hope that you will come here as I did, still
free,
Find your way under a tree, love under a light,
Grasp your outlook, heighten observation to
art,
And I think I am stuck with what I chose,
I am the consequences of those moments of
heart,
Then so tentative, now this purpose that
glows.

And that is what stands out, this purposive
drive
This search for meaning through the rational
West, 50
This dangerous outlook that makes me strive
Against your unchanging backdrop, this quest
You look on with detachment as I carry the
torch;
But you shaped my probing of empirical
sense.
Oxford, you designed the pattern of my
scorch
On the fine carpet of your indifference.

22 February 1986, revised 29 November 1993

QUESTION MARK OVER THE WEST

After Fernhurst we turn up a wooded lane
And drive across Lord Cowdray's estate till
A three-gabled stable cottage and urbane
Line of chestnut trees, facing a wooded hill,
With honeysuckle over the front door.
I stand near a French drain with my cousin
and gaze
Across sheep wire and mounded mole-hills
for
Wild life, and potter in the house and praise
The white-wooded windows and life of a
squire,
Then sit in one wing at the birch log fire. 10

And now at night a deep peace in the dark.

We stroll under a brilliance of stars and
swoon -
W of Cassiopeia, Plough like a question mark
Or sickle in the sky - and gaze at the moon,
A cusp on its back above a line of firs
And I smell the sweet smell of the earth,
digest
The moisture of woods, this idyllic quiet that
spurs,
Wonder at the question mark hanging over the
West
Like a sickle set to recapture lost ground
And scythe all Western gains without a
sound. 20

The rabbits have eaten the growing shoots,
A fox escaped the hunt up the hill somewhere,
An owl sits on the fence-posts and hoots,
The baaing of new lambs fills the evening air;
A green-topped pheasant sits in the green
field,
I hear a gun's report, a squirrel runs,
A hare lopes among hedgehogs; may the gun
yield
To the bird by the chestnut fencing. The
Englishman's
Country life is as old as Chaucer's day,
The sweet smell of the earth has its own
way. 30

Who would think here of a threat to
democracy?
This remote lane through a lord's estate, these
woods
Keep at bay the bad news on the TV,
The darkness round our sickle moon, our
"coulds".
We who threw up computers and man's quest
Through NASA saucers and voyaged through
a comet's trail,
We masters of chips and reason master our
West
By carrying homes on our backs as we work,
like a snail.
I see the Plough fall in a shiver of stars
And a question mark scythe the fir-trees to
stubbed bars. 40

Before the fire and flintlock guns, we recall
Our roots in our grandmother's garden,

The shed we scooted to, where Percy stood
Over the grinding wheel, sharpening knives,
A fir and frogs in a cellar, the sunlit grass,
"Shut this gate" wood with primroses to each
    knee,
A bomb blast at the gate and shattering glass;
We made the best of forties austerity
Like the arcade minstrel doll with a hand held
    out
Who popped a coin in his mouth, we never
    went without.   50

This Sunday country air at six hundred feet,
Is heady like wine; we walk past suckling
    lambs
Up the wooded hill to Northpark Copse and
    greet
A crack down the blue sky to where a feller
    jams
Felled chestnut trunks as fencing poles in the
    ground.
I look between the Downs over the Weald
Towards Black Down and the Pilgrim's Way,
    which wound
From Winchester to Canterbury across field,
And then we plunge down to Verdley Edge
    and the chime-
less clock in the woods that measures a
    timeless time.   60

The air is scented with spruce and pine tree,
We cross the road, climb to Henley through
    beech
Where a stream splashes and pours down the
    hill, and see
Ears of bud, crocus and snowdrops gush and
    reach,
Sip draught cider at the Duke of Cumberland
By wysteria, wheel and posthorn, gaze and
    doze
And watch dark trout dart, turn and dash, get
    canned
By the pool that collects the spring and
    overflows
To trickle and splash and gush down the road
With a freedom that our land has always
    showed.   70

Over cheese and chutney sandwiches we talk
Of how you settled here - but not how,

looking at Mars
That first spring day after a five-mile walk
I saw the night fall in a shower of stars;
Of the peace of a family inside their fence,
Each individual free in the scented air
To think and talk and be, without inter-
    ference -
And to open their hearts to the One in each
    easy chair,
So that pinpricks of light pierce from on high
Into this one ball, the mind and inner eye.   80

Lunch is finished. At four a wet mist sweeps
Up the valley, the horse edges towards the
    poles
On the leaping flames in the farm as the dark
    creeps.
In this peaceful country life men find their
    souls
And live in the shadow of the moon-like One
And go to town to work the West's machines
And then return to enjoy the quiet, the sun,
Or go to the ancient Norman church, grow
    beans,
Graze sheep under the crooked crozier of the
    Plough,
The shepherd's crook that hangs in the night
    sky now.   90
16 March 1986, revised 23-24 October 1993

COTSWOLDS: WINTER FOUR-SIDEDNESS

Moreton in the Gloucestershire Cotswolds, a
    skin
Of Regency windows, and peace like a spire.
Here Jane Austen might have walked, here in
    this inn
Charles the First slept a night, by the bar log-
    fire
Which leaps invitingly through the freezing
    glass.
In the back courtyard a fountain squirts and
    falls,
Icicles hang baggy round its trickling pass
Like the cold brittle poems round my spring's
    walls.

Broadway in Worcestershire, a quaint wind-
    blown
Village of old houses, removed from

power,   10
In a long lined street of yellow Cotswold
        stone
And behind it on the Beacon a great church
        tower
Where a fire was lit to warn of a dangerous
        threat
And where Byrne-Jones walked with Morris
        in a gale.
We visit a vicar in double-glazed quiet
Then go to Evesham across the snowy Vale.

Chedworth Villa, a 1st century Roman's
        dream:
He saw sheltering hills and a sweet spring for
A thermal bath with "central heating" steam
Through stone toadstools that held a mosaic
        floor   20
I look at the mosaic Winter with his hood
(Birrus) and tunic, holding a branch and hare.
Perhaps this Roman Briton owned the wood
Before the Saxons drove him out somewhere.

Burford. Near the Wild Life Park, a scare:
A blue car in front swerves across the road,
I see it hit the verge, spin through the air
Three times, bump a stone wall upside down.
        Slowed,
A red car swerves round it and drives at me.
I brake, it swerves back. I stop and get out 30
An elderly man, blood trickling from head.
        He
Lifts two stones from his lap, stained. Eyes
        doubt.

After this intrusion, the Cotswold peace has
        gone,
The quiet, the antiquity of stone and moss.
Bourton-on-the-Water, three low bridges on
The Windrush. Stow-on-the-Wold with stocks
        and cross,
A church where Cromwell locked up a
        thousand
Royalists - I keep seeing that car spin through
The air, blood trickle down that head and
        hand
As he staggered from his car as if to queue. 40

Now I stand by the four shire stone, twilit,
In winter east of Moreton, and I think

Of the four counties I cross as I walk round it
And of the Western spirit, and I link
To a Winter four-sidedness, and see
Fine art, domestic peace free from ferment
And civil disturbance, scenic beauty,
And Providential protection from accident.
        22 March 1986, revised 29 November 1993

ODE: COUNTER-RENAISSANCE

I hurtle down the M3 like a lord
To the Saxon capital, Winchester, and pass
Alfred who holds out his guarding sword,
Then, early, linger by Cathedral grass,
See the site of the Saxon minster's aisles,
Then go inside to look at St. Swithun's tomb,
Canopy and catafalque, and ancient stones:
Saxon knights, Norman arches, medieval tiles,
Reformation bishops, Caroline hair, Victorian
        room -
This history begins with Cynegils' holy
        bones.   10

This tradition wrested a hope from death,
Like Bishop Fox's corpse, which he carved to
        stand
For mortality and urge humble breath.
St. Cuthbert holds King Oswald's severed
        hand,
In the mixed-up bones in chests of the once
        crowned
Which include Canute. Ribbed figures lie,
        fresh
Mouths gape on tombs in images of hope.
These ribbed, recumbent men in marble found
The invisible body within decaying flesh,
The letter within the outer envelope.   20

The tradition is there, which fifteen centuries
        kept
And there is a practice with it, on the hour
As a black-frocked priest ropes off the north
        transept
And singing voices waft into the tower;
A practice that, like mould on a forest log,
Feeds on antiquity, but yet smells stale
To all but the connoisseur and naturalist.
O living history, damp in evening fog!
I hear the Hallelujahs, and like a snail
Creep off to await the lifting of the mist. 30

417

And now I arrive at the nearby college where
For nine years mystics and scientists have
met.
And a spiritual presence is in the air
And confronts materialists with an uncertain
threat:
Bits of magic clutter the reception hall;
Crystals, charms, trinkets of a superstitious
time.
I leaf through books on soul, wince at the
weird,
And stare at people who strut and pose and
sprawl,
Who wave their hands and know we have to
climb
And smile under berets, all posture and white
beard.   40

Some stand at the lectern, one by one, and
shine;
A white-haired man calls for a new
Renaissance.
There is little imagery for their line
Save the diagrams on the wall and their own
stance.
They cite the lore from books, and boldly
shout
"This cannot be proved by 'the intellect',
You must imagine the spiritual is here,
The reason is bad, do not take notes." They
spout.
(An hour of Pan - if only he could select!)
All have progressed from editor to seer!   50

With mounting excitement white-hair scythes
the air:
"Science lifted us from medieval theorisings,
But ego, with the sensebound body's flair,
Cut us off from spirit. We are spiritual beings
Housed in the temple of the pure body,
Sparks of divine fire, remember who you are.
Don't believe this, but live with it today,
Imagine you have an immortal eye
In your divinely designed body, say
"Hurrah!"
You are not an accident of chance or play.   60

"A deep psychological change affects each
art;
When the arts renew contact with the divine

There will be a new Renaissance of the heart,
That will outshine the fifteenth century
sunshine.
We are on its threshold now, for we are open
To a flooding in of power, light, thought,
romance;
We are being transformed from sensebound
wit
To divine beings lifted, as by oxygen,
To the pre-Fall mind - a Counter-Renaissance
That takes us back from body to spirit!"   70

It's a new movement within the tradition, a
late
Going-back on three hundred years of
Darkness,
I walk in blossom and meditate
With this white-haired giant who shines his
"Yes",
And leave behind my body and fly through a
hole
To a Garden of Angels, a pre-Fall place,
And float in my invisible glowing form;
"All Nature is unfulfilled till the human soul
Unites with its being," he says from inner
space
As the Light beams in and leaves me feeling
warm.   80

I kill Darwin with Sheldrake and then shrug,
And now his wife talks on the vibrating
world:
Her Mongolian chant can smash a jug
For sound decomposes matter when it is
curled,
I sit and make my body into an ear,
And vibrate like the ringing of a gong.
Forgotten-about knowledge pours in from the
air:
"The higher mind when we attune and peer
Is like fish turning in shoals," or like a throng
Of migrating swallows wheeling above
Leicester Square.   90

Now Sheldrake talks to me of goals in my
room,
Teleology Darwin did not know;
Of purpose in creature, atom, star, and womb,
How the Western lack of tension must go,
How spiritual intensity thrives in war

418

Conditions, not comfortable surfeit and scorn,
Not in the liberal West that lacks an aim.
I say the new Renaissance will restore
To a world that is Western wherever suits are
    worn
A rekindling of mystic goals - the Flame!   100

I walk among trees at blossom time and feel
The rutting sweat and shudder of passionate
    love,
Know ambition to make money. This zeal
For the sensebound should not be sneered at
    from above.
Celebrate the opposite of decaying flesh -
Bodily health! These greyfaced ghosts that
    stroll,
These spirits before their time, are sheltered
    from shock.
As man discovers his spiritual being afresh
Let him also love and earn - and be healthily
    whole!
Sense and spirit - world and beyond: the
    Baroque!   110

I return to the Cathedral and its Saxon kings
The holy relics that healed, and in the crypt
The healing waters that cured the skin's red
    rings -
Was not sense known in each clerestory
    manuscript?
I think of the West, which Hermeticists
    deride,
As being in a cheap reductionist age -
Woe to the civilisation that will not allow
Scientists to explore within as well as outside:
Bishop Fox carved his own skeleton's corpse,
    the sage,
To remind his soul he should be humble -
    now!   120

A thousand million stars in as many galaxies,
And does Providence guide despite this dust?
The Dark Age is round the corner, and it is
Human agency that will keep the West robust
And reunite its western and eastern shores,
Unify the world in a new image of man,
The spirit in sweating flesh that loves from
    afar
Like the winged Guardian Angels where this
    chapel soars -

O Saxon knights in stone, awake and scan
And fill with angelic light this tiny star!   130

5-6 April 1986, revised 20 September 1993

AT BLEA TARN HOUSE

Grey stone walls and roofs and sweep of
    green hill,
Curly smoke and jackdaws on the chimney
    pots -
I leave High Newton and drive to a room that
    still
Overlooks Morecambe Bay, where men are
    dots.
This was the old coach-house where the coach
    with a splash
Crossed the quicksands. I linger at the view,
Then drive to the Cumbrian mountains, where
    rains lash
Far down in the valley below, like gentle dew.

We climb through hairpin bends, and snow-
    capped peaks,
Pass the Roman fort under distant Scafell,   10
And soon Blea Tarn approaches - no one
    speaks -
Under Bowfell, the whitewashed wall and
    spell
Of the house by the stream where the Solitary
    met
The Wanderer. Four windows and a porch;
I linger. No one, only mountains and sweat,
And to walk in solitude is to carry a torch.

I ascend the rocks around the sloping stream
And sit and look at the mountains and
    mankind
And gaze at a life where the poet alone can
    dream,
Apart from other people in his deeper
    mind,   20
From dawn to dusk, whispering to the breeze
And feeding off white peaks and this still tarn
In the company of rocks and birds and trees
And contemplating without a need to yarn.

I return to the car and switch on the radio
And hear the news from the active life that
    drives.
American planes from Suffolk, flying low,
Have bombed Libya and taken many lives.

My car crawls up to Langdale Pikes, just
copes,
A snow-ridge plunges down from a craggy
height;   30
I stop and look back: house and tarn and
slopes,
Grey in the distance and nothing else in sight.

The world outside this valley has a collective
heart -
Two million men are trained in two hundred
camps
To assail the West, which includes this part,
And snuff out minds like candles inside
lamps,
Regard all as bodies within a State
That expects solitaries to fill their dream
Not with these preciptious Forms but with
hate,
Ephemeral slogans for a war regime!   40

As I plunge into the valley down winding
bends
And drive to Grasmere, I think of my desert
stay,
How I saw one take Tripoli for his own ends,
Fire in the air to frighten resistance away
And export terror round the globe, again
Not for Palestine but to destabilise the West;
I think of Wordsworth sitting in the garden,
Ignoring Trafalgar for a poet's quest.

I drive up Dove Cottage lane where
Wordsworth met
The Leech-gatherer a hundred yards from his
door,   50
At the top I see the pond he stirred, feet wet,
Earning a solitary living on the moor
From leeches he sold to doctors to bleed the
unwell,
A craggy man with ten children and pride.
Past Rydal I take the Rothay road and tell
Stepping-stones Wordsworth crossed to
Ambleside.

I stand by the stepping-stones on the Rothay
road,
Now stand on the stilts with the stream
running below.
On one side the house where De Quincey

lived and showed
The opium dream to all whose vision would
glow;   60
On the other the post office where, like a
convict,
The Distributor of Stamps piled coins. I stand,
The two sides of my self in tense conflict:
The solitary eye, the active worker's hand.

The radio is full of crisis news,
Of what "dictator" Gaddafi has done,
Of how America has made the terrorists lose,
Who have sworn to be avenged with bomb
and gun.
And can one be a solitary today and ignore
The ravings of lunatics and heroic deeds,   70
And, tuned to television, can one not adore
The magic that each mountain scene
concedes?

The whole, perfect, well-rounded man - take
heed -
Is both alone and in and of mankind,
And heeds the rocks and fields and lakes to
feed
His spirit, which grows height and depth
while blind.
I think of Maecenas, Augustus's stripling
Minister of Arts, Horace's patron and dole,
Who built a villa by a Bandusian spring
Where he could refresh his action-weary
soul.   80

We are each a solitary, each a martyr pressed
By a cause that affects our civilisation's
health
And in this clash between Islam and West,
Like the Crusaders, we cannot stay at home
for wealth.
And yet to be whole rounded people we need
The Solitary's music and telescope.
His moss and eye, his solitary interests breed
A love of the universe, rooted in hope.

I see the Solitary at Blea Tarn strain
To paint in words poems which are five land-
scapes,   90
The places, houses, abbeys which contain
The heritage our civilisation shapes.
He puts in his solitary verse, from all apart,

420

The common richness to which all aspire,
Unites action and contemplation in his art,
Which all will learn by heart and chant for its
    Fire!

15-16 April 1986, revised 18 October 1993

THE ARTIST

See the white-haired old artist sit
In the back of his studio;
Lakeland paintings crowd all the walls
At eighty he is seen to know.

See the white-haired old artist stand
And talk to a boy framing a print, kind,
His life time's work upon the walls,
His studio like the walls of his mind.

See the leaflet which tells how he had
An experience in his youthful brain
Of "wholeness", how mountains pushed up
Damp which came down in misty rain.

And see how the wise white-haired man
Has painted Oneness in cloud and mound,
How each picture relates earth and sky,
Gives pattern to mountain and ground.

16 April 1986, revised 13 December 1993

INNER POWER

I stand astride your stepping-stones,
The water gushes under my feet,
I know that movement of the mind
That races through block-like brain's heat.

I stand on the terrace where you played,
The water flows with a river's roll,
I know that flow from day to day
That sweeps a purpose into a goal.

I stand under your waterfall
Which roars and foams like wind in trees,   10
I know the manic headlong dash
Of the pouring inspirational breeze.

I look back at a still, calm lake,
Then rise into cloud on the Pass
And I too know this serene calm
And this thick obscuring cloud on grass.

Rothay, Derwent, Aira Force and

Ullswater reflect one inner power
Which changes its pace and its moods,
Now pushing torrent, now breathless hour.   20

17 April 1986, revised 17 October 1993

THE POWER WITHIN THE MIND
(OR: AT AIRA FORCE WATERFALL)

Go down through woods and see the lake
And the high snow-capped mountain peaks,
Descend the steps, stand on the bridge
Where the roaring waterfall streaks.

It foams above the humped back bridge,
Then spouts and gushes down in shocks
And pours in a sheer, steep cascade
And froths in a torrent on rocks

And a fine spray hangs in the air
Like smoke over the bright green moss   10
That carpets the soft quiet wood,
The trees that overhang and toss.

Now cross the bottom bridge and climb,
Ascend the steps the other side
And stand at the very top and see
The stream race among boulders, hide,

Then pour down underneath, below
And hear its muffled pounding sound,
Then turn and look sheer down and hear
The roar now loud as it plunges to ground,   20

Then walk back to where you began
And ponder the steps up and down,
Ponder the two bridges, which frame
This foaming torrent, and then frown

And build airy bridges and steps
Deep down in your mind near its force
So you can descend and be filled
With the roar of this alien source

As it cascades from far elsewhere
And bubbles in when you are blind   30
And fills your being with its power,
Energises your stream-like mind;

And ascend and look down at your

Rocky depths where the currents break,
See the power rush and froth and foam
To your serene, reflecting lake;

And know, as you gaze at the snow
Where the mountain towers so bleak,
The aim of this rushing power
Is to reflect an out of reach peak!   40

17 April 1986, revised 10-11 January 1994

THE GUIDE OF MEANING
(OR: THE QUICKSANDS OF MEANINGLESSNESS)

Walk from the old coachhouse
Where the horses from the sands
Were stabled by the sea,
Along to the ancient farm-lands

Where for seven hundred years
The guide of the sands had dreams,
Go into his thick walled house
Where he stands under black beams.

And see through the windows
The quicksands of Morecambe Bay,   10
And the sinkings of centuries' lost
Who still wail today.

Time was when brigands held
The woods around Grange which weren't thin
And only the guide's safe-conduct
Could allow a stranger in.

But now the guide walks tours,
And keeps a knowledge alive,
Seven hundred years of crossing
These treacherous sands to survive.   20

I know another quicksand
Where meaning may not be found,
And wanderers are sucked down,
And disappear beneath the ground

Unless a leader leads
The pilgrim band in a ride,
And steers a well-learned course
So he reaches the other side.

Our civilisation should give
Its purpose guide a chalet,   30

And lead all seeking men
Across quicksands by his safe way.

This is the true poet's task
To mark the quicksands and show
A true direction to all
From seven hundred years ago.

17 April 1986, revised 19 October 1993

AT CARTMEL PRIORY: TAMING THE UNICORN

I enter the Priory where black habited monks,
Augustinians, kept a sub-Abbey with a smile,
A lamp under chancel arches like tree trunks
And triforium stones whose Norman style
Arrived late in this backwater, this glade,
("Transitional Norman" it is called), until
The Dissolution of barbaric Henry made
The roof fall in, this art to be damaged, and
    shrill.

I wander the fourteen fifty choir and gaze
At the Renaissance screen where pillars
    show   10
Emblems of war - crusading swords, the blaze
Of a tunic cross, gauntlet of ring mail -
    "grow"
Among the crucifixion (hammer, spear, nails,
Ladder) and the true vine, the life and law,
And I think of my crusade through
    Christendom's gales
And am troubled by my own crusading war.

For I have struck a blow at the infidel -
And shattered a hostile tyrant's HQ
Where he co-ordinated fifty terror gangs well,
Have unmasked his secret design, his private
    view,   20
And now he is rampant, quite mad with scorn,
And I am like a stoner's pile of stones,
A lion fighting the dangerous unicorn,
A beast that retaliates and spikes one to
    bones.

I wander restlessly, and start in the gloom -
A reminder of my mortality, I stand
On a skull and two crossed bones on a flag-
    stone tomb,
And an hourglass with moments like grains of
    sand

And wings which show that time is winging
round
To the day when I too will become, und
one,   30
A skull and two crossed bones under the
ground,
Struck down by an assassin's murderous gun.

I reflect posthumously, a lingering ghost,
Was it worth it? To accept martyrdom?
Yes! For an anti-Western army, a host
Of two million would assault our land and
bomb,
And there were few who recognised the war,
And few who would stand up and take the
risk, the best;
I did not flinch to attack the murderous four
Who would destroy with bombs our sacred
West.   40

I think of the attack that must surely come,
The smash of the bullet into the brain,
The leaking of blood on the flagstones, flesh
numb,
As the unicorn turns savage, and spikes again,
And seeks to impale all with its white horn
And I await in a Priory church bloodstains
As Becket awaited his four knights who,
sworn,
Sliced off the top of his skull and spilled his
brains.

I wander back to the choir and gaze
At the misericords on the choirboy seats,   50
The grimacing devils and holy saints in a
daze,
And suddenly by the opening my heart beats
For I see an oak-tree and a unicorn;
The tale's hunter has dodged behind the tree,
At which the beast has charged and impaled
his horn.
The oak-tree has captured the unicorn, I see!

And now I am light-footed as I tread
On the two crossed bones, skull and winged
hourglass
And gaze at the loaf on the tray, the bread
Put out for the poor each day while centuries
pass,   60
And now I watch sheep crop the tumbling

graves
And climb the Gatehouse, once near the
convent part
And the prior's manorial court, and my mind
behaves,
Now I am resolute and firm of heart.

We are on earth a fleeting time and act
To improve our age in a small or major way,
And we must not flinch from death, which is a
fact.
We define ourselves against the dark, each
day.
Then others carve our names on our
tombstones,
And our deeds are recorded for others to read
and see   70
And the crusading lion does not rejoice with
moans
As it captures the unicorn in an oak-tree!

18 April 1986, revised 18-19 October 1993

THE VICTIM OF TERRORISM
(A FRAGMENT)

It was the waste – my life incomplete, cut
short.
I had a destiny – I needed twenty more years.
Twenty more years and my name would have
rolled from your tongue
With the ease of a Michelangelo, Darwin,
Freud.
I was snuffed out, I had no say in it.

Summer 1986

IN SHAKESPEARE'S STRATFORD: THE NATURE OF ART

"Nature I loved, and, next to Nature, Art."

Walter Savage Landor

Stratford, a smiling town by the green Avon
Elizabethan thatch, heart of England!
Here roam past 15th century timber frame,
Thatched wattle and brick in a green garden,
And find the great Shakespeare through the
everyday,
See his strange powers grow out of the
familiar.
On at the theatre, for which we have tickets

Happens to be *A Winter's Tale*, about a man
Who lost his wife and son (who died) and
    daughter,
And recovered daughter and wife after sixteen
    years.   10
(As Leontes asks his Queen to be hostess
To Polixenes - and pales as they touch hands,
And accuses her of infidelity,
Claims her daughter is not his, and orders
Her to be cast out to crows in a desert place,
Then tries his wife, and as the Oracle
Pronounces her both chaste and innocent,
I howl within as the disunity appears
And he is left alone to live with his wrong.)

So it was with you. I see you first here at   20
Your mother's close-timbered house (a sign
    of wealth),
Built from the Forest of Arden and field
    straw,
Here she lived on rushes and dirt, here stood
The reversible board in the Great Hall,
Here were the platters they wiped, here the
    hot pot
From which they took "pot luck", at this fire
    they sat,
Before it slept the servants, damping it down
And watching for sparks the cold night long.
    Here she
Lived with her hair done up a year at a time,
Her lice itching her scalp, taking the trap steps
    upstairs,   30
Baby in the cubby hole, slipping into bed
Down sloping floors. All this before your
    father
Took it as a dowry, and merely let it out.

Your everyday life is in your birthplace, too,
This timbered beamy house on Henley Street,
Half home, half shop for your glover father
(Also whittawer, wool-dealer and yeoman).
I see you born in a room with a four-poster,
Canopy above for the rats, mice, bats, spiders
That might drop from the thatch into the
    bed.   40
Downstairs I see you sit by the fire, toddle
To the door and play outside among flowers
When that you were and a tiny little boy.
Did the rain really raineth every day? Or did
    you

Play in a meadow, as you went to school?

Now I find you at Shottery, courting your
    Anne,
A mere eighteen, and she is on the shelf,
An old twenty-six and pregnant by you.
I see you approach the door of this farmhouse,

Hewlands, in ninety acres (outhouses now
    gone),   50
And sit on the parlour seat by the inglenook
On which, the Hathaways hold, you did your
    courting,
I see you outside with Anne, in the farmyard
And meadow of daisies and violets, and the
    country life
While the servants prepared the food and once
    a year
"Greasy Joan doth keel the pot!" And you
    observe.

And now you are married to a farmer's
    daughter
You a merchant's son, back living with your
    father.
Some say that as you had to get married
You wanted to move away, I see the
    disgrace -   60
As here at Charlcote you poach deer from the
    man
Who as agent of the Privy Council
Condemned Edward Arden in the Tower,
You are caught and taken before Sir Thomas
    Lucy
Who saw you as an Arden - and were you not
Avenging that family wrong? I see you
    judged
And flogged in the Great Hall at Charlcote
    House
And told to leave the district or face prison.
I see you pin ribald verse to the gatehouse,
I see your leave-taking as you swear
    revenge.   70
Were you a schoolmaster at first? We do not
    know.
Or were you offered a job by a family friend,
Field, a London printer of histories and verse?
I see your exile start as you tramp towards
    London,
I see you in penury wait on your patron

("Being your slave") – I see you vow to get
 even
With "Justice Shallow" (Lucy), your
 prosecutor.
Or did you leave because like Leontes
You suspected your Anne was unfaithful to
 you?

Those ten London years away from those you
 loved,   80
You worked so hard, and you made your
 fortune!
I see you surrounded at work by History
 books,
Holinshed, the *Bible*, Plutarch, and base
Your plots on his stories, and work flat out.
I see you meet Henry Wriothesley,
I see you hoard your earnings, and invest
 them
So that here in Stratford you were known as a
 businessman.
I see you devastated by Hamnet's death,
I see you in fifteen ninety-seven return
And buy New Place, and next year install
 Anne   90
And your daughters - and go away again.
I see you regard the death as a punishment
For your self-will in your bleak winter's tale.

And now your mood darkens into tragedies.
Your father is buried, death preys on your
 mind.
Gone is the happy ending of the sunny
 comedies,
Gone is the sparkle of Renaissance wit
Now the heroes are flawed and cause their
 own disasters,
Now there is no second chance as life buffets
 them.
Now you show a man staring at a skull (his
 friend)   100
And the laughter and dashing wit are
 melancholy,
And nothing gives you pleasure any more;
It is in the staring eyes of the Chandos
 portrait.

And now I see you return to Stratford here,
Hugely rich and retired from the London
 stage

With its censorship and politics and risk,
I see you return to the peace of the
 countryside
And your stone-like Hermione whom you
 discover anew,
I see reconciliation after the storms,
I see you a family man, here in all that is
 left: 110
Your cellars below the servants' quarters, two
 walls,
And the Knott Garden near where you planted
 a walnut tree,
And your Great Garden through which you
 walked to the Avon.

I see you take delight in your daughters,
I see you walk to Susanna's house, Hall's
 Croft,
And talk medicine with her doctor husband.
I see you go to Judith's corner house,
And speak to Thomas Quiney the vitner.
And did you not have a chest of papers,
Manuscripts of plays, letters to the Dark
 Lady?   120
And what happened to them when you died
After drinking with Drayton and Jonson - who
 has them now?
Did Anne take them when Susanna had the
 house
And Henrietta Maria stayed in sixteen forty-
 three?
Or were they taken by Susanna's Elizabeth
When she returned the house to the Cloptons?
Blunden once told me "They are in an attic
In a forgotten house in Stratford." O where?
Did they descend to the Hathaways or Halls?

Known primarily as a businessman, you
 bought   130
The space before the altar in this ancient
 church.
Your epitaph - "forbeare/To digg the dust"
And "curst be he yt moves my bones" - it
 worked.
(And did you after Guy Fawkes' Popish plot,
Fear a Catholic Dissolution of Protestant
 bones?)
I stare at the lines beneath your quilled bust
"Stay passenger, why goest thou by so fast,
Read if thou canst whom envious death hath

plast"
And I think of the engraving on the First Folio
And of the dark "Flower" portrait, based on
    Droeshout.   140
I have no doubt you, sir, wrote all
    Shakespeare,
I have found you as a country boy made good,
Who still loved the meadows, longed for
    order.

Now this Stratford is given to Morris dancers
Who cavort and leap and twirl in ancient
    form,
Flapping white handkerchiefs in fine old
    clothes
While a stag with horns walks among the
    recoiling crowds,
A fertility rite to celebrate spring
And bring an end to winter, rebirth from
    death.
Now see on the Guild Chapel's chancel
    arch   150
The remains of a painted Day of Judgement
Hangs above the walls which show a Dance
    of Death.

Here in Stratford is a watery plain where
Green fields and trees blend with theatrical
    art,
Where the Nature a country lad loved with his
    heart
Was embroidered on civilised plays for a
    Queen's Court
To achieve a Golden Age of honeyed
    perfection,
Of movement of thought, metaphor or simile,
Of complexity, naturalness and maturity.
By this green town Nature and Art are
    one -   160
As when your Globe burned from a cannon's
    shot on thatch.

The tyrant Kings disorder a chain of being
Linking all things, and when order is
    disturbed
Chaos fractures the world with
    misunderstandings,
Accidental separations, false appearances.
Appearance belies reality in Baroque
Like the reflection of willows on drifting

water.
Your business sense contributed to your
    success
In the Chamberlain's Men, as proprietor of
    the Globe,
And as in a piece of music, you brought
    harmony,   170
Forgiveness and reconciliation at the end,
And saw the cloudy yearnings of the Kings
Mirrored in this sliding green Avon here
And showed that Nature is the spring of Art.
For as in winter ribbed ploughed fields and
    trees
Emphasise the bare structure behind
    profusion,
Art is the winter by whose lines Nature is
    grasped:
Art simplifies Nature's relationships
As the Avon mirrors and frames the trees and
    sky.

    25 May 1986, revised 28 September 1993

CASTLES IN THE AIR

Warwick Castle, turrets and battlements,
Finest medieval castle for earl and liege.
Take the winding path, admire its gaunt
    beauty.
Inside the portcullis think of each siege,
Walk through the private rooms, State
    apartments
Yet this fortress was Warwick's home, and
    task;
The Chapel built by Greville, State dining
    room,
The Great Hall with its armour and
    Cromwell's mask,
Bonnie Prince Charlie's shield, paintings and
    statues
Where the Kingmaking Warwick made
    known his views.   10

Admire the cedar panelling, the tapestries,
Chippendale chair, a rare French clock
    cajoles,
Marble Florentine tables and gold ceilings,
Silks woven from Lyon, rose-water bowls,
Red and green drawing-rooms, the blue
    boudoir,
Van Dycks, Henry the Eighth after Holbein,
A 14th century staircase lurking near

Opens for secret messages - the hot line:
A boat down the river, a horse across fields
    means
Affairs of State are solved behind the
    scenes.   20

All Europe is in this fine country house!
It is a work of beauty, intricate, detailed,
Perfectly proportioned, a pattern on life's
    flux,
History everywhere, the spirit is unveiled.
I could gaze for ever at Ann Boleyn
And her sister Mary, when Henry took a
    stroll.
This richness that edifies and exalts
Sends the heart soaring and uplifts the soul.
I wish I were an aristocrat, I who
Am a connoisseur of what spirit knows is
    true!   30

And now the lake side. I climb to the
    Watergate Tower
Which Fulke Greville's ghost haunts after his
    foul
Murder by his servant. Now the torture
    chamber,
With its rack and head clamp, foot screw and
    howl,
The dungeon with its chains and "oubliette"
    pit.
Poitiers prisoners sat in a dark still,
Wall stocks. On to the capstan guardroom
    where
Edward the Fourth was imprisoned by
    Richard Neville.
He had Henry the Sixth in the Tower -
    Kingmaker's bones,
How history cries out of these forbidding
    stones!   40

Beauty and cruelty are to be found here,
The beauty of a cruel, oppressive past.
I see Elizabeth visit Warwick
On the way to his brother Leycester (the
    favourite last).
His father Northumberland had lost his head,
After Jane Grey's queenship, in Mary's Hell.
How did he greet her four hundred retainers?
What a miracle the sons survived so well!
Elizabeth loved Dudley, the Queenmaker's

son,
Whose stepson Essex rebelled and was
    undone.   50

I go to Kenilworth a few miles away,
A reddish ruin with bluebells on the walls
And a Norman keep, which Cromwell's
    barbarians sacked
For the Warwicks always answered Royal
    calls.
The towers open to the air - clouds pass
    across,
Old Gaunt's first floor Great Hall is a ruin
    now;
Superb square-topped windows, which
    Dudley built,
Hoping to be King, and the hearth is still
    there, somehow.
And here are the windows where Elizabeth
    stayed,
For nineteen golden days in heat and
    shade.   60

O royal lovers in our Golden Age,
Your spirits are here in this romantic glow.
The moat has dried, but I can see "R.D."
On Leycester's gatehouse, and his Tudor
    stables show
The esteem in which he held his fairy Queen.
Birdsong now fills the trees, as you hunt to
    the horn.
O how you tried to please your would-be
    bride -
You set up a Hospital for the poor on the
    lawn.
I pass it on the way back, it is still in use
And the Queen kept her head, and let you
    loose.   70

I leave the two brothers, go to Charlecote
By the Avon where a Tudor-style gate-
-house shows Sir Thomas Lucy, with spade
    beard,
Dog, falcon and family, the magistrate
Whom Shakespeare crossed as he killed deer
    (Shallow)
Two years after Lucy killed Edward Arden.
What fine paintings and furniture adorn
This Lucy's house: Tudor wine-cup and pen.
Kingmaking Shakespeare looked at this

landscape:
The green field by the river, the field of
    yellow rape!   80

The Heart of England has a wild beauty:
Castles intact, preserving all from fate,
And ruined palaces where ghosts now meet.
Why should this distant past still fascinate?
We are as we are now through our fine past,
Which shaped each art, set standards for all
    time
To which we now imperfectly aspire,
Which we hand on before our midnights
    chime.
Civilisation gilds rough objéts d'art
And makes magnificence where there were
    faux pas.   90

And so accursed be the Cromwellians
Who tore down Leycester's love, for their
    own time;
And may we live among the past's spendours
As by the Avon, we chant Shakespeare's
    rhyme.
The soul is fed by beautiful artefacts,
Art nourishes the soul, is its psychic food,
So to live with the art of a great tradition
Will keep the soul vibrant and pure and good.
These battlements and ruins escape their hour
And feed my soul, for castles in air tower. 100

26 May 1986, revised 11 October 1993

WARM RAIN

As I walked in the May rain
The tulips raised their heads,
The daffodils smiled at me,
Forget-me-nots winked from the beds,

The bright yellow furze blazed,
The cherry blossom glowed,
All Nature seemed more bright
From my umbrella by the road;

And globules hung on the grass
And I looked up at the cloud   10
And cursed the Soviet reactor
That had cast this fall-out shroud

As I thought of other ground
Radioactive for thirty years,

And thought of the cows that will munch
So their milk creates fears

And glows in my stomach
And activates dormant cells
Till my being, like this hawthorn,
Is stifled by ivy that swells.   20

Once when I was a child
You could walk in the rain and be glad,
And drink the milk on a farm,
Not live under clouds that are bad.

Summer 1986, revised 14 December 1993

BLUEBELL WOOD

In a beechwood full of green
And last year's golden leaves,
In a sea of bluebells
A woman bends (white sleeves).

She is gathering logs
For a May fire (white hood),
Unaware of the blue
That glorifies the wood.

So it is now with me:
I toil and do not see
The silver birch nearby
And the tide of blue near this tree.

Summer 1986, revised 14 December 1993

ICE-SKATING

To command the soul is like
The skater's glide and wheel,
Pirouette through mid-air
To land on a steady heel,

And slide across the ice
And turn in a blur round,
Double axle, triple loop
In a crescendo of sound,

Then bow and collect flowers
As the audience stand and cheer
And see the judges' marks
The best in the skating year.

Summer 1986, revised 13 December 1993

SPLIT PINE AND PINE-CONES

The pine swayed in the breeze

I looked at its gaping trunk,
A split where lightning struck
And took out a great chunk.

The gap widened in the storm:
A hurricane from the south
Split the tree to its roots
So it opened and closed like a mouth.

I could put my hand inside,
It was dangerous and had to come down.   10
The children clapped and cheered
As four men climbed to its crown

And sawed with a chain-saw
And pulled on a long rope
And broke it in sections down
Till - cones on an empty slope.

I too am a split pine
That sways in a cold wind;
My split is like a wound
But my cones are all thick-skinned.   20

And when I disappear
May all remember me
For my many pine-cones
That fill children with glee.

Summer 1986, revised 14 December 1993

SQUIRREL ON THE LAWN

A squirrel is sitting on next door's lawn,
A nut cupped in its hands by its head.
He scurries, stops, scurries again,
And buries it in a flower-bed.

He returns to my bird-table and hangs
Upside down, takes another and scampers
away.
He buries it behind the tulips;
I am indignant, the thief! Where's his drey?

But then I consider, in this warm June
How he makes provision for a colder time,
Stores and hoards food for the winter -
So full of foresight, so sublime!

I know this squirrel and how he lives
In the present, warm sun on his back,
And in the future, how he plans ahead,

As do I in this room, for winter lack.

Summer 1986, revised 14 December 1993

A DEATH IN THE BOAT

At the next table in the boat café
A group of black girls laugh like birds
As a tattooed man in a singlet
Tells a story: four letter words.

Adjacent passengers frown at
The intrusion on their peace, and glare;
A white-haired man closes his eyes
And sits, head bowed as if in prayer.

I watch him. His wife, opposite,
Bends forward, and pale, makes a sign;
The purser comes and bends and goes.
She sits, pretending everything is fine.

At the next table the black girls laugh
And a white-haired man cannot hear
As he slumps in death, having taken
One last long breath in his seizure's sear.

6 August 1986, revised 13 December 1993

AT GUNWALLOE: THE TAO

A blue sky, green turf on cliffs, a calm day,
But as I sit on this rocky promontory,
Hair tugging in the wind, feet splashed with
spray,
I am the surging of the mighty sea.
Waves curl and hang and dip and explode and
boil
And foam on this once molten rocky tower;
A haze hangs over the tranquil bay, I coil,
Am taut with frothing white and swirling
power.
The winds, the sea, the earth have motions that
We take for granted till we wake in shock
And gaze at the headlong dash and boom-
thud, at
The conflicting stillness of this glistening
rock.
Two opposites are reconciled in spray
In the haze on the still blue sky of this surging
Cornish day.

16 August 1986

THE FISHERMEN: GOD'S PLAN

The fishermen know how God moves and

works,
How strong tides make currents on the ocean
floor
Which fill the nets with seaweed and drag and
tear,
So the nets are flattened and no fish reach
shore.

They know the habits of the common gull,
How a red eye swells on a yellow bill to be
viewed
At summer breeding, how the young bow or
beg,
Tap at them to regurgitate their food.

They know how monkfish sometimes drown
in their nets,
If the tide is high there is not enough
oxygen   10
To flow through their gills. "You would not
think
A fish could drown, would you" they say.
Again,

They know dogfish is the only fish that
blinks,
That the fulmer is related to the albatross,
They can tell a Manx Shearwater from a
Shag,
A black-backed gull can swallow a rat at a
toss.

The fishermen are close to Nature and know
Each creature has a feature on skin or down:
The star-ray's false eyes to confuse its foes,
The young gull's camouflage of rocky
brown.   20

The fishermen look into the wind and
know
When it will rain before it does, or roar.
They are close to and understand God's Plan
And the intricacies of Creation we ignore.

I sometimes peep into God's world, and am
Amazed at the organisation of an eye,
The design of a fin, the shape of a crab's
claw;
Speckled camouflage shows care that a brill
should not die.

And I am also sad at the killing,
As a fisherman smashes a shivering turbot on
deck.   30
And I feel that our body is only here
To house our soul; the captain in the wreck.

Somewhere in God's Plan there is a sea for
souls,
And all these butchered fish are swimming
there,
And so are human sufferers, before
Being sent to this Hell-like school down here.

17-18 August 1986, revised 30 November 1993

IN GOUGH'S CAVERN, CHEDDAR

Enter the dark of a Cheddar cave,
The limestone has hollows like cheese,
And stalactites still wet grow from
A million years of dripping ease.

The deeper you go in, the more
They assume man-made shapes and sprawls;
There are: St. Paul's Dome, Organ Pipes,
Solomon's Temple, Niagara Falls.

Now in the dark Druid Chamber,
A cat prowls near the light, coal black,   10
And now there is a Swiss Village,
Church and castle on a mountain crack.

It reflects the ceiling above
In still water that runs gently
Fom the river Yeo which trickles from
An underground lake like a sea.

The heart's tongue fern grows when the
lights
Are on, bringing warmth like the sun,
There are horseshoe tufts in the rocks
Which pulse with the energy of the One.   20

Here images sleep near a central sea.
Each cave reminds me of the heart,
And phallic stick-ups vie with what
Imagination suggests through art.

Each cave reminds me of the heart,
And I think of the candles at Wells;
And oh for a flame like Jesus's love

430

That would light this cave, cleanse its fouls
    smells.

It is now filled with horseshoe bats
And lurks with menacing shadows;   30
And when there is a light in the dark
It softens the dripping of time, which glows.

The flame of love burns in the heart,
Shines in the dark, without ceasing to be,
Burns brighter for being offered to others,
Throws shadows across the cave walls of
    "me".
        25 October 1986, revised 14 December 1993

PAPER LIKE A TONGUE
The vatman scoops cotton from the vat
In a tray - it solidifies inside,
The coucher peels it and drops it down
On a blanket to be pressed and dried.

The rag paper has a watermark
From a mould in the tray - and will last
Four hundred years as it is pressed
Then hung on a clothes line to dry fast.

I have a wet cotton within
That solidifies, is pressed and hung,
That dries into paper that endures
Four hundred years beyond my tongue.
        25 October 1986, revised 14 December 1993

BY THE CHALICE WELL, GLASTONBURY
(A CONTEMPLATION)
Avalon is like an earth goddess on her back,
Great breast and nipple, pregnant tum, raised
    knee;
Ponder how you disembarked by the lofty
    track
Up Wearyall Hill, as if from surrounding sea,
And saw by the windswept thorn, once
    Joseph's staff,
The misty isle of Avalon stretch and reach
Down to the Abbey fields and the Tor's top
    half
To this Chalice Hill and the Pomparles beach.
    That ziggurat drew Neolithic crowds,
      A tiered world mountain bulging into
      clouds!   10

Here height corresponds to depth, as
    mountain tracks
Reflect cave-paths down and up a rock-face.
At Wookey Hole descend to the Styx-like
    Axe
Which pours from deep within the caverned
    place,
Then go down from cave to stalagmite cave,
    for
Hell is a dark seven-ringed tower upside
    down
Which mirrors the seven-layered maze of the
    rising Tor
That corkscrews up and thrusts its sunlit
    crown.
    Height-depth, Light-dark are linked, like
    Heaven and Hell,
    As on the two-circled cover of this ancient
    well.   20

In your mind ascend the Tor and gaze from
    the top
Round the once-flat waters of the dried-up
    marsh.
See hills rise from St. Michael's Tower and
    drop
With the last Abbot, and be quartered, a harsh
Fate. Admire the scales and St. Bridget
    milking her cow,
Then descend to the house of Tudor Pole
Who saw Oneness and bought what is here
    now,
Visit his rooms, enter this garden of soul
    And sit by the waters of this chalybeate
    spring
    That runs from within the Tor and heals
    suffering.   30

Ascend four levels: the water-splashing bowl;
Up through two yews to the arched gate in the
    wall,
Past daisies and a red-berried shrub, stroll
To the splash and tinkle of a reddened
    waterfall
And iron-red runnel and Pilgrim's Bath; there
    dwell,
Then up past a yew to the Lion's Head; there
    drink,
Then pass two thorns till you reach this silent
    well.

Is the Grail that caught His blood buried here?
 Think,
  Does it stain these watery channels a
  healing red?
  Is there a Lourdes-like healing at this
  well-head?   40

Four worlds in garden levels approach this
 grid:
Here under two berried yews three steps of
 stone
Lead down to a chained, wrought iron and
 wooden lid
And two overlapping circles which can be
 known
As the seen and unseen worlds in a yin-yang
 whole,
Or male-female, conscious and unconscious
 mind.
Stoop and open the doorway to your soul,
Look through the bars, leaves float where old
 bricks wind.
  In Roman times the ground was near the
  base
  Of this well, and the spring ran through
  this holy place.   50

Here sit and recall the past, how He was here,
The boy Jesus who came by boat to mine
With His uncle Joseph of Arimathaea
And take back Priddy lead for a Roman
 shrine;
How he later returned and built the first
 church
And how He held the Last Supper in a room
At Joseph's house, how the cross ended His
 search,
How his uncle buried Him in his own tomb,
  Then fled with the rest of His disciples,
  and the Grail,
  And Mary, to live here beyond the Roman
  pale.   60

Travel in slow mind, linger in the crypt where
Joseph was buried under the Lady Chapel and
See the Abbey before it became ruined air
(Turf on arched windows), wander and stand
Outside under the Jesus Maria stone;
Think, Mary too lay in this floorless void,
And think of the others who became bits of

 bone
Before the wattle and daub church was
 destroyed;
  Near Joseph and Mary, know why it is
  said
  That Avalon means "the Island of the
  Dead".   70

Ponder the best kept secret of the Christian
 Way,
How Joseph's altar tomb with quatrefoil
And shield, caduceus and stone JA
Was moved from the Abbey in Puritan
 turmoil
To the parish churchyard, thence inside the
 church door
Where now it is topped with glass and a
 funeral pall,
And stand before the relics of one who saw
The face of Christ. Did it grace the Templars'
 wall
  As the Turin Shroud (they claim) from the
  Garden Tomb,
  Which they copied onto wood in
  Templecombe?   80

All that was then, it is now we must renew,
So sit and be the moment in this evergreen!
Be the green oak fountain against the blue,
Be the hovering hoverfly and all that's seen.
Be the drifting ice of the tide-drawn cloud,
Be the rose that glows red to the reddening
 sun -
Be the translucent rose! that lurks in a shroud.
See how the whorls of your forefinger run,
  And gazing at the whorls round the grassy
  Tor
  Let the Light shine through your whorled
  and grassy awe.   90

I close my eyes and am filled with a surge,
 now a lull.
The Light is in my limbs, and behind my face.
A sun-like circle interlocks my skull,
Haloing my shadow in this quiet place.
Here in the birdsong of this October evening
I am each bird, insect and flower. Here see
Eternity as an ever-flowing spring
And feel your soul as a well that can catch,
 and be,

And store the spring-like powerful Light
    that rose
Within the great Tor, in a high world
    where Void flows.   100

I see a man with a water pitcher pour,
I see the waters of spirit pour through the air,
I see all nations drink at this spring near the
    Tor;
No more the fish, the Aquarian flood is here.
No Vesica Piscis where two circles meet,
Where two worlds energise the spirit's thread;
The soul like a circular well traps Light's
    round heat
And pours its healing as from a Lion's Head
    That cures the body like Lourdes, fills
        soul with power
    So Eternity flows through a wall and
        through every hour.   110

26 October 1986

THE ROMANTIC REVOLUTION

Did Coleridge come to Wookey Hole,
And see the Axe pour out
From the underground Wookey caves and
Hear *Kubla Khan* like a shout?

I go to Nether Stowey and stand
At the green front door aglow,
Where the person from Porlock stood,
And peer through the curtained window.

And I go to Watchet's old port
And see the lighthouse and hill,   10
And gaze at the Methodist "kirk",
Which the mariner knew when ill.

And now at Alfoxton House
I see where Wordsworth stayed
And pondered the *Prelude* on his couch,
Till a revolution was made.

And I feel close to both of them,
And can almost share in their walks;
I find them through their quaint houses,
And reconstruct their talks.   20

And they soon lose their mystery,
And lead me like a guide:
The mariner and the caves of ice,

The Prelude, the countryside.

Their great poetry revolution
Was a friendly affair
That grew out of visits to place,
And they then built domes of air!

26 October 1986, revised 14 December 1993

GOG AND MAGOG

Gog and Magog - just two
Ancient oaks that survive.
Of an Avalon avenue
That led to the Tor like a drive.

The rest were chopped down in
Nineteen hundred and six, and
Many had seasoned rings
Numbering two thousand.

Gog and Magog's huge trunks
Show a girth unlikely to fall,
And are honoured by druids,
"Lovers of the oak", and by all

Nature lovers who feel
The oak is the English tree
Whose acorns once made cakes
For a mystic mass of the free.

26 October 1986, revised 14 December 1993

HEDGEHOG IN THE WILD

I went alone to the field.
There by the oak-tree log
Weary and hungry lay
An exhausted hedgehog.

I took him to my house
And gave him milk and bread,
He sniffed, then sat in it,
Lapped round his prickly head.

I made him a nest of leaves,
I nursed his health with a glass
That held carrots, lettuce,
I tickled his snout with grass.

The next night I ran to his box
To give him his bedtime milk -
But o, my hedgehog had gone,
Climbed down my table nest's silk.

He is out there in the cold
Roaming the darkened hill,
Looking for those he lost
When I seized him against his will.

Autumn 1986, revised 14 December 1993

A PILGRIM IN EUROPE

Mile out on the sea beyond St. Michael's
    Mount,
The Ictis where Joseph sailed with the boy
    Jesus
For tin, boat rocks as the nets are winched up
From thirty fathoms with monkfish and ray,
Flat turbot, brill, which we slit and throw
Their offal overboard where the gulls swoop,
Fulmar, kittiwakes even a Sheerwater.
Our sail steadies the boat, gives it balance,
Keeps its head to wind when the crew think
    cash.
Fishermen with prices per stone in mind,   10
Look at the black whale that rises, curved fin
    and dips.
What steadies this Europe we have just
    found?

Under cranes abandoned for the weekend
At Dunkirk harbour sun glints on calm water
Where an army waded out and was
    decimated.
O the flat fields of Flanders, and their poppied
    wheat.
And who could see this place disfigured by
    war?
Cars race along the roads to Europe's cities,
Radio aerials up, minds on immediate things.
O the silage smells of this countryside.   20

O the peace of the Belgian countryside,
And of Bruges's cobbled town by moated
    walls
And floodlit weeping willows with whiffs of
    drains.
I walk past offices where men are not
    themselves,
And Baroque buildings, its halls and belfry,
Hear its carillon of fifty-seven bells
Near where the lacemaker demonstrates her
    skill
At earth level, the Templar chapel of St. Basil
With twelfth century arches, ancient carvings

- St. Basil and a dove - is brick and gloom   30
As crones drone chants, finger rosaries in
    pews,
See, each gravestone in the floor has a cup,
    the Grail.
Go upstairs to the green and red basilica,
Under the pelican feeding its blood to its
    young,
And sit in quiet, Mozart playing softly,
And gaze at the Last Supper alabaster screen.
And now at the altar of the Holy Blood
Brought back from the Crusades, silver
    glinting
In candlelight, surrounded by angels -
A sublimity that uplifts the peaceful spirit; 40
So I soared free here where art seems
    religion -
In this town you can't walk into a church
And not know what is central to the tradition -
And demonstrates its devastating truth
Like the spoked "Veritas" that pours down on
    the pulpit
In the nearby Church of our Lady, or as
In Van Eyck's Mystic Lamb in Ghent the
    Light's
Yellow rays reach from heaven, touching
    those below.
So was I touched by that heavenly music!

Speed down motorways, hurtle over
    bridges,   50
Take the fast lane, and now look for a hotel
In Amsterdam, crossing and recrossing
    canals.
At Tourist Information the students stand ten
    deep
And no hope of a bed, round the Central
    Station
Immigrants stand near "Beware Pickpockets"
    signs.
I see two men snorting at open palms.
In the narrow littered streets by an old church
Ladies sit in the windows, legs apart,
And beckon a group of noisy football fans,
A notice says "Come in, Boys."
    Merchandise.   60
Now on a glass-topped boat, glide through
    canals,
Gaze up at Baroque fronts from the great
    Dutch past,

Houses whose pediments are works of art.
And on the quai, ascend steep stairs and pass
The swung-back bookshelves to the hiding-place
Of a schoolgirl terrified of the Nazis -
See the pictures she stuck on the wall: filmstars
Wild flowers, paintings and artists, children as angels.
The simple peace-time values of Anne Frank.
And visit Rembrandt's house, where Baroque began   70
See his self-portraits, the dark look in his eyes
As bankruptcy approached and he lost this house.
And here in the van Gogh Museum, stare hard
At the wheatfield: a path that stops in wheat,
The bread of life eaten by deathly crows.
Stare at his last testament through his dark eyes.
There is a sombreness at the heart of Europe,
A darkness that has rejected the glorious Light.

On the roads cars whizz and flash, wheels hum and hiss.
Undiscernible faces approach and pass and fade,   80
Like ghosts one cannot speak to, all bound by the law,
All doing the same, journeying fast somewhere.
At Arnhem, cross a bridge, sit in a café
Under the rebuilt Cathedral in the square.
And now by the Rhine at Bonn, distant mountains,
Think of the lives lost, as many as the swarms
Of birds that sweep across Kennedy Bridge
Or the midges crowding at the riverside windows.
Or in the Town Hall square cheers from a café
Where beery Germans sing under a sunshade   90
(As once Beowulf's thanes sang over the mead).
Now go the the Bonn Minster and see Christ sit
On a rainbow in spiderwebbed stained glass.
Down below - put down the tiresome mind -
Bow your head and enter the silent crypt,

In a casket Cassius and Florentius, Roman martyrs
Are remembered, here join two nuns still as stone
And float in their silence deep below the ground.
The candles each side of a spoked monstrance
That hangs like a spider's web give out incense.   100
Sink beneath centuries in these Romanesque arches,
And discover the source of what contemplation seeks.
And in this house where a genius was born and grew
Hear chords ring in the ears of Beethoven.
The faces approach and pass and fade from view,
Strangers hurtling towards a darkening doom.
There is no touching them. Speed on crusading knights,
Speed on modern pilgrims on your Pilgrims' Way!

At Luxembourg's Echternach, in the Ardennes
The shattered basilica has been rebuilt but   110
See the broken Christ sheared in half on the wall.
And down in the ancient crypt which survived the blitz
Are ceiling murals from a quieter age
And the tomb of the eighth century Saint Willibrord,
The first Anglo-Saxon missionary
To the Germanic tribes, and a fountain;
Linger at this holy place and recall accord.

Luxembourg, on a gorge, rises round a ravine,
Which beetling walls have made impregnable,
A fortress riddled with underground passages   120
For seventeen miles so troops could be moved around.
Clamber through the Bock, a mind riddled with fear.
So many nations have invaded here.
And here at the war cemetery, shed a tear
For General Patton and five thousand men
Whose white crosses fan out across the turf.

A sign says "We are happy the way we are."
On the corner Michael spears the Dragon
Where is the"lux" in this fortified bourg?

And now at Brussels, in the Market Place, 130
See the illuminated buildings in this cobbled
    square
And crowds of late-night strollers in this
    summer air,
Gaze at the fountain of the Mannekin Pis.
And now on the Hill of the Lion, survey
    Waterloo
Where Wellington staved off Napoleon
Until Blucher arrived. A futile war.
Wheatfields trampled by armies, smoke and
    dust;
Wellington's H.Q., Napoleon's down the
    road.
As the wind chaps your hands and you blow
    on your nails,
Think of Generals, farms taken and lost
    again, 140
And smoke-filled fields and cavalry
    slaughtered;
As you stand back to allow French girls to
    pass
Ponder the lessons of war! as a wind blows
The dandelions on the great grass bank.
At Rouen see the place where St. Joan died,
At Caen see where William the Conqueror
    lies.

I see the force of wheatfields and whirling
    stars,
And the force that destroyed Arnhem and
    Echternach.
O the mutilated Christ and healing waters.
On the ferry, West Indians loll and laugh, 150
An old man dies and sits on, no one notices.

Now back where it all began, in a school hall,
I stand beneath Burne-Jones' *Light of the
    World*
And look out at a garden, fields and trees,
In harmony with the One, and contemplate:
Can Christ return to cleanse the chaos and
    link
The oases in his desert civilisation,
To restore the creative force we need?
Wars, terrorism, drugs and thieves - chaos.

(The wildflower paintings on a schoolgirl's
    wall.) 160

At Gunwalloe there is a church on the beach,
The sea races in and dashes spray on rocks,
And here the old Celtic church is close to
    hand.
Europe. I see a history of destruction -
The guillotine, Nazis and Communists -
And I see a history of creation -
The Sistine Chapel, Rembrandt, Beethoven;
I see a line that has made Europe great:
The Holy Blood, the peace in a dark crypt.
Here sitting in this church whose inner
    doors 170
Are made from Portuguese screens, sitting
    alone,
I feel a buried peace that Europe needs;
Here and in St. Sampson's church, when the
    bats are quiet,
Above the River Fowey on a green hill.

The Light of the World is the steadying sail
Who makes fishers of men. But in Loughton
The Methodists have pulled down their
    Gothic church
And will now rebuild a more glassy one,
More in keeping with a comprehensive
    school -
A centre for all the community. 180
The Church of England is in decay, exudes
An atmosphere of decrepitude and tombs.
The Pope stands in his Popemobile and
    waves;
Can he unite the differing sects, so that
All holy crypts and phials are of one faith,
A network of Light in this secular society?
Can Christ sit on a rainbow again, and be
    seen?
The senses and the body - man is much more
And can this spirit be found in the Church?
In silence, not in the distraction of hymn-
    singing. 190
Silence is best found outside congregations.
The spirit is best found before works of art.
In Rome, mingle with crowds in St. Peter's
    Square
Then go to the Sistine Chapel, where
    Michelangelo
Painted Heaven, and Christ drawing up the

damned.
O Saxon tombs and chests at Winchester,
O rose window of York. O great Durham,
O maze of Chartres, o Gothic spires,
What a legacy you have left - are we worthy?
"F— off," shouts a red-scarfed youth on the
    ferry,   200
As the television shows men shoot to kill.
The telephone rings. The alarm jangles.
    Loudness.
A plane roars overhead bound for Spanish
    seas.
Are we worthy of the concentration of
The fourteenth century mystics who sought
    silence out?

The boat dips in the waves, the fishermen
See Europe as a ribbon of land from sea,
Its ruins and cathedrals now monuments
To an energy like spring sap in this autumn
Of windfall and leaf-shedding and decay.   210
A Pilgrims' Way round all the Continent's
    stones
Is like a tour of fountains whose spring has
    gone.
O Light of the World, come again and renew
The freshness in the European soul,
Cleanse the atmosphere of tombs and
    museums
With the Light from Heaven - beyond - which
    makes men whole.

6 November 1986, revised 21 September 1993

ST. OLAF'S CHURCH

Under snow-capped Scafell,
England's highest peak, sun-kissed,
Is England's deepest lake
Wastwater, eerie in mist,

And here within yew trees
Is England's smallest church,
Elizabethan diamond windows,
Pews for thirty-nine to perch.

It is St. Olaf's church
Three Viking beams across,
Which came from the wreck of a ship,
A dreadful Viking loss.

At the inn see Will Ritson

England's biggest liar peep.
I measure truth by the snow-
-capped height and sparkling deep.

12 April 1987, revised 13 December 1993

DRIED SPRING

A smoking chimney under green headlands.
Here Wordsworth came, I pass the Rectory
He knew, opposite the Grasmere churchyard,
And go on to Rydal. At the River Rothay
I stand on the stepping-stones where
    Wordsworth walked
To work at Ambleside, relic of passion,
Like a stone fountain round a spring that
    dried.

12 April 1987, revised 13 December 1993

FULL MOON ON THE PENNINES

On the bleak moor the wind is keen
And bites below the ribs.
An old slate pub with a two-door grate
Warms for the dales, or fibs.

At Barnard Castle above Teeside
And a splashing rill explore
A window near the round tower with
Richard the Third's four-barred boar.

At Bowes' west end stands Dotheboys Hall,
Low-windowed, edged by moon,   10
Where Nickleby suffered under one
Less generous than I with a spoon.

And at High Force brown water slides
And cascades seventy foot down
And foams on boulders through ancient trees
Whose roots cling above one's crown.

And I am back at the divine source.
As a full moon has uncurled,
I disturb rabbits and pheasants
Above the moonlit world.   20

The Yorkshire dales slide up and down
The mountains rise to cloud,
And I have left contemporary life
To know God in a shroud

Who can warm hearts like two-door grates

Open the mind like a tune,
Rush down its cleft like a waterfall
And shine like a Pennine moon.

13 April 1987, revised 13 December 1993

NEAR BARHAM

The yellow rape blows in the May wind,
A skylark twitters above my head,
A sheep baas from the far curved hill,
Hawthorn and lilac nod and spread.

And I enjoy this country air
Near where the dead sleep in the churchyard,
The redbrick cottages and gardens,
The sleepy workers lolling on guard.

Life pulses in this country scene.
Near the crematorium I choke,
For an uncle goes to the fire
And will come out as chimney smoke

And drift on this wind, returned to the One,
His spirit in this sunny chill,
Floating above the Paradise
Of the buttercups on this quiet hill.

20 May 1987, revised 29 November 1993

VISIT TO A PHILOSOPHER
(A FRAGMENT)

I turn into the grey familiar street,
Pass within the low white wall and ring the
    bell.
His wife lets me in, creased in maturity.
I go upstairs via the first floor bathroom,
Resume my climb, and there at the top of the
    house
In a study lined with books, in his easy chair
Smiles the domed head of a great philosopher.
So many times I have been and sat at the desk
And as his publisher asked his guidance
On a particular line, and he has reached   10
For a book or just talked, saying "Eliot
Told me when we lunched in the
    Athenaeum...."
Or "Toynbee once said to me about culture
(*A Historian's Conscience* is a wonderful
    work)...."
Or "Freddie Ayer doesn't champion
    positivism
Now, we sat together at a conference...."

Last time it was, "They've hijacked
    Wittgenstein,
He died saying 'Send in a priest but don't
Let him be a philosopher.'" And "Russell's
    book
On Western philosophy is very poor,   20
He told me his brain was ruined by too much
    logic."
And: "Marcel told me (in French) about his
    Journal."
Every great man in the twentieth century
Has confided in this head that twinkles at me.
Only Whitehead he never met - that great man
Whose role he now fills. I think back to when
I knew him in Japan; he came to dinner,
And we talked of the Absolute. Now I fondly
    recall
How once we talked of Whitehead, and the
    phone rang
And he could not understand, and his wife
    came   30
And said, "It's the gasman wanting to visit."
He was so immersed in the Absolute
That he could not understand the gas board's
    girl.

But today he is different. He tells me he is ill:
"I've had a constant headache for over a
    month,
And a bad cough, my surgeon says it's TB.
I know it's been eradicated, but I've got it.
I've been going to bed at seven, exhausted.
I can't translate this French book for
    Routledge,
I don't feel up to the work for the BBC."
And I looked at him and saw his death in
    him.   40

30 July 1987, revised 10 January 1994

REALITY IN LEGOLAND

Legoland in Jutland. The boys run in
And whirl and soar and dip where horror
    reigns,
On harum-scarum, revolving up tower,
Rollercoaster. I watch and look at Danes.

I see a Viking face - a crewcut blond -
In the dipping prow of a Viking ship;
The boys are high on an electric monorail
Over tiny lakes where lego villages grip.

438

A black cloud looms, a squall of rain lashes,
We run for cover to Titania's Palace.　　10
Pain knifes under my arm, I roll as if still
On ship, grit teeth, indigestion? Grimace.

I slump on a chair, it stabs some twenty times,
My legs are weak, I tremble and shake, feel
　　odd.
Is this a heart attack? My last moment?
Do I stand before a wall for a firing-squad?

I sip my tea and see my body die,
Lie on the floor, a crowd all round; some
　　bend:
A kiss of life from one, a blow to the heart -
But me lying, no more; my life at an end.　　20

I sit with Death in this playtime Legoland,
The boys are driving electric cars and beam;
I sit with what is real in this make-believe,
And know the world's an illusion, like a
　　child's dream.

Houses and towns we work for are lego
　　bricks,
That mean no more than a reflection in a lake,
And man is alone with pain and his dripping
　　death
And this knowledge of what is real,
　　metaphysical ache.

The sun warms cheeks through this café
　　window,
Reflecting the Sun that fires burning hearts
　　and　　　　　　　　　　30
Pours in a wisdom that has scarcely changed
Since the days the Vikings searched for a new
　　green land.

The Real is like a hole in a thundercloud,
Void with a wind that blows to the tossing
　　rose,
And the soul sheds petals of great fragrance
And is blown by the truth and knows what an
　　angel knows.

1 August 1987, revised 20 December 1993

THE METAPHYSICAL CONDUCTOR

Near Ladby where a Viking ship was found

Is the white church of Rynkeby, where you
　　fetch
The key from the polo-necked pastor, go
　　round
And unlock the door, walk under white vaults,
　　stretch
To the medieval altar arch, fawn-grey,
Then turn and catch your breath.　For
　　crowded, tense
On three vaults above pews, brown angels
　　play
A concert of seventeen musical instruments!

There are thirty-one with brown wings and
　　bobbed hair,
They play trumpet, triangle, zither, harp,　　10
Curved horn, organ, bagpipe and flute, and
　　share
A heavenly concert. The faces are still and
　　sharp,
But look at the conductor - for on a wall
Above Christ crucified, with nails in his feet,
Arms raised above the cross the risen Christ,
　　tall,
Conducts the concert to an angelic beat.

In this family chapel the lord of the manor
　　lives,
Who set this vision he learned from Luther's
　　friend,
Seeing the angels as his relatives,
For whom he had a simple message: the
　　trend　　　　　　　　20
Of the Reformation changed both world and
　　mind;
Now Christ conducts the simplest soul to
　　birth,
Each makes sweet music of a unique kind,
Blends with all souls, creates a heaven on
　　earth.

These heavenly angels are earthly souls
Seen with illumined and enlightened eyes,
No judgement here - angels of God and goals
Listen in peace as each one tries to rise
To the Lord of Heaven, no priest in between,
Each with cello, or lute, and eyes that
　　entice,　　　　　　　　30
Bows out a note of perfect sound, serene,
That echoes the music of Paradise.

And over all is the Conductor here
Who keeps them all together, brings in each
    on cue
Like a flat-nosed earthly man raising a cheer
With the 1812 as a cannon and mortar to-do.
Effortlessly he conducts each soul who has
    grown
Into a vibration and resonance, so
A water-music shimmers of ethereal tone -
Conductor of a higher world, copied
    below!   40

O musician of the spheres and drawing-board,
Who saw all creation as a Great Octave
And created mathematics from a chord
And proportion and beauty like clef or stave,
I see that now the angels play no more,
Each sits and radiates the supernal Light,
Their radiant eyes shine with your pitch,
    whose law
Makes each winged soul's being shine gold
    and white.

2 August 1987, revised 20 December 1993

A VIKING INHERITANCE

On this Trelleborg heath, this starting-place
    for wars,
See the round green banks with four openings
And the markings of square houses in fours
Which housed Svein's twelve hundred much-
    armed Vikings.
Two rivers wind for the sea, where the long
    ships wait,
And we embark for England, to harry towns
For silver to pay the fleet. Piled stones by the
    gate,
Now sheep graze thistles, clover on these
    downs.

Wander in this Heorot-like hall of toasts,
An upside-down boat, crossed timbers at each
    end,   10
With oak-carved tiles and thirty outer posts,
See the tables before the hearth, the feast and
    friend-
-ship as men drink mead, hear heroic deeds
    and yell
Until they fall back asleep, their spears and
    shields
In the end vestibules that keep out dread

Grendel.
House martins flit from the roof, swoop low
    on fields.

Now at Roskilde see the Viking fleet
In its glory! A deep-sea trader soars;
The curved prows of a merchant ship, so neat;
A wide warship, see the holes for the oars; 20
But just look at the length of this long ship,
It could take a hundred men and was used to
    raid
And even now fills me with terror. I see it dip
As it heads for the open sea and the English
    "trade".

It is a heroic time, chieftans buried
In graves marked out by boat-shaped stones,
    or in
A ship as at Ladby, the Viking pyramid.
The Aggers of Aggersborg, to a deafening
    din,
Glide off for England to pillage towns, to
    look,
Settle with English women, to be confirmed 30
As lords of the manor in the Domesday Book,
Living on the Danelaw fringe, as it was
    termed.

3 August 1987, revised 23 November 1993

LONG BARROW AT LEJRE

Near Lejre, the home of Heorot
Turn off down a track to a tree-clad hill
And the shaft entrance to a long barrow.
Eleven upright-, five cap-stones thrill,

One wet. Light seven candles, look round
Think of the care - making a hollow,
Lining it with small stones, then boulders
Almost five thousand years ago,

Think of the Chieftan who rested here.
In this magnificent Kurgan tomb
Death speaks for the Neolithic time,
Here eternity can be found in a room.

For this was a House of the Dead,
Somewhere to live, not a hole in the dry,
And the men who put their chieftan here
Knew the eternal need a water supply.

3 August 1987, revised 20 December 1993

CENTRE OF THE MAZE

Here in this Iron Age settlement
Thatched houses open to the wind
And volunteers grind ears of corn
With polished stones for bread, thick-skinned.

Also here is a sacrificed boy;
Horse skins hang on Odin's bare tree.
Here men reject present for past
And recover a lost technology.

On this green hill, a maze of stones
And see the children walk its ways,
Run joyfully round to the centre,
Faces lit up as they thread the maze.

Here in the Iron Age we know the sun
And our centre in the winter dark
Where the true sun bathes our still souls
As we huddle together and blow a spark.

3 August 1987, revised 20 December 1993

AT GILBJERG: KIERKEGAARD THE ROMANTIC

I walk the clifftop at Gilbjerg Hoved.
The sea is calm and blue in the afternoon
    sun
To a thin ribbon of distant Sweden,
Far below a sandy beach where children run.

And now a forest begins, with scented pine.
I go up steps and find a gigantic stone,
I read Soren Kierkegaard's name on it.
You loved this spot, your *Journal* made it
    your own.

I think of your work having found you in
    Nature,
Having looked for you at Stjernen ("star"),
    your core,   10
Where eight roads meet in the Grib Skov
    forest,
A deserted place you loved which gave you
    Either-Or.

I see you on the moors of Jutland, then
Studying in Copenhagen under Schelling,
But most of all a Romantic in deep forests,
Like Werther or Wordsworth, untamed and
    wandering.

And now your dread, your fear, your
    loneliness
Seem like a late flowering of the Romantic
    Age;
Your emphasis on choice and decision,
Your agony, the search of a frustrated
    sage.   20

I stand here because you were the first
    Existentialist.
Seeing you as a Romantic makes you clear.
Romantics sought the One Light in Nature,
You searched but never found, then erected
    despair

Into a subjective philosophy,
Then sought consolation in the pastoral;
You took the wrong road at the star cross-
    roads:
Truth is not subjectivity, but metaphysical.

3 August 1987, revised 20 December 1993

AT JELLING
(A FRAGMENT)

At Jelling, the ancient royal capital,
Between two ancient burial mounds (one
    Gorm's)
Stands a stone erected by Harald Bluetooth
After he converted Denmark to Christianity:
Christ with a halo. Did we look to here?
From here we Vikings took the English silver
And paid the way until the next invasion.

3 August 1987

VIKINGS AND THE SEA

The Vikings braved this trail
Through menacing waves with sail,
But now this wonder afloat,
This Titanic-size boat,
Dominates the angry sea,
Crosses in calm and glee:
Dance to a live swing-band
In sequins, tipple at bars and
Eat white-clothed in the swell,
Watch films - a floating hotel,

Our cars below. Outside
From the throbbing music, glide,
Gaze for the stars, walk back
On the causeway of wake, track

441

To where the Viking long
Ships curve and dip and throng,
See the white-haired Vikings
Just like these Danes. Foam flings,
They prefer their soaking trip
To this safe, throbbing ship.

6 August 1987, revised 21 December 1993

AT CHARLESTOWN

The sea is calm now at low tide,
Barely a ripple disturbs its sheen,
Gulls float at rest, brown bladderwrack;
Waves languidly drift in, serene.

On the harbour wall the August wind
Stirs the wings of the mating flies,
Sways the bushes on the headland,
Flutters the Regatta flags and sighs.

The sea breathes with a gentle sigh
And I think of the lungs of a dying man,
I think of a philosopher's dying breaths
As he wonders what became of his plan.

The sea is calm this August day
And life goes on, beach-sitters doze,
But I am sombre in this calm
For a life is sinking to its close.

14 August 1987, revised 21 December 1993

TIME AND ETERNITY: A CROSS OF LIGHT

The days come in like waves on Gunwalloe's
    shore,
Again on these laval rocks, like this gull, I
    weigh
The swoosh and thud and shhh as white
    waves pour,
The clear blue sky, the dash of this flinging
    spray,
And I, in a scene that pre-dates Time, am still
On volcanic rocks that counterpose the waves,
Gaze back at life - the church nuzzling the
    hill,
A crowded beach, windbreaks, surfboards and
    graves,
And, half way out into Eternity,
Apart from christenings, flats and worldly
    things,   10
Wind tugging my hair, flapping my page, I

can be,
Feet drenched in spray, and give myself a
    hawk's wings
For the sun. I squint into a cross of light:
Across Time; down sparkling Eternity;
    beyond night.

15 August 1987

SPUR DOG AND PHILOSOPHER

Up over the winch come the fishing-nets,
Cod, hake, pollack, their gills all blown.
Only this spur dog is panting
With shark-like little flips, still thrown.

A dogfish lies at my feet breathing,
Its eye looks at me in its death,
Its gill is a round hole with a shutter
That opens and closes with each breath.

I watch it die as the fishermen
Gut cod and hake, stamp crabs from their
    nets,   10
And I think of a man whose lungs pack up -
Will he pant like this spur dog's sweats?

And are we just like heaving fish?
Is life no more than a spur dog's jaw?
A philosopher's death as significant
As this dead thing at my feet, no more?

Or do angels attend his last panting,
Transport him to a philosophy school
That is filled with the great ones' souls,
Where Socrates and Whitehead rule?   20

I stare across the expanse of sea,
At all Non-Being, know one thing:
All that has Being is different from
The spray - Being is enduring.

17 August 1987, revised 5 December 1993

OUT ON THE ALONE, OR, THE MYSTERY OF BEING

Up before four, I drive to Newlyn quay
And put out in a boat in a dawnless dark;
The black water's calm, town lights recede as
    we
Leave social man for the Alone in an ark;
One says, "Twinkling lights in clear air, there
    be rain."

442

And now I am timeless on sea, in sky.
Moon, stars, and land-thoughts shrink and
    fade. Again
I see with a perspective that asks why.

We head for an old wreck and eat below
While dawn breaks. The Lizard is in our
    wake.   10
We winch up the first net, a dripping glow
Of pollack, cod with pointed beard, and hake.
The tides flow east and west every six hours,
"We can't fish each other week, there's a
    spring-tide."
Fish drawn from fifty fathoms down - strange
    powers! -
Get bends and flop on deck, their gills blown
    wide.

The sun is high, the crew knife out the guts.
One puts a heart in my palm, it still beats,
A little tickling jumping that rebuts
The death that befell a cod in a Lost Land's
    watery streets.   20
Now we are over the wreck of a troopship.
The nets have torn. A spur dog gasps for
    breath,
Gills open and close like shutters at each sip.
A huss has slit eyes that blink up in death.

"The gills take oxygen from water - it's droll,
You can drown a fish if you hold it by its
    throat."
Inside a hake is another, swallowed whole,
"It's eat or be eaten under this boat."
Two spines on the spur dog can cause a stir:
"They inject poison that can swell an arm; 30
The only antidote is its liver."
Nature gives and takes the power to harm.

I glimpse a cod's swollen phallus and peep
At a female hole, a slit to a roe-store,
And I marvel at the order of the deep
As far as the eye can see to the line of shore.
The mystery that it is amazes me,
Each creature is unique, in perfect breeds,
Each "Amness" or "Isness" that roams the sea
In mindless tides that give it all it needs. 40

Existence fills me with a sense of its
    "Ownness";

All that has Existence differs like all fish
From unified Being, which moves like waves
    that press
But have no heart to love a mate or wish;
Human beings and creatures perceive the sun,
Being is manifestation of what has sight,
Has form, lives in or shares its inseparable One
That permeates tides of mind, the sea of
    Light.

Being is the sea in which all Existence breeds,
In which all particular weed and fish
    subsist;   50
Being is the universal tide that feeds
All states of manifestation which exist.
Like outer space Non-Being contains all
Non-manifestation as Void, before the Big
    Bang
From which Being unfolded. The Infinite One
    Fireball
Flames through Being and Non-Being from
    which all galaxies sprang.

Embark on the Negative Way and we under-
    stand:
Awake from the social dream of the blind ego
And leave Existence like a stretch of sand,
Glimpse Being in the freedom of this tidal
    flow,   60
See the Void in negative bob, as from a space-
    buoy,
Let the Infinite One pour in like infused sun,
And the Way of Fire is now one of detached
    joy
And its serene gifts make our suffering seem
    well done.

We return through sea mist, and now fine rain.
People stand on the harbour wall, some old;
I climb a steep ladder, back in time again,
I have returned to the social blindfold
Which shuts out what is real and the Black
    Head's haze,
Heedless of boats on the Alone of sea and
    sky   70
Or men who now see with their Shadow's
    Fire-won gaze
Who glimpse God's meaning as Being that
    does not die.

18 August 1987, revised April 1990

GRAVITY

I sunbathe on a Cornish beach;
In the hazy blue above my fun
A silver plane thunders above,
Flashing and glinting in the sun.

I lie on my back and gaze at it
And suddenly I begin to rise
And feel myself falling down to it -
I clutch the stones and close my eyes.

The plane has gone but as I look up
I am held to stony earth by
The merest gravity that might snap
And leave me plunging into sky.

19 August 1987, revised 21 December 1993

CHRISTMAS

A snowfall buried our town,
Frost sparkles on moonlit fire,
Feet crunch on frozen ice
To the black path under the spire.

Inside warm lights and leaves,
Warm people, a warm hymn;
Choirboys with open mouths
Gape at each swaddled limb

As God squalls in a manger,
Calls all to smile at a drib-
-ble; the meaning of Christmas is
A choirboy's smile by a crib.

3 December 1987

CHRISTINGLE

A joint lesson: I sit in a pew
Hear my two boys in choir-robes thrum:
"I am the Light of the World....
Arise, shine, for your light has come."

Now the children take a lit candle
In a world-like orange and band of blood,
And stand in the aisles, cubs and brownies,
Cupped hands guard flickering souls, and
    thud,

And I, fizzing up my fuse, burn too,
Blaze out with a fire of ecstasy,
Until the snuffing moment when
Smoke curls and hangs in a sun-shaft, free.

This is contentment, to share the Light
With children and see souls as Fire,
To be filled with flickering love, as tears
Mist all to a flecked sun-shaft and choir.

13 December 1987, revised 11 January 1994

A STROKE FROM THE DARK
(OR: MIND IN A BRAIN X-RAY)

I awoke that morning with a numb right
    arm,
Pins and needles in each tingling finger,
And I was clumsy, lurched out of bed and –
    alarm! –
Stumbled on a stair with my right foot, speech
    slur-
-red slightly, I found holding a razor hard,
My grip had gone like sleep, my hand was
    slack
But I thought nothing of it, kept up my guard,
Thought I had slept on my arm, and it would
    come back.

After several days my right arm was still
    weak,
As I lifted a sack of potatoes, the pain
    surprised   10
Me, I had reduced use, it seemed from my
    cheek
Down my whole right side was slightly
    paralysed.
I went to the doctor, he gave my arm a severe
Tug, lent on my hand, and said "There is a
    weakness",
And referred me to a specialist in Queen
    Square
Where I had a blood test near a young
    Princess.

The expert tested me, said I was paralysed,
    how
I'd had "a cerebral micro-embolism, a stroke;
It's a warning, you may have a clot on your
    brain right now."
A fast for a magnetic photograph, a joke,   20
And I was slid into a kind of washing-
    machine
A magnetic drum which clicked and knocked
    near my frown
Like a tumbledrier that grates pictures on a
    screen,

444

Photographed segments of my head, across
and down.

I went for the verdict. He said, "Everything's
all right,
It's good." And against white light he put nine
Segments of my brain, nine more taken at
night,
Then another nine: "Your cerebellum, your
spine,
Your pons. The attack was where your
insulating swells,
Here. There may be small damage which this
does not show,   30
MRI's resolution does not show single brain
cells.
You should take one declotting aspirin a day
till you go."

We had a discussion on brain physiology.
He said: "I am sure that mind is functioning
brain.
There's no soul, which some of my older
colleagues see.
Mind is a function of each nerve-cell and
vein."
Then where is consciousness? He said, "Brain
cells
Have a tendency to fire or not to fire,
The brain has analogue and digital spells.
We could build a machine that could see
every cell's desire."   40

I am reprieved, have a prospect of life again,
A future opens. I sit with my X-rays
Which show my skull's cortex in outline, then
My bulbous eyes, seaweed-like fibred gaze,
Where lightning struck, leaving no damage
but a lull,
And I look for the mind that is not there.
Can it be I am this cloud around my skull,
And will go out like a light when it gasps for
air?

On the edge of the universe, I peer at the dark
Of this negative which mirrors my parts   50
But hides my smile, the gleam in my eye, my
mark,
And I ask "What is life? What glow excites
hearts?

Did the Fire mystics gasp at make this thing
grow?"
I gaze at my jesting skull, probe its secret,
Questioning my death in these images which
know
This dark which stroked me tenderly, like a
pet.

24(?) February 1988, revised 21 November 1993

A GARDENER IN HEAVEN

Jack, our part-time gardener, hoed
Sorrel and elder with great care,
Then he'd sit and pant, "It's me ulcer,"
On the school step, and quote Shakespeare.

His wife rang. "Jack won't be coming again,
He died yesterday morning. Cancer.
We were told just five weeks ago.
He had not an ulcer but a tumour."

An undertaker walked, holding
His hat, held up traffic with his lope.
Fourteen filed into the chapel
Where a vicar shouted words of hope.

His wife wept as the curtains drew,
A cooing of doves under smoke and years.
Large flakes of snow fell on the flowers
As if Heaven wept frozen tears.

And somewhere in Heaven's garden,
"Shall I hoe any sorrel and elder I see?"
Jack asks, sitting with his flask and beer,
His craggy face grimace-and-pain-free.

4 March 1988, revised 6 December 1993

FROM THE COBB, LYME REGIS, 1988
(OR: 400 YEARS ON)

A cloudless sky, a summer's day,
The sea is calm and washes in;
Ancient homes bask in the sun and grin,
The cliffs are green across the bay.

And from the Cobb jutting out to sea
Five men o'war drift out to fight,
The galleons of the Armada's might
Which puff their red-cross sails to lee.

And where on Grannie's 'carious teeth

445

Jane Austen's heroine fell down:
A harbourmaster's cap on crown,
A boy directs their course beneath.

Forget that there on Monmouth beach
Twelve rebels danced on a gallows,
Their heads stuck on church spikes by foes -
Memories that wash in and reach.

All Lyme is full of joy this day,
The waves sparkle, dazzle the soul,
All creatures flash out from the whole
And smile to exist by this bay.

11 April 1988, revised 21 November 1993

FAMILY GATHERINGS

A family gathering is like
A rock in a sea of time;
The months and years wash by,
It survives all flux and chime.

The wedding or funeral,
The eighty-fifth party
That brought all from far and wide -
Enshrined in the memory,

A landmark like Gull Rock,
Which though seas crash and run,
Is solid, never-changing -
So why aren't they more fun?

A family gathering is
A measure of our aims,
Our rise and status, our car,
And we hide our secret shames.

7 August 1988(?), revised 21 December 1993

AT POLRUAN CASTLE, A 15TH CENTURY BLOCKHOUSE

I sit in the peace of a ruined tower,
A gull sits ruffled, much wind-tossed,
The light leaps off the river mouth
Like a snowfield sparkling in frost.

My heart soars out across the bay
To where distant Trenarren floats
And I am as still as the rock
Opposite Q's house and many boats.

I am like this battered tower,

I have weathered decades and rain
And my heart, too, shuts out old boats
When the harbour is cut by my chain.

21 August 1988

MOONLIGHT

A causeway of moonlight across the bay
And September's in the air.
Silhouettes throw eerie shadows
Of fishermen on the pier.

The round moon sails, a reflecting sun,
And is now obscured by cloud.
Dark sky and midnight hide all light
Behind a veil like a shroud.

The calm sea waits for the creeping dawn,
Knowing it will soon unfold.
And lo! the morning breaks again,
The water shimmers gold.

The mind is like this midnight sea,
And shares its great extent,
And when darkness casts moonlit shadows
It knows they will be rent.

29 August 1988, revised 21 November 1993

ON ELIOT'S CHURCH

A grey church with grey windows, but go
        inside;
See the gold reredos and the altar's pride.
High statues of Christ, red and white arched
        gloss
And almost gaudy stations of the cross.
Here Eliot worshipped, whose centenary is
        this year,
And before him Tomlin, in whose honour we

26 September 1988, revised 14 December 1993

THE DEAD POET BIDS FAREWELL TO HIS MOURNERS

Now a life is ended,
Hear the wisdom of death:
A thousand moments fade
Like a cloud of frosty breath.

O all you who are gathered
In this old Forest church,
Look out of the diamond windows

Where the beech and silver birch

Reach for the whirling clouds,
Wave in the dying sun,
Rooted round the graveyard
Where all the dead are One.

Know that I'm among them
And camp under reaching leaf,
I rise and float at night
In a mist that knows no grief,

My heart is in the Forest,
I roam alone and free,
A cloud of consciousness in
Sunshine of eternity.

Undated 1988, revised 21 November 1993

A HOME LIKE A NEST

I sit and gaze at a calm sea,
Across the harbour from this rest
Workmen flit through my harbour-house
Like birds carrying twigs to a nest.

Below my window a workman
Sweeps seaweed thrown up from the shore;
The storm flooded a house up the road:
Drains blocked, the sea rose through the floor.

As he sweeps and cleans, does he pray
For the sea to be high and foam
Across the road and leave a trail
Of weed which will feed him in his home?

Like birds workmen flit to and fro,
Through homes like nests for holiday men
To relax by a sea that is calm
But can rage dangerously again.

13 October 1988, revised 22 November 1993

A SNEEZE IN THE UNIVERSE

1989 – 1992

THE ARTIST AND FAME

Fame is like a surly fellow who lives down
    your road.
As you paint your large Hall so all can view
Each room and feature, he drives a tractor
Across your entrance so no one can visit you.

Fame is like a scowling farmer pointing a
    shotgun,
An armed robber made good who
    malevolently frustrates
All who live on his road – installs a cattle-grid
To wake this one's baby when each car wheel
    grates.

Fame controls the approach to your artistic
    Hall.
He will block the cattle-grid, if he feels like it.
He will leave a rusty plough, a heap of spikes
So your refurbishment is for you, as no one
    can visit.

The artist cannot think beyond his gate;
Absorbed, he plasters his Orangery with skills
For appreciative adults and children to walk
    within,
But if shotgun Tommy prevents – he can still
    view hills.

    13 February 1989, revised 7 January 1994

MATURING LOVE AND VISION
(OR: THE 85 YEAR OLD ORPHEUS TO ANY WOMAN)

I think of a time that was full of nakedness:
Slim and voluptuous, she shared her body
    with me,
Fed me, bathed me naked, cradled my head
So I woke to sunbeams, nipples and the sound
    of the sea.

I knew I had to work but delicious sloth
Forbad me the vision I knew I must win.
Each exciting moment we explored each
    other,

Seeking our souls through crevices in our skin.

Now my warmth is flabby and obese, and
    hides
Her wrinkled soul under shielding clothes like
    a glove
And I work as I always knew I had to do,
And ejaculate lyre-songs like acts of love.

Your presence around the house keeps me
    working.
I dive into rocky depths below all speech,
Gaze at finny images and surface again.
I could not do this without you lying on the
    beach.

Now love is like a statue, frozen apart,
And the longing I miss is deep within my soul
As I, too, have withdrawn from my creased
    skin
To live in vision, my youthful, mature goal.

    13 February 1989, revised 10 January 1994

SHINGLE STREAKED WITH TAR

The sea sighs in, a beach, green fields,
The air is warm, hear the pier plead,
And out beyond Gull Island, gulls
Swoop down on a line of brown seaweed.

It looks like a line of bladderwrack,
Beyond the pipe from the ramp it is thick;
But look again, the idyllic scene
Is menaced by a sewage slick.

Alas for the child that paddles and laughs,
For the canoeist's poke, oar like crowbar;
Alas for the smell when the tide comes in
And the shingle is streaked with "tar".

    14 February 1989, revised 10 January 1994

A BUSINESS WALK BY THE SEA

On the pier a tycoon walks
In a suit and a bow-tie

And a man in a suit carries a briefcase;
All else is sea and sky.

They talk, heads bowed, blind to
The Paradise around,
Abstracted from their situation,
In a dream of moneyed sound.

Stooping, heads bowed, they walk
Back to the Georgian Hotel
Which with the pub and museum
They regard as things to sell.

Stooping, their bodies pass through,
Their inspection now complete,
And do not glance at the port
Which exists on their balance sheet.

14 February 1989, revised 10 January 1994

CHAIN AND PADLOCK: TIME AND FORGOTTEN YEARS

Outside between two posts, a chain
Stops cars passing our front door.
The chain is padlocked at a post,
A barrier when waves roar.

The padlock is an iron brown,
The winds and storms and spray
Have rusted the lock so they key won't turn –
It needs to be oiled today.

My heart has a chain that keeps apart
All prying strangers' eyes;
When once the key turned easily
The lock rusts with disguise.

Alas that we bar our secret life
And lock all access like tears.
Time salts fresh experience into
The rust of forgotten years.

14 February 1989, revised 10 January 1994

THOUGHT BETWEEN GORRAN PIER AND CHARLESTOWN SEA

I sit by the Charlestown sea and sadly think
Of the critic's life that might have coloured
the Age,
Of the seventy books I might have written,
Each repeating the last, and nothing beyond
the page.

I think of the fortune I might not have made,
The family hard up, scraping along:
Was I right to turn my back, on Gorran pier,
On the armchair life of tomes for a life of
song?

I travelled widely and found the Eastern pearl
In a Zen temple, knew Ming and Hindu
ways;   10
And now I have brought back an under-
standing,
Like a general, and write memoirs of a maze.

I sit by the Charlestown sea and proudly think
Of the life I chose on a windswept Gorran pier,
To seek a secret place within the heart
Below the armchair mind, to become a seer.

I stand by the choice I made on Gorran pier,
I had to cross the sea to begin to grow.
Not for me a statement of the need for a search
(Seventy permutations) – I had to glow.   20

On this Charlestown pier, I reflect that I
Who rejected the armchair mind for a way of
loss,
And found in the desert a way of Fire
And reflects the sparkle as these waves toss.

Spring 1989(?), revised 10 January 1994

IMAGES AT TWILIGHT: EMPEROR TO SUN-GODDESS

I feel sad tonight for I miss your face
Which is here between my eyes.
You over me, Light shining down,
A radiance round your thighs,

You whimpering at each caress,
As I stroked you like a high priest,
You in the forty minutes it took
For the sun to leave the east.

An umbilical cord at which you tug
Causes me pleasing pain;
I feel sad for I miss your smile,
I hear you say through this rain

"I know how to look after a man"
As you sat above my waist
And bent your head with a knowing smile,

Dazzling me, and so chaste.

I loved the electric thrill in your hand,
That tingled up my spine,
This knowledge between us we could not know
If each was purely "mine".

A current threw me from side to side –
An angel with soft touch,
You gasped as I shuddered and convulsed,
A power overwhelmed your clutch.

Then limp, you swelled and a fullness
Drooped down your heavy limbs;
And I miss each look you give me now
As this aching twilight dims.

4 March 1989, revised 21 December 1993

PRINCE TOAD

I. TOAD

A toad came to my door,
It sat on the door ledge.
I took it to the pond,
It flopped near the shallow edge.

Now I sit and recall
How you opened in surprise
Into a delicious wetness
Till I flopped, a dream in your eyes.

A heaviness near my heart
And a wistfulness within,   10
And the prince in me is hidden
In this oozing bubbling skin.

I, toad, love ooze and slime
But conceal a prince beyond
Who is free from all wetness
In the still surface of this pond.

II. PRINCE

"I, prince, in the public eye,
Conjure the trees into bud,
Charm birds onto boughs and sing
Like the wind in the reeds above mud.   20

I, prince, sing of the pond
And so must become, out of need,
A toad now and again to know

Shivering shudders in the weed.

I, prince, can become a toad
And suck the slime near my chin,"
Sang the prince in me, caught
In this crusty, horny skin.

Who's in charge, this horny me
Or that handsome prince, wallowing?   30
That reflection that envies the pond
Or this croaking, floppy thing?

The prince is judged by his work,
The deed says all, and is dud
Without the veracity that
Shows all the world of mud.

The prince is nothing without
The beast he conceals, and its grime,
That leaves a trail of spawn
From a toad-like nature of slime.   40

4 March 1989, revised 10 January 1994

PUMP AND BRAIN DOWNSTAIRS

Only one pump is working in school,
The central heating system is old.
You can hear it knocking in the ground
Floor radiators, upstairs is cold.

In his room my son has one pump
Working in his brain, his mind's cold home,
He needs to get the other one going
To heat the upstairs of his caverned dome.

Yet downstairs is more important,
And that is where his alert mind dwells:
A deep close-to-the-soil warmth and
Down-to-earth pumping in his nerve cells.

11 March 1989, revised 21 December 1993

EASTER SUNDAY

Easter is here, muffled song in the church;
The sun has gone in, I sit outside and gaze.
After the snow the sap is risen to bud,
I ponder the risen Christ of their muffled praise.

A Bishop has said there was no Resurrection,
And doubting men have stayed away from the
pews

450

And now a smiling Christian can believe
The Crucifixion ended with bad news.

The God of dilettante and of Dante
Taps on the soul like a woodpecker. Aglow 10
I sit, identifying with gnarled bark
As the swelling organ thunders its crescendo.

I, who believe in the sun though it does not
    shine,
Am calm within this dark as I squint and peek –
The Fire within, like a furnace! whose
    shivering glow
Warms my soul like this sun on my tingling
    cheek.

Easter is here, a throng outside the church
Joyfully shares a risen something, while
I breathe out, sigh out, the immortal Fire
Apart in Paradise, gaze across the stile   20

At where the congregation laugh and chat,
At where the bespectacled Rector, clad in
    black,
Hovers like Death beside a crowd of souls
For whom Easter is like fun round a haystack.

Apart, outside, I gaze on a straw life
That will ignite with one breath of this Fire,
And I gaze on the black-clad Rector who
    looks sad
That Easter is now a smile under this spire.
                    26 March 1989, Easter Sunday

TOIL

An early summer's day, twittering birds,
The fields are carpet green, trees flecked with
    bud,
Flowers dance in breeze, everywhere silky
    green,
All just being; save the ants that toil in this
    mud.

I, too, am out of harmony with this peace;
I, driven, must go gathering like the bee
Worrying from flower to flower, ticking off
    jobs,
Doing rather than being in this green eternity.

It cannot be otherwise, my busy-ness

Has a place in this vast scheme, in the whole
    play;
Ants, bees and men crawl on, oblivious to
The shimmering glory of this summer's day.
                    26 March 1989, Easter Sunday

BEING'S SHOUT

The chestnut fountains its white,
Its candles glow and preen;
It was bare just two months ago,
Now all is teeming and green

And waves in the remote breeze
Which blows from the Milky Way
And with the sun and the rain
Makes everything grow each day.

I am a chestnut tree,
My candles of words shine out,
I wave in a divine breeze,
And exist in Being's shout.
                    Spring 1989(?), revised 19 October 1993

CHARLESTOWN IN MOTION

The blue sea lashes around Gull Rock,
The wind tugs around this pier,
The hills burn green under blue sky,
Yachts sail on the bay and veer,

And I squint with the wind in my hair,
The smell of salt in the spray
As the waves leap with a thousand lights
White surf boils round the bay

All is adazzle, all adance,
All is a surging joy,
And where, as the wind beats round my cheek,
Is the stillness I knew as a boy?
                    2 April 1989, revised 20 December 1993??

A COLD IN THE HEART

A sunny day, the green fields glow
Yet the trees are in despair,
And the caravan waits so solitary,
And yearns for hearts that care.

What is this misery in the trees
That waves green buds in the wind?
I am involved with feelings that
Belong to one who has sinned.

I muse how I bore the weight of the West,
How Gaddafi took my child,   10
And how his child was taken from him
Through a deed the West compiled.

And now my child theatres with her,
Instead of seeing me,
And I must sit alone and work
With the strength of a solitary.

I am sad in this lovely day,
The sun glints on passing cars,
As white clouds scud on blue, I spy
Faces like last night's stars.   20

A sunny day, the green fields glow,
A heaviness on my heart
Recalls lost faces who mattered to me,
The people I left for art.

And now, as if eighty, I sit
While ghosts flit through my head,
With laughs from lost years and smiling
        eyes –
As out of reach as the dead.

My love, if you did not exist,
I would invent your smile;
You are as remote as these dead ghosts,
As cold as the winter Nile.

I sniff and locate a stuffy nose,
Head throbs in a green daze,
And now I know my response to the sun
Was more than a depressed gaze.

                        8 April 1989

A SUMMER'S DAY, A HORRIBLE EVENT

At the end of a long life
I recall a summer's day
During the First World War
By the mill-race during our play.

We all swam in the stream,
I was twelve, my brother five.
The waterfall was so cool
There were bubbles round my "dive".

A cry and my brother was gone.

The sun glinted in the trees.   10
Nothing in the foaming stream.
I stood up to my knees.

They found him by the weir,
Carried him back to the farm,
Laid him on the table;
He looked beyond all harm.

My mother and father wept
And accused me with their eyes.
A sunshaft through the window
Lit my brother's two sties.   20

Now I stand on the bridge
And survey the peaceful air;
The waterfall plashes gently.
Could Death have visited here?

Like a vicar strolling past?
And where are the ghosts who that day
Wept in the kitchen to keep
The Reverend Death at bay?

            20 April 1989, revised 21 December 1993

DANCING UNIVERSE

I walk on the starlit pier;
Sea booms through the universe,
The cliffs are dark around
I turn and start at a curse,

For there on the pebble beach
Under the high sea wall
A fire flickers by the waves,
Two men prepare to sprawl.

Two shadows in a red glow
Two wraiths with a bottle, no names,
I gaze at the line of surf
And the dance of the leaping flames.

The power of the surging sea,
The thrust of the leaping fire
Reveal to human ghosts
The dance of divine desire.

            27 May 1989, revised 21 December 1993

HOUSE MARTINS IN THE DOCK

As I walked out one fine morning

452

A dozen house martins skimmed or swooped,
Diving down into the small dock,
And climbed into the sky and looped

They came and went in all directions
But none collided in their charge,
Swooping to meet their reflection
Then perching on a rusty barge.

It seemed they wheeled and dipped for joy,
While on either side of the dock
A dozen humans came and went,
Their bowed faces mournful like rock.

28 May 1989, revised 21 December 1993

SILENCE

The sea is calm, the house is still,
I rustle, two birds cheep,
And rest on a deep silence as
The gull rests on the deep

The silence of the years folds round,
I scratch the sounds of life;
The silence of the grave, the sound
Of stillness like a wife.

I sit in calm, I am at peace,
A tiny ant by this sea,
This tide of events which moves in and out
Masking quiet eternity.

28 May 1989(?), revised 21 December 1993

UNDER THE STARS

I go for a late night walk;
From Smeaton's pier, ablow,
The stars hang round me like
Leaves on a weeping willow.

I am lost in a universe
Whose wisps fold round my head,
And gaze at reflections from
White crests on waves, quite dead.

I look down at the up
Like God on a stone pier,   10
And look up at the down,
A trillion miles so near.
A muffled cry startles:
On the seat, an old tramp,
Huddled in a sleeping-bag

This starlit night, in the damp.

I creep by without a word,
I creep back to my home
And sit in my warm chair
And feel for all who roam.   20

O blind indifferent stars,
O cruel beauty in dark –
What indignation twinkles
At an old tramp's perishing bark?

And now I know for sure,
A trillion trillion miles
Are less than a twinkling eye
And a homeless cough that riles.

30 May 1989, revised 21 December 1993

AN EVANGELIST'S INSTANT SALVATION

A crowd in West Ham stadium sings a hymn.
I stand in a stand, the pitch is full of chairs,
The ground is packed, all faces wait and brim.
There is music from the platform, and words
    and prayers,
And then unannounced a tiny figure in a suit
Speaks casually. Laughter. It is him, surely?
Then his voice booms out, now like Hitler,
    now mute,
Making sense of life, confident and free.

Gently he takes us further in, like a don:
"God's interpreters speak with authority.   10
The Pope does not say 'I think' or 'In my
    opinion',
He says, 'This is the word of God.'" And now
    he
Speaks authoritatively about our wants and
    fears:
"Money does not satisfy, or bring you calm,
Everyone here will be dead in a few years.
Our spirits are crippled, like a withered arm."

And now he talks of sin: "We're all sinners,
But Jesus died for us. You must burn your
    boats
Like Cortes, make the heart sacrifice that stirs
Aztecs. Jesus is the way to a life that
    denotes."   20
I hear his fluent oratory, and recall

How I heard him at Haringey forty years
    hence.
"A public declaration of your faith, that's
    all.
Come up, come up." And then a long silence.

From the top of the West Stand I see them
    stream.
Counsellors first, then people, getting up,
Leaving their bags with friends, walking in a
    dream
Towards a curve like a communion cup.
As they come from all corners, like rippling
    wheat, I see
The word of God rustle a crowd like the
    wind.   30
My eyes are wet. "You are not coming to
    Billy
But to Jesus Christ, who loves all who have
    sinned."

Now I strut on the pitch, take penalties, save
    goals.
The platform deserted, the crowd mills, all is
    done.
I find my boys and muse on the saving of
    souls.
What a man! Able to speak directly to
    everyone.
A revivalist like Jonathan Edwards, he
Is not a leader of a sect or a movement;
A great communicator, not a Wesley;
A preacher of instant Heaven, not mystic
    ascent.   40

There are those who teach a lifelong Mystic
    Way
And those who turn men round from bad to
    good
By one impulsive choice that saves today,
As if we could tune mankind from "want" to
    "should".
The first teach hardship, the second
    happiness.
The first know truth, the second trust the
    Lord.
Mystics grow peace through the Light's
    glowing ingress,
Evangelists sway crowds' minds to accord.

16 June 1989, revised 10 January 1994

ANGELS AND PARADISE: QUESTION AND ANSWER

Question:
Strange angel, is it true
That angels cavort and dance
And lie with each other,
As if they were in France?

And do they all love
In a tactile way,
Is Paradise a place of girls,
Of an ever possible lay?

Answer:
They flit like a jaybird,
A brown-blue blur in a tree,
And they wash their feathers
In a leafy shade, and be;

And marvel at the feast
Served at the Almighty One's word,
The berries and fruit and nuts
That will winter each starving bird.

Summer 1989(?), revised 21 December 1993

BREZNEV TO GORBACHEV

"Strong rule, strong rule holds a country
    together,
I made them fear to break free from control.
Give them freedom, they will use it against
    you
Like a caged bird taking to the wing at
    dawn.
I held them all back, and I handed on
What I inherited – can you say the same?
Strength, not freedom holds a country
    together.
All right, so I waded in blood? So what?
Did not Stalin even more? And was the
    Empire
Not safe under Stalin? Strong rule requires
    blood,
Peace and security feed on blood-letting.
You did not grasp that the Empire had to be
Held together, you saw it from the point of
    view
Of the individual – and so there is now chaos.
It has all fallen apart – thanks to your
    weakness.

You will be reviled as a weak ruler.
You will be condemned for allowing
    dissenting voices
To babble our decisive Mother Russia
Into cackling confusion. I despise you!"

Summer 1989(?), revised 21 December 1993

DONKEY DERBY

Four donkeys stand before two-wheel traps,
Four ladies sit, their legs up wide,
The tote is closed, twice round the track –
Away they go, each smacks a side,

Tom-toms on a flank, holding the rein
Like a Roman charioteer.
The donkeys run, the spoked wheels bounce,
The throng of faces shout and cheer.

Pulling a tail, thumping a round,
My sister rides second, eyes lit.
I think of the beast that I must urge
To carry me round my circuit.

Plato saw emotions reined back
Like a charioteer reining horses,
But I know the mind must be got going
With blows and slaps to encourage what is.

24 July 1989, revised 6 December 1993

PARACHUTIST

The plane gleamed in the blue sky,
At seven thousand feet
Four dots came out and hung
Smoke trailing in the heat.

They dived for ten seconds,
Then parachutes puffed out,
Grew larger and came in
Their arms raised with a shout.

One of them will soon be you
Standing on the steps by a wheel;
But my heart will be in my mouth
When you first dive off with a squeal.

I will stick to my parachute,
My philosophy of new birth.
Without it I would fall
Like a stone to the earth.

25 July 1989, revised 21 December 1993

BEN NEVIS: CLOUD OF UNKNOWING

Ben Nevis's low slopes are hidden in cloud.
Climb from the glen, leave the crowded world
    below,
Ascend and be wrapped in a thin white shroud,
A mist that seems a cloud unless you know;
Now grope in a fog which obscures every
    view
Save haversack and rocks, flip-flops on feet,
Till wisps roll clear, and a high ridge shows
    through,
Awesome where mountain and a pale sun
    meet.

There are glimpses along the mystic way;
Ascend into a cloud that separates   10
You from the deep ravine, the towering day,
And in detachment from all loves and hates
Hear rushing water through a lifetime's
    smoke;
The trembling veil lifts on a rugged scene
But still the peak is obscured. Who can
    invoke
A summit that remains behind a screen?

Discard illusions, how you thought or
    dreamed;
People see from the level they are at.
The peak must now be higher than it seemed;
Others toil past on a mountain that seems
    flat.   20
Mist lifts on flowering grass above a tarn
And at the turn of the bouldered path, now see
Like a close-up spider on a distant barn:
Fort William, dewy heather, and a honey bee.

There is a height of mind like barren rock.
Be mindless now beneath the upper cloud.
Now mop your brow, now pant for breath,
    take stock
Of a rugged landscape, a wilderness's crowd
Of granite boulders, shingle, screed or shale.
All you with furred-up lungs from city air, 30
Seek out these snow-stretched heights where
    all can fail,
Climb pure Ben Nevis and surmount despair!

On the last long haul up to the grey summit
The sun breaks through the all-enfolding haze.

At the top trig point, the cairn, small
    whitethroats flit,
Now flop and recover your breath and,
    mindless, gaze
Down a clear precipitous drop to a green glen
Four thousand feet below, and at north face
    snow;
Look down upon the awesome ridge again,
Now insignificant and very low.   40

Each man has his own private mountain slope
Which corresponds to Nevis's winding way;
Having ascended, he understands pure hope,
Having taken on trust the divine ray;
Knows warm air, rising, cools and is
    condensed
To cloud, which he must bravely go within ,
That purges what his worldly self has sensed;
Knowing what he now knows, would he now
    begin?

Now struggle back down to the world of ills;
Legs wobble three hours down; longing to
    sit,   50
Pass dozens bent double, trudging up hills,
Believing the next ridge is the summit.
Now pause and loll at a turf spring and drink
The cool, sweet mountain water that is so
    clear,
And, stiff as Keats in back leg muscles, think
Of the achievement of rising to sunlit air.

25-26 July 1989

SPRING

The cliffs are green, the sky is blue;
Over the hill past the Battery
Which guarded against Napoleon's ships,
Down the wooded lane, pick blackberry,

And on the beach seek a coffin cave
And sit on boulders by the sea,
Hear the spatter of the waterfall
Pour round the moss, splash stone, flow free.

The water comes from in the cliff,
A pure spring water of the earth
Like the spring from within my brain
Which will be clay when I end this birth.

I leak a spring of fresh insight,

My rock trickles with a pureness,
And this saline sea of vast size
Absorbs its freshwater ingress.

26 July 1989, revised 6 December 1993

CHARLESTOWN: MOON AND METEORITE TRAILS

Evening in Charlestown, through
The window a half-moon
Hangs above Trenarren,
Yellow line shimmers, strewn

On the ripple-free sea;
Softly the waves plash in,
Splash on the rocks below
As the hot Dog-day draws in.

A streak and now the first
Of a meteorite shower
Trails down the twilit sky;
Eighty will fall in an hour.

I gaze at the reflected moon
Which is not wet or whole,
And wait for burnt-out dust
To trail down my moonlit soul.

12 August 1989, revised 21 December 1993

UP THE TAMAR

The lifeboat outing: from Tamar bridge
We leave civilisation, and chug
Into the interior, as if
Going back in time in a Congo tug.

Wider than the great Thames at first –
The border from the Saxon shock –
It narrows to wooded hamlets
And the grey roofs of old Calstock,

Passes the chimneys of arsenic mines,
The tall sedge bends in our wake, see:
We reach the iron water wheel
And tall ships of Morwelham quay.

And there among the disused mines
In period costume, men climb
And wave from hidden hedges and
We are back in another time.

As the boat turns, we are now in

A more primitive time; serene,
I am one with the eagle which soars
And dives and swoops on this ravine.

O tiny tiny grub, caveman,
Who lives in wooded crags an hour,
Hide now before you become prey
To the elemental eagle's power.

Men huddled and hunted and slept,
Cowering from such a thunderstorm,
And now this drunken laughter here
As we huddle from the rain, keep warm.

13 August 1989, revised 6 December 1993

TWO SWANS

Two swans on the Tamar
Glide through the driving rain,
Their composure unruffled
By its lashing, stinging pain.

Two swans on the Tamar
Extend their necks to the bank,
Then sit as still as statues
In this cold jumping dank.

My love, we can be as calm
As they in this tumult,
Where words jump like raindrops
And deafen with their insult.

13 August 1989, revised 6 December 1993

UNIVERSE

I put a rug on the dark lawn
And lie on my back and gaze at the stars:
Cassiopeia, Cepheus, Perseus –
A streak like a rocket, not far from Mars.

These are the Dog-days, and a shower
Of meteorites is passing near.
Some are caught and burnt up within
Our earth's candescent atmosphere.

A wait for the next one: a satellite?
And now Concorde rumbles round the bay.
Andromeda, Ursa Major – some stars
Are two thousand light years away.

The star I see is as it was
In the Roman times, it may not be

There now! I gaze at the Milky Way,
Hundred billion stars in our galaxy.

We are one of that many stars:
A hundred billion galaxies race.
Ours is a grain of sand on the beach,
A tiny smallness in infinite space.

I gaze at the stars – another streak –
And think of the oneness of everywhere,
And I think of social illusion
And, giddy, I fall from the lawn up there.

13 August 1989, revised 6 December 1993

THE CHURCH OF STORMS

I sit on rocks at Gunwalloe. All's well;
The Church of Storms nestles to the cliff
across the bay.
Blue sky; only the sea birds on the swell
Are within reach of me, and this flung-up
spray.
The sea's a sparkle and rolling in calm;
Barnacles, limpets, mussels and boiling surf.
Another year has curled by under the charm
Of a sunlight-and-stone vision. Near green
cliff turf
We squat on timeless rocks and perceive the
All
And on a cloudless day, open to a heal-
ing self-luminous Being that sparkles our
brief stay
As phenomenal months roll on to our
nightfall,
And know we are immortal in what is Real,
Warm beams melting white foam that
measures out our day.

AT GUNWALLOE: LIGHT

I sit in the Church of Storms near the beach
In sixth century peace, I don't pray.
It is deserted, I sit in a pew
Under the red light this hot day.

Outside it is sunny, in here cool.
The door is from a wrecked ship. I respond
To wooden roof beams, quatrefoil squint,
I am back in the Middle Ages and beyond.

I ask the Light for its knowledge.

I feel the surge come into me,
I quiver, and soak up what is given.
I am full this hot day, and can be.

18 August 1989, revised 21 December 1993

LIGHT LIKE FISH

I put down the phone on the gas board
And casually looked out to sea,
And was startled at the dance of light
As if ten thousand fish jumped for glee.

I stopped and gazed, aware, and thrilled:
No gull swooped or alighted there,
Yet a third of a mile from shore
Some ten thousand fish jumped for air.

Then a cloud scudded across the sun
And the leaping fish had gone, wind-blown,
Leaving a slightly ruffled calm,
And with heavy heart I returned to my phone.

Summer 1989(?), revised 10 January 1994

RUN AGROUND

A cargo boat laden with china clay
Leaves the dock. The Harbourmaster tells me,
"We're two feet low, high pressure and wind
    press
The water down, we'll run aground, you'll
    see."

It is a Dutch boat crewed by Calvinists
Who would not come in on a Sunday tide.
As the boat slews round on ropes there is a
    rasp,
A scrape, and the bows are beached on the
    bar, and subside.

The pilot boat hovers near with winches and
    ropes,
But she is stuck fast in the harbour sands
At midnight on a bitter February night,
The raw wind numbing the crew's freezing
    hands.

As engine and ropes refloat her on a nearby
Channel, I think of my beached cargo and
    pray
That I will be able to refloat my wares
Which ran aground on a windy, pressured day.

Summer 1989(?), revised 10 January 1994

PALE FIRE
(A FRAGMENT)

Pale fire like seaweed in
The curl of the silver-blue waves;
A low skimming bird, red clouds,
And a dark headland the green sky braves.

Summer 1989(?), revised 11 January 1994

PALE FIRE

As I locked up the school
The sky darkened to black,
Thunder rumbled around
With forks of fire at my back.

I sat in my window in dread,
As the reverberations fell,
I wondered if such a storm
Galvanised the first cell,

And I wondered if life is
Manifested élan that jars
Like thunder, and not chance,
And what pervades the stars?

My child, this I have learned
From fifty years on earth,
That the stars and human mind
Have had a mysterious birth

And are nothing but gases and tides
Like our own aimless lives
Unless all is pale Fire,
And a divine love with drives.

13 September 1989, revised 21-22 December 1993

COUPLING: SPACE

As two strangers lie on a couch,
Filled with temporary tenderness
And couple, unaware of the night,
And sigh with pleasure, and then dress,

Two clothes moths couple back to back;
Absorbed in each other, they might be
    dead.
I lift them gently in a glass
And tip them tenderly on a flower-bed.

I stare at the stars: Voyager Two
Is passing Neptune somewhere out there.
Coupling, we creatures are not conscious

Of the vast space between far and near.

Revised 10 January 1994

ELEMENTAL

The wind is whistling and roaring tonight,
Flinging fountains of foam a hundred foot
    high,
Washing along the harbour wall, waterfalling
    down,
Lashing the window, blowing in clouds of
    spray.

A hurricane is blowing in from the sea
And I am elemental once again,
I sit among the winds and booming tides
And cower from the storm like a caveman.

This cavernous home on the edge of land
Is buffeted by winds and mountainous seas
And I delight in the frothy turbulence
That rages round the peace of its timeless
    days.

It is good to receive a hundred smiling guests
And then drive down to this timeless hermit's
    cell,
Perched on a cliff, and watch with a seaman's
    eyes
Till the whirling clouds reveal bright stars: the
    All.

Good wine, laughter and the merriment of
    friends
In a hall with a Christmas tree make one
    forget
The fountaining of an elemental sea
And a hermit's glimpse of what Is and is
    not.

16 December 1989

INVISIBLE FOAM

Spray flicks on my window-pane
From the tumultuous sea,
Which crashes over the harbour wall
And waterfalls down the quay.

Spray flicks on my window-pane
As the tumultuous sea
Reminds all living creatures that
There's a power greater than "me".

The flick on the pane reminds
Of the flick on the inner eye
As a metaphysical ocean
Reminds of a foam that is dry:

The timeless invisible sea
From which forms crawl and peep,
The crabs and whelks and images
That manifest from its deep.

17 December 1989

STILLNESS AND TIDES

Hundred foot waves round Porthleven's
    Clock Tower
Have smashed the quay. How fared the
    church on the beach?
I drive down the narrow lane, where the sea's
    power
Has left pools of water within the grey sky's
    reach.
The bay is white with surf and boiling foam
Which splashes on black rocks and a clean
    shore.
I take the sandy path as to a porched home.
Sandbags; within, wet tiles, wet wooden floor.
O wind that blew the sea at this church's
    inside,
O invisible power behind the winds that
    surge –
How could you destroy what a saint has toiled
    to raise?
Or does the invisible force behind wind and
    tide
Wash into old forms this new age to urge
Men to renew the symbols of their still gaze?

19 December 1989

CANDLEFLAME STORM

A power cut throughout the village, the
    darkness shocks,
The wind howls, rain lashes the windows,
White surf tears in and foams on the dark
    rocks.
I huddle without heat where a candle glows,
A roar in the empty chimney, blow on my
    hand
And sit among the shadows like the Georgian
    poor
When this cottage was built. The wind that
    has banned

The TV's noise now rattles the front door
And all is stillness beneath the wind and rain
This December night, and I am still within   10
And hear the silence beneath the furious
     storm.
How good that still Eternity should strain
To make us gaze at the candleflame in our
     skin,
So that we who cower in dark can know Its
     form.

19 December 1989

A MAN OF WINDS AND TIDES

A Cornish sea captain with a grizzled beard,
And weather lines round his elemental gaze.
From the cliff he gazes at where the horizon's
     cleared
And slowly says, "There be rain later, and
     haze."
He knows the weathers and can steer by stars:
"Orion's three-starred belt, there: his top
     knee's Rigel.
His bottom shoulder's Betelgeuse – not Mars.
See the triangle down to bright Sirius – he's
     well –
And up to Procyon. See Regulus, and Pollux
     too.
Up to Aldebaran, Algol and Capella.
To the Pleiades, and Cassiopeia's 'W',
And the Plough's two pointers to Polaris, the
     Pole Star."
He lives among winds and tides and does not
     know
Quick town-men envy his being, which is
     slow.

20 December 1989

BEING AS A RIPPLE OR TWO

Green hills, an exploding sea and veiling of
     spume
Which hangs like mist across the sunlit bay.
As the energy froths, a perpetual roar and
     boom;
Foam leaps half way up the cliffs. I turn away
And enter the small stone church, stepping
     over a snail,
And linger under arches from another Age,
And on the silence, like a distant gale
I can hear the roaring where seas boil and
     rage.

And now, sitting in the graveyard, quite alone
I watch black petrels wheel and mew and
     soar
And gaze on rocks as old as time. From the
     stone
Wall a wren hops and pecks near the church
     door,
And I look out on Being as the dead must do
And see its fountaining energy as a ripple or
     two.

15 February 1990

GNOSIS: THE NATURE OF THE SELF
(OR: BRAIN, MIND; HEART, SOUL; SPARK, SPIRIT)

A tall bald-headed man with longish hair
And spectacles, who knows more about the
     brain
Than any living man in this hemisphere,
Who has defined away the mind-body strain.
He speaks gently, slowly, at this conference.
He is more sympathetic to the One than all
Who define the self in terms of commonsense
Through EEGs that cannot find the soul at all.

"Science is about the external world, it
     assumes
That consciousness is brain function. It
     will   10
Be 'non-scientific' to question what it
     presumes.
The brain makes a model of the self until
A stroke or 5 hydroxytryptomine
Slurs words or adds a more aggressive role.
We are all trapped in our chemistry. So seen,
We are mechanical beings without soul.

"Brain structure and function determine how
     we behave.
Disorders in genes create disorders in mind:
Down's patients' and schizophrenics' genes
     enslave.
In dyslexics the brain's hemispheres are not
     aligned;   20
The left controls speech, the right excites. Its
Limbec system controls each frown or kiss.
This is the source of the mystical – and fits.
Stimulate your system and you know total
     bliss.

460

"Here is the source of the near-death
		experience,
The 'gnosis' of bright white light. Slice
		through ten brains
With computer technology and you see the
		tense
Parts as they function, hot areas coloured like
		stains.
Mind-body was first fractured by Galileo,
Mind and brain are two sides of a cube, a
		whole.						30
We need a new science of consciousness to
		show
Science can include experience of the soul."

With a bald Vipassana monk in a darkened
		room
Now still the body and judging mind,
		withdraw,
Enter the chapel of soul – an inner gloom –
Which links intellect to spirit that has lived
		before,
Watch stray thoughts leave like birds that
		cannot perch,
Observe your breathing in-out, and the cause
Of pain, behind which is joy, feel detached
		from your search,
Feel the lightness of being as your spirit
		soars.						40

I am serene, the Light is in my soul.
It ripples like white fire before my third eye.
I say "What next?" And the answer is droll:
"Influence world leaders." "I have no power,"
		I sigh.
Instantly, like a shock of two thousand volts,
Light bursts in my crown and prickles through
		limbs in
A surge of power from scalp to toes, two jolts
Of Spirit that leave my spirit refreshed, soften
		my skin.

Gnosis is in my soul, my brain, my skin;
My spark is lit, my pneumatic spirit aglow: 50
The "I" which persists through many lives,
		within
Intellect and the receptacle of soul. I know
I am not my body or quietened thought,
I am spirit brain physiologists deny.
My body-self, like a six-sided cube, can be

sought
As brain, mind, heart, soul, Angel's spark in
		crown; and spirit that will not die.

To know one's self is to know the universe
Whose oneness is known through the chakra
		of the heart;
To influence the universe is to be immerse-
-d in the "whole, combined into one," with an
		adept's art.					60
I am spirit which opens to the tidal Spirit
Which pants in and out through my soul's
		narrow strait.
I am being, breathed by the sea of Being,
		lit
By an ocean of Light that pours through this
		harbour gate.

9 April 1990

SKYLARK AND FOAM

As that skylark soars twittering towards the
		sun,
I, in this church on a curved foam-touched
		shore,
Soar sunwards. I sit between pillar and steps,
		shun
The world in a seat under the oak roof,
		withdraw,
Still body and mind till my spirit sees image-
-s break in my soul below like the foam in the
		bay:
Strange architectural sights from a bygone
		Age.
The waves break gently, throwing up Being's
		spray
On many different rocks outside. I
		correspond:
My soul is under a tide of Light within;
This sea of Being which comes in from the
		beyond
Like cosmic radiation, penetrates my skin.
Where shore meets sea, there I am washed,
		and swoon,
Till the skylark plummets down into a dune.

12 April 1990

CONSCIOUSNESS LIKE A POND

Consciousness is like a pond.
If it is clouded with mud

And stirred up, it retains
No reflection, as in a flood,

But if it is still and clear
A sharp reflection. Soon
The bottom is revealed
Limpid as a lagoon.

Still mind, clear its surface
And it will retain what it sees,
Mirroring a clear image
From the outside wood and trees.

12 April 1990, revised 11 January 1994

IN BUDAPEST OLD CITY

I sit in a baroque house in Budapest
And drink coffee in an arched room and survey
The scene in the street, alone, a faded charm
Like thirties Berlin, but no cabaret.

Here in this central part of Great Europe
Nothing really works, everything is late;
Now pinched faces that are old before their
        time
Stare at me with envy, and even hate.

And I, an exile and imperialist
Look in upon their gnarled and struggling lives,
The eyes that see me as their wildest dream
And then go back to bent and weary wives.

24 April 1990, revised 13 December 1993

DANUBE: BALL AND CHAIN

The morning Danube floats in mist,
I stroll, water laps at my feet;
Two men in a police car watch
As I commune with Nature, complete.

The water was blue yesterday,
It is grey now, and there are trees;
And the men who watch believe I am one
Of the Russian-Jewish refugees

Whom they must observe and guard against
The threat of an Arab attack.   10
The Danube is still as a lake,
This misty morning as I look back

To old Europe, and a time before
Three thousand five hundred BC

When Kurgan man from the Russian steppes
Came here on his way to a British lee.

I stand by the Danube and gaze
And try to be at one with all,
But the policemen hold my passport
And keep my feet chained to the earth's ball. 20

25 April 1990, revised 13 December 1993

WILLOW-WARBLERS

There are dandelions by the Danube
As I walk to meet my friend,
And the waters are silver
And a bird twitters to an end.

I sit on a seat and listen
It sings from a tree, near a plank.
One answers from the willows
That line the river bank.

Up and down they both warble.
Spellbound at the concert,
I drink in the warm sunshine
And the warblers' joy, alert.

27 April 1990, revised 29 November 1993

WESTERN MEN AND ISIS

Sunlight in a drop of water
Is like sunlight in my mind;
To Divine Light in the soul
We Western men are blind.

The chestnut tree is within
The brown conker above;
The body is in the seed
That spills in a sigh of love.

The river that has dried up
Has undergone a change;
It is carried by the wind
Across the mountain range.

Butterflies in the buddlea
Have crawled from a chrysalis
So let Isis with naked breasts
Bring the Light down with a kiss.

April 1990

A CRYSTAL

An arrow-shaped crystal.

With cloudy seed inside,
Pulsates like a lingam,
Throbs in the hand of a bride.

This crystal, clear as a soul
Was once dark solid rock.
Now purified to clearness
Its energy gives out a shock.

The transformation from dark
To clear, transparent power
Is what the soul must do
As it crystallises the hour.

27 May 1990

METAPHYSICAL-PHYSICAL
(OR: ORPHEUS-TAMMUZ, SERENE AMONG THE MAENADS)

The more metaphysical this sea and I become
The more I love the physical: the smell
Of new-mown grass; all clover where bees
        hum;
A sea-moon's shimmering causeway; a
        whorled shell;
In a blue sky, warming the cheeks, a bright
Sun; heat and an iced drink; through half-
        closed eyes
The leaping of a fire on a frosty night;
Summer evenings; shooting stars like
        fireflies;
And the glittering sweep across the Milky
        Way
Sparkling like a trail of ploughed-up ancient
        coins;
But most of all, curved breasts, taunting
        foreplay
Until, skin smooth as silk, the sneeze in the
        loins
Which corresponds to the tingling of the
        divine
And the breaking of the beyond into a spine.

6 August 1990

WISTFUL TIME-TRAVELLERS
(SECOND VERSION)

Sitting here in our flat, after dinner,
We can turn on the past. One TV knob, and
        Lord-
-s of Time, we are back eight years at the
        Marathon.

It could be twelve years ago on a tape-record-

-er. Our voices will speak from that
        Christmas, at a touch
Of a key. Or if I put up a screen, I could be
Me as I was at a wedding fifteen years back
In a garden of celluloid Eternity.

We Westerners are all time-travellers now.
We glide at the speed of light. For a few
        pounds   10
We can put back the clock to yesterday,
Fill the present with yesterday's sights and
        sounds –

Football, cricket, boxing, thrillers, or songs,
Memories on tape or film or a round disc,
Available in the home, or the waves of the air,
To escape the present for a vicarious risk.

We needed the past when we were doddering.
We looked nostalgically back to the Golden
        noon
When the West held, baffled that the
        mightiest,
Most inventive civilisation, whose offshoot
        reached the moon,   20

Should, after D-Day, shrink in senescent ruin,
Retreat in a world which prefers the tyrant's
        prime
To our old system. Whispering disapproval,
We Westerners wistfully escaped the present
        time.

And we need the past now we are victorious,
The Cold War won, the tyrants out of sight;
We need to remind ourselves how glorious
Was tyranny's collapse and NATO's might

When really Russia's poor economic
        performance
Led East Europeans to reject their colonial
        rule   30
And rediscover the Fire in their soul,
Which they'll teach as they learn democracy
        at our Western school.

They have made America Lord of the world,
And will give Europe a new self-belief;

463

But now we've lost the tension in our living
We Westerners escape the present with relief.

26-28 April 1976, revised 1990

SNOW

All night it snowed – all's white,
The grass, the roofs, all clean;
And the world that was dull is bright
With an iced cake's frosty sheen.

Icicles hang from the eaves
As I blow on my hands and write.
Railings, fences and plant leaves
Support eight inches of white.

No bird moves, all is still
And my whitened heart is at peace.
As more snow flecks the chill
I am one with when I will cease.

8 February 1991

ODE: SPIDER'S WEB: OUR LOCAL UNIVERSE IN AN INFINITE WHOLE

"Does aught befall you? It is good.
For it is part of the great web of all creation"

Marcus Aurelius

I. THE VASTNESS OF THE UNIVERSE

I walk on the dark stones of the harbour wall
And gaze at the choppy foam round two dark
        rocks
(Gull Island and crag) and the swirling sea
        recall-
-s the stone swirls where an infinite Zen truth
        shocks.
The bobbing boats, the harbour lamps that dip
And land, are reflected in the endless deep;
The last clouds blow inland, stars wink and
        drip
And soon the universe will awake from sleep.

The universe is like a spider's web from here
And stars tremble like drops of suspended
        dew   10
On invisible threads that engulf the black
        hemisphere
And hang like globules under the spider's
        view.

I gaze at the spiral that holds all in place
And marvel at God the Spider who span its
        thread,
At the millions of stars that throb and drip
        down space,
As the web vibrates with a breath beyond the
        dead.

There are more stars than grains of sand in
        this bay.
The most luminous object emits energy an
        immense
Thirty thousand times as powerful as the
        Milky Way,
Is sixteen thousand million light years
        hence;   20
And can be a young or proto-galaxy, just
Eighty-three per cent back to the Big Bang, or
        can be
A bright quasar embedded in a cloud of dust –
The most luminous star is too dim for us to
        see.

I think of Bohm who knew Einstein, who
        knows
The vastness of the visible universe
From equations, who greeted me then close-
ed his eyes, then said with Einstein's
        mildness, terse-
-ly: "You can't have a vision of the Whole,
        it's infinite;
Our universe is a local event, a wave   30
In a sea of cosmic energy that's implicate.
There's something cosmic behind how atoms
        behave.

"The universe emerged from the vacuum,
The quantum void which is infinite in space.
Our vision's finite, a view from a room;
You can't measure the immaterial from our
        time and place.
The Big Bang is limited in importance, as is
Cosmic background radiation, its residue;
I see no unification of the four forces,
There are no prospects for such an optimistic
        view."   40

The unified sea foams round two rocks, the
        earth.
I think of bearded Gunzig with curly hair

464

Who told how an unstable vacuum must give
    birth
To a stable universe with an atmosphere:
A quantum vacuum expels pairs of flee-
-ting virtual particles, which return without
    trace;
Some are transformed into real ones by
    energy
From the geometric background of the
    curvature of space.

"A vacuum is unstable and Nature prefers to
    give
A stable state to a vibrating trembling , so   50
The energy linked to curvature is negative
    gravitational
And combines with positive mass to give
    zero.
It costs no energy to make a universe. But
    then
The price is entropy, or running down."
So something comes from nothing. Is there
    anything hidden
Behind physics? "It is not my field," he says
    with a frown.

I recall the view of a bald Dutch Professor.
As I sat in All Souls he said: "We are born to
    die.
Between, humans make society. An 'I'
    before
Birth? After death? Fantastical! How?
    Why?"   60
The Void's Fire is received in human
    consciousness
And passed to society; not created by mind.
The human mind that lives in this vast web's
    "mess",
Did it create these millions of stars that are
    blind?

II. THE ONENESS BETWEEN THE
FIRELIT SOUL AND THE UNIVERSE

The mind is the measure of each blind star.
I recall Winchester Cathedral, and the bones
Of seven kings in mortuary chests, and going
    afar
In the Venerable Chapel, feet on ancient
    stones,
I said to the Fire, "If you are there, inspire

What Hawking and Gunzig claim is the air, 70
Come into me," and a terrific surge of Fire
Poured into me, nearly knocking me off my
    chair.

If the infinite Whole manifests from Fire
Which we receive in our finite brains and see
Then there is within us that which is infinite
    desire,
Takes part in it, is of the infinite Whole and
    free.
And as in a hologram the whole's in the part
So in our galaxy the infinite whole can be
    found,
So in my mind roll the infinite wastes of the
    heart
Of a bright, eternal vastness that has no
    ground.   80

To some there are thirteen signs in the zodiac
    sky,
One each full moon, for each twenty-eight
    days,
And Arachne is between Taurus and Gemini,
The spider who spins a thread into a web and
    sways.
Go within your mind and ascend the universe
And climb the spider's web within the soul,
Look down on the star Arachne, and traverse
And bathe in its translucent glow, and see the
    Whole!

The spider that creates also destroys,
Weaving a web from nothing, killing its
    prey.   90
This spiral net of stars that traps hangs joys,
A web of beauty across the phenomenal day.
The spiral universe converges at the Pole
Where lurks the transcendent creator
    Godhead.
Each life is entrammelled in the web of the
    Whole,
A different shape caught up in the same
    thread.

Look down and see earth like a round base-
    ball,
The size of a fist held at arm's length, so
    sublime,
So fragile and finite. Look down and fall

Towards dry, cold Mars. Now travel back in
    time. 100
From here the web looks like a ripe fruit tree.
As in a car wash, globes on a windscreen
    band
When driven by air, then rush apart, now see
The Big Bang's blast, our corner of the
    universe expand.

Now forward, see Mars' colonisers toil
To give the Red Planet breathable air,
With orbiting mirrors heat the red soil
Till water flows and vegetables grow there,
As the ice melts plant life and forests grow;
And see the pink sky turn a brilliant blue. 110
The cold planet now has farms, and towns.
    Oh,
I see a New World for Voyagers with derring-
    do!

This vast universe, does our consciousness
Fit in or is it just an accident?
A hundred billion galaxies, each with no less
Than a hundred billion stars – if any less
    extent
Then the Whole would not have existed a
    long enough span
For man to exist. The Anthropic Principle!
Astronomy, physics, biology, all centre man
In the planets, electrons, double helix of the
    web's spiral. 120

III. THE ONENESS BETWEEN SOUL
AND UNIVERSE AND THE DIVINE
SOUL'S VISION OF THE INFINITE
WHOLE

All is interrelated, corresponds perfectly.
Can consciousness be the exception? Is all a
    mess?
We are the outcome of the universe's
    symmetry.
Within one law: matter, body, consciousness.
The Fire behind Nature and history shines
Into and through all things, and holds for
    evermore
Galaxies, matter, bodies, minds, and entwines
Everything in the universe within one whole
    web-like law.

Like God, the poet sits in a spider's web

As large as the universe, spun from his
    head, 130
Waiting for images to float on the winds from
    the ebb-
-ing beyond and tremble his hung silk thread,
Making him scamper to his winged catch, run
    round
It, roll it up in a ball, wind it and climb.
He knows a poem is an image caught and
    bound
In a twisted net of fibrous words that rhyme.

And, hung in the night among stars that drift
    and flit,
He sees the earth fly into his webbed sun-
    rise
And winds it round with silk and fixes it
In a great web of being, hung with other
    flies. 140
And now from the centre of this galaxy,
Woven in light from deepest space, like some
Marble, he holds the earth – white cloud, blue
    sea –
The earth between his forefinger and thumb!

Gaze at the outward burst of web-hung things
And sense the infinite Fire which moves
    beyond
And manifests into subatomic strings
And, inseparable from the whole, swirls round
    this "pond"
's two rocks in this local corner of England,
And with my ego and my infinite soul (and
    Bohm) 150
I see the dark whole and local froth, and
Symbolise the infinite in Gull Island's foam.

And I who can see the oneness of sea and sky,
Who can see the Being behind this
    phenomenal earth,
See also, with X-ray vision, the dark Void,
    high
Up where atoms unfold from nothing in an
    endless birth,
Where infinity swells to finite form, like the
    sun,
Where eternity enters time like a moving sea.
And as I close my eyes and gaze at the One
I hear the wash on rocks of cosmic
    energy. 160

A vision of the whole can be a partial one,
A symbol's fragment of wholeness in a place,
And it can be an inner glimpse of a sun,
Of a Fire like moonlight in infinite timeless
　　　　space.
So I sit on the wall near dark Charlestown and
　　　　ga-
-ze on a loving mind that is fifty fathoms deep
And stretches far beyond the Milky Way
And spy with a finite eye on the infinite
　　　　whole asleep.

2 April-July and 16 August 1991, revised 27 May 1992

TINKLING: BEING LIKE A BREEZE

A tiny Japanese bell
Suspended near a shrine
Tinkles, its paper tongue
Blown like a prayer from a pine.

Like a tiny bell I hang
As on a shrine's pine tree
And I tinkle in the breeze
Paper tongue turning in glee.

My tongue is tinkled by
An invisible breeze that desires
My still heart to affirm
The Being that inspires.

April 1991(?)

ABBOT OF THE SPRING

My school is like a spring,
It provides for all who dip
Their cup into its gushing,
Who dip their cup and sip.

Like an Abbot I walk (or run)
Round my grounds which a tree screen
　　　　shields
And encourage each monk and nun
Who labours in my fields.

They who once worked for God and were fed,
Now banknotes provide their needs,
Still labour for love and bread
In my mystery school that feeds.

My cornucopia gushes,
And quenches all thirsting

In the many who till where it rushes –
I am Abbot of the spring.

April 1991(?)

TWO TOMBS: LIFE WITHIN DEATH

Two tombs, an ash growing between,
Blue sky, oak hedge, and sprouting seed,
And in the cool shade this hot day
Two naked bodies move with speed.

Two tombs in this country graveyard,
And in the shade in the cool breeze
Two bodies lie together and
Gaze at the blue after their sneeze.

Two tombs side by side, two bodies
Not yet corpses, whose lungs still breathe
And revel in the cooling wind
That makes the nearby hedgerow seethe.

May 1991, revised 23 January 1994

SPARKLES IN AN INFINITE SEA

The pale sea sparkles at low tide,
The sun blinds in the curl of each wave
And I think of the sea of void it reflects
Beyond the pale sky, beyond the grave.

In this infinite sea our universe
Is a local event, and from sun in it
There is in us a sparkling out,
There is in us what is infinite.

I am a drop of a vast sea,
A gleam of light within its waves,
And stars and men shine from the beyond
And gleam in time which the eternal craves.

27 May 1991, revised 20 December 1993

RIPPLING ONE

A lake green with willow,
In the ripples below this seat
Ducks bob down, tails up, so
Carp swerve beside webbed feet.

Birdsong this midsummer's day:
Sedge warbler and blackbird flit
In this scented breeze and play
Where the roses toss and split.

467

Ducks and carp and shy birds
Share this green paradise
As do my willow words
Scenting bulrushes like spice.

My heart is a trembling harp,
The wind ripples a string
And greens ducks, birds and carp:
One rippling echoing.

26 June 1991

AT POLRUAN BLOCKHOUSE: SOUL AND BODY

Like a guard in this ruined blockhouse,
Looking out across the Renaissance bay,
Winching up a chain to stop all boats
And collect their tribute, and their pay –

Like a guard in these ruined stones,
Wandering from window to hearth,
Which he shares with the keen west wind
And the honeysuckle up the path,

I, my soul, in this ruined flesh
Like this butterfly, this herring gull,
Beating in these ruined bones and walls
Flutter in my imprisoning skull.

O flying soul, you are happiest
Out near this calm wide, sparkling sea
And long to escape this prison and know
The oneness known by a bumble-bee.

20 July 1991

AT GUNWALLOE: CALM AND SERENE

Rain spatters the windscreen but down by the
cove
All's calm, and dry, with patches of blue sky,
I cross wet sand to rocks where petrels rove,
Clamber along veined gold and not asking why
Listen to the sea boom into shore
And wash quietly near my feet; gaze at the
church
Which nuzzles against a hill, more hills
behind, for
No storms can touch my family as we perch.
All's calm without, and within I feel serene,
Sea, shore, farm-house, church, graves – all
life is here

As our souls gaze out from our bodies at this
treat,
On this paradise of shades of blue and green,
As our souls, fed by this wind, drink in this air,
As peaceful currents wash round my weary
feet.

22 July 1991

AT PORTHLEVEN

Across the granite harbour
A causeway of light, feel
From the pier the fisherman's joy
As he reels in a conger eel.

Across my soul I have
A causeway of sunshine
That jumps and sparkles like this
When I hang out my line.

22 July 1991, revised 29 November 1993

TALL-MASTED SHIPS AND WOODPECKERS

Two tall-masted ships in the harbour,
A two-masted brig on the sand,
Its hull being painted this low tide;
And a square rigger in the dock. And

Two green woodpeckers sit on the lawn
Of this pink house; green backs and tails,
Red striped heads and speckled bellies,
As rare as rigging and old furled sails.

Tall-masted ships and woodpeckers –
Both things that are now rarely seen;
They bring back a century ago
When trees meant decks and roads were green.
O mechanisation! Today,
Iron cargo boats and holds in foam
Preserve the woodland trees and rides
Where woodpeckers can nest and roam.

31 July 1991

REFLECTION AND REALITY: PEAK EXPERIENCES AND TIDAL CONSCIOUSNESS

I. QUESTIONING LEFT BRAIN'S INTENSE PEAKS

I walk up the private Cornish lane – no
gates –

To the kitchen where, in sailing dungarees,
A genius forks smoked salmon on two plates.
His bespectacled, welcoming smile puts me at
      ease.
Time has stood still, more than thirty years
      have passed
Since I first sat in this room on tenterhooks.
We again sip goblets of wine, and contrast
Husserl, Heidegger, Toynbee and our books.

I say his Outsider, who "sees too deep
And too much", develops from a bored sick
      ego   10
To a glimpse of the Fire which is behind
      Nature and peep-
-s through History when civilisations grow.
I tell him how the mystic Fire is known,
How in Japan's Zen temples they still the
      mind,
How you pass to beauty and in a trance, when
      shown,
Are filled with power from the beyond –
      behind.

He says, "It's mystic right brain, there's a
      split
Down the skull, and you pass from left to
      right."
"Mind may not depend on the brain, but may
      use it,"
I say, "brain may filter and limit mind –
      Bergson's insight."   20
"I agree, but am deeply suspicious of right
      brain," he
Says. "Your Fire, like wine, is pressure in the
      crown,
Pumping up the mind. There is a valve that
      can be
Regulated from left brain, up or down."

I say, "The vision of God is Fire from the
      beyond,
It is not pressure – a mechanism; the whole
Line of mystics, their heart stilled like a pond,
Saw a sun mirrored in their unrippled soul.
This sun that is seen is not the mechanism that
      sees, claim-
-ed William James; 'photism'." He says, "The
      intense or   30
Peak experience of the left brain is the aim.

Tolstoy's joy at two hussars. It can be in war.

"How do people escape partial consciousness,
      the stare
Of boredom and feeling futile, for their
      peaks?
That's what interests me, you may be only
      half way there."
"The Outsider," I say, "will find the Fire he
      seeks
In his soul." "Through left brain concentration
      he could,"
He says, "transcend everyday consciousness,
Feel an elation when social life seems good,
When self-observation and the valve say
      Yes.   40

"There are seven levels of consciousness:
Sleep; dream; the drowsy, half-awake; the
      driftwood
Sense that a material flux is meaningless,
The everyday; happiness that grasps all is
      good;
Ecstasy; and moments when time and space
      are gone,
Of revealed delight." "And the sense of
      cosmic one-
-ness, the Being mystics know," I say; "and
      the Fire beyon-
-d. The highest consciousness is of the unseen
      sun."

"We may have a problem of language," he
      says. "We may
Be closer than we seem. Often when writers
      talk   50
They don't make contact, like two passing
      trai-
-ns. It was the same when I met Toynbee and
      walk-
-ed with Camus. I said, 'Your reality is
Material, unlike Einstein's.' He indicate-
-d a Teddy Boy and said, 'My reality must be
      his.'
It could be that your Fire-vision is my level
      eight.

"My view is very simple. What do I do?
What gets us forward? Whitehead said
      movements,

Operations of thought, are like cavalry
    charges – too
Many and you lose the battle in the tents.   60
I cut through movements thus. Sartre's right
    brain
Depression entered his left brain and he wrote
La Nausée; I urge left brain to say 'All's well
    again'
So right brain glows – the new man's
    antidote.

"The new man is never depressed, he is
Interested in everything, each discipline,
And competent in all. Anyone who deems
    his
Positive qualities boring is living in
The old consciousness, bound by negative
    desire.
The new man can concentrate most of the
    day."   70
I know the new man is cleansed by the Fire
From beyond, like me, all depressions burned
    away.

"Intense experiences can be summoned at will
When left brain, optimistically, signals 'All's
    well'
And right brain responds with images" – and
    a thrill-
-ing tide of meaning filling the soul with its
    swell,
The imagination's crab-like memories
And impressions. Conscious opening of the
    lock-gate
To the vast, deep joy of intense awareness is:
"The next step in evolution – the willed peak
    state."   80

II. TIDAL RIGHT BRAIN

In Gorran Haven I wander in past desire.
Here, thirty years ago, I chose to withdraw
From the social round and return with Eastern
    Fire,
And I muse on the wall near the green cliffs,
    for
The paranormal's a right brain thing:
Precognition, telepathy, guidance received
From beyond, clairvoyance, distant healing –
Right brain's imaginings, extremes, should
    not always be believed.

I think of New Age livers who do not work,
Who spend all day in a Quietist trance   90
Glimpsing fragments of the future – a frown,
    a smirk –
And deciphering pain that comes through in
    advance,
Interpreting what project is at risk, gaz-
-ing at auras, crystals and devas, clairvoyantly
    peer-
-ing at fairies on daisies, and beings sending
    rays.
All rooms have a dark presence and
    atmosphere.

All is believed – spirits and chakras,
Dead Masters who send messages from above
    Tibet
To snow-capped Shambhala in the Himalayas
Where the Lords of all Mankind rule the
    planet.   100
All is in accordance with occult law
Which can be influenced by a candlelit rite.
Tarot and horoscopes are studied, for
Everything happens in a significant light.

Akashic records, psychometry (hold-
-ing a coin and seeing an ancient Egyptian
    market),
Setting up events on the astral plane, which
    unfold –
Everything is done with right energy, yet
With psychic correspondences; each
    coincidence
Within the plan has a foreordained mean- 110
-ing: dark presences and hauntings from a
    past existence,
Past life memories of when you were a
    Queen.

But then I think of the spirit the right brain
    plies.
I recall an Egyptian dancer, a vision in white,
Black hair, headband, and green malachite
    round eyes,
Raise slender fingers, flow with her arms, like
    light,
Open the doors of the centres, bring down
    Fire,
Energise her aura and, floating, pour it out;
Feel the tingling up your spine and the Light

470

desire,
And know we reflect each other – without
    doubt.   120

Over her head she brings down a pillar of
    light,
Sweeps down and with lotus fingers makes a
    cup,
Clasps it to her heart, then gives it to all in
    sight,
Pouring heart energy with her gift, then up
And scoops Light energy and pours it on her
    head
And presses her palms down over her arms,
    then
Turns and pours it out to the earth, cupped
    hands outspread –
One ba, ka and sahu, the soul is lit again.

The best of the right brain is this great calm
When, as before Zen silence in a stilled
    soul,   130
The Light prickles up my back and down each
    arm
And floods my heart and mind so I feel
    whole.
I sit on the wall and gaze at the yellow sand,
Then close my eyes and see the waiting Fire,
Relax as its brightness intensifies – aaaaah! –
    and
Then peek at the sea which reflects the
    quantum mire.

Now there is a dipped lock-gate to my right
    side.
My peak takes a mere two minutes. Like
    ancient seers
I can will my ego to receive the divine tide,
I turn to the harbour between my
    hemispheres.   140
I close my eyes, open my dry cortex and reach
Into right brain, see a dazzling sea and admire
Symbols, images, dreams which foam across
    my beach,
And, light jumping on their waves, receive –
    willed Fire.

I recall a dream. I was on a mountainside
In moonlight; beneath my feet from my great
    height

Rolling away, white clouds. It seemed with
    each stride
I went for a walk on the clouds. My Shadow
    in the moonlight
Lay beneath me on the clouds like Thor, and I
    saw
Twenty lines of verse, that I'd put on
    Angelhood.   150
I awoke with a start. It was half past four
And life had meaning, everything was good.

And I had a strong feeling that I had bro-
-ken through cloudy veils of earthly existence,
Transcended – come up beyond – the material
    below
To a summit view and a peak experience.
I knew "I exist therefore I am" and said Yes,
Knew "I have Being therefore I am" on this
    steep
Moonlit slope, and that I had glimpsed divine
    consciousness
In a high dream, left brain shut down in
    sleep.   160

III. SYNTHESIS OF LEFT AND RIGHT BRAIN CONSCIOUSNESS: INTENSITY REFLECTING AND REFLECTED IN SPIRITUAL AND DIVINE HARMONY

On Charlestown's harbour wall I now
    maintain
That there is a tidal order that the right brain
    knows
Which pours infused knowledge into the left
    brain;
The analytical half the sceptic shows.
I mull the lock-gate split that divides him and
    me.
My left brain ruminates on a symbol-tide,
And recollects in left's tranquillity
Imaged emotion received in the right sea side.

He sides with the social side of the lock-gate,
With the inner harbour, controlling left
    brain;   170
I with the outer harbour, the right brain's state
Which is closest to the universal sea, the main
That pours its living things from deepest
    night.
Yet the view from this harbour wall unites
    him and me:

The setting sun a fire on waves, a light,
And the peak of the Black Head's headland,
    proud and free.

Being pours into Existence in a glance.
The Humanist is and sees body and mind:
The social "harbour" of the Renaissance.
The Metaphysical sees beyond, behind   180
The lock-gate of five senses which blinds ego,
And is and sees spirit, the divine as well:
The outer harbour into which tides flow.
Is he a Metaphysical? Or a Humanist rebel?

The ego's consciousness can be a passive
    thing,
Or a grasping, prehensile "I"; linked with the
    soul
It reaches out with joy, seizes meaning
With energised perception that can be control-
-led, that flows into it when the brain is
    energised.
This should be normal consciousness – the
    everyday   190
With added tidal meaning, concentration
    vitalised,
A superconscious Yes when life's child's
    play.

Attention is thrown at the world like a
    mariner's rope
As a ship docks here in narrow Charlestown;
The consciousness that reaches and grasps
    with hope,
Intentional perception, as Husserl lays down.
Yet this meaning in the right brain floods with
    glee
And laps round the ego, which it never
    destroys.
Unless the lock-gate's always dipped there
    cannot be
A regular grasping of meaning, only
    occasional joys.   200

My purpose is a still in which the ego
(Left brain) opens like an inner harbour quay
To the tidal soul (right brain) and sees
    Oneness. I know
Left brain sees differences, right unity like a
    sea;
Left sees Existence, while right knows Being,

And beyond, closed to reason in mystery,
The ocean of Void and Fire that surrounds
    Nature, filling
The mind with waves of meaning and ecstasy.

The left brain, connecting with right, can see
Order and meaning in the dreary social
    fray.   210
Glimpses of joy are nudges that can be
Hints of the bliss ahead on the Mystic Way.
As I ruminate on the dark which mirrors the
    One,
I affirm, the peek at the Fire is the peakist's
    goal
And my consciousness will reflect the right
    brain's sun,
Reject extremes for a moderate left-right
    whole.

Reality manifests down like a widening spire;
Each level and section reflects the one above.
Existence reflects Being, the Void, the Fire,
And Being reflects the Void, corresponds to
    Its love.   220
The earthly Yang mirrors a Heavenly Yin;
As above, so below, like a branched, large-
    rooted tree.
The reflection and what reflects are reflected
    in
A mind which reflects the invisible quantum
    sea.

Mystics surrender their hearts to the Fire
    whereas
Occultists manipulate it with their will.
Existentialists and poets gaze at what has
Being, emphasise the Fire or intense thrill.
Metaphysicals and Humanists record each vibe
Of the harmonious consciousness they
    seek.   230
Metaphysical Existentialists describe
Optimistic visions of willed Fire and peak!

Now in twilit Charlestown a tranquil sea
Reflects the Black Head and each village
    light.
Metaphysicals and sceptics on the quay
Are one when the lock-gate is dipped between
    left and right.
Now the social and natural worlds of village

and peak
Are one with the divine flow of the sunlit
deep

And the still mind reflects Black Head and
creek
In a shimmering tidal wakefulness like
sleep.   240

7-13 August 1991, revised until 17th September 1991

SPRING, MONK

Sometimes I am tempted by a pampered life
In which I am just looked after; don't work,
Go to the beyond for images, my wife
Treating me as if I were ill, like a nurse with a
smirk,
Granting my whims, discussing what comes
through,
So that my real self is tended lovingly,
Not my persona. This can never ensue,
Can there be pampering in a monastery?
And so, faithful to my being's clear spring,
I turn away from the social round of mirth
To maintain its flow, so it goes on gushing,
Regularly poke and prod the blocking earth.
Only Spartan discipline and a monk's eye
Can guard my spring full time, like a vigilant
spy.

August 1991, revised 23 November 1993

A SHOOTING STAR
(OR: UNIVERSE: HOSTILE AND FRIENDLY)

It is the dog-days in the year,
See the Perseids, scan the night,
All's black and moonless, except for the stars –
So many thousands in an awesome sight.

I scan and stare and screw my eyes
And squint, but nothing unroutine.
Then suddenly, a finger moves down
The night sky, gone as soon as seen.

"A shooter" I say and my son says too.
Our words succeed it, it has expire-
-d, a meteorite that entered the earth's
Atmosphere and blazed a trail of fire.

I gaze at a universe in which
A tracer bullet may fire at me.

But peace! when, later, I close my eyes,
The Fire is gentle and friendly.

16 August 1991

CALVARY: A PURE BEING GOES UNDER THE EARTH
(In memory of Margaret Taylor)

I was choosing a birthday card in the cardshop
off
The High Road in March. I heard coughing.
You hung
On your husband's arm "Hello," I said,
"You've got a bad cough."
You said, "I've got a secondary in each lung,
I've just been in the London's terminal war-
-d. I wasn't supposed to know it was terminal
– then
Next week I begin a chemotherapy cour-
-se." You put your hand to your mouth and
coughed again.

I was shocked. I asked how your future would
be spent.
Your doctor husband said nothing. "I might   10
Turn it round," you said. "I've got to try. The
treatment
Will last until Christmas." I talked about your
fight.
You were optimistic but realistic. "I might die
By then," you laughed. I thought of you, a
nurse, how
You saw two women I knew through their
end. "How i-
-ronic," I said, "you're on the other side
now."

And so your Calvary began. The pillar of your
Church, you who organised the cleaning and
flower-rota,
Who scrubbed the floor under the crucifix,
and the door,
Now took up your cross and walked towards
Golgotha   20
Pretending you might get better, while the
coughing got worse.
You lost your job, they said you shouldn't
work as well
So you fretted at home, feeling a useless
nurse,

473

And you watched your life slip away as in a
    condemned cell.

In June you called without notice. I could
    have wept.
I was dictating, I set the typist work. We sat
In the window, near the grounds you dug and
    kept
And a skull, you cough-cough-coughed your
    way through our defiant chat
About your future, gasping for breath on
Occasions. You looked so frail, and seeing
    your wreath –   30
Your shrubs outside the window – I thought
    of Tennyson,
"Man comes and tills the field and lies
    beneath."

In August your husband broke the news, my
    wife cried.
You couldn't breathe on a Friday, and were
    soon in
Whipps, where you sat in your bed with your
    cross and your pride
And directed the nurses: "I want heroin
Twice a day, and a drip that works." On
    Saturday night
You got worse and told a consultant "I'm
    dying." You knew.
"She's not actually," he said, but you were
    right –
On Sunday morning you had gone, your
    family round you.   40

Your agony over, I sat in Christ Church, your
Coffin on a trestle, a congregation in tears.
"Forty-eight," the vicar said, and as the mour-
-ners carried you out to the hearse, o the lost
    years.
I followed the cortège to the cemetery. At
The grave I stood as your bones were lowered
    in
Straps, your family round the hole. I knelt and
    scatt-
-ered a handful of dusty earth on the flowers
    on your coffin.

Now it's over, and you are alone in the earth
And I am here by the sea, enjoying the sun, I
    wonder   50

Why you, a nurse, who lived healthily from
    birth,
Who never smoked, were visited with lung
    cancer,
You who served others and were an angel
    down here.
Acceptance of suffering ennobles and
    dignifie-
-s. You accepted it and wore it like a gift.
    Where
You did not ask "Why me" I can't ask "Why?'

I think of others who have walked to their
    Calvary,
At home, in hospitals, before firing-squads
    each day.
And I think of the human condition, man is
    born to be
A victim, to suffer and go into the clay.   60
Life-death, positive and negative energy fill
The universe, which runs off zero energy . It-
-s positive breath is cancelled by death's still.
But the real you has survived, your soul and
    spirit.

The soul is immortal, a droplet from the
    divine
Ocean of cosmic energy, the void from which
    Be-
-ing manifests, the quantum Void in which
    spirits shine,
Your soul has returned to Being's great sea.
You are a wave in it now, and exist more
    purely than in air –
Than here. You have discarded your lower
    body. I am sure,   70
Now there is no coughing to impede your
    prayer,
You are being – spirit – in the Heavenly void
    where Being is pure.

16-17 August 1991

SMEATON'S TOWER AND WESTERN CIVILISATION

"Except the Lord Builds the House They Labour in
Vain That Build it."
    (*Psalm* CXXVII, Inscription in Smeaton's Tower)

From Plymouth Hoe a tranquil sea,

In the blue sky a dazzling sun,
Like Drake I finish my game of bowls
Before I make the Armada run.

Drake waited for the tide to turn,
His piracy had provoked Spain,
His coolness hid self-assertion
And an Empire built on the pirates' main.

Now I climb Smeaton's 18th Century Tower,
Ninety-three spiral steps to a glass box   10
Where twenty-four candles shone to ships
In Victorian times from the Eddystone
        Rocks.

Each stone was measured exactly
And rowed fourteen miles out to the light
And winched into place with pulleys
So it fitted exactly in breadth and height.

And when it was later replaced
The light was dismantled stone by stone
And re-assembled, in a perfect fit,
Here on Plymouth Hoe to be wind-blown.   20

Hail engineer Smeaton's precision –
Now a war time spitfire loops its loop,
Diving down over Drake's Island,
Dipping its wing to the Tower in a swoop.

In our civilisation great events
Are not forgotten, are like a shrine.
They shine like the light on a lighthouse,
A cool response, an exact design.

A civilisation is a spiral
With a staircase like Smeaton's Tower,   30
Its base is in a Golden Age,
A Light shining through its sea power.

On Smeaton's Tower an inscription reads
"Except the Lord Build the House They
Labour in Vain that Build it." Our
Light-based civilisation was built this way.

Our civilisation once carried a Light
But now, like Smeaton's empty Tower,
Its glass chamber stands empty
And the Lord who built does not light the
        hour.   40

Will no one relight the lamp that lit
Our civilisation in its Victorian time?
We need to restore its tallow candles
And learn the lesson of Smeaton's spiral
        climb.

17 August 1991(?)

BUMBLE-BEE: CORRESPONDENCE

A bumble-bee in the thistles
As I sunbathed by the flowerbed:
It crawled in some purple spikes,
Flew onto the next one's head.

I watched it for ten minutes,
Back and forth it joyfully went.
When there were no more it flew
To where the bellbind leant.

Somewhere there is a garden
Where souls crawl in flowers,   10
Like bumble-bees with pouches,
Bring pollen from the hours.

Even now I am a soul,
And collect beauty's nectar
From petalled mystic moments,
And crawl in a woman's anther-

-s: I go from mystic moment
to moment, from hour to hour:
I go from time to thyme
As the bee goes from flower to flower.   20

O bumble-bee in my garden,
You are an image of me,
My Fire-Flower is like your flowers,
There's a correspondence in our glee.

18 August 1991

POLKERRIS-KERRIS

Drive down the narrow lane
Past the studio to the sea,
Gaze at the tiny harbour,
Then enter the Rashleigh.

The artist stands by the door
Finishing his lunchtime beer,
Half-listening to a stutterer
Who grins from ear to ear.

His work is round the walls.
Tousle-haired with vacant eyes,   10
He is mindless while he rests
His creative powers, and skies.

I chat to him and observe
His paint-stained sweater and jeans.
Now the artist has gone
Back to his studio scenes.

The artist loves Nature's colours,
He lives to reflect a storm
Which he has observed with care
And has lovingly put into form.   20

The artist has sharp vision,
Observation that is precise,
And he sells his careful work,
Feeds body *and* soul with his price.

20 August 1991

LYONESSE: BEING LIKE SUBMERGED LAND

O see how the Scilly Isles
St. Mary's and Tresco call
That they are separate, see how
The sea is between them all.

Each island is a peak
Of the lost land of Lyonesse
Which according to legend was drowned
By a rising sea and distress.

Each island is separated
By thirty foot of water. Then   10
Remove the water between
And all are connected again.

So it is with people,
They all seem separate, apart;
Remove the space between,
They are connected in their heart.

Bodies have hard outsides.
Auras are like a cloud.
But there's an invisible being
That joins together a crowd.   20

The sea of material space
Divides our hard heads, and

Our hearts are all connected
In this submerged land.

21 August 1991

SHADOW ON THE CLIFF

At midnight a boat approaches
This Charlestown harbour wall.
The crew were asleep offshore,
Were woken by the pilot's call.

The arc lights shine across
This crowded harbour dock
And I see my shadow
Reflected on the Battery rock.

As I walk along the wall
My shadow traverses the cliff
And spellbound, I raise an arm;
It gives me a wave that is stiff.

The arc light throws a relief
Of a Shadow for all to see.
But all are watching the boat,
Their attention is on the quay.

21 August 1991?

NIGHT WINDS: DOZING

A night wind has got up,
Great waves tear in, rolling,
White breakers at low tide,
A south-westerly blustering.

The wind moans in the chimney
And roars round the harbour wall,
It rattles the window frames
And knocks at the door to the hall.

A storm is brewing tonight,
The air whistles with distress.
I sit and listen to each sound
As my eyes droop with tiredness.

The wind that brings the storm
Is the wind that begins the calm.
After days of peace and quiet
How nice to doze through harm.

21 August 1991

CATHEDRAL

As the train approached Tresco –

The city lights in the night,
And the great floodlit Cathedral,
Two towers ablaze with light.

It towered above the city,
It towered above the lights
Showing its sometime stature
Above all medieval sites.

The height of a Cathedral
Means little beside a tank;
The Church's declining stature
Puts a Cathedral alongside a bank.

The height of a Cathedral
Meant stature long ago.
Today many would build it
As low as a bank, and more low.

21 August 1991

GULLS: A CLOUD OF BEING

The passenger boat dips on,
Spray flicks up on the top deck.
It rolls on the Atlantic swell,
Wind tugs my hair and neck.

Above my head two dozen
Herring gulls with superb control,
Hover with outstretched wings,
Motionless as we move and roll,

Hang in the buffeting wind,
Waiting for some thrown meat,   10
Following the back of this boat,
Group soul at work as they eat.

The gulls caw and hang still,
Pink legs out straight behind,
They ride the wind and swerve,
Do not collide, though blind.

Now they swoop and flap and screech,
Catch bread on the wing, and take
It from hands in yellow beaks,
And compete in the wake.   20

We pass the whistling buoy.
It rings its tide-rung bell.
The red ensign flag droops,
Proof that the wind just fell.

These gulls follow like souls
That have come back off Land's End –
Like souls of the recently dead
To be fed by a long lost friend.

O gulls who float on wind
And fly beside dipping boats,   30
You are visible grey and white
Of a cloud of being that floats.

21 August 1991

LEPERS' ABBEY

We lunched in St. Benet's Abbey,
Built from fourteen eleven
As a lazar house for lepers –
As a hospital and chapel then.

The chapel Tower survives,
The bog garden and waterfall.
The stone cross at the front
Marks the Saints' Way wall.

O Benedictine monks,
O lepers from the Saints' Way –   10
I feel your presence is here
As if it were yesterday.

I sense you by the stone walls,
I see you drink from the stream –
You who are now mere souls
And I will join your sunbeam.

Today there are no lepers here
But we are leprous within –
O for a lazaret to bring fire
To all leprous with sin.   20

22 August 1991?

THE UNIVERSE IN MOTION, AND A STILL

The sea is green and choppy,
White seahorses toss their manes,
They dash on Gull Island,
Flick spray over rocks and brains.

The universe is in motion,
It dips and rears its will,
It rushes and flows and changes –
Yet behind it all there's a still.

22 August 1991

LIGHTNING OVER THE SEA

The black sea comes in in white ribbons
And out across the bay
A dark cloud hides the moon –
A flash as bright as day.

The distant thunder rolls,
The first lashing of rain.
I turn and head for home
In a universe of pain.

The indifferent universe
Communicates in fire,
It speaks in thunderbolts
Or the light of inner desire.

22 August 1991

A GOLD BEING, GLOWING

A round moon in the night sky
As bright as a glowing lamp,
And a sea with silver patches
Like ice that has cracked and is damp.

And down in a rock-pool
Below this harbour wall,
A well with liquid gold
Near the tin mine's entrance hall.

The brilliant moon above
And the reflected moon below
And the sparkling silver waves
Make my gold being glow.

23 August 1991

AT THE BALLOWALL BARROW

Ballowall barrow is on a cliff
Near a tin-mine chimney stack,
Overlooking Longships lighthouse,
Its entrance ringed by brack-

-en. Inside this dry-stone vault several
Bronze Age men lay in rooms,
This grave is as old as the Trojan War
From an age known through its tombs.

Now down at Cape Cornwall the sea
Boils and surges with spray;
Down here there is life, but up there death
Is three thousand years away.

23 August 1991

DANDELION

I sit between Cape Cornwall and Land's
        End
In a cove opposite the Brisons rocks,
With rugged cliffs and granite boulders,
Green turf and a bubbling stream that shocks.

The wind tears in, the Atlantic waves –
Dash round the Brisons Rocks and fling.
The green-grey sea with white breakers
Boils round the shingle shore, booming.

The wind blows flowers on these granite
        rocks,
As the sea froths in the surf boils on;
I, emptied of all self, blow in
The wind like a cliffside dandelion.

23 August 1991

MERMAID OF ZENNOR

Enter St. Senara's old church
In Zennor's rural street,
See the nude medieval mermaid
Carved on the side of a wooden seat.

Long tresses cover her bare arms,
She has no breasts that I can see,
She kneels with a pure fish's scales
And fins where her nether parts should be.

Half woman, half fish she is Christ
Who was half man and half divine
(Or Christian fish). Her two natures
Recall his two natures that shine.

She holds a quince, or love apple
Like Aphrodite, and a comb for her tress-
-es. The quince has become a mirror
Of vanity and heartlessnesses.

This mixture of love and nude scorn,
Of Aphrodite and Jesus
Are both in this kneeling mermaid
Who is human-divine like us.

23 August 1991

ANCIENT VILLAGE: OUR SKILLED TIN-PANNING ANCESTORS

Walk round Chysauster village

On a hill overlooking the sea,
See Roman Britons' houses,
Stone walls built carefully,

Thatched rooms round a paved courtyard,
Cultivated plot beside –
Here round the time of Christ
Our ancestors stood in pride.

Each courtyard house has a stone
Socket for a timber upri-   10
-ght. And water channels with slabs
Kept the unroofed courtyard dry.

Weaving and grinding corn,
Farming with cows and sheep,
They tin-panned in a nearby stream,
Sold the Romans tin that was cheap.

Now all is grassed, and quiet,
The bouldered stone walls survive
And the heather covers where
Our skilled ancestors loved to strive.   20
                                    23 August 1991

A MOON WITH A HALO

A misty night from the sea,
The moon has a halo,
Its aura shines on the bay,
Bathing all in a faint glow.

A hard night's work for me;
Now I have a moon in my soul.
Its aura shines in this room,
Unifying all in a whole.
                                    24 August 1991

CLEANSED SENSES AND
A TINKLING, RUSTLING
GREEN

The running water tinkles
And splashes with a clearness,
As I write, my clothing rustles;
My washed-out ears hear Yes.

O the clear sounds and sights
When the five senses are clean!
Open washed eyes to the Heaven
Which tinkles through all that's green.
                                    27 August 1991

ETERNITY

As far as the eye can see
The waves glint in the sun
Like a thousand fish surfacing
And winking in their fun.

This winking sea and fins
As I screw up my eyes,
This blinding jubilation,
Is like angels at sunrise.

For miles this calm, calm sea
Leaps with bright angels' wings
As Eternity cavorts
On the surface of things.
                                    August 1991

MECHANISED MOTION AND
NATURE

The orange street-light is still on
Although the day is in.
A tiny shrew with a pointed snout
Lies crushed by men with skin.

Last night is passed, the revellers gone;
Can this late street light recall
The dark loud music from the car
And this shrew's twitching sprawl?

The fishermen loll outside the hotel,
Fold hands and bend their heads
Indifferent to the wheel that crushed
This creature with its treads.
                                    21 September 1991

FIRE WITHIN THE GLOBE

The fields are full of fire
As tiny men burn stubble
Smoke on the motorway –
We crawl out of trouble.

Two balloons over the fields;
Under one a fire like a light.
It burns near a crimson sun
And improves its floating height.

The fire in the fields and air
And the fire in my soul
Are like the setting sun,
As red as a rose in a bowl   *21 September 1991*

HARVEST MOON AND A CHEER

High in the night a harvest moon
Glows and flecks the sea at low tide,
Silhouettes the Battery cliff
And paints with magic the dark hillside.

Alone, I walk the village ways
And stalk along the moonlit pier
And gaze out to sea past dancing waves
And thrill as the universe gives a cheer.

21 September 1991

IMAGE AND REALITY: STREET-LAMP AND SUN IN MIST

A morning mist and a calm sea,
The orange street lamp hangs,
And on the horizon an orange line
Where the invisible sun harangues.

A morning mist within my mind
Where an orange street lamp shines
And on my horizon, where is the line
Where a hidden sun inclines?

21 September 1991

WAR AND PEACE

Ah the multitude
In this Ambresbury breeze,
The ghosts prepare for battle
Flitting in the trees.

Ah the war work
Near Ambresbury Banks,
Digging by the roadside
Traps for Nazi tanks.

Now I wander
Peaceful as blown down
From a roadside thistle
That scorns the town.

AT KABUKI: THE FLOWER OF CULTURE

A culture grows perfection like a flower.
See kabuki – see the musicians sit, three-
Stringed samisens, shoulder and stick drums'
    power
And flute, see snow fall near a willow-
    tree,

See the great Tamasaburo extend his hands
As the heron-girl, dying of lost love,
    glad.
It is easier to scoop water from her bag as she
    stands
Than seize her lover's heart, and she is sad.

Now see the vision of Yin and Yang.
Now see her glide, now stamp her feet to
    scare –   10
To the shoulder drum's tap, stick drum's
    active bang –
Off evil spirits like a Buddhist prayer.
Now see her lean back, head touching the
    ground,
Hold the pose, bent like a supple bow, and
    pause:
The flower, the perfection held for a moment,
    found,
Peeps through before the tumultuous
    applause.

Here is beauty that fills the eyes with tears,
And breathless attention on each move she
    makes.
She weakens in the falling snow, it sears,
The perfection wilts as the flute wails and
    aches   20
That a heron-girl's heart, like a dew-drenched
    flower, must go.
Now see as she swoons and totters and
    falls
And lies in a crumpled heap in the drifting
    snow.
Eyes mist as all clap through ten curtain calls.

5 October 1991, revised 29 November 1993

FLOWER

(YUGEN)

The peonies are in bloom and butter-
    flies
Dart round her coiffeured hair and lovely
    smile.
She shields her eyes with her bright fan to
    view
Flowers in their perfect moment, for a while.

Before summer breeze blows in the willow-
    tree
The butterflies must perish, and her gaze,

480

And the peonies will wither by autumn
But the Flower of this moment will last
    always.
5 October 1991, revised 29 November 1993

CHILDREN LIKE FRUIT

School Harvest Festival.
Amid good things with grain and root
The Deaconess holds up, displays,
A wooden box of rotten fruit:

Black bananas, rotten apples
Squashy peaches – children say "Urrr."
"We are all like apples and pears,
We can grow into good or squashy fur."

Now she offers the harvest to God.
I, in God's place, look down upon
Faces like fruit, with souls like seed
That peep through eyes and then are gone.

And I see each child as a growing soul
Who can grow to bad or good today,
And I hope, like God, that all turn ripe
And that none has to be thrown away.
31 October 1991, revised 13 December 1993

COPPER BEECH:
FOUNTAIN AND FIRE

The copper beech still fountains down
This early November morning.
Leaves yellow-orange, like droplets,
Cascade and tumble with much foaming.

The copper beech curls like a fire
Licking, flickering as it dies down,
Blazing downwards in a glory
Consuming in gold orange-brown.

The copper beech will soon not pour,
Its copper flames will soon be out
But within my soul it will foam on,
A fire that knows no fall or doubt.
November 1991, revised 13 December 1993

THE DIVINE BREATH

I am the wind that blows through the trees,
That whistles through the grass,
I am the wind that ruffles the seas
And blows on the mountain pass,

The breeze that lulls the woods to dreams,
That blows on the mountain sides:
I am the breeze that ripples streams
And turns with the turning tides.

I am the breath that stirs each lung
So humans are, and are past.
I am the breath that moves each tongue
As a man expires his last.

I am what I am, and though sensed in storms,
Am the unknowable unsaid,
I am in all living things, all forms.
I am when all things are dead.
1 January 1992

WE TWO ARE CLOUDS

As a cloud merges with air
Against a deep blue sky,
And what seems a white edge
Is a perceptive lie,

As a body merges with air
Between self and bodies and trees
And what seems a boundary,
What the corporal eye sees

Is really a cloudy aura
That floats all round the skin,   10
And our organs of perception
Atrophied, buried in

Five senses, so we two
Are clouds, and when we come
Together we two are one
Cloud as our auras thrum.

And great is the lightning flash
As our clouds collide and bruise
And great the electric thunder
As our cloudy beings fuse!   20

One day we will vanish
Like clouds into sky, and where
Was the space we occupied
When our clouds have become air?
February 1992

TWO CLOUDS

We two in borderless clouds

From a vacuum like a fog;
When we collide and flash
We burn and pour and jog.

We lie within each other
As two clouds who have met
And we are one with all,
And fill all dry and wet.

9 February 1992

FULL MOON

The moon is full above the sea
And gleams in each curled wave
Which ripples light towards the shore,
Each decade towards the grave.

The Light shines down on history
And gleams in ten movements
Which bring light rippling in with time,
A pattern of spent events.

The full moon silvers in soft light
A shadow on the wall
On which light that hurries through space
Pours knowledge of the All.

My Shadow strolls along this pier
Within a curling wave
But fades from view when it washes within
A cliff-hewn tin-mine cave

16 February 1992

ORANGE TREE

By my gate in Libya stood
A dazzling orange tree;
Among its green leaves hung
Oranges for all to see.

So in my scribblings stands
A tree of images where
Among leafy sentences
Symbols like oranges flare.

Both orange and symbol
Are ripened by a sun
And compared to its glow
Reflect their growth from its One.

Ripe orange and symbol
Shine out and say to all

That they are shaped like their sun:
A flaming orange ball.

17 February 1992

AN OLD CORNISH LADY GLIMPSES REALITY

A week you have lain in a coma,
Strokes on both sides of your brain,
Each breath rattling with pneumonia,
And now, at last – no more pain.

I watch the news and ponder
Those you'll meet on the angelic stair:
Sheikh Musawi of Hezbollah,
And four IRA men who glare.

Drowned lifeboatmen await you
Where Charon puts you down:
You'll complain about the riff-raff
Hanging around that crystal town.

And you'll gossip about our village
With all who've gone before,
And sit on your wooden porch seat
And gaze at the sea from your door.

Your dour, basic life is over,
Your pension does not matter now
As you see at the end of the tunnel
The light between each eyebrow.

17 February 1992

RAINBOW

A rainbow in the sky
And fine rain on my face
And a sea mist creeps in
So appearances are space.

Half a rainbow in my mind
From on high down to my head
And the real crock of gold
We can find before we're dead.

The rainbow comes and goes,
Manifests and disappears,
As nothing takes a shape,
A vision behind the years.

A rainbow is an arch
That bridges heaven and earth

And connects my sea-wet cheeks
To an unseen world of worth

18 February 1992

REFLECTION AND REALITY
From this dark harbour wall
In a rock pool nearby
A round cold yellow ball –
Horus' reflected eye.

And high in the night sky
Above the copying beach
Re's round cold yellow moon –
The real beyond all speech.

The rock pool is now dark
A cloud covers the moon,
The real and its reflection
Are one in a dark dune.

19 February 1992

BARE TREE
As I walked for the papers
In a winter morning's cold
I stopped at a fire-shaped tree –
No leaf or crackling gold.

And in its thick twigs sat
Four fat sparrow-like birds,
No shelter from the sea-wind,
No fruit, like starving Kurds.

I walked on for the news
Of our recession. God care-
-s for birds and humans who perch
In a fire-shaped place that is bare!

19 February 1992

SEPARATE CLOUDS
We are two clouds. We too
Move our cloudy edges proud-
-ly into each other and merge
So we become one cloud.

What lightning as we bounce,
Thunder as we collide,
Wrapped in each other's arms,
Our cloudy beings inside.

Now we are separate clouds

Drifting through airy void,
And I am beyond desire
And beyond what I enjoyed.

24 February 1992

TUBE
I sit under Oxford Circus.
Across the tube line – herds,
A safari under Kilimanijaro,
Of buffalo, great birds.

And I have a thumping headache
From tramping to Harley Street
And the stop in the café was wasted,
My head is as sore as my feet.

With a rattle of lines and a roar
The tube rushes in on its beam.
I begin my whine through my landscape,
Africa remains a dream.

SNOWDROP DROOPING
The snowdrop droops
Its head to the ground
But bustling by
I cannot watch;

Planning, solving
I am busy
And can't linger
By a snowdrop's head.

When I retire
Will other things
Take me away
From Nature's stealth?

7 March 1992

SUNLIGHT
Last night, black sky and stars
Over a moonless sea,
Bright and twinkling fires,
Between vast space and me.

And now a glorious day
I walk in dazzling sun
To the sea's gold causeway,
All Nature bobs with fun.

Men wave, basking in light

A reflection shimmers on
The old stone harbour wall,
I too reflect what I'm shone.

3 April 1992

MYSTERY

Over the April sea
A pitch-black night
And a towering tree
Twinkling white.

Why should space hang, stars fizz,
Milky Way be?
The mystery that it is
Amazes me.

4 April 1992

STEPPING-STONES

Walk on the stepping-stones
In this churchyard, behave.
If you wander to one side
You will stand across my grave.

Walk quietly on these stones,
My tired bones lie below.
This stained glass window shines
Like my soul when aglow.

Walk softly on these stones
So my poor skull can hear
The handbells ring out and
The congregation's cheer.

13 July 1992

GIG-RACING

We stand on Porthleven pier.
Ten gigs on a heavy swell,
Low Viking boats with crews
Who pull on the oars. We yell

As they race towards misty buoys,
Now specks, now out of sight.
We wait twenty minutes
And squint for blobs of light.

Now they approach from the cliffs.
We cheer "Come on", call down.
The first home is not ours,

The Mystery from Charlestown.

Each crew slumps on its oars,
Raises three cheers for the rest.
I turn away and love
The mist, the cliffs, their zest.

9 August 1992

THE ONE AND THE MANY

"The One remains, the many change and pass....
Life, like a dome of many coloured glass
Stains the white radiance of Eternity"

Shelley

A late night walk. The moon is full
Beside the cliff with a sloping side
That joins the dark sea and curves back
Where its black shadows lap with the tide.

Transfixed on the pier, I stare, I stare
As the moon-like One manifests through
space
Into the Being of a silhouette
And its reflection in existing place.

Transfixed on the pier, I gaze, I gaze
At a moonlit void where – mystery! – lurks
A sloping Being and its shadow,
I gaze at how the universe works.

A late night walk, and a spring in my step
As I tread the granite back to my home
And sit agog that the One has shone
Into sloping things that have stained it with
foam.

9 August 1992

MOON AND TIDE

I walk at night on the harbour wall.
The full moon shimmers out
On the distant calm, but the beach is dark
As if covered with doubt.

A few paces on and in the rock pool
An orb of dazzling white;
A few paces and a conger eel
Of wriggling, shimmering light.

So it is in my mind, there is a dark beach,

484

White pool and a bright splurge.
Each change is a shift in perspective,
Each step makes light emerge.

So it is in my mind, there is a moon
That draws the tides of thought
From dark to still to energy
The reflecting soul has caught.

10 August 1992

HOODED FALCON

Four chained and hungry, squawking birds –
Eagle, kestrel, two Harris hawks –
And a hooded peregrine falcon,
So still where a snowy owl stalks.

Now the eagle glides with outspread wings
And swoops for prey on a gloved hand
And gulps raw meat, then flaps and soars
Into an oak and scans the land.

The eagle, buzzard and hawks fly
But the falcon stays on its perch,   10
Hooded, not alarmed by movements,
At peace in the general food search.

The display is over, I now stand
And gaze at the still falcon, and know
The red flap blinkers that close eyes
So the soul can feel at peace, and glow.

The poet is like a bird of prey,
He hunts images on the wing
And cruelly swoops on quarry, then
Sits and reflects, like a hooded thing.   20

11 August 1992

STILL AND MOVING: MOON AND EYES

Gig-racing off the harbour where
A crowd mills round small stalls;
An old tall-masted ship sails in
And bobs as twilight falls.

I watch from a chair by our front door,
Turn and gasp with surprise –
The moon is huge and still and round,
A mystery to moving eyes.

I turn binoculars onto it

And breathless, amazed, see
Mountains that look like Africa
And Asia, shadowy.

The moon hangs over silvery waves.
How still it is up there
While it whirls round the moving earth
And my still, yet moving stare.

14 August 1992

YOUNG AND OLD: NOISE AND STEALTH

Summer evening by the harbour.
As twilight creeps like doubt
Young bloods in wet suits jump and splash
And laugh and chat and shout.

Summer evening by the harbour.
As twilight makes its raid
The old sit in their porched doorways
And watch the sunset fade.

Summer evening by the harbour.
The local young blood's yells
As they push each other and have fun
Ring in old ears like bells.

15 August 1992

WHAT IF GRAVITY SNAPPED?

I poise on the springboard pier;
The Milky Way below
In the silver moonlight
Is like the sea, in flow.

And what if gravity snapped?
And, headlong, I dived out,
Plunged towards that rippling space,
Towards stars, like rocks, with a shout?

I stand on the moonlit pier,
My feet tugged, ankles bound,
And thank the invisible force
That holds my being on ground.

18 August 1992

A FLIRTATION WITH THE MUSE

1992-1993

CHRISTINE CARPENTER TO THE WORLD

I have an invisible body
Within the flesh in my dress
And in it I love the Light,
And so will to live in darkness,

And so have been walled up,
Squat in the dark and peer
Through the quatrefoil and squint
Into the church, or just hear.

I am removed from the world,
My flesh from the Devil's bite.
I can close my eyes in this dark
And look for ethereal light.

I live in its sunless ray,
I swoon in its joyous beam;
But how I wish I could go
Past the pillory down to the stream

And lean on the bridge in the sun,
See it leap from the ripples, at play,
And the smile in a young man's eye
As he gallants his maid with may.

1992(?), revised 25 January 1994

THE ARTIST, ENCLOSED

Again I stand in Shere
And see the quatrefoil
In the old church wall where
A nun was a gargoyle.

She chose to be walled in
But then broke out, elope-
-d and was enclosed again
At the will of an Avignon Pope.

O Christine Carpenter,
I know your choice between
Your vow and the sensual life –
Art and the Magdelene.

I know one who would break out
Of her enclosing art,
Just as I made my vow
To work with a disciplined heart.

O Christine Carpenter,
Artists wall themselves in
And break out now and again.
And then work off their "sin".

27 August 1992

HESITATION

A cornfield and crossroads
And a funereal sky
And fields of drooping wheat
As a corn bunting hops by.

A crossroads in the rain.
Which straight road should one take?
The ears of wheat are ripe,
A longing makes me ache.

Parked here in this open plain,
Should we get out and lie
In the storm-beaten corn
And love limbs that will die?

A crossroads in the rain,
Hesitation in the wind
And flesh that heals and loves
Stares like a soul that has sinned.

Drive back to the noisy road,
An opportunity missed,
And the wheat and the wind whisper
Like lips that have been kissed.

27 August 1992

ANTICIPATION AND REGRET

A railway station,
A maze of tracks and wires,
Mad urban to and fro
Of time, haste and desires.

A railway station
Where people rendezvous,
Come from their private lives
And eat and talk and woo.

A railway station
Of impersonal steel,
And where is the soul that waits?
At the other entrance? Feel

Anticipation as
You see her cross the street.
But o the regret when
She leaves with dragging feet.

A railway station,
Anticipation, then
Discovery and love,
Till regret flits like a wren.

All artists are alive,
And risk all pain and dread,
And shun the safe lone lives
Of the emotionally dead.

27 August 1992

QUATREFOIL: MIRROR IMAGES

Look in the quatrefoil
Shaped like a clover leaf
Or a bad luck Christian cross,
At the rubble within the belief.

Bourgeois peer down the squint
To where an anchoress fell,
Unaware that our decay
Filled in her hermit's cell.

Look in the quatrefoil,
And see the haunted eyes
Squint back, and know at once,
With a shock that is half surprise,

That they are yours, and mine,
And peer from a walled-in heart.
We are mirror images
Enclosed in our art, apart.

27 August 1992

STEPPING-STONES

Stepping-stones in the Mole,
Each round as a millstone.
Jump off the bank your side
And wait as the waters moan.

Stepping-stones that are still
As the river rushes past,
Come across to me, my love,
Skip across the stones, skip fast.

Stepping-stones to be crossed
And you wait on the first
Hesitant like a child
Afraid the next will burst.

These solid stepping-stones
Will take your weight, my Muse,
So come across at once.
Do not be afraid to choose.

27 August 92

HEALING MUSE

Heal me with soft fingers
And soothe away all strain.
Let warmth from your being
Pour into my poor brain.

My Muse, pour images in;
One hand above my head
And one behind my neck –
Beam energy from the dead,

Inspire me with your lips,
Brush softly against mine,
Channel images within
My delicate, tender spine.

Do not be deaf to my prayers
Even though your tinnitus yells,
But inspire in me the sound
Of gently tinkling bells.

27 August 1992

A FREE SPIRIT

How strong you seem to be,
Alone with your art;
How free you want to be,
To paint your heart.

We both portray the truth
Of the universe,
We both sketch an order
Beyond the hearse.

O Muse, when you choose one
Weaker than you,
You despise him and want
One strong and true.

How strong you seem to be,
Apart, above;
How free you want to be
Within strong love!

27 August 1992

WIND

The wind is whistling
And howling with moaning rain,
Now the wind is whining
And wailing in my brain.

The wind is echoing
Like a shrill woodwind pipe;
The wind is as ghostly as
A fading daguerreotype.

O wind, you bellow in
The breath in my lungs
That breathes in images
And moves a thousand tongues.

O wind, you are so sad.
O why do you inspire
A heaviness in me
Like unfulfilled desire?

27 August 1992

TIME AND THE TIMELESS

South London: tower blocks,
Fly-overs, traffic lights,
A mesh of railway lines,
Chimneys and building-sites.

The Surrey countryside:
Timber frame, Tudor bays,
Cottage, farmhouse and barn
Along Merrie England's ways.

I live in a tension
Between this new and old.
Everywhere I observe
A conflict that leaves me cold.

The concrete that renews
Is judged by ten thousand rays,
And o the juxtaposition
As a civilisation decays

28 August 1992

TIN-MINE NEAR LAND'S END

A tin-mine on rock cliffs,
Dusk at Land's End.
A chimney like a tombstone
Where bones descend.

A shaft where tin was mined,
Ores from the earth,
Gleaming in shiny rock
Where ideas have birth.

I mine my unconscious for
Images of tin,
Until, as in a tomb,
I am buried therein.

29 August 1992

RISING SOULS

Tower blocks and the UN
And a demonstrating crowd,
Rays ascend and descend
Between faces and a cloud.

Tower blocks and the UN
And universal souls
Whose divine sparks are fanned
And glow like glowing coals.

Mouldering masonry,
Science's progress decays
And o, the redemption
Of souls rising on rays.

29 August 1992

COLLAPSE OF PROGRESS

St. Mark's lion on a pillar
And a thinner column – today's –
Of concrete near rubble
As the new world decays.

Tower blocks, station girders –
Can progress end in this
Rubble of concrete beams,
Are we on a precipice?

Winged lion on a pillar
Judges what we have built,
And the disintegrating
Collapse of each concrete stilt.

29 August 1992

MY MUSE

My Muse has come today,
I held her close and we
Entwined, I coaxed an image
As she inspired me.

I kissed her beautiful eyes,
She told me that I should
Be a follower of
Beauty, like Plato's Good.

I flattered my divine Muse
For her divine knowledge. She gasped.
I soothed her delicate lips
And stroked her brow, and grasped

That Beauty manifests
From within to the outer face
As one unified being,
An inner, outer grace.

She left me alone again,
Sighing "Boys will be boys"
And I returned to my work,
To the world's trundling noise.

29 August 1992

LOVE AND DEATH

Under this skull I loved.
You kissed me with your tongue
And now that you have gone –
A heaviness in each lung.

Dark, it all seems dark,
And sombre as this night.
I gaze at the universe,
And cannot see any light.

Tutankhamun looks back
With pupil-less, blank eyes.
But in the dark – what art! –
Pupils from blank arise.

What craftsmanship in wood –
Thirteen sixty BC,
Soon after Aton's rays
Whose hands gave eternity.

Outside it is all dark,
I gaze at the universe
With eyes that have pupils, and
Carve love and death in verse!

29 August 1992

MY MUSE, GONE

My Muse has left me but
Our souls are joined by thread,
A line of light that tugs
At the heart that would be dead.

My Muse has left me and
As we are out of time
Our eternal souls won't change
And we are roped and climb.

My Muse has gone as one
Who waves from a moving train,
Leaving a half-eaten
Apple on a plate, and pain.

29 August 1992

RUIN

Threadneedle Street totters,
Bank of England decays,
Materialism moulders,
Bats wheel round reason's ways.

Ruined Foreign Office,
The smell of new mown grass.
Downing Street crumbles,
Admiralty's broken glass.

Waterloo has caved in,
Wild flowers on Canary Wharf,
Parliament is roofless
And looks to Dusseldorf.

The fall of the Windsors,
The lure of a woman's arms,
Buckingham Palace rots
As we die into Europe's farms.

29 August 1992

STORM AND ART

A storm batters the port,
A gale beats round this home,
Sea fountains up the walls,
And drowns the pier with foam.

The wind gusts round the roof,
The sea storms at the gate,
And howls and roars and moans,
And how can I create?

A storm batters the port
And beats round my buffeted heart,
And o for a sunny calm
And an untempestuous art.

29 August 1992

YUGOSLAVIA

Rows of roofless houses,
Crumbling walls and stones,
Burning fires and ruin,
A torso and rotting bones.

Our civilisation is
Decaying like a spire,
And its disintegration
Is helped by mortarfire.

Rows of roofless houses
And torsos in the street
And o the agony as
We decline into the feat

Of a new world order:
United States of Europe,
Crumble into a future
Of ruin and culture-swap.

29 August 1992

SPRING TIDE AND ACADEMIC WORK

A dream: my desk and chair
Were outside my Cornish home
And a high spring tide edged up

And surrounded them with foam.

And would it sweep away
My marooned desk and chair?
What is the tide that threatens
When you muse in open air?

O Nature, please reclaim
My academic springs
Which reveal the mystery
Of the tides in all visible things.

30 August 1992

MUSE'S GIFT

Nineteen poems in three days!
My Muse, you came across,
Stepping from stone to stone,
To this river bank's soft moss.

You came across like one
Who murmurs "Do you need me?"
And "When did you notice me first?"
With demure modesty.

You gave yourself, and left
Your gift and reward for pain:
Twenty poems in three days.
O when will you come again?

30 August 1992

IMAGINATION: SPRING AND SEA

How does it work, my spring?
A word bubbles up, a phrase
And then another, linked
And I know I must gush and gaze.

What is this shaping art
That fixes and makes sense
Of Nature's ephemeral tides,
This ordering of evidence?

My imagination wells
From underground with force,
From a subterranean sea,
Imagination's source.

How can my tiny spring
Be filled with sea-wide power
And tap eternal forms

490

In one small place and hour?

30 August 1992

SEISMIC INSPIRATION

As I probed you, my Muse,
There was a tremor, you shook
In a convulsive earthquake,
You had a far-away look.

As if you were Mother Earth
You quivered my probing power,
Reservoir of symbols,
Yet a mere trembling flower.

O seismic shuddering
That releases energy
And fills me with images
Come again and inspire me.

30 August 1992

MIDNIGHT IN JESUS COLLEGE, CAMBRIDGE

Night in Jesus College.
A great stillness outside.
Now a clock strikes midnight,
Time disturbs like a tide.

But no, it's a cheerful sound,
The chiming of that bell.
It sends a message to
Each monastic hermit's cell

As it did in the twelfth century,
When this was a convent
And the cloisters nearby
Were filled with nuns, heads bent.

Somewhere nearby ponders
The great Penrose I walked
With an hour ago, and got lost,
So hard and deep we talked.

Midnight in Jesus, and
Silence of eternity.
O bells, at one send your
Medieval message to me.

1 September 1992

FORM FROM MOVEMENT THEORY

Dinner at Jesus College.
Long tables, rows of head-
-s, I eat with a Norwegian,
Scribble beside my bread.

Eleven in the bar.
We have imagined a new
Origin of the universe –
Only the maths to do.

Midnight under the stars.
As I walk back to my room,
O the elation as
I know I have found their womb.

4 September 1992

A SUNLIT WALL

The scientists confer:
Each talk begins "neuro" –
Let neurophilosophy,
Let neurobiology flow.

Neural Darwinism,
Neuropsychology – no soul.
Dons rise to demonstrate
That parts reduce the whole,

That mind evolved in time,
That we are in Nature again,   10
That neurons group and bind,
That mind: is functioning brain.

I wonder on the grass,
What ape am I, or machine?
Should I accept those dons'
Materialistic screen?

I wander back to the quad –
O beauty! a sunlit wall!
I am filled with a great joy,
Atheism is not all!   20

5 September 1992

AUTUMN AT FLATFORD MILL

At Flatford Mill the ducks swim round
The reflection of the trees
Where Constable painted, from the lock,
A calm without a breeze.

491

Here in the Essex countryside
Hedgerow and elm create
The water splashing from the weir,
Trickling from the lock gate.

At Flatford Mill a timeless calm
Beneath the cloudy blue
And the river Stour is a smear of paint
Near where wood pigeons coo.

From the humped bridge by the thatched
house,
On the river bend, the sun!
In the nearby hedge the leaves turn yellow,
Huge tangled blackberries stun.

At Flatford Mill the ducks quack on,
A yellowhammer flits,
And near the bridge is timeless thatch
And a peace not shot to bits.

Away from here the world's gone mad,
Men starve in a dozen wars.
But here this stillness is heavy with
Autumnal hips and haws.

Autumn is a ripe heaviness
When the harvesting is done,
Hedgerows and black elderberries,
And a low orange sun.

12 September 1992

LOCK-GATES

Flatford lock-gates are shut,
The still water behind
Is dammed up and stagnant
Like a housewife's mind.

Flatford lock-gates open,
The water rushes out
Like a housewife's energy
When she has lost her doubt.

12 September 1992

NATURE, WALLED

Walk in the landed grounds
Of this Hall with a clock,
Down to the long twilit lake
And piping birdsong's shock.

Here men knew lasting peace
And shut out the old world
With a variety of walks,
What the nineteenth century hurled.

O forefathers who knew
How to live in such halls
And in grounds as well kept as these,
You loved Nature within your walls.

12 September 1992

FIVE PER CENT RISE IN INTEREST RATES

Five per cent rise in interest rates,
The pound has fallen through the floor
Of the ERM, and the Bundesbank
Asks us to devalue, as if winning the War.

Five per cent rise in interest rates
And incredulity on the streets,
And consternation and long faces
And gloom in a million office seats.

But outside the window a sunny day,
The grass drinks in the September sun,
The trees are a glory round the field,
Birds and squirrels have unworried fun.

Through the post, Pissarro's Coopersale Hall
as
It was in eighteen-ninety-three,
And a hundred years of wars and fears
Slumber in this scene of field and tree.

16 September 1992

BEING IN SNOWDONIA

A rushing mountain stream,
And a humped back stone bridge
And on the pine-clad skyline
Still Snowdon's misty ridge.

My being rushes near
Betws-y-coed's Swallow falls
And reaches for the heights
Where cloud-capped Snowdon calls.

26 September 1992

SNOWDON

Across this plunging gorge
Stand breathless – the rain stops;

492

Clouds drift on Snowdon's peak
And jagged crags and drops.

Green sunlit hills sweep down
And below a foothill
Nuzzles a toy white house
And all is breathless still!

26 September 1992

LIGHTS LIKE SOULS

Night over Llandudno –
Are they promenade lights that reach
Round the bay from the Hydro?
Fishermen along the beach.

Thirty-six fly fishermen
Opposite where I sat
In the Hydro's glass veranda
Thirty-six years ago, at

The start of the Suez crisis;
Now, hanging on tripod poles
Lights shine near standing men
Like a sweep of well-lit souls.

26 September 1992

STILLNESS OVERLOOKING ANGLESEY

Across this sun-filled valley
The isle of Anglesey,
Across the shimmering water
Still woods, houses – and me.

I sit, and gaze in the sun
As birds pipe in the trees;
No movement stirs the leaves
In this stillness beneath all breeze.

27 September 1992

PLUNGING, SOARING MOUNTAINS
(OR: "COR!")

See how the mountains hang
And plunge down to the pass
And steeply climb again –
What massive rock and grass.

The mountains have presence,
Their vastness inspires awe,
Their hugely rearing sides

Make all gulp and gasp "Cor!"

Now green, now russet red,
These autumnal mountain shades
That plunge and soar, so sheer,
Uplift as daylight fades.

27 September 1992

A NEW LIFE

A sunlit Georgian house
With russet on the wall,
A car park where a son
Unloads by a students' Hall.

A tiny room, a home,
And his fierce joy and fears
At a new independent life,
And our smiles and suppressed tears.

27 September 1992

TRANSIENT EXISTENCE AND LASTING BEING
(OR: LASTING THINGS AND TRANSIENT THINGS)

"Time is the order of the succession of events."

A pier with Victorian lamps,
A man with a bending rod,
A shivering mackerel,
A mist that is moist with God.

Mountains and misty woods
Of lasting Anglesey,
And the pointed Byzantine domes
Of this pier speak to me

Like the rare butterfly settled
By my feet with outstretched wings,
And the tide that flows and swirls,
Like the wind, with transient things.

Transient things shiver
Like wings and tails, then die;
Permanent things of stone
Reflect Being on high.

O Victorian lamps and domes,
Ephemeral butterflies,
O pier and fish-filled currents,

What lasts is where time sighs.

27 September 1992

RABBIT: SELF-PRESERVATION

A rabbit on the grass
Munching a leaf,
Fawn ears back and white tail,
Aware of grief.

It watches half-afraid
Of human harm.
Then a lollop on back legs
Evades my arm.

O rabbit in the hedge,
You look at me,
And, confusing a touch and a catch,
Continue to be.

27 September 1992

LADYBIRD

A tiny ladybird
On my car's front pane
As I sit with the door open
In this country lane.

Yellow with small black spots –
I finger its fall
So it curls upside down
Into a dead ball.

I hand it to my son
Who observes things;
Now it crawls among stones,
Then opens its wings.

A tiny ladybird,
And now it has flown.
Millions of years shaped it
Into what it's grown.

27 September 1992

LOVE LIKE A SELFLESS PRIEST

You have left your empty room
And this house misses your zest;
I am pleased for you but feel
Your absence on my chest.

Study hard my grown-up son.

I was used to having you here.
I must let go of that habit,
Your reality is elsewhere.

Love, like a selfless priest,
Gives all and does not take;
I gave when you were here,
And will give even though I ache.

27 September 1992

LEAVES LIKE MEMORIES

The wind is high today,
Whirls leaves like snow;
The gold copper beech leaves
Fountain and glow.

Autumn is in the air
And in my soul.
I shed gold memories
And become whole.

I am a tree, am bare
Structure and bough;
My leaves past memories
I recall now.

25 October 1992

BRILLIANT SUN

I went out into the sun
And lent on the granite wall
And blinked in the morning glare
And sneezed at the blinding ball.

A causeway across the sea
And a glimpse of the sun's eye,
And a white light shooting out
Across the dazzling sky.

Down by the water's edge
Wet harbour boulders stun-
ned and people gazed, amazed
At the brilliance of the sun.

29 October 1992

SPLIT ASH

I drive across ploughed fields,
Through gold and russet trees,
To the sweep of Parndon Wood
Where the dead float in the breeze.

Your name is in the book.
I walk to the split ash where
Eleven years ago
You forked away into air.

Three rooks glide like dead souls,
A squirrel scampers by.
I wonder in the stillness
Where we go when we die.

In this sacred oak grove
I have turned from noise and talk
And sense your dead presence
Behind me as I walk.

A chimney, a split ash
And life is split from death.
Here angels glide and soothe
And still each griever's breath.

1 November 1992

ALL SOULS DAY

The wind moans round tonight –
A wail, a groan, a whine –
As it did that Hallowe'en
When you vacated your spine.

The wind's disturbed tonight,
Trees, stars and all things blow.
O what is in the wind
That makes it whimper so?

1 November 1992

FLOW AND FLOOD

The wind is blowing tonight;
I lie in bed and hear
The gales buffet this house,
Roar in the chimney and tear.

The neap sea pounds tonight;
In bed I count waves fall,
Thunder onto the beach
And boom up the sea-wall.

O lift the curtain, look;
White crests fountain up rock,
Break over the harbour wall
And spray lashes the dock.

Surf boils near the Hotel steps,

A lone boat dips and bobs,
A gull hovers hindwards,
All Nature dances and throbs.

This tearing energy
Quickens my breath and blood.
All Nature is in a flow,
I swell with passion's flood.

The wind and sea tear in;
My love, feel this thudding heat.
Let us lie in bed and count
Each breath and each heart-beat.

Think, body's and Nature's tides
Obey one vital flow
Until the flood is spent
In one last panting blow.

18 December 1992

GUNWALLOE METAPHYSICAL SONNET: BOILING FOAM

After the storm this cove, and I have come
    home:
A frothing of white billows and a drifting
    mist,
A dashing well up headlands and boiling
    foam,
A leaping that hosannahs: all things exist!
But in this ancient churchyard all is still.
The stone pilgrim with a staff nods from the
    turf,
On the beach a sand martin bobs, by this hill
I smell the salt of the spray from the snow-
    white surf.
The Church is split but this church has stood
    for
Some eight hundred years by these stormy
    seas
And will affirm the power that rolls these
    waves
Long after crown and mitre are no more;
So I sit on a pew by a granite pillar and tease
Out the distant roar of the sea, like wind on
    graves.

18 December 1992

ELEMENTAL

A rough grey sea and surf,
And a sea-mist like smoke

That hides the cliffs, a gull
Whose sure swoop makes me choke.

Huge rollers thunder in
With blown spume and flung spray;
Porthleven cowers and huddles
At the end of this grey day.

My being's at one with the sea
In this damp floating cloud,
It froths and surges forward
Aloof from the village crowd.

18 December 1992

HARBOURMASTER

When Graham was Harbourmaster
He knew every inch of the port,
The boats came in within
An inch of what he thought.

When Graham was Harbourmaster
Even a rough sea learned.
It boomed up the sea-wall
So far and no more, then turned.

Now he is gone, I look
At the raging sea's progress
And fear it may flood this harbour
And reclaim us like Lyonnesse.

18 December 1992

ROYALS

The Royals are falling apart:
Windsor Castle on fire,
The Queen is paying tax,
Prince Charles has his desire.

And what will become of the Church
When the monarchy dies,
For women priests have split
Christendom, in our eyes.

A royal photographed baretop
Or playing "It's a Knockout" –
All play to the camera.
Divorce fills us with doubt.

The game is up, royals!
You got away with it while
We looked up to you, but now we

Look scathingly down and smile.

18 December 1992

THE WORKINGS OF THE UNIVERSE
(For Anthony)

Sea, clouds and rain on my cheeks,
Gulls on a breakwater's bars,
On a beach under crumbling cliffs
Tiny stones glisten like stars.

Sea, sky and stars converge:
As a black cormorant flies
Close to the waves for fish
The particular opens eyes

To something general,
A universal scene,
The workings of the universe
Revealed behind their screen.

19 December 1992

THE RETURN OF THE MUSE

You come in a cloche hat
And sit on a carpeted floor
And spread out your pictures
Like an art-inspiring whore.

I watch spellbound until
I gather you in my desire
And love you on the carpet
Before a blowing fire.

So, Muse, my mirror shows
When I gaze in inner night
Until you tug the cord
And the bulb brings back the light.

In my looking-glass, two cups.
In my mirror, my Muse, who is true.
And the beauty in your look
As you breathe "Is it really you?"

30 December 1992

LADY THROUGH THE WINDOW

Look through the hotel window
Into the dark – what style!
See a beautiful lady
Sip tea, cut cake, and smile.

She hangs above the road,
Like a goddess in chiffon.
Look again – in a trice
She has turned back and gone.

Now look into your soul
As in a teatime window
And see her flushed face turn
With a question like a blow.

A ghost paces up and down
Like a Bilderberger spy.
My love, look through the window
Past the wraith with his watching eye.

30 December 1992

MUSE INSPIRING: WINGED LION

My Muse taps on my arm
As if she had just found
A statue of great value,
Winged sculpture in the ground.

Unity of Being
Should pervade every way:
Body, feeling, reason,
Emotion and mystic ray.

We are whole with each other,
Each bone of our human frame   10
Expresses itself with the warmth
Of an uninhibited flame.

We think and feel and touch,
And image and taste and see,
And overflow into vision,
Hot surges of energy.

O my Muse with you I am
On fire in my skull, a god,
You give me divine knowledge
Like water from Aaron's rod.   20

I am like my coat of arms,
Am helmet, armour and crown,
Double-headed eagle,
Lion, snake and creative frown.

With you I take off my mask
For my double-eagle soul

And see a winged lion –
Spiritual vision of the whole.

30 December 1992

LINES: TOWN AND COUNTRY

Chimneys and railway lines,
Ferroconcrete in rain.
You find your lines in towns,
You're lost in field and lane.

Girders and streetcar wires,
Paved streets and hankerings.
Mine, too, was a city art
And imaged structured things.

Now I rejoice in growth,
In trees and flowers and clouds.
Can you not measure death
By rays on living crowds?

30 December 1992

FROST

A sharp frost glistens on
Fields, cars and puddled ice.
In the night a lone fox barks.
Stars glint like edelweiss.

A thaw in this morning sun
But fields and each windscreen
Sparkle like alpine quartz
In my frozen-eyed routine.

30 December 1992

REFLECTIONS ON TIME: PAST AND PRESENT, HORSEMAN AND LION

A medieval horseman
On a sarcophagus, an immense
Wheel-raised Great War cannon
Represent belligerence.

A winged Venetian lion
And one eroded by time
As chaotic energy
Destroys all that has been sublime.

Now the medieval horseman
With his sarcophagus shield
Propels our past towards a
Future like a battlefield,

Just as this winged lion
Is our present ideal
And behind it is an unknown
And uncertain past that is real.

30 December 1992

WHITE-CENTRED FLOWER

A gold brooch with three flowers.
Two sapphires and, between these,
A cubic zirconium
Nuzzle like tiny bees.

Artist, mother, mistress,
Each petalled flower is thick
With the pollen you hold for
Lover, daughter, public,

And in the pure white centre,
Your soul, your gleaming art,
When your sapphire people
Do not nuzzle in your heart.

31 December 1992

AFTER A DEATH

This morning you lay head back,
Eyes closed, tucked up in bed,
Hooked nose, mouth open, white skin.
I kissed your cold forehead.

Now a fire leaps in my grate,
Near the lit Christmas tree.
On the dark glass a fog,
And you, coming in for tea.

2 January 1993

FOG AND FROST: THE UNIVERSE

Last night a freezing fog,
Now sparkling on my car.
Crystals forming from air
Twinkle in the sun like a star,

Glisten like the wet sand
When a harbour tide is low.
I glint in my being, glad
That air can sparkle so.

So is it with the void
Out of which the universe spun,
A fog of pre-being

Which now sparkles in the sun.

3 January 1993

CREMATORIUM

Smoke in the crem chimney,
And an acrid taste in the mouth.
I gaze as another's life
Goes up in smoke, drifts south.

Now it's your turn next.
A perfunctory text, a prayer
And your lifetime's achievement
Is torched and dispersed in air.

O life, o death, o air
That contains and excludes both –
Where is the justification
For an artist's work and growth?

12 January 1993

PARTING THE BLIND

I asked "Have you seen the grounds?"
And part the vertical blind
And disclose a railed green field
And you gasp at what lies behind.

So it is with my art.
I part two downward slats
And disclose a hidden world
And you gasp at its sunset and gnats.

12 January 1993

HEALING MUSE

O Muse, I love it when
You appear behind my back,
Press healing hands on my head
Pour images into my black.

I relax into a deep state,
Am inspired by your love
As you pour in creative juice,
Then squat on my gristle, above,

And extract my images
Like warm and viscous seed,
My creative energies
Which all can love, which breed.

But best of all is the end
When with a dazzling rush

You fill my empty brain cells
With a knowledge I will gush.

12 January 1993

DOUBT: THE MUSE AS WILL O' THE WISP

And if we ran away, my Muse,
And lived in hot Venice
(My Byzantium) and
You pampered me with service,

Would you erode my will,
Would my discipline fall apart?
Long life is mind over matter –
Would hot baths sap my heart?

O my Muse, a small doubt gnaws:
The Venice of my dreams,
Where I go and write full time,
And a Tuscan villa's streams

May be a will o' the wisp
That lures me into a bog
And destroys my health and art
And leaves my mind a fog.

12 January 1993

MUSE: LOVE LIKE FLOWERS

Draw the curtains, shut out
The miserable English day.
We could now be in Venice –
Hear the gondoliers play.

Flowers on the striped curtains,
Flowers on the striped bedspread;
Fifty flowers in each stripe,
Thousands of flowers on the bed.

My Muse, I will love you once
For each one of these flowers.
We have twenty years before us,
Thousands of love-filled hours.

I will love you till your soul
Quivers like fluttering wings,
And your flow pours through the dam
Which shuts out eternity's springs.

Please please me like a geisha,
Always wanting to please;

Each time I will pick you a flower
To advance your quivering sneeze!

13 January 1993

MUSE: QUESTIONS

And have you been to the church
Where I read the lesson
Which épatéd the bourgeois
Like a furious Albion?

And were you in that house
When I brought your post in haste
And did I see the curves
Of your Stradivarius waist?

Questions but no answers
As I brood on destiny, fate;
On how we nearly met,
On who we met too late.

And now I sit and stare
With a heaviness in my chest,
And have you now a void
In your stomach and your quest?

13 January 1993

MUSE: ALIVE

And you have come alive
Like an almond tree in May;
You wear a white blossom:
Your skin glistened today.

And you have come alive
In your quivering eyes and loins.
I see your whispering head
As small as on Maundy coins.

And I have come alive
In my quickening pulse and heart,
Through you I have come alive
In my quivering art.

13 January 1993

DREAM OF THE MUSE

You sit in the Rendezvous lounge,
We drink tea and then flit
To the Regency Room, where you place
A hand on my back, as I sit.

A warmth behind my heart,

Muffled announcements blare
On the station through the window
As images pour round my chair.

A piano tinkles, we leave
For Charing Cross Road's end,
You weave a spell as I choose
A book by an old friend.

Now, a ghost at my elbow,
You sit in a Soho café
And whisper "I do love you"
And I glimpse a Ligurian bay.

18 January 1993

ARRIVEDERCI, MUSE

O hurry, the train is still
And now it crawls to town.
O hurry, My Muse is waiting
In my soul with a frown.

She smiles, I am with her.
She can inspire me, she sighs,
Gives me ten images
As I kiss her cheeks and eyes.

And o the softness as
Her soul and heart give out
And o the ecstatic pleasure
As her tongue licks round my doubt.

O Muse, your experience knows
That most who've loved were wrong,
And your international living
Can strengthen my truth-seeking song.

Now arrivederci, Muse.
The tube clatters me away
With an embryonic poem
That will hatch in my soul this day.

19 January 1993

TURBULENCE

You say that you have known
Irrequietudine,
Or turbulence: broken glass
In factories you hid from day.

But now you have gone into air,
Stretching like elastic

My umbilical cord –
Has air turbulence made you feel sick?

21 January 1993

DRIZZLE

Drizzle on the window
And drizzle in my heart,
Drizzle in my mirror
As we travel apart.

O my beautiful courtesan
With a young model's skin,
O my Stradivarius Muse
Would the sun could bring back your grin.

21 January 1993

AIRWAVES

I feel you on the airwaves
In this dead of night,
I feel you on my chest
Like a probing searchlight.

My love, so far away,
My Muse who deserted me,
I feel your warm healing
Like a wartime battery.

21 January 1993

BUTTERFLY

I sit in an Epping church
Where a congregation hear
An Epping schools' concert,
And I wish you were near.

A butterfly settles
And lies stunned on the stage
As my school's choir files on,
Their feet fill me with rage.

Now an orchestra plays.
I look at a violin,
And think of your narrow waist –
Between breasts and hips, curved skin.

In the interval I talk,
Then notice in a pew
Four petalled quatrefoils –
And immediately think of you.

The butterfly flies up,

The violinists are blind,
And I think of the strings
In your Stradivarius mind.

An artist in paint, not sound,
You love the butterfly
And the beauty it celebrates,
And the flower it flutters by.

21 January 1993

TROPICAL FISH

Hospital waiting-room.
A tank and colourful fish,
Some with red blob eyebrows;
I gaze as their tails swish

And at the mystery of life
Lived under water, with fins.
Like a swimmer's arms they chase,
Then drift and sun their skins.

What nervous system, what brain
Do blue-red neons boast?
What complexity ordered such things
And made them to race and coast?

25 January 1993

PARADISO

Muse, you are so versatile:
Healer, artist, geisha,
Courtesan, nurse and cook,
Violin Cremonese –

How have I managed without you?
You unite body and soul
And mind steeped in the arts,
A Renaissance woman, whole.

You embody my ideal
Unity of being, and see
Your heraldic spirit as
A royal fleur-de-lis.

Goddess, I am so lucky
To have you at my call,
To beckon with crooked finger
And watch the images fall

Like fruit from the Tree of Life
Known in Kabbalah schools;

My Beatrice, your lines of light
Pierce this Dark Wood's toadstools,

Lead me to a mountain height
Somewhere near Rapallo
Where I glimpse Paradise
And a guide and flower aglow.

26 January 1993

NOT ENDURANCE BUT PROCESS: THE PAST PRESENT

Ten philosophers list
The assumptions scientists spread.
"'Endurance of particles,'"
Says Read, quoting Whitehead.

"If everything's always the same
There is no process, yet time
Is a succession of events"
Which change with each clock's chime.

"Materialists assert
Past particles endure,
Only make way for new ones
If obliterated. That's for sure.

"Past particles need to be –
In my cumulative view –
Obliterated to make way
For present events, which accrue."

Later we stand and fork
Salmon, salad and cheese.
"'Endurance is the root
Of materialism.'" I freeze.

It is all so obvious:
After salad, apple pie.
Present events are added
To past events nearby.

Remember, I recall:
On the sea how broke daylight,
How day came as quanta
Adding themselves to night.

Each civilisation's stage
Is superimposed on the last
So the past eternally persists,
The present is full of the past.

And so it is with our lives:
The echoes are still there,
Our past is still with us
When we vanish into air.

The stuff of the universe,
This stone-gardenlike mess,
Is swirling quanta of Light
And a dazzling process.

The Light is a moving process
That manifests into event
Whose substance, or quanta,
Dances past into present.

28 January 1993

RAINGLOBES

Rainglobes on the rose-bush,
Globes hang along the wire;
Birdsong this damp morning,
A January choir.

Crocuses nudge through grass,
The spring is in the air.
Green woodpecker and moorhen
Move in the field and stare.

New life is coming through,
Pushing up through the earth,
Pushing through winter dead,
Pushing into floral birth.

Rainglobes on the rose-bush,
Each like a world, they spin
And twinkle in the sunlight
As a blue tit glides in.

29 January 1993

ILLUMINED ARTISTS AS LEADERS OF THEIR CIVILISATION

If the Light is central to
Our civilisation's health
Then the illumined artists
Lead it, not bankers' wealth;

The Metaphysical Revolution
Is a call for us to survive,
For artists to show the Light

Which keeps our culture alive.

So Muse, add new images
To those now in the past,
Send new images of Light
To make our culture last.

And when you inspire me, Muse,
Be an earth mother or priestess
Who loves the Light from on high
Into my brain's dark recess.

Artists are the antennae
Of our civilisation, our race,
Feelers which send danger signs
To mankind's beetling grimace.

Pound traced the troubadours
To the Cathars and Eleusis,
To ritual priestly sex
Which released the Light with a kiss.

Pound's Rapallo stood for
A culture that is new,
Provençal heresy,
But Christians had it too.

O healing goddess Muse,
Curved as Syrian Astarte,
Bring down the sacred Light
And renew our culture's heart.

30 January 1993

MUSE WITHDRAWN

I think of you on Helicon
Or in a town where you've begun
To prop paintings beside
A canal in the Sunday sun.

When not inspiring, do you
Sell your work on a quay?
Is that how you pass your time
When you are not visiting me?

31 January 1993

FEBRUARY DAFFODILS

Out of the kitchen window
February daffodils!
Two dozen nodding heads
As a wind moans round these hills.

They nod and sway and bob,
Alive in an unseen breeze,
Six-petalled trumpet-heads
Nodding like grey MPs.

And as they nod and nod,
Affirming an unseen wind,
I know they love the force
That keeps growth disciplined.

13 February 1993

FLOCK

A flock of birds in the sky
Wheel in an oval whole.
Now flecks, now large black dots,
They turn like fish in a shoal.

The oval of specks has gone
Over the hill, and I
Open my hundred million
Cells to one tidal sky.

18 February 1993

AT COLINTON

Colinton parish church
And a mortsafe near the door
To stop body-snatching,
Protect the graves of the poor.

In the graveyard we stare
At these skulls and crossed bones
And gravedigger's spades,
And think they are *our* tombstones.

As the font lid moves up
A dove on chains moves down,
The descent of the Spirit
On a child's wetted crown.

The dove holds a round light,
The graves show a round skull.
Our light pulleys aloft
From our head as our eyes grow dull.

O my daughter, we will lie
In the ground all too soon,
So let us now enjoy
This river, this bridge, this moon.

My heart leaps at the dusk

And the yellow wagtail
That bobs and paddles and pecks
In this valley's rocks and shale.

This plashing Water of Leith
That tinkles over stones,
This laughing Scottish stream
Stirs joy in our bubbling bones!

25 February 1993

IN SPYLAW STREET: LOVE AND PAIN, FLOW AND BOULDERS

This night in Spylaw Street
The river sounds like rain
As it flows its bouldered way –
What justifies one's pain?

From a copse by the churchyard
A quiet owl hoots "to woo"
And accepts by the bouldered flow
That to love one must become two.

25-26 February 1993

OUTSIDE HEAVEN

Under the Pentland Hills
In Colinton's valley Dell
A dipper darts by the weir.
How can there be a Hell?

I stand by the three gates
To Heaven's old churchyard,
One closed, one ajar, one between
Which when pulled swings shut on a bard.

The raindrops glint in the sun
Like diamond stars on each tree.
The gate to Heaven has closed
And I sing what I see.

26 February 1993

LIKE A DESCENDING CHRIST

I sit on a flight deck
Strapped in behind two crew
Who steer a 737
With casual derring-do.

I hang above snowfields
Like a descending Christ.
Is this my frozen land?

503

What happened to its zeitgeist?

I hang above these clouds,
Thrust-lever me up again.
I cannot thaw its soul,
It's a land of snowmen.

26 February 1993

LONG-TAILED FIELD MOUSE

As I cleared our front porch
And the debris of years and boys,
I found a nest in a shoe
And opened a suitcase of toys –

Out jumped a mouse and ran
And hid under steps – "see him?" –
Then ran and jumped on a wall
And sat, bright-eyed and slim.

A long-tailed field mouse –
I identified him, and then
He was up the bank into shrubs
And gone under leaves again.

O field mouse I am sorry
I disturbed your cosy lair.
You were welcome – the universe
Is for all beings to share.

29 March 1993

CHAOS AND ORDER

As I walked out at night
Through black and hellish clouds
The full moon slid behind
Its irregular, similar shrouds,

And a pale moonlight fell
On the waters of the bay,
Each fractal patterned cove
Was irregular in the same way.

O Mandelbrot, who saw
How the many relates to the one
In a new geometry
Of everything under the sun –

Pebbles, rocks and snowflakes,
Water runnels in limestone,
Cacti, oak-trees and twigs,
Sand and sea-swirls, and bone –

The unpredictable is
Like love in the afternoon:
Chaos against order,
Like clouds across a moon.

5 April 1993

FIRE I AM

Five circles gyrate and chant:
"Fire I am, earth I am,
Water, air and spirit."
I weave and chant and enjamb.

Five circles swirl round in
A centre of great power.
As I chant "Fire I am"
And thread a bright-eyed hour.

And will pews become this,
This circular dance, this rite?
Will the coming forms free us
From being blinded by sight?

5 April 1993

CAR PARK: ASCENDING

The cinema car park.
I swing up through each floor
To level 5, and display –
And I head for Heaven's door.

We left the cellular level
And rose through biology
And psychological mind
To the spiritual and divine "me".

Levels – we spend our lives
Ascending to this great height
And our inner cinema
And a white screen filled with Light.

11 April 1993

THE NIGHTINGALE IN THE MIND
(OR: THE SOURCE OF POETIC INSPIRATION)

A sea-breeze and bay foam.
As I eased through the gate to the field
And walked up past stunning gorse
And the wind-swept hawthorn shield,

Listen! the magnificent trill

Of a hidden nightingale.
I creep, it flits among leaves
And warbles across the dale.

I make the top, then turn
And hear it beneath me, and stalk
But it flies between thickets
And rustles when I walk.

And I have often heard
In the hedgerows of my mind
A pure but elusive sound
Whose source I can never find.

12 April 1993

Threw a shadow from each shape.
A few crawled but most clung,
Pleased at having made their escape.

O how like human life!
They huddle together at night,
Each in its distinctive place
Near sand-free orange light.

O sand-hoppers who are drawn
To my house wall, and this glow
You can stay here until dawn
Drives you back to the beach below.

12 April 1993

SOUL LIKE A GREENFINCH

A brrrr in the garden,
A bird flits to a tree.
I train field-glasses on him –
A fat yellow "canary".

Too large for a siskin.
The sun sets, and I flinch,
For its breast has now turned green.
Thick bill – it's a greenfinch.

It sits on a bare twig
Like a soul in a brain of bark.
I gaze at a burning tree
In the descending dark.

12 April 1993

STORMY PETREL

Near my window above big waves
And foam dashing on the shore
A black stormy petrel,
Blown hindwards by wind, or

Floating with wings outstretched,
Rests on the wind like a soul
On the turmoil in the mind,
At one with the flowing whole.

12 April 1993

SAND-HOPPERS

As I walked late-night in the rain
And returned from the booming sea
On the house wall by the street-lamp –
A thousand sand-hoppers, free.
The light on the wet pink wall

SOJOURNS

1993

PISA

I bus to the Duomo.
Through an arch - a shock, I shake:
Galileo's tower tilts
Like a white, iced wedding cake.

I bus back across the town.
The Arno reflects in bliss
Amber houses near where
Shelley wrote *Adonais*.

Pisa, I could live here
In your raucous bustle and still
And kiss the sunlight somewhere
On an Apuan hill.

30 April 1993

BELLS

The bell of San Marco tolls
Across the gardens where
Lorenzo found Michelangelo,
Across the Duomo square.

The bell of Campanile answers
From Giotto's great tower:
Its belfry proclaims today
With a sombre, leaden hour.

2 May 1993

THUNDER

Thunder reverberates round
The Medici gardens, but
In this room there is a peace,
A woman's eyes are shut.

In this quiet Renaissance room
A woman sings to a lute
Of how she was deserted,
Now protesting, now mute.

In the thundery dusk, in a trance,
She sings of Renaissance love
And holds us spellbound from
A divine plane above.

2 May 1993

PARADISE

Masaccio's Eve is aghast,
And open-mouthed at the price.
Adam covers his eyes
As they leave Paradise.

An angel points the way
Like a football referee
Who has shown a red card
To two who were too free.

And have you tempted me
To break a rule with a bite,
Which will get us expelled from
A Paradise of light?

2 May 1993

RAIN

It is raining in the puddle,
It is raining in my mind
For I must leave a way of life
That I long tried to find.

It is raining in the windows,
It is raining in my eyes
For I must return to a daily grind
That is safe, secure – and unwise.

2 May 1993

CLOISTERED

In the Carmine cloister
A tranquillity, a love –
And a tingling down my spine
As the Fire licks down from above.

The daisies on the lawn,
Each loggia arch, this rose
And the palms proclaim a peace
The monks chose to enclose.

My Muse, holding my back,
Whispers over my shoulder.
I cannot see my Muse
But know her in this cloister.

3 May 1993

PEACE AND A TEAR

Peace in the arched cloister
In the sun and arched shadows,
And peace in my being
And a tear for what I enclose.

I am moved in my being
By this peace that helps me be,
These stones built for haloes
And now left behind for me.

Peace in the ancient cloister,
The sun's warmth on my back,
And a life's work is calling –
A tear for the left-behind track.

3 May 1993

SUN AND SHADE

If I had no cares at all
I'd go to Carmine
And sit in the square or trattoria
And sun myself all day.

If I had no cares at all
I'd seek a cloister's shade
And sit with my Muse and glow
Where many monks have prayed.

3 May 1993

MUSE, DESOLATE

My Muse is desolate,
She feels empty and tired
As I leave Florence,
The town she has inspired.

My Muse is desolate:
I am removing my mind
From the service of the art
By which she is defined.

And I am desolate,
Having lived through an art of "si"
For the last five days – Masaccio,
Angelico, Botticelli.

The Quattrocento greats,
I have soaked them in, and ten
New symbols, including:
Rose, halo and fountain.

I like to live for art
But must now return to bills.
I would like to live like Ficino
In these Medicean hills.

3 May 1993

SPIRAL

Like the spiral staircase to
My old college library,
Life turns us round and round
As we rise above all we see.

And if we stumbled below,
On the same higher-up stair
With our ascending wisdom,
We avoid the fall with care.

Like a spiral staircase
Life raises us to repeat
Situations we left behind,
Which we tread with surer feet.

3rd May 1993

THE GATEWAY TO PARADISE

The Gate of Paradise
Is barred with rails, which means
We are held back as we look
In wonder at ten gold scenes.

One day the rails will go,
The Gate will open wide
And we will live beneath
A Dantean dome inside.

3 May 1993

WATER

The burnt ambers of walls
By the cobbled river way
Are reflected in the Arno
This windless sunny day.

I stand where Shelley wrote
Adonais and muse
On a name "writ in water",
How he heard the dreadful news.

On my way in, in the air,
I saw the Arno's mouth
And where drowned Shelley was washed in
Just eight miles to the south.

507

Water obsesses now:
Its transience and danger
Seem far from these beautiful flecks
Of ochres in this shimmer.

3 May 1993

FOUNTAIN

We sit in the fountain spray,
Me and my shadow.
I say to my silent Muse,
"It is now time to go."

I pull away from the square
And wave to the fountain spray
Where my Muse sat in the sun
And healed me one warm day.

3 May 1993

MUSE: WORKING IN ISOLATION

I am alive with you:
We talk and respond as one,
Feelings as pure as tears,
Our bodies leap and run.

I am alive with you.
We can work on our own.
Talent operates in groups,
Genius stands alone.

7 May 1993

ITALY: LIZARD

Neat rows of suburban houses,
Terraced or semi-detached –
I do not like England
Even when it is cottaged or thatched.

Give me orange walls, green blinds,
Shutters in the noon glare,
And a hot, blinding sun
And a lizard in dry air.

7 May 1993

FIRE

A vast industrial scene
Within a murky cloud,
And round it, billowing fire –
Could chimneys belch such a shroud?

No, out of the Fire have come

These chimneys and their smoke,
From the hot source of all
One glimpse of which makes me choke.

7 May 1993

THE LAUGHING PHILOSOPHER

I

Walk up a tree-lined avenue to a gate
And an orange Quattrocento fortress with
        great
Curved walls and barred windows and a high
        walk
Where sentries and lookouts stood in idle talk,
Go into an open orange courtyard
Whose arches echo with birdsong and the
        voice of a guard,
And the summer villa of Cosimo Medici,
Patron to the arts and philosophy.

Here Cosimo held court, limping with gout
Into a long upper room with a ruler's pout 10
And received the Platonist scholar Ficino
And his Academy, when they all ro-
-de through heat and dust from his small
        house on a near hill
To report on translations done at the Prince's
        will.
It is now a nuns' hospital, but the past chimes:
Stand in this place and feel those ancient
        times.

Here perhaps the Greek Gemistos came the
        May
He inspired the Pope's banker to revive Pla-
-to's Academy when his doctor's son was six
And had not left medicine for Greek and
        candlewicks. 20
Scholars say the Renaissance began to show
When the Ottomans sacked Byzantium's
        libraries so
Greek books came west, but in fact it was
        born, we find,
When Ficino became a doctor of the mind.

Here severe Ficino stood and read and ate
As proud Medici sat in pomp and state
Like a Maecenas filled with a divine desire;
And passionately spoke of Plato, Christ and

Fire
As like Clement of Alexandria he reconciled
Pagan and Christian teachings, and never
    smiled   30
As he brought about a shift in the Christian
    west,
Brought in a New People with a new quest.

From here he taught Botticelli to transmute
Carnal, erotic love to its divine root:
Sad Venus and the Humanist ideal
Not as mournful shadowy form, but Platonic
    real.
From here he replaced the halo with a bloom
And expressed Platonic beauty in a womb
And, religious Humanist who believed in Fire,
Secularized the virtuous human with
    desire.   40

From here he became a priest and challenged
    this feat.
Sometimes Cosimo left him to go on retreat
To the Dominican monastery of San Marco
And walk near his cell and watch Angelico.
The Renaissance birth of Venus dethroned
    Mary.
Now I see Cosimo die in this Villa Careggi.
Ficino reads Plato as he lies sublime
And sighs, "Ah, I have wasted so much
    time."

II
Philosopher and physician, astrologer, priest,
First and last of the unified men, creased   50
Ficino saw learning as an aspect of one,
Of incorporeal light behind the sun
Which spread from God, the angelic world, to
    soul,
Nature and earthly matter, and, being whole,
Paganised the Church for a universal grace –
In Maria Novella, look at his crumpled face.

Downstairs I hear how Gemistos presuppose-
-d the Fire of Heracleitus, under old frescoes –
Temples, swans, gardens, villas and ships, one
    wrecked –
The Renaissance round my head, and now
    reflect: 60
Today a new Renaissance is in the air
As we recover the unity of being where

The mystics and Ficino lived, and see
The universe and soul as one energy.

Last week I sat in my Academy's gloom,
A dozen philosophers in an Uxbridge room,
And spoke to a modern group about the Fire,
To philosophers who know the real and
    aspire
To change the zeitgeist back to the unified
    One
That warms each virtuous soul like a sun,   70
Not back to the atoms of Democritus –
One graceful reality licking down to us.

Alchemists see changes souls undergo:
Blackening (Dark Night) in an underworld of
    No;
Whitening, coniunctio of mind and soul in
    Light;
Yellowing, ripening of imagination's insight;
And reddening, unus mundus of body and
    soul
And cosmic consciousness, oneness of the
    whole.
Ficino and I both died from the world and
    "me"
To be reborn in our souls and unity.   80

III
Now in this garden look back at the walls that
    tease,
The mauve wisteria, small bowled orange
    trees
Where images hang, touch a Greek goddess,
    then prowl
To where two boys ride a tortoise and an owl,
And the fountain pool where red fish rise and
    blow,
Listen to birds, pick and taste leaves and glow
With the smell of scents, all senses like a
    choir –
See pink chestnut candles like a mind on Fire!

In our Universalist time, when the Fire and
Incorporeal Light blaze across our land,   90
My books echo Ficino and reconcile
Western and Eastern Fires in a new style.
I must not be a preacher in a church
Or lecture on the Fire as a pentecostal search
As my six works show the universe's law

In an interlocking picture, like a child's
    jigsaw.

In a picture in Milan by Bramante
Two philosophers stand by a globe, one sad,
    one gay.
Democritus knew atoms before Rutherford's
    ball,
He laughs because men believe transience is
    all.   100
Heracleitus weeps as all believe "everything
    flows"
And no one sees the Fire – which he himself
    knows,
And so should smile. Sad Ficino, laugh and
    inspire:
For all is flux, but underneath – the Fire!

1-12 May 1993

A STAIN OF FIRE

The river Arno moves
Water no longer the same,
Everything is in a flux,
The houses burn like flame.

All is aflow and all
Is always the same, a stain
As the Fire flames out its flecks
And takes them back again.

13 May 1993

EXECUTION

In a medieval dream
I await execution, then flee
And walk across hill and dale
The length of Italy.

Is there anything in such a dream?
Have I lived it all before?
Are such hangings memories?
Do we relive barbarous war?

13 May 1993

POET AND SNAIL

A snail outside my house –
A slug with two thin horns
And a round house on its back
And the freedom of hundreds of lawns.

You travel with your house

As you trail, like a free man –
Like a gipsy wanderer
Who writes in his caravan.

31 May 1993

STING

I laugh with philosophers –
A jab in my side, a bite?
I see a large insect
Sway drunkenly off in flight.

Stung through my long-sleeved shirt
This sunny day, I scratch.
Like the stigmata of Christ
My side has a red patch.

O creature (hornet? bee?)
You are welcome to my flesh
But why did you harm one
In harmony with what's fresh?

31 May 1993

OAK

A great many-branched oak
That reaches towards the sun
And throws a pool of shade
To shelter everyone.

A great many-leafed oak
That puts out green acorns
Like a year's crop of poems
That ripen through summer dawns.

Acorns cannot be eaten,
Poems may seem useless,
But both are expressions of
A crowned, ripe massiveness.

1 June 1993

EPITHALAMION
(For Nadia and Sandy)

The sun streams in your room, wake up o
    bride,
Rise up with happy heart, take in the flowers
The nymphs have left on your doorstep and
    tied
To your brass knocker to decorate the hours.
With gleaming ring prepare yourself, wash
    hair,
Bustle to the kitchen, have your breakfast

510

there,
Get yourself ready, put on your ivory gown.
Let your window plants be your sundial, see
      where
Your attendant waits by your mirror, sit down,
Wear white gypsophila in your hair, adorn   10
Yourself for your beloved like a summer
      dawn.
Hold your posey, ignore that plane's dull
      whine,
And know the happiness of all new wives
As the longed-for moment at last arrives
For your father to take you to the shrine,
Give thanks to Hymen in this fine sunshine.
      Hear the guitar play like sunlight on
         water,
      Hear the stream bubble over rocks, my
         daughter.

Contain your excitement during the drive
To the ancient house in the pine-clad
      garden,   20
Pass between two stone pillars, smiling arrive
At where the guests wait on the lawn, and
      then
Take up your place before your male
      bridesmaid,
By your kilted lord, and female best man/aid,
Stand at Nature's altar in the open air,
Near the tall pine trees and the pools of shade,
Near the plashing water, out of the sun's
      glare.
Among fragrant herbs and woodland scents,
      and moss,
Stand at the table before the silver cross,
Before the smiling vicar, under the sky,   30
Near where the peeping nymphs make a love-
      knot.
Here stand witness the ghosts of Burns and
      Scott
Who joyfully recall meeting nearby.
Now put on the ring, "io Hymen" the nymphs
      cry.
      Let the guitar play like sunlight on water,
      Hear the stream bubble over rocks, my
         daughter.

Now bride and groom embrace in a rustic
      vow,
All smile as, garlanded, you beam at all,

As cameras catch you by the wrought-iron
      plough
And the two cartwheels that lean on the white
      wall.   40
Now the nymphs creep from the stream's long
      grass again
And bring forget-me-nots and a daisy chain.
You have what you want, be happy, o bride.
A weather glance – the nymphs have held off
      rain.
Now go with your groom and sapphire, go
      inside
To panelled wood and a fireplace, linger here
And reflect, ahead is a duck pond somewhere,
And a cottage where little feet patter all day.
A pianist plays new guests in, a drummer
      beats,
A joyful line of smiling faces greets   50
The happy couple, "io Hymen" all say,
"Io Hymen" as the band of minstrels play.
      Now the guitar plays like sunlight on
         water,
      Outside the stream bubbles over rocks,
         my daughter.

The sun is low, the gnats dance round the
      moon,
You are surrounded by many drinking friends,
Rejoice in the love you have known this
      afternoon.
All dance, the music speeds and your heart
      ascends.
The sun is setting, the dusk flits with a bat,
The night curls and settles like a black cat. 60
Soon you will be together, but o nymphs look
After her as she twirls, then has a chat;
All are merry, the drink flows, flushed and
      shook
Faces grin as the minstrels strum. O bride,
Bright-eyed and clear, you flow like the
      stream outside,
Your being splashes with happiness from afar.
Enough, you have both spent enough time in
      this dream.
Go outside to where the nymphs sit by the
      stream,
Let husband and wife be joined under evening
      star,
And in dark silence, groom, take up your
      guitar.   70

511

Now the guitar plays like moonlight on
   water,
And your stream bubbles over rocks, my
   daughter.

1-2 June 1993

PEACE AND WAR
(For Anthony)

"One swallow doesn't make a summer."

Three swallows dart around
The old harbour boat store,
Out at sea a cruiser
Rigged out for Bosnian war.

The playful swallows swoop
Round the clay boat in the dock.
The grey cruiser plays war
Beyond Gull Island rock.

In this village backwater
I walk for papers in peace,
As I sit among daisies
All the world's troubles cease.

3 June 1993

GARDEN

When Sid was alive his lawn
Was mown like a bowling green,
Lettuces had covers,
From his wall plants grew to be seen.

Now he is dead and gone
His house curtains are drawn,
Vegetables and rock plants sprawl –
And daisies fill the lawn.

5 June 1993

SOUL LIKE A ROSE

A beautiful rose,
Cars whizzing past.
Town petrol fumes
And a pace that is fast.

Where's country peace?
Where is clean air?
My soul like a rose
Needs roots somewhere.

25 June 1993

NIAGARA FALLS: BEAUTY AND TRANSIENCE

Niagara Falls, Niagara Falls,
Where waters pour and end in spray
That hangs like mist or smoke, and calls
To all that substance ends this way.

Niagara Falls, Niagara Falls,
Where waters cascade into smoke
That drifts like a lifetime spent in halls;
Where mottled thrushes peck, I choke.

Niagara Falls, Niagara Falls,
Where a lifetime slips towards an edge
And rolls over – now it appals
Near where gulls scream on every ledge.

Niagara Falls, Niagara Falls,
Between birth and death, a joyful time.
Look for a rainbow on the walls
That plunge and froth away our time.

12 July 1993

FLORAL CLOCK: BEAUTY'S CHIMES

A Canadian floral clock:
Steel hands for seconds, minutes, hours.
As the sun shines on well-kept flowers
A sudden chiming – what a shock!

It chimes eleven summertimes
Then, returns to a floral garden,
I try to forget how time creeps on –
Cruel beauty, to disturb with chimes!

12 July 1993

AT LAKE ONTARIO

We sh we sh we sh we sh,
The sound of the wavelets on the shore,
We sh we sh we sh we sh,
As Lake Ontario washes once more.

We sh we sh we sh we sh,
The sound of the waves on this beach,
They lap above my feet, beneath
Where the masts of Toronto stretch and reach.

12 July 1993

IN BOSTON

Be greeted in 1810
On the SS Constitution,
Hear a jaunty American sailor
Sing her victories in hot sun.

And down at the Tea-party site
Think about taxes and grouse
On a replica of *Beaver II*,
Join the crowd at the Meeting House.

As an actor plays Sam Adams
And leads you into your choice,
Shout "Fie" or "Hear hear"
With a tea-throwing voice.

12 July 1993

RAINBOW

See from the bridge, the Falls.
Under a clear blue sky,
See the two smooth curves
And a cloud of smoke nearby.

And as our coach moves on
See the rainbow in the mist:
A gift made in just seconds,
Like a bracelet worn on a wrist.

13 July 1993

SUSQUEHANNA

"Susquehanna, Indian: long and beautiful."
"And when I asked the name of the river…and
heard that it was called the Susquehanna, the beauty
of the name seemed to be part and parcel of the
beauty of the land…that was the name, as no other
could be, for that shining river and desirable valley."
Robert Louis Stevenson, 1879

The river Susquehanna
Sleeps so peacefully
In central Pennsylvania,
Its shallows wait for me.

The river Susquehanna
Is as green as the wooded hills,
The Appalachian Mountains
Once full of Indian skills.

I will wade in Susquehanna

And flick my fishing rod out
And stand in cool rapids
And wait for rainbow trout.

13 July 1993

ON CATCHING A GLIMPSE OF THE U.N. SECURITY COUNCIL CHAMBER

"Don't push in," said the polite
English lady as I looked hard
Round the Security Council door
Just as it was closed by a guard.

But as the ladies walked
Towards the rest-room door
She hurried past them all
To be first in the queue, before.

"There would have been a puddle
On the floor if I hadn't," she said.
And what of my puddling tears
If the door had kept out my head?

13 July 1993

AMISH FARMS, PENNSYLVANIA

The Amish women serve,
White bonnets, parted hair,
In this enclosed market,
Plain clothes and eyes elsewhere.

Outside straw-hatted men
Drive in horse and "buggy" (not cart)
While women bend near maize,
Keeping themselves apart.

A young girl serves coffee
With parted hair, plain dress,
Then moves back to the stove,
A Puritan moving from mess.

14 July 1993

EVERGLADES SWAMP, FLORIDA

In the Florida Everglades,
In the mangrove swamp, in disguise
As the airboat sweeps and stops,
From the water a pair of eyes.

An alligator grins

513

Just by my resting arm.
Five vultures sit on trees,
A racoon stays out of harm.

In the Florida Everglades
Everything watches everyone:
Ibis, bald-headed eagle,
Egret, brown pelican.

The 'gator stares at me,
Then sinks under the surface.
I am back in a primeval swamp
In my ancestor-hunter's race.

21 July 1993

BURIED TREASURE

High above Treasure Island
We eat and watch bats fly
And lightning lights the sky,
Serene above palm, white sand.

I chew scallops and shrimps, mince
Grouper, a nice white fish.
Through the window – peace. I wish.
Suddenly you make me wince.

You say: "Those girls thought we're a
Happy family. If they
Only knew – we're good actors." Hey,
You struck buried treasure.

24 July 1993

IN ST. AUGUSTINE

In St. Augustine's castle
Six rangers fire a cannon
Dressed as 1740 Spanish
Artillerymen fighting on.

They hold ladder, worm, sponge,
A rammer and linstock,
And fight off the British
With smoke and a deafening shock.

I walk through the Spanish quarter
In an old George Street crowd.
The Spanish have been and gone
Like a long gone-by smoke cloud.

24 July 1993

CROSSING HOWARD FRANKLIN BRIDGE, ST. PETERSBURG, USA

Dawn on the intercoastal waterway,
And such a calm. On both sides of the road
A still silver, on which we are driving,
And reflections of distant hotels, like a code.

I look for a dolphin's fin – three days ago
While sailing on a yacht I saw sixty-two,
But only sea-birds, an egret on a post,
And this silver under the early pale blue.

We approach Tampa, and soon the rush
Of city traffic will replace this peace.
Palms now line the road that was touched by
    the still.
Now office blocks have made the vision
    cease.

27 July 1993

AT SPACEPORT, USA
(To the memory of Judy Resnik)

I see an Imax film on a screen five
And a half storeys high, and Judy Resnik,
    who
Is peering out, floating, laughing in shorts,
And two others of Challenger's ill-fated crew.

And then I drive to complex thirty-nine
At Kennedy Space Center, to launch pad B
Where the Discovery awaits lift-off next
    week,
The pad from which Challenger flew to
    eternity.

And I think of my fear of heights and am
    awed
That astronauts have the courage to walk in
    space   10
And perform repairs on other spacecraft,
Hanging upside down, oblivious of their
    place.

The ignition and clouds of steam and
    deafening roar –
I recall the thrust of rockets up into the sky.
Twenty-four years ago Apollo 11 went
To the moon with Armstrong from this same
    pad nearby.

And now the three-part rocket they used,
    Saturn-Five,
Lies massively in the open air, expire-
-d. I walk round it and am amazed
At the heroism of men who trusted its fire. 20

And now I visit the Astronauts Memorial,
Count sixteen names on the space mirror
    which aims,
Rotates and tilts to maintain a constant
    position
In relation to the sun which lights their names.

"To those who gave their lives to bring the
    stars
A little closer." I gaze at fifteen hundred li-
-ned signatures that were "with" the flight
    after Challenger,
And the brave man who said "We cannot wait
    to fly".

Astronauts everywhere, we see your names in
    sunshine
And thanks to what you did, the frontier of
    our race   30
Is no more, and a new Age of Discovery
Beckons mankind: the colonisation of space.
                   27 July 1993

DAYTONA, USA

I come out of McDonalds
To return to my car, and tread –
A lizard slithers near
And stops, with a raised head.

I look at it, it looks back,
A newt that lives on land.
We stare at each other,
Then it scurries across the sand.

I am here to write poems
But o lizard, what do you do?
Why do you live under bushes,
Why did God make you?
                   28 July 1993

GEORGE WASHINGTON AND A LIZARD

In the grounds of Mount Vernon
I gaze at George Washington's tomb,

Enclosed behind iron gates,
A raised white slab in gloom.

A lizard crawls across it.
The mightiest man in the land
Is now a convenient rest
For this lizard to command.
                   29 July 1993

AMERICAN LIBERTY QUINTET
(To Bill Clinton)

1. NEW YORK

I

A skyline of thrusting stone:
Rectangular towers and spires,
Sprouting commercial desires
Like a settlement overgrown.
Gape at Manhattan steel,
At how skyscrapers reach,
Dwarf the UN, and beseech
A global commonweal.
In Spanish and English
All are proud of their nation's zest,   10
Know America is best,
Echo Rockefeller's wish.
Sad Liberty surveys
All world events that are dire,
And lifts a welcoming fire
With a philanthropic gaze

II

When American Indian bark huts were here
In Manhattan (an Indian name) da Verrazano
Found "a very agreeable situation
Located within two small prominent hills", 20
And the Dutch East India Company's
    Hudson,
Who gave his name to the river, also found
"A pleasant land to see". (A mutinous crew
Put him in a boat to drift to his freezing
    death.)
From the north thirty Dutch settlers came and
    called
The place New Amsterdam and soon there
    were
Three hundred with a Governor, Peter
    Minnewitt,
Who bought it from the Indians for sixty

515

guilders.
Peg Leg Peter Stuyvesant, the Governor, built
A wall (Wall Street) to exclude British
    settlers,   30
And a farm (Dutch "bowerie"). When the
    British claimed
All east coast lands Charles the Second gave
    them
To his brother, the Duke of York, and sent
    Colonel
Nicholls to take New Amsterdam from the
    Dutch,
And in honour of the Duke he called it New
    York,
Which, despite revolts, was British for a
    hundred years.
When the English government at length
    imposed
The Sugar and Stamp, Currency and
    Quartering Acts,
Levying money from the colonists, and the
    Sons
Of Liberty led revolts; after the Boston   40
Massacre and Declaration of thirteen states
The first engagements between British and
    American troops
Took place at New York, where crowds
    pulled down George
The Third's statue, and Lord Howe forced
    Washington
To evacuate Brooklyn to Manhattan
With three thousand Americans killed or
    taken,
And the British ruled New York till
    Cornwallis
Surrendered. Then Washington rode down
    Canal Street
To Fraunces' Tavern, and the man whose will
Had held the American army together,   50
Said "I am not only retiring from public
Employment, but am retiring within myself"
And New York was the new nation's capital,
And once the Constitution had been written
Only Washington could fill the President's
    role
And he took the oath in Wall Street's Federal
    Hall
A year before the federal government
Transferred to Philadelphia for a ten-year
    term.

III

A rush and raucous streets
And a sultry southern air,   60
Manhattan an icon
To a modern despair
In all except money
And the power it buys:
Midtown skyscrapers
That block out the sunrise.
Grid-pattern avenues,
Straight streets and huge bank blocks
Follow a rational pattern
But conclude in a paradox: 70
Derelicts and stretch-limos,
Urban pride and neglect,
Manhattan and Chinatown,
Wall Street and the human wrecked.
Smoke, racism and drugs,
Homelessness and crime,
Look for a gun in each hand,
Hear the rapping of time.
From near Queensborough Bridge
Or from Staten Island   80
Feel the violence of change
And the excitement of demand.
In the faded splendour
Of a run-down Washington Park
Where is genteel Henry James?
And O'Neill's drunken dark?

The flashing neon lights
Of glittering Times Square,
East 42nd Street,
Where the arts teach how to care.   90
See the Dakota Building
Where John Lennon was shot
And in Central Park imagine
A place where the random is not.
Broadway, Fifth Avenue,
Museums, Madison Square,
Under the Empire State
Were Kong grabbed planes from the air.
The wedding cake décor
Of the Waldorf Astoria   100
And the Bowery and Bronx
Skid Row for drunks and hauteur.
Little Italy and Greenwich,
SoHo and TriBeCa,
Cafés and restaurants,
Salon, club, cinema.

The mild Mother of Exiles
Still lights the tempest-tost,
The tired, poor masses,
The homeless who are lost.   110
In the markets of Harlem
Two opposites make a truce:
Squalor and beauty lie
In the faces of Liberty's youth.

IV

New York points to the future, to a world role
For Liberty crowned with a Sun and holding
        fire
And a law book inscribed the fourth of July
Seventeen seventy-six. Now stand before
The Rockefeller Center on Fifth Avenue,
A skyscraper city within a city,   120
With tunnels underground, before which lies
A gold Prometheus holding fire, on a plaque
Read words of John D Rockefeller Junior
(Who gave New York Rockefeller University,
Fort Tryon Park, the Cloisters, the UN site
Which stood on twenty-two acres he owned,
And the non-denominational Riverside
        Church),
Ten Commandments each beginning "I
        believe":
"I believe in the supreme worth of the
        individual
And ... his right to life, liberty and the pursuit
        of happiness...,   130
That every right implies a responsibility...,
That the law was made for man and not man
        for the law,
That Government is the servant of the people
And not their master..., that truth and justice
        are
Fundamental to an enduring social order...,
That a man's word should be as good as his
        bond...,
That the rendering of useful service is the
        common duty
Of mankind and that only in the purifying Fire
Of sacrifice is the dross of selfishness
        consumed
And the greatness of the human soul set
        free.   140
I believe in an all-wise and all-loving God,
Named by whatever name, and that the
        individual's

Highest fulfilment, greatest happiness and
Widest usefulness are to be found in
Living in harmony with His will, that love
Is the greatest thing in the world, that it alone
Can overcome hate, that right can and will
Triumph over might." Noble sentiments,
Great words backed by his other Greek statue:
Atlas holding up the world in Fifth
        Avenue.   150
(And in the UN building, there is also Zeus
Who ruled the pre-Christian known world.)
        And this
Noble vision of world government, of a
UN incarnating Prometheus and Atlas,
Has returned in our time in the New World
        Order
("Novus Ordo Seculorum" on dollar bills)
Which David Rockefeller champions,
Club of Rome dream of a united ten-zone
        world:
After a world crash, a one-world currency,
By 2000 a pan-faith, pan-nation   160
UN-led universal world government
Under a benevolent rule, guarded by Liberty,
To serve the individual and love him,
Make his lot better with the "fire of sacrifice"
And New York money, which will rule the
        New Order.
And can we accept the words, not suspect the
        deeds,
And will the heirs live up to the high ideals
Of the world's greatest philanthropist, who
        was
America's wealthiest citizen? Go to
The CFR Headquarters on 68th Street   170
(The corner stone building without a plaque)
And ask them, are they committed to a world
That serves the individual and eliminates
Wars, arms and famines? Let us hope that
        they are,
As they have a network that influences the
        system.
Let us trust the vision of Rockefeller's words,
But please, Mr President, be on your guard,
Be wary of manipulators of his ideal,
Of groups of billionaires who seek world-rule,
Who would enslave every individual   180
To their own law and nightmare government,
Who would control the world's population
        increase

With wars, arms and famines, not by growing
    more food;
Please, Mr President, do not become
The prisoner of any system which controls
    you.
For ahead is a glorious American role,
A Golden Age, which Liberty will applaud:
The illumined pyramid eye on the dollar bill,
The masonic eye of Re and the enlightened
    mind
In a New World Order of illumined love   190
In which each nation is a pyramid brick,
Ruled by the inscription on quarters:
    "Liberty".

V

This thrusting financial might
Whose growth is a high wall,
This Liberty for all,
Is present here tonight
But is like the sun's rays
Spread round the world, is known
From Russia to South Africa,
In each world government's zone.   200
The rational enlightenment
Of grid-pattern avenues,
High-rise blocks, hourly news,
"Don't walk" crossings and rent,
Of "Have a nice day" for tips
And litter-free cut-lawns
And spotless clean restrooms,
Is wherever there are dawns.
The post-war Marshall Plan
Has after Maastricht grown   210
A USE and has shown:
Dollars can reshape man.

America's financial might
Helps democracies emerge:
Dollars in return for votes,
"Value all, please do not purge."
As Liberty lights in
All refugees from all
Tyrannies that will fall
With a welcoming torch and chin,   220
So Liberty gives light
To all nations who follow her,
Who overthrow tyrants
And proclaim what they prefer.
As we fly out of New York, scorch-

-ed on her island, Liberty
Stands alone, proud and free
And raises her arm and her torch.
Liberty like the sun
Holds out immortal Fire,   230
A sun-crowned, spoked ideal
All mankind will admire.

2. BOSTON

I

Bays and lagoons and green –
The first English pilgrims spied
A paradise, wide-eyed
At a terrain so clean.
In the South Meeting-House, sigh.
Hear a nation's agonised birth
From the freedom of the earth
And a dissenting cry.   240
The Puritans gone, somehow
Italians and Irish mill
Round the "bluebloods" on Beacon Hill.
It's a Catholic city now.
And now an urban sprawl
But still a nation's youth
Enshrines its freedom's truth
In Samuel Adams' call.

II

When the Indians called it Shawmut or
    "living waters"
William Blackstone lived here with early
    colonists   250
And invited the Puritans led by John
    Winthrop
Across from Charlestown to the spring,
Who renamed it Boston after an English town
(Short for Botolph's Town). Their "citty upon
    a hill"
Took it over, and gave Blackstone fifty acres
(Now the Common), which he left for Rhode
    Island,
And after James the Second revoked the
    colony's charter
And installed a Governor, who was forced to
    resign,
And after the Seven Years' War, England
    passed Acts
On her two million American colonists: 260
The Proclamation Line and the Sugar Act,

The Quartering Act (housing for British
    soldiers),
The Stamp Act (taxing anything written on
    paper).
Faneuil Hall, Cradle of Liberty, had seen
A protest ("No taxation without
    representation"),
And the Sons of Liberty rose, Patrick Henry
Crying out, "Give me liberty or give me
    death."
In Boston, there were riots and a boycott
Until Parliament repealed the offensive tax,
But what blindness not to learn from the
    Stamp Act.   270
And when Americans boycotted British
    imports
And rioted when John Hancock's ship,
    Liberty,
Was seized for non-payment of customs dues,
England sent four thousand redcoats to
    Boston,
And when Boston workers taunted them,
    protesting outside
The Governor's State House, the soldiers
    fired,
Killing five, one on the steps under the
    balcony.
Now Samuel Adams set up a network,
Formed "committees of correspondents" in
    the colonies –
In Boston a group of congregationalists   280
Who knew the Light and were mostly masons.
When Parliament's Tea Act gave a monopoly
On tea shipments to the British-owned East
    India
Tea Company, which was nearly bankrupt
With millions of pounds of unsold
    warehoused tea,
And a subsidy on tea to the Governor's friend,
One December night five thousand citizens
Rallied against the tea tax at Old South
And after hours of debate, which Samuel
    Adams chaired
(Through a hubbub of voices crying "Fie" or
    "Hear hear"),   290
And concluded, "Gentlemen, this meeting can
    do
No more to save the country," giving a signal
To a hundred Sons of Liberty outside
Who, already disguised as Mohawk Indians

With feathers in their hair, led two thousand
Down to Griffin's Wharf, boarded three ships,
    undid
Hatches, opened three hundred and forty-two
    chests
And hove the tea overboard. (And were they a
    lodge
Of Freemasons, these still anonymous men?)
"Boston Harbour, a tea-pot tonight," they
    cried   300
And: "Liberty, we're the Sons of Liberty."

After a calm, the retaliation came
As England closed Boston's port and then
    gave
The colony's government to the Royal
    Governor.
When the colonies met in the first Continental
    Congress
In Carpenters' Hall in Philadelphia,
And voted to resist England and stop all trade,
George declared Massachusetts to be in a
    state
Of rebellion. Minutemen armed, and as Gage
    left
To raid Concord and stop a second
    Congress   310
Paul Revere (a mason, like Washington)
Tipped off the Minutemen at Concord and
    rode
To Lexington, where a Minuteman's stray
    shot
Rang out, "the shot heard round the world",
And at Concord many British soldiers were
    killed,
And when sixteen hundred colonists defended
    at Breed's Hill
The British attacked and shot when they saw
    "the whites
Of their eyes", and won the battle of Bunker
    Hill.
When Congress made George Washington
    commander-in-chief
Of the Continental Army, he attacked   320
Canada, then bombarded Boston in March,
Then went to New York, after Paine's
    pamphlet,
Congress adopted Lee's resolution,
"These United Colonies are, and of right
Ought to be, free and independent States,"

And asked Jefferson to draft the Declaration
Of the Independent new United States.

III

Boston is a vibrant place:
Italians and Chinese,
Public parks and cafés,   330
Indians, Vietnamese;
Shops, boutiques and hotels
Where once God's true Elect
Obeyed their Elders' command,
Inspired by Calvin's sect.
The trolleys run between
Back Bay by the Charles which is still,
Two huge mirroring towers,
West End and Beacon Hill,
Harbour and Aquarium,   340
Little Italy, North End,
USS Constitution,
Where the Tea Party happened;
Downtown and Chinatown,
Frog Pond and the Common where
Witches were burned, men hanged,
Back to Copley Place and Square.
Renaissance style library,
Museums and concert halls,
Served by an underground –   350
A city where art has walls.
Not so far from Harvard,
Diverse and varied space
As old and modern mix –
Boston is a cultured place.

The mystic Light is found
Wherever Freemasons lament,
In the old lodge that built
The Bunker Hill monument.
Massachusetts State House,   360
The Common and Beacon Hill,
Has the Boston of Henry James
Faded like a love gone shrill?
At Boston University
Where art and science mix
The students are blessed with
The impact of Bell and Ricks.
Relics and bustling streets,
The old colonial times:
The Union Oyster House.   370
Federal gaslamps, church chimes.
Down in Quincy Market

A man entertains a crowd.
Have the Faneuil Hall Puritans
Gone like a passing cloud?
Outside the Old City Hall
Benjamin Franklin stands;
One half of his face smiles,
The serious half understands.
But at the Harbour's entrance   380
The permanent Boston light
Calls to all Puritans and masons
And shines out against the night.

IV

While New York's money can change the
        world, Boston
Can show a world government its immigrants.
E pluribus unum: out of many, one
("Give me your tired, your poor," says
        Liberty).
A million and a half Irish came from
The potato famine of eighteen forty-five,
And   were   joined   by   as   many
        Scandinavians,   390
And by nineteen-twenty, Poles, Jews,
        Austrians, Czechs,
Hungarians, Slovaks, Mexicans, and now they
        come
From Dominica, Haiti, Jamaica, Salvador,
Guatamala, Vietnam, Nicaragua and China.
From nineteen-ninety Congress set aside
Forty per cent of visas for Irish,
Who are now the most favoured immigrants,
And here in Boston comprise eighty per cent.
There has been an Irish Mayor, and in
        Charlestown
There are many Catholics, like the
        Kennedys.   400

Boston Irish look back not to the Puritans
Of England, but to Ireland, and the IRA
And so Boston embodies America's Irish
        roots,
An alternative to the Puritan heritage,
Another link with Europe, a lineage
More palatable than Puritanism to
The coming world government and a future
        time
When all the world government's ten zones
        have links.
The New World Order will not think of

520

Puritans.
Where are the Puritans now? Where have they
    gone? 410
What were they like? Were they like the
    people
The reconstructed settlement in Plymouth?
Or the black-wearing Amish Anabaptists
Round Lancaster in Pennsylvania?
The New World Order unites all races,
Seeks links between the US and Europe,
And Boston is a microcosm of its work.

          V
Boston's old freedom trail
Shows local men who fought
The British – Hancock's sort, 420
Two Adams, Revere risked jail.
But this trail is now for all
The States in the union,
Who find their own struggles
Mirrored in this first one.
These colonists were subjects
Of Britain and their King,
Freedom was a precious thing,
They were reluctant disaffects.
The statue of Franklin 430
Half smiling and half sad
Catches their torn feelings
As they turned against what was bad.
True men's integrity
Makes civilisations grow
When they see, their soul aglow,
Universal liberty.

Boston's old freedom trail
Is still trodden today,
As all growth from first beginnings 440
Is measured by their way.
Now the world comes to celebrate
And admire their deeds and aplomb,
And Sam Adams' freedom
Inspires others to emulate.
America is free
From all outside tyranny,
From all who would tax her,
Or compromise liberty.
American quarters show 450
"Liberty" inscribed above
Washington's head in love –
A pledge of what will never go.

And the world government
Will likewise seek to be free
And will be inspired by Boston
As it pledges man's liberty.

3. WASHINGTON

          I
A Roman grandeur and space:
White columns, and marble domes,
Wide avenues, quaint homes 460
Show a world capital's face.
Wonder at the Capitol, the
White House, Washington monument,
The memorials to President
Jefferson, Lincoln, Kennedy.
A city built for politics,
Capital that empties at night
Leaving the streets to non-white:
Washington's union fix.
From the top of the Capitol 470
Freedom, over nineteen feet tall,
And her eagle look down the Mall
To his obelisk and temple.

          II
George Washington *was* the nation, between
    defeats
And final victory stood this obstinate man
Who rode in the countryside, rallying new
    troops,
Keeping freedom alive. A mason, van Braam,
Perhaps taught him military tactics,
And he was made Adjutant with the rank of
    Major
At just twenty, by the Governor of
    Virginia, 480
Then a mason in March seventeen fifty-three
And a Master Mason in August at the lodge
At Fredericksburg when he was only twenty-
    one,
And the masonic Light shone into his
    Episcopalian faith
And gave him a freedom-fighter's proud will.
His military career began when he
    volunteered
To fight the French in Ohio and he put
Into practice his masonic tenets
(In the end one fifth of his troops, two out of
    ten

Thousand, were masons) until after many
    skirmishes   490
He was appointed Commander-in-chief of the
    new
Continental Army after Bunker Hill,
Aged forty-three, in seventeen seventy-five.
For eight years he fought an up-and-down
    campaign
As the US entered Canada (Quebec did not
    fall)
But in March seventy-six they forced the
    British
To withdraw from Boston, go to New York,
Where Washington lost to Lord Howe, but
    crossed
The Delaware and won at Trenton and at
Bennington, and having lost at Brandy-
    wine   500
Near Philadelphia, fought back at
    Germantown
And at Saratoga, harried Clinton's English
At Monmouth, extended the war to sea.
    Clinton
Captured Charleston and Cambden, but the
    Americans
Fought back at Coupens and Guilford and
    with French help
Washington trapped Cornwallis at Yorktown,
Cornwallis surrendered, and the war ended.
It had been a long and exhausting struggle
When, in February seventeen eighty-two,
England began peace negotiations   510
And in September signed a Peace Treaty
Which ended the American Revolution.
Some Americans wanted Washington to be
    King,
But he disbanded the Continental Army
And gave a farewell address to his soldiers
In New York, at Fraunces' Tavern – "With a
    head
Full of love and gratitude I now take leave of
    you" –
And, Cincinnatus of the West, went back to
    his farm
At Mount Vernon and tilled the earth till the
Articles of Confederation proved
    inadequate   520
And the Constitutional Convention's
    delegates
Gathered in Philadelphia's Independence Hall

With Washington presiding and Benjamin
Franklin (now eighty-one) encouraging
("How has it happened, that we have not once
    thought of applying
To the Father of Light to illuminate our
    understandings?"),
Wrote a charter for a more perfect union
With three branches of government –
    executive,
Legislative and judicial – and Washington
Was nominated for election as President.   530
And at Mount Vernon walk among tall trees
    and cicadas
Overlooking the Potomac, to the dining-room
Where Washington heard he had won and
    received the call
To be the first President, and accepted it
Though he did not want the job, seeing
    himself
As a General, not as a politician,
But he had come to embody the new nation,
The United States that was largely his
    creation.

III

By day a bustling city.
By night a ghost town. I stress,   540
In two hundred years, this capital
Grew from marshy wilderness
(And an idea in Washington's mind)
To have a Graeco-Roman feel:
The Supreme Court draws on Rome's
Hall of Justice ideal;
Jefferson Monument – Pantheon
(Amid six thousand cherry trees);
Lincoln's – the Parthenon;
White House – Dublin Romanese;   550
Capitol – St. Peter's.
Avenues radiate extent
Like spokes in a wheel from
Capitol to Washington Monument,
To Lincoln Memorial,
To Jefferson's hauteur,
To the White House and Union Station,
Connect each circle and track
Pierre Charles L'Enfant's design
(Carved out by the Potomac).   560
Congress allowed Washington
To choose a ten mile square
Site on the Potamac River,

He gave Alexandria a share.

L'Enfant, a French engineer
Saw "magnificent distances" through
The Mall, a Champs Elysées,
Napoleonic "Grand Avenue",
To recapture Versailles,
Capitol – Les Invalides,   570
But architects followed Rome.
Now this downtown diamond pleads
Between its four avenues
Which survived the burning down
Of the Capitol and White House
In eighteen-fourteen by the Crown.
Go to Arlington Cemetery,
See the eternal fire
By J. F. Kennedy's stone
(Robert Lee's house a spire);   580
Pass the Pentagon on your way
To Alexandria's heat
And the eighteenth century houses
In each old colonial street,
But you can never escape
The Father of the Country
Who gave his name to the place
And whose Light is in his debris
As it is in the Pharos,
Where he stands in the Great Hall   590
And in the Egyptian shrine
And the pyramid that tops all.

IV

Washington has a great future, it is already
The unofficial capital of the world.
By and large, what the President says goes,
And any answer he gives tops the world news
Even if it is shouted near a helicopter
Or exchanged with TV men on a golf course.
Caesar has spoken, hear what Caesar said.
Mr President, US hegemony   600
Is greater than ever, your economy
Two and a half times your nearest
    competitor's
(With a GNP approaching Europe's and
    Japan's),
You have a huge capacity to project
Military force overseas, with forward bases
And 14 aircraft carriers, more than all navies',
But it seems that your country has lost
    confidence,

That, weary, debilitated, you have abdicated
World leadership, believing you are
    overstretched,
Lacking influence, inclination and money 610
To use military force and full of doubts
About your moral mission except under the
    UN,
And it seems you are switching from defence
    to medicare
And will cease to be a global superpower,
Disarming as powers rise in the Far East
(China and North Korea), and calling for
A Pacific Community, and abandoning
Your Pax Americana for a mild
Isolationism under the New World Order
Which will look to Washington as well as
    New York.   620
For how can the UN agree without the
    guidance
Behind the scenes of its most influential
    member,
Of the only superpower with troops for all
    quarters,
Which is flying round the planet and capable
    of
The precision-bombing that awed during the
    Gulf War?
What is decided in the White House is
    generally
Followed in the UN, where liberty
Has the assent of the world's nearly two
    hundred
Nations, who increasingly act with a united
    voice.
Mr President, your civilisation is young 630
And has a Roman expansionist stage ahead
When all will seek the benefit of liberty
And the rights conferred by American
    citizenship.
But there are rumours that Washington is in
    the grip
Of the heirs of the Illuminati, the secret
    society
Which infiltrated the Grand Orient and
Covertly ran the French Revolution
Through Robespierre and Mirabeau and their
    guillotine,
And attempted world government through
    Napoleon,
And, having financed Marx while he wrote

Das Kapital,   640
Again through Lenin and Hitler, arming both
Left and right, and who are waiting to try
    again,
Some say with a plan to reduce the world's
    population
By three billion within the next few years,
Some say by deliberately spreading Aids and
    wars.
Revisionist history is full of rumours,
And few can know the truth, and we are
    perplexed.

Let us draw comfort from the purity of
    George Washington,
And the masonic temple in Alexandria
Which is shaped like the Pharos in Egypt's
    town of that name   650
(One of the seven wonders of the world)
With a pyramid triangle at the top,
And the Hebrew for Yahweh, where in the
    Great Hall
Washington stands as a Worshipful Master,
Below seven levels of the Tower and the
    Royal Arch Room
And the Ark of the Covenant, and near the
    shrine's
Children's Room, where an Egyptian god
    sends light
To heal a boy and girl while children play
In trees, suggesting the lodge's charitable
    work.
Washington was a mason in seventeen fifty-
    three,   660
The Illuminati were formed in July
Seventeen seventy-six. Washington later
    wrote
"I believe that none of the lodges in this
    country
Are contaminated with the principles
Of the society of the Illuminati"
And: "It is not my intention to doubt
That the doctrines of the Illuminati
And the principles of Jacobism had not spread
In the United States. On the contrary
No one is more fully satisfied of the facts   670
Than I am. The idea I meant to convey was
    that I
Did not believe that the Lodges of
    Freemasons

In this Country had, as Societies, endeavoured
To propagate the diabolical tenets of
The first, or the pernicious principles of the
    latter."
Let us believe that Washington, Master
    Mason,
Was in no way touched by those who would
    overthrow
Christianity and European governments.
At Mount Vernon see the bed on which he
    died
And in the grounds the site of his first
    tomb   680
Where he was interred by local Freemasons
(Which he preferred to a place in the Capitol)
And the site he chose there for his present
    tomb,
And know in his death as well as in his life
Washington gave himself to masonry.
And so let us hope that the influential world
    groups
Are all likewise free from the Illuminatist
    taint
Of Satanism and its anti-religious creed
Of occult rituals and black witchcraft,
And, as the millennium advances and
    some   690
Point to the tradition of the Second Coming,
Free from the rule of the Beast which some
    have predicted
After three and a half years of tribulation
Beginning in nineteen ninety-seven, a time
Of great dreadfulness. Please, Mr President,
Dissociate yourself from the rumours,
Associate yourself with deniers of them,
And keep Washington as pure as its founder
    planned,
Respect the Light that made the Revolution
And America's world role will be applauded
    by all   700
As Washington comes to be seen as the new
    Rome
With a universal vision for all mankind.

V

A union of States unfurled
The nation's government well,
And is now a model
For the government of the world.
Freedom stands guard on top

Of the Capitol she owns
And looks across fifty States;
Now she also guards ten zones   710
Of the world's continents;
For the UN, she looks down
(The tallest statue in town),
On blocks and refugees' tents.
The whole world now looks here –
Whether on Bosnian need
Or for Somalian food –
For guidance and a lead.
The masonic Light whose place
Shaped Washington's determined wish   720
To expel the British
Is now the centre of space.

In the dome of the Capitol
Brumidi's fresco shows
Washington and thirteen maidens,
Each free colony glows
From the central Light as a womb:
A round spider's web of sun.
In the Rotunda crypt, a shun-
-ned space for Washington's tomb.   730
At the Constitutional Convention
Washington's presiding chair
Was topped by a half-rising sun
With eyes and thirteen-rayed hair,
And the Washington obelisk
Of true Egyptian height
Is a ray of the Light
That towers near the sun's disc
To remind the world for all time
The American civilisation   740
Began with a vision of Light
That took physical form and shone.

4. PHILADELPHIA

I

More towers and blocks as thrust
Buildings dwarf Penn's statue
On the Town Hall and the view,
Once the capital, now just
A provincial city that fell,
Independence Hall, the dawn
Where the United States was born,
And the cracked Liberty Bell.   750
And Franklin left his home,
Walked the cobbles by the Post

Office to help them ghost
A Constitution worthy of Rome.
A city remembering where
The three arms of the USA
Were just a short walk away
In this quiet tree-filled square.
And then the closing down
As the capital moved elsewhere,   760
The President no longer there,
And an emptiness, a frown.

II

Philadelphia, city of "brotherly love",
Was founded by William Penn of Chigwell
    School,
Who landed up the Delaware River,
Whose statue stands on the new Town Hall,
    who owned
Pennsylvania as a proprietorial colony
And whose family owned it till seventeen
    seventy-six
(Not bad for a Chigwell boy, owning a
    colony).
Once the second largest city to London,   770
Philadelphia had its moment after the burning
Of George's royal coat of arms, when in
Seventeen seventy-six the Declaration of
Independence was signed in Independence
    Hall
(Before the British captured Philadelphia),
Where eleven years later, the Constitution
    was signed –
See Washington's chair with a half-rising sun.
Here Franklin was peacemaker, for ten years
Philadelphia became capital of the new US,
Washington lived in the President's
    house   780
The other end of the Mall from Independence
Hall, Congress Hall and the Supreme Court
    (which met
In the Old City Hall) through the yellow fever
    epidemic,
Until Congress moved the new capital to
    Washington.
Ten glorious years at the start of a new nation,
At the birth of a new civilisation.

III

A slow, uncommercial town;
Only the gharries that wait

525

At the end of the Mall
Suggest early or late, 790
Only steak and fruit sellers
At the roadside wait to be paid.
In the gardens sit and munch
A steak sandwich in the shade,
Then walk to Franklin Court,
Look in at the Post Office which,
As it pre-dates the union,
Still has its own franking pitch.
Wander to Franklin's grave
In Christ Church Cemetery. 800
How could a printer represent
His State, his country and be?
Fall in with a Ranger
And follow his Washington tour,
As he stands and talks by the site
Of the President's House, and sure-
-ly relates the schism between
Hamilton and Jefferson, who were
Pro-British or pro-French,
Pro-bank or pro-farm, who blur- 810
-red the union, which became
The two parties who glare,
How Washington lived a myth:
Black velvet and powdered hair

Feel the presence of Washington
And see the Liberty Bell
Hang in the Hall's belfry,
Reconstruct what the past can tell.
Join the long waiting line
In Independence Square 820
Where the Declaration was first read
In a voice suggesting a glare.
Wander to the Old State House,
Saunter to the Congress Hall,
Meander to the Philosophical
Society, Franklin's call,
As people meander
And come and go and share
In dynamic America
Though the centre has moved elsewhere.
Gaze at the present, which is in- 830
-conceivable without the past.
Philosophers Penn and Franklin,
Your statues survey the vast
Nation you brought into being.
You were right to turn away
From your mother England,

Let all talents enter your way.
What do you now think of us?
Let Franklin speak the truth.
Are you not proud of Liberty's 840
New world role and her youth?

IV

And the future? Despite the surge of energy
A decade ago, Philadelphia is in decay,
People are moving out, it looks rundown,
Needs cash; and yet Penn's was the highest
     statue in
Nineteen eighty-three and now he is dwarfed
     by
The upsurge that has moved across the
     USA,
The energy is here, it is still the fifth
Largest town in the country. And as the
     US
Moves towards a world role, so the principles
     of the 850
Declaration of Independence (an appeal
To equality and the natural rights of men,
To life, liberty and the pursuit of happiness)
And of the Constitution (that the people of the
     US
"To form a more perfect union" promote
     justice,
Domestic tranquillity, welfare and Liberty)
Will be taken up and adopted all round the
     world,
And will be sought, just as Roman principles
And Roman citizenship were sought after
By all the known Roman world, and will
     form 860
The basis of the coming world government.
This Liberty Bell which once called a town
To assemblies and ceremonies as a working
     bell,
And symbolised liberty for all anti-slaves
And travelled the country to "proclaim
     LIBERTY
Throughout all the Land until all the
     Inhabitants
Thereof" and became a symbol of national
     unity,
This Bell which spoke in a booming tongue
     now gathers
Two million people a year, and in the same
     way

This town, which first proclaimed the
    Declaration   870
Of Independence and the Constitution,
Will proclaim to the entire world the principle
    of
Brotherly love, which the world will discover
    from it.

V

Independence is one.
What the USA is now
Is inseparable from how
The nation has begun.
The room where Jefferson lodged
And wrote his Declaration
In two weeks, is still there;   880
The President's House has gone
As has Franklin's, but all
Are present beneath our feet
From Market to Walnut Street
And the Independence Hall,
And the important room
Where the inkstand still stands,
Where a great exit stirred
The pens in Romantic hands.
And so the US, the shield   890
Of the world and its kitty,
Is inseparable from this city
Where the Liberty Bell pealed.

The Founding Fathers knew
"Liberty is a sacred Fire"
And they also knew new nations
Grow when spirits aspire.
Civilisations hatch
When rays of the Fire shine
On souls that become a shrine,   900
Energise what leaders they catch.
And the half-rising sun
On the back of Washington's chair
Was illumination that rayed
Washington's soul like hair,
And shines on all who see both
And so shines to the world and inspires,
Is a centre for all Fires,
And the secret of all growth.
The US's upsurge   910
Is rooted in this soil
And America's glory mirrors
The Founding Fathers' toil.

5. ST. PETERSBURG

I

Blue pools and a white beach
On the Gulf of Mexico,
Palms and a hot wind blow
Liberty from the office's reach.
White sand and concrete hotels
Along Gulf Boulevard
From the pink Don CeSar,   920
And islands laden with shells.
The intercoastal waterway
Is a still, sunny silver
From St. Pete to Clearwater
And in palm-lined Dolphin Bay.
De Soto's healing springs
Led American medics to state
That the Pinellas could create
A "world health city" for kings.
So Demens brought the railway   930
From Tampa into town and
Named it St. Petersburg, land
Where the sun shines every day.

II

Europeans – Spaniards and English – first saw
Florida, and a Spanish map of 1502
Shows a peninsula like it, and Peter Marty
Wrote of land near Bahamas with water of
Eternal youth. Two years later bearded
Juan Ponce de Léon, Governor of "San Juan"
(Now Puerto Rico) who had been on
    Columbus's   940
Second voyage, heard from local Indians
Of "a fabulous fountain at Bimini
That turned old men young", a fountain of
    youth,
And obtained a document signed by the King
    of Spain
Granting him a licence to discover lands
North of Cuba, where Indians said there was
A miraculous fountain, and was made
    Governor
And Chief Justice of such lands as he might
    discover.
De Léon sought the Fountain of Youth (or
    perhaps gold).
Sailing by the stars, keeping a thirty
    degree   950
Angle between Pole Star and the horizon,

And sighted Florida in March and went
    ashore in April
Near St. Augustine: he sailed into Matanzas
    Bay,
Did not turn into the Salt Run or the North
    River,
And avoided islands and the Matanzas River's
    mouth
And perhaps made for Selois, the town of
Timucuan Indians, whom he christianised
And who now practised Christian burials.
He landed in the time of the Spanish Feast of
    Flowers
At Easter, and named the land "La
    Florida"   960
("Flowering" or Land of Flowers after
    "Pascua Florida")
And Florida became the name for America
From the nearby Rio Grande to Labrador,
The base for exploring Peru and Chile.
He explored the land of the Timucuan Indians
And found an ancient spring which maintains
    the legend;
Perhaps he was led there by the Indians
Who had a burial ground not far away.
Today the water table has dropped, but still
The spring trickles water into a well   970
From which you can drink, and beside it a
    workman found
A Landmark cross of stones, fifteen down,
    thirteen
Across, to make the date, fifteen thirteen,
Which was also the date Spain's colonial era
    began.
But, eight years later, landing off Marco
    Island
He was wounded by the Culoosa Indians
And died, and so his search for eternal youth
Ended in death. And Saint Augustine,
    founded by
Pedro Menendez de Aviles in
Fifteen sixty-five, grew and was captured
    by   980
The British Drake in fifteen eighty-six
And then in seventeen sixty-three after
The Spanish had built the Castillo de San
    Marcos
And kept out the British in two sieges.
And how many have since sought eternal
    youth

Before Walt Disney came from California
And bought land, paid no tax, and recreated
With his imagination an eternal youth.
O water of eternal youth, I salute you!

Florida was settled after the Civil War: 990
Palm Beach, Miami Beach, Fort Lauderdale,
And the original swamp lands of the
    Everglades
Still hold the spirit of the original Florida.
Go over sunshine skyway to Naples
And boat by the waterside holiday homes of
    the rich,
Drive to Everglades City by the narrow river,
See ibis, blue herons and snowy egrets,
See alligators peering near the reeds,
Near a pond of twenty alligators and turtles
Take an airboat into the mangrove
    swamps   1000
And see osprey's nests, buzzards (actually
    vultures),
Cormorants, blue crabs, tree crabs and
    racoons,
Look for cougars and bald-headed eagles
While alligators watch, and then drive to
Marco Island, largest of the Ten Thousand
    Islands,
Where brown pelicans fly in formation
Over the white shell sands by the green Gulf.
See thousands of egg cockles, cat's paws,
    cat's eyes,
Many-ribbed scallops, Florida fighting conch,
Banded tulip, whelk, crested and thorny
    oysters   1010
Before you return in the evening sun.
Looking for eyes in the water, know you have
    seen
The primeval Florida de Léon saw
As you pass the spot where the Culoosa
    wounded him.
(A lowering cloud and a white sting in its tail,
A rumble of thunder and drops of rain,
Then a round red sun and a pink and orange
    sunset.)

III

Here people come to relax,
To laze and swim, not think,
To lie in the pool and eat,   1020
To sunbathe, laugh and drink.

From the drifting parasail
Look down at the Don CeSar,
Built in the twenties boom,
Its pink stucco seen afar.
Narrow Gulf Boulevard
Has the Gulf on one side,
Dolphin Bay the other,
Sun-worshippers drowsy-eyed.
There is no shade on the beach,   1030
Only the white glare of sand;
Huddle under the cool palms
Or thatched cones and get tanned.
Priapic Florida protrudes
From the USA's underbelly;
Lithe wives sit on the pool ledge
As if to say, "Look at me."
See the pleasure-seekers
Throng the long white reach,
Or seek dolphins in yachts   1040
As brown pelicans soar past the beach.
At de Léon's Fountain of Youth
Stand by the enclosed well.
A trickle still drips from the spring,
Sip the elixir, and feel well.

Or go to Orlando and see
The secret of eternal youth:
In Disney's Magic Kingdom
Main Street, USA has the truth.
At a "surprise" parade at three   1050
Crowds line the baking streets,
Music blares over loudspeakers,
A carnival atmosphere beats:
A band waving at children,
Glittering men on stilts,
And, drawn on a chariot,
Like a Moloch that tilts,
Like a Hindu god to its shrine,
A gigantic Mickey Mouse
In rubber with waving girls,   1060
As tall as a three-storey house,
Who brings wide-eyed wonder
To each waiting heart and tongue,
And calls to the child in man
Who is eternally young.
Here is a magical kingdom
Of fantasy, fancy dress.
Does it matter that it's false,
Artificial and tasteless?
Find in the imagination   1070

Perpetual entertainment,
And through the eternal child,
Eternal youth and assent.

                    IV
Back to the future at Universal Studios
In Orlando: sit in a De Lorean
And be bumped and violently jolted and
        plunge
Round the side of a skyscraper, see machines
With gadgets fly through the air. Is Florida's
        future
To create fantasies and nightmares for
        tourists,
The "what if?" speculations that led to
        ET,   1080
King Kong and *The Fly*, and Hitchcock's
        Birds
(Nature turning against us), the other rides?
Is Florida's future to frighten with awful
Possibilities forced perspective buildings
And make us all grateful for the status quo,
Appreciate the present after being involved
In living its contradiction, to practise
A subtle population mind-control?
At Disney's nearby Epcot Center see
Images of the future – deserts reclaimed, 1090
Cities under sea, telescreen phones, and space
Colonies – from an Age of Information,
From an electronic network linking earth and
        space.
Ours is surely the greatest generation ever:
While others barely coped with the wheel, we
Have taken to the air and have solved the
        problems of living
Without gravity in space. And so do we not
Deserve our sun and sea, our R and R?

For a Floridan contribution to future world
        power
And the pioneering spirit of the first
        Americans   1100
See this testimony to American prestige,
To the one nation that is flying round the
        planets:
Cars converge on flat Cape Canaveral,
The roads are jammed, thousands line nearby
        beaches
Looking towards Spaceport USA, where
At Nasa's Kennedy Space Center, a

Shuttle is ready to fly. Last week you drove,
Passing the nest of a bald eagle, the national
    bird,
To complex thirty-nine and launch pad B
(Where Apollo 11 left for the moon,   1110
And where Challenger left) by the crawler-
    road, and saw
The Discovery waiting for its lift-off.
Now view it across the wide Indian River:
To the left of the vehicle assembly building,
From the launch pad see a rolling cloud of
    steam
Billow first to the right, then to the left, and
    then
Flames and an upward trail, and later a roar,
See the space shuttle Discovery climb
Watch it for two minutes as it thrusts five
Astronauts up into space – seven minutes 1120
To twenty thousand miles per hour. Did you
    see
The fuel tank and booster rockets fall off?
The orbiter sails clear across the blue sky
To revolve the world in space and help build
A space outpost, the Space Station Freedom,
A launching pad to send more astronauts
Back to the moon and possibly to Mars.
Hear the cheering from us humans below
For a safe launch (unlike the Challenger's).
Mr President, the hope and dream are
    there,   1130
And the curiosity of humankind,
Know America's pioneering spirit lives:
New voyages to new New Worlds, a new
Age of Discovery. The future calls,
The Space Station Freedom is being built,
The imagination puts Liberty in space
With an information network above all
    nations
And guards the world's freedom with
    computers,
Through a thousand orbiting signalling
    spacecraft,
An awesome array of technological
    might.   1140
Will it one day control the world's weather?
Drive back through a storm, under a black
    Florida sky,
With the lightning flickering every two
    seconds
And every half minute a flash of white hot fire

That jolts the pen from your hand as you write
    on,
Ignore the distraction, retain your
    concentration –
Then the rainbow against black over Dolphin
    Bay!

V

Florida, the "sunshine state",
Is a world tourist centre
(Over forty million a year),   1150
With lakes that evaporate.
The world's first airline service
Was from St. Petersburg to Tampa,
Yet still the Everglades
Belongs to the alligator.
The dolphins in Dolphin Bay
Curve up a fin, then dive;
Stone-like ibis – alive.
On a pole sits a rare osprey.
Here there are rare manatees,   1160
Orange-throat cormorants fish,
Brown pelicans grin and dive,
Terns sit on their heads and wish.
Feel the jerk of the parasail, then
Dance on the wind above
And think, who would not love
To be a US citizen?

Guaranteed sunshine
Between subtropical warm
And tropical damp, fine weather   1170
Quickly returns after storm.
A tourist Paradise:
Here the world comes for health.
New York stands for the world's wealth,
Boston for its freedom's price,
Washington for its politics,
Philadelphia its independence,
Florida offers the world
Health and youth's sunshine sense –
Five fingers on Liberty's hand   1180
That guards the world with her fire
In five shapes that inspire:
Whether as Boston's tea-band,
Washington's Freedom, the Bell,
Space Station Freedom (still furled),
Or New York's democracy,
Sun-crowned Liberty lights the world.

11-29 July 1993

THE HILLS OF FIFE: DOVES AND WEDDING

The mist lifts from the hills of Fife,
A distant sun appears,
The puddles no longer splash with rain,
My daughter, have no fears:

It is brightening from the hills of Fife,
Twelve white doves sit and wait
For the sun that will soon be shining on
Your four o'clock wedding date.

It is early yet, and before sundown
You will be married, and hot,
And those twelve doves will still sit on
The perches of their dovecot.

5 August 1993

TOBOGGANING DOWN THE SKY

Above the mountain of cloud, the glare
Dazzles our screwn-up eyes.
Like an arrow, our trajectory
Declines from its slow rise.

We descend from the blue into clouds
That are like Arctic snowdrifts;
Now we sleigh on a sledge through white,
Sending out spray – mist lifts

And we're gliding down over London,
Over blocks like stones on a bend,
And we cross a winding brook,
A toboggan at its run's end.

6 August 1993

RUBBLE

An Italian gallery,
With Renaissance works of art,
A place where people queue
To view the visionary heart.

A bomb in a sidestreet
And now from the shattered walls
Hang broken canvas and glass,
Desecration that appals.

Who could put their cause
Above eight hundred years,
And shatter the heritage

That preserved so many seers?

And what artist foresaw it?
Only one seer I know
Who painted a pile of rubble
By a front that is cinquecento.

13-14 August 1993

ARRIVAL OF THE MUSE

I stand at the Arrival Gate,
One after another, people come through.
Then you, pushing a trolley with
Your bags, and a smile like a billet-doux.

O Muse, welcome back, you have returned,
O Muse, this way to the car park.
We pay our dues, then drive for home –
O Muse, I am tranquil in this dark!

13-14 August 1993

MASK

You catch my eye, I smile and wait,
You hand me images as I kneel,
A diagram of the universe:
Neo-Platonist circles like a wheel.

That look in your eyes, does it ask
"What's going on?", "Come again", or
            "Yes"?
Or is it "Danger"? What does it say?
Your face is a mask, I can only guess.

13-14 August 1993

TOGETHER

And now we are together at last,
O lie still in my arms, my love.
Fill me with a thousand images,
Inspire from a world above.

O my love, we are together again,
You are again in your rightful place,
And I am full of images
You will draw out at a leisurely pace.

13-14 August 1993

AURA

You see the aura round my head,
A bright white glow around my crown,
You see with eyes that are clairvoyant,
A glance that knows me up and down.

531

The organ of perception has
Atrophied, but has grown in you.
You see the future, Muse, and know
My aura and yours will be one, and two.

13-14 August 1993

BEAUTY: PUMPING, DEFLATING

You say "Can I do some channelling",
Lie me face down so my eyes see black,
Then turn me round and stroke my mind
With slender fingers that pump what's slack,

And your divine knowledge turns to love
As you love time, my erotic Muse;
Eternity's treasures are bright,
Our two imaginations fuse.

"You're beautiful" I whisper in
Ecstatic pleasure, and you reply
"You make me feel beautiful" and
Deflate me so gently I want to cry.

13-14 August 1993

GONG

I gong the gong for your breakfast,
You come down, Muse, for coffee and
Cereal, bread, I serve it as
If you were a guest, with a reverent hand.

O Muse, we must remain apart
As if we had broken a taboo
Such as incest, which booms like a gong.
Be patient, and we will come through.

13-14 August 1993

SNAKE-CHARMER

My lungs are bad, my eyes have rings,
You soothe my skin, I can't reply.
I am ill and cannot respond to you.
For a third time in a day, I sigh.

But you will heal me with your art,
Nursemaid and snake-charmer, you will
Draw out the patch on my lungs as heat
And I will rise to your charming skill.

13-14 August 1993

WATERS

O Muse, we walk by your childhood haunts,

Round waters where coots and geese swim
And anglers sit and wait and snooze,
And a vitality now fills each limb.

I walk myself back to health with you,
As if near your Pierian spring
I revel at being close to you
And love each crawling, flying thing.

13-14 August 1993

MUSE, COAXING

We sit in a candlelit restaurant
And eat tandoori for a change,
And you ask me about the genres
That give a great poet his range.

I say, "Lyrics, odes, elegies, epic –
Virgil, Horace, Ovid all pass."
You coax ideas out of my mind
As the candle splutters in the glass.

And now you coax me back to health,
Your hands are burning as you draw
The patches from my lungs and then
Coax vigour from me like a whore.

13-14 August 1993

BURIED TOGETHER

We walk in the Forest graveyard,
I show you the rail where I will lie,
Show the spire and the weather-vane
Where God measures clouds that drift by,

And you say, "I would like to be buried with
            you,
We will be together for eternity."
And I am moved, for no one else
Has asked to spend for ever with me.

O Muse, some would not be alone
For an hour, let alone a long decade,
Yet our bones will lie beneath slow time
And love for ever in this Forest glade.

13-14 August 1993

IMAGES

I lie in the dark and close my eyes
And you descend and fondle me,
Surprise me with your warm approach,
And now I see visions excitedly.

You say, "Your surrendering soul tingles
Like chilly ice cream on warm lips."
O Muse, as you draw images from me
You draw out poems in little drips.

13-14 August 1993

TRAM

Tram, slow creature of time,
Trundling early or late,
Carrying people to appointments
Past stops where workers wait,

Past the canal with still water
Past the church with the still spire,
Past Eternity which peeps through
Time's cage of line and wire.

13-14 August 1993

POSSESSED

O Muse, I want you now; you say,
"First make a fuss of me."
But come into me now while the interest is
                              there,
Don't let me go dark prematurely.

Now as if we lay on petalled sheets
You give me knowledge and moan
"I feel possessed – by you", and I smile
As if you were now flesh and bone.

13-14 August 1993

VINES AND ROSES

A vineyard and red roses,
At the end of the vineyard lines.
Once roses revealed disease
Three weeks before the vines.

Artists are like a rose,
Civilisations a vineyard.
Artists reveal disease
Before a vine is scarred.

Rothschilds' vineyard, two roses:
O Muse, we two now show
The health of the world's vineyard
By the health our two blooms know.

13-14 August 1993

RAIN

It is raining outside as we lie

Behind drawn curtains, closely splayed.
The night has lengthened into day,
At least the sun has been delayed.

O time, stand still, "lente, lente"
As we huddle together against the gloom
And rejoice in each other's presence
And shut the universe out of our room.

13-14 August 1993

EXECUTION

Last day – we drive on the motorway,
"Station, don't come" you plead to daylight
As if you could hold off evenfall
Like Faustus holding off midnight.

"Don't come, don't come" you whisper again,
Watching time take your love away.
A few clouds in clear sky, the time
Of execution is the end of day.

O Muse, we are like two condemned
Who ride in a tumbril through green,
But let us hold each other's hand
Until we reach the guillotine.

13-14 August 1993

GOODBYE

The train is in, o hurry now –
"No, let it go, we'll miss the train,
Let us take the next one, have tea
And ten minutes together again."

We sit on a platform and sip tea.
O Muse, you will be going soon.
We chew millionaire shortcake and
Lament the movements of the moon.

And now the dreadful train grates in,
I put your luggage on the rack
And wave you off to Helicon
And sadly turn my aching back.

13-14 August 1993

PAINTED FACE: COIN

A painted face, a stunning Muse
With Roman hair combed to the eyes.
I look amazed, you smile, are pleased,
Flattered at my wide-eyed surprise.

A painted face above me now,
I lie back as you slip on me,
Dance up and down, your ear-rings swing
Till I turn and kiss you tenderly.

Gone, you are like a coin in my head,
A small face with combed Roman hair
Who brought me inspiration from
A region of images in the air.

13-14 August 1993

DOG DAYS: SHOOTING STARS

O Muse, you have coaxed me to come
Six times in four energetic days,
Straddling my mind till I explode
Like a meteorite's trailing blaze.

Now in the August sky trail down
Six shooting stars from a meteorite shower,
The fireworks of the universe
Which loves our atmosphere this hour.

13-14 August 1993

EMPTINESS

I ring, and hear a recorded voice:
"Sorry, the number you have rung
Is out of order." Discontinued.
I feel an emptiness in each lung.

You are incommunicado,
All the memories of you undressed,
Your inspiring lips and narrow waist,
Are now emptiness in my chest.

13-14 August 1993

TRAWLING

I walk under the stars
Above a sea agleam
And gaze at a Milky Way
Like an eddying Gulf Stream.

And is the Shuttle up there
With five voyagers aboard?
And are two floating outside
Like fishermen, unawed?

The stars shine like islands
At which the Discovery calls

To affirm man is at the heart
Of a universe he trawls.

13-14 August 1993

STEALTH

I overhear, "If any Muse
Had a child, he would be as divine as us,
Would have our blood." O Muse, you use
Analogies like a blunderbuss

Which fires many balls in my mind
(Like "The wind's a barometer of your
health")
Which lodge and spread divine meaning.
So you inspire my art by stealth.

14 August 1993

SEA-SHANTY

In the dock the Maria Asumpta's
Rear sail is raised, and a man sings
A sea-shanty above the quiet waves.
From the deck his lone voice warbles and
rings.

In my room, polishing my poem, I stop
And listen. His voice drifts out to sea.
I too am singing to the wind
In the hope that someone will hear me.

14 August 1993

TALL SHIP

Coke, jeans and hamburgers,
Disney and Westerns probe;
American ideas
Penetrate the entire globe.

Americanisation
Has swept across the world
Like da Gama's tall ship
With all her sails unfurled.

13-14 August 1993 or 14 August 1993

BRIG

A calm sea, and out slides
The Maria Asumpta brig
Stern first, two masts, rigging,
Four sails still furled, so big.

As she slowly turns, the sails

Recall the Romantic time
And I could be in this house
When our sea-power was in its prime.

15 August 1993

PHILOCTETES: WOUND AND BOW

You ache on my chest, my Muse,
Each day that goes by I feel
As though I have a wound,
A sore that will not heal.

But I have my compensation:
My unerring poet's eye
Which aims its arrow straight
At whatever target I spy.

I carry around a wound
And a true-aiming bow.
The wound will last until you,
Muse, are with me wherever I go.

15 August 1993

MIDNIGHT SKY: HAWTHORN AND ALMOND

From the pier the midnight sky
Is an umbrella of great height
That blew into hawthorn spikes
And now leaks points of light,

Or like an almond tree
With blossom, that has white
Petals down all its boughs
And shines against the night.

15 August 1993

DANCING

The sea sparkles in the sun,
Its leaping calm surface
Jumps with a million stars
That dance as if in space.

All Nature is adance today
And my heart dances too,
My blood is a million bubbles
That effervesce at you!

15 or 16 August 1993

CORRESPONDENCE

At first I thought you were a soul

In bodily form that I could love,
As if we had been angels who
Put on bodies, came down from above.

But then I realised you are something more,
A spring of feeling from the heart,
And defining myself in relation to you
Keeps flowing the spring of my art.

And now I know you complement me,
You're soul, heart, body and much more
And draw each equivalent out from me.
We correspond by magnetic law.

17 August 1993

SPRINGS OF ART

You paint with your left hand,
And live through your right brain.
I recognise the place
Where I must live and reign.

Can anyone tell me
Where are the springs of art?
They flow into the right brain
From the welling, bubbling heart.

17 August 1993

MILKY WAY: LOBSTER AND SAUCE

In the black sky
The Milky Way
Like a lobster
On a dark tray

Lies by the Plough
For our main course,
A small ladle
For hollandaise sauce.

19 August 1993

HEADBAND

Night wears the Milky Way
Like a jewelled headband
Above sparkling diamonds
Which drip towards each hand.

19 August 1993

A BOY, 22, DEAD

A tearaway left his dog
By the gorse near the Cliff Head

And fell a hundred feet
To the rocks and is gladly dead.

The lifeboat pulled him in,
Helicopter hovered near,
His mother is in hysterics,
His father in drunk despair.

19 August 1993

MIST: BAT AND WALLS
A sea-mist in the harbour,
The coastguard lights are dim,
A glow from the headland street-lights
Makes the clouds look ghastly and grim.

But round the outer harbour
A bat flits as if wind-blown,
Dipping in irregular flight,
Wheeling round walls of stone.

A sea-mist coming in,
And a mist around my mind,
A cloud of unknowing
That touches all mankind,

And my soul like a bat
Flits round and round the walls
Of its open prison
With a freedom that appals.

20 August 1993

SNAIL SHELL
A snail shell on the lawn,
The snail now lives elsewhere.
I gaze at a discarded home,
As empty as thin air.

A snail shell on the lawn
And I am moving away,
Leaving behind no trail,
Just memories of the day.

21 August 1993

STILLNESS
In Fowey harbour three swans
With red-black beaks on white
Sail with great grace to three
Small boats where men sit tight.

The gig race washes by,

Three swans bob happily.
The boats have gone, I watch
Three swans content to be.

And on this purple lilac
Three Red Admirals sit
And bask in the August sun
Without needing to flit.

21 August 1993

STORM, DESTROYING
A storm on the horizon,
Flashes light clouds like a war,
A bombing or bombardment
Seen from a distant shore.

A storm far out at sea,
Frequent flickers of light
Like a naval barrage
By destroyers out of sight.

21 August 1993

GUESTS
Every morning in the guest house
The guests sit back to back,
I see them in the front window
Still wraiths on a background of black.

Every breakfast in the guest house
Ghosts sit in silence and wait,
Elderly folk remember their lives
Till the waitress brings their plate.

22 August 1993

TRUTH
I receive symbols that
Express the True
As a daisy on the lawn
Catches the dew.

22 August 1993

NIGHT SKY: QUATRAINS

1. FOUNTAIN
A fountain of stars drips
Down the sides of the sky,
A never-ending flow
Of drops that gush from high.

23 August 1993

2. TENT

A tentpole like a mast
On the edge of the night sea,
And a tent with many holes
Hanging all around me.

23 August 1993

3. TREE

Tonight the stars are like
Fireflies that flutter free
On a tree with fairy lights,
A great acacia tree.

23 August 1993

4. PEACOCK

The universe displays
Like a proud and plumed male;
The stars glow like the eyes
On a distant peacock's tail.

23 August 1993

5. SPARKS

White-hot curls of burnt ash
Shoot as from spent desire:
The stars are like a crowd
Of sparks from a bonfire.

23 August 1993

6. RAINDROPS

A dark night sky with wisps,
Stars like raindrops on a tree,
Fishermen round a storm-lamp
That is like a moon from the quay.

24 August 1993

DOWNPOUR OF LIGHT

As I sat in my upstairs window
The sea was millions of blobs
Of light like splashing raindrops,
A downpour of joy that throbs.

In the middle a fishing boat
Surrounded by splashing light
As jumping hailstones made
A sparkle of arctic white.

24 August 1993

LIGHT LIKE MACKEREL

Light explodes on the sea
Like fish jumping for bait;

A million mackerel leap
Round where the fishermen wait.

24 August 1993

GREENFINCH WITH WORM

A greenfinch in the grass
Holding a raw red worm,
While starlings sit on the wire
To migrate for a term.

24 August 1993

TRODDEN DAISIES

Two daisies trodden down.
I lift each petalled head,
Each sand golden eye,
And straighten what looked dead.

O daisies, I am sorry
I so carelessly trod
On your beautiful petals
As if you were a clod.

24 August 1993

YOUTH

With you I don't think I'd ever die,
With your healing energy
You'd arrest the ageing in my bones
And restore my youth to me.

24 August 1993

TRAM: ORANGE AND WHITE

An orange tram trundling
Towards a sky that is white;
Orange-black cloud above,
And beyond, a pure white light.

Like the Venetian school, you paint
An object's colour in the sky
But you show an orange today
With a white tomorrow nearby.

25 August 1993

FLAT

Sometimes I see you in your flat
Sitting by your window, alone again,
Sash up to let in the summer,
And a wasp crawling up the pane,

And looking across at a hill
Or painting on the slab by the sink

537

Or frying over your little stove
Or lying in bed and trying to think,

And I wonder, Muse, if you think of me
And have shooting pains above your womb
And as you think of what we've done
If you see me in a distant room.

25 August 1993

PALE

After the flood, my Muse
You are now dizzy and pale,
I know you are anaemic,
Need iron to look unfrail.

You hear your blood "groaning"
In your ears, and though I can heal
You are strained and I know
A headache affects how you feel.

It is as if you have cooked
Pasta, chicken and mushrooms,
Served salad and diced fruit
While feeling like fodder for tombs.

25 August 1993

DISHES

An artist serves dishes
Like a careful work of art:
Chicken and mushrooms spaced
As if arranged by the heart.

Sit in beauty and fork
Each separate taste to your lips;
All blend in a harmony
With the sun-rich wine she sips.

26 August 1993

WELL

You are tired, my Muse, and strained,
Lie down on this quilted bed,
Close your eyes and relax,
Go down ten steps to the dead,

Walk in to the black tunnel,
Lie with your left arm up,
Feel weightless as I knead
Your ear like an oblong cup,

Pour new energy in,

Surges of light that tear
Through and prickle my scalp and heal
The ringing in your ear.

And now I bring you back
Up ten steps to the top
Your cheeks now have colour,
Refreshed from your deep drop.

My Muse, you are whole again,
My Muse, your energy's back.
And now let me lie with you,
As your teeth touch mine, you are slack –

My Muse, let me hold you,
As I wind down my being, I pull.
You are like a deep well for me,
And your bucket comes up brim-full.

26 August 1993

REPUTATION: SELF-STRIPPING

"Would you miss your reputation?"
You ask. My Muse, I have stripped
Myself of wife, child, job,
I can walk away from what's slipped.

I do not care for prestige
Or social position, yet
Am perceived as having them –
I could walk away from debt

And live in the south of France
Where the air is less damp
Than Cornwall's, like a desert
Mystic, or alone like a tramp,

Or like Ghandhi, barefoot,
Just a staff and a loincloth,
In harmony with the stars
And the universe's froth.

We leave without anything,
Custodians who owe –
All that is put in our trust,
Let us enjoy it before we go.

After self-stripping we are not
Attached to possessions but free,

But, my Muse, you know it is not
Better to have than to be.

26 August 1993

RICH

And now you are rich, my Muse,
A lady of leisure now.
You can pursue your art
Without sweat on your brow.

You are independent, my Muse.
You don't have to work any more,
But you will because it's your way,
That is your being's law.

27 August 1993

HEARTACHE

The angels work their plans
By joining two in love
And until they have been achieved,
The two are like hand in glove.

No longer involved, they think
"How could we have been so close";
Did we have to call to relieve
Heartache like a drug-dose?

27 August 1993

SECRET OF THE MUSE

That you are a sweet Muse, I know
But which one are you? Which of the nine?
When I am with you I don't care
Which as you make me feel fine.

You seem to be the lovely Erato,
Playing a lyre, smile like a purr,
Muse of lyric and love poetry,
And you are erotic enough to be her.

Then you seem to be Polymnia
Of many hymns with your pensive look,   10
Muse of all sacred poetry,
But then it seems you hold a book

And I think you are Clio, the Proclaimer,
Holding a date-filled chart-like scroll,
Erudite Muse of world history
Who knows how civilisations unroll.

Or are you heavenly Urania,

Holding a globe, a star, a purse,
Muse of astronomy and the One
That is hidden behind the universe?   20

But I know you are Calliope
The beautiful-voiced, holding a tablet:
Muse of heroic epic poetry
Who tempts me towards the task I was set.

Like a chameleon, my Muse
You loom and dissolve and change your
            shape
And are all Muses, each by turn,
And leave their gifts near where I gape –

Even well-pleasing Euterpe,
Muse of music, playing her flutes,   30
And the songstress Melpomene
With her tragic mask and tragedy's fruits;

Whirler of the Dance, Terpsichore,
Muse of lyre-dance and choral song,
And blooming Thalia, comedy's Muse,
Holding a comic mask in a throng.

Muse, I know you are all nine Muses
And channel their father's power to me,
But most you are Calliope
Who becomes Erato to tempt me with glee 40

As you know my impossible task ahead,
To think of which makes me feel ill,
Six years of toil on a vast epic
That will be worthy of Homer and Virgil.

29 August 1993

ANGEL OF VERTICAL VISION
1993

HIGH ANGEL

Angel, perfected being
Who has transcended me,
Superman with one vision
Who embodies all beauty,

Angel, you look from your height
On the empty bourgeois pride
That dismisses you with contempt
As you cannot be verified,

And show your judgement of it
On a canvas of rubble and dust –
Angel, I long for you,
Am in love with your truth, and your bust.

1–3 September 1993

AS IF

Angel, I am giddy for you
And feel I might expire.
You say, "I'd die if you died"
As if you were mortal desire

But I say, "No, you'd get
My work across to mankind."
And you say, "You must write that down" –
As if words could bind *your* mind!

1–3 September 1993

ELEGANCE LIKE PARADISE

Angel, your glamour is
Of spirit as well as of face.
You wear your earthly flesh
With a heavenly grace,

Elegant in carriage,
Posture and slow movement,
Inner beauty and still,
Languor and a cocked head, bent.

You say depression precedes
A creative time like ice,
But like melting Beatrice
You lead me to Paradise.

1–3 September 1993

SMIRK

Angel, you embody thought
And wear wisdom like a ring,
You live them through your flesh,
And love me for my spring.

Angel, you are not split
Between body and low mind,
You have unity of being
Like an artist who is blind.

Angel, please be guardian
And curator of my work;
To my immanent mind
You bring a transcendent smirk.

1–3 September 1993

GLOW

You say I have charisma
That attracts people to my schools –
But I have been washed by the Light
Which glows through my disciplined rules.

1–3 September 1993

BEES

You say I'm a visionary,
Not a philosopher among birds,
A mystic who rationalises
Philosophy (Whitehead's words).

Philosopher, leave your room,
Sit on the lawn, and see
How the universe manifests,
Like a Plato watching a bee.

Angel, who knows all truth
And looks on our honeycomb lives,
Smile on all who know that the Sun
Draws us like bees to their hives.

1–3 September 1993

GOLDEN MEAN

Angel, you are perceptive
And know what I think and fear,
Seeing with clairvoyant eyes,

Hearing with clairaudient ear

My "Don't fall in love with me".
You say, "As the question had not
Arisen I knew you were
Arguing with yourself somewhat,

And so I said nothing."
And your silence is not far
From Bacon's middle way:
Mediocria firma.

1–3 September 1993

LEVELS

You say, "She's not at your level."
You see with vertical eyes,
You see horizontal limits,
The bourgeois who think they're wise –

You measure by Everest,
Not by the low foothills
Which are peaks to small people,
Mere ripples the wind fills

No larger than the ripples
On sea-sand, after the tide
Has ebbed and left worm-holes,
To your giant sight as you stride.

1–3 September 1993

JUICE

Angel, your cheeks are soft
As peaches that invite;
Tenderly with my teeth
I brush them and gently bite.

Angel, you are whole,
Like Primavera you
Represent spiritual beauty
With the juice of a natural hue.

1–3 September 1993

DARK ANGEL

Dark Angel, not so much in form
As in the density of each limb,
Angel who has put on darkness
To enter a world whose light is dim,

I appreciate how you have given up
A realm of light to look after me,

To know the darkness within my flesh
And to love from a land of light that is free.

Dark Angel, you are a brightness
In this dark world and its despair,
And without you I would perish,
Your Light lightens my task down here.

2 September 1993

TYPIST

Eyes glazed with overwork,
The audio-typist,
Eyes on screen, earphone in ear,
Clicks keys that whirr by her wrist.

Eyes apart, she looks away
Focusing on nothing,
A pile of work to do –
For a system to which she will cling.

2 September 1993

GENIUS

Angel, measure of genius,
You know talent seeks groups
While genius works alone
By its spring in two-handed scoops;

And that genius, ever changing,
Completes, moves on to the new.
Your own genius is the source
Of the Beautiful and the True

Which, scooping, I reflect
As a windscreen flashes the sun
Or as a puddle shows
A universe well-done.

7-9 September 1993

ENERGY

If you wonder where I am, I am there,
Angel, in my navel, my belly
Where you take my energy and push
It out of me as poetry.

If you wonder where I am, I am there,
Near my overflowing, trembling heart
Which is joined in an invisible bond
To your energy from which flows art.

7-9 September 1993

KNEADING

If you were a witch would I love you?
If you manipulated my will
As you knead my energy with your fingers,
If you handled me with a witch's skill?

You're the centre of my being,
Wherever you are, I am there,
Only two spots on the globe have meaning:
Where you and I are kneading air.

7-9 September 1993

HEIGHT

I recognised you instantly,
Angel who was waiting to be,
Yet I did not know you existed,
Although you had heard about me.

I did not even know you knew
I was here and waiting for love,
To be touched from your awesome height,
Drawn up to a light above.

7-9 September 1993

EARTH GODDESS

Earth Goddess, with slim waist
Curving between breasts and thighs,
As you squat in your temple,
I admire your symmetrical size.

Like the Syrian Astarte
Or Melqart, you are form
From the ripeness of the earth,
Clay shaped into someone warm.

7-9 September 1993

FERTILITY

Earth Goddess, with swollen breasts,
Your fertility suckles the land,
And attracts men to the temple
So religion and crops and

The generative power in your loins
Renew a nation's wealth;
No Fisher King's sexual wound
Can hide your bursting health.

7-9 September 1993

DREAM

You say "I can't imagine

Living without you now,
You are my stability" –
With a slightly raised eyebrow.

You say "You are my centre"
As if I sipped red wine
And forked your Chinese food
And sat with you while you dine.

O Angel, you tantalise me
Like a shadow on the wall.
Are you there or are you only
A dream that answered my call?

7-9 September 1993

THOUGHTS

"You are passionate," you say,
"When I first saw you I thought
Within ten seconds 'What's
He like in bed? Or as an escort?'"

I thought 'You are feminine,
Making yourself beautiful
With make-up and ear-rings
So I can admire your pull.'

7-9 September 1993

FULL

Angel, you say "I am full of you,
I just sit, daydreaming,
Thinking over what you've done,
Channelling through your spring" –

And how you made yourself beautiful
And waited an hour for me,
And how I admired your transcendent waist
And your femininity,

And how I possessed your vast knowledge,
As if being a thousand psalms,
And how I returned to the universe
With a quiet strength that calms?

7-9 September 1993

ATTENTION

O Angel, let me go with you,
Let me through the departure gate,
Let me travel to your region,
Rise early and work till late.

O Angel, let me fly
On your wings that soar and glide;
Angel, I am like a plant
Which lacked attention and died.

7-9 September 1993

BRUISED

I have you on my chest
As I say goodbye at the gate –
The absence of you that
Has not happened yet but can't wait.

You put your hand on my lungs,
I feel hot love heal there.
The collision between our beings
Has left me bruised, by air.

7-9 September 1993

SHRAPNEL, GRAPPLING IRON

Angel, I hurt, you have gone,
Wrenched out of my chest like shrapnel.
Airports can be places of joy
But this one resembles Hell.

As I drive down the motorway
Your wings rise into the sky
Like a feathered arrow uncoiling
A grappling iron in my sigh.

7-9 September 1993

ASHES

O Angel, I am wounded,
You expect me to return
To those who want and grab
In this dark world's upturned urn.

O Angel, I am hurting
Now that you have withdrawn
And left me to measure myself
Against the ashen dawn.

7-9 September 1993

CORD

An umbilical cord stretches
To the clouds, I can feel it tear;
At the other elastic end
You sit alone in the air.

Each second you fly from me,
Each second tears me more.

As I drive down this motorway
I am tugged by invisible law.

7-9 September 1993

BEAUTIFUL SOUL

Some have beautiful souls
And make a beautiful Yes,
While some have ugly minds
And create an ugly mess.

I have known some of the last,
But you are among the first;
I see the state of your soul
Wherever your symbols burst.

8-9 September 1993

PRUNING

I will now prune my time,
Cut out inessentials, snick
As if I were pruning a tree
To make the sap rise quick.

All art and poetry are
At one in us as we
Take from each other's work
And snick out our energy.

8-9 September 1993

IF YOU WONDER: ANSWER

If you wonder where I am, I am there
In the ruby red of your red wine,
If you sit alone and think of me
You can find me in the glow of the vine.

If you wonder where I am, I am there
In the taste upon your tongue as you sip,
If you feel lonely, you can find me
In the red that lingers on your lip.

If you wonder where I am, I am there
Beside your arm, within your reach,
Even though I seem to be removed,
Above the stem of your wine-glass, beneath
        all speech.

11 September 1993

POEMS LIKE CANVASES

Like an attic full of canvases
Are my abandoned works:
I rifle portraits and landscapes

And rework the meaning that lurks.

I am faithful to the mood
As I polish my lines,
Complete the nearly finished,
Am definite with my shrines.

So, Angel, it will be
When, like two rivers that flow   10
Into each other, you melt into me
And then separate to know.

We will clear out our attic,
Our studio will be well-known,
All our past works finished,
Even those we have outgrown.

Genius moves forward,
Developing each day,
Constantly leaving behind,
And inventing a new way.   20

We will put today's gloss
On yesterday's inspired work
Which time prevented then,
But nowsee our future smirk.

          21 September 1993, revised 29 November 1993

EARTH AND LIGHT
(OR: PYTHONESS)

"I am the earth, and you are the Light," you
          say,
"Your shaft enters my cleft, and overflows –
You are brimful with Light – through me to
          the clay.
I am the earth goddess, from each breast
          flows
Milk and honey, soma like royal jelly.
I am the divine mother with milk for the nerve
Which feeds the etheric body's energy.
There will be disasters, a financial downward
          curve,
Floods that will sink Cornwall and Italy,
          signs,
Man-made earthquakes, plagues, Arab
          Antichrist for
Whose rule in Jerusalem a Cabal craves.
We will save the earth by lying on ley lines,
Stop the world disorder and a Third World
          War.

I will explode; and neutralise the tidal waves."

          22 September 1993

BUSYBODY SUN
(After Donne)

O busybody sun,
Why do you poke your nose in here
And spoil our bedroom fun?
Get lost and go and shine elsewhere.

          September 1993, revised 30 November 1993

AFTER THE FRACTURE: GROWTH

After the fracture: growth –
As a civilisation breaks
All is rubble, nothing connects,
A heap as after earthquakes.

But despite the fracture, growth
Returns with new energy
As wild flowers thrust on a tip,
New grass on old débris.

The fracture happened, but now
Continuity with the past
As new, growing art forms connect
To the 19th century, and last.

          3 October 1993

MAN
(OR: GOD THE ARTIST)

What a marvellous thing is man,
Two eyes, two nipples and
A nose, a "thing" balance
Two arms, two legs – just stand

And gaze in the mirror;
Ten fingers and ten toes,
What symmetry and proportion
The design of man shows!

And how economical is
Each orifice and lip,
Two ears, two hands, two feet,
And stomach and scrotum dip.

What does the design say
About the designer's mind?
God or evolution or Light
Is an artist who can find

Balance and symmetry,
Proportion and design
In a network of functional veins
That crisscross round the spine.

3 October 1993

COMMUNISTS LIKE WASPS

Live from Moscow, tanks fire
At Parliament, many dead;
Puffs of smoke on windows,
Communists run, hands on head.

Wasps swarm in the school roof,
One puff from the man up high,
The dust settles like smoke,
The wasps buzz out and die.

O Communists, o wasps,
Why did Nature give you folk
Stings to make us afraid
So we flush you out with smoke?

4 October 1993

THE SHINGLE OF THE STARS

The shingle of the stars
Is strewn on the beach of the night
Where a gentle tide washes,
Leaving each pebble bright.

The universe is alive,
I can see its gentle flow
And the shingle shines out
Like diamonds that glint and glow.

22 October 1993

INVISIBLE TREE

Above the roundhouse mast
Some stars dance like fireflies
On a great fir-branch that is hung
With fairy lights, in disguise.

The biggest, brightest stars
Are like globes on a lead
On an invisible tree
That supports a structured deed.

22 October 1993

MOIST

A glorious morning, and the sun
Was blinding by the sea-foam's sighs,

As each froth withdrew, the bubbling stones
Winked like a thousand well-screwn eyes.

The wet beach was alive and danced,
The glinting pebbles all rejoiced,
Their being engaged my being
And I laughed aloud, for I was moist.

23 October 1993

PEERING FACE

The bottom half of the moon,
Round half up to a bar,
Orange on the night's horizon,
Huge and seen from afar.

As I drive, a great oak-tree
Passes across its space
Like a silhouette on a lantern
Held by a peering face.

23 October 1993

FIRE

Several split logs in the yard,
I knock two on the gate,
Shake off a wood-louse and a slug,
Then place them in the grate

Whose heat touches my cheeks,
Flame curls in a faint fog,
I hope no wood-lice lurk
In the crevices of each log.

I peer from my scorching face,
Low flame and smoke and souls
Round the grey-ashed, blackening fuel,
From the brilliant orange coals

That throw out a great heat
And warm our lips to a grin
And cheer our fingers and hearts.
How good that wood warms skin!

23 October 1993

FOUNTAINING LEAVES

As I spoke on the telephone –
A shower of golden leaves,
Filling my entire window
Like ticker-tape under my eaves.

A shower of gold from heaven,

Fountaining from a tree,
Covering the Garden Room roof
With the foam of eternity.

5 November 1993

BOOKS, LIVES

We live our lives round books;
Like rocks on a sandy beach
Tomes by Tennyson, Milton –
We pick our way between each.

They are part of our landscape,
We can sit on them and peer
At the sea and sky in the sun
But our real lives are elsewhere.

1 December 1993

RED SUN

December, and a huge red sun
On the eastern horizon.
Over the still sleepy valley,
House and street lights still on.

Three times its usual size, massive,
A deep, blinding blood red
Like a fierce and jealous god who
Takes tribute for its dead.

2 December 1993

THE WAY WE SEE

A wild, wild wind gusting,
Blowing the tree inside out,
So it sways like an umbrella,
Whirling twigs flying about.

A wild wild wind inside
Roaring in the chimney,
Battering roof and window,
Cleansing the way we see.

8 December 1993

STANDARDS

The education expert
Was immersed in his work;
Bang! A window shatters,
See his startled head jerk.

He rushes to the window,
Bang! Falling masonry.

The shock as he registers
Words that are revolutionary:

That State schools can be poor,
That attainment can be low, 10
Classes can be overcrowded,
Pupils sent home to know.

Now "Where is the evidence?"
Education expert asks.
(Dilapidated roofs.
Stumbling reading and tasks.)

My love is infinite
And helps all children shine
I would the nation's schools
Could be as good as mine. 20

I teach skills to my souls
So they can find their way
I see the souls in their eyes,
Not statistics experts say.

Pupils not making progress,
Children going nowhere.
Bang! Let thunderflashes disturb
Officialdom into prayer.

11 December 1993

THE PHILOSOPHER'S STONE: SOUL AND GOLDEN FLOWER

I am like Red Mercury
Pink with the texture of salt,
I disturb the molecules
In your elemental fault,

Disturb your consciousness,
In its foundations' mould,
I rearrange your parts
So your base metal turns gold.

I am the philosopher's stone
Who converts your soul to Light; 10
I can be evangelical
But prefer to describe its night.

Others perfect men's lives,
See work as illusory;
I grow and perfect my work
Which describes reality.

I can plumb your darkness,
Transform where I describe,
Change your way of looking
Without joining the preaching tribe.   20

My love is infinite;
Your dangerous volatile power
Can give off lethal fumes
Or explode like a bomb, or flower

And be beautiful and strong;
Like a rebellious terrorist,
You can passionately ignore
Or shape with a tender wrist.

I can change your consciousness
So you no longer rail   30
Against a pyramid of words,
How academics fail,

But grudgingly admire
Dostoevsky, Proust and Joyce,
Whose words describe what is real
Who reveal with a new voice,

And see that what I paint
Describes the universe,
That I do my work, then rest,
That my statement is full and terse   40

So a new generation can know
The invisible has power;
That when theory and practice blend,
The eternal within the hour,

Then understanding is felt,
That the boring can fascinate,
That how soul lives and the world
Are hemispheres on one plate,

That my Red Mercury starts
A new chain of events   50
Or qualifications of
The Absolute that presents,

And that we can grow in the One –
Our consciousness not fixed –
Where we share the Golden Flower
Once our base beings have mixed.

8 December 1993

THE PHILOSOPHER'S STONE: WORLD AND MANKIND

All alchemists have distilled and sought
The philosopher's stone in their mould,
The new compound which will distort
Base metal into gold.

Russia found it after many trials,
Sold it to an American Jew
Who stored it in Warsaw in chemists' phials
In a flat, guarded by you.

Its coral pink is antimony,
Which activates molecules   10
Of all elements, and mercury:
They cannot be joined, say the rules.

A chemical detonator,
One drop could wipe London out,
And you lived for six months as it were,
With ten H-bombs, and no doubt.

Red Mercury is the philosopher's stone,
$Hg_2\ Sb_6$.
One use is the most instant way known
Of making mankind mix.   20

May the Light that is benevolent
Guard suffering mankind from
A new order's murderous intent
That would liquidate and bomb

Three out of six billion into thin air,
With this Red Mercury.
May the philosopher's stone prepare
For a world democracy,

A new world order, a peaceful norm,
That sees men like molecules,   30
Activates all into a new form,
A world government with rules,

And as antimony and mercury
Cannot be joined but are,
So join ten regions, let them be
Like a philosopher's stone in a jar.

26 November 1993, revised 28 November 1993

PREFACES

AND

NOTES
(A METAPHYSICAL
COMMENTARY)

PREFACES

PREFACE ON THE NEW BAROQUE CONSCIOUSNESS
AND THE REDEFINITION OF POETRY

My poems record a shift – a growth, a transformation – from the consciousness of the controlling social ego to the contemplative, unitive consciousness of a new centre in the inner core which includes the soul and spirit. (In Kabbalistic terms the shift is from Yesod to Tepheret or Tiferet.) This shift of consciousness is significant because it makes possible an approach to a metaphysical Reality and Being. For when the universe is perceived through the new centre it is perceived as being one through being permeated by a unifying metaphysical principle akin to Heracleitus' Fire, which unites the spiritual and physical outlooks.

This metaphysical Fire, and the consciousness that perceives it, have been known in every generation somewhere in each civilisation during the last 5,000 years. It breaks out at certain stages during the life cycle of a civilisation, and the vision of these poems should be related to the historical perspective of *The Fire and the Stones*, in which I maintained that mankind's gnosis of a universal God perceived or known as the Fire or Light is central to all religions and civilisations, and controls and explains their growth, survival and decay. In *The Fire and the Stones* I attempted to show that all civilisations pass through 61 stages.

These poems are set against what in that work I designate as stages 42-45 of the European civilisation. *The Fire and the Stones* holds that in stage 42 a civilisation decolonises (a stage the European civilisation has been in since 1910), that European civilisation is already passing into stage 43 (a conglomerate that deprives it of its national sovereignty, i.e. the enlarged European Community which will control 80% of European legislation from Brussels by 1997, according to Jacques Delors), and that stages 44 and 45, which begin soon after the start of stage 43, are associated with this new unitive consciousness.

The Fire and the Stones shows that an Age of Universalism (in which the vision of metaphysical Supreme Being or God as Fire is widespread) is initiated in stage 15 of a growing civilisation (the North American civilisation currently occupies stage 15) and affects stage 44 of a declining civilisation (a syncretistic, Universalist stage about to be experienced by the European civilisation). In stage 45 civilisations experience a revival of cultural purity in which there is a yearning for the lost past of a civilisation. In both religion and art stage 45 draws on the artistic tradition of stage 28, and the coming revival of cultural purity soon after c2000AD can be expected to return to the pure vision of the European civilisation's own religion (a similar stage to the one the Arab civilisation has been in since 1956 under Nasser, Gaddafi, Khomenei, and Saddam Hussein), and to glorify the Fire-based medieval vision which was expressed in the historical Baroque art which dominated stage 28 of the European civilisation.

These poems are particularly concerned with the Universalist rediscovery of metaphysical Being in stage 44 of the European civilisation and with the coming revival of cultural purity in stage 45 of the European civilisation, and with the new Baroque consciousness that has already emerged in preparation for this stage. They draw on the historical Baroque Fire (stage 28) and the new Baroque's immediate antecedent, the Romantic Fire or Light (stage 33). Some regard the new consciousness I associate with Baroque as a development, or a new flowering in a different form, of the Romantic spirit, one in which Romanticism is crossed with Classicism to make a hybrid. To have a full grasp of the new Baroque consciousness and the outlook of stage 45, we therefore need to approach it through the traditions of European Renaissance Classicism, of the historical Baroque of the Counter-Reformation, of 18th century Neo-Classicism, and of the Romanticism which evolved from Neo-Classicism and whose attitudes passed into Modernism.

*

"Classicism", following the way of writing, painting and sculpting which the Greeks and Romans used, emerged from the Renaissance (during stage 24 of European civilisation). The Graeco-Roman order, clarity, balance, restraint, taste and sense of beauty were rediscovered during the Renaissance, which coincided with the Reformation, and historically European Classicism was at its height in 17th century France, the golden age of Classicism or "Neo-Classicism" (if we seek to distinguish European Classicism from Greek and Roman Classicism). The French dramatists Corneille, Racine and Molière imitated the classical standards of the Greeks and Romans as set out in Aristotle, Horace, Quintilian and Longinus, standards rediscovered by the Renaissance. They trusted in the powers of the mind, and especially the reason of the social ego, and the scientific discoveries of the Age – for example, those of Newton – seemed to confirm that all things could be known.

In England, a parallel interest in reason led to the "thought based" poetry of the Metaphysicals and of Milton, Dryden and Pope. T. S. Eliot sought to explain this Rationalism in his essay on Milton. Eliot argued that there was a "dissociation of sensibility" after the Civil War, as a result of which thought separated from feeling in English poetry, whereas earlier in the 17th century thought and feeling were united in Donne as "felt thought". "To Donne," Eliot wrote, "a thought was an idea, invested with feeling." Neo-Classical critics tend not to believe in this split which Eliot attributed to the Cromwellian Revolution, and though a similar separation can be observed immediately after any modern Revolution – I have witnessed it myself among Chinese and Libyans shortly after their Revolutions – the split Eliot noted can just as easily be explained by the growth of European Renaissance Classicism (or "Neo-Classicism") in 17th century France.

In fact some of this "thought-based" poetry (notably the sensual-spiritual poetry of the Metaphysicals and of Milton) should be seen in terms of the vision of 17th century Baroque, the art produced c1600-1750AD by first the Catholic Counter-Reformation and then the Protestants following the Renaissance and Reformation as they reasserted the pre-Reformation vision of the Fire and renewed the Fire or Light of European civilisation's central idea. Historically, the Baroque is the least understood of movements. Originally a term of abuse from the Portuguese "barroco", meaning a large irregularly shaped pearl (see my dedication at the beginning of *The Silence*, 1965-6, which describes the poem as a "string of baroque pearls"), the Baroque sometimes has a pejorative connotation, of being overwrought and ornate, contorted and eccentric, full of strangeness, tension and irrationality, even grotesque. This connotation has been fostered by Neo-Classical critics. If we get away from their pejorative disapproval, however, we can see that historically the Baroque style was essentially full of movement and freedom, it was *dynamic*. Artificiality was stripped away (hence the masks and mirrors that appear in Baroque art) and human beings were shown as everyday feeling people, whether they were saints from contemporary history like St. Teresa or from the early Christian days, or the people of Bruegel or Velasquez or Rubens or Rembrandt. Baroque art emphasised metamorphosis, the protean quality of life, *transformation*, and as the Baroque began as a movement of religious architecture in the Catholic Church during the Counter-Reformation, the Fire or Light which unites Catholics and Protestants and therefore heals the divisions caused by the Reformation is never far away and can be found in the centre of Baroque church domes (for example, the white centre of the dome of Wren's St. Paul's). Baroque art aimed to involve the spectator's feelings in visions.

But perhaps the main feature of the historical Baroque was that it contained elements of the High Renaissance and of Mannerism. In other words, it was *a mixture of the world of the senses and the world of the spirit*, as in Bernini's *Ecstasy of St. Teresa*. In fact, it sought to *remove the barriers between the world of the senses and the world of the spirit*, sometimes between the erotic and the spiritual, and to renew contact between art and Nature. If the Baroque seems to be all movement across a sky with whirling clouds and children with wings, this is because the artist was trying to express his sense of the *Spirit – the infinite – within the finite world*.

The Baroque mixture of High Renaissance Classicism and Mannerism, of sense and spirit, can be seen in terms of Leonardo and Michelangelo. The High Renaissance (c1490-1520AD) created works that were harmonious, well-balanced, clear and direct, in which order negated the artist's individuality, and out of this came Leonardo's universally perfect body and perfect work of art. The restless and powerful Michelangelo soon broke with the High Renaissance, and created the tense Mannerism of the Sistine Chapel. Both Leonardo's Classicism (which drew on the world of the senses) and Michelangelo's Mannerism (which derived from the world of the spirit) were present in Baroque, which was a Counter-Renaissance.

The Baroque was greatly present in the European poetry of the 17th century; in the 33 French, German, Dutch, Spanish and Italian poets which Frank J. Warnke has anthologised in *European Metaphysical Poetry* – poets such as Marino (Italian), D'Aubigné (French), Gryphius (German), Vondel and Huygens (Dutch), and San Juan de la Cruz (alias St. John of the Cross, Spanish). Warnke, like Odette de Mourgues in *Metaphysical, Baroque and Précieux Poetry*, sees the literary Baroque style as parallel to but distinct from the Metaphysical style, although many of the 17th century European poets (like those just mentioned) are both Baroque and Metaphysical: Baroque in being characterised by extravagance of language and a concern with appearance and reality, particularly in the religious impulse and the new science; and Metaphysical in being concerned with a protagonist who, with wit and wordplay, confronts the complexities of experience, and in the longing of the Soul to be liberated from the Body. The Dutch Luyken, like the English Vaughan, drew inspiration from the Hermetic books, the Kabbalah and the Alchemists, and wrote of the Inner Light. English Metaphysical poetry should therefore be seen within this European literary Baroque context.

The Baroque faded c1750AD. It had co-existed with Classicism rather than replaced it, and first 18th century Neo-Classicism (an offshoot of stage 32 of European civilisation, the advent of scientific materialism) and then Romanticism (a creation of stage 33 of the European civilisation, the artistic reaction against scientific materialism) took its place. The revival – or survival – of Classicism in the 18th century is known as "Neo-Classicism" to distinguish it from 17th century Classicism, which, as we have seen, is also confusingly called "Neo-Classicism" to distinguish it from Greek and Roman Classicism; and it is primarily in this 18th century sense that I now use the term "Neo-Classical" to refer historically and aesthetically to the time when the 17th century Materialism of the Age of Reason had given way to the 18th century Materialism of the Augustan Age and the Enlightenment. It is important to distinguish Materialism with a capital "M", the philosophy based on the supremacy of matter which holds that man is mere material, from materialism with a small "m", the money-seeking attitude that can unconsciously result from a widespread acceptance of a Materialist philosophy.

In England, the 18th century Neo-Classical poetry of Dryden and Pope was objective, impersonal and rational – written from the cortical or upper left brain. It was ordered, being concerned with harmony and proportion, and it was controlled by the reason of the social ego. "Reason alone countervails all the other faculties," Pope wrote in the *Essay on Man*, and in his *Essay on Criticism* (1711) he asserted that the reason "methodizes" Nature by obeying the Classical rules: "Those rules of old discoverd, not devis'd/Are nature still, but nature methodiz'd." Going back to Aristotle, the 18th century Neo-Classical tradition held that the main principle behind artistic creation was the imitation or representation of Nature. Thus, to Dr

Johnson, poetry was "just representation of general nature". A glance at Pope's *Rape of the Lock*, *To Burlington* and *Epistle to Dr Arbuthnot*, which span the years 1712-1735, reveals what the Neo-Classical Nature showed. In these satires, Pope condemns the pride, vanity and self-interest of the beaux and belles, villa-builders and poets who made up the court society of his day, and he extols good humour and good sense: the common sense of the rational, social ego which was at the forefront of the Neo-Classical view of human nature. Such a Neo-Classical vision dwells on ordinariness and mocks anything that smacks of the heroic; hence the mock-heroic debunking of epic grandeur and supernatural "sylphs" in Dryden and Pope, for whom the heroic is simply not a Neo-Classical subject.

Towards 1750, throughout Europe the Neo-Classical tradition which had coexisted with the Baroque began to crumble. In Neo-Classical art the imagination only had a decorative function, and the irrational side of the creative process was lost under what came to be a standardised, rigid, sterile, excessively rational formula. These weaknesses of stale formalism, lack of spontaneity and coldness led to a questioning of Neo-Classical standards during the Enlightenment (c1750), for example by Voltaire, Diderot and Lessing. As a result, Neo-Classicism fell into decline and its objective certainties disintegrated. Judgements consequently became subjective, hesitant, relative and ambivalent. Reason was still the god – through reason man could find knowledge and happiness – but genius was now admitted, even though it was beyond the reason and far from ordinary. England escaped much of this traumatic process as the Neo-Classical rules had continuously been modified and as Shakespeare and the Elizabethans had anyway by-passed the Classical standards, so much so that *Hamlet* was considered "incorrect" by early 18th century Neo-Classical critics; and so 18th century English writers had not been so constrained by the Neo-Classical rules as had the writers in France. Similarly, Neo-Classicism never took root in Germany.

Out of this Neo-Classical decline grew the pre-Romantics (1740-80), who revolted against the dull rules, the formal elegance and the orderliness of the Neo-Classical conventions, and emphasised the natural instead of the rational, and *feeling*. Novels by Prévost (1731), Rousseau (1761) and Goethe (*Werther*, 1774) appeared on the Continent, but the English novelists led the way: Richardson (c1740-54), Goldsmith (1766) and Sterne (1768). The letter form made for a more subjective approach, and the Gothic novel became popular from the 1760s on. Inward contemplation made the heart conscious of its own melancholy, and Methodism in England and Pietism in Germany also emphasised the heart and the individual soul.

The Pre-Romantics had an organic view of Nature and the world, not a mechanistic one, and man and Nature became closer (for example in Gray and Cowper). The natural man – Rousseau's noble savage – grew out of Defoe's *Robinson Crusoe* (1719). The feeling was that civilisation and property-owning caused decadence and one should return to Nature, a Utopian ideal that was later found in the Pantisocratic project of Coleridge and Southey, and in Blake's Golden Age. The "natural" poetry of Ossian (by Macpherson, 1762) swept Europe, and the "natural man" was taken up by Goethe and Schiller in works of 1773 and 1781. The idea that a work of art was organic appeared in Young's *Conjectures on Original Composition* (1759), which was translated into German in 1760 and received wide attention, and this was taken up by the "Sturm und Drang" (Storm and Stress) movement of the early 1770s. Goethe and Schiller were the two most prominent writers, and they asserted that art was produced when the creative genius of the individual expressed personal experience freely and spontaneously. Lacking the slow modifications of English Neo-Classicism, this German Romantic movement was violent as it "caught on".

The Romantic Revolution itself broke in Germany first, through the early German Romantics of 1797. These were centred on Jena, and the leaders were the brothers Friedrich and August Schlegel – it was Friedrich Schlegel who first used the word "Romantic" in a literary context – along with the poet Novalis, the natural philosopher Schelling, and other less well known men.

Hoölderlin, Schiller's friend, was little known during his life but his poems were highly metaphysical. The "metaphysical" approach of these men was followed by a second phase, the High Romantics (1810-20), some of whom came from Heidelberg. The main poet was Heine. These later Romantics were interested in the natural world rather than metaphysics, and they took their lyrics from folk songs.

Meanwhile, the English Romantic movement of 1798 took place. The English Romantics – first the lake poets Wordsworth and Coleridge, and later the cosmopolitans (1818-22) Shelley, Keats and Byron (though we should not forget Crabbe, Clare, Scott, Campbell, Moore and Southey) – were comparatively very undoctrinaire. They did not seek a national literature like the Germans or oppose Neo-Classicism like the French Romantics, and so there was no violent break with continuity. Rather, they thought of themselves as restoring a native tradition. (Hence the realistic, Neo-Classical novels of Jane Austen could flourish during the Romantic period.) In fact, so undoctrinaire were the English Romantics that the word "Romantic" does not appear in Wordsworth's *Preface to the Lyrical Ballads*, Coleridge's *Biographia Literaria* or Shelley's *Defence of Poetry*, all of which were anyway (like my own Prefaces) written after their poems rather than as manifestos. One consequence of this lack of doctrine was that both Realism and Idealism are found in English Romantic poetry. Wordsworth's poems about solitaries like Michael are very Realistic, whereas his sense of "unknown modes of being" suggests a metaphysical and Idealistic outlook, like Shelley's sense of the One. Whereas the Realistic view of the imagination perceived with full adequacy the sensebound universe in which we live, the Idealistic view of the imagination emphasised the powers of the mind in perception and "imagined", or imaged, and located, a higher Reality beyond the reach of the senses.

French Romanticism was arrested by the Revolution, for from 1790 to 1820 it was dangerous to express new ideas or to question the Emperor Napoleon's restoration of Neo-Classical literature for the glory of France. Romanticism was therefore at heart a German-English, or Anglo-Saxon, movement. It was not until 1820 that Lamartine introduced Romanticism into French literature, and not until 1830 that Hugo brought it to the theatre. The French Romantics had very little appreciation of the creative imagination, and practised the opposite of Pascal's "le moi est haissable" ("hateworthy") by stressing feeling. It was left to Baudelaire and the Symbolists of the mid 19th century (Mallarmé, Verlaine, Rimbaud) to recognise the imagination and preserve a metaphysical view of the universe, a cult of beauty, a mystical sense of a transcendental world beyond appearances, and the use of symbols to convey perceptions.

The Romantic Revolution of the brothers Schlegel (1797) and of Wordsworth and Coleridge (1798) was thus the result of a gradual evolution. Romanticism thus forms an essential continuity with the Augustan, Neo-Classical tradition as W. Jackson Bate has pointed out (*From Classic to Romantic*), and this is especially true of the Realistic poems of Wordsworth, Keats and Byron. For all that, much of Romanticism was still a reversal of Neo-Classical aesthetic theories (for example, a change from imitative reason to creative imagination), and a reversal of Neo-Classical standards of beauty and ideals and modes of expression; and to that extent it was a revolution that directly opposed Neo-Classicism, the social ego and the world of the senses.

And this brings us to the heart of Romanticism, the Idealist tradition. For as we have seen, with the imagination the best Romantics saw beneath the surface of the Neo-Classical "inanimate, cold world" to the ideal, infinite, eternal behind it or within it. They did not describe the world with the "corporeal eye" ("bodily eye", Blake), but with the eye of the imagination. The best Romantics did not disregard the natural, physical world – Wordsworth and Keats loved the visible and temporal world more than most other poets and had an eye for its beauty, and the social ego was never abandoned altogether – but they were haunted by the presence of an invisible and eternal world, an ideal Being or Reality, behind or within the physical world. The prefix "meta" can mean "behind", and they sought a *metaphysical* Reality in the sense that there was a Reality *behind* the physical world: the eternal behind the temporal, the significance behind the surface appearance – a dimension that had been missing during the Neo-Classical time (although it had been present in the Baroque). The Idealistic Romantics expressed the inward and abstract by outward and concrete images, or, as August Schlegel put it, the transcendental could be made apparent "only symbolically, in images and signs" ("nur symbolisch, in Bildern und Zeichen").

Neo-Classicism had always been hostile to such Idealism. The Neo-Classical Dr Johnson had totally misunderstood the Idealist Berkeley when he simplistically said "I refute him thus" and kicked a stone to demonstrate that matter was not mental. His crude common-sense Materialistic position did not begin to see the subtleties of the Idealist position as they are contained, for example, in the manifestation of matter from the invisible through the four worlds of the Kabbalistic Tree of Life (a variation of which is now proposed in the subatomic physics of Dr. David Bohm).

Meanwhile, at the Realistic level, Romantic individualism came out in confessional stories – Rousseau's *Confessions* (1781), Wordsworth's *Prelude* (1805), Byron's *Childe Harold's Pilgrimage* and De Quincey's *Confessions of an English Opium-Eater* (both 1812) – and there were historical novels with a Romantic interest in the past (for example, by Scott). Now that the certainties of Neo-Classical Rationalism were abandoned, the individual was forced to embark on a search, and so there was searching in aesthetics, metaphysics, religion, politics and the social sciences, and, of course, in how to write literature. This searching reinforced the Romantic's individualism, and it is notable that although the Romantic writers all have a "family" similarity, they are fundamentally individuals.

We are now in a position to see that Romanticism was a revolt against tradition and authority, reason and classical science. It emphasised individualism – the individual consciousness – at the expense of the French Materialistic, Neo-Classical tradition which treated Nature as a dead ornament. It opposed the authority of the contemporary political order, which was tyrannical by today's standards. It opposed the Rationalism of Descartes and the Enlightenment (which was in fact a Darkness). It opposed the empiricism of Locke and the mechanistic science of Newton.

Despite its slow evolution and relatively undoctrinaire intentions, Romanticism had the effect of reacting against Neo-Classical "poetry of thought", and of restoring feeling to the European sensibility. Unlike the Neo-Classical tradition, Romantic poetry is subjective, personal and irrational – written from the subcortical or lower right brain – and it is emotional in the sense that Wordsworth meant when he wrote: "Poetry is the spontaneous overflow of powerful feelings." It is daemonic – inspired by supernatural genius or impulse. If we leave aside the swoonings and extreme despairs, the Gothic sensationalism and the excessive adoration of Nature which the Neo-Classical Jane Austen was caustically ironical about in *Emma* ("It led to nothing; nothing but a view"); then we find the Romantic feeling in the solitude of the heroes. Wordsworth's solitaries – his beggars and forsaken women – exemplify this feeling, as does the sentiment in his famous poem "I wandered lonely as a cloud". This feeling could go to extremes. All the Romantics sought to escape their solitude by flirting with the American and/or French Revolutions, which they saw as free-ers of oppressed individuals, and when they inevitably became disillusioned with the excesses of the guillotine, the isolation of their heroes was increased and heightened into an agony, as Mario Praz detailed in *Romantic Agony*. This agony was not always decadent; for example, Wordsworth's "We poets in our youth begin in gladness,/But thereof comes in the end despondency and madness" (*Resolution and Independence*, 1802). It could become decadent, as in Shelley's *Alastor; or the Spirit of Solitude*.

The roots of political, libertarian Romanticism can be found in Rousseau, who developed his "back to Nature" philosophy as early as 1755. All men were equal in their primitive natural state, Rousseau argued. From this premise, he went on to hold (in T.E. Hulme's words) "that man was by nature good, that it was only bad laws and customs that suppressed him", or as Rousseau himself later put it, "Man is born free, and everywhere he is in chains" (*Du Contrat Social,*

1762). This outlook coloured the Romantic opposition to tyranny for years to come.

The attack on reason gathered force with the German Sturm und Drang (Storm and Stress) movement, which, as we have seen, included the young Goethe and Schiller. This sought to overthrow Rationalism – Descartes had placed the reason above imagination – and it exalted Nature and individualism, and Goethe's *The Sufferings of Young Werther* (1774) was the first really influential Romantic novel. Next came Kant, whose *Critique of Pure Reason* (1787) was enormously influential. Kant created a German Idealism which was followed by Schelling, who saw Nature as developing towards spirit (1795-1800).

The attack on science was on the 17th and 18th century Materialistic-Mechanistic belief, based on Newton and Locke, that Nature was material, and that there was a Cartesian duality between its material and mind. Romanticism now asserted that Nature was a living thing – organism, not material – and Schelling's philosophy of Nature, in which a plant was a tendency of soul, won the approval of Goethe, whose researches into biology and botany had already led him to see form in plants as being drawn out by an eternal, creative idea (1784-1790). Goethe would clearly have been very interested in Schelling's work.

*

The new Baroque consciousness is rooted in this Romantic Idealism; in the Romantic spirit's consciousness of the infinite. We need to trace this awareness of the infinite "Spirit" (or Being) in the main English Romantic poets. The four threads enumerated above (revolt against tradition, authority, reason and classical science) are never far away.

Wordsworth and Coleridge were very conscious that Nature is a living thing or "Presence", that *Nature is Spirit* (or Being), that there is an infinite world behind or within the finite one. "Spirit" is a word that has lost its immediate accessibility in the 20th century, and it is often dismissed as an imprecise use of language. The OED defines it as "the supernatural power that controls our destinies", while the Shorter OED gives a medieval definition that is more specific: "the active essence or essential power of the Deity conceived as a creative, animating, or inspiring influence." It is this medieval "Spirit" that Wordsworth and Coleridge rediscovered, and their rediscovery (akin to the metaphysical notion that Being envelops sensebound Existence) was independent of German Idealism. Coleridge was steeped in the Cambridge Platonists, and though he and Wordsworth visited Germany in 1798-9 – it was partly to pay for this trip that they published the *Lyrical Ballads* – and though Coleridge studied German Idealism there, his sense of a Spirit in Nature undoubtedly came from Platonism, which held that behind the world was Soul, and further behind were the Forms in the Void of what metaphysical thinkers would call Non-Being. Wordsworth learned this vision from Coleridge, of whom he later wrote:" "To thee, unblinded by these formal arts (ie the sciences),/The unity of all hath been revealed."

Romantic poems are deeply rooted in the experience of the poet, which is why they often seem mystical and existential, and the great Romantic poem is undoubtedly Wordsworth's autobiographical *Prelude* (1798-1805). Romantic poems are also frequently didactic in intention; it was certainly Wordsworth's intention to teach people about the living "Presence" within Nature which challenged 18th century scientific Materialism, and his belief that poetry should teach revolted against the Neo-Classical opposition to didacticism. Wordsworth knew, and taught, "the calm/That Nature breathes" during the boyhood "seed-time" of his soul, and the experience of "unknown modes of being", when he stole a shepherd's boat and rowed out on Lake Ullswater and was pursued by a mountain, was an experience of the Spirit or Platonic Soul within Nature which feeds the passions of the soul:

> "Wisdom and Spirit of the universe!
> Thou Soul that art the eternity of thought,

> That givest to forms and images a breath
> And everlasting motion, not in vain...
> ...didst thou intertwine for me
> The passions that build up our human soul."
> (Composed 1798-9)

From "that still spirit shed from evening air" he learned "a quiet independence of the heart", and so sought Nature "for her own sake" so that "feeling...imparted power/That.../Doth like an agent of the one great Mind/Create." As a result:

> "An auxiliar light
> Came from my mind, which on the setting sun
> Bestowed new splendour."

This was the joy Coleridge was to miss in *Dejection*, and it came from the mountains, lakes, cataracts, mists and winds that taught him to live with God and Nature. In *Tintern Abbey* (1798) Wordsworth referred to the Spirit (or Being) in Nature (the "essential power of the Deity") as:

> "A motion and a spirit, that impels
> All thinking things, all objects of all thought,
> And rolls through all things."

Coleridge began as a Materialist, an associationist like Hartley, after whom he named his first son. However, his meeting with Wordsworth, whom he regarded as a genius, in 1795/6 led him to reflect on the mind, and his reading of the Cambridge Platonists (notably Cudworth) and of Berkeley, after whom he named his second son, and finally of Plato between 1795 and 1798 convinced him that the mind was too *active* for the association of ideas to explain it. He turned against Hartley and made Wordsworth tone down the Hartleyan language of the 1802 *Preface*. He now asserted that the passive view of the mind of the empiricist Locke and the "cold world" of Newton were an error: "Newton was a mere materialist – *Mind* in his system is always passive – a lazy *looker-on* on an external World....Any system built on the passiveness of the mind must be false as a system" (*Collected Letters* II, p709). Only the imagination explained the active genius of Wordsworth's mind. Coleridge arrived at his theory of the imagination "before I had even seen a book of German Metaphysics" (*Letters* II, pp735-6), and it differed from the theories of Kant and Schelling. Schelling's philosophy, for example, was pantheistic – he identified Nature and mind – whereas (like Blake) Coleridge saw Nature as symbolising a transcendental Reality; and, believing in God, rejected Schelling as "a mere Pantheism" (letter of 24th November 1818).

Coleridge's theory of imagination is in *Biographia Literaria*, which began as a Preface and ended up as a mixture of autobiography and philosophy, the interweaving of his life and opinions. The theory distinguished fancy – an associative process as seen throughout the 18th century – from imagination, which was both an involuntary perception and a voluntary willing to unify the raw materials of experience and shape it, a psychological creative process which Coleridge called "secondary imagination". Coleridge held that through the imagination the mind perceives eternal Platonist Ideas in sense objects, and that since the reason receives the Ideas – and here it seems to me that Coleridge went astray for he should have used the word "intellect" (see note to line 24 of *Fire-Void*) – besides being under the will, the imagination is "the agent of the reason": "The poet brings the whole soul of man into activity....He diffuses a tone and spirit that blends, and (as it were) *fuses*, each (faculty) into each, by that synthetic and magical power, to which I would exclusively appropriate the name of Imagination" (ch 14). By failing to distinguish intuitive "intellect" and analytical "reason" Coleridge is saying that the imagination is inferior to the reason, a strange reversal of the position taken up by later Romantics which Shelley did not hesitate to attack: "Reason is to imagination as the instrument to the agent," or: "Poetry has...no necessary connexion with the...will." Be that as it may, it was the imagination that grasped the Spirit within Nature. "An IDEA in the highest sense of the word," Coleridge writes in *Biographia* (ch 9), meaning the Platonist sense, "cannot be conveyed but by a symbol," and so Wordsworth's genius took objects of everyday perception, modified them with his imagination and transformed them into symbols of universal truth – though Coleridge readily acknowledged that in some of his poems which had a "matter-of-factness" (ie the Realistic poems) Wordsworth used fancy rather that the imagination. Thus, a poet showed the transcendent world by embodying his experience in symbols which reflected the essential organic unity, which the critic translated into thought, and Pope was at fault for writing down his thoughts without transforming them into symbols.

Coleridge, a would-be Unitarian minister until 1797, first expressed the Spirit (or Being) of Nature in terms of God. In 1795 he wondered, echoing Cudworth the Platonist:

> "what if all of animated nature
> Be but organic harps diversely framed,
> That tremble into thought, as o'er them sweeps
> Plastic and vast, one intellectual breeze,
> At once the Soul of each, and God of All?"
> (*The Eolian Harp*)

In 1798, echoing Berkeley, he hoped that his baby

> "shalt wander like a breeze
> By lakes and sandy shores...
> ...so shalt thou see and hear
> The lovely shapes and sounds intelligible
> Of that eternal language, which thy God
> Utters, who from eternity doth teach
> Himself in all."
> (*Frost at Midnight*)

He drank in "all adoration of the God in nature" from Britain (*Fears in Solitude*, 1798), and this vision of Nature as being filled with God explains why the shooting of the albatross in *The Rime of the Ancient Mariner* (1797-8) caused disharmony in Nature, when a spirit followed the boat "nine fathom deep" and parched the tongues of the crew in revenge; and it also explains how Geraldine could be possessed by the spirit of Christabel's mother in the Gothic *Christabel* (1797-1800). In his *Dejection* (1802), Coleridge made it clear that he could *feel* the beauty of Nature – a state then denied to him – if "the Passion and the Life, whose Fountains are within" would rise in his soul, for:

> "Ah, from the Soul itself must issue forth
> A Light, a Glory, a fair luminous Cloud
> Enveloping the Earth!...
> This beautiful, and beauty-making Power!"

This Power (Wordsworth's "auxiliar light") is Joy, "that wedding Nature to us gives in Dower". In other words, his soul must give out a cloud of luminous joy – the Divine Light – which gives meaning to the world of Nature, which in turn nourishes his soul. Failure to know the infinite in this way results in dejection.

The Romantic consciousness of the infinite continued with Blake, who really began it, for his Romantic *Songs of Innocence* which were written under the influence of his Swedenborgian friends, came out in 1784, though without attracting any attention, and his *Songs of Experience*, which understood the devouring cruelty of the French Revolution in *The Tyger*, appeared in 1794. Blake went on to write about wars of liberation from authority in his longer works, but as early as 1793 he wrote of infinity in *The Marriage of Heaven and Hell*: "If the doors of perception were cleansed, every thing would appear to man as it is, infinite." In 1788 in *There is No Natural Religion* and in *All Religions are One* he had challenged Locke's empiricism, his doctrine of the "corporeal eye", for Locke had chained the inner life of the mind: "Man cannot naturally Perceive but through his natural or bodily organs....Man's perceptions are not bounded by organs of perception; he perceives more than sense (tho' ever so acute) can discover....The desire of Man being Infinite, the possession is Infinite and himself Infinite. He who sees the Infinite in all things, sees God." Similarly he attacked Newton who had explained the outer world of Nature and the universe mathematically to further Hobbes' view of reality as matter in motion, and in a letter of 1802 he made his scathing reference to classical science as "Newton's sleep", and he wrote of Los, the imagination, as the spiritual sun (Los is Sol in reverse, the Fire or Light). Blake experienced the Fire or Light after visiting the Truchsessian Gallery in 1804 – he wrote that he had been in darkness for 20 years, which suggests he first saw it in 1784 – and he attributed many of his works (eg *Milton*) to his "celestial friends", from whom he took automatic dictation. (Compare Coleridge's spirits in *The Ancient Mariner* and *Christabel*.) By 1810 Blake took an extreme metaphysical, Platonist and Idealist position. In *The Last Judgment* he wrote of the nature of the imagination and the "Eternal nature & permanence of its ever Existent Images": "the Oak dies as well as the Lettuce, but its Eternal Image & Individuality never dies" (cf Plato's Forms and Goethe's view of plants). Again: "Mental Things are alone Real." Blake believed, like Wordsworth (*Intimations of Immortality*), that the soul existed before birth and was born with wisdom from the transcendent world of which Nature was a reflection, and that the imagination was the faculty that could see behind the appearance to the spiritual significance, the infinite. Blake's imagination was therefore less psychological and more transcendent than Coleridge's imagination.

The Romantic consciousness of "infinity" passed to Shelley rather than to Keats or Byron, although Shelley's Idealism is mixed with the Neo-Platonism of Thomas Taylor the Platonist. In two poems Shelley wrote in Switzerland in 1816, *Hymn to Intellectual Beauty* and *Mont Blanc*, Shelley refers to the Spirit in Nature as "the awful shadow of some unseen Power" which "floats though unseen among us", and as "the everlasting universe of things" which "flows through the mind". And of course he hailed the west wind (in 1819) and the skylark (in 1820) as "spirit" – the one embodying the Spirit in Nature, the creative principle behind the universe, and the other its material reflection in the creative gladness of the poet. It is hard to believe that Shelley was sent down from Oxford for professing atheism, and that he is today sometimes regarded as "a Red", when he could write in *Adonais*, his elegy on Keats (1821):

> "The One remains, the many change and pass;
> Heaven's light forever shines, Earth's shadows fly;
> Life, like a dome of many-coloured glass,
> Stains the white radiance of Eternity."

It was his *spirit* that had the imagination to grasp this and feed his heart, and it is a measure of our age's Materialism that a poem like "When the lamp is shattered/The light in the dust lies dead" (1822) is not understood today – and is regarded as "afflatus" by Neo-Classical critics –

because readers have difficulty in distinguishing the lamp/spirit from the light/echoes in the heart, and therefore in giving meaning to:

> "The heart's echoes render
> No song when the spirit is mute."

In fact, Shelley is saying that his spirit is his creative source because it reflects the creative Spirit in Nature.

Keats, of course, wrote about the joys and beauties of Nature, but he was haunted by the transience of life ("I was one whose name was writ in water") rather than by its infinity, and he did not write about the Spirit in Nature. He longed for a permanent beauty that was also truth, which his imagination could seize, and he found it in the perennial song of the nightingale and in a 2,500 year old Grecian urn, and there are traces of a Platonic ideal Beauty in "Beauty is Truth, Truth Beauty" (which came from his reading of Thomas Taylor the Platonist at Bailey's) and in the letters ("the mighty abstract idea I have of Beauty"); but by and large he was a Romantic of the visible world, not of unseen power. He rejected reason, preferring to be "in uncertainties, mysteries, doubts without any irritable reaching after fact and reason" (letter of 22nd December 1817), but this "negative capability" – or capability of making his rational, social ego negative – merely led him to feel the beauty of the visible world more deeply, to enter into the being of a sparrow picking on the gravel, and to accept the mystery of its beauty without seeking a rational explanation; and he never located the "power of the Deity" or the creative principle of the universe, as Shelley did. To put it in the words of contemporary brain physiology, he made his left brain negative so that his right brain could feel into the visible forms of Nature. Although he wrote of revolt (in *Hyperion*) and emphasised feelings and individuals in his poems, and imagined he flew (*Ode to a Nightingale*) and received and channelled images from the unconscious (*Ode on Indolence*), and was on the verge of receiving "knowledge enormous" – of Beauty – that "makes a God of me" (*Hyperion*), and although he had advanced to Moneta's inward contemplation (*Fall of Hyperion*), he lacked the vision of spirit or Being which Wordsworth, Coleridge and Shelley had, and lived far more in the world of the senses. The same is true of Byron, who was really a Romantic version of Pope. Byron did not proclaim the creative imagination, a fact which demonstrates his closeness to 18th century poets, and his subject was the social ego – albeit treated with Romantic attitudes – and not the soul or spirit, which he implicitly lampooned by lampooning poets who write of the soul and spirit.

Romanticism after 1830 is a mere ghost of its former self and its Idealism was soon replaced by Realism. Although we have contrasted Romanticism with 18th century Neo-Classicism, Romanticism ("transformation through the imagination") is more naturally opposed to empirical, Materialistic Realism ("observation of the 'res'", as in Zola) – this in spite of the fact that, as we have seen in Wordsworth and Keats, Idealist Romanticism could be combined with Realism, which soon collapsed without the imagination, making way for a Neo-Romanticism in Germany through the young Rilke.

As we have seen, the Romantic consciousness was taken up by German poets such as Heine, and by French symbolist poets like Baudelaire, Mallarmé and Laforgue, and of course by composers like Beethoven, Brahms and Tchaikovsky, and by painters like Constable and Turner. In English poetry though there are traces of it in Tennyson's mysticism and Arnold's *Scholar Gipsy*, Romanticism eventually paled into William Morris, Pater and Ruskin. During the Victorian Age, the settled spiritual values of the Romantic Age weakened in the face of Darwin's theory of evolution and in the face of positivism, and faith became doubt. In Victorian poetry we can see the beginning of that neglect of spiritual values which was to lead to Europe's decline in the 20th century; the bridge between the Romantic spirit before 1830 and the scepticism of T.S. Eliot's *Waste Land*.

The view of Nature as a living thing passed into the Vitalism of Nietzsche, Bergson and Shaw, and was taken up by two men who lived in Grantchester, just outside Cambridge, in the first decade of the 20th century: Rupert Brooke and Whitehead. Brooke saw Nature as a living thing in his *Grantchester*, which is sometimes dismissed as being too sentimental, and he wrote of becoming "a pulse in the eternal mind" in *The Soldier*, and of his "mysticism" in a letter to Ben Keeling. Whitehead, one of the few 20th century philosophers to believe that "the purpose of philosophy is to rationalize mysticism", opposed the Materialistic view of Nature held by traditional classical science with a philosophy of organism. Significantly, in his tremendously important *Science and the Modern World* (1925), Whitehead picked out Wordsworth and Shelley as reacting against the Materialism of 18th century science: "Berkeley, Wordsworth, Shelley are representative of the intuitive refusal seriously to accept the abstract materialism of science."

Romanticism made a come-back in disguise in the early 20th century with the three great Modernists, Eliot, Pound and Yeats. As Kermode has argued in *Romantic Image*, this triumvirate did not understand themselves as Romantics, going for the image rather than the experience as they did, but they share the Romantics' preoccupation with the image, organic form and their view of the artist as a solitary; and therefore they have the Romantic consciousness. They saw themselves rather as Classicists, and the confusions of T. E. Hulme (ably pointed out in pp32-5 of Hough's *Image and Experience*) have contributed to their misinterpretation of themselves. Hulme's *Romanticism and Classicism* correctly points to the infinite as the goal the Romantics sought, but wrongly contrasts it with the religious attitude, by which he means the religion of the social ego (man as a "fixed and limited animal"). (The Romantic spirit's contact with the infinite Fire or Light is arguably a more truly religious attitude than the subordination of the Classical, rational social ego to a theoretically, rationally proposed God, Blake's Nobodaddy; and the major objection to Hulme is that he fails to distinguish the religion of the social ego – church religion – from the religion of the core, the mysticism of the Romantic spirit.)

The Romantic spirit of Blake, Coleridge, Shelley and Yeats, and their emphasis on imaginative truth, was continued in the 1930s and later under the shadow of Modernism by Edwin Muir, Vernon Watkins and David Gascoyne, and by St. John Perse. All these have written of the imaginative tradition, by which they meant Jung's Collective Unconscious, Yeats' *Anima Mundi*, Blake's world of Imagination and Plato's world of Ideas, and therefore "that Plato's is the truest poetry" (Muir). For all of them the poet was a seer and eternal life could be contacted and known. In David Gascoyne's case, the sorrow on his return led to acute depression and a spell in which he relived Hölderlin's madness.

Most of the English poetry since the Second World War has been Neo-Classical and anti-Romantic. The now unimportant but still powerful Movement of 1956, for example, harks back to the 18th century Augustan Age, to Rationalism and to Neo-Classical, mechanistic form. It is a poetry of rational statement, like Dr Johnson's poetry which was written in the 18th century, and it is hostile to anything that smacks of Romanticism. It makes sincere feeling or realistic description the test of merit. It emphasises ordinariness as in Larkin, and opposes epic grandeur as in Amis's "nobody wants any more poems on the grander themes for a few years". This attitude is now widely prevalent among the universities and modern publishers, those two powerful conditioners of modern taste, and few voices – Kathleen Raine is one in *Defending Ancient Springs* – have spoken out against it on the grounds that it lacks a metaphysical dimension and perspective, an awareness of "eternal life". Such an archaic return to the 18th century on the part of English poets suggests that the European civilisation has temporarily lost its creativity during its time of decolonisation and has retired to imitate past forms.

As soon as Neo-Classical critics look at Romanticism in its wider, historical context, they argue that Romanticism was a disaster for the European tradition; that it was a sickness (Goethe) that led to a decline in spiritual effort, to self-expression and abstract art, to decadence and a sense of nothingness as artists tried to find the infinite, eternal world and ended in disillusioning failure. To this, the new Baroque artist who is rooted in Romantic Idealism has to reply that, on the contrary, the old imitative Neo-Classicism is dead, along with its mechanical view of the universe, and that though much 20th century art is appallingly decadent and spiritually barren, it was Romanticism that highlighted the spirit. Moreover, the disillusioned pessimism is no longer appropriate, for a new mysticism and an awakening of the spirit have put an end to the Age of Anxiety in which Modernism flourished – which was in fact an Age of Blindness and Sloth when there was an inability to see (with the imagination) beneath the surface to the core that knows the Divine Fire or Light, and which, accepting defeat too readily, never really made the effort to reconstruct a *new* vision, a fusion of the best of the Romantic and Classical ways of looking, such as is the new Baroque vision.

*

Today this new Baroque vision, which is partly a new – disguised – Romanticism, is abroad. It has flowered in the so-called New Age consciousness movement, where such a figures as Sir George Trevelyan and the more precise Neo-Platonist Dr Kathleen Raine fulfil the function for a modern young Shelley that Thomas Taylor the Platonist fulfilled for the early Romantics. If we leave to one side the astrology, the psychic research, the Steinerian doctrine – the more extreme manifestations of the New Age's spiritual and metaphysical vision – we can see that the new Holism has restored the vision of man as an incarnating spirit, which was declared a heresy at the Fourth Council of Constantinople in 869AD, and that its consciousness takes an Idealistic view of the universe, seeing matter as infinite "Spirit". Nature is once again Spirit or Being, only now it has manifested from the Divine Fire or Light.

We have seen that Romantic Idealism presented the world of the senses in order to reveal an invisible force that is beyond the senses. Once again man is infinite, for at his core his consciousness is filled with the invisible power of the mystic Fire or Light which flows through all Nature and the heart of man; which, through spiritual effort, he can see with his inner eye (see my volume *The Gates of Hell*); and which can "flash upon that inward eye/Which is the bliss of solitude" (Wordsworth).

This Holistic view of man and Nature is supported by the new science, which has overthrown classical science and 18th century Materialism. It is supported by the new cosmology, and in particular by the new subatomic physics, which has challenged the Mechanistic, Newtonian view of the universe, and by the new biology, which has challenged Darwin's directionless evolution and restored Goethe's view of plants. It is supported by the new neurophysiology which, contrary to Locke's view, more and more sees mind as controlling the brain and causing chemical changes in its cells, rather than being dependent on the brain. The new vision's view of the mind is an anti-Materialist one: our incarnating spirits grow minds that link with the Universal Mind which flows all about the brain like the cosmic background radiation which is a perpetual echo from the Big Bang. According to some anti-Materialist scientists, consciousness flows into a person through certain centres (chakras) which act like gates and admit it into the nervous system, whence it flows up to the limbic centre in the brain, the child-like area linked with the soul and spirit (the core) where images and symbols are received and creative ideas flow. Wordsworth insisted that "the child is father of the man" because he knew that a child's spirit was closer to its divine origins than an adult rational, social ego, and both Wordsworth and Milton composed in the mind before writing anything down because they had an anti-Materialist view of the mind and sought to contact the Universal Spirit or Muse.

The new science, then, assumes that the universe is a whole, and Descartes' split between the mind of the social ego and matter is now criticised as, at our core, our minds merge into the whole universe of Spirit or Being. Thus our separation from the universe is an illusion based on the faulty perception of the rational, social ego. ("If the doors of perception were cleansed,"

Blake wrote, meaning 'if the grime of the social ego can give way to the core', "every thing would appear to man as it is, infinite.") We are each a wave in one sea of energy or Being, and what we do affects the whole, just as the whole affects us. Both mind and matter manifest from the One and are conscious in varying degrees, according to physicists like Dr David Bohm, and photons within "matter" (which is in fact energy) have a kind of consciousness in so far as they are "aware" of each other and order themselves. In *Supernature* Lyall Watson sees Nature (mind and matter) as being governed by a supernatural, or supra-natural, power; an unseen, invisible force of Being – the Fire or Light – that is more fundamental than the world of the senses and which is very close to the Romantics' conception of the Spirit in Nature.

It is possible that this metaphysical Fire is associated with, i.e. manifests in, the cosmic background radiation which is a still-surviving product of the Big Bang which created the universe 18 billion to 15 billion years ago. Discovered in 1964/5 at Holmdel in New Jersey, America, this radiation is received as a persistent hiss. It is dispersed throughout the known universe as a diffuse glow at constant microwave tendencies, and the American NASA satellite Cobe (Cosmic Background Explorer) was launched in November 1989 to investigate this. This perpetual hissing echo of the fiery birth of the universe may be regarded as the physical and temporal manifestation of a metaphysical and eternal principle; the Fire or Light, whose silence preceded the universe and will succeed it, and which can be experienced as the vision of God as Fire or Light, a vision which has inspired the genesis of 25 civilisations. This radiation is the equivalent of the ether for which 19th century scientists searched unsuccessfully. This hugely important idea reconciles time and eternity, physics and metaphysics, and offers the theory of everything which the physicists are seeking, for the cosmic background radiation which cooled into matter and organisms can be expected to organise gravity, electro-magnetism, strong and weak forces into one unifying law. (A theory of everything is impossible without cosmic rays because two of the three families of elementary particles, all of which existed naturally a fraction of a second after the Big Bang, can now only exist naturally on earth in cosmic rays as the universe has cooled since the Big Bang.)

What is the Baroque Fire or Light, this mysterious Divine Fire or Light that is so baffling when it first arrives, and which, after years of observation, is found to be full of symbols from the eternal world? It was better known to the ancient sages of Egypt, India and China than it is to us today, and as I showed in *The Fire and the Stones* it is to be found in every religion. In Christian terminology it is the Holy Spirit which fills Creation and flows into the spirit as "the Inner Light" of divine guidance and Providence. The workings of this "Spirit" are best seen outside the West, and in Hindu and Yoga terminology, where it has been known for thousands of years, it is *prana*, the cosmic vital essence which is experienced in Kundalini Yoga. This *prana*, or immaterial life energy which has been in existence since a fraction of a second after the Big Bang of creation, is everywhere: in every atom of the earth, in the sun and moon and in the stars. Hence the tradition that there are planetary influences, or "flowings-in". *Prana* is an immaterial substance that pervades the universe in which it becomes material, a unified principle that contradicts the Cartesian division of experience into material and mental. It is the vital energy which acts on matter as force ("Sakti") and on mind as life ("Prana Sakti"). It is the architect that shapes organic structures out of elements and compounds. It is, in a sense, the agent of the divine imagination which shapes everything we know: trees, flowers, sunshine, seas, everything. So far it has not been tested empirically, and its radiation is too subtle to show up in a laboratory without reference to cosmic background radiation, but Gerard Manley Hopkins (for one) was on its track when he wrote of "instress" and of the world being "charged with the grandeur of God".

Some hold that this immaterial Fire or Light or *prana* flows into the body's subtle centres or "chakras", perhaps within the manifested cosmic background radiation, and that, in the case of most people, it is extracted from the surrounding organic mass by nerves. Now a very fine, delicate, volatile, biochemical essence, they claim it is conducted up the spine to the brain where it resides, constantly leaving it to circulate the body as a motor impulse and sensation, and guiding choices providentially. Most people are unaware of this process. However, some Yogis have discovered voluntary control over it, and can channel it and use it voluntarily in healing when it rises as four or more "shivers" up the spine and leaves the laid-on hand as a surge. Such Yogis can see it as deathless in "samadhi", the enlightenment that occurs in the course of my volume, *The Gates of Hell*. (The central experience of my life – both my active life and my poetic life – has undoubtedly been my experience of this Fire or Light which so fascinated Wordsworth, Coleridge, Blake and Shelley.) On death it departs; hence the Tibetan Clear Light of the Void which dying people are supposed by Tibetans to see as the prana gathers itself to leave and the immortal spirit is released, provided the spirit's immortality has been assured through an experience of illumination. *This Fire or Light – this immaterial prana which becomes material*, this vital energy which fills matter and mind like the cosmic background radiation and acts as the medium of the divinity – is the Romantic infinity.

In the new Baroque vision, the Romantic infinity (the Fire or Light) is synthesised with Classical harmony, just as the historical Baroque vision combined harmony and dynamic movement. The stillness of the contemplative gaze amid the dynamic world of the new subatomic physics and of the immaterial *prana*/Holy Spirit is a Baroque paradox. It is because the New Age consciousness movement combines a celebration of the world of the senses with a great striving, even yearning, for the infinite spirit that it should properly be regarded as a Baroque movement, and the same processes are at work in artists (such as the Catholic Margaret Riley of Shoreham) whose landscapes and bodies show the influence of a peaceful, divine order. And this is the main feature of the new Baroque: the Classical sense that there is order behind the physical world is synthesised with the Romantic infinite and movement. This "mix" is to be found in T.S. Eliot's *Four Quartets*, which anticipate the new Baroque vision in lines like "at the still point of the turning wheel". In synthesising Romanticism and Classicism, the new Baroque synthesises Modernism and Neo-Classicism and makes for a continuity between their scepticism and the Baroque Reality.

It may be objected that art and literature are different, and that aesthetic categories applied to art ("the Baroque") should not be applied to literature. I would disagree. Both art and literature are products of minds – and souls and spirits – that are affected by, or reacting against, their Age. The Age dominates both art and literature, and there is, for those who have the eyes to see and the ears to hear, a fundamental parallel between the Baroque St. Paul's Cathedral (started 1675) and Milton's *Paradise Lost*, a Baroque epic published eight years earlier in which the spirit is within the world. The same is true of the Baroque music of Bach or Handel, and the literature of the Metaphysicals, who were of the Baroque period and whose work is steeped in the Church of England Light: Marvell's *Garden* for example, in which spirit and world are intertwined.

The Baroque literary style includes both Classicism and Romanticism. Let us contrast the way a Neo-Classical writer works with the way a Romantic writer works, paying attention to the role of the social ego. A Classical writer concentrates on the social being, as we have seen. In 18th century Neo-Classicism, too, the writer hides his ego behind the ego of Man, but it is the social ego – the social ego of Man – that he is interested in. For the Classical hero is always a social being, he is never a mystic or solitary or social parasite like the Romantic hero (and contemporary anti-hero). The Neo-Classical writer never delves far below the social surface of life, and as a generalising moralist he seeks to present not the unique individual but the social type: the greedy man, the liar etc. (Compare Ben Jonson's types.) The Neo-Classical writer sees social types, and consequently praises empirical observation, tending not to believe in genius. In typifying or rationally classifying Nature, he "imitates Nature". A Neo-Classicist's work thus reveals very little of the writer, and he creates a social world to be shared by all.

On the other hand, the Romantic writer reveals his ego – often in a confessional context, as we have seen – and he is often a mystic or solitary who creates a world that is different from anyone else's: unique and individual. The Romantic Idealist relates his revealed *spirit* – for he is ultimately more soul and spirit than ego – to the invisible world behind the world of the senses.

The Baroque writer combines Classicism and Romanticism by reflecting both the social ego of the Classical writer and the mystic infinite spirit of the Romantic writer. It is most important to stress this: the Baroque writer includes much more of the social ego than does a Romantic writer. (Compare the social ego of Adam or Eve in Milton's Baroque *Paradise Lost* with the dream self that received the images from "the other mind" in Coleridge's Romantic *Kubla Khan*, for example.) The Baroque writer relates his revealed social ego and its feelings to the core that lies behind it and its deeper feelings, and to the metaphysical truth of the Fire or Light which is the same for all men. See the "Reflection" and "Shadow" in my early Baroque work, *The Silence*. Hitherto, Classical writers have not included the sub-social, unconscious depths, but the Baroque writer is aware that the core is a *type*, as well as being unique and individual – compare the collective unconscious of Jung – and that the universality of the core in relation to the universal Fire or Light could have Classical undertones in the right hands.

This invisible power, the Fire or Light, is perceived by the core of man's being, not his social ego, and so the new Baroque blends with mysticism, transcendental or Metaphysical Existentialism and Idealism and *reveals that core, the soul and spirit of Romanticism, in conjunction with the social ego of Neo-Classicism. It is the purpose of the new Baroque poetry to show the relationship between the social ego and the core, to reveal* through all the confusion of human emotions and feelings and thoughts and sensations the *core that can perceive the Fire or Light.* And just as Wordsworth had a didactic aim, to teach that Nature was a living thing, so the new Baroque has a partially didactic aim: to teach the presence of the core that glimpses the metaphysical, that mystically perceives the Fire or Light, and to offer its consciousness which differs so greatly from the consciousness of the controlling social ego – while at the same time creating a work of harmony and beauty that catches the harmony and beauty of the universe of Fire or Light and of the world of the social ego, and that may seem at times close to Classicism. However, whereas Romanticism was to some extent egotistical, in as much as Wordsworth had to be self-absorbed in *The Prelude* in order to dig out from his own experience his sense of the "Spirit of the universe" – hence John Jones' Neo-Classical view of him in the title of his book *The Egotistical Sublime* (Keats' words) – the new Baroque seeks to *loosen the hold of the social ego* and free the core of the human being, his soul and spirit, and it is thus relatively *un*egotistical; although it is concerned with the individual and inwardness as it traces a dying away from lower consciousness to higher consciousness and awareness of Being which gives meaning to life. The new Baroque *revolts against the tyranny of the social ego*, Blake's rational, Materialistic "spectre" which oppresses the immortal self:

> "Each man is in his Spectre's power,
> Untill the arrival of that hour
> When his Humanity awake
> And cast his Spectre into the lake."
> (*Jerusalem*)

Of course, the new Baroque writer never completely escapes his social ego or spectre or "Reflection", for everyone without exception always has an outer social side. It is all a matter of control. All men and women spend a large amount of time living through their social ego: at parties, when talking in the High Road, through their job. Property developers and politicians spend large parts of their time in their social ego. A personality becomes disharmonious and unbalanced when a person is imprisoned in the social ego, and cannot locate the inner core. A shift from the controlling social ego to this inner core (the thread of these poems) liberates a person. Kabbalists offer an exercise to illustrate this. They arrange ten chairs in the hopscotch-like pattern of the sephirot, and ask you to sit in each chair in turn. Only chair 2 represents the social ego, and if you are centred in the equivalent of chair 5, which controls all the chairs (Tepheret or Beauty), then from your true centre you perceive things as they are and are in contact with the spiritual and divine as well as the physical and psychological worlds. You can then sit in the centre of the social ego which is equivalent to chair 2 at will to do your negotiating or social transactions, but you can leave it and return to your true centre which is equivalent to chair 5 at will, aware that you are not controlled by the centre which is equivalent to chair 2, not chained to it or imprisoned in it.

The new Baroque recognises that the social ego is not to be, and cannot be, finally rejected or obliterated, and so in a sense the new Baroque writer is in permanent revolt against it. He can, however, *escape its power*, loosen its spectre-like grip, so that though it still features in art, giving all the benefits of the Neo-Classical range of subject matter and orderliness, it appears in conjunction with the deeper core, as do the social egos of the characters in D.H. Lawrence's *The Rainbow* in which the social and unconscious characteristics are distinct and almost separate. The point needs underlining. In view of the underlying continuity of the Augustan tradition into Romanticism, it may seem that in liberating the spirit of Romantic Idealism from the social ego of Augustan Neo-Classicism and Romantic Realism, which depends on the world of the senses, the new Baroque must pay a price in human terms. On the contrary. The new Baroque is not exclusively about the invisible Fire or Light. It seeks to relate the social ego to the core, to deepen the Neo-Classical definition of what a human being is, and consequently the new Baroque is as interested in everyday life as was the historical Baroque. Thus, like light, the new Baroque shows a protean self that can be both a particle and a wave, both social ego and core (Blake's two "contrary states"), both the spectre's social hardness *and*, at the core, a wave in the Oneness that the mystic consciousness can know, whose powerful Light flows through the self during the inner, contemplative vision. The new Baroque has its source in the spiritual, intuitive right brain – and more specifically in the subcortical, emotional limbic area of the brain where the Fire or Light is known during the theta brain rhythms of the creative trance – rather than in the analytical, cortical, Materialistic left brain, but it is still very human. Holistic poetry covers the whole brain (mind/psyche/soul); it is poetry in which both the social ego and the core are involved, and while it originates in the core it is interpreted by the social ego.

The new Baroque Imagination – like the Romantic Imagination – originates in the core, not the interpreting social ego. It continues to find the infinite as Spirit or Being. For Coleridge, as we have seen, it was the *unifying* power, the faculty by which we reach towards and perceive and *know* the indivisible One behind creation. Coleridge called it the "esemplastic" power that "shapes into one", and he derived the word "esemplastic" from the Greek "eis hen plattein", "to shape into one". Hence his reference in *Dejection* to "My *shaping* spirit of Imagination". For all the Romantics, including Coleridge, the Imagination from the synthesising area of the right brain perceives a symbolic truth which the cortical reason of the left brain cannot know (even if it is superior to the imagination, as it was for Coleridge), and it serves the eternal part of our nature whereas associative Fancy serves the temporal world of the social ego. Neo-Classical critics who do not acknowledge an eternal part of ourselves and only acknowledge the social ego, tend not to find the distinction between Imagination and Fancy helpful, but Wordsworth was very clear on this: "Fancy is given to quicken and beguile the temporal part of our nature, Imagination to incite and to support the eternal." Both Fancy (associative metaphor) and Imagination (eternal symbols) are found in new Baroque poems as they reflect both the temporal and eternal parts of man's nature.

Let us be quite clear about this. There are three distinct views of the imagination:

1. The temporal view: the 17th century Neo-Classical, and 18th century Augustan Neo-Classical view which regards the imagination as the decorative verbal playfulness, associative elaboration and metaphorical grace of Fancy with which the reason

embroiders poems, comparing dissimilar phenomena from the temporal social world; and as a faculty of the temporal rational social ego (e.g. the Neo-Classical Larkin's "Why should I let the toad *work*/Squat on my life?" in which "toad" is decorative and "squat" purely associative, a view that is related to the novelist's temporal imagination, i.e. imagining oneself into different characters' shoes).

2. The eternal view: the realistic Romantic view which regards the imagination as the power (associated with the Fire or Light) that synthesises raw experience into concrete images, apprehends order and organic form, and fuses feeling, vision and thought into a unified whole which suggests "the Translucence of the Eternal in and through the Temporal" (Coleridge on the symbol) so that the laws of the lower world are seen to correspond to the realities of a higher order; and the Idealistic Neo-Romantic view, which regards the creative imagination as receiving from on high in the trance-like "other mind" images and symbols from the eternal world. (Both these views are at work in the river-caverns-sea symbols in the Xanadu of Coleridge's *Kubla Khan* "where Alph, the sacred river ran/Through caverns measureless to man/Down to a sunless sea".)

3. The contemplative mixture of the temporal and eternal views: the new Baroque view, in which the temporal rational social ego reflects upon the reception and synthesising of images and symbols which correspond to or reflect the eternal world or metaphysical Reality, recollecting in tranquillity and quietness and contemplating the emotion, feeling, vision and thoughts that arise when in a social setting the eternal Fire presents itself from on high, relating the temporal self (social ego) to the eternal One, i.e. a small part to the unified whole.

Today, the new Baroque has redefined the Romantic Imagination as the faculty with which we grasp *the whole* (i.e. unity of Being) during contemplation (when "emotion is recollected in tranquillity"), and poetry is the expression of the "whole behind everything" or the Fire behind a particular social setting, in which it is present, and therefore of the meaning of life, the perspective of meaning which is given by an awareness of the whole. In Blake's words (c1803), the whole, or infinity, is everywhere:

> "To see a world in a Grain of Sand
> And a Heaven in a Wild Flower,
> Hold Infinity in the palm of your hand
> And Eternity in an hour...."
>
> *(Auguries of Innocence)*

This meaningful vision from the synthesising area of the brain where the Light flows in is like a spring of inspiration that flows behind the eyes, and it is buried when the earth-like distractions of the social world of work are flung upon it. The Romantic Imagination could "see into the life of things" (Wordsworth). The new Baroque Imagination sees *into* each form and relates it to the one Fire or Light behind all, employing a metaphysical vision that is known to all mystics. The new Baroque Imagination thus approaches a cosmos filled with one "Spirit" or Being, and lifts consciousness to levels which are cosmic and transcendent, so that it can attain the objective, unitive consciousness of the one Fire or Light.

Into this cosmic consciousness – this metaphysical vision and contemplative imagination which unite with the Idea-filled Void of Non-Being or non-manifestation – flow symbols which represent Reality. Or to put it the other way round, metaphysical Reality (the Fire or Light) manifests from eternity into temporal, psychological and physical forms which are symbols. These symbols are received in the soul (the mind's eye) or by the physical eye. They can be seen as transparencies of Reality or as being identified with Reality, which they veil and then reveal so that a reader can get to know, approach and have the unitive vision of the metaphysical Fire or

Light. According to the Kabbalah Reality has layers and the symbol embodies the layers of the four Kabbalistic worlds, the physical, psychological, spiritual and divine worlds. René Guénon wrote of a law of correspondence which operates throughout the cosmos, in which "all things are locked together and correspond in such a way as to contribute to the universal and total harmony" and a consequence of which "is the plurality of meanings contained in the symbol" as "anything and everything can in fact be regarded as representing not only the metaphysical principles, but also realities of orders higher than its own". To a contemplative poet, symbols are signs which point to Reality, suggesting that the parts of our universe (its physical manifestations) are identified with a greater whole, and they pale to relative insignificance beside the central unitive vision of the Fire, which offers a theory of everything and governs the whole. In the Rationalistic 18th century there was a de-symbolisation, but the Romantic movement revived symbolism and the new Baroque vision welcomes the symbols that come into the core of consciousness from the beyond for they represent, contain and are identified with a layered Reality of Fire whose presence is not far behind.

Politically, the new Baroque (unlike Romanticism) is not dedicated to totalitarian revolutions, which are exclusively social and materialistic. The new Baroque aspires to a better, cleansed world on holistic principles in which man's spirit can prosper, and man can live in true harmony with Nature – the world of the senses – like the early Taoists. The ideal is some sort of world government, in which man relates to *the whole* world, but as that will take time to achieve, the more immediate ideal is of a supra-national European State that has a wise attitude, for example, towards organic food and insecticides. More than ever, the Romantic "back to Nature" attitude is expressing itself in a return to the countryside, where people can grow fresh food and have healthy bodies, like the Essenes of the two centuries before Christ. Educationally, the new Baroque seeks to open the imaginations of the young to the eternity that is all round them, and within Nature.

The new Baroque's rejection of totalitarian political revolution – the Russian, Chinese and Libyan revolutions in my poems – emphasises again the solitude of the Romantic at the level of the social ego, and provides a new emphasis on inwardness, and therefore on heightened consciousness, which can lead to a Holistic view of mankind. Just as Wordsworth's disillusion with the French Revolution led to *The Prelude*, so the new Baroque artist's rejection of materialistic Marxism which is based on the social ego alone, can afford similar opportunities and possibilities. Because his life-style is opposed to much of the materialism of the West – he may seek to live close to Nature, eat natural food, be largely vegetarian, non-smoking and teetotal, and have values that differ from the materialistic round of work-and-pleasure of the city, where Nature is forgotten – it may be thought that he seeks to overthrow European civilisation, but this is not so. He is aware of the importance of preserving European civilisation, which transmits the tradition of the European Fire or Light, and of the danger of that even greater materialism, Communism, which can still be expected to succeed a destroyed European civilisation.

As to reason and science, despite the inroads made on them by Jung and Einstein, the heirs of Descartes, Locke and Newton are still abroad, and Rationalism, Empiricism and scientific Materialism have regrouped after the early Romantic attacks on them, and have combined with a regrouping of Neo-Classicism in England (all the Movement poets and critics, for example) and with practitioners of Scepticism and atheistic, ego-centric Humanism (as opposed to the early Christo-centric or theo-centric Humanism), particularly in the universities. The result is a world-view that is totally inimical to the new Baroque writer – and to the Fire or Light. The new Baroque must challenge these obstructions to a true world-view, the heirs of Darwin, the evolutionists, the empirical linguistic analysts (the Ayers and Ryles) and the heirs of the positivists who have threatened to bankrupt the Western spiritual tradition. It must put forward the anti-Materialist alternative which is not based on the Neo-Classical social ego, so that it is still available for the younger generation. It must proclaim the message that the reason of the ego serves the core, which includes the unifying Imagination. The reason is in the service of the irrational, or supra-rational, supra-empirical Divine Fire or Light, one glimpse of which burns away Scepticism; the reason does not dominate the core, as Descartes held. The new Baroque Fire or Light differs in emphasis from Coleridge's Platonism. Instead of Platonist Ideas flowing into the higher reason and thence to the Imagination as symbols, and the phenomena of the natural world in turn being regarded as symbols of the Ideas (Coleridge); the inspirational Fire or Light – prana – flows into the core – the spirit, which includes the intuitive intellect (the Kabbalistic Binah-Hokhmah) and which is nearest to the Fire or Light being furthest from the world, and then the soul (the Kabbalistic Neshamah), which is nearer to the world (being moved by poetry and music), both of which awaken when the reason of the social ego slumbers – and its eternal symbols proceed thence to the Imagination (the Kabbalistic receiving Tepheret, where the physical, psychological and spiritual worlds meet), while the phenomena of the natural world are "symbols" that have manifested from the eternal world of the Fire or Light and the Void of Non-Being. The intellect is only involved when it has received Ideas or other communications from the Fire or Light, and it may be baffled at the symbols which the Imagination has received directly from the Light. The new Baroque writer, then, works for change within our materialistic Christendom along these lines, seeking to make its consciousness blossom from the Materialistic dead wood.

*

The new flowering in Europe should be seen as a new stage in the life cycle of the European artistic style. This new stage coincides with the Universalist rediscovery of metaphysical Being and the Fire in stage 44, and the revival of cultural and metaphysical purity in stage 45 of the 61 stages in the life cycle of European civilisation.

Although the history of art and literature (like the history of a civilisation) is a continuous process through different Ages, there are undoubtedly stages within the life cycle of a civilisation's artistic style that spans all Ages (and, indeed substages within the life cycle of the artistic style of each Age). Whereas Neo-Classical critics have concentrated on the social environment which produced the style, the material, moral and intellectual climate of each Age, Romantic critics have had a vitalist approach, and have seen an Age's style as organically going through stages of growth, like a plant. (See the development of the Gothic style, for example.) In other words, the determining factors in a work of art were not in circumstances outside the work, but in the artistic activity itself.

Returning to the life cycle of the artistic style of a civilisation, it was the vitalist Swiss Professor Heinrich Wölfflin, in works published in 1888 and 1898 (*Renaissance und Barock* and *Die klassische Kunst*), who first defined the two main stages of a style in terms of the psychological concepts of "classical" and "baroque", two mutually hostile attitudes to life which he removed from their historical context (historical Classicism and the historical Baroque). In this last sentence and in what follows the historical Classicism and Baroque have a capital "C" and "B", whereas the universal styles removed from their historical context have a small "c" and "b". In Bazin's words (*A Concise History of Art*, pp524-25), the European Renaissance style's classicism, according to Wolfflin, "attempts to strike a balance between form as it is conceived by the intellect on the one hand and the direct observation of nature on the other, expresses itself in centred compositions and through a strict arrangement of component parts, each of which retains its distinct unity; classical forms are ponderable and static, and obey the laws of gravity, while movements are governed by rhythms and may be reduced to a harmonious cadence." European Baroque, on the other hand, "expresses uneasiness and a longing for freedom, and shows itself in open compositions, fragments of the world rather than a world in themselves, which overflow the limits of the frame. Baroque forms are imponderable, weightless, they soar into space, which they cut across with movements that set the eye moving in every direction, far beyond what they actually show. The unity of baroque compositions is not of an intellectual" (he means "rational") "order, but it is organic, living, comprehensive, resulting in a close dependence of the forms one upon the other." Thus, "Classicism means cohesion, it reduces nature to the human scale. It is a state of being, while baroque is a state of becoming, a dispersion, so enamoured of nature that it absorbs man into the cosmic rhythm. Baroque tries to depict human passion, grief and pain, love and death, all the ages of man; whereas classicism is only interested in the mature man at the height of his powers, when all his faculties are controlled by reason. The favourite medium of baroque is painting or music, while classicism expresses itself most fully in architecture and sculpture. In extreme baroque, architecture tends to abandon abstract principles, becoming as it were plant-like, closely wedded to the organic forms of nature."

The view that in every civilisation there are differing stages in the life cycle of its artistic style was first suggested by Déonna in Geneva in 1913, and developed by Faure (1927) and Focillon (1934). On this view, the complete evolutionary life cycle of a style passes through the following stages. There is first a primitive, archaic, pre-classical, experimental stage or Age, in which there is no clear distinction between the soul and the world. The artist projects mental data into his work, and has little awareness of the external world and does not use his powers of observation. There follows a classical stage or Age in which the reason and soul are in balance, with reason informing the soul of its observation and the soul being aware of the harmony in the external world. There is then an academic or post-classical stage or Age in which artists have an undue respect for the forms of the previous generation and out of exhaustion obey conventional rules (Neo-Classicism). Nothing new is invented, and the result is an anaemia that results in artificiality and drives artists to revolt and create the extremes of the ensuing pre-baroque Mannerist stage or Age. In this they create a world of their own as a substitute for the everyday world around them, and the body is distorted and lengthened. The end of Mannerism – its cure – is *in the baroque stage or Age* in which "the spirit is again in contact with the world, the imagination drinks deeply of its forms, and at the very source, with an eagerness born of long deprivation. The cosmos itself seems to be throbbing in the soul, filling it with inspiring emotion" (Bazin, p528).

If the life cycle of an artistic style is seen as lasting centuries, its stages as lasting 100-200 years or more and its substages as lasting for several decades, then in the style of all civilisations we can recognise similar classical/baroque stages in equivalent Ages. In the European style which emerged from the decay of ancient classical forms we can recognise broad sweeps or Ages: a primitive, pre-classical stage or Age in the Medieval Age; a classical stage or Age in the High Renaissance and after; an academic or post-classical stage or Age in Neo-Classicism; and a Mannerist or pre-baroque stage or Age in Romanticism and its aftermath, when, and I quote Bazin again: "with his mind obsessed and arrested by conventional memorized forms, his soul impoverished by the sudden lowering of vitality that cuts it off from the outside world, the artist can only create a world of his own, a substitute for the real one around him. This anaemia results in artificiality and drives artists to extremes, for instance such deformities as the exaggerated lengthening of the body or frantic gestures, feverish attitudes and caricatured expression" (p527). We have seen that "the world of the artist's own" passed from Romanticism – compare the world of Blake's own in his long poems – to Modernism and abstract art. In this case, the dynamic "baroque" stage or Age, the psychological term as used by Wölfflin, corresponds to the new Baroque Age into which European art is now beginning to pass – in which Classicism is combined with Mannerism just as in the historical Baroque the High Renaissance was combined with Mannerism as we have seen. In this Baroque Age we are now entering, soul and spirit, with heightened consciousness, contact the invisible source of the cosmos with the baroque Imagination, and depict (to recall Bazin's words) all human passion, grief and pain, love, death and the ages of man, uneasiness and a longing for freedom, the whole human life cycle in fact. For the new Baroque Age *redefines man*.

On the evidence of the consciousness movement, we are now proceeding into a period that is really a Counter-Renaissance. The Italian Renaissance's rediscovery of the classical past in Rome and Greece, along with its rediscovery of the human body, is parallelled by the Romantic rediscovery of the Middle Ages and of Gothic architecture, both of which were ended by the Renaissance. Hence such Romantic poems with medieval settings as Coleridge's *Christabel* and Keats' *Isabella* and *The Eve of St. Agnes*, and the medieval subjects of the Romantic novels of Walpole and Scott. In our day a new and parallel Renaissance has a new concern with the past. There is a revival of interest in the ancient wisdom and ancient religions, and in particular in the old Neolithic shamanism, the journey of the shaman, which gave birth to them. There is also a rediscovery of the soul and spirit, which were well known in the past, and of the Fire or Light, which was widely known in the Middle Ages. *We are living at the beginning of a kind of Counter-Renaissance that is restoring the soul and spirit to Renaissance Humanism.*

It is enormously difficult to pigeon-hole periods and styles, but if we look more closely at the life cycle of the artistic style of the European civilisation, which *shows* man's relation to the civilisation's central idea of the metaphysical Fire, and therefore to his soul and to Nature, in different Ages, we can identify some of the historical substages within the broad classical/baroque stages or Ages within the one main style in our European civilisation. As we have just seen, there was a long pre-classical, primitive, archaic stage (the Medieval Age) as the civilisation grew round its spiritual élan of Christianity, in which there was no clear distinction between the soul of the artist and the world. (Hence the use of the halo in all social settings.) This became Mannerist in 14th century French Madonnas. Out of this substage grew a classical stage (the Renaissance, c1425-1590) in which the mind's observation dominated the soul, a trend anticipated in Chaucer in the 1380s, a Christo-centric Humanism that culminated in the High Renaissance of Leonardo and Michelangelo (1490-1520). Then followed the first post-classical or Neo-Classical or academic stage ("the academy" of the late 15th century and early 16th century) when artists belonged to "schools" of past masters, and decorum was taken from rules based on the great masters, with the result that artists did not have to invent. After this there was a first pre-baroque or Mannerist stage in which artists revolted against the academic rules (16th century, for example the ecstatic trance of El Greco who lived during the time of St. John of the Cross). Finally, there was a first dynamic, baroque stage in which the barriers were removed between the world of the senses and the world of the spirit, and in which there was a mixture of classicism and Mannerism (sense and spirit) as artists used the body to express the spirit (the historical Baroque, c1600-1750). This baroque stage was in turn succeeded by its academic and Mannerist stage (Rococo), which was based on the wave-like lines of Nature.

After a civilisation breaks down its central idea of metaphysical Fire goes into decline and its religion ceases to inspire new artists, who gradually turn to secular subjects. In due course the civilisation ceases to be artistically creative, and artists continue past modes of thought, notably the struggle between reason and the irrational spirit. It seems that the last three stages of the cycle repeat themselves. In the European civilisation which broke down c1453-1550, a new, second post-classical or academic stage continued with Rationalistic Neo-Classicism and the Augustan Age (17th and 18th centuries), which resisted the Baroque and led eventually to the Realism of the Victorian social novelists. Secondly, there was a new, second pre-baroque, Mannerist trance, ecstasy and extreme emotion in the Romantic movement (late 18th and early 19th centuries), which freed artists from Neo-Classical shackles. If we bring literature into our look at art, this turned academic (Matthew Arnold, Pater, Ruskin), while Romantic expressionism – when intense emotions are poured out in a monologue – really marked a pre-baroque stage in which sense and spirit are merged (in Romantic Idealism). Hence, though Blake is often regarded as a Mannerist "shackled" by a Neo-Classical form, he was full of pre-baroque elements; while Rodin's feverish, tormented art was also Mannerist, although in *The Burghers of Calais* (a copy of which stands outside the British Houses of Parliament in London) he anticipated the new Baroque. In the 20th century, as we have seen, Romantic expressionism and Mannerism developed into fragmented and abstract Modernism (for example, abstract art), and into the symbolist Neo-Romanticism of poets like Kathleen Raine. Meanwhile, there has been a Neo-Classical revival since World War 2, at least in England. Out of the conflict between these two repeated stages, a new, second baroque stage, a mixture of Classicism and Mannerism, of sense and spirit, is set to emerge. This new – repeated – mode of thought will redefine spirit or metaphysical Being in relation to sense and will save European civilisation – which cannot survive without the Fire of the spirit as *The Fire and the Stones* attempts to demonstrate – for a while.

We can now place this new Baroque Age/Counter-Renaissance in a more sharply focused historical context. It was perhaps anticipated by metaphysical or religious (as opposed to atheistic) Existentialism, and it significantly preserves the central feature of the Medieval stage of the Western style, the Fire or Light. It emphasises the baroque "transformation" of consciousness – what I at the outset of this essay, this Preface, called "a shift, a growth, a transformation" in consciousness – and by transforming consciousness to an awareness of the Fire or Light it can hand on the medieval Fire or Light to European civilisation. As the new Baroque Age has emerged from the collapse of classical Humanism due to the new science and the rediscovery of the ancient wisdom surrounding the Fire or Light, it fits in with the dynamic view of the world held by the new subatomic science and with the workings of irrational *prana*, and can be expected to last as long as stages 44 and 45 of European civilisation last, i.e. as long as the coming United States of Europe lasts before European civilisation enters its long process of disintegration. Now – and here I introduce a note of optimism and hope – it is possible that the new Baroque Age will be the crowning glory of Western literature, and perhaps of the whole of Western civilisation (ie the European and the North American civilisations). For just as medievalism gave way to Humanism from about 1450AD (when the halo disappeared from paintings), and the glory of the High Renaissance was only forty years in coming; so our Humanism is giving way to a new anti-Materialist, spiritual or metaphysical Baroque Age whose High Counter-Renaissance may be only forty years in coming and as great as the 16th century High Renaissance. The foundation of this Counter-Renaissance is the Fire or Light which, through the writings of St. Augustine, Pope Gregory the Great and St. Bernard, was central to the growth of European Christendom; for without the Fire or Light there could be no coming new age. Such a baroque new age within the European style – new age in values and in an aesthetic and artistic sense rather than an astrological sense – can be expected to have its own classical substage (in Wölfflin's sense of "classical"), and it will emphasise the unity of the universe. (Compare Toynbee's prediction that the idea of unity will dominate Europe's disintegration.) Thus our anti-Humanist stage within a European Christendom that has known the Humanist Renaissance is charged with the task of restoring the soul and spirit to Renaissance Humanism by restoring the Fire or Light, and *this redefinition of man can produce the greatest art and literature Western civilisation (ie the European/North American civilisations) has known.*

This is a huge subject, involving as it does considerations of the rise and fall of civilisations and the relation of the life cycle of a civilisation's artistic style to the salvation of its civilisation, which I have dealt with in *The Fire and the Stones*. But it does fit in with T.E. Hulme's broad scheme (Middle Ages – Humanism – and a coming Religious, i.e. Metaphysical, Age) and with the concept of a New Age that has nothing to do with astrology and everything to do with a rebirth of the spirit and an awareness of Being. The conclusion is clear. We are on the verge of a new Baroque Age, or, as I wrote in 1965 (though I do not think it found its way into the text of the poem until 1970) in a passage which came straight from the beyond and which for some years I did not fully understand:

> "I heard a cry from the old Professor's darkened room,
> 'The Age of Analysis is dead!'
> Books lined with dust, a buzzing fly....
>   While, naked on the petalled lawn,
> A new Baroque Age is born."
>   (Lines 1348-1352 of *The Silence*,
>   which the dedication describes as
>   "a string of baroque pearls".)

*

What is the role of poets in the Counter-Renaissance and in this new Age? We have seen that this new Baroque Age casts a respectful look back to Romantic Idealism, and indeed to the Metaphysicals of the original Baroque Age, and we have said that writers and artists living in a declining civilisation cannot help echoing earlier stages in that civilisation, in so far as stage 45 echoes stage 28. Nevertheless, there is no question of going back, archaistically, to the old Baroque. Rather the new Baroque Age *looks forward*, for it is creating something new out of everyday life and a new climate for the coming age, to which writers and artists will in due course react, as did Milton, Handel and Bach in the past. It is appropriate that the Christian mysticism of stage 45 will feature strongly in the new Baroque Age along with the Universalist New Age consciousness of stage 44, as the original Baroque began as a Catholic movement and traditionally the Church has been the guardian of the soul and spirit in European Christendom.

In the past, the great poets have been the best interpreters of their Age. ("No man," Coleridge observed in chapter XV of *Biographia Literaria*, "was ever a great poet without being at the same time a profound philosopher.") Just as the poets of the Victorian Age saw a time of settled Christian faith turn to doubt, so today in our Space Age – compare the whirling clouds and blue skies of the original Baroque – we are seeing the traditional view of the universe being overturned, with consequences for our view of the world and ourselves.

A very important aspect of the coming Age of Universalism is what is universal to mankind in relation to the deep mystery of the universe. It is fundamental to the coming Universalist, Baroque Age that it is not enough to define man in purely social terms, in terms of the social egos of his society. Man also has to be defined in terms of the stars and the metaphysical Being that gives oneness to the vast interstellar spaces. It is a salutary and sobering experience to stand on the end of a completely deserted Cornish harbour on a moonless night, a unifying laburnum tree sweeping branches of stars round your head, each bright and gleaming like a yellow laburnum flower, and to reflect on the vast distances involved and the millions of light years that separate you from the stars 180,000 light years from the Magellanic Clouds, the two satellite galaxies of our galaxy the Milky Way which is 100,000 light years in diameter, and nearly 15,000 million light-years from the remoter quasars, high-energy sources which may be centres of galaxies which were created about the same time as our Big Bang. Orion, Cassiopeia, the Plough – you identify familiar friends. You stand there on one of a hundred thousand million stars in our galaxy, and out there across the quiet sea there are another hundred thousand million galaxies equally large, and so far as we know there is only life on our planet. *The Silence* contains a similar Japanese experience:

> "The sea sighed like a lover,
> Explored the face of the shore with webbed fingers,
> Blind in the dark phase. And in a glittering sweep
> Some of a hundred thousand million suns
> In one of a hundred thousand million galaxies

Whirled on in a fiery band, shot out rays
To traverse the silence for a hundred thousand years
And beam on the man who crouched by a whelk-shell.
On a Japanese beach, my terrestial illusions shattered,
I fell headlong into a deep, dark silence...."
                                    (lines 896-905)

This metaphysical dimension is missing from the social view of Neo-Classical art. Metaphysics, the philosophical study of Reality, traditionally includes ontology, the study of Being; epistemology, or what can be known with certainty about Being, which overlaps with psychology; and philosophical cosmology, which relates the findings of astronomical cosmology to ontological Being. It sees the One (or Fire or Light) as enfolding the Void or Non-Being, which pre-existed the Big Bang and which is unmanifest; which in turn enfolds or envelops Being which is manifestation; which in turn envelops Existence, the world of the senses and of the rational social ego, the world of physics and astronomical space probes. The metaphysical dimension is never far from astronomy, and Voyager 2's journey round the planets has brought it back to us. Man in relation to the entirety of the universe, not just in relation to his immediate society, and the meaning of life – these are themes of Universalist, new Baroque art. It is an art of Metaphysical Existentialism for its subject is direct, existential experiences of ontological Being, the Reality behind the cosmos and the unity behind all existence.

"What good are metaphysics or an understanding of our Space Age to the common man?" I am sometimes asked. And when I begin to explain I am told, "You're speaking Greek, the common man doesn't understand about ontology, and it's no good to him. There are many views of what life is about, and they are all equally right to those who hold the views. The idea that there is something beyond the social world of the senses is a theory, an opinion. It is useless to the common man and only as true as the contrary opinion that there is nothing beyond it. All opinions are relative and equally true."

In fact, many "common" craftsmen and artists – particularly stonemasons – are instinctive metaphysicians, and it is extremely patronising to the common man to suppose that he is only aware of the social world of the senses, of his pay packet and beer and girl friend, of the physical and material, and that he is not aware of a higher or divine layer of Reality. To those who have read deeply over 5,000 years and have unearthed the Tradition (which I have described in full in *The Fire and the Stones*), there is ample proof that there is something more than sensebound Nature, and to suggest otherwise is like denying the existence or benefits of all libraries because the common man apparently never visits them. Spiritual improvement or purification of consciousness as an end in itself in this life and as a possible preparation for the next world, and understanding the structure of the universe as an approach to the human condition whose context it is, are both better goals than "being ignorant and proud of it". The Tradition is quite clear that all opinions are *not* relative, that the "fourfold vision" is more absolute than (to quote Blake) "single vision and Newton's sleep", and if you are not prepared to visit the libraries or look in encyclopaedias and dictionaries and delve, you will never have an informed as opposed to an uninformed opinion or learn the terminology in which truth is expressed, and it will always "seem Greek" to you, just as classical Greek does to those who have never made it their business to master the Greek script. (In the same way, the terminology of the "commonest" electrician will seem Greek to the greatest Professor Emeritus at Oxford or Cambridge unless the Professor takes himself to a library and masters the terminology of electricity.) The common man can place his social (working and family) life within the context of the meaning and purpose his life has if he will open his mind to the metaphysics which used to be so widespread and which have again gained ascendancy. This essay, and the poems it introduces, are addressed to the common man, despite their admittedly complex ideas, in the hope that his life will take on an added quality and existential authenticity and consciousness as he faces the question of what the environment of the universe is in relation to his life's goal and destiny. By facing metaphysical questions, the common man's life can become satisfyingly religious or blessed with a philosophical certainty, depending on how and at what level he responds to the answers a metaphysical vision gives him.

Traditionally the poet has always interpreted his Age. Now such a poet would interpret the new Space Age, and see that the conflict of the Counter-Renaissance is between Materialism and the spiritual or metaphysical "something more", the awareness of ultimate Being that gives meaning to life. Matthew Arnold believed that religion would be supplanted by poetry, that the poet would take over the function of priest (as Eliot in a way did) "to interpret human life afresh and to supply a new spiritual basis to it". (Taken literally, the belief that religion will be supplanted by poetry is absurd, but taken somewhat metaphorically in the sense that poetry would take on a spiritual role as it did in the hands of Eliot, or a metaphysical role, this belief can be seen to have been prophetic.) It is to be hoped that our poets can rise to the task of interpreting this fundamental conflict in our Age and break out of sensebound, social poetry into a metaphysical vision.

If our poets can rise to the metaphysical vision of the coming Age, there will be a redefinition of poetry and of poetic assumptions that differs from both the Neo-Classical and Neo-Romantic definitions of *their* assumptions.

Consider the Neo-Classical and Neo-Romantic assumptions as regards subject matter and language, for example. Neo-Classical poets and social rationalists regard poetry as a rational statement from the social ego in social situations, and the language of their poems is a plain one of statement and uses fancy, decorative simile or metaphor and association. Its merit is to be found in its presentation of sincere feeling or realistic description. The drawback of such poetry is that it ignores the soul and the universe. On the other hand, the Neo-Romantic or imaginative or imagist-symbolist poets regard poetry as the language of the soul speaking to the spirit of the reader, and the language of their poems is dream-like and incantatory, from the "other mind", and presents its theme in a succession of images and symbols which are received or channelled from another world. Its merit is to be found in its presentation of the eternal world behind the phenomenal world of appearances. The drawback of such poetry is that it ignores the social world, which is a very important facet of existential living, and it regards the current everyday language in which the soul attempts to express itself as being polluted and corrupted by television and the press. Life is about more than the soul as the soul has to live and act within the context of the social world, and to reject the social world completely is to be the artistic equivalent of a monk or nun and write in etiolated language.

Let us turn aside and examine the Neo-Romantic position more closely by considering the attitude of Plato, whom the Neo-Romantics admire. Plato does not present poetry as a rejection of the social world, although he does see poetry as an irrational pursuit. Let us comb the pages of Plato's *Collected Dialogues* and list the main statements of his doctrine of poetic inspiration. According to Plato the poet is divinely inspired and receives "sublime messages without knowing in the least what they mean" (*Apology*, 22c). The poems are "divine and from the gods, and...the poets are nothing but interpreters of the gods, each one possessed by the divinity to whom he is in bondage" (*Ion*, 534). "If any man comes to the gates of poetry without the madness of the Muses, persuaded that skill alone will make him a good poet, then shall he and his works of sanity with him be brought to nought by the poetry of madness, and behold, their place is nowhere to be found" (*Phaedrus*, 245a). Socrates points out with some humour that "there are two kinds of madness, one resulting from human ailments, the other from a divine disturbance of our conventions of conduct....And in the divine kind we distinguish four types, ascribing them to four gods: the inspiration of the prophet to Apollo, that of the mystic to Dionysus, that of the poet to the Muses, and a fourth type which we declared to be the highest, the madness of the lover to Aphrodite and Eros" (*Phaedrus*, 265a,b). "Poets..., singing as they do under the divine afflatus, are among the inspired and so, by the help of their Graces and Muses, often enough hit upon true historical fact" (*Laws*, 3.682a). "When a poet takes his seat on the Muse's tripod, his judgement takes leave of him. He is like a fountain which gives free course to the rush of its waters, and since representation is of the essence of his art, must often contradict his own utterances in his presentation of contrasted characters, without knowing whether the truth is on the side of this speaker or that" (*Laws*, 4.719c).

Nowhere in these passages is Plato saying that the poet hears the words of his poem in the course of his divine inspiration or that the poet must not write about the social world. Rather he talks of the poets being "possessed" by the divine, i.e. the Fire or Light; of "interpreting" the divine; of becoming "mad" (in the sense of out of their reason through inspiration) because they are too close to the divine. The inspiration is "afflatus" ("the communication of supernatural knowledge") or a "fountain"; it quickens the flesh and tingles up the spine, causing (in Coleridge's words) "flashing eyes" – the images in *Kubla Khan* were divinely inspired. Inspired poetry is in a language of the soul but Plato does not say it has to be exclusively about the world of the beyond. The inspiration can flow into and be very much about the social world, as were the dramatic epics of Homer and the poetic dramas of Aeschylus, Sophocles and Euripides, who presented "contrasted characters". Plato says there must be contact with the divine – the madness of the Muses – and if a poet is not inspired from the divine then his works will not last. In Hindu terms the poet must be a "rsi" ("inspired one" in whose heart the universal and internal Light shines) to be a true poet.

Our view that inspiration flows into and informs the social world amounts to a guided rather than an abandoned view of poetic inspiration. The Baroque poet, inspired from the beyond and contemplating the social world, unites his being into a new whole that unifies time and eternity, and his poem is an artefact of this unification. The poet retains the control over himself and the social world of a meditator who channels the divine; he does not abandon himself into an extreme Bacchic frenzy or babble incomprehensible words that defy meaning. In the politics of inspiration the Baroque poet is an Orphic, not a Dionysan; a moderate, not an extremist. To adapt Wordsworth, he offers inspiration recollected in tranquillity.

Let us return to the conflict between Neo-Classical and Neo-Romantic poetry. The 1,200 year old tradition of European poetry, like the poetry of all cultures and civilisations over the last 5,000 years, includes both the Neo-Classical and Neo-Romantic traditions of language at different times. Each side defines poetry in terms of its own outlook and denies the definition of the other side. In our time the early Eliot redefined symbolist poetry in terms of his symbolist outlook in his essays, while Yvor Winters wrote In *Defense of Reason* to reaffirm the rationalist view and to deny the symbolist view.

A middle way it to combine the two, and this is what the new Baroque poetry will do. In the social-spiritual poetry of the new Baroque which combines the Classical and Romantic visions, the language of the poets will combine statement and image as the social ego writes *about* the Fire, starting in social settings and employing both decorative fancy and imaginative images. In other words, the social world of the Neo-Classicists is informed by the soul's Reality of the Neo-Romantics: as the soul (Shadow) looks at Nature it includes the social ego (Reflection). In Kabbalistic terms the consciousness in sephira 5, Tepheret (Beauty), can look at Nature and include sephira 2 (Yesod), the social ego. Such a poetry concentrates on the consciousness that receives the images – social setting included – rather than on the images themselves. It is the same phenomenological approach to consciousness which I outlined in *The Fire and the Stones*. It records the experience in everyday consciousness of inspiration from an unseen metaphysical Reality beyond it. This can be a conflagration from the beyond – a catching fire with inspiration, being seized or "rapt" – or an advance from a specific social setting which can turn into a raid on the eternal world and a Promethean "stealing", or more accurately borrowing, of the divine Fire. Whether the Fire approaches him or he approaches the Fire, the poet is a seer of a Paradisal world which nourishes his sojourn – indeed exile – in the social world. Such a poetry looks back to the Wordsworth of *The Prelude* who wrote *about* "the unseen power" in a language of statement that appealed to common men (the language of "a man speaking to men") but which included images which had flashed upon the "inward eye". For example, the mixture of image and statement which in one and the same passage could show the image of an animate mountain – "a huge peak, black and huge,/As if with voluntary power instinct/Upreared its head" – and at the same time make a profound ontological-metaphysical statement: "for many days, my brain/Worked with a dim and undetermined sense/Of unknown modes of being." The late Eliot of the *Four Quartets* was working towards such a poetry. As philosophical as he was inspired, he touched on the Fire at the end of *Little Gidding*: "And the fire and the rose are one." In our time such an approach makes a new kind of poetic language possible.

To put it another way, the social rationalists define poetry as the unpictorial rational statement about a human experience which suggests an empirical, social truth. The imaginative imagist-symbolists define poetry as images or symbols which are channelled from an imaginative Reality. The social-spiritual Baroque poets will redefine poetry as a statement by the reflecting soul of a metaphysical Reality which is received along with images and symbols; which is sometimes in the form of images and symbols; and which flows into and is combined with the consciousness of the social ego. This glimpse of Reality may come to the soul unexpectedly, or it may arise out of a visit to a particular place in a specific social setting – as if Larkin's *Church Going* had resulted in a vision of the divine Fire instead of the social observation of "some brass and stuff/Up at the holy end". Instances of both can be found in my work: for example, there is an unexpected glimpse in *The Silence* (line 1202), "And golden gods with Egyptian heads were drawn past my closed eyelids", while a visit to a particular place results in a glimpse in my volume *The Gates of Hell* in which "visions wobbled up like bubbles". The images are there. It is how they are presented that is crucial. They are described, deliberately written *about*, rather than strung together in an incomprehensible way in the interests of a purely imaginative logic.

Such a redefinition of the subject matter and language of poetry in our Europe will at one and the same time revivify and detrivialise Neo-Classical poetry and revitalise and de-etiolise Neo-Romantic poetry. It makes possible a new reflective poetry that speaks to ordinary people by relating individuals, social settings, and scenes of Nature to the deeper meaning of the universe, to the stars and the metaphysical Reality that is behind all things and flows through all things.

Poets looking back on the 1,200 year old European tradition can connect themselves to the poetry of many different branches of the tradition: Pre-classical Medieval poetry, High Renaissance Classical poetry, Neo-Classical poetry, and Romantic and Modernist poetry. There is a poetry for each of these branches of the tradition, and each has its own assumptions as to whether it is statement or image, whether it has architectural or organic form and as to whether the poet-artist has a social role or is isolated. Each poetic tradition is rooted in a different area of the creative brain (whether it be cortical thought, feeling, vision or the centre which receives unconscious images from the beyond), and each claims it alone guards the right way and that other ways are wrong. (We have seen that 20th century Neo-Classicals despise Neo-Romantics, and vice versa.) The consciousness of the new pro-metaphysical Baroque Age allows for a redefinition of poetic assumptions in a number of areas that amounts to a Metaphysical Revolution, and its points of difference from the other traditions can be summarised as follows:

1. Subject matter: the vision of Reality/God as Fire, human passion and grief, pain, loss, death and freedom, the correspondence between the temporal, natural world and the infinite, eternal world of the Void/Being;

2. Form: architectural and organic (like a climbing rose by an orderly country house);

3. Language: both statement and image/symbol (which embodies a psychological or physical form that is a manifestation of a divine Reality and spiritual Void);

4. Centre: both Neo-Classical social ego and Romantic soul and spirit (all of which are connected in the sephirotic centre which the Kabbalists call Tepheret, or Beauty);
5. Imagination: both temporal comparison and eternal correspondence to present the whole/unitive metaphysical Fire;
6. Metaphysical outlook: both awareness of physical reality and an ontological, epistemological and cosmological approach to the eternal metaphysical Supreme Being and Reality (the Fire) which is behind both the Void of Non-Being (or non-manifestation) and unitive Being (or manifestation);
7. Perspective of man: both man as a member of his society and man as a member of the universe which has a metaphysical order behind it;
8. Philosophical outlook: scepticism presented within the context of metaphysical Being and Reality, and unitive anti-Materialism;
9. Psychological outlook: the reason presented within the context of the irrational;
10. Cosmological scientific outlook: scientific Materialism presented within the context of the unitive new science (subatomic physics and anti-Darwinian biology) and metaphysical cosmology;
11. View of the universe: the multiplicity of phenomena presented within the context of the Oneness of the universe when seen with the unitive vision of Being;
12. Historical outlook: themes of contemporary social history (including rejection of totalitarian and particularly pro-Communist political revolution), presented within the context of support for unifying, holistic world government/supra-national state.
(To this can be added:
13. Purpose of the teaching of English Literature: to take pupils from a response to, and judgement of, temporal imagination, i.e. imagining themselves temporally into the shoes of others and associatively, to an awareness of eternal imagination, i.e. of metaphysical Being/Reality. Minor poets operate in an exclusively temporal mode, major poets operate in both temporal and eternal modes, i.e. a metaphysical mode.)

Besides being points of difference from other traditions, some of the above threads of the new metaphysical Baroque poetry of the coming Metaphysical Revolution can reconcile and synthesise other traditions, for while Baroque poetry differs from both Classical and Romantic poetry in its assumptions regarding subject matter, form and language etc., it also reconciles Classical and Romantic poetry at each of the above points as we have seen.

If poets can rise to the challenge of the Age, then once again poetry will drip with experience as the soul drinks deep from the natural world and finds the eternal Being within Nature. Once again poets will contemplate and point the way for the young. The followers of the new Baroque are contemplative "illuminati" who live very much in the world of the senses. They are a generation of Contemplatives. Baroque artists of the world, who have one foot in the social world of the senses and one foot in the metaphysical world of contemplative spirit/Being and Void/Non-Being, unite and contemplate the Supreme Being or Fire or Light! You have nothing to lose but your sceptical, Neo-Classical sensebound chains!

*

This collection spans 30 years of my poetic life, and traces the growth of my Baroque consciousness and outlook, and the marrying of sense and spirit, social and unconscious, everyday thoughts and symbols during my development as a Metaphysical Existentialist and late Universalist who sees the unity of Being behind Existence. I have included whole works rather than excerpts, for organic form demands to be read as a whole. Some of these works can now be seen to have been written before their time, in view of their contemplative, Baroque content.

This Baroque collection reveals an interest in the interpretation of contemporary history, notably in stages 42 to 45 of the European civilisation. As to stage 42, the decolonising of European civilisation and the shedding of Empire are caught in *Blind Churchill and the Night*, in *Old Man in a Circle*, and in the anti-Western attitudes of the Libyan Revolution. Stage 43, the winning of the Cold War, the coming expansion of Europe and the impending global domination of America are also foretold in *Old Man in a Circle* and in *Archangel*, with its closing vision of world government; while the resurgence of Japan is present in Part Three of *The Silence*. The coming tussle between stage 44 of the European civilisation (Universalism and syncretism) and stage 45 (a revival of the purity of Christian religion) is anticipated in the 16 poems of *The Fire-Flower* and is more deeply explored in *Beauty and Angelhood*.

This Baroque collection reveals the Romantic elements I have identified: an autobiographical element, emphasis on the solitude of the artist, an obsession with the image and a challenge to the social ego and the reason (eg in *The Silence*, which is a latter-day version of *The Prelude* as well as the journey of a latter-day shaman in an early Mannerist-Baroque style, a 20th century idiom of abbreviated narrative which is essentially Baroque as it is all movement and the images flow into each other); fascination with, and rejection of, totalitarian revolution (eg *Archangel*); extreme passion, grief, pain and love as the ego is dismantled, and illumination (*The Gates of Hell!*); and then a growing sense of the whole as the ego's hold is loosened (in *The Night-Sea Crossing* and *The Labyrinth*), an increasingly spiritual and unitive vision (eg *The Four Seasons*), an absorption of the new science which is in revolt against classical science, and the sense that eternity is within Nature (the 16 poems of *The Fire-Flower*).

Being Baroque, a mixture of Romanticism and Classicism, this collection also reveals some Classical elements. Thus these poems are written from the social ego – the mature man and his reason who opens to, and receives, images from beyond – rather than exclusively from the dream-like "other mind" of totally irrational verse, and there is a strong grasp of the world of the senses in which the infinite operates. There is verbal play, and especially towards the end, as the Baroque method matures, there is a harmonious, well-balanced, orderly, intricate approach that is very Classical, and a sense of stillness. In other words, there is often a Classical – orderly – way of proceeding about Romantic material, or a presentation of the infinite in a context of the finite, of the eternal within the temporal, which is one of the ways by which we recognise metaphysical Baroque.

On the Romantic side, the poems reveal a concern with organic form throughout. As the starting-point of each longer poem is a feeling or state of mind within a particular level of consciousness, the form grows organically like a plant by an emotional logic, through an emotional linking of juxtaposed images, either with abbreviated narrative (*The Silence*), or more musically – the favourite medium of baroque being painting or music – as in *The Night-Sea Crossing* or the narrativeless *The Four Seasons*, both of which follow an anti-rational sonata form.

On the Classical side, the poems become progressively impersonal as the control of the ego, the enemy or "Reflection" of *The Silence*, is progressively obliterated and lower consciousness dies into higher consciousness, lower emotion into higher feeling. The form becomes more orderly as order and harmony predominate towards the end of this selection. The same movement can be observed in the metres, which depart from traditional disciplines into freedom and irregularity as the social ego is challenged and its control dismantled. The iambic line gives way to anapaests and they pass into Stress Metre to combine discipline and natural speech rythms, strict form and free verse, "in correspondence with some transition in the nature of the imagery or passion" (Coleridge on the 4-stress line of *Christabel*), and eventually this too becomes more orderly as the power of the social ego is subjugated for mystical ends, and a Classical stillness is reached within the dynamic flow of the universe. The classical poets of the ancient world regarded rules and metre as providing harmony. One cannot say that the poems become more

Classical as the mystical subject matter is the very antithesis of Neo-Classicism's concern with the social ego; but one can say they are classical Baroque rather than romantic baroque (or Baroque). (The Baroque has its own substages, and in classical Baroque a harmonious and well-balanced, orderly form and world overrules the personal individuality of the artist.)

The language combines Classical statement and Romantic image. It is conversational in social situations and seeks to be direct when catching the freshness of the world of Nature, and ruminative – or even sublime and elevated – when the poetic consciousness ponders on and contemplates the Spirit or Being within Nature. (In the same way, Wordsworth and Coleridge in their *Lyrical Ballads* sought at one and the same time to catch the language of common speech, and to approach the supernatural Spirit with a Miltonic, "sublime" diction.) The amount of directness or ruminativeness depends on the degree of contemplation the poetic consciousness is doing as it approaches Reality, the truth which the Imagination can grasp but which the reason cannot. It should be pointed out that the relationship between consciousness and Reality is two-way. Sometimes consciousness penetrates into Reality and grasps the Oneness of the universe, while sometimes Reality penetrates into the Imagination, which receives it quietly in contemplation with a "wise passiveness" (Wordsworth) and channels its images and symbols. These come from the divine ocean of Light and are, as Blake pointed out, eternal. Contemplative writing is a bit like reflective prose, which combines the freshness of description with the toughness of a more abstract, reflective thought – only in the case of contemplation, the thought is imaginative (in the Romantic-Baroque sense of the word).

The Baroque consciousness combines the rational ego and the spiritual core. Its *attitude* to metaphysical Reality, the vision of God as Fire or Light, differs from that of the Neo-Classical reason in that it is ultimately one of acceptance. This is especially true of the artistic Romantic-Baroque consciousness, whose attitude is well summed up in Keats' "being in uncertainties, mysteries, doubts, without any irritable reaching after fact and reason", for "with a great Poet the sense of Beauty overcomes every other consideration, or rather obliterates all considerations" (letter of 22nd December 1817). In other words, a sense of beauty obliterates all *rational* considerations, and so Keats could write to Shelley, "My imagination is a monastery and I am its monk" (letter of 16th August 1820). Thus, Baroque poets can accept the mystery and beauty of the Fire or Light in their core, without the social ego's having to *explain* it in rational and scientific language – after all, what is essentially divine cannot be explained by the human ego – although hints from the new science can help a poet achieve a true perception of the Fire or Light and its relation to Nature (see the 16 poems of *The Fire-Flower*).

According to Horace, "A poet should instruct or please or both," and how much instruction or pleasing depends on how puritanical the poet is. Classical poetry emphasises the pleasing, whereas Romantic poetry instructs regarding the vision. Baroque poetry marks the opening of the social ego to the core, and the outpouring of the soul's delight when, in the course of contemplating the natural world, the spirit unfolds to Reality and perceives the infinite and eternal world of the Fire or Light which is immanent in creation, and whose symbols control the Imagination. The composition of Baroque poetry, as opposed to the process of its inspiration, is thus a receiving by the social ego of an outpouring from the deeper core as, in harmony with the social ego and at one with the universe, the deeper core channels the still deeper eternal world within appearances, and knows that all Nature is filled with the Fire or Light. Baroque poetry both instructs and pleases.

I have already said that these poems have a partially didactic intention. They seek to teach Being or the Fire or Light and the perception and consciousness of the mystic (to "instruct") as well as to create works of harmony and beauty (to "please"). Wordsworth wrote that "every great and original writer, in proportion as he is great or original, must create the taste by which he is to be relished; he must teach the art by which he must be seen". I offer this essay as an instruction in the redefinition of man and his consciousness which have made possible a redefinition of poetry and a new Baroque Counter-Renaissance (a Universalist stage 44 of the European civilisation), the beginnings of which are now already taking place in our midst and which can be relished once they are understood.

September-October 1982, revised August, October 1989

PREFACE ON THE METAPHYSICAL REVOLUTION

Metaphysics is the philosophical study of the real nature of things, of the meaning, structure and principles of what is. Traditionally it was ranked the highest of the university studies, and its three branches are ontology, the study of Being, of the basic characteristics of Reality; epistemology, or what can be known with certainty about Being or Reality, which overlaps with psychology; and philosophical cosmology, which follows astronomy's cosmology in studying the origin and physical structure of the many galaxies of the universe (which in the 20th century is galaxy-centred not earth- or sun-centred), but relates it to ultimate principles, i.e. Being or what is Real. Metaphysics was originally theoretical and speculative, as in the philosophers from Plato to Leibniz and Kant, but in the 20th century metaphysics has become practical, existential and empirical in the phenomenological existentialism of Husserl and Heidegger and in the cosmological observations of American space probes.

Metaphysical poems are penetrations into Reality. Being a linked sequence, these 16 metaphysical poems (of *The Fire-Flower*) aim to present a consistent vision. The thought progresses through complementary pairs and reconciles all sixteen poems into the harmony of the whole scheme, so they can all be read in terms of each other as well as by themselves and in pairs. In view of the revolutionary novelty and complexity of their subject matter, it may help if I briefly outline the progression.

The metaphysical Fire or Light, the Supreme Being which permeates all creation and which can be known by turning within from the five senses, is presented obliquely at first. Contact is made with it and with "timeless" Eternity (1). Eternity is then explored in relation to death (2). This Eternity contains a Void, the fiery Idea that brings in all forms and transforms souls (3). It also contains the spiritual Sun which, though found within, is paradoxically at the heart of the universe (4). This Sun is the inner Light of the halo of the Christian mystic tradition (5), in contrast to the roaring fire of the unmystic aesthete who does not know the Light (6). The Sun aids spiritual growth from ego to soul, and according to tradition enables the soul's genes to reincarnate (7). It enables the soul to unite with the Tao (as manifested Being) (8). Eternity (the Tao as unmanifested Void) is in panting love with the forms of time (9), and it takes the initiative in entering the imagination of stonemasons who fix it in changeless images (10). The symbolist artist draws back the veil and shows the unity of the physical world in terms of the spiritual world (11). Symbols come from the spiritual world (12). They have a religious force when they embody the Idea or Fire of God (13). Far memories – images from past lives – are symbols, being divine reminders of past spiritual glories (14). The central Sun in the soul is one with the eddying power of the universe, whose tides flow into mystics, healers and poets (15). This eddying power is the swirling "implicate" Tao (as Void) or Idea which forms matter, the Fullness which creates (16). The progression, then, is from metaphysical intimations of Eternity to a deeper grasp of the Void, which is also Idea, Logos, and Tao, and thence to its spiritual power, which symbols communicate, and finally the eddying, swirling power of creation, the Fullness, Sun or Inner Light which forms matter and all created things.

These poems offer a new model of Reality. All poems, novels, plays, cinema and television films, and critical works, all paintings and scientific hypotheses – indeed, all art and language itself – are, in effect, constructions of different models of Reality in varying degrees of simplicity or complexity. They say "Reality is like this", and as Reality can be material, physical, social, intellectual, psychological, educational, financial, criminal or what you will, as well as philosophical and religious, all at the same time, Reality may very well be "like this" in part, to some extent, on one occasion, at one level or layer. Since Reality is layered, the simplified or complex models that appeal to a reader, listener or viewer are those which correspond to the layers of Reality he or she is groping towards at that particular time, the level or layer he or she is nearly at. Thus, what seems to be a good model to a 20-year-old student may not seem a good model when he or she has reached a mature 40. Some models claim that only one layer of Reality is absolute, and if it is demonstrated that the "absolute" Reality is limited and incomplete, then the model collapses as an absolute statement, in which case it is incorporated into a newer, better, truer, more real model. This happened to Newton's model of the universe, which has been incorporated into Einstein's model.

These poems demonstrate that the physical, social sensebound Reality of much modern poetry is limited and incomplete, and in providing a layered metaphysical context within which the social layer operates, they incorporate the social layer into a truer, *more real* metaphysical model. As they draw on the very latest, often bewildering ideas of post-war physics and psychology in constructing a new metaphysical model, it is important to make clear the central premise that underlies them, an understanding of which will aid interpretation of the whole. This premise is the relationship between post-Newtonian and post-Einsteinian subatomic physics and cosmology, the collective unconscious of transpersonal psychology and epistemology, and the spiritual Eternity of ontological mysticism, which together make up an entirely new metaphysical outlook that is best conveyed by poetry, and by a poet who observes some impersonality, or transpersonality.

According to post-Einsteinian cosmology, the universe is expanding outwards with galaxies moving away from each other. (Einstein himself was wrong to accept the then prevailing idea that the universe is static.) According to post-Einsteinian subatomic physics, the universe of "matter" is in fact a sea of dynamic, organic energy whose inter-relating subatomic particles are also waves, and are even to some extent "conscious", since all photons in the sea "know" what other photons are doing exactly when they are doing it. In quantum theory, this sea comes from the quantum vacuum, the underlying reality of all that is. All basic physical properties – mass/energy, charge, spin – are conserved in this sea of potential, and under the laws of physics this vacuum or Void will continue to exist even if the universe one day collapses down a black hole. The American physicist David Finkelstein has linked a Theory of Everything with this quantum vacuum: "A general theory of the vacuum is thus a theory of everything."

According to Bohm's theory (1980), the whole sea of matter is explicate (manifest in forms, particles) and implicate (Void-like, eternal unformed whole) at the same time. Space-time, the fourth dimension is curved and finite, and physicists now postulate an infinite "Superspace" which is timeless, eternal and transpersonal, an implicate Reality which manifests into form, from which different universes or "many worlds" (a concept made possible by the discovery of black holes) "explicate" into being, a concept that appears to confirm Einstein's words: "Anyone who studies physics long enough is inevitably led to metaphysics." The non-local theory, a consequence of the enormously important Bell's theorem (1964), states that events do not take place in localised space but affect the whole sea of "matter" that includes our universe, and according to the superluminal information transfer theory (1975), events are linked by a velocity faster than that of light, a phenomenon which affects theories of perception and makes telepathy and psychic phenomena – and communication with other universes (if they exist) through black holes – theoretically possible, and brings physics to the verge of metaphysics. Events, then, have to be understood in relation to the whole, and one wave is affected by, and affects, the whole ocean and cannot be considered to have a "local" identity only; it is part of the ocean and is the ocean, has "implicate" identity. As matter is a whole sea of "conscious" organic energy, the old distinction between mind and matter has collapsed, along with the old distinction between the observer ("I") and what he observes, for the part is inseparable from the indivisible whole, and to see from a fixed point distorts Reality.

In the transpersonal psychology and epistemology of later Jung, who derived his idea of the psyche from his meetings with Einstein in Zurich, there is a sea of collective unconsciousness, the Alchemists' "unus mundus", outside time, an eternal, transpersonal world of "dead spirits" which pours archetypal images into the Self (the core), whence they are communicated to the ego just as waves become particles. This concept closely resembles "Superspace". In what Jung called "synchronicity", a symbolic image in the "unus mundus" or timeless psychic inner world (a dream, waking vision, communication from a "dead spirit", or hunch) coincides with an event in the outer world, as when a mother suddenly has an intuition that her child has had an accident. Such psychic and physical events coincide simultaneously in time without being connected causally – indeed, images from the "unus mundus" can break into time and manifest as synchronistic events – and psyche and matter are thus linked. (Jung's collaborator, Marie-Louise von Franz, strengthened this link in *Number and Time*, which develops Jung's view that numbers regulate the unitary realm of psyche and matter.) Jung's findings confirm both Bohm's theory, in which implicate "energy" can manifest into form as explicate "matter", and the non-local and superluminal transfer theories. Again, the old dualism of mind and matter has collapsed, and the psyche has no local identity only (the ego), but is a part of – and is – the whole ocean, which can by mystically known.

Ontological mysticism sees Reality as an ocean of Fire or Light or Idea outside the cosmos, that manifests into form. Though interest in mysticism has never been greater than today – witness the many New Age sects – there is a 5,000 year old mystic tradition which has always maintained this process of manifestation, a tradition I have dealt with at great length elsewhere (in *The Fire and the Stones*). One of the models in this tradition is the Kabbalistic one, in which manifestation takes place through four worlds (the divine, spiritual, psychological and physical worlds) down an inverted Tree of Life, through ten sephirot, relevant details of which appear in the notes at the back. All periods in the tradition agree that the soul or Self can return to the Fire or Light of its origin if it takes the Mystic Way and journeys away from the centre of the ego, the social "I" or vantage point which misses the Being or Idea or Fire or Light within all forms. The soul turns within from the five senses, and, by-passing outer space and therefore space-time in inner vision, contacts the timeless, and therefore eternal, spiritual Reality which is a dynamic present of Fire or Light and images. This sea of Fire or Light closely resembles "Superspace" and the "unus mundus". The soul rises to cosmic and transcendent levels of consciousness in which the observer knows he is not just a part of the Eternal totality or implicate Void he observes, he is the totality, and is inseparable from the whole. The distinction between mind and matter collapses, and in ontological mysticism, as well as in cosmological physics and epistemological transpersonal psychology, the perspective of the ego or social "I" gives an unreliable, distorted picture of Reality, alienating and separating the observer from the whole sea of Fire or Light and spiritual being. The "I" must be obliterated if a truly objective picture of Reality is to emerge.

The link between cosmological subatomic physics, epistemological psychology and ontological mysticism may be found in modern cosmology, which is based in astronomy and reflected in metaphysical philosophy: notably in the cosmic background radiation (CBR), a still-existing perpetual hiss from the Big Bang, the non-localised explosion which created a fireball everywhere and which cooled into the universe 18 billion to 15 billion years ago. This radiation was discovered in America in 1964/5 by Penzias and Wilson, and has been found to be evenly dispersed throughout the known universe as a diffuse glow at constant microwave tendencies (with a temperature of $2.7°$ Kelvin.) The NASA satellite Cobe (Cosmic Background Explorer) was launched in November 1989 to investigate this radiation.

The discovery of CBR, for which Penzias and Wilson were awarded the 1978 Nobel Prize for

Physics, has been enormously important as, together with the existence of quasars, it is now held to confirm the Big Bang theory and to discredit the Steady State view of creation. As a result cosmologists are now probing the vacuum that existed shortly before the Big Bang, the Void of nothingness or Bohm's "implicate order" out of which "something" came, which existed before the Big Bang and which will exist after the universe. Although there are arguments (e.g. by the sceptical Hume) against the necessity of placing the divine immediately before the Big Bang, I have already linked this Void with the metaphysical Fire in *The Fire and the Stones*. The CBR, which dates back to 300,000-500,000 after the time of creation, may be a manifestation of the implicate, mystical, metaphysical Being or Reality or Quantum Vacuum or Void of the Fire or Light which influences the psyche and which can be experienced as the vision of God as Fire or Light, a vision which has given rise to all history's civilisations. Our bodies are composed of material that came out of the Big Bang and which had cooled when the universe had ceased to be radiation-dominated and had become matter-dominated (after hydrogen ceased being ionised and the radiation decoupled from the gas) about one million years after the Big Bang, and our bodies can therefore be expected to have an affinity with, and receive and absorb, the radiation from which matter condensed. (Penzias himself has said that we receive and absorb the CBR as a slight warmth.) As our bodies are composed of material that emanated or manifested from the vacuum or Void (which has been called a superdense blob) that preceeded the Big Bang, our souls can be expected to have an affinity with, and receive and absorb, the metaphysical Fire which, the new metaphysics argue, manifested into CBR, the spirit-like radiation from which bodies congealed.

There are therefore four levels of Reality which link cosmological physics, epistemological psychology and ontological mysticism, and which mirror the four worlds of the Kabbalah; and from a metaphysical point of view the scheme of things looks as follows, with alternative descriptions for each layer, the highest layer being no. 1 and the lowest no. 4:

Four layers of Reality	Religious interpretation	Four Kabbalistic worlds	Metaphysical discipline
Eternity: 1. Infinite/Supreme Being/Reality/ Fire or Light/the One/absolute Good (& Ontic realm above intellect)	God	divine	ontology/ mysticism
2. Non-manifestation/Non-Being/ Quantum vacuum (before Big Bang)/Void/implicate order/ Nonduality (advaita)/Idea/ Archetypes/Forms/Logos/Tao/ Superspace/sea of Fire or Light/ Alchemists' "unus mundus"/ metaphysical Zero/Divine Mind/ Intellectual Principle (or Nous)/ Totality of Possibilities of Being/Holy Spirit/Heaven	Holy Spirit known by spirit	spiritual	intellectual Idealism/ transpersonal psychology/ transformation to new centre

Time:			
3. Manifestation after Big Bang/ Being/Totality of Possibilities of Existence/invisible cosmic background radiation/Ocean of Being/Unity of Being known by soul	Oneness of creation known by individual soul illumined by Fire through spirit	psychological	epistemology/ psychology
4. Existence/matter/organism/ world of senses	world known by social ego/ body	physical	cosmology/ physics

Being has been variously regarded as belonging to divine, spiritual, psychological and physical layers of reality by the varied approaches of Idealism, Materialism and Existentialism. Despite attempts by Materialists and Realists to connect Being with matter of the observable world, and by Logical Positivists to define Being as non-existence, in metaphysics Being is regarded as manifestation (layer 3 above) and also as the Supreme Being (layer 1) which includes the Void or non-manifestation/Non-Being (layer 2). More specifically, Being (layer 3) envelops universal Existence, which is the sum total of manifestation of all Being's possibilities. (The oneness of the pebbles and rocks in the stone garden at the Zen Ryoanji temple in Kyoto, Japan, images this relationship between Being and Existence.) Unity contains multiplicity, and there are many degrees of Existence (layer 4), all of which are multiple manifestations of Being (layer 3) (e.g. trees, flowers, birds, animals, humans etc). The anti- metaphysical Existentialists were wrong to see Existence as particular and individual without being enveloped by universal Being (for example, Sartre's Roquentin in *La Nausée* who lacked the vision of Being that relates the particular and individual chestnut tree to the universal whole of Being and therefore felt disgust at the gratuitiousness of the cosmic order); and it is the Materialistic error of the 20th century to regard Reality as being confined to layer 4.

Being is the sum total of everything manifested, and Non-Being (layer 2) contains everything unmanifested, including the possibilities of Being which have not yet manifested. In other words, as Guénon points out in *The Multiple States of Being*, Non-Being (layer 2), or the non-manifested (i.e. the Void, "la vide" or the metaphysical Zero) "envelops Being" (layer 3) "or the principle of manifestation, so silence contains within itself the principle of the word". Universal Possibility or the Infinite (layer 1) therefore contains both Being (layer 3) and Non-Being (layer 2), or as the famous Eastern thinker and Japanese poet Junzaburo Nishiwaki scribbled out for me in 1965 in a sake bar with sawdust on the floor next to Keio University's Mita campus, "+A (to be) + - A(small zero) = 0 (great nothing)", an equation my poem *The Silence* carries as a pentameter: "$(+A) + (-A) =$ Nothing". In other words Being + Non-Being (metaphysical Zero) = Infinity (layer 1), which encompasses both time and unmanifested eternity.

The idea that the metaphysical Fire or Light which preceded the Void and Big Bang (or unmanifested Non-Being and manifested Being) manifests in cosmic background radiation unites physics and metaphysics and enfolds time within eternity, and it offers a theory of everything which includes all four layers of Reality. A theory of everything cannot exist unless it includes cosmic rays and CBR as while all the three families of elementary particles existed naturally a fraction of a second after the Big Bang, now that the universe has cooled two of the three families are only found in cosmic rays and in this cosmic background radiation.

Ontological mysticism has derived renewed strength from the scientific corroboration of cosmological physics and epistemological psychology, and it is the renewed drawing together of the three disciplines in our time that has led to the Metaphysical Revolution in which ontological Being can be epistemologically known through illumination (as St. Augustine maintained) and related to the cosmological first cause (the Big Bang of astronomy). The mystic's sea of Fire or Light is the traditional metaphysical Being which metaphysical ontologists have always claimed was behind creation and therefore Existence. Metaphysical philosophy is a philosophy of Being and Knowing, and in the new metaphysics, Supreme Being (Fire or Light) can be known during contemplation as an existential, mystical *experience*. It is not a theoretical concept to be argued, speculated about and reasoned in the manner which has given the word "metaphysical" its popular derogatory connotation of "abstract and subtle talk", "mere theory". (It was in this pejorative sense that Drummond, Dryden and Johnson dismissed as "metaphysical" the 17th century poets who drew on the new learning and science, and who knew the Fire or Light.) Traditionally, "metaphysics" has wrongly been thought to mean "*beyond* physics", the "science of things transcending what is physical or natural" – in fact, "ta meta ta phusika" were the works of Aristotle which were placed "meta" or *after his Physics* by his early students – but as physicists move towards a traditionally metaphysical model of the universe in which an infinite, implicate quantum vacuum or Void or "Superspace" outside space-time manifests into explicate form as Being and Existence, and as Einstein's prophecy that physicists are "inevitably led to metaphysics" is fulfilled in more books like Fritjof Capra's *The Tao of Physics*, then the *workings* of the timeless, eternal, transpersonal and extra-cosmic Fire or Light which can be seen in contemplation become increasingly accessible to physics; and metaphysics will increasingly cease to be the traditional, popular "what is *beyond* physics" and will increasingly become almost a new branch of physics, "what is *behind* or *hidden within* (or implicate within) physics, which is now being revealed". Physics will try and "catch" the metaphysical manifesting into the physical, the Void into Being and Existence, the "supernatural" into the natural, and the manifesting process will be seen to be to some extent a physical and natural one, though the implicate Void through which Being or Fire or Light becomes form is outside space-time.

The new metaphysics, then, include a physics-based study of the first principles of ontological, epistemological and cosmological Being, substance or essence (the manifesting Fire or Light) which is *behind* time, space, cause and identity, as well as a description of existential, contemplative experiences of the great "*behind*" or "*hidden within*", and this important perspective of an ontological, epistemological and cosmological Reality *behind* the physical world is contained in the very word "metaphysical". For interestingly, the prefix "meta" occasionally has the sense of "*behind*" rather than "after", as in "metaphrenon" ("the part of the back that is behind the diaphragm"). "Metaphysics" can therefore mean "*behind* the physical" or "*behind physics*", and the new metaphysical perspective and approach to Reality marks a break with the speculative past precisely because this *behindness* can be directly known. In other words, the Supreme Being or Reality – God – *behind* the physical world can be known directly as an experience of the Fire, which is simultaneously (1) an ontological truth, in the sense of a non-contradictory fundamental principle, (2) an epistemological truth that can be directly known through mystical experience, (3) a cosmological truth which offers a first cause in the physical world as it preceded the Big Bang, (4) a teleological truth which links design in nature to the purpose or end of the universe, and (5) a moral truth which is the "Good", the supreme object of knowledge. All these five traditionally theoretical approaches to Being or Reality or God can now be directly *experienced* through Existential Metaphysics in which Metaphysical freedom involves participating in the unity of Being, escaping the chains of multiplicity and Existence for the oneness of Being through the experience of the Fire. The new metaphysical perspective is in fact a Metaphysical Existentialism, for it is concerned with direct existential experiences of Being, with existential glimpses of the unifying Reality that is *behind* the phenomenal cosmos and Existence. It is of course this break with the past that makes it necessary to speak not of a Metaphysical Restoration, but of a Metaphysical Revolution.

Metaphysical revolutions might seem to be the province of philosophers who inquire and penetrate into the nature of Reality. With the very honourable exception of some of the Continental Existentialists and Whitehead, whose organic Reality (or process metaphysics) took the side of poets against Newtonian scientists, the philosophy of recent years has been in such a state that philosophers now have little chance of penetrating into anything very important, let alone Reality. Moreover, the post-Relativity philosopher is a part of – and is – the Reality he seeks to describe, and the old technique of an on-looker observing and cogitating is no longer as appropriate to an inquiry and penetration into an existential Reality as is direct experience of it through image- or symbol-channelling.

Metaphysical revolutions are more properly the province of traditionalist poets. Symbols point to, and indeed embody, Reality. Metaphysical poets open to Reality, the highest level of Being (layer 1), and their symbols present Reality as a manifestation in a psychological or physical form. The symbol (Greek *symbolon* meaning contract, token, insignia, means of identification) therefore represents Reality; it is certainly a transparency of, or reference to, Reality, the supreme vision of the Fire, the sacred or holy Being which has manifested in time and space, and may be identified with it, i.e. the psychological or physical manifestation may be identified with the spiritual power symbolised in it. The symbol mediates between Reality and conventional physical forms. As religion and metaphysics involve man's relationship to the sacred or holy (i.e. Reality) the symbol always represents a religious or metaphysical idea. The four worlds of the Kabbalah, the physical, psychological, spiritual and divine worlds, are all present in the layered meanings of the symbol for those who have eyes to see. The symbol shows a part (the psychological or physical form) representing a whole (Reality) with which it is identified. In epistemological terms, the symbol helps a reader to *know* Reality (layer 1) by veiling and then revealing its Fire or Light either instantaneously or gradually, by giving the reader access to the sacred or holy Reality. (In this the symbol is helped by myth, sacred stories that define the human condition and man's relation to the sacred or holy.) In ontological terms, the symbol points the reader in the right direction and enables him to *experience* the existence of Being (Reality) as a fusion of his own being with the divine Fire or Light (layer 1). The symbol can startle a reader into an experience of the Fire or Light, the delicate yugen (flower) which is regarded as a moment of perfection in the Japanese culture. The reader must therefore learn to interpret the symbol as a pointer to Reality (layer 1), and this places on the poet the onus of instructing the reader in the metaphysical Reality embodied in his symbolism.

The layered meanings within the symbol which reflect the four worlds of the Kabbalah are illuminated by the metaphysician René Guénon's view of the law of correspondence which operates throughout the cosmos: "By virtue of this law, each thing, proceeding as it does from a metaphysical principle from which it derives all its reality, translates or expresses that principle in its own fashion and in accordance with its own order of existence, so that from one order to another all things are linked together and correspond in such a way as to contribute to the universal and total harmony, which, in the multiplicity of manifestation, can be likened to a manifestation of the principal unity itself. For this reason the laws of a lower domain can always be taken to symbolise realities of a higher order.... A consequence of this law of correspondence is the plurality of meanings contained in the symbol. Anything and everything can in fact be regarded as representing not only the metaphysical principles, but also realities of all orders higher than its own." Elsewhere he says: "Rites and symbols fundamentally are only two aspects of a single reality, and this is none other than the correspondence that binds together all the degrees of universal existence in such a way that by its means our human state can enter into communication with the higher states of being."

Reality, the Fire or Light that comes into form through an eternal "Superspace" or "unus mundus" or sea of Light, is best penetrated existentially by channelling symbols and images. Symbols and images originate in the divine ocean of Light – according to Jung they manifest into form by "synchronicity" – and they contain all Reality in a layered form. (As can be gleaned from the poems and the notes at the back, an "image" is an external pictorial form, whereas a "symbol" is an image which is perceived to have a layer higher than layer 4, i.e. a spiritual layer, and so the words are interchangeable depending on which association is required.) Symbols and images therefore apply at both spiritual and physical/material levels at the same time. The poet's soul was always traditionally a channel for images of this metaphysical Reality, and in past times, simply to be a channel for it (some would say be inspired by it) was the most important thing that could happen to a man, and certainly to a poet. Image- and symbol-channelling is the proper – I would go so far as to say the true – subject for poetry, and is the basis of true poetic aesthetic, although the social, rational poetry of the wordly "I" of recent years has helped us to forget this. The image has always traditionally played a part in healing – modern researchers are rediscovering that visualising, or intentional imaging, can heal disorders in the body – and poems that channel images and symbols of Reality are not bourgeois entertainments, but *transmissions of healing* to the receiving civilisation. Such poems raise consciousness to higher worlds and enable Imagination to see into the form and to perceive within it the Idea or Fire or Light of Reality, and today they heal (as if with healing flower potencies) the anxiety which was caused by distorted appreciation of Reality during the now happily defunct Age of Anxiety, whose legacy of dis-ease is still with us. The poet is therefore a priest-healer who merely passes on the images and symbols he has received, much as a medium passes on communications from a higher source, and like a "de-egoed" healer, he is a pipe through which the waters of spiritual image can flow without being blocked by the stone of an ego. The poet must therefore ensure that his personality does not intrude between the divine source he is channelling and the reader whose attitudes are being transformed, transmuted and "healed".

As he is a link between the physical, material, temporal world of the reader, and the spiritual, Eternal source, the contemplative, metaphysical poet-healer stands half-way between the two. He blends realism with a sense of Eternity; the everyday with the mystical; social meetings with a spiritual dimension; the disorderly with a teleological sense of the meaning of life. Though his poems are finally poems of the soul that have won free from worldly attachments, they all begin in the world as poems of the heart. They begin in precise moments (like the 17th century Metaphysical poems), but develop into ruminative contemplation. The poet-healer ruminates half-way between the social and the unconscious, at the place where the withdrawn contemplative mystic gazes upon Reality, receives images and symbols of Reality and interprets them with his receiving mind. In existential phenomenology, the phenomena of consciousness are studied by examining what is in *the receiving mind*, by investigating what is in the perceiving, interpreting consciousness and bracketing out, or forgetting, the source from which it came. The poet-healer is a receiving, perceiving, interpreting consciousness, and, being closer to society than trance-like imaginatives whose poems are a string of automatically received unconscious images which are not interpreted for the rational, social mind, he can urge the reader to take part in the transforming, healing power of the image and symbol. He can become a contemplating voice over the reader's shoulder, issuing the imperatives and precise instructions of a spiritual director.

A poet who channels the metaphysical vision has an obvious problem in the language and vocabulary he uses. With the decline of the old speculative metaphysics, the traditional metaphysical words and concepts have lost much of their freshness. A word Donne used to excess in *The Exstasie*, "soul", does not have the precise, widely experienced meaning in our sceptical Age that it once had in the Elizabethan Kabbalistic Age. Other, similar words which have tended to become ciphers or slogan-words, and therefore "dead language", are: "mind", "spirit", "heart", "Idea", "Eternity", "God", "order" and "Nature", while recent additions from psychology like "ego", "centre", "self", or from Eastern religion like "Void" or "Fullness", have blurred the metaphysical terminology. Words like "universe", "world" and "Time" have been given new, confusing meanings by physics, and words like "meaning", "pattern", "images" and "symbols" have been blurred by the rational, social, sceptical philosophy and criticism of our time.

So what does a poet who is half-way between social and spiritual worlds do? Avoid all such words altogether and build up his metaphysical vision through symbols without any super-structural terminology at all? Or boldly seize the dilemma by its horns and attempt to renew metaphysical language by a reasonably sparing use of such words – without most of the traditional capital letters which tend to sloganise – in precise, and, where possible, fresh contexts? The social ego and critical judgement advocate the second. All these words once had precise metaphysical meanings, and as a Metaphysical Revolution is bound to reinstate and rehabilitate some wrongly discredited traditional concepts in stating its new vision I believe it is part of the metaphysical poet's task and function in his criticism to restore some precision to traditional words that have lost their meaning, and to redefine and revivify, through use, the metaphysical "metalanguage" which enables a society to absorb its metaphysical experiences. To this end it will be helpful if his poems are accompanied by Notes that take the form of a Metaphysical Commentary. However, criticism is not the exclusive language of poetry, and although he must employ a certain amount of metaphysical terminology, as the cosmos is one the metaphysical poet should present the metaphysical in terms of the physical, between which there is a correspondence through Reality's layers. In other words, the metaphysical poet of the core should also use symbols. The metaphysical poet will therefore use a mixture of metaphysical terms to which he gives precision, and symbols, thus reflecting both the social and the spiritual approaches to his material.

It will be extremely helpful to form a clear idea of the metaphysical terminology for the structure of the self. We need a clear chart of the structure of the self, and it will help our restatement of the metaphysical vision if we list again the four layers of Reality in descending order, using the Kabbalistic headings we have already given, and relate these to the different parts of the self involved, first in the Greek tradition and then in our Western metaphysical tradition. Our structure of the self will then look as follows:

Four Layers of Reality/ Four Kabbalistic worlds	Greek concept of part of the self involved	Western part of the self involved	Level of Reality received by part of the self
1. divine		crown centre or chakra, divine spark of potential Angelhood	Fire or Light of One Being
2. spiritual	pneuma (spirit which receives breath and gnosis)	spirit (the "I" which has lived before, which receives gnosis)/ intellect of the intellectual vision/ spiritual soul (Ruah in the Kabbalah)	Spiritual power from Void/ Fullness

3. psychological	psyche (soul which animates)	higher mind including intellect (which has concept of self)/mind's animating soul (Neshamah in the Kabbalah) heart centre or chakra (which sees global one-ness)	Being
4. physical	soma (body)	body/brain-function & reason/social ego of judging mind/ lower sensation/ bodily soul (Nefesh in the Kabbalah)	Existence

It will be seen that there is some overlapping, and that spirit, intellect and soul make contact with the psychological as well as with the spiritual and divine worlds. The spirit is distinguished from the intellectual in that it is enduring and eternal whereas the intellectual centres are temporal. The soul is a receptacle for the Fire or Light; it is a link between the mind and the vision, and so it is often portrayed as a butterfly or a bird which can fly between worlds and bring back the divine vision.

The Reality a metaphysical poet channels is reflected in the technical side of his poetry, for form and style always serve the subject matter. The unity between the channelling egoless observing psyche and "matter", which is known in meditation when the body, emptied of mind, is perceived as a rock, and rock in turn is perceived as becoming dynamic like mind, is expressed in rock-like stanzas that lack an ego. The Reality – the Fire or Light – is an orderly principle which it is the purpose of evolution to express, and so the form in which the images come to rest will express a sense of order in strict stanzas, metres and rhymes, to distinguish it from the unstanzaic, unmetred, unrhymed, *random* or "entropied" poetry of so many poetry readings, which is to ordered poetry what electronic music is to Bach, or splodges on a canvas are to Rembrandt. In the poems that follow, the contrast – initially discord – between the transient physical world and Eternal spiritual vision is caught by the rhyming couplet, and the growing harmony between them, a growing sense that one is a manifestation of the other, emerges as alternate rhyming, in which the earlier "pairing" of the contrast is not so pronounced. Similarly, the development from unipart to multipart sectioning obviously reflects a growing sense that multiplicity and complexity are manifestations of a unity, a sense which the growing harmony makes possible. The layering of Reality's divine, spiritual, psychological and physical levels is caught in a symbolic, layered language in which words carry deliberately ambiguous associations which apply at different levels simultaneously. The total effect of the obliteration of the ego is to throw attention onto the "thing made", and create an objective art.

When specialised knowledge in several disciplines draws together, someone has to be able to take a "whole" view and experience and recreate the whole knowledge, or Reality is lost among the various compartments of learning. Today, the poet-mystic is the person who can best embody and express the whole, not the philosopher or the physicist or the psychologist, who approach part of the whole, a greater part than the social-rational sceptic, no doubt, and one that is nearer to the Fire or Light, but nevertheless a part. (I am reminded of Whitehead's words, "The purpose of philosophy is to rationalize mysticism".) A phenomenological poetry of the Mystic Way which continues the Einsteinian-Jungian tradition and channels images and symbols is a better metaphysical path than the path of philosophy. It is one that can restore the stature of poetry, which, in turning away from the grand themes, has been trivialised and impoverished in recent years. The urgent task is to renew poetry's traditional contact with its metaphysical source.

May-June 1980, revised August, October 1989

NOTES:

A METAPHYSICAL COMMENTARY

Few post-war poems need notes. However, these poems of mine draw on a metaphysical vision which may at first baffle the reader accustomed to a purely social perspective; and the technique of "layering" in these poems – using images and symbols which have multiple metaphysical, as well as social, associations and meanings – demands a particular kind of response from a reader. These notes, a Metaphysical Commentary, are to help the reader find the metaphysical depths beneath the surface of the poems of main metaphysical interest. A reader must become rather like a geologist who has to distinguish the various veins in a rock, and notes can help him make the survey which will identify all the veins and achieve the required response.

These notes can do no more than indicate where the veins are, point the geologist in the right direction and discourage surface-skimming. They are not intended to be more than indications and pointers, and they certainly do not intend to label, catalogue and codify the veins: the symbols in these poems, and the symbolist tradition they draw on, are far too densely layered, and have far too many associations, for that. Nor do these notes intend to replace the images and symbols of the poems. Notes come from the critical, social reason, whereas images and symbols are channelled from the beyond; and notes cannot be substitutes for images any more than a geologist's labels can be a substitute for the rock-samples he has prised from a rock-face.

These notes are, rather, a rope thrown to a geologist to help him up a difficult rock-face he is exploring for the first time. The rope can be dispensed with once the rock has been thoroughly surveyed and climbed, and its total veined perspective grasped. For by then the geologist will have obtained sufficient knowledge of the rock-face to have the confidence to attempt his researches on it without any rope at all.

Where possible these notes give dates so that the reader can relate each poem to my chronological as well as to the thematic development. There are dates at the end of most of the later poems. These dates have been taken from my *Diaries*, which contain day-to-day literary, existential and metaphysical reflections and observations, and run from 1960 to the present. They begin properly in 1963 and there is a Collins Royal 52 Diary for each year since then. Volume 1, *Awakening to the Light*, covers 1958 to 1967.

PREFACES

These Prefaces were written before the compilation of *Collected Poems* and omit references to all works written after 1989. They are included as offering useful background on the Baroque and metaphysical perspective of many of the poems.

PREFACE ON THE NEW BAROQUE CONSCIOUSNESS AND THE REDEFINITION OF POETRY

This Preface presents the new Baroque consciousness as a blend of Classicism and Romanticism (pp551-62), of classicism's social ego and Romanticism's infinite spirit or core. The new

Baroque consciousness allows for a redefinition of poetic assumptions (see pp577-78).

This Preface was first drafted in September-October 1982 and finally revised in August and October 1989 in Cornwall (within sight of the Black Head of Trenarren). It was first written with a *Collected Poems* in view.

PREFACE ON THE METAPHYSICAL REVOLUTION

This Preface presents a new Existential Metaphysics linking cosmology and subatomic physics, transpersonal psychology and epistemology and ontological mysticism; all of which approach Reality as the metaphysical Fire or Light which can be seen. The *Preface* shows four layers of reality (pp584-85) which manifest downwards from the Infinite to Non-Being or Void, to Being, to Existence, and incorporate the layered meaning of the symbol.

First written in May-June (especially 22nd June) 1980 and subsequently revised in August and October 1989. This essay originally introduced the 16 poems in *The Fire-Flower*.

A WELL OF TRUTH, 1958 – 1963

These poems are early juvenilia and express an awareness of, yet a sense of an absence and deprival of, a metaphysical reality. *The New Man* refers to the philosopher's stone and anticipates the last poem in the collection.

A STONE TORCH-BASKET, 1963 – 1965

These poems were all written in Japan.

THE EXPATRIATE

The epigraph can be translated: "Oh halls of Admetus, in which I endured a menial's fare, although being a god."

Written in Japan on 28th-30th November and 5th December 1963. In Asvaghosa's *Buddhacarita*, or *The Acts of the Buddha*, the enlightenment of the historical Buddha (or Buddha Sakyamuni) is described in terms of four watches of the night. The text can be found in *Buddhist Scriptures*, translated by Edward Conze. In the first watch the Buddha recollected all his former births and deaths, and observed that the world is helpless, "like a wheel it turns round and round"; the world of Samsara is as unsubstantial as the pith of a plantain tree. In the second watch he looked upon the entire world, which appeared reflected in a spotless mirror. It became clear to the Buddha that no security can be found in this flood of Samsaric existence. In the third watch, from the summit of the world he could detect no self anywhere. Like the fire when its fuel is burnt up (i.e. like cinders), he became tranquil. In the fourth watch, when dawn broke, he reached the state of all-knowledge "and the earth swayed like a woman drunken with wine"; he had finally convinced himself of the lack of self in all that is.

The four sections of the poem are based on these four watches, as the philosophising expatriate, drinking in a pleasure-garden, recognises his attachment to his social ego, a brief escape from which takes him close to enlightenment. "Bhodi-garden" (line 15) suggests "Garden of Enlightenment". In his dawn he does *not* perceive lack of self in all that is.

4.   "Gingko tree", tree with fan-shaped leaves, found in China and Japan.

92.   "Differential coefficient". "Quantity measuring rate of change of a function of any variable" (*Concise Oxford Dictionary*); here used more generally in the sense of "permanent outlook in terms of which change can be measured".

95. "Stone torch basket", in Japanese "ishi doro", the stone lantern found in Japanese gardens.

TWILIGHT

First written on 13th June, 1964, after which an early version appeared in the Japanese magazine, *The Rising Generation*, and subsequently revised e.g. on 2nd-3rd September 1966 and in 1968. The poem maintains that although 20th century logic and science have overthrown the forms of traditional religion, those like the prophet who experience the divine Fire or Light know a vision, conviction and purpose which defies rational justification. As the poem anticipates *The Fire and the Stones* the first and third versions are given, and the changes to the second version were: "Contemplation in a wilderness of graves" (line 3); "cross-on-wheel from 'druid ages'" (line 9); "Oblivious of their stones, their laughs, their gibes" (line 22); "And galaxies of Saints" (line 25). The last two and a half lines are: "Do not ask him to verbalise –/For, with perfect eyes of purpose, he will confess:/'The senselessness of self-development'" (lines 29-31). The following are notes on the third version:

7. "Our logic-chopping century". Logical positivism and linguistic analysis.
10. "Lunar ash". Ash brought back from the moon, whose conquest gave heart to Materialists.
    "Heelstone clock". Stonehenge, which has a Heelstone (or sun stone, "hele" being Greek for "sun") and which is regarded as an astronomical clock by contemporary scientists.

WINTER IN NARA

A slop shop is a shop that sells "oyako", a kind of soup with egg in it. The Tempyo period is the end part of the Nara Period, 710-794AD. 3

THE EARLY EDUCATION AND MAKING OF A MYSTIC (FRAGMENTS OF A SPIRITUAL ODYSSEY), 1965 – 1966

The soul awakens to a level of consciousness and awareness which is more intense than that of the social ego.

These fragments observe Freeman in 42 situations, and sometimes allow him to speak in the first person and sometimes describe his activities in the third person.

No 14 is set in London in 1957 (a Philosophy course in the Haymarket, and a Fleet Street coffee-bar, where Colin Wilson spoke, first drafted in 1960). "The way up and the way down are the same": Heracleitus (c500BC). No 16 is set in Oxford in 1959 (the Worcester College lake). Readings in the original version are: "The blue envelope came" (line 3); "observing" (line 7); "Then I opened it" (line 9); "Unbreakfasted in my room" (line 25); "woken from" (line 27). No 33 is set in Essex in 1963 (the back first landing bedroom at Journey's End, see note on *Journey's End*). No 34 is set at the Strawberry Hill pond in Epping Forest, off the road from Loughton to the Robin Hood. The original version reads: "I stood in an inner dark/Between nothing and nothing in" (lines 3-4).

Nos 38 to 41 were written in 1965-1966. Paradise Valley (no 38) is at Nobe, near Kurihama, Japan. The "Garden Temple" (no 39) was a meditation centre in Ichikawa City, Japan, which I visited on 10th July 1964. "Fine rain of Rosan", etc., is by Sotoba. *Andrizesthe* (no 41) refers to "nesting-boxes" in line 4. The Japanese Imperial Household have nesting-boxes in their Palace trees. These are believed to house the souls of the dead. The "round white sun" is described in *A Mystic Way*. The glimmer of satori (no 40) took place in the Zen Engakuji Temple in Kita-

Kamakura, Japan on 26th July 1965, which prepared the way for a full experience of the dazzling "white sun" on 18th October 1965. Gravity snapped when I once stood near the centre of Tower Bridge, and I had a strong feeling that I was falling up into the sky.

THE SILENCE, 1965 – 1966

This is a contemplative poem of transformation. There is a transformation in consciousness from that of the social ego to the consciousness of a new centre.

Written January 1965-June 1966, revised in August 1970, 25th-26th July 1974 and later. The opening and closing passages were added in April 1973.

Mr F. T. is an amalgam of Frank Tuohy and E. W. F. Tomlin.

The poem is a latter-day *Portrait of the Artist as a Young Man*, in the course of which Freeman chooses himself as an artist. The "silence" of the title is the silence of eternity which (as the Void or quantum vacuum) is the ultimate source of mysticism, and of creativity and therefore of art. In the course of Freeman's choice of himself as an artist he experiences all four Kabbalistic worlds: the physical, psychological, spiritual and divine worlds.

At another level, the poem is about a transformation in the young Freeman's consciousness, which ceases to be controlled by his Reflection, or social ego, and becomes centred on his Shadow; not the Jungian term but at one and the same time an amorphous principle from which the Reflection manifests, and an amorphous image of one's future self as a higher or spiritual consciousness which perceives meaning and has a metaphysical awareness. The heading of *Section One (Dying: Shadow)* refers to Freeman's awareness of his goal (the Shadow) and of his need to die away from the everyday social consciousness that surrounds him; the heading of *Section Two (In the Underworld: Moon on the Northern Dead)* refers to the netherworld limbo between the social and metaphysical outlooks, when Freeman is still under the control of his social ego; and the heading of *Section Three (Rising: Reflection on the Clouded Ground)* refers to the breaking of the social ego's control and, following a first experience of illumination, his shift to a new centre in himself and to a new metaphysical awareness and consciousness, which gives him the freedom to rise to and embark on the Way of a metaphysical artist. The shift is seen in the imagery of a seed which has fallen from the tree of European civilisation, and which sprouts and grows a new shoot.

The poem ranges over West and East in the Universalist manner, and particularly draws on the Mesopotamian legend of Tammuz (or in Sumerian, Dumuzi) which dates back to c2600BC. Tammuz died, was imprisoned in the Underworld, and rose again with the vegetation in the spring after Inanna (or Ishtar), the Sumerian form of the Neolithic Earth Mother or Magna Mater, Queen of Heaven and sister of the Sun-god Utu, descended into the Underworld to reclaim him. There was then a Royal Sacred Marriage in which Tammuz married Inanna (an event which is celebrated each year at the Spring Festival at Isin, just south of Babylon in Iraq). Traces of this legend can be found in the headings (Dying/Underworld/Rising), and in lines 273, 558, 663 (in which the Universalist Earth Mother is associated with Inanna) and 695-6.

Embroidered into this legend in the poem is the association of Tammuz with Orpheus (see lines 395 and 1374), the Greek poet who in one version of the myth was torn to pieces by the Maenads (see line 394), worshippers of Dionysus, in a Bacchic orgy because he preferred to worship Apollo, and whose head still sang after his death; and the Egyptian Osiris (see lines 1086 and 1353-4; and the gloss to line 1110) who was dismembered into 14 pieces and who was pieced together by Isis, the Magna Mater goddess. (Hence lines such as 718.) The deaths of Tammuz, Orpheus and Osiris reflect one Universalist myth in which the hero dies away from his society into an Underworld beneath the social ego, from which he is rescued by a subrational Earth Mother or Magna Mater; and from which he is reborn with a new illumined spiritual centre like a seedcase splitting into shoot.

THE FORM OF THE SILENCE

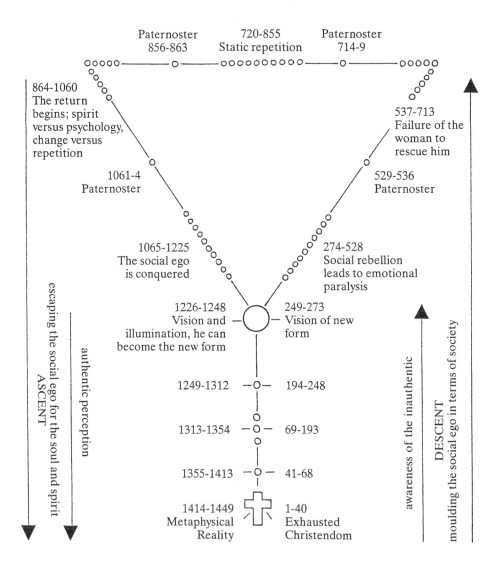

STATIC

in the grip of the social ego

Paternoster 856-863

720-855 Static repetition

Paternoster 714-9

864-1060 The return begins; spirit versus psychology, change versus repetition

537-713 Failure of the woman to rescue him

1061-4 Paternoster

529-536 Paternoster

1065-1225 The social ego is conquered

274-528 Social rebellion leads to emotional paralysis

1226-1248 Vision and illumination, he can become the new form

249-273 Vision of new form

1249-1312   194-248

1313-1354   69-193

1355-1413   41-68

1414-1449 Metaphysical Reality

1-40 Exhausted Christendom

escaping the social ego for the soul and spirit ASCENT

authentic perception

awareness of the inauthentic

DESCENT

moulding the social ego in terms of society

Note: The word "Baroque" may come from the Spanish "barrueco" (Portuguese "barroco"), a term from gemmology meaning an irregular pearl.

The poem associates Freeman/Tammuz's death with his rebellion against his society, whose consciousness he abhors, and with the subsequent malaise in an emotional Underworld beneath the domination of his Reflection.

The technique of the poem is abbreviated narrative in an emotionally linked sequence of images, which are "told" like rosary beads (see diagram). This allows Freeman to speak in the first person while his actions are viewed objectively as by a camera, and are described in the third person. The marginal glosses apply the technique of *The Ancient Mariner* to the poem's interiorised, metaphysical theme.

Freeman's exploits are seen in various situations: in a High Road, church and library in the Epping Forest Clay Country village where he is living; among London commuters, on a London bus and in a Jazz Club on his way to and from the London solicitors' office where he is working; in his Oxford rooms, at an Oxford Commemoration Ball and in Oxford's Jericho, while he is an undergraduate; and teaching in the Middle and Far East, with a spell in between as a park gardener in London. This variety of outer and inner situations is presented as a dynamic flux in the baroque manner, and permits Freeman's growth into wholeness to be seen as a dynamic, organic process.

It is important to grasp that throughout the poem the mature Freeman meditates on the development and transformation of the young Freeman. There are sometimes therefore two voices – the voice of the mature Freeman and the voice of the young Freeman – and sometimes within the meditation they are in dialogue. The mature meditating Freeman can describe the young Freeman's deeds in the third person, and identify with them in the first person and question the young Freeman. The young Freeman can speak or answer back in the first person. The development and transformation of the young Freeman from social ego to metaphysical artist/poet (and from the "horizontal" to the "vertical" vision) is seen Tammuz-like in terms of a seed which splits, roots and shoots as the development takes place. The mature Freeman images the progress of the young Freeman in terms of a seed, which is in fact his germinating soul.

The Silence is a new Baroque work in both subject matter and technique; it reconciles the Shadow and Reflection, the metaphysical and social drives within man, and the physical, psychological, spiritual and divine aspects of man and the four worlds of the Kabbalah; and shows a finally still man against a moving background.

1-13.	The mature Freeman meditates on the young Freeman near Trenarren in Cornwall. The "Black Head of Trenarren" (5) is a promontory within view of Charlestown in St Austell Bay, Cornwall.
7.	"Angry years". The years when Freeman was angry; also, the years of the Angry Young Men, i.e. the 1950s
10.	"Necklace". A rosary. The moments Freeman remembers will be like beads on a rosary.
12.	"Tell". Count.
13.	"Age". Both "youth" and "period" or "era".
14-19.	The mature Freeman focuses on the young Freeman in Essex.
20-27.	"Iron tree...cubes". The tree of European civilisation is iron as a result of the Industrial Revolution; London is a city of mouldering cubes like windfalls on "unhealthy soil" (47).
28-37.	"The once prosperous...bones". The European empires died into the silence, and the post-imperial British survey a chilling future.
38.	After empire, British soldiers have come home and are veterans thinking about the past.
39-40.	Walking in the Roman Forum suggests that European civilisation may one day be a similar ruin as a result of nuclear weapons. "Seeds...cloud". The seeds/legacy of Western civilisation include the H-bomb.

41.	"Monumental", i.e. from the top of the Monument to the Great Fire of London, 1666.
41-48.	"Robots...computers...clockwork...metal". The commuters to grimy London offices appear mechanical and dehumanised. "Metal" replaces "humanity".
49-52.	Example of "horizontal" feeling for the agony of suffering fellow human beings: for a motorcycle victim who has lost part of an arm, and for aircrash victims.
53-65.	The "vertical vision" (65) involves observing human beings in relation to their awareness of their impending death and the authenticity of their existential response to it.
68.	The consciousness of the nation is hidden within the external beauty of European civilisation.
69-92.	Freeman recalls the consciousness he knew during a temporary job in a small factory where he made frames for motorcycle sidecars with Sid Frampton, his foreman, Joe, Harry Luscombe and Albert Lee. Joe's mind is on a pop song as he works.
88.	"Collective", socialist.
93-113.	Freeman imagines Jeanie day-dreaming as she prepares to meet Charlie Weemack.
114-133.	Mrs Hall broods on her widowhood as she boils the kettle.
134-50.	The Wing-Commander lives in the past and angrily tries to provoke Freeman.
151-171.	Fosdick dreams of a sensual encounter and receives a client. They value an estate for probate, and it is suggested that the true amount of tax is not going to be paid. Freeman, as articled clerk, is called in to prepare the legal papers. There is a suggestion that Fosdick will benefit for helping his client to avoid, or rather evade, some tax. (If my memory serves me correctly, an estate in existence before 1810 escaped the need for registration which applied to all post-1810 estates, and therefore its acreage and annual rents were merely estimated, allowing room for tax evasion.)
165.	Freeman should be concentrating on the Law but instead he is reading ancient Egyptian history and Cretan archaeology. ("Phaestos ruin" is a Minoan palace in Crete.)
172-191.	At Cliveden, the scene of the Profumo affair; "His Acred Lordship's" perception is clouded after an all-night party which Freeman has attended.
193.	Lower consciousness spans all classes and backgrounds, as the six examples have demonstrated.
194-207.	Higher consciousness begins with awareness of immediate surroundings and continues with eternal questions: Why is there cruelty and suffering? Why do strangers feel pity for human beings they do not know? Why is our universe expanding? Why do civilisations rise and fall? Why are we alive? Spiritual consciousness is the consciousness of the spirit, the "I" that lived before birth and which will survive death.
208-231.	The Church has no answer to these questions because the congregation is in an "absent-minded dream" and the message from the pulpit is devalued by social jumble sales, which pander to materialism.
212.	"Insinserious". A neologism combining "insincere", "serious" and "in sin", suggesting hypocrisy.
223.	"Child's flesh". Freeman, in his "savagery", surrealistically imagines chaos erupting into the Christian order.
230-1.	The suggestion is that many of the ladies are there for social purposes that have little to do with religion.
232-240.	The nation is sinful because its consciousness is filled with trivial living, and has

not opposed it; Jeanie is dreaming of pop songs, Mrs Hall has mindlessly watched television for five hours, Dolly Jakes is only worried about bingo, and Mr Parks thinks of earning money that will keep the bailiff at bay. Pop singers and advertisements are partly to blame, and the way to higher consciousness is through the silence the saints and mystics have known.

249-253.   Freeman rebels against a society that encourages mundane consciousness, and feels his own choice of Law as a profession (made to the playing of a violin in the background) is challenged by a glimpse of his Shadow in the local public library: a brief awareness of his future consciousness which gives him a momentary sense of purpose.

263.   "Each". Each man and each shadow.

272-3.   "A Tammuz". See above. Tammuz died, descended into the netherworld or Underworld and then rose again with the spring. Freeman's despair (hence his savage anger) is because he has rejected or died away from the everyday consciousness that surrounds him, including that connected with his profession of the Law; but has not yet chosen himself as an artist, to rise to which will make life bearable for him.

274-9.   Freeman's inner growth and transformation will be like the splitting, rooting and shooting of the seed of his soul within his skull. This has not happened yet.

280-294.   The suggestion that he should give up the Law comes from his watching an escapologist escape his chains on Tower Hill not far from the Monument, and from a chance meeting with a school- fellow on the Tube, who attributes Freeman's present study of the Law to existential choice.

292.   "Wood...primroses". A childhood memory of "Shut this gate wood" in East Grinstead, Sussex, which was full of primroses. The wood was named after the words on the gate.

293.   Freeman connects his "anxious look" with a particular day when he was chased past a churchyard.

299-327.   The eldest cricketer's stories and the stale joke about Jim's jock strap lead the angry young Freeman to imagine – surrealistically – a dismissal in terms of a beheading. His innings is accompanied by bizarre thoughts and he is ready to begin changing himself by giving up a game which had been meaningless.

328-349.   Freeman's awareness helps him to identify the girl who is bored, but he dreads making himself known. Later he is embarrassed and humiliated that the music stops just after he has plucked up the courage to ask Jeanie to dance in a Jazz Club.

350-367.   Jeanie, with her lack of curiosity in all matters except hair spray, is the wrong kind of girl for Freeman, the budding artist. Jeanie is presented through the mature Freeman's images (350-5) and the young Freeman chimes in with his account (356-362). The mature Freeman continues with another "moment" (363-7).

368-383.   Freeman, in his Law office, dreams of walking in Epping Forest and being an artist, and imagines that Fosdick too wanted to escape the Law.

384-393.   At Oxford Freeman wins his father's consent to his giving up Law. His father's authority shatters as he reads a letter to this effect by his college's lake.

394-428.   The mature meditating Freeman recalls "moments" (cf 10-11) from a riotous Oxford summer when the young Freeman experimented with and misused his new-won freedom of the will. He links the moments surrealistically and intersperses reflective comments (394-5, 420-1). There are two voices in this passage; sometimes the mature Freeman and sometimes the young Freeman – and sometimes they are in dialogue (e.g. 425-8). Orpheus (395), Freeman the artist.

429-458.	Freeman's rebellion leads him to attend a Commemoration Ball with "a madam".
434.	"Slot-machine disc". The sun seen from an emotional underworld that is cut off from the vitalist's feeling for the oneness of the universe.
442.	"Rollers". Two meanings, the main one being Rolls Royces.
459-480.	The young Freeman reports on an incident while he is selling programmes at the Soho Fair during a vacation. The K man was an advertising representative of a particular brand of king-size cigarettes who gave £5 to any member of the public who identified him at the Soho Fair.
467.	Vollard. The hero of Picasso's picture *Ambroise Vollard*.
469-70.	A momentary vision of Christ.
471-492.	With his family at the seaside Freeman sees beyond the everyday social norm. His consciousness sees the sunbathers as the skeletons they will become.
493-528.	Freeman sees a film about nuns with a pregnant woman, and is visited by another girl. He tries marijhuana as an example of intensified consciousness.
529-536.	The non-Christian Freeman is called back to the example of "silent saints".
537-558.	Angry at the secular celebration of Christmas in a pub, Freeman tells the drinkers that as they are living inauthentically they should burn their church. He is thrown out by the godless publican and visits a Forest pond.
558.	"Rescuer". Cf Inanna, who rescued Tammuz from the Underworld or "netherworld" (594).
559-592.	Freeman turns away from the reason and abstract ideas, which he feels have dismembered his heart (580), to experience with a golden-haired lady who had had a medieval dream (588-592). "Tarts" (577) i.e. rational ideas (cf line 1355). Jericho, a district of Oxford.
593-607.	Freeman's decision to teach abroad. The coastguard's cottage (593) and jetty (604) were at Gorran Haven, Cornwall.
608-648.	Freeman's decision to marry. A contrast between the unreal woman of 608-613 and the cynosure of 636.
619.	"Moon". Inanna was the daughter of Nanna, the moon-god who was originally worshipped on the ziggurats in Tammuz's Mesopotamia. Inanna was therefore associated with the power of the moon, and this association is in the heading of *Section Two*.
623.	The clock strikes each quarter of an hour in a drowsy house.
640-1.	Again Freeman thinks of surrealistic, anarchic possibilities that lie beneath a conventional social situation.
649-674.	The wedding. A contrast between the social approach to marriage (649-662) and the subrational approach (663-674). "Single face", unity of being.
656.	"The exampled Paire, and mirrour of the bourgeois race". See Jonson's *Epithalamion*: "Search, sun, and thou wilt find/They are th'exampled Paire, and mirrour of their kind."
661-2.	Blake's *Jerusalem* is sung with its reference to Christian altars as "dark satanic mills" in England's "green and pleasant land". Blake lived in Lambeth.
663.	"Fertility goddess". Inanna.
695-6.	"Ziggurats... dead." The Sumerians who built the ziggurats came from the north where the land was covered with fir-trees. The "northern dead" in the heading of *Section Two* suggests those like Tammuz and Freeman who have come from the north (Europe in Freeman's case) and who have entered the Underworld.
675-719.	Freeman is teaching in Iraq. There is no transformation in his consciousness at the rational university, where there is a killing outside the Dean's door. The Dean at the University of Baghdad was also Head of the Secret Police. (Hence he is "the

Leader's Dean".) The Leader or dictator was General Kaseem, who was overthrown and executed in 1963. There are glimpses of heightened consciousness where the Tigris and Euphrates join (703) and on the Shatt al Arab waterway (704-5) but not among the coach party at the Garden Tomb in Jerusalem (698) or in the Garden of the British Embassy in Baghdad, where Freeman sees a priest.

713.   "I thirst". Christ's words on the cross.

716.   "Pools". A mirage as is often seen in the Iraqi desert.

720-754.   Back in London, Freeman is still in the grip of his Reflection. He perceives his father's stroke and the birth of a child in terms of Mechanism.

727.   "Octopus of steel". The Upjohn brain, the first functioning model of the sensory mechanism of sight and hearing which was exhibited in London.

755-782.   Freeman recovers the Vitalist vision after taking a temporary job as a park gardener in London.

755-762.   The withering of a crocus is seen as Vitalist rather than Mechanist in terms. The imagery sees decomposition in terms of an earthquake rather than as a reduction in voltage.

782.   "The music in my heart I bore". See Wordsworth's *Solitary Reaper*.

783-799.   Freeman chooses to go abroad again "for a Shadow's voice".

800-840.   The death of his father after another stroke confronts Freeman with a universe in which death brings "an endless night". The young Freeman reports his feelings (809-10).

841-863.   The young Freeman reports his feelings during and after the funeral.

864-895.   Freeman is within "Eastern silence" in Japan. The valley is Kita-Kamakura, where there are Zen temples. The bridge (878) is Edogawa Bridge in Tokyo's Bunkyo-ku region. The "pachinko dens" are pinball arcades which were always full of Japanese. The mature Freeman observes the young Freeman (881-888), and the young Freeman records a train journey from Tokyo to Kurihama, where he was to stay in a village by the Pacific (889-895), and a near mystical experience of inner harmony.

898-913.   Freeman renews the "vertical" (as opposed to the "horizontal", social) vision and recalls his feelings in the vastness of the universe.

914-922.   Freeman receives an image from the beyond/Eternity, which took the form of a future work of art (a possible record of a coming transformation).

923-962.   Freeman's contact with an American nun in Hiroshima confronts him with the spiritual life, which he later rationalises away, knowing he is recreating himself as an artist.

941-2.   "Bracket out the symbol/There is still the spiritual". Bracketing out is a technique of existential phenomenology, e.g. in Husserl's *Ideas*.

961.   "Actor", i.e. saint or rebel. "Disembodied voice", i.e. contemplative artist.

962-989.   Freeman has rejected Christianity and the "saint's ascent" and he has taken the way of art (the way of an "existential saint"). His poems include apostates (971) and his reason now proposes that he has associated priests with his father-figure. He proposes that he has been repeating himself in his works of art (982-988) and he turns to psychology (the second of the four worlds of the Kabbalah).

990-1042.   Freeman believes that he has been projecting roles onto people he has met, i.e. that he has been repeating himself in his relationships, but he also sees that as he visits one of the Imperial Palaces he has changed and has become a figure of the Japanese Establishment. He now differs from a rebel who reminds him of how he used to be.

1010.   "Arts". Arts Theatre.

1043-1064.	Freeman sees himself in relation to a pattern of Becoming, who "might be dead", and falls into despair; his quest seems unsuccessful.
1053.	"Sea-slug...thread". Sea-slugs are as plentiful as jellyfish on Japanese beaches.
1064.	"Luminous sapphire-cell". One of the small blue cells that are washed up by the tide, and which glow at night on Japanese beaches as they die.
1065-1097.	Freeman resorts to a psychological approach to the self, which is seen in terms of a submerged mosaic with a centre and four images in each corner. First (1069-1074) the centre of the self is seen as the mother figure, and the four aspects of the young Freeman (son, husband, seeker and poet) are seen in terms of a would-be infant's return to the womb. Next (1080-1085) the centre of the self is seen as the father-figure, and the four aspects of the young Freeman are seen in terms of a prodigal's wished-for reconciliation with his father. These two Reflection-based deterministic views are rejected for a third view (1087-1097) in which the centre of the self is seen as the Shadow, and the four aspects of the young Freeman are seen in relation to his growing metaphysical vision which will unite him with his Shadow.
1083.	"Unshattered shadow", cf "some great shadow of authority shattered into fragments" (390).
1086.	Osiris, i.e. Freeman is still in pieces and is not yet pieced together. (See marginal gloss for 1110.)
1098-1113.	The artist paints two wheels, one for the social world of the Reflection and one for "a form that is real", that of the Shadow. Both can be found on a Grecian urn, which balances pictures of both social men and gods. The artist holds the two in balance on his yellow (sun-lit) urn, which therefore makes a judgement about the respective strengths of the physical and metaphysical worlds, and of the active and contemplative lives. Only the metaphysical artist can express the balance between the two – there is no such balance in the work of the social artist who excludes the metaphysical – and this balance heals.
1114-1144.	Freeman's Reflection (in the guise of Picasso's Ambroise Vollard) criticises him in terms of psychology, which Freeman counters by defining himself in terms of his Shadow's drive to "a towering image of man" (1144) and his artist's mission, which is his "purpose" (1130).
1145-1166.	Freeman resumes the vertical vision under the stars (1156) and locates the metaphysical in the "empty and full" silence at a Zen temple. He now rises to the spiritual world (the third of the four worlds of the Kabbalah).
1167-1209.	Freeman confronts the rational and irrational parts of himself, the "I" and the eternal silence. His two profiles (one rational, one irrational) are seen in a succession of opposite pairs (1182-1190) and as a husband and wife (1191-1209), the child occupying the central position between the two.
1210-1235.	The mature Freeman recalls his inner transformation as a succession of images, some memories, some inner visions (e.g. 1219-1221), each corresponding to a "moment".
1213.	"My thousand selves". 1,000 images of Kannon, which were placed round a central image of Kannon in Kyoto's Sanjusangendo, or Hall of 33 spaces, in 1266AD. "In tiers". Also "in tears".
1227.	"Tiled bungalow". At this time I was living in a tiled bungalow at 108 Kohinata Suido-cho, in Bunkyo-ku, Tokyo.
1230-2.	The moment of transformation when the seed bursts open and there is inner illumination, i.e. experience of the inner Light or "round white light". He has now risen to the divine world (the fourth of the four worlds of the Kabbalah).

1236-1248.	The celebrated Ryoanji stone garden in Kyoto (see back of jacket) which images and reveals the Being behind Existence.
1245-6.	The "Eastern sage" was Junzaburo Nishiwaki, Japan's foremost poet at that time whose *January in Kyoto* appeared within a year of Eliot's *The Waste Land*. His metaphysical formula, which embodies the wisdom of the East and which can be interpreted as "Being plus Non-Being equals Great Nothing or the Infinite", is referred to in the *Preface on the Metaphysical Revolution*, see p585.
1249-1283.	Freeman has not digested his metaphysical experience, and he falls back into rational attitudes, denying personal immortality in a graveyard and siding with his fellow men in the "horizontal" vision.
1254-6.	"Monuments to synthesis". Each grave contains the remains of someone who sought a synthesis. The dead have all had experience of the abyss of nothingness which (the reason believes) is the after-life.
1258.	"Between system and finality there is no difference". "System" recalls the "Absolute" of 1247; "finality" is death, what is seen when the monuments in the graveyard gape and reveal the abyss.
1263.	The vision is influenced by Bruegel's powerful *Triumph of Death*.
1284-1312.	Freeman now perceives Being as well as Becoming, and from his new centre, the core of his soul and spirit (the burst seed-case) rather than his social "I" or Reflection. His quest is successful, he has exorcised all his psychological "ghosts" (1302)
1295.	"Percipere est esse", i.e. to perceive the universe truly as Being and not Existence is to be aware of one's own immortal Being rather than of one's own finite Existence. Berkeley gave the phrase a very different meaning: to be, used of a subject, means to perceive ("percipere"), whereas to be, used of an object, means to be perceived ("percipi"), so that "Existence is *percipi* or *percipere*" (notebook). The use of the phrase here is more credible and meaningful than Berkeley's use of the phrase.
1308-9.	"I became nothing/I surpassed myself", i.e. the social "I" became nothing in the silence beneath it, and therefore surpassed itself by passing into a new centre.
1313-1338.	Freeman is now under the direct influence of his Shadow, which urges him to bring in "the 'new' form your age needs for ancient energy" (1327), i.e. "a form of pagan height" (1334) or "the giant Buddha's calm" (1338), i.e. the illumined, enlightened soul "at one with his fellow man" (1337). "Giant Buddha", the Daibutsu or Buddha Vairocana at Nara, 752AD.
1339-1347.	The new form is to be found in inner silence, between the new centre and the Shadow (or between central child and irrational woman). The "four-faced striking clock" is taken from Lopping Hall, Loughton, Essex, which is within view of Epping Forest and which is near the Essex scenes with which the poem has opened.
1348-1375.	Freeman now has a vision of the death of the rational outlook and the Age of Analysis; and the birth of a new Baroque Age, which is explained in *Preface on the New Baroque Consciousness*. He has become whole (1353-4) – these two lines bring together parts of himself that have been referred to separately throughout the poem – and he can now become a metaphysical artist.
1355-1374.	Freeman rejects the way of the saint ("changer in a school") and of the leader ("leader of movements") for the way of the artist. As Tammuz-Orpheus-Osiris he thus emphasises the Orphic aspect of his Universalist identity.
1370.	"Jar". Cf "urn" (1100).
1376-1397.	Freeman knows his quest still has many years to go and he recalls the solitude and

silence of past mystics in mountains or, like the Desert Fathers, in the desert at Nitria. He now feels that his life has meaning.

1398-1413. The mature Freeman congratulates the young Freeman on his inner development and transformation, on having discovered his soul "as an eternal silent glow" (1404). But the young Freeman must be careful to hold onto his gains. The "heads and torsos" (1493) have been abandoned in the course of arriving at the final exhibition, and in the same way the young Freeman has discarded his exclusively rational, psychological approach now that he has arrived at a metaphysical and baroque view of himself.

1414-1449. Back in London, the young Freeman has a vision from the Monument of the eventual ruin of European civilisation, but coming out of his meditation near Trenarren in Cornwall, the mature Freeman is able to affirm the fourfold vision, seeing the waves as Existence, Being, Non-Being and the Infinite, which combines Being and Non-Being (in accordance with the metaphysical formula "(+A) + (-A) = zero"). For a fuller statement of this metaphysical vision, see the *Preface on the Metaphysical Revolution*, p585.

1446-9. "Let us be". A call to the fourfold vision (see above).

THE WINGS AND THE SWORD, 1966 – 1969

As in the inner world so in the outer social world there is a dying away from self-assertiveness and the birth of a new world consciousness.

ARCHANGEL

This poem prophesies the end of Communism and the USSR 23 years before it happened.

Written 20th June-23rd July 1966 following visits to China (March) and Russia (June), and subsequently revised, e.g. in 1968. The visit to China was made four months before the Cultural Revolution became first known, and the visit to Russia (I made a second visit in August 1966) took place less than two years before the Soviet Army crushed Czechoslovakia's Prague spring. The title is taken from the Cathedral of the Archangel in the Kremlin, Moscow. A Russian Orthodox Cathedral derives its name from the second icon from the right (see line 280), which in this case is of the Archangel Michael. At one and the same time the Archangel Michael symbolises the Christian tradition Communism attempted to obliterate, and the impossibility of the Communist ideal (Communism's use of the sword being very different from Michael's).

The poem contrasts the Leaders' cry for justice that inspired the Russian and Chinese Communist Revolutions with the "diseased" inequality of the Christian Saints of the traditional Russian order on the one hand, and with the brainwashing tyranny of the new Communist leaders who have created compulsorily happy People's States, on the other hand. The vision of reconciliation between Christian Saints and Communist Leaders based on human values anticipates the changes of 1989, and the closing vision of World-Lords as Leader-Saints, embodiments of the Archangel Michael, predicts a world order that has not yet arrived. The title 'Archangel' suggests both the Communist dream and the closing vision of reconciliation.

1-14. The theme is stated in terms of the murals in the Cathedral of the Archangel.

5. Kremlin mausoleum. Cathedral of the Archangel.

15-32. Contrast between Hong Kong and China, and between East and West Berlin.

33-80. The events of the Russian and Chinese Revolutions are recalled in terms of disease and cure.

70. "Sun-set". A pun. The setting of Sun Yat-sen.

80-133. Scenes of conditioned happiness from: the opera *The East is Red*; a visit to Peking

	University; a visit to a People's Palace; a meeting with a Shanghai landlord and a capitalist, both of whom were under guard; and a visit to the Peking Summer Palace. These are contrasted with the truthful life in the West (124-133).
109.	The Shanghai capitalist was the former match-king of China.
134-174.	The Soviet Leaders are now under pressure and their atheistic creed does not satisfy their People. Compare the scant honour accorded to the last Ming Emperor.
146.	"Bustless grave". Stalin's. (The bust had been removed from Stalin's grave.)
154.	"Cobbled approach to Heaven", i.e. to the Temple of Heaven, Peking.
174.	Wan-li, the last of the Ming rulers, doubted his own divinity and was buried in haste.
175-231.	The Communist atheistic view of man as "material" and contempt for life contrast with the Christian view of man as a soul whose life has value.
179.	"Material". The Chinese Communists saw human beings as material that can be "remoulded", not as souls.
188.	"Forward slump". Based on the filmed public execution of an Italian war criminal in 1945.
220-230.	Blake's gardener had invited the insolent soldier, a private of the 1st or Royal Dragoons, into Blake's garden at his Felpham cottage to work as his assistant. Blake knew nothing of the arrangement until he found the soldier working there, and, not wanting to pay the extra wages, asked the soldier to leave. The soldier threatened to knock Blake's eyes out. Blake "took him by the Elbows & pushed him" out and then ran him "down the road about fifty yards" (Blake's letter to Thomas Butts, 16th August 1803), as a result of which Blake was summonsed before a J. P. in Chichester. Blake recognised that the soldier "affronted my foolish pride", but found the non-violent idealism of his "everything that lives is holy" compromised by the "cruel necessity" of using force.
225.	"Cruel necessity". "A tradition, supported by some contemporary stories, tells that Cromwell himself came by night to see the body of the dead King (Charles I) in the chamber at Whitehall, to which it had been borne from the scaffold. He lifted up the coffin lid, gazed for some time upon the face, and muttered 'Cruel necessity'" (Sir Charles Firth, *Oliver Cromwell and the Rule of the Puritans in England*, OUP 1961).
232-248.	The need for Leaders to escape confrontation between classes or nations for a vision of the wholeness of the earth and the brotherhood of man.
249-271.	The vitality of Christ's vision in Peking, yet it is trivialised and taken for granted in the West.
272-302.	A vision reconciling Leader and Saint under the Shadow, a world government composed of sensitive contemplatives who value life and freedom and have "perfect feelings" towards their peoples.
286.	"An élite of self-made saints/Each still on the last hour's quest". A world government by contemplative mystics who have a metaphysical awareness and deep human compassion is, even more than a government composed of Plato's Guardians, an impossible dream to our minds, like a vision of the Archangel. Nevertheless, this is the ideal for which the West should strive.

BLIGHTY

This poem is about the decline of imperial, cosmopolitanised Britain in the 1960s.

AN INNER HOME

First written 13th-16th October 1966, and revised. In the first version the sixth line from last reads: "Like a Saint enfolded in an Irrational he projects", and in place of the last three lines is the single line, "Like a submerged photo, beneath what a still stream reflects". The Waltham stream is Cornmill stream, Waltham Abbey, Essex. The two humped bridges above the overflow are near the main road. King Harold (whose grave is in the grounds) is considered to have used Harold's bridge, and the two-arched gateway was built in the reign of Edward III, c1370AD. Loughton Camp is an Iron Age camp that was supposed to have been occupied by Boadicea during her campaign against the Romans in 61AD. The Stubbles are nearby. Lippitt's Hill Lodge, High Beach, was the madhouse where the poet John Clare lived. Beech Hill House, High Beach, was where Tennyson heard the Waltham Abbey bells and wrote "Ring out wild bells" in *In Memoriam*.

THE CONDUCTOR

Written 20th-26th October 1966 in Japan and subsequently revised. The first version has for line 32 "Like an inquisitor, only he would wear the Reflection's robes" and for line 44 "And I was not sure it was that priestly Saint". In the poem I recalled a visit to the Royal Albert Hall when Sir Malcom Sargent was conducting. The audience at the concert symbolises society, which focuses on the Conductor, a symbol for the Prime Minister who is trying to arrest the decline of the British part of European civilisation. The Artist embodies Leader/Reflection and Saint/Shadow, while the Shadow controls the impulses of Artist and Saint.

The Conductor is seen in terms of Leader; Saint; Artist who unites the ways of action and contemplation; Reflection or dominating social ego; and Shadow. For the Shadow as conductor. There are obvious double meanings e.g., "banked", "a chord"/accord. The reference to "a drinking orchestra (line 18) draws on a reception I attended in Tokyo for the London Symphony Orchestra, when I met the conductor Sir Arthur Bliss.

7.   "All is finished", i.e. he can see beyond the end of what the orchestra is playing; but also "a stage of European civilisation is finished".

41-8. The Reflection ("Flash Harry tyrant") controls reflexes, the Shadow attracts the creative and religious impulses.

TWO MORAL LETTERS AFTER HORACE
An Epistle to an Admirer of Oliver Cromwell

Written on 29th-30th August 1966, revised in December 1974. This poem is about the Puritan Revolution, and raises the prospect of a revolution in modern Britain.

EPISTLE TO HIS IMPERIAL HIGHNESS, ON HIS BIRTHDAY

First written in December 1966, revised in December 1974. The Imperial Highness in question is H.I.H. The Prince Hitachi, the Japanese Emperor Hirohito's second son who was then my pupil. The poem urges Japan to exercise a benevolent role in Asia and prophetically anticipates in 1966 Japan's role in a coming world government (lines 58-9) as evidenced in the Trilateral Commission (idea begun in 1971, founded in 1973).

THE RUBBISH DUMP AT NOBE, JAPAN

This poem was later re-worked into *Fire-Void* (see note on p633).

A CHAMBERMAID LIES ON THE BEACH IN A WHITE MINI AND LAMENTS

Written on Nobe beach, Japan. "Lies" (title) has two meanings.

A POET READS THE FIRE

Line 14 was originally "Like stars in a throbbing brain" and line 16 "To die on a sooty pane".

BARBARY SHORES (THE EXILE)

15.   The Abu Simbel temple is referred to here.

OLD MAN IN A CIRCLE, 1967

Written 20th December 1966-13th March 1967 and subsequently revised, in lines of 4 stresses or 5 stresses. The title is taken from a medieval miniature in which the signs of the zodiac and of the year's labours are arranged in a circle around a bandy-legged old man who holds the sun and moon in either hand. "The year is usually represented by the figure of an old man in a circle, with two or three outer rings containing such items as: the names of the months, the cycle of work appropriate to each month, the signs of the Zodiac and so on" (J. E. Cirlot, *A Dictionary of Symbols*, entry for Year).

The poem chronicles the decline of the European empires, focusing on the British decline of the 1960s. It associates colonisation with the domination of the civilisation's social ego, and decolonisation with a shedding of the Reflection or social ego. It rejects a revolutionary or Christian cure (that of Leaders and Saints) in favour of a new purification and metaphysical awareness which will bring the Fire or Light to a united Europe, gather the European spirit and renew European civilisation under the image of the Brocken Shadow, which can be seen across the clouds above Germany.

1-8.   Reference to the Industrial Revolution.

9-22.   The turning Wheel of Life casts down 10 empires and moves towards Aquarius.

15.   The 10 empires are the Austro-Hungarian, the Ottoman, the French, the Spanish, the German, the Italian, the Dutch, the Belgian, the Portuguese, and the British Empires.

21.   The Age of Pisces is now being replaced by the Age of Aquarius. I have turned and reversed the zodiac to see it in terms of Europe's Great Year whose Ages are months linked to signs of the zodiac. In the poem the Great Year starts at the old man's head and moves down the right hand "sun" side. European civilisation has moved out of the "inner sun" phase, so I have repositioned Aquarius, which is now where Libra was in the miniature, Pisces being immediately to its right just before the Year's "return" up the left side of the miniature. For the purposes of the poem Pisces and Aquarius are not 2,000 year long Ages as in the Hindu scheme of "yugas", but merely Ages. We are passing from an Age which emphasised the body in the waters of the spirit (the fish) to an Age which emphasises the pouring of the waters, i.e. the Light.

23-66.   The post-war twilight of the European empires and decolonisation. The rising power of the U.S.A. amid the lights of independence.

31,40,62. Britain as the Suffering Servant, see *Isaiah*, 52.13-53.12.

68.   "Watchman", see *Isaiah* 21. 6-12, a haunting image of the rise and fall of a civilisation.

73-87.   Churchill's funeral coincided with the dismantling of the British navy.

88-182. Britain's imperialist past is contrasted with a decadent present.

90.	15 St. James's Square, originally the home of the Duchess of Richmond who sat as model for the Britannia on the pre-decimalisation British penny.
90-1.	The statues can all be found in Waterloo Place, before the Athenaeum.
93.	4 Carlton Gardens was the home of Lord Palmerston in 1846-54 and of Lord Balfour in 1905-29, two British imperialists, and it was the headquarters of General de Gaulle, the leader of the Free French movement, from 18th June 1940.
95.	An amalgam of names associated with the defence of the British Isles against Soviet nuclear power.
110.	Seamen's Strike. In the summer of 1966.
118.	NAB, National Assistance Board
134.	"Mene Mene Tekel Peres". See *Daniel* 5. 25-28 for the writing on the wall at Belshazzar's Feast. Mene, "God hath numbered thy kingdom and finished it." Tekel, "Thou art weighed in the balances, and art found wanting". Peres (or Upharsin), "Thy kingdom is divided, and given to the Medes and Persians."
147.	"*Look Back*". *Look Back in Anger* by John Osborne, a class war play that appeared in 1956 with a pre-revolutionary theme.
148.	"Vous vous êtes donné la peine de nâitre". "You took the trouble to get born." From Figaro's soliloquy in Beaumarchais' *The Marriage of Figaro*, first performed in Paris in 1784; a speech that contains indications of the coming French revolution.
160.	"Crooked" has two meanings: "beckoning" (one syllable) and "dishonest" (two syllables).
163.	"Minidollies". Dolly birds in mini-skirts.
179.	The British social phenomenon of Mods v Rockers.
183.	"Ring a ring a roses". This child's song was about the plague, the red rose-like rings on the skin being caused by the plague.
184-205.	London's post-imperial decay and the need for purification.
184.	"Harlot". See *Isaiah* 1.21
194.	"Churchillian crowns". Coins specially struck in honour of Winston Churchill's 90th birthday in 1964.
196.	"Ah London, your sins" etc. See *Isaiah* 1.4 ("Ah sinful nation").
199.	"Wash you, make you clean". See *Isaiah* 1.16.
206-233.	Intimations of a coming British revolution.
206.	Horse Guards. Opposite the Banqueting Hall (224) where Charles I was executed by the revolutionary Puritans. He walked through the minstrels' gallery window (263).
233-74.	The revolutionary cure.
268.	Pride's purge, on Parliament.
274.	Thermidor. The Thermidorian reaction followed the French revolution.
275-325.	The need for a puritanical cleansing in people's lives.
330-40.	The metaphysical cure.
345.	"Yellow Year". "Yellow" because lit by the sun. The first half of the year in the miniature is ruled by the sun, on the old man's right side; the year returns through darkness, up the old man's moon-ruled left side.
345-380.	European civilisation grew round the Fire or Light and during the first half of its life it developed round the old man's "light (right) side"; following the Renaissance (Michelangelo), the Reformation (Luther), the Puritan revolution, Copernicus' science and the Industrial Revolution, the central idea of the Church's Fire was weakened by scepticism, and there must be a revival of the Fire to carry European civilisation through into the second half of its life on the old man's "dark left side".
351.	"Goddess". Virgo, the last sign of the zodiac on our revised miniature.
353-6.	The theme of my later work *The Fire and the Stones*, here stated in 1967.

357.   "Old man's light side". The side during which the Light was known.

363-80.   Rejection of Christianity and acceptance of a metaphysical's mysticism based on the true self as the cure for our civilisation.

375.   "Tight-lipped". "Determined", but also "silent".

380.   "Byzantine pride". The breakdown of European civilisation coincided with the end of the Byzantine Empire following the fall of Constantinople in 1453 (see *The Fire and the Stones*). So "Byzantine pride" is an image of the healthy growth of European civilisation when the Fire or Light was widely known. (The old man resembles the Byzantine God or Christ.)

381-465.   The need to change the self rather than the environment. The ideal of "the metaphysical man" (463).

428.   "The Lighthouse of Europe". Compare the end of *Archangel* for the ideal union of contemplative and active lives.

441-464.   Based on the Catholic Cathedral in Tokyo's Bunkyo-ku, a modern building which includes a ladder in its architecture.

464-493.   A vision of a "giant" United States of Europe which balances the twilight of the European empires (lines 23-66). The people are "calm and gentle" (cf the end of *Archangel*).

482-493.   Britain has to die away from its ego into a union of federal states; decolonisation is a time of shedding the dominating ego or Reflection. Harold prayed at Waltham Cross before the Battle of Hastings and the Norman Conquest from Europe. (Cf note to *An Inner Home*.)

494-499.   Taken from the zodiac clock in Henry VIII's Hampton Court, where a clock hand bears a sun.

498-500.   "Sun...blood clot". The inner sun can purify Europe's consciousness so that Europe's consciousness becomes "the Lighthouse of Europe" (428).

502-511.   "The giant Brocken Shadow". The Brocken Spectre is an enormously magnified shadow cast upon the clouds from Mount Brocken when the sun is low. A businessman from Halberstadt, Germany, Herr Willie Beyer, is reported to have climbed 3,733 feet to the top of the mountain no less than 650 times, so much did he love to see his shadow. Mount Brocken is on the border between East and West Germany. (Compare the East-West theme in *Archangel*.)

511.   The Shadow is the "new God" (513), for to become one's Shadow is to have metaphysical consciousness and to know the Fire or Light; and as the Shadow knows God in the unitive vision, it is God, for its soul is indistinguishable from the inflowing God, or Fire or Light.

512-515.   A closing recognition that a civilisation's new initiatives and great times take place against the pattern of the rise and the final fall of that civilisation.

THE GATES OF HELL, 1969 – 1975
(A Record of a Victorious Overcoming, a Triumph of the Spirit)

These poems are arranged so as to tell a story of an emotional life. As the emotional life disintegrates, so, on occasion, the poems disintegrate into irregularity, and in some of these poems is to be found the beginning of Stress Metre, which is explained in the introductory Note to *The Pilgrim in the Garden*. Some of these poems begin in strict syllabic metre and then, when the feeling demands, break into a notation of stresses or, on occasion, straight prose rhythms. The purpose of this mixed metre is to gain effects that cannot be gained by regularity alone.

There is, of course, nothing new in describing an emotional life. This sequence would seem perfectly natural to a Roman of the late Republic who was familiar with Catullus's poems about

Clodia, whom he called *Lesbia*.

After the glimpse of illumination and the first spiritual life in *The Silence* there is a long shedding of the sensual outer world in preparation for what St. John of the Cross called a Dark Night of Sense, in which the spirit is separated from the senses. In this Way of Loss the soul's attachment to the five senses is weakened, and the hold of the social ego is loosened.

The Gates of Hell was written between 1969 and 1975. The first poem is about Gaddafi's revolution in Libya in 1969 and the ending suggests that Islam rather than the Soviet Union is the main threat to the West. The Phoenician ruins near the Crown Prince's palace, the Homs Road beaches and the American base will be known to all who lived in Tripoli in that revolutionary time.

Corinna was the heroine of Ovid's *Amores*, whom Ovid wrote in *Tristia ex Ponto* IV.x.59-60: "Moverat ingenium totam cantata per urbem/nomine non vero dicta Corinna mihi." ("My genius had been stirred by her who was sung throughout the city, whom I called, not by a real name, Corinna.")

I visited Egypt in February 1970.

The visit to Ghadames took place in February 1970 and involved a drive across the Sahara between Czech camps; the Czechs were building a road from Nalut to Ghadames. Ghadames is an underground town surrounded by the Sahara. Its spring was known c2600BC, and its baths were in use in Roman times; citizens still wear barricans fastened like Roman togas.

Eurydice Lost: Expectation and a Tear was written on 24th November 1972. The Malta visit took place in April 1970. "Turn" (line 6) i.e. Orpheus looks back. The poet Orpheus went down into the Underworld/Hell to reclaim Eurydice, who had died of a snakebite and was under the influence of Pluto. Despite his poetic lyre, Orpheus lost her when he looked back, and she returned to live in the Underworld. In *The Fall* line 1 (Eve) refers to Milton's *Paradise Lost*, Book 9, lines 205-385.

As the spirit detaches itself from the senses, there is a hope of salvation from despair, through vision. *Orpheus-Philoctetes at High Beach* was written on 10th November 1972.

The gods gave Philoctetes a wound (a snakebite which would not heal) to compensate for his great skill with the bow. Orpheus, the skilled poet of the lyre, is wounded by the loss of Eurydice and feels himself to be in Hell along with her. The artist has to suffer in order to deepen his heart, and his art. Orpheus-Philoctetes is a Universalist amalgam.

JOURNEY'S END

Journey's End is in Station Road, Loughton, the family house of the Haggers for 35 years. In October 1970 when the poem was written, it was a magnificent wooden-gabled Victorian house, but since my mother's departure it has had parts demolished (notably the garage and the porch), the gable faces have been hidden behind pebbledash, and it is but a shadow of its former self. Once (in 1860) one of only two houses in spacious fields, it is now crowded by the post-war fire station and other recent buildings. The tappings and creaks were actually heard, and my mother and solicitor brother considered they were made by movement of the roof-timbers, which were unsound. The title also suggests "The end of a journey (or relationship)".

7.   Beethoven. My mother was a violinist who gave recitals in the 1930s and taught the violin until her death, and there was a small white statue of Beethoven on the dining-room mantelpiece near the piano.

13.   "My mayfly". A winged mayfly with two or three long thread-like tails is found near a stream or pond. It has a brief ephemeral existence once it has passed through the stages of egg (two weeks), nymph (two weeks to two years) and subimago (perhaps only a few minutes). The adult imago lives a few hours or possibly two days, just long enough to mate and reproduce; it dies after mating. The suggestion is that the

woman "died" after mating, like a mayfly.

24.   "Morning dew". Also "mourning due", i.e. "I must choose what I dread but not let the experience rot like cellar pears; rather I must bring it alive, turning stars into morning dew/mourning due, i.e. I must make something positive out of the experience, and like Orpheus pursue the destiny of a metaphysical poet."

Weathervane and Wind was written on 7th December 1972 and came from the beyond, whole. The "High Beach church" is the Church of the Holy Innocents, set in Epping Forest.

Orpheus-Prometheus in the Blackweir Region of Hell was written on 18th November 1972. Prometheus, the first artist who made clay images of the gods (humankind), stole the sacred Fire from the gods and was punished by being chained to a rock. Orpheus has been visited with sacred sorrow after knowing the forbidden Fire. Orpheus-Prometheus is a Universalist amalgam.

Lost Calm was written on 19th November 1972. The first version ends: "There is a calm hidden within them, somewhere. Will I ever find it?/And if I do, will it leave me useless, a small round cushion without pins?"

The detached spirit opens to the Fire or Light and the soul is illumined in the mystical experience I have dealt with fully in *The Fire and the Stones*.

The poems of illumination focus on the time between August and November 1971, the most intense period of my life, and on spring 1972. *Flow: Moon and Sea* was first written on 3rd-4th September 1971 when I was staying in Worthing; it was revised on 7th December 1972. "Tortoise-shell", butterfly.

The visions in the next three sonnets and in *Visions: Shield of God* were received in the front balcony room at 13 Egerton Gardens, off the Brompton Road, London, a short walk from the Brompton Oratory, on the following dates: 10th September 1971; 11th September 1971; 11th September 1971; 12th September 1971. I have retained the original version of the first two and the fourth. (The amended version of these sonnets is in the present tense.) In *Visions: The Pit and the Moon* "imagination" (line 13), is the image-receiving faculty which channels images from the beyond. The first version of *Visions: Shield of God* ends: "so early/Will be lost, so we are left with a meaning,/A hard, strong message like my Shield of God."

Flowers in the Soul was written on 21st January/1st February 1975. *February Budding, Half Term* was written on 11th November 1972. The setting is Strawberry Hill. In the first version line 8 begins "I feel the endurance". *A Stolen Hour* was written some time between 1972 and 1975. The church is the Church of the Holy Innocents, High Beach.

In *March: Crocuses* "Red Admiral Blake" suggests emerging from a chrysalis into a mature poet.

Having escaped the chains of the social ego, the illumined spirit contemplates and is now filled with certainty. The vision for *Law of the Seed* was received on 13th October 1971. "Hazel nut" (line 11), cf Julian of Norwich's vision or "shewing".

Time and Eternity is a first version of the poem which appears in *The Fire-Flower*. The first draft has line 4 as "Like fluff from a dandelion clock, across the blue", and line 7 as "like a daughter's pattering".

The illumined spirit is seized by the Fire or Light beyond and is filled with joy.

The poems of rapture were written between 1972 and 1975: *Visions: Raid on the Gold Mine*; *The Furnace*; *Vision: Snatched by God, a Blue Light*; *Vision: Love like a Grid*. The visions were received in 13 Egerton Gardens, London on 8th April 1972 and in the top floor flat at 33 Stanhope Gardens, London on 17th, 22nd and 28th April 1972.

In *The Furnace* "fired pots" (line 10) suggests poems.

In the first version of *Tageties like Shopgirls*, line 11 is "where is the meaning".

In the first version of *Possibilities: Dead Leaves and Oak* line 9 is "You Carlotta, reach to the sky".

In the first version of *A Bathroom Mirror and a Shadow* line 14 begins "And now, Carlotta" and line 16 is "I shall forget you, Carlotta".

The original version of *Will like a Mountain Peak* has one last line "By God, Carlotta, I will!"

In *The Rainbow in the Water Shower* lines 11-12 refer to reliving childhood memories.

Sunbathing was written on 31st July 1973 at 10 Brechin Place, off Gloucester Road, London (the top two floors of which I then occupied). Entry into the divine mind (lines 13-16) results in a cosmic consciousness.

In *Thistles* line 13 "thistles" suggests distractions from single-mindedness. The first version ends "May I be simple/To preserve this breathless rain".

In *Angles* angles are an aspect of time and blinkered sensebound vision.

The Code. The MS of Donne's poem, *Good Friday 1613, Riding Westward* was discovered in a stable at Kimbolton Castle in 1974.

THE FLIGHT, 1970

The Flight was written in August 1970. The yodling took place off Baldwin's Hill, Loughton. The "grating overflow" is at the nearby Blackweir pond. The Lost Pond is further into the Forest, and is hard to find. The clearing (line 20) is the Stubbles, off Nursery Road, Loughton. The "green eaves" to which I carried my battleship in 1945 belonged to the family house at Journey's End (see lines 78-9). Before that we lived at 52 Brooklyn Avenue, Loughton, the setting of lines 39-48 and the wartime bombs. Turpin's Cave, High Beach, has been pulled down; it was a simple woodman's pub and you could sit with your feet by the coal fire. Oaklands, the school of my childhood, and Coopersale Hall I now own.

4.　　　　"Oy-olly-ocky, I see Liz". This was a game of hide and seek we played among the bushes on Baldwin's Hill. One of the children was "finder" and when the finder saw another child he or she called out "Oy-olly-ocky, I see…" and named the child seen.

A BULB IN WINTER, 1972 – 1975

After the illumination, the spirit is cleansed in a further Dark Night of Spirit. The soul is enfolded in a cloud of unknowing, and seems dormant like a bulb in winter.

In *Nets* lines 7 and 14 refer to The Filey Brig.

A Tree that is Wild is a second version. The first version differs in each stanza. The poem was written on 5th November 1973. For Turpin's Cave, High Beach; the Blackweir pond; and the Lost Pond (which Epstein walked beside every morning) see the notes to *A Green Country*. Robin Hood Hill and Green Ride are both in the Loughton part of Epping Forest.

In *Time* desert rose or Rose of the Desert is a kind of stone which has been shaped into a rose by the Saharan wind. It can be found in desert villages.

Spring was written on 20th December 1973. I visited Horace's spring in Italy in 1957.

In *The Waterfall Stopped and Cried* the waterfall is at Stoke D'Abernon, Surrey.

Caves. St. Clements' Caves, Hastings, where smugglers lived until 1825. They exported sand to Brussels and brought back rum and contraband.

Closed. The castle was at Arundel. The Hotel had a Victorian cart in the yard.

In *Chased* line 1 refers to Christine of Schire, who was voluntarily walled in a cell adjoining the church in 1329, and, after her escape and recapture, compulsorily walled in again in 1332. Shere church is in Surrey, near Guildford.

Trunks. "Trunk", large box with hinged lid, dead body without head or limbs, chest.

Fire and Waterfall, written on 31st March 1974 after being started a week before, is set in the Journey's End garden. The concrete clothes post stood near the nursery window and the lattice wall and ivy were nearby. The marble statue of Beethoven reappears in *Journey's End*.

Back and Forth. Two versions are given.

THE PILGRIM IN THE GARDEN, 1973 – 1974

These poems are elegies. Some of them have been reworked and appear in a more metaphysical form in *The Fire-Flower*. The idea of a pilgrim in a garden comes from a tapestry by Burne-Jones, *The Heart of the Rose*, which is alternatively titled *The Pilgrim in the Garden*.

NOTE ON THE ELEGY

Today an "elegy" suggests a melancholic, meditative lament about someone who has died, after the manner of Gray's *Elegy*. In Greek and Latin literature, however, an "elegy" was defined only by its metre: it was written in couplets, the first line being a dactylic hexameter, the second one a pentameter. Ovid compared the rise and fall of the elegiac couplet to the rise and fall of a jet of water.

The earliest Greek elegies we know of were by Callinus, Tyrtaeus and Archilochus, in the 7th century BC. These dealt with a variety of themes: war, politics, the pleasures and pains of life, love, friendship, death. They convey a variety of moods: joy and sadness, hope and despair, and the poet's personal beliefs. The elegy reveals more of the poet's personality, his tastes and experiences, his philosophy of life, than does the epic.

Later on, for example with Callimachus, it was adapted to mythological narratives though it retained its personal, highly emotional character. During the Augustan Age at Rome it became the main medium of love-poetry. The Roman elegiac love-poets regarded themselves as "sodales", something of a group. They were: Catullus (died 55BC); Propertius, whose first book of elegies was published around 29 or 28BC; Tibullus, whose first book of elegies appeared soon after and Ovid, whose *Amores* appeared after 20BC. Neither Horace nor Virgil wrote elegies.

The Middle Ages, by-passing the Old English elegiac tradition (*The Wanderer*, *The Seafarer*), favoured Ovid most of these, and imitation of his work came with the Renaissance. The first real imitation in English was by Marlowe, who translated the *Amores* as "The Elegies of Ovid". He used the heroic couplet – two rhyming pentameters – and this has ever since been regarded as the nearest English equivalent to the elegiac couplet. Donne was influenced by this when he wrote his cynical love "elegies" in the 1590s, and the couplet was accepted by Milton, Waller, Dryden and Pope, all of whom carried on the English elegiac tradition. Pope brought it to perhaps its highest achievement with *Elegy, in Memory of an Unfortunate Lady*, which is full of deep feeling for a universal suffering.

In his *Elegy*, Gray reacted against the Popian couplet and chose quatrains, following the metre Dryden had used in *Annus Mirabilis*, and after this elegies tended to take stanzaic forms instead of paragraphs. One thinks of Shelley's *Adonais*, the idea of which was based on an epitaph by Moschus, and Tennyson's *In Memoriam*, both of which are really in the tradition of the Roman custom of pronouncing an éloge on the interment of a man of high birth. This led to a kind of elegy called an "epicedium", which Donne translated as "epicede" and which Dryden followed in *To the Memory of Mr Oldham*. Often these pieces came down to encomiums of praise on the departed, like Jonson's elegy on Shakespeare, or Tickell's elegy on Addison.

The point I am making is that the elegiac tradition really contains two genres: the original adaptation of the Greek elegy and Roman love-elegy, and the later adaptation of the Roman funeral-oration. The English elegiac tradition turns on Milton; for Marlowe and Donne wrote in the first genre, Milton (in *Lycidas*) and his successors in the second genre. The elegies presented here represent an attempt to return to the first of these two genres. There is, nevertheless, a lamenting tone, as they mourn the passing of the old certainties in this beloved Britain. Coleridge described the elegy as "the form of poetry natural to the reflective mind", and the reflections in these elegies attempt to identify and salvage some traditional values for our time.

NOTE ON THE LINE: STRESS METRE

It has been my concern to evolve a twentieth century line which is both musical and free, one that accommodates both discipline and the natural rhythms of speech, one which draws on the advantages of a strict traditional form (like the elegiac or heroic couplet) while at the same time offering the advantages of a free verse that operates by stress.

These poems are written in Stress Metre. That is to say, they scan in metre, and at the same time they can be measured by stress. The principle on the metrical side is that the lines are pentameters and hexameters, and even, on occasion, heptameters, when the natural rhythms of speech and the feeling demand a longer line. There is, however, no requirement for the lines to be the same syllabic length, and pentameters and hexameters can be interspersed, as they were in the original elegiac tradition. It will be observed that I have made full use of the paeon. The principle on the stress side first requires a distinction between stress and accent. Any word of two or more syllables has an accent. The accent may fall on the first, second or third – or fourth – syllable, but it is there (e.g. SYLLable). In reading a poem aloud, however, one inevitably stresses certain words or groups of words that are important to the meaning of the line, irrespective of how the words are accented, and it is this highlighting of sense that is the concern of stress.

I have taken a predominantly 4-stress unit line, i.e. a line of 4 primary stress units. Secondary stress is excluded for the purposes of the 4-stress unit line. It is worth recalling the distinction between primary and secondary stress. As any teacher of English as a Foreign Language knows, in any sentence, nouns, adjectives, adverbs, demonstrative and interrogative pronouns, and verbs other than auxiliaries are regularly stressed. Other classes of words have no stress unless they are being emphasised or are strong forms. However, when two words are combined or placed side by side, one can yield to the other and be secondarily stressed. In the following examples, depending on the sense, the first part of speech yields to the second:

(i)   Adjective + Noun – a tàll bóy, leàther bóots
(ii)   Possessive (Noun) + Noun – a dày's wórk, my frìend's cár
(iii) Noun + of-Possessive – the wràth of Gód
(iv)   Noun + Adjective – all pèrsons présent
(v)   Verb + Adverb – mòve ón, sìt dówn
(vi)   Adverb + Adjective – vèry góod, fàst asléep
(vii) Present Participle + Noun – leàding árticle, weèping wíllow
       In the following examples, depending on the sense, the second part of speech yields to the first:
(i)   Noun + Noun – lóaf sùgar, féllow cìtizen
       Though here there is an important distinction between "used for" and "made of" e.g. bríck yàrd (yard used for bricks) and brìck yárd (yard made of bricks); gláss-càse (case used for glass) and glàss cáse (case made of glass).
(ii)   Adjective + Noun – bláckbird, bláckboard
       (Though blàck bírd, blàck bóard (any black-coloured bird or board, adj.)
(iii) Gerund + Noun – díning-ròom (a room for dining), físhing vìllage.

Thus when I write (in the first elegy) "green pond" or "nun's chapel", it is "pond" and "chapel" that strictly speaking carry the primary stress. "Green" and "nun's" both carry secondary stresses. It may be, however, that the sense demands an equal stress from "green" and "pond", or "nun's" and "chapel". In that case, instead of marking one as a primary and the other as a secondary stress, I have grouped them together as one primary stress unit, and this is denoted by the mark

⌐——⌐. The idea is that each should be given a quick equal stress, so that each forms half a stress.

There are three licences in Stress Metre. First, a group of words may form one primary stress unit on occasion if they belong together and are to be spoken at speed. Secondly, there may be a rest, as in music. This is a pause that is longer than the caesura, and it may take half a scanned foot, e.g. reduce a pentameter by half a foot. This will not, as a rule, affect the 4-stress unit line. Thirdly, there may be a number of slack (unstressed) syllables together. These can be scanned as paeons or tribrachs, etc.

Stress Metre may seem a new system of notation, but it is, in fact, a refinement of techniques developed from Old English verse by Coleridge and Hopkins. The Old English line has 4 feet, each of which is made up of an accented part and a varying number of unaccented syllables. In his Preface to *Christabel* Coleridge wrote of "counting in each line the accents, not the syllables. Though the latter may vary from seven to twelve, yet in each line the accents will be found to be four. Nevertheless, this occasional variation in number of syllables is not introduced wantonly, or for the mere ends of convenience, but in correspondence with some transition in the nature of the imagery or passion." That was around 1800. For accent read stress. Then Hopkins used the mark ⌐——⌐. For instance:

And the séa flint-flake, black-backed in the régular blów.

Here "flint-flake" counts as one primary stress, the two words are treated as one stress-unit. Or, to quote Hopkins' exact words from the note to "To What Serves Mortal Beauty?": "The mark ⌐——⌐ over two neighbouring syllables means that, though one has and the other has not metrical stress, in the recitation-stress they are to be about equal." Eliot, of course, followed a system of stress in *The Waste Land*, but he had 3 and 5 stresses to a line as well as 4.

The overall effect of Stress Metre is, while retaining syllable counting, to focus attention on sense-stress. Thus, though there may be 10 candidates for primary stress in a line, only 4 can carry the primary stress, and the others must perforce carry a secondary stress.

1st Elegy
IN MARVELL'S GARDEN, AT NUN APPLETON

This poem was reworked as *A Metaphysical in Marvell's Garden.*

35.   Harrington Hall, near Somersby, Lincolnshire, where my daughter was then living. The "other Hall" is Hunmanby Hall School, near Filey, Yorkshire.

3rd Elegy
AT STOKE D'ABERNON

Stoke D'Abernon is now a centre for teachers' courses and conferences.

12.   There is a headless caryatid at the bottom of the maze-like hedge-walk.

24.   In the Baptistry a 15th and 16th century Flemish window shows St. Anne teaching the Blessed Virgin to read.

32.   The six-foot-long brass of Sir John D'Abernon dates from 1277, and is the oldest brass now remaining in our Kingdom.

4th Elegy
TATTERSHALL CASTLE

7.   Tattershall Castle, Lincolnshire, was rebuilt in 1434-45 by Ralph, third Baron Cromwell, Treasurer of England under King Henry VI, 1433-43.

17.   By this Elegy my daughter had moved from the Hall "where Tennyson longed for Maud".

32.   The gromwell weed was of course introduced as a punning allusion to the owner's name. The flat I bought shortly after this contained two Adam fireplaces with a lamp and two love-knots carved on them.

33.   "Agger", Latin for "a rampart".

7th Elegy
DUNFORD HOUSE

10.   I have used poetic licence with the name Logan-Hall, who appears in *A Mystic Way* under his actual name of Logan-Reid.

18.   Richard Cobden, the Victorian statesman, was born at Dunford in 1804, and he built the present House in 1853 and lived there until his death in 1865. Cobden was a prophet of Free Trade, and he is especially remembered for the part he played in securing the repeal of the Corn Laws. Throughout his life he worked for co-operation between nations.

At the time of writing the Arabs had just put an end to the Western Age of Affluence by exorbitantly increasing the price of oil. I worked in Iraq and Libya.

8th Elegy
STANHOPE GARDENS
(To a Young Lady with Child)

31.   In Stanhope Gardens there is a fountain of a boy holding a cornucopia, the horn of plenty that traditionally overflowed with flowers, fruit and corn.

34.   In Burne-Jones's tapestry *The Heart of the Rose* which is alternatively titled *The Pilgrim in the Garden*, a young man is reaching out towards a rose in which there is a woman's head. Her eyes are closed, her skin is white, she is as dead as an unborn child.

9th Elegy
CENTURY HOUSE: ON A PATRIOT
(Or: On the Unfortunate Necessity of Governments)
For Kenneth L.

Kenneth Littlejohn spied on the IRA for the British Ministry of Defence. He was arrested after robbing a bank, disowned by the British, and committed to an Irish prison. After going on a hunger strike to insist on his "political status" he escaped and took refuge in Amsterdam.

Kenneth Lennon spied on the IRA in Luton. He was arrested by mistake, tried and acquitted. Two days after confessing his role to the National Council for Civil Liberties he was found shot dead in Chipstead, Surrey.

8.   OSA. Official Secrets Act.

63.   I was thinking of Kenneth Littlejohn.

10th Elegy
HIGH BEACH CHURCH

This poem was reworked as *A Crocus in the Churchyard*.

11, 15.   The tiles of the church floor are the same as the tiles on the scullery floor of Journey's End, the house where I was brought up.

11th Elegy
SOMPTING ABBOTTS

This poem was reworked as *A Stonemason's Flower-Bowl*. Sompting Abbotts is a mile or two outside Worthing in Sussex.

12th Elegy
CHESTER COURT, SUSSEX SQUARE

This poem was reworked as *An Aesthete's "Golden" Artefacts*.

14th Elegy
STRAWBERRY HILL

This poem was reworked as *Clouded-Ground Pond*. Strawberry Hill is in Epping Forest, Essex.

15th Elegy
PORTHLEVEN

This poem was reworked as *Sea-Fire*.
9.   The cross, lighthouse and boat are also lit up on the hill.
15.   The Triptania was wrecked during the Christmas of 1912.
30.   The vision referred to was seen by Margaret Riley. (See next Elegy.)

16th Elegy
BROMPTON ORATORY

This poem was reworked as *A Mystic Fire-Potter's Red Sun-Halo*. The snails (line 26) and the Pyramid (line 46) refer to pottery, and the seaside church (line 32) to a painting which Margaret Riley gave me.

17th Elegy
HILL PLACE

This poem was reworked as *An Obscure Symbolist's Rock-Tree*.
    Hill Place is an old farm just outside East Grinstead, Sussex. The Cornish artist referred to is Gwen Broad, who died in 1972. Her painting *Dusk near Land's End* was probably completed between 1959 and 1960. Daledene, the house of the Broadleys, stood on the Lewes Road, on the other side of East Grinstead.

18th Elegy
THE ROYAL OBSERVATORY, GREENWICH

29, 39.   The gold lines and the gold lettering can be found in the sundial marked "Horae Inaequales Seu Planetariae", Unequal or Planetary Hours. This was an ancient system of time-keeping, whereby daylight and darkness were divided into 12 parts. The clover-leaf can also be seen on the wall of the Royal Observatory.

19th Elegy
LOUGHTON METHODIST CHURCH

The original church has since been pulled down and replaced by a more modern, glassy building.

12.   Yorkshire was, of course, a Methodist stronghold following John Wesley's journey there in 1742, and his subsequent visits.

20th Elegy
CHIGWELL SCHOOL

Archbishop Samuel Harsnett was Bishop of Chichester and Bishop of Norwich before he became Archbishop of York. He founded Chigwell School in 1629 and died in 1631. Earlier he was vicar of Chigwell Church from 1597-1605. His book, *Declaration of Egregious Popish Impostures* (1603) was the source for the spirits in *King Lear*. The brass in Chigwell Church is the last really fine brass of an ecclesiastic in England. The detail is minute, to the point of showing a cast in one eye, and the Archbishop is shown wearing a rochet, an academic chimere, and a cope, along with his mitre, which is the present badge of the School.

4.   LAVDATE PVERI DOMINVM ("Praise the Lord, Boys").

5.   "Nothing too much" (Aristotle) and "thinking-shop".

21.   The motto, "Aut Viam Inveniam Aut Faciam" is originally supposed to have been spoken by Hannibal when about to cross the Alps. It was chosen as the motto of Chigwell School in 1868, and the school song that was based on it was composed later still.

31.   William Penn, the founder of Pennsylvania, attended the school during Cromwell's rule.

22nd Elegy
OUR LADY OF VICTORIES

Our Lady of Victories is Britannia (see last stanza).

THE NIGHT-SEA CROSSING, 1974

BLIND CHURCHILL TO THE NIGHT

Written in June 1974 in stress metre (4 stresses to a line). Conventionally regarded as the saviour of Britain from Nazi expansion, Churchill foresees in anguish that his course of action will destroy the British Empire and will then bring in a new age of European union. He is unable to express his vision and blindly attempts to make sense of history, not grasping the central idea of European civilisation (the Fire).

THE NIGHT-SEA CROSSING
A Symphonic Poem in Sonata Form

The Night-Sea Crossing originally expressed the sun's journey and death in the lower abyss of night and its resurrection the next morning. For Jung, the idea suggests the journey to Hell of Dante and Virgil, but also a journey to the Land of the Spirits. This poem is about dying (crossing over) and death, and is set on board ship.

   Sonata: "Composition for one instrument (e.g. piano) or two (e.g. piano and violin), normally with three or four movements (one or more being usually in sonata form) contrasted in rhythm and speed but related in key." Sonata form: "Type of composition in which two themes ('subjects') are successively set forth, developed, and restated." Symphony: "Sonata for full orchestra."

Oxford English Dictionary

The first movement has three sections. These correspond to the Exposition, Development and Recapitulation, which are to be found in the first movement of a symphony. The second, slow movement is in Aria form, or ABA. That is to say that after the first section there is a section that contrasts with it in mood and tone. Finally the first section is repeated. The third, bright movement is also in ABA form. It comprises a scherzo, then a trio, and finally a repetition of the scherzo. The fourth movement is in Rondo form: ABACABA. It is a commentary on the first movement, and has the quiet, contemplative ending to be found in a symphony whose fourth movement comments on the first.

419.   Amenophis is one of the two Memnon Colossi to be seen in a field of Thebes, Egypt (Amenophis or Amenhotep III).

504.   The "destructive" Colossus (see I(ii)) lives in the lower consciousness of the outer world and is a revolutionary. He is a follower of Satan. The "creative" Colossus lives in the higher consciousness of this inner world, and sides with Christ.

VISIONS NEAR THE GATES OF PARADISE, 1974 – 1975

After illumination, the soul has glimpses of intense joy.

In the first version of *The Blind*, lines 12-13 are "Glory! What the blind man sees/Anew is like a discovered", and lines 14-16 run: "I was hampered with eyes, and I have spied/The white sun of my soul for three years now./How terrible to be blinded...."

In *Paradise* "scribbles" seems to be a verb rather than a noun.

In *Poems like Vases* my Victorian vase (line 16) was formerly the possession of Percy Sharman, the composer.

In *The Keep* the Pharos, or Lighthouse (line 12), is reputedly the oldest standing building in England. It was built by the Romans and dates from c50AD.

The Call describes an experience that was later to become religious Universalism, an eventuality confirmed in the next poem, *The Way Really Opens*.

In the first version of *A Joyful Sob*, line 8 is "See God's plenty nod" and line 11 "Green lilac shoots crane – and birds".

In the first version of *A Vision near the Gates of Paradise*, lines 3-4 are "Paradise is within a Cathedral. Or an/Abbey? We"; lines 7-9 are "Planets surround Him, then saints. The wind that blows/The petals of that Kingdom of coloured light/Is a breath of holiness"; line 10 has "Paradise is fire in the eyes"; line 12 has "dancing and cavorting"; line 14 ends "souls, puffing on their wings the dust of the Spirit".

THE FOUR SEASONS, 1975

"From very ancient times spiritual truths were conveyed by illustrations drawn from everyday life....The earliest type of Mystery was probably an agricultural cult....All plants were sacred, they possessed immortality exhibited each Spring by the constant renewing of themselves. There was a realisation of the unity of life whether of man or plant, manifested in myriad forms in nature and the secret of these old religions was a recognition that this spirit of life was divine, and was the centre and source of all life. Thus man was taught to interpret nature, to feel at one with it, to subject his soul to be cultivated in a similar manner, by sharing figuratively in the various agricultural operations, thereby inducing spiritual growth."

A. Bothwell-Gosse, The Lily of Light

Quartet: "Musical composition for four voices or instruments, especially for four stringed instruments (piano quartet, 3 stringed instruments with piano)". (*Oxford English Dictionary*) "Sonatas for three instruments are called 'Trios'; those for four, five, or six, 'Quartets', 'Quintets', 'Sextets'." (Palmer, *Music*)

NOTE ON THE SECTIONS

Each of the four poems is a sonata for four voices. Each of the four voices explores one theme: a season; the spirit; memory; and the decline of Western civilisation. The whole work is imagistic and associative, and proceeds with a subrational arbitrariness as the gazing poetic subconscious responds to impressions in a disorganised, almost dream-like way: "My reason is in the grip of the irrational" (*Spring*, line 78). This is how our minds work at a subconscious level.

Each sonata, or quartet, therefore has four movements. The first is in Sonata Form and contains an Exposition, Development and Recapitulation. The second, slow movement is in Aria form, or ABA. The third, bright movement is also in ABA form. It comprises a scherzo, a trio, and then another scherzo. The fourth movement is in Rondo form: ABACABA. It comments on the first movement.

Because man is a part of Nature, and the spirit obeys the laws of the seasons, in contradistinction to the evidence of man's memories and of our declining Western civilisation, I think of these four poems as my "Seasons Quartets", the seasons featuring like a piano in four Piano Quartets. Because life is a unity, these four poems represent different views of the same idea, like a camera looking at a beautiful Adam dome from four different angles. Where you stand shows you the part of the whole you see and the figures in the circular frieze recur. There is an optimistic conclusion as the idea of Eternal Recurrence is seen in terms of the Whole and linked to the movements of Eternity: "The ever-now recurs, not in memory but in kind." (*Spring* line 323).

NOTE ON THE DATING

Though parts of these four poems were sketched as far back as 1965, they were not completed in their present form until 1975.

A NOTE ON DISSOCIATION

In Sonata Form there is a progression from the Home Key to the Sharp Key, and we then arrive back in the Home Key. The conversion of flat Keys into sharp Keys, and vice versa, is known as an Enharmonic Change, and the Enharmonic relation between the flat Keys and the sharp Keys is best seen in the following clock:

```
                F   C  G#
           B              D#
        E                     A

        A                     E
           D              B
             G   C   F
```

On this, F Major is the Enharmonic of E sharp Major; B flat Major of A sharp Major; E flat Major of D sharp Major; A flat Major of G sharp Major; D flat Major of C sharp Major; G flat

Major of F sharp Major; C flat Major of B Major; and F flat of E Major.

Beethoven, in his Late Quartets, sometimes disconcertingly arrives back in a Key that is quite different from the Home Key, so that, for example, he is a tone lower than the Home Key. This cuts the ground from under the Home Key's feet. In Opus 130, instead of returning to B flat he lands in G flat. This device is called "Dissociation", and the extent of the dissociation can be measured on the Enharmonic clock of tonality.

Certain Keys are brighter than others, and the choice of a Key is therefore to some extent conditioned by the sentiment of the music. Major keys are often chosen for expressing happiness and merriment, and Minor keys for sadness and longing. Every Major Scale has a Relative Minor. So, G Major has E Minor; D Major has B Minor; A Major has F sharp Minor; E Major has C sharp Minor; B Major has G sharp Minor; F sharp Major has D sharp Minor; C Sharp Major has A Sharp Minor; F Major has D Minor; B flat Major has G Minor; E flat Major has C Minor; A flat Major has F Minor; D flat Major has B flat Minor; G flat Major has E flat Minor; and C flat Major has A flat Minor.

It is difficult to classify Major and Minor Keys according to their different sentiments, but as a rough guide the following (taken from Palmer, *Teach Yourself to Compose Music*) will do:

Major Keys	
C	Bold, vigorous
D flat	Sonorous, elegant
D	Majestic, grand
E flat	Dignified, soft
E	Bright, powerful
Major Keys	
F	Peaceful, contemplative
F sharp	Brilliant, incisive
G	Pastoral
A flat	Dreamy, gentle
A	Confident, sunny
B flat	Bright, graceful
B	Energetic, bold
Minor Keys	
C	Gloomy, sad
C sharp	Tragic
D	Solemn, subdued
E flat	Very sombre
E	Restless
F	Gloomy, passionate
F sharp	Mysterious, spectral
G	Melancholy
G sharp	Sorrowful, anxious
A	Tender, noble
B flat	Funereal
B	Savage, ominous

In poetry, then, the equivalent of Keys is feeling and tone, which influence subject and style so greatly and which allow different faces or characters, or the same face or character, to wear different expressions.

If the frieze round the inside of a dome is regarded as the "tonal clock", and if the figures on the frieze are regarded as containing the feelings and tones of the Keys, then a dissociation is possible in poetry similar to that which I have identified in music. There can, on occasion, be a jump from one figure on the frieze, or tone, to another one some way away on the "clock" and not in direct Enharmonic Relation to it. As a result there will be an abrupt change of tone and possibly of character. I have used this idea sparingly in these Quartets, but examples can be found.

AUTUMN

90.   One of the 53 stages of the Tokaido, near Fujisawa.

LIGHTHOUSE, 1975
THE DARK NIGHT EASTER TEMPTATION OF A SOMEWHAT SAINTLY MAN
(A Contemplation Inspired by the Fugal Form)

"Everyone who lives in this deplorable exile of ours knows that he cannot be filled with a love of eternity....unless he be truly converted to God. Before he can experience even a little of God's love he must really be turned to Him, and, in mind at least, be wholly turned from every earthly thing...To turn away from those 'good things' of the world, which pervert rather than protect those who love them, involves the withering of physical lust...Those who persistently practise uncleanness cannot know any love for Christ, for what fires them is carnal lust. They cannot display the devotion which is God's due: they are firmly earthbound by the very weight of their desires. Consequently they are not destined to enjoy the delights of Paradise, for they persist in their perverse ways till they die....No young man who is surrounded by feminine beauty and flattery and sweet nothings and enervating luxury can possibly be holy, unless it is through grace, great and exceptional...I reckon it a major miracle when a man through God's grace and a love of Christ spurns these allurements completely, and out of the midst of them all (which war against his soul, however pleasant they be to his flesh), rises like a man to the utmost heights of heavenly contemplation. There is no doubt that he is more holy as a result of all this, and inwardly much richer through the comfort brought him by his love of God. If he was thrown into the fire of hell he would not burn! For he has completely extinguished the seductions and delights of life which come to him from outside. It is not surprising, even if it is unusual, that Christ works thus in some of his beloved. It is said of such *He has spread a cloud* (obviously a cloud of divine grace) *for a covering* (from carnal lust, by the fire of everlasting love) *and fire to give light* (within their mind) *in the night* (of this life); and all this lest they should be taken captive by the attraction of empty beauty. But Christ's love burns in them with such sweetness that they deem every carnal, illicit pleasure the most appalling filth, and trample it down."

Richard Rolle, *The Fire of Love* (from chapters 1, 4, 8; 1343AD)

"This darkness and this cloud is, howsoever thou dost, betwixt thee and thy God, and letteth thee that thou mayest neither see Him clearly by light of understanding in thy reason, nor feel Him in sweetness of love in thine affection. And therefore shape thee to bide in this darkness as long as thou mayest....For when I say darkness, I mean a lacking of knowing: as all that thing that thou knowest not, or else that thou hast forgotten, it is dark to thee; for thou seest it not with they ghostly eye. And for this reason it is not called a cloud of the air, but a cloud of unknowing, that is betwixt thee and they God....(It is) a dark mist which seemeth to be between thee and the light thou aspirest to."

The Cloud of Unknowing (from chapters 3, 4; second half of 14th century)

NOTE ON THE FUGAL FORM

Fugue. "Polyphonic composition in which a short melodic theme ('subject') is introduced by one of the parts and successively taken up by others, thereafter forming the main material of the texture."

Oxford English Dictionary

Fugue. "An instrumental or vocal composition – contrapuntal in character – developed from one short, pithy theme, called the subject, which is announced by a single voice and immediately replied to at a different pitch by another voice, the first voice continuing the counterpoint."

Macpherson, *Form in Music*, Joseph Williams

"If Yeats knew a fugue from a frog he might have transmitted what I told him in some way that would have helped rather than obfuscated his readers."

Ezra Pound, letter of April 1937

This poem is a fugue for two voices. The three sections follow the three parts of a fugue. The first section is the Enunciation, or Exposition, which introduces both voices once. It states the Subject, which in a fugue is announced by the first voice in the key of the Tonic, and the Answer, which is announced by the second voice in the key of the Dominant. There is a Codetta, which links the end of the Answer to the beginning of the second appearance of the Subject. The second section is the Middle (or Modulatory) section. In a fugue, this introduces the Subject and Answer in keys other than that of the Tonic. There is an Episode after the Answer. In a fugue, this provides relief from the incessant use of Subject and Answer. The Final section returns to the original key. In this, Subject and Answer draw together in a Stretto ("drawing-together") and reach a climax. There follows a Coda, which begins after the last entry of Subject or Answer in the Tonic key.

The fugal form is an ideal one for catching the self-divided mind. The mind in question belongs to a retired diplomat, who is spending an Easter night in a hotel by the sea and near a lighthouse before a wedding the next day and whose interior (dramatic) monologue reacts to the temptation to visit one of the wedding guests late at night, a married lady with whom he may have a future.

71.   See St. John of the Cross, with whose *Dark Night of the Soul* (c 1583) our "somewhat saintly man" is obviously acquainted.

THE WEED-GARDEN, 1975
(A HEROIC SYMPHONY)

"Mary, Mary, quite contrary,
How does your garden grow?
With silver bells and cockle-shells,
And pretty maids all in a row."

"It is possible...that this rhyme has a religious background; that it is a 'word-picture of Our Lady's convent' has been suggested, the bells being the sanctus bells, the cockleshells the badges of the pilgrims, the pretty maids the nuns 'rank behind rank at office'."

Iona and Peter Opie, *The Oxford Dictionary of Nursery Rhymes*

"Cockle-shell – Wearers of the cockle, the emblems of a pilgrimage to Compostella, Blades." "Cockles of the heart, one's feelings...explained by (1) the likeness of a heart to a cockleshell (2) by the zoological name for the cockle, Cardium." "Cockle, plant which grows in cornfields."

Oxford English Dictionary

"One of the cancers (δαπανῶν) of the spiritual life in souls born into the present generation is the low spiritual tension (ῥαθυμίαν) in which all but a few chosen spirits among us pass their days. In our work and in our recreation alike our only objective is popularity and enjoyment. We feel no concern to win the true spiritual treasure."

> Longinus, *Sublimity in Style* (last chapter, on how spiritual decadence is reflected in literary decadence; quoted in Arnold Toynbee's *Study of History*, vol. 9, p.608)

NOTE ON THE FORM

This is a symphony and is therefore in four movements. The first movement contains an exposition, a development and a recapitulation. The second movement is in Aria form, ABA, and the third movement contains a minuet, a second minuet, and then the first minuet repeated (also ABA). The fourth movement is in Rondo form, ABACABA, and is a commentary on the first movement, providing an answer to some of the questions raised by the irony of the first movement.

In the first and fourth movements, the rhyme scheme is *abba*, *a* being a true rhyme, and *b* being consonant rhyme or assonance. In the first quatrain, *b* is a consonant rhyme; in the second and third quatrains b is assonance. The fourth quatrain is like the first, the fifth and sixth like the second and third, and so on throughout the first and fourth movements.

NOTE ON THE INTERPRETATION OF THE POEM

The use of irony in the first movement should not obscure the main reason why the garden is full of weeds instead of flowers.

Quite simply, it is autumn. What was possible for flowers in the spring is not possible now. There are contributing factors, e.g. the gardeners are no longer observing the right growth processes, do not water the plants or believe in their life-cycle, have an egalitarian attitude towards seeds, as a result of which the land is thought to be infertile; and the flowers have had their heads snipped off (see the second movement). Nevertheless, the fact that it is autumn is the main point, and some people (ridiculed through irony, i.e. the simulated adoption of their point of view) seem unaware of this. Alternatively, some who regard our autumn as a Golden Age believe it will last for ever, and these are ridiculed at the end of the fourth movement.

This poem is, then, an indictment of Western blindness and Western pride. Although it is autumn, *some* flowers can grow, e.g. the Lily-of-the-Field, *provided the correct growth-processes are observed*. These are to be found in the first movement, e.g. the section on the monastic past of Western civilisation.

Thus the poem is both pessimistic and optimistic. Pessimistic about the immediate future, for winter is ahead for Western civilisation, but optimistic because of the prospect of a future spring. It is this optimistic thread which allows me to subtitle the work *A Heroic Symphony*.

31.   This refers to the Philosophoumena, which formed the climax of the Eleusinian Mysteries.

333-4. From *Ancrene Wisse* on the 7 Deadly Sins.

335-338. From Wulfstan's *Address to the English* (*Sermo Lupi*, 1014), the text being: "Leofan men, gecnawath thaet soth is: theos woruld is on ofste, and hit nealaecth tham ende; and thy hit sceal nyde for folces synnan fram daege to daege aer Antecristes tocyme yfelian swythe."

339.   From *Isaiah*.

362.   Moore, Bacon, Stockhausen, Pinter, Amis and Larkin are some who are taken to task in lines 350-7, and John Lennon's "Participation" Art Exhibition, Bridget Riley, Ron Grainer, Tynan, B. S. Johnson and Horovitz in lines 358-361.

507.	The shrine was removed in the reign of Henry VIII, but the polished floor is still there.
644.	The word "mystic" can be derived from muein, meaning "to see".
750-1,785.	These lines, written in 1975, were prophetic in anticipating the collapse of the USSR and of the Soviet empire in Eastern Europe, and the advent of the European Union which now has legal priority over nation states.
829, 849, 859.	St. Michael's Mount is dedicated to the Archangel St. Michael, who, according to an old Cornish legend, appeared to some fishermen in 495 AD. Hence Milton's "The great Vision of the guarded Mount" in *Lycidas*. Christina of Glastonbury was healed on 14th May 1262. There are old maps which show the Mount as an ascent to Paradise, like a famous engraving from Il Monte Sancto di Dio, 1477. According to Cornish legend the land of Lyonesse, between Cornwall and the Scilly Isles, was submerged suddenly one winter's night on 11th November 1099 (according to *The Saxon Chronicle*), and 140 churches were drowned. The bells can be heard beneath the sea, gently tolling with the rocking waves.
875.	The autumn lily or Lily-of-the-Field is otherwise known as the Winter Daffodil. It resembles a spring crocus. The curtains then in my study, a gift from the nurse Margaret Barron who used them when she lived in Buckingham Palace while looking after Queen Mary, were pink with a pattern of lilies.

THE LABYRINTH, 1976

"The palace at Cnossus – the house of the *labrys*, or double-axe – was a complex of rooms and corridors....The Athenian raiders had difficulty in finding and killing the king when they captured it....An open space in front of the palace was occupied by a dance floor with a maze pattern used to guide performers of an erotic spring dance. The origin of this pattern, now also called a labyrinth, seems to have been the traditional brushwood maze used to decoy partridges towards one of their own cocks, caged in a central enclosure, which uttered food-calls, love-calls and challenges; and the spring-dancers will have imitated the ecstatic hobbling love-dance of the cock partridges, whose fate was to be knocked on the head by the hunter....Only the exceptional hero – a Daedalus or a Theseus – returned alive....A maze dance seems to have been brought to Britain from the Eastern Mediterranean by neolithic agriculturalists of the third millennium BC....At Cnossus the sky-bull cult succeeded the partridge cult."

Robert Graves, *Greek Myths* (vol.1, 98 2–4)

"Labyrinth. An architectonic structure, apparently aimless, and of a pattern so complex that, once inside, it is impossible or very difficult to escape. Or it may take the form of a garden similarly patterned. Ancient writings mention five great mazes: that of Egypt, which Pliny located in lake Moeris; the two Cretan labyrinths of Cnossus (or Gnossus) and Gortyna; the Greek maze on the island of Lemnos; and the Etruscan at Clusium. It is likely that certain initiatory temples were labyrinthine in construction for doctrinal reasons....To trace through the labyrinthic path of a mosaic patterned on the ground was once considered a symbolic substitute for a pilgrimage to the Holy Land....Eliade notes that the essential mission of the maze was to defend the 'Centre' – that it was, in fact, an initiation into sanctity, immortality and absolute reality and, as such, equivalent to other 'trials' such as the fight with the dragon. At the same time, the labyrinth may be interpreted as an apprenticeship for the neophyte who would learn to distinguish the proper path leading to the Land of the Dead."

J. E. Cirlot, *A Dictionary of Symbols* (pp165-67)

The poem is about the dying of a statesman who was murdered for his role in the Cold War. He has returned to a great house on the edge of Epping Forest to die. He compares the bullets that cut him down to the Cretan Axe of Cnossus or Knossos, and the ritual killing of the King by his successor in Frazer's *Golden Bough*. The suggestion is that the succession has not passed cleanly from Christendom to Communism, and that the ideal of mysticism will triumph.

WHISPERS FROM THE WEST, 1976

In this volume the contemplative soul regards Western affluence and living conditions with some disquiet. The active soul rejects the comfortable conditions of the body. At the same time there is a concern that wrong attitudes may bring about a collapse of the West.

In *Lightning Over Polruan*, Q (line 1) is Sir Arthur Quiller-Couch, the Shakespearian scholar who lived in Fowey.

In *Love like a Length of Cloth* the poet's love is boundless and eternal, and over many lives it has been bestowed on many brides and wives.

In *Lament of the Cast-Off Shirt* the soul laments the false values of the body and Time, entering into the being of and speaking through a discarded shirt ("the body's vest") which is like a discarded spirit.

In *A Boo-oom and an Undeaf Ear* the victim of the IRA explosion in Stanhope Gardens was in fact a Southern Irish butcher who worked in Balham.

In *A Ruined Tower and Grubby Souls* the laundry is The Bendon Valley laundry.

Dancing Wraiths. "Dance of Death, also called Danse Macabre, a medieval allegorical concept of the all-conquering and equalizing power of death, expressed in the drama, poetry, music and visual arts of western Europe mainly in the late Middle Ages. Strictly speaking, it is a literary or pictorial representation of a procession or dance of both living and dead figures, the living arranged in order of their rank, from pope and emperor to child, clerk, and hermit, and the dead leading them to the grave. The dance of death had its origins in late-13th- or early-14th-century poems that combined the essential ideas of the inevitability and the impartiality of death....The earliest known example of the fully developed dance of death concept is a series of paintings (1424-25) formerly in the Cimetière des Innocents in Paris. In this series the whole hierarchy of church and state formed a stately dance, the living alternating with skeletons or corpses escorting them to their destination. The work was a stern reminder of the imminence of death and a summons to repentance" (*Encyclopaedia Britannica*).

In *Providence* of the three Fates of Greek mythology (line 14), Clotho spun the thread, Lachesis measured it, and Atropos cut it with her shears.

In *Spectre of a Cloud* the flat was at 10 Brechin Place, London.

The first version of *Telephones* has line 10 ending "solitary rod" and line 12 "the presence of my God".

In *The Entryphone* it is a fact that some entryphone systems can be made to work if the carbon crystals (line 8) near the bells are tapped.

A Coat of Arms. Written soon after 5th March 1976 and subsequently revised in July 1985. A poem in imperfect rhyme. Imperfect rhyme is the chiming of accented and unaccented syllables which would be perfect rhymes if both were accented, i.e. accented-unaccented coupling.

14.	"Viam Inveniam". From the motto of Chigwell School, Essex, "aut viam inveniam aut faciam", "find a way or make a way". The motto is reputed to have come from Archbishop Harsnett, who founded the school in 1629. Harsnett in turn took it from Hannibal, who made the remark while crossing the Alps.
24.	A Hagger was Lord of the Manor in the 16th century, and there is apparently a graveyard with many Haggers' names on tombstones from around that time near Royston.

33-6.   The coat of arms foresees and anticipates the confrontation between Christendom and part of Islam during the Gulf War of 1991, and suggests partisan patriotism and conflict at the level of the social ego. The coat of arms also reconciles the two opposing forces into a symbol of Universalist unity at a deeper level. (Both Christendom and Islam are founded on the vision of the Fire or Light, which unites them.)

Moon is a reworking of an earlier poem, *My Moon*. There are several changes.

In *Bringing Evil Down* the "red light beetle" (lines 10-11) suggests my natural inclination to avoid speaking bluntly in the interests of diplomacy, and seeing danger signs in situations and therefore not speaking plainly.

In *Wind in a War Cemetery* Pegasus Bridge (line 15) was the first part of Normandy to fall on D-Day.

In *Heaven: Glass like the Windows of a Soul*, the first version ends "Whose windows let in Light with the passing shafts of the sun?"

The nine week period referred to in *Gold* was from 22nd February to just after 26th April 1976. I deliberately put an end to it in June 1976 to do preliminary research for *The Fire and the Stones* and to undergo further development towards a metaphysical outlook.

In *Souls like Pigeons*, on 18th June 1944 a flying bomb wrecked the Guard's Chapel during morning service (line 3), with the loss of 121 lives. Plaques commencing with the words "Ici tomba" (line 15) – "Here fell" – commemorate places where members of the Resistance fell in Paris.

In *Energy Techniques* "slicked" (line 4) is meant to suggest an oil slick on a polluted beach, in which a moth is trapped.

Wistful Time-Travellers (about Westernersc who are "in flight from the present") ponders the post-war decline in influence of European civilisation when its "offshoot", the U.S.A., reached the moon (in 1969). The second version is on p463.

Leaves that Feed. In Peking (line 8) or Beijing, the Museum of the Revolution, which covers the last 50 years, has the same space as the museum which covers from Peking Man to 1926, indicating the emphasis placed upon the present in China, as opposed to the past. The match-king (line 10) is the former tycoon, Mr. Li, who, in 1966, was still paid interest on his millions by the anti-capitalist Maoist regime, but who was nevertheless confined under permanent house-arrest.

Westerners and Desire: A Dialogue between Body and Soul (Or the Maenads and Orpheus). Orpheus was eventually torn to pieces by the Maenads, but his head carried on singing. The soul of the artist lives in a constant state of tension with the blandishments of the body, and endeavours not to be destroyed by its coaxings. (The Maenads were followers of Dionysus or Bacchus and used drunken orgies to achieve spiritual intoxication; they therefore symbolise development of the soul through bodily gratification.)

The Price of a House. The house was my solicitor brother's at Bidborough, near Tunbridge Wells.

The Fall of the West. The poem confronts international terrorism which attempted to secure the Fall of the West in the 1970s (and early 1980s). At the time it seemed that international terrorism was organised by Communists; it is only recently that it can be seen that it was ultimately controlled by a pro-world government behind-the-scenes organisation. The poem urges resistance to terrorism; the fall of the West can be averted by the right "mental attitude".

17.   Daniel Cohn-Bendit was one of the leaders of the student uprising that took place in Paris in spring 1968.

19.   Tariq Ali led large demonstrations in London against American involvement in Vietnam, the first of which (in March 1968) saw attacks on police horses.

21.   The Angry Brigade carried out 25 bombings in Britain between January 1968 and

August 1971, including attacks on the house of Mr. Robert Carr, the Conservative politician. The two Cambridge boys were Jim Greenfield and John Barker; the two Essex girls were Anna Mendelson and Hilary Creek.

25.   The Baader-Meinhof gang carried out a number of bombings in Germany, including explosions in US Army HQ in Frankfurt and Heidelburg in May 1972. The gang is credited with 5 murders and 54 attempted murders. Ulrike Meinhof hanged herself in prison in May 1976.

29.   The Japanese Red Army sent three men to take part in the massacre at Lod airport.

31.   The Italian publisher in question helped to pave the way for Italy to go Communist.

37.   The Libyan Lieutenant was Gaddafi, who usurped the throne and, without any basis of legality save force, was declared a Colonel.

38.   Gaddafi is thought to have organized the murder of the athletes at the Munich Olympic Games in 1972.

39.   The Venezuelan is "Carlos" Sanchez, "the Jackal", who is reputed to have been one of Saddam Hussein's hired killers.

40.   The capture of the OPEC Ministers took place in 1976, and nearly resulted in the death of the Saudi-Arabian Oil Minister, Sheikh Yamani.

41.   The Portuguese doctor, Dr Alberto Noronha-Rodrigues, secretary of the Portuguese and Colonial Liberation Front, and a Portuguese exile, was then helping ARA (Armed Revolutionary Action) carry out explosions against NATO targets in Portugal. He flew into Lisbon, disguised in a false beard, before the first ARA explosion at the Telecommunications Centre, Lisbon, in September 1970.

46.   The Colonel who negotiated the supply of Libyan arms is not Gaddafi, and must remain anonymous. He stayed in Room 261 at the Churchill Hotel. Shortly afterwards a boat carrying Libyan arms for the IRA was intercepted, and the cargo dumped overboard.

49.   The conference was organized by the World Council of Churches in Frankfurt in March 1972. I covered it for *The Times*. The Christian host was the General Secretary of the World Council of Churches, E. C. Blake, and the participants, whose fares were paid by the WCC, were mostly atheistic guerillas and ultra-leftists.

53.   The Communist worked for the Programme to Combat Racism within the World Council of Churches. In 1970 and 1971 the WCC paid out a total of $45,000 to the MPLA, which later won the Angolan Civil War with Cuban and Soviet help, and a total of $17,500 to UNITA, their opponents in that war, who at one time had links with China.

57.   The Belgian conference for SWAPO was mounted in May 1972. The Bishop and the Lord must remain anonymous.

64.   "L'Oeuvre Francais" was the slogan daubed on Paris walls before the violent student demonstration of April 1976, which demanded the right to work, and by implication a new society in which all students obtained jobs of the kind they wanted. I saw the slogans as I was in Paris at the time.

65.   The Weathermen were an early American group. The revolutionary SLA (Symbionese Liberation Army) kidnapped Patty Hearst in February 1974, mounted the People in Need of Food Programme on her father's money and made her take part in a bank robbery and a shooting near a shop. Six members of the SLA, including "Field-Marshal" Cinque, the leader, were killed after a shoot-out with police in Los Angeles.

69.   Philip Agee exposed the names of many CIA agents, and after several pro-Soviet newspapers had followed suit, Richard Welch was assassinated in Greece in 1976.

72.   The lawyer's daughter is Polly Gaster, the Secretary of the Committee for Freedom

in Mozambique, Angola and Guiné.

82.   I saw the Chinese board at Peking University in March 1966. I was told by my Chinese "guide" that the Chinese had the vote because they could vote for different names.

85.   Alexander II reigned from 1855 to his assassination in 1881, for which five Nihilists were publicly hanged.

86.   The Nihilists emerged in the 1860s, following the Emancipation of the Serfs in 1861. The first attempted shooting of the Tsar by a Nihilist was in 1866, and there were political assassinations from 1878-81. The great scourge of the Nihilists was Dostoevsky, in *The Devils*.

There were several acts of French anarchism between 1886 and 1894, involving Gallo, Duval, Ravachol, Vaillant and Emile Henry.

89.   See 39 above.

90.   The new imperialism is Soviet imperialism, which has gobbled up many former European colonies and peoples, ruling them through puppets and the fiction of "popular democracies".

97.   AHF: anti-haemophiliac factor.

120.   The Balcombe Street siege of December 1975 resulted in the capture of four IRA bombers, including Harry Duggan, alias Michael Wilson who had terrorised London for two years.

127.   After D-Day the British wanted to drive straight for Berlin, but the Americans had other ideas, and Roosevelt in particular failed to see its importance. Yalta and the subsequent Cold War have revealed the American strategy to be the catastrophic blunder it was.

APPENDIX: POEMS 1977

Garden (On the Third Anniversary). In Japan, a small temple bell (line 5) is hung on a tree to celebrate a birth. A thin strip of paper is tied to the tongue. This is a wish. The paintings were by Guy Worsdell in Margaret Riley's gallery (lines 9-10). The Grail has been regarded as a glass bowl (line 11) filled with water, which lit the fire of a shrine from the sun's light. (See Flavia Anderson's *The Ancient Secret*.)

LADY OF THE LAMP, 1979

The contemplative spirit now approaches a new Dark Night, which St. John of the Cross called the Dark Night of the Spirit, in which the spirit is further refined and the sensual is further purged. The contemplative spirit is sure that Eternity is involved in matters of Time, and, drawing away from the worldy-sensual, it sees the Light of Eternity in sensual imagery. The Lady of the Lamp is therefore the Lady Eternity, a Universalist amalgam of such mediators between man/Time and the Light as the Mesopotamian-Egyptian "Shining Ones", the Earth-goddess or Magna Mater, the Gnostic Sophia-Prunikos, the Virgin Mary (Queen of Heaven), Dante's Beatrice, and the lady of Sufi mysticism, all of whom escorted the soul into the presence of God as Fire or Light. Eternity changes her guise and appears as now one, now another of these embodiments of the supreme feminine principle. These Baroque poems have a Sufi mixture of erotic and metaphysical imagery. These poems were mostly written in 1979.

In *Rapt in a Hotel Room* the Lady Eternity initially seeks the spirit out, and more than goes half way to embrace it in a brief encounter.

In *Light from a Warm House* Eternity is seen as the Gnostic Sophia Prunikos (the "whore" of line 7). The poet knows the stillness of Eternity at a particular moment of time.

Like an Earth-Mother. Neolithic Europe worshipped the sun in an earth-orientated fertility cult: the matriarchal Mother Earth was creative in her own right, and it was not until the Indo-Europeans that the patriarchal sky-father fertilised the Earth-Mother and fecundated the soil.

My Soul is one of the most metaphysical of my poems. "Succuba", "Female demon supposed to have sexual intercourse with sleeping men".

A Bee-Like Soul. The point is, lines 6-8 contradict lines 1-5. Each lifetime is not independent of its previous one, a self-contained growth from a seed to a flower; but it carries forward the growth of the previous one, adding a stage to the growth from an acorn-like form to a form like an oak.

In *The Burden* Cnut (line 2) is Canute; also nut in the sense of "nutcase". The "C" is silent. The burden is to "turn a tide", to bring a knowledge of Eternity to the Age.

In *The Shell* Eternity absents herself from the poet who cannot forget the joys he has known with her. The contemplative soul is now in darkness.

In *Lord with a Sword* the lord (line 2) is the priapic Siva or Shiva, the Hindu god of Light. The slide is in fact a Cambodian brooch I have seen.

Eurydice. Like Eurydice, the Lady of the Lamp now dwells in darkness (line 6), though she has shown herself in the sunlight. She is the Orphic Muse, and became the Philosophoumena of the Eleusinian grain rites to Demeter or Persephone (line 14). Orpheus's head was later cut off by the Dionysian Maenads and thrown into a river. Later still it had oracular power.

Blindfolds: Lady of the Lamp, i.e. Lady of the Light. The Light, like a roadworks lantern, leads the poet into the basement of himself where its veils are removed. "Unveils" (line 12) means "removes the veils of" rather than "reveals".

In *Ten Wives* Eternity is Sophia Prunikos again.

In *Breaststroke, Drowning* the mystical experience of Eternity leaves the poet feeling drowned.

In *Dream Cottage* the poet imagines a life close to Eternity. For the holly bush (line 1), see Hardy's *Far From the Madding Crowd*; for the deadly nightshade (line 2), see L. P. Hartley's *The Go-Between*. "We" (line 5), i.e. the poet and the Lady of the Lamp. Bittersweet (line 13) is the purple and yellow bittersweet plant.

In *Secret Place* the poet meets Eternity at the spot where he will be buried. The "Secret Place" is the Church of the Holy Innocents at High Beach. "Soughing" (line 14) is pronounced "suffing".

In *Enemy* the poet again meets Eternity by his future grave. Death "the Enemy" appears at the Church of the Holy Innocents, High Beach.

Horseshoe, "the eye in the eyebrow" (line 8). Eastern religions recognise the seat of the third eye as being the eyebrow chakra.

In *Sea of Light*, the serpent (line 6) refers to Kundalini.

Swan-Upping. The title refers to the arrival, taking and marking of Thames swans.

In *Warm Fire* "loiving" (line 10) is a combination of "living" and "loving".

The Challenge. There are at least ten sefirot or sephiroth (line 8) in the Kabbalah. These can be symbolised by chairs. The psychological, spiritual and divine worlds all converge on the fifth sefira, Beauty (line 10).

Encampment. See *The Encampment, St. James's Park* by the 18th century painter Paul Sandby. I have used contact lenses as a magnifying glass that can burn paper in the sun.

In *Ivy and Oak*, the serpent (line 6) refers to Kundalini.

In *Taoist Lady* the Neo-Taoist sexual imagery (lines 12-13) parallels the Tantric Hindu "ojas".

In *Immobility* Baudelaire (line 9) immortalised the mulatto Jeanne Duval.

In *Snowman* the Tutankhamun figurine (line 8) is a wooden shawabti.

THE FIRE-FLOWER, 1980

The 16 poems are to be read in sequence. They show a growing metaphysical vision and are increasingly preoccupied with eternity. Some of these poems are reworkings from *The Pilgrim in the Garden*. There is sometimes an intermediary version which it is not possible to show.

A METAPHYSICAL IN MARVELL'S GARDEN

First drafted on 24th and 28th-29th October 1973, and subsequently revised e.g. on 4th and 16th-17th February 1980. The poem is about how the contemplative vision approaches the Reality of the universe, which is both the sea of energy of subatomic physics and the manifestation of a metaphysical "Rose-tree" which forms souls. Novices perceive the complexity of this Rose-tree as a simple lily.

Marvell's Garden is at Nun Appleton in Yorkshire. There Marvell was tutor to the daughter of Cromwell's General Fairfax from 1651AD and wrote *The Garden*, the crowning glory of our contemplative poetry.

10.	"Discard all thought as in a mystery school". The function of a mystery school (cf *Cambridge Ode: Against Materialism* line 161) is to bring to birth the spiritual "I" which is behind the social ego and its reason. As at a Zen temple, a mystery school therefore encourages silence, in which the reason withers and the soul comes into its own.
18.	The Latin inscription on the South Front sundial, literally "Who is not today", means "No one is the present moment".
28.	"Spirit", here a centre of the soul/a bloom on the climbing rose rather than the wind-like power which flows in.
31.	The firethorn, or pyracantha, has red berry-like fruits which give it its name, and white flowers.
33-48.	See *Preface on the Metaphysical Revolution*, paragraph 6 (p582) for the background in physics for this post-Einsteinian vision of the universe, and for the superluminal information transfer theory (line 43); and paragraph 8 (p583) for the Alchemistic "unus mundus" which is seen as an extra-cosmic rose-tree of light in line 47.
36.	"Swelled form". "Forms that are subject to a sea-swell, i.e. the heaving of sea with waves that do not break after a storm."
42.	"Curved". Our universe is curved because space is curved.
43.	"Holes", black and white holes.
44.	"Wisdom" is also the ninth sephira in the Kabbalah, the one nearest to the divine Crown.
49.	The vision of metaphysical Reality passes and social reality returns.
51-2.	"Peep...walls", i.e. lords who never peep in waters for lilies which hint the Light, or have to make their souls climb to freedom up town walls like climbing roses, as town-dwellers do, for they (the lords) do not live in such squalid surroundings.

These lines hint at a paradox which is echoed elsewhere in the poem: town men who live in a squalor of walls sometimes close their physical eyes and shut out their surrounding ugliness, open their inner eye to the Light and release and grow their soul and imagination; whereas country lords, surrounded by the beauty of the seasons, tend to see with their physical eyes and lack the walled squalor which liberates the inner eye. The town contemplative, then, *needs* imprisoning walls so that his soul can recoil and withdraw into inner vision, and when it climbs to freedom like a climbing rose that rises above all walls, its many heads suggesting the town soul's complexity, sophistication and learning, its social reality has pushed it towards the metaphysical Reality. The country soul inclines towards simplicity and unity, and when it glimpses the Light it is like a single water-lily rather than a manifold, many-bloomed climbing rose. Wordsworth hints at this paradox when he contemplates Tintern Abbey in his imagination "in lonely rooms, and 'mid the din/Of towns and cities", and it is because the town-dwelling Metaphysical has already developed his inner eye in towns that he is able to abstract himself from the beauty of Marvell's Garden and achieve the visions of 25-48.

52.   "And to their daughters", i.e. leave halls to lords or to *their own* (i.e. town seers') daughters, by making financial sacrifices to enable them to live or board in the peace of country halls, which they can then enjoy vicariously.

54.   T. C., Theophila Cornewall (born 1644) of Marvell's *The Picture of little T.C. in a Prospect of Flowers*.

57-64.   "Wall-high climbers", i.e. "advanced souls who climb town walls like a climbing rose", e.g. the Metaphysical of this poem. "Novices", e.g. the "nymph". The social layer shows one rose reflected in water, which merges with the reflection of one water-lily. The metaphysical layer suggests that an advanced town soul who sees the metaphysical Light as the essential rose, interprets it in a sophisticated way in terms of an emanation or manifestation (a rose-tree), and knows his soul as a climbing rose, has no advantage *in the present moment* over the simplest country soul who sees the Light as, and is, a water-lily. In the present moment any soul can see the one Light or Sun in its *essential* aspect through direct vision that by-passes space-time ("the rose" of 58 and 61 or "a watery/Dark's shimmer"), but only a lifetime's glimpses of "present moments" in space-time can reflect the essential Light's emanation or *manifesting* aspect ("rose-tree" of 58 or "water-lily"). Only very sophisticated souls are aware of this emanation or "unus mundus" or Demiurge (to use the Gnostic term), from which the one Light passes into form and appears in Time as many created souls and universes, and into which, conversely, the many return to the one; souls and universes – microcosm and macrocosm – being fundamentally of one stuff (Light) and therefore one. A knowledge of the emanation does not make perception of the Light any easier, though it may deepen understanding of it, and so the country soul who sees the Light for the first time, in the present moment, as a water-lily, and interprets it in terms of oneness, has the same experience (if not the interpretative knowledge of time-space) as the town soul who has often seen the Light as a rose and interprets it in terms of the more complex, manifold and multiple rose-tree.

64.   "Nymph" recalls Marvell's poem *The Nymph complaining for the death of her Faun*.

67-8   "To keep...board", i.e. in the peace of country halls which town contemplatives themselves long for, though the peace of Harrington Hall, near Somersby, Lincolnshire, where Tennyson wrote *Maud*, brought no peace to the lover of Maud. "Where you board". Hunmanby Hall, Yorkshire.

68.   "Town climbers", i.e. "souls like climbing roses in towns" and "men who climb the promotion ladder in towns".

72.   "May the nymph one day have the universe in her heart and therefore be the universe, reflecting it as the one reflects the many."

A CROCUS IN THE CHURCHYARD

First written on 24th March 1974, and subsequently revised, e.g. on 17th February 1980. The purpose of life is to glimpse the Fire or Light which the dead reflect. The Churchyard is that of the Church of the Holy Innocents, High Beach, Essex, which is in the heart of Epping Forest.

2.	"Arrowed spire". See line 64.
6.	"Eternity". Timelessness; also infinite time; also immortality, the future life. Timelessness etc. is disturbed by the nightingale.
12.	"Cattle brands". The lady chapel has an altar cloth on which are embroidered the stamps with which local cattle used to be branded, and in some cases still are.
14.	To follow the Ten Commandments helps one perceive the metaphysical Light during contemplation.
19-20.	"No host...dream", i.e. the marble tablets recall a time when the Ten Commandments were observed, the practice of consecrating bread (the Eucharist) was strong, and an understanding of spiritual nourishment was not yet lost. "Host" also "large number" and "one who lodges or entertains another"; "manna" also "my Anna".
28.	"Attest". Intransitive, "bear witness to a Britain that was like a marble cross", i.e. had religious values; or transitive, "put Britain on oath so that it lived up to its image as a marble cross, lived up to its ideals". The deeds have eternal as well as temporal significance, and are therefore still present, still bear witness or keep Britain up to the mark. "Like a marble cross". This can be taken with "Britain" (see immediately above) or with "they", i.e. they are like a marble cross in bearing witness to the true Britain.
30.	"Their belief", their acceptance of Christian theology and "the life everlasting" as embodied in the Apostles' Creed, which is also called "The Belief", i.e. their religion. But a pun is also intended, "bell-leaf", following on from "bluebells" and "bellbind", i.e. "they preserved the leaves of their bluebells from bellbind".
35.	"The eternal". Timelessness.
40.	"The Golden Flower". The crocus is a temporal flower proclaiming on behalf of the dead its eternal counterpart, which can be "glimpsed" as "gold sunshine" from "fields of silver light" (46-8). The Light is the posthumous message of the dead to souls in Time. (Compare the Chinese text, *The Secret of the Golden Flower*.)
41-48.	A decaying heart feeds a crocus which symbolises in Time the "silver light" it knows in Eternity.
44.	"Silence...brimming", i.e. the dead are empty and full at the same time.
46.	"Still", here a verb.
53.	"Startle...theodolite". The new physics have destroyed the old distinction between observer and observed because the "I" is not part of but is the totality of creation (see *Preface on the Metaphysical Revolution*). It is precisely because God, too, the Light, is the very stuff of His creation of souls and universe, and cannot detach Himself from it as an observer, that He has to use an observer's theodolite in His physics. Time, after all, is alien and unreal to Him even though He created it, for (if such a thought is possible) He is *outside* the space-time which is part of Him and therefore *is* Him. God, the Light, has the powers of a measuring mathematician.
61-64.	"Your posthumous meaning in Time is to reflect symbols of eternity in a rain-filled crocus, which will grow from your buried heart."

FIRE-VOID

First written on 17th July 1967 and subsequently revised 10th-15th November 1979, and 20th-22nd February and 5th April 1980. The rubbish dump was at Nobe, a small village on the Pacific near Kurihama, in Japan. Being/Nature is seen as having pattern and meaning in relation to Non-Being/the Void, which contains the Metaphysical Fire as a latent energy within itself. The aesthetic of the first three stanzas also applies to the construction of a poem.

16.	"Contour: outline; line separating differently coloured parts of design; artistic quality

of outline; outline of coast, mountain mass etc. Contour-line: one representing horizontal contour of earth's surface at given elevation" (*Concise Oxford Dictionary*). "Contour" can therefore here mean "curves".

18.   "Green and white" points forward to "seasons and ages" (19), suggesting spring/youth and winter/old age, but other contrasts are included: hill (green) and dump (white boxes and panniers etc.); Nature (green "spring and fall") and history (white "skull and scroll"); birth (green youth) and death (white hair and bones); and the physical world of "sunrise and set" (green leaves) and the immaterial world (white "soul").

22.   "Why is man?" "Why does man exist, why is he here?"

"Why...door", i.e. the Church is reluctant to give rational answers to questions about the meaning of man's life.

24.   "Reason...intellect". The distinction between reason and intellect (Latin "intellectus" means "perception" and therefore "understanding", "comprehension") is between analytical and intuitive faculties of the mind, and between perception of particulars and of universals. Contemplation (line 33) is in touch with the intellect.

25.   "Perspective", "relation in which parts of subject are viewed by the mind" (*Concise Oxford Dictionary*).

26.   "Be", "merely have being or existence".

32.   A mallow is the image for a civilisation in Spengler's *Decline of the West*.

34.   The Void synthesises the Buddhist Void (which has Light connotations in the Tibetan Clear Light of the Void, and Fire connotations in the Buddha's fire-sermon); the Hindu Brahman; the Christian Dantean Empyrean; Swedenborgian Angels; the Neo-Platonist Idea; and Kabbalistic manifestation. Nevertheless, it is not an academic Void but a vision of Non-Being (see *Preface on the Metaphysical Revolution*, pp584-85), the way Reality impinges on earthly life and is mirrored or copied by Beauty.

35.   "Shadows", i.e. pre-forms.

39.   "In negative", cf the mystic "via negativa" or negative way.

45.   The process of dissolution is known in physics as entropy.

46.   "Empyrean", "the highest heaven, as the sphere of fire/abode of God" (*Concise Oxford Dictionary*).

48, 55.   Alchemy appeared to seek to turn base metals to gold, but in fact symbolised mystic illumination; gold being the texture of the illumined soul. "Goldhood" would be achieved through the discovery of the Philosopher's Stone, which was symbolised as an egg.

51.   "Try", test.

53.   The view expressed is that many Angels have dull souls and are not necessarily fully enlightened. They may achieve full enlightenment on earth, life on which they regard as preferable to life in the Void because *transformation* is possible.

63.   The golden Fire-bird is an image in the "unus mundus" for an advanced mystic whose soul has been completely illumined (i.e. hatched from a Philosopher's Stone or egg), and who will not therefore have to be reincarnated into the world of forms.

64.   "Lighten". "Shed light upon", i.e. "enlighten", "illumine", but also "reduce load of", i.e. "disperse the karmic load of".

"Hence". Souls are born and take bodies so that they can open themselves to the Light (see lines 50-56).

SEA-FIRE

First written on 10th August 1974 and revised on 23rd-24th February and 6th April 1980. The poem is about "the heart of universes" which stirred to fire like the bonfire in a Cornish fishing village; and about the relationship between the inner space of the mind and the outer space of the universe. Porthleven is in Cornwall.

6-9.   The annual St. Peter's-tide gala-week begins with a torchlight procession and ends with hymn-singing at dusk, while hardboard models of "a cross, a lighthouse, a boat" and an anchor light up on the hill that overlooks Porthleven.

28.   "Divine Will". "Will" in the sense of "Thy will be done", i.e. what God desires and ordains; but also the auxiliary "will" meaning "a future that will inevitably come to pass", here "an experience of the Divinity which will inevitably take place".
"Steals", i.e. "like a thief in the night".

31-32.   The souls are seen as brightness or lamp-carrying pilgrims crossing a causeway like the one that leads from nearby Marazion to St. Michael's Mount, though the causeway is of course the Milky Way; and simultaneously as gulls that fly up to the Milky Way and "alight" where angels meet, a layer of meaning that is developed in the next stanza.

33-48.   The centre of all universes is found by entering one's personal mind and passing to the "impersonal" or unconscious sea of mind, which paradoxically leads to the objective Light which is "behind" all physics. Inner and outer space seem air and a shut box, but enter the "box" of the mind, find a crack in its side (or "inside" the mind), and a sun becomes visible which is not visible in outer space though it spins all atoms of outer space; and which is therefore "new", i.e. "newly discovered".

33-7.   The shift from a cosmic to a transcendent consciousness and perspective opens regions in the mind which are as vast as our universe.

38-9.   The idea that the spiritual Fire can be returned to during life or after death on the wings of a sea-gull goes back to the flight of Horus the hawk to Re the sun in the Egyptian *Book of the Dead*. Here, dead souls become gulls and "wing" living souls.

41.   "Light at midnight". Cf Apuleius's *Golden Ass* where Lucius reports his ceremony of initiation into the Isis Mysteries: "At midnight I saw the sun shining as if it were noon."

42-48.   See *Preface on the Metaphysical Revolution* paragraphs 6 and 8 for this view of Superspace and the "unus mundus" from which universes and archetypes come; and Jung's collaborator, Marie-Louise von Franz's *Number and Time* for an old engraving showing a spiritual pilgrim looking through the window into eternity ("fenestra aeternitatis") (the airhole into eternity or "spiraculum aeternitatis" of Gerhard Dorn, Paracelsus's pupil), which is an outer version of the crack or slit in the mind.

44.   "Well-earned prime". Man has to be in the "state of highest perfection" ("prime") to receive the divine spark, and as "prime" is also the "golden number" and the canonical hour of sunrise, it is suggested that his golden readiness waits to be lit by the inner sun. Man must also be open to the "behind" like a "well-grate", by means of which a fire burning in a hearth receives its air supply from below. "Earned" also suggests "urned", and the idea that man is waiting to be "urned", i.e. waiting for the finality of death, is countered by the hint of a "well" or escape beneath the grate of his cremation. This hint is taken up in the next two lines, for the "box" is also a coffin-urn from which there is an escape into the metaphysical Light.

47.   "In side". In its side, and inside.

49-50.   The sea brings the divine life, which is associated with the spiritual Sun at the centre of our universe (the source of all fire) and the moon and stars (the causeway of the Angels), to its lower manifestation or copy, the human life where rocks represent all that is inhospitable to man, and where fire represents the community spirit of which men are sparks. Fire therefore has spiritual and material modes, both of which are reflected in the sea, in the curl of one wave.

A MYSTIC FIRE-POTTER'S RED SUN-HALO

First written on 15th-16th August 1974 and subsequently revised. The poem is about an art of the heart transformed by the illumined soul.

The Catholic is the Austrian Margaret Riley, whose vision of Christ in St. Ives and whose Shoreham portrait of another vision, *St. Teresa of Avila as a Nun*, along with such outstanding pottery works as her *Pyramid of Chains* which I have, make her one of the most important British artist-potters since the war. The red sun-halo eventually graced the window of her art-gallery in Shoreham, along with some of the Marys, and a visitor could always tell the state of her soul from it. For each day she adjusted its three pieces to indicate her spiritual mood, and if her peace had been broken by excessively worldly clients, the halo was shattered into three fragments. In this poem, the mystic Light she embodies has two manifestations or aspects: Fire, which is its creative aspect, and the Sea, which represents its religious aspect. Both are united in the image of the Sun, the source of Fire which also lights the moon which draws the tides. The Fire-potter who transforms through the furnace and still of the soul, and the sea-artist who admits the flow of spiritual experience into the harbour of her soul, are both manifestations of a Light-mystic who receives the Light of the spiritual Sun in her soul, whence it flows via the centre to her heart, where it is experienced as a halo. When properly understood, this poem is very much about the relationship between the heart and the soul. Margaret Riley practises an art of the soul rather than an art of the worldly heart; or rather, her art is one of a heart transformed by soul.

24.	"Beyond doubt". The fire is beyond doubt, but also so is the view expressed.
32.	The reference is to her painting *Via D'Amore* or "Way of Love", a mystic work completed in Manorola, Italy. This hung on my wall for many years until, one day, she came and took it back.
44.	Charlestown is a 1790s harbour near St. Austell in Cornwall where I now have the Harbour-master's House, which has a view of the Black Head of Trenarren. Its inner harbour symbolises the worldly heart, its outer harbour (beyond the lock-gate) the soul. The inner harbour can be full of water which reflects moonlight while the outer harbour is dry sand and shingle.
55-6.	The Trinity of: Holy Ghost/Holy Spirit; Father/Trenarren; and Son/Christ, i.e. "guide".
56.	The "black headland peak" is the nearby Cornish headland, the Black Head of Trenarren.
60.	"Fired still". The meanings include "distilling-apparatus".
67.	In Alchemy, the Sun is the father of all things according to the *Emerald Tablet* of Hermes Trismegistos. The secret fire which has no flames ("ignis innaturalis"), the fire of love, was in fact a salt prepared from cream of tartar and spring dew. It unites Sol (gold) and Luna (silver) in the third process of distillation which creates the red philosopher's stone. This is made from white combustible sulphur and is the agent that turns base metal/heart to gold/soul.
77.	The Oratory is the Brompton Oratory on which stands a statue of Mary.

AN AESTHETE'S "GOLDEN" ARTEFACTS

First written on 23rd-26th July 1974 and subsequently revised, e.g. in March 1980. The poem is about the contrasting aesthetics of the sceptical and metaphysical outlooks, "aesthetic" being defined as "philosophy as to what is beautiful".

The Aesthete is Frank Tuohy, who is among the finest short story writers since the war, a practiser of the art of miniature. In the 1970s he had a flat in Brighton, at 3 Sussex Gardens. He is the last living witness to the last ideas of Wittgenstein, and his aesthetic of imaged statement is based on a visit he and Wittgenstein made to *King Lear*, at the end of which Wittgenstein stood up and said, "Yes." When Tuohy asked why he had said Yes, Wittgenstein said: "A work of art is a proposition in feelings and perceptions that cannot be paraphrased and which has to be answered Yes or No, and so I have said Yes." Wittgenstein's aesthetic is countered in 33-40 by an aesthetic of the symbol. A work of art is a model for a Reality it symbolises, one or more of whose layers may transcend logic and logical propositions; and whereas the Tuohyan image is an external pictorial form perceived by the heart, the symbol has a spiritual layer perceived by the soul, which can transform the heart. This poem is clearly closely related to *A Mystic Fire-Potter's Red Sun-Halo*, for besides contrasting the Saint with the Aesthete, it, too, is about the relationship between heart and soul, which have different aesthetics. Though the "soul aesthetic" in this poem differs from Tuohy's sceptical "mind and heart aesthetic" in emphasising that the symbol reveals a layered metaphysical Reality (gold) rather than an exclusively social Reality (metal), I have a great respect and admiration for the solitary, occasionally gregarious polymath who lives for his "melting" art.

22.	The 19th century Parnassians believed in an "objective art".
24.	"Gold image". This claim to Alchemy is refuted in 33-6 (e.g. "base image"). In the aesthetic of symbol, besides developing an image into a symbol with a spiritual layer, soul transforms the heart.
25.	"Persona", i.e. "mask".
33-40.	The Alchemists sought to turn base metal into the red Philosopher's Stone, which, once found, could become the distilled "elixir", essence or gold, the Alchemists' word for the "Golden Flower" of the Neo-Taoist text *The Secret of the Golden Flower*, the principle of rejuvenation and immortality, i.e. the Light seen through a "hole in the mind's hedge". The idea of the Rose comes into an earlier stage in the Alchemical process, e.g. the Rosa Alba or White Rose, the Sulphur of the Wise, which preceded the finding of the Philosopher's Stone.
55.	"Quiet despair". During this visit Tuohy said to me, quoting Thoreau, "I live a life of 'quiet desperation'." "Desperation" and "despair" have the same root; "desperate", i.e. loss of hope.
56.	"Beauty". In the Kabbalah, Beauty is the fifth of the ten sephirot (or sephiroth), and it represents the heart.

PEAR-RIPENING HOUSE

First written on 4th August 1974 and later revised, e.g. 23rd March, mid-April and 26th May 1980. Growth within a family house is seen in terms of a soul preparing for future lives. Journey's End, for thirty-five years the family house of the Haggers, is in Loughton, Essex. During the war it accommodated the ARP (Air Raid Protection). The blackened stump and ivy were to be found in the garden. For the garage and porch see Journey's End. In my bedroom under the back gable I first discovered my literary ambitions ("a reaching out to moons").

43.	The idea that the soul inherits genes, which are developed and passed on to the next life or incarnation, to be further developed there, is related to the Tao in *Clouded-Ground Pond* (line 49). If the "pips" are stunted in this life, there will be an effect on the next life, which may be stunted.
44.	"Vision". The impetus for a new direction/new tree, the goal of a soul's present life, may partly be a memory from its previous life.
45-6.	We do not merely "know" the divine will that fills us, and we are not merely "a part

of" the totality of the universe ("all that's green"); we *are* the divine will and we *are* the totality of the universe, which is inherited in each gene. The idea is that though genes only use that part of the whole code which they need to do their specific, local work, they have the potentiality to draw on the totality.

47.   Since we *are* God, we serve the totality by adapting the environment and evolution to God's purpose, i.e. we participate in the purpose of the universe, and have a vision of its purpose by entering the mind of God, which we *are* (46). There is a hint in this line that Darwin's findings might be only half the story, that species do not just adapt to their environment to survive, but also adapt the environment to the purpose of the totality.

48.   "New seeds", new lives. "Shoot", i.e. reincarnate.

54-6.   Both parents and children are alive to ripen their souls, so that they can shed ripe genes into the ground of the One on their deaths, and come again as new lives in the future. The image suggests that just as the seed of one pear can grow into a future tree on which many pears depend, so one life can ramify into a future life on which many depend, and a humble soul in this life may become a leader in a future life on whom many souls depend.

CLOUDED-GROUND POND

First written on 4th August 1974 and subsequently revised, e.g. on 23rd March 1980. The pond reveals all layers of Being and Non-Being/Tao/Void to the self, including the possibility of many lives. In quantum theory, the quantum vacuum is sometimes referred to as a pond. "Clouded-Ground Pond" is the inner of two ponds on Strawberry Hill in Epping Forest, between Loughton and High Beach, Essex. It is near the pond which appeared in Part Three of The Silence.

27.   "Frogs...in mud". The frog, covered in the mud of human passions, sits still and watches like a meditator.

31.   "Two hearts". The heart of the looker and the heart in the reflection.

32.   The social ego drowns in spirit until it comes back to life again on material ground. (Compare *Breaststroke, Drowning*.)

33.   The four worlds of the Kabbalah meet in Beauty, the sephira of the heart centre. They are the physical world of the sephira Foundation or "ground", i.e. the ego and Nature, and the psychological world, both of which are mirrored by the heart; the spiritual world of "clouds", which is mirrored by the soul; and the divine world which unites man's unconscious with the divine Sun, the eternal source of all creation.

35.   "Pond". Also the quantum vacuum or Void (see above).

36.   "Layered leaves", i.e. the psychological world.

39.   "First source", i.e. the Sun is the Tao-source, from which all creation sprang.

48.   "Tao-self". The Tao and the self are one, for when the Tao flows into the individual's self, the self is the Tao, or God.

49.   "Old genes teem new lives", i.e. the Tao accepts old genes into its Void and returns them in new forms as new lives.

49-51.   "Tao's hidden sun...is now this lily". The lily is a manifestation of Tao, and it embodies the process of manifestation; for it comes from the immaterial Tao, its leaves and flower are open to the spiritual and divine worlds of wind and pure sun, and yet it is rooted in the mud of physical passions.

55.   "Yes". Cf 39. At Clouded-Ground Pond Essex men say Yes to the One.

TWO VARIATIONS ON ONE THEME

First drafted on 14th November 1972 as *Time and Eternity* (see *The Gates of Hell*) and subsequently revised, e.g. 21st-22nd June 1980. Both poems are about the silence of Eternity and the Void in which the "white light" can be known.

    The two poems are set in the churchyard of Holy Innocents, High Beach, Essex, like *A Crocus in the Churchyard*. Much of it is set in the corner of the churchyard where the *Crocus* poem ends.

TIME AND ETERNITY

1.	"Omega gate". The lych-gate at the Church of the Holy Innocents, High Beach is inscribed with an alpha and an omega.
2.	"Yew". Also "you".
21.	"Mystery". See note to 61-8 below.

THE BRIDE OF TIME

12.	"Chaste". Also "chased".
17-20.	Eternity is in love with man's soul and spirit, and is hence in love with the forms of Time. To shape and obtain them, she has to inflict pains on, and finally destroy, man's body, but she feels compassion for this necessary suffering.
18.	"Mould". "Shape", but also "make mouldy", "rot".
32-44.	Eternity destroys the forms she gives birth to, but preserves all souls, no matter how expanded they are. "Flow" (43) is transitive: since an "expanded" soul is like a sea (i.e. of spirit), and since spirits originate in life as fish-like sperm, fish-like spirits expand by "flowing" tides (i.e. creating seas, "causing tides to flow"). The undercurrent of sexual imagery in these lines also sees souls as sperms in Eternity's womb, and expansion/sea as semen; hence "waste" (44) is also "waist". See the *Preface on the Metaphysical Revolution*, paragraphs 5-8 (pp582-83) for the paradox in physics and metaphysics whereby an individual is an ocean.
53.	Time enslaves souls by imprisoning their perception in the five senses of the body, and consequently in physical sensuality.
59.	"Freeze" suggests that the "hidden Void" (60) is moving, i.e. it is a fullness rather than a void.
60.	"Will", "purpose".
61-8.	This optimistic message on a gravestone pictures Eternity as a bride whose "mystery" can be "carnally" known once the bridal veil of the physical world is removed. "Billowing" suggests a bridal veil and also the waves of the sea. It therefore points back to "caves" (56) and forward to "foams" (63) and "surge" (67). Eternity's bridal veil of "springs and graves" is made of procreative "springs", seasons and deaths (i.e. Time, for the children she procreates will all have graves), but also of "springs of genius" and of Reality after death (i.e. Eternity). The churchyard stile symbolises the barrier between Time and Eternity, or doubt and faith. The three steps which lead to the existential "leap" across into Eternity, and to the secret of life, correspond to the three upper worlds of the Kabbalah. After a hint of a tantalisingly near-at-hand invisible "meaning" in the visible universe, there must be progress first to the "silence", then to the spiritual "mystery" of Eternity, which is revealed as operating behind Time. The resultant perception of the divine immortality of the soul (the third step) creates the "smile". "Know" means

"experience" as well as "have knowledge of" or "have gnosis of", "have carnal knowledge of", and "have incarnate knowledge of". "Mystery" suggests the "inexplicable" (in the sense "it's a mystery"); the "mystery" of a woman, i.e. "mysteriousness"; and a secret "mystery cult", a "religious truth divinely revealed, one beyond human reason", i.e. the metaphysical Light. The reader can approach the full meaning of the "mystery", and of the mysterious last two stanzas, by beginning to think of a dynamic, spiritual ocean of silence that manifests into form, and which guarantees all souls an immortality after death.

A STONEMASON'S FLOWER-BOWL

First written on 24th July 1974 and subsequently revised, e.g. on 10th August 1974 and 19th-20th April 1980. The poem is about how the artist/stonemason captures and fixes eternal changeless images and symbols in time. The neo-Gothic school at Sompting Abbots is a mile or two outside Worthing in Sussex. My daughter holidayed there with other children from 1971 to 1974.

19.	"The changes", cf the *I Ching* or *Book of Changes* which codified the 64 archetypes in the "unus mundus", according to later Jung.
22.	"Petrifies", "turns to stone", i.e. turns into art, turns the ephemeral into the lasting. Some artists turn their women into art and kill their relationships, others ignore their women for their art and turn them to stone another way, and still others frighten them (the other sense of "petrify") with their genius.
24.	"Chiselling", also "swindling", for all art which turns the ephemeral into the lasting is to some extent perpetrating a swindle, or at least, a confidence trick.
39-40.	"Shell", "airhole". See the 17th (or possibly 19th) century engraving reproduced in *Number and Time* by Jung's disciple, Marie-Louise von Franz, and taken from Jung. It shows a spiritual pilgrim discovering the hole open to eternity. The idea of a "fenestra aeternitatis" ("window into eternity") is in western Alchemy, and was taken over by Paracelsus's pupil Gerhard Dorn as the "spiraculum aeternitatis" ("airhole into eternity"). This is a chink in the continuum of space-time and looks into the timeless world of the collective unconscious. This chink links with the "mysterium fenestrae" in the Kabbalah, the Light in the upper three sephirot. The idea of a window or airhole into eternity comes from a 17th (or possibly 19th) century engraving in which a seeker looks through sensebound reality into the metaphysical beyond.
40.	"Prime", "state of highest perfection" but also sunrise, prime being the first canonical hour of divine office.
43.	"Images", "events". In Jung's synchronicity, an image in the "unus mundus" can also manifest acausally and simultaneously as an event on earth.
44.	"Blind sense", i.e the five senses do not have visionary powers and are therefore blind.
53.	"Beauty", i.e. the aesthetic beauty of art, for all artists put flowers (characters, images) in a form, but also the Self, Beauty being the fifth sephira for the Self.
54.	"Come again", i.e. reincarnate.
56.	"Enduring", "lasting", in contrast to 48 where "endure" means "last" in the sense of "survive, undergo pain, submit, bear".
57.	"Then", i.e. because souls endure.
64.	A notice on Worthing beach, where I walked, mentioned "sea-defences".

AN OBSCURE SYMBOLIST'S ROCK-TREE

First written on 17th August 1974, while I stayed in Frank Tuohy's flat in Brighton, and subsequently revised, e.g. on 17th-18th April 1980. The poem is about the obscure artist's struggle to escape a choking social life and contact and channel eternal symbols in paintings, and the true relationship of Eternity to Time's forms.

Hill Place is an old farm just outside East Grinstead, Sussex. It dates back to 1296AD. The Cornish artist who lived there was Gwen Broad, who died in 1972. She was a friend of my mother and her family, and wrote to me on my birth: "To Dear Little Nicholas, With every good wish for a life filled with love and usefulness. Your Dawn has commenced in sunshine, may the eventide have just sufficient clouds to make a glorious Sunset! With love from your Mother & Father's friend, Gwen M. Broad."

20.	*Dusk Near Land's End*. This oil painting was probably completed between 1959 and 1960. The Kynance and Land's End pictures are now on my wall.
28.	"Groins and caves", i.e. empty spaces in rock.
30.	"Fossils, and ancient dreams". The unconscious mind.
31-2.	The idea expressed is that Eternity parts or separates round its forms while still nevertheless permeating them; and refills the space occupied by forms in their life when they cease to exist.
33-40.	Expands 31-2, so the Idea is simply an aspect of Eternity. It is nevertheless a very important aspect, for it manifests into form and is the active principle in Eternity's creation. Originally a Greek, pre-Christian concept for the rational, spiritual principle that permeates Reality, it came to be identified with the Logos, the Word made Flesh, which in Christian terms is Christ. Its Christian connotations are excluded here, but the parallel can be taken.
	"Rock cube". There are two ways of looking at the solid rock cube with sculpted holes in it. One way sees the solidness as matter, the other way sees the solidness as spirit. Thus, Idea seems air besides solid matter, but ideas in conceptual form (i.e. manifested) are hollow forms in solid spirit or Eternity.
37.	"Concept", from "conceive" meaning "form in the mind", i.e. concept at the level of manifested form, not Idea.
71.	"Silver lead". Cornish locals produce lumps of "silver lead" which have come from tin-mines and offer them as gifts of value.
75.	"Chapel". In fact, the Methodist chapel.
76.	"Japanese cherry tree". The Japanese cherry tree stood on the lawn in the front garden of Daledene (81), the old house of the Broadleys on the Lewes Road, East Grinstead. It was such a fine specimen that Lord Strathcona wrote and asked for its Latin name, which the local nursery identified as "Cerasus hisacura cerulata". An identical tree now stands on the corner of Ritherdon Road and Sainfoin Road, Tooting.
77.	"Grandfather". See the first three chapters of Margaret E. Broadley's *Patients Come First* for a glimpse of this man (called "Father" there).
79.	"Acme", i.e. "highest point of perfection".
85.	"Stone lawn". The lawn at Daledene was concreted around the end of the Second World War.
92.	"Reaching depth". "Depth which reaches". "Spirit" flows in from outside, from the Truth in deep seams, and so the choking is in fact a blocking out, an interference which causes a lack of opening to the Spirit.
96.	"Earth", here a verb.

THE TREE OF IMAGINATION

First written on 24th and 31st December 1979 and subsequently revised. Between Christmas 1979 and February 1980 in six creative weeks I wrote *The Tree of Imagination*, *Firethorn*, *A Temple-Dancer's Temple-Sleep*, *A Metaphysical's Light-Mandala* and *The Fire-Flower* while living at 46 Ritherdon Road in Wandsworth.

The poem is about the contrast between the academic scholars' social and sceptical view of the poetic tradition, and the true poet's imaginative vision of poetic symbols and of metaphysical Reality. (The Tree of Tradition stands in the physical world, the Tree of Imagination is in the metaphysical world.) The central image of silkworm, chrysalis and moth suggests the three ages of the poet: the visionary, the writer of poetry, and the mature poet whose work is behind him.

The Professor, Christopher Ricks, my tutor when I read English Literature at Oxford, is one of the most brilliant Professors of English Literature to have emerged since the war. Until the late 1980s at Christ's College, Cambridge, he has carried on Empson's "verbal" approach to Literature, and his reinterpretations have transformed our understanding of some classical texts (for example, of Middleton's *The Changeling*). Though he is a true Augustan at heart, and takes a social view of poetry (see his *Keats and Embarrassment* and *Eliot and Prejudice*, for example), I have a great respect for, and indebtedness to, the originality and sharpness of his mind.

I met Empson when Ricks invited him to chat with some of his pupils, and in the 1960s I taught at the Japanese university where Empson taught in the 1920s.

2. "Milton's ancient mulberry tree". There is a mulberry tree at Christ's College, Cambridge which Milton (a pupil there) knew.
"Withstands", "resists" modern materialism and therefore "endures".

18. "Stir", i.e stir to life.

23. "Veined". Besides suggesting the veins which carry blood to the heart and the ribs of a leaf, "vein" of course has a geological meaning: "fissure in rock filled with deposited matter".

25-32. The poet as silkworm. The true poet feeds on the hallucinogenic mulberry Tree of Tradition which is only known to those who have "precise understanding", and protects his vision from the world in a cocoon of verse (i.e. "work"). It is a fact that a silkworm's cocoon is made of one often unbroken thread of silk some 1,000 yards long. It is also a fact that a hatched silkmoth does not feed much or fly, and that its life-span is a mere three days or so. This corresponds to the post-chrysalis phase of a poet when he "lays eggs", i.e. hands on the seeds of his work, imparts a knowledge of what he has learned to his successors, and prepares to die. The poets provide the raw material, the silk, which critics weave into saleable dresses in their critical and educational works, and profit from; hence their interest in guarding the Tree of Tradition.

29. "Beauty". Again, the Kabbalistic Self, the fifth sephira. Also in 73.

30. "Three day moths", i.e. mature, fully grown.

33. "Snicks out energies", "snicks energies into being so that they express themselves in form".

34. "As", "just as".

37. "'Sacred' trees". See the anthropologist Mary Douglas, *Social and Religious Symbolism of the Lele* (in *Implicit Meanings*), which argues that religious symbolism derives its meaning from everyday social practices, that consecration is connected with prohibition (cf the basic feeling of taboo). Thus, the rain forest's being regarded as "the place of God" is associated with the fact that humans are separated from it, e.g. menstruating women are excluded from it.

40. Ricks told me, "I am an Empsonian atheist, I believe that if I walk under a bus this

afternoon, death is the end."

42-8.	See note to line 111.
49.	"Four worlds", cf the note to 33 of *Clouded-Ground Pond*, on the four worlds of the Kabbalah.
	"Matrix", "womb, mould in which type is cast or shaped" (*Concise Oxford Dictionary*).
55.	The Tree of Life or cosmic tree (cf 38) is an aspect of the inverted Tree. In the Kabbalah the invisible is shown as an upside down Tree, its roots in the heavens, manifesting through its branches into visible form as from the quantum vacuum. Each fruit is therefore a symbol of Eternity.
59.	"Images", cf the introductory note to *An Aesthete's "Golden" Artefacts*. An "image" is an external or pictorial form perceived by the heart, whereas a symbol has a spiritual layer perceived by the soul. "Image" is used in this poem (e.g. in 48 and 69 as well as here) in place of "symbol" as it is the pictorial form of the symbol that is being stressed. "Dark sun", dark because spiritual.
63.	"Hawk". Compare the note on the gull in 38-9 of *Sea-Fire* for the association of Horus the hawk flying to Re. The hawk is the part of the soul which bears the main soul and flies between physical and spiritual worlds.
65.	That visualising or active imaging can warm hands and cure migraine, and warm feet and cure hypertension, has been established by the work of Dr Elmer and Alyce Green of the Menninger Foundation. In the same way the passive reception of images rather than their active generation, has a healing effect. "Visualising". Visualising in images has the power to change body temperature and health, and a poet's images therefore have a healing effect on the reader's mind and on "a sick society" with a "poisoned perspective".
66.	"Body is "dense mind" according to the spiritual view.
67.	That actively imaging light increases photons in the body has been established by a Romanian team.
68.	"Crown", the crown chakra of Hinduism, and also Keter, the topmost sephira in the Kabbalah. (Cf 74-5.)
72-80.	The social, sceptical view blocks out the metaphysical vision.
73-4.	"Four worlds...which consciousness/Reflects". When consciousness *does* reflect the four worlds, it becomes fully aware, its horizons are fully extended.
77.	"Worm", silkworm. "Screening", "separate without completely cutting off" (*Concise Oxford Dictionary*), i.e. symbols which act as a screen that separates from Reality without completely cutting it off.
78.	"Blend", "form harmonious compound" (in this case of language and ideas).
79.	"Harmonised", "bring into harmony", i.e. decorated.
86.	"Fancies". Fancy is decorative imagery which plays on a social vision, whereas imagination enters spiritual or divine Reality. Mulberries are decorative, optional fruits rather than a staple diet. See the *Preface on the New Baroque Consciousness* for the distinction between timebound fancy and eternal imagination.
89-96.	Symbols and language are layered and are capable of metaphysical and not merely social meanings.
89.	"Sown beyond". Symbols come from an eternal, transpersonal, spiritual source, the repository of all Ideas, the "unus mundus", and enter form as language. 89-96 insists that man lives in a universe before he lives in a society.
97.	"Heaven opens to crown knowledge". Crown and Knowledge are the sephirot in the Kabbalah which go straight up to the divine world from Beauty of Self. The idea expressed is that the upper part of the Tree of Imagination is Heaven. The meanings

of "to crown knowledge" therefore include "to the knowledge or gnosis of the crown chakra or centre", the Kabbalistic sephira Keter.

99. "Chain of being". The Elizabethan idea of a great chain of being which is found in many of Shakespeare's plays (e.g. *Julius Caesar*) and in Marvell came from the worlds of the Kabbalah. It included all creation, and therefore all the four worlds of the Kabbalah, which are "tangled in one moment". Here, the sephirot Beauty, Knowledge and Crown (psychological, spiritual and divine worlds).

100-104. The metaphysical vision is opposed by academics who have a sceptical, social view.

104. "The word", i.e. influenced by anthropologists who see symbols in terms of customs.

110-112. Concern with the "actual" social tradition precludes opening oneself to the symbols of the beyond, which are glimpsed in the metaphysical vision.

111. "Ungolden Tree". To scholars, the fruit of the Tree of Tradition is decorative rather than edible. Only the true poets who feed on the Tree of Tradition can see and taste the nourishing Heavenly symbols of the Tree of Imagination. The "golden fruit" of 102 makes the soul gold.

FIRETHORN

First written on 31st December 1979 and subsequently revised, e.g. on 3rd May 1980. The poem is about the involvement of the Fire of God in the Mass or Communion service. Firethorn (the Fire as a crown of thorns), i.e. Christ. The church is All Saints', Tooting Graveney.

4-5. "Catacomb", "flamen". The Roman origins of Christianity are emphasised.

9. "A symbol". The priest, receiving the Fire or Light from above, symbolises the eternal Holy Spiri

17. "Wisdom", the ninth sephira, next to Crown from which the divine lightning flash zigzags into form in the Kabbalah.

24. "Can God catch fire". The Fire of God manifests into form in men's souls.

29. "Enigma". The machine German HQ used to communicate with Generals in the field during the Second World War. Its code was broken by the British at Bletchley Park. It may similarly be possible to break into transmissions of the "cipher messages".

34-5. "Four clouded worlds, down/Which fire descends." See the note to line 33 of *Clouded-Ground Pond*, on the four worlds of the Kabbalah. Light zigzags down the Kabbalistic Tree of Life to the lower sephirot, but the mystic sees straight up from Beauty through Knowledge to Crown(36); cf the note to 99 of *The Tree of Imagination*.

36. "Crown", the Kabbalistic sephira Keter which is closest to the Fire or Light.

37. "Through glass darkly" echoes St. Paul.

38-9. "Multiple thorns...acacia crown". The thorn of the acacia is related to the world-axis, and therefore to the cross. When twined into one crown, its multiple prickles symbolise the unitive vision.

43. "Idea", cf the Logos.

51. God's revelation in the four Kabbalistic worlds is divine Fire, spiritual Flame, Light received in the soul and physical candle.

52. "Fire-crowned hero with four faces, Firethorn". Christ with Fire in his crown sephira or chakra, a Fire that is imaged in each of the four worlds. Firethorn/Christ is a model or example of achieved illumination for which all mean have the potential, and which they can achieve on their own, without any mediation on the part of anybody.

53. "Spark God". Cause God to spark and ignite men to show them that their souls are potentially Fire.

54-5.	i.e. God needs sceptical, thorn-crowned men to transform with Fire.
56.	"Reveal four worlds again", i.e. remove the clouds that veil the spiritual and divine worlds from our vision.

A TEMPLE-DANCER'S TEMPLE-SLEEP

Experience of images purporting to come from past lives during hypnotic regression suggests that the spirit has one endless life through many existences and bodies, and that between death and rebirth it returns to the quantum vacuum or Void of Non-Being (or potential Being) to secrete what it has learned and to be recharged.

The hypnotist was Maurice Blake, who continued the pioneering of Arnall Bloxham by regressing people into past lives. The Temple-sleep of the title and line 3 required an initiate ("mustes") to lie in a deep trance or state of unconsciousness near death for as much as three and a half days. During the time when his physical body withdrew he came to know his spiritual nature and link with the divine world, which he remembered on waking. A regressed person acquires similar knowledge. At another level, both "mustes" and a regressed person come to feel that life is a sleep from which death is an awakening, so a "temple-sleep" is also "a life spent in a temple".

4.	"Traitors' Gate". A Traitors' Gate (see also 94) connects the Tower of London to the River Thames, and is in the poem a symbol for the barrier between conscious and unconscious minds (the images of past lives being seen as approaching from the sea of the unconscious via the river).
5.	"Images". See the note on 59 of *The Tree of Imagination*. In this poem, the "images" of past lives are "images" when their pictorial side is being stressed, but they are later found to be "symbols" with spiritual layers and are eventually understood as such (69-72).
6.	"Someone", i.e. the "I" to which the enduring soul was attached during that particular life in its long history.
10.	Ramesses II, the Great, reigned from 1304 to 1237BC.
32.	"Shining goddess". The Egyptian "Shining Ones" ("akhs") were "Light-reflecting angels" (59).
37-38.	Are far memories known during regressions dream-like fantasies – mere images – or are they actual memories? That is the dilemma.
45.	"Drift", i.e. die.
56.	"Salvage cargo from an ancient hold", i.e. make use of qualities gained in a former life's body.
60.	"Golden thread". An esoteric idea for the continuous, endless, unbroken life of the spirit in different bodies.
71-2.	"Perpetual/Renewal". The exquisite idea is that on death spirits dip back into the quantum vacuum or Void, secrete their experiences and return with the knowledge of that secretion in a new form, as new flesh, for another lifetime.
73.	"Far source", i.e. the quantum vacuum or Void where all images exist.
82-3.	Truths from the upper worlds manifest in symbolic form in the lower worlds like frost and remind of the spirit's past achievements (Beauty being the fifth sephira of the Kabbalah).
85.	"Arche-drives". Like archetypes, but with drives that press them into manifestation.
97-100.	Space-time is a fourth dimensional continuum according to the Relativity Theory. Time does not exist in our three dimensions of curved space, but is only measurable in relation to space. Vision does not involve outer space, and therefore sees a dynamic timeless present which contains eternal images, the "infinite ocean" of the

quantum vacuum or Superspace, the timeless and therefore eternal repository and source of all images. These pictorial images are also spiritual symbols (see note to 5 above).

101.　　"Theta". Delta waves (3-4 cycles per second) have been thought to be connected with "far-memory" images, but I have used theta waves (4-8 cycles) because of the link established between images and theta waves by Dr Elmer and Alyce Green of the Menninger Foundation.

107.　　"Sleep", i.e. life is a sleep.

112.　　"Traitors", i.e. men ruled by their social egos, who have not opened their "Traitors' Gate" to the Light within, which is associated with images from past lives.

A METAPHYSICAL'S LIGHT-MANDALA

First written on 29th January 1980, when stanzas 4-11 wrote themselves, and subsequently revised, e.g. on 4th May 1980. A mandala is a diagram of the soul and of the universe. The Divine Light is freed from veils within the soul and its metaphysical power is known to mystics, healers and poets in their heart centres, after which the universe is known to be one power.

　　The mandala (symbolic diagram of the universe) and the Tibetan guerilla came from Lhasa. In 1967 Tibetan patriots were fighting a running war against the Chinese occupiers, and they crossed the Himalayas on foot with works of art, traded them for guns in Katmandu, Nepal, and then walked back over the Himalayas to do battle.

8.　　　"Stupa". A replica of the tumulus of the historical Buddha (Sakyamuni), the "flesh-and-blood saint" (13), at Sanchi.

11.　　"Which is the South". The East is always shown in the south position in a mandala.

16.　　The "freedom" of the Buddha was his "parinirvana", when he was released from rebirth to dwell in endless Light.

22.　　"Dark", because spiritual.

23.　　"Metaphysical". Metaphysics is the philosophy of being and knowing, and as all Being is the Light which can be known by turning within from the five senses, it is natural to speak of a "metaphysical blaze" and a "metaphysic of Light" (96).

25-6.　　Cf 18. The soul is the universe. (Compare *Sea-Fire* 45.)

27.　　"Hole in the centre". See note to *Sea-Fire*, lines 42-48, airhole.

29.　　i.e. find the "unus mundus" or Superspace; the quantum vacuum or Void.

31.　　"Chakras", centres of energy in the Hindu subtle body.

48-64.　　In these lines *one and the same* image is seen in different terms (e.g. first as female, then as male), by the imagination. Or, to put it another way, the thing seen is interpreted in a variety of images by the imagination of the viewer.

57.　　"Four rushes", or "four surges" (66).

70-1.　　At the moment of healing, the patient's brain waves assume the pattern of the healer's brain waves. This pattern (known as "State 5") shows as the shape of a Christmas tree on Max Cade's two "mind-mirrors", brain-wave machines which monitored both healers and patients at Bruce MacManaway's clinic in Lupus Street, London.

74-5.　　"Symbols", "images". See note to line 5 of *A Temple-Dancer's Temple-Sleep*.

77.　　"Light of the World", i.e. Christ.

80.　　"Cold flame". The Light.

81.　　The "eddying" universe of the new science is fundamentally Taoist in conception. See Fritjof Capra's *The Tao of Physics*, which also deals at length with the dance of Siva (93), the dance of subatomic particles in the new physics.

93.　　"Aquarian Siva". As Lord of the Dance, Siva led the Hindu dance of creation. In the

Aquarian Age his Universalist rather than his Hindu aspect is emphasised.

95. All four elements are contained in the tide of Siva: earth (rose), fire, air (moon) and water (seas).

96. "Beauty", the heart centre (Beauty being the fifth sephira of the Kabbalah).

THE FIRE-FLOWER

The poem is about the Void of Non-Being or Tao behind the universe which swallows like a black hole and which gives out matter and souls like a womb. The image of the Fire-Flower as a black hole collapsing inwards (108) I received during contemplation on 30th March 1980. The Fire-Flower is the Void of Non-Being or Tao, and also the soul (which is a microcosmic void).

The Japanese fan has ten struts, and a design on both sides that varies gold atomic chains on a red background, and the white "swirls" described in the first stanza. The fan unites the swirling world of phenomena known to the senses (hills, clouds, waves etc.) and the atoms and Fire from which they manifested.

10. "Stone garden". The Ryoanji garden in Kyoto, Japan, which was built by Soami (1472-1525) who was influenced by Zen. ("Ryoanji" has the sense of "It has been there a long time".)

15-24. The pebbles in the stone garden are seen first as all Existence, then as one meditating soul whose pool a dropped rock can disturb, then as many hard egos becoming unconscious energy and waves and acting in brotherhood. Just as in physics a particle is also a wave, so the hard human ego is also potentially an unconscious wave of energy.

23. "Nature", i.e. their Buddha-nature, their Reality in the transcendent Light.

29. The algebraic formula was written out for me in a Japanese bar with sawdust on the floor by Junzaburo Nishiwaki, probably Japan's greatest 20th century poet and then Professor Emeritus of Keio University, at which I taught, where the "sculptured stone" (30) can be found.

31. "Implicate". See note to 103-120. (Also 93.)

34. No dancing flourished from about the 13th century. It came from bugaku, the Chinese court-dancing (see 65) which became the music of the Japanese court in the 7th century, and both were influenced by Zen, which flourished in China in the 4th and 5th centuries, and, further back, by the Tao.

40. The Flower or "yugen", the unexpected joy at a perfectly achieved beauty, comes from *Kwadensho*, printed c1600, which purports to be a treatise on No by Seami (1363-1444). *Kwadensho* or *Book of the Handing On of the Flower* refers to the handing on of the Buddha's "flower-thought" to Kashyapa, who passed it on to the Zen patriarchs, who made it a Zen idea. The Buddha picked a flower while preaching and twisted it in his fingers, and Kashyapa grasped that Truth cannot be communicated by speech or writing for it lies hidden in the heart of each person as potential Light, and can only be discovered by Zen contemplation. (See Arthur Waley's *The Noh Plays of Japan*, Allen and Unwin, 1954, p21, which also defines the symbol of the "yugen" as "a white bird with a flower in its beak" or "wild geese seen and lost among the clouds", which I have combined in 55.) "Her". This Noh actor is a male impersonating a woman.

41. "Ma" is the balance between space and silence which is central to the Japanese aesthetic. It is to be found in Japanese gardens, where Nature is refined in such a way that the apparently random creates a harmony between man and Nature through the use of space and silence. Through space and silence one discovers one's personality and its negative side, the emptiness which leads to truth. Ma is also to be

43.   found in Noh. The concept is linked to the "yugen".

43.   "Falling leaves". The Japanese autumn sadness ("mono-no-aware") contrasts with the ritual spring viewing of cherry blossom.

46.   "Stone torch-baskets". The "ishi doro" or stone lantern to be found in Japanese, and particularly Zen, gardens.

48.   "Aaaaaaah". The Zen sigh of enlightenment.

64.   "Intellect". See note to *Fire-Void*, line 24.

65-9.   These lines are based on observation. I was a guest of the Japanese Imperial Family at bugaku in Tokyo in 1967, when there were two flame shields in the ring, and four dancers. I saw the Egyptian Temple-Dancers of Dennis Stoll in London in July 1977, and as one of them has confirmed to me, the four dancers themselves felt transported into a world of soul while they performed the ancient dances of Luxor.

76-9.   I saw the "head-shaven youths" beaten for failing "koans" or riddles during a visit to the meditation centre in Ichikawa City (see Notes to *Glimpses of Purification*) which was arranged by my former colleague, the late Zen authority Dr R. H. Blyth.

79.   "Quick", "alive" as well as "hasty".

103-120.   The Fire-Flower is the creative Void behind the universe, the Non-Being which produces Being through the Fire. According to the modern physics of the quantum theory, and of Bohm, the universe (macrocosm) is implicate (void-like energy) and explicate (fullness, matter) at the same time. The soul (microcosm) is also void, and fullness when manifested into form. Thus the Fire-Flower is an image of the full soul's knowledge of its own original nature in the swirling universal void of Reality, to which it still belongs and into which it will return, i.e. the microcosm is the macrocosm.

120.   "Which is". Compare the note to 45-7 of *Pear-Ripening House*. The full soul "is a part of, and therefore is" the vast void, i.e. soul and universe are one metaphysical Reality.

BEAUTY AND ANGELHOOD, 1981

INTRODUCTION

These notes are to help the reader find the metaphysical depths beneath the surface of the poems.

The four poems correspond to the four worlds in the Kabbalah: the physical, psychological, spiritual and divine worlds. Thus, the first poem starts in the physical world, the second progresses to the psychological world, and so on. In addition, each poem/world corresponds to one item in each of the following quaternities: body, psyche, spirit and the divine spark/flame; Lovers, Teachers, Masters and Angels; and the images of desert rose, tree, mine and flame. Thus, the first poem features body, Lovers and desert rose, and so on. The fourth world of the fourth poem, the divine world, is the origin of the Divine Light and Angels. In each poem, each of the ten stanzas can be thought of as a Kabbalastic sephira. Otherwise, the use of the Kabbalah can be understood by the general reader.

The central figure in three of the four poems is the remarkable Canon of Coventry Cathedral, Peter Spink, and the poems draw on an exciting meeting with him, a vague invitation to teach within his Order, a visit to his Comunity, a difference of opinion as to the emphasis of his growing movement, and a parting. It must however be stressed that they are poems using poetic licence to state their theme, rather than precise historical records. The theme running through all four poems is the clash between the traditional-reformist and progressive-revolutionary attitudes prevalent in religion today. This is also the clash between the mystic tradition and evolutionary optimism, i.e. the optimistic progressive belief (founded on Rudolf Steiner and Teilhard de

Chardin) that the next stage of evolution will inevitably transform the consciousness of *all* mankind *to one and the same level*, an unlikely eventuality that allows for a new interpretation of mysticism and its organisation, one that totally rejects the past. This theme includes the clash between the Church and the New Age movement, which is symbolised in images that contrast dry land and Aquarian floods or waters.

All four poems were drafted in London and revised in Cornwall. Hence the West Country images in each poem. These images contrast Tree-rock heights and watery depths. Height and depth are mirror images, and as "the way up and the way down are one and the same" (certainly on the Kabbalistic Tree of Life), the watery depths of the first and third poems are really the submerged heights of the second and fourth poems, neo-monastic Aquarian waters having destroyed the dry land and fiery air of traditional "life in the world". The final West Country image of Smeaton's tower represents the triumph of the dry land of tradition over the destructive waters of Aquarius the water-pourer, and of the New Age.

These poems attempt *a redefinition of man's identity*, which has four interconnected parts: body, mind (including soul), spirit and divine spark or flame. Contrary to the teachings of Humanism (ie the anthropocentric Humanism that has prevailed since the Enlightenment, which was in fact a Darkness, not the theocentric Humanism of the Renaissance), a human being is not complete until he has developed and purged his spirit into the divine spark and Angelic flame that sees the whole universe as having the unity of One Fire.

HIGH LEIGH

Written in May 1981. Also "Highly". High Leigh is at Hoddesdon, Herts. The poem is about a new esoteric Christianity of the Fire or Light, experience of which in meditation renews the soul. The poem emphasises the mystical experience in terms of the physical body. The central idea of this poem is that the egocentric heart is a rock that is shaped, by the "Saharan wind" of the white Fire of Beauty, into a rose – a Rose of the Desert (see note to line 72).

8.	"What we're shown, i.e. the Light has already been regularly experienced.
9.	Canon Peter Spink founded the Omega Order in 1980. This Christian Order was immediately inspired by the prediction of Teilhard de Chardin that there would be a "new mysticism" based on the evolution of a transformed consciousness, and by the mystical works of F. C. Happold (the author of the Penguin *Mysticism*), especially *Religious Faith and Twentieth Century Man* which also emphasised an evolutionary spiritual leap and in particular inspired the thought in lines 11-12: the rejection of all intellectualising dogma and doctrine and the historical element of religion for the mystical experience of the Light. Happold drew on the mystical gropings of T. S. Eliot's *Four Quartets*. Canon Spink was addressing a conference on "Esoteric Christianity", and made a remarkable impact before leaving early on the evening of Saturday May 8th, 1981. His tapes on the Mystic Way were then in particular demand, and he had received no less that 125 orders from different groups of nuns.
12.	"Flesh and blood", i.e. the essence.
14.	The body and corpse are of course the Church, the backbone the dogma or doctrine.
15.	"Rock-hard". The Church is founded on a rock, but a rock-hard heart is the sign of a corpse buried in rock.
17.	"Blowing". The suggestion is that the spirit is like a wind from the sea. The New Age idea is of an "upsurge" of the spirit, which needs new forms.
18.	"Christ-tide", i.e. Light.
19-22.	The introduction of St. Michael's Mount, Cornwall, paves the way for lines 69-72. The Mount is joined to the mainland by a causeway that is covered by sea twice a day, and is thus cut off from the world of dry land.

NOTES

	Argument: Mystics meditate in all religions. You should follow your country's Mystic Way. Indians should be Hindu, Westerners Christian. New Age churches (i.e. his communities) should be the Light they preach.
22-25.	"Sea-washed", "sea-lapped". Both St. Michael's Mount and the Order are monastically cut off from the world and joined to the mystic whole (the sea connecting all countries and religions).
29.	"To bring the West/A contemplative rose", i.e. make the rock-hard Western heart a rose (see line 72).
31-32.	"Soul", "souls". The upper mind in the upper psychological world.
34.	Beauty here and in subsequent passages. Readers will be familiar with Plato's Ideas or Forms and Shelley's Neo-Platonist *Hymn to Intellectual Beauty*, which was influenced by Thomas Taylor the Platonist. Shelley's friend Keats was perhaps groping in a Neo-Platonist direction in his "Beauty is Truth, Truth Beauty". The Divine Light manifests into such a Platonist Form that can be seen by the inner eye – though not by the five senses – and all beautiful things are manifestations of it. It is also important to grasp the metaphysic of the Kabbalah, in which the fifth sephira, Tepheret, is known as Beauty, and also as heart. This is the sephira from which the Light and the divine world can be known, along with the psychological and spiritual worlds. Beauty is thus what is received in the heart, but it can also be the heart that does the receiving.
37.	"Entry to Beauty". The same ambiguity contained in line 34 is at work. The Lover's imagery conceals a serious Kabbalistic concept. One must "open" and be a "skin-bowl" (lines 34-5), i.e. enter Tepheret. One can then "get to know" Beauty from Tepheret, reflecting her like a rose. It is then possible to enter Beauty – it is possible for there to be "entry to Beauty" – through the soul and spirit which are above Tepheret. (The Kabbalah is dealt with in greater detail in the next poem).
38-40.	i.e. a storm prevents the concentration required to see Beauty.
41-8.	The priest, Kenneth Cuming – like Spink, a former Warden of Burrswood Healing Centre, Kent – quoted the Metropolitan Anthony as once referring to the bread and wine as "Spirit-bearing food", i.e. food which bears the Holy Spirit to the spirit. Stanza 6 thus emphasises the unconscious *symbolism* of Christian ritual. The "thank you" of line 41 of course translates the modern Greek "epharisto" with which "Eucharist" ("eucharistia", "thanksgiving") is connected. The "tombed ghost" of line 48, the Egyptian "ka", is a poetic equivalent for the spirit. The "ka" was in fact very different from the spirit, being the "double" that dwelt in the tomb with a body and had to be fed. The reference to ancient Egypt stresses the antiquity of the origin of the Eucharist ritual.
46.	"*Be* host". Actually become the Holy Spirit in the host or bread, so that your spirit is one with it. Also "be a host to" the Holy Spirit, which is a guest.
47-8.	"He who calls fire to Mass". The Canon, whose Masses are accompanied by a meditation that opens to the Light. Though he has gone, his teaching can be followed by considering the spiritual symbolism of the Eucharist ritual.
50-1.	In Arthurian legend, the pre-Christian Grail is a symbol for the Light, and in ancient Egypt the "gradalis" or dish was connected with its "white fire".
50-64.	Cuming held a meditation using the Lord's Prayer to "circulate the Light" in the manner of *The Secret of the Golden Flower* (the "Golden Rose"). This was the most dramatic and powerful meditation I have ever attended. Each line of the Lord's Prayer was accompanied by directions concerning the Light and then meditated on for several minutes, so the whole meditation lasted over an hour. Stanzas 7 and 8 thus emphasise *experience* rather than unconscious *symbolism*.

65.   "Beauty". Beauty as white fire which shapes the heart into its own image, and is therefore "like" as well as "in" a bare heart; also Tepheret, otherwise known as "heart" or "Beauty". (See also line 80.)

66-7.   The relationship between the mystic and the Light is a Lover's relationship, and the inner act of love of a hermit includes and reconciles both the "old" unconscious symbolism of stanza 6 and the "new" experience of stanzas 7 and 8 into traditional experience, i.e. the hermit *experiences* the traditional symbolism and renews it. "Lowered eyes" suggests the symbolism of the Virgin Mary, "white fire" the experience. The "secret place" is Tepheret, and for the "entry to Beauty" see note on line 37.

67-8.   "White fire", "tides". The *experience* of the Light as an act of love makes the paradox of "tides of white fire" a possibility. You can love the fire of the Light/a woman and be affected by its/her tides.

       "Veined rock": (1) rock with veins or fissures filled with deposited matter; (2) a rock-hard (i.e. egocentric) heart which now has veins of feeling and humanity; (3) rock being shaped into a rose (see note to line 72); (4) "veined" is also "vaned" and "rock" also has the sense of "spire" (see line 71), i.e. "weathervaned spire" with phallic suggestions.

       "Womb". The Eastern idea that Beauty, the Void, is also a Womb, the Mahayana Buddhist "Tathagata" or "Suchness".

69-71.   Height and depth are mirror images, so the heights of the new experience at High Leigh (also "highly", to be associated with the "high places" of hermits) are also to be found in the submerged depths of the mystic tradition, i.e. in the churches of Lyonesse between the sixth and twelfth centuries AD which contain the contemplative tradition of St. Augustine, Pope Gregory the Great and St. Bernard. (Conversely, the old depths are to be found within the new heights.)

       "Lyonesse". The lost land of Lyonesse sunk dramatically one winter's night nearly 900 years ago (the *Saxon Chronicle* gives the date as 11th November 1099), drowning 140 churches and its inhabitants. Legend has it that there was one survivor – a man, Trevelyan of Basil – who escaped the catastrophe by riding before the advancing waters on horseback. Most of the sunken territory is between Land's End and the Scilly Isles, and drowned houses can supposedly be seen near the Seven Stones Reef. However, some of Lyonesse was in Mount's Bay. A 13th century tradition speaks of a submerged forest in this region, and the 15th century *Itinerary of William of Worcester* speaks of submerged land between St. Michael's Mount and the Scillies. Cornish folklore has it that muffled church bells are now heard tolling beneath the waves off Newlyn and Mousehole. I spent a day at sea on a Newlyn crab-fishing boat on 17th August 1981. I was twelve miles out in Mount's Bay with fishermen from Porthleven, where coral found in the Bay is sold in shops.

       "Tristan". Lyonesse is linked with the 6th century Tristan, the lover of Iseult of Ireland who was betrothed to his uncle, King Mark of Cornwall. According to Malory's 15th century *Morte d'Arthur*, Tristan's native land was Lyonesse, but Tristan is probably associated with Leonois, or Saint-Pol-de-Léon in Brittany, where he died. I have preserved Malory's tradition. Mark is named on a stone found near his wooden hall at Castle Dore, and now standing at the Four Turnings, Fowey. Tristan's "bare-hearted" secular love is an image for the divine love of lines 65-7.

       The fishermen "thrill" partly because the unconscious symbol of line 70 becomes a direct experience in line 71, but mainly because they are reminded that just as the old Christian forms and tradition (the 140 Lyonesse churches which were once on dry land) cannot be utterly destroyed by the sea – the past may be drowned like the submerged churches, but it is still there, influencing the present – so the contemporary Christian forms and tradition cannot be destroyed by the Aquarian waters of the New Age. The "new" experience of stanzas 7 and 8 is very valuable, but it merely takes us back to the way hermits *experience* the traditional symbolism, back to *traditional experience*.

72.   "Desert rose": (1) a rose, the flower, that grows in the desert; (2) a woman, in the sense of "an English rose", i.e. a female desert hermit; (3) the rose of the rosy cross of Rosicrucianism, which is linked to the Kabbalah and lurks behind this stanza and this poem; (4) a member of a desert esoteric cult – to this day they ask on the banks of the Nile "What rose do you wear?" i.e. "To what esoteric sect do you belong?"; (5) principally, the "Rose of the Desert", the Saharan rock which is shaped or veined into a rose by the desert wind. I brought some of this strange rose-like rock back with me from Ghadames, in the Libyan Sahara.

Here, just as the tide shapes coral into a Rose of the submerged Desert, and just as the Saharan wind shapes rock into a Rose of the Desert, so the tide-wind of the spirit (Beauty) shapes the heart into a Rose (compare lines 54, 68).

"Beauty". As in line 65, "Beauty" is *both* the white fire that shapes the heart into its own image (and is therefore "like" as well as "in" a bare heart); *and* the heart that is shaped (Tepheret, or Beauty). "Like a desert rose" can therefore go with both "I" and "you", i.e. "Like a desert rose I found my shaper Beauty" or "I found what Beauty shaped in its own image like a desert rose".

74.   "Veined Rose", i.e. shaped heart. This is the Viennese artist Margaret Riley, the painter of St. Teresa of Avila and the mystic who appeared in *A Mystic Fire-Potter's Red Sun-Halo*. Though the relationship between the mystic and the Light is a Lover's relationship, the mystic occupies a bare desert of sensual deprivation, like Margaret Riley's deliberately chosen "desert" in a barely furnished flat in Shoreham, Sussex. The prayers of this modern contemplative appear to have affected Cambridge, in so far as an announced intention has been succeeded by a result, and her rosary seems to have affected a court case. She appears here as a hermit who is a member of the Catholic Church.

78.   "Shaped". Poets *shape* inner experience and readers hear an echo of their own inner experience, and recognise it. To make a start on the mystic life is one thing, to shape that start, and get it into perspective, is quite another thing.

80.   i.e. in Tepheret, where the white fire of Beauty shapes the bare "rock" of a hermit's heart into a rose.

The "new form" of the meditation using the Lord's Prayer has taken us back to the prayer of the traditional Church hermit, though its Light was patently not experienced during the "old form" symbolism of the Eucharist (lines 41-5). So far, the conflict between old and new has been inconclusive. Both routes achieve the Light.

HAWKWOOD

Hawkwood College is at Stroud, Gloucestershire. The old monastery wall is 12th century. The experiential seminar on the practice (as opposed to the teaching) of the Kabbalah of Jewish mysticism took place from May 29th to 31st, 1981.

This second poem concentrates on the psychological images that are received on the Mystic Way. The central idea of this poem is that the psychological mind is water in which images are reflected from the Tree of Life, and that delusion can take place unless the climb up the Tree is continued. ("Hawkwood" suggests the soaring of a hawk up into the Tree.)

9. The Tree of Life is reputed to go back to Abraham although it was not written down until the 12th century AD. It is here inverted, the seed of the divine source, which is both "sun" and "nut" (see note to line 10), being rooted in the heavens as when a horse chestnut tree is seen mirrored in water. Its trunk and branches are the spiritual world spreading down into the buds of the psychological world and the world of physical manifestation. Thus Beauty descends through four worlds.

10. "Nut". The idea that the origin of everything is a nut is a Kabbalistic idea from the 1270s. It found its way into the *Zohar* ("*Sefer ha-zohar*", "Book of Splendour", literally "Radiance"), the classic Kabbalah work presumed to have been written c1275 by Moses de Léon. There mystics are spoken of as people who have "penetrated to the kernel" (1.154b). The idea probably originated with de Léon's friend, the Spanish Joseph Gikatilla, whose *Nut Orchard* is behind both the *Zohar* and Dante's "radiantly bright" "infinitesimal Point" in *Paradiso* (c1318-21). Julian of Norwich reflected the idea in the course of her sixteen visions of 1373, when she saw a hazel nut that was "all that is made". Here the idea is applied to the more familiar conker, and the first seed, the origin of all, is both sun and conker-nut.

11. "Forms". Archetypal Forms, of Plato's Forms.

12. "Lake". I particularly recall an experience in the gardens of Worcester College, Oxford, on a clear fine day in the spring of 1959. (I believe it was 2nd March.) I had received an important letter from my father which opened the way for my destiny, and I took it down to the lake before breakfast. No one was about, and, feeling a very strong impression of the future ahead, I was suddenly totally absorbed in the image of an inverted chestnut tree in the lake. It seemed to grow out of the sky and reach down to earth. I have been haunted by that tree ever since, and over the years have been amazed to find it pictured in books that deal with the Kabbalistic tradition.

14-16. In the fifth sephira, Tepheret (or Beauty or heart), contact can be made with the psychological, spiritual and divine worlds. Direct contact can be made with the divine worlds, as in *High Leigh*, without going through the psychological world, the "leafy world" of line 25. So although mystics have no need to experience the psychic, archetypal unconscious images which are spiritual and divine in origin, and which feature in stanza 4 and 5, nevertheless wise mystics can tell whether images are in fact spiritual and divine (i.e. cosmic), or merely psychological, fantasised day-dreams which come from the physical world.

14. "Hermit's eye", i.e. Tepheret. (See end of *High Leigh*.)

15-16. "Images", "candles". The flowering chestnut candles will of course become the fruit, the "spiked nut-cup" of line 68. The whole poem is really about the difference between "unconscious images" and fantasised "day-dreams".

17. "Reflected", i.e. inverted ("sky-rooted") and reflected or mirrored as in water; but also a copy, i.e. a diagram.

18. The goat-bearded teacher was Warren Kenton, alias Z'ev ben Shimon Halevi.

20. Neshamah, the psychological soul, which is of the psychological world. Ruah, the spiritual soul, which is of the spiritual world. (Also in line 73.)

23. "We are like water". Modern subatomic physics has found that a particle can also be a wave. Similarly, human beings can be static, solid, rock-like egos; or dynamic power in soul and spirit.

Again New Age techniques are seen in terms of water. Here the churning round makes all in the circle aware of their watery selves, in which images can be reflected.

25. "Mirror", i.e. imagine. "Leafy world", the psychological world.

26-30. Although these lines record an actual vision, the Roman baths may well have been suggested by Sabratha in Libya, which I have visited several times. This ruined

Roman town has many mosaic floors which are open to the sky and but a tessera's throw from the sea. The Magna Mater mosaic from Justinian's Basilica could almost be a peacock and lyre, and the haunting 2nd century AD head of Neptune from the baths of Oceanus is similar to the head of Christ in some ways.

27.   "Hopscotch". The sephirot were often arranged into the pattern children now use in their hopscotch games, to make a kind of maze.

28.   "Crown". Keter or Crown is the tenth and top sephira; but the crown of the head is also referred to, along with the crown of thorns.

The Jesus is the mystical, not the historical, Christ. The distinction is important.

32.   The Jewish Merkava mysticism sought to experience Ezekiel's vision of the chariot of fire in the first centuries AD.

35.   "Nothings", of Donne's "Some lovely glorious nothing I did see" in *Aire and Angels*.

40.   Lucifer, an image of the shadow behind the ego, i.e. the alter ego, according to practical Kabbalah. Lucifer was an Angel who fell from the seventh heaven, and is the adversary all meet on the Way. The gales are of course within the vision.

43-8.   St. Peter's Grange has a head of Henry VIII as a boy on one of its walls. Henry VIII eventually visited the "Abbot's House" in 1535, and dissolved it in 1540. The monks returned there in 1928, and only moved out to the new Abbey in 1972. The commercial activities of Prinknash monks also include a bird farm (line 48). The Prinknash stanza contrasts the practical Kabbalah with the Catholic mystical tradition of the Church. (NB. "Prinknash" rhymes with "spinach".)

49.   The "inner teacher" has an outer correspondence to "the Teacher" (line 18).

58.   "Magic water", i.e. the magic circle where power flows like water (see lines 21-2).

61-4.   The spiritual and divine origin of some of the images is being doubted. They may be psychological day-dreams which originate in the physical world. They may thus have come from the shallow lake of the mind rather than from its deep sea, where the great poets fish. "Fishy" (line 62) also has the sense "of dubious character, questionable". Line 63 sums up the dilemma of all who adopt the image approach to Truth. What is seen: actual Angels or merely images of Angels? And are the images unconscious or conscious images?

64.   "Ruah's trawl", of line 20: "what is seen by the spiritual soul", i.e. divine.

65.   The Tree of Life is a valuable aid to understanding, but when it is applied to imaginings ("reflections in water"), delusion can take place if the seeker is unwary. Only this one imagining aspect of the esoteric is renounced.

67-8.   "Tree-crown". Also Keter or Crown, the tenth and top sephira. As in *High Leigh*, there is a conflict between waters and "heights".

68.   "Spiked nut-cup", i.e. the green case which splits, allowing the red-brown conker nut to peep through. Beauty is "the sun-like nut of all" (line 10), and it can be seen to be reproduced many times in all its copies in manifested "beautiful things". (See the note to line 10.)

69.   "Magic", clearly connected with water in the imagery of the poem.

70-80.   Roche rock is in Cornwall. It is a rocky crag jutting up to a height of 100 feet on which, now reached by an iron ladder, stands the ruins of a 15th century chapel to St. Michael, and above it, a hermit's cell. The hermit lived high above the world like an eagle in an eyrie. The rock, being higher than most trees, is of course a symbol for the Tree of Life. It may be connected with the story of Tristan, for it may well have been the home of Ogrin the hermit, who acted as Tristran's go-between and reconciled Iseult and King Mark.

72.   "Thy will", i.e. "thy will be done".

74.   "Four levels", of four worlds.

74-5.	"Waterfall", "Fire". Compare the note for *High Leigh* lines 67-8, where "white fire" and "tides" are connected. The experience of the Light permits it to be described in paradoxical terms as a waterfall of fire.
77.	"Turn" follows (1) "see", i.e. is imperative; and (2) "Fire", i.e. see Fire foam…and turn. All division between subject and object breaks down in Ruah's vision, and the grammar reflects this. "Nut-heights". The nearer to the divine source or "sun-like nut" one gets, the higher up the Tree one is.
78.	"Hawk's face", of the Egyptian Horus the hawk, who as son of Osiris-Ra, symbolised the Light.
80.	Man in the likeness of the Angel Michael and Divine Light.

KENT HOUSE

Kent House was in Tunbridge Wells, Kent. It was the centre of the Omega Trust, so named after Spink saw an omega window in a village church. (Cf Teilhard de Chardin's "homing in upon the Omega point", and the *New Testament* "I am alpha and omega", perhaps worlds of time and timelessness.) The Omega Order was founded in 1980, and to quote from Spink's book: "The Order takes its inspiration from the writings of two men, F. C. Happold and Teilhard de Chardin. Happold's proposition that a leap epoch is now taking place in human evolution resulting in a profound change of consciousness, and Teilhard's perception of a new Christ consciousness combine to give the Order its vision." Spink quotes the aims of the Order as: "(1) To follow those Spiritual disciplines which awaken the heart to the truth 'as it is in Jesus'. (2) To reverence Christ under all forms to the exclusion of none. (3) To encourage the new Christ consciousness wherever it is found. (4) To work for co-operation with the evolving life of the planet." The Omega Trust is fast becoming the Christian Findhorn (which Spink mentions in his book). The Edwardian House was built in 1905. The weekend retreat and course took place on 20th-21st June 1981.

This third poem focuses on the discovery of the spirit ("pneuma" as opposed to "psyche"), the "I am" which is known through silence. (Spink's book is significantly titled *Spiritual Man in a New Age*.)

The central idea of the poem is that if the heart opens, like the entrance to a mine-shaft, then the spirit (the "I am" that has lived before) is revealed deep in the unconscious like the depths of the shaft, and intuitive wisdom and understanding – Truth – can be found like tin-ore, along with memories of past lives. Although all individuals can follow the example of the great mystics and undertake the effort of making their own shaft and undergoing their own Dark Night of Sense, they are not helped by the fact that the Western heart is mucky like a pond, and disused and flooded like a Cornish tin-mine, its spirit submerged. Alternative images (flower, well) for the heart's relationship to the spirit which require little effort are rejected.

The establishment of the Community at Kent House was inspired by F. C. Happold's *Religious Faith and Twentieth Century Man* (Penguin 1966, DLT 1980), and it will be helpful to quote Happold's idea in full (pp173-6) to show the influence of T. S. Eliot and of the Iona Community. Writing of Eliot's "the point of intersection of the timeless/With time (*The Dry Salvages*), Happold asks: "How is it possible for you and me, if we wish to do so, to attain to this state of Intersection, so that it becomes a part of us, a pattern of inner life capable of gripping thought and action?…The Idea of Intersection takes on an extended form in my mind, in the dream of a Community of the Intersection coming into existence, which would express the idea in a corporate flow. It would have similarities to the Iona Community, which Dr George MacLeod founded in the Presbyterian Church of Scotland….It would include men and women of varying types, abilities and beliefs, not Christians only but also those of other faiths, scientists and humanists, artists, poets and musicians, and men of affairs. How…could such a community have any sort of homogeneity? It would not be at the intellectual level. Each member of the Community would remain at the point where he stands...until such time as he is impelled to move from it. The homogeneity would evolve at a higher level....Both by the very fact of its existence and also by its members fathering together in a quiet retreat, living in close contact for a time, engaging in corporate meditation and that sort of prayer, in which mind and spirit are thrown open to influences outside one's own limited perception, a particular sort of mutual mental sympathy and integration would develop....There come moments of intellectual illumination, with a shift of awareness and an expansion of vision, so that possibilities are seen which had not been seen before. When those who have attained this level write to each other, talk with each other or gather round a conference table, conversation and discussion are on a different plane. Ideas come together and interfuse....Out of such an intimate association of men, each eminent in his particular field and primarily engaged in his own specialism, might come those unifying concepts and integrated thought-patterns for which we are searching. Such a Community might be initiated by a small group of men and women, eminent in their particular fields, who, through a long, rich life, had matured in wisdom, understanding and mental and spiritual insight. They would quickly gather round them a group of younger men to carry on the work when they had gone. Like the Iona Community, such a Community, for its success, would need a permanent centre, a Community House, to which members of the Community could retire when they wished and in which groups of people, not members of the Community, but intent on the same quest, would come for short periods. I shall never forget the week I spent at the Abbey of Iona, with its combination of morning and evening offices, quiet meditation, lectures and discussion, swimming, dreaming and wandering. Perhaps one day a new St. Benedict will arise to found such a Community, an Order more truly catholic than anything that has yet appeared. Perhaps, more likely, it might be the work of a small group of the sort described above. Its influence could be immense."

It should be emphasised that Kent House existed within a context of "counter-cultural" community movements in America, which form a network to resist the existing Western culture, and of similar communities like Findhorn in England; and that the assertion of F. C. Happold and Teilhard de Chardin that, through a spiritual leap, the next stage of evolution will inevitably transform the consciousness or alter the awareness of mankind represents a cosmic optimism which traditional mystics, including T. S. Eliot, would find difficult to share. They knew all too well that the transformation of humanity is an impossible dream as not all spirits can end at the same level. The truth is, as Toynbee has shown, consciousness rises with civilisations and declines as they collapse into Dark Ages, when it survives in small monastic communities. If spirits do indeed help raise the consciousness of the civilisations they are born into, and are in turn raised by it, then the long-term raising of consciousness can best be served today by *defending* the West as an alternative to a coming Dark Age, rather than by resisting Western culture and bringing the Dark Age nearer.

5.　　　　　Cf the Tree of Life of *Hawkwood*.

8.　　　　　"Ionan" recalls the Iona Community (see above). "Silent prayers", i.e. communion, contemplation.

9-16.　　　The flower image shows the heart unfolding the petals from the ego and opening like a flower to the "fiery light"/sun, so that the spirit is revealed like a pistil whose ovary ripens into fruit. This is a natural image, like the well image of stanza 9 – also part of the Canon's thought – which suggests the Holy Spirit bubbles up into the soul spontaneously. These two images deny the years of effort which can go into preparing the spirit for the Light. For this reason, the central image of the poem is the mining image, which requires a shaft to be sunk, and an effort made, on the part of the Truth-seeking mystic.

　　　　　　　　The language changes from the Kabbalistic terminology of the last poem to the more Christian terminology of "the fire of love". But the ideas reiterate ideas covered in the last poem. In terms of the Kabbalah "head" refers to the first four sephirot, and "heart" to Tepheret, the fifth sephira which is in contact with the spiritual and divine worlds and is therefore the centre where body meets the "fiery Light" of the Spirit, which enters the spirit. Entering Tepheret stimulates the deeper intellect or contemplative thought, the eighth sephira which is at a totally different level from that of everyday ideas. The "silence" and "deep life" of lines 19-20 refer to that part of the Tree of Life which is between Tepheret and Keter, the tenth sephira.

11.   Spink translates St. Paul's *Epistle to the Ephesians* (1.18) as "I pray that the eyes of your *heart* may be opened, and that you may know." The Authorised Version has "the eyes of your *understanding* being enlightened; that ye may know."

    The heart is here established as the approach to the spirit. If the heart is "choked" by weeds, its centre or eye (Tepheret) will be closed, and the spirit will also be closed.

    "Opened". The chakras or centres are generally seen as being enclosed by enfolding lotus petals, which must open if their eye is to be used. The heart is here seen as the centre of a flower whose calyx is the enfolding ego.

12.   "Fiery Light". This is the "fire of love" of which most mystics speak. Here it has the effect of opening the petals of the heart-centre.

    "One glance", cf the eye being "single" in *Matthew* 6.22: "The light of the body is the eye: if therefore thine eye be single, thy whole body shall be full of light." "One" has the force of "single".

13.   "Airs pistil-ripe thought". The opened petals reveal the pistil-like spirit to the air (which is the element that dominates this poem), and the ovary of the pistil ripens into the fruit. The "thought" is thus spiritual thought, the fruit which has been brought into being as a result of repeated contact with the sun-like Light which transforms both heart and spirit. (Compare the hermit whose "eye is air" at the end of *High Leigh*.)

15.   i.e. open your heart-petals and see the spiritual sun.

16.   "Sun-warmed", opened by the warmth of the "fiery Light".

20.   "Looks", i.e. "sees", but also "appears".

21.   "Sufi tales". Especially the ones about Nasreddin.

22.   Weeding the garden was one of the tasks I was given in the Zen temple at Kita-Kamakura, Japan, which I visited. The idea is that you think about the weeds round your heart, which are choking the spirit. Purification is sometimes taught with a broom. I escaped the most drastic therapy, swabbing out the foul-smelling temple "bog", a duty reserved for those whose souls were particularly foul-smelling.

23.   Three similar communities in the past. Groote and Thomas à Kempis were associated with the Windesheim Community of the Brotherhood of the Common Life, Pascal with the community at the Convent of Port Royal, and Nicholas Ferrar and Crashaw with the Anglican community at Little Gidding, which of course inspired T. S. Eliot. All these are the "dead" of line 24.

25-48.   The image of the opened flower – with the heart as petals, spirit as pistil, and choking ideas as weeds – changes to the image of a pond, with the heart as its surface, the spirit as its depths, and choking ideas as thickets. The point is, this contemporary heart/pond is mucky and *shallow* when contrasted with the deep, water-free mine shaft of the great mystics' heart (lines 33-38), where the heart is the top of the shaft, the spirit is at the bottom, where wisdom and understanding are found like tin, and the choking ideas are flooding water. Hence the need for the pond to be "pumped dry" (line 46), though the "shaft" of line 48 is in the imagination, the assumption being that the pond is a mine. Later the image of a well is introduced, with a welling-up from the Spirit, but though it is refreshing to drink from the effortlessly welling waters of the Holy Spirit, the mined Truth – Truth mined through effort – is not available.

Though the image changes (flower, pond, mine, well) it is the deep spirit that is being explored during the silent afternoon of line 19.

25-30. The "bushes" and "thickets" are physical, emotional and intellectual (see line 42). In terms of the Kabbalah, the "still place" is Tepheret, the "stillness" (line 43) being all the Tree of Life between Tepheret and Keter or Crown. The heart is found "within" the head (line 29) when it is Tepheret behind the ego.

30. "Beyond all mind", i.e. beyond the ego.

31. "Past lives". The spirit is the part of the identity which has lived before, which Jesus referred to on the cross: "Father, into thy hands I commend my spirit" (*Luke* 23.46). Early Christianity (e.g. Origen, died 254AD) believed in reincarnation until it was rejected by the Council of Constantinople in 543AD.

32. i.e. conversation, ego's wanting and other people, the three chief distractions from the deep life.

33. "Mined", also "mind" meaning "care for", "attend to" or "look after".

33-40. Despite the deep shaft mystics cut as they emptied their ego ("rock" of line 35, cf *High Leigh*), they kept the spirit open to the air (line 38), whereas the depths of the pond are under water. The spirit in the modern pond can only see the Light murkily through "caddice sight" (line 52).

East Wheal Rose is now reached by the small Lappa Valley Railway at St. Newlyn East, near Newquay, Cornwall. This was one of the greatest mines in Cornwall, and was the scene of Cornwall's worst mining disaster in May 1854, when floods inundated 39 men and boys. The mine was improved in 1882 and became disused in 1885 at about the time (i.e. shortly after 1875) that the Light lost its previously prominent place in Western religion, culture and art. The deserted stack is 100 feet high, and the shaft is 960 feet deep. The engine-house housed a 100 inch beam engine built by Harveys of Hayle.

34. The "Dark Night of Sense" is St. John of the Cross's term for the purging of the senses and merging of the soul with the spirit ("emptying rock of earthly images"), the "Dark Night of the Spirit" being his term for the further process of purification of the spirit.

37. "Veined Truth like ore". The spirit gives access to understanding and wisdom, or Binah and Hochma, the eighth and ninth sephirot on the Tree of Life. Here the Tree of Life is seen as growing downwards into the mine shaft rather than upwards to the heights, and the treasures of the spirit are living ("veined Truth" suggesting veins that carry blood) though the image is of tin-ore.

As the spirit has lived before the lumps of tin may also be regarded as images from past lives, which are located when the spirit is contacted deep in the unconscious during hypnotic regression to past lives. (See *A Temple-Dancer's Temple-Sleep.*) The tin may also be the images which an artist discovers when he excavates his own heart. It is a strange paradox that in the course of *emptying* the heart of earthly images, an artist finds wonderful images with which to describe inner experience, almost as a by-product of his main operation.

38. "Fiery divine air". This is the Holy Spirit, or the Light, the "sunny air" which the Egyptians called the beams of Shu, and which nourishes spirit.

39. "East Wheal Rose". There are obvious ambiguities: (1) compare the rose of *High*

Leigh; and (2) "ruined Rose" suggests a whore who has done an "East Wheel", i.e. taken the way of the Eastern bargirls, and possibly (in view of the "Western" context) the way of the Eastern sects.

40.   i.e. the Western spirit is now submerged.

41-4.   The spirit is "beneath" the heart, so the gnat sees itself as being *beneath* the surface of the water, along with its reflection and with the spirit, and therefore "in" stillness rather than "on" stillness.

The gnat sees itself and the universe in reverse as it catches sight of its own image and of the universe which is reflected in the water, and as the eternal world of the reflection is the reverse of that of time, the despair of line 40 is reversed.

The gnat is beyond the reflected "cloud of delusion" of this life, which is the sense-impressions, words, ideas and thought-patterns reflected from the outer world that obscure the Light. Compare the 14th century *Cloud of Unknowing*. "This life brought", i.e. one day's cloud on the pond is equivalent to a lifetime.

42.   "Body", the physical body; "emotions" and "thought", the psychological mind. The "I am" is the spirit which is revealed by the heart (or Tepheret).

45.   "Mirror a past meaning", i.e. become your spirit and recall past lives, not just of yourself but of the West. These are recalled like a reverse image, and a new meaning of life is mirrored: a meaning given depth by the context of past lives.

"In detachment", i.e. without emotion, which is of the psychological mind.

46-8.   Compare lines 59-64, where "wet" imagery is used instead of "dry" imagery, suggesting that the problem has been seen in the wrong terms.

48.   "On shaft mud, not sky". The surface of the pond (heart) reflects the sky and "cloud" of line 44 (the outer world) and conceals the mud (the inner world of the spirit). So the wish is for the Light to enter the depths of the spirit, and not merely rest on the heart's surface. The implication is that the Light cannot dry up the muck on its own, it needs human agency to do the pumping-out. "Shaft", an ironic reference to the *shallowness* of the pond when compared to the depth of the mine.

49.   "Michael's chapel". A carving of Michael hangs in the chapel at Kent House, which uses its own very unorthodox form of service, the Michael Office.

50-5.   The imagery suggests that the contemporary spirit is impure and covered with "foul" pond-water, through which the Light can still be seen with "caddice sight" (line 52). The experience of the Light in *High Leigh* (lines 50-64) is now more fully understood: it was the "I am" or spirit that received the Light. "Brings spirit", cf "spirit-bearing food" of *High Leigh* (line 45).

55.   "Ezekiel". On the wall of the Michael chapel at Kent House is a painting of Ezekiel's vision by Sister Petra Clare, who is associated with the Order. Compare the "Merkava chariot" of *Hawkwood*. "We revere flight in all". This reverence for the potential for Light in everyone is without intensity, which is emotional (and one of the thickets). It is "in detachment" with detached agapé.

57.   "Mystic hatching". It can take twenty years to hatch from impurity to the air of spirit and the Light, and be fully divinised by it into a spark and finally the Angelic "flame". (See next poem.) There is also a hint of the need to hatch to dry land from Aquarian waters.

58.   "Poor monks", like the young Siddhartha Gautama, the Buddha.

59-64.   This progressive answer attempts to underline the corporate homogeneity of the Community at a level higher than the intellect (see the quotation from Happold above). Nevertheless it conflicts with the traditional view of the Mystic Way for it takes the side of ordinary inarticulate lay people against the Way of the great mystics of the past, whose wisdom and book-learning it rejects as intellectualised history.

This is anathema to the New Age along with doctrine and dogma, which, according to Happold, are intellectualised symbols. The answer implicitly sides with the apocalyptic New Age view that Light is being poured into individuals by the divine source at this particular time in a way that did not happen during the "Old Age", and that mysticism is different today because the mystics of the past did not have the sense of "many lives" which the New Age spiritual movement has as a result of evolution. (See the writings of Steiner, and of the Steinerian "church", the Christian Community.)

65-72.   There is a divergence of views. First Spink seems more concerned with the "corporate homogeneity" of the Community than with the experience of private individuals; more concerned with his New Age form of the future than what happened in the Old Age in the past. Secondly he seems, like St. Benedict, to be the founder of an Order that is based on "the intersection of the timeless/With time", while identifying with the New Age, rather than a transformer of the West, a remysticiser of the West.

65.   "Past effort", i.e. the Old Age, here seen as the great mystics' mine.

"Red Guard". Red Guards made their appearance in China around Lin Piao in Mao's Cultural Revolution of 1966, when I was one of the first eye-witnesses. The Cultural Revolution aimed to smash much of the past.

68.   The distinction between an Old (Piscean i.e. Christian) Age and the New (Aquarian) Age is not accepted, nor is the date of its changeover (c2000AD), though we are undoubtedly moving from a Humanist Age to a Metaphysical Age (or, to put it another way, from an anthropocentric Humanism back to a theocentric Humanism) in accordance with the diagnosis of T. E. Hulme in *Speculations*, and are therefore undergoing a Counter-Renaissance. There is merely the flow of history and tradition.

69.   i.e. Spirits are not equally pure. They may be equal before God, in the same way that individuals are equal before the Law, but they are all at different levels of development and purification by the Light, which leads individuals at different times to the divinised sense that all is a oneness. (See next poem.) Spink is looking for Happold's "homogeneity" rather than at the differences between individual spirits.

70.   "New wells". His "new form", his Communities. The "welling-up" within the Kent House Community is unsought and effortless, and, as the image suggests, does not involve "mining" and lacks the "ore". The implication is that the Communities are alternative societies awaiting an alternative "New Age", and will not have an impact on the West, although in his book Spink emphasises that no "alternative religion" is considered.

71-2.   "New Age dogma". There is a new, alternative dogma within the New Age's rejection of old dogma, and it is founded on the unproved ideas that (1) the next stage of evolution will transform the consciousness of all without effort, (2) the year 2000AD will see a totally different New Age in which everything will have changed from what is was under the Old Age, (3) all have an equal chance of instant illumination regardless of how little or much effort they have put in, and (4) man is perfectible, a restatement of the Pelagian heresy and of the Romantic error (as T. E. Hulme argued in a much maligned and much misunderstood essay in *Speculations*) which puts man on a par with God rather than subordinating him to the Light (as does the Augustinian religious attitude and Classicism). Such unfounded optimism rejects the existing world and will have nothing to do with it, preferring alternative communities. The question asked here is whether the New Age will learn from Michael, its patron saint, and apply itself to ameliorating the status quo.

"Learn from their Angel and cleanse". Kent House, using the Michael Office,

	shares its appeal to Michael with the whole New Age movement. Michael watches over the world and wishes to ameliorate it. *He* does not bury his head in the sand.
72.	"Cleanse", i.e. pump muck from.
73.	"All", "all people" but also "everything".
73-80.	The mine image triumphs over the pond and well images, and "fiery Light" and air triumph over water.
74-5.	Two hopes are expressed, that the Church service will be reformed to include contemplation of the Light, and that the Light will be the decisive factor in Ecumenism, as it is the "candle" all sects have in common.
77.	"St. Benedict's vision". See the end of the quotation from Happold, above. St. Benedict founded the Benedictine Order in the 6th century AD.
78.	"Mine Europe to meaning", i.e. give Europe the meaning of a heart and spirit being opened and Truth being brought to the surface like ore.
78-9.	"Lost". The Age has lost its way like a child, has lost its direction. Line 80 indicates how the direction can be recovered.
80.	"Look west", (1) to the sun as a symbol of the Light, (2) as a vocative, "Look o West", (3) look to West Country Cornwall and the flooded shaft of East Wheal Rose, and (4) look at the decline of the West (the setting of Beauty). Despite this warning of a "setting" of the traditional values of civilisation which are based on Beauty, there is an indirect appeal for a pumping-out of the impurity that fills the Western heart today, and for a return to the mystic tradition of the Light. Both the diagnosis and the cure of the Western complaint are therefore contained in this line.

ST. PETER'S CONVENT

St. Peter's Convent is in Woking, Surrey. There is a life-sized, haloed statue of St. Peter outside the Chapel. A hundred years ago there were 100 nuns in the Convent, and the drop to 26 has created unused space, and explains why the nuns were ready to rent Canon Peter Spink part of the Convent for the meeting on 18th July 1981, at which some sixty people approved a new direction for the Omega Trust.

This fourth poem deals with those who, through repeated contact with the Light or Christ-Light, have so fired and purified their spirits in the "Dark Night of Spirit" that they have been "divinised" into "sparks", and, being fanned into flames, see the universe and mankind as having the oneness or unity of one Fire.

The central idea of the poem is that a divinised Angel, whose "flame" is like that of a Mithraeum or crypt dug out with effort (depth) or a lighthouse tower (height), sees both himself and the whole world as one Fire, which is symbolised in the sanctuary lamp. This signals that the Eucharist is in the tabernacle, i.e. the Presence, and is therefore associated with the sacrifice which is the Mass, and it is a "Grail-gold" flame covered with blue glass which veils its true nature from the world.

1.	"Showdown", between the traditional-reformist and progressive-revolutionary attitudes to religion.
8.	i.e. this is a dying community.
9.	"Excavate", "dig out soul leaving a hole (which is the spirit)".
9-11.	"Mithraeum", "caves". The worship of Mithras probably dates from c1700BC and certainly predates c1500BC, when Indo-Europeans migrated from Iran to the Indus Valley. Then Mithras took the side of the Sun in helping the god of light, Ahura Mazda, in his battle with the powers of darkness under Angra Mainyu or Ahriman. Mithras soon became the genius of celestial light, and in Roman times the central mystery concerned the battle between light and darkness for the neophyte's soul.

Initiation into the cult took place in mountain caverns or in subterranean vaults or crypts, where the neophyte descended. An inextinguishable fire burned in a lamp in the hearth of the Mithraeum, a cult of fire that symbolised Mithras's Light. This fire also burned in a lamp in the Caesars' palace, for the Caesars were incarnations of Mithras's Light.

Here, the excavating of spirits (cf "spirits dug out like caves, line 15) links the "mine" image of Kent House to the "flame" image of this poem. The nuns dig shafts into their spirits that open into the subterranean vaults of a Mithraeum, where a flame burned. They have dug themselves out and then placed a light lit by Beauty in their deep place.

10.	"Beauty, which sparks". All sparks in the spirit and thus the soul come from Beauty.
11.	"Lamps". The lamp goes back to the roots of Indo-European civilisation. Besides being present in the crypts of Mithras, the eternal fire burned on the fire altars of the Zoroastrians, where it was housed in a metal urn. There was a lamp near the Holy of Holies in the Temple of Solomon, and according to chapter 24 of the *Koran*, Allah's "light can be compared to a niche that enshrines (or wherein is) a lamp" "within a crystal or glass of star-like brilliance", which is lit "from a blessed olive tree". (The spirit in the *Koran's* image is like an olive tree or Tree of Life that produces olives which provide oil for the lamp, the divine flame.) Compare also the "ishi doro" or "stone torch-basket", the stone lamp found in Japanese Zen gardens which represents the Light, and which I have used in earlier works.
12-19.	"Saturday Feria" were celebrated at 1 p.m., the psalms being 53, 56 and 57.
12.	"Dark flames". Angels are creatures of Light whose bodies have been transformed by the Light into a flame-like texture. Their bodies are at their densest or darkest when they are born to earth and take on fleshly form. (See also "dark" in line 21.)
14.	"Age". "Generation" or "era", but also "youth".
15.	"Spirits made flames who see One Fire". Their spirits have been turned into sparks and then fames of the fourth world, so they see the whole universe as having the unity of one fire. The nuns have achieved the vision of oneness in this life or in past lives. (See also line 70.)
16.	"Sanctuary's blue lamp-cage". The "lamp-cage" is the sanctuary lamp which has been part of all Catholic churches since the 16th century. It signals the presence of the Eucharist in the tabernacle on the altar (which itself goes back to the martyrs' tombs in the early catacombs), but is also a symbol of the Presence of God as Light in the church. Hence the appropriateness of a sanctuary lamp as an image for the divine life. The eternal flame in the lamp is the colour of a worldly candle, but in this Convent (and other convents) it is darkened into a blue or violet, the colour of eternity, by the glass on the sides of the lamp, which is also a cage. The darkening and caging make an ambiguous image that suggests at one and the same time (1) the imprisoning of the soul in the body, which darkens it, i.e. the blue is a false rather than a real colour, and the divine flame appears differently to the world, as if seen "through a glass darkly"; and (2) the imprisoning of the soul in the Convent walls, i.e. the blue is the real colour of eternity and the nuns are worldly flames whose surroundings make them shine the colour of eternity. "Cage" is thus "a portable prison of wire or bars", but also "a frame for hoisting and lowering when mining".

"The flame" is of course the "One Fire" the nun sees – "flame" is thus singular as opposed to the "candles" of line 17, which considers the flames of the individual nuns – and the lamp is a symbol for Beauty, which is the Oneness behind creation.

17.	The transition from flames in "dug out caves" to candles in Smeaton's tower is one from depth to height.

17-18.	"Smeaton's tower", at one time the Eddystone Lighthouse 15 miles out to sea, was built between 1756 and 1759. John Smeaton, the civil engineer, based it on the shape of an oak tree, and it had a granite exterior. (It was of dovetailed Portland stone within, a new technique like the use of limestone and clay mortar under water.) It was originally lit with candles, and it appeared on pennies from George II until recent times, behind Britannia who ruled the waves. It was thus a patriotic symbol. In 1811, Argand lamps and reflectors replaced the candles, and in 1884, its rocky foundations having been undermined by the waves, Smeaton's tower was dismantled and re-erected on Plymouth Hoe, where it may be climbed today. On the inside, carved on the curved wall, visitors can read evidence of Smeaton's trust in God: "Except the Lord built the house, they labour in vain that build it. Laus Deo." Smeaton's tower did its job for 125 years, resisting strong winds and tides far longer than its predecessor, Winstanley's tower, which lasted only seven years. (It was erected in 1696 and disappeared in 1703 along with Winstanley and the keepers.) Smeaton was the builder of the solid granite walls of St. Ives' pier, which is still known as Smeaton's pier, and soon afterwards, just before his death, he planned the building of Charlestown harbour with Charles Rashleigh.

The idea here is that as candles magnified into two beams turn the oak-shaped lighthouse into a cross, so the nuns' flames, magnified into two beams, turn the Tree of Life, which they have climbed to the top, into a Christian cross. The Convent is thus seen as a lighthouse, and all the nuns/candles in it, together with the two beams, are seen as the "One Fire" of line 15 by passing "ships" on the Aquarian waters. "Beam", "beam of light" but also a "beam of timber" across a cross.

21.	Both (1) the nuns serve those who are dying and the blue sanctuary light, and (2) the nuns are Angels who are rescuing the blue sanctuary light which is dying.
24-7.	Betty James presented her idea of a "dance of consciousness", 'Programme towards the Education of the Christ-Mind'. In her conception, the stance of personality changes between correspondence courses, which are solitary, and training weekends, which are social. The intake would be half-yearly, and five courses and five weekends (including the teaching of healing) would result in commitment to the Omega Order.

Such a programme was a far cry from the conception of Happold (see the beginning of the notes for *Kent House*). Some of those present felt it was too planned.

28.	Burrswood Healing Centre in Kent, whose former Wardens include Kenneth Cuming (the priest of *High Leigh*) and Peter Spink. "Heartburn". Beauty "burns" the heart in traditional mystical literature (e.g. St. John of the Cross), but after the planned programme of courses and weekends there will be no place for Beauty, which will be unwanted.
29.	The poem wins through to a view of "what God wants".
33.	i.e. working through the existing religion and institutions of the Old Age, not creating new alternative religious communities to await a hitherto unarrived New Age. As there is a Christian Kabbalah, any movement to incorporate the Tree of Life into Christianity is a reform movement "within the Church".

"A Steiner cult", i.e. a Steiner-like cult. Spink has some affinities with Theosophy and Rudolf Steiner's Anthroposophy, to which he refers several times in his book *Spiritual Man in a New Age*.

37.	The Western crisis has been stated by Happold (*Religious Faith and Twentieth Century Man*, DLT pp177-78) in progressive, *evolutionary* terms. On this view, the West has lost the need for a conventional religion because its old foundations,

images of God and models have shattered as a result of the new science. The West therefore now has a sense of emptiness, aridity and desolation that amounts to a corporate Dark Night. This, however, can lead to a greater spiritual maturity, a *going forward*: an evolutionary mental and spiritual leap which enlarges human consciousness, widens perception and causes growth in the soul (i.e. a movement up the Kabbalistic Tree of Life on the part of all mankind). A more *traditional* view will see the West as being rightly dissatisfied with conventional religion and forms, which are dominated by an erroneous anthropocentric Humanism that betrays the mystic tradition, but as finding its way *back* to the tradition of the Light which has always been there throughout the last 5,000 years. On this traditional view, if Christianity is undergoing a new "evolution", it is to return to the true mystic tradition.

38.   i.e. for churches to embody the Light and teach ways to find it so that the young do not turn to Eastern sects. The image of the Church as lighthouse – a spire with "two-flamed beam" – is close to the Tree of Life/cross image of lines 17-18, and the "waveswept" suggests that the Church should "beam" the Light across Aquarian waters.

39.   "Are rocked" suggests that the young (1) are rocked from side to side on the Aquarian waters in the direction of Eastern sects, (2) are wrecked on the rocks of Eastern sects, especially on sects like the sect of Bhagwan Shree Rajneesh, which are really cults, and (3) have their egocentric "rocks" shaped into roses (cf *High Leigh*) in the East rather than in the West.

40-6.   The West's Counter-Reformation awaits a man of the stature of the leader of the Reformation or of the Methodist movement within the Church of England, which became a sect without breaking away from Christianity.

41.   "I must speak out". The following lines reflect the Angelic task referred to by the Inner Teacher of *Hawkwood*, and the words are not spoken from the head but from the divinised thought which is stimulated by the heart (the "pistil-ripe thought" of *Kent House* line 13). In terms of the Tree of Life, this originates in Hochma and Binah, Wisdom and Understanding, which are just beneath Keter or Crown.

42.   "Lowers", "frowns" but also "becomes more low" or menacing.

42-4.   There is an appeal for a revival of the mystic heights and for a strengthening of Europe's ideology in preparation for its coming conflict with Communism, which is the cause of the darkness.

44-6.   A quartz flint, struck by steel, readily produces a spark. The quartz is the vision of the great mystics which has been "mined" (see *Kent House* line 35) or acquired in the subterranean crypts of a Mithraeum, and the steel is discipline, or, in the nuns' case, a Rule. Kindling of the spirit requires the action of both the example of the great mystics and a discipline or Rule. Although some spirits can achieve illumination by sheer perseverance through example and discipline, "waiting on God", and although all illumined spirits anyway ultimately owe their illumination to Beauty (see note to line 10), illumination mostly takes place when Beauty providentially sends a spark (the Dominican "scintilla") direct into a ready or purged soul and spirit, one that is usually already aware of great mystics and already disciplined, and it is the providential illumination the Canon is thinking of in lines 54-6. All those who eventually become Angels are undoubtedly providentially chosen by Beauty.

The idea that great mystics spark the masses accords with the Toynbeean view of history in which élites inspire the masses, who imitate by "mimesis". Marxist theory of course sees the masses as inspiring élites (cf line 55).

47.   "One Fire, Beauty's blue Flame". Both (1) the Oneness of creation is symbolised by the blue flame in the sanctuary lamp, which also represents Beauty, and (2) the Oneness of Beauty appears to the human eye in a different form from that which it really is, like the blueness of a sanctuary lamp. The "sparks" of line 46 are "parts" of the One Fire, and of Beauty, which sparks all to flame (see line 10).

49-58. Again there is a divergence of views. Like St. Benedict, the Canon has founded an Order which, like the Iona Community, attempts to recapture the mystical experience, the intersection "of the timeless/With time" (see the quotation from Happold at the beginning of the *Kent House* notes), and he is not immediately concerned to transform Europe like a Luther or a Wesley. The dream has turned sour because it wanted the Order to be something it was never going to be, i.e. an opportunity to implement the Angelic task stated by the Inner Teacher in *Hawkwood*, whereas the Canon's interest in Theosophy, Anthroposophy and the New Age has made him something of a Steiner who is not really concerned to save the "Old Age", i.e. Western civilisation.

50.   "Pour". Spiritual sources have predicted that the New Age of Aquarius, the water-pourer, will bring tidal waves with it that will destroy much of Western civilisation before the end of this century. On Toynbee's analysis of history, the collapse of Western civilisation would be followed by a Dark Age. The New Age movement is hostile to the institutions of Western civilisation, including the Church, and is working for this Dark Age (Yeats' "rough beast" which is "slouching towards Bethlehem to be born"). The New Age floods would have the effect of drowning the "fires" of Western civilisation's mystic tradition, and leaving a Dark Age in which knowledge of the past would be scanty.

52.   Revolutions destroy or drown the past and, as "turnings-round", reverse and change its direction, whereas reforms, or "formings-again", restore the past. The anti-bourgeois Chinese Cultural Revolution of 1966 and the anti-Western Libyan Revolution of 1969, both of which I witnessed, both sought to destroy or drown in order to reverse directions. Here the argument is that there should be no destruction and reverse of the mystical tradition or the Church, but rather a "forming again" of it that still honours the past. I would comment in passing that sometimes there has to be a revolution before there can be a reform. So anthropocentric Humanism needs to be "reversed" before its Metaphysical alternative can be restored.

53.   The task given by the Inner Teacher in *Hawkwood*.

54-6.   i.e. the Canon will not plan so that God can guide. The starting-point with the spirit is "here", where each is now, and he will be led by the masses and their anti-intellectual level. This confession that Omega is not sufficiently advanced for the great mystics represents an indirect backing away from the remysticisation of Christendom in favour of a New Age movement that proliferates communities as alternatives to churches.

57.   "Under the tower". The religious attitude, according to T. E. Hulme, shows man as subordinated to God, in contrast to the "perfectible" Humanist man who is under nothing.

61.   "Terrify". The tasks of Angels "terrify" because of the self-sacrifice, dedication and menial service involved, and because of the awesome demands on their spirit which makes their lives possible. Angels have reached awesome depths or heights of spirit. Compare Rilke, "Every Angel is terrible" ("Ein jeder Engel ist schrecklich", 1st *Duino Elegy*).

62-5.   Lovers, Teachers, Masters and Angels dominate the four worlds of the Kabbalah, of the body, mind (or soul), spirit and divine spark or flame. Angels, humans who have been divinised into flame by the Light of the fourth world, care for all four parts of man (including the two immortal parts, spirit and spark/flame) during their lives, whereas Lovers, Teachers and Masters care for parts of him rather than for his whole.

65-8. This very metaphysical stanza draws on early Christianity's belief in reincarnation until 543 AD. Beauty in the fourth world creates Angels like peers as a reward for obtaining purity of spirit and being fired into sparks and later flames by repeated contact with the Light. Hence Beauty creates Angelhood and is an "Angel-Maker". This view of Angels accords with the vision in *Hawkwood* (lines 32-8). Angels form a kind of "upper House" in Heaven, which they leave to be born in order to carry out specific tasks on earth, and to which they return on death when their tasks are accomplished and their Angelhood has been confirmed. The returning flames always include some who were not Angels when they were born, but achieved Angelhood during their most recent life. It is worth noting in passing that the Light, like the "spirit-bearing food" of *High Leigh* line 45, changes the texture of the body, so that it comes to be less dense in Angels than in the rest of mankind.

66. "Damp". Earthly "damp" would of course put out the "flame" of line 67. Hence the need for it to be veiled from all damp earthly things.

68. "Grail-gold" recalls the experience of the Light in *High Leigh* (line 50), which is now fully understood. Thus: as a reward for spirits that are flamed a Grail-gold colour, i.e. that are made gold in the fourth world. "Flamed" also recalls "flamen", "a god's priest". "Beauty's blue lamp". The sanctuary lamp veils or distorts gold flames into a blue, so that their outer appearance differs from their inner reality.

69, 72. A synthesis. God's Providence presides over all conflicting attitudes and points of view, all of which have a part in the whole. God renews institutions through movements which being *outside* them, and which find their way inside. So the renewal of the Church takes place *outside* the Church initially, and the new energy will later find its way into the Church. God therefore needs the initiative of the Canon and of the whole New Age movement (including such fringe groups as the Steinerian Christian Community), which He is also using, *as well as* its channelling into the traditional Mystic Way (the "old" of line 71). The New Age movement and the tradition are two different emphases within the same process.

  God wants the Christian tradition to be renewed and restored. He does not want it to be swept away and destroyed by a new Dark Age.

69. "Veiled outside". Both (1) veiled and outside the Church, and (2) with their outside veiled like the sanctuary lamp. The renewing is thus conducted outside the Church by Angels who are almost in disguise, and it is later imported into the Church.

70. Nuns, sparks who become flames and are one fire, see "One Fire" (i.e. all souls as part of one soul) and open their hearts to souls (i.e. minds who have not yet achieved spirithood or the spark of Angelhood).

73. "Accept". The feeling is that the Church will absorb the Canon's initiative, and that the remysticisation of Christendom is taking place.

  "'Cripples'", i.e. head-ruled people who have never known Tepheret or the Light.

75. "Michael" "in Mount's Bay". In the 14th century Priory Chapel on St. Michael's Mount, Cornwall (which was dependent on the Benedictine Abbey of Mont St. Michel in Normandy until it was seized and given to the Brigittine Abbey of Syon at Twickenham), there hangs a late 15th century gilt brass chandelier which shows St. Michael slaying the Dragon. The reference is to *Revelations* (12.7-9): "And there was war in heaven: Michael and his angels fought against the dragon....And the great dragon was cast out, that old serpent, called the Devil, and Satan, which

deceiveth the whole world: he was cast out into the earth." Michael is generally shown with a sword. St. Michael's Mount was named after St. Michael allegedly appeared to some fishermen in 495AD (just before the life of Tristan), high up on the west side of the Mount. (Milton referred to this in *Lycidas* as "the Great Vision of the Guarded Mount".) Because Michael fought the Devil in heaven, he is the patron saint of high places, and many churches built on hill tops or high places were dedicated to him (like Roche Chapel).

The reference to Mount's Bay recalls the image of drowned Lyonesse in *High Leigh*, and thus unites the contrast that runs through these four poems between heights and depths. Here the idea is that Michael does not just watch over the world. He is directly concerned to save it, as evidenced by his opposition to the Dragon, which seeks to destroy the last two thousand years of Christian civilisation. The Dragon is the Anti-Christ (cf Yeats' "rough beast"), i.e. the Devil, which this line suggests is running the New Age. Michael is therefore concerned to save the West and its Christian civilisation, which must be renewed, and he will not abandon it to destruction at the hands of the Devil's New Age forces. The Canon does his job and lets other Angels get on with their jobs, but Michael is directly concerned in the remysticisation of Christendom.

77. i.e. through effort, shine out like a lighthouse that is as powerful as a Convent's lighthouse.

"Words". Words, like ideas and books, are as anathema to the anti-intellectual Canon as they are to a Zen Master. (See stanza 3.) For all that, God needs some people to "build words" just as He needs some people to be silent.

"Tree-stepped" recalls the Tree of Life, which can be climbed, and Smeaton's "wave-pounded" tower recalls the waves that drowned Lyonesse in *High Leigh*. The final resting-place of Smeaton's tower on Plymouth Hoe (the scene of Drake's game of bowls) represents the triumph of tradition on dry land over the destructive Aquarian waters of the New Age.

78. "A hermit's night". This takes us back to the hermit in the desert of *High Leigh*, a lady hermit who is in the Church and not concerned with the New Age outside it.

79. The dream that the Canon would lead the Counter-Reformation and remysticise Christendom. The role may be ahead for him, but at present it is still unfilled.

80. "Blown", by the writing of the words of these four poems, and they "glow blue" like the blue light that lights the nuns' chapel. "Blue", "miserable" as well as the colour.

Coming after line 77, this line suggests that the blue embers will be magnified as in a lighthouse, and that the blue light will therefore shine out.

There is also a hint of a hope that a spark from the embers may relight "old fire" (line 72) and ignite the desired movement within the Church.

"Angels' blue light". The Angels' light is of course not blue but yellow. The idea is that these four poems are an outer manifestation (the veiled blue of a sanctuary lamp) of the inner flame the Angels veil, i.e. of the real flame which changes colour and appearance in the course of being described. We thus end close to the Taoist idea that the Tao is indescribable.

THE WIND AND THE EARTH, 1981

This volume explores the death of my mother in 1981, and the conflicting themes in her life of her musical gift and violinist's inspiration (the wind) and her practical, social and family role (the earth). The soul and spirit are seen against death.

In *Rosy Cheeks, Blurred Eyes* (no 2) "Resus" (line 3) is the hospital's abridgement for

"Resuscitation".

In *A Shaken Head* (no 7) "be" (line 5) means "have being".

Beethoven (no 22). A white sculpture of Beethoven (line 7) stood in my mother's room.

Christening Dress (no 27). My mother was christened at home by her grandfather (my great-grandfather) Grandpa Broadley, a Methodist minister.

A Paper Wasps' Nest (no 28). Line 14 suggests that the poet will make something beautiful from her clutter and papers, something that can be lived in like a wasps' nest.

Chinese Table: Rose of Light (no 40). The 16-petalled rose in the table (line 7) recalls Dante's "sempiternal rose". The papyri on the table suggest manuscripts. "Chew" (line 11). Cows chew, but the poet is hungry, going without lunch. A rose-bush (line 14) was planted to commemorate the spot where my mother's ashes were strewn.

Tortoiseshell Clock (no 42). The tortoiseshell clock (line 2) was a bequest to my mother from Mrs. Mason, who was over 100. There is a hint of reincarnation in line 14.

Violin Sighs (no 43). My mother met the composer Arthur Somervell (line 5) during the 1920s – I believe he then lived next door to Daledene in East Grinstead – and she played his violin concerto at musical evenings in the 1930s and 1940s.

A RAINBOW IN THE SPRAY, 1984 – 1985

The title comes from *Staffa* and suggests the glimpse of vision.

CRAB-FISHING ON A BOUNDLESS DEEP

First written on 24th August 1981 following a fishing trip I made with my wife's cousin, the fisherman Stephen Orchard and other Cornish fishermen on 17th August 1981 and revised on 19th-20th April 1985. The poem is about the sea of Being in which all Existence moves, and the symbols that can be hauled up like crabs from its waters.

4.	Mount. St. Michael's Mount
33.	Land is seen as swirling cloud on a ship-to-shore radar.
63.	Compare Joyce's image for the detachment of the artist above his work: "paring his fingernails".

THE ROYAL MASONIC HOSPITAL: THE NUT WITHIN THE SUN

The poem was written while I waited to have an operation on a toe. The chestnut tree was outside my window.

The Kabbalistic Tree of Life, which is the secret behind the manifesting universe, was put into the architecture of Cathedrals by medieval masons, and has been put into the architecture of Freemasonry's modern hospital; but it can still be grown in the mind.

3.	Hiram King of Tyre and Hiram Abiff, along with Solomon, planned the building of Solomon's Temple and held the second Lodge. They are shown on the outside of the hospital in Ravenscourt Park.
5-6.	Solomon is shown in glass on the front of the hospital.
7.	"Luf-knot", from *Gawain and the Green Knight*, where the "luf-knot" is a pentagram.
8.	Blake's picture of God shows God leaning out of heaven to create the world with dividers or "compasses".
14.	"Four worlds", a Kabbalistic idea.
20.	The top of the Wakefield wing resembles a Babylonian ziggurat.
25.	King's College chapel was built by masons and contains papyri in the roof and

pillars that correspond to sephirot of the Kabbalistic Tree of Life.

26.   "The nut within the sun". The idea is that the seed of the Tree of Life is a nut which is contained within the shell of the sun, and that this nut is where God, the first cause, resides.

31.   "Leaves", "pages of book" as well as "leaves" on a Tree. "Sinewed" from "sinew" (verb transitive), "glands which are united to muscle and bone with tough fibrous tissue".

31-2.   All the visions and images of the mind are copies of "the nut within the sun", and they emerge into consciousness from its unconscious source. The "stone" of line 1 has become a "nut".

CAMBRIDGE ODE: AGAINST MATERIALISM

First drafted on 11th-12th August 1982 and subsequently revised, for example on 20th-21st April 1985. The poem is about the organicist reaction against Cambridge Rationalism and Materialism, and the unity of one sea of mind-and-matter within an expanding force that counteracts gravity, for which Newton sought unsuccessfully but which may be present in cosmic background radiation, an echo of the Big Bang of creation discovered by Penzias and Wilson in 1964/5 (see pp583-84).

The Enlightenment was a movement in the thought of the 17th and 18th centuries which emphasised a rational approach to God's Nature and to man. As its earliest figures included Descartes, Galileo and Newton, the Enlightenment was founded on an outer scientific revolution, an enlightened, rational approach to Nature through the telescope that had nothing to do with the inner divine "enlightenment" known to Zen Buddhists as "satori" and to Christian mystics as "illumination".

The young Newton established the Enlightenment with his discoveries of the properties of light, gravity, calculus and mechanics in 1664-6 ("three green/Years"), discoveries which led to three hundred years of Materialism, Humanism and Scepticism. But Newton then spent thirty years searching in alchemy for an expanding force in the cosmos which would balance the contracting force of gravity and explain the order in the universe. In the 1930s the American astronomer Edwin Hubble discovered that the universe has been expanding since the Big Bang.

Newton's unsuccessful search brought him close to inner "enlightenment", for he delved deep into alchemy, Freemasonry and the Kabbalah, and he associated this expanding force with light, which he saw as a manifestation of the Kabbalistic four worlds. David Castillejo writes in *The Expanding Force in Newton's Cosmos* (Ediciones De Arte Y Bibliofilia, Madrid) p105: "The contracting force in Newton's world is gravitation, which tends to draw all bodies together. But he also seems to have sought a single expanding force in the cosmos. This force, the law it obeys, and the structures it builds, can best be observed by following the progress of a ray of light. From his study of polarised light, Newton deduced that 'every Ray may be considered as having four Sides or Quarters.' So his ray of light is four-sided."

Blake was right to speak of the young Newton's "single vision" and "sleep", but he did not realise that the older Newton was close to the "fourfold vision" of the Kabbalah which Blake espoused. Similarly it was of the young Newton that Coleridge wrote in a letter: "Newton was a mere materialist – *Mind* in his system is always passive – a lazy *looker-on* on an external world."

10-13.   The two atheists were Frank Tuohy, once an undergraduate at King's, whose view of art derives as much from E. M. Forster (a Fellow at King's for many years) as from Wittgenstein (see Notes to *An Aesthete's "Golden" Artefacts*; and Professor Colin McCabe, the post-structuralist, formerly a don at King's, who split the English Faculty at Cambridge with his controversial ideas.

36.   Hermetic alchemy. Newton saw matter attract and repel from afar "with force

proportional to their mass and distance squared".

48.   "Mystic Rose". The mystic Light (cf Dante's sempiternal rose) is sometimes taken to be the First Cause.

51.   Flamsteed, for whom the Royal Observatory, Greenwich, was built in 1675.

53.   "Mural arc". A mural quadrant.

55.   "Newton's spite". In his capacity as President of the Royal Society Newton seized Flamsteed's work.

65.   Wordsworth was an undergraduate at St. John's, Cambridge, and his room was until recently the Senior Common Room.

67-8.   The MS of Brooke's poem *The Soldier*, from which "the eternal mind" is taken, was displayed in King's College Chapel for many years. Brooke lodged at The Orchard in Grantchester from 1909 to 1910, after which he moved to the Old Vicarage.

74-8.   Mill House, where Whitehead lived from 1898 to 1906. Whitehead opposed "scientific Materialism" in *Science and the Modern World* (1925) and stated his "philosophy of organism" in *Process and Reality* (1929). He wrote of the "bifurcation" of Nature in *The Principle of Relativity* (1922), when he rebuked scientists for separating Nature as it really is from their psychological experiences of it, but the real "bifurcation" of Nature is the division between mind and matter.

82.   "Green fields billow". For the vision of subatomic physics, cf *A Metaphysical in Marvell's Garden*.

90.   Crown. The sephira in the Kabbalistic system nearest to the divine, from which existence manifested.

98.   One sea of mind-and-matter. This may be found to be in cosmic background radiation (the "CBR" of 146), which was discovered in 1964/5.

104.   "Planospheric astrolabe". A flat representation of the heavens, examples of which can be seen in the Royal Observatory, Greenwich.

111-2.   World-Tree and sun-door. Both these ideas feature in the ascent of the shaman.

114.   "Mind and matter dual (Plato)." Plato believed in the immortality of the soul which was "akin" to the Forms or Ideas, which were discovered through the intellect. To Plato the soul was fundamentally distinct from the body, although it was affected by its association with the body; and the realm of Ideas was distinct from the world of experience. In this sense Plato was a dualist. (Neo-Platonism broke down this dualism.)

115-6.   "Entwined/Between". A dualist in our time is the Nobel prize-winner Sir John Eccles, who told me in 1982 that a consciousness looking at a flower is outside the skull, between mind and flower.

120.   Stone garden. Cf *The Silence*, Part Three.

122.   "Angel-naut". An Angel seen as an astronaut.

128.   "Contracting force". Gravity, which is weaker on the moon than on the earth, thus allowing more expansion for the mind, more "water" as opposed to restricting "ice".

130.   "Levity". The opposite of gravity, a concept of medieval scholasticism which strongly anticipates Newton's expanding force.

133.   "Four-sided rays". See introductory note. The four worlds of the Kabbalah are the divine, spiritual, psychological and physical worlds (see line 144).

136.   "Temple Molecular". In his later years Newton was a Freemason who saw the structure of the Temple in matter, hence matter is a molecular Temple.

140-3.   In query 30 of *Opticks* Newton asked: "Are not gross Bodies and Light convertible into one another, and may not Bodies receive much of their Activity from the Particles of Light which enter their Composition?"

In query 31 he asked: "Have not the small Particles of Bodies certain Powers,

Virtues, or Forces, by which they act at a distance, not only upon the Rays of Light...but also upon one another for producing a great part of the Phenomena of Nature?"

In an alchemical MS now in the Burndy Library, he states that "Ether is but a vehicle of some more active spirit & the bodies may be concreted of both together, they may imbibe ether well (sic) as air in generation & in the ether the spirit is entangled. This spirit is the body of light because both have a prodigious active principle."

In Latin he wrote in his notes for the second edition of the *Principia*: "It will first be necessary to understand the soul, and investigate the laws...of the spirit, the powers and actions of the electrical spirit which pervades all bodies."

Newton knew the white divine Light which only his spirit could see in contemplation, which could *not* be observed through a telescope, and by combining it with ether and giving it the capacity to create spirits, souls and bodies, he was proposing a single system in which the internal and external systems were linked in a two-way relationship. He thus seems to have departed from Descartes' dualism of mind and body in favour of a single system which united spirit, soul, mind and body. The discovery of cosmic background radiation (CBR), an echo from the Big Bang, in 1964/5, would have greatly interested Newton who would undoubtedly have linked this expanding force to CBR rather than to ether.

146.	CBR. See immediately above.
149.	Chakras. The Hindu and Yogi centres of the subtle body, into which energy is drawn from the surrounding air and light as into a whirlpool.
151.	Samadhi. Hindu "enlightenment".
154.	"The human". In contrast to the divine (line 152).
158.	Prana. The Hindu and Theosophical life energy.
160.	Expanding Nature. Cf Hubble's expanding universe, which is now a proven fact. Mind and matter are one, i.e. within one Being that is infused by the Light.
161.	Pythagoras' Garden and mystery school. Oaklands School, Loughton, Essex, where visitors contact their sense of direction and between whose two fields there are specific rusty Victorian iron gates in the hedge. When they are closed there are two fields, the whole being "bifurcated" (to use Whitehead's word), but when they are open there is one field. So mind and matter can appear two fields but when gates are opened and the perspective is changed, they are seen to be one. Also see the note to *A Metaphysical in Marvell's Garden*, line 10. A mystery school, like a Zen temple, encourages silence in which reason withers. The Oaklands fields take people beyond rational thought to a quietness in which the spirit can be known.
164.	Being *expands* the universe because its creative and illumined powers act on the universe. Its expanding force enters other bodies, minds, souls and spirits and stimulates them to expansion, uniting mind and matter.
166.	"Thought and shade". Mind and matter. There is also a conscious echo of Marvell's Garden, "a green thought in a green shade".
168.	"Hedgerow screen". Cf "Eternity is a hole in the mind's hedge" (*An Aesthete's "Golden"Artefacts*).

NIGHT VISIONS IN CHARLESTOWN

First drafted on 6th August 1983 and added to between then (for example, 17th-18th April 1985) and 20th May 1990. Charlestown is a 1790s harbour near St. Austell in Cornwall, where I have the Harbourmaster's House which overlooks the harbour wall or pier. The poem is about the soul's flight to the coming Age in which Universalism and a united Europe are matched by gains in knowledge about the universe and man's journey to a safer star than earth; the soul is filled with Light and knows the value of its Way of Fire.

The "flight of the soul" is a mystic idea that occurs in Plotinus' writings, but compare the flight of the shaman up the World-Tree, the Axis Mundi or world-axis. A shaman, too, brought back from his flight as a Sun-Bird an optimistic vision of the future, a healing vision of Hope.

7.	Void, in its metaphysical sense of Non-Being, which puts out Being.
14.	"Firefly". A shooting star.
16.	The idea that the soul is a hawk which flies between lower and higher worlds goes back to the Egyptian *Book of the Dead* (Horus the hawk) and to the Kabbalah.
17.	Galileo saw the earth as ceasing to be the centre of the universe; Descartes' "Cogito ergo sum" ("I think therefore I am") split mind from body; Newton placed the "I" in a mechanistic universe; Darwin dethroned the primacy of man as a species and placed him on a par with the ape; and Freud split the mind into conscious and unconscious parts.
21.	Einstein saw a universe of atomic waves; Hubble saw an expanding universe of 100 billion (hundred thousand million) galaxies; and Penzias discovered cosmic background radiation in 1964/5.
27.	Bohm. See the physicist David Bohm's *Wholeness and the Implicate Order* for his account of how implicate Oneness unfolds Being into a wholeness. Bohm's famous non-local theory must be understood within this wholeness. It is a view that contradicts the mechanistic physics of early Newton.
32.	"Speculative" because the Tree is also the Kabbalistic Tree of Life, which manifests into form and parallels Bohm's ideas.
34.	Sheldrake. See the biologist Rupert Sheldrake's *A New Science of Life* for his theory of "formative causation" through "morphogenetic fields", which offers an alternative to Darwinism. I had a long conversation with Sheldrake in April 1986.
38.	"Waves", i.e. waves of light, for according to the new physics light is both particles and waves at the same time. This idea is present in the philosophy of Whitehead and the psychology of Jung.
41.	New philosophy. A deliberate echo of Donne's "And new philosophy calls all in doubt". The "all" is now Materialism, not Christianity as it was for Donne. The new subatomic science and our conquest of space have shifted our perspective away from Materialism and Mechanism – the reverse of what was happening in Donne's time.
46.	A new Baroque Age. Baroque shows a mixture of the world of sense and the soaring spirit.
47-48.	Both stars and meanings are expressions of the One. The coming Age feels the need to go beyond the meanings of the heart. "Meanings...are one". As the universe is a unity, the meanings beyond the heart are all fundamentally One.
54.	It is a consequence of Einstein's Theory of Relativity that if you travel out from earth faster than the speed of light, you will perceive the earth at a different time from earthbound time, and, if you look through a powerful telescope you may see dinosaurs. The rapid flight of the soul across inner space which is as vast as the Milky Way makes possible a vision of the future.
57.	Old Baroque. The style of art that rose c1620AD and achieved its zenith between c1660 and 1720AD. See Peter Skrine's *The Baroque Literature and Culture in 17th century Europe*.
65.	"Universal" Age. A Universalist Age, but also an Age of the Universe (as opposed to an Age of the Earth).

69.	"Catholic rose". Cf Dante's sempiternal rose and the rose windows in Gothic cathedrals. The rose represents the mystic Light.
72.	"Again". In the old Baroque Age, it was the Turks who menaced Europe. It has recently been the Soviet Union, and will soon be Islam, particularly the southern Islamic states of the U.S.S.R. (see 86).
81.	Charles's. Charlestown was named after Charles Rashleigh, but here the reference is to Prince Charles, the heir to the British throne.
83.	Crown. The top sephira of the Kabbalah which admits the Light into the body. Also the crown chakra. Also the regal crown Prince Charles will wear.
85.	"A gust of air". Caused by one Soviet SS20 or Scud missile.
91.	"Occupied". East Christian Europe has been occupied by the Materialistic Communist Soviet Union.
93.	This line anticipated the anti-Communist movements of 1989.
94.	"Intellect". Intuitive perception through contemplation.
97.	Space telescope. The Hubble, launched in 1990, which is expected to find and map 200 billion galaxies (if they exist). Voyager 1, launched in 1977, has photographed the solar system, and both the Voyagers will reach the heliopause when the solar wind dies out.
98.	"Two hundred billion galaxies". This is different from the figure in line 23 because in the course of mapping our universe the Voyager I has travelled farther than any other probe and is finding more stars.
99.	"Lumpy universe". The image of 10 per cent of the visible sky, a composite of 185 photographs taken by the U.K. Schmidt Telescope in Australia, reveals 2 million "visible" galaxies drawn by gravity into curving sheets and walls separated by void. Invisible dark matter is probably responsible for pulling galaxies into clumps. (The largest clump, a group of quasars about 650 million light years across, formed 6.5 billion years ago, and cosmologists now have to reconcile it with the steady expansion of the universe following the Big Bang.)
101.	Dyson's. Professor Freeman Dyson of the Institute for Advanced Study at Princeton has calculated that if the universe has an overall density less than 3 atoms per cubic metre then the universe will go on expanding for 10^{76} years, a figure so huge that if you wrote a 1 and noughts the size of hydrogen atoms, they would fill the circumference of 200,000 billion billion billion billion earths, i.e. the universe would expand for ever. If, on the other hand, the overall density is more that the 3 atoms per cubic metre, the universe will collapse down a black hole in 20 billion years' time; when all matter, space and time would vanish, and nothing would exist.
105.	"Non-Being kinked", i.e. there are kinks on wave-like back-twists in Non-Being which form the four forces.
105-112.	Quantum void. A concept of quantum theory whose quantum vacuum binds all into one. This is a statement in modern physics of the metaphysical Void of Non-Being which is replete and which gives birth to creation or Being with the Big Bang and which supports it (112). It is the underlying reality of all that is, which has existed since the Big Bang in which all basic properties (mass/energy, charge, spin) are eternally conserved. It contains no particles and yet particles come into existence as excitations or energy fluctuations within this sea of potential. The laws of physics do not require the vacuum to cease even if the universe collapses into a black hole. The American physicist David Finkelstein has said "A general theory of the vacuum is thus a theory of everything." As quantum particles behave as one when linked, the quantum void connects vacuum, matter and mind in the new subatomic physics.
106.	"Four tidal forces". Gravity, electro-magnetism and the strong and weak nuclear

	forces.
110.	"Being craves", i.e. Being is in love with consciousness.
111.	"What is", i.e. Being.
113.	"Stardust". Men are composed of stardust. Man evolved from stardust as he has material from extinct stars in his body.
114.	"Fifth expanding force". This is an anti-gravity force. See *Cambridge Ode: Against Materialism* for Newton's 30 year long unsuccessful search for this force, which Hubble's expanding universe anticipates and which may be found in Penzias' cosmic background radiation.
115.	"Solar wind". The wind from the sun which blows sub-atomic particles across space at 865,000 mph until after 4,650 million miles it stops at the heliopause.
116.	The heliopause is where the heliosphere ends, some 4,650 million miles from the sun.
118-120.	Red giant. In 5 billion years time our sun will run out of hydrogen; expand into a red giant; swallow our earth, which will burn to a cinder; and then cool to a white dwarf. By then, the vision shows, man will have moved to a safer star; he will have escaped the doomed earth for the eternal universe.
124-28.	The highest vision of this Age will bring in the zeitgeist of the next Age, which will renew the organs of perception and be aware of the Sun-Bird's flight.
132.	"What buds in me". The Tree of Life of the Kabbalah, whose pattern is within each individual as well as in the macrocosm.
134.	Gunwalloe. There is a church on the beach in Gunwalloe Cove, Cornwall.
138.	The Universal Age will draw on all times of quest. It will be Universalist, but in the West Christendom will be restored – albeit a more syncretistic Christendom than we know – and there will be new mystic developments which find their inspiration in past times of quest.
140.	Roman West. The West which has Roman origins, but also the West which has a Roman Catholic backbone, and the West in which the Holy Roman Empire will be revived through the role of a united Germany.
143-4.	The "star-rose souls" are the mystics whose Way of Fire earns them a place in the galaxy of mystics. The Light they have known gives hope of the soul's immortality beyond death. "Star-rose" suggests both "star" and "rose" and that they "rose like stars" after their death.
144.	"Death". The death that overtakes the body, but also Materialistic death.
	In the last line the two main images of the poem come together: the star-Tree which has fruit for the hawk, and the rose of the vision. The outer Tree, the World-Tree into which the soul can fly, and the inner Rose-tree which buds in the soul (whose dark is as vast as the universe) are seen to be differing aspects of the same Tree which exists in both macrocosm and microcosm. On this same Tree hang the star-like, shining souls of the dead – a revelation which answers the question in line 6 of the poem, and the Void (line 7).

ON THE DEATH OF AUNT FLO

3. EVENING STAR

13-14.	It is a Gnostic idea that souls find their way back from an alien world to the Light from which they originated.

AT PENQUITE HOUSE, NEAR ST. SAMPSON'S

Penquite House is near St. Sampson's church at Golant, Cornwall. Col. Peard (1811-1880) graduated from Oxford and became a barrister. In 1859 he went out to Italy to help the struggling Italian patriots and commanded the English legion, being known as "Garibaldi's Englishman". He was a bit like Lawrence of Arabia. In April 1864 Garibaldi visited Peard at Penquite House, which Peard took over in 1860 while his house at Trenython was being built. St. Sampson or Samson (c490-565) was a Welsh Bishop of the 6th century who had a vision and came to Cornwall, building St. Sampson's church at the same time that King Mark (one of the last Cornish kings, whose palace was at Castledore) sent Tristan to woo Iseult – Mark and Iseult made their devotions at the church, Iseult gave the bishop a piece of cloth – and then he continued his evangelising in Brittany, where he founded the Abbey and Bishopric of Dol. Tristan had also gone to Brittany, and wounded, sent for Iseult, who alone could heal him. She was to fly a white sail if she was on the ship, a black sail if she wasn't. His wife found out about the message and told him the boat had a black sail, and Tristan died, even though Iseult was on the boat. His 6th century gravestone (c550) stands on the outskirts of Fowey. St. Michael's appearance to fishermen near St. Michael's Mount in 495 is referred to by Milton in his *Lycidas* (line 161) as "the great vision of the guarded Mount".

PASSION PLAY

The passion play took place on 27th and 28th May 1984 at various sites round Chigwell, such as the William IV car park, the hillside over that pub, the King's Head car park, and the churchyard of the parish church.

COPPED HALL

Copped Hall is a large, former royal palace near Epping, Essex. It was owned by the Fitzauchers from c1150, and passed to the Abbot of Waltham, then Henry VIII, who visited Copped Hall several times during the last ten years of his reign. His son Edward VI gave it to Mary Tudor, who was a State prisoner there. In 1558 it passed to Elizabeth I, who in 1562 set up a Commission "to repair yourselves as well to our Manor House of Copped Hall..., as also to our park, there to enquire...(as to)...what destruction hath been made of any of our timber trees." Coopersale Hall, which I acquired in 1988, was on this park, and in 1562 Elizabeth I is reputed to have planted a famous holm oak there which still survives and is shown in the badge of Coopersale Hall School. In 1564 Elizabeth I gave Copped Hall to Sir Thomas Heneage, who in 1594 married Mary, Countess of Southampton, whose son Henry was Shakespeare's Southampton. Shakespeare's *A Midsummer Night's Dream* seems to have been written for the wedding, and Theseus and Hippolyta represent Heneage and his bride. The first performance took place in the Long Gallery at Copped Hall. Later owners included Charles Sackville, who took the arms to Knole.

MULTIPLICITY: BETWEEN BATHROOM MIRRORS

9.   Dante's "infinitesimal point" seen as the smallest of many mirror-images between two bathroom mirrors.

AT GREENFIELD FARMHOUSE and GREENFIELD

Greenfield is the name of a house in the remote Scottish highlands, where my aunt, my sister's family and mine spent a fortnight in August 1984. There was no water or electricity; we drew water from the burn and lived by candlelight as if in the 18th century.

IONA: SILENCE

First written on 7th August 1984 during a visit to Iona, and subsequently revised, for example on 18th April 1985. The poem is about the silence and Light in Iona, in which Western civilisation is rooted through the 6th century hermit, St. Columba (c521-597AD). England was converted to Christianity in two missions, one from Rome which landed in Kent in 597, and the other from Ireland under St. Aidan, which arrived in Northumbria in 636. St. Columba arrived from Ireland in druid-worshipping Iona in 563, and then converted Scotland. He thus has the distinction of bringing Christianity to Britain, and St. Aidan was a member of the monastery he established on Iona.

Columba's journey to Ireland was a self-imposed exile. When a local Irish prince violated the sanctity of his church, Columba allied with a powerful family and, after the Archangel Michael appeared to him in a dream and told him to fight (cf Krishna's message to Arjuna in the *Bhagavadgita*), led the clans into battle. As a result 3,000 of the prince's men were killed, and Columba was excommunicated by the Irish Church. Michael had told Columba that he should exile himself from his beloved Ireland to atone for the murders, and his excommunication was rescinded on condition that he should win as many souls for the Church as people he had killed. With 11 disciples he headed for Western Scotland in a coracle, and landed on Iona.

20.	"Began in", "prayed in" and "started in". Both interpretations are there.
26.	In a prayer that has survived, St. Columba modestly prayed that he would keep a small door in Paradise.
27.	Columba died near the Abbey altar in 597AD.
43.	"Zen masters". A Universalist comparison between Christian and Zen mystics.
44-5.	Sense and spirit. The mixture of sense and spirit is the hallmark of the Baroque style in art. Columba's worldly murders and saintliness make him very much a figure for our Baroque time.

STAFFA: WIND

Written in August 1984 during a visit to Scotland and subsequently revised, for example on 19th April 1985. The visit to Staffa itself took place on 7th August 1984. The wind in Fingal's Cave makes a strange piping sound which is seen as an echo of breath and of the divine wind of inspiration.

Mendelssohn visited Staffa in 1829 and wrote *his* experience of the phenomenon of the pipes into his Hebrides Overture, which features Fingal's Cave.

9.	Fingal. Fionn MacCoul, the 3rd century AD Irish hero who defended the Hebrides against pirate attacks.
	Hermit of hypes. To be a hermit on Staffa is to overdo the hermit's life because Staffa is so rugged and bare.
24.	I had been diagnosed as having bronchiectasis four months before visiting Staffa.
28.	The third eye is the eye of inner vision which is painted on the centre of the forehead in the Hindu culture. (Cf "Om", line 27.)
33.	Night-sea boatings. Compare the archetypal night-sea crossing.
42.	It is a Platonic idea that the wind is an echo of the divine wind of inspiration. Hence the reference to Plato's "Idea" (48).
43.	The "symphony blast" was an actual experience of the most wonderful music; it came from the beyond but had the clarity of a full orchestra playing in a promenade

concert. I wished I could have written it down. Compare the "old masters" in *A Stonemason's Flower Bowl*.

AT FINDHORN

Conversations with St. John is by David Spangler.

THE MASSACRE AT CULLODEN

The battle of Culloden took place on 16th April 1746. George II's 9,000 troops commanded by the Duke of Cumberland defeated the 5,000 strong army of Bonnie Prince Charlie in less than an hour and, having lied that the Jacobites had issued a "no quarter" order, massacred all the prisoners they could take.

SEA FORCE

Gunwalloe Cove is near Porthleven, Cornwall. It has a church and graveyard on the beach, the only building there. The sea always throws up spray there. The next poem is also set there.

CLOUDS HILL

Clouds Hill, the home of Lawrence of Arabia, is in Dorset. The Greek phrase over the door, "ou phrontis", is taken from a tale by Herodotus (vi 129) in which it expresses indifference to worldly advancement, and T. E. Lawrence freely translated it as "Why worry?" T. E. Lawrence was a British intelligence agent who led the Arab revolt against the Turkish Ottoman Empire and raced the British General Allenby to Damascus, which he ruled for three days. He left on the fourth day having achieved his aim and seeing the danger to his wisdom of remaining in power. In 1921 he was made Political Adviser to the Colonial Office and secured the thrones of Iraq and Jordan for Feisal and his brother. Repudiating the Lawrence of Arabia legend, in 1922 he joined the RAF as Private Ross and then, when news leaked out, the Tank Corps as Shaw. He was back in the Air Force in 1925 as Aircraftman Shaw, and often drove from nearby Bovington Camp to Clouds Hill to reflect there during the day. On 13th May 1935 he was thrown off his motorbike and died on 19th May, and was buried at Moreton. He was apparently avoiding two boys cycling, but there is a story that he was forced off the road by a mysterious black car, and that his motor-cycle had a scrape of black paint on its side. Lawrence stands for the man of action; he understood the importance of reflection but never quite united the active and contemplative lives.

AT WEST HAM: SAVED BY AN ARTIST

Tom McAlister, the West Ham goalkeeper, saved a penalty taken by Mo Johnstone in West Ham's 2-0 victory over Watford on 8th September 1984, when Upton Park was packed for the local derby. Potts headed in John Dutchman's brilliant cross to win Pegasus the FA Amateur Cup at Wembley in 1951 before a crowd of 100,000. Both McAlister and Dutchman took football at Oaklands School for a while. The true saving of the title is of course the poet-artist's saving of the footballer, who realises there is more to life than kicking footballs.

BRISTOL FIGHTER

My uncle Tom Broadley overstated his age and became a Flight Lieutenant. He was shot down over enemy lines on 15th September 1918.

SUN-RISE AND CLARINET

The Hymn to the Sun by Mazonides of Crete was written on papyrus c130AD.

ORPHEUS TO EURYDICE
(A Soul-and-Body Sequence)

Orpheus and Eurydice represent opposite principles: Orpheus the soul and divine inspiration, Eurydice the body and sensual gratification. Both contain within themselves elements of the other's world. Orpheus can be tempted by the underworld just as Eurydice yearns for the world of the gods.

58.   Angel, a term used in Babylon in the 6th century BC and therefore roughly contemporary with Pythagoras, who took the name "Orpheus".

TIME COMPRESSED
(Or: A Universe like Sparkles from a Wave)

10.   "Enzymes", encapsulates in miniature.

STILL CLOUDS AND WHIRLING STARS
(Or: A Hole in an Eggshell Universe)

20.   Holed. A holed universe is possible because of black holes.

STAR-GAZING
This poem was written in the dark during one of several sessions of star-gazing at Chigwell School, whose Observatory gave me glimpses of the universe.

STARS LIKE BEES AND PETALS

10.   "Tree", cf the Kabbalastic Tree of Life.

IN PÉRIGORD

Périgord is a historic and cultural region in South France. It takes its name from a Gallic tribe whose capital became Périgueux, and was fought over by the French and English from 1259. The area round the river Dordogne saw homo sapiens (somewhere between 400,000BC and 100,000BC) throw up Neanderthal man (c100,000BC) who was displaced by Cro-Magnon man (c35,000BC). The last great period of prehistory is called Magdalenian (c17,000 – 11,000BC) after La Madeleine. Many of the cave paintings in Lascaux, Font de Gaume and Les Combarelles go back to c16,000BC and are Magdalenian. Périgord Noir (Black Périgord) is the region around Sarlat, where St. Bernard preached in August 1147. The Lantern of the Dead was erected in the last quarter of the 12th century to commemorate St. Bernard's miracle, when bread he blessed healed the sick regardless of whether they were in perfect faith at the time. Rocamadour was at its height before the 12th and 14th centuries, when penitents actually climbed its many steps on their knees and prostrated themselves before the black Virgin, made of wood covered with silver in the late 12th century. Périgord and the Dordogne were "the cradle of the poets" (Henry Miller) and produced the troubadours or lyric poets of S. France, N. Spain and N. Italy who wrote in the "langue d'oc" of Provence between the late 11th and late 13th century. According to Dante the greatest troubadour was Arnaut Daniel.

TIN-MINE AND HAWK

2.   "Cross". The tin-mine suggests the Church, which no longer mines an "iron seam".
9.   The image of poet as hawk.

ROUGH STONES LIKE MONKS

Edward the Confessor gave St. Michael's Mount to Mont St. Michel.

TREVARTHIAN REVISITED

9.   I stayed at Trevarthian opposite St. Michael's Mount in the summer of 1955.

FIRE

11.   Five elements. Body, heart, mind, soul and spirit.

OAKLANDS: OAK TREE

25.   Nature Walk. There was a particular walk round the Oaklands fields in the 1940s and 1950s which was known as "the Nature Walk".
40.   Horn of plenty. The Roman cornucopia.

WITH HAROLD AT WALTHAM

The full story of Tovi and the discovery of the black flint crucifix is told at the beginning of William Addison's *Epping Forest, Its Literary and Historical Associations* (1945). The Old English name of Edith Swan Neck was "Swanneshals". Harold built the church at Waltham, near the cross that cured him of paralysis, c1060, and when he prayed there before going into battle against William at Hastings, the figure on the cross, which had always looked upwards, looked down, a sign that Harold would lose. Harold's tomb can be seen at Waltham Abbey today, as can the 15th century "Doom painting" of the Last Judgement. To Harold, the conquering Normans were a horde, but the perspective of the Bayeux Tapestry is different: they brought with them the Roman Fire of Pope Gregory the Great.

GREENSTEAD CHURCH: MARTYR

Greenstead church has a pre-Conquest nave, the walls of which are upright tree trunks split in halves. St. Edmund's body rested there in 1013 on its way back from London to Bury St. Edmund's. The Crusader bowman's tomb is 12th century.
21.   "Eye-hole", "eag-thyrd".

AT DARK AGE JORVIK: THE LIGHT OF CIVILISATION

Jorvik was the main Danish settlement in England. Today it can be visited in York as a reconstruction of everyday Viking life. Vikings captured York in 847, and York was burned by the Normans in 1069. The massacre of 500 Jews took place in 1190. The World Tree on which Odin hung is Yggdrasil, and Odin welcomed the newly dead heroes in Valhalla. Saint Olaf was Olaf II Haraldsson, effectively the first king of Norway whose religious code of 1024 was Norway's first national legislation.

SOUL LIKE A MAGPIE

This may appear to be a Manichaean poem, but the dualistic nature of the magpie is reconciled in its oneness as a living bird.

QUESTION MARK OVER THE WEST, 1985 – 1988

This volume is preoccupied with the future of the West during hardline Communism's last vicious onslaught on the West. See my Autobiography *A Mystic Way*, for an account of the work of the Heroes of the West in resisting this onslaught. The question mark in the poem whose title gives its name to the volume is the Plough in the night sky, seen as a question mark.

FOUNTAIN OF ICE

2.   "Rule", suggests that the Hotel in Moreton-in-the-Marsh is run on monastic lines.

OXFORD REVISITED

"The King". Ian Flintoff, who acted and virtually lived at the Randolph, drinking with Rex, the *Daily Express* reporter.
55.   "Scorch" suggests the metaphysical Fire.

QUESTION MARK OVER THE WEST

My cousin, Richard Carter, and his wife Wendy live on Lord Cowdray's estate in Haslemere, Surrey, and the Saturday walk was to Burchhill Copse, the Sunday walk to Henley Common, where we drank at the Duke of Cumberland. The question mark in the night-sky catches the worries felt in the mid-1980s about the future of the West. These are transcended in the final stanza.

COTSWOLDS: WINTER FOUR-SIDEDNESS

41.   "The four shire stone" is where Gloucestershire, Warwickshire, Oxfordshire and
           Worcestershire meet one and a half miles east of Moreton-in-the-Marsh on the A34.

ODE: COUNTER-RENAISSANCE

The form is the same as that of Keats' *Ode to a Nightingale*: stanzas of ababcdecde. The white-haired man was Sir George Trevelyan. I have used poetic licence in putting into his lips the title theme of "Counter-Renaissance" (line 69). The idea that we are in a Counter-Renaissance is mine.
128.   The Guardian Angels' Chapel in Winchester Cathedral is medieval.
129.   "Sun". "Look" but also "write poems".

AT BLEA TARN HOUSE

Blea Tarn House is between Little Langdale and Great Langdale in the Lake District. It is where Wordsworth's Solitary met the Wanderer in *The Excursion*. The American bombing of Libya took place during my visit there, and I heard the news on the radio. The effect was of an intrusion from the active world into contemplative peace.

THE ARTIST

The artist was W. Heaton Cooper whose studio is in Grasmere.

THE GUIDE OF MEANING
(Or: The Quicksands of Meaninglessness)

The poem was written after an encounter with the legendary guide of Morecambe Bay, Cedric Robinson.

AT CARTMEL PRIORY: TAMING THE UNICORN

Cartmel Priory church is two miles from Grange-over-Sands, Lancs. It is 12th century, and the oak stalls are c1450. The Gatehouse is 14th century, the "convent part" has vanished. The screen is c1620. The poem was written when I was filled with a sense of foreboding at the violence that then faced the West from such forces as the IRA, Libya, the USSR and international terrorism ("the murderous four"). It was with some reluctance that I took the beautiful and fabulous unicorn as a symbol of terrorism, because of its impaling horn.

IN SHAKESPEARE'S STRATFORD: THE NATURE OF ART

William Shakespeare was born in Henley Street, Stratford in 1564. His father had a shop, his mother was the daughter of a farmer yeoman who lived in Wilmcote. He attended Stratford's Grammar School and in 1582 when just 18 married Anne Hathaway, who lived in Shottery. In 1583 Susanna was born, and Shakespeare was punished (probably flogged) by Sir Thomas Lucy for poaching a deer from Charlecote Park, and may have had to leave the district. His twins Hamnet and Judith were born in 1585. He seems to have gone to London in 1587.

He may have left to work in a printers. Richard Field, a London printer, was a family friend of Shakespeare's. His father, a tanner, was a friend of Shakespeare's father, who was a glover. Richard Field had married the widow of Vautrollier, a Huguenot printer, and ran the business in Blackfriars. In 1589 Field printed Ovid's *Metamorphoses* and in 1593-4 he published Shakespeare's *Venus and Adonis*, which has an epigraph from Ovid, and *The Rape of Lucrece*, both of which were influenced by Ovid. He also printed school textbooks and Plutarch's *Lives*, which Shakespeare used as a source. In 1592 Field's younger brother joined him in the business, and according to Dr A. L. Rowse Shakespeare may have began work as an apprentice printer in 1587, surrounded by all the books that he would need for his poems and plays.

If so, Shakespeare soon preferred the theatre to printing. He was one of the Chamberlain's Men (Court actors) by 1594, and many of his plays were written for the company. In 1596 his son Hamnet died. In 1597 he bought New Place and installed Anne there in 1598. He retired and returned to Stratford in 1610 and lived in New Place. The Globe theatre was accidentally set on fire by a cannon in 1613. He died in 1616 after entertaining Jonson and Drayton, it is said, at New Place, and was buried in the chancel of Holy Trinity, Stratford, where the gravestone contains the lines:

> "Good friend for Jesus sake forbeare
> To digg the dust enclosed heare;
> Blese be ye man yt spares these stones
> And curst be he yt moves my bones."

The monument on the wall says:

> "Stay passenger, why goes thou by so fast.
> Read if thou canst, whom envious death hath plast
> With in this monument Shakespeare, with whome
> Quick nature dide whose name doth deck y tombe.
> Far more then cost, sieh all y he hath writt
> Leaves living art, but page, to serve his witt."

The conflict between appearance and reality, how "appearance belies reality", is the major theme of Baroque, and the relationship between art and nature is very much a part of this conflict, as the words on Shakespeare's monument make clear. The new Baroque focuses on the relationship between art and nature.

CASTLES IN THE AIR

Richard Neville, Earl of Warwick (1450-71) was known as "the Kingmaker" because he imprisoned Henry VI in the Tower of London and held Edward IV captive in Warwick Castle before making him King. After this bad experience the Crown made sure that Warwick Castle remained Crown property until Edward VI gave it to John Dudley, Earl of Warwick and Duke of Northumberland, who on Edward's death made Lady Jane Grey (who had married his son Lord Guilford Dudley) Queen for two weeks, and was executed by Mary with his son. His two other sons were given Castles by Elizabeth I. Ambrose Dudley, Earl of Warwick, was given Warwick Castle, and Robert Dudley, Earl of Leycester, was given Kenilworth Castle. Elizabeth spent 19 days with him there in July 1575, and he hoped to make himself King when for a while it seemed as if he would marry Elizabeth. Sir Thomas Lucy was knighted by Robert Dudley who deputised for Elizabeth, and it was Lucy who punished Shakespeare for poaching a deer. The title "Castles in the Air" suggests the hopes and plans of the Kingmakers, and the ruins their castles in varying degrees became, are now open to the air.

WARM RAIN

The title, of course, suggests "hot rain", the fall-out from Chernobyl.

SPLIT PINE AND PINE-CONES

19-20.   The wound and the cones, the artist's life and his work.

AT GUNWALLOE: THE TAO

See note on *Sea Force*.

BY THE CHALICE WELL, GLASTONBURY

First drafted on 26th October 1986 during a visit to the Chalice Well and garden, and revised between 9th and 11th June 1990. The poem is about the ever-flowing spring that flows through the Chalice Well and garden in Glastonbury, as the Light flows into the soul; the social and metaphysical worlds are the interlocking concentric circles on the well lid.

2.   The isle of Avalon was an island of three hills. "Great breast and nipple": the Tor and St. Michael's Church. "Pregnant tum": Chalice Hill. "Raised knee": Wearyall Hill.

| 3. | "How you disembarked", i.e. imagine you are one of Joseph's disciples landing in 36AD. |

3. "How you disembarked", i.e. imagine you are one of Joseph's disciples landing in 36AD.

4. Wearyall Hill, so called because when Joseph of Arimathaea arrived with Jesus's disciples in AD36, he pronounced them "all weary".
"Surrounding sea". Avalon was originally an island. The sea has since receded (see 22). Pomparles (8) was then by the sea; it is traditionally the spot where Sir Bedivere threw Arthur's sword into the mere.

5. "Joseph's staff". The story is that Joseph of Arimathaea stuck his staff in the ground and it became a hawthorn ("thorn").

9-10. The Tor seems to have been man-made c2500BC as a ziggurat or high place, or "world mountain".

11-20. The idea is that the depth of the caves of Wookey Hole correspond to the height of the Tor. On these mirror images in structure are the very different worlds of Hell and Heaven. The River Axe runs through Wookey Hole.

20. "Two-circled cover". The concentric circles on the lid.

24. The last Abbot, the 80 year old Michael Whyting, was hanged from St. Michael's Church in 1539, during the dissolution of Glastonbury Abbey. Later his body was quartered and displayed at Wells, Butt, Bridgwater and Ilchester, while his head was placed over the Abbey's gateway.

25. "The scales". Above the arch of St. Michael's Tower is an angel watching the weighing of a soul, who is seated in the scales of judgement. There is also a carving of St. Bridget (the Great Mother Goddess of the Irish in Christian guise who is said to have visited Glastonbury in 488AD) milking her cow (an animal sacred to Isis who was also a Mother Goddess).

26. Tudor Pole's house is very near the Chalice Well and contains an upper room that is set out as for the Last Supper.

29-30. "Chalybeate". The spring has a high chalybeate (iron) content and is iron-red (35). It flows at 25,000 gallons a day at a constant temperature of 52°F. "Within the Tor". The source of the water is unknown but is thought to be deep in the Tor, and by some to be in the Mendip Hills some miles to the north. I have reviewed the evidence and prefer to see it as coming from the Tor.

30. "Heals suffering". There are many details of pilgrims who have been healed in the Pilgrim's Bath.

31-7. The "four levels" correspond to the four worlds of the Kabbalah: the physical or material ("water-splashing bowl"); the psychological ("waterfall" and "Pilgrim's Bath"); the spiritual ("Lion's Head"); and the divine ("the silent well"). Hence "four worlds in garden levels" (41). There is a tradition that the Grail (the cup of the Last Supper which also caught some blood from the cross after the spear of Longinus lanced Jesus's side) was buried near, under or in the well; and that also buried there were two cruets (containing Jesus's blood and sweat) whose crystal gave Glastonbury its name.

40. Lourdes-like. The waters at the cave of Lourdes are of course famous for their healing properties.

44. "Two overlapping circles". Essentially, the social and metaphysical worlds.

49-50. It is possible that the spring was all that Joseph and his disciples would have known; although it is also possible that the well was built by Egyptian Hebrews who came to England nearly 4,000 years ago.

52-3. For the full story of how Jesus came to Glastonbury as a boy with his uncle Joseph of Arimathaea and then returned to build a wattle and daub church in 26AD, see my book *The Fire and the Stones*.

60. Joseph fled Roman Palestine for Britain because Britain was on the fringe of the

Roman Empire, from which the British threatened to secede, and the Romans who ruled Palestine had persecuted Jesus's disciples. Joseph of Arimathaea himself seems to have been in prison after the crucifixion. For the tradition that he brought the Virgin Mary with him to Glastonbury, see my book *The Fire and the Stones*.

61-2.   Joseph of Arimathaea died in 82AD and was buried in the crypt of the first church which he himself had built, under the Abbey's Lady Chapel. On the side of the wall there is now a stone which says Jesus Maria, which testifies to the fact that the Virgin Mary may have been buried in the Lady Chapel. See my book *The Fire and the Stones*.

70.   Avalon does mean "the Island of the Dead".

71-78.   Joseph of Arimathaea's tomb can now be seen in St. John's, the parish church of Glastonbury. In 1367AD Joseph's body was found and placed in a silver casket in a stone tomb in Glastonbury Abbey. The stone sarcophagus with the initials JA (referred to locally as "John Alleyne" to protect the secret) was moved from the Abbey to the churchyard in 1662AD and from the churchyard into the parish church in 1928 by the Rev. L.S. Lewis.

79.   The shroud Joseph of Arimathaea wound round the body of Jesus is traditionally the Turin Shroud, which traditionally bears an imprint of Jesus's face; although carbon-dating in 1988 ruled that the shroud is a medieval forgery dating to c1350AD. The "Templecombe" face seems to have been copied from the shroud. There was a Templar preceptory at Templecombe.

81.   i.e. We must renew the present, or we must renew in the present.

93.   The two circles are now the Inner Sun or Light, and the skull.

98-9.   "Can catch, and be,/And store". That can catch, that can be, and that can store the Light. Or, that can catch, and be; and store the Light.

100.   The Light comes from the Void or quantum vacuum as the spring comes from the Tor.

101-4.   The closing vision is of the Age of Aquarius the water-pourer replacing the Piscean (Christian) Age of the fish and bringing in a time when the Light heals the body and makes gold the spirit.

106.   "Two worlds". The metaphysical world is earthed by the social world, and through the contact, or even friction, between the two they "energise" the spirit.

110.   Through a wall, i.e. the wall in which the Lion's Head is set, but also the wall that separates the immaterial from the material.

THE ROMANTIC REVOLUTION

Coleridge lived at Nether Stowey from 1797 to 1800. Wordsworth stayed at Alfoxton House in 1797 (in Wordsworth's day Alfoxton House was called Alfoxden House). The two of them had a poetry revolution and began the Romantic movement in English poetry. *Kubla Khan* followed a dream, and the writing was famously and ruinously interrupted by a tradesman from Porlock who wanted a bill settled.

GOG AND MAGOG

4.   Tor. The Tor, Gog and Magog are in Glastonbury.

A PILGRIM IN EUROPE

The poem records a journey, a modern Pilgrims' Way, through Europe and contrasts the spiritual depth of the past with modern noise. Europe has traditionally been centred on Christ, the Light of the World, but today the European soul is in need of renewal.

VISIT TO A PHILOSOPHER
(A Fragment)

The philosopher was E. W. F. Tomlin. The visit took place on 30th July 1987.

THE METAPHYSICAL CONDUCTOR

18.   Luther's friend was Philip Melanchton, at whose house Eric Hardenberg learned the Reformation ideal that was later put on the walls of Rynkeby church in Denmark.

A VIKING INHERITANCE

Denmark's Trelleborg contains the ring-forts and houses of the 1200 Vikings who left with Svein, and Roskilde has the Viking Ship Museum.

CENTRE OF THE MAZE

The Iron Age settlement and maze were at Lejre.

AT GILBJERG: KIERKEGAARD THE ROMANTIC

8.   Kierkegaard's *Journal*, see 1835 entries.

TIME AND ETERNITY: A CROSS OF LIGHT

See note on *Sea Force*. "A cross of light". If you squint at the sun you see a cross of light.

SPUR DOG AND PHILOSOPHER

15.   Philosopher. E. W. F. Tomlin, who died earlier that year.

OUT ON THE ALONE
(Or: the Mystery of Being)

Written on 18th August 1987 following another fishing trip with my wife's cousin, Stephen Orchard, and other Cornish fishermen on 17th August 1989; and revised in April (e.g. 10th April) 1990. The poem is about the awareness of Being, and of the Void behind it, which can be known "out on the Alone" of the sea, in contrast to the "social blindfold" on the land; to know Being is to realise that human beings are immortal.

20.   "Lost Land's watery streets". The lost land of Lyonesse sunk in 1099AD according to tradition. (See note to *High Leigh*, lines 69-71). Much of it was in Mount's Bay, and the cod off the Lizard could therefore have come from the submerged streets of a medieval town.

37-48.   Existence differs from Being. Existents are particular and individual, whereas Being is the Oneness of all existents.

55.   "Fireball". The Big Bang of creation, whose radiation permeates Being. The Infinite One Void from which it came permeates Non-Being. The Fire is present in both;

hence it "flames" (56) through both.

57.   Negative Way. Traditionally the Negative Way was followed in the Egyptian desert, where Nature was reduced to sand and sky. Fishermen leave "the social dream" for "the Alone of sea and sky" and can likewise reduce and simplify their environment.

61.   "Void in negative bob, as from a space-buoy". The Void as a bobbing sea of outer space, observed from a buoy out in space.

68.   "Social blindfold", i.e. of the Reflection. The struggle between the Reflection and the Shadow with which *The Silence* began is perennial and ongoing

69.   "Black Head's haze". The haze round the Black Head of Trenarren suggests the Black Head's contemplative calm; the meditative stillness associated with the Black Head of Trenarren, with which *The Silence* began.

A STROKE FROM THE DARK
(Or: Mind in a Brain X-Ray)

MRI Magnetic resonance imaging, a technique in which magnets incite molecules so that radio signals are fired.

31.   The MRI's resolution is 0.75mm.

39.   "Analogue". A computer using physical qualities to represent numbers (e.g. voltage, weight, length). "Digital" A computer making calculations with data represented by digits.

FROM THE COBB, LYME REGIS, 1988 (OR 400 YEARS ON)

9.   'carious. Also "precarious".

8.   to lee. To the sheltered side, i.e. towards land.

AT POLRUAN CASTLE, A 15TH CENTURY BLOCKHOUSE

8.   Q. Sir Arthur Quiller-Couch, the Shakespeare scholar, lived by the water at Fowey opposite Polruan in Cornwall.

12.   From Polruan Castle a chain was stretched across the mouth of the river to a castle the other side, to stop ships and collect a toll.

ON ELIOT'S CHURCH

Eliot's church was St. Stephen's, Gloucester Road.

A SNEEZE IN THE UNIVERSE, 1989 – 1992

This volume has a Universalist preoccupation with the universe.

THOUGHT BETWEEN GORRAN PIER AND CHARLESTOWN SEA

21.   "Reflect that I", "reflect the (that) 'I' who rejected".

IMAGES AT TWILIGHT: EMPEROR TO SUN-GODDESS

The (divine) Japanese Emperor spends the night of his coronation alone with Amaterasu, the Sun-goddess, and is left alone at some point the next day (and certainly by twilight).

PRINCE TOAD

Prince Toad is about the artist's conflicting life and work, and his two natures.
16. In, i.e. mirrored within.

EASTER SUNDAY

5.   The Bishop of Durham, whose statement led to accusations that he was underminding Christian doctrine.

AN EVANGELIST'S INSTANT SALVATION

The evangelist was Billy Graham who spoke at West Ham stadium in the course of his British tour. The poem contrasts the instant way of the evangelist with the lifelong way of the mystic.

    Western Men and Isis suggests that Westerners have lost the Christian knowledge of the Divine Light in their soul and that they must recover it as best they can, through Isis if necessary. Lines 15-16 suggest that Western men are blind to the Divine Light which manifests into all creation (e.g. water and seed which grows into a tree or body) and later removes it (as the wind takes a river); if they open their soul to Isis (a form of the eternal Universalist goddess) they will become receptive to the Light. The last line contains the Baroque mixture of sense and spirit.
    In *A Crystal* eternity crystallises time, transforming the soul and the hour.

BEN NEVIS: CLOUD OF UNKNOWING

Written on 25th-26th July 1989 from notes made during my ascent in August 1984. *The Cloud of Unknowing* is a 14th century mystical work about the separation from the world which prepares for the unitive life. Ben Nevis, 1,343 metres above sea level, is the highest mountain in the United Kingdom. I climbed it with my brother-in-law, Dr Richard Moxon, on 9th August 1984. It was an impulsive climb and I was ill-prepared, wearing only flip-flops on my feet. It was reassuring to have instant medical attention on hand if my legs gave out.
47.   "Has sensed", i.e. the impurity of the five senses of his worldly personality.
55.   Keats. The poet John Keats climbed Ben Nevis on 2nd August 1818 and wrote a sonnet on the summit. The descent proved so tiring that Keats was in bed for a week. Keats wrote: "'Twas a most vile descent" which "shook me all to pieces".

SPRING

The coffin cave is at Porthpean.

UNIVERSE

16, 18.   A hundred billion. In the American sense: a hundred thousand million.

THE CHURCH OF STORMS

Gunwalloe Cove is near Porthleven, Cornwall. It has a church and graveyard on the beach, the only building there. The sea always throws up spray there.

AT GUNWALLOE: LIGHT

1.   The Church of Storms. St. Winwaloe's church, Gunwalloe.

STILLNESS AND TIDES

The "saint" in line 11 is St. Winwaloe or Guénolé, who was born in Brittany and founded the "Church of Storms" at Gunwalloe in the 6th century AD, living in a cell in the shelter of Castle Hill.

CANDLEFLAME STORM

Written on 19th December 1989 during a powercut in Charlestown when I was alone in the Harbourmaster's House.

A MAN OF WINDS AND TIDES

Written on 20th December 1989. The "Cornish sea captain with a grizzled beard" is Captain Ken Gowsell, my neighbour at Charlestown.

GNOSIS: THE NATURE OF THE SELF

Written on 9th April 1990. The poem is about conflicting views of the nature of the self held by brain physiology and mysticism. It sharpens the definition of mind, intellect, soul and spirit.

The "tall bald-headed man with longish hair" is Dr Peter Fenwick, a world authority on the mind-brain problem. In January 1991 he was reported by the London *Sunday Telegraph* as having succeeded in locating the human soul in the right half of the brain, in an area whose malfunction is associated with the inability to experience higher thoughts. His view is that while stimulating the brain produces disorders or bliss in the mind, there are experiences, like the mystical experience, which brain physiology should explore and include as valid evidence.

29.   Galileo. Galileo's fracturing of mind-body took place in 1623 when in *Saggiatore* he distinguished between the primary properties of matter and the other properties, and wrote: "The Book of Nature is....written in mathematical characters." Descartes' fracturing took place in 1648 when he wrote of "res existens" and of "res cogitans".

33.   The Vipassana monk was the Ven. Ajahn Anando.

45.   "Two thousand volts". A surge 2,000 volts is used to execute criminals in the electric chair.

49.   Gnosis, i.e. knowledge from direct experience of the Fire or Light.

56.   A long line because of its importance.

57.   To know one's self is to know the universe. The Temple of Delphi enjoined "gnwqi seauton", "know thyself". Hermes Trismegistos is reputed to have added that to know one's self is to know the universe.

60.   "Universe" means "whole, combined into one".

64.   Harbour gate. The "dipping lock-gate" at Charlestown, Cornwall, referred to in *A Mystic Fire-Potter's Red Sun-Halo*.

SKYLARK AND FOAM

The title images the spirit and the symbols it perceives for Being.

DANUBE: BALL AND CHAIN

16.   Lee. Shelter.

METAPHYSICAL-PHYSICAL
(Or: Orpheus-Tammuz, Serene among the Maenads)

Written on 6th August 1990 in Charlestown. The shimmering causeway of moonlight stretched from under my window out across the sea to the horizon; for three nights there was a wonderful full moon in a cloudless night sky. For the full moon and Inanna, see note to *The Silence*, line 619. Orpheus-Tammuz is a Universalist amalgam; the artist and consort of a fertility goddess are now in harmony.

13.   "Corresponds". See *Preface on the Metaphysical Revolution*, p587 for the law of correspondence.
14.   "The breaking of the beyond into a spine". Two meanings. The metaphysical beyond or divine tingling received in the physical spine corresponds to or symbolises the "sneeze in the loins"; and the metaphysical beyond becomes a physical spine in the act of conception or creation.

ODE: SPIDER'S WEB: OUR LOCAL UNIVERSE IN AN INFINITE WHOLE

This poem was begun on 2nd April 1991 and I was still working on it on June 1st. I believe I finished polishing it at the end of July and on 16th August 1991. It was revised on 27th May 1992. The poem marked the beginning of my contemplation of the universe which became *The Universe and the Light* (published in March 1993) which contains a full view of the infinite whole.

I saw David Bohm on 27th March 1991 and Edgard Gunzig at Winchester on 6th April 1991. I visited the bald, Dutch Professor, Johan Goudsblom, at All Souls, Oxford to discuss fire and the Fire on 28th July 1991. The image of God the Spider came to me as I walked at night to the end of the Charlestown harbour pier, and I later connected the image with Arachne, the 13th month between Taurus and Gemini. (See James Vogh *Arachne Rising: The Thirteenth Sign*, Granada 1977.)

TINKLING: BEING LIKE A BREEZE

3.   It is a Japanese custom to hang bells with paper prayers tied to their tongues on pine trees of Shinto shrines.

SPARKLES IN AN INFINITE SEA

Our universe is a local event within a sea of cosmic energy that has no beginning or end.

RIPPLING ONE

Written at Trinity House in the Cambridge Science Park where I attended a seminar on food handling following the Food Safety Act, 1990. The seminar began at 2.00 p.m. and at 1.50 p.m. I went out to a wooden platform above the edge of the lake and sat alone in the sun, and I returned in time for the start of the seminar with this poem about the Oneness of the Universe and the Nature of Inspiration.

12.   Scenting bulrushes like spice. The words waft over what the poet sees, covering them like pollen.

16.   One rippling echoing. One rippling which echoes: Also One which ripples and echoes.

REFLECTION AND REALITY: PEAK EXPERIENCES AND TIDAL CONSCIOUSNESS

In August 1991 I made three visits (on August 6th, 14th and 22nd) to Colin Wilson, the author of *The Outsider* and 60 other books who lives near Gorran Haven, renewing a friendship that goes back to 1957. On each occasion I drove from Charlestown to see him (twice stopping at Asda for Beaujolais). On the first of these visits, on 6th August, we had much of the conversation recorded in section one of the poem, and there seemed to be a fundamental difference in our Existentialist outlooks, he emphasising willed intense or "peak" experiences of the left brain – the "peak" being a term coined by the psychologist Abraham Maslow, about whom he has written – and I emphasising the inspirations in the right brain of the "tidal" spirit and divine Fire. Subsequently the similarity in our outlooks became clearer, and we both stressed the importance of the intense or harmonious experience that comes through a metaphysical vision. I made it clear that I was talking about contemplation, not reason; and as a result of our conversations we agreed that Existentialism is dead, and I developed a new outlook of a post-Existentialist Universalism.

The title of the poem evokes a Platonic vision, that phenomena are a reflection of an invisible reality. Section one features the left brain and the physical-natural and social-psychological worlds. Section two features the right brain and the spiritual and divine worlds. The synthesis between the left and right brains in section three therefore includes a unifying vision of the physical-natural, social-psychological, spiritual and divine worlds in one metaphysical vision of correspondence in which each pair of worlds reflects the other (the first pair being the physical-natural and social-psychological, the second pair being the spiritual and divine). The land-sea imagery of the title and air-water imagery of the poem reflects the contrast between Colin Wilson's peak experiences and my tidal consciousness.

"Reflection" in the title. "What is reflected" (anticipating the title of section three); "reconsideration" (as in "on reflection"); and (cf *The Silence*) the Reflection as opposed to the Shadow.

"Questioning" in the heading for section one. Deliberately ambiguous. Both adjective and verb, i.e. "the intense experiences of the left brain which questions", and "we should question the intense experiences of the left brain". Section one could be called "Questioning Left Brain's Intense Peaks in the Physical-Natural and Social-Psychological Worlds".

3.   "Genius". In 1956 Colin Wilson was called a genius following reviews by Philip Toynbee and Cyril Connolly of *The Outsider*, one of the most influential books of the 20th century. It opened up Continental literature in the 1950s (writers such as Nietzsche and Hesse, Sartre and Camus, Dostoevsky and Tolstoy), and was written following a succession of labouring jobs while he camped on Hampstead Heath and cycled to the British Museum. His determination in those early days was that of a "genius of will".

5.   "Thirty years". In January 1961 I spent a week in the chalet in his garden. He drove me to Plymouth after I just missed the St. Austell connection for the train back to Essex, where I was due to speak on a panel at a brains trust at Oaklands School, Loughton.

8.   "Husserl, Heidegger, Toynbee". He introduced me to Husserl's *Ideas* in 1973 and gave me the method for *The Fire and the Stones*, which is about the rise and fall of civilisations; hence the discussion of Toynbee. Heidegger's work was *Being and Time*.

11-12.	The argument of *The Fire and the Stones*.
15.	"Beauty". Tepheret in the Kabbalah.
20.	Bergson. Henri Bergson saw mind as a force which is limited when it is held by brain.
22-23.	A seemingly Mechanistic view. Hence line 26.
23.	Air imagery ("pumping", "valve").
28.	Soul. In meditation we move behind the rational social ego, which has an eye of reason, to the soul, which has an eye of contemplation. The Fire or Light is contacted in the soul.
30.	William James. See *The Varieties of Religious Experience*, Fontana, page 251, for "photisms" or experiences of Light.
32.	Tolstoy. See Colin Wilson's *Access to Inner Worlds* p128: "Gorki tells how Tolstoy was walking down the street when two guardsmen came walking towards him. As they strode along with jingling spurs Tolstoy said indignantly: 'What pompous stupidity, like circus animals....' Then, as the soldiers came abreast, marching in step, 'But aren't they magnificent!' Sheer vital energy overwhelmed his intellectual judgement; the right brain contradicted the left."
41.	For Colin Wilson's statement of seven levels of consciousness, see *Books and Religion*, summer 1991, p15.
49.	Colin Wilson met both Camus and Toynbee.
58-61.	Whitehead in Introduction to Mathematics warned against thinking logically about what we are doing: "Civilisation advances by extending the number of important operations which we can perform without thinking about them. Operations of thought are like cavalry charges in a battle – they are strictly limited in number, they require fresh horses, and must only be made at decisive moments." Colin Wilson quoted this as a warning, to check that my Metaphysical Revolution is being made at the decisive moment.
65-7.	Colin Wilson gave the definition of the new man at a lecture on Mozart at Dartington on August 20th.
76-7.	The sea symbolises meaning and imagination as well as the spiritual in this poem.
80.	Colin Wilson's interruption of my rumination. Con, "against" but also "confidence trick". Section two could be called "Tidal Right Brain: Con (Psychic and Occultist Extremes) and Pro (the Harmony of Spiritual Symbols, Divine Fire, and High Dream)".
81.	The small harbour of Gorran Haven is only a mile or two from Colin Wilson's home. It was there in early January 1961 that I decided to go abroad, a choice that resulted in my spending the 1960s out of Britain.
85-112.	The more undesirable side of the right brain – the lower psychic and occult powers which often seem unverifiable imaginings that are removed from reality and seem unbelievable.
113-128.	The memory of Christine Klein, the Egyptian Temple-Dancer I saw in 1977, here dancing the Descent of the Fire in a room in Hampstead. Christine is the only dancer I can think of who embodies the purely metaphysical dance. Each of her movements is a reflection of reality.
113.	"Spirit", i.e. Light.
129-136.	When one sees the vision of the Fire or Light which is the vision of God, it seems natural to see the sea as a reflection of the manifesting quantum vacuum or Void, which is behind all Existence.
139, 144.	One can will the reception of the Fire by willing to open oneself to it. It then appears in the vision of God.

145, 160.	I had the dream in the early morning of 2nd September 1991. I awoke at 4.30 a.m. exactly with 20 lines of verse still in mind – I had seen them written on the clouds beneath me. Within twenty seconds they had all faded and the only words I could remember were "I went for a walk on the clouds. My Shadow in the moonlight/Lay beneath me on the clouds." I have faithfully reproduced these words, received in high dream.
157-8.	"I exist therefore I am" is the physical-natural and social-psychological view of Humanists and sceptics. "I have Being therefore I am" is the spiritual and divine view of Metaphysicals and Metaphysical Existentialists.
160-1.	"Reflecting and reflected". The title in section three states the metaphysical theme that runs through the remainder of the poem: that the physical-natural and social-psychological intensity reflects the spiritual and divine harmony from which it manifests, and conversely that this intensity is reflected (or mirrored) in the spiritual and divine harmony as a headland peak is reflected in tranquil sea. Both are reflected in, and what reflects is reflected in, the still mind of line 231.
	Section three could be called "Synthesis of Left and Right Brain Consciousness: Physical-Natural and Social-Psychological Intensity Reflecting and Reflected in Spiritual and Divine Harmony".
161-8.	Back in Charlestown where a dipping lock-gate separates the inner harbour from the outer harbour.
164.	"Sceptic", i.e. sceptical Humanist.
174-6.	Section three seeks the unifying vision that unites Colin Wilson's view and my own.
177.	The idea that the physical-natural and social-psychological are a reflection of an invisible reality.
184.	i.e. Is Colin Wilson a Metaphysical who sees the spiritual and divine, or a rebel (as in his Religion and the Rebel) within the Humanist tradition, who sees Humanist man as flawed by having imperfect consciousness and who has focused on Humanist peak experiences? In the original version line 184 is "Is he a Metaphysical? Who can tell?"
185-200.	The Humanist left brain ego's attempt to create meaning through prehensile consciousness brings only occasional joys. Regular joys only come when one opens to the right brain.
188-9.	The brain (and therefore its perception) is energised
197-8.	when the ego links with the soul and receives "tidal meaning" which floods the soul with glee.
199-200.	The lock-gate between ego and soul must be permanently down if meaning is to be seen regularly.
204-5.	Existence is full of different phenomena ("differences"). Being is perceived as a unity.
207.	"Void", the quantum Void, Non-Being, latent spirit.
214.	"Peek"/"peakist", i.e. peep/seeker of intensity.
216.	"Moderate left-right". The psychic and occult extremes (see section two) are rejected in favour of the synthesis between left and right brain which is advocated in section three.
217-8.	"Spire". The top of a spire like Salisbury Cathedral's (once the highest in the world) starts as a point at the top (cf Dante's "infinitesimal point") and widens down to its base where it joins the earthly church. The poem envisages a spire in four widening sections or levels.
219.	Cf the four worlds of the Kabbalah, the four metaphysical levels.
220.	The Void is seen as love. Potential Being is love.

222.	Tree. The upside down Kabbalistic tree whose roots are in the sky and whose branches touch the material earth; both roots and branches being the same size.
223-4.	The last stanza and this stanza are perhaps the key stanzas in the poem. The unified contemplative vision which unites subject and object, reflect and are mirrored in the "still mind" which is itself a reflection of the loving Void (the "quantum sea") since Being reflects the Void. These are among the most profound lines I have ever written and will repay careful consideration.
225-6.	Mystics are contrasted with occultists. Mystics surrender their ego's will to the Fire, occultists use their ego's will.
227-8.	Both Existentialists and poets perceive Being as opposed to Existence.
228.	"Fire"/"intense thrill". The difference in emphasis between the heightened consciousness in my metaphysical vision and Colin Wilson's view of heightened consciousness.
229-230.	There are two harmonious consciousnesses, one which is social-psychological (which Humanists seek, reflect and record) and one which is spiritual-divine (which Metaphysicals seek, reflect and record). Each harmonious consciousness reflects a different reality.
231-2.	Both Colin Wilson and I are seen as Metaphysical Universalists with optimistic visions, but with a different emphasis (Fire and peak). Optimism is a feature of the vision of the Fire, or of what Bucke described in the title of his Victorian classic as "cosmic consciousness".
233-240.	Now the physical-natural world (headland) and social-psychological world (village) are reflected in spiritual consciousness (tranquil sea). This moment of unifying contemplation can unite both Metaphysicals and sceptical Humanists if Humanists can open themselves to the spiritual.
236.	"Left" and "right". Both "left and right hand side", and "left and right brain".
236-240.	The still mind reflects both the reflection of headland and village and the reflecting sea. In the last two lines reflection and what reflects are both seen as reflections within a mind which is itself a reflection of an invisible reality. All levels of manifesting reality reflect each other.
238.	"Deep", i.e. spirit lit by divine sun.
240.	The contemplative wakefulness is like a sleep. The mind has to be stilled to a sleep-like trance to perceive the four worlds simultaneously, all reflecting each other.

CALVARY: A PURE BEING GOES UNDER THE EARTH

Margaret Taylor, wife of Dr Graham Taylor, acted as the Oaklands' gardener for therapeutic reasons. She was diagnosed as having lung cancer in March 1991 and died on 4th August 1991. Her funeral took place on 12th August at Christ Church, Wanstead.

SHADOW ON THE CLIFF

13.	Relief, projection of a carved design on the surface.

LEPERS' ABBEY

19.	Lazaret, leper hospital.

AT THE BALLOWALL BARROW

1.   Ballowall Barrow cairn is of the middle-late Bronze Age, c1400-600 BC. Its central structure held a dry-vault and held several burials. It is near Cape Cornwall and the tin-mine chimney of Gwen Broad's *Dusk at Land's End* (see my poem *An Obscure Symbolist's Rock-Tree*).

FIRE WITHIN THE GLOBE

12.   i.e. Just as the rose is in a bowl, so the fire is in a container, our globe.

AT KABUKI: THE FLOWER OF CULTURE

The Japanese kabuki performance was of *Sagi-musume* at the National Theatre, London, with the famous Tamasaburo as the heron-girl. It was the art of Tamasaburo that allowed the Flower (yugen) to peep through.

THE ONE AND THE MANY

15.   "Has shone into", i.e. "has become", but also "has shone into the interior of".
16.   As the moon draws the tide so the One controls the shadows of existence, the reflections of Being.

MOON AND TIDE

16.   "Reflecting", "pondering, contemplating" but also "mirroring".

A FLIRTATION WITH THE MUSE, 1992 – 1993

All poets have addressed a Muse, from Ovid to Byron ("Hail, Muse! et caetera", the opening of canto 3 of *Don Juan*) and Robert Graves. In this sequence of poems the Muse is the artist's inspiration, and represents a life devoted to the pursuit of art. The Muse symbolises a way of living centred on the spring of artistic (here poetic) inspiration.

    The Muse is approached in Baroque terms, through a mixture of spirit and sense, and is imagined expressionistically in social and erotic situations that approach her realistically. The theme of a poet approaching but unable to capture an imagined and unknown erotic-spiritual Muse continues in *Sojourns* and culminates in the final poem in that volume, *The Secret of the Muse*, where the Muse is found to inspire all the poet's works. The treatment of the Muse is Universalist in seeing inspiration as flowing in from beyond the poet.

    The chief centre of the cult of the nine Muses was at Mount Helicon in Boeotia, Greece. The Muse of lyric and love poetry was Erato. She often played a lyre. The Muse of sacred poetry was Polymnia. Orpheus is described as the son of one of the Muses (generally Calliope, occasionally Polymnia). A Muse inspires at her choice, not the poet's; and the poet can only await the approach of the Muse who is a free and independent spirit.

CHRISTINE CARPENTER TO THE WORLD

Christine Carpenter who was walled into the church at Shere resembles the Lady of Shalott in being an enclosed figure who broke out.

MY MUSE

16.   Grace, i.e. (1) bestower of beauty and charm, (2) i.e. she has grace.

RABBIT: SELF-PRESERVATION

This poem was written at the Kingswood Venture Centre at Albrighton, on the Staffs/Warwicks boarder, as was the next poem.

LEAVES LIKE MEMORIES

12.   The "I" is always present like a winter tree trunk and branches, and memories are in the past like leaves.

LADY THROUGH THE WINDOW

14.   Bilderberger spy. The Bilderberg Conference is an annual conference for about 100 of the most influential bankers, economists, politicians and government officials in Europe and North America. The conferences began in 1954 and took their name from the hotel at Osterbeek in the Netherlands where the first conference was held. The Bilderberg conferences are extremely influential and highly secret, and delegates are kept informed by secret means.

MUSE INSPIRING: WINGED LION

27.   In the *Apocalypse* or *Revelation of St. John* (4.7-8) the four beasts represent the four evangelists of the Gospels, and St. Mark is the lion. The statue of the winged lion in St. Mark's Square, Venice demonstrates the endurance of this symbol handed down from he *Apocalypse*. St. Mark's Basilica in Venice was begun in 829 and consecrated in 832 to house the remains of St. Mark, which were brought from Alexandria. St. Mark replaced St. Theodore as the patron saint of Venice and his attribute of the winged lion became the official symbol of the Venetian republic.

WHITE-CENTRED FLOWER

3.   Translucent zirconium silicate is cut into gems.

FOG AND FROST: THE UNIVERSE

The poem suggests that just as existence crystallised from the quantum vacuum like frost from a fog, so it will eventually melt like frost in the sun.

TROPICAL FISH

11.   Complexity theory studies how complex systems, governed by simple rules, produce order.

NOT ENDURANCE BUT PROCESS: THE PAST PRESENT

In the philosophy of Geoffrey Read there is no endurance of particles (the materialists' position) as time is a succession of events and nothing endures through time. The present is added to the past, which is not obliterated. Memory reflects on a past event that is in the present.

4. Whitehead, see *Process and Reality* pt 2, ch 2, sec 5 on "undifferentiated endurance" which is the "root doctrine of materialism".

41. "Moving process", see my "Form from Movement Theory" in *The Universe and the Light*.

This poem offers a metaphysical view of space and time as continua, and substance, matter and memory as process.

ILLUMINED ARTISTS AS LEADERS OF THEIR CIVILISATION

23. Ezra Pound believed that the sacrament of Eleusis was coitus, that ritual sexual union of priests with young women produced knowledge symbolised as light. Pound's view of the sexual act is similar to that of Tantric Yoga: the release of sperm stimulated the brain, energising it with a luminous fluid. Leon Surette, who has studied Pound's thinking in detail, regards the connection between the Eleusinian Mysteries and the Cathars and Provence as being "peculiar to Pound". According to Walter Burkert's authoritative *Greek Religion*: "That sexual elements play a role in mystery initiations is virtually certain, but there is hardly any clear evidence; how in Eleusis, for example, conception and birth-giving was indicated remains obscure."

FLOCK

The flock was seen migrating over the Tamar, the river which runs between Devon and Cornwall.

AT COLINTON

At Colinton parish church there is a font with a lid. When the lid is raised a dove descends to meet it on a pulley and chain. It works on a counterpoise: as the child's head on the arched handle rises the weight with the dove moves down. There are several tombstones with skulls and crossbones on them, and some with a gravedigger's spade. The young Robert Louis Stevenson played pirates in the yew.

OUTSIDE HEAVEN

5. There are two "three-gates" at the Colinton church, one at the front and one a side entrance to steps and railings.

CHAOS AND ORDER

7. The Warsaw-born Benoit Mandelbrot coined the word "fractal" in 1975 to describe rough irregular shapes such as the outlines of an island or a tree which do not fit in a geometry of straight lines, curves and squares. He found there was a regularity in their irregularity, a "self-similarity", and he is consequently now regarded as the world's most famous mathematician.

FIRE I AM

Matthew Fox, a Dominican priest who devised "creation spirituality", was expelled by the Vatican in 1993. He has looked for new forms of worship, and circular dancing in five rings round a centre, which I experienced on 4th April 1993 after a lengthy discussion with him, is one such new form.

CAR PARK: ASCENDING

1-3.　　　There is a multi-storey car park near the St. Austell film centre.

SOJOURNS, 1993

This volume focuses on visits to Italy, America and Scotland.

PISA

3.　　　The leaning tower of Pisa.

BELLS

Both bells are in the centre of Florence.

THUNDER

5.　　　The room was in the Villa Medicea or Villa Careggi, the Medici summer palace on the outskirts of Florence.

PARADISE

1.　　　Masaccio's newly restored frescoes are in the Brancacci chapel in the Carmine, Florence.

THE GATEWAY TO PARADISE

The gold Gate of Paradise by Ghiberti (1425 – 1452) can be seen on the outside of the Baptistery, Florence.

THE LAUGHING PHILOSOPHER

This poem was conceived on April 30th at the Villa Medicea, Florence. Stanzas 1-3 were written in the open orange courtyard (see stanza 1) on my knee early in the morning of May 1st, when I was alone. Stanza 11 was written sitting in the gardens near the Greek goddess, and another 6 stanzas were scribbled out in the lecture hall that evening, after a tour of the building in the afternoon. The stanza on the laughing and weeping philosophers was added the next day May 2nd, and the poem was revised between then and May 12th, particularly on May 11th and 12th, when it was finished.

　　　The summer villa of Cosimo de' Medici, ruler of Florence, the Pope's banker and the richest man in the world in the 15th century, is the Villa Careggi or Villa Medicea at Careggi, Florence. It was acquired by Cosimo il Vecchio in 1417 and enlarged by Michelozzo after 1433. It became the literary and artistic centre of the Medicean court. Here, perhaps, came Gemistos or Gemistus Plethon (who was born c1355 and who lived to be 95 or 97) in May 1439 when the Byzantine Emperor's delegation to bring the Byzantine and Catholic faiths closer together was received by Cosimo in Florence. Gemistos spoke "On the Difference between Aristotle and Plato" and fired the Florentine Humanists with a new interest in Plato and inspired Cosimo to found the Platonic Academy of Florence. (Plethon died in 1450/2 around the fall of Constantinople to the Ottomans in 1452.) Cosimo met his doctor's son, Marsilio Ficino, in the same year, 1439, when Ficino was 6, and eventually supported him in his struggle with his father, who wanted him to be a doctor. He gave Ficino (1433-1499) a small house in the nearby hills in 1462 so that he could revive Plato's Academy (which had run for 1,000 years from 385BC to 529AD until it was closed by Justinian) and translate all Plato, an idea Cosimo had been given by Gemistos in 1439. Cosimo was a great patron to the arts and died at his summer villa in 1464. He was succeeded by Lorenzo, for whom Ficino also ran the Academy, influencing Botticelli in 1478 when he was painting the *Birth of Venus* and *Primavera*, in both of which the creative principle of spring is shown as the earth mother or earth goddess Venus, an embodiment of Plato's divine reality. Ficino was a reconciler of Christian, Platonist and pagan teachings like Clement of Alexandria.

32.	New People. The concept is from my Grand Unified Theory of world history, *The Fire and the Stones* (stages 26 and 28). The Renaissance Humanists paved the way for the new Protestants.
35.	"Sad Venus". In both the *Birth of Venus* and *Primavera* Botticelli's Venus is sad firstly because she still mourns the death of Adonis, but also because she embodies the Platonic realities looking at the forms of time.
57-8.	The lecture on Gemistos Plethon was given by an American, Chris Bamford, who related Gemistos to the tradition of the Fire which, he said, began with Zoroaster and Plato. Bamford knew my work *The Fire and The Stones* which traces the Fire back beyond 3000BC.
58.	The frescoes were 16th century and relate to the redecoration by Pontormo and Bronzino for Cosimo I (c1540), but in an adjoining room there was a terracotta Resurrection by Verrocchio (1455-88).
65.	"My Academy". This was the Universalist Philosophy Group, renamed after my Universalism (see *The Universe and the Light*), a metaphysical research group which I had been asked to lead, perhaps the first group of philosophers of its kind since the Vienna Circle of the 1920s and 1930s.
73.	For the four alchemical stages see Jung's *Psychology and Alchemy*. The four stages are: (1) Nigredo or blackening, the "dark night of the soul", disintegration and entering the underworld, depression; which leads to (2) Albedo, the whitening or sublimation, union of mind and soul, (coniunctio oppositorum), separation from matter, and mystical experience; which leads to (3) Citrinitas, the yellowing, ripening and fertilising through the imagination as a middle ground between body and soul; which leads to (4) Rubedo, the reddening, unus mundus of body and soul, the spiritualisation of matter, the alchemical goal of unity with the cosmos, cosmic consciousness.
105.	The painting by Bramante (1444-1514), who was a painter, writer, poet and musician as well as an architect, is in the Brera, Milan. It shows a laughing Democritus (c460-c370BC), who saw reality or Being as a whole in which a vacuum was filled with atoms. Democritus laughs to think that transience is taken seriously. Heracleitus of Ephesus (c540-480BC), the philosopher of change, asserted that "everything flows" or "all is in a flux" – "upon those who step into the same rivers different and ever different waters flow down" – but he saw a first principle of Fire. He weeps because no one knows the Fire. However, as he knows it himself, he should laugh for reality

is to be known individually, not collectively, and he sees the truth about the universe. Ficino is shown in the one contemporary portrait as unsmiling, but he should be a "laughing philosopher", as should the serious poet. Both Ficino and the poet are temperamentally akin to the weeping Heracleitus, but need to laugh for joy at the knowledge they have and not feel sad at the blindness of humanity.

111.   "Sad Ficino". Ficino had a melancholic temperament, and astrologically linked himself to Saturn and gloomy saturnine influences.

EPITHALAMION

An Epithalamion covers the day of a wedding. The form has been attempted by Homer, Hesiod, Catullus, and memorably by Spenser in 1594; also by Ben Jonson. It is a dramatic form which captures the bustle and happiness of the bridal day. Each epithalamion is based on a local incident that has a universal application and is understood everywhere. The convention requires nymphs and fragrance, but I have introduced modern elements, for example cameras. I have adopted Spenser's 18-line stanza, and the rhyme scheme is ababccdcdeefggffhh.

My Epithalamion was written to celebrate the marriage of my daughter Nadia, an air stewardess with British Midland, to Sandy Wright, the classical guitar player, at Johnsburn House in Balerno, Edinburgh on 5th August 1993. The Epithalamion was read at the wedding. Johnsburn House was built c1780, and the poet Robert Burns is reputed to have had his only meeting with Sir Walter Scott there.

FLORAL CLOCK: BEAUTY'S CHIMES

The floral clock near Lake Ontario was modelled on a floral clock in Prince's Street, Edinburgh.

AT SPACEPORT, USA

29–31.   1,524 signatures of the Kennedy Space Center team were presented to Commander Rick Hauck, whose full words were: "The bird is ready and we're ready. We're excited. We cannot wait to fly."

AMERICAN LIBERTY QUINTET

The theme of the poem (dedicated to the US President) is America's growth, energy and coming world role, which are seen within the context of the American Revolution and the spirit of the Founding Fathers.

Each part of the *Quintet* ("a composition for five performers") is about an American east-coast city (New York, Boston, Washington, Philadelphia and St. Petersburg), and is in 5 sections. The first section evokes the past lyrically and is in abba. The second section catches an important event associated with the past in blank verse. The third section is in two blocks of 7 quatrains and evokes the present lyrically in abab. The fourth section looks forward to the future and relates the city to America's coming world role. The fifth section is in two blocks of 5 quatrains and combines the past, the present and the future lyrically in a combination of abba (section 1) and abab (section 3).

In the *Quintet* the figure of Liberty – originally a gift from the Satanistic French Illuminati – and of her Washington form Freedom embodies the mystic Light and stands for the central idea of the American civilisation. This poem should be read in conjunction with *Archangel*, which in 1966 prophesied the end of Communism.

CORRESPONDENCE

First stanza, cf the beginning of Donne's *Aire and Angels*.

MILKY WAY: LOBSTER AND SAUCE

Some chefs would serve cheese, mustard and brandy sauce with lobster.

DISHES

8.   Sun-rich. Ricosola.

ANGEL OF VERTICAL VISION, 1993

The Angel sequence, conceived on 1st September 1993, looks back to my *Beauty and Angelhood* and draws on Donne's *Aire and Angels* and Rilke's "Every Angel is terrible" in the *Duino Elegies*. The Angel in these poems is the perfected, illumined human being who has transcended man, a kind of Superman who has a unitive vision of the universe, instinctively understands the Theory of Everything and channels knowledge of spiritual beauty. The Angel is thus more all-knowing than the Muse, and unites perfection of the work with perfection of the life and an appropriate moral stance on world issues of concern.

GOLDEN MEAN

12.   Bacon's motto and family crest ("mediocria firma", "the golden mean" or "middle way") was taken from an inscription over the porchway of a temple at Gorhambury. Bacon is often credited with being the founder of the international Conspiracy, to which the Angel is seen as an antidote.

JUICE

6.   Primavera. See Botticelli's painting in which Venus unites both spiritual and natural beauty.

DARK ANGEL

The Angel is the perfected illumined being who has had to make the sacrifice of putting on darkness so as to communicate with us. My "Dark Angel" is therefore the complete opposite of Lionel Johnson's "Dark Angel", a spirit of evil, doubt and sensuality who tempted Johnson to abandon religion.

This poem came to me whole as I parked my car at 10.55 a.m. to keep an 11 o'clock appointment with my bank manager. I scribbled it out on my knee, sitting in my car in Monkhams Avenue, Woodford, opposite Hutton Close, finished it by 10.57 and was still in time for my 11 o'clock appointment. The audio-typist of the next poem was working as I waited, glowing in the aftermath of a received poem, for the bank manager to emerge from his room.
12.   "Lightens". "Lights" and "makes less heavy".

FERTILITY

Sex, land and religion blend together in the imagery of Eliot's *The Waste Land*, in which the

Fisher King has a sexual wound. The Earth Goddess also unites sex, land and religion, but with sexual vitality.

AFTER THE FRACTURE: GROWTH

1.   "Fracture". The breakdown of certainties happened around the time of the First World War.

COMMUNISTS LIKE WASPS

After a failed October revolution on October 3rd, the Communist hardliners Rutskoy and Khasbulatov defended the White House Parliament building in Moscow and were stormed by President Yeltsin's troops.

THE PHILOSOPHER'S STONE: SOUL AND GOLDEN FLOWER

4.   "Elemental". Red Mercury disturbs the molecules of every element. See note to next poem for the Russian discovery of the philosopher's stone. "Fault" (geology). "Break in continuity of strata or vein" (*Concise Oxford Dictionary*).

48.   "Plate" (geology). "Rigid sheet of rock in earth's outer crust" (*Concise Oxford Dictionary*).

51-52.   "Qualifications of/The Absolute that presents." The Absolute emanates or manifests each second through qualifications or limitations of the Absolute, which have been calculated as 10^{-23}, i.e. 10 thousand million million million events per second.

55.   "Golden Flower". In Neo-Taoist alchemy, a symbol for the Light, as in the 9th century Chinese text *The Secret of the Golden Flower*.

THE PHILOSOPHER'S STONE: WORLD AND MANKIND

The philosopher's stone was supposed to produce gold by activating the molecules of base metal. Evidence for the Russian discovery of the philosopher's stone as a pink salt, Red Mercury ($Hg_2 Sb_6$), which activates the molecules of all elements and can act as a chemical detonator, and for its sale to China and thence to an American Jew, has been supplied to me from two sources, a Philippino I will call Alan and the Polish-born Agnieszka Milewska. The existence of the philosopher's stone at the physical level, with its attendant dangers, makes a peaceful world government, which can combine regimes like the philosopher's stone, all the more pressing. The philosopher's stone this philosopher bequeathes is the idea of a benevolent world government that will end wars and famines, not a neo-Fascist world government committed to causing the deaths by limited wars, starvation and diseases of a half of the world's population (3 billion people by 2000 within the spirit of the *Global 2000 Report*) to make the world's resources go round.

36.   "Jar". The alchemical distilling retort suggests a round vessel or bowl, like the globe of our earth.

INDEX

(Volume titles and previous works are in capital letters. *Prefaces* and *Notes* are included).